Encyclopedia of Law and Economics
Volume V

Encyclopedia of Law and Economics
Edited by Boudewijn Bouckaert and Gerrit De Geest

Volume I	The History and Methodology of Law and Economics
Volume II	Civil Law and Economics
Volume III	The Regulation of Contracts
Volume IV	The Economics of Public and Tax Law
Volume V	The Economics of Crime and Litigation

Encyclopedia of Law and Economics Volume V

The Economics of Crime and Litigation

Edited by

Boudewijn Bouckaert

Professor of Law, University of Ghent, Belgium

Gerrit De Geest

Professor of Law and Economics, University of Ghent and University of Antwerp, Belgium and Researcher, Economic Institute/CIAV Utrecht University, The Netherlands

Edward Elgar

Cheltenham, UK • Northampton, MA, USA

Published by
Edward Elgar Publishing Limited
Glensanda House
Montpellier Parade
Cheltenham
Glos GL50 1UA
UK

Edward Elgar Publishing, Inc.
136 West Street
Suite 202
Northampton
Massachusetts 01060
USA

Reprinted 2001

A catalogue record for this book
is available from the British Library

Library of Congress Cataloguing in Publication Data

Encyclopedia of law and economics / edited by Boudewijn Bouckaert,
Gerrit De Geest.
Contents: v. 1. The history and methodology of law and economics — v. 2. Civil law and economics — v. 3. The regulation of contracts — v. 4. The economics of public and tax law — v. 5. The economics of crime and litigation.
Includes bibliographical references.
1. Law and economics Encyclopedias. I. Bouckaert, Boudewijn.
II. Geest, Gerrit De.
K487 .E3E53 2000
330—dc 21 99–38062
CIP

ISBN 1 85898 988 4
1 85898 565 X (5 volume set)

Printed and bound in Great Britain by MPG Books Ltd, Bodmin, Cornwall

Contents

EDITORIAL BOARD

Board of Referees

Foreword

Richard A. Posner
Chief Judge, US Court of Appeals for the Seventh Circuit
Senior Lecturer, University of Chicago Law School

The law and economics movement was for a long time regarded as an American movement. This was never completely correct. Its origins, certainly, are international. British economists, Adam Smith and Jeremy Bentham to begin with, and later A.C. Pigou and Ronald Coase (among others), played a founding role, as did Max Weber - himself both a lawyer and an economist. Friedrich Hayek and Bruno Leoni are other examples of scholars from outside the Anglo-American sphere whose thought has had an influence on the movement. And there are others. Today, at any rate, it is plain that the movement is international. There are law and economics associations in Europe and Latin America as well as in North America, law and economics scholarship is being produced in every major country and in many minor ones, and several of the leading journals are published outside the United States. Improvements in transportation and communications, and the rapid diffusion of English as the international language of scholarship, has fostered the internationalisation of law and economics. And there is growing recognition that comparative studies are an indispensable tool for gaining a better understanding of the economic nature and consequences of law. It is, for example, most unlikely that we will ever gain an adequate understanding of the efficiency of the Anglo-American 'adversarial' system of legal procedure without comparing it to the 'inquisitorial' system that prevails in Continental Europe; or understand the role of property rights in economic growth without studying the experience of the Central and European nations that have recently emerged from Communism.

Along with the internationalisation of the field has come an extraordinary growth in breadth of coverage and in specialisation of focus. Few areas of legal scholarship remain untouched by economics. Apart from the obvious examples - areas such as taxation and antitrust and securities regulation and (other) regulated industries and commercial law, all areas where the law is explicitly engaged in regulating economic activity - recent decades have seen a broadening of interest to include tort, contract, family, intellectual property, constitutional, criminal, admiralty, labour, arbitration, and antidiscrimination law, among others. But not only have more and more areas of law been brought under the lens of economics; more and more of the increasingly technical tools of economics - itself a field undergoing rapid growth and increased specialisation - have been brought to bear on the law, along with the latest in game theory. An immense and difficult body of monographic and journal scholarship is the result.

When a field becomes large, diverse and technical, it cries out for encyclopedic coverage. Thirty years ago one person, in one book, could map most of the terrain of law and economics. That is no longer possible. It has become infeasible for any single individual to keep fully abreast of the field of law and economics. He or she cannot be fully expert in every area of the field. And yet from time to time the scholar will find it necessary to cross the boundary that demarcates his own area of primary interest. For such a person, the opportunity of getting a quick overview of another part of the field by reading an encyclopedia article is welcome and even essential. It is even more welcome to those scholars, consultants, and practitioners who do not consider themselves 'law and economics' people, but whose work intersects the law and economics field. Law and economics has had interesting things to say about virtually every area of law, and this makes it of potential relevance to anyone working in one of those areas, who might be a practising lawyer, an economic consultant, a sociologist, psychologist, historian, or philosopher. For these 'outsiders', facing a research or practical task to which law and economics may be relevant, the opportunity to consult an encyclopedia article as the initial port of entry into the law and economics field is of immense potential value - as it is to students, and to scholars who are beginning to work in law and economics and want a broader view of the field before they decide where to specialise within it.

The *Encyclopedia of Law and Economics* endeavours, I think very successfully, to provide the kind of encyclopedic coverage - comprehensive and sophisticated but lucid, international without being esoteric, uniform without being monochrome, collective but individual - that the field of law and economics requires. It will help to make the field accessible to outsiders and to promote mutual intelligibility among insiders. It provides a meeting place for and an overview of a vast activity of scholarship, and will thus help to unify and advance the field. It is a milestone in an advancing field.

INTRODUCTION

Boudewijn Bouckaert and Gerrit De Geest
General editors

General Aims

The *Encyclopedia of Law and Economics* is an ambitious reference work that attempts to survey the whole law and economics literature in nearly 5,000 pages. Most entries contain two elements: a review of the literature, written by an authority in the field, and a quasi complete bibliography (not just a selection).

Economic analysis of law has expanded dramatically in recent years. In many branches, the literature is now at a 'mature' stage, where scholars agree on basic concepts, theories and even on policy recommendations. Yet, this scholarship does not reach many policymakers, lawyers or judges. Outside the USA, it even does not seem to reach law professors. This is not so much due to the fact that policymakers, judges or law professors are not interested in the economic consequences of legal rules, but rather to the fact that the literature is too inaccessible. There is a clear need for reference works that give a reliable overview of the literature in a way that is understandable also for non-specialists. This is the primary purpose of the *Encyclopedia of Law and Economics*.

Reviews of the Literature

The reviews are relatively lengthy articles (on average nearly 10,000 words) in which the basic questions and items of discussion are explained, the literature is summarized, critical reflections on these publications and on the evolution of the discussion in general are developed, and perhaps suggestions for further research are made.

The authors have been asked not to make their surveys too technical in order to make sure that readers without a mathematical training can still understand them. The result is in-depth and up-to-date syntheses of the literature that are still accessible for non-specialists, like judges, politicians or undergraduate students. All review articles have been anonymously refereed.

Bibliographies

The *Encyclopedia of Law and Economics* is to a great extent also a bibliographical work. In most cases, authors have tried to be quasi-complete.

The bibliographical lists at the end of all entries are not a 'list of cited works'. They list many more references than could be discussed in the text. Beside the bibliography of law and economics studies on the topic itself, many entries contain a second list, entitled 'Other References', which are references cited in the text, but either purely legal, philosophical, sociological, or cited law and economics publications that are not directly related to the very topic (for instance, many authors have cited Coase, 1960).

There is no doubt a need for these such specialized bibliographies. The law and economics literature has exploded in recent years (this Encyclopedia lists over 20,000 law and economics publications). However, to date it has not been so easy for readers to find the relevant publications, because they are spread out over law reviews, economics journals, conference volumes and so on. The fact that economic analysis of law is an interdisciplinary approach means that the specialized bibliographies in economics (like Econlit) or the specialized sources on law (like Lexis or Westlaw) give a very incomplete overview. Moreover, titles of articles or books do not always make clear whether the research was purely legal, purely economic, or truly interdisciplinary.

Quotation Style

As anyone can experience every day, there is no uniformity concerning the quotation style in law and economics, nor in economics or legal science. To make the bibliographies useful for as many scholars and students as possible, it is the policy of the *Encyclopedia of Law and Economics* to provide the maximum of information, but within certain limits. More specifically, the references to articles contain in principle the volume number of the journal and the year of publication, as well as the number of the first and the last pages of an article. Journal titles are written out in full. Titles of works in languages other than English are translated into English.

Structure

The *Encyclopedia of Law and Economics* has a pyramidal structure. The question was what structure had to be chosen. The general division of legal rules into branches differs fundamentally among legal systems. Most continental (European) legal classification systems are based, for instance, on the division between public law and private law. They also unify contract law, tort law and the law on restitution into one branch of law, called 'law of obligations'. American lawyers would have a hard time trying to find their way in such a system. The classification system of Econlit (where K is 'law and economics') was in our opinion no perfect alternative either, since it is not detailed enough and not much common-law oriented to satisfy continental lawyers.

Therefore we decided to elaborate a new, detailed classification system, inspired by both legal theory and law and economics insights. After a methodological and historical part (0000-0900), the law is divided into substantial norms (1000-6000) and meta-norms.

Substantial norms are divided into property (private property 1000 ff., common property 2000 ff.) and the transfer of property (involuntary transfer between private parties - tort law and restitution - 3000 ff.), voluntary transfer of property between private parties (general contract law, 4000 ff., and the regulation of contracts, 5000 ff.) and involuntary transfers between citizens and the state (taxation, social security, takings, 6000 ff.).

Meta-norms include litigation and evidence law (7000 ff.), criminal law (putting some additional incentives on legal rules defined in other branches of law) and rules on the production of legal rules (9000 ff.).

A correct classification system can improve analyses by suggesting what kind of models are to be applied. Medical malpractice, for instance, is considered by Anglo-American rules as a branch of tort law. It is more correct from an economic viewpoint to consider it as a regulation of contracts between physicians and patients (therefore it is treated in the volume on the regulation of contracts and not in the general part on tort law). Marriage law is according to many legal systems a part of 'family law'. Again, it is better to see it as the regulation of a specific contract. Modern economic scholarship on marriage law tries to apply the models on optimal contract remedies to the problem of unstable marriages.

Acknowledgments

A massive undertaking requires the help of an enormous amount of people. We would like to thank, first of all, the members of the editorial board and the board of referees. Second, we owe a lot to the publisher, Edward Elgar, and his staff - especially to Dymphna Evans for supporting the project in many ways. Third, we would like to acknowledge the financial support of the Economic Institute/CIAV of Utrecht University and of the Department of General Jurisprudence and History of Law of the University of Ghent. Finally, we can give no more than a sample of the people that have substantially contributed to this project: Luc Bosman, Olivier Delbecque, Ben Depoorter, Anja De Wilde, Niky D'Hulster, Wim Dubois, Regine Goemaes, Ghislain Hoffman, Steven Mels, Geert Premereur, An Saerens, Gianni Trovisi, Frieda Van Caneghem and Nancy Van Nuffel.

7000
CIVIL PROCEDURE: GENERAL

Bruce H. Kobayashi and Jeffrey S. Parker
Associate Professor of Law and Professor of Law
George Mason University School of Law

Abstract

The economic analysis of civil litigation has focused on the action of the litigants and on the effects of substantive and procedural rules on their behavior. This chapter focuses on the economic analysis of procedural rules and how these rules alter the incentives of the litigants to file, settle and litigate disputes. Such procedural rules affect the private costs and benefits of litigation through altering the net expected value and loss faced by the plaintiff and defendant. Procedural rules also affect the social costs and benefits of litigation by affecting the both the direct and error costs of litigation. The analysis in the chapter is organized around the US Federal Rules of Civil Procedure, and in reverse chronological order to reflect the economic analyses use of backwards induction to examine civil litigation. Topics examined in depth include sequencing rules, rules that affect the capitalization of litigation over parties and claims, the rules of discovery, and juries.
JEL classification: K4, K40 K41
Keywords: Civil Procedure, Civil Litigation, Settlement, Trials

1. Introduction

The economic analysis of civil litigation, following upon the pioneering work of Landes (1971), Gould (1973), and Posner (1973), has proven to be a fruitful area. Economic analyses of litigation have focused both upon the actions of parties in civil litigation and upon the effects of substantive and procedural rules on the litigants' behavior (see Cooter and Rubinfeld, 1989, for a previous survey of the field). This chapter focuses on the economic analysis of procedural rules. Papers in this field generally have examined the effects procedural rules have on error costs and the direct costs of litigation. The length of the reference list annexed to this chapter indicates the extent of academic interest in studying the economic effects of procedural rules, and the consequences of alterations to those rules.

2. Organizing Framework

The organizing framework for this chapter generally follows the US Federal Rules of Civil Procedure (FRCP). The FRCP, as supplemented by statutory and decisional standards concerning the jurisdiction of courts and the preclusive effects of judgments, regulate most aspects of the civil litigation process, from the general statement of the purpose of the rules to the particularized standards regarding process, pleadings, lawyer sanctions, discovery, the allocation of legal costs, the relationship between multiple parties (including the regulation and certification of class actions), motions, trials and judgments. Since their promulgation in 1938, the FRCP have provided generally uniform rules for the conduct of litigation in the US Federal courts, and similar rules have been adopted in a majority of American states (for a comparison of federal and state procedural rules, see Oakley and Coon, 1986). In addition, the Federal Rules have been frequently revised, and the process of rulemaking itself has become a topic for economic and legal analysis. However, we do not discuss the rules and related topics in numerical order. Rather, because the economic analysis of litigation must be forward looking, and thus proceed using backwards induction, our chapter is organized in reverse chronological order.

3. Topics Covered

Topics reviewed in depth in this chapter include sequencing rules, rules that affect the capitalization of litigation over parties and claims, the rules of discovery, and juries. Related areas not addressed in detail in this chapter are treated in other chapters of this volume and earlier volumes. These areas include: other areas of civil procedure, including fee shifting (7300), the litigation/settlement decision (7400) and class actions (7600); the organization of the courts, including jurisdictional issues (7100-7200); criminal procedure (7700); the economics of crime and punishment (8000-8600); arbitration and the private enforcement of law (7500); bankruptcy proceedings (7800); legal error, rules versus standards, and accuracy in adjudication (Volume I, 790), punitive damages (Volume II, 3700), the computing of damages, including the allocations of damages via contribution and indemnity rules (Volume II, 3500); and the production of legal rules and precedent (9000-9900). In addition, issues relating to evidence and information in litigation, including the rules of discovery, attorney client privilege, and advice for litigation, are examined in a companion section on evidence (7900).

4. The Economic Analysis of Procedural Rules

Economic analyses of procedural rules generally have proceeded within Posner's (1973) framework, which conceives the purpose of such rules to be the minimization of the sum of error costs and direct costs. See also Tullock (1975) and Posner (1992) for a general analysis of procedure. Consistent with this framework, Rule 1 of the FRCP directs that the rules be construed and administered to secure the just, speedy, and inexpensive determination of every action. Economic analyses of procedural rules focus on the effect such rules have on the incentives of potential and actual litigants. Thus, the economic analysis of procedural rules must begin with an economic model of litigation.

5. The Economic Model of Litigation

The basic economic model of litigation has two parties, a plaintiff (p) that has a potential claim against the defendant (d). The plaintiff's estimate of the net expected value (NEV) of the claim equals his estimate of the probability (P) that he or she will prevail (P_p) multiplied by the expected award (D_p), net of the marginal costs to the plaintiff of proceeding to the next stage of litigation (C_p). The defendant's objective function for estimating expected loss (EL) is developed in parallel fashion, as equaling the defendant's estimate of the probability the plaintiff will prevail (P_d) times the expected award (D_d) plus the defendant's marginal costs of proceeding to the next stage of litigation (C_d).

In the more developed models, several of the variables may be endogenously determined. For example, both litigants' selections of C may affect their estimates of the outcome, and one litigant's choice of C may affect the other litigant's estimate of its own cost of proceeding to the next stage. Most analyses use sequencing models, for which the definition of marginal cost given in the text is the most general case. In the most basic models, this cost is conceptualized as the marginal cost of 'trial' over 'settlement', though obviously it can be generalized to any of the multiple stages of litigation, and can refer to cooperative, decisional, or unilateral withdrawal outcomes, as developed by Cornell (1990). In processes without discrete formal stages, such as the American discovery process and some Continental trial processes, the most general case will be continuous updating of NEV and EL as each new item of information (for example, each witness or investigation) becomes available.

In addition, the litigants can be influenced by effects external to the current litigation - for example, by the precedential or preclusive effects of the judgment in the current litigation on future litigation. In such cases, a current plaintiff's judgment will produce an external gain to the plaintiff (G_p) while the defendant will suffer external loss (L_d). Likewise, a defendant's judgment will produce external gain (G_d) while the plaintiff will suffer an external loss (L_p).

The *NEV* and *EL* are the primary determinants of the incentives given to litigants in the economic model, including the amount of effort expended during litigation, the trial/settlement decision, the decision to file a suit, and the decision to avoid behavior that would give rise to legal liability. Because procedural rules alter the *NEV* and *EL*, these rules will have a central role in determining litigation incentives and outcomes. Because decisions made at earlier stages of litigation are dependent upon the parties' expectations of the outcomes (and their own and opposing parties' decisions) during later stages of the litigation, economic analysis begins from the last stage of trial and judgment, and proceeds by backward induction. Thus, we list and discuss topics in reverse chronological order.

6. Trial Courts

The last stage of a civil litigation in the court of first instance is the trial and judgment (Cooter and Rubinfeld, 1990). This discussion suppresses the possibility of appellate review, which in the US federal system is governed by a separate set of Federal Rules of Appellate Procedure. Appellate review in the United States is concerned primarily with the correction of legal error and secondarily with factual error. For a discussion of the economic analysis of those topics, see Volume I, Chapter 0790 in this volume.

7. The Choice Between Judge and Jury Trials

Trials and judgments are governed by Sections VI and VII of the FRCP (Rules 38-63). Subject to certain motions for the court to set aside the verdict (Rule 50) or order a new trial (Rule 59), judgment is entered as given by the factual findings and legal conclusions of a judge (see Rule 52) or the verdict of a jury (Rule 58). The federal rules allow any party to demand a trial by jury of any issue triable as a matter of federal constitutional right by a jury (Rule 38). Although most American states also provide by state law or constitution for a right to trial by jury in some or all cases, the state courts generally are not bound by the federal constitutional right to jury trial, except in certain cases where they are adjudicating federal claims for which federal law requires a right to jury trial. Rule 39 allows the parties in these cases also to have a trial by the court, by joint consent. Gay, et al. (1989) examine the choice between judge and jury under the assumption that juries are 'noisier' adjudicators than judges. Clermont and Eisenberg (1992) examine empirically whether the choice of judge versus jury produces differing verdicts in product liability cases tried under state law, finding that - contrary to the popular belief - judges, not juries, are more generous to plaintiffs. Further, they do not find that these results are explained by selection bias.

In addition to explicit choices by the parties, several of the Rules allow the judge to exercise certain powers even when the case is tried by jury. Rule 49 allows the court to require a jury to return a special verdict, which involves explicit findings upon each of several elements of the claim at issue rather than allowing the jury to return the more common general verdict (see Lombadero, 1996; James, Hazard and Leubsdorf, 1992, p. 377). Rule 50 provides for judgment as a matter of law, which can be used by the judge to preempt or overrule a jury upon the determination that, after being fully heard, there is no legally sufficient basis for a reasonable jury to find for a party on an issue (see McLauchlan, 1973). Rule 56 provides for an equivalent ruling in the pretrial stage by summary judgment, on the basis of pretrial discovery material and written submissions by the parties (see McLauchlan, 1977), and Rule 12 permits a judgment as a matter of law at the earlier pleading stage, in cases where the plaintiff's claim is legally deficient on its face.

8. Jury Structure and Decision Rule

The rules also regulate the size and decision rule used by civil juries, as well as the process through which jurors are selected. Rule 48 specifies that, unless the parties otherwise stipulate, a civil jury shall be not fewer than six nor more than twelve, and that the verdict shall be unanimous. Economic analyses of jury decision making include an examination of how juries process information (Klevorick, Rothschild and Winship, 1984; Froeb and Kobayashi, 1996), and the effect of jury size and alternative decision rules (Klevorick and Rothschild, 1979). Finally, Rule 47 (as supplemented by federal statutes) controls the selection of jurors, including the procedures for examination of jurors during the selection process, and the use of peremptory challenges (see, for example, Schwartz and Schwartz, 1996).

9. Litigation Expenditures

A separate literature has bypassed explicit consideration of the jury versus judge decision-making process by modeling the outcome of a trial as being determined by the litigants' expenditures on litigation. The most common model of litigation expenditures is where the both litigants expend resources to alter the probability of prevailing (see Posner, 1973; Goodman, 1978; Tullock, 1980;

Wittman, 1988; Katz, 1988; Hay, 1995; Kobayashi and Lott, 1996). That is, in these models, the marginal cost of future litigation stages C_p and C_d (usually conceptualized as 'trial versus settlement') are endogenous choice variables that determine the probability that the plaintiff will prevail $P(C_p,C_d)$. The equilibrium amounts of litigation expenditures depend upon the relative stakes of the parties, and upon the relative merits of the case. The litigation expenditures and probability determined by solving for the Nash equilibria are used as the expected values for earlier stages of litigation. Other articles have examined the relationship between the burden of evidence or decision standard and litigation expenditures. In these models, litigation expenditures that allow a litigant to meet the burden of proof or decision standard serve as a costly signal of liability (see, for example, Rubinfeld and Sappington, 1987).

10. The Trial/Settlement Decision

The major decision preceding commencement of a trial is the decision whether to settle the case or proceed to trial. The relative magnitudes of the plaintiff's *NEV* and the defendant's *EL* are the primary determinants of whether a case settles or whether trial occurs. As noted above, this modeling can be generalized to any stage preceding a decision by the court, or a further commitment to incur litigation expense. Under risk neutrality, the *NEV* sets the plaintiff's minimum acceptable settlement offer and the *EL* the defendant's maximum settlement bid. In the absence of lawyer-client agency costs, a sufficient (but not necessary) condition for litigation is the perceived absence of a bargaining range, which occurs when the plaintiff's minimum acceptable offer is greater than the defendant's maximum bid, that is, $NEV > EL$, or equivalently:

$$P_p(D_p + G_p + L_p) - P_d(D_a + L_d + G_d) + G_d - L_p > C_p + C_d \qquad (1)$$

The above condition identifies two reasons why parties choose to forego settlement and proceed to trial. The first is based on prediction failure. The second is based on consideration of external effects, specifically precedential or preclusive effects of the current litigation on future litigation.

A. The Optimism Model

11. The Prediction Failure Model

Under the simplifying assumptions that the litigants have symmetric stakes ($D_p = D_d = D$) and that there are no external effects ($L_d = L_p = G_d = G_p = 0$), the condition for trial rather than settlement reduces to the following expression:

$$(P_p - P_d)D > C_p + C_d \tag{2}$$

This condition illustrates the optimism model of litigation. In such a model, settlement fails to occur because of prediction failure - that is, settlement fails because the parties have mutually inconsistent and relatively optimistic estimates of the probability that the plaintiff will prevail (that is, $P_p > P_d$). The litigants' erroneous predictions lead them to behave as if there were no room for a mutually beneficial settlement.

12. The Priest-Klein Selection Model

Economists also have modeled the process through which such mutually inconsistent and optimistic predictions are generated. The Priest and Klein (1984) model of case selection is based on the optimism model, and has two major hypotheses. The first and more general hypothesis is that the cases selected for trial are not representative of the population of disputes. Specifically, under the assumptions of symmetric stakes and specific distributional assumptions about the litigants' estimates of P (specifically that each litigant's estimate of P is an independent draw from a unimodal distribution centered around the true P), the basic Priest-Klein model predicts that a disproportionate number of cases selected for trial will come from cases that are close to the decision standard. The second hypothesis is a specific prediction for observed case outcomes in the limiting case where the litigants accurately estimate P. Priest and Klein show that under these circumstances the distribution of filed cases around the decision standard becomes approximately symmetric, and the generated plaintiff win rate approximately equals 50 percent.

A large number of articles have examined the limiting prediction of a 50 percent win rate, and have presented evidence where the win rate differs from 50 percent. See, for example, Priest (1985), Wittman (1985), Ramsayer and Nakazato (1989), Eisenberg (1990), Hylton (1993), Thomas (1995), Waldfogel (1995), Shavell (1996). See Kessler, Meites and Miller (1996) and Kobayashi (1996) for recent surveys of the literature. While generally rejecting the specific fifty percent hypothesis, this evidence may simply reflect the fact that the assumptions underlying the limiting case do not hold. Further, empirical studies examining the more general predictions of the Priest-Klein model have found evidence consistent with model (see Kobayashi, 1996).

13. Settlement Failure and Discovery

Because the prediction failure model predicts settlement failure because litigants lack information at the time of the final trial/settlement decision, it suggests procedural reforms aimed at increasing pre-trial information. The management of pre-trial information is addressed in Section V of the FRCP (Rules 26-37). The primary rule is Rule 26, which contains the general provisions governing civil discovery. Under Rule 26, litigants are required to respond to requests for information by the adverse party, on the theory that such requests and responses would increase pre-trial information and increase settlement and accuracy in adjudication. However, economic models of discovery have pointed out several problems with the rules. First, the rules shift the costs of gathering information from the requesting to the responding party, and thereby introduce both a potential moral-hazard problem and strategic behavior into the demand for pretrial discovery. Because the costs of responding to a discovery request are, in many cases, larger that the cost of making a request, this externalization predicts that parties will request information well past the point where the marginal value of information outweighs the marginal costs of gathering the information. In addition, the process of discovery can decrease, rather than increase, settlement by making parties more optimistic (see Cooter and Rubinfeld, 1994). Finally, discovery can potentially decrease the amount of information in litigation by providing disincentives for the production and retention of information that might be subject to extensive legal discovery (see Kobayashi, Parker and Ribstein, 1996; see also Hay, 1994 and Sobel, 1989).

14. Amendments to the Discovery Rules

The perceived problems of 'overdiscovery' predicted by the economic model of litigation have been addressed in several amendments to the discovery rules. In 1983, Rule 26(b) was amended to embody an explicit cost-benefit test that could be applied by the judge to limit discovery. At that same time FRCP 16 was amended to expand the judge's power to manage the pretrial process in general. However, the economic model suggests that these managerial solutions may be inferior to forcing each litigant to internalize the costs of its own information requests, or at least to pay for the marginal cost of extensive discovery requests (Cooter and Rubinfeld, 1994).

In 1993, Rule 26 was further amended, again in response to concerns regarding litigants' overinvestment in discovery activity. However, the major change to the rules was to institute a regime of initial disclosures to be made without any request for information from the adverse party (see FRCP Rule 26a; Brazil, 1978; Schwarzer, 1989; Cooter and Rubinfeld, 1995). Applying the economic model, this change is likely to make matters worse. To the extent that cost-shifting is the source of 'discovery abuse', these rules exacerbate the problem by allowing the requesting party to externalize the costs of both requesting and responding to requests for information. This effect is magnified by abandonment of code pleading in favor of the broad notice pleading rules contained in the FRCP (Section III, Rules 7-15; see Epstein, 1973a, 1973b, 1974, 1986; Posner, 1973; Katz, 1990; Bone, 1997). Further, to the extent that this rule moves the costs of pretrial discovery into an earlier phase of the litigation, this may have the effect of increasing total costs, and decreasing the marginal costs of trial over settlement. The 1993 amendment was subject to a local option in US federal districts, which has reduced some of the effects of the rule change. Empirical analysis has shown that the busiest federal districts have opted out of the new rule (Kobayashi, Parker and Ribstein, 1996).

B. The External Effects Model

15. External Effects

Relative optimism is not the only way in which to generate the absence of a perceived bargaining range. The existence of external effects can cause litigation to occur even if the parties to the litigation agree on the likely outcome of the case. Examples of external effects include the precedential and preclusive effect of litigation, both of which serve to affect litigants' prospects in future cases (see Galanter, 1974; Rubin, 1977; Che and Yi, 1993 and Kobayashi, 1996; see also Landes and Posner, 1979; Blume and Rubinfeld, 1982; Priest, 1987, 1980; Cooter, 1987; Galanter, 1987). For a more complete discussion of precedent and legal change, see Chapters (9000-9900) of this volume.

To illustrate this point, consider the case with symmetric stakes and where the litigants agree on the probability the plaintiff will prevail, that is, $P_p = P_d = P$. According to the simple optimism model, such a case will settle in order to save the costs of a trial. However, even under these assumptions, litigation may be generated if the current case has implications for future behavior of the litigants involved. The *NEV* of the lawsuit to the plaintiff equals $P(D + G_p) - (1 - P)L_p - C_p$, and the defendant's $EL = P(D + L_d) - (1 - P)G_d + C_d$. The condition for litigation $NEV > EL$ becomes:

$$P(G_p - L_d) + (1 - P)(G_d - L_p) > C_d + C_p \tag{3}$$

Condition (3) shows that, even when the prospective outcome of a trial is agreed upon by the parties, trials can be generated when the external gains to the winning litigant outweigh the external losses to the losing litigant. In contrast to the sources of trial in the prediction failure and settlement failure models (where information costs prevent litigants from achieving a settlement within an existing bargaining range), external effects cause trials by preventing the existence of a bargaining range due to asymmetries in external effects. Because no mutually beneficial bargain is foregone, these trials are not a failure. In fact, the existence of external effects focuses on the positive and valuable rulemaking function of trials.

16. External Effects and Procedural Rules

The model of trial based on external effects also suggests the relevance of a different set of procedural rules - one that focuses on the effects of litigation on future claims and third parties. The FRCP addresses the packaging of claims and parties generally in Rules 13-14 and 17-25. These rules serve as inclusive packaging devices, which operate by giving litigants incentives and opportunities to join parties and claims in order to internalize external effects and to achieve economies of scale in litigation. They include the permissive joinder rules (Rule 18-20), impleader (Rule 14), interpleader (Rule 22), intervention (Rule 24), the rule governing counterclaims (Rule 13), and the rule governing class actions (Rule 23). For an economic analysis of counterclaims, see Landes (1994). For a discussion of various aspects of class actions, see Dam (1975), Rosenfeld (1976), Bernstein (1978), Friedman (1996), and Chapter 7600 of this volume.

17. Common Law Packaging Rules

A second major category of packaging rules include the common law rules of precedent, or stare decisis, and the rules of preclusion, or the law of res judicata. The common law rules of res judicata include the doctrines of claim preclusion (also known as merger and bar) and issue preclusion (also known as collateral estoppel). Under the rule of claim preclusion, parties or their privies (that is, predecessors or successors in interest) are precluded from relitigating issues that were or could have been raised in the first action (see, for example, Kobayashi, 1996; Landes and Posner, 1994). Claim preclusion prevents the splitting of claims based on the same out-of-court transaction, thus functioning as mandatory joinder-of-claims rules by their prospective effect on future litigation. In contrast, issue preclusion (collateral estoppel) is limited to issues that were actually litigated, actually decided, and necessary to the judgment in the first case. In addition, while application of claim preclusion is generally limited symmetrically to persons who were either parties or successors to parties on both sides of the initial litigation, collateral estoppel can operate non-symmetrically, or, as it is termed in legal doctrine, non-mutually, in the sense that collateral estoppel can operate in favor of strangers to the first action, but can operate against only parties or their successors (see Spurr, 1991; Hay, 1993). The existence of non-party preclusion has led to the attempted use of settlement conditioned on vacatur (the eradication of a prior public decision) as a means to eliminate the effect of preclusion (see Fisch, 1991).

18. Offensive Non-Mutual Collateral Estoppel

To see the effect of the application of non-mutual collateral estoppel, consider the case where a single defendant faces two different plaintiffs sequentially. Suppose for simplicity that both cases turn on a single issue that determines the outcome. First consider offensive collateral estoppel. If the first plaintiff prevails against the defendant, the defendant is precluded from relitigating the decisive issue against the second plaintiff. Thus, a loss in the first case results in the loss of both cases, and the external effect $L_d = (1 - P)D$. In contrast, a win by the defendant against the first plaintiff does not preclude the second plaintiff from relitigating the issue, if the second plaintiff is neither a party nor a privy to the first action. Thus, the only effect on the second litigation would be the precedential gain $G_d = (dP\ D)$, where dP equals the change in P in the second litigation. If there are no novel issues of law, this gain is likely to be close to zero. And under the assumption that the plaintiffs are not repeat litigants, $L_p = G_p = 0$.

Substituting into the condition for litigation (equation (3)) yields:

$$(1 - P)D(dP - P) > C_d + C_p \qquad (4)$$

If the precedential change dP is close to zero, condition (4) is unlikely to be satisfied. Thus, there will be little incentive to take such cases to trial. This incentive for settlement has led some to object to offensive non-mutual collateral estoppel on the grounds that such a rule will allow plaintiffs to repeatedly extract large settlements from a common defendant. However, the total effect on settlement amounts from such a rule is unclear (see Hay, 1993). First, the effect of estoppel causes the repeat litigant to capitalize all future litigation into the first litigation. This increase in the stakes causes the repeat litigant to spend a larger amount of resources when he goes to trial. This has the effect of lowering P, thus moving the bottom of the bargaining range downward. Further, the repeat litigant is likely to take a harder bargaining stance in the first litigation by anticipating its effects on future litigation.

19. Defensive Non-Mutual Collateral Estoppel

In contrast, consider the use of defensive non-mutual collateral estoppel with multiple plaintiffs. Again, assume that $L_p = G_p = 0$. Now $L_d = dP\,D$ and $G_d = PD$. Substitution into the condition for litigation (equation (3)) yields:

$$PD\,((1 - P) - dP) > C_d + C_p \qquad (5)$$

In contrast to the rule of offensive non-mutual collateral estoppel with multiple plaintiffs, such a rule increases the likelihood of litigation. In addition, use of such a rule would apply preclusion against a non-party that was represented by a party in the first litigation with low relative stakes, which may increase legal error and increase the amount of litigation (see Spurr, 1991). Thus, the court's rejection of the latter rule because of due process concerns is consistent with the predictions of economic analysis.

C. The Bargaining Failure Model and Asymmetric Information

20. Bargaining Failure

Even within the basic optimism model of litigation, condition (2) is not a necessary condition for litigation. Even if a positive bargaining range is perceived to exist, the parties may fail to settle due to bargaining failure (see, for example, Cooter, Marks and Mnookin, 1982; Gross and Syverud, 1991; Shavell, 1993) or due to the existence of asymmetric information (see, for example, P'ng, 1983, 1987; Bebchuk, 1984; Schweizer, 1989; Spier, 1992, 1994b; Daughety and Reinganum, 1993; Froeb, 1993; Wang, Kim and Yi, 1994). In the former case the litigants fail to agree on a specific bargain even if both litigants agree that a positive bargaining range exists. In the latter case, trials are a necessary cost of avoiding adverse selection problems. In both of these cases, the potential for costly trials represents a calculated cost of strategic behavior aimed at obtaining a better expected settlement.

21. Bargaining Failure and Procedural Rules

The existence of asymmetric information in litigation again points to the discovery rules (see the discussion in Part B, above). In addition, economists have examined procedural rules that would increase the incentives for settlement. Under FRCP Rule 68, the defendant can make an offer of judgment. If this offer is not accepted by the plaintiff, and the subsequent judgment is less favorable to the plaintiff, the plaintiff is responsible for the defendant's costs after making the offer (see Miller, 1986; Anderson, 1994; Anderson and Rowe, 1996; Chung, 1996). However, liberal and early use of Rule 68 is limited by the requirement that the defendant offer not merely settlement but judgment, which can have a preclusive effect in subsequent litigation. Further, under the current rules, it does not allow the plaintiff to recover marginal fees (although many statutes provide for one way fee recovery by plaintiffs). In addition, economists have analyzed contractual settlement devices such as settlement escrows (see, for example, Gertner and Miller, 1995), and the use of mediation and arbitration techniques (see Shavell, 1995).

D. Lawyer-Client and Client-Client Agency Costs

22. Lawyer-Client Agency Costs

Finally, trials can be generated due to agency costs between lawyer and client and by agency problems between co-interested clients. A large literature has modeled the consequence of attorney compensation arrangements that give rise to the agency problems in settlement (see, for example, Miller, 1987). Articles examining the incentive effects of contingent fees include, Clermont and Currivan (1978); Danzon (1983); Lynk (1990, 1994); Miceli and Segerson (1991); Thomason (1991); Dana and Spier (1993); Rubinfeld and Scotchmer (1993); Miceli (1994); Watts (1994); Hay (1996, 1997). Potential solutions to such problems include enforcement of ethical rules or the use of reputational mechanisms (see Gilson and Mnookin, 1984; Smith and Cox, 1985; Yang, 1996).

23. Contribution, Indemnity and Agreements with Multiple Defendants

Similarly, litigation and settlement are affected by the rules which allocate liability among multiple defendants. These include the rules of contribution and indemnity (see Easterbrook, Landes, and Posner, 1980; Landes and Posner, 1980; Hause, 1989; Kornhauser and Revesz, 1989, 1990, 1994; Klerman, 1996) and agreements between plaintiffs and defendants (see Bernstein and Klerman,

1995).

E. Effect of the Decision to File a Suit and the Decision to Avoid a Lawsuit

24. Incentives to Avoid Litigation

Finally, the *NEV* and the *EL* provide incentives during the earlier stages of litigation. The *EL*, discounted by the probability that a suit will be filed and by the likelihood of settlement, provides deterrence of and incentives for avoidance of behavior subject to legal liability (Polinsky and Rubinfeld, 1988a, 1988b; Cooter and Rubinfeld, 1989; see also Ordover, 1978, 1981, and Hylton, 1990).

25. The Decision to File a Lawsuit

Similarly, the *NEV* of a lawsuit is a primary determinant of whether or not a plaintiff chooses to file a suit. While many analyses of litigation limit their examination of legal claims to those whose NEV is positive, this is not a necessary condition for a suit to be filed. Negative NEV suits may also be filed in order to extract a settlement, and such strategies can be successful when the threat to litigate is credible (see Rosenberg and Shavell, 1985; Nalebuff, 1987; Bebchuk, 1988, 1996; Katz, 1990; Klein, 1990; Miceli, 1993; and Bone, 1997). For general analyses of the relationship between the cost of litigation and private and social incentive to bring a suit, see Schwartz and Tullock (1975); Priest (1982); Shavell (1982b); Menell (1983); Trubek, et al. (1983), Kaplow (1986); Rose-Ackerman and Geistfeld (1987); Hazard (1989); Williams and Williams (1994).

26. The Role of Sequencing of and Exit from Litigation

Perhaps one of the most salient features of the FRCP, and one that has been only recently addressed by the economics literature, is the effect of the rules on the timing and sequencing of litigation. While many economic models treat litigation as a timeless decision, the procedural rules lay out a sequence of events that determine how litigation will proceed over time. The timing and sequence of litigation has been shown to have important implications for the *NEV* of a lawsuit and the behavior of litigants.

For example, the ability of litigants to sequentially litigate motions or to separate liability and damage phases of trials have been shown to affect both the cost of litigation and the value of the litigation if litigants are allowed to exit.

Sequencing with easy exit increases the 'option' value of litigation by allowing plaintiffs to avoid conditional negative NEV outcomes by exiting the litigation (see Cornell, 1990; Landes, 1993; Chen, Chien and Chu, 1997). In addition, the ability to take motions sequentially can affect the credibility of negative expected value suits (Bebchuk, 1996).

Under the FRCP, exit is controlled by Rule 41. Under Rule 41, the plaintiff can unilaterally dismiss an action without order of the court at any time before the adverse party answers. After this, dismissal requires mutual stipulation by all parties, or an order of the court. The application of Rule 41 is a prime example of the tension between the *ex ante* and *ex post* effects of procedural rules. *Ex post*, it is unlikely that a defendant will prevent a plaintiff from abandoning a claim. However, the willingness of the court or the adverse party to allow the plaintiff to easily exit the litigation may be the primary reason the suit was filed in the first place.

27. Lawyer Sanctions

The FRCP address this inability to commit through Rule 11, which allows the court to impose sanctions on parties and their attorneys for filing frivolous suits. This rule addresses the commitment problem by allowing the motion for sanctions to survive the dismissal or mooting or the original claim. Thus, Rule 11 allows the motion for sanction to survive as separate action with the sanctions as the incentive to litigate. Economic analyses of sanctions under Rule 11 include Kobayashi and Parker (1993); Polinsky and Rubinfeld (1993); Bebchuk and Chang (1996); and Bone (1997).

However, recent amendments to Rule 11 may have reduced the value of Rule 11 as a commitment device. In the 1993 Amendments to the FRCP, the rules were amended to allow the a litigant twenty-one days to withdraw his pleading upon being served with a Rule 11 motion by the adverse litigant. In essence, the new rules allows for free exit, and thus weaken the commitment and deterrent effect of the rules. While the amendments to Rule 11 were designed in large part to decrease the volume of 'satellite' litigation over alleged Rule 11 violations, the effect of the rule change may be to increase the number of filed cases, the rate of Rule 11 challenges, and total litigation costs (Kobayashi and Parker, 1993).

28. Fee Shifting

Economists have also examined the use of two-way fee shifting (often referred to in America as the 'English' rule, in contrast with the general 'American' rule that each party bears its own fees, regardless of outcome) to deter low or negative value lawsuits. Because two-way fee shifting imposes extra costs on the losing party, it disproportionately affects low probability lawsuits (see Shavell, 1982a). However, the FRCP has not incorporated two-way shifting of fees and costs, and state experiments have not proven successful or long lived (see Snyder and Hughes, 1990; Hughes and Snyder, 1995). In addition, almost all fee-shifting statutes require the imposition of a judgment. Thus, the use of fee shifting would not necessarily reduce the option value of litigation. That is, if exit is routinely allowed prior to judgment, fee shifting will not serve as a deterrent. Indeed, to the extent that two-way fee shifting would increase the variance in final outcomes, use of such a system would increase the option value of litigation, and thereby increase the supply of filed cases (Cornell, 1990). For a more complete discussion of fee shifting, see Chapter 7300 of this volume. See also, Dewees, Prichard and Trebilcock (1981); Braeutigam, Owen and Panzar (1984); Reinganum and Wilde (1986); Bowles (1987); Katz (1987); Plott (1987); Donohue (1991); Graville (1993); Spier (1994a), and Katz and Beckner (1995).

F. Procedural Rulemaking

29. The Process of Procedural Rulemaking

Finally, both the process of procedural rulemaking and the adversarial system itself have been the subject of economic analyses. Indeed, the controversy over the relative merits of party-controlled adversarial presentation and a more 'managerial' system of litigation was at the heart of the controversial amendments to the discovery rules, and has been the subject of debate in the academic literature (see McChesney, 1979; Tullock, 1980, 1988; Langbein, 1985). For a recent report of experimental results, see Block and Parker (1996). For a public choice treatment of the common law of procedural rules, see Macey (1994).

The controversy over the recent amendments to Rule 11 and 26a have drawn attention to the process through which the rules are revised (see Kobayashi and Parker, 1993; Kobayashi, 1996), and have highlighted the lack of empirical evidence on the performance of procedural rules and systems (see, for example, Galanter, 1983; Walker, 1994). Indeed, the amendment to Rule 26a, which allows individual district courts to opt-out of the discovery rules, the Civil Justice Reform Act of 1990, which encouraged local variations in each district, and variation in local Federal Court rules and state court rules all provide substantial challenges to the traditional centralized system of rule making that existed in the federal system prior to 1990 (see Kobayashi, Parker and Ribstein, 1996; Solimine and Pacheco, 1997; and Subrin, 1989).

Bibliography on Civil Procedure: General (7000)

Anderson, David A. (1994), 'Improving Settlement Devices: Rule 68 and Beyond', **23** *Journal of Legal Studies*, 225-246.

Anderson, David A., and Rowe, Thomas D. (1996), 'Empirical Evidence on Settlement Devices: Does Rule 68 Increase Settlement?', **71** *Chicago-Kent Law Review*, 519-545.

Bebchuk, Lucian A. (1984), 'Litigation and Settlement Under Imperfect Information', **15** *RAND Journal of Economics*, 404-415.

Bebchuk, Lucian A. (1988), 'Suing Solely to Extract a Settlement Offer', **17** *Journal of Legal Studies*, 437-450.

Bebchuk, Lucian A.(1996), 'A New Theory Concerning the Credibility and Success of Threats to Sue', **25** *Journal of Legal Studies*, 1-26.

Bebchuk, Lucian A. and Chang, Howard F. (1996), 'An Analysis of Fee Shifting Based on the Margin of Victory: On Frivolous Suits, Meritorious Suits, and the Role of Rule 11', **25** *Journal of Legal Studies*, 371-404.

Bernstein, Lisa and Klerman, Daniel (1995), 'An Economic Analysis of Mary Carter Settlement Agreements', **83** *Georgetown Law Journal*, 2215-2270.

Bernstein, Roger (1978), 'Judicial Economy and Class Actions', **7** *Journal of Legal Studies*, 349-370.

Block, Michael, and Parker, Jeffrey S. (1996), 'Some Experimental Evidence of the Efficiency of the Adversarial System', mimeo, George Mason University School of Law.

Blume, Lawerence E. and Rubinfeld, Daniel L. (1982), 'The Dynamics of the Legal Process', **11** *Journal of Legal Studies*, 405-419.

Bone, Robert G. (1997), 'Modeling Frivolous Suits', **145** *University of Pennsylvania Law Review*, 519-605.

Bowles, Roger A. (1987), 'Settlement Range and Cost Allocation Rules', **3** *Journal of Law, Economics and Organization*, 177-184.

Braeutigam, Ronald, Owen, Bruce and Panzar, John (1984), 'An Economic Analysis of Alternative Fee Shifting Systems', **47** *Law and Contemporary Problems*, 173-185.

Brazil, Wayne D. (1978), 'The Adversary Character of Civil Discovery: A Critique and Proposals for Change', **31** *Vanderbilt Law Review*, 1295-1361.

Che, Yeon-Koo and Yi, Jong Goo (1993), 'The Role of Precedents in Repeated Litigation', **12** *Journal of Law, Economics and Organization*, 399-424.

Chen, Kong-Pin, Chien, Hung-Ken, and Chu, C.Y. Cyrus (1997), 'Sequential versus Unitary Trials with Asymmetric Information', **26** *Journal of Legal Studies*, 239-258.

Chung, Tai-Yeong (1996), 'Settlement of Litigation under Rule 68: An Economic Analysis', **25** *Journal of Legal Studies*, 261-286.

Clermont, Kevin M. and Currivan, John D. (1978), 'Improving the Contingent Fee', **63** *Cornell Law Review*, 529-599.

Clermont, Kevin M. and Eisenberg, Theodore (1992), 'Trial by Jury or Judge: Transcending

Empiricism', **77** *Cornell Law Review*, 1124-1187.

Cooter, Robert D. (1987), 'Why Litigants Disagree: A Comment on George Priest's "Measuring Legal Change"', **3** *Journal of Law, Economics and Organization*, 227-234.

Cooter, Robert D. and Rubinfeld, Daniel L. (1989), 'Economic Analysis of Legal Disputes and Their Resolution', **27** *Journal of Economic Literature*, 1067-1097; reprinted in Richard A. Posner and Francesco Parisi (eds) (1996), *Law and Economics*, Edward Elgar.

Cooter, Robert D. and Rubinfeld, Daniel L. (1990), 'Trial Courts: An Economic Perspective' **24** *Law and Society Review*, 533-548.

Cooter, Robert D. and Rubinfeld, Daniel L. (1994), 'An Economic Model of Legal Discovery', **23** *Journal of Legal Studies*, 435-463.

Cooter, Robert D. and Rubinfeld, Daniel L. (1995), 'Reforming to New Discovery Rules', **84** *Georgetown Law Journal*, 61-89.

Cooter, Robert D., Marks, Stephen and Mnookin, Robert (1982), 'Bargaining in the Shadow of the Law: A Testable Model of Strategic Behavior', **11** *Journal of Legal Studies*, 225-251.

Cornell, Bradford (1990), 'The Incentive to Sue: An Option Pricing Approach' **19** *Journal of Legal Studies*, 173-187.

Dam, Kenneth W. (1975), 'Class Actions: Efficiency, Compensation, Deterrence, and Conflict of Interest', **4** *Journal of Legal Studies*, 47-73.

Dana, James D., and Spier, Kathryn E. (1993), 'Expertise and Contingent Fees: The Role of Asymmetric Information in Attorney Compensation', **9** *Journal of Law, Economics and Organization*, 349-367.

Danzon, Patricia M. (1983), 'Contingency Fees for Person Injury Litigation', **14** *Bell Journal of Economics*, 213-224.

Danzon, Patricia, M. and Lillard, Lee (1983), 'Settlement Out of Court: The Disposition of Medical Malpractice Claims', **12** *Journal of Legal Studies*, 345-377.

Daughety, Andrew F. and Reinganum, Jennifer F. (1993), 'Endogenous Sequencing in Models of Settlement and Litigation', **9** *Journal of Law, Economics, and Organization*, 314-348.

Dewees, Donald N., Prichard, J. Robert S. and Trebilcock, Michael J. (1981), 'An Economics Analysis of Cost and Fee Rules for Class Actions', **10** *Journal of Legal Studies*, 155-185.

Donohue, III, John J. (1991), 'The Effects of Fee Shifting on the Settlement Rate: Theoretical Observations on Costs, Conflicts and Contingency Fees', **54** *Law and Contemporary Problems*, 195-222.

Easterbrook, Frank H., Landes, William M. and Posner, Richard A. (1980), 'Contribution among Antitrust Defendants: A Legal and Economic Analysis', **23** *Journal of Law and Economics*, 331-370.

Eisenberg, Theodore (1990), 'Testing the Selection Effect: A New Theoretical Framework with Empirical Tests', **19** *Journal of Legal Studies*, 337-358.

Epstein, Richard A. (1973a), 'A Theory of Strict Liability', **2** *Journal of Legal Studies*, 151-204.

Epstein, Richard A. (1973b), 'Pleadings and Presumptions', **40** *University of Chicago Law Review*, 556-582.

Epstein, Richard A. (1974), 'Defenses and Subsequent Pleas in a System of Strict Liability', **3** *Journal of Legal Studies*, 165-216.

Epstein, Richard A. (1986), 'The Temporal Dimension in Tort Law', **53** *University of Chicago Law Review*, 1175-1218.

Fisch, Jill E.(1991), 'Rewriting History: The Propriety of Eradicating Prior Decisional Law

Through Settlement Conditioned on Vacatur', **76** *Cornell Law Review*, 589-642.

Friedman, David D. (1996), 'More Justice for Less Money', **39** *Journal of Law and Economics*, 211-240.

Froeb, Luke M. (1993), 'The Adverse Selection of Cases for Trial', **13** *International Review of Law and Economics*, 317-324.

Froeb, Luke M. and Kobayashi, Bruce H. (1996), 'Naive, Biased, Yet Bayesian: Can Juries Interpret Selectively Produced Evidence?', **12** *Journal of Law, Economics and Organization*, 257-276.

Galanter, Marc (1974), 'Why the "Haves" Come Out Ahead: Speculations on the Limits of Legal Change', **9** *Law and Society Review*, 95-160.

Galanter, Marc (1983), 'Reading the Landscape of Disputes: What We Know and Don't Know (And Think We Know) About our Allegedly Contentious and Litigious Society', **31** *UCLA Law Review*, 4-71.

Galanter, Marc (1987), 'Conceptualizing Legal Change and its Effects: A Comment on George Priest's 'Measuring Legal Change'', **3** *Journal of Law, Economics and Organization*, 235-242.

Gay, Gerald D., Grace, Martin F., Kale, Jayrant R. and Noe, Thomas H.(1989), 'Noisy Juries and the Choice of Trial Mode in a Sequential Signalling Game: Theory and Evidence', **20** *RAND Journal of Economics*, 196-213.

Gertner, Robert H. and Miller, Geoffrey P. (1995), 'Settlement Escrows', **24** *Journal of Legal Studies*, 87-122.

Gilson, Ronald and Mnookin, R. (1984), 'Disputing through Agents: Cooperation and Conflict Between Lawyers in Litigation', **94** *Columbia Law Review*, 509-566.

Goodman, John C. (1978), 'An Economic Theory of the Evolution of the Common Law', **7** *Journal of Legal Studies*, 393-406.

Gould, John P. (1973), 'The Economics of Legal Conflicts', **2** *Journal of Legal Studies*, 279-300.

Graville, H.S.E. (1993), 'The Efficiency Implications of Cost Shifting Rules', **13** *International Review of Law and Economics*, 3-18.

Gross, Samuel R. (1987), 'The American Advantage: The Value of Inefficient Litigation', **85** *Michigan Law Review*, 734-757.

Gross, Samuel R. and Syverud, K.D. (1991), 'Getting to No: A Study of Settlement Negotiations and the Selections of Cases for Trial', **90** *Michigan Law Review*, 319-393.

Hause, J.C. (1989), 'Indemnity, Settlement, and Litigation, or I'll be Suing You', **18** *Journal of Legal Studies*, 157-179.

Hay, Bruce L. (1993), 'Some Settlement Effects of Preclusion', **1993** *University of Illinois Law Review*, 21-51.

Hay, Bruce L. (1994), 'Civil Discovery: Its Effects and Optimal Scope', **23** *Journal of Legal Studies*, 481-515.

Hay, Bruce L. (1995), 'Effort, Information, Settlement, Trial', **24** *Journal of Legal Studies*, 29-62.

Hay, Bruce L. (1996), 'Contingent Fees and Agency Costs', **25** *Journal of Legal Studies*, 503-533.

Hay, Bruce L. (1997), 'Optimal Contingent Fees in a World of Settlement', **26** *Journal of Legal Studies*, 259-278.

Hazard, Geoffrey C., Jr (1989), 'Authority in the Dock', **69** *Boston University Law Review*, 469-476.

Hughes, James W. and Snyder, Edward A. (1995), 'Litigation and Settlement under the

English and American Rules: Theory and Evidence', **38** *Journal of Law and Economics*, 225-250.

Hylton, Keith N. (1990), 'The Influence of Litigation Costs on Deterrence under Strict Liability and under Negligence', **10** *International Review of Law and Economics*, 161-171.

Hylton, Keith N. (1993), 'Asymmetric Information and the Selection of Cases for Litigation', **22** *Journal of Legal Studies*, 187-210.

James, Fleming, Hazard, Geoffrey C. and Leubsdorf, J. (1992), *Civil Procedure*, Boston, Little Brown.

Kaplow, Louis (1986), 'Private versus Social Costs in Bringing Suit', **15** *Journal of Legal Studies*, 371-385.

Katz, Avery (1987), 'Measuring the Demand for Litigation: Is the English Rule Really Cheaper?' **3** *Journal of Law, Economics and Organization*, 143-176.

Katz, Avery (1988), 'Judicial Decisionmaking and Litigation Expenditure', **8** *International Review of Law and Economics*, 127-143.

Katz, Avery (1990), 'The Effect of Frivolous Lawsuits on the Settlement of Litigation', **10** *International Review of Law and Economics*, 3-27.

Katz, Avery and Beckner, Clinton F. (1995), 'The Incentive Effects of Litigation Fee Shifting when Legal Standards are Uncertain', **15** *International Review of Law and Economics*, 205-224.

Kessler, Daniel, Meites, Thomas and Miller, Geoffrey (1996), 'Explaining Deviations from the Fifty-Percent Rule: A Multimodal Approach to the Selection of Cases for Litigation', **25** *Journal of Legal Studies*, 233-260.

Klein, Cristopher C. (1990), 'Predation in the Courts: Legal Versus Economic Analysis in Sham Litigation Cases', **10** *International Review of Law and Economics*, 29-40.

Klerman, Daniel (1996), 'Settling Multidefendant Lawsuits: The Advantage of Conditional Setoff Rules', **25** *Journal of Legal Studies*, 445-462.

Klevorick, Alan, and Michael Rothschild (1979), 'A Model of the Jury Decisionmaking Process', **8** *Journal of Legal Studies*, 141-164.

Klevorick, Alan, Rothschild, Michael and Winship, C. (1984), 'Information Processing and Jury Decision Making', **23** *Journal of Public Economics*, 141-164.

Kobayashi, Bruce H. (1996), 'Case Selection, External Effects, and the Trial/Settlement Decision', in Anderson, David A. (ed.), *Dispute Resolution: Bridging the Settlement Gap*, Greenwood, JAI Press, 17-49.

Kobayashi, Bruce H. and Lott, John R., Jr (1996), 'In Defense of Criminal Defense Expenditures and Plea Bargaining', **16** *International Review of Law and Economics*, 397-416.

Kobayashi, Bruce H. and Parker, Jeffrey S. (1993), 'No Armistice at 11: A Commentary on the Supreme Court's 1993 Amendments to Rule 11 of the Federal Rules of Civil Procedure', **3** *Supreme Court Economic Review*, 93-152.

Kobayashi, Bruce H., Parker, Jeffrey S. and Ribstein, Larry E. (1996), 'The Process of Procedural Reform: Centralized Uniformity versus Local Experimentation', George Mason University School of Law Working Paper.

Kornhauser, Lewis, and Revesz, Richard (1989), 'Sharing Damages Among Multiple Tortfeasors', **98** *Yale Law Journal*, 831-884.

Kornhauser, Louis and Revesz, Richard (1990), 'Apportioning Damages among Potentially Insolvent Actors', **19** *Journal of Legal Studies*, 617-651.

Kornhauser, Lewis and Revesz, Richard (1994), 'Multi-Defendant Settlements: The Impact of Joint and Several Liability', **23** *Journal of Legal Studies*, 41-76.

Landes, William M. (1971), 'An Economic Analysis of the Courts', **14** *Journal of Law and Economics*, 61-107.

Landes, William M. (1993), 'Sequential versus Unitary Trials: An Economic Analysis', **22** *Journal of Legal Studies*, 99-134.

Landes, William M. (1994), 'Counterclaims: An Economic Analysis', **14** *International Review of Law and Economics*, 235-244.

Landes, William M. and Posner, Richard A. (1979), 'Adjudication as a Private Good', **8** *Journal of Legal Studies*, 235-284.

Landes, William M. and Posner, Richard A. (1980), 'Joint and Multiple Tortfeasors: An Economic Analysis', **9** *Journal of Legal Studies*, 517-555.

Landes, William M. and Posner, Richard A. (1994), 'The Economics of Anticipatory Adjudication', **23** *Journal of Legal Studies*, 683-719.

Langbein, John H. (1985), 'The German Advantage in Civil Procedure', **52** *University of Chicago Law Review*, 823-866.

Lombardero, David A. (1996), 'Do Special Verdicts Improve the Structure of Jury Decision Making', **36** *Jurimetrics Journal*, 275-324.

Lynk, William J. (1990), 'The Courts and the Market: An Economic Analysis of Contingent Fees in Class-Action Litigation', **19** *Journal of Legal Studies*, 247-260.

Lynk, William J. (1994), 'The Courts and the Plaintiffs' Bar: Awarding the Attorney's Fee in Class-Action Litigation', **23** *Journal of Legal Studies*, 185-210.

McChesney, Fred S. (1979), 'On the Procedural Superiority of a Civil Law System', **30** *Kyklos*, 507-510.

McLauchlan, William P. (1973), 'An Empirical Study of Civil Procedure: Directed Verdicts and Judgments Notwithstanding Verdict', **2** *Journal of Legal Studies*, 459-468.

McLauchlan, William P. (1977), 'An Empirical Study of the Federal Summary Judgment Rule', **6** *Journal of Legal Studies*, 427-459.

Macey, Jonathan R. (1994), 'Judicial Preferences, Public Choice, and the Rules of Procedure', **23** *Journal of Legal Studies*, 627-646.

Menell, Peter S. (1983), 'A Note on Private versus Social Incentive to Sue in a Costly Legal System', **12** *Journal of Legal Studies*, 41-52.

Miceli, Thomas J. (1993), 'Optimal Deterrence of Nuisance Suits by Repeat Defendants', **13** *International Review of Law and Economics*, 135-144.

Miceli, Thomas J. (1994), 'Do Contingent Fees Promote Excessive Litigation?', **23** *Journal of Legal Studies*, 211-224.

Miceli, Thomas J. and Segerson, Kathleen (1991), 'Contingent Fees for Lawyers: The Impact on Litigation and Accident Prevention', **20** *Journal of Legal Studies*, 381-399.

Miller, Geoffrey P. (1986), 'An Economic Analysis of Rule 68', **15** *Journal of Legal Studies*, 93-125.

Miller, Geoffrey P. (1987), 'Some Agency Problems is Settlement', **16** *Journal of Legal Studies*, 189-215.

Nalebuff, Barry (1987), 'Credible Pretrial Negotiation', **18** *RAND Journal of Economics*, 198-210.

Oakley, John B. and Coon, Arthur F. (1986), 'The Federal Rules in State Courts: A Survey of State Court Systems and Civil Procedure', **61** *Washington Law Review*, 1367-1427.

Ordover, Janusz A. (1978), 'Costly Litigation in the Model of Single Activity Accidents', **7** *Journal of Legal Studies*, 243-261.

Ordover, Janusz A. (1981), 'On the Consequences of Costly Litigation in the Model of

Single Activity Accidents: Some New Results', **10** *Journal of Legal Studies*, 269-291.

Perloff, Jeffrey, Rubinfeld, Daniel L. and Ruud, P. (1996), 'Antitrust Settlements and Trial Outcomes', **78** *Review of Economics and Statistics*, 401 ff.

Plott, Charles R. (1987), 'Legal Fees: A Comparison of the American and English Rules', **3** *Journal of Law, Economics, and Organization*, 185-193.

P'ng, Ivan P.L. (1983), 'Strategic Behavior in Suit, Settlement, and Trial', **14** *Bell Journal of Economics*, 539-550.

P'ng, Ivan P.L. (1987), 'Litigation, Liability, and Incentives for Care', **34** *Journal of Public Economics*, 61-85.

Polinsky, A. Mitchell and Rubinfeld, Daniel L. (1988a), 'The Deterrent Effects of Settlements and Trials', **8** *International Review of Law and Economics*, 109-116.

Polinsky, A. Mitchell and Rubinfeld, Daniel L. (1988b), 'The Welfare Implications of Costly Litigation for the Level of Liability', **17** *Journal of Legal Studies*, 151-164.

Polinsky, A. Mitchell and Rubinfeld, Daniel L. (1993), 'Sanctioning Frivolous Suits: An Economic Analysis', **82** *Georgetown Law Journal*, 397-435.

Posner, Richard A. (1973), 'An Economic Approach to Legal Procedure and Judicial Administration', **2** *Journal of Legal Studies*, 399-458.

Posner, Richard A. (1992), *The Economic Analysis of Law,* 4th edn, Boston, Little Brown.

Priest, George L. (1980), 'The Selective Characteristics of Litigation', **9** *Journal of Legal Studies*, 399-422.

Priest, George L. (1982), 'Regulating the Content and Volume of Litigation: An Economic Analysis', **1** *Supreme Court Economic Review*, 163-183.

Priest, George L. (1985), 'Reexamining the Selection Hypothesis: Learning from Wittman's Mistakes', **14** *Journal of Legal Studies*, 215-243.

Priest, George L. (1987), 'Measuring Legal Change', **3** *Journal of Law, Economics and Organization*, 193-226.

Priest, George L. and Klein, Benjamin (1984), 'The Selection of Disputes for Litigation', **13** *Journal of Legal Studies*, 1-55.

Ramsayer, J. Mark and Nakazato, M. (1989), 'The Rational Litigant: Settlement Amounts and Verdict Rates in Japan', **18** *Journal of Legal Studies*, 263-290.

Reinganum, Jennifer F. and Wilde, Louis L. (1986), 'Settlement, Litigation and the Allocation of Legal Costs', **17** *RAND Journal of Economics*, 555-566.

Rose-Ackerman, Susan and Geistfeld, Mark (1987), 'The Divergence between Social and Private Incentives to Sue: A Comment on Shavell, Menell, and Kaplow', **16** *Journal of Legal Studies*, 483-491.

Rosenberg, David and Shavell, Steven (1985), 'A Model in Which Suits are Brought for Their Nuisance Value', **5** *International Review of Law and Economics*, 3-13.

Rosenfeld, Andrew (1976), 'An Empirical Test of Class-Action Settlement', **5** *Journal of Legal Studies*, 113-120.

Rubin, Paul H. (1977), 'Why is the Common Law Efficient?', **6** *Journal of Legal Studies*, 51-63.

Rubinfeld, Daniel L. and Sappington, David E.M. (1987), 'Efficient Awards and Standards of Proof in Judicial Proceedings', **18** *RAND Journal of Economics*, 308-315.

Rubinfeld, Daniel L. and Scotchmer, Suzanne (1993), 'Contingent Fees for Attorneys: An Economic Analysis', **24** *RAND Journal of Economics*, 343-356.

Schwartz, Edward P. and Schwartz, Warren F. (1996), 'The Challenge of Peremptory Challenges', **12** *Journal of Law, Economics, and Organization*, 325-360.

Schwartz, Warren F. and Tullock, Gordon (1975), 'The Costs of a Legal System', **4** *Journal* *of Legal Studies*, 75-82.

Schwarzer, William W. (1989), 'The Federal Rules, The Adversary Process, and Discovery Reform', **50** *University of Pittsburgh Law Review*, 703-723.

Schweizer, Urs (1989), 'Litigation and Settlement under Two-Sided Incomplete Information', **56** *Review of Economic Studies*, 163-178.

Shavell, Steven (1982a), 'Suit, Settlement, and Trial: A Theoretical Analysis Under Alternative Methods for the Allocation of Legal Costs', **11** *Journal of Legal Studies*, 55-81.

Shavell, Steven (1982b), 'The Social versus the Private Incentive to Bring Suit in a Costly Legal System', **11** *Journal of Legal Studies*, 333-339.

Shavell, Steven (1993), 'Suits versus Settlement when Parties Seek Nonmonetary Judgments', **22** *Journal of Legal Studies*, 1-13.

Shavell, Steven (1995), 'Alternative Dispute Resolution: An Economic Analysis', **24** *Journal of Legal Studies*, 1-28.

Shavell, Steven (1996), 'Any Frequency of Plaintiff Victory is Possible', **25** *Journal of Legal Studies*, 493-501.

Smith, Janet K. and Cox, Steven R. (1985), 'The Pricing of Legal Services: A Contractual Solution to the Problem of Bilateral Opportunism', **14** *Journal of Legal Studies*, 167-183.

Snyder, Edward A. and Hughes, James W. (1990), 'The English Rule for Allocating Legal Costs: Evidence Confronts Theory', **6** *Journal of Law, Economics and Organization*, 345-380.

Sobel, Joel (1989), 'An Analysis of Discovery Rules', **52** *Law and Contemporary Problems*, 133-159.

Solomine, Michael E. and Pacheco, Bryan (1997), 'State Court Regulation of Offers of Judgement and its Lessons for Federal Practice', **13** *Ohio State Journal on Dispute Resolution*, 51-78.

Spier, Kathryn E. (1992), 'The Dynamics of Pretrial Negotiation', **59** *Review of Economic Studies*, 93-108.

Spier, Kathryn E. (1994a), 'Pretrial Bargaining and the Design of Fee-Shifting Rules', **25** *RAND Journal of Economics*, 197-214.

Spier, Kathryn E. (1994b), 'Settlement, Bargaining, and the Design of Damage Awards', **10** *Journal of Law, Economics, and Organization*, 84-95.

Spurr, Stephen J. (1991), 'An Economic Analysis of Collateral Estoppel', **11** *International Review of Law and Economics*, 47-61.

Subrin, Stephen N. (1989), 'Local Rules, and State Rules: Uniformity, Divergence and Emerging Procedural Patterns', **137** *University of Pennsylvania Law Review*, 1999-2051.

Thomas, Robert E. (1995), 'The Trial Selection Hypothesis without the 50 Percent Rule: Some Experimental Evidence', **24** *Journal of Legal Studies*, 209-228.

Thomason, Terry (1991), 'Are Attorneys Paid What They're Worth? Contingent Fees and the Settlement Process', **20** *Journal of Legal Studies*, 187-223.

Trubek, David M., Sarat, Austin, Felstiner, William L.F., Kritzer, Herbert M. and Grossman, Joel B. (1983), 'The Cost of Ordinary Litigation', **31** *UCLA Law Review*, 72-127.

Tullock, Gordon (1975), 'On Effective Organization of Trials', **28** *Kyklos*, 745-762.

Tullock, Gordon (1980), *Trials on Trial: The Pure Theory of Legal Procedure*, New York, Columbia University Press.

Tullock, Gordon (1988), 'Defending the Napoleontic Code over the Common Law', **2** *Research in Law and Policy Studies*, 3-27.

Waldfogel, Joel (1995), 'The Selection Hypothesis and the Relationship Between Trial and Plaintiff Victory', **103** *Journal of Political Economy*, 229-260.

Walker, Laurens (1994), 'Avoiding Surprise from Federal Civil Rule Making: The Role of Economic Analysis', **23** *Journal of Legal Studies*, 569-593.

Wang, Gyu Ho, Kim, Jeong-Yoo and Yi, Jong-Goo (1994), 'Litigation and Pretrial Negotiation under Incomplete Information', **10** *Journal of Law, Economics and Organization*, 187-200.

Watts, Alison (1994), 'Bargaining Through an Expert Attorney', **10** *Journal of Law, Economics and Organization*, 168-186.

Williams, Philip L. and Williams, Ross A. (1994), 'The Cost of Civil Litigation: An Empirical Study', **14** *International Review of Law and Economics*, 73-86.

Wittman, Donald (1988), 'Dispute Resolution, Bargaining, and the Selection of Cases for Trial: A Study in the Generation of Biased and Unbiased Data', **17** *Journal of Legal Studies*, 313-352.

Wittman, Donald (1985), 'Is the Selection of Cases for Trial Biased?', **14** *Journal of Legal Studies*, 185-214.

Yang, Bill Z. (1996), 'Litigation, Experimentation, and Reputation', **16** *International Review of Law and Economics*, 503-521.

Other References

Adams, Michael (1981), *Ökonomische Analyse des Zivilprozesses* (Economic Analysis of Civil Procedure), Königstein/Ts, Athenäum, 130 ff.

Adams, Michael (1983), 'Eine wohlfahrtstheoretische Analyse des Zivilprozesses und der Rechtsschutzversicherungen (An Economic Analysis of Civil Procedure and Legal Aid Insurance)', **139** *Zeitschrift für Schweizerisches Recht*, 187-208.

Adams, Michael (1986), 'Der Zivilproze als Folge strategischen Verhaltens' (On Civil Procedure as a Consequence of Strategic Behavior)', **7** *Zeitschrift für Rechtssoziologie*, 212-225.

Alexander, Janet Cooper (1994), 'Judges' Self Interest and Procedural Rules: Comment', **23** *Journal of Legal Studies*, 647-665.

Bone, Robert G. (1994), 'The Empirical Turn in Procedural Rule Making: Comment', **23** *Journal of Legal Studies*, 595-613.

Bowles, Roger A. (1981), 'Economic Aspects of Legal Procedure', in Burrows, Paul and Veljanovski, Cento G. (eds), *The Economic Approach to Law*, London, Butterworths, 191-209.

Broder, Josef M. (1978), 'Citizen Participation in Michigan District Courts', in Randall, Allan (ed.), *Citizen Participation in Natural Resource Decision Making*, North Central Research Strategy Committee for Natural Resources, Department of Agricultural Economics, University of Kentucky. Reprinted in Samuels, Warren J. and Schmid, A. Allen (eds) (1981), *Law and Economics: An Institutional Perspective*, Boston, Nijhoff, 166-178.

Brown, John Prather (1985), 'Alternatives to the Present System of Litigation for Personal Injury', in Baily, Mary Ann and Cikins, Warren I. (eds), *The Effects of Litigation on Health Care Costs*, Washington, Brookings Institution, 69-79.

Carrington, Paul D. (1979), 'Adjudication as a Private Good: A Comment', **8** *Journal of*

Legal Studies, 303-317.

Carroll, Sidney L. and Gaston, Robert J. (1981), 'A Note on the Quality of Legal Services: Peer Review and Disciplinary Service', **3** *Research in Law and Economics*, 251- 260.

Chiorazzi, Michael et al. (1988), 'Empirical Studies in Civil Procedure: A Selected Annotated Bibliography', **51** *Law and Contemporary Problems*, 87-207.

Conference (1987), 'Conference on the Law and Economics of Procedure', **3** *Journal of Law, Economics, and Organization*, 143-372.

Cooper, Edward H. (1994), 'Discovery Cost Allocation: Comment', **23** *Journal of Legal Studies*, 465-480.

Cooter, Robert D. and Ulen, Tom (1989), *Law and Economics* (Scott Foresman, 1988; 2nd edition, 1996, Japanese translation by Prof. Shozo Ota, introduction by Prof. Koji Shimdo, published by Shoji-Homu.

Davis, Otto A. (1979), 'Public and Private Characteristics of a Legal Process: A Comment', **8** *Journal of Legal Studies*, 285-293.

Denzau, Arthur (1979), 'Litigation Expenditures as Private Determinants of Judicial Decisions: A Comment', **8** *Journal of Legal Studies*, 295-302.

Getman, Julius G. (1974), 'A Critique of the Report of the Shreveport Experiment', **3** *Journal of Legal Studies*, 487-497.

Goldberg, Victor P. (ed.) (1979), 'Discussion by Seminar Participants', **8** *Journal of Legal Studies*, 323-398.

Huang, Peter H. and Wu, Ho Mou (1992), 'Emotional Responses in Litigation', **12** *International Review of Law and Economics*, 31-44.

Linder, Douglas O. (1989), 'Some Doubts Concerning the Selection Hypothesis of George Priest', **37** *University of Kansas Law Review*, 319-347.

Miller, Geoffrey P. (1977), Note, Aldinger v. Howard and Pendent Jurisdiction, **77** *Columbia Law Review*, 127-152.

Miller, Arthur R. (1984), 'The Adversary System: Dinosaur or Phoenix', **69** *Minnesota Law Review*, 1-37.

Miller, Geoffrey P. (1989), 'Comment: Some Thoughts on the Equilibrium Hypothesis', **69** *Boston University Law Review*, 561-568.

Miller, Geoffrey P. (1994), 'Economic Analysis of Civil Procedure: Introduction', **23** *Journal of Legal Studies*, 303-306.

Nederlands Juristen Blad (1990), *Rechtshulp anno 1990*, Special Issue, (a number of articles).

Nederlands Juristen Blad, (1987), *Tussen Kwaliteit en Efficiency in de Rechtspraak* (Between Quality and Efficiency in Case Law), Special Issue (a number of articles).

Polinsky, A. Mitchell and Che, Yeon-Koo (1991), 'Decoupling Liability: Optimal Incentives for Care and Litigation', **22** *RAND Journal of Economics*, 562-570.

Posner, Richard A. (1988), 'Comment: Responding to Gordon Tullock', **2** *Research in Law and Policy Studies*, 29-33.

Rowe, Thomas D., Jr (1994), 'Repealing the Law of Unintended Consequences? Comment', **23** *Journal of Legal Studies*, 615-626.

Sarokin, H. Lee (1989), 'A Comment on Geoffrey Hazard's Authority in the Dock', **69** *Boston University Law Review*, 477-479.

Schwarzer, William W (1988), 'Rule 11 Revisited', **101** *Harvard Law Review*, 1013-1025.

Shavell, Steven (1989), 'The Sharing of Information Prior to Settlement of Litigation', **20** *RAND Journal of Economics*, 183-195.

Symposium (1987), 'Conference on the Law and Economics of Procedure', **3** *Journal of Law, Economics, and Organization*, 143-447.

Symposium (1989), 'Issues in Civil Procedure: Advancing the Dialogue', **69** *Boston University Law Review*, 467-779.

White, Lawrence J. (1988), 'Litigation and Economic Incentives', **11** *Research in Law and Economics*, 73-90.

Yeazell, Stephen C. (1989), 'The Salience of Salience: A Comment on Professor Hazard's Authority in the Dock', **69** *Boston University Law Review*, 481-486.

7100
JUDICIAL ORGANIZATION AND ADMINISTRATION

Lewis A. Kornhauser
Professor of Law, New York University School of Law

Abstract

This chapter surveys the economic literature on the functions and structure of courts. Issues concerning appellate courts and collegiality are addressed in a companion chapter.
JEL classification: K4
Keywords: Judicial Administration, Court Organization, Judges, Adjudication

1. Introduction

Economic analyses of substantive legal rules generally suppress the adjudication of factual and legal disputes that a legal rule might engender. The nature of adjudication, however, will influence greatly both the content of the substantive law and the costs of dispute resolution. An understanding of the structure of adjudication is thus central to an understanding of the effects of legal rules on behavior and on the identification of socially desirable legal rules. In addition, adjudication is a complex task implemented through institutions that vary across time and jurisdiction. The structure of adjudication and questions of judicial organization and administration thus present a rich field of study in their own right.

These two approaches to the study of judicial organization raise different, though equally interesting, questions. As yet, no unitary theory has developed to explain the structure of adjudication. The initial economic analyses of these institutions have raised several important questions: (1) What are the functions of adjudication? (2) Why is adjudication public rather than private? (3) Should there be only one system of courts or should there be many? (4) What is the relation among courts, legislature and executive? (5) How do we explain the organizational features of courts such as their jurisdiction and their hierarchical relation?

The questions presented by judicial organization and administration are contiguous with those presented by appeal and supreme courts. I adopt a somewhat arbitrary division of topics and relegate discussions of the reasons for appeal, explanations of hierarchy and collegiality to Chapter 7200 Appeal and Supreme Courts.

2. The Functions of Courts

2.1 What Do Courts Do?

Adjudication resolves disputes. Dispute resolution itself consists of at least four different tasks. First, courts must determine the facts of the dispute. Second, they apply the law to those facts. Third, the court may, in some instances, enforce its judgment against one of the parties. Finally, in some instances, the court may have to compel one or more of the parties to submit to the jurisdiction of the court.

In some legal systems, the judicial function is limited to these four tasks; in others, courts also make law. In civil law theory, for example, courts simply apply the law announced by legislatures to resolve disputes. Legal theorists in common law countries, by contrast, resolve disputes through the application of law but also promulgate new legal rules; courts thus play a lawmaking function as well.

This difference between civil and common law perceptions of adjudication, as well as various structural differences between the two systems, presents a challenge to economic analysts which has yet to be answered.

2.2 Public vs. Private Adjudication

Adjudication is commonly considered a quintessential function of government. In recent years, however, there has been a substantial privatization of at least some of these functions through a growing use of arbitration and other 'private judges'. This phenomenon has prompted scholars to study the extent to which government must supply judicial functions. Landes and Posner (1979) provide one of the earliest inquiries into the choice between private and public provision of adjudicatory services. Working within a common law framework, they identify the judicial functions as both dispute resolution and rule generation. They argue that only the dispute resolution function is suitable for (partial) privatization. Some public provision of dispute resolution might be necessary because (1) enforcement of judgments might require public authority and (2) in some instances, public authority may be necessary to compel one or more parties to submit the dispute to adjudication in the first place. A private market in adjudicatory services, however, would meet all other requirements of a dispute resolution system. They argue that a competitive market would produce competent and impartial judges because both qualities would be necessary to induce all parties to a dispute to consent to adjudication of their dispute by a given judge. Cooter (1983) offers a similar argument.

Landes and Posner, however, argue that private provision of rules will not, in general, be desirable. Rule generation is a public good and a private judge who announces a rule will not capture all the benefits that the announcement of a rule creates. Therefore, in a system of private adjudication, rules will be undersupplied. In addition, competing judges may generate competing sets of rules. They do not, however, explain why rules cannot be adequately supplied by legislatures.

Shavell (1995) considers the choice of private dispute resolution in the context of an established public system of courts. He addresses two questions: why would parties resort to private dispute resolution? and when is it socially desirable? He distinguishes *ex ante* invocation of private dispute resolution, in which the parties agree prior to the emergence of a dispute to resort to private resolution of their dispute, from *ex post* invocation of it, in which the resort to these private methods occurs after the dispute arises. He argues that *ex ante* invocation is socially desirable for three reasons: (1) it may lower the costs and risks of dispute resolution; (2) it may create better incentives to perform because of the greater accuracy of private resolution; and (3) it may reduce the number of litigated disputes. He argues that *ex post* invocation of private dispute resolution is not desirable.

3. The General Organization of Courts

3.1 Judicial Motivation

Economic models of judicial behavior and of court organization require an assumption concerning the motivations of judges. This requirement presents the central challenge to the economic analysis of courts. Several approaches have been adopted, most of which are surveyed here. A supplementary discussion that emphasizes a distinction between 'team' and 'political' models of judges appears in Chapter 7200 on Appeal and Supreme Courts.

The literature has focused primarily on adjudication in common law jurisdictions. This focus has implied that lawmaking is the judicial function that has received the most motivational attention. In this context, the literature has advanced three different types of answers to the question of judicial motivation. First, one can assume that judges meet their obligations as articulated in some jurisprudential theory of adjudication. Put differently, judges 'follow the law'. Team models, discussed in Section 2 of Chapter 7200 Appeals and Supreme Courts attempt to ground this adherence to norms in a more economic framework. Second, one can assume that judges seek to implement their own policy preferences subject to constraints such as review by other judges or by legislatures. This political model is discussed at greater length in Section 3 of Chapter 7200. Third, one may assume that, as in political models, judges act self-interestedly but define self-interest differently. The literature surveyed here has largely attempted to infer judicial motivation from the structure of incentives within which the judge works.

Aranson (1990) surveys the political science literature that applies the spatial theory of voting to courts and compares it to law and economics approaches to judicial motivation. He suggests three competing views of judicial motivation. The first, that it is rule governed, parallels the first strand mentioned above and discussed at greater length in Section 2 of Chapter 7200. The second, that judicial motivation is rent redistributing, and the third, that it is wealth maximizing, describe systemic tendencies rather than the motivation of particular judges. One might understand 'rent redistribution' consistently with the political model discussed in Section 3 of Chapter 7200. Wealth maximization, by contrast, assumes that Posner's claim that the common law maximizes wealth can be explained in terms of judicial success in pursuit of their common aim.

Posner (1973) sketched an approach to the problem of identification of the preferences of judges. He assumed that judges were self-interested and then briefly examined different incentive structures from which he inferred the underlying preferences of the judges. In particular he compared the structure in many states in which judges lack life tenure and aspire to higher political office to the structure of the federal courts in the United States in which the judges have life tenure. These themes were developed in the subsequent literature.

Landes and Posner (1980) argue that utility maximizing judges will primarily seek to maximize their power because their performance is too weakly linked to income and promotion for those concerns to have much effect on judicial behavior. They then adopt the number of times a judge is cited in other cases as a measure of his power. They then argue that judges with higher salaries and more secure tenure will have greater power (and hence be cited more often) because higher salaries both attract more competent judges and reduce the judge's incentives to distort his decisions and because longer tenure reduces turnover and the influence of politics. They then provide an ingenious test of their hypotheses. They create two samples of common law appellate opinions rendered in 1950. First they looked at all 246 tort, contract and property cases decided by the federal appellate courts under their diversity jurisdiction. Second they drew a random sample of 241 tort, property or contract cases decided by state supreme courts in 1950. The number of cases drawn from a specific state matched the proportion of federal cases decided under the law of that state. They then compared the citation rates of state and federal decisions in the two systems. They found only weak support for their hypothesis concerning higher salary and more secure tenure. Federal decisions were more likely to be cited in the state supreme courts of 'other' states (that is, states other than the one of which the federal court applied the law) than the decisions of state courts.

Cooter (1983) adopted a procedure similar to that of Landes and Posner (1979). He developed a theory of behavior of private judges and used that as a benchmark from which to infer the preferences of public judges. He argued that both public and private judges would care about their reputations among other judges and the bar.

Higgins and Rubin (1980) addressed the concern for promotion somewhat more directly. They argued that judges have preferences over policy 'discretion' and wealth; these preferences are conditional on their age. They argue that a judge's ability to satisfy her preferences are constrained in two ways. First, the reversal rate depends on the judge's policy preferences and the policy preferences of the higher court. Second, wealth depends on the reversal rate (because that affects each judge's prospect of promotion) and age. They then derive a test for the relative effects of discretion and wealth.

They study two samples. The first sample consists of those active district court judges in the eighth federal circuit in 1974 who permitted the release of data on the total number of cases they decided in 1973 and 1974. The second sample consisted of all active district court judges in the fifth federal circuit in 1966. They found that neither age nor seniority explained the reversal rates of the eighth circuit judges. They did find however that the estimated parameter on reversal rate had the predicted sign and was significant at the 10 percent level in a logit estimation of the probability of being promoted.

Greenberg and Haley (1986) argue, contrary to the conventional wisdom in general and to Posner (1985) in particular, that low judicial salaries are socially desirable because they signal a greater willingness to accept the non-pecuniary benefits of the judiciary; moreover, they argue that individuals who derive greater non-pecuniary benefits from judging make better judges.

Elder (1987) identifies two distinct mechanisms for monitoring judges: political and administrative mechanisms. These mechanisms create different incentives so that one should observe different behaviors in systems with different monitoring mechanisms. Without specifying the judicial objective function precisely, he nevertheless argues that judges deciding criminal cases will produce more trial verdicts under political monitoring than they would under administrative monitoring. He then tests this claim on 1977 data drawn from state criminal courts in 247 districts in seven states. His parameter estimates are consistent with his hypothesis.

Cohen (1992) followed up Elder's approach. He argued that Elder implicitly assumed that each judge sought to maximize his preferences defined in terms of minimizing his workload and his reversal rate. He argues that these preferences also imply that, when the penalty range increases, a judge will increase the penalty of those defendants who request a trial more than they increase the penalty of those who plead guilty. He also argues that judges will be concerned about promotion and that this too will influence the pattern of sentencing. He then considers a sample that consists of all federal antitrust indictments from 1955 through 1980. In 1974, Congress increased the maximum penalties for antitrust violations from $50,000 to $100,000. He finds that promotion concerns are explanatory with respect to fines but not with respect to incarceration.

Cohen (1991) exploited the data generated by a 'natural experiment' presented by the adoption of new sentencing guidelines by the United States federal courts. He examined 196 decisions by federal district courts that considered the constitutionality of the guidelines. He estimated a probit model of the probability of upholding the guidelines as a function of judicial ideology, caseload, promotion potential and the number of prior decisions for constitutionality. Promotion potential was measured by an index that reflected the (per district court judge) number of open seats on the appellate circuit. He found that the parameters on workload and promotion potential had the predicted sign and were highly significant.

Katz (1988) adopts a behavioral approach. He assumes that judges decide cases on the basis of the arguments presented to it. Each party offers arguments in its favor and the court decides in favor of the plaintiff if the plaintiff's arguments, in light of the 'underlying' (or, perhaps, *ex ante*) merits of the case, outweigh the defendant's arguments and some random error. He then shows that, when cases are more evenly balanced *ex ante*, expenditures of each party on litigation rise; and, if judicial decision is more random or variable, each party's expenditures fall.

3.2 Independence of the Judiciary

Economic analysts have devoted much attention to explanations for, and implications of, 'independent' judiciaries. An independent judiciary is one that is free from external influence, primarily, political influence. This conception of independence is somewhat at odds with the ascription of a political motivation to judges themselves because independence is generally seen as guaranteeing a more 'objective' resolution of disputes. Though the literature has not attended much to this specific problem, there are suggestions that a more general model of constitutional structure might justify an independent branch of politically motivated judges.

Most industrialized countries assert the independence of their judiciaries but the structures that guarantee independence differ greatly. In the federal system in the United States, for example, judges have life tenure and their (nominal) salaries cannot be decreased during their lifetime. In many states of the United States, however, judges serve for a term of years; moreover, in many states, they may be elected in either partisan or non-partisan elections. In both the state and federal systems, as in common law jurisdictions generally, judges are, however, drawn from the general bar. In many civil law countries by contrast, law graduates choose to enter practice or the judiciary at the outset of their career; a judicial bureaucracy then creates incentives for that judge. The insulation of that bureaucracy from 'normal' politics then determines the extent of judicial independence. This institutional variation across jurisdictions permits a comparative study of judicial independence. As a consequence, studies of independence, unlike studies in other areas of judicial organization, have been primarily comparative in nature.

Landes and Posner (1975) offered the earliest discussion of independence. Their argument rests on the claim that an independent judiciary will, in statutory interpretation, enforce the original legislative understanding. Individual legislatures accede to this practice because they want to increase the time a statute prevails. Landes and Posner then claim that the degree of independence should increase with the size of the jurisdiction because larger jurisdictions provide broader scope for rent-seeking. They then attempt to test their theory on data concerning 97 statutes declared unconstitutional by the United States Supreme Court between 1789 and 1972.

Ramseyer (1994) extends the analysis of Landes and Posner (1975) by drawing on a comparison of Japan and the United States. Ramseyer defines judicial independence as the extent to which politicians do not manipulate careers of sitting judges. He asks why some politicians provide an independent judiciary and others do not. He claims that a political structure will provide for an independent judiciary if (i) politicians believe that elections will continue indefinitely and (ii) politicians believe that their prospects of continued victory are low. He then does three case studies: the United States which satisfies both antecedent conditions and has an independent judiciary; contemporary Japan which satisfies the first condition but not the second and does not have an independent judiciary; and imperial Japan which satisfied condition (ii) but not condition (i) and did not have an independent judiciary.

Cooter and Ginsburg (1996) also deploy comparative data to study the question of judicial independence. They work with a different conception of independence than Ramseyer. Ramseyer's definition referred to the structure of appointment, pay, promotion and tenure in the judiciary. Cooter and Ginsburg have a more substantive view of independence; they look to the courts' ability to make law that diverges from the views of the legislature. They argue that the degree of judicial independence will depend on both political and constitutional features of a society. In particular they argue that societies in which a cohesive party dominates politics will be less likely to have judicial independence. On the other hand, the more 'legislative vetoes' that the constitution builds into its political process the more independence the courts have. They then asked experts in comparative law to rank the daringness of the judiciary of various countries. They then regressed daringness on the number of vetoes and the duration of the governing coalition. Despite the small sample size, the parameters on both independent variables had the predicted sign and were statistically significant; moreover they explained a substantial part of the variance.

3.3 Jurisdiction

Case and controversy requirement Courts generally resolve disputes but the dispute must generally be, in some way, 'live' and 'real'. In the United States, this requirement of the existence of a real dispute is embodied in the 'case or controversy' requirement of Article III of the Constitution. The requirement, however, is not a peculiarity of United States federal courts. With the exception of some constitutional courts, such as those of France and Germany, that have jurisdiction to issue opinions on the constitutionality of legislation prior to its enactment, most judicial systems require some similar trigger. Why should this be so? And who should be allowed to press a claim concerning a 'real' dispute?

Jensen, Meckling and Holderness (1986) address this latter question of who should be allowed to press a claim in a live dispute. They argue for limited rules of standing because, they claim, a liberal standing rule increases the costs of engaging in any rule-governed transaction.

Landes and Posner (1994) address the first question concerning the justification of a requirement of a concrete case to trigger the adjudicatory power. They extend a model of legal advice developed by Shavell (1988, 1992) and Kaplow and Shavell (1992) to investigate questions concerning the use of attorneys to the question the case or controversy requirement. They focus on the distinction between type 1 and type 2 error - the wrongful attribution of liability to defendants versus the wrongful excusal from liability of defendants. They argue that this distinction can be deployed to explain much of the observed pattern of exceptions to the case or controversy requirement. Specifically, they note that anticipatory adjudication, in violation of the concreteness requirement, increases both errors. They then examine in detail the institutions of declaratory judgments, res judicata, advisory opinions, and preliminary injunctions.

Stearns (1995, 1996) argues that the case or controversy requirement serves to restrict the occurrence of cycling that plagues institutions of social choice. For a fuller discussion, see the section on collegiality in Chapter 7200.

Specialized courts vs. courts of general jurisdiction Over what disputes should a court have jurisdiction to decide? Two methods for defining the subject matter jurisdiction of courts predominate. First, and most commonly, a court might have jurisdiction over any dispute that arises within a specified geographic area. Virtually all court systems consist primarily of these courts of general jurisdiction. Second, a court might have jurisdiction over disputes with a specified subject matter. Notice that these organizational patterns could be applied to courts of first instance (that find facts as well as apply law) only, to appellate courts only, or to both courts of first instance and to appellate courts. Moreover, in a system with specialized courts of first instance but appeal to courts of general jurisdiction, one could limit appeal to a single general court of jurisdiction or one could allocate non-exclusive jurisdiction to a number of appellate courts. In the United States, one may understand the administrative law structure as establishing administrative agencies as specialized courts to determine the facts and make initial legal rulings that are then appealed to courts of general jurisdictions. Thus most labor disputes, welfare disputes and immigration disputes are first heard in administrative agencies and then, if necessary, appealed to the federal courts of appeals. In these instances, each of the federal courts of appeal has jurisdiction to hear appeals from these specialized tribunals. Many environmental disputes, by contrast, may only be appealed to the US Court of Appeals for the DC Circuit. Finally, there are some specialized courts of appeal such as the tax court and the federal circuit for Court of Appeals for the Federal Circuit which has jurisdiction over patent and other intellectual property disputes. What is the appropriate way to allocate jurisdiction among courts?

Posner (1985) argues that specialized appellate courts are likely to be more ideological than courts of general jurisdiction because judges on specialized courts are likely to be more focused on the subject matter of their jurisdiction and hence more likely to be sensitive, and responsive, to controversy.

Revesz (1990) analyzes the desirability of vesting appellate authority over administrative agencies in specialized courts. His analysis emphasizes the effect of the nature of the appellate court's jurisdiction on legislative ability to control agencies. He argues that review by specialized courts reduces the effectiveness of congressional delegation to administrative agencies. He develops a simple principal-agent model in which Congress is the principal and the administrative agency the agent. They have different policy preferences because commissioners in agencies have terms that do not correspond to the terms of the commissioners and because there may be a divergence in preferences between Congress and the President who appoints the head of many agencies. Congress has three mechanisms for the control of agencies: it may overrule particular decisions, it may exercise oversight through one or more committees, and it may alter the agency's budget. Congress, however, might also use the courts to monitor the agency. Revesz argues that a court of general jurisdiction is a better monitor.

3.4 Court Congestion

Comparative law scholars have often noted the variation in 'litigiousness' across countries. There is little economic literature that seeks to explain this cross-cultural variation but there is a substantial literature analyzing the causes of 'congestion' in the courts of one notably litigious society, the United States.

Virtually every proposal to reduce court congestion in the United States federal courts recommends the abolition of diversity jurisdiction which grants federal courts the authority to resolve disputes between citizens of different states, even when they involve only questions of sate law. One justification for diversity is that it prevents discrimination against out-of-state residents. Goldman and Marks (1980) tested this claim by looking at two samples of attorneys drawn from the US District Court for the Northern District of Illinois in 1976. They randomly sampled 200 attorneys tied to specific questions and asked them their reasons for litigating in federal court. They had a 62 percent response rate. In addition they randomly sampled 205 attorneys from the law division of Cook County District Court in 1976; this court had a $15,000 amount a controversy minimum so that the cases within its jurisdiction were reasonably comparable to those within the jurisdiction of the federal court. This survey had only a 37 percent response rate. Only 40 percent of the attorneys in federal court listed local bias as a reason for choosing federal court. Attorneys drawn from state court cases were asked to consider a hypothetical case identical to the one litigated but in which their client was an out-of-state resident. Roughly 25 percent said they would file in federal court. Local bias thus had very little influence on the choice of forum.

Noam (1981) attempts to assess the social cost of court congestion by calculating the effects of congestion on criminal sentences and then on the crime rate. He argues that plea bargain reached between prosecutor and defendant will depend on the caseload of the court. The higher the caseload per judge, the lower the average sentence. Moreover, he argues that the per capita crime rate is a function of the average sentence. Using simple specifications of these functional relations he derives an equation that represents the marginal effect of additional resources devoted to the criminal courts. He then estimates his equation using FBI data on crime rates for four types of crimes against property in the District of Columbia. This estimation yields very high marginal returns to increased investment in the court system.

4. Fact-Finding

To resolve disputes, courts must determine the facts. A substantial portion of procedural rules govern the fact-finding process. Each of these rules influences the structure of the judicial system because each influences the cost of litigation relative to the cost of settlement and to self-help remedies. (The literature on evidence and the choice between settlement and litigation are summarized elsewhere in this volume.) Some procedural rules play a more central role in the organization of court systems. In this section, I examine the structure of trials and the use of juries, a characteristic element of many but not all court systems.

4.1 Sequential vs. Unitary Trials

Most disputes present more than one factual issue for resolution. Should these be resolved simultaneously or sequentially? In the United States, factual issues are generally resolved simultaneously, but often the question of liability and the question of remedy are decided sequentially, sometimes by different fact-finders.

Landes (1993) presents the primary investigation of this issue. He modifies his own, early model of the choice between settlement and litigation (see Landes, 1971) to analyze several issues concerning the effect of trial structure on the settlement rate. The analysis rests on the insight that a sequential structure to the litigation reduces the expected cost of litigation. Hence, the plaintiff's incentive to sue increases, which implies that the number of lawsuits will increase. Landes argues further that sequential trials reduce the probability of settlement because they narrow the range of acceptable settlements.

4.2 Juries

Many legal systems divide the law-finding (or law-applying) and fact-finding functions of trial courts. These systems delegate fact-finding to a *jury*, generally a group of lay individuals chosen more or less randomly to decide one case. This procedure raises several questions.

Jury selection Bowles (1980) compares the cost of jury trials in Britain to the cost of a system of fact-finding by a three-judge court. The cost of a jury trial consists primarily of the production foregone by persons serving on the jury. Bowles notes that high wage earners will attempt to avoid jury service more vigorously than low wage earners. He concludes that a jury trial will be less expensive if the cost of a judge is more than three times the cost of a juror. He does not, however, correct for the speed of the trial.

Martin (1972) also estimates the social cost of the jury system in the United States. He first estimates the occupational distribution of jurors on the assumption that juror days of service are distributed identically to jurors. He then multiplied by the median daily wage rate for each occupation and estimated the social cost at $233 million ($135 million) in 1958 dollars. He then compares the cost of two systems of jury selection: random selection and a 'keyman' procedure in which lists are constructed through consultation with community leaders. He finds that random selection is significantly less expensive because community leaders are more likely to draw jurors from high wage occupations than random selection. Finally Martin argues that voluntary service would reduce costs even further.

Jury size and jury voting rules Models of jury size and the effects of jury voting rules must specify how juries deliberate and vote. Many models assume no deliberation. Moreover, until recently, the literature assumed that each juror voted conscientiously; her vote expressed her view of the guilt or innocence of the defendant. When one assumes in addition that each juror is more likely than not to decide correctly and that jurors' judgments are independent of each other, the Condorcet jury theorem applies and one can easily show first, that a unanimity rule minimizes the probability of wrongful convictions; second, that majority rule maximizes the probability of a correct decision; and third, that, as the number of jurors increases, the probability of wrongful conviction under a unanimity rule decreases towards zero and the probability of a correct decision under majority rule increases towards one. Recently, however, analysts have introduced models of strategic voting by jurors and these models yield dramatically different results.

Austen-Smith and Banks (1996) and Feddersen and Pesendorfer (1996) show how radically the assumption of strategic behavior by jurors undermines the Condorcet Jury Theorem. When a juror acts strategically, the information aggregation feature of the Condorcet Jury Theorem disappears because each juror now decides how to cast her vote in light only of those instances in which her vote will be pivotal. As a consequence, as Austen-Smith and Banks show clearly, a juror's vote may not reveal her actual view concerning the case. Feddersen and Pesendorfer show, more dramatically, that the probability of wrongful conviction may be higher under a unanimity rule than under a different voting rule.

These models raise important questions about the appropriate way in which to model juries. These questions parallel those presented in the study of collegial courts, discussed in Chapter 7200, where team models in which judges act in a fashion somewhat analogous to the assumption underlying the naive Condorcet Jury Theorem models contend with political models in which judges act strategically.

In the United States, until the 1970s, juries typically consisted of twelve individuals and required unanimity to render a verdict. Then, the United States Supreme Court ruled that neither the number twelve nor unanimity were constitutionally required in state criminal proceedings. These decisions spurred research into the importance of these requirements.

Klevorick and Rothschild (1979) provide a model of jury deliberation in order to determine whether non-unanimous juries or unanimous juries of fewer than twelve jurors would yield different verdicts than the 'standard', twelve-person unanimous jury. Their analysis uses a stationary Markov model to provide a dynamic model of the majority persuasion hypothesis, derived from Kalven and Zeisal (1966), that the final verdict is the same as the majority position on the first ballot. They offer both a discrete and continuous model of jury deliberation.

The cores of the models are identical. The jurors enter the jury room with a view on the merits and cast an initial ballot. The vote then changes incrementally as time passes with one person changing her vote at each instant until unanimity is reached. The transition probabilities are given by the current vote: the probability of one more vote for the plaintiff equals the percentage of jurors who favor the plaintiff's case. In this model one can calculate both the expected number of jury ballots until unanimity is reached (conditional on the initial vote) and the probability that a non-unanimous jury will agree with a unanimous one. Klevorick and Rothschild show that a move to a requirement of ten votes for judgment rather twelve always alters the probability of conviction by less than 0.0055. Their result, of course, depends critically on the manner in which majority pressure operates in the jury room. When they adopt a different assumption concerning transition probabilities, they calculate that the move to ten for judgment may lead to as many as 1/6 of the cases decided differently. Klevorick and Rothschild also show that this shift substantially reduces the expected number of ballots prior to judgment.

Schwartz and Schwartz (1992, 1995, 1996) offer a somewhat different approach to jury decision making. The earliest paper addresses three questions concerning the decision rules of juries. First, why do juries fail to reach a verdict? Second, what verdict will a jury reach when it may convict for lesser included offenses or when multiple offenses are litigated simultaneously? Third, how, if at all, will the jury decision rule alter the charges filed by prosecutors? To this end, they assume that a defendant might be charged with any number of counts within some interval. They consider two regimes. In one the prosecutor chooses one count in the interval, and the jury must choose among three outcomes, conviction on that count, acquittal, or no decision. In the second regime, the prosecutor chooses two counts, one entailing a lesser punishment than the other, and the jury chooses among four outcomes, acquittal on both counts, conviction on the lesser count, conviction on the more severe count, or no decision. In the event of no decision, a retrial before a different jury occurs. Each jury consists of four people, chosen randomly from a population. Each potential juror is an expected utility maximizer, characterized by spatial 'preferences' for punishment of the defendant; that is, each juror has an ideal outcome that represents the crime for which she believes the defendant should be convicted. The simple model implies that a defendant always prefers a non-unanimous, super-majority rule to unanimity because his expected verdict is lower under the non-unanimous rule. This result occurs because, though the probability of conviction is greater under non-unanimity, the probability of acquittal rises more rapidly. When the jury may convict on a lesser included offense, the analysis is more complex and less clear-cut.

Schwartz and Schwartz (1995) extend the analysis of their prior article in the context of the liability and punishment phases of capital offenses in the United

States. They argue that the decision process for fact finding has three elements: the voting rule, the jury selection process, and the characterization of the set of outcomes among which the jury may choose. They argue that, in a multi-stage fact-finding process, the voting rule must be the same in each stage in order to avoid the jury at one stage nullifying the law governing the jury at a different stage. In addition, only *reciprocal* voting rules will avoid hung juries (where a rule is reciprocal if 'conviction' requires c of n votes then 'acquittal' requires $n - c$ of n votes).

Schwartz and Schwartz (1996) carries the argument of the prior two papers further. They argue that any voting rule should satisfy at least two properties: (1) it should be decisive; and (2) it should satisfy the 'one person/one vote' criterion. This second property does not eliminate any anonymous voting rule, whether majority, supermajority, or submajority. (Super and submajority rules would violate neutrality). The first criterion identifies majority rule as the unique decisive voting rule when there are only two possible outcomes. To satisfy the desire to minimize wrongful convictions that the unanimity rule is said to promote, Schwartz and Schwartz argue that the size of the jury should be increased perhaps to 15.

5. Concluding Remarks

Economic analysis of judicial organization and administration, though it has greatly increased understanding, is only in its infancy. No question has received an exhaustive treatment and many have not been examined at all.

This area suggests a multitude of comparative questions, most of which have not received any attention at all. They are ripe for analysis.

Bibliography on Judicial Organization and Administration (7100)

Aranson, Peter H. (1990), 'Models of Judicial Choice as Allocation and Distribution in Constitutional Law', *Brigham Young University Law Review*, 794-826.

Austen-Smith, David and Banks, Jeffrey S. (1996), 'Information Aggregation, Rationality and the Condorcet Jury Theorem', **90(1)** *American Political Science Review*, 34-45.

Backhaus, Jurgen (1992), 'General Legislation and the Budget: Commentary', **12** *International Review of Law and Economics*, 209-210.

Barnard, David (1977), *The Civil Court in Action*, Butterworths, London, 350 ff.

Bowles, Roger A. (1980), 'Juries, Incentives and Self-Selection', **20** *British Journal of Criminology*, 368-376.

Brunet, Edward (1985), 'Measuring the Costs of Civil Justice', **83** *Michigan Law Review*, 916-938.

Casper, Gerhard and Posner, Richard A. (1974), 'A Study of the Supreme Court's Caseload',

3 *Journal of Legal Studies*, 339-375.

Casper, Gerhard and Posner, Richard A. (1976), *The Workload of the Supreme Court*, Chicago, American Bar Foundation.

Casper, Gerhard and Zeisel, Hans (1972), 'Lay Judges in the German Criminal Courts', **1** *Journal of Legal Studies*, 135-191.

Cohen, Mark A. (1991), 'Explaining Judicial Behavior or What's 'Unconstitutional' about the Sentencing Commission?', **7** *Journal of Law, Economics, and Organization*, 183-199.

Cohen, Mark A. (1992), 'The Motives of Judges: Empirical Evidence from Antitrust Sentencing', **12** *International Review of Law and Economics*, 13-30.

Cooter, Robert (1983), 'The Objectives of Private and Public Judges', **41** *Public Choice*, 107-132.

Cooter, Robert and Ginsburg, Tom (1996), 'Comparative Judicial Discretion: An Empirical Test of Economic Models', **16** *International Review of Law and Economics*, 245-313.

Ebner, P. (1982), *Reducing Pretrial Delay... A Look at What State and Local Courts Are Doing to Break the Logjam*, Santa Monica, Rand Institute of Civil Justice.

Elder, Harold W. (1987), 'Property Rights Structures and Criminal Courts: An Analysis of State Criminal Courts', **7** *International Review of Law and Economics*, 21-32.

Feddersen, Timothy J. and Pesendorfer, Wolfgang (1996), 'Convicting the Innocent: The Inferiority of Unanimous Jury Verdicts', Northwestern University Center for Mathematical Studies in Economics and Management Science Discussion Paper No. 1170.

Feeley, Malcolm (1983), *Court Reform on Trial: Why Simple Solutions Fail*, New York, Basic Books, 251 ff.

Flanagan, Robert J. (1987), *Labor Relations and the Litigation Explosion*, Washington, DC, Brookings Institution, 122 ff.

Friedman, David (1979), 'Private Creation and Enforcement of Law: A Historical Case', **8** *Journal of Legal Studies*, 399-415.

Galanter, Marc (1986), 'The Day After the Litigation Explosion', **46** *Maryland Law Review*, 3 ff.

Gely, Rafael and Spiller, Pablo T. (1990), 'A Rational Choice Theory of Supreme Court Statutory Decisions with Applications to the *State Farm* and *Grove City* Cases', **6** *Journal of Law, Economics, and Organization*, 263-300.

Gillespie, Robert W. (1976), 'The Production of Court Services: An Analysis of Scale Effects and Other Factors', **5** *Journal of Legal Studies*, 243-265.

Goldman, Jerry, Hooper, Richard L. and Mahaffey, Judy (1976), 'Caseload Forecasting Models for Federal District Courts', **5** *Journal of Legal Studies*, 201-242.

Goldman, Jerry and Marks, Kenneth S. (1980) 'Diversity Jurisdiction and Local Bias: A Preliminary Empirical Inquiry, **9** *Journal of Legal Studies*, 93-104

Gravelle, Hugh S.E. (1983), 'Judicial Review and Public Firms', **3** *International Review of Law and Economics*, 187-205.

Greenberg, Paul E. and Haley, James A. (1986), 'The Role of the Compensation Structure in Enhancing Judicial Quality', **15** *Journal of Legal Studies*, 417-426.

Griffiths, J. (1991), 'De Rechtbank als Fietsenfabriek' (The Court as Bicycle Manufacturer)', **66** *Nederlands Juristenblad*, 129-130, 445.

Hazard, Geoffrey C., Jr (1965), 'Rationing Justice', **8** *Journal of Law and Economics*, 1-10.

Higgins, Richard A. and Rubin, Paul H. (1980), 'Judicial Discretion', **9** *Journal of Legal*

Studies, 129-138.

Jensen, Michael, Meckling, William H. and Holderness, Clifford (1986), 'Analysis of Alternative Standing Doctrines', **6** *International Review of Law and Economics*, 205-216.

Kalven, Harry and Zeisal, Hans (1966), *The American Jury*, Boston, Little Brown.

Kaplow, Louis and Shavell, Steven (1992), 'Private vs Socially Optimal Provision of Ex Ante Legal Advice', **8** *Journal of Law Economics and Organization*, 306-320.

Karotkin, Drora (1994), 'Effect of the Size of the Bench on the Correctness of Court Judgments: The Case of Israel', **14** *International Review of Law and Economics*, 371-75.

Katz, Avery (1988), 'Judicial Decision Making and Litigation Expenditures', **8** *International Review of Law and Economics*, 127-143.

Klevorick, Alvin K. (1977), 'Jury Composition: An Economic Approach', in Siegan, Bernard H. (ed.), *The Interactions of Economics and the Law*, Lexington, Lexington Books.

Klevorick, Alvin K. and Rothschild, Michael (1979), 'A Model of the Jury Decision Process', **8** *Journal of Legal Studies*, 141-164.

Kornhauser, Lewis A. and Sager, Lawrence G. (1986), 'Unpacking the Court', **96** *Yale Law Journal*, 82-117.

Landes, William M. (1971), 'An Economic Analysis of the Courts', **14** *Journal of Law and Economics*, 61-107.

Landes, William M. (1993), 'Sequential versus Unitary Trials: An Economic Analysis', **22** *Journal of Legal Studies*, 99-134.

Landes, William M. and Posner, Richard A. (1975), 'The Independent Judiciary in an Interest Group Perspective', **18** *Journal of Law and Economics*, 875 ff.

Landes, William M. and Posner, Richard A. (1979), 'Adjudication as a Private Good', **8** *Journal of Legal Studies*, 235-284.

Landes, William M. and Posner, Richard A. (1980), 'Legal Change, Judicial Behavior and the Diversity Jurisdiction', **9** *Journal of Legal Studies*, 367 ff.

Landes, William M. and Posner, Richard A. (1994), 'The Economics of Anticipatory Adjudication', **23** *Journal of Legal Studies*, 683-720.

Levin, Martin A. (1975), 'Delay in Five Criminal Courts', **4** *Journal of Legal Studies*, 83-131.

Martin, Donald L. (1972), 'The Economics of Jury Conscription', **80** *Journal of Political Economy*, 680-702.

Melumad, Nahum D. and Thoman, Lynda (1990), 'On Auditors and the Courts in an Adverse Selection Setting', **28** *Journal of Accounting Research*, 77-120.

Miller, Arthur R. (1984), 'The Adversary System: Dinosaur or Phoenix', **69** *Minnesota Law Review*, 1-37.

Miller, Geoffrey P. (1989), 'Comment: Some Thoughts on the Equilibrium Hypothesis', **69** *Boston University Law Review*, 561-568.

Noam, Eli M. (1981), 'A Cost-benefit Model of Criminal Courts', **3** *Research in Law and Economics*, 173-183.

Noll, Roger G. (1992), 'Judicial Review and the Power of the Purse: Comment', **12** *International Review of Law and Economics*, 211-13.

Pastor, Santos (1990a), 'Economia de la Justicia (I) y (II)' (Economics of the Judicature), **5** and **6** *Revista de Economia Pública*.

Pastor, Santos (1990b), 'Economia de la Justicia en España (The Spanish Courts and the

Economic Analysis)', *Revista de Economìa*, 4 ff.

Pastor, Santos (1991), 'Informe sobre la Litigación, Recursos y Acceso de los Cuidadanos a la Justicie' (Report on Litigation, Courts Inputs and Access to Justice)', In Ministerio De Justicia, *Materiales para una Reforma Procesal*, Madrid.

Posner, Richard A. (1973), 'An Economic Approach to Legal Procedure and Judicial Administration', **2** *Journal of Legal Studies*, 399-458.

Posner, Richard A. (1983), 'Will the Federal Courts of Appeals Survive until 1984? An Essay on Delegation and Specialization of the Judicial Function', **56** *Southern California Law Review*, 761-791.

Posner, Richard A. (1984), 'The Meaning of Judicial Self-Restraint', **59** *Indiana Law Journal*, 1-24.

Posner, Richard A. (1985), *The Federal Courts: Crisis and Reform*, Cambridge, Harvard University Press, 365 p.

Posner, Richard A. (1986), 'The Summary Jury Trial and Other Methods of Alternative Dispute Resolution: Some Cautionary Observations', **53** *University of Chicago Law Review*, 366-393.

Posner, Richard A. (1989), 'Coping with the Caseload: A Comment on Magistrates and Masters', **137** *University of Pennsylvania Law Review*, 2215-2218.

Priest, George L. (1989), 'Private Litigants and the Court Congestion Problem', **69** *Boston University Law Review*, 527-559.

Ramseyer, J. Mark (1994), 'The Puzzling (In)dependence of Courts: A Comparative Approach', **23** *Journal of Legal Studies*, 721-47.

Revesz, Richard L. (1990), 'Specialized Courts and the Administrative Lawmaking System', **138** *University of Pennsylvania Law Review*, 1111 ff.

Scheiner, Alan Howard (1991), 'Judicial Assessment of Punitive Damages, the Seventh Amendment, and the Politics of Jury Power', **91** *Columbia Law Review*, 142-226.

Schwartz, Edward P. and Schwartz, Warren F. (1992), 'Decision making by Juries Under Unanimity and Supermajority Voting Rules', **80** Georgetown Law Journal, 775-907.

Schwartz, Edward P. and Schwartz, Warren F. (1995), 'Deciding Who Decides Who Dies: Capital Punishment as a Social Choice Problem', **1** *Legal Theory*, 113-148.

Schwartz, Edward P. and Schwartz, Warren F. (1996a), *Simple Majority Rule for Criminal Jury Trials: The Verdict is Now In*, manuscript.

Schwartz, Edward P. and Schwartz, Warren F. (1996b), 'The Challenge of Peremptory Challenges', **12** *Journal of Law, Economics and Organization*, 325 ff.

Shanley, Michael G. (1991), 'The Distribution of Posttrial Adjustments to Jury Awards', **20** *Journal of Legal Studies*, 463-481.

Shavell, Steven (1988), 'Legal Advice about Contemplated Acts: The Decision to Obtain Advice, Its Social Desirability, and Protection of Confidentiality', **17** *Journal of Legal Studies*, 123-150.

Shavell, Steven (1992), 'Liability and the Incentive to Obtain Information about Risk', **21** *Journal of Legal Studies*, 259-270.

Shavell, Steven (1995), 'Alternative Dispute Resolution: An Economic Analysis', **24** *Journal of Legal Studies*, 1-28.

Sociaal Cultureel Planbureau (1990), *Doelmatig Rechtspreken* (Efficient Administration of Justice), S.C.P. **88**, 's-Gravenhage, Staatsdrukkerij, 74 ff.

Stearns, Maxwell (1995), 'Standing Back from the Forest: Justiciability and Social Choice', **83** *California Law Review*, 1309-1413.

Stearns, Maxwell (1996), 'How Outcome Voting Promotes Principled Issued Identification: A Reply to Professor John Rogers and Others', **49** *Vanderbilt Law Review*, 1045-1067.

Straussman, Jeffrey D. (1986), 'Courts and Public Purse Strings: Have Portraits of Budgeting Missed Something?', **4** *Public Administration Review*, 315-351.

7200
APPEAL AND SUPREME COURTS

Lewis A. Kornhauser
Professor of Law, New York University School of Law

Abstract

This chapter surveys the economic literature on judicial appeals and collegiality of courts. More general issues concerning judicial administration and court organization are surveyed in a companion chapter.
JEL classification: K4
Keywords: Appellate Courts, Appeals, Adjudication, Supreme Courts

1. Introduction

This chapter reviews the literature concerning several issues raised in the economic analysis of appeal and of supreme courts. These issues overlap those considered in Chapter 7100, Judicial Organization and Administration. Appellate courts in general and supreme courts in particular exist only in hierarchically organized court systems.

Most of the literature has focused on courts in common law countries. Indeed, most models that extend beyond the simplest features of adjudication do so in the context of the political system of the United States. This review consequently shares the parochial focus of the literature. Analyses of appeal in civil law systems and in the context of different political systems would greatly advance understanding of the subject as they often present different institutional features. At least some civil law systems, for example, allow an appellate court to make an independent assessment of the facts of the case, a judgment denied common law courts. Similarly, the highest courts in some civil law jurisdictions hear substantially more cases than the highest courts in common law countries, a fact that may explain, or be explained by, differences in precedential practice and in the style and content of judicial opinions.

2. Explanations of Hierarchy

Appeal, and supreme courts, only arise in court systems which are organized hierarchically. Why does hierarchy occur? Posner (1985) suggested that the primary function of a supreme court was law creation and the insurance of uniformity of application of law among the lower courts. In addition, he argued that, in the United States, concerns about unreviewable power implied that trial courts would be subject to some supervision. These ideas have not been much elaborated in the literature. Rather, two distinct research strategies have emerged from two different models of adjudication. The 'team' model assumes that all judges in the system share a common objective function - to maximize the number of 'correct' decisions rendered by the system. Hierarchy emerges because it somehow promotes the goal of error minimization. The 'political' (or 'principal-agent') model assumes that judges differ in their objective functions. Hierarchy arises in this model so that the small set of politically dominant judges can enforce their views on recalcitrant judges lower in the hierarchy.

Kornhauser (1995) provides an informal team model that explicitly addresses the question of the optimal organization of n judges into a judicial system. Judges share the goal of minimizing the number of errors; the likelihood of a correct decision depends on the amount of effort the judge invests in deliberation on the case. Moreover, deliberation on a specific case also provides a signal about the correct resolution of 'nearby' cases. Because the court faces a resource constraint, the question of optimal organization of judges arises. Kornhauser argues that, in appropriate circumstances, a hierarchy will emerge in which there is (a) division of labor between trial judges who find facts and appellate judges who determine the law; and (b) strict vertical *stare decisis* so that lower court judges will always adhere to the decisions of higher court judges. Models of hierarchy that emphasize the need for consistency as in Rogers (1995) and Dorf (1995) are team models in which the 'correct decision' requires consistency.

3. Team Models of Error Correction

Shavell (1995) is the earliest formal model of error correction. Shavell assumes that the state must decide first, whether to establish both trial and appellate courts or trial courts only; and second, how many resources to devote to each level of court that it establishes. The probability of correct decision by a court increases with increased allocation of resources to that court. The state seeks to minimize social costs which consist of the costs of the judicial system and the costs created by wrongly decided cases. A trial court is characterized by the probability (as a function of state resources) that it will render the wrong decision. Litigants know for certain whether a court has correctly decided their case. An appellate court is characterized by two probabilities (as functions of state resources devoted to appeal): the probability $q(y)$ that an incorrect trial decision will be reversed on appeal and the probability $r(y)$ that a correct trial decision will be reversed on appeal. Litigants know with certainty whether the court has rendered a correct decision. Litigants face a cost to appeal. It is straightforward to see that, if $q(y) > r(y)$ and if the court can impose fees or give subsidies for appeal, then the state can insure that only cases wrongly decided at trial will be appealed.

Shavell then characterizes the state's optimal strategy by showing when appellate courts should be created and how resources should be divided between trial and appellate levels. He also shows that litigant selection of cases is superior to the random review of trial court decision. When a court undertakes random review of lower court cases, it unnecessarily uses resources to reconsider some correctly decided cases; under litigant selection (with the appropriate subsidies and fees), by contrast, only cases that should be reconsidered are in fact reviewed.

Cameron and Kornhauser (1996) offer a more strategic model of error correction that formalizes a portion of the argument in Kornhauser (1995). Their paper divides into two distinct parts. First, they identify conditions under which it would be desirable to add an additional level of appeal to a court structure. They define the selectivity of a process as the ratio of the proportion of wrongly decided cases that would be appealed to a new tier to the proportion of correctly decided cases that would be appealed to a new tier. They define the error correction ratio as the ratio of the probability that the new appellate court would reverse a wrongly decided case on appeal to the probability that the new appellate court would uphold a rightly decided case on appeal. They prove that an additional tier of review is desirable if the appeals process is sufficiently selective or sufficiently error correcting.

The second part of Cameron and Kornhauser's argument considers a particular technology of review. The correct decision of a case depends on the defendant's type which, initially, is known to the defendant but not to the plaintiff. At trial, the plaintiff, but not the court, becomes fully informed about the defendant's type. A court's ability to discriminate among defendant types is a function of the effort it invests in the case. Litigants incur a cost each time they appeal. Judges seek first to maximize the number of correct decisions; in addition a judge prefers not to be reversed. Cameron and Kornhauser show that, when litigants select cases for appeal, the hierarchy will have three tiers. They also study the process when the appellate courts select cases for review.

4. Political Models of Review

4.1 Models of Pure Adjudication

Political models generally justify appellate review in terms of law making. They do this in large part because the structure of the model requires that interpretation. Each court usually has preferences over policy space. Thus, to decide a case is to announce a policy, or, put differently, to announce a new legal rule.

Cameron (1993) presents the political model of review in its starkest form. There is one supreme court and n lower courts. Each court has spatial preferences over a one-dimensional policy space. There is complete information so that each lower court knows the supreme court's ideal point and the supreme court knows the location in policy space of the decision of each lower court. Each lower court seeks to maximize its utility which depends only on the final decision in the case it decides; the supreme court wants to maximize its utility which is a function of the decisions in all cases. The game has two stages: in stage 1, each lower court issues a decision; in stage 2, the supreme court selects at most only one case for review. There is a unique equilibrium to this game in which each lower court decides its case by announcing the ideal policy point of the supreme court as its decision and the supreme court reviews no case because it has already achieved its optimum utility. No other pattern of lower court decisions is an equilibrium because, in any other pattern, the lower court that will be reversed on appeal has an incentive to alter its strategy.

McNollgast (1995) offers a more elaborate political model, which focuses on conflicts in the policy views of the supreme court, the legislature and the lower courts. To enforce its views the supreme court must both induce lower courts to adhere to its 'doctrine' and avoid reversal through legislation. McNollgast extends the model of Cohen and Spitzer (1994). They consider a three stage game in which the supreme court first identifies the range of acceptable decisions in policy space. In stage 2, the lower courts decide whether to adhere to supreme court 'doctrine'. In stage 3, the supreme court reviews some subset of the lower court decisions; the number of cases reviewed is determined by the supreme court's budget. Each case presents a single issue in a K-dimensional policy space. Each judge has separable, spatial preferences over this policy space, an assumption that reduces a decision in any given case to the framework outlined in Cameron. That is, each judge's preferences can be represented by an ideal point in each dimension such that she prefers any decision closer to that ideal point to one further away. The supreme court has preferences defined over the outcomes of all cases decided within the system but each lower court has preferences defined over its case load only. Moreover, the supreme court does not know either the ideal point of any specific court nor the actual decision rendered by a lower court. The supreme court does know the distribution of ideal points of lower courts and it does know whether a lower court has complied with supreme court doctrine. It will thus choose to review some random sample of non-complying lower courts; upon review it will learn their actual decisions. Several results flow from this model. First, in general, some but not all lower courts will comply with supreme court doctrine; compliance, however, results from the threat of enforcement. Second, the game has a unique Bayesian equilibrium. Third, as the costs of enforcement rise, the supreme court may expand the range of acceptable lower court decisions.

4.2 Models of Adjudication Embedded in a Constitutional System

Many if not most cases on the appellate docket do not present common law issues; rather they raise issues of statutory or constitutional interpretation. The decisions of the courts thus rely on, and affect, the decisions of other political actors including administrative agencies, legislatures and the executive. Most applications of the political model to adjudication have concerned these institutional relations.

The two earliest applications to adjudication appear to be Ferejohn and Shipan (1990) and Gely and Spiller (1990). They adopt similar but not identical frameworks. Specifically, Ferejohn and Shipan assumed that all political actors had preferences over a one-dimensional policy space while Gely and Spiller assumed that institutional actors had preferences over a multi-dimensional policy space. I set out the Ferejohn and Shipan model here because of its simplicity and because most subsequent models exploit their formulation. Gely and Spiller (1990) is discussed in Section 5 in the context of its interesting model of doctrine.

Ferejohn and Shipan analyze the effects of judicial review on the activities of administrative agencies. In addition to the assumption of a one-dimensional policy space, their results depend critically on the sequence in which the institutions act. In their model, the agency acts first. It is then subject to judicial review. The court, in turn, is subject to potential legislative overrides. (They study both the case of overrides that require a presidential veto and those that do not.) They show that judicial review may shift the equilibrium policy towards the policy preferred by the legislature.

Eskridge and Ferejohn (1992a, 1992b) use the model in Ferejohn and Shipan to analyze the balance of powers in the US Constitution in general and the effect of *INS vs. Chadha*, on that balance of power. *Chadha* ruled that legislative vetoes of administrative action were unconstitutional. According to Eskridge and Ferejohn this ruling shifted power to the agencies; put differently, the decision made Congressional delegations of power to administrative agencies less desirable.

The literature employing variants of this political model have proliferated. For instance, Gely and Spiller (1992) present a three-stage game in which, in the first stage, an administrative agency announces an interpretation of a statute; in the second stage the court reviews the agency interpretation; and in the third stage the legislature decides whether to overrule the Supreme court and announce its own policy outcome. Note that in each stage the interpretation is an announcement of a policy. Each actor has spatial preferences over a one dimensional policy space. The model predicts that the court will always pick that policy that is best for it and just avoids legislative overruling. Gely and Spiller investigate several variants of this structure in which the legislature is modeled somewhat differently. They then test their model on data from the United States National Labor Relations Board and subsequent review.

Cohen and Spitzer (1994) apply this political model to the analysis of the effects of another Supreme Court decision, *Chevron U.S. A. Inc. v. Natural Resources Defense Council Inc*, which required courts to grant more deference to an administrative agency's own interpretation of statutes it implemented. They assume political actors have preferences over policy-deference pairs. They then show that the Supreme Court's rulings on deference respond to the relative pattern of policy preferences among the other institutional actors: president, congress, and the appellate court.

Toma (1991, 1996) has argued that the congressional budgetary process serves as a means to control the decisions of the Supreme Court by signaling approval or disapproval of the Court's behavior. Again, both justices and Congress have spatial preferences over policy space. She examines two times series of decisions of the Supreme Court of the United States: one consists of civil liberties cases decided from 1946 through 1988 and the other of economic liberties cases decided over the same time period. She determines the 'average degree of liberality' of each of these two yearly portfolios of decision and similarly takes the average ADA rating of the members of the judiciary subcommittee of the Senate and House appropriations committees. For each group of cases, she then regresses the size of the yearly Supreme Court budget on the divergence between the judicial and congressional liberality ratings; she finds a statistically significant pattern with the budget rising when Supreme Court opinions conform more closely to the views of Congress. She then regresses the liberality of the judicial portfolio against the Supreme Court budget, the parameter of which is also statistically significant.

4.3 Some Other Empirical Studies

There is a vast American political science literature that seeks to determine the effects of the 'ideological' views of the judges on judicial decisions. This literature in general implicitly accepts the political model of adjudication and it generally finds at least some influence of 'ideology' on outcome, where the judge's ideology is measured either by her political affiliation or the affiliation of the appointing president. In this section, I consider three recent studies within the legal-economic framework.

The first study, Eisenberg and Johnson (1991), examined 118 federal district court opinions and 66 federal circuit court opinions in racial discrimination cases decided under the fourteenth amendment to the US Constitution. These opinions constituted all opinions on this issue published between 7 June 1976 and 6 February 1988. Eisenberg and Johnson found no effect of ideology, measured either by party of judge or of appointing president, on outcomes at either the district or appellate level. They attempted to evaluate the effects of the selection of cases for trial on their results by comparing trial success rates and success rates on appeal in the class of cases that they studied to these success rates in other classes of cases.

Ashenfelter, Eisenberg and Schwab (1995) ('AES') also found no effects of ideology. In a clever research design, they studied 2258 federal civil rights and prisoner cases *filed* in three federal districts courts in fiscal 1981. Unlike most prior studies, AES examined the effects of ideology not only on cases with published opinions but on all case dispositions. AES determined whether a case settled and, if it did not settle, which party prevailed. They also collected data, including party and party of appointing president, on each of the 47 different judges who sat on some case in the sample. AES then analyzed this data by district. This district analysis permitted them to exploit the federal practice of random assignment of cases to judges. Any observed differences in behavior across judges could be attributed to differences in judges rather than differences in cases. They found that judges had relatively little effect on case disposition. Moreover, 'ideological' variables did not explain the small effects observed.

Revesz (1997) studied the industry and environmental challenges to EPA rulemaking in the 1970s and the late 1980s through early 1990s. This sample of cases has two features that make it a nearly ideal sample for analysis. First, all such challenges were heard in the Court of the Appeals for the District of Columbia. Second, virtually all challenges to EPA rulemaking are appealed. Given the legal context, there is no opportunity for the agency to settle with dissatisfied litigants. Following AES, Revesz focused on time periods in which a large number of judges had continuous tenure on the Circuit; he restricted his analysis to these judges. He measured the judge's policy preferences by the party of the appointing president, assuming that Republicans would favor industry challenges and disfavor environmental challenges relative to Democrats. For the late 1980s through early 1990s, he observed that ideology had a clear effect on industry challenges and a more ambiguous effect on environmental challenges. (A different statistical test, however, would likely reveal a stronger ideological effect in environmental challenges.)

5. Modeling Doctrine

Courts in common law systems do more than announce an outcome 'upheld' or 'reverse' to an appeal. An opinions offers a rationale for the decision and it is this rationale which guides the decisions of lower courts. To study appeal, then, the analyst must model this 'doctrinal' structure. The literature reveals two distinct approaches to modeling doctrine, approaches that have already been alluded to in the prior discussion. The importance of the issue, however, merits a brief exposition of the two approaches.

One approach, first set forth in Kornhauser (1992b), describes a case as a vector of fact characteristics. Kornhauser then defines a cause of action as a pair (**S**,**f**) where **S** is a class of subsets S of the fact space and **f** is a collection of functions f_S from each subset S into a two-element set that might be interpreted as (proven, unproven) or (for plaintiff, for defendant). Each S in **S** is an issue. A case is then a collection of causes of action. For plaintiff to prevail on a case, she must prevail on at least one cause of action; to prevail on a cause of action, the plaintiff must prevail on every issue. The approach models doctrine essentially in terms of a partition on the fact space and sees the development of the law in terms of changes in this partition. The approach has been followed in Kornhauser (1995), Cameron and Kornhauser (1996) and Cameron, Siegel, and Songer (1996).

The second approach, which adapts the framework of Ferejohn and Shipan and has been employed by Schwartz (1992), Cohen and Spitzer (1994) and McNollgast (1995), assumes that the Supreme Court has preferences over a two-dimensional space. One dimension remains the policy space in the original political model. The second dimension, variously called 'deference' or 'precedent', explicitly measures the judge's level of tolerance for deviation from her optimal policy choice. In one sense, this modeling strategy parallels that of the first approach; it also yields a partition of the policy space. More fundamentally, however, this second approach remains inherently 'political' and non-legal; it makes no reference to the facts of a case or features of legal discourse that appear in an opinion.

Gely and Spiller (1990) offer a variant of this political model of doctrine that acknowledges some of the structure captured in the legal model. In their model, justices (and other political actors) have preferences over a multidimensional policy space. They seek to explain the Court's choice of grounds - constitutional or non-constitutional - for the Court's review of agency action. They argue that a constitutional decision restricts the discretion of the agency (or of other political actors) by lowering the dimensionality of the policy space from which the agency may choose a policy. This ingenious idea captures the effect of doctrine without requiring that one model the legal attention to facts and explicit doctrinal structure.

In political models, 'doctrine' generally serves to explain the extent of discretion granted to lower courts (or administrative agencies). Thus, Cohen and Spitzer (1994) argue that the amount of discretion is a function of the ideological alignment of the Supreme Court relative to other political actors. McNollgast (1995) prove that, as the number of cases in a particular area increases, the amount of discretion granted lower courts never decreases and it may increase.

6. Collegiality

Generally, an appeal is decided by a panel of judges rather than a single judge. In the United States, the three judge panels that sit on federal intermediate appeals courts are drawn from a larger bank of judges while the nine justices of the Supreme Court sit en banc. The inverted pyramidal structure of the federal hierarchy in the United States in which the size of the panel deciding a case increases as the case rises through the system is a nearly universal feature of court systems. The highest courts in some civil law countries (for example, the Cour de Cassation in France), however, function similarly to the federal intermediate courts, with each case decided by a panel drawn from a larger bench.

Collegiality presents several puzzles. First, why are appellate courts collegial and why does the number of judges increase as one proceeds up the hierarchy? Second, what consequences for adjudication does collegiality have? The economic literature began with Easterbrook (1982) which addressed the second question.

6.1 Why Are Appellate Courts Collegial?

Posner (1985, p. 12) offered several reasons for the existence of collegiality on the Supreme Court: (a) multiple judges reduce the costs of poor appointments; (b) a multiplicity of judges reduces the power of any single judge on a court which has vast power; (c) a multiplicity of judges allows the court to benefit from deliberation; and (d) a multiplicity of judges permits the division of the labor of opinion drafting and hence increases the productivity of the court.

Kornhauser and Sager (1986) provided a more systematic analysis of the reasons for collegiality. First, they distinguished two conceptions of adjudication: the rendering of judgment and the expression of preferences. They then suggested three different models of collegial adjudication, each of which identified a distinct standard against which to measure judicial performance. (1) One might view collegial courts as engaged in the aggregation of the preferences of the judges on the court and one would measure the quality of the court by its *authenticity*, the extent to which the court's judgment correctly reflects the preferences of the judges. (2) One might view collegial courts as engaged in the aggregation of judgments and one would evaluate the court's procedures in terms of their *accuracy*, that is, their ability to 'get the right answer' however one defines the right outcome. (3) One might view collegial courts as representative institutions that seek to reach the outcome that the represented body would have reached had they deliberated and voted. This representative model suggests two different evaluative measures: *fit*, which is simply the tendency to arrive at results that the represented group would have reached and *reliability*, which is the absence of bad surprises.

Kornhauser and Sager reject preference aggregation as an appropriate understanding of adjudication. This eliminates authenticity as an evaluative measure. They then argue that increasing the numbers of judges improves accuracy, fit and reliability. They focus specifically on accuracy and rely on the Condorcet Jury Theorem.

Good and Tullock (1984) offers a representation model of Supreme court collegiality. The Justices of the Supreme Court are treated as a representative sample of the population of competent lawyers. Good and Tullock calculate the probability $p(r,s)$ that a case decided by a vote of r to s will fit the decision of the represented group. They determine that $p(5,4) = 0.62304$ and $p(9,0) = 0.99902$.

6.2 Consistency and Coherence

In the first model of collegiality, Easterbrook (1982) relied on simple social choice arguments to argue that one could not expect the Supreme Court of the United States to generate a consistent body of case law. Easterbrook assumed that each case presented the Court with a choice between two legal rules to govern a particular doctrinal realm. When more than two legal rules were possible and no rule was a Condorcet winner, the Court's case law would cycle as successive cases challenged the prevailing rule with an alternative that a majority of the Court preferred.

Kornhauser and Sager (1986) distinguished between *consistent* and *coherent* patterns of decisions. A court that decides cases consistently will decide identical cases identically. The definition of coherence was less clear; a court that decides coherently creates a body of law that exhibits the quality of conceptual unity. They then argued that a panel of judges, each of whom had a consistent view of the law would produce a consistent body of law; but a panel of judges, each of whom had a coherent conception of the law, need not yield a coherent body of decisions.

Kornhauser (1992a) extended this analysis. Kornhauser identified three different bases of judicial decision: result-bound, rule-bound, and reason-bound decision. In a result-bound decision process, the court is obligated to respect the results of the prior decisions of the court; in a rule-bound process the court is obligated to respect the rule announced in prior cases while a reason bound court respects the reasons provided in prior decisions. He then argued that, with a rule of strict stare decisis, law in a result-bound judicial system will generally be path dependent and consistent.

Stearns (1995) offered an analysis of the development of the law in a collegial court that contained elements of both Easterbrook's and Kornhauser and Sager's analysis. Stearns, like Easterbrook, viewed adjudication as rule-bound though he abandoned Easterbrook's assumption that a case presented only two rules. Stearns, however, emphasized the role of both *stare decisis* and standing doctrine in ameliorating any cycling problems.

6.3 Voting on Collegial Courts

The doctrinal paradox Kornhauser and Sager (1986) noted a paradoxical feature of collegial adjudication which later attracted extensive comment. Specifically, they considered a case that presented two distinct issues for decision. Legal doctrine determines the relation between the decisions on each issue and the decision on the case. In some circumstances, the procedure the court adopts for aggregating votes will determine the outcome of the case. They discussed two procedures: *case-by-case* adjudication in which each judge registers her view of how the *case* should be decided and the court aggregates these votes to reach a majority judgment. Alternatively, each judge may register her view on each *issue* in the case should be decided; the court then aggregates the votes on each issue and applies the legal doctrine to the issue-by-issue results to reach a judgment in the case.

Kornhauser (1992b) named this conflict 'the doctrinal paradox' and extended this analysis in several ways. Recall the formalization of doctrine in this article that was summarized in Section 5. A single judge decides a case by deciding each legal issue in each cause of action. To prevail on a cause of action, the plaintiff must prevail on each issue; to prevail in the case, she must prevail on at least one cause of action. On a multi-member court, the two different aggregation methods may lead to different results. Kornhauser showed that the doctrinal paradox was distinct from the Condorcet cycle. When the judges' orderings of outcomes (described as the vector of outcomes on each issue) yield a Condorcet cycle issue-by-issue and case-by-case voting might not conflict. Conversely, when the judges' orderings produced a Condorcet winner over outcomes, the issue-by-issue result might differ from the case-by-case result. Finally, he analyzed several actual instances in which the doctrinal paradox arose.

Rogers (1991) examined and classified all plurality opinions of the United States Supreme Court. He counted approximately 150 such cases. Of these he identified only eight cases in which the vote of one or two justices effectively resulted in a court aggregation of votes on an issue-by-issue, rather than a case-by-case, basis. He argued further that the limited doctirnal incoherence of case-by-case aggregation was normatively preferable to the inconsistency and indeterminacy that may result from issue-by-issue adjudication. Leonard (1984) found a similar paucity of instances of issue-by-issue aggregation in a study of decisions in criminal cases by the highest courts of Alabama, California, Indiana, and New York. Rogers based his argument for case-by-case voting on the grounds that issue-by-issue adjudication may lead to unfair results.

Post and Salop (1992) argued that collegial courts should always aggregate votes issue-by-issue. They did so on several grounds. First, they disputed the unfairness of case-by-case aggregation. Second, they argued that case-by-case aggregation led to path-dependent decision making; framed more positively, they argued that an aggregation procedure should yield the same results regardless of the order in which cases arrive before the court. Third, issue-by-issue aggregation promotes collegial deliberation by inducing the judges to join issue. Post and Salop (1996) expand and clarify their argument in favor of issue-by-issue voting. They note that issue-by-issue voting clarifies the law more quickly than case-by-case voting. Kornhauser and Sager (1993) then extended their earlier analysis of the doctrinal paradox. They emphasized the peculiar nature of actual Supreme Court practice which permitted each judge to count votes as he wished and which suppressed discussion of the aggregation procedure. they argued that the Court should justify its decision on whether to resolve case issue-by-issue or case-by-case because the appropriate decision procedure was context-dependent.

Rogers (1996), Stearns (1996) and Post and Salop (1996) then recapitulated the debate over the appropriate aggregation method. Rogers noted importantly that issue-by-issue voting required the Court to identify a set of issues on which each judge should vote and illustrated the complexity of this task. Stearns (1996) argues that in fact agreement on issues is not as difficult as Rogers suggests. Post and Salop (1996) also argue that the identification of issues is less problematic than Rogers asserts.

Sincere vs. sophisticated voting Analysis of the doctrinal paradox assumed that each judge voted 'sincerely' on each issue regardless of the method of aggregation of the votes on the court. (Defining 'sincerity' in the context of multiple issue cases presents difficulties that are addressed in a different voting context in Benoit and Kornhauser (1995).) An assumption of sincerity comports well with a team model; it does not easily fit into a political model. In a political model, a self-interested, rational judge should foresee the results of sincere votes that might be detrimental to the realization of her interests.

Spiller and Spitzer (1995) ask whether judges are voting sincerely or with sophistication. They assume a court with one sincere judge and show how that judge can be manipulated by sophisticated judges. In their model, the judges and the legislature play a two-stage game. In stage 1, the Court interprets a statute and in stage 2, the legislature decides whether to overrule the court's interpretation. All judges and legislators have preferences over a one-dimensional policy space. The model predicts that (1) the legislature will frequently overrule the court and (2) coalitions of extremes will often form. They then contend that, as these phenomena are not observed, one should assume that all judges vote with sophistication.

Revesz (1997), in his study of environmental decisions by the DC circuit, tested for effects of panel composition on the voting behavior of individual judges. In particular, he asked whether the reversal rate of a judge depended on whether she was in the minority or a majority on the panel. He identified judicial policy preferences with the party of the appointing president and found substantial differences between the voting behavior of judges in an ideological minority on a panel from those in an ideological majority.

Schwartz (1992) does not explicitly address the question of sincere vs. sophisticated voting. He does, however, present a political model of 'doctrine' in which each justice acts in a strategic manner. As discussed in Section 4, 'doctrine' here refers to a feature of vertical precedent: the probability that a lower court will respect the Supreme Court's policy announcement in the case. Thus, in this model, justices have preferences over a two-dimensional space. Each justice has an ideal policy; the second dimension measures the degree of precedent that the justice attaches to the policy. The justice's preferences are for less strict precedent the more distant the announced policy is from his ideal policy.

Each case presents the Court with a choice between two policy alternatives. The sequence of the game is as follows. First, the justices vote in reverse order of seniority for one of the two policy alternatives. Second, the senior member of the majority designates an opinion writer who voted for that alternative; the senior member of the minority also designates an opinion writer. Third, each opinion writer drafts an opinion that specifies a level of precedent for the proposed policy. In the fourth stage, the Justices vote between the two policy/precedent pairs represented by the two opinions. The majority vote determines the outcome.

Schwartz restricts his analysis to the case in which the Court initially divides five to four between the two policy alternatives. He calculates the range of precedent that is invulnerable to invasion by the minority. The senior member of the majority can then pick an opinion writer that will draft an opinion with the optimal level of precedent from the senior members point of view. Schwartz then illustrates his analysis through a discussion of some reapportionment cases.

7. Discretionary Review

The United States Supreme Court has a largely discretionary jurisdiction. This discretion cannot be explained in a team model of error correction when litigants select which cases to appeal, for, as Cameron and Kornhauser (1996) show, the optimal hierarchy will have only three tiers and the highest tier will hear no cases. Discretionary review, however, might be explained in a team model in which the Supreme Court has lawmaking powers.

Cameron, Siegal and Songer ('CSS') (1996) use a political model to study the Supreme court's certiorari procedure. They assume that the Supreme Court serves only to correct error. As is typical in political models, both higher and lower courts have preferences over a one-dimensional policy space. As in

Cameron and Kornhauser (1996), each case is characterized by a single parameter and each court is characterized by an ideal point so that defendant should prevail if the value of the case parameter is less than the court's ideal point. For ease of exposition, CSS assume that the ideal point of the Supreme court lies to the right of the lower court's ideal point. Consequently, the two courts disagree about the appropriate resolution of the case if its parameter lies in the interval between the two ideal points. The Supreme court has discretionary authority to review but it decides to review the lower court decision on the basis of an index of the parameter rather than the true value which is both known to the lower court and would be revealed to the Supreme Court in the course of a review on the merits. Each court wants to maximize the number of correct decisions (from its point of view); lower courts get disutility from reversal and the Supreme court incurs cost in the event it decides to review a case on the merits. CSS characterize the equilibrium strategies of both lower court and Supreme court. They then present an exploratory analysis of Supreme Court certiorari practice in search and seizure cases between 1972 and 1986.

Discretionary review in the US Supreme Court employs a submajority rule of four of the nine justices to trigger review. This submajority review raises interesting legal and strategic questions concerning the behavior of the Justices themselves. Revesz and Karlan (1988) presented a largely legal analysis of this rule (and a 'Rule of Three' governing the granting of stays) but their analysis raises a number of issues for economic analysis. They argue that the rule of four creates a legal process with less stable precedent than a process in which discretionary review required a majority.

8. Stare Decisis

Stare decisis refers to a set of practices peculiar to Anglo-American courts in which one court adheres to its own prior decisions or to the decisions of a higher court. For a fuller discussion of the legal aspect of these practices, references to the legal literature and the modeling questions they present, see Kornhauser (1998).

Several models of horizontal and vertical stare decisis have appeared in the literature. In this section, I shall focus primarily on models of horizontal stare decisis in which a court follows its own prior decisions. Discussions of vertical stare decisis are implicit or explicit in most political models of hierarchy because these models pose as one of the key questions the extent to which lower courts comply with the rulings of higher courts. Vertical stare decisis in a team model is discussed in both Kornhauser (1995) and Cameron and Kornhauser (1996). Kornhauser (1995) argues that vertical stare decisis arises because of the benefits presented by specialization of labor between fact finding and law making and for error-correction reasons. Cameron and Kornhauser (1996) investigates the error-correction justification in detail.

Heiner (1986) argues that stare decisis arises because courts only observe the 'correct' answer to specific cases with error. A judge might then do better to announce a decision that is best 'on average' (for some class of cases) and adhere to that decision rather than to make a series of errors on a case-by-case basis.

Kornhauser (1989) characterized horizontal stare decisis as a practice in which a court adheres to a decision it believes to be wrong. He offers two informal models based on two distinct justifications for the practice. The first model applies to a 'panel court' in which each case is decided by one or more judges drawn from a larger bench. If judges have different views of the law then stare decisis serves to reduce legal uncertainty faced by actors governed by the legal rule. The second model assumes a unitary court with an unchanging social objective; the court however faces a world in which the optimal behavior (as viewed from its perspective) changes because some underlying parameters change. Kornhauser's model modifies that in Blume and Rubinfeld (1982) in which the court, through its announcement of standards of care, seeks to minimize the costs of accidents and the costs of adjustment to new standards. In the Blume and Rubinfeld model, the court does not adopt a practice of stare decisis; rather, as the technology of care shifts, the court adjusts gradually towards the standards that would be optimal in an unchanging world with the new technology. In Kornhauser's version, a court must announce standards of care in a world in which the technology of accident care is improving at a known rate. The court adheres to stare decisis as long as the standards of care optimal under the new technology are not too far from the old standards. Otherwise it announces new standards that overshoot those currently optimal.

Rasmusen (1994) presents a political model for horizontal stare decisis. Rasmusen's model provides a formal justification for an argument implicit in O'Hara (1993). The court consists of a single judge who decides $n + 1$ cases and is then replaced by another judge who also decides $n + 1$ cases. Each judge has preferences over the outcomes of all cases and these preferences differ. Assume that only one of these $n + 1$ cases is a case of first impression. Under a practice of stare decisis each judge would adhere to the n prior decisions governing n of his cases and n subsequent judges would adhere to the decision he announces in his case of first impression. Rasmusen shows that a practice of stare decisis is an equilibrium to this game.

9. Concluding Remarks

The study of judicial organization in general and the nature and function of appeal in particular is in its infancy. Though analysts have begun to investigate the reasons for hierarchy, the nature of the interaction among courts and other political branches, and the internal workings of the courts themselves, most questions remain open or even unaddressed.

Bibliography on Appeal and Supreme Courts (7200)

Ashenfelter, Orley, Eisenberg, Theodore and Schwab, Stewart J. (1995), 'Politics and the Judiciary: The Influence of Judicial Background on Case Outcomes', **24** *Journal of Legal Studies*, 257-282.

Blume, Larry and Rubinfeld, Daniel (1982), 'The Dynamics of the Legal Process', **11** *Journal of Legal Studies*, 405 ff.

Cameron, Charles M. (1993), *New Avenues for Modeling Judicial Politics*, University of Rochester Wallis Institute of Political Economy Working Paper.

Cameron, Charles and Kornhauser, Lewis A. (1996), 'Litigant Selection and the Structure of Judicial Hierarch', mimeo, August.

Cameron, Charles M., Siegal, Jeffrey A. and Songer, Donald R. (1996), 'Signals and Indices in the Supreme Court's Certiorari Decisions', mimeo.

Cohen, Linda and Spitzer, Matthew (1994), 'Solving the *Chevron* Puzzle', **57** *Law and Contemporary Problems*, 65 ff.

Dorf, Michael C. (1995), 'Prediction and the Rule of Law', **42** *U.C.L.A. Law Review*, 651 ff.

Easterbrook, Frank (1982), 'Ways of Criticizing the Court', **95** *Harvard Law Review*, 802-832.

Eisenberg, Theodore and Johnson, Sheila Lynn (1991), 'The effects of Intent: Do We Know How Legal Standards Work?', **76** *Cornell Law Review*, 1151 ff.

Epstein, Richard A. (1987), 'Judicial Review: Reckoning on Two Kinds of Error', in Dorn, James A. and Manne, Henry G. (eds), *Economic Liberties and the Judiciary*, Fairfax, George Mason University Press, 39-46.

Eskridge, William N. and Ferejohn, John (1992a), 'The Article I, Section 7 Game', **80** *Georgetown Law Journal*, 523-564.

Eskridge, William N. and Ferejohn, John (1992b), 'Making the Deal Stick: Enforcing the Original Constitutional Structure of Lawmaking in the Modern Regulatory State', **8** *Journal of Law Economics and Organization*, 165-189.

Ferejohn, John and Shipan, Charles (1990), 'Congressional Influence on Bureaucracy', **6** *Journal of Law Economics and Organization*, 1-20 (Special Issue).

Gely, Rafael and Spiller, Pablo T. (1990), 'A Rational Choice Theory of Supreme Court Statutory Decisions with Applications to the *State Farm* and *Grove City* Cases', **6** *Journal of Law, Economics and Organization*, 263-300.

Gely, Rafael and Spiller, Pablo T. (1992), 'The Political Economy of Supreme Court Constitutional Decisions: The Case of Roosevelt's Court Packing Plan', **12**

International Review of Law and Economics, 45-67.

Good, I.J. and Tullock, Gordon (1984), 'Judicial Errors and a Proposal for Reform', **13** *Journal of Legal Studies*, 289-298.

Heiner, Ronald (1986), 'Imperfect Decisions and the Law: On the Evolution of Legal Precedent and Rules', **15** *Journal of Legal Studies*, 227 ff.

Koppen, P.J. van (1990), 'Cassatieadvocaten en de Selectiekamer (Cassation Lawyers and the Chamber of Selection)', *Nederlands Juristen Blad*, 14-26.

Kornhauser, Lewis A. (1989), 'An Economic Perspective on Stare Decisis', **65** *Chicago-Kent Law Review*, 63 ff.

Kornhauser, Lewis A. (1992a), 'Modeling Collegial Courts I: Path Dependence', **12** *International Review of Law and Economics*; 169-85.

Kornhauser, Lewis A. (1992b), 'Modeling Collegial Courts. II. Legal Doctrine', **8** *Journal of Law, Economics and Organization*, 441-70.

Kornhauser, Lewis A. (1995), 'Adjudication by a Resource-Constrained Team: Hierarchy and Precedent in a Judicial System', **68** *Southern California Law Review*, 1605 ff.

Kornhauser, Lewis A. (1998), 'Stare Decisis', in Newman, Peter (ed.), *New Palgrave Dictionary of Economics and the Law*, London, MacMillan.

Kornhauser, Lewis A. and Sager, Lawrence G. (1986), 'Unpacking the Court', **96** *Yale Law Journal*, 82-117.

Kornhauser, Lewis A. and Sager, Lawrence (1993), 'The One and the Many: Adjudication in Collegial Courts', **81** *California Law Review*, 1 ff.

Leonard, David P. (1984), 'The Correctness Function of Appelate Decision-making: Judicial Obligation in an Era of Fragmentation', **17** *Loyola of Los Angeles Law Review*, 299-352.

McNollgast (1995), 'Politics and the Courts: A Positive Theory of Judicial Doctrine and the Rule of Law', **68** *Southern California Law Review*, 1631-1683.

O'Hara, Erin (1993), 'Social Constraint on Implicit Collision?: Towards a Gane Recretic Analysis of Stern Decisis', **24** *Seton Hall Law Review*, 734 ff.

Posner, Richard A. (1982), 'Toward an Economic Theory of Federal Jurisdiction', **6** *Harvard Journal of Law & Public Policy*, 41-50.

Posner, Richard A. (1985), *The Federal Courts: Crisis and Reform*, Cambridge, Harvard University Press, 365 ff.

Post, David and Salop, Steven (1992), 'Rowing Against the Tidewater: A Theory of Voting by Multi Judge Panels', **80** *Georgetown Law Journal*, 743 ff.

Post, David and Salop, Steven (1996), 'Issues and Outcomes, Guidance, and Indeterminacy: A Reply to Professor John Rogers and Others', **49** *Vanderbilt Law Review*, 1049-1085.

Rasmusen, Eric (1994), 'Judicial Legitimacy as a Repeated Game', **10** *Journal of Law Economics and Organization*, 63-83.

Revesz, Richard L. (1997), 'Environmental Regulation, Ideology, and the D.C. Circuit', **83** *Virginia Law Review*.

Revesz, Richard L. and Karlan, Pamela (1988), 'Non Majority Rules and the Supreme Court', **136** *University of Pennsylvania Law Review*, 1067 ff.

Rogers, John M. (1991), '"I Vote This Way Because I'm Wrong": The Supreme Court Justice as Epimenides', **79** *Kentucky Law Journal*, 439-475.

Rogers, John M. (1995), 'Lower Court Application of the "Overruling Law" of Higher Courts', **1** *Legal Theory*, 179 ff.

Rogers, John (1996), '"Issue Voting" by Multi Member Appellate Courts: A Response to Some Radical Proposals', **49** *Vanderbilt Law Review*, 997-1039.

Schwartz, Edward P. (1992), 'Policy, Precedent, and Power: A Positive Theory of Supreme Court Decision Making', **8(2)** *Journal of Law, Economics and Organization*, 219-52.

Shavell, Steven (1995), 'The Appeals Process as a Means of Error Correction', **24(2)** *Journal of Legal Studies*', 379-426.

Spiller, Pablo and Spitzer, Matthew (1992), 'Judicial Choice of Legal Doctrines', **8** *Journal of Law, Economics and Organization*, 846 ff.

Spiller, Pablo and Spitzer, Matthew (1995), 'Where is the Sine in Sincere? Sophisticated Manipulation of Sincere Judicial Voters (With Applications to Other Voting Environments)', **11** *Journal of Law, Economics, and Organization,* 32-63.

Stearns, Maxwell (1995), 'Standing Back from the Forest: Justiciability and Social Choice', **83** *California Law Review*, 1309-1413.

Stearns, Maxwell (1996), 'How Outcome Voting Promotes Principled Issue Identification: A Reply to Professor John Rogers and Others', **49** *Vanderbilt Law Review*, 1045-1067.

Stith, Kate (1990), 'The Risk of Legal Error in Criminal Cases: Some Consequences of the Asymmetry in the Right to Appeal', **57** *University of Chicago Law Review*, 1-61.

Toma, Eugenia (1991), 'Congressional Influence and the Supreme Court: The Budget as a Signaling Device', **20** *Journal of Legal Studies*, 131-146.

Toma, Eugenia (1996), 'A Contractual Model of the Voting Behavior of the Supreme Court: The Role of the Chief Justice', **16** *International Review of Law and Economics,* 433-447.

Other References

Benoit, Jean-Pierre and Kornhauser, Lewis A. (1995), 'Assembly-Based Preferences, Candidate-Based Procedures, and the Voting Rights Act', **68** *Southern California Law Review,* 1503 ff.

Cases

INS vs. Chadha, 462 U.S. 919 (1983)

Chevron U.S.A. Inc. v. Natural Resources Defense Council Inc, 467 U.S. 837 (1984)

7300
INDEMNITY OF LEGAL FEES

Avery Wiener Katz
Georgetown University

Abstract

This chapter surveys the effects of legal fee shifting on a variety of decisions arising before and during the litigation process. Section 2 provides a brief survey of the practical situations in which legal fee shifting does and does not arise. Section 3 analyzes the effects of indemnification on the incentives to expend resources in litigated cases. Section 4 examines how indemnification influences the decisions to bring and to defend against suit, and Section 5 assesses its effects on the choice between settlement and trial. Section 6 addresses the interaction between the allocation of legal fees and the parties' incentives for efficient primary behavior. Section 7 considers two important variants on simple indemnification: rules that shift costs based on the parties' settlement negotiations (such as US Federal Rule 68 and the English practice of payment into court), and rules that shift costs based on the margin of victory (such as US Federal Rule 11 and the common law tort of malicious prosecution). Section 8 reviews the brief but instructive empirical literature on legal cost shifting, and Section 9 summarizes the discussion and offers conclusions.
JEL classification: K40, K41
Keywords: Litigation, Legal Costs, Legal Fees, Legal Fee Shifting

1. Introduction

In most Western legal systems, a party who prevails in litigation is generally entitled to indemnification from the losing party for at least part of his or her economic costs of prosecuting the lawsuit. The amount of litigation expenditures that can be recovered, however, varies substantially both among and within individual regimes. In the United States, the predominant rule awards a prevailing litigant what are officially termed 'costs' - typically defined by statute to include filing fees, court reporter charges, printing, copying, and witness fees, and the like - but does not entitle him or her to recover expenditures on attorneys' fees, which are of far greater magnitude in the usual case. Consequently, US litigants can bear significant expense even when they are ultimately vindicated on the merits. In the other common-law countries, in contrast, and indeed in most of the rest of the Western world, winning litigants are entitled to recover attorneys' fees as well as other out-of-pocket costs of litigation. As a result, they come closer to being made whole than do winning litigants in the US.

The substantial increase in expenditures on litigation and dispute resolution in the United States in recent years has led both policymakers and scholars to advocate a variety of substantive and procedural reforms in the legal system. The rules for allocating attorneys' fees in civil litigation have drawn particular attention in this regard, with a number of influential commentators recommending a move in the direction of fuller indemnification - or what in the US is usually called, for historical reasons, the 'English' or 'British' rule. Such recommendations have begun to have influence on both public and private lawmakers; indeed, one of the more prominent and widely supported provisions in the Republican Party's 1994 'Contract with America' platform would have adopted a modified form of the English rule for federal cases brought under the diversity jurisdiction. But the political debate over litigation costs in the US does not seem to have assimilated the main lesson of the economic literature on the topic - that the effects of cost shifting on the amount and intensity of litigation are substantially more complicated than a superficial consideration of the matter might suggest. Indeed, the current state of economic knowledge does not enable us reliably to predict whether a move to fuller indemnification would raise or lower the total costs of litigation, let alone whether it would better align those costs with any social benefits they might generate.

The reason for this agnostic conclusion is straightforward. Legal costs influence all aspects of the litigation process, from the decision to file suit to the choice between settlement and trial to the question whether to take precautions against a dispute in the first place (for a survey of such effects, see Cooter and Rubinfeld, 1989). Furthermore, as Shavell (1982b) has shown, an individual litigant's incentives to bring suit in a costly legal system do not generally conform to the social optimum; and the divergence between private and social incentives to sue are complex. A plaintiff's decision to sue imposes an obvious cost on the defendant and on the taxpayers who foot the bill for public legal institutions. Less obviously, it affects litigants in other cases by crowding the courts, by delaying the resolution of other disputes in the system, and, through informational externalities, by altering the expected costs of settlement. It also affects future litigants by increasing the stock of legal precedent, and potential litigants (as well as those who never intend to resort to the courts at all) by influencing the perceived likelihood of sanctions for violating substantive legal duties. Similarly, the decisions to pursue a lawsuit to trial rather than settling, and to litigate more rather than less intensively, generate analogous external costs and benefits. The combination of all these external effects are too complicated to be remedied by a simple rule of 'loser pays'. Instead, indemnity of legal fees remedies some externalities while failing to address and even exacerbating others.

This chapter, accordingly, surveys the effects of legal fee shifting on a variety of decisions arising before and during the litigation process. Section 2 provides a brief survey of the practical situations in which legal fee shifting does and does not arise. Section 3 analyzes the effects of indemnification on the incentives to expend resources in litigated cases. Section 4 examines how indemnification influences the decisions to bring and to defend against suit, and Section 5 assesses its effects on the choice between settlement and trial. Section 6 addresses the interaction between the allocation of legal fees and the parties' incentives for efficient primary behavior. Section 7 considers two important variants on simple indemnification: rules that shift costs based on the parties' settlement negotiations (such as US Federal Rule 68 and the English practice of payment into court), and rules that shift costs based on the margin of victory (such as US Federal Rule 11 and the common-law tort of malicious prosecution). Section 8 reviews the brief but instructive empirical literature on legal cost shifting, and Section 9 summarizes the discussion and offers conclusions.

(N.B.: The scholarly literature on fee shifting has flourished in recent years, to the point where it is no longer feasible to discuss every pertinent contribution. For recent surveys of work in the area, see Cooter and Rubinfeld (1989), Anderson (1996), and the symposia appearing in *Law and Contemporary Problems* (1984) and *Chicago-Kent Law Review* (1996) respectively.)

2. The Practical Extent of Legal Fee Shifting

This chapter does not attempt to survey the law governing fee shifting, either in the US or elsewhere. For such surveys, see Pfennigstorf (1984), Note (1984), or Tomkins and Willging (1986). It should be recognized, however, that there are significant areas of US legal practice that do not follow the traditional American rule. Most important among these are the various federal and state statutes that entitle a successful plaintiff, though not a successful defendant, to court-awarded attorneys' fees as part of a recovery. Similar 'one-way' fee-shifting policies have also been established in both federal and state courts through a combination of statutory interpretation and common law development, though the scope for such interpretations at the federal level was substantially limited by the Supreme Court in *Alyeska Pipeline Service Co. v. Wilderness Society*. Such provisions and policies, which make up a central part of litigation practice in such fields as civil rights, consumer, and antitrust law, have only some of the effects of the traditional two-way English rule. Second, both federal and state courts have authority to award indemnification to parties who are victimized by abuse of process, though such authority is typically exercised only in response to egregious behavior. Examples include the provisions in Fed. R. Civ. Proc. 11 dealing with frivolous or improper pleadings, and those in Fed. R. Civ. Proc. 37 relating to discovery abuse. US practice also provides litigants with an 'offer-of-judgment' procedure under which a defendant can make a settlement offer to the plaintiff which, if rejected and filed with the court, creates a trigger for partial indemnification. Both of these specialized types of provisions - sanctions for abuse and offers of judgment - are discussed separately in Section 7 below.

Conversely, even in jurisdictions following the majority or 'English' rule, indemnification for legal costs is substantially less than complete. Court-awarded attorneys' fees obviously do not compensate for the nonmonetary and psychic costs of litigation. Even the monetary amounts awarded, furthermore, are limited by the judge's view of what expenditures are reasonable and, in some jurisdictions (for example, British Columbia), by statutory schedule. Such judicial and statutory caps can and often do hold fee awards below the going market rate for legal representation, forcing winning litigants to pay the difference out of anticipated recoveries or their own pockets (indeed, Leubsdorf, 1984, presents evidence that such court-imposed price ceilings were responsible for the historical development of the American rule in the first place). Accordingly, the pure English and American rules discussed below should be understood as ideal polar cases, and the differences among actual jurisdictional practices as ones of degree along a spectrum ranging from lesser to greater indemnification .

Additionally, Donohue (1991b) points out that the American rule is a default rule rather than a mandatory one, in that parties are generally free to provide for indemnification through private contract - either at the time they begin their litigation or, for those disputes arising out of a consensual relationship, in their original agreement. He presents anecdotal evidence that such *ex ante* indemnification terms are widespread, though the provisions he cites seem primarily to be drawn from standardized form contracts and tend to operate asymmetrically in favor of the drafting party: for instance, apartment leases that indemnify landlords but not tenants for attorneys' fees in the event of a dispute over unpaid rent. The scope for fee shifting in the US, therefore, may be significantly greater than is ordinarily supposed. Conversely, there is no apparent bar in England or in the other jurisdictions following the English rule to a partial settlement or stipulation in which the litigants agree in advance to give up their rights to indemnification *ex post*. Donohue's further conjectures that such contractual terms are likely to be efficiency-enhancing and that the pattern of such terms will help reveal whether the English or American rule is more efficient, however, are more problematic. To the extent that indemnification is provided by a one-sided standardized term, there is no guarantee that it promotes the joint interests of the parties. The nondrafting party may fail to notice the indemnification provision at all; and if he does notice it, he may avoid raising it as an issue for fear of revealing himself as someone who anticipates a dispute. Even when such agreements arise out of arms-length bargaining, furthermore, this does not imply that they are efficient. As Bernstein (1993) and Shavell (1995) have observed in their respective analyses of alternative dispute resolution, because of the divergence of private and social incentives in litigation, the fact that a particular agreement is in the litigants' *ex post* interest does not necessarily mean that it is socially efficient. The fact that the parties have come to litigation in the first place, moreover, casts doubt on the presumption that they are bargaining in a Coasian fashion.

3. The Effect of Fee Shifting on Trial and Pretrial Expenditures

The standard economic theory of litigation, as developed by Landes (1971), Posner (1973) and Gould (1973), models litigating parties as rational actors who seek to maximize their returns from the litigation process. From this perspective, amounts spent on trial preparation can be seen as a type of private investment. An additional hour of legal research or argumentation is profitable, in this view, only if the marginal return, measured by the change in the expected outcome of trial or settlement, outweighs the cost of the attorney's time. Plaintiffs, accordingly, will choose to spend legal resources up to the point where their expected recoveries, net of expenses, are maximized; defendants will act so as to minimize total payouts. The precise outcome of this contest depends on how the parties react and adjust to each others' decisions. One simple and natural assumption is that the litigants reach a Nash equilibrium in expenditure; that is, that each takes the other's expenditure as given when choosing his own. Whatever the nature of the parties' strategic interaction, however, the parties' expenditures are determined in equilibrium by a host of economic and technological factors including the stakes of the case, the marginal cost of legal resources, and the sensitivity of trial outcomes to the parties' individual efforts. In high-stakes cases in which the outcome is heavily dependent on the parties' work product, expenditures will be high; in petty cases where the outcome is largely predetermined by legal precedent, expenditures will be low.

As Braeutigam, Owen and Panzar (1984) first proved and Katz (1987) subsequently explained, it follows from the standard model that fee shifting encourages greater expenditure in litigated cases. The reasons are twofold.

First, fee shifting increases the stakes of the case by making legal expenditures part of the potential damages. Second, it lowers the expected marginal cost of legal expenditure. Each party, when deciding whether to purchase an additional unit of legal services, will discount its cost by the probability with which she expects to win and to be reimbursed by her opponent. More formally: if we let p denote the probability of liability, A the amount awarded if the plaintiff wins, and x and y the amounts spent by the plaintiff and defendant respectively, then under the American rule a plaintiff will expect to recover $p(x, y)\ A(x, y) - x$. Assuming risk-neutrality for the sake of simplicity, it follows she will choose x to satisfy the first-order condition, $p_x A + pA_x = 1$. The defendant, conversely, expects to pay out $pA + y$, and will select y to satisfy his first-order-condition, $p_y A + pA_y = -1$. Under the English rule, in contrast, the plaintiff's expected recovery is $pA - (1 - p)(x + y)$; so her first-order-condition is $p_x(A + x + y) + pA_x = 1 - p$. Similarly, the defendant's expected payout is $p(A + x + y)$, and his first-order-condition is $p_y(A + x + y) + pA_y = -p$. In all of these equations, the left-hand side represents the marginal private benefit of expenditure, and the right-hand side its marginal cost. Inspection of the equations reveals that the marginal private cost of legal expenditure is lower for both parties under the English rule. If the parties' expenditure affects the probability of liability (that is, if p_x and p_y are positive), the marginal private benefit is also higher; if expenditure affects the amount awarded rather than the probability of liability, marginal benefit is unchanged. Other things being equal, therefore, the English rule makes expenditure more attractive.

It should be noted that the marginal-cost effect depends not on the actual probability of liability, but on its perceived probability. It follows that the increase in expenditure under the English rule will be greater the more optimistic are the litigants. In the extreme, parties who regard themselves as very likely to win will perceive litigation as virtually costless and will increase their expenditures accordingly. To the extent that such efforts increase the probability of prevailing, therefore, such optimism will be partially self-fulfilling. Similarly, in other than even cases, the marginal-cost effect will be stronger for the party with the stronger probability of prevailing *ex ante*. For instance, if both parties regard the initial probability of liability as 90 percent, the plaintiff will discount the expected marginal cost of legal services to 10¢ on the dollar while the defendant discounts it only to 90¢. The stimulus to the plaintiff's expenditure will accordingly be ten times greater than the stimulus to the defendant's. Fee shifting, accordingly, reinforces the advantages of the party who is initially favored in litigation.

Because of the interaction between the parties' expenditure decisions, it is not possible to prove that both sides will increase their expenditures under the English rule. The reason for this ambiguity is that a marginal increase in one side's expenditure has an ambiguous effect on the other's; it could either provoke the opponent to respond in kind, or intimidate him into reducing his own efforts. Braeutigam, Owen and Panzar, however, showed that in Nash equilibrium the sum of the parties' expenditures must increase. The extent of the increase depends on how sensitive p and A are to litigation expenditure, as Plott (1987) has demonstrated. Using a Nash equilibrium model and making some simplifying technical assumptions regarding functional form, he found that if the case outcome depends entirely on factors out of the litigants' control, the English rule has no effect on expenditure. If case outcome is determined solely by their efforts, conversely, the English rule will cause expenditure to increase without limit.

Such effects are mitigated in regimes that limit the amount of fees that can be shifted. For example, under both English and US practice, indemnification is limited to reasonable expenditures. Similarly, some recent US proposals provide that a losing party need not pay any indemnification in excess of his or her own litigation costs. Both of these variations reduce the private benefits of legal expenditure relative to the pure English rule; and as Hughes and Woglom (1996) show, the latter actually operates as a tax on the weaker party's expenditure, since increases in his spending raise the cap on the indemnification potentially payable to his opponent.

Furthermore, while most of the economic literature on litigation expenditure has assumed a Nash equilibrium, a few authors (for example, Hersch, 1990) have argued that it is not reasonable to expect litigants to ignore the effect on the other side's expenditure when choosing their own. The Nash specification is most appealing when expenditure is simultaneous, when each side must choose how much to spend before learning the opponent's decision, or when the expenditure decision is largely determined by one's initial choice of an attorney; it is least appealing when one side can commit to a given level of expenditure and communicate that commitment to the opponent in advance. One can analyze the latter situation using the more general model of conjectural variations - so-called because it allows a party's decision to depend upon his conjectures regarding how the opponent's decision varies with his own. Formally, let v_x denote the rate at which the plaintiff expects the defendant to respond to her expenditures. This rate could be positive (in which case expenditure would be provocative), negative (in which case expenditure would be intimidating), or zero (as in the Nash model). The plaintiff's first-order condition then becomes $(p_x + v_x p_y)A + p(A_x + v_x A_y) = 1$ under the American rule, and $(p_x + v_x p_y)(A + x + y) + p(A_x + v_x A_y) = (1 - p)(1 + v_x)$ under the English rule. (The analysis for the defendant is symmetric and is omitted for the sake of brevity.) Comparing the first term of each equations, one can see that the stakes effect is still present. The direction of the marginal-cost effect, however, is now ambiguous. Under the English rule, an additional dollar spent on legal services will cost the plaintiff only $1 - p$, after she discounts for the probability of prevailing. But if the plaintiff loses, she will also have to pay the defendant's costs, and the additional dollar induces him to change his expenditures by v_x. If the plaintiff's expenditure is intimidating, this will lower her marginal cost even further. If her expenditure is sufficiently provocative, however, her marginal cost of legal resources will rise; if it is provocative enough to outweigh the stakes effect, her equilibrium expenditure will fall.

It is difficult to judge the empirical importance of the conjectural-variations model. Katz (1988) has shown that in the typical case one party is in a provocative position and the other in an intimidating one. In particular situations, however, expenditure may be very provocative. One such context may be civil discovery, the process through which US litigants are permitted to request information from their adversaries before trial. Expenditures on discovery have risen substantially in recent decades, and it has been widely alleged that much of this increase is an abuse of the system, encouraging both frivolous suits and unfair settlements. The underlying problem, however, may simply be one of incentives. As Cooter and Rubinfeld (1994, 1995) and Cooper (1994) explain, a party seeking discovery can under current American practice impose significant costs on her adversary at relatively low cost to herself - for instance, by issuing a formulaic though burdensome list of interrogatories and document requests, or by resisting requests that could be complied with cheaply. For such types of expenditure, the conjectural variation v_x is very large; fee shifting, accordingly, may substantially deter 'abusive' behavior of this sort.

The analysis in this section has focused on the amount of resources expended in litigated cases. Total expenditures on litigation, however, are the product of two factors: expenditures per litigated case, and the number of cases that are actually litigated. Fee shifting can influence the number of litigated cases in two ways: by influencing the decision to bring the dispute to court in the first place, and by influencing the parties' incentive to settle cases before trial. The next section of this article discusses the former effect, and Section 5 discusses the latter.

4. Effects of Fee Shifting on the Decisions to File and Contest Lawsuits

Consider the case of a consumer who has purchased a defective ballpoint pen and who is in theory entitled to a refund. Because the value of the pen is exceeded by even the most streamlined judicial proceeding, the consumer's threat to litigate is not credible; and absent procedural devices such as a class action that can allow aggregation of her claim with others, she will be forced to rely on nonlegal incentives such as the seller's interest in its reputation for goodwill. If the consumer can recover legal fees along with the value of her refund, however, her threat to sue becomes credible. Shavell (1982a), extending the work of Landes (1971) and Gould (1973) on the incentives to sue, generalized this argument to show that the English rule, and indemnification in general, works to encourage lawsuits by plaintiffs with relatively small claims but relatively high *ex ante* probabilities of victory. The American rule, conversely, encourages plaintiffs with relatively large claims but lower probabilities of victory.

The formal logic of the argument is as follows: let p represent the probability of a plaintiff victory, A the expected award if the plaintiff wins, and c the cost of litigation for each litigant. (To simplify the argument, suppose that this cost is the same for both sides; this will affect the specific point at which the incentives switch, but not the basic intuition of the argument.) Under the American rule, litigation is profitable if (and only if) $pA > c$; thus, a plaintiff will bring suit if she views her chances as better than the threshold probability p_{US} c/A. Under the English rule, however, the plaintiff's expected litigation cost is not c but $(1 - p)2c$, since she pays no costs if she wins but $2c$ if she loses. She will accordingly wish to litigate if $pA > (1 - p)2c$, or equivalently, if she views her chances at better than $p_{ENG} 2c/(A + 2c)$. Algebraic manipulation reveals that $c > A/2$ implies $p_{US} > p_{ENG} > ½$, and $c<A/2$ implies $p_{US} < p_{ENG} < ½$. Thus, when costs are high or stakes low, the English rule encourages some better-than-average suits that would be deterred under the American rule; when costs are low or stakes high, the English discourages some worse-than-average suits that would be brought under the American rule.

An identical line of argument shows the effect of indemnification on the incentives to defend against a lawsuit once it has been brought. If it costs the defendant c to put up a defense that will succeed with probability p, it is worthwhile to defend (rather than suffer a default) only if the expected savings pA exceed the expected costs of litigation. Under the American rule these expected costs are c, and under the English rule they are $(1 - p)2c$. The logic is as before; the American rule encourages long-shot defenses in high-stakes and low-cost cases, while the English rule encourages high-probability defenses in high-cost and low-stakes cases.

Such arguments lend support to the frequently expressed view that the English rule is superior on grounds of corrective justice, since the claims and defenses that it promotes are relatively meritorious ones - at least when viewed from an *ex ante* perspective. Similarly, as Rosenberg and Shavell (1985) have shown, indemnification can help discourage certain frivolous or 'strike' suits, by emboldening defendants to put forward costly defenses against them (assuming that the frivolous nature of the suit is common knowledge; as Katz (1990) argues, the English rule may do little to discourage strike suits that cannot be identified as such without a trial).

But there is a cost to this ostensible increase in justice. The claim and defenses encouraged by the English rule are low-stakes and high-cost - that is, expensive to try relative to their importance. The claims and defenses encouraged by the American rule may be relative longshots on the merits, but they are relatively cheap to resolve. Moreover, some suits, including those brought to test or clarify the law or to settle matters of principle, may be socially desirable notwithstanding a low *ex ante* probability of success. Accordingly, legal policy in this area may present a tradeoff between justice and more narrow conceptions of efficiency.

Any conclusions regarding the effect of litigation fee shifting on incentives to sue must also take account of the litigants' expected response to risk. As has been widely recognized, the English rule magnifies the private risk arising from litigation by increasing both the returns from success and the losses from defeat. Thus, it tends to discourage risk-averse parties from bringing or defending lawsuits, regardless of the merits of their positions - a factor that has been stressed by partisans of the American rule. What has been less well recognized, however, is that this same increase in variance can encourage more litigation by the risk-neutral. The reason is that most lawsuits are divided into a series of procedural stages, at each of which it is possible to decide whether to continue depending on how the case is going. Because of this flexibility, as Cornell (1990) has shown, the decision to litigate can be interpreted as the purchase of an option. Just as financial options can sell for a positive price even if the probability of exercising them is low, the option value of litigation can make it profitable to put forward claims with negative expected value. Because the value of an option increases with its variance, the English rule, by increasing both the upside and the downside of litigation, intensifies this incentive. Indeed, if parties can drop arguments before trial without penalty, such enhanced option value could increase litigation even by the risk-averse.

Additionally, as the previous section indicated, the English rule indirectly alters incentives to sue through its effects on the expected cost of the individual case. Because indemnification encourages parties to litigate their disputes more intensively, it increases the expected cost of bringing and defending suits *ex ante*. This will deter parties on the margin of litigation from pursuing their cases, whether they are on the margin because of low stakes, high cost, or low probability. This effect is essentially analogous to a tax on litigation; as both Bowles (1987) and Hause (1989) have observed, to the extent it is empirically significant it could outweigh the effects described above. Unless such increased expenditures improve the quality of judicial decision making, however, they must be counted as a disadvantage of the

English rule. Even if it is deemed desirable to deter litigation by raising its private cost, it is plainly more efficient to do so with an excise tax, which merely transfers wealth from litigants to the public fisc, than by wasting real resources. The same objection applies to any policy of deterring litigation through increased risk, which constitutes a real loss for those on whom it is imposed.

5. Effects of Fee Shifting on the Settlement of Litigation

Because the great majority of civil cases are settled rather than tried, and because trial substantially increases the cost of disputes, effects on settlement are a critical factor in any comparison of the English and American rules. As a result, the economic literature on fee shifting has focused on this issue more than any other. The conventional wisdom among practicing attorneys appears to be that a shift toward fuller indemnification would encourage settlement. The conclusions of the scholarly literature, however, cannot be said to offer strong support for this proposition; at best the effects are ambiguous.

As a first approximation, fee shifting magnifies the effect of litigants' optimism, making them less likely to settle. As Landes (1971) and Gould (1973) observed, since litigation is a negative-sum game *ex post*, parties who accurately assess their chances of victory have a strong collective incentive to avoid the costs of trial. Indeed, in a world of purely Coasian bargaining, there would be no trials at all, since full sharing of information would eliminate any differences of opinion. Because of random variations in information, judgment and temperament, however, some fraction of litigants will inevitably overassess their chances; and it is these optimistic litigants who have an incentive to go to trial. Pessimistic or unbiased parties, in contrast, would prefer to settle. But the degree of optimism necessary for a trial to result depends on how litigation costs are allocated, as the following argument (suggested by Mause, 1969, and formally demonstrated by Shavell, 1982a) shows: under the American rule, a plaintiff who perceives the probability of liability as p_P, her stakes as A_P, and her costs as c_P will insist on receiving a settlement of no less than $S_P\ p_P\ A_P - c_P$. Similarly, a defendant who perceives the probability of liability as p_D, his stakes as A_D, and his costs as c_D will be willing to pay no more than $S_D\ p_D\ A_D + c_D$. Settlement is thus possible if (and only if) $S_P < S_D$, or equivalently, if the total litigation costs, $c_P + c_D$, exceed the difference between the parties' reservation settlement values, $p_P\ A_P - p_D\ A_D$. Parties whose litigation costs are below this cutoff level, conversely, will prefer to go to trial. Under the English rule, however, the plaintiff's reservation settlement value becomes $S_P\ p_P\ A_P - (1 - p_P)(c_P + c_D)$, and the defendant's becomes $S_D\, p_D\, (A_D + c_P + c_D)$. Now settlement is possible only if $c_P + c_D > (p_P\, A_P - p_D\, A_D)/(1 - p_P + p_D)$. If the plaintiff's probability estimate p_P exceeds the defendant's probability estimate p_D, the parties' reservation prices will diverge, making settlements less likely.

The economic intuition underlying this result is that indemnification internalizes one externality while creating another. Under the English rule, a litigant is forced to take into account the other side's litigation costs to the extent that she risks losing the case, making her more willing to settle. But conversely, she is freed of her own litigation costs to the extent that she hopes to win, making her less likely to settle. Since litigants are disproportionately drawn from the population of optimists (else they would settle however costs are allocated), the latter effect tends to outweigh the former. Indeed, in the limiting case when both parties are fully confident of winning, neither expects to pay any costs at all and settlement is impossible. This line of argument, however, suggests an important exception to the basic result: in some cases, parties might choose to litigate due to a difference of opinion not over liability but over stakes. A plaintiff who regarded the stakes as sufficiently higher than did the defendant - for example, because she hoped to establish a favorable precedent that could be drawn on in later cases - might refuse all settlements even if the parties agreed on the probability of liability or were both relatively pessimistic. If the parties' relative optimism about the stakes were enough to outweigh their relative pessimism about probability, fee shifting would encourage settlement and discourage trial.

The Landes-Gould model of settlement bargaining (often called the 'optimism model' in subsequent literature) is open to the criticism that it is not rigorously grounded in the modern theory of imperfect information games. In particular, it does not explain how the parties can maintain their inconsistent perceptions of the case in the face of negotiation; and its conclusion that nonoptimistic parties will always settle ignores the possibility of strategic behavior and depends on the assumption of collective rather than individual rationality. Accordingly, subsequent writers have often preferred to base their analyses on an alternative bargaining model based on Bayesian inference and on the assumption of rational expectations. In this model, due to Harsanyi and Selten (1972) and introduced into the law and economics literature by Cooter, Marks and Mnookin (1982), trials are caused not by optimism but by uncertainty over the opponent's reservation settlement value. The logic is that parties uncertain of their opponents' bottom line will find it individually rational to balance the probability of settlement against its terms - making offers that more combative opponents will reject, in order to improve the return from settlements with those who are more conciliatory, Whether cases settle, therefore, depends on a number of factors, including the stakes, the cost of litigation and, most importantly, the extent of uncertainty between the parties. A high variance of reservation settlement values means that taking a marginally tougher position sacrifices fewer bargains - lowering the opportunity cost of hard bargaining. More uncertainty thus means less settlement.

Despite their differences from the optimism model, however, Bayesian models of settlement (see, for example, Bebchuk, 1984; Reinganum and Wilde, 1986; Talley, 1996) tend to confirm its conclusion that the English rule tends to discourage settlement in disputes revolving around liability, though not in disputes revolving around stakes. The reason is that indemnification magnifies uncertainty in the former set of cases but not in the latter. More precisely, uncertainty about opponents' reservation values can stem from numerous sources: variations in the private cost and stakes of litigation, in attitudes toward risk and delay, and in private information relevant to the trial outcome. Differences in risk aversion, time preference and stakes are not affected by fee shifting, but differences in private cost and in information relevant to liability are. Fee shifting thus increases the difference between the reservation values of parties with favorable private information and high litigation costs on one hand, and parties with unfavorable information and low litigation costs on the other. This increase in uncertainty leads all types of parties to toughen their overall bargaining positions, lowering the probability of settlement. Ironically, as Polinsky and Rubinfeld (1997) point out, this implies that the English rule actually lowers the average quality of tried cases, since the marginal parties it sends to trial have relatively less favorable private information than those who would litigate absent the prospect of indemnification.

The foregoing discussion of both optimism and Bayesian models, however, has assumed risk neutrality and has taken the cost of litigation as given. As the previous sections have observed, indemnification both increases the risks of litigation and raises litigation costs generally. Both effects tend to encourage settlement, thus mitigating and perhaps counteracting the effects of optimism and asymmetric information. Whether indemnification increases or decreases settlement on balance, accordingly, depends on the relative magnitude of competing factors, and cannot be settled theoretically.

Even if fee shifting does not alter the probability of settlement, however, it can still influence its amount. As Cooter and Rubinfeld (1994) have argued in the context of legal discovery and Bebchuk and Chang (1996) have argued in the context of offers of judgment, fee shifting can, by equalizing the bargaining power of parties with asymmetric litigation costs, help to move the settlement amount closer to the expected trial outcome. To the extent that trial outcomes are deemed to be just, fee shifting thus may help promote equity;

to the extent that trial outcomes reflect substantive legal norms, fee shifting helps promote incentives for proper primary behavior - a subject more fully explored in the following section.

6. Effects of Fee Shifting on Substantive Behavior

The discussion thus far is in a fundamental sense incomplete, since it has focused largely on the procedural costs of litigation. If such costs were one's only concern, of course, they could be eliminated entirely by abolishing the legal system and all publicly enforceable rights to relief. A central purpose of having a public system of courts, however, is to redress wrongs and to encourage compliance with primary substantive norms such as taking precautions against accidents and keeping one's promises. Indemnity of legal fees, accordingly, must ultimately be judged on these latter criteria - or more accurately, on whether it increases the social value of substantive enforcement net of process costs.

Viewed from this perspective, the English rule initially appears attractive, since it tends to encourage high probability suits and discourage low probability ones. Assuming that the probability of liability is correlated with the actual violation of substantive norms, therefore, indemnification increases the net expected punishment for such violations and thus helps promote substantive compliance. This is easily seen in the case where courts' liability determinations are error-free, as Rose-Ackerman and Geistfeld (1987) and Polinsky and Rubinfeld (1988) have shown. Consider a potential tortfeasor who can take precautions against an accident that will cause an uncertain amount of damage. Suppose that the possible damage ranges from zero to A, and that the cost of establishing liability following an accident is c. Under the American rule, it follows that the tortfeasor will have inadequate incentives for precaution. In the event that damages turn out to be less than c, the victim will not sue, so the tortfeasor will escape responsibility for a portion of the damages caused. Under the English rule, however, the victim will always have the incentive to sue, so that all accident costs will be fully internalized. Under a rule of negligence as opposed to strict liability, indeed, complete cost internalization can be achieved without incurring any litigation costs at all: defendants will be induced to take optimal care by the threat of litigation, so plaintiffs will never actually have to sue. Conversely, under the American rule, defendants may rationally decide to take excess care - or to abstain from risky though optimal activities - in order to avoid the greater expense of having to defend their behavior in court. Indemnification protects them from such expenses, thus preventing overdeterrence.

This happy outcome, however, depends on the assumption that deserving plaintiffs and defendants always win their cases. In the presence of legal error, as P'ng (1987) and Polinsky and Shavell (1989) have shown, neither the American nor the English rule provides incentives that are first-best optimal. Optimal incentives, rather, require at least two separate policy instruments - one to motivate efficient substantive behavior, and another to promote an efficient amount of litigation. Polinsky and Che (1991) demonstrate that, in general, this means decoupling the amounts paid by losing defendants from those received by victorious plaintiffs. (Indeed, as Polinsky and Rubinfeld (1996) show, decoupling is generally necessary even to achieve the lesser goal of minimizing the litigation costs associated with achieving a given level of deterrence.) Devices combining fines, punitive damages and taxes (positive or negative) on litigation accomplish such decoupling, but the English rule, which merely re-allocates costs between the parties in zero-sum fashion, does not. Furthermore, it is not even the case that the English rule is second-best efficient within the category of zero-sum policy instruments. Kaplow (1993) shows that damage multipliers, such as the treble damage provisions of US antitrust law, provide a cheaper method of achieving any given amount of deterrence. The reason is that damage multipliers provide incentives for private law enforcement to be undertaken by those plaintiffs whose litigation costs are lowest; fee shifting, in contrast, encourages plaintiffs to bring lawsuits without regard to their costs of litigation.

One might still ask whether the English rule does better than the American in promoting efficient substantive behavior, notwithstanding the potential availability of alternatives that are superior to both. The answer to this question, however, is ambiguous, as Gravelle (1993), Hylton (1993a, 1993b), and Beckner and Katz (1995) demonstrate in independent formal models. It is possible to draw generalizations regarding when the English rule improves matters, but they depend on the subtle interaction of a number of factors, including whether substantive precaution affects the magnitude of injury or just its probability, the extent to which precaution affects the probability of liability, whether damage awards are sufficient to compensate plaintiffs for their losses, and whether defendants have the opportunity to act strategically by taking just enough care to foreclose litigation. Hylton, for instance, concludes that a one-way fee-shifting rule operating in favor of plaintiffs would be best, but this conclusion depends upon several features of his model (including, perhaps most importantly, the assumption that plaintiff's care does not affect the expected cost of accidents). Applying such generalizations to individual cases or categories of cases is probably beyond the capacity of either courts or legislatures. As Gravelle concludes, '[i]t seems more promising to pursue other, more direct means of correcting the inefficient incentives for care provided by a costly and imperfect legal system'.

7. Variations on Simple Fee Shifting

The foregoing discussion has been premised on the assumption that 'costs follow the event' - that is, that any fee shifting that takes place is based solely on who wins the case. Much recent discussion in policy and scholarly circles, however, has focused on two more complicated forms of indemnification.

7.1 Fee Shifting Conditioned on Offers Made in Settlement

Both England and a number of American jurisdictions provide a mechanism through which a defendant who would otherwise be obliged to pay for legal expenses can partially avoid the obligation by making a suitable offer of settlement. In England this procedure is called 'payment into court' and requires the defendant actually to deposit funds with a court officer; while in the United States, Federal Rule of Civil Procedure 68 and similar court rules merely require the formal filing of what is labeled an 'offer of judgment'. Under either provision, a defendant who makes such a formal offer is considered the prevailing party for purposes of cost allocation if the plaintiff rejects the offer and then is subsequently awarded a lesser amount at trial. In such an event, the defendant avoids having to pay any costs incurred by the plaintiff subsequent to the offer, and is entitled to indemnification for his own subsequent costs as well. By all accounts, defendants avail themselves of this procedure much more frequently in England than in the US - probably because the prospect of shifting liability for 'costs' is likelier under the broader English definition of the term to outweigh the disadvantages of making a settlement offer. Similarly, within the US, Rule 68 appears to be used more widely in disputes covered by one-way pro-plaintiff fee-shifting statutes such as Title VII, since the Supreme Court held in *Marek v. Chesny*, that attorney's fees shifted under such statutes are to be considered 'costs' under Rule 68.

Because of the relatively infrequent use of Rule 68 in US courts, a number of American critics have in recent years supported its expansion - either by extending its coverage to attorneys' fees generally, or by making the procedure available to plaintiffs as well as defendants. (It should be noted, however, that providing the procedure to plaintiffs is meaningless to the extent that they are already entitled to collect costs when they prevail; in such circumstances, the opportunity to make an offer of judgment can only advantage defendants.) The recent GOP 'Contract with America', for example, would have established just such a generalized offer-of-judgment rule in federal diversity cases. Such proposals have commonly been supported by the claim that they will reduce expenditures on litigation by encouraging parties to make more reasonable settlement offers and to accept such offers when they are made. Their proponents have also argued that it is fairer to charge the costs of trial to the party who, by refusing a reasonable settlement, causes those costs to be incurred.

In general, the economic literature on offers of judgment is substantially less developed than that on pure indemnification; and many interesting questions remain to be fully investigated, including the effect of the procedure on strategic behavior in negotiations. The place to begin any analysis of the offer of judgment, however, is with the observation that it is essentially an option to convert disputes over damages into disputes over liability. To see this, compare two cases: one in which it is clear that the defendant has acted negligently but unclear whether the plaintiff's injuries are 1000 or 3000 (with the two possibilities being equally likely), and a second in which it is clear that damages are 4000, but an even gamble whether the defendant is liable at all. In both cases, expected damages are 2000, but absent an offer-of-judgment procedure the plaintiff's position is stronger in the former. She is certain to prevail at trial and to recover some fraction of her costs, even if it is only court fees. In the latter case, she runs the risk of paying both her costs and a portion of the defendant's. Under Rule 68 or a similar procedure, however, the defendant can convert the former dispute into a partial settlement of 1000 combined with a dispute over whether the defendant is liable for an additional 2000. In this converted dispute, the defendant stands an even chance of avoiding liability for the plaintiff's costs and of recovering his own. This improves his expected position to what it would be in the case of pure liability, at the plaintiff's expense.

The example illustrates two lessons. First, a rule authorizing defendants but not plaintiffs to make offers of judgment redistributes wealth from plaintiffs to defendants in disputes that are entirely or partly over damages, as both Priest (1982) and Miller (1986) have suggested. Second, such offers have no effect in disputes that are purely over liability. If the only possible trial outcomes are verdicts of zero or 4000, for instance, there is no advantage to the defendant in making a Rule 68 offer of less than the full 4000. If he offers a lesser amount, he will be liable for costs in the event of a plaintiff's verdict and certain to receive costs in the event of a defendant's verdict - just as he would if he made no offer at all. Similarly, a less-than-full offer does not affect the possible payoffs for the plaintiff. The defendant could of course offer to settle for the full 4000, but the plaintiff should be happy to accept such an offer whether or not Rule 68 is in force. The offer-of-judgment procedure, accordingly, cannot affect whether an offer is made or accepted in such cases.

With these points taken as caveats, the effects of offer-of-judgment rules are roughly analogous to those of indemnification in general. The possibility that costs will be shifted following a settlement offer both raises the stakes of the case and lowers the perceived marginal cost of legal expenditure, thus increasing incentives to expend resources at trial. The effect is less than under the pure English rule, however, since only post-offer expenditures are liable to be shifted. Similarly, the opportunity to make an offer of judgment increases expected payoffs for plaintiffs who expect to win large awards at trial, and lowers expected payouts of defendants who expect awards to be low, emboldening such parties to pursue litigation.

The effect of offers of judgment on the settlement decision depends, like the effect of indemnification generally, on the parties' attitudes toward risk and on the model of settlement that one thinks appropriate. Under the Landes-Posner-Gould optimism model, offers of judgment tends to lower the chances of settlement between risk-neutral parties, since, as Priest (1982) suggests and Miller (1986) and Chung (1996) confirm, such offers lower the reservation values of optimistic defendants more than they do those of optimistic plaintiffs, thus reducing the potential settlement range. Offers of judgment also increase the risk of litigation, though not as much as pure indemnification does; this encourages risk-averse parties to settle, but risk-preferring parties to litigate. Anderson (1994), who extends the optimism model to include the possibility of bargaining stalemate, reaches similar results. Within Bayesian models of settlement, the outcome appears more complicated. Cooter, Marks and Mnookin (1982) conjecture that an offer-of-judgment rule, by effectively taxing hard offers and subsidizing soft ones, should encourage settlement. Spier (1994), however, in a model in which defendants make offers to plaintiffs with private information, finds that the procedure leads to more settlement than the pure American rule in cases where the plaintiff's private information relates solely to the size of the award, less settlement than the American rule in cases where the plaintiff's private information relates solely to the probability of liability, and an ambiguous effect in other cases. She also demonstrates a similar result using a mechanism-design model that, instead of specifying any particular bargaining process, assumes that the parties use a Pareto-efficient trading mechanism in the style of Myerson and Satterthwaite (1983). As with pure indemnification, accordingly, the effect of offers of judgment on settlement probabilities appears to depend on the sources of the underlying dispute.

7.2 Fee Shifting Conditioned on the Margin of Victory

In the United States, a variety of statutory and judicially created rules allow courts to award partial or full indemnification in lawsuits in which the losing party's case is deemed after the fact to be of sufficiently low merit. Such rules include the common-law torts of barratry, abuse of process, and malicious prosecution, the traditional authority of courts of equity to exercise their discretion in the interests of justice, the sanctions for discovery abuse provided by Federal Rule of Civil Procedure 37, and the (just amended) provisions of the Internal Revenue Code requiring the government to pay a taxpayer's reasonable litigation costs upon a court finding that the government's position in a tax dispute was substantially unjustified. Similarly, as Pfennigstorf (1984) reports, indemnification awards in most other Western legal systems are likely to be more generous in cases where the loser's legal or factual position appears weak.

The possibility of tying indemnification to the merits of the losing case has attracted increased attention in recent years, in part as a response to the growth of litigation practice under US Federal Rule of Civil Procedure 11. This rule requires persons filing court papers to warrant that their filings are well grounded, and authorizes courts to impose monetary sanctions on parties whose filings are found to be frivolous, harassing, or made for purposes of delay. Limiting fee shifting to cases of particularly low merit has seemed to many commentators an attractive compromise between the English and American rules, since it protects clearly deserving litigants without imposing unnecessary risk on those who bring colorable claims in good faith.

As Bebchuk and Chang (1996) have pointed out, the effect of policies such as Rule 11 is to condition fee shifting on the winner's margin of victory; those who win in a rout receive indemnification, while those who win narrowly do not. They confirm the conventional wisdom in a formal model, showing that such policies, if designed properly, can do a better job than either the English or the American rule at encouraging meritorious suits (and by analogy, defenses) and discouraging frivolous ones. The reason is that such policies make use of the parties' private *ex ante* information regarding the merits of the case. A party who loses by a large margin is less likely to have believed *ex ante* that her case had merit; conversely, one who wins by a large margin is less likely to have believed that her case lacked merit. While the optimal fee shifting rule depends on the distribution of judicial and litigant error, it is possible by altering the threshold for fee shifting to regulate the proportion of potential claims and defenses that are actually brought into the system. Because its effects are zero-sum, however, margin-based fee shifting is still less efficient than policies that decouple one side's payments from the other side's recovery (see generally Polinsky and Rubinfeld, 1993). Policies that tax or subsidize individual parties based on the *ex post* quality of their case may be best of all; they may also, of course, be the most difficult to administer.

While other incentive effects of margin-based fee shifting have not been formally explored, it appears likely that it has analogous consequences to indemnification generally, though in lesser degree. These consequences recapitulate the discussion in earlier sections of this article and can be surveyed in brief. First, to the extent that such policies succeed in encouraging meritorious claims and defenses and discouraging frivolous ones, they will tend to improve incentives for primary substantive behavior. The complications described in Section 6 above, however, remain to be analyzed. It is possible, for instance, that the prospect of shifting litigation costs to the other side following a commanding victory will induce excessive caretaking *ex ante*, though the benefits of doing so are less than under the pure English rule.

Second, margin-based fee shifting will both raise the stakes of litigation and decrease its expected marginal cost, inducing the parties to intensify their efforts at trial. Schmalbeck and Myers (1986) argue that this effect will be relatively minor, since in a truly frivolous case there is little that the parties can do to change the outcome. Their argument is open to question, however, as the substantial amount of litigation effort under Rule 11 illustrates (see, for example, Kobayashi and Parker, 1993, who discuss the incentive effects of recent amendments intended to reduce such 'satellite' litigation). While margin-based indemnification has little effect on cases that are clearly contestable or clearly frivolous, in many disputes the colorability of the losing case is less obvious. Parties in such intermediate cases, thus, will have an incentive to increase their expenditures in order to influence the size of the margin of victory.

Third, margin-based fee shifting will decrease the likelihood of settlement to the extent that the parties have a difference of opinion regarding the chances of indemnification. Optimistic parties will exaggerate the likelihood that they will win by a large margin and underestimate the likelihood that they will lose by a large margin. The prospect of indemnification will cause such parties to toughen their settlement demands, reducing the range for settlement. Since pessimistic and unbiased parties will have an incentive to settle in any event, the net consequence will be an increase in trials. Similarly, given private information regarding the probability of a one-sided outcome, margin-based fee shifting will increase the variance of the parties' reservation settlement values, encouraging tougher bargaining and hence fewer settlements. The increased risk of trial, however, works to counteract such effects for risk-averse litigants.

In sum, however, the case for at least some margin-based fee shifting appears stronger than the case for indemnification generally, on grounds of both fairness and efficiency. Parties who lose lawsuits decisively are probably more deserving of sanction than those who lose barely. The social value of litigation is probably higher in close cases, whether measured by the public benefits of legal precedent or by more libertarian considerations. And margin-based fee shifting seems to do a better job at providing improved incentives for primary behavior, and has lower costs in terms of incentives for increased expenditure at trial. In light of the relatively limited theoretical and empirical work on this particular topic, however, these conclusions must be regarded as tentative.

8. Empirical Evidence on the Effects of Fee Shifting

Given the complexity and ambiguity of the aforementioned considerations, it would plainly be desirable to have some hard empirical evidence to bring to the policy debate. Unfortunately, such evidence is sparse. Critics of the American rule commonly point to the larger numbers of disputes and higher expenditures on litigation in the US to support their case for reform. But such a crude comparison does not seem especially fruitful in light of the many other significant features that distinguish the American legal system from its counterparts in other Western countries, including economic and demographic factors, differences in substantive rights, procedural practice, the structure of courts and the legal profession, the availability of other financing arrangements such as the contingent fee and prepaid legal services, a high degree of rights-consciousness among individual citizens, and the absence of a comprehensive program of social insurance that would help to channel demands for compensatory relief away from the private legal system.

The proper question to ask, therefore, is what effect fee shifting has on litigation expenditures and primary behavior, holding constant other features of the legal environment. But again, answers to this question are hard to come by. Although the US legal system contains a number of pockets of indemnification, these examples have for the most part escaped systematic quantitative inquiry. The evidence on fee shifting, rather, falls into three categories: laboratory research on bargaining behavior by experimental subjects, numerical simulations of litigation behavior based on empirically obtained parameters, and econometric evidence primarily drawn from a single policy experiment: Florida's experience with the English rule in medical malpractice cases from 1980 through 1985.

8.1 Laboratory Experiments

Coursey and Stanley (1988) tested the effects of fee shifting within an experimental setting they designed to simulate the process of bargaining under threat of trial. They divided their subjects (students at the University of Wyoming) into pairs and instructed them to attempt to divide between themselves a number of tokens that were subsequently convertible into cash. If time expired before the subjects reached agreement, the tokens were divided through a random drawing, intended to represent an uncertain court award. To simulate rational expectations, the subjects were presented with the probability distribution of awards arising from the random drawing, and to simulate the costs of trial, the subjects were collectively fined an amount equaling 40 percent of the total value of the tokens in the event the drawing had to take place.

The experimenters conducted negotiations using three different cost allocation rules. Under the simplest procedure, the fine was divided between the two parties equally, in an intended simulation of the American rule. A second group of subjects negotiated under a rule whereby the fine was paid entirely by the party who received the smaller portion of the token in a random drawing; this was intended to simulate the English rule. Yet a third group negotiated under an offer-of-judgment rule intended to simulate Rule 68: the plaintiff paid the entire fine if the draw awarded her an amount less than or equal to the defendant's last proposal; and the fine was otherwise split equally.

The result of this experiment were that subjects settled more frequently under the English than under the American rule. Under Rule 68 settlement was likeliest of all; and in addition the plaintiff was much more likely to be the accepting party. The authors also found that settlements were more favorable to the defendant under Rule 68 than under the English rule, consistent with the theoretical predictions outlined in the previous section. The American rule was most favorable of all for the defendant, though the authors ascribed this result to the behavior of one especially risk-averse individual. These findings are consistent with theoretical models that predict increased settlement on the basis of simple risk aversion. Because the experimental design ruled out the possibility of optimism or private information, however, its results cannot be extrapolated to situations in which such phenomena, which could cause the English rule to reduce settlement, are present.

In a separate series of survey experiments, Rowe and various co-authors studied the effects of cost allocation rules on lawyers' and law students' responses to a variety of bargaining situations presented by hypothetical tort and civil rights cases. While this experimental design suffered from the weakness that the subjects were not provided with any direct financial incentives, the more realistic nature of the problems and the subjects' professional status and experience provided at least some motivation to bargain seriously. The results of the experiments, however, were mixed. Rowe and Vidmar (1988) found that there was little difference between the American rule and a modified Rule 68 (enhanced to cover attorneys' fees and to allow plaintiffs as well as defendants to make offers) on law students' willingness to accept offers of settlement, although they did find an effect on the size of counteroffers as well as a difference in plaintiff acceptance rates between modified Rule 68 and a one-way pro-plaintiff rule. Anderson and Rowe (1996) replicated this experiment with practicing lawyers, also examining the subjects' behavior under an alternative fee shifting rule in which the maker of a rejected offer had to pay the rejecting party's subsequent reasonable attorneys' fees. They found that while modified Rule 68 did not appreciably affect plaintiffs' minimum asks relative to the American rule, it did raise the maximum amounts that defendants were willing to offer. Finally, Rowe and Anderson (1996) considered the effects of a modified Rule 68 on hypothetical bargaining in civil rights cases otherwise governed by a pro-plaintiff rule. They found that replacing this one-way rule with an enhanced Rule 68 significantly lowered plaintiffs' minimum asks, as well as the gap between plaintiff asks and defendant offers. In all, these results suggest that fee shifting has its strongest effect when it is one-sided and when the favored side is risk averse or liquidity constrained.

8.2 Simulations

A number of authors have attempted to estimate the quantitative effects of fee shifting by numerically simulating the behavior of theoretical models. Katz's (1987) approach is illustrative. He developed algebraic formulas, based on a linear approximation to the standard model of litigation expenditure, that relate the difference in expenditure per case between the English and American rules to two empirical parameters: the ratio of total expenditure to the stakes of the case, and the elasticity with which parties increase their expenditures in response to higher stakes. Using empirical estimates of these parameters taken from the University of Wisconsin's Civil Litigation Research Project (Trubek et al. 1983), he calculated the likely effects of switching from the American to the English rule, concluding that such a switch would increase expenditures per case in the neighborhood of 125 percent.

Such a large increase in cost per case, however, could be expected to lead to a reduction in the number of cases or to increased settlement. In an attempt to measure this anticipated reduction, Hause (1989) extended the Landes-Gould optimism model to allow for variable expenditure, and calculated its numerical behavior for a range of possible parameter values. He concluded that the increased costs per case under the English rule were sufficient to outweigh any effects of optimism, resulting on balance in an increased frequency of settlement. Hersch (1990) recalculated Hause's simulations under the assumption that trial expenditure is determined in a conjectural-variations rather than a Nash equilibrium. He found that both settlement and costs per case rose, though by a lesser amount than Hause had estimated. The parameter values Hause and Hersch used, however, were not based on any empirical data. Donohue (1991a) recalculated Hause's simulations using what he argued were more plausible parameter estimates, and concluded that the English rule would increase trials on balance.

Finally, Hylton (1993a, 1993b) used numerical simulation to estimate the effects of fee shifting on primary behavior. He concludes that while litigation is more frequent under the English than the American rule, levels of substantive compliance under the two rules would be similar. Best of all, according to his calculations, is one-way pro-plaintiff fee shifting, which leads to the highest level of compliance and least amount of litigation. These conclusions, however, depend both on the functional form used in his simulations, and on the specific assumptions of his theoretical model.

8.3 Econometric Evidence of Actual Disputes

The statistical and econometric evidence on fee shifting, as well as on litigation and settlement more generally, has unfortunately been rather limited. Schwab and Eisenberg (1988) report on a 1976 statute that established one-way pro-plaintiff fee shifting in federal constitutional tort cases (that is, cases in which where the federal government is sued for violating the plaintiff's constitutional rights). They find some evidence that the statute was followed by a decline in plaintiff success rates at trial and by an increase in trials relative to other federal civil actions, but little evidence of any increase in the number of lawsuits filed. These results suggest that the statute had its primary effect in encouraging plaintiffs to bargain more aggressively in settlement negotiations, consistent with Rowe et al.'s survey experiments as well as with the theoretical predictions of the optimism and Bayesian settlement models discussed in Section 5 above. Because of the relatively low magnitude of their quantitative estimates, however, and because their observations were muddied by the fact that some courts shifted fees on a discretionary basis before the statute was passed, the authors present their findings as tentative.

Fournier and Zuehlke (1989) develop an econometric model of settlement behavior in which the plaintiff's settlement demand and the probability of settlement are jointly determined. Using nonlinear methods that correct for data censoring (that is, the fact that the amount of the demand is only observed when settlement takes place), they estimate their model using data from a nationwide survey of civil federal filings between 1979 and 1981. The data classifies disputes according to the type of legal claim at issue (for example, tort, copyright, antitrust) and includes information regarding the alleged damages and the number of litigants in each case, the mean and variance of trial awards in litigated cases within each subject-matter classification, and separately prepared estimates of government litigation costs in each case classification, which the authors argue serve as a reasonable proxy for private litigation costs. The coefficients of the resulting equations suggest, not surprisingly, that settlement demands are positively correlated with mean trial awards and alleged damages, and negatively correlated with litigation costs. More interestingly, they also suggest that settlement is more likely in cases and categories with high alleged damages, high mean and variance of trial awards, multiple parties, and low (!) litigation costs. These latter results are at odds with the theoretical predictions of most models of settlement, although the negative relationship between settlement and potential trial awards is consistent with a hypothesis of risk aversion.

Because a fraction of the sampled filings were subject to the English rule, Fournier and Zuehlke were able to estimate its effects as well. They find that fee shifting is negatively correlated with both the probability of settlement and the size of the settlement demand, although the latter effect is not statistically significant. This finding lends some support to the predictions of both the optimism and Bayesian models. The filings in their sample governed by the English rule, however, were few in number and concentrated in a few specialized areas, so this evidence cannot be regarded as especially strong. It is possible that this correlation reflects differences in the types of disputes covered by the rule, rather than effects of indemnification. The authors' unusual findings regarding the other determinants of settlement also call this result into question.

More instructive is Hughes' and Snyder's research on Florida's experiment with the English rule in medical malpractice cases. The Florida statute, passed in 1980 with the support of the state medical association, also provided an offer-of-judgment procedure and exempted insolvent parties from the obligation to pay indemnification; it was repealed in 1985 with the support of its original proponents following a series of expensive and well-publicized plaintiff verdicts. In Snyder and Hughes (1990), the authors use a bivariate probit procedure to analyze insurance company data on closed claims filed before, during, and after the period in which the rule was in effect, and estimate the effects of indemnification on plaintiffs' decisions to drop claims, settlement, and defendants' expenditure on lawyers. Their findings lend support to several of the theoretical predictions outlined in previous sections of this article. Specifically, they find that in cases governed by the English rule, (1) a significantly higher percentage of claims were dropped at an early stage of the litigation, consistent with the proposition that fee shifting encourages risk-averse and low probability plaintiffs to exit the system; (2) defendants spent significantly more per case, in amounts consistent with Katz's simulations, in both settled and in litigated cases; (3) holding other case characteristics constant, the likelihood of litigation increased, consistent with the optimism model. Because dropped cases tended disproportionately to have characteristics that would have made them likelier to go to trial had they remained in the system, however, the authors conclude that the English rule decreased the frequency of litigation on balance. Because of greater expenditure per case, however, total expenditures on litigation still increased.

In a subsequent article analyzing the same data set (Hughes and Snyder, 1995), the authors find that the English rule was associated with an increased frequency of plaintiff success rates at trial, increased jury awards, and larger out-of-court settlements. These increases were significant not just statistically but in absolute terms; for instance, the average judgment in litigated cases increased from $25,190 in cases governed by the American rule to $69,390 in cases governed by the English rule. These results appear to be driven by the case selection effects detailed in the first article. The authors suggest that their results vindicate the proposition that indemnification improves the quality of claims brought, although they admit the possibility of an alternative explanation that low-damage cases are merely being driven away by the higher costs of litigation. They conclude that fee shifting, contrary to the assertions of some legal practitioners, is not necessarily an antiplaintiff policy. Rather, it benefits plaintiffs with high-quality or high-damage claims at the expense of those with low-quality or low-damage claims, and possibly at the expense of defendants. These conclusions, if valid, would explain why the financial advantages expected by the Florida statute's original proponents did not appear to materialize; they would also suggest that the statute improved the deterrent effect of civil liability. Whether such an improvement would be worth the increased litigation expenditures it occasioned, however, and whether it would be replicated in other areas of law with different substantive and procedural characteristics from medical malpractice, remain open questions.

9. Conclusion

It is worth mentioning two relatively underinvestigated aspects of fee shifting, the first of which is its interaction with attorney/client fee contracts. US practice is unusual not only in its allocation of costs between plaintiff and defendant, but also in its tolerance of a variety of cost-sharing arrangements between attorney and client, including the contingent fee, which is widely used by tort plaintiffs. While an analysis of the contingent fee is beyond the scope of this article, it is apparent that many of the incentive effects of fee shifting would be altered in its presence. To give just one obvious example, any deterrent effect of indemnification on risk-averse litigants may be substantially lessened in the presence of contingent fees, since it may be possible to shift some of the increased risk from indemnification to the attorney through adjustments in the contingency arrangement. For another example, the effect of indemnification on trial expenditures may be different under contingent than under hourly fees, since under the former arrangement the attorney's incentives to devote time to the case are dependent on the trial outcome, while under the latter they are independent. Halpern and Turnbull (1983) discuss some of the incentives of contingent fee contracts under both the English and American rules, and Dewees, Prichard and Trebilcock (1981) analyze some of the additional complications that can arise in class actions, but neither article explicitly focuses on the effects of indemnification. Donohue (1991b) discusses the combined effect of the English rule and contingent fees, but his analysis is limited to effects on the settlement range within the optimism model of settlement, and he presents only numerical examples based on a few parameter values. A systematic analysis of the effects of fee shifting under contingent fee contracts, accordingly, remains to be undertaken.

Second, it would be useful to know more about the effects of the English rule on incentives for investigation prior to the onset of litigation. One commonly cited advantage of fee shifting is that, by increasing the penalty for losing at trial, it encourages potential litigants to spend more resources investigating the merits of their claims before officially entering the legal system. This claim is plausible, but the developing economic literature on pre-trial investigation has not yet formally addressed it. While it is possible that this effect could help to make the English rule more efficient than the American, such a conclusion turns on a number of unknown propositions, including whether litigants' investigative incentives are currently adequate, and whether, given the availability of civil discovery, it is cheaper for investigation to take place before rather than after a lawsuit has been filed.

All in all, despite the substantial scholarly and popular attention that the question of indemnity for legal fees has attracted, the number of robust conclusions that can be drawn regarding its consequences are few. Fee shifting does appear to increase legal expenditures per case, in some cases significantly. It also encourages parties with poorly grounded legal claims to settle or to avoid litigating them in the first place, and has a similar effect on litigants who are averse to risk, regardless of the merits of their cases. Aside from these generalizations, most of the other propositions commonly asserted about fee shifting can neither be verified nor rejected. It is unclear whether fee shifting increases the likelihood of settlement, whether it decreases total expenditures on litigation or total payouts by defendants, or whether it on balance improves incentives for primary behavior. It is even unclear whether fee shifting makes it easier for parties with small meritorious claims to obtain compensation, in light of the increased costs per case that it induces. In this regard, the relative lack of systematic empirical investigation of these questions is particularly lamentable.

In light of this state of affairs, and in light of the numerous theoretical demonstrations that fee shifting is a less effective way to promote optimal behavior than other available procedural devices such as decoupling or damage multipliers, one is tempted to conclude that the amount of scholarly attention directed to this topic exceeds its actual social importance. The continued popular and political interest in fee-shifting rules, however, makes this conclusion problematic. While some support for fee shifting arises from its relative simplicity and its status as the international majority rule, much of its continued appeal undoubtedly stems from its association with deeply held notions of corrective justice - and specifically, from the idea that a party who is determined *ex post* to be in the right should be made financially whole. Counterarguments based on economic efficiency, or indeed on any *ex ante* perspective, can never entirely rebut this simple yet powerful intuition.

Whether the English rule is more just than the American rule, or whether its greater fairness justifies its incentive properties, cannot be settled by lawyers or economists alone. The citizenry as a whole must decide whether the principle of full compensation for victorious litigants outweighs the procedural values of providing citizens with an open forum for grievances and an opportunity to be heard, the uncertainty imposed on those who cannot predict the outcome of court decisions, and the political implications of regulating legal fees through a system of bureaucratic oversight rather than through private contract between attorney and client. Moreover, as Prichard (1988) and Hylton (1996) have observed, rules of cost allocation feed back through the selection of cases to influence the development of other areas of substantive and procedural law. Rules that encourage parties to raise relatively innovative claims and defenses help to break down precedent, while rules that penalize risk-taking and novel arguments help to preserve traditional formal categories. Given the pervasive influence of ostensibly procedural rules on substantive outcomes, it may not be possible to separate the policy of fee shifting from deeper questions of what the law should be.

Bibliography on Indemnity of Legal Fees (7300)

Anderson, David A. (1994), 'Improving Settlement Devices: Rule 68 and Beyond', **23** *Journal of Legal Studies*, 225-246.

Bebchuk, Lucian Arye and Chang, Howard F. (1996), 'An Analysis of Fee Shifting Based on the Margin of Victory: On Frivolous Suits, Meritorious Suits, and the Role of Rule 11', **25** *Journal of Legal Studies*, 371-403.

Beckner, Clinton F. and Katz, Avery (1995), 'The Incentive Effects of Litigation Fee Shifting when Legal Standards Are Uncertain', **15** *International Review of Law and Economics*, 205-224.

Bowles, Roger A. (1987), 'Settlement Range and Cost Allocation Rules: A Comment on Avery Katz's Measuring the Demand for Litigation', **3** *Journal of Law, Economics, and Organization*, 177-184.

Braeutigam, Ronald R., Owen, Bruce M. and Panzar, John C. (1984), 'An Economic Analysis of Alternative Fee Shifting Systems', **47** *Law and Contemporary Problems*, 173-185.

Chung, Tai-Yeong (1996), 'Settlement of Litigation Under Rule 68: An Economic Analysis', **25** *Journal of Legal Studies*, 261-286.

Cooper, Edward H. (1994), 'Discovery Cost Allocation: Comment', **23** *Journal of Legal Studies*, 465-480.

Cooter, Robert D. and Rubinfeld, Daniel L. (1989), 'Economic Analysis of Legal Disputes and Their Resolution', **27** *Journal of Economic Literature*, 1067-1097. Reprinted in Posner, Richard A., Cooter, Robert D. and Rubinfeld, Daniel L. (1995), 'Reforming the New Discovery Rules', **84** *Georgetown Law Journal*, 61-89.

Coursey, Don L. and Stanley, L.R. (1988), 'Pretrial Bargaining Behavior within the Shadow of the Law: Theory and Experimental Evidence', **8** *International Review of Law and Economics*, 161-179.

Dewees, Donald N., Prichard, J. Robert S. and Trebilcock, Michael J. (1981), 'An Economic Analysis of Cost and Fee Rules for Class Actions', **10** *Journal of Legal Studies*, 155-185.

Dnes, Antony W. and Rickman, Neil (1998), 'Contracts for Legal Aid', **5(3)** *European Journal of Law and Economics*.

Donohue, John J. (1991a), 'The Effects of Fee Shifting on the Settlement Rate: Theoretical Observations on Costs, Conflicts, and Contingency Fees', **54** *Law and Contemporary Problems*, 194 ff.

Donohue, John J. (1991b), 'Opting for the British Rule; or, If Posner and Shavell Can't Remember the Coase Theorem, Who Will?', **104** *Harvard Law Review*, 1093 ff. Reprinted in Levmore, Saul (1994), *Foundations of Tort Law*, p 160.

Fournier, Gary M. and Zuehlke, Thomas W. (1989), 'Litigation and Settlement: An Empirical Approach', **71** *Review of Economics and Statistics*, 189-195.

Gravelle, Hugh S.E. (1993), 'The Efficiency Implications of Cost Shifting Rules', **13** *International Review of Law and Economics*, 3-18.

Halpern, Paul J. and Turnbull, Stuart M. (1983), 'Legal Fees Contracts and Alternative Cost Rules: An Economic Analysis', **3** *International Review of Law and Economics*, 3-26.

Hause, John C. (1989), 'Indemnity, Settlement, and Litigation, or I'll Be Suing You', **18** *Journal of Legal Studies*, 157-179.

Hersch, Philip L. (1990), 'Indemnity, Settlement, and Litigation: Comment and Extension', **19** *Journal of Legal Studies*, 235-241.

Hughes, James W. and Snyder, Edward A. (1995), 'Litigation and Settlement under the English and American Rules: Theory and Evidence', **38** *Journal of Law and Economics*, 225-250.

Hughes, James W. and Woglom, Geoffry R. (1996), 'Risk Aversion and the Allocation of Legal Costs', in Anderson, David A. (ed.), *Dispute Resolution: Bridging the Settlement Gap*, Greenwich, JAI Press, 167-192.

Hylton, Keith N. (1993a), 'Litigation Cost Allocation Rules and Compliance with the Negligence Standard', **22** *Journal of Legal Studies*, 457-476.

Hylton, Keith N. (1993b), 'Fee Shifting and Incentives to Comply With the Law', **46** *Vanderbilt Law Review*, 1069-1128.

Hylton, Keith N. (1996), 'Fee-Shifting and Predictability of Law', **71** *Chicago-Kent Law Review*, 427-459.

Kaplow, Louis (1993), 'Shifting Plaintiffs' Fees versus Increasing Damage Awards', **24** *Rand Journal of Economics*, 625-630.

Katz, Avery (1987), 'Measuring the Demand for Litigation: Is the English Rule Really Cheaper?', **3** *Journal of Law, Economics, and Organization*, 143-176.

Katz, Avery (1990), 'The Effect of Frivolous Lawsuits on the Settlement of Litigation', **10** *International Review of Law and Economics*, 3-27.

Kobayashi, Bruce H. and Parker, Jeffrey S. (1993), 'No Armistice at 11: A Commentary on the Supreme Court's 1993 Amendment to Rule 11 of the Federal Rules of Civil Procedures', **3** *Supreme Court Economic Review*, 92-152.

Leubsdorf, John (1984), 'Toward a History of the American Rule on Attorney Fee Recovery', **47(1)** *Law and Contemporary Problems*, 9-36.

Mause, Philip (1969), 'Winner Takes All: A Re-Examination of the Indemnity System', **55** *Iowa Law Review*, 26-55.

Miller, Geoffrey P. (1986), 'An Economic Analysis of Rule 68', **15** *Journal of Legal Studies*, 93-125.

Note (1984), 'State Attorney Fee Shifting Statutes: Are We Quietly Repealing the American Rule?', **47** *Law and Contemporary Problems*, 321-346.

Pfennigstorf, Werner (1984), 'The European Experience With Attorney Fee Shifting', **47** *Law and Contemporary Problems*, 37-124.

Plott, Charles R. (1987), 'Legal Fees: A Comparison of the American and English Rules', **3** *Journal of Law, Economics and Organization*, 185-92.

Polinsky, A. Mitchell and Che, Yeon-Koo (1991), 'Decoupling Liability: Optimal Incentives for Care and Litigation', **22** *Rand Journal of Economics*, 562-570.

Polinsky, A. Mitchell and Rubinfeld, Daniel L. (1993), 'Sanctioning Frivolous Suits: An Economic Analysis', **82** *Georgetown Law Journal*, 397-435.

Polinsky, A. Mitchell and Rubinfeld, Daniel L. (1996), 'Optimal Awards and Penalties When the Probability of Prevailing Varies Among Plaintiffs', **27** *Rand Journal of Economics*, 269-280.

Polinsky, A. Mitchell and Rubinfeld, Daniel L. (1997), 'Does the English Rule Discourage Low-Probability-of-Prevailing Plaintiffs?', **26** *Journal of Legal Studies*.

Prichard, J. Robert S. (1988), 'A Systematic Approach to Comparative Law: The Effect of Cost, Fee and Financing Rules on the Development of the Substantive Law', **17** *Journal of Legal Studies*, 451-475.

Priest, George L. (1982), 'Regulating the Content and Volume of Litigation: An Economic Analysis', **1** *Supreme Court Economic Review* , 163-183.

Reinganum, Jennifer F. and Wilde, Louis L. (1986), 'Settlement, Litigation, and the Allocation of Litigation Costs', **17** *Rand Journal of Economics*, 557-566.

Rosenberg, David and Shavell, Steven (1985), 'A Model in Which Suits are Brought for their Nuisance Value', **5** *International Review of Law and Economics*, 3-13.

Rowe, Thomas D. (1984), 'Predicting the Effects of Attorney Fee Shifting', **47** *Law and Contemporary Problems*, 139-171.

Rowe, Thomas D. and Anderson, David A. (1996), 'One-Way Fee Shifting Statutes and Offer of Judgment Rules: An Experiment', **36** *Jurimetrics Journal*, 255-273.

Rowe, Thomas D. and Vidmar, Neil (1988), 'Empirical Research on Offers of Settlement: A Preliminary Report', **51** *Law and Contemporary Problems*, 13-39.

Schmalbeck, Richard L. and Myers, Gary (1986), 'A Policy Analysis of Fee-Shifting Rules Under the Internal Revenue Code', **6** *Duke Law Journal*, 1986, 970-1002.

Schwab, Stewart J. and Eisenberg, Theodore (1988), 'Explaining Constitutional Tort Litigation: The Influence of the Attorney Fees Statute and the Government As Defendant', **73** *Cornell Law Review*, 719-784.

Shavell, Steven (1982a), 'Suit, Settlement and Trial: A Theoretical Analysis Under Alternative Methods for the Allocation of Legal Costs', **11** *Journal of Legal Studies*, 55-81.

Snyder, Edward A. and Hughes, James W. (1990), 'The English Rule for Allocating Legal Costs: Evidence Confronts Theory', **6** *Journal of Law, Economics and Organization*, 345-380.

Spier, Kathryn E. (1994), 'Pretrial Bargaining and the Design of Fee-Shifting Rules', **25** *Rand Journal of Economics*, 197-214.

Symposium on Attorney Fee Shifting (1984), **47** *Law and Contemporary Problems*, 1-354.

Symposium on Fee Shifting (1996), **71** *Chicago-Kent Law Review*, 415-697.

Talley, Eric (1996), 'Liability-Based Fee Shifting Rules and Settlement Mechanisms Under Incomplete Information', **71** *Chicago-Kent Law Review*, 461-503.

Tomkins, Alan J. and Willging, Thomas E. (1986), *Taxation of Attorneys' Fees: Practices in English, Alaskan, and Federal Courts*, Washington, Federal Judicial Center.

Trubek, David M., Grossman, Joel B., Felstiner, William L. F., Kritzer, Herbert M. and Sarat, Austin (1983), *Civil Litigation Research Project: Final Report*, Madison, Wisconsin, Institute for Legal Studies.

Other References

Anderson, David A. (ed.) (1996), *Dispute Resolution: Bridging the Settlement Gap*, Greenwich, CT, JAI Press.

Anderson, David A. and Rowe, Thomas D. (1996),'Empirical Evidence on Settlement Devices: Does Rule 68 Encourage Settlement?', **71** *Chicago-Kent Law Review*, 519-545.

Bebchuk, Lucian A. (1984). Litigation and Settlement Under Imperfect Information, **15** *Rand Journal of Economics*, 404-415.

Bebchuk, Lucian A. and Chang, Howard F. (1996), *The Effect of Offer-of-Settlement Rules on the Terms of Settlement*, Manuscript, University of Southern California.

Bernstein, Lisa (1993), 'Understanding the Limits of Court-Connected ADR: A Critique of Federal Court Annexed Arbitration Programs', **141** *University of Pennsylvania Law Review*, 2169-2259.

Cooter, Robert D. and Rubinfeld, Daniel L. (1994), 'An Economic Model of Legal Discovery', **23** *Journal of Legal Studies*, 435-463.

Cooter, Robert D. and Rubinfeld, Daniel L. (1995),'Reforming the New Discovery Rules', **84** *Georgetown Law Journal*, 61-89.

Cooter, Robert D., Marks, Stephen and Mnookin Robert (1982), 'Bargaining in the Shadow of the Law: A Testable Model of Strategic Behavior', **11** *Journal of Legal Studies*, 225-251.

Cornell, Bradford (1990),'The Incentive to Sue: An Option Pricing Approach', **19** *Journal of Legal Studies*, 173-187.

Gould, John P. (1973), 'The Economics of Legal Conflicts', **2** *Journal of Legal Studies*, 279-300.

Harsanyi, John C. and Selten, Reinhard (1972), 'A Generalized Nash Solution for Two Person Bargaining Games with Incomplete Information', **18** *Management Science*, 80-106.

Katz, Avery (1988), 'Judicial Decisionmaking and Litigation Expenditure', **8** *International Review of Law and Economics*, 127-143.

Landes, William M. (1971), 'An Economic Analysis of the Courts', **14** *Journal of Law and Economics*, 61-101.

Myerson, Roger B. and Satterthwaite, Mark A. (1983), 'Efficient Mechanisms for Bilateral Trading', **29** *Journal of Economic Theory*, 265-281.

P'ng, Ivan P.L. (1987), 'Litigation, Liability, and Incentives to Take Care', **34** *Journal of Public Economics*, 61-85.

Polinsky, A. Mitchell and Rubinfeld, Daniel L. (1988), 'The Welfare Effects of Costly Litigation for the Level of Liability', **17** *Journal of Legal Studies*, 151-164.

Polinsky, A. Mitchell and Shavell, Steven (1989), 'Legal Error, Litigation, and the Incentive to Obey the Law', **5** *Journal of Law, Economics, and Organization*, 99-108.

Posner, Richard A. (1973), 'An Economic Approach to Legal Procedure and Judicial Administration', **2** *Journal of Legal Studies*, 399 ff.

Rose-Ackerman, Susan and Geistfeld, Mark (1987), 'The Divergence Between Social and Private Incentives to Sue: A Comment on Shavell, Menell, and Kaplow', **16** *Journal of Legal Studies*, 483-491.

Shavell, Steven (1982b), 'The Social Versus the Private Incentive to Bring Suit in a Costly Legal System', **11** *Journal of Legal Studies*, 333-339.

Shavell, Steven (1995), 'Alternative Dispute Resolution: An Economic Analysis', **24** *Journal of Legal Studies*, 1-28.

Cases

Alyeska Pipeline Service Co. v. Wilderness Society, 421 US 240

Marek v. Chesny, 105 S.Ct. 3012 (1985)

7400
SETTLEMENT

Andrew F. Daughety
Department of Economics and Business Administration, Vanderbilt University

Abstract

This survey of modeling of pretrial settlement bargaining organizes current main themes and recent developments. The basic concepts used are outlined as core models and then a number of variations on these core models are discussed. The focus is on papers that emphasize formal models of settlement negotiation and the presentation in the survey is organized in game-theoretic terms, this now being the principal tool employed by analyses in this area, but the discussion is aimed at the not-terribly-technical non-specialist. The survey also illustrates some of the basic notions and assumptions of information economics and of (cooperative and noncooperative) game theory.
JEL classification: K41, C70
Keywords: Settlement Bargaining

1. Introduction

This survey of the modeling of pretrial settlement bargaining organizes current main themes and recent developments. The basic concepts used are outlined as core models and then a number of variations on these core models are discussed. The emphasis in the survey on main themes and modeling of basic concepts is for two reasons. First, Cooter and Rubinfeld (1989) provide an excellent survey of this literature (in the context of a broader consideration of the economics of dispute resolution and the law) up to that date, while Miller (1996) provides a recent non-technical review addressing policies that encourage settlement. Second, as with much of law and economics, a catalog of even relatively recent research would rapidly be out of date. The focus here is on papers that emphasize formal models of settlement negotiation and the presentation is organized in game-theoretic terms, this now being the principal tool employed by analyses in this area. The discussion is aimed at the not-terribly-technical non-specialist. In this chapter some of the basic notions and assumptions of game theory are presented and applied, but some of the more recent models of settlement negotiation rely on relatively advanced techniques; in those cases, technical presentation will be minimal and intuition will be emphasized. For the interested reader, a recent source on game theory applications in law and economics is Baird, Gertner and Picker (1994); extensive reviews of that book appear in Huang (1995) and Salant and Sims (1996). Two quite readable books on game theory, modeling and a number of related philosophical issues are Binmore (1992) and Kreps (1990). Finally, chapters seven through nine of Mas-Colell, Whinston and Green (1995) provide the technically sophisticated reader with a convenient, efficient and careful presentation of the basic techniques of modern (non-cooperative) game theory, while chapters thirteen and fourteen provide a careful review of the basics of information economics.

What is the basic image that emerges from the settlement bargaining literature? It is that settlement processes act as a type of screen, sorting amongst the cases, presumably causing the less severe (for example, those with lower true damages) to bargain to a resolution (or to do this very frequently), while the more severe (for example, those with higher damages) may proceed to be resolved in court. The fact that some cases go to trial is often viewed as an inefficiency. While this survey adopts this language (as does much of the literature reviewed) one might also view the real possibility of trial as necessary to the development of case law and as a useful demonstration of the potential costs associated with decisions made earlier about levels of care. In other words, the possibility of trials may lead to greater care and to more efficient choices overall. Moreover, the bargaining and settlement literatures have evolved in trying to explain the sources of negotiation breakdown: the literature has moved from explanations fully based on intransigence to explanations focused around information. This is not to assert that trials do not occur because of motives outside economic analysis, just that economic attributes contribute to explaining an increasing share of observed behavior.

In the next few sections (comprising Part A) significant features of settlement models are discussed and some necessary notation is introduced; this part ends with a simplified example indicating how the pieces come together. Part B examines the basic models in use, varying the level of information that litigants have and the type of underlying bargaining stories that are being told. Part C considers a range of 'variations' on the Part B models, again using the game-theoretic organization introduced in Part A.

A. Basic Issues, Notions and Notation

2. Overview

In this part the important features of the various approaches are discussed and notation that is used throughout is introduced. Paralleling the presentation of the models to come, the current discussion is organized to address: (1) players; (2) actions and strategies; (3) outcomes and payoffs; (4) timing; (5) information and (6) prediction. A last section provides a brief example. Words or phrases in italics are terms of special interest.

3. Players

The primary participants (usually called litigants or *players*) are the plaintiff (P) and the defendant (D); a few models have allowed for multiple P's or multiple D's, but for now assume one of each. Secondary participants include attorneys for the two litigants (A_P and A_D, respectively), experts for the two participants (X_P and X_D, respectively) and the court (should the case go to trial), which is usually taken to be a judge or a jury (J). Almost all models restrict attention to P and D, either ignoring the others or relegating them to the background. As an example, a standard assumption when there is some uncertainty in the model (possibly about damages or liability, or both) is that, at court, J will learn the truth and make an award at the true value (the award will be the actual damage, liability will be correctly established, and so on). Moreover, J is usually assumed to have no strategic interests at heart, unlike P, D, the A's and the X's. Section 15 considers some efforts to incorporate Js decision process in a substantive way.

Finally, uncertainty enters the analysis whenever something relevant is not known by at least one player. Uncertainty also arises if one player knows something that another does not know, or if the players move simultaneously (for example, they simultaneously make proposals to each other). These issues will be dealt with in the sections on timing (6) and information (7), but sometimes such possibilities are incorporated by adding another 'player' to the analysis, namely nature (N), a disinterested player whose actions influence the other players in the game via some probability rule.

4. Actions and Strategies

An *action* is something a player can choose to do when it is their turn to make a choice. For example, the most commonly modeled action for P or D involves making a *proposal.* This generally takes the form of a demand from P of D or an offer from D to P. This then leads to an opportunity for another action which is a *response* to the proposal, which usually takes the form of an acceptance or a rejection of a proposal, possibly followed by yet another action such as a counterproposal. Some models allow for multiple periods of proposal/response sequences of actions.

When a player has an opportunity to take an action, the rules of the game specify the allowable actions at each decision opportunity. Thus, in the previous example, the specification of allowed response actions did not include delay (delay will be discussed in Section 18). Actions chosen at one point may also limit future actions: if 'good faith' bargaining is modeled as requiring that demands never increase over time, then the set of actions possible when P makes a counterproposal to Ds counterproposal may be limited by P's original proposal.

Other possible actions include choosing to employ attorneys or experts, initially choosing to file a suit or finally choosing to take the case to court should negotiations fail. Most analyses ignore these either by not allowing such choices or by assuming values for parameters that would make particular choices 'obvious'. For example, many analyses assume that the net expected value of pursuing a case to trial is positive, thereby making credible such a threat by P during the negotiation with D; this topic will be explored more fully in Section 16.1.

In general, a *strategy* for a player provides a complete listing of actions to be taken at each of the player's decision opportunities and is contingent on: (1) the observable actions taken by the other player(s) in the past; (2) actions taken by the player himself in the past; (3) the information the player currently possesses; (4) any exogenous relevant actions that have occurred that the player is aware of (for example, speculations about the award a specific J might choose). Thus, as an example, consider an analysis with no uncertainty about damages, liability, what J will do, and so on, where *P* proposes, D responds with acceptance or a counterproposal, followed by P accepting the counterproposal or choosing to break off negotiations and go to court. A strategy for P would be of the form 'propose an amount x; if D accepts, make the transfer and end while if D counterproposes y, choose to accept this if y is at least z, otherwise proceed to court'. P would then have a strategy for each possible x, y and z combination.

An analogy may be helpful here. One might think of a strategy as a book, with pages of the book corresponding to opportunities in the game for the book's owner to make a choice. Thus, a typical page says 'if you are at this point in the book, take this action'. This is not a book to be read from cover-to-cover, one page after the previous one; rather, actions taken by players lead other players to go to the appropriate page in their book to see what they do next. All the possible books (strategies) that a player might use form the player's personal library (the player's strategy set).

There are times when being predictable as to which book you will use is useful, but there can also be times when unpredictability is useful. A sports analogy would be to imagine yourself to be a goalie on the A team, and a member of the B team has been awarded the chance to make a shot on your goal. Assume that there is insufficient time for you to fully react to the kick, so you are going to have to generally move to the left or the right as the kicker takes his shot. If it is known that, in such circumstances, you always go to your left, the kicker can take advantage of this predictability and improve his chance of making a successful shot. This is also sometimes true in settlement negotiations: if P knows the actual damage that D is liable for, but D only knows a possible range of damages, then D following a predictable policy of never going to court encourages P to make high claims. Alternatively, D following a predictable policy of always going to court no matter what P is willing to settle for may be overly costly to D. *Mixed strategies* try to address this problem of incorporating just the right amount of unpredictability and are used in some settlement models. Think of the individual books in a player's library as *pure* strategies (pure in the sense of being predictable) and think of choosing a book at random from the library, where by 'at random' we mean that you have chosen a particular set of probability weights on the books in your library. In this sense your chosen set of weights is now your strategy (choosing one book with probability one and everything else with probability zero gets us back to pure strategies). A list of strategies, with one for each player (that is, a selection of books from all the players' libraries), is called a *strategy profile.*

5. Outcomes and Payoffs

An *outcome* for a game is the result of a strategy profile being played. Thus, an outcome may involve a transfer from D to P reflecting a settlement or it might be a transfer ordered by a court or it might involve no transfer as P chooses not to pursue a case to trial. If the reputations of the parties are of interest, the outcome should also specify the status of that reputation. In plea bargaining models, which will be discussed in Section 17.4, the outcome might be a sentence to be served. In general, an outcome is a list (or vector) of relevant final attributes for each player in the game.

For each player, each outcome has an associated numerical value called the *payoff*, usually a monetary value. For example, a settlement is a transfer of money from D to P; for an A or an X the payoff might be a fee. For models that are concerned with risk preferences, the payoffs would be in terms of the utility of net wealth rather than in monetary terms. Payoffs that are strictly monetary (for example, the transfer itself) are viewed as reflecting risk-neutral behavior on the part of the player.

Payoffs need not equal expected awards, since parties to a litigation also incur various types of costs. The cost most often considered in settlement analyses is called a *court cost* (denoted here as k_P and k_D, respectively). An extensive literature has developed surrounding rules for allocating such costs to the litigants and the effect of various rules on the incentives to bring suit and the outcome of the settlement process; this is addressed in Section 17.2. Court costs are expenditures which will be incurred should the case go to trial and are associated with preparing for and conducting a trial; as such they are avoidable costs (in contrast with sunk costs) and therefore influence the decisions that the players (in particular P and D) make. Generally, costs incurred in negotiating are usually ignored, though some recent papers reviewed in Sections 11.2 and 18 emphasize the effect of negotiation costs on settlement offers and the length of the bargaining horizon. Unless specifically indicated, assume that negotiation costs are zero.

The total payoff for a player labeled i (that is i = P, D, ...) is denoted $\$_i$. Note that this payoff can reflect long-term considerations (such as the value of a reputation or other anticipated future benefits) and multiple periods of negotiation. Generally, players in a game maximize their payoffs and thus, for example, P makes choices so as to maximize $\$_P$. For convenience, D's payoff is written as an expenditure (if D countersues, then D takes the role of a plaintiff in the countersuit) and thus D is taken to *minimize* $\$_D$ (rather than maximize -$\$_D$). While an alternative linguistic approach would be to refer to the numerical evaluation of D's outcome as a 'cost' (which is then minimized, and thereby not use the word payoff with respect to D), the use of the term payoff for D's aggregate expenditure is employed so as to reserve the word cost for individual expenditures that each party must make.

Finally, since strategy profiles lead to outcomes which yield payoffs, this means that payoffs are determined by strategy profiles. Thus, if player i uses strategy s_i, and the strategy profile is denoted s (that is, s is the vector, or list $(s_1, s_2, ..., s_n)$, where there are n players), then we could write this dependence for player i as $\$_i(s)$.

6. Timing

The sequence of play and the horizon over which negotiations occur are issues of timing and of time. For example: do P and D make simultaneous proposals or do they take turns? Does who goes first (or who goes when) influence the outcome? Do both make proposals or does only one? Can players choose to delay or accelerate negotiations? Are there multiple rounds of proposal/response behavior? Does any of this sort of detail matter in any substantive sense?

Early settlement models abstracted from any dynamic detail concerning the negotiation process. Such models were based on very general theoretical models of bargaining (which ignored bargaining detail and used desirable properties of any resulting bargain to characterize what it must be) initially developed by Nash (1950). More recent work on settlement negotiations, which usually provides a detailed specification of how bargaining is assumed to proceed (the strategies employed and the sequencing of bargaining play are specified), can be traced to results in the theoretical bargaining literature by Nash (1953), Ståhl (1972) and Rubinstein (1982). Nash's 1950 approach is called *axiomatic* while the Ståhl/Rubinstein improvement on Nash's 1953 approach is called *strategic*; the two approaches are intimately related. Both approaches have generated vast literatures which have considered issues of interest to analyses of settlement bargaining; a brief discussion of the two approaches is provided in Sections 10 and 11 so as to place the settlement applications in a unified context. The discussion below also addresses the institutional features that make settlement modeling more than simply a direct application of bargaining theory.

When considered, time enters settlement analyses in two basic ways. First, do participants move simultaneously or sequentially? This is not limited to the question of whether or not P and D make choices at different points on the clock. More significant is whether or not moving second involves having observed what the first-mover did. Two players who make choices at different points in time, but who do not directly influence each other's choices (perhaps because the second-mover cannot observe or react to what the first-mover has done) are viewed as moving simultaneously: that my choice and your choice together influence what each of us receives as a payoff (symbolized in the payoff notation as $\$_i(s)$ for player i) does not make moving at different points in time significant in and of itself. The real point here is whether all relevant decision makers must conjecture what the others are *likely to do*, or whether some can observe what others actually *did*. This is because the second-mover is influenced by the first-mover's choice and because they *both* know this, which affects the first-mover's choice as well. Asymmetry in what choices depend upon (in this sense) is modeled as choices being made in a sequence; symmetry is modeled as choices being made simultaneously. As will be seen in the example to be discussed in Section 9, who moves when can make a very significant difference in what is predicted. Note that a sequence of simultaneous decisions is possible (for example, P and D both simultaneously make proposals and then both simultaneously respond to the proposals, and so on).

A second way that time enters is in terms of the length of the horizon over which decisions are made. The main stream of research in the strategic bargaining literature views the horizon as infinite in length; this is done to eliminate the effect of arbitrary end-of-horizon strategic behavior. Settlement models, on the other hand, typically take the negotiation horizon as finite in length (and often very short, say, two periods). This is done for two reasons. First, while some cases may seem to go on forever, some form of termination actually occurs (cases are dropped, or resolved through negotiation or meet a court date). While setting a court date is not an iron-clad commitment, few would argue that an infinite number of continuances is realistic. Second, in the more informationally complex models, this finite horizon restriction helps provide more precise predictions to be made than would otherwise be possible. Thus, in most settlement models there is a last opportunity to negotiate, after which either the case proceeds to trial or terminates (either because the last settlement proposal is accepted or the case is dropped). This is important because court costs are incurred only if the case actually proceeds to trial; that is, after the last possible point of negotiations. If negotiations were to continue during the trial, the ability to use the avoidance of these costs to achieve a settlement obviously is vitiated: as the trial proceeds the portion of costs that are sunk become larger and the portion that is avoidable shrinks. This problem has not been addressed generally, though papers by Spier (1992) and by Bebchuk (1996) consider significant parts of this issue; this is discussed in more detail in Section 18.

7. Information

In Shavell (1982), the range over which litigants might bargain when assessments about outcomes may be different is analyzed as a problem in decision theory (a game against nature, N); this raises the issue of who knows what, when, why and how. Shavell's paper indicated that differences in assessments by P and D as to the likelihood of success at trial, and the likely award, can lead to trial as an outcome. While Shavell's paper did not consider strategic interaction among the players (for the first paper to incorporate strategic behavior, see P'ng, 1983), the role of information has become a central theme in the literature that has developed since, with special emphasis on accounting for informational differences and consistent, rational behavior. Moving momentarily from theory to empirical analysis, Farber and White (1991) use data from a hospital to investigate whether seemingly asymmetrically distributed information influenced settlement rates and the speed with which cases settled; they find that it did.

Informational considerations involve what players individually know and what they must guess about (where such guessing presumably involves some form of organized approach). Many of the analyses in the literature use different informational structures (who knows what when) and in this survey a variety of such structures will be presented. As a starting example, consider Pat, who developed an improved framitz (a tool for making widgets). Pat took the tool to the Delta Company (D), with the notion that Delta would manufacture the tool and Pat would become rich from her share of the profits. Delta indicated that the tool was not likely to be financially viable and Pat went back to work on other inventions. Some years later Pat noticed that many people who made widgets were using a slightly modified version of her tool made by Delta. Pat (P) decided to sue Delta (D) for misappropriation of intellectual property, and for convenience assume that while D's liability is clear, the assessment of a level of compensation to P is less clear. D's familiarity with the profits made (and experience with creative accounting procedures) means that D has a better idea of what level of total profits might be proved in court. Both P's attorney and D's attorney have (potentially similar) estimates of what the court is likely to do with any particular evidence on the level of profits of the tool (how the court, J, might choose to allocate the costs and revenues of the tool to P and D). Simplifying, there are two sources of uncertainty operating here: uncertainty by P and D about J and uncertainty by P about what D knows.

First, both P and D cannot perfectly predict what J will choose as an award: here each faces an essentially similar level of uncertainty (there is no obvious reason to assert the presence of an asymmetry in what is knowable). Moreover, we will assume that this assessment of J's likely actions, while probabilistic, is *common knowledge*. Common knowledge connotes the notion that were P and D to honestly compare their assessments of J's likely actions for *each possible* set of details about the profits made by D, their assessments would be exactly the same, and P and D know that the other knows this, and P and D know that the other knows that the other knows this, and so on (see Aumann, 1976; Geanakoplos and Polemarchakis, 1982, and Binmore, 1992 for two early technical papers and a recent game theory text with an extensive prose discussion of this topic).

Thus, P and D have the same information with regard to J; we might call this *imperfect* or *symmetrically uncertain* information to contrast it with the clear asymmetry that exists between P and D with respect to the information about revenues and costs that D knows. This latter notion of uncertainty is referred to as *asymmetric* information, and it is a main attribute of much of the recent work on settlement. Finally, if actual damage was common knowledge and if P and D truly knew exactly what J would choose as an award and *that* were common knowledge, the resulting information condition is called *perfect*.

A nice story which makes the differences in informational settings clear is due to John Roberts of Stanford University. Consider a card game played by at least two people, such as poker. If all hands were dealt face up and no more cards were to be dealt, this would be a situation of perfect information. If, instead, hands are dealt with (say) three cards face up and two cards face down, but no one can look at their 'down' cards, this is a setting of imperfect information. Finally, asymmetric information (also called *incomplete* information) would involve each player being able to privately look at their down cards before taking further actions (asking for alternative cards, betting, and so on). Note that in this last case we see the real essence of asymmetric information: it is not that one party is informationally disadvantaged when compared with the other (as in the case of Pat and Delta) as much as the players have *different* information from each other.

One caution about the foregoing example. The perfect information case seems to be rather pointless: players without the best hand at the table would choose not to bet at all. Perfect information models are really not as trivial, since they significantly clarify what the essential elements of an analysis are and they provide a comparison point to evaluate how different informational uncertainties affect the efficiency of the predicted outcome.

Timing in the play of the game is also a potential source of imperfect information. If P and D make simultaneous proposals (which might be resolved by, say, averaging), then when they are each considering what proposal to make they must conjecture what the other might choose to propose: what each will do is not common knowledge. Even if all other information in the analysis were perfect, this timing of moves is a source of imperfect information.

The incorporation of informational considerations (especially asymmetric information) has considerably raised the ante in settlement modeling. Why? Is this simply a fad or an excuse for more technique? The answer is revealed in the discussion of the basic models and their variations. As indicated earlier, the problem with analyses that assumed perfect or imperfect information was that many interesting and significant phenomena were either attributed to irrational behavior or not addressed at all. For example, in some cases negotiations fail and a trial ensues, even though both parties may recognize that going to court is very costly; sometimes cases fail to settle quickly, or only settle when a deadline approaches. Moreover, agency problems between lawyers and clients, discovery, disclosure, various rules for allocating court costs or for admitting evidence have all been the subject of models using asymmetric information.

7.1 Modeling Uncertainty

Models with perfect information specify parameters of the problem with no uncertainty attached: liability is known, damages are known, what J will do is known, costs are known, and so on. Imperfect information models involve probability distributions associated with one or more elements of the analysis, but the probability distributions are common knowledge, and thus the occurrence of uncertainty in the model is symmetric. For example, damages are 'unknown' means that all parties to the negotiation itself (all the players) use the same probability model to describe the likelihood of damage being found to actually have been a particular value. Thus, for example, if damage is assumed to take on the value d_L (L for low) with probability p and d_H (H for high) with probability $(1 - p)$, then the expected damage, $E(d) = pd_L + (1 - p)d_H$ is P's estimate $[E_P(d)]$ as well as D's estimate $[E_D(d)]$ of the damages that will be awarded in court. Usually, the court (J) is assumed to learn the 'truth' should the case go to trial, so that the probability assessment by the players may be interpreted as a common assessment as to what the court will assert to be the damage level, possibly reflecting the availability and admissibility of evidence as well as the true level of damage incurred. Note that such models are not limited to only accounting for two possible events (for example, perhaps the damage could be any number between d_L and d_H); this is simply a straight forward extension of the probability model. On the other hand, since P and D agree about the returns and costs to trial, there is no rational basis for actually incurring them and the surplus generated by not going to trial can be allocated between the players as part of the bargain struck.

With asymmetric information, players have different information and thus have different probability assessments over relevant uncertain aspects of the game. Perhaps each player's court costs are unknown to the other player, perhaps damages are known to P but not to D, or the likelihood of being found liable is better known by D than by P. Possibly P and D have different estimates, for a variety of reasons, as to what J will do. All of these differences in information may influence model predictions, but the nature of the differences is itself something that must be common knowledge.

Consider yourself as one of the players in the version of the earlier card game where you can privately learn your down cards. Say you observe that you have an Ace of Spades and a King of Hearts as your two down cards. What can you do with this information? The answer is quite a bit. You know how many players there are and you can observe all the up cards. You can not observe the cards that have not been dealt, but you know how many of them there are. You also know the characteristics of the deck: four suits, thirteen cards each, no repeats, and so on. This means that given your down cards you could (at least theoretically) construct probability estimates of what the other players have and know what estimates they are constructing about what you have. This last point is extremely important, since for player A to predict what player B will do (so that A can compute what to do), A needs to think from B's viewpoint, which includes predicting what B will predict about what A would do.

To understand this, let us continue with the card game example and consider a simple, specific example (we will then return to the settlement model to indicate the use of asymmetric information in that setting). Assume that there are two players (A and B), a standard deck with 52 cards (jokers are excluded) and the game involves two cards dealt face up and one card dealt face down to each of A and B; only one down card is considered to simplify the presentation. Table 1 shows the cards that have been dealt face up (available for all to see) and face down (available only for the receiver of the cards, and us, to see). For expositional purposes, H, D, C and S stand for hearts, diamonds, clubs and spades while a K represents a King, and so on.

Table 1
Hands of Cards for A and B

	Up	Down
A	4S, KD	KH
B	QH, AC	2C

(Note: entries provide face value of card and suit)

By a player's *type* we mean their down cards (their private information), so A is a KH while B is a 2C, and only they know their own type. A knows that B is one of 47 possible types (A knows B cannot be a KH or any of the up cards) and, for similar reasons, B knows that A is one of 47 possible types. Moreover, A's model of what type B can be (denoted $p_A(t_B|t_A)$) provides A with the probability of each possibility of B's type (denoted t_B) conditional (the vertical line) on A's type (denoted t_A). The corresponding model for B that gives a probability of each possibility of A's type is denoted $p_B(t_A|t_B)$. Note that all the probability models are formally also conditioned on all the upcards (for example, if we are especially careful we should write $p_A(t_B|t_A$, 4S, KD, QH, AC) and $p_B(t_A|t_B$,4S, KD, QH, AC)), which we supress in the notation employed.

In the particular case at hand t_A = KH, so once A knows his type (sees his down card) he can use $p_A(t_B|\text{KH})$ to compute the possibilities about B's down card (type). But A actually could have worked out his strategy for each possible down card he might be dealt (and the possible up cards) *before* the game; his strategy would then be a function that would tell him what to do for each possible down-card/up-card combination he might be dealt in the game. Moreover, since he must also think about what B will do and B will not know A's down card (and thus must use $p_A(t_B|t_A)$, instead of $p_A(t_B|\text{KH})$, as his probability model for what A will use about B's possible down cards) then this seemingly extra effort (that is, A working out a strategy for each possible type) is not wasted, since A needs to do it anyway to model B modeling A's choices. What we just went through is what someone analyzing an asymmetric game must do for every player.

Finally, for later use, observe that these two probability models are *consistent* in the sense that they come from the *same* overall model $p(t_A, t_B)$ which reflects common knowledge of the deck that was used. In other words, the foregoing conditional probabilities in the previous paragraph both come from the overall joint probability model $p(t_A, t_B)$ using the usual rules of probability for finding conditional probabilities.

So what does this mean for analyzing asymmetric information models of settlement? It means, for example, that if there is an element (or there are elements) about which there is incomplete information, then we think of that element as taking on different possible values (which are the types) and that the players have probability models about which possible value of the element is the true one. For example, if P knows the true damage level, then it has a probability model placing all the probability weight on the true value. If D only knows that it is between d_L and d_H, then D's model covers all the possible levels of damage in that interval. The foregoing is an example of a *one-sided* asymmetric information model, wherein one player is privately informed about some element of the game and the other must use a probability model about the element's true value; who is informed and the probability assessment for the uninformed player is common knowledge. *Two-sided* asymmetric information models involve both players having private information about either the same element or about different elements. Thus, P and D may, individually, have private information about what an independent friend-of-the-court brief (still in preparation for submission at trial) may say, or P may know the level of damage and D may know whether the evidence indicates liability or not (this latter example will be discussed further in Section 12.4).

7.2 Consistent versus Inconsistent Priors

The card game examples above, in common with much of the literature on asymmetric information settlement models, involve games with consistent priors. A few papers on settlement bargaining appear to use 'inconsistent' priors. In this section we discuss what this means.

A game has *consistent priors* if each player's conditional probability distribution over the other player's type (or other players' types) comes from the same overall probability model. In the card game example with A and B, we observed that there was an overall model $p(t_A, t_B)$ which was common knowledge, and the individual conditional probability models $p_A(t_B|t_A)$ and $p_B(t_A|t_B)$ could have been found by using $p(t_A, t_B)$. This was true because the makeup of the deck and the nature of the card-dealing process were common knowledge. What if, instead, the dealer (a stranger to both A and B) first looked at the cards before they were dealt and chose which ones to give to each player? Now the probability assessments are about the dealer, not the deck, and it is not obvious that A and B should agree about how to model the dealer. Perhaps if A and B had been brought up together, or if they have talked about how to model the dealer, we might conclude that the game would have consistent priors (though long-held rivalries or even simple conversations themselves can be opportunities for strategic behavior). Thus, if there is no underlying $p(t_A, t_B)$ that would yield $p_A(t_B|t_A)$ and $p_B(t_A|t_B)$ through the standard rules of probability, this is a model employing *inconsistent priors.*

Thus, if P and D both honestly believe they will win, they have inconsistent priors, because the joint probability of both winning is zero. While such beliefs might be held, they present a fundamental difficulty for using models which assert fully rational behavior: how can both players be rational, both be aware of each other's assessment, aware that the assessments fundamentally conflict, and not use this information to revise and refine their own estimates? The data of the game must be common knowledge, as is rationality (and more, as will be discussed in the next section), but entertaining conflicting assessments themselves is in conflict with rationality. Alternatively put, for the consistent application of rational choice, differences in assessments must reflect differences in private information, not differences in world views. Presented with the same information, conflicts in assessments would disappear.

To understand the problem, consider the following example taken from Binmore (1992, p. 477). Let A and B hold prior assessments about an uncertain event (an election). A believes that a Republican will win the election with probability 5/8 and the Democrat will win it with probability 3/8. B believes that the Democrat will win with probability 3/4 and the Republican with probability 1/4. Now if player C enters the picture, he can offer A the following bet: A wins \$3 if the Republican wins and pays C \$5 if the Democrat wins. C offers B the following bet: B wins \$2 if the Democrat wins and pays C \$6 if the Republican wins. Assume that A and B are risk-neutral, are well aware of each other's assessments, and stick to the foregoing probabilities and that C pays each of them a penny if they take the bets. Then both A and

B will take the bets and for *any* probability of the actual outcome, C's expected profits are $2.98 ($3 less the two pennies). This is derisively called a 'money pump' and works because of the inconsistent priors; that is, neither A nor B update their assessment in response to the assessments that the other is using and is willing to bet with.

Now inconsistent priors may occur because one or the other or both think that the other player is irrational. Recent laboratory experiments (see Babcock et al., 1995) have found seemingly inconsistent priors that arise from a 'self-serving' bias reflecting anticipated opportunities by players in a settlement activity. However, in an analysis employing incentives and rational choice, introducing something inconsistent with rational behavior creates a problem in terms of the analysis of the model and the comparison of any results with those of other analyses.

How important consistent priors are to the analysis has been made especially clear in work on analyzing asymmetric information games. Starting from basic principles of rational decision making, anyone making a choice about something unknown must make some assumptions about what characterizes the unknown thing (usually in the form of a probability distribution). To have two players playing an asymmetric game means, essentially, that they are playing a family of games, one for each possible pair of types (that is, one game for each pair of possible players). But which one are they playing? This is solved by superimposing a probabilistic choice by Nature (N), where each game is played with the probability specified by the overall distribution over types (denoted earlier in the card examples as $p(t_A, t_B)$). If this distribution does not exist (that is, if priors are inconsistent), we cannot do this and players are left not properly anticipating which game might be played. This transformation of something difficult to analyze (an asymmetric information game) into something we know how to analyze (a game with imperfect information) won John Harsanyi a share (along with John Nash and Reinhard Selten) of the 1994 Nobel Prize (the original papers are Harsanyi, 1967, 1968a, 1968b).

Thus, while players may hold different assessments over uncertain events, the notion of consistent priors limits the causes of the disagreement to differences in things like private information, and not to alternative modes of analysis; thus, players cannot paper-over differences by 'agreeing to disagree'. It is through this door that a literature, initially spawned by dissatisfaction with the perfect (and imperfect) information prediction that cases always settle, has proceeded to explain a variety of observed behavior with asymmetric information models.

One last point before passing on to prediction. Shavell (1993) has observed that when parties seek nonmonetary relief and the bargaining involves an indivisible item, settlement negotiations may break down, even if probability assessments are the same. An example of such a case would be child custody in a state with sole custody laws. This survey restricts consideration to cases involving non-lumpy allocations.

8. Prediction

The main purpose of all of the settlement models is to make a prediction about the outcome of bargaining, and the general rule is the more precise the prediction the better. The main tool used to make predictions in the recent literature is the notion of *equilibrium*. This is because most of the recent work has relied upon the notion of *non-cooperative* game theory, whereas earlier work implicitly or explicitly employed notions from *cooperative* game theory. The difference is that in a cooperative game, players (implicitly or explicitly) bind themselves *ex ante* to require that the solution to the game be efficient ('no money is left on the table'), while the equilibrium of a non-cooperative game does not assume any exogenously enforced contractual agreement to be efficient, and may end up not being efficient. We consider these notions in turn (for a review of laboratory-based tests of bargaining models (see Roth, 1995).

8.1 Nash Equilibrium in Non-Cooperative Games

A strategy profile provides an equilibrium if no individual player can unilaterally change their part of the strategy profile and make themselves better off; this notion of equilibrium is often called *Nash equilibrium* (after Nash, 1951), but its antecedents go far back in history. Using the notation introduced earlier, let s^* be an *equilibrium profile*; for convenience, assume the game has two players, named 1 and 2, so $s^* = (s_1^*, s_2^*)$ and s_1 and s_2 are all the other strategies that 1 and 2, respectively, could use. Then player 1 is prepared to stay with s_1^* if:

$$\$_1(s_1^*, s_2^*) \geq \$_1(s_1, s_2^*)$$

for every possible s_1 player 1 could choose. Player 2 is prepared to stay with s_2^* if:

$$\$_2(s_1^*, s_2^*) \geq \$_2(s_1^*, s_2)$$

for every possible s_2 player 2 could choose. As stated earlier, no player can unilaterally improve his payoff by changing his part of the equilibrium strategy profile.

Without generating more notation, the above conditions for a Nash equilibrium in a perfect information setting can be directly extended to the imperfect information setting. Here, the payoffs shown in the above inequalities are replaced by expected payoffs (the expectation reflecting the presence of uncertainty in one or more elements in the payoff function). Finally, in the case of asymmetric information, strategies and expectations are dependent upon type, and thus the equations must now hold for every player type and must reflect the individual player's conditional assessment about the other player(s). This last version is sometimes called a Bayesian Nash equilibrium to emphasize the role that the conditional probability distributions have in influencing the strategies that players use (for more detail, see Mas-Colell, Whinston and Green, 1995, Chapter 8).

Note that in all the variations on the definition of Nash equilibrium, there is a reference to no individual choosing to 'defect' from the strategy profile of interest. What about coalitions of players? Class action suits involve forming coalitions of plaintiffs, joint and several liability impacts coalitions of defendants and successful ('real world') bargaining strategy sometimes requires building or breaking coalitions (see Lax and Sebenius, 1986). Issues of coalitions have been of great interest to game theorists and equilibrium notions have been developed to account for coalition defection from a purported equilibrium strategy profile (see Binmore, 1985; Bernheim, Peleg and Whinston, 1987; Binmore, 1992; Greenberg, 1994, and Okada, 1996 for a small sample of recent work), but this is still an emerging area.

8.2. Cooperative Solutions

If two people are to divide a dollar between them (and both get nothing if they do not come to an agreement), then *any* allocation of the dollar such that each player gets more than zero is a Nash equilibrium, meaning that there is no predictive 'bite' to our definition of equilibrium in this bargaining context (prediction improvements, called refinements, exist and often have considerable bite; more on this later). In yet another seminal contribution, Nash (1950) provided a remarkable result that still provides context, and a reference point, for many analyses (cooperative and non-cooperative) of bargaining. His approach was to focus on the outcome of the bargaining game and to ignore the details of the bargaining process entirely, thereby also skipping the notion of requiring an equilibrium as the prediction mechanism. He posed the question: what desirable properties (called axioms) should a bargaining solution possess in order that a problem have a *unique* prediction? As mentioned earlier, by *solution* we mean that, *ex ante*, the two players would be prepared to bind themselves to the outcome which the solution provides. This approach is presented in more detail in Section 10.

Nash's axioms can be summarized as follows (see Binmore, 1992). First, the solution should not depend on how the players' utility scales are calibrated. This means that standard models of utility from decision theory may be employed (see, for example, Baird, Gertner and Picker, 1994). If payoffs are in monetary terms, this also means that players using different currencies could simply use an exchange rate to convert everything to one currency. Second, the solution should always be efficient. Third, if the players sometimes agree to one outcome when a second one is also feasible, then they never agree to the second one when the first one is feasible. Fourth, in a bargaining game with two identical players, both players get the same payoffs. The remarkable result is that whether the game is in utilities or money terms, the four axioms result in a *unique* solution (called the *Nash Bargaining Solution* or NBS) to the bargaining game. We return to this in Section 10.

There is a very important linkage between predictions using refinements of Nash equilibrium and predictions using a cooperative solution. One of the most remarkable and far-reaching results of game theory which emerged over the 1970s and 1980s has been the delineation of conditions under which the equilibria for properly structured non-cooperative games would be (in the lingo, would *support*) solutions to properly related cooperative games. In our particular case, there are conditions on the data for the strategic approach which guarantee that the equilibrium predicted for that model is the NBS of the associated bargaining problem. In other words, under certain conditions, the non-cooperative equilibrium is an efficient outcome.

Since we have not explored the axiomatic or strategic approaches in detail yet, let us consider an example likely to be familiar to most readers: the classic model of the conflict between group and individual incentives captured in the 'Prisoner's Dilemma' (see, Baird, Gertner and Picker (1994)). A variety of non-cooperative formulations have been developed wherein individual choices of strategies lead to the socially optimal outcome. The same techniques have been applied in a variety of settings, including bargaining. Thus, we now have a better understanding of how institutions, incentives and behavior may or may not substitute for artificially imposed binding agreements in achieving an efficient outcome. This also means that sources of inefficiencies ('money left on the table', and thus wasted) brought about by institutional constraints, incentives and non-cooperative behavior can be better understood.

9. An Example of a Model of Settlement Negotiation

Before venturing into the section describing the range of settlement models, a brief example will help clarify the concepts raised above. Reconsider Pat and Delta's negotiation with the following further simplifications and some numerical values. First, assume that the only source of uncertainty is Delta's liability. Damages are known by all, as are court costs. Moreover, there are no attorneys or experts and J will simply award the actual damage if Delta is found to be liable. Second, we will consider two simple bargaining stories.

(1) P makes a demand of D, followed by D accepting or rejecting the demand. Acceptance means a transfer from D to P; rejection means that J orders a transfer from D to P (the two transfers need not be the same) and both parties pay their court costs. Third, it is also common knowledge that if D is indifferent between accepting the proposal and rejecting it, D will accept it.

(2) D makes an offer to P, followed by P accepting or rejecting the offer. Acceptance means a transfer from D to P; rejection means that J orders a transfer from D to P (again, the two transfers need not be the same) and both parties pay their court costs. Third, it is also common knowledge that if P is indifferent between accepting the proposal and rejecting it, P will accept it.

Let d = 100 be the level of damages and L = 0.5 be the likelihood of D being found liable by J for the damage d. Let court costs be the same for both players with $k_P = k_D = 10$. Note that the expected compensation Ld exceeds the plaintiff's court cost k_P, so that should D reject P's demand in case (1), or offer too little in (2), it is still worth P's effort to go to trial. Note also that this ignores the possibility of bankruptcy of D. All of the above, that both players are rational (that is, P maximizes, and D minimizes, their respective payoffs) and the bargaining story being analyzed are common knowledge. One final bit of notation: let s be a settlement proposal.

9.1 Analyzing the Case Wherein P Makes a Demand

The first task is to find out if settlement is possible (the *admissible* settlements). We start with D, as P must anticipate D's choice when faced with P's demand. D and P know that if the case goes to trial, D will expend either $d + k_D$ or k_D (110 or 10), the first with probability L and the second with probability (1 − L); thus D's expected expenditure at trial (payoff from the outcome go to trial) is $Ld + k_D$ (that is, 60). Note that in this circumstance, P's expected payoff from the outcome labelled trial is $Ld - k_P$ (that is, 40). Thus, D will accept any settlement demand not exceeding this expected expenditure at trial:

$$s \leq Ld + k_D. \qquad (*)$$

P wishes to maximize her payoff which depends upon P's demand and the choice made by D: $\$_P = s_P$ if D accepts the demand s_P or $\$_P = Ld - k_P$ if D rejects the demand.

More carefully, using our earlier notation that the indicated payoff depending upon the strategy profile, we would have $\$_P(s_P, \text{accept}) = s_P$; that is, the payoff to P from her using the strategy 'make the settlement demand s_P' and D using the strategy 'accept' is the transfer s_P. Similarly, we would have $\$_P(s_P, \text{reject}) = Ld - k_P$. In the rest of this example we will suppress this notation when convenient, but understanding it will be of value later.

Observe that the maximum settlement demand that P can make ($s_P = Ld + k_D$, as shown in inequality (*)) exceeds P's payoff from court. Thus, P maximizes the expected payoff *from the game* by choosing $Ld + k_D$ as her settlement demand, which D accepts since D cannot do better by rejecting the proposal and facing trial. Thus, to summarize: (1) the players are P and D; (2) the action for P is the demand s_P (this is also P's strategy) while the action for D is to accept or reject and D's strategy is to accept if s_P satisfies the condition (*) and to reject otherwise; (3) the outcomes are settlement and transfer with associated payoffs $\$_P = s_P$ and $\$_D = s_P$, or proceed to trial and transfer with associated payoffs $\$_P = Ld - k_P$ and $\$_D = Ld + k_D$; (4) the timing is that P makes a demand and D chooses accept or reject; (5) information is imperfect in a very simple way in that P and D share the same assessment about the trial outcome with respect to liability. Note that it is unnecessary to model a choice for P about going to court if her demand were rejected because of the assumption that the expected compensation exceeds plaintiff trial costs. Moreover, since nothing in the settlement phase will influence the trial outcome itself should trial occur, J is not a player in a meaningful sense. The prediction (the equilibrium) of this game is that the case settles, the resulting transfer from D to P is $Ld + k_D$ (in the numerical example, 60) and the game payoffs are $\$_P = \$_D = Ld + k_D$ (60).

9.2 Analyzing the Case Wherein D Makes an Offer

We now start with P in order to find the admissible settlements. Given the foregoing, P will accept any settlement offer that yields at least what she would get in court:

$$s \geq Ld - k_P. \qquad (**)$$

D wishes to minimize its payoff, which depends upon the offer it makes and the choice made by P: $\$_D = s_D$ if P accepts the offer s_D or $\$_D = Ld + k_D$ if P rejects the offer. Thus D minimizes its payoff from the game by choosing $Ld - k_P$ as its settlement offer, which P accepts since P cannot do better by rejecting the proposal and going to trial. Thus, to summarize: (1) the players are P and D; (2) the action for D is the offer s_D (this is also D's strategy) while the action for P is accept or reject and P's strategy is to accept if s_D satisfies the condition (**) and to reject otherwise; (3) the outcomes are settlement and transfer with associated payoffs $\$_D = s_D$ and $\$_P = s_D$, or proceed to trial and transfer with associated payoffs $\$_D = Ld + k_D$ and $\$_P = Ld - k_P$; (4) the timing is that D makes an offer and P chooses to accept or reject; (5) information is imperfect in the same way as in the first case. The prediction (the equilibrium) of this game is that the case settles, the resulting transfer from D to P is $Ld - k_P$ (40) and the game payoffs are $\$_P = \$_D = Ld - k_P$ (40).

9.3 Bargaining Range and Bargaining Efficiency

A clear implication of the foregoing analysis is that who moves last has a significant impact on the allocation of the surplus generated by not going to court. One could think of the process in the following way. D pays L*d* to P no matter what procedure is used. P and D then contribute their court costs to a fund (called surplus) which they then split in some fashion. If the bargaining process involves P making a demand and D choosing only to accept or reject, then P gets all the surplus. If the roles are reversed, so are the fortunes. This might suggest that the two cases studied provide the extremes (the *bargaining range*) and that actual bargaining will yield something inside this range. The answer, we shall see, is maybe yes and maybe no. In the preceding analysis bargaining was efficient (no cases went to trial; again the reader is cautioned to recall the earlier discussion of the use of the word 'efficiency') since all information was symmetric and the first mover could make a take-it-or-leave-it proposal (cognizant of the second-mover's ability to go to trial). Efficiency will fail to hold when we allow for asymmetric information. This will occur not because of mistakes by players, but because of the recognition by both players that information which is asymmetrically distributed will impose a cost on the bargaining process, a cost that often falls on the better informed party.

B. Basic Models of Settlement Bargaining

10. Perfect and Imperfect Information Models: Axiomatic Models for the Cooperative Case

The perfect information model (and its first cousin, the imperfect information model), versions of which appear in Landes (1971), Gould (1973) and Posner (1973), is an important starting place as it focuses attention on efficient bargaining outcomes. Many of the earlier models employed risk aversion, which will be addressed in Section 17.1. For now, and so as to make the presentations consistent with much of the more recent literature, payoffs will be assumed to be in dollar terms with risk-neutral players.

10.1 Perfect Information

We start with the perfect information version. In keeping with the earlier discussion, the following model emphasizes final outcomes and suppresses bargaining detail. While the analysis below may seem like analytical overkill, it will allow us to structure the problem for later, more complex, discussions in this part and in Part C.

The players are P and D; further, assume that the level of damages, d, is commonly known and that D is fully liable for these damages. Court costs are k_P and k_D, and each player is responsible for their own court costs. Each player has an individual action they can take that assures them a particular payoff. P can stop negotiating and go to court; thus the payoff to P from trial is $\$_P{}^t = d - k_P$ (note the superscript t for trial) and the payoff to D from trial is $\$_D{}^t = d + k_D$. Under the assumption that $d - k_P > 0$, P has a *credible threat* to go to trial if negotiations fail. For the purposes of most of this paper (and most of the literature) we assume this condition to hold (the issue of it failing will be discussed in Section 16.1). By default, D can 'assure' himself of the same payoff by stopping negotiations, since P will then presumably proceed to trial; no other payoff for D is guaranteed via his individual action. The pair ($\$_D{}^t$, $\$_P{}^t$) is called the *threat or disagreement point* for the bargaining game (recall that D's payoff is an expenditure).

What might they agree on? One way to capture the essence of the negotiation is to imagine both players on either side of a table, and that they actually place money on the table (abusing the card-game story from earlier, this is an 'ante') in anticipation of finding a way of allocating it. This means that D places $d + k_D$ on the table and P places k_P on the table. The maximum at stake is the sum of the available resources, $d + k_P + k_D$, and therefore any outcome (which here is an allocation of the available resources) that does not exceed this amount is a possible settlement.

P's payoff, $\$_P$, is his bargaining outcome allocation (b_P) minus his ante (that is, $\$_P = b_P - k_P$). D's payoff, $\$_D$, is his ante minus his bargaining outcome allocation (b_D); thus D's *cost* (loss) is $\$_D = d + k_D - b_D$. Since the bargaining outcome ($b_P + b_D$) cannot exceed the total resources to be allocated (the money on the table), $b_P + b_D \leq d + k_D + k_P$, or equivalently, P's gain cannot exceed D's loss: $\$_P = b_P - k_P \leq d + k_D - b_D = \$_D$. Thus, in payoff terms, the outcome of the overall bargaining game must satisfy: (1) $\$_P \leq \$_D$; (2) $\$_P \geq \$_P{}^t$ and 3) $\$_D \leq \$_D{}^t$. In bargaining outcome terms this can be written as: (1') $b_P + b_D \leq d + k_D + k_P$; (2') $b_P \geq d$ and (3') $b_D \geq 0$. For the diagrams to come, we restate (2') as $b_P - d \geq 0$.

Figure 1(a) illustrates the settlement possibilities. The horizontal axis indicates the net gain ($-\$_D$) or net loss (that is total expenditure, $\$_D$) to D. The vertical axis indicates the net gain ($\$_P$) or net loss ($-\$_P$) to P. The sloping line graphs points satisfying $\$_P = \$_D$ while the region to the left of it involves allocations such that $\$_P < \$_D$. The best that D could possibly achieve is to recover his ante $d + k_D$ and get k_P too; this is indicated at the end of the line at the point (k_P, $-k_P$), meaning D has a net gain of k_P and P has a net loss of k_P. At the other extreme is the outcome wherein P gets all of $d + k_P + k_D$, meaning P has a net gain of $d + k_D$ which is D's net loss.

Note also that points below the line represent inefficient allocations: this is what is meant by 'money left on the table'. The disagreement point ($-(d + k_D)$, $d - k_P$) draws attention (observe the thin lines) to a portion of the feasible

Figure 1 Settlement Under Perfect Information

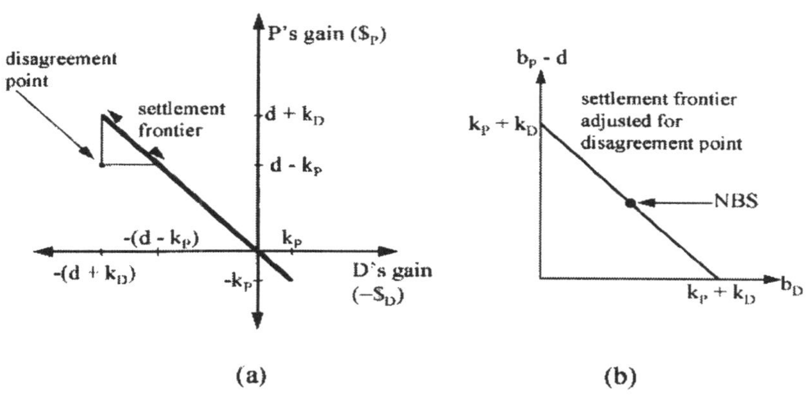

set that contains allocations that satisfy inequalities (2) and (3) above. The placement of this point reflects the assertion that there is something to bargain over; if the point were above the line $\$_P = \$_D$ then trial is unavoidable, since there would be no settlements that satisfy (2) and (3) above. This triangular region, satisfying inequalities (1), (2) and (3), is the *settlement set* and the end points of the portion of the line $\$_P = \$_D$ which is in the settlement set are called the *concession limits*; between the concession limits (and including them) are all the efficient bargaining outcomes under settlement, called the *settlement frontier*.

Figure 1(b) illustrates the settlement set as bargaining outcomes, found by subtracting the disagreement point from everything in the settlement set. Doing this helps adjust the region of interest for asymmetries in the threats that P and D can employ. This leaves any remaining asymmetries in power or information in the resulting diagram. In the case at hand, the only power difference might appear in the difference between the costs of going to trial; other power differences such as differences in risk preferences, patience, and so on will be discussed in Section 17.1, while informational differences will be discussed in the sections on asymmetric information in Parts B and C.

Notice that, in view of (2') and (3'), the vertical (non-negative) axis is labelled $b_P - d$ while the horizontal (non-negative) axis is labelled b_D. Moreover, since aggregate trial costs determine the frontier in Figure 1(b), the bargaining problem here is symmetric. The Nash Bargaining Solution (NBS) applies in either picture, but its prediction is particularly obvious in Figure 1(b): recalling the discussion in Section 8.2, requiring the solution to be efficient (axiom 2) and that, when the problem is symmetric the solution is too (axiom 4), means that splitting the saved court costs is the NBS in Figure 1(b). Thus, to find the NBS in Figure 1(a), we add the disagreement point *back into the solution from Figure 1(b).* Therefore, P's payoff is $d - k_P + (k_P + k_D)/2 = d + (k_D - k_P)/2$. D's net outflow is $-(d + k_D) + (k_P + k_D)/2$. In other words, D's payoff (his expenditure) is $d + (k_D - k_P)/2$. The result that players should 'split the difference' is always the NBS solution for any bargaining game with payoffs in monetary terms.

Observe that if court costs are the same, then at the NBS P and D simply transfer the liability d. If D's court costs exceed P's, P receives more from the settlement than the actual damages, reflecting his somewhat stronger relative bargaining position embodied in his threat with respect to the surplus that P and D can jointly generate by not going to court. A similar argument holds for P in the weaker position, with higher costs of going to court: he settles for less than d.

10.2 Imperfect Information

This is essentially the same model, so only the variations will be remarked upon. Assume that P and D have the same probability assessments for the two court costs and assume that they also have the same probability assessments over expected damages. This latter possibility could reflect that the level of damages is unknown (for example, as discussed in Section 7.1) but that liability is taken to be assured. Then they both see expected damages as E(d). Alternatively, perhaps damages are known to be d but liability is less clear but commonly assessed to be L; that is, L is the common assessment that D will be held liable for damages d and (1 - L) is the common assessment that D will not be held liable at all. Then E(d) = dL (an admitted but useful abuse of notation). Finally, if there are common elements influencing the values that d might take on and the likelihood of D being held liable, and if the assessments of the possible values and their joint likelihood is common knowledge, then again we will write the expected damages from trial as E(d).

Again, this is abusing the notation, but avoids needless technical distinctions. The point is that in an imperfect information setting we simply take the preceding analysis and replace all known parameters with their suitably constructed expectations, yielding the same qualitative results: no trials occur in equilibrium, strong plaintiffs settle for somewhat more than their expected damages, and so forth.

11. Perfect and Imperfect Information Models: Strategic Models for the Non-Cooperative Case

Again, we start with the perfect information case. Furthermore, since the actual bargaining procedure is now to be specified, the length of the bargaining horizon now enters into the analysis. The generic style of the models to be considered is that one player makes a proposal followed by the other player choosing to accept or reject the proposal. Concatenating as many of these simple proposal/response sequences as we choose provides the basic story.

Some questions, however, remain. First, is the proposer the same player each time? In general we will assume that if there is more than one round of proposal/response, then proposers alternate (an important exception is Spier, 1992, where the plaintiff always proposes; this will be discussed in Section 18). If there is more than one round, the next proposal is often thought of as a counterproposal to the one before it.

Second, how many periods of proposal/response will there be? This turns out to be a very significant question. Recall that in the cooperative model P and D were committed to finding an efficient bargaining outcome. Here, no such commitment is made; instead, we want to know when non-cooperative bargaining will be efficient. However, certain types of commitments in strategic models still may occur. The reason this is of interest is that commitment generally provides some power to the player who can make a commitment. For example, if there is one round of proposal/response, then the proposer has the ability to make an all-or-nothing proposal (more carefully put, all-or-court proposal). As was seen in the examples in Section 9, this led to a settlement that was efficient but rather one-sided. In particular, the proposer was able to achieve the point on the settlement frontier that is the responder's concession limit. This is a reflection of the commitment power that the proposer enjoys of *not* responding to any counterproposals that the responder might desire to make: these are ruled out by the structure of the game analyzed. This is why this game is often referred to as an *ultimatum game.* Ultimatum games form the basis for many of the asymmetric information settlement analyses we shall examine.

Almost at the other end of the spectrum of theoretical bargaining analyses is the Rubinstein infinite-horizon model (Rubinstein, 1982). In this model an infinite number of rounds of proposal/response occur wherein the proposer's identity alternates. In the settlement setting, each round allows P to choose to break off negotiations and go to trial. Here there are two somewhat more subtle forms of commitment in place of the power to make all-or-nothing proposals. First, if there is a positive interval of time between one round and the next, and if 'time is money', meaning (for example) that costs are accruing (perhaps experts are being kept available, or lawyers are accruing time), then the fact that during a round only one proposal is being considered (the proposer's) provides some power to the proposer.

Second, who goes first is still significant. Rubinstein considers a simple 'shrinking pie' example wherein each player discounts money received in the future relative to money received now. This encourages both players to want to settle sooner rather than later (all else equal). Thus, delay here yields inefficiency. Rubinstein uses a notion of Nash equilibrium that incorporates the dynamics of the bargaining process (this extra property of equilibrium is called *sequential rationality,* which will be discussed in more detail in Section 11.1) which results in a unique prediction for the bargaining game. In particular, there is no delay and, if both players are identical, then the player who goes first gets more than half of the amount at stake.

Models that shrink the time interval associated with each round find that both sources of power go away as the time interval between proposals becomes vanishingly small. Note that, even with positive intervals, the effect of commitment (in this case, a short-run commitment to a proposal) is not as strong as in the ultimatum game, since counterproposals can occur and players generally cannot bind themselves to previous proposals they have made. In other words, such infinite horizon models can generate efficient settlement at points on the frontier other than the concession limits. In fact, under certain conditions they predict the NBS as the unique equilibrium of the strategic bargaining game. Note that the fact that a strategic model employs perfect information does not guarantee that the predicted outcome is efficient. A particularly striking example of this is contained in Fernandez and Glazer (1991) who consider wage negotiations between a union and a firm under perfect information and yet get inefficient equilibria. The source of the inefficiency is a pre-existing wage contract. This is an unexplored area for settlement bargaining which might yield some interesting results.

Finally, a further difference between settlement applications and the general literature on bargaining concerns the incentive to settle as soon as possible, all else equal. Generally, in the settlement context, P wants to settle sooner but D wants to settle later. While countervailing pressures, such as costs that increase with time, may encourage D to settle as early as possible, the fact that payment delayed is generally preferred by the payor (due to the time value of money) means that D's overall incentives to settle soon can be mixed and delay may be optimal. Moreover, as observed in Spier (1992), unlike the Rubinstein model, if both P and D have the same discount rate then the pie itself is *not* shrinking (assuming no other costs of bargaining). This is because the effect of the opposed interests and the same discount rates is to cancel out. Therefore, in a multiperiod settlement model, delay due to the time value of money does not, in and of itself, imply inefficiency. We will return to this shortly.

11.1 Sequential Rationality

Note that in much of the preceding discussion an implicit notion was that a player's strategy anticipates future play in the game. A strategy is *sequentially rational if* it is constructed so that the player takes an *optimal* action at each possible decision opportunity that the player has in the future. Earlier, in the discussion of the disagreement point, sequential rationality was used by P. The threat to go to trial if bargaining failed to satisfy (2) was sequentially rational: it was a credible threat because if P got to that point, he would choose to fulfill the threat he had made. Applying sequential rationality to the strategies players use, and to the analysis players make of what strategies *other* players might use, means that strategies based on threats that a rational player would not carry out (incredible threats) are ruled out. Many of the improvements in making predictions for asymmetric information models that have occurred over the last fifteen years have involved employing sequential rationality, generally in conjunction with further amplifications of what rational behavior implies. Rubinstein finds a unique prediction in the infinite-horizon alternating offers game (for short, the Rubinstein game) because he predicts Nash equilibria which enforce sequential rationality (called *subgame perfect equilibrium*; for a discussion of some applications of subgame perfection in law and economics, see Baird, Gertner and Picker, 1994). In the Rubinstein game, even though the horizon is infinite, the (sequentially rational) Nash equilibrium is a unique, specific, efficient bargaining allocation which is proposed and accepted in the first round. Thus, efficiency (both in terms of fully allocating what is available to bargain over as well as doing it without delay) is a *result,* not an assumption.

11.2 Settlement Using Strategic Bargaining Models in the Perfect Information Case

The discussion in Section 9 provides the details of the ultimatum game version of settlement. Since that application technically involved imperfect information (the assessment about liability), a careful treatment means that we would take L = 1, yielding the payoffs for the ultimatum model with P as proposer (the P-proposer ultimatum model) to be $\$_P = \$_D = d + k_D$, while the D-proposer ultimatum model's payoffs would be $\$_P = \$_D = d - k_P$. The rest of this section is therefore devoted to the analysis in the infinite horizon case.

The tradeoff between D's natural interest to delay payment and any incentives to settle early (in particular, P's credible threat to go to court and any negotiation costs borne by D) is explored in the settlement context in Ho Wang, Kim and Yi (1994); they also consider an asymmetric information case which will be discussed in Section 12.4. In the perfect information analysis, D proposes in the first round, but is subject in each round to an additional cost, c, which reflects per period negotiating costs but is charged *only* if the negotiations proceed to the next period. One could include a cost of this sort for P, too, but it is the difference between P's and D's negotiating costs that matters, so letting P's be zero is not a meaningful limitation.

Let f (a fraction between zero and one) be the common discount rate used by the players for evaluating and comparing money flows at different points in time; that is, a player is indifferent between receiving \$1 next period and \$$f$ this period. Note that this effect could be undone if, at trial, damages were awarded with interest from the date of filing the suit; this does not occur in their model. Wang, Kim and Yi show that if $fc/(1 - f^2) > d - k_P$, then the unique subgame perfect equilibrium is for D to offer $f^2c/(1 - f^2)$ to P; if instead $fc/(1 - f^2) < d - k_P$, the unique subgame perfect equilibrium involves D offering $f(d - k_P)$ to P. For a careful proof of this, see Wang, Kim and Yi; for our purposes, let us use some crude intuition (sweeping all sorts of technical details under the rug) to understand this result.

Consider D's viewpoint. The only reason for D to be indifferent between an expenditure in one period and an expenditure in the next period involves the delay cost and the discount rate: indifference as to when to spend s in one of two adjacent periods means the discounted value of waiting, incurring c and then spending s (which is $fs + fc$) should just equal the expenditure of s now (that is, $fs + fc = s$). Of course, since D only makes a decision every *other* period this relationship affects P more directly than D. P will find this to be advantageous if c is large enough and if $fs + fc > d - k_P$. Assume it is; this means that if costs are high enough to get D to not want to delay (or make an offer that would have P choose to go to trial) the worst that P would get would be $f(fs + fc)$, which should be the most D would offer; that is, s. Solving $f(fs + fc) = s$ for s yields $s = fc/(1 - f^2)$. If this is large enough, D will make an offer that P will prefer to the payoff from going to trial. Since the offer only has to make P indifferent between two adjacent time periods (when D offers and P accepts or rejects, and when P decides about going to trial or counterproposing), D can offer $f(fc/(1 - f^2))$ and P will accept in the period in which the offer is made if next period $fc/(1 - f^2) > d - k_P$ (the equality between the two sides is eliminated as it provides multiple predictions, while the strict inequality yields a unique solution; see Rubinstein, 1985). In this sense, $fc/(1 - f^2) > d - k_P$ really is a statement that the cost of delay is high from D's viewpoint, which is why D must offer something higher than the discounted value of going to trial, that is, $f(d - k_P)$.

Even if costs are low (that is, $fc/(1 - f^2) < d - k_P$), D must still worry about P's choice of going to court, but P can no longer exploit D's cost weakness to further improve the bargain in his favor. Thus, D can offer the discounted value of P's concession limit, namely $f(d - k_P)$, since P cannot choose to go to court until next period and therefore might as well accept $f(d - k_P)$ now.

To summarize, the players are P and D, actions in each period involve proposals followed by accept/reject from the other player, with P able to choose to go to court when it is his turn to propose. Payoffs are as usual with the added provisos concerning the discount rate f reflecting the time value of money, and the per period cost c, for the defendant, which is incurred each time negotiators fail to agree. The bargaining horizon is infinite and information is perfect. The result is that: (1) P and D settle in the first period; (2) the prediction is unique and efficient; (3) if negotiation costs are sufficiently high then the prediction is on the settlement frontier, between the discounted values of the concession limits and (4) otherwise it is at the discounted value of P's concession limit, reflecting the fact that D moved first.

11.3 The Imperfect Information Case

The extension of the ultimatum game results of Section 9 to the imperfect information case parallels the discussion in Section 10.2. This is similarly true for the multiperiod case, which is why this issue has not received much attention.

12. Analyses Allowing for Differences in Player Assessments Due to Private Information

In this section we consider models that account for differences in the player's assessments about items such as damages and liability based on the private information players possess when they bargain. We focus especially on two models: one developed by Bebchuk (1984) and one developed by Reinganum and Wilde (1986). Most of the analyses in the current literature are based on one of these two primary settlement models, both of which analyze ultimatum games and both of which assume one-sided asymmetric information; that is, that there is an aspect of the game (typically a parameter such as damages or liability) about which P and D have different information, and only one of the players knows the true value of the parameter during bargaining. Since the model structure is so specific (the ultimatum game) and the distribution of information is so one-sided, we also consider what models with somewhat greater generality suggest about the reasonableness of the two prime workhorses of the current settlement literature. For a survey of asymmetric information bargaining theory, see Kennan and Wilson (1993). For a recent discussion of the settlement frontier under inconsistent priors, see Chung (1996).

12.1 Yet More Needed Language and Concepts: Screening, Signaling, Revealing and Pooling

Reaching back to Section 7, a one-sided information model is like a card game where only one player has a down card and knows the value of that card. That player is privately informed and, because of consistent priors, both players know that the probability model being used by the uninformed player is common knowledge.

Since the basic bargaining process involves one round of proposal and response, the fact that only one of the players possesses private information about something that is important to both means that *when* the informed player acts is, itself, important. A *screening* model (also sometimes called a *sorting* model) involves the uninformed player making the proposal and the informed player choosing to accept or reject the proposal. A *signaling* model involves the reverse: the informed player makes the proposal and the uninformed player chooses to accept or reject it. Note that the word 'signaling' only means that the proposal is made by the informed player, not that the proposal itself is necessarily informative about the private information possessed by the proposer. Bebchuk's model is a screening model and Reinganum and Wilde's model is a signaling model.

These are non-cooperative models of bargaining, so our method of prediction is finding an equilibrium (rather than a cooperative solution). In both cases sequential rationality is also employed. Generally, in the case of a screening model this yields a unique prediction. In the case of a signaling model sequential rationality is generally insufficient to produce a unique prediction. The reason is that since the uninformed player is observing the informed player's action in this case, the action itself may reveal something about the private information of the proposer.

To understand this, consider a modification of the card game story from Section 7.1. Here are the hands for players A and B and, as before, only A knows his down card.

Table 2
Hands of Cards for A and B

	Up	Down
A	AD, QD, JD, 10D	2H
B	10C, 10S, 9S, 5D, 2C	

(Note: entries provide face value of card and suit)

To fill out the story, all the above cards have just been dealt, after players put some money on the table, from a standard 52-card deck. The rules are that player A may now discard one card (if it is the down card, this is done without revealing it) and a new card is provided that is drawn from the undealt portion of the deck. A can also choose not to discard a card. If he does discard one, the new card is dealt face up if the discard was an up-card and is dealt face down otherwise. After this, A and B can add money to that already on the table or they can surrender their share of the money currently on the table ('fold'); for convenience, assume that a player must fold or add money (a player cannot stay in the game without adding money to that already on the table). The cards are then compared, privately, by an honest dealer, and any winner gets all the money while a tie splits the money evenly amongst those who have not folded. The comparison process in this case means that, for player A, a down card that matches his Ace, Queen or Jack card with the same face value (that is, A ends up with two Aces or two Queens or two Jacks) will beat B's hand, as will any Diamond in conjunction with A's up cards currently showing. Other draws mean that A will either tie (a 10H) or lose.

Before A chooses whether and what to discard, B knows that the down card could be any of 43 cards with equal likelihood. Now if A discards his down card, based on sequential rationality, B knows that it was not an Ace, a Queen, a Jack or a Diamond. This information can be used by B *before* he must take any action. He may choose to fold, or he may choose to add money, but this decision is now influenced by what he believes to be A's private information, A's new down card. These beliefs take the form of an improved probability estimate over A's type (adjusting for what has been observed). In fact, these assessments are called *beliefs*, and in an asymmetric information model, players form beliefs based upon the prior assessments and everything that they have observed before each and every decision they make. The addition of the need to account for what beliefs players can reasonably expect to hold makes the signaling game more complex to analyze than the screening game.

A few more observations about the card game are in order. First, even though this was a signaling game, the signal of discarding did not completely inform the uninformed player of the content of the private information. A strategy for the informed player is *revealing* if, upon the uninformed player observing the action(s) of the informed player, the uninformed player can correctly infer the informed player's type. In this sense, each type of player has an action that distinguishes it from all the other types. For example, in the settlement context where P is privately informed about the true level of damages but D only knows the prior distribution, a revealing strategy would involve each possible type of P (each possible level of damages) making a different settlement demand, such as P demands his true damages plus D's court costs. If instead P always asked for the average level of damages, independent of the true level, plus court costs, then P would be using a *pooling* strategy: different types of P take the same action and therefore are observationally indistinguishable.

In the card game above, A choosing to discard his down card has some elements of a revealing strategy (not all types would choose this action) and some elements of a pooling strategy (there are a number of types who would take the same action). This is an example of a *semi-pooling* or *partial pooling* strategy. Notice that if the deck had originally consisted of *only* the eleven cards AD, KD, QD, JD, 10D, 10C, 10S, 9S, 5D, 2C, 2H, then B could use the action 'discard' to distinguish between the private information 'initial down card = KD' and 'initial down card = 2H' because discarding the down card is only rational for the player holding a 2H. Thus, discarding or not discarding in this case is a fully revealing action. In this particular example we got this by changing the size of the deck (thereby changing the number of types), but this is not always necessary. In many signaling models, extra effort placed on making predictions, even in the presence of a continuum of types, leads to fully revealing behavior; we will see this in the signaling analysis below.

Finally, a *revealing equilibrium* means that the equilibrium involves the complete release of all private information. In a revealing equilibrium the privately informed player is employing a revealing strategy. In a *pooling equilibrium* the private information is not released. In other words, at the end of the game, no more is necessarily known by the uninformed player than was known before play began. More generally, in a *partial pooling equilibrium*, some of the types have been revealed through their actions and some of the types took actions which do not allow us to distinguish them from one another.

12.2 Where You Start and Where You End

As will be seen below, a typical screening model produces partial pooling equilibria as its prediction; in fact, the equilibrium is often composed of two big pools (a bunch of types do this and the rest do that) and is only fully revealing if each pool consists of one type. In other words, if the private information in the model takes on more than two values, some pooling will typically occur in the equilibrium prediction of a screening model. On the other hand, a typical signaling model has all three types of equilibria (revealing, fully pooling, partial pooling) as predictions, but with some extra effort concerning rational inference (called *refinements* of equilibrium) this often reduces to a unique prediction of a revealing equilibrium. Either one of these types of prediction may be desirable, depending upon the process being analyzed.

12.3 One-Sided Asymmetric Information Settlement Process Models: Examples of Analyses

In the subsections to follow we will start with the same basic setting and find the results of applying screening and signaling models. Bebchuk's 1984 paper considered an informed defendant (concerning liability) responding to an offer from an uninformed plaintiff; Reinganum and Wilde's 1986 paper considered a plaintiff with private information about damages making a demand of an uninformed defendant. Initially, information will be modeled as taking on two levels (that is, a two-type model is employed) and a basic analysis using each approach will be presented and solved. The result of allowing for more than two types (in particular, a continuum of types) will then be discussed in the context of the alternative approaches.

Since most of the discussion earlier in this survey revolved around damages, both approaches will be applied to private information on damages, suggesting a natural setting of an informed P and an uninformed D (note, however, that the earlier example of Pat and Delta was purposely posed with Delta as the informed party to emphasize that the analysis is applicable in a variety of settings). More precisely, the level of damages is assumed to take on the value d_L (L for low) or d_H (H for high), meaning that P suffers a loss and it takes on one of these two levels, which is private information for P. Moreover, $d_H > d_L > 0$. The levels are common knowledge as is D's assessment that p is the probability of the low value being the true level of damages. If the case were to go to trial then J will find out the true level of damages (whether the damages were equal to d_L or equal to d_H) and award the true damages to P. Thus $E_D(d) = pd_L + (1 - p)d_H$ is D's prior estimate of the expected damages that he will pay if he goes to trial; P knows whether the damages paid will be d_L or d_H. Should the case go to trial each player pays his own court costs (k_P and k_D, respectively) and, for simplicity again, assume that $d_L > k_P$; relaxing this assumption is discussed in Section 16.1. Finally, in each case the structure of the bargaining process is represented by an ultimatum game. In particular, the player who responds will choose to accept the proposal if he is indifferent between the payoff resulting from accepting the proposal and the payoff resulting from trial. *Without any more information*, D's a priori (that is, before bargaining) expected payoff from trial is $E_D(d) + k_D$; P's payoff from trial is $d_L - k_P$ if true damages are d_L, and $d_H - k_P$ if true damages are d_H.

12.3.1 Screening A Two-Type Analysis In this model D offers a settlement transfer to P of s_D and P responds with acceptance or rejection. For the analysis to be sequentially rational (that is, we are looking for a subgame perfect equilibrium) we start by thinking about what P's strategy should be for *any* possible offer made by D in order for him to maximize his overall payoff from the game. If $s_D \geq d_H - k_P$, then no matter whether damages are high or low, P should accept and settle at s_D. If $s_D < d_L - k_P$, then no matter whether damages are high or low, P should reject the offer and go to trial. If s_D is set so that it lies between these two possibilities, that is, $d_H - k_P > s_D \geq d_L - k_P$, then a P with high damages should reject the offer, but a P with low damages should accept the offer. This last offer is said to *screen the types*; note that the offer results in the revelation of the private information. Thus P's optimal action is contingent upon the offer made; we have found P's strategy and it involves rational choice. D can do this computation, too, for each possible type of P that could occur, so from D's viewpoint he models P as having a strategy that depends both on P's type and upon D's offer.

As always, D's objective is to minimize expected expenditure and he must make an offer before observing any further information about P; thus, D cannot improve his assessments as occurred in the card game. D knows, however, that some offers are better than others. For example, the lowest offer in the range $d_H - k_P > s_D \geq d_L - k_P$, namely $s_D = d_L - k_P$, is better than any other offer in that range, since it does not change the result that H-type P's will reject and L-type P's will accept, and its cost is least when compared to other possible offers in this range. The expected cost of screening the types is $p(d_L - k_P) + (1 - p)(d_H + k_D) = E_D(d) + k_D - p(k_P + k_D)$, since the offer elicits acceptance with probability p (the probability of L-types) and generates a trial and attendant costs with probability $(1 - p)$. The payoff from making offers that both types reject is $E_D(d) + k_D$. Finally, the expected cost from making an offer that both types will accept is simply the cost of the offer that the H-type will accept, namely $d_H - k_P$.

A comparison of the payoffs from the different possible offers that D could make indicates that it is always better for D to make an offer of at least the L-type's concession limit (that is, the value of s_D specified above, $d_L -$

k_P). It may be optimal to pool the types; that is, to make an offer at the H-type's concession limit ($d_H - k_P$), which will therefore be accepted by P independent of his actual damages incurred. Finally, comparing the expected cost to D of the screening offer, $E_D(d) + k_D - p(k_P + k_D)$, with the expected cost to D of the pooling offer, $d_H - k_P$, it is optimal to screen the types if $E_D(d) + k_D - p(k_P + k_D) < d_H - k_P$; that is, if:

$$p > (k_P + k_D)/(d_H - d_L + k_P + k_D). \qquad \text{(SSC)}$$

Inequality (SSC) is the *simple screening condition* (simple because it considers two types only); it indicates that the relevant comparison between screening the types or pooling them involves total court costs ($k_P + k_D$), the difference between potential levels of damages ($d_H - d_L$) and the relative likelihood of H- and L-types. Given court costs and the gap between high and low damages, the more likely it is that P has suffered low damages rather than high damages, the more likely D should be to screen the types and thereby only rarely go to trial (and then, always against an H-type). If the likelihood of facing an H-type P is sufficiently high (that is, p is low), then it is better to make an offer that is high enough to settle with both possible types of plaintiff. Therefore, with pooling there are no trials, but with screening trials occur with probability $(1 - p)$. Condition (SSC) also suggests that, for a given probability of low-damage Ps and a given gap between the levels of damages, sizable trial costs auger for pooling (that is, settling with both types of P).

Finally, the model allows us to compute the efficiency loss and to recognize its source. To see this, imagine the above analysis in the imperfect information setting; in particular, for this setting both P and D do not know P's type, and they agree on the estimate of damages, $E_D(d)$, and that liability of D for the true damages is certain. In the imperfect information version of the D-proposer ultimatum game, D's optimal offer is $E_D(d) - k_P$, P's concession limit under imperfect information. Since in that setting P doesn't know his type, he would settle at $E_D(d) - k_P$ rather than require $d_H - k_P$ (which is greater than $E_D(d) - k_P$) to avoid trial if he is an H-type. Thus, the difference in D's payoff under imperfect information ($E_D(d) - k_P$) and that under the asymmetric information analyzed above ($E_D(d) + k_D - p(k_P + k_D)$) is $(1 - p)(k_P + k_D)$. This extra cost to D comes from the fact that D recognizes that P knows his own type and will act accordingly. Note that this is not a transfer to P; it is an efficiency loss. This loss is a share of the surplus that, under perfect or imperfect information, would have been avoided by settling rather than going to trial, and is a loss that is due to the presence of an asymmetry in the players' information.

12.3.2. Screening with Many Types The principle used above extends to settings involving finer distinctions among levels of private information. In particular, this subsection will outline the nature of the model when applied to a continuum of types, such as a plaintiff whose level of damages could take on any value between two given levels of damages (that is, d may take on values between, and including, d_L and d_H; $d_L \leq d \leq d_H$). This is formally equivalent to Bebchuk's original model (Bebchuk, 1984), even though his analysis presented a D who was privately informed about liability in a P-proposer setting with known damages. Thus, differences in the presentations between this discussion and Bebchuk's are due to the shift of the proposer and the source of private information; there are no substantive differences between the analyses.

As always, D's probability assessment of the likelihood of the different possible levels of damages is common knowledge and is denoted $p(d)$, which provides the probability that damages are no more than any chosen value of d. Figure 2 illustrates the intuition behind the analysis. The distribution of possible levels of damages as drawn implies equal likelihood, but this is for illustrative purposes only; many (though not all) probability assessment models would yield similar qualitative predictions. Figure 2 illustrates a level of damages, x, intermediate to the two extremes, d_L and d_H, and that the fraction of possible damage levels at or below x is given by $p(x)$. Alternatively put, if D offers $s = x - k_P$, a P who has suffered the level of damages x would be indifferent between the offer and the payoff from going to trial. Moreover, this offer would also be accepted by any P with damages less than x, while any P with damages greater than x would reject the offer and go to trial. The expected expenditure associated with offers that are accepted is $sp(x)$. Note that the particular value x that made the associated P indifferent between settling and going to trial depends upon the offer: $x(s) = s + k_P$. This is accounted for by explicitly recognizing this dependence: if D makes an offer s_D, then the expected expenditure associated with accepted offers is $s_D p[x(s_D)]$.

Figure 2 Screening with a Continuum of Types

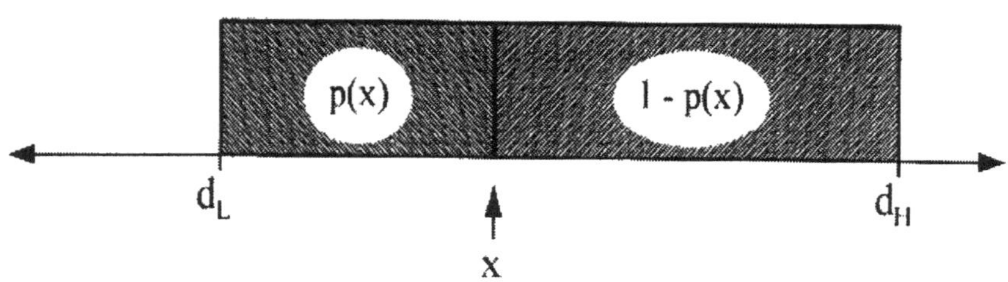

Two observations are in order. First, as s_D increases, the 'marginal' type $x(s_D)$ (also known as the 'borderline' type; see Bebchuk, 1984) moves to the right and this would increase $p(x(s_D))$. Thus, this expected expenditure is increasing in the offer both because the offer itself goes up and as it increases, so does the likelihood of it being accepted. Second, while the types of P that reject the offer and go to trial are 'revealed' by the award made by J (who learns the true d and awards it), as long as x does not equal d_L there is residual uncertainty in every possible outcome of the game: the offer pools those who accept, and their private information is not revealed (other than the implications to be drawn from the fact that they must have damages that lie to the left of x in Figure 2). The fact that the equilibrium will therefore involve only partial revelation is the main difference between the two-type model (where screening reveals types) and the model with a continuum of types.

To minimize expected expenditure, D trades off the expected expenditure from settling with the expected expenditure for trial, since the fraction $(1 - p(x(s_D))$ goes to trial. Under appropriate assumptions on $p(x)$, this latter expenditure is declining in s_D, yielding an optimal offer $(s_D{}^*)$ for D that makes the type of P represented by the level of damages $x(s_D{}^*)$ the marginal type. Thus, 'P has been screened'.

As an example, if all levels of damages are equally likely, as illustrated in Figure 2 above, then as long as the gap between the extreme levels of damages exceeds the total court costs (that is, $d_H - d_L \geq k_P + k_D$), the equilibrium screening offer is $s_D{}^* = d_L + k_D$ and the marginal type is a P with level of damages $d_L + k_D + k_P$; Ps with damages at or below this level accept the offer while those with damages in excess of this level reject the offer. Note that should the gap in levels of damages be less than aggregate trial costs ($d_H - d_L < k_P + k_D$), then D simply pools all the types with the offer $d_H - k_P$.

12.3.3 Signaling: A Two-Type Analysis This approach employs a P-proposer model in which P makes a settlement demand followed by D choosing to accept or reject the proposal; given the assumptions made in the discussion before subsection 12.3.1, a rejection leads to P going to trial, at which J learns the true level of damages and awards P their value.

As discussed in Section 4, in the circumstances of this ultimatum game, D should use a mixed strategy: if demands at or below some level were always accepted, while those above this level were always rejected, some types of P would be compensated more than might be necessary and D would go to court more often than necessary. Here a mixed strategy should respond to the demand made: low demands should be rejected less often than high demands, if only because a high demand is more advantageous to a greater percentage of possible types of Ps, and therefore requires D to be more diligent.

The notion that lower types (those with lesser damages) of P have an incentive to try to be mistaken for higher types (those with greater damages) plays a central role in the analysis. D's use of a mixed strategy, dependent upon the demand made, provides a counter-incentive which can make mimicry unprofitable: a greedy demand at the settlement bargaining stage, triggering a greater chance of rejection, may therefore more readily lead to much lower payoffs at trial (where the true level of damages is revealed with certainty and P then must pay his court costs from the award) than would have occurred at a somewhat lower demand.

P's demand is s_P, which D responds to by rejecting it with probability $r_D(s_P)$ or accepting it, which occurs with probability $1 - r_D(s_P)$. Clearly, if the demand is $d_L + k_D$, then D should accept this demand as D can do no better by rejecting it. For convenience, we will define s_L to be this lowest-type demand, and thus, $r_D(s_L) = 0$. On the other hand, if P were to make a demand higher than what would be D's expenditure at trial associated with the highest type, namely $d_H + k_D$, then D should reject any such demand for sure. It is somewhat less clear what D should do with $d_H + k_D$, which for convenience we denote as s_H. As will be shown below (in both the two-type and the continuum of types models) D's equilibrium strategy will set $r_D(s_H)$ to be less than one. This will provide an incentive for greedy Ps to demand at most s_H (technically, this is for the benefit of specifying an equilibrium, and it turns out not to hurt D). Since P knows what D knows, P can also construct the $r_D(s_P)$ function that D will use to respond to any demand s_P that P makes. P uses this function to decide what demand will maximize his payoff.

While there are demand/rejection probability combinations that can generate all three types of equilibria (revealing, pooling and partial pooling), the focus here is on characterizing a revealing equilibrium. To do this we take our cue from the appropriate perfect information ultimatum game. In those analyses, if it was common knowledge that P was a high type, he could demand and get s_H, while if it was common knowledge that P was a low type, he could demand and get s_L. Making such demands clearly provides an action that could allow D to infer that, should he observe s_L it must have come from a low type, while if he observed s_H, it must have come from a high-type. While wishing does not make this true, incentives in terms of payoffs can, so that a low-damage P's best choice between s_L and s_H is s_L and a high-damage P's best choice between s_L and s_H is s_H. In particular, consider the following two inequalities (since $r_D(s_L) = 0$, the following inequalities employ the notation r for the rejection probability; we will then pick a particular value of r to be the value of D's rejection strategy, $r_D(s_H)$):

$$s_L \geq (1 - r)s_H + r(d_L - k_P) \quad \text{(ICL)}$$

and

$$s_L \leq (1 - r)s_H + r(d_H - k_P). \quad \text{(ICH)}$$

The first inequality, called ICL for the *incentive compatibility condition for the low type* states that D's choice of r is such that when P has the low level of damages, his payoff is at least as good when he demands s_L as what his payoff would be by mimicking the high-damages P's demand s_H, which is accepted with probability $(1 - r)$, but is rejected with probability r (resulting in the P of either type going to court). Note that, since J would learn the true type at court, a low-type P gets $d_L - k_P$ if his demand is rejected. In other words, on the right is the expected payoff to a P with the low level of damages from misrepresenting himself as having suffered high damages. Inequality ICH *(the incentive compatibility condition for the high type)* has a similar interpretation, but now it is for the high types: they are also no worse off by making the settlement demand that reflects their true type (the expected cost on the right side of the inequality) than they would be if they misrepresented themselves. When r, s_L and s_H satisfy *both* (ICL) and (ICH), then these strategies for D and the two types of P yield a revealing equilibrium.

Substituting the values for s_L and s_H and solving the two inequalities yields the following requirement for r:

$$(d_H - d_L)/[(d_H - d_L) + (k_P + k_D)] \leq r \leq (d_H - d_L)/(k_P + k_D).$$

While the term on the far right is, by an earlier assumption, greater than 1, the term on the far left is strictly less than one. In fact, for *each* value of r (pick one arbitrarily and call it r' for now) between the value on the left and one, there is a revealing equilibrium involving the low-damages P demanding s_L, the high-damages P demanding s_H and D responding via the rejection function with $r_D(s_L) = 0$ and $r_D(s_H) = r'$. In the equilibrium just posited a low-damage P reveals himself and always settles with D at $d_L + k_D$ and a high-damage P always reveals himself, possibly (that is, with probability $(1 - r')$) settling with D at $d_H + k_D$ and possibly (with probability r') going to court and achieving the payoff $d_H - k_P$. Note that the strategies for the players are very simple: P's demand is his damages plus D's court costs; D's strategy is to always accept a low demand and to reject a high demand with a given positive, but fractional, probability.

For what follows we will pick a particular value of r in the interval, namely, let $r_D(s_H) = (d_H - d_L)/[(d_H - d_L) + (k_P + k_D)]$, the smallest value. There are technical reasons (refinements) that have been alluded to earlier, concerning extensions of notions of rationality, to support this choice, but another motivation is that the smallest admissible r, $r_D(s_H)$, is the most efficient of the possible choices. All the r values that satisfy the incentive conditions (ICL) and (ICH) provide the same expected payoff to D, namely $E_D(d) + k_D$. P's expected payoff (that is, computed before he knows his type) is $E_D(d) + k_D - (1 - p)(k_P + k_D)r$, for *any* r that satisfies both incentive compatibility conditions, so using $r_D(s_H)$ minimizes the efficiency loss $(1 - p)(k_P + k_D)r$. Note also that using the specified $r_D(s_H)$ as the rejection probability for a high demand means that the likelihood of rejection is inversely related to total court costs, but positively related to the difference between possible levels of damages. This is because while increased court costs minimize the threat of going to court, an increased gap between d_H and d_L increases the incentive for low-damage Ps to claim to be high-damage Ps, thereby requiring more diligence on the part of D. D accomplishes this by increasing $r_D(s_H)$.

12.3.4 Signaling with Many Types While the principle used above extends to the case of a continuum of values of the private information, the extension itself involves considerably greater technical detail. The presentation here will summarize results in much the same manner as used in Section 12.3.2 to summarize screening with a continuum of types. This presentation is based on the analysis employed in Reinganum and Wilde (1986), though that model allows for non-strategic errors (that is, exogenously specified errors) by J and awards that are proportional to (rather than equal to) damages.

The basic results developed in the two-type model remain: (1) a revealing equilibrium is predicted; (2) P makes a settlement demand equal to damages plus D's court cost and (3) D uses a mixed strategy to choose acceptance or rejection. The likelihood of rejection is increasing in the demand made, and therefore in the damages incurred, and is decreasing in court costs. This means that the distribution of levels of damages that go to trial involves, essentially, the entire spectrum of damages, though it consists of preponderantly higher rather than lower damages (relative to the initial distribution).

Figure 3 shows an example which starts with the same assessment over damages as envisioned in the continuum screening model in Section 12.3.2. As is shown in the graph displayed in the upper left of Figure 3, again assume that each possible level of damages is equally likely. Following the gray arrow, the graph in the upper right shows the equilibrium settlement demand function for P: it is parallel to the 45° line (the dotted line) and shifted up by the amount k_D. Thus, P's settlement demand function $s_P(d) = d + k_D$, where d is P's type (level of damages actually incurred). Thus, for example, $s_P(d_L) = d_L + k_D$ (this is s_L on the vertical axis). The graph below the settlement demand function (follow the fat gray arrow) displays D's rejection function.

Demands at or below s_L are accepted and demands above s_L are rejected with an increasing likelihood up to the demand $s_H = d_H + k_D$. This is rejected with a positive but fractional likelihood (the dot is to show the endpoint of the curve); anything higher yet is rejected with certainty. Finally, following the gray arrow to the lower left of Figure 3, the posterior assessment of damages for cases going to trial is shown. The word posterior is used to contrast it with the assessment D used before bargaining commenced (the prior assessment). The effect of settlement bargaining is to create an assessment model at the start of the next stage of the legal process which is shifted upwards; that is, which emphasizes the higher-damage cases. This contrasts with the resulting distribution of cases that emerge from a screening process. The result of the screening model applied to the 'box-shaped' prior assessment shown in Figures 2 and 3 would be a box-shaped posterior assessment model over the types that rejected the screening offer.

Figure 3 Signaling with a Continuum of Types

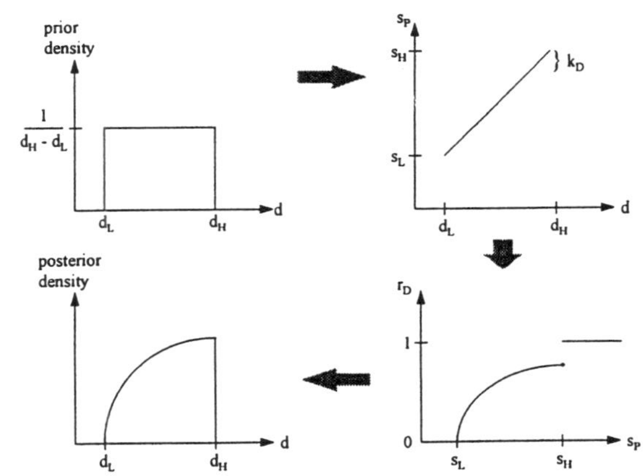

12.4 How Robust are One-Sided Asymmetric Information Ultimatum Game Analyses?

As the earlier discussion of the various approaches used in perfect information suggests, model structure and assumptions play an important role in the predictions of the analysis. Is this a problem of 'tune the dial and get another station'? In some sense it seems to be. Such models seem to provide conflicting predictions which: involve proposing one or the other player's concession limit (not in between, as the Nash Bargaining Solution provided); sometimes fully reveal private information, other times do not; and strongly restrict when and if players can make proposals at all.

However, some consistent threads emerge. Asymmetric information will generally result in some degree of inefficiency in the bargaining process due to some use of trial by the players. The extent of inefficiency is related to the nature of the distribution of the information, the range of the possible values that the private information can take on and the level of court costs. Higher court costs encourage settlement and influence the transfer between P and D. Asymmetric information means that the relatively less informed player needs to guard against misrepresentation by the more informed player, and must be willing to employ the threat of court. The signaling model indicated another aspect of this: even though P was informed and made the proposals, it was P who bore an inefficiency cost (D's expected payoff was what it would have been under imperfect information). This is because the private information that P possesses cannot be credibly communicated to D without a cost being incurred by P via the signaling of the information.

Clearly, both models use a highly stylized representation of bargaining. How restrictive is this? While this question is difficult to address very generally, some tests of the robustness of the model structure and the predictions exist. These analyses are of two types. (1) Would changes in sequence matter (who moves when, whether moves must be sequential, what if there were many opportunities to make proposals)? (2) Is the one-sided nature of information important; would each player having information on a relevant attribute of the game affect the outcome in a material way?

Papers by Daughety and Reinganum (1993), Wang, Kim and Yi (1994) and Spier (1992) address aspects of the first question above. Daughety and Reinganum provide a two-period model that allows players to move simultaneously or sequentially. Here, P and D can individually make (or individually not make) proposals in the first period and then choose to accept or reject whatever comes out of the first period during a second period; a rejection by either individual of the outcome of the first period means going to court. What comes out of the first period is: (1) no proposal, which guarantees court; (2) one proposal, provided by whomever made it; or (3) an intermediate version of two proposals if both players make one; the intermediate proposal is a general, commonly known function of the two individual proposals. An example of such a 'compromise' function would be one that averaged the proposals. Note that this means that if both players make proposals then intermediate outcomes are possible candidates as equilibria of the overall game. The model allows one-sided asymmetric information, but examines both possible cases in which a player is informed. The general result is that players do not choose to wait: they both make proposals in the first period. Thus, formally, the ultimatum structure wherein only one player makes a proposal is rejected as inconsistent with endogenously generated timing. However, the unique equilibrium of the game has the same payoffs as either that of the ultimatum signaling game or the ultimatum screening game; which one depends only on the compromise function used and which player is informed.

The Wang, Kim and Yi (1994) paper discussed earlier in Section 3.2.2 also contains a continuum-type, one-sided asymmetric information model based on Rubinstein (1985). Wang, Kim and Yi consider the case of an informed P and an uninformed D, with D as first proposer. In subsequent periods proposers alternate. They show that the settlement outcome is consistent with a one-period D-proposer screening ultimatum game as discussed above. Finally, Spier (1992) (discussed in more detail in Section 18 below) also employs a dynamic model (in this case a finite horizon model) with negotiating and trial costs. In her model if negotiating costs are zero then all bargaining takes place in the last period. Together, the three papers provide some limited theoretical support for using the ultimatum game approach to representing one-sided asymmetric information settlement problems.

The second issue, concerning one-sided versus two-sided information, is addressed in papers by Schweizer (1989) and Daughety and Reinganum (1994) (Sobel, 1989, also considers a two-sided model, but his interest is discovery; this paper will be discussed in Section 19). Both Schweizer and Daughety and Reinganum consider ultimatum games where P is privately informed about damages and D is privately informed about liability. Schweizer considers a P-proposer model with two types on both sides while Daughety and Reinganum consider both P- and D-proposer models with a continuum of types on both sides. The results are fundamentally the same: the proposer signals and uses the signal to screen the responder. Thus, proposer types are revealed fully and responders are partially pooled.

In sum, it would appear that the screening and signaling models have reasonably robust qualitative properties that survive relaxation of some of the underlying structure and that the intuition derived from the separate analyses survives the integration of both types of models in a more comprehensive analysis.

13. Comparing the Two-Type Models: Imperfect and Asymmetric Information

This section provides two means of comparison. First, employing specific numerical values, Table 3 presents computations for the same data from imperfect, screening and signaling analyses; it also acts as a convenient summary of the strategies and payoffs for the different models. While the results do not purport to indicate magnitudes of differences in the predictions made, it will suggest directional differences. The directional differences will be amplified, based on the two-type analyses provided earlier, as the second means of comparison.

Table 3
Ultimatum Game Results Under Imperfect and Asymmetric Information

Data: $d_H = 75$, $d_L = 25$, $L = 1$, $k_P = k_D = 10$, $p = 0.5$.
Thus, $E_D(d) = 50$ and (SSC) is met: $p = 0.5 > (k_p + k_D)/(d_H - d_L + k_P + k_D) = 0.29$

Model	D-Proposer	NBS	P-Proposer
Imp. Information		$\$_D = \$_P = 50$	
	$s_D = E_D(d) - k_P = 40$		$s_P = E_D(d) + k_D = 60$
	$\$_D = 40$		$\$_D = 60$
	$\$_P = 40$		$\$_P = 60$
	efficient		efficient
	no trials		no trials
Asy. Information			
Screening	$s_D = d_L - k_P = 15$		
	$\$_D = ps_D + (1 - p)(d_H + k_P) = 50$		
	$\$_L = d_L - k_P = 15$		
	$\$_H = d_H - k_P = 65$		
	inefficient: loss $= (1 - p)(k_P + k_D) = 10$		
	$\$_D = E_D(d) + k_D - (1 - p)(k_P + k_D) = 50$		
	$\$_P = p\$_L + (1 - p)\$_H = 40$		
	probability of trial $= (1 - p) = 0.5$		
Signaling			$s_L = d_L + k_D = 35$
			$s_H = d_H + k_D = 85$
			$r_D(s_L) = 0$
			$r_D(s_H) = (d_H - d_L)/(d_H - d_L + k_P + k_D) = 0.71$
			$\$_D = ps_L + (1 - p)[(1 - r_D(s_H))s_H + r_D(s_H)s_H] = 60$
			$\$_L = s_L = 35$
			$\$_H = (1 - r_D(s_H))s_H + (r_D(s_H))(d_H - k_P) = 70.71$

inefficient: loss = $(1 - p)(k_P+k_D)r_D(s_H)$
= 7.14
$\$_D = E_D(d) + k_D = 60$
$\$_P = p\$_L + (1 - p)\$_H = 52.86$
probability of trial = $(1 - p)r_D(s_H) = 0.36$

Table 3 considers a two-type model wherein P is informed of the true level of damages and D is not. D's prior assessment on the two levels of damages is that they are equally likely (this is to make comparisons easier). Court costs are the same for the two players and liability by D for damages is certain. Specific values of the data are provided at the top of Table 3. Note that (SSC) holds as shown. D's expectation of damages [$E_D(d)$] is the common expectation under imperfect information.

Table 3 concentrates on the ultimatum game predictions, but the relevant imperfect information NBS is also provided, as shown near the top. Given the information endowments, the only asymmetric information D-proposer model is a screening model and the only P-proposer asymmetric information model is a signaling model. The table provides the proposer's proposal, the responder's strategy in the signaling case and the payoffs to the players. Note that $\$_L$ provides the payoff to a P with low damages while $\$_H$ provides the payoff to a P with high damages. Finally, in the asymmetric case $\$_P$ provides the expected payoffs to a P before damages are observed so that *ex ante* efficiency can be evaluated. The statement 'efficient' means that the outcome is on the settlement frontier, while 'inefficient' means that the solution lies below the frontier, with the efficiency loss calculated as shown. Finally, the source of inefficiency, that some cases go to trial, is indicated by providing the probability of trial derived from the model used.

The example and the formulas in the table indicate that the efficiency losses predicted by the screening and signaling models, as compared with the efficient solutions in the imperfect information model, differ from one another. More generally, as long as p meets the simple screening condition (SSC) of Section 12.3.1, the signaling model predicts less of an efficiency loss than the screening model. This is because while a low-damage P settles out of court in both models, a high-damages P always goes to court under a screening model while they only go to court with a fractional likelihood under the signaling model. Note also, however, that when p does not satisfy (SSC), then the screening model predicts full efficiency while the signaling model still predicts an inefficient outcome.

A similar type of comparison could be performed for the ultimatum games involving asymmetric information about the likelihood of liability (with damages commonly known). Typically, such analyses assume that D has private information about the true likelihood of being found liable. In the screening model, the higher-likelihood Ds settle and the lower likelihood Ds reject P's offer and proceed to trial. In the signaling model, the higher likelihood D makes an offer that P accepts while the lower likelihood D makes a lower offer that P rejects with an equilibrium rejection probability. Most notably, in the case wherein there is a continuum of types, the distribution of cases that go to trial include essentially all the D-types (with the preponderance of types being less likely to be held liable).

This is worth contrasting with a vast literature which has grown out of a paper by Priest and Klein (1984). Reviewing the literature in this area (mainly empirical studies with a variety of predictions) would take us too far from our main purpose, but a few words are appropriate. The Priest-Klein model employs an inconsistent priors approach to examine the selection of cases that proceed to trial. Their results imply that, as the likelihood of proposal rejection by parties becomes small, then among those cases that do not settle, the likelihood that either P or D wins at trial approaches 50 percent. As Shavell (1993) shows for the two-type screening case, and as is clearly also true for the signaling case (as described above) and the continuum screening case, by varying parameters one can get essentially any prediction about case selection that is desired.

C. Variations on the Basic Models

14. Overview

This part locates and briefly reviews a number of recent contributions to the settlement literature. Two cautions should be observed. First, no effort will be made to discuss unpublished work. This is primarily motivated by the fact that such work is, generally, not as accessible to most readers as are the journals that published work has appeared in. There are some classic unpublished papers (some of which have significantly influenced the existing published papers) that are thereby slighted, and my apologies to their authors. Potentially, such a policy also hastens the date of the succeeding survey.

Second, the selection to be discussed is a subset of the existing published papers: it is not meant to be comprehensive. Instead, the selection is meant to show ideas that have been raised, or how approaches have been revised. A limited number of papers that address relevant issues, but which are not focused on settlement itself, are also mentioned.

Following the outline of Part B, papers will be grouped as follows: (1) players; (2) actions and strategies; (3) outcomes and payoffs; (4) timing and (5) information. Not surprisingly, many papers could conceivably fit in a number of categories, and a few cross-references will be made.

15. Players

15.1 Attorneys

Watts (1994) adds an attorney for P (denoted A_P) to the set of players in a screening analysis of a P-proposer ultimatum game; D is privately informed about expected damages at trial (for a discussion of agency problems in contingent fee arrangements, see Miller, 1987). The main role of A_P is expertise: A_P can engage, at a cost, in discovery efforts which release some predetermined portion of D's information. The cost to A_P is lower than the cost of obtaining the same information would be to P. Moreover, more precise information about D's likely type costs more to obtain (for either P or A_P) than less precise information (precision is exogenously determined in this model). Before bargaining with D, P can choose whether or not to hire A_P, and attorneys are paid on a contingency basis. If hired, A_P obtains information about D's type and then makes a settlement proposal to D. Given the precision of obtainable information and the expertise of A_P (that is, A_P's cost of obtaining information as a fraction of P's cost of obtaining the same information), Watts finds a range of contingency fees that P and A_P could agree upon (a settlement frontier for P *and* A_P to bargain over), and that their concession limits decrease as the expected court award in the settlement problem with D increases.

15.2 Judges and Juries

As mentioned earlier, J is generally modeled in this literature as learning the truth and making awards equal to the true damages. Early models have allowed for unsystematic error on the part of J. Since the informed player usually computes payoffs at trial on the basis that their true type will be fully revealed in court, something here is needed to indicate how J learns the true type, or if J does not learn the true type, what J does in that event. Thus, what J will know could influence the settlement strategies and outcomes.

Daughety and Reinganum (1995) consider a J whose omniscience is parametric (that is, with an exogenously specified probability, J learns the truth; if not, J must infer it based upon P and D's observable actions) in a continuum-type ultimatum game signaling model, wherein P is informed about damages and D is not. J is a second 'receiver' of a signal. If all that is observable to J is the failure of settlement negotiation, then when J observes that a case comes to trial, he can infer the distribution of such cases (using the posterior model shown in Figure 3) and pick a best award (note that this means that all the elements of the settlement game are common knowledge to J, as is this fact to P, D and J). If J can also observe P's settlement demand, then he uses that information, too. The result is that this feeds back into the settlement process, resulting in P making demands to influence J. As J's dependence on such information increases (omniscience decreases), revelation via the settlement demand disappears as more and more types of P pool by making a high demand (P 'plays to the judge'). The result can be that, for sufficiently high reliance on observation instead of omniscience, J has even less information than if he could not observe P's settlement demand at all (and must rely on the posterior distribution of unsettled cases).

Influencing J is also the topic of Rubinfeld and Sappington (1987), which while not focused on settlement *per se*, does model how effort by players can inform J. The setting is nominally a criminal trial, but the point potentially applies to civil cases, too: if innocent Ds should be able to (more readily than guilty Ds) obtain evidence supporting their innocence, then the amount of effort so placed can act as a signal to J of D's innocence or guilt. This is not a perfect signal, in the sense that the types of D are not fully revealed. As in much of the literature dealing with criminal defendants (this is discussed in more detail in Section 17.4 below), J here maximizes a notion of justice that trades off the social losses from punishing the innocent versus freeing the guilty and accounts for the costs incurred by D in the judicial process.

One final note on this topic. There is an enormous literature on jury and judicial decision-making spread across the psychology, political science, sociology and law literatures that has yet to have the impact it deserves on formal models of settlement bargaining.

15.3 Multiple Litigants

Many settings involve multiple litigants (for example, airline crashes, drug side-effects, and so on). Che and Yi (1993) and Yang (1996) consider games with two Ps who D faces sequentially; partly these are models of precedent and partly these are models analyzing game-to-game informational links. Damages are correlated over plaintiffs and thus information obtained in bargaining with the first P (P_1) influences bargaining with the second P (P_2). Che and Yi concatenate two D-proposer ultimatum games, where D faces informed P's in the two games. Note that when D plays the second ultimatum game, the correlation of levels of damages over plaintiffs means that learning in game one affects D's strategy in game two, thereby feeding back into D's game one strategy choice. By allowing for effort applied by all parties to influence the probability of winning, Che and Yi get a 'front-loading' effect to influence the precedent-setting case.

In a two-P model, the outcome of the settlement process with P_1 (which can include trial) influences P_2's decisions. Employing a model similar to that of Che and Yi, Yang includes the decision by both informed Ps to initially file their respective cases. Thus, D's actions with respect to P_1, and the likely outcome from going to trial, may deter P_2 from filing. Yang finds conditions under which this causes D, in dealing with P_1, to be more or less aggressive than the one-P model would find. While more aggressive play (being 'tough') against P_1 may seem intuitive, less aggressive play is also reasonable if going to trial will reveal information (such as, that P_1 had high damages) that encourages P_2 to file. Why would this encourage P_2, who knows his damage? Assume that P_2 is a low-level-of-damages plaintiff. By making a pooling offer to P_1, D does not learn P_1's type, which ignorance P_2 would be aware of. Thus, P_2 knows that D is still uninformed, and cannot capitalize on D having received 'bad news' that P_1 is a high-level-of-damages plaintiff, shifting his prior assessment about P_2 up (recall that D takes damages as correlated). There is a strategic advantage to not being informed if the knowledge of the information places you at a disadvantage. If D remains uninformed then if P_2 is low he cannot expect D to overestimate him as high and make a second pooling offer.

Kobayashi (1992) considers a two-D model in a plea-bargaining setting; because of the change in payoffs, this will be discussed in more detail in Section 17.4 below.

16. Actions and Strategies

16.1 Credibility of Proceeding to Trial Should Negotiations Fail

In the screening examples in Section 12.3 above, an uninformed D made an offer to an informed P with liability commonly known but the level of damages the source of the informational asymmetry. For convenience of exposition, consider the reversed setting with D informed about the likelihood of being found liable at trial, P uninformed, but both commonly knowledgeable about the level of damages (this is the original Bebchuk example). Thus, a screening analysis means a P-proposer ultimatum model. In this context Nalebuff (1987) examines the assumption that P is committed to proceeding to trial after bargaining fails (alternatively put, Nalebuff relaxes the assumption that there is a minimum positive likelihood of liability that, multiplied by the level of damages, would exceed P's court costs; this is the analogy to our earlier assumption that $d_L > k_P$ holds).

Nalebuff considers cases that, initially, have 'merit': $E_P(d) > k_P$. Nalebuff appends a second decision by P (concerning whether or not to take the case to trial) to the P-proposer ultimatum game screening model. After observing the response by D to the screening demand made by P, P recomputes $E_P(d)$ using his posterior assessment; denote this as $E_P(d|$ D's response), meaning P's expectation of the level of damages which will be awarded in court given D's choice to accept or reject the offer. Since all types whose true likelihood of liability implied levels of expected damages in excess of that associated with the demand (that is, the more likely-to-be-liable types of D) have accepted the demand, the collection of types of D who would reject the demand by P are those with stronger cases (that is, those that are less likely to be held liable). Thus, P's new expected payoff from proceeding to trial, $E_P(d|$ D's response) $- k_P$, is lower than before the bargaining began ($E_P(d) - k_P$). The decision by P as to whether or not to actually litigate *after* seeing the outcome of the screening offer results in a reversal of some of the predictions made by the original screening model about the impact that changes in the levels of damages and court costs will have on settlement demands and the likelihood of trial.

For example, Nalebuff shows that the settlement demand in the relaxed model is *higher* than that in the model with commitment. Why would this happen? To see why, consider what happens in stages. When P is making his settlement demand, he is also considering the downstream decision he will be making about going to trial and must choose a settlement demand that makes his later choice of trial credible. If P can no longer be committed to going to trial with any D who rejects his screening demand, this means that he will use $E_P(d|$ D's response) to decide about going to trial, and this is now heavily influenced by the presence of 'tough' types; those types that are 'weak', that is, who have high likelihoods of liability, have accepted P's offers. Thus, if P raises his settlement demand, some of the intermediate types will pool with the tough types, resulting in $E_P(d|$ D's response) $- k_P > 0$, making the threat of trial credible. Thus, the effect of relaxing the assumption that P necessarily litigates any case that rejects his settlement demand actually results in an increased demand being made.

16.2 Filing a Claim

One potential effect of a cost associated with filing a suit is to provide a disincentive for a P pursuing what is known as a 'nuisance' suit. The definition of what a nuisance is varies somewhat, but generally, such a suit has a negative expected value (NEV) to P; that is, $E_P(d) < k_P$; such a suit is not one that P would actually pursue to trial should negotiations fail (note that this ignores any psychic benefits that P may derive from 'having his day in court' which might make such a suit have a positive expected utility). Clearly, the reason for consideration of NEV suits is the perception that Ps can pursue NEV suits and obtain settlements: the asymmetry of information between an informed P and an uninformed D allows Ps with NEV suits to mimic PEV suits (positive expected value suits) and extract a settlement. Two questions have arisen in this context: what contributes to the incentive for plaintiffs to pursue NEV suits and what attributes of the process might reduce or eliminate it.

An example may be of use at this point. Consider a D facing three possible types of P, with possible damages $d_N = 0$, $d_L = \$10{,}000$ and $d_H = \$50{,}000$, respectively and with associated likelihoods $p_N = 0.1$, $p_L = 0.3$ and $p_H = 0.6$ (N here stands for 'nuisance'). Further assume both P and D have court costs of \$2,000. The screening equilibrium involves the firm offering \$8,000 and settling with the nuisance and the low-damages type and going to court against the high-damages type: the nuisance-type benefitted from the presence of the low-damage type and the expected costs to the firm are higher (an average expected cost of \$34,400 per case) than would obtain if the nuisance type had not been present (an average expected cost of \$33,600 per case).

P'ng (1983), in one of the earliest papers to consider strategic aspects of settlement bargaining, endogenizes both the choice by P to file a case and the choice to later drop the case should bargaining fail; NEV suits are considered, but the level of settlement is exogenously determined in this model. Rosenberg and Shavell (1985) found NEV suits can occur if filing costs for P are sufficiently low when compared with D's defense costs and if D must incur these costs before P must incur any settlement or trial costs. Bebchuk (1988) provides an asymmetric information (P is informed), D-proposer ultimatum game that specifically admits NEV suits (that is, no assumption is made that all suits are PEV). Filing costs are zero. Bebchuk shows how court costs and the probability assessment of the possible levels of damages influences settlement offers and rates. He finds that when NEV suits are possible, a reduction in settlement offers in PEV cases and an increase in the fraction of PEV cases that go to trial, when compared with an analysis assuming only PEV suits, is predicted.

Katz (1990) considers how filing and settlement bargaining affects incentives for frivolous law suits. By a frivolous suit, Katz means one with zero damages and positive court costs; the numerical example above involved a frivolous suit. Katz appends a filing decision made by an informed P to a D-proposer ultimatum game. This is a two-type model (the paper also includes a continuum-type extension) with $d_L = 0$. The modification of the D-proposer model is that the offer is either the high-damage P's concession limit or zero, so the strategy for D becomes the probability of making the high-damage concession limit offer. P's filing strategy is whether or not to file; if he files P incurs a cost f_P. Of course, once incurred this cost is sunk. Under the assumption that $d_H - k_P - f_P > 0$, and if a condition similar in notion to (SSC) is violated, then in equilibrium both types of Ps file cases, D pools the Ps by offering the high-damage P's concession limit, $d_H - k_P$, to all Ps and all Ps accept. Katz also addresses a case selection issue: such a policy by D will attract frivolous cases, changing the likelihood that a randomly selected case is a frivolous. Thus, the profits from filing a frivolous case will be driven to zero. In this 'competitive' equilibrium, Katz shows that the likelihood of trial is not a function of p or k_D, but it is increasing in f_P and decreasing in $E_D(d)$.

16.3 Counterclaims

Using an imperfect information model, Landes (1994) shows that counterclaims (suits filed by D against P as part of the existing action by P against D, rather than filed as a separate lawsuit) do not always reduce P's incentive to sue, and may (by raising the stakes in the game) actually increase the likelihood of the case going to trial. This is based on mutual optimism about each player's own claim (mutual optimism involves each player expecting to win the action that they initiated; this need not involve inconsistent priors, as discussed in Section 6). Under these conditions the counterclaim reduces the size of the settlement frontier (and possibly eliminates it).

17. Outcomes and Payoffs

17.1 Risk Aversion

Most of the earliest analyses allowed for risk aversion by assuming that payoffs were in utility rather than monetary terms. The Nash Bargaining Solution can be applied to such problems (now all four axioms come into play), again yielding a unique solution, though not necessarily where the 45° line crosses the frontier. The solution is efficient (due to axiom 2; see Section 8.2) in perfect and imperfect information cases. The divergence of the solution from the 45° line reflects the relative risk aversion of the two players, with the more risk-averse player receiving a smaller share of the pie (see, for example, Binmore, 1992, pp. 193-194).

There is a similar analysis in the perfect information strategic bargaining literature, where risk is introduced into an infinite horizon game by ignoring the time value of money but incorporating a probability of negotiations breaking down. Once again, for players whose preferences over outcomes reflect aversion to risk, the less risk averse player gets the greater share of the pie (see Binmore, Rubinstein and Wolinsky, 1986).

In the settlement context, Farmer and Pecorino (1994) view a player's risk preferences as private information. While trial outcomes are uncertain, the likelihood of the outcomes themselves is common knowledge. P is taken to be risk averse (that is, privately informed of his risk preferences) and D is risk neutral and uninformed; the model allows for two types of P (extension to three types is also considered). This is a D-proposer ultimatum model; if the roles of proposer were reversed, then P's risk aversion would not interfere with an efficient settlement solution, so the order here is crucial to obtaining the possibility of trial. A standard screening condition is found (not unlike (SSC)), but more interesting is the result that increases in the uncertainty of the trial outcome result in the screening condition being more readily met, thereby increasing the likelihood of trial (a result consistent with the earlier analysis involving risk aversion). This occurs because it is the most risk-averse Ps that settle, and the greater the uncertainty the more they are prepared to accept a settlement in lieu of court, which encourages D to make tougher offers.

17.2 Offer-Based Fee Shifting Rules

Many settlement papers consider the allocation of court costs (fee shifting) as part of their overall analysis. Typically, comparisons are made between the 'American' system (each player pays their own costs) and the 'British' system (the loser pays all costs). The very common association in the literature of loser pays with Britain potentially understates the contrast; see Posner (1992) who uses the term 'English and Continental' to emphasize that a significant portion of the world uses loser pays. All the discussions in this survey have employed the pay-your-own system. The allocation of court costs is an extensive topic, with a typically suggested result that the loser-pays system discourages low-probability-of-prevailing plaintiffs more than the pay-your-own system (see Shavell, 1982), but other observations are that it may (or may not) adversely affect the likelihood of settlement (see Bebchuk, 1984 and Reinganum and Wilde, 1986). A recent extension of the basic fee-shifting discussion to making fee-shifting dependent upon the magnitude of the outcome is discussed in Bebchuk and Chang (1996). Since the general area of fee shifting is a separable topic of its own interest (which is likely to be addressed in a number of other surveys in these volumes), this survey will not attempt to cover it.

A related issue is recent work on Rule 68 of the US Federal Rules of Civil Procedure, as an example of a variety of *offer-based* fee-shifting rules which directly address settlement offers made by defendants and rejected by plaintiffs. First, it should be noted that, under long-standing practice, and also under many state rules of evidence and US Federal Rule of Evidence 408, information on settlement proposals and responses is not generally admissible as evidence at trial; a similar type of restriction usually applies in criminal cases to information about plea bargaining. Rule 68 includes restrictions on the use of settlement proposals at trial.

Thus, in the case of offer-based fee-shifting, offers are not used in court to infer true damages or actual liability; rather they influence the final payoffs from the game *after* an award has been made at trial. Rule 68, for example, links settlement choices to post-trial outcomes by penalizing a plaintiff for certain costs (court costs and, sometimes, attorney fees) when the trial award is less favorable than the defendant's 'final' proposal (properly documented). As Spier (1994a) points out, the stated purpose of such a rule is to encourage settlement (Spier also provides other examples of offer-based rules similar in nature to Rule 68). Spier employs screening in a D-proposer ultimatum game. In comparison to the likelihood of settlement without Rule 68, she finds that under Rule 68: (1) disputes by P and D over damages are more likely to settle; and (2) disputes over liability or the likelihood of winning are less likely to settle. Spier also finds that the design of a bargaining procedure and fee-shifting rule that maximizes the probability of settlement yields a rule that penalizes either player for rejecting proposals that were better than the actual outcome of trial, providing some theoretical support for offer-based fee shifting rules such as Rule 68.

17.3 Damage Awards

In previous sections of this summary the award at trial has been the level of damages associated with the plaintiff who goes to court. This, minus court costs, becomes P's threat. This is based on J choosing an award that best approximates P's damages. Other criteria for choosing awards are also reasonable. For example, J might choose awards that maximize overall social efficiency or that minimize the probability of trial.

Polinsky and Che (1991) study decoupled liability: what the defendant pays need not be what the plaintiff receives. By decoupling, incentives for plaintiffs to sue can be reduced, while incentives for potential injurers to improve the level of care can be increased; that is, both goals can be pursued without necessarily conflicting. In particular, they show that the optimal award to P may be less or more than the optimal payment by D. Spier (1994b) considers coupled awards in an asymmetric information setting, and finds that the level of settlement costs influences the nature of the award that minimizes social cost (precaution costs plus litigation costs plus harm). Note that, here, precaution is one-sided: precaution on the part of a potential P is not included. Spier considers a two-type screening D-proposer ultimatum game and allows for two awards, a_H and a_L, for circumstances where the level of damages is High or Low, respectively, and thus the payoff from trial is the award minus court costs. Spier uses a condition such as (SSC) and shows that, if total court costs are low enough the socially optimal award is equal to the level of damages *plus* P's court costs (as D will make a screening offer in those circumstances), while if total court costs are sufficiently high, the optimal award is the *expected* damages plus P's court costs (as D will be making a pooling offer). Therefore, simply compensating for actual damages is not socially optimal (recall also that court costs are fixed). Moreover, 'fine tuning' the award to reflect P's actual level of damages is socially optimal only if total court costs are not too high.

17.4 Other Payoffs: Plea Bargaining

As an example of a significantly different payoff measure, consider negotiations between a defendant in a criminal action and a prosecutor. This type of settlement bargaining, called plea bargaining, has been addressed in a number of papers over the last quarter-century. Early papers in this area are Landes (1971) and Grossman and Katz (1983) who model settlement bargaining between a prosecutor and a defendant. In Landes the payoffs are expected sentence length for the prosecutor versus expected wealth (wealth in two states: under conviction and under no conviction) for the defendant, who is guilty. In Grossman and Katz some defendants may be innocent; the defendants know their guilt or innocence (a two-type model). The defendants seek to minimize the disutility of punishment (they are risk averse) while the uninformed prosecutor maximizes a notion of justice that trades off the social losses from punishing the innocent versus freeing the guilty; the Grossman and Katz analysis is a screening model with innocent defendants choosing trial.

More recent work includes Reinganum (1988, 1993) and Kobayashi (1992). Reinganum's 1988 paper involves two-sided asymmetric information: defendants know their guilt or innocence (two types), while the prosecutor knows the strength of the case; that is, the probability that the case will yield a conviction at trial (a continuum of types). Guilt and evidence are correlated, so there is a relationship between the two sets of types. A special case of this relationship appears in Grossman and Katz and was also employed in Rubinfeld and Sappington, discussed in Section 15.2: innocent defendants can more readily obtain supporting evidence than can guilty ones. The prosecutor's payoff is social justice minus resource costs while the defendant's payoff to be minimized is the expected sentence plus the disutility of trial. Reinganum's 1993 paper uses a similar payoff for D but takes all Ds as guilty and therefore takes the prosecutor's payoff as expected sentence length minus resource costs. In this latter model the probability of conviction is determined in the equilibrium, influencing the initial choice to engage in criminal behavior by D.

Finally, Kobayashi considers conspiracies: there are two defendants (for example, a price-fixing case) who face different (exogenously determined) initial probabilities of conviction based on the existing evidence. Each D can, however, provide information on the other D which increases that second D's likelihood of conviction. Kobayashi assumes that the D with the higher initial conviction probability (the 'ringleader') also has more information on the other D (the 'subordinate'). Here the prosecutor makes simultaneous offers to each D so as to maximize the sum of the expected penalties from the two Ds. Litigation costs are taken to be zero so as to focus on plea-bargaining as information gathering.

18. Timing

Four papers have focused especially on the implications of changing the timing assumption in the models used: Spier (1992), Daughety and Reinganum (1993), Wang, Kim and Li (1994) and Bebchuk (1996). The papers by Daughety and Reinganum and by Wang, Kim and Yi were discussed in Section 12.4 above. These two papers (along with Spier's) analyzed models that contributed some support for the one-sided asymmetric information ultimatum games. The papers by Spier and Bebchuk examine what happens if the settlement interval is subdivided. We consider these two papers in more detail in turn.

Spier considers a finite-horizon concatenation of P-proposer ultimatum games, with D informed about damages for which he is liable (a continuum-type model). Spier finds a 'deadline effect' in which some cases settle in the last period, and that the distribution of settlements over time can be U-shaped in the sense that some cases settle immediately, some settle in the last possible period and a few settle in between. Spier's main analysis is different from the other multiperiod models discussed in that the horizon is finite, not infinite, and the model does not allow alternating offers (an infinite horizon model is also considered; see below). Moreover, P, the (initially) uninformed proposer, cannot choose to go to court during the horizon. P incurs two costs: (1) each extra period incurs a negotiating cost and (2) going to trial incurs a court cost. D incurs neither cost, which is not a restrictive assumption in this analysis. Both P and D discount money in future periods at the same discount rate. Thus, the analysis involves subdividing the bargaining period into a sequence of periods and associating a delay cost for each period that settlement is not reached. Since the pie is not shrinking, the delay cost provides a clear incentive to P to settle sooner. On the other hand, P is uninformed and may need to use the approach of the end of the horizon to get D to reveal information. This tradeoff leads to some settlements being made immediately and some being made in the last possible period when D faces the imminent possibility of trial. Spier also considers an infinite-horizon extension, where P may now choose to go to court in each period; this provides a model that allows for an endogenous date for trial. The model yields a range of equilibria (this is not unusual in strategic bargaining games with outside alternatives); the range runs from efficient to fully inefficient (all cases go to trial in the second period). Finally, Fournier and Zuehlke (1996) have recently tested the predictions of Spier's finite horizon model with data from a survey of civil lawsuits from 1979-1981 in US federal courts. They found results that were consistent with computer simulation predictions based on Spier's analysis.

Bebchuk (1996) also examines the effect of subdividing the settlement interval into parts. Costs accrue somewhat differently in his model than in Spier's. In particular, a player's costs of negotiation and court are fully subdivided by the number of intervals. Thus, the level of costs incurred is influenced by when an agreement is reached. Bebchuk concatenates a series of settlement predictions using the average of the (one-period) concession limits under perfect information; filing costs for P are zero. Sequential rationality does the rest: with costs subdivided so as to make it credible for P to continue to bargain, Bebchuk finds that NEV suits can be successful if there are a sufficient number of periods and the difference between k_P and k_D is not too great. Note that D cannot commit not to respond to demands; if he could, then P's NEV strategy would be unprofitable.

While the number of periods in the model is exogenously set, this is suggestive of a strategy for P: increase the number of settlement periods. The notion of credible commitments should work both ways, however. What if D could hire a busy lawyer? Delegation of bargaining authority or the requirement for advice, if credible, is one way for D to make the number of periods smaller. After all, each time P makes a proposal, D must have an attorney carefully evaluate the proposal, a costly and time-consuming activity. This would create credible delay, which is beneficial from the viewpoint of D's direct monetary interests and now beneficial from the viewpoint of repelling some NEV cases. Thus, this suggests that a game wherein the proposal/response period length and frequency is endogenously determined would be of interest. To the degree that the overall horizon is sub-divided, however, Bebchuk's main point will still hold: there will be NEV suits that could be successful (again, assuming that filing costs are zero).

19. Information

19.1 Acquiring Information from the Other Player: Discovery and Disclosure

Shavell (1989) examines the incentives for informed players to voluntarily release private information in a continuum-type, informed-P, D-proposer ultimatum game. Before D makes a proposal, P can costlessly reveal his hidden information to D; he may also choose to stay silent. Shavell shows that silence implies that P's information involves low types (for example, that P's level of damages is low). Shavell considers two possibilities: claims by P are costlessly verifiable by D or some types of P cannot make verifiable claims; for convenience, call the first analysis an *unlimited verifiable claims* (UVC) model and the second a *limited verifiable claims* (LVC) model (in the LVC model those types of P unable to make verifiable claims is an exogenously specified fraction u). In the UVC model, all Ps whose true type is less than or equal to a given value stay silent while all those above that value make their claims. Since the claims are verifiable, D settles with those types by offering their concession limit and settles with the silent types by offering a settlement offer designed to reflect this group's types. Thus, there are no trials in equilibrium. Under discovery rights for D that provide mandatory disclosure, all types of P reveal, resulting in a reduced expenditure for D: each type of P settles for their concession limit.

In the LVC model there will be trials. The reason is that the silent Ps now include those types who cannot make verifiable claims; some of these will have higher levels of damages than the offer made to the group of silent types, and will thus reject the offer and then go to trial (this relies on the assumption that u is independent of the level of damages). The rest of the silent types will settle, as will those whose claim is both greater and verifiable. Discovery now means that D can settle with $(1 - u)$ of the possible types of P at their concession limit and must screen the silent types, all of whom have unverifiable claims and, thus, some of whom will proceed to court (if the continuum-type version of (SSC) holds). Again, total D expenditures will generally be reduced from the original LVC payoff. Mandatory disclosure in the LVC case raises the screening offer for the silent group, since those lower types with verifiable claims have settled at their concession limit. Thus, the probability of trial will be reduced relative to the original LVC outcome. Moreover, those with verifiable claims would have settled with or without mandatory disclosure.

Sobel (1989) provides a two-sided asymmetric information model that examines the impact of discovery and voluntary disclosure on settlement offers and outcomes; significantly, discovery generates costs and this affects results. He sandwiches one of two possible discovery processes between an initial D-proposer ultimatum game and a final P-proposer ultimatum game. Settlement in the D-proposer model ends the game, while rejection leads to the possibility of either mandatory discovery or no discovery of D's private information by P. This is then followed by the P-proposer ultimatum game. The cost of disclosure to D is denoted c. In a voluntary disclosure setting, D's choice to disclose is costly, and therefore might be used by D to signal that the information was credible. By making P the final proposer, P is able to extract all the surplus from settlement. Thus, D has no reason to voluntarily disclose information if $c > 0$. This contrasts with results, for example, by Milgrom and Roberts (1986) who model costless voluntary disclosure and find that such disclosure can be fully revealing. As Sobel observes, this suggests that such a conclusion is sensitive to the assumption that $c = 0$. Sobel also finds that mandatory disclosure reduces the probability of trial and may bias the selection of cases that go to trial, generating a distribution in which P wins more often.

Cooter and Rubinfeld (1994) use an analysis based on an axiomatic settlement model with prior assessments that may be inconsistent; discovery may or may not eliminate inconsistency. For example, discovery may reveal a player's private information or it may cause a player to adopt an alternative perspective about what may come out of trial. Either way, an NBS is applied to a settlement frontier adjusted by the difference in expected trial payoffs. One of the main results is the proposal of an allocation of discovery costs so as to provide disincentives for abuse by either player. The proposed allocation assigns discovery costs to each party up to a switching point, at which point incremental costs are shifted to the requesting player.

19.2 Acquiring Information from Experts

As discussed in Section 15.1, Watts (1994) considers a model with an agent that provides expertise in the sense that they can acquire information for a player more cheaply than the player can themselves. She shows how to view the problem as one of bargaining between the player and the agent and provides some comparative statics about their settlement frontier.

In Daughety and Reinganum (1993) a model allowing simultaneous or sequential moves by both players (this is discussed in more detail in Section 12.4) is embedded in a model which allows uninformed players to acquire information from an expert before settlement negotiations begin. The information, which is costly, is what an informed player would know. Thus, a player may start the game already informed (called *naturally informed*) or start uninformed but able to acquire the information at a cost $c > 0$; for convenience, assume that court costs are the same for the two players and denote them as k. If both players are uninformed then, in equilibrium, neither will choose to buy the information. This is because informational asymmetry results in some possible cases going to trial while symmetric uncertainty involves no trials. With one of the players naturally informed and one uninformed then, as discussed earlier, depending on the form of the compromise function, the equilibrium involves either payoffs consistent with an ultimatum screening model or payoffs consistent with an ultimatum signaling model. In those conditions which lead to the screening game payoffs, the uninformed player will choose to buy the information if $c \leq k$.

Alternatively, in those conditions which lead to signaling game payoffs, the uninformed player will *not* acquire the information. Thus, uninformed players will not always choose to 're-level the playing field' by purchasing information; signaling will provide it if a revealing equilibrium is anticipated.

D. Conclusions

20. Summary

The modeling of settlement bargaining has been influenced primarily by law, economics and game theory. In many ways it is still developing and expanding, and hopefully deepening. The more recent analyses employ, primarily, a mix of information economics and bargaining theory (both cooperative and non-cooperative) to examine, understand and recommend improvements in legal institutions and procedures.

There has been a tug-of-war between the desire to address interesting behavior and the current limited ability to relate seemingly irrational acts to rational choice. As the development of technique has progressively allowed this to be accomplished, and as the intuition as to why seeming irrationality may be rational has driven improvement in technique, a broader picture of what elements contribute to, or impede, dispute resolution has evolved.

In this area, I think, it is fair to claim that issues have led techniques, a good thing. If there is an aspect that could use improvement, it is the fact that, to date, there are few empirical or laboratory studies of the details of the settlement process. In an area where 93 percent of the outcomes are partially or totally unobservable by researchers, empirical studies are hard to do, and the few that have been done have undoubtedly involved hard work. The development of improved summary data sources, some available on the Internet, is very exciting, but more studies of settlement bargaining at the actual process level (as in, for example, Farber and White) would also be most helpful.

Laboratory studies (experimental economics and related efforts in sociology and psychology) are expanding but the more subtle predictions of some of these models means that laboratory studies have to walk a fine line between being a test of a particular model's prediction or ending up mainly gauging a subject's IQ. Such studies are also very labor-intensive (on the part of the researcher), though the recent increased entry of researchers into this area bodes well.

Most of the work in this area (covering the last quarter century) has occurred in the last dozen years (and most of that has occurred in the last half-dozen years), indicating an accelerating interest and suggesting that the next survey will have a lot more new, useful theory and detailed empirical and laboratory tests to report, a good thing, too.

Acknowledgements

Support from NSF grants SBR-9223087 and SBR-9596193 is gratefully acknowledged. I thank Jeremy Atack, A. Mitchell Polinsky, Richard Posner, Robert Rasmussen, David Sappington, Steven Shavell, John Siegfried and Kathryn Spier for helpful comments and suggestions on (and corrections of) an earlier draft. I especially thank Jennifer Reinganum for many helpful comments and discussions.

Bibliography on Settlement (7400)

Bebchuk, Lucian Arye (1984), 'Litigation and Settlement under Imperfect Information', **15** *Rand Journal of Economics*, 404-415.

Bebchuk, Lucian Arye (1988), 'Suing Solely to Extract a Settlement Offer', **17** *Journal of Legal Studies*, 437-450.

Bebchuk, Lucian Arye (1996), 'A New Theory Concerning the Credibility of Success of Threats to Sue', **25** *Journal of Legal Studies*, 1-26.

Bebchuk, Lucian Arye and Chang, Howard F. (1996), 'An Analysis of Fee Shifting Based on the Margin of Victory: On Frivolous Suits, Meritorious Suits, and the Role of Rule 11', **25** *Journal of Legal Studies*, 371-404.

Che, Yeon-Koo and Yi, Jong Goo (1993), 'The Role of Precedents in Repeated Litigation', **9** *Journal of Law, Economics and Organization*, 399-424.

Chung, Tai-Yeong (1996), 'Settlement of Litigation under Rule 68: An Economic Analysis', **25** *Journal of Legal Studies*, 261-286.

Cooter, Robert D. and Rubinfeld, Daniel L. (1989), 'Economic Analysis of Legal Disputes and Their Resolution', **27** *Journal of Economic Literature*, 1067-1097.

Cooter, Robert D. and Rubinfeld, Daniel L. (1994), 'An Economic Model of Legal Discovery', **23** *Journal of Legal Studies*, 435-463.

Daughety, Andrew F. and Reinganum, Jennifer F. (1993), 'Endogenous Sequencing in Models of Settlement and Litigation', **9** *Journal of Law, Economics and Organization*, 314-348.

Daughety, Andrew F. and Reinganum, Jennifer F. (1994), 'Settlement Negotiations with Two Sided Asymmetric Information: Model Duality, Information Distribution, and Efficiency', **14** *International Review of Law and Economics*, 283-298.

Daughety, Andrew F. and Reinganum, Jennifer F. (1995), 'Keeping Society in the Dark: on the Admissibility of Pretrial Negotiations as Evidence in Court', **26** *Rand Journal of Economics*, 203-221.

Farber, Henry S. and White, Michelle J. (1991), 'Medical Malpractice: An Empirical Examination of the Litigation Process', **22** *Rand Journal of Economics*, 199-217.

Farmer, Amy and Pecorino, Paul (1994), 'Pretrial Negotiations with Asymmetric Information on Risk Preferences', **14** *International Review of Law and Economics*, 273-281.

Fournier, Gary M. and Zuehlke, Thomas W. (1996), 'The Timing of Out-of-Court Settlements, **27** *Rand Journal of Economics*, 310-321.

Gould, John P. (1973), 'The Economics of Legal Conflicts', **2** *Journal of Legal Studies*, 279-300.

Grossman, Gene M. and Katz, Michael L. (1983), 'Plea Bargaining and Social Welfare', **73** *American Economic Review*, 749-757.

Katz, Avery (1990), 'The Effect of Frivolous Lawsuits on the Settlement of Litigation', **10** *International Review of Law and Economics*, 3-27.

Kobayashi, Bruce H. (1992), 'Deterrence with Multiple Defendants: an Explanation for "Unfair" Plea Bargaining', **23** *Rand Journal of Economics*, 507-517.

Landes, William M. (1971), 'An Economic Analysis of the Courts', **14** *Journal of Law and Economics*, 61-107.

Landes, William M. (1994), 'Counterclaims: An Economic Analysis', **14** *International Review of Law and Economics*, 235-244.

Miller, Geoffrey P. (1987), 'Some Agency Problems in Settlement', **16** *Journal of Legal Studies*, 189-215.

Miller, Geoffrey P. (1996), 'Settlement of Litigation: A Critical Retrospective', in Kramer, Larry (ed.), *Reforming the Civil Justice System*, New York, NY, New York University Press.

Nalebuff, Barry (1987), 'Credible Pretrial Negotiation', **18** *Rand Journal of Economics*, 198-210.

P'ng, Ivan P.L. (1983), 'Strategic Behavior in Suit, Settlement, and Trial', **14** *Bell Journal of Economics*, 539-550.

Polinsky, A. Mitchell and Che, Yeon-Koo (1991), 'Decoupling Liability: Optimal Incentives for Care and Litigation', **22** *Rand Journal of Economics*, 562-570.

Posner, Richard A. (1973), 'An Economic Approach to Legal Procedure and Judicial Administration', **2** *Journal of Legal Studies*, 399-458.

Priest, George L. and Klein, Benjamin, (1984), 'The Selection of Disputes for Litigation', **13** *Journal of Legal Studies*, 1-56.

Reinganum, Jennifer F. (1988), 'Plea Bargaining and Prosecutorial Descretion', **78** *American Economic Review*, 713-728.

Reinganum, Jennifer F. (1993), 'The Law Enforcement Process and Criminal Choice', **13** *International Review of Law and Economics*, 115-134.

Reinganum, Jennifer F. and Wilde, Louis L. (1986), 'Settlement, Litigation, and the Allocation of Litigation Costs', **17** *Rand Journal of Economics*, 557-566.

Rosenberg, David and Shavell, Steven (1985), 'A Model in which Suits are Brought for their Nuisance Value', **5** *International Review of Law and Economics*, 3-13.

Schweizer, Urs (1989), 'Litigation and Settlement under Two Sided Incomplete Information', **56** *Review of Economic Studies*, 163-177.

Shavell, Steven (1982), 'Suit, Settlement and Trial: A Theoretical Analysis under Alternative Methods for the Allocation of Legal Costs', **11** *Journal of Legal Studies*, 55-81.

Shavell, Steven (1989), 'Sharing of Information Prior to Settlement or Litigation', **20** *Rand Journal of Economics*, 183-195.

Shavell, Steven (1993), 'Suit Versus Settlement When Parties Seek Nonmonetary Judgments', **22** *Journal of Legal Studies*, 1-13.
Sobel, Joel (1989), 'An Analysis of Discovery Rules', **52** *Law and Contemporary Problems*, 133-160.
Spier, Kathryn E. (1992), 'The Dynamics of Pretrial Negotiation', **59** *Review of Economic Studies*, 93-108.
Spier, Kathryn E. (1994a), 'Pretrial Bargaining and the Design of Fee-Shifting Rules', **25** *Rand Journal of Economics*, 197-214.
Spier, Kathryn E. (1994b), 'Settlement Bargaining and the Design of Damage Awards', **10** *Journal of Law, Economics and Organization*; 84-95.
Wang, Gyu Ho, Kim, Jeong Yoo and Yi, Jong Goo (1994), 'Litigation and Pretrial Negotiation under Incomplete Information', **10** *Journal of Law, Economics and Organization*, April, 187-200.
Watts, Alison (1994), 'Bargaining through an Expert Attorney', **10** *Journal of Law, Economics and Organization*, 168-86.
Yang, Bill Z. (1996), 'Litigation, Experimentation and Reputation', **16** *International Review of Law and Economics*, 491-502.

Other References

Aumann, Robert J. (1976), 'Agreeing to Disagree', **4** *Annals of Statistics*, 1236-1239.
Babcock, Linda, Loewenstein, George, Issacharoff, Samuel and Camerer, Colin (1995), 'Biased Judgments of Fairness in Bargaining', **85** *The American Economic Review*, 1337-1343.
Baird, Douglas G., Gertner, Robert H. and Picker, Randal C. (1994), *Game Theory and the Law*, Cambridge, MA, Harvard University Press.
Bernheim, B. Douglas, Peleg, Bezalel and Whinston, Michael D. (1987), 'Coalition Proof Nash Equilibria, I: Concepts', **42** *Journal of Economic Theory*, 1-12.
Binmore, Ken (1985), 'Bargaining and Coalitions', in Roth, Alvin E. (ed.), *Game-Theoretic Models of Bargaining*, Cambridge, Cambridge University Press.
Binmore, Ken (1992), *Fun and Games: A Text on Game Theory*, Lexington, MA, DC, Heath and Company.
Binmore, Ken, Rubinstein, Ariel and Wolinsky, Asher (1986), 'The Nash Bargaining Solution in Economic Modelling', **17** *Rand Journal of Economics*, 176-188,
Fernandez, Raquel and Glazer, Jacob (1991), 'Striking for a Bargain Between Two Completely Informed Agents', **81** *American Economic Review*, 240-252.
Geanakoplos, John and Polemarchakis, Heraklis (1982), 'We Can't Disagree Foreever', **28** *Journal of Economic Theory*, 192-200.
Greenberg, Joseph (1994), 'Coalition Structures', in Aumann, Robert J. and Hart, Sergiu (eds), *Handbook of Game Theory, Vol. 2*, Amsterdam, North Holland-Elsevier.
Harsanyi, John C. (1967, 1968a, 1968b), 'Games with Incomplete Information Played with "Bayesian Players"', **13-14** *Management Science*, 159-182, 320-334 and 486-502.
Huang, Peter H. (1995), 'Strategic Behavior and the Law: A Guide for Legal Scholars to *Game Theory and the Law* by Douglass Baird, et al. and Other Game Theory Texts', **36** *Jurimetrics Journal of Law, Science and Technology*, 99-114.

Kennan, John and Wilson, Robert (1993), 'Bargaining with Private Information', **31** *Journal of Economic Literature*, 45-104.

Kreps, David M. (1990), *Game Theory and Economic Modelling*, Oxford, Oxford University Press.

Lax, David A. and Sebenius, James K. (1986), *The Manager as Negotiator*, New York, NY, The Free Press.

Mas-Colell, Andreu, Whinston, Michael D. and Green, Jerry R. (1995), *Microeconomic Theory*, New York, NY, Oxford University Press.

Milgrom, Paul and Roberts, John (1986), 'Relying on the Information of Interested Parties', **17** *Rand Journal of Economics*, 18-32.

Nash, John F. (1950), 'The Bargaining Problem', **18** *Econometrica*, 155-162.

Nash, John F. (1951), 'Non-Cooperative Games', **54** *Annals of Mathematics*, 286-295.

Nash, John F. (1953), 'Two-Person Cooperative Games', **21** *Econometrica*, 128-140.

Okada, Akira (1996), 'A Noncooperative Coalitional Bargaining Game with Random Proposers', **16** *Games and Economic Behavior*, 97-108.

Posner, Richard A. (1992), *Economic Analysis of Law*, Fourth Edition, Boston, MA, Little, Brown and Company.

Roth, Alvin E. (1995), 'Bargaining Experiments', in Kagel, John H. and Roth, Alvin E. (eds), *The Handbook of Experimental Economics*, Princeton, NJ, Princeton University Press, 253-348.

Rubinfeld, Daniel L. and Sappington, David E.M. (1987), 'Efficient Awards and Standards of Proof in Judicial Proceedings', **18** *Rand Journal of Economics*, 308-315.

Rubinstein, Ariel (1982), 'Perfect Equilibrium in a Bargaining Model', **50** *Econometrica*, 97-110.

Rubinstein, Ariel (1985), 'A Bargaining Model with Incomplete Information About Time Preferences', **53** *Econometrica*, 1151-1172.

Salant, Stephen W. and Sims, Theodore S. (1996), 'Game Theory and the Law: Ready for Prime Time?', **94** *Michigan Law Review*, 1839-1882.

Ståhl, Ingolf (1972), *Bargaining Theory*, Stockholm, Economics Research Institute.

7500
ARBITRATION

Bruce L. Benson
DeVoe Moore Professor and Distinguished Research Professor
Department of Economics, Florida State University

Abstract

Within the economics literature on arbitration, some studies, generally considering commercial disputes, emphasize arbitration-litigation relationships. For instance, commercial arbitrators often rely on customary commercial law rather than national law, suggesting that arbitration can be a jurisdictional alternative to litigation rather than simply a procedural one. In support of this, the literature demonstrates that arbitration is a potential source of precedent, and is viable without judicial backing. Others studies, mostly dealing with labor disputes, focus on negotiation incentives given alternative forms of compulsory interest arbitration. Arbitration selection processes' implications for arbitrator behavior and the relative 'quality' of arbitration are also considered.
JEL classification: K41, J52
Keywords: Arbitration, Customary Law, Private Sanctions, Precedent, Interest Arbitration, Exchangeability

1. Introduction

The law and economics literature on contracts and contract enforcement has focused almost exclusively on judicial adjudication (Rubin, 1995, p. 113), despite the fact that the vast majority of contracts are never adjudicated. Outside the realm of law and economics there is a large literature on alternative dispute resolution (ADR) including arbitration, for instance, indicating that even when disputes cannot be resolved through negotiation or mediation, they are directed away from national courts and into arbitration, at least for some large categories of contracts. Lew's (1978, p. 589) detailed examination of the evidence on international commercial contracts concludes that around 80 percent of these contracts had arbitration clauses at the time of his study, for example, and that over time, 'more and more [international traders] ... turn to arbitration'. More recent studies confirm this trend: Casella (1992, p. 1), Berger (1994, p. 12) and others report that about 90 percent of all international trade contracts contain arbitration clauses. Similarly, within the United States, arbitration under the auspices of various commercial organizations, or by independent arbitrators, perhaps from the American Arbitration Association (AAA), resolve at least three times as many commercial disputes as the common law courts do (Auerbach, 1983, p. 113).

Arbitration of disputes between employers (both government and private) and unionized employees has also been routine (and even compulsory for government employees, as well as for some private sector employees, when negotiation proves inadequate) for several decades in the United States. Furthermore, while non-union employees' disputes were almost never arbitrated before 1970, growing numbers are now resolved by arbitrators (Ware, 1996, p. 1). Arbitration is also used for disputes between businesses and customers. For instance, the New York Stock Exchange formally provided for arbitration in its 1817 constitution, and it 'has been working successfully ever since', primarily to rectify disputes between Exchange members and their customers (Lazarus, et al., 1965, p. 27). The Council of Better Business Bureaus (BBB) operates arbitration programs for consumers in many parts of the United States, several automobile manufacturers have contracts with the BBB to arbitrate car owners' complaints, AAA arbitrators annually resolve thousands of insurance claims, the National Association of Home Builders offers AAA arbitration of buyers' complaints against association members, medical malpractice arbitration, begun in 1929, is on the rise, and so on (Denenberg and Denenberg, 1981). Non-contract civil disputes are also shifting to arbitration in the United States, in part to avoid litigation costs such as delays due to congested government courts (Bloom and Cavanagh, 1987, p. 35). Indeed, a new private-for-profit court industry, developing since 1979, offers a wide variety of ADR procedures to resolve all kinds of disputes (there were more than 50 such firms in the United States 1992, most with offices in several states (Ray, 1992, p. 191)). These firms are attracting growing numbers of customers (as well as profits and investors (Phalon, 1992, p. 126)), including many who do not contractually stipulate ADR prior to the dispute arising.

While arbitration has not attracted much attention in the core of the law and economics literature, there are some exceptions (for example, Landes and Posner, 1979; Bernstein, 1992; Shavell, 1995). Furthermore, expanding 'law and economics' to include some contributions from 'new institutional economics' and labor economics, reveals considerable analysis of various aspects of arbitration, thus providing the foundations upon which a law and economics approach to understanding arbitration's functions can be built. There is a much larger literature on arbitration outside of economics, of course, including several journals exclusively concerned with arbitration or ADR, but this review focuses on research by economists or by legal scholars who have adopted a law and economics approach (and at times, contributions from the larger literature referred to in this research), thus leaving out some issues that may be attracting attention in the larger literature and/or of potential but yet unexplored interest from a law-and-economics perspective.

The economics literature on arbitration divides, roughly, between labor arbitration and commercial arbitration. However, within this literature, a different (but correlated) division is also apparent. In particular, some studies, mostly concerned with commercial arbitration, emphasize relationships between arbitration and litigation, while other economics research, primarily in the labor literature, focuses on arbitration's influence on negotiation incentives (explorations of the arbitration process are found in both literatures). The following presentation is organized in reflection of this division. It appears that the reason for the differences in focus arises, at least in part, because commercial arbitration is generally an *ex ante* voluntary decision by both parties to contractually specify arbitration over litigation in the event of a dispute, while the most widely studied examples of labor arbitration by economists (interest arbitration dealing with public sector employees) are compulsory under statute law. This is probably due to the fact that data on some compulsory arbitration systems can be obtained relatively easily, while data on general grievance arbitration is not nearly as accessible. As a consequence, however, within the economics literature, voluntary commercial arbitration is often depicted as a cooperative endeavor to minimize the costs of dispute resolution, while labor arbitration tends to be characterized as a much more adversarial process. In reality, like commercial arbitration, most private-sector labor arbitration arises through collective bargaining contracts rather than through compulsory statutes, the primary exception being parts of the transportation industry governed by the Railway Labor Act so, as indicated below, the impression taken from the labor economics literature on arbitration may be quite misleading.

First, some of the reasons for why law and economics scholars should be interested in arbitration are discussed in Part 2. An important one, at least for commercial law, is that arbitrators often resolve disputes under customary commercial law and/or trade association rules rather than under the statute and/or precedent law of a particular nation. That the choice of arbitration is a jurisdictional issue rather than simply a procedural one might not be accepted if, as is frequently claimed, arbitration is not viable without judicial enforcement of arbitration agreements and rulings, and/or arbitration is simply a compromising process and not a source of legal interpretation and precedent. Therefore, the arguments and evidence regarding these two 'arbitration versus litigation' issues are explored in Sections 3 through 6. The arbitration/negotiation relationship as it is depicted in the labor economics literature, primarily in consideration of the effect of alternative forms of compulsory arbitration on incentives to negotiate, is examined in Sections 7 through 10. Arbitration selection processes and their implications for arbitrator behavior and the relative 'quality' of arbitration are examined in Section 11, and concluding comments appear in Section 12.

2. Why Should Arbitration be Studied?

There are many reasons for more careful consideration of arbitration in the law and economics literature. For instance, the similarities between arbitration and civil litigation are considerable, so perhaps we can learn something about more complex dispute resolution processes by studying arbitration (Ashenfelter, 1987, p. 342; Bloom and Cavanagh, 1987, p. 353). The differences between arbitration and litigation may also be instructive. For example, unlike judges and juries, arbitrators tend to specialize in particular types of disputes. A knowledgeable specialist can render a decision more quickly and with less information transfer from, and therefore less costs incurred by, the disputants, and is less likely to make an error, but Ashenfelter (1987, pp. 342-343) raises another point: since disputants typically have veto power in arbitrator selection, arbitrators competing for business have incentives to develop expertise and render unbiased decisions echoing those of past arbitrators. Thus, as explained below, considerable empirical evidence suggests that arbitrator decisions are statistically 'exchangeable'. In contrast, US juries are selected for their lack of knowledge in an effort to assure 'unbiased justice' (fairness), but the exchangeability of expert arbitrators' decisions suggests an alternative way to achieve bias-free justice while reducing the likelihood of error or bias: competition between 'experienced jurors'.

Perhaps a more important reason for considering arbitration is to gain a fuller understanding of contracting and contract law. In this regard, the focus on judicial adjudication in the law and economics literature on contracting would be appropriate if court precedents and statutes as interpreted by a nation-state's courts (as well as court-interpreted trade agreements between nations) was the exclusive source of law shaping contracts. This is not the case, however, at least in the area of commercial contracting (Rubin, 1995; Benson, 1989, 1998a, 1998b; Bernstein, 1992, 1996). For instance, Lew's (1978, pp. 582-583) examination of international commercial arbitration records demonstrates that arbitrators often 'denationalize' disputes, looking instead to a 'non-national and generally accepted rule or practice appropriate to the question at issue ... developed through the concerted efforts of those concerned with and participating in international commerce' (Lew, 1978, pp. 582-583). That is, as Berman and Dasser (1990, p. 33) explain, international arbitrators 'refer to international commercial custom, including contract practices in international trade, as a basis for their award', and no nation's law is applied unless the contract specifies it or the parties expect it (also see Trakman, 1983, and Benson, 1992b).

Standards of business practice and usage within trade associations and other commercial groups (or a trade association's explicit internal 'legislation' (Bernstein, 1996)) are also the sources of many of the basic rules under which contracts are drawn up and disputes are arbitrated within many countries. Bernstein's (1992, p. 126) examination of the systematic rejection of state-created law by the diamond industry in favor of its own internal rules (including arbitration institutions and privately produced sanctions) provides a very revealing example: the New York diamond merchants' 'Board of Arbitrators does not apply the New York law of contracts and damages, rather it resolves disputes on the basis of trade custom and usage'. Furthermore, despite Bernstein's (1992, p. 116) contention that 'the diamond industry is unique in its ability to create and, more important, to enforce its own system of private law', the same abilities actually exist in many other commercial groups. The fact is that commercial arbitration makes 'the courts secondary recourse in many areas and completely superfluous in others' (Wooldridge, 1970, p. 101). Thus, while many contend that law is what judges say it is, this is only true in contracts to the extent that a judge is expected to have the last word on the contract; when adjudication is not sought, perhaps due to the availability of arbitration and the benefits it produces (and/or private sanctions to discourage adjudication, an issue discussed at length below), other behavioral rules can and often will control the contracting parties' conduct (Rubin, 1995, pp. 118, 124; Bernstein, 1992, 1996; Benson, 1998b, 1998c, 1998d).

Furthermore, if government courts are occasionally called upon, thus influencing the expectations of parties to particular kinds of contracts, 'influence is different from control... [and] One cannot assume, moreover, that the influences flow only in one direction' (Rubin, 1995, p. 124). Some of the new rules for business behavior that develop through evolving practices, contractual negotiations, and arbitration are likely to be recognized and adopted by judges (Chen, 1992; Benson, 1989, 1990a, pp. 227-229, 1998b), for instance. But even when the courts do not recognize custom as a relevant source of law (perhaps because they conflict with precedents or statutes), a judicial decision does not have to be treated as a permanent determinant of behavioral rules. A contract can specify different types of behavior along with a general arbitration clause, thereby nullifying the future application of the judicial ruling (De Alessi and Staaf, 1991). Thus, an understanding of the evolution of contract law, at least in many areas of commercial activity, requires recognition of arbitration, not only as an ADR, but at least in conjunction with contracts, as a mechanism for nullifying statutes and precedents - that is, as an alternative to legislation and judge-made precedent (Wooldridge, 1970, p. 101; Benson, 1989, 1990a, 1990b, 1992a, 1992b, 1995a, 1998b, 1998c, 1998d; Bernstein, 1992, 1996; Rubin, 1995). This is in sharp contrast to the view that arbitration is essentially a procedural issue (for example, Brunet, 1987), of course, but it is reinforced below when the potential for precedent setting through arbitration is discussed. Before this potential for law creation through arbitration can be fully appreciated, however, an understanding of what motivates the use of arbitration in commercial contract disputes is required.

3. Why is Commercial Arbitration Chosen Rather than Litigation?

Any dispute is 'adversarial' of course, but in the commercial area, the voluntary use of arbitration is motivated by positive economic incentives. Private arbitration appears to be an attractive substitute for litigation, in part because arbitrators can be selected on the basis of their expertise in matters pertinent to specific disputes, as noted above. Government judges need have no such expertise, so arbitration reduces the uncertainty associated with judicial error and/or bias. This specialization also means that arbitration can be accomplished faster, less formally, and often with less expense than litigation because the parties do not have to provide as much information to the arbitrator as they would to a judge/jury. Another benefit arises when government court time is allocated by waiting, since delay can be devastating to a business. Other potentially important benefits include: (a) arbitration is generally less 'adversarial' than litigation so it is more likely to allow continuation of mutually-beneficial repeated-dealing relationships; (b) if desired, privacy can be maintained; and (c) businessmen may wish to avoid the application of state-made law by agreeing to something in a contract that would be overturned in a government court, since an arbitrator looks to the contract first and the contract can specify the relevant law for deciding a case (for example, business practice and custom rather than the statutes or judicial precedents of a particular nation). For elaboration on some or all of these points, see Mentschikoff (1961), Lazarus et al. (1965), Williamson (1979), Trakman (1983), Ashenfelter (1987), Berman and Dasser (1990), Benson (1989, 1990b, 1992b, 1995a, 1998a, 1998b, 1998c), Bernstein (1992, 1996), Currie (1994), Shavell (1995), and Rubin (1995). The potential of mutual gains (lower costs of dispute resolution and/or a larger 'pie' to share in the long run) means that there clearly is a 'cooperative' element to arbitration as compared to litigation.

Despite widespread recognition of at least some of the benefits listed above, a frequent contention is that the defendant can always refuse to engage in arbitration or to accept an arbitration ruling, so the plaintiff must be willing and able to seek judicial (government) enforcement in order to have a credible threat to induce acceptance (see, for example, Willoughby, 1929, p. 56; Lazarus et al., 1965, pp. 31, 125; Landes and Posner, 1979, p. 247; Domke, 1984, p. 27; and Shavell, 1995, p. 3). If this is correct then the contention that arbitration often involves a choice between legal systems may be at least partially undermined.

After all, if the primary threat backing arbitration is litigation, then for it to be credible arbitration procedures and awards will have to be acceptable to judges.

In sharp contrast, Charny (1990, pp. 409-412) maintains that when a 'community of transactors recognizes an authoritative nonlegal decisionmaker' such as an arbitrator, 'nonlegal sanctions' will induce the members of the community to accept arbitration and comply with the arbitrator's judgement; thus, arbitration and nonlegal sanctions are 'a perfect substitute for legal enforcement'. These nonlegal sanctions are essentially the 'private' (as apposed to government-imposed) sanctions discussed in the large economics literature suggesting that bond-posting or hostage-taking (for example, Klein and Leffler, 1981; Williamson, 1983; Kronman, 1985), including the potential loss of reputation (for example, Kreps, 1990; Ellickson, 1991; Milgrom, North and Weingast, 1990; Klein, 1997), provides powerful sources of credibility, and Charny (1990) explains that this analysis also applies for commitments to arbitrate (also see Wooldridge, 1970; Trakman, 1983; Auerbach, 1983; Bernstein, 1992; Benson, 1989, 1992b, 1995a, 1998a, 1998b, 1998c). Perhaps more important than these negative threats, however, are various positive incentives associated with relation-specific reciprocities that arises in repeated dealings (Fuller, 1964, p. 24; Axelrod, 1984; Ellickson, 1991; Trakman, 1983, p. 10; Benson, 1989, 1998c). Indeed, one potential long-term benefit from accepting an unfavorable arbitration award is the reciprocal commitment by a trading partner to accept low cost arbitration and abide by an unfavorable judgement in any future dispute. Of course, private sanctions reinforce such incentives, so the combination can provide strong incentives to arbitrate even without an added 'legal' (that is, government-imposed) threat (indeed, reciprocities are valuable assets which can be threatened, and therefore, part of the private sanctions arsenal).

4. Does Commercial Arbitration Rely on Reciprocities and Private Sanctions, or on Legal Sanctions?

Those who see legal sanctions as necessary to back arbitration cite United States arbitration history as 'evidence' in support of this view. In light of the competing hypotheses that reciprocities and private sanctions create strong incentives to arbitrate, Benson (1995a) re-examines this alleged 'historical evidence': that arbitration supposedly was not in widespread use in the United States prior to passage by New York (1920), New Jersey (1923), the federal government of Pennsylvania (1927) and California (1925), Oregon (1925), Massachusetts (1925, 1927) of statutes commanding the common law courts to enforce arbitration agreements and rulings (examples of this contention include Willoughby, 1929, p. 56, and Lucas, 1987, p. 55). Prior to this, it is often alleged (incorrectly, as explained below) that agreements to arbitrate were generally not considered binding under common law until these statutes were passed, and that hostile judges felt free to overturn arbitration decisions if one of the parties chose to litigate (examples include Lazarus et al., 1965, p. 18; Horwitz, 1977; Murray, Rau and Sherman, 1989, p. 435; Allison, 1990, p. 11).

A relative lack of litigation in the United States regarding arbitration issues appears to be the evidence that many have looked to in contending that commercial arbitration was not widely used before 1920. It is true that litigation over issues arising in arbitration increased dramatically following passage of the 1920s statutes (see Sturges, 1930), but court records do not provide a clear picture of the historic level of arbitration because the vast majority of arbitration decisions are never appealed, and the statutes themselves may have increased the propensity to appeal rather than the propensity to arbitrate, as explained below. Moreover, an examination of newspapers, merchant letters, and the records of organizations providing arbitration services, such as the New York Chamber of Commerce, clearly demonstrate that commercial arbitration actually was in widespread use in each of the British Colonies almost three centuries before modern arbitration statutes were passed (Auerbach, 1983; Jones 1956; Smith, 1961, pp. 180-188; Odiorne, 1953, 1954). After the revolution, arbitration remained in wide use in all of the states (Auerbach, 1983; Jones, 1956, p. 219; Smith, 1961, pp. 180-188; Odiorne, 1953, 1954). Why? Because 'Not only did courts, according to one New York merchant, dispense "expensive endless law"; they were slow to develop legal doctrine that facilitated commercial development' (Auerbach, 1983, p. 33).

Common law judges in America were hostile toward arbitration during the eighteenth and early part of the nineteenth century, as they exhibited an increasing willingness to overturn arbitrators' decisions for issues relating to either law or fact is evident (see Benson, 1995a for cases and references). The use of commercial arbitration developed during the colonial and post-revolutionary periods in spite this hostility, however, suggesting that court backing is not a prerequisite for such arbitration. Later in the nineteenth century, a trend toward less hostility can be detected in several state courts (MacNeil, 1992; Benson 1995a), but arbitration continued to evolve both in states where the courts were relatively receptive and states where judicial acceptance was evolving more slowly (Benson, 1995a). For instance, as New York merchants organized into various associations and exchanges, provisions were always made for the arbitration of disputes among members (Jones, 1956, p. 214), despite New York's maintenance of the common law doctrine of revocability of arbitration clauses in statutes longer than many other states.

The volume of evidence regarding the widespread and growing use of arbitration is particularly heavy for the last four decades of the nineteenth century (Jones, 1956, pp. 214-215; Wooldridge, 1970. p. 101; Auerbach, 1983; Macneil 1992; Benson, 1995a). Indeed, these developments suggest that arbitration was being substituted for litigation, since this period witnessed rising litigation costs due to court congestion and trial delay, as well as increasing uncertainty costs regarding the credibility of state courts' implicit commitments to support business contracts as 'the growth of the regulatory state unsettled advocates of commercial autonomy who turned to arbitration as a shield against government intrusion' (Auerbach, 1983, p. 101; also see Benson, 1995a). Rising litigation costs increased incentives to establish contractual arrangements and organizations (for example, trade associations, commercial exchanges) to govern the process of dispute resolution and insure against litigation (for example, arbitration clauses, arbitration institutions, institutionalized private sanctions). Thus, by the end of World War I, arbitration had clearly made the courts irrelevant for contract disputes by a large segment of the business community in the United States (Wooldridge, 1970, p. 101).

Perhaps private sanctions and reciprocities are sufficient to encourage disputants to live up to most *ex ante* agreements to arbitrate, but to date, most arbitration apparently arises under preexisting agreements (or mandates in the case of compulsory interest arbitration discussed below). Does this mean that arbitration cannot be agreed to after a dispute has already developed, unless a strong (that is, state-backed) sanction can be brought to bear? An alternative explanation for the apparent lack of *ex post* arbitration may simply be Shavell's (1995, p. 9) point that the benefits of arbitration are greater when agreed to *ex ante* than when established *ex post*. However, he also notes that an *ex post* agreement to arbitrate can still reduce dispute resolution costs (Shavell, 1995, p. 9). Other potential benefits from *ex post* arbitration agreements include the possibility that the dispute will be resolved more amicably (arbitration is a less adversarial procedure), that risks of judicial error are reduced, and/or that the parties prefer the application of alternative law (for example, custom, the rules designed in a trade association). Thus, arbitration should also be attractive *ex post*, and perhaps legal sanctions to explicitly encourage such arbitration would be beneficial. However, there appears to be an evolving trend toward more *ex post* arbitration even without direct efforts to encourage it through legal sanctioning. For instance, nonmembers of the diamond merchants' organization who have a dispute with members often request *ex post* that the diamond industry's arbitration board hear their cases, and this is done if both parties sign an *ex post* agreement to arbitrate (Bernstein, 1992, p. 126). Furthermore, the recent and rapid development of private for-profit courts that resolve business disputes, personal injury disputes, divorces, construction warranty disputes, disputes over loan defaults, and so on, as they arise (Pruitt, 1982; Benson, 1990b; Ray, 1992; Phalon, 1992), and the growing scope of arbitration of non-contract civil disputes, both suggest that arbitration can be quite attractive even for disputants who do not precommit, and that private institutions are evolving to provide such services.

Additional evidence that reciprocities and/or private sanctions are sufficient to support a great deal of commercial arbitration at least, comes from international commerce. International contracts often expressly exclude litigation and almost always refer disputes to arbitration, and international trade disputes that cannot be resolved through negotiation are almost always arbitrated (for example, Lew, 1978; Trakman, 1983; Berman and Dasser, 1990; Casella, 1992; Berger, 1994; Benson, 1990b, 1992b, 1998c). Certainly, statutes in several nations, as well as various international treaties and agreements mandate court enforcement of international arbitration agreements, but the fact, as David (1985, p. 357) stresses, is that:

> A sense of fair dealing on one hand, the respect for public opinion on the other, also the fear of being criticized by one's own community or that non-performance may be interpreted as evidence that one's business is in a critical financial situation are reasons why arbitral awards are most generally promptly and willingly executed by business people. Such conduct may also be encouraged if the losing party is led to believe that the community will not remain passive in case of non-performance, but that sanctions may be imposed if the award is not executed.

Arbitration is also attractive because international traders generally assume that national courts will not enforce obligations derived solely from customary commercial law (Chen, 1992, p. 100). Indeed, during the medieval period this was particularly true, and as a result, the medieval 'Law Merchant' was an almost pure system of privately-arbitrated customary commercial law backed by private sanctions (for example, Trakman, 1983; Berman, 1983; Benson, 1989, 1990b, 1998b, 1998c, forthcoming; Milgrom, North and Weingast, 1990).

5. What are the Consequences of Legal Sanctions for Arbitration?

Rejection of the hypothesis that government sanctions are necessary for all successful commercial arbitration does not definitely follow from the refutation of the evidence typically supporting it. Indeed, a middle ground is obviously also possible that may well be consistent with all of the evidence. Rubin (1994, p. 4), for example, suggests that 'private parties can use many available mechanisms to make agreements self-enforcing ... [but] the law can facilitate the use of these mechanisms ... [by enforcing] arbitration clauses in contracts if parties insert such clauses'. Perhaps positive incentives from reciprocities and/or private sanctions are not strong enough to support arbitration for some (many?) commercial transactions and, therefore, statutes mandating court backing are, on net, beneficial, as is often claimed (for example, Rubin, 1994; Shavell, 1995a; Ware, 1996)? Frequently, however, those who call for arbitration agreements and awards to be enforced by the judicial system look only to the benefits of state backing without considering potential costs. The fact is that when reciprocities and private sanctions provide sufficient sources of credibility for transactors, state-imposed sanctions may actually raise transactions costs (Ashe, 1983; Auerbach, 1983; Trakman, 1983; Benson, 1989, 1990b, 1995a, 1998b; Charny, 1990, pp. 426-429; Bernstein, 1992, pp. 154-157) (note that this appears to be consistent with a similar argument from the labor arbitration literature discussed below, that the availability of compulsory arbitration can raise the transactions costs of negotiations). For instance, an enormous number of court cases were filed as businessmen tried to determine what characteristics of arbitration would be considered "legal" by the courts (Sturges, 1930), and this has continued: the early 1980s were still witnessing a 'growing number of court challenges to arbitration awards' (Ashe, 1983, p. 42).

Ashe (1983, p. 42) suggests that the increase in appeals reflects the increasing use of lawyers in arbitration because losing attorneys have a stronger tendency to circumvent the arbitrator's decision than does the losing party who tends to have greater 'allegiance to the system of arbitration itself' when lawyers' 'advice' is not involved (that is, there is a principal/agent problem between attorneys and their clients). It is clear that lawyers were rarely involved with commercial arbitration in the United States before the 1920s (indeed, Auerbach, 1983 and Benson, 1995a, contend that the arbitration statutes were passed due to the lobbying efforts of Bar Associations, because lawyers saw arbitration as a growing threat to their business and sought to 'legalize' it in order to gain a role in the arbitration process), but as Charny (1990, pp. 388, 403-405) explains, when state-imposed sanctions are available, the demands placed on formal contract writing are increased. If reciprocities and private sanctions alone apply, particularly within narrowly focused commercial organizations, less formality in contracting is required because the parties are intimately familiar with business practice and custom in their particular area of transactions; they understand what a general statement in a contract means, *and* they can choose an arbitrator with similar intimate understanding. However, a judge is much less likely to have such an understanding, so a contract that may face judicial scrutiny will have to be much more specific and formal in order to avoid a high probability of judicial error (Charny, 1990, pp. 385, 404). Thus, after the modern statutes were passed, some businesses, forced to pay attention to the prospect of judicial review, had to make their arbitration processes compatible with statute and precedent law including court procedure. In order to do so, they had to consult lawyers in drafting contracts and involve lawyers in arbitration (for instance, lawyer representation before AAA arbitration tribunals rose from 36 percent in 1927 to 70 percent in 1938, 84 percent in 1942, and 91 percent in 1947 (Auerbach, 1983, p. 111; Benson, 1995a); also see

Bernstein, 1992, p. 156 for related discussion about the growing use of lawyers in diamond industry arbitration).

The increased likelihood of appeal reflects more than the increasing reliance on lawyers, however. Cohen (1921, p. 150) observed, after New York Arbitration Act's passage in 1920, that this statute

> establishes legal machinery for protecting, safeguarding and supervising commercial arbitration. Instead of narrowing the jurisdiction of the Supreme Court it broadens it ... Instead of being ousted of jurisdiction over arbitration, the courts are given jurisdiction over them, and ... the party aggrieved has his ready recourse to the courts.

When the state asserts that it is the source of authority and sanctions for arbitration agreements it implies that rulings from arbitrated commercial disputes are less decisive than they otherwise would be, weakening incentives to abide by arbitrated settlements explicitly subject to potential appeal. Furthermore, there is the possibility that upon appeal a judge will find private sanctions themselves to be illegal (for example, as a restraint of trade). For instance, in *Paramount Lasky Corporation vs. United States* (282 U.S. 30 (1930)) an explicit agreement to boycott designed to back an arbitration system was struck down. A group of motion picture producers had agreed to place an arbitration clause in all contracts with motion picture exhibitors, *and* to boycott any exhibitor who refused arbitration or refused to accept an arbitration ruling. Thus, government sanctions can undermine the ability or incentives to use private sanctions (Ashe, 1983, p. 42; Bernstein, 1992, p. 156; Benson, 1989, 1995a, 1998d), and even stifle the development of trust relationships and organizations from which reciprocities and private sanctioning mechanisms often spring (Benson, 1989, 1995a, 1998d; Charny, 1990, p. 428). So the possibility that government sanctions to back arbitration may benefit some parties for whom reciprocities are uncertain and private sanctions provide weak threats does not imply that such sanctions are, on net, beneficial, because they may raise costs to others for whom reciprocities and private sanctions are or could be strong enough.

6. Are Precedents Produced Through Arbitration?

Even if the net effect of court backing of arbitration is negative, however, there may be another reason for judicial review. For instance, Brunet (1987, p. 19) contends that 'the output of conventional litigation should be viewed as a public good - society gains more from litigation than would be produced if litigation were left to the private market'. This presumably is the case because the results of arbitration and other forms of ADR are 'internal' to the parties involved (Brunet, 1987, pp. 14-15) so they will either not produce precedent, or will underproduce precedent. Similarly, Landes and Posner (1979, pp. 238, 239, 245) argue that 'because of the difficulty of establishing property rights in a precedent, private ... judges might deliberately avoid explaining their results because the demand for their services would be reduced by rules that, by clarifying the meaning of the law, reduce the incidence of disputes'; that 'a problem is that a system of voluntary adjudication is strongly biased against the creation of precise rules of any sort'; and further, that commercial arbitration is 'not a source of rules or precedents'. Thus, the increasing use of arbitration apparently is eroding 'the guidance function of the law' (Brunet, 1987, p. 23).

Secrecy is often a characteristic of arbitration. For instance, Bernstein (1992, p. 124) explains that within the diamond industry 'As long as judgments are complied with, the fact of the arbitration as well as its outcome are officially kept secret'. But this 'official' secrecy does not mean that precedents are never created, or that too few rules exist. The parties to the dispute will certainly consider the arbitration result in future dealings under similar circumstances, for instance, and probably have to explain them to trading partners. But more importantly, a diamond bourse (trading club) is 'an information exchange as much as it is a commodities exchange'. As one author put it, 'the bourse grapevine is the best in the world. It has been going for years and moves with the efficiency of a satellite communications network. ... Bourses are the fountainhead of this information and from them it is passed out along the tentacles that stretch around the world' as each local bourse is part of an umbrella organization that, among other things, arbitrates disputes between members of different bourses, enforces arbitration judgments from other bourses, and facilitates the establishment of uniform trading rules throughout the industry (Bernstein, 1992, p. 121). Under such a circumstance, 'official' secrecy is probably not much of a constraint on the spread of important information about an arbitration ruling that might provide new precedent. It is clear that in the diamond industry arbitration results do 'become known through gossip' (Bernstein, 1992, p. 126) at any rate.

Bernstein (1992, pp. 126-127) contends that when diamond industry arbitrators hear complex cases 'it is difficult to determine what substantive rules of decisions are applied', and such observations may appear in support of the view that arbitration does not produce effective precedent. However, as Fuller (1981, p. 90) explains, '[e]ven if there is no statement by the tribunal of the reasons for its decision, some reason will be perceived or guessed at, and the parties will tend to govern their conduct accordingly'. Thus, precedent of a sort may well be produced even in such an environment. Furthermore, and importantly, it must be recognized that within a customary legal system there are a number of ways for new rules to evolve (for example, through unilateral adoption of behavior that is observed and emulated, through bilateral negotiation and contracting with resulting contract clauses spreading and becoming standardized), besides through precedent (Benson, 1998b), so when a particular arbitration process does not appear to be designed to produce precedent it simply may mean that precedent is a relatively unimportant source of new rules for the relevant group, or that circumstances do not change often enough to require new rules. And importantly, if situations change, making precedent more important, the group is also free to change its arbitration procedures. Thus, as Bernstein (1992, p. 150) explains, diamond dealers have begun to recognize that 'The lack of written decisions and a tradition of stare decisis makes it difficult to determine in advance the type of sanctioned behavior. In order to increase predictability, many bourses in the world federation have relaxed the norm of complete secrecy. Arbitrators publish written announcements of the principles used to decide novel cases while keeping the parties and other identifying facts secret'. Private dispute resolution mechanisms are very flexible and diverse. They can even accommodate the demands for precedent setting while still meeting demands for privacy. However, privacy is not always as important as some critics of arbitration seem to believe.

Landes and Posner (1979), Brunet (1987) and others who see in arbitration a failure to create external benefits appear to take the characteristics of some arbitration and extrapolate them to all arbitration, assuming that arbitration is a much more homogeneous commodity than it really is. But if external benefits are significant there are strong incentives to internalize them, so when precedents become important institutional adjustments are likely to be made. Indeed this provides traders with one of the incentives to form groups such as trade associations and diamond bourses which clearly can internalize the benefits of precedents. Within such an organization, it is easy to imagine a contractual arrangement that creates incentives to minimize disputes by setting clear precedents (for example, consider arbitrators who compete to receive a lump-sum fee under a contract to handle all of the disputes between members of a particular organization over a particular period of time, or arbitrators chosen from the membership of an association who have high opportunity costs if they encourage excessive disputes in the form of time spend away from their business pursuits, and who also personally benefit from clear precedents). Thus, those arbitrators who, as characterized by Landes and Posner (1979, p. 240), 'tend to promulgate vague standards which give each party to a dispute a fighting chance' actually do less business. Fuller (1981, pp. 110-111) contends that incentives are exactly the opposite, for instance: 'Being unbacked by state power ... the arbitrator must concern himself directly with the acceptability of his award. He may be at greater pains than a judge to get his facts straight, to state accurately the arguments of the parties, and generally to display in his award a full understanding of the case'.

An obvious hypothesis is that when the environment is a dynamic changing one in which the need for existing rules may be frequently inadequate guides for a new dispute, arbitration rulings are likely to be recorded and/or made known to the relevant group (which certainly is not likely to be the entire 'public', of course, but in general, that is not necessary or even desirable - the idea that a single universal system of law is somehow superior to polycentric law with parallel, as well as overlapping and competitive jurisdictions is not consistent with either theory or reality (Benson, 1990a, 1990b, 1992a; Berman, 1983)). This in turn creates incentives for arbitrators to make careful rulings based on past business practices, customs and precedents established within the relevant group. For support of this hypothesis, consider international commercial arbitration. When no clear rule applies from the 'private international law systems from which the parties come' arbitrators must determine the appropriate new rule (Lew, 1978, p. 584). To do so, 'in their desire to 'denationalize' the award and make it acceptable and fair, arbitrators often try to show the inherent correctness of their decision in the award itself... arbitrators may refer to several rules to show how they all lead to the same result' (Lew, 1978, pp. 584-585). Thus, international arbitration has characteristics often attributed to the common law, as arbiters look to past rulings, practices, traditions, and usage in extending the law to new issues - that is, in producing new precedent based on older law. In fact, the general view of international arbitrators is that, 'owing no allegiance to any sovereign State, international commercial arbitration has a special responsibility to develop and apply the law of international trade' (Lew, 1978, p. 589).

It appears that the misallocation of resources under arbitration is not be as great as Landes and Posner (1979) and Brunet (1987) predict. Indeed, the law-making consequences of private arbitration led Wooldridge (1970, p. 104) to suggest that its substantial growth in this century has involved a 'silent displacement of not only the judiciary but even the legislature'. Furthermore, Bernstein (1992, p. 117) points out that 'nonlegal norms trump legal rules in a given [voluntary] market only where market participants find that keeping to the industry norms advances their own self-interest. The private regime must be Pareto superior to the established legal regime in order to survive'. (In addition to their contentions that private judging underproduces precedent, however, Landes and Posner, 1979 and Brunet, 1987, p. 21 argue that the common law produces efficient rules as contended by Rubin, 1977 and Priest, 1977, but the validity of this argument has also been subject to considerable attack; this literature is not discussed here, but see for instance, Rizzo, 1980a, 1980b; Aranson, 1986, and Benson, 1990a, 1990b, 1992a, 1996).

7. Are there Important Differences in Labor Arbitration Institutions?

Non-compulsory labor arbitration in the private sector is also growing, as collective bargaining agreements include arbitration clauses much like many contracts between businessmen do. The development of repeated dealings between unions and firms with institutionalized collective bargaining along with strike and lockout options appears be a sufficient stimuli for arbitration of many grievances and perhaps even contract disputes when negotiations break down. The incentives of the decision-makers must also be recognized. Arbitration may be relatively attractive to union leaders, for instance, because of their legal status. They are in a position of representing everyone in the union, including those who opposed their election and perhaps even campaigned against them. Indeed, they have a legal duty to represent all members, and therefore, in order to avoid a breach of fair representation lawsuit, union officials may pursue grievance arbitration in cases that they would prefer not pursue or would negotiate in the absence of the antagonistic position held by the member with the grievance. Arbitration of such cases is clearly more attractive than the alternatives (a strike or a lawsuit) that may be much more costly for the union as a whole, including the union leader's supporters. Thus, grievance arbitration may offer union leaders an effective way to avoid controversy and maintain the appearance (and indeed, the reality) of fairness (this suggests that the availability of grievance arbitration may reduce strikes, litigation, and negotiation - the latter is a subject that is widely considered in the labor arbitration literature, and discussed below).

There also appears to be incentives to structure grievance arbitration so that benefits of precedents can be internalized. After all, both labor unions and corporate management are likely to recognize that repeated disputes over the same type of issues are costly, and therefore that arbitration which establishes clear precedent is desirable. In this light, consider the incident reported by Bloom and Cavanagh (1986, p. 412): 'a system known as expedited arbitration was adopted by labor and management in the basic steel industry in 1971. Under this system, unresolved employee grievances that do not require precedent-setting rulings are arbitrated by a rotating panel of young, inexperienced arbitrators (mostly lawyers) who decide the case for a relatively small fee within two weeks of the decision to arbitrate'. When a resolution is expected to be particularly valuable because it will set a precedent, more experienced, more expensive arbitrators are chosen (factors determining the choice of arbitrators are discussed below). This system was established because of rising costs and increasing delays due to a relative shortage of experienced arbitrators. While it has not yet attracted 'an in-depth study', it is spreading (Bloom and Cavanagh, 1986, p. 412). United Steel Workers contracts outside the basic steel industry now include it, and it has also been included in some United

Mineworker contracts, and is employed in the US Postal Service. Thus, it is instructive for at least three reasons. First, it points to the fact that within an 'industry' (the group of employers and the union, not simply the two parties in a particular dispute) the benefits of precedent can be recognized and internalized, even in some types of labor arbitration. Second, it reinforces the fact that arbitration is flexible enough to produce a mix of dispute resolution procedures and outcomes. Third, it suggests that even labor arbitration may have a cooperative element, in contrast to the perception one draws from the economics literature on the subject (Non-union employees' disputes are also being resolved by arbitrators in growing numbers (Ware, 1996, p. 1)). This perception reflects the fact that the focus of the economics literature on labor arbitration has been on compulsory interest arbitration.

Compulsory interest arbitration is almost exclusively a 'public sector' phenomena (baseball arbitration and some transportation sector arbitration are among the few exceptions). Yet many of the publications in this interest-arbitration literature begin with a brief discussion of the widespread use of arbitration in commercial areas, perhaps also recognizing that arbitration between individuals and their employers is frequently used to resolve private-sector labor grievances, implicitly suggesting that inferences from their empirical and/or theoretical examination of compulsory public-sector arbitration apply under other institutional arrangements as well. This clearly is not always the case, however. For instance, the compulsory-arbitration focus of the literature might create the impression that labor arbitration in general must rely on state backing or mandates. Much of the literature does not appear to recognize that the institutional environment might create different incentives, although there are a few exceptions. Bloom and Cavanagh (1987, p. 355) and Currie (1989, pp. 365-366) note that private sanctions and expectations of reciprocities may be quite weak for some government employers whose incentives are tied to particular constituencies that may not view an arbitrated (or negotiated) outcome as desirable, for example. Currie (1989, p. 366) also suggests that significant principal/agent problems may arise when imperfectly-monitored self-interested union leaders are bargaining with imperfectly-monitored self-interested government officials (private-sector managers are not perfectly monitored either, but the incentives to monitor public officials are much weaker (Benson, 1995b)). When publicly employed laborers are protected by civil service 'tenure' the potential for reciprocities and private sanctions influencing their behavior may also be sharply limited. Thus, the institutional background may be very important, and expanding the scope of the statutes (for example, to mandate arbitration in place of private sector strikes and lockouts) might alter incentives to develop and use labor arbitration institutions voluntarily, as evidenced by some of the things that have happened in commercial arbitration since arbitration statutes were passed in the 1920s.

Compulsory arbitration can take different forms, but it often means that strike and lockout options are precluded for public employees by the state, so if one party requests arbitration the other can be forced to accept it. Thus, Stevens (1966), in an early and influential contribution to this literature, describes compulsory arbitration as a bargaining tool in a purely distributional dispute (for example, a zero-sum dispute over the distribution of a fixed 'pie' to be divided between employers and a union) that has much in common with a strike or a lockout. In particular, if arbitration is costly then when it is threatened, it can induce the other party to negotiate. Furthermore, he explains that arbitration mechanisms can be designed to encourage negotiated settlements (discourage arbitration), and as demonstrated by the empirical research discussed below, this clearly appears to be the case. He then suggests that arbitration should be designed to impose costs on bargainers in order to encourage voluntary settlements. In fact, following Stevens, it is often contended that the most successful form of compulsory arbitration 'is one that is not used' (Long and Feuille, 1974, p. 202). A recommendation that arbitration be made more costly in order to encourage negotiation obviously requires a strong normative belief that negotiated settlements are more desirable than arbitrated settlements (Bloom and Cavanagh, 1987, p. 354; Currie, 1989, p. 364). This norm seems to permeate the economics literature on labor arbitration (with important exceptions, like Bloom and Cavanagh, 1986, 1987; Ashenfelter, 1987, and Currie, 1989). Indeed, as Currie (1989, p. 364) explains, 'most industrial relations experts believe that settlements reached by the parties themselves are superior to those imposed by an arbitrator', but without much theoretical basis for the belief. There is some theoretical basis for the conclusion, of course. In particular, as Stevens (1966) alleges, standard interest arbitration as a compromising process tends to 'chill' bargaining as it creates incentives for negotiators to misrepresent their true underlying profit- and/or utility-maximizing positions, expecting arbitrators to split the difference between their extreme demands. However, there are alternative theoretical explanations for the relationship between arbitration and negotiation that can produce the same empirical fact and quite different normative implications.

Law and economics scholars might anticipate that arguments for encouraging negotiations are based on Coase's (1960) famous theorem, that if the transactions costs of bargaining are not prohibitive an efficient allocation of resources is achieved through voluntary negotiation. However, the decision to arbitrate obviously implies positive transactions costs for bargaining (perhaps in the form of uncertainty for the union representative regarding the 'political' or legal consequences of a negotiated settlement that might be perceived as biased or unfair to some of the membership), and in that context the typical inference drawn from Coase is to lower the cost of negotiating (for example, by clarifying property rights, or in labor arbitration, perhaps by allowing the aggrieved party rather than the elected union leaders to choose a negotiator), not raise the cost of the alternative. Thus, for instance, in the diamond industry, Bernstein (1992, p. 124) explains that parties who submit a dispute to arbitration must first participate in a conciliation proceeding before a conciliation panel that attempts to help the parties negotiate a settlement. Only if such third-party aided negotiation fails can the dispute go to arbitration. This is clearly a mechanism intended to encourage negotiation without raising the cost of arbitration, in sharp contrast to Stevens' (1966) proposal, and an estimated 85 percent of the diamond-industry disputes submitted to arbitration are settled during this conciliation procedure.

Moreover, as Williamson (1979) explains, characteristics of the transaction that determine transactions costs (for example, degree of asset specificity, frequency of the transaction, uncertainty) determine the efficient organizational choice, given 'market', 'bilateral' (direct negotiation and contracting), and 'trilateral' (use of a third-party), or 'ownership-integration' governance options. Under these circumstances, if arbitration is used it may be because the transactions costs of negotiation are relatively high, so fair arbitration is a more efficient means of achieving a settlement. Thus, encouraging negotiation by raising the costs of arbitration can reduce efficiency. As Posner (1986, p. 366) notes in his discussion of summary jury trials and other ADR options, the objective should not be to maximize negotiated settlements but to minimize the total costs of the system of achieving settlements, whether voluntarily or through third-party procedures.

Perhaps the points made here do not apply to Stevens' (1966) arguments about compulsory labor arbitration, however. The disputants themselves presumably have not voluntarily designed this governance arrangement if it is mandated by statute (in all likelihood, public sector unions and employers lobbied to influence the statutes, of course, but the statutes may not allow the transaction-specific adjustments in governance organizations that would lead to efficient outcomes (Benson, 1995b)). Compulsory arbitration still may be a cooperative outcome if it is the low-cost dispute resolution mechanism relative to a particular high-transactions-cost negotiation, however. Indeed, Bloom and Cavanagh (1986, p. 409) point out that 'labor practitioners place greater emphasis [than economic theorists] on arbitration as a mechanism for helping disputants identify and reach efficient outcomes. In their view, arbitrators are professional gatherers and processors of information who play a highly constructive role in a bargaining process which is better treated as a cooperative attempt at problem solving than as direct economic conflict'. Furthermore, Bloom and Cavanagh (1986, p. 421) conclude, from their study of the selection of arbitrators (discussed below), that 'the similarity of union and employer preferences for different arbitrators suggests that collective bargaining functions more cooperatively than most existing models indicate'. Doubt is cast on the theoretical underpinnings of this hypothesis by considering the assumption that arbitrators split the difference between offers. Farber (1981) raises important theoretical questions regarding the assumption, noting that even empirical evidence of difference splitting would not be sufficient to prove that this is the objective of the arbitrator since parties are likely to position their offers around the expected arbitration award. That is, 'the expected arbitration outcome shapes the parties' bargaining positions rather than the reverse' (Farber, 1981, p. 70). Gibbons (1988) goes even further, modeling arbitration in the context of a three-party game in which arbitrators also learn about the state of the employment relationship from the parties' offers.

8. Does Final Offer Arbitration Encourage Negotiation (or Discourage Arbitration)?

Stevens (1966) and several others propose what has come to known as final offer arbitration (FOA) to overcome the hypothesized tendency for compromising arbitration to 'chill' negotiation. FOA requires the arbitrator to choose one or the other of the two sides' final offers rather than choosing some compromise between them. The idea is that the negotiators will have incentives to move toward relatively reasonable positions before arbitration, but in doing so they are presumably more likely to reach a negotiated settlement on their own. FOA has been implemented in labor arbitration through statute law in a number of places, and as a consequence, it has attracted a good deal of theoretical analysis.

Crawford (1979) provides one of the earliest formal theoretical examinations of FOA. He notes that if the arbitrator's exogenously determined notion of what a settlement should be is known to the two parties then FOA and conventional arbitration will lead to the same outcome in a zero-sum distributional game. Under conventional arbitration neither party would settle for a distribution different from the arbitration outcome so all awards have to correspond to that outcome whether they are achieved through negotiation or arbitration. If the arbitrator selects the final offer closest to his preferred outcome, the same is true, as one party can always improve on any final offer by offering the arbitrator's preferred settlement. Of course, given positive arbitration costs (that is, if use of arbitration makes the process a negative-sum game), arbitration should actually not be used at all. This might appear to desirable, given the arguments by Stevens (1966), Long and Feuille (1974) and others, but in this case the parties are simply agreeing on what the arbitrator would award anyway, so arbitration is actually the determining factor, not negotiation (Ashenfelter and Bloom, 1984, p. 112).

Crawford (1979) also draws on Schelling's (1963) model of commitment, suggesting that parties find it advantageous to commit to a position that is costly to disavow. Given uncertainty about the strength of the parties' commitments, the potential for commitment by both parties can lead to a disagreement and therefore to arbitration. Factors that increase the payoff to commitment increase the likelihood of disagreement. Still, the model predicts that FOA should not increase the likelihood of negotiation. Indeed, Crawford (1979, p. 152) suggests that 'FOA may create a Prisoner's Dilemma situation and thereby prevent agents who would otherwise cooperate from agreeing on an efficient settlement'. Of course, in a repeated game setting the prisoner's dilemma outcome of non-cooperation is less likely (Axelrod, 1984), so if the interaction generating the dispute is not viewed by the negotiators as a one-shot game this result may not hold. Nonetheless, Crawford's framework does not appear support the contention that FOA should increase the propensity to bargain.

Actually, Crawford (1979) does raise one point that implies that FOA can be relatively 'costly'. If negotiations break down, neither final offer may actually be efficient (or equitable, depending on the objectives of the arbitrator and/or the nature of the dispute - the outcome of a zero sum dispute may reflect the arbitrator's view of equity, for instance). If there are multiple issues involved in the dispute, for example, both final offers may involve inefficient mixes of solutions. Constraining the arbitrator to choose one or the other would, therefore, guarantee an inefficient solution. Crawford (1979) concludes that 'multiple FOA' is superior to single FOA arbitration, but under conventional arbitration the arbitrator has a full range of outcomes to consider, so an efficient solution is also possible. If conventional arbitrators are expected to search for an efficient solution (or an equitable distribution in a zero-sum bargain) rather than to split the difference, and if bargaining costs are high, FOA could easily 'encourage' more bargaining and more costs than conventional arbitration does, but in this case, the result actually involves higher transactions costs. Thus, whether FOA is desirable or not depends on what bargainers expect arbitrators to do, which in turn should depend on what they actually do Bloom (1981, p. 243).

Farber and Katz (1979), and Farber (1980, 1981) offer a different view of compulsory arbitration than Crawford (1979). They assume that the parties are uncertain about arbitrators' preferences and explain that the likelihood of a bargain depends on the parties' expectations about the arbitration award and their risk preferences. For instance, similar expectations about arbitration outcomes and significant arbitration costs can produce a contract zone, and Farber and Katz (1979) suggest that a larger the contract zone increases the probability of a bargaining settlement. Divergent expectations (for example, overly optimistic expectations by at least one party), on the other hand, can prevent successful bargaining. However, Farber and Katz (1979) conclude that uncertainty about arbitration's outcome coupled with risk aversion on the part of at least one party, can also produce a contract zone, while greater certainty about the arbitration award, and hence less risk, may mean that no contract zone exists and arbitration results. Thus, in keeping with Stevens' contention that arbitration should be structured to encourage negotiation, Farber and Katz (1979) express concern that uncertainty will decline as parties gain experience with arbitration, and that arbitration will become more prevalent over time (this is one variant of the 'narcotic effect' hypothesis discussed below). In addition, the relative impact of FOA and conventional arbitration depend on the parties' attitudes toward risk and their expectations about arbitrator preferences, among other variables.

In line with Stevens (1966), Kochan (1980) contends that FOA is more effective at imposing costs on parties if they fail to reach a negotiated settlement. After all, the expected award from FOA is a probability weighted average of two points while the expected conventional award is a probability weighted average of a distribution of potential awards, and by removing the ability of an arbitrator to compromise, the relatively low risk middle part of this distribution is removed. FOA appears to be riskier, and as Farber and Katz (1979) emphasize, uncertainty regarding the behavior of the arbitrator is a source of arbitration costs. But this reasoning is flawed (Farber, 1980; Crawford, 1982; Farber and Bazerman, 1987, 1989). For instance, Farber and Bazerman (1989) point out that the risk of FOA can be manipulated by manipulating offers, and FOA eliminates the high-risk tails of the distribution as well as the low-risk middle. Indeed, they use existing estimates of arbitration behavior, assuming constant absolute risk aversion utility functions and identical normal prior distributions on the arbitrator's concept of an appropriate award, and conclude that contract zones are unambiguously larger under conventional arbitration than under FOA. Given that identical-expectation contract zones are relatively large, it should take a greater degree of divergent expectations to offset the potential for bargaining under conventional arbitration. Thus, if larger contract zones imply that a voluntary settlement is more likely, negotiation should be more prevalent under conventional arbitration.

In contrast to the standard view, however, Bloom (1981) explains that wider contract zones do not necessarily imply a greater likelihood of successful negotiations (a point also made by Crawford, 1981). After all, there may be substantial direct costs of negotiations, as well as uncertainty about settlement points within the contract zone. Indeed, it may be easier to agree if there is one point in the contract zone that both parties prefer to arbitration than if there are a large number of alternatives. Thus, raising the costs and/or uncertainty associated with arbitration may not lead to more negotiated settlements. In this light, Farber and Bazerman's (1989) finding of larger contract zones under conventional arbitration does not necessarily imply more negotiations, a fact that they recognize. However, they point to another of their results, contending that the best explanation for relatively more negotiated settlements under FOA, as hypothesized by Stevens (1966), comes from their finding that the expected-utility-maximizing-Nash-equilibrium last offers given to an arbitrator (where a negotiator is indifferent between the last offer and the expected arbitration award) are closer under FOA than conventional arbitration. Thus, they conclude that strategically, when equilibrium offers are farther apart the parties are more reluctant to make concessions. If this is the case, then FOA does not appear to raise the cost of arbitration, although it does influence bargaining behavior.

An alternative hypothesis, apparently not found in the literature but tentatively proposed above, is that when bargaining costs are high arbitration becomes relatively attractive because arbitrators are expected to search for the efficient (or equitable) solution to a dispute rather than simply splitting the difference, and that FOA constrains such a search so FOA is less attractive (more costly) than conventional arbitration. Note that this hypothesis is consistent with recent empirical findings by Burgess and Marburger (1993) that 'FOA awards tend to be of "low quality" in the sense that they lie outside the range of negotiated settlements' in their study comparing baseball player salaries determined through negotiation versus those determined through FOA arbitration. Indeed, A number of empirical testable hypotheses follow from this theoretical literature, and a growing body of empirical research addresses many of them.

9. Do Arbitrators Split the Difference?

The 'split-the-difference' assumption appears to be key to the conclusion that conventional arbitration chills negotiations (Feigenbaum, 1975; Feuille, 1975; Anderson and Kochan, 1977; Starke and Notz, 1981). In this regard, Bloom (1986) finds that on average, arbitration decisions in his sample appear to be mechanical compromises between the parties' final offers, but he also emphasizes that there is in fact a substantial amount of unexplained variance in arbitration awards, so that the overall conclusion need not apply to any particular case. His examination of written arbitration decisions also finds a correlation between final offers and the facts in each case (a finding supported by several studies discussed below). That is, negotiators tend to adjust final offers to be consistent with the facts that arbitrators are expected to look at, as Farber (1981) suggests, and therefore arbitrators can use the parties' final offers as a source of information about facts. Furthermore, Bazerman and Farber's (1985) study of wage awards by 64 actual arbitrators in 25 simulated conventional arbitration cases clearly suggests that arbitrators look at both final offers and the facts of the case, weighing the facts more heavily than the offers. The facts also are increasingly important as the offers diverge, contradicting 'the naive split-the-difference view of arbitrator behavior' (Bazerman and Farber, 1985, p. 76).

Farber and Bazerman (1986) report the results of a similar study comparing arbitrator behavior under FOA and conventional arbitration. They assume that the same criteria, determining awards based on facts rather than offers, characterizes arbitrator behavior under different arbitration schemes. Their findings support the assumption: again, conventional arbitration awards are weighted averages of the facts and offers with weights depending on the reasonableness of the offers, and final offer awards are also determined by the facts and the offers. Thus, it appears that arbitrators are generally consistent in their behavior under different arbitration regimes (Farber and Bazerman, 1986, p. 842). Ashenfelter and Bloom (1984) reach similar conclusions about the virtually identical decision processes for arbitrators under conventional arbitration and FOA, using a data sample drawn from New Jersey where public employee disputes can be decided under conventional arbitration if the parties agree to it, but FOA if they do not. Arbitrators, it seems, do much more than split the difference.

10. Does Conventional Interest Arbitration 'Chill' Negotiations?

Despite the significant evidence that arbitrators do not simply split the difference, there does appear to be empirical evidence of a chilling effect to conventional arbitration. One source of evidence (although there is in fact no strong theoretical linkage (Currie, 1989, p. 364)), is the hypothesized 'narcotic effect' (Kochan and Baderschneider, 1978, p. 431) of third-party dispute resolution. It is contended that when compulsory arbitration is available parties become reliant upon it rather than negotiating. Early studies conclude that such an effect exists because, for example, wage settlements appear to be less responsive to market conditions when third-party procedures are employed (for example, Kochan and Baderschneider, 1978; Butler and Ehrenberg, 1981, and Auld, et al., 1981). Bloom and Cavanagh (1987, p. 355) point out that the simple descriptive statistics which appear to support the hypothesis are far from conclusive (also see Anderson, 1981), however, as a complete test of the hypothesis would require establishing serial correlation in the use of arbitration after controlling for heterogeneity across bargaining units.

Currie (1989) provides what may be the most sophisticated empirical analysis of the 'narcotic effect' hypothesis to date. She finds, controlling for a number of other factors, that bargaining units who used arbitration in the previous round of negotiations are at least 10 percent more likely than other bargaining units to use it in the current round, thus supporting the narcotic-effect hypothesis. Yet, the total number of arbitrations in previous years (her sample included 35 years of compulsory arbitration by teachers in British Columbia) has a negative effect on the probability of arbitration, and variables intended to capture attitudes toward risk, changes in the degree of uncert associated with arbitration awards, and differing beliefs about awards do not have significant effects on the probability of using arbitration. Thus, Currie (1989, p. 378) concludes that the typical explanations for a narcotic effect do not appear to hold, so 'A theoretical explanation of this "stylized fact [positive state dependence]", perhaps in the context of a dynamic model of arbitration, is badly needed'. Indeed, the result is consistent with the idea suggested above that an experience with arbitration simply reveals that the net benefits of arbitration are higher than previously believed, so when the transactions costs of negotiation prove to be high, those with experience tend to opt for arbitration relatively more quickly. A very similar point is made by Bloom (1981, p. 243), when he observes that if the split-the-difference hypothesis does not hold and arbitration appears to chill negotiation it may be because 'the parties view this mechanism [compulsory arbitration] as the least costly alternative for establishing a contract'. Of course, if this is the case, the 'chilling' of negotiations may well be appropriate from an efficiency perspective, and designing arbitration mechanisms to raise the cost of arbitration is inefficient (another possible explanation for increasing relative use of arbitration might be that union leaders perceive an increasing probability of breach of fair representation lawsuits in light of the perceived increases in the propensity to litigate in the United States, leading union officials to pursue more grievance arbitration in cases that they would prefer to negotiate in the absence of this perceived threat).

There is yet another set of studies that probably provides the strongest evidence of a potential chilling effect of conventional arbitration: the growing literature comparing negotiation under FOA and conventional arbitration. It appears that FOA increases the probability of a negotiated settlement (Feuille, 1975; Neale and Bazerman, 1983; Farber and Bazerman, 1989). Thus, Stevens (1966), Farber and Katz (1979), and others who suggest that the nature of the arbitration process influences the likelihood of a bargained outcome appear to be correct. But does this support the contention that arbitration should be structured to encourage negotiation or that FOA is desirable? The answer still depends on the relative costs and benefits of negotiated and arbitrated settlements, as Bloom (1981) suggests. In this regard, the evidence of arbitrator behavior, including evidence from the FOA literature, is instructive. Some characteristics of arbitration behavior have already been discussed, such as the fact that they apparently do not split the difference. However, in order to fully appreciate the reasons for this and other characteristics of arbitrator behavior, we must first look at the arbitrator selection process.

11. How are Arbitrators Selected?

Many critics of arbitration and other forms of ADR contend that these private alternatives to litigation will be biased. The proposed reasons for such bias vary, however. Some contend that arbitrators are easily corruptible, so the bias is in favor of the disputant with the most financial resources: 'If the rendering of verdicts is to be independent of the relative wealth of the litigants, then the provision of judicial services naturally requires separation of the decision-makers gain from that of each litigant. This fact either requires heavy regulation or it requires public provision of the judge directly' (Mabry, et al., 1977, p. 83). A different bias is seen by Landes and Posner (1979, p. 254) who contend that 'it might seem that competition would lead to an optimal set of substantive rules and procedural safeguards. But this is incorrect. The competition would be for plaintiffs, since it is the plaintiff who determines the choice among courts having concurrent jurisdiction of his claim. The competing courts would offer not a set of rules designed to optimize dispute resolution but a set designed to favor plaintiffs regardless of efficiency'. Brunet (1987, pp. 31-40) simply concludes that arbitration's procedures bias results away from 'quality', 'accurate' results because they do not incorporate as much information as litigation does (Currie, 1994, makes a similar point except that she focuses on the relative use of information in arbitration and negotiation, and she is much more tentative in her normative conclusions). Essentially, he sees ADR procedures as too 'informal, ambiguous, and not administered in a managerial fashion' and lacking effective discovery processes (Brunet, 1987, pp. 31-33).

All such arguments involve a failure to recognize the potential for creating an arbitrator selection process to avoid such biases. Indeed, as Bloom and Cavanagh (1986, p. 409) explain, 'one of the most important characteristics of arbitration systems is that they may be designed in different ways'. Not surprisingly, arbitration selection mechanisms actually vary widely. For example, within some organizations a single arbitrator or panel is appointed for a set period to arbitrate all disputes between members. Of course, prescreening occurs because these arbitrators are chosen from a competitive pool by the association through its membership approved selection process. For instance, in the diamond industry, arbitrators are elected from the organization's membership for two year terms (Bernstein, 1992, pp. 124-125). A different alternative is that contracting parties or organizations preapprove a list of arbitrators, and if a dispute arises, an arbitrator is chosen from the list by some preset mechanism (for example, random selection, rotating selection, selection by a third party such as a governing board of the association). Yet another common selection system gives the parties to a dispute the resumes of odd numbered list of arbitrators from a larger preselected group (for example, preselected by a trade association, or provided by the AAA), with each party having the power to successively veto names until one remains. Thus, a second level of prescreening is added at the disputant level, contributing 'to the legitimacy of the arbitrator and his award in the eyes of the parties' (Bloom and Cavanagh, 1986, p. 409). The parties are also given the arbitrator's résumés, so they know about experience, training, the nature of awards given in the past, and so on. A similar practice, the subject of Bloom and Cavanagh's (1986) empirical study discussed below, is also common: the parties are given a list and résumés of seven potential arbitrators with the power to veto three and rank the other four, and the arbitrator who is not vetoed by either party and has the highest combined rank is chosen. Another common practice is for both sides of the dispute to provide a list of, say, six arbitrators, and each can then veto any or all of the names on the other party's list; if all names are vetoed each provides another list and the process is repeated (clearly, this procedure requires that both parties want to arbitrate, so they do not continue to provide unacceptable names). All such systems guarantee the appointment of an arbitrator without requiring explicit agreement by the two parties while still allowing for prescreening of the potential arbitrators.

In light of the fact that selection mechanisms allow veto, each party might be expected to support at least some candidates that are expected to be unbiased. In fact, it is widely contended that arbitrators are chosen for their expertise, reflected by their experience and training, as well as for their consistency in deciding cases solely on their merits, and for their impartiality (for example, Elkouri and Elkouri, 1985), but before Bloom and Cavanagh's (1986) study, little statistical evidence existed to verify this. They examine the selection of arbitrators for 75 public employee disputes in New Jersey. A number of findings are of interest. First, in many cases the union and the employer have similar rankings, suggesting that their preferences for arbitrator characteristics are at least moderately similar. Second arbitrators with perceived biases tend to be eliminated. Thus, arbitrators that exhibit a tendency over time to favor labor are given poorer rankings (generally vetoed) by management and vice versa. Similarly, economists get low rankings by labor, relative to lawyers and labor relations practitioners, perhaps because 'economists are likely to be heavily influenced by efficiency conditions' (Bloom and Cavanagh, 1986, p. 418) such as the advantages of competition, mobile labor, and other factors that labor unions tend to undermine. Third, both employees and employers show significant preferences for experience, controlling for impartiality and training. Clearly, while it is not possible to prove that experience reflects arbitrator-specific characteristics such as expertise, it probably does because experience both adds to expertise and is a reflection of past popularity. Fourth, while a number of variables representing impartiality, experience and training appear to be significant, their magnitudes are small, suggesting 'that the parties are relatively indifferent to many of the arbitrators in the New Jersey system' (Bloom and Cavanagh, 1986, p. 419). It would appear that the preselected group of 70 arbitrators that each panel of seven in this sample is drawn from are actually perceived to be quite similar. As Ashenfelter (1987) explains, this is precisely what should be expected.

12. Conclusions: 'Exchangeability' and the Benefits of Arbitration

Given that disputants have the same information about arbitrators and the power to veto any arbitrators that are expected to be biased (Ashenfelter, 1987) explains that arbitrator decisions should be statistically 'exchangeable'. Furthermore, a number of independent empirical studies tend to verify this exchangeability hypothesis (for example, Ashenfelter and Bloom, 1984; Bazerman and Farber, 1985; Farber and Bazerman, 1986; Ashenfelter, 1987; Bloom, 1986; Faurot and McAllister, 1992; Burgess and Marburger, 1993). Consider for example, Faurot and McAllister's (1992) study of salary arbitration in major league baseball. They hypothesize that an arbitrator will attempt to base decisions on the same criteria with the same weights as other arbitrators in order to avoid being vetoed, and find that the expected value of the arbitrator's notion of a fair settlement is significantly influenced by a number of fact-based variables specified in the contract (the Basic Agreement): player performance in the last year, career performance and consistency, recent club performance, and previous compensation (Faurot and McAllister, 1992, p. 710; also see Burgess and Marburger, 1993).

Furthermore, while some evidence might appear to suggest that arbitration is biased, a careful examination generally reveals the opposite. For instance, Ashenfelter (1987, pp. 343-345) discusses a sample of New Jersey's FOA system for police disputes in which the employers win only about a third of the decisions. However, both conventional arbitration and FOA are used in this system, so they can be compared. Recall the evidence discussed above that arbitrators choose conventional awards using a consistent criteria based on the facts, and that FOA arbitrators use the same criteria, choosing the final offer closest to their preferred award. In this light, Ashenfelter (1987) compares conventional and FOA awards and finds that on average, union offers were more reasonable than the employee offers (perhaps because union bargainers were more risk averse, or perhaps because employers were making unreasonable offers for political reasons), so the disproportionate number of union wins reflects bargaining positions, not arbitrator bias, and is actually consistent with the exchangeability hypothesis. He also examines a set of data from the Iowa

FOA system for public employees where, in contrast to New Jersey, the employer offers were more frequently chosen, but in this case it appears that the employers' offers were, on average, the 'more reasonable'.

It is exchangeability, Ashenfelter (1987, p. 341) suggests, that underlies the continued acceptability of labor arbitration systems. Indeed, given the political influence of unions and bureaucratic organizations (Benson, 1995b), it is hard to imagine that compulsory arbitration statutes could survive if they were not perceived by both parties to be beneficial relative to alternatives (strikes, lockouts, litigation, negotiation when transactions costs are high). The view in the commercial arbitration literature that arbitration is a positive-sum process appears apply to compulsory labor arbitration as well.

The private sector is responding to the demand for resolution of a wide variety of disputes by offering a wide variety of specialized dispute resolution options. Specialization has desirable consequences in the production of most goods and services. It is reasonable to expect that this is also true for the production of justice. Indeed, many of the efficiency-based arguments against arbitration (for example, that it will produce 'low quality' biased judgments, that it cannot efficiently produce precedent) are undermined by the flexibility of arbitration and other ADR options. Furthermore, while there is evidence that appears to support some arguments against at least some arbitration, such as the hypothesis that its availability raises the transactions costs of negotiation, it appears that the evidence is also consistent with other hypotheses. Thus, the evidence to date does not provide strong reasons to be discouraged by the fact that arbitration is being substituted for litigation and legislation.

Acknowledgements

I wish to thank Barry Hirsch, Brad Smith, Stephen Ware, Lisa Bernstein, and an anonymous referee for very helpful comments.

Bibliography on Arbitration (7500)

Allison, John R. (1990), 'The Context, Properties, and Constitutionality of Nonconsenual Arbitration: A study of Four Systems', **1** *Journal of Dispute Resolution*, 1-101.

Anderson, John C. (1981), 'The Impact of Arbitration: A Methodological Assessment', **20** *Industrial Relations*, 129-148.

Anderson, John C. and Kochan, Thomas A. (1977), 'Impasse Procedures in the Canadian Federal Service', **30** *Industrial and Labor Relations Review*, 282-301.

Ashe, Bernard F. (1983), 'Arbitration Finality: Myth or Reality?', **38** *Arbitration Journal*, 42-51.

Ashenfelter, Orley (1987), 'Arbitration Behavior', **77** *American Economic Review. Papers and Proceedings*, 342-346.

Ashenfelter, Orley and Bloom, David E. (1983), 'The Pitfalls in Judging Arbitrator Impartiality by Win-Loss Tallies Under Final-Offer Arbitration', **34** *Labor Law Journal*, 534-539.

Ashenfelter, Orley and Bloom, David E. (1984), 'Models of Arbitrator Behavior: Theory and Evidence', **74** *American Economic Review*, 111-124.

Auerbach, Jerold S. (1983), *Justice Without Law?*, New York, Oxford University Press.

Auld, D.A.L., Christofides, L.N., Swidinsky, R. and Wilton, David A. (1981), 'The Effect of Settlement Stage on Negotiated Wage Settlements in Canada', **34** *Industrial and Labor Relations Review*, 234-244.

Bazerman, Max H. and Farber, Henry S. (1985), 'Arbitrator Decision Making: When are Final Offers Important?', **39** *Industrial and Labor Relations Review*, 76-89.

Benson, Bruce L. (1989), 'The Spontaneous Evolution of Commercial Law', **55** *Southern Economic Journal*, 644-661.

Benson, Bruce L. (1990a), 'Customary Law with Private Means of Resolving Disputes and Dispensing Justice: A Description of a Modern System of Law and Order Without State Coercion', **9** *Journal of Libertarian Studies*, 25-42. Reprinted as 'Law and Order Without State Coercion', in Veljanovski, Cento (ed.) (1991), *Regulation, Regulators and the Market*, London, Institute of Economic Affairs, 159-179.

Benson, Bruce L. (1990b), *The Enterprise of Law: Justice Without the State*, San Francisco, Pacific Research Institute for Public Policy.

Benson, Bruce L. (1992a), 'Market Failure versus Government Failure in the Production of Adjudication', in Bowman, Gary W., Hakim, Simon and Seidenstat, Paul (eds), *Privatizing the United States Justice System: Police, Adjudication, and Corrections Services from the Private Sector*, Jefferson, NC, McFarland & Co., 203-225.

Benson, Bruce L. (1992b), 'Customary Law as a Social Contract: International Commercial Law', **2** *Constitutional Political Economy*, 1-27.

Benson, Bruce L. (1995a), 'An Exploration of the Impact of Modern Arbitration Statutes on the Development of Arbitration in the United States', **11** *Journal of Law, Economics, and Organization*, 479-501.

Benson, Bruce L. (1998a), 'Arbitration in the Shadow of the Law', in Newman, Peter (ed.), *The New Palgrave Dictionary of Economics and the Law*, London, Macmillan Press; New York, Stockton Press.

Benson, Bruce L. (1998b), 'Evolution of Commercial Law', in Newman, Peter (ed.), *The New Palgrave Dictionary of Economics and the Law*, London, Macmillan Press; New York, Stockton Press.

Benson, Bruce L. (1998c), 'Law Merchant', in Newman, Peter (ed.), *The New Palgrave Dictionary of Economics and the Law*, London, Macmillan Press; New York, Stockton Press.

Benson, Bruce L. (1998d), 'How the SECEDE in Business Without Really Leaving: Evidence of the Substitution of Arbitration for Litigation', in Gordon, David (ed.), *Secession, State, and Liberty*, New Brunswick, New Jersey, Transaction Publishers.

Benson, Bruce L. (forthcoming), 'Law Without the State: The Merchant Courts of Medieval Europe', in Beito, David T. (ed.), *Voluntary City: New Directions for Urban America*, Oakland, California, Independent Institute.

Berger, Klaus P. (1994), 'Aufgaben und Grensen der Parteiautonomie in der Internationalen Wirtschaftsscheidsgerichtsbarkeit', **40** *Recht der Internationalen Wirtschaft*, 12-18.

Berman, Harold J. and Dasser, Felix J. (1990), 'The "New" Law Merchant and the "Old": Sources, Content, and Legitimacy', in Carbonneau, Thomas E. (ed.), *Lex Mercatoria and Arbitration: A Discussion of the New Law Merchant*, New York, Dobbs Ferry, Transnational Juris Publications, 21-36.

Bernstein, Lisa (1992), 'Opting Out of the Legal System: Extralegal Contractual Relations in the Diamond Industry', **21** *Journal of Legal Studies*, 115-157.

Bernstein, Lisa (1996), 'Merchant Law in a Merchant Court: Rethinking the Code's Search for Immanent Business Norms', **144** *University of Pennsylvania Law Review*, 1765-1821.

Bloom, David E. (1980), 'Customized Final-Offer: New Jersey's Arbitration Law', **103** *Monthly Labor Review*, 30-33.

Bloom, David E. (1981), 'Is Arbitration Really Compatible with Bargaining?', **20** *Industrial Relations*, 233-244.

Bloom, David E. (1986), 'Empirical Models of Arbitrator Behavior Under Conventional Arbitration', **68** *Review of Economics and Statistics*, 578-585.

Bloom, David E. and Cavanagh, Christopher L. (1986), 'An Analysis of the Selection of Arbitrators', **76** *American Economic Review*, 408-422.

Bloom, David E. and Cavanagh, Christopher L. (1987), 'Negotiation Behavior Under Arbitration', **77** *American Economic Review. Papers and Proceedings*, 353-358.

Brinig, Margaret F. (1995), 'Why Can't a Woman be More Like a Man? Or Do Gender Differences Affect Choice?', in Simon, Rita J. (ed.), *Neither Victim nor Enemy*, Lanham, MD, University Press of America.

Brunet, Edward (1987), 'Questioning the Quality of Alternate Dispute Resolution', **62** *Tulane Law Review*, 1-23.

Burgess, Paul L. and Marburger, Daniel R. (1993), 'Do Negotiated and Arbitrated Salaries Differ Under Final-Offer Arbitration?', **46** *Industrial and Labor Relations Review*, 548-559.

Butler, Richard and Ehrenberg, Ronald (1981), 'Estimating the Narcotic Effect of Public Sector Impasse Procedures', **35** *Industrial and Labor Relations Review*, 3-20.

Casella, Alessandra (1992), 'Arbitration in International Trade', **721** *Center for Economic Policy Research Discussion Paper*, London.

Charny, David (1990), 'Nonlegal Sanctions in Commercial Relationships', **104** *Harvard Law Review*, 373-467.

Chen, J.C. (1992), 'Code, Custom, and Contract: the Uniform Commercial Code as Law Merchant', **27** *Texas International Law Journal*, 91-135.

Cohen, Julius H. (1921), 'The Law of Commercial Arbitration and the New York Statute', **31** *Yale Law Journal*, 147-160.

Crawford, Vincent P. (1979), 'On Compulsory Arbitration Schemes', **87** *Journal of Political Economy*, 131-160.

Crawford, Vincent P. (1981), 'Arbitration and Conflict Resolution in Labor-Management Bargaining', **71** *American Economic Review. Papers and Proceedings*, 205-210.

Crawford, Vincent P. (1982), 'Compulsory Arbitration, Arbitral Risk and Negotiated Settlements: A Case Study in Bargaining Under Imperfect Information', **49** *Review of Economic Studies*, 69-82.

Currie, Janet (1989), 'Who Uses Interest Arbitration? the Case of British Columbia's Teachers, 1947-1981', **42** *Industrial and Labor Relations Review*, 363-379.

Currie, Janet (1994), 'Arbitrator Behavior and the Variance of Arbitrated and Negotiated Wage Settlements', **12** *Journal of Labor Economics*, 29-40.

David, René (1985), *Arbitration in International Trade*, Deventer, The Netherlands, Kluwer Law and Taxation Publishers.

Denenberg, Tai Schneider, and Denenberg, R.V. (1981), *Dispute Resolution: Settling Conflicts Without Legal Action*, New York, Public Affairs Committee, Inc.

Domke, Martin (1984), *Domke on Commercial Arbitration*. Revised Edition by Wiker, Gabriel M., Willmette, Ill., Gallaghen & Co.

Elkouri, Frank and Elkouri, Edna Asper (1985), *How Arbitration Works*, Washington, DC, Bureau of National Affairs, Inc.

Farber, Henry S. (1980), 'An Analysis of Final Offer Arbitration', **24** *Journal of Conflict Resolution*, 683-705.

Farber, Henry S. (1981), 'Splitting-the-Difference in Interest Arbitration', **35** *Industrial and Labor Relations Review*, 70-77.

Farber, Henry S. and Bazerman, Max H. (1986), 'The General Basis of Arbitration Behavior: An Empirical Analysis of Conventional and Final-Offer Arbitration', **54** *Econometrica*, 819-844.

Farber, Henry S. and Bazerman, Max H. (1987), 'Why is there Disagreement in Bargaining?', **77** *American Economic Review. Papers and Proceedings*, 347-352.

Farber, Henry S. and Bazerman, Max H. (1989), 'Divergent Expectations as a Cause of Disagreement in Bargaining: Evidence from a Comparison of Arbitration Schemes', **104** *Quarterly Journal of Economics*, 99-120.

Farber, Henry S. and Katz, Harry C. (1979), 'Interest Arbitration, Outcomes, and the Incentives to Bargain', **33** *Industrial and Labor Relations Review*, 55-63.

Faurot, David J. and McAllister, Stephen (1992), 'Salary Arbitration and Pre-Arbitration Negotiation in Major League Baseball', **45** *Industrial and Labor Relations Review*, 697-710.

Feigenbaum, Charles (1975), 'Final Offer Arbitration: Better Theory than Practice', **14** *Industrial Relations*, 311-317.

Feuille, Peter (1975), 'Final Offer Arbitration and the Chilling Effect', **14** *Industrial Relations*, 302-310.

Gibbons, Robert (1988), 'Learning in Equilibrium Models of Arbitration', **78** *American Economic Review*, 896-912.

Holzhauer, Rudi W. and Teijl, Rob (1988), 'Geschillenbeslechting als economisch alternatief (Dispute Settlement as Economic Alternative)', in Snijders, H.J., et al. (eds), *Overheidsrechter gepasseerd*, Arnhem, Gouda Quint, 489-499.

Horwitz, Morton J. (1977), *The Transformation of American Law, 1780-1860*, Cambridge, MA, Harvard University Press.

Jones, William C. (1956), 'Three Centuries of Commercial Arbitration in New York: A Brief Survey', **33** *Washington University Law Quarterly*, 193-221.

Kerkmeester, Heico O. and Mulder, R.V. De (1988), *Overheidsrechter Gepasseerd* (Theoretical Decisionmaking Criteria in Settling a Legal Dispute by a Third Party), Arnhem, Gouda Quint.

Kochan, Thomas A. (1980), 'Collective Bargaining and Organizational Behavior Research', in Staw, B. and Cummings, L. (eds), *Research in Organizational Behavior, Vol. 2*, Greenwich, CT, JAI Press.

Kochan, Thomas A. and Baderschneider, Jean (1978), 'Dependence on Impasse Procedures: Police and Firefighters in New York State', **31** *Industrial and Labor Relations Review*, 431-449.

Landes, William M. and Posner, Richard A. (1979), 'Adjudication as a Private Good', **8** *Journal of Legal Studies*, 235-284.

Lazarus, Steven, Bray, John J., Jr, Carter, Larry L., Collins, Kent H., Giedt, Bruce A., Holton, Robert V., Jr, Matthews, Phillip D. and Willard, Gordon C. (1965), *Resolving Business Disputes: The Potential for Commercial Arbitration*, New York, American Management Association.

Lew, Julian D.M. (1978), *Applicable Law in International Commercial Arbitration: A Study in Commercial Arbitration Awards, Dobbs Ferry*, New York, Oceana Publications.

Long, Gary and Feuille, Peter (1974), 'Final-Offer Arbitration: Sudden Death in Eugene', **27** *Industrial and Labor Relations Review*, 186-203.

Lucas, Malcolm M. (1987), 'The Future of Arbitration', **42** *Arbitration Journal*, 55-59.

Mabry, Rodney H., Ulbrich, Holly H., Macauley, Hugh H., Jr and Maloney, Michael T. (1977), *An Economic Investigation of State and Local Judiciary Services*, Washington, DC, National Institute of Law Enforcement and Criminal Justice, Law Enforcement Assistance Administration.

MacNeil, Ian R. (1992), *American Arbitration Law*, New York, Oxford University Press.

Mentschikoff, Soia (1961), 'Commercial Arbitration', **61** *Columbia Law Review*, 846-869.

Milgrom, Paul R., North, D. and Weingast, B. (1990), 'The Role of Institutions in the Revival of Trade: The Law Merchant, Private Judges, and the Champagne Fairs', **2** *Economic and Politics*, 1-23.

Murray, John S., Rau, Alan Scott and Sherman, Edward F. (1989), *Processes of Dispute Resolution: the Role of Lawyers*, New York, Westbury, The Foundation Press.

Neale, Margaret A. and Bazerman, Max H. (1983), 'The Role of Perspective Taking Ability in Negotiating Under Different Forms of Arbitration', **36** *Industrial and Labor Relations Review*, 378-388.

Odiorne, George S. (1953), 'Arbitration Under Early New Jersey Law', **8** *Arbitration Journal*, 117-125.

Odiorne, George S. (1954), 'Arbitration and Mediation Among the Early Quakers', **9** *Arbitration Journal*, 161-169.

Phalon, Richard (1992), 'Privatizing Justice', *Forbes*, 126-127.

Posner, Richard A. (1986), 'The Summary Jury Trial and Other Methods of Alternative Dispute Resolution: Some Cautionary Observations', **53** *University of Chicago Law Review*, 366-393.

Pruitt, Gary (1982), 'California's Rent-a-Judge Justice', **5** *Journal of Contemporary Studies*, 49-57.

Ray, Larry (1992), 'Privatization of Justice', in Bowman, Gary W., Hakim, Simon and Seidenstat, Paul (eds), *Privatizing the United States Justice System: Police Adjudication, and Corrections Services form the Private Sector*, Jefferson, NC, McFarland & Co.

Rubin, Edward L. (1995), 'The Nonjudicial Life of Contract: Beyond the Shadow of the Law', **90** *Northwestern University Law Review*, 107-131.

Rubin, Paul H. (1994), 'Growing a Legal System in the Post-Communist Economies', **27** *Cornell International Law Journal*, 1-47.

Shavell, Steven (1995), 'Alternative Dispute Resolution: An Economic Analysis', **24** *Journal of Legal Studies*, 1-28.

Smith, Joseph H. (1961), *Colonial Justice in Western Massachusetts*, Cambridge, MA, Harvard University Press.

Starke, Frederick A. and Notz, William W. (1981), 'Pre- and Post-Intervention Effects on Conventional vs. Final Offer Arbitration', **24** *Academy of Management Journal*, 832-850.

Stevens, Carl M. (1966), 'Is Compulsory Arbitration Compatible with Bargaining?', **5** *Industrial Relations*, 38-52.

Sturges, Wesley A. (1930), *A Treatise on Commercial Arbitrations and Awards*, Kansas City, Vernon Law Book Company.

Trakman, Leon E. (1983), *The Law Merchant: The Evolution of Commercial Law*, Littleton, Colo., Fred B. Rothman and Company.

Ware, Stephen J. (1996), 'Employment Arbitration and Voluntary Consent', Cumberland School of Law Working Paper, Birmingham, AL, Samford University.

Willoughby, William F. (1929), *Principles of Judicial Administration*, Washington, DC, Brookings Institute.

Wittman, Donald A. (1986), 'Final Offer Arbitration', *Management Science*, 1551-1561.

X (1979a), 'Conference: 'Private Alternatives To the Judicial Process. Proceedings of a Seminar Sponsored by the Liberty Fund and Administered by the Law and Economics Center of the University of Miami School of Law', **8** *Journal of Legal Studies*, 231-415.

X (1979b), 'Seminar: Process Private Alternatives to the Judicial', **8** *Journal of Legal Studies*, 231-418.

Other References

Aranson, Peter H. (1986), 'Economic Efficiency and the Common Law: A Critical Survey', in Graf von der Schulenberg, J.-Mathais and Skogh, Goran (eds), *Law and Economics and the Economics of Legal Regulation*, Dordrecht, Kluwer Academic Press, 51-84.

Axelrod, Robert (1984), *The Evolution of Cooperation*, New York, Basic Books.

Benson, Bruce L. (1995b) 'Understanding Bureaucratic Behavior: Implications from the Public Choice Literature', **8** *Journal of Public Finance and Public Choice*, 89-117.

Benson, Bruce L. (1996), 'Uncertainty, the Race for Property Rights, and Rent Dissipation due to Judicial Changes in Product Liability Tort Law', **8** *Cultural Dynamics*, 333-351.

Berman, Harold J. (1983), *Law and Revolution: The Formation of Western Legal Tradition*, Cambridge, MA, Harvard University Press.

Coase, Ronald (1960), 'The Problem of Social Cost', **3** *Journal of Law and Economics*, 1-44.

De Alessi, Louis and Staaf, Robert J. (1991), 'The Common Law Process: Efficiency or Order?', **2** *Constitutional Political Economy*, 107-126.

Ellickson, Robert C. (1991), *Order Without Law: How Neighbors Settle Disputes*, Cambridge, MA, Harvard University Press.

Fuller, Lon (1964), *The Morality of Law*, New Haven, Conn., Yale University Press.

Fuller, Lon (1981), *The Principles of Social Order*, Durham, NC, Duke University Press.

Klein, Benjamin and Leffler, Keith (1981), 'The Role of Market Forces in Assuring Contractual Performance', **89** *Journal of Political Economy*, 615-641.

Klein, Daniel B. (ed.) (1997), *Reputation: Studies in the Voluntary Elicitation of Good Conduct*, Ann Arbor, MI, University of Michigan Press.

Kreps, David (1990), 'Corporate Culture and Economic Theory', in Alt, James and Shepsle, Kenneth (eds), *Perspectives on Positive Political Economy*, New York, Cambridge University Press.

Kronman, Anthony T. (1985), 'Contract Law and the State of Nature', **1** *Journal of Law, Economics, and Organization*, 5-32.

Priest, George L. (1977), 'The Common Law Process and the Selection of Efficient Rules', **6** *Journal of Legal Studies*, 65-82.

Rizzo, Mario J. (1980a), 'Law Amid Flux: The Economics of Negligence and Strict Liability in Tort', **9** *Journal of Legal Studies*, 291-318.

Rizzo, Mario J. (1980b), 'The Mirage of Efficiency', **8** *Hofstra Law Review*, 641-658.

Rubin, Paul H. (1977), 'Why is the Common Law Efficient?', **6** *Journal of Legal Studies*, 51-64.

Schelling, Thomas C. (1963), *The Strategy of Conflict*, London, Oxford University Press.

Williamson, Oliver E. (1979), 'Transaction-Cost Economics: The Governance of Contractual Relations', **22** *Journal of Law and Economics*, 233-261.

Williamson, Oliver E. (1983), 'Credible Commitments: Using Hostages to Support Exchange', **83** *American Economic Review*, 519-540.

Williamson, Oliver E. (1991), 'Economic Institutions: Spontaneous and Intentional Governance', **7** *Journal of Law, Economics and Organization*, 159-187.

Wooldridge, William C. (1970), *Uncle Sam, The Monopoly Man*, New Rochelle, New York, Arlington House.

7600
Class Actions - Representative Proceedings

Charles Silver
Cecil D. Redford Professor
University of Texas Law School

Abstract

A class action is a representational lawsuit that binds all persons with related claims, including those who were not parties to the proceeding. The procedure enables parties and court systems to enjoy certain benefits that are lost when claims are heard separately. These include reduced litigation costs per claimant, cost-internalization, and improved litigation incentives. The procedure generates these benefits by eliminating the need for collective action and giving class counsel control over claims held by non-parties. Because market discipline is lacking and judges regulate class actions inappropriately, this transfer of control entails serious risks of agency failure and opportunism that are often dealt with inadequately. The contemporary challenge is to reform the procedure in ways that preserve its advantages while reducing its risks and costs.
JEL classification: K41
Keywords: Class Action, Consolidation, Representative Litigation, Collective Action, Agency Costs

1. Introduction

Most litigation is representative in nature because it is handled by agents, typically though not always attorneys, who advocate and otherwise act on the parties' behalf. Ordinarily, parties hire their agents directly, using market pressures and contracts to encourage good performance and to mitigate the risks and costs that are predicted to beset any relationship of principal and agent (Stiglitz, 1987).

In a percentage of the cases, judges appoint attorneys in the absence of market transactions. This happens mainly when a party is a child, an incompetent, or a person in need of charity. It also happens in certain situations where bargaining impediments prevent lawyers and clients from coming to terms despite perceived opportunities for mutual gain or systemic needs to aggregate claims. The class action is the paradigm of judicial appointment of representation in this situation.

Numerically, class actions make up a small part of an average court's civil docket. Of the 272,027 civil lawsuits filed in all federal district courts in the United States in 1997, only 1,475 or one-half of one percent were class actions. If all 647 authorized judgeships had been filled, federal district court judges would have received an average of only two new class actions apiece in 1997 (Administrative Office of the United States Courts, 1997).

Though comparatively rare, class actions are disproportionately important. They consume far more of judges' time than other civil suits. Judges have been estimated to spend eleven times as many hours on certified class actions and twice as many hours on non-certified class actions as they do on non-class civil cases (Willging, Hooper and Niemic, 1996). Because class actions also involve far more claimants than other civil suits, these judicial investments can yield enormous economies of scale. Class actions brought to remedy economic harms often encompass thousands or even millions of consumers. Personal injury class actions can also be quite large, especially those that attempt to resolve claims held by persons who may become ill in the future. When judges' time is amortized across claimants, the economy of the class action is revealed (Bernstein, 1978).

Class actions also involve unusually large financial stakes. A study of securities class actions reported that the 105 lawsuits in its sample for 1995 generated settlements averaging US$10,619,174 and totaling US$1,115,013,250 (Martin et al., 1996). Many personal injury class actions have generated settlement funds or settlement offers of US$100,000,000 or more. In 1998, a single antitrust class action yielded a proposed settlement in excess of US$1,000,000,000.

Not all class actions seek money damages. Many are brought to achieve social, political, or legal reforms. Targets of reform lawsuits include mainly public and private institutions, such as school districts, large employers, manufacturing plants, welfare agencies, prisons and legislatures, whose operation affects large numbers of individuals.

Given their potential to transfer massive amounts of wealth and to reorganize important institutions, it should surprise no one that class actions are politically controversial. Although the federal rule that governs the conduct of these lawsuits in the United States retains the basic structure it received in 1966, there have been many attempts to reform the rule and to reduce the rate at which class actions are brought. Statutes now restrict prisoner class actions, securities cases, consumer cases and lawsuits by legal aid organizations that receive public support. Federal common law also deals with matters like subject matter jurisdiction, notice, and attorneys' fees in ways that make class actions more difficult to bring.

Reflecting the importance of class actions, the scholarly literature discussing them is enormous. The history of the procedure, which has its roots in England, its trunk in the United States, and new branches in other countries, has been carefully studied (Yeazell, 1987). Developments in the case law are followed closely. A large and growing empirical literature studies trends in filings, dismissals, settlements, and fee awards (Alexander, 1991; Garth, Nagel and Plager, 1988; Hensler et al., 1985; Martin et al., 1996; Rosenfield, 1976; Willging, Hooper and Niemic, 1996b). The impact of class actions on issuers of securities and securities markets has also been studied (Strahan, 1998; Bohn and Choi, 1996). Finally, a literature emphasizing microeconomics and game theory considers normative justifications for class actions, examines agency problems that arise in them, and suggests avenues for reform (Coffee, 1987b, 1995; Hay, 1997a; Macey and Miller, 1991; Perino, 1997; Rosenberg, 1984, 1987).

A. Legal Basics: What a Class Action is and How One Works

2. The Class Action is a Representational Device, Not a Joinder Device

The class action is a procedural device that expands a court's jurisdiction, empowering it to enter a judgment that is binding upon everyone with covered claims. This includes claimants who, not being named as parties, would not ordinarily be bound. A class-wide judgment extinguishes the claims of all persons meeting the class definition rather than just those of named parties and persons in privity with them, as normally is the case.

Judges and scholars sometimes treat the class action as a procedure for joining absent claimants to a lawsuit rather than as one that permits a court to treat a named party as standing in judgment on behalf of them. This is a mistake (Hutchinson, 1983). Class members neither start out as parties nor become parties when a class is certified.

3. How a Class Action Commences

A named party begins the process of having a class recognized by filing a pleading in which a class is preliminarily described. Later, a named party files a motion for certification. The motion refines the class definition and requests entry of an order allowing a class action to proceed. In theory, a named plaintiff can ask to have a class of plaintiffs or of defendants certified, and a named defendant has the same two options. In practice, requests by named plaintiffs to certify plaintiff classes greatly outnumber all other requests.

Defendant classes comprise fewer than 1 percent of all certified class actions, and named defendants rarely ask judges to certify classes of any kind (Willging, Hoper and Niemic, 1996b).

A named plaintiff who seeks to stand in judgment for a class is called a putative or actual class representative, depending upon whether the motion for certification has been granted. An attorney appointed to act for a class is called class counsel. Usually, the attorney representing the named plaintiff is appointed class counsel in the order that certifies the class. A person who is not a named party but who falls within a class definition is called an absent class member or an absent plaintiff.

4. The Certification Decision

For a lawsuit to proceed on behalf of a class, a judge must certify that certain criteria are met. The named plaintiff must be a member of the class. It must be impracticable for the named plaintiff to join all absent plaintiffs to the lawsuit as named parties. Common questions of law or fact must connect the named plaintiff's claims with those of the absent plaintiffs. The named plaintiff must also be a typical claimant who, having no significant conflicts of interests with the absent plaintiffs and being assisted by competent counsel, can be relied upon to represent adequately all members of the class. These criteria are repetitive and overlapping.

At least one of the following additional criteria must also be met to secure class certification. There must be a risk that an opposing party will be subject to multiple, duplicative, or inconsistent obligations unless a class is certified. There must be a chance that an absent claimant's ability to protect his interests will be impaired unless a class is certified. The defendant must have subjected all class members to a common practice or course of conduct, justifying a class-wide grant of declaratory or injunctive relief. Or, questions of law or fact common to all class members' claims must predominate over any individual questions that may arise and the class action must be superior to other available procedures for handling the block of complaints.

Judges certify common question class actions far more often than they find any other criteria apply. Approximately two-thirds of all certified class actions fall into the common question category (Willging, Hooper and Niemic, 1996b), which is used for all manner of economic harm cases, including securities and insurance fraud and other deceptive trade practices. These cases typically involve large numbers of claimants who incurred small losses and require mainly evidence about the conduct of defendants (Issacharoff, 1997).

The law encourages judges to decide certification motions 'as soon as practicable' (Federal Judicial Center, 1995). Even so, judges usually decide dispositive substantive motions first. A plaintiff who prevails on a substantive motion will find the chances for certification greatly improved (Willging, Hooper and Niemic, 1996b). Judges also frequently consider class certification and settlement at the same time. This occurs in about one-third of all lawsuits where classes are certified (Willging, Hooper and Niemic, 1996b).

5. Post-Certification Procedures

Certification usually triggers additional procedures that are specific to class actions. In common question cases, absent plaintiffs are entitled to notice of the lawsuit and to an opportunity to exclude themselves from it. They also may appear in the lawsuit if they wish. When certification and settlement occur concurrently, absent plaintiffs are entitled to notice, to a complete description of the settlement including attorneys' fees and expenses that may be paid, to file objections, and usually to exclude themselves. Any settlement that is proposed also must be judicially approved for a judgment to bind all class members.

A class action that has been certified for all purposes proceeds toward trial much as any other lawsuit does, and trial rates for certified class actions are comparable to those for other civil suits (Willging, Hooper and Niemic, 1996). The named plaintiff uses ordinary discovery tools to gather information about the merits of class members' claims. Admissions and dispositive motions are used to remove factual and legal issues from dispute and to identify any remaining factual issues that must be tried. At the trial itself, the named plaintiff must offer evidence sufficient to prove all elements of his individual claim and to support favorable findings on all class-wide issues, including damages (Issacharoff, 1991). The stakes being larger in class actions than conventional lawsuits, the parties devote greater effort to these matters and incur greater expense, but the differences are matters of degree not of kind.

Settlement rates for certified class actions also are generally comparable to those for conventional lawsuits, with securities class actions settling more frequently than class actions involving other complaints (Martin et al., 1996; Willging, Hooper and Niemic, 1996b) . Empirical studies have not borne out the charge, often heard in policy discussions, that a judge's decision to certify a class forces even an innocent defendant to surrender (Priest, 1997).

As explained above, judges must review and approve class action settlements after giving absent plaintiffs notice and an opportunity to object. Historically, objections have been infrequent. Few absent plaintiffs take the trouble to attend fairness hearings. More file written objections, but the number who write in also is small. As might be predicted, these meager efforts rarely prevent settlements from proceeding. In the past, judges approved without alteration 90 percent of all proposed class settlements to which objections were filed (Willging, Hooper and Niemic, (1996b).

Recently, certain abusive or allegedly collusive class action settlements have received widespread press coverage and extensive academic scrutiny (Coffee, 1995a; In Camera, May-June 1993, July-August 1993; Koniak, 1995; Koniak and Cohen, 1996). As a result, judges, who are charged to act as guardians for absent class members, have begun to examine settlements more closely. They have paid special attention to proposed settlements that resolve immature claims of personal injury, that offer class members coupons or discounts instead of cash, or that abridge the right of dissenting class members to opt out. Although these settlements are not impermissible *per se* (Miller and Singer, 1998), they often signal that class counsel and a settling defendant colluded to the detriment of a class.

B. The Basic Microstructure of the Class Action

6. Separation of Ownership from Control

Class actions contain far more class members than class representatives. Consequently, most of the economic value of a class action is attributable to absent plaintiffs' claims. If a single class representative were to sue on behalf of ninety-nine absent plaintiffs with identical claims, the absent plaintiffs collectively would account for 99 percent of the value of the case.

Because representatives with minority interests manage class actions, it is useful to think of classes as litigation groups in which ownership and control of assets are in different hands (Jensen and Meckling, 1976). In this respect, classes resemble stock companies, mutual funds, and innumerable other economic undertakings in which investors play relatively passive roles (Coffee, 1998; Shapiro, 1998; Silver and Baker, 1998). Seeing this resemblance, judges have subjected named plaintiffs to fiduciary duties like those that customarily apply to managers of other enterprises.

Judges have also subjected class counsel to fiduciary duties. From an economic perspective, this makes sense. The regulation and incentivizing of counsel affects the likely success of class actions far more than anything having to do with named plaintiffs. As explained, a named plaintiff holds a tiny fraction of the entire economic interest possessed by a class. Often, a named plaintiff's claim is far too small to justify the expense of litigation, and it is always too small to motivate a named plaintiff to invest resources at a level that is optimal for a class. By comparison, class counsel's interest is usually far larger. Counsel is paid on a contingent basis an amount that reflects the value of the relief recovered by the entire class. In most cases, the fee is a fraction - between 20 and 40 percent - of the common fund (Lynk, 1990, 1994; Martin et al., 1996; Willging, Hooper and Niemic, 1996). Because class counsel holds the largest single stake, it is not surprising that class counsel is the primary decision-maker and the moving economic force in class litigation (Kane, 1987; Miller, 1998).

The concentration in class counsel's hands of economic interest and managerial control accounts both for the attractiveness of class action lawsuits and the risks associated with them. The attraction derives from the possibility of placing a large block of claims, including many that may be too small individually to warrant conventional lawsuits, under the control of someone who is in a position to maximize their value. The risks derive from the possibility that control will be abused for the benefit of the agent in charge.

7. Comparing Class Actions and Other Group Lawsuits

Class actions are involuntary or nonconsensual group lawsuits. They begin and, for practical purposes, end without class members' consent.

Other group lawsuits are consensual. They involve multiple clients all of whom contract for representation with the same attorneys. Small voluntary groups greatly outnumber large ones, but entrepreneurial attorneys have built enormous groups with tens of thousands of plaintiffs by using mass-marketing techniques and by actively working referral markets (Resnik, Curtis and Hensler, 1996; Silver and Baker, 1997; Spurr, 1988). Entrepreneurial lawyers play the same role in large voluntary group lawsuits that organizers play in other collective actions (Hardin, 1982). They also use the same techniques as organizers to reduce their costs. For example, they use existing associations, such as labor unions, trade associations, and homeowner groups, to recruit individual plaintiffs and to serve as representative plaintiffs.

Still other group lawsuits straddle the consensual/non-consensual divide. These lawsuits are called consolidations. Consolidation occurs when pending cases are routed to a single court for coordinated management. Usually, this occurs when lawsuits involve common facts. For example, claims arising out of airplane crashes, explosions, and other disasters are frequently consolidated. The perception is that such cases can be processed efficiently in tandem (Steinman, 1995a, 1995b).

Consolidations begin consensually. Plaintiffs employ attorneys and authorize them to file lawsuits. Thereafter, plaintiffs lose control. Judges frequently consolidate cases at defendants' request and over plaintiffs' objections. In effect, they force together plaintiffs who would rather remain apart. In federal multi-district litigation, a consolidation order may transfer cases to distant jurisdictions where plaintiffs' chosen lawyers rarely practice. Judges then subject transferred cases to the control of managing committees. These consist of several lawyers who are selected to handle most tasks for all plaintiffs, including the preparation of master complaints and motions, discovery and settlement negotiations. These lawyers receive supplemental compensation, usually as a result of judicial orders entitling them to shares of other lawyers' fees (Resnik, Curtis and Hensler, 1996; Silver, 1991b).

From an economic perspective, all three kinds of group lawsuit can be analyzed in similar terms. In all, control is separated from ownership and placed in the hands of lawyers with large financial interests. From a practical perspective, however, the three cases differ. When litigation groups form voluntarily, plaintiffs use contracts to govern them. They select attorneys, set their compensation, allocate responsibility for expenses, establish procedures to govern individual and group-wide decision making, create incentives to keep the collective action going, and otherwise take care of the group's constitutional needs. They also waive conflicts of interests, retain withdrawal rights, and can fire attorneys who perform poorly (Silver and Baker, 1997). By contrast, class actions and consolidations are created by regulation. Judges form them and decide how they will operate. Class actions and consolidations thus operate outside the reach of market forces. Absent plaintiffs cannot fire their appointed representatives when they are dissatisfied with their performance. They cannot sell their interests or join new groups when they disagree with fundamental strategies or decisions, as shareholders in publicly traded corporations can. Nor can they rely on anything analogous to the takeover market to police inefficient management of their claims. Consequently, agency problems can be far more serious in class actions and consolidations than in voluntary group suits (Silver and Baker, 1998; Silver, 1991b).

C. Advantages of Aggregation

Litigation groups offer plaintiffs several important advantages. These include economies of scale in litigation costs, greater leverage in settlement negotiations, and conservation of defendants' assets, all of which can increase plaintiffs' recoveries.

8. Economies of Scale

Group lawsuits enable plaintiffs to reduce litigation costs per capita by sharing the burden of litigation services that can be used by many plaintiffs. Plaintiffs who sue individually must separately pay for legal and factual investigations, for representation at trial and in settlement negotiations, and for litigation support services such as document preparation, expert witness testimony, and computer simulations. A group of plaintiffs need pay for these services only once, the services being non-rival goods insofar as members of the group are concerned. Plaintiffs who sue together also gain by taking advantage of the specialization of labor when performing tasks such as monitoring counsel's performance, answering interrogatories, and attending hearings and depositions. By assigning these tasks to claimants who can best handle them, performance can be improved and savings generated that make all plaintiffs better off than they would be if each were responsible for performing every task.

9. Enhanced Bargaining Leverage

Most group lawsuits settle. Bargaining power is therefore as important in group lawsuits as in conventional cases. In theory, plaintiffs can often gain leverage in settlement negotiations by joining forces. This happens, most straightforwardly, because groups of plaintiffs will often find it rational to litigate more intensively than individuals.

The impact of economies of scale on bargaining power is clearest when individual claims are too small to justify the expense of litigation. In this situation, claims pressed by individual plaintiffs have little settlement value because plaintiffs cannot make credible threats to try their cases. By comparison, the threat value, and therefore the settlement value, of groups of small claims may be relatively great, owing to the feasibility of trying small claims *en masse*.

Economies of scale can increase the settlement value of large claims too. On the standard economic model of the decision to settle or sue, a plaintiff's minimum demand falls as litigation costs rise. Because aggregation reduces plaintiffs' litigation costs per capita, it should increase their minimum demands and, correspondingly, the settlement value of their claims.

Aggregation also can increase plaintiffs' demands by increasing the expected value of claims at trial. A claim's expected value is partly a function of the probability that a plaintiff will prevail in a trial against a defendant. In turn, the probability of winning is a function of the level and quality of litigation support services obtained. If members of plaintiff groups save money by sharing the cost of non-rival litigation services, they can afford to purchase more services or services of better quality than plaintiffs who sue by themselves. They can thereby raise the expected value of their claims at trial and improve their prospects in settlement. This may explain why class members have won sizeable settlement payments on claims that failed to generate payments in conventional cases. The class action can bring 'compensation and closure' to persons who are otherwise poorly served by the tort system (Tidmarsh, 1998).

Even when plaintiffs sue separately, their fortunes often intertwine. Plaintiffs' attorneys share information about trials and settlements. Factual findings, legal rulings, and verdicts in decided cases inform assessments of the settlement value of cases yet to be resolved (Hensler and Peterson, 1993). Predictably, these connections between separate lawsuits give defendants an edge in litigation. A defendant facing a test case knows that the stakes are greater than just the amount likely to be won by the litigating plaintiff. The amount paid in settlement or lost at the trial of the test case will affect the value of claims held by other plaintiffs who are waiting in the wings. The defendant may therefore find it rational to invest far more in the lawsuit than the litigating plaintiff's claim alone would warrant. Manufacturers of tobacco products maintained an unbroken record of success in personal injury litigation for four decades by outspending the opposition.

When claim values intertwine, a defendant almost certainly will find it economically rational to outspend an attorney who represents a single client. Ordinarily, a plaintiff's attorney's fee is a percentage of the client's recovery Clermont and Currivan (1978). This compensation arrangement gives an attorney no incentive to spend even an amount equal to the expected value of the plaintiff's claim, the expected fee being far smaller. By itself, the possibility that the trial or settlement of a test case may affect the value of other plaintiffs' claims will not induce the attorney to spend more. Unless other plaintiffs or their attorneys agree to share litigation expenses, these external effects will be ignored.

Aggregation brings the parties' stakes more nearly into balance and improves the incentives of plaintiffs' counsel as well. When all claimants participate or are represented in a single lawsuit, the defendant's exposure is the sum of the expected values of all the claims (or the defendant's total assets, whichever is less). As a group, the plaintiffs' stake is the same amount. The investment incentives are still unequal because the attorney representing the plaintiff group stands to earn only a fraction of the plaintiffs' recovery, usually one-third (Martin et al., 1996). Even so, the plaintiffs' attorney can credibly threaten to invest significant resources in litigation services that, from the plaintiffs' perspective, are joint goods. If, as seems likely, litigation investments have declining marginal value, the threat to spend heavily will give the defendant pause.

Group counsel's predominant financial interest is and must be the economic force that drives group litigation. The expectancy of receiving a fee that far exceeds the typical class member's recovery motivates attorneys to make the enormous financial commitments these lawsuits require and to incur the correlative risks. Even so, the size of counsel's interest has sparked political controversy. Because counsel's interest dwarfs that of all but the largest class members, for example, institutional investors in securities fraud cases, it often seems that group lawsuits have more to do with paying attorneys than compensating victims.

From an economic perspective, this imbalance is not a source of concern. Attorneys who manage large litigation groups are not distinguishable from managers of widely held companies or mutual funds. It would be foolish to limit a manager's compensation to the amount any individual investor earns in a given period. It would be equally unreasoning to limit class counsel's fee to the amount recovered by the largest claimant. Such a limitation would undermine counsel's incentive to invest. This would harm group members, not help them.

Of particular concern to a defendant facing a group lawsuit is the possibility that a single trial will adjudicate its entire liability. Ordinarily, a defendant can handle risk far more easily than a plaintiff can. The plaintiff will have an undiversified risk of loss associated with a claim that may be his single largest asset. By contrast, the defendant will face hundreds or thousands of claims, some of which will succeed, some of which will fail, and none of which taken individually will pose a serious threat to the defendant's solvency. In this situation, the defendant can more easily tolerate the risk of trying cases than can any individual plaintiff. Aggregation turns the tables on defendants. It puts them in the position of being rendered insolvent by a single trial (a high variance event), thereby saddling them with a large, undiversifiable risk. It also forces defendants to go to trial knowing that plaintiffs' attorneys have strong incentives to invest. Many defendants are willing to pay large sums to avoid facing the prospect of a real trial followed by liquidation.

10. Conservation of Defendants' Assets

When a defendant's assets (including insurance) are insufficient to cover all plaintiffs' claims, a group lawsuit can make plaintiffs better off by conserving the defendant's resources and preserving the going concern value of the defendant's operations. When claims are litigated in separate forums, defendants must retain local counsel in each venue, pay experts to testify concerning the same scientific issues at each trial, suffer the expense of repetitive depositions of managerial personnel, and bear other duplicative costs. These expenditures, which can be reduced when plaintiffs sue in a single proceeding, consume resources, making them unavailable for transfer to plaintiffs.

The value of a defendant's assets also can be diminished when a defendant's business is liquidated piecemeal rather than as a unit, so that the value of the operation as a going concern is lost. Speaking less than strictly, competing plaintiffs participate in an *n*-person Prisoner's Dilemma. If each strives independently for a share of the defendant's resources, the defendant's operations will be liquidated piecemeal, going-concern value will be lost, and plaintiffs as a group will net a smaller recovery than they could have realized by keeping the defendant's operations intact. Just as the possibility of avoiding this race to judgment supports some scholarly justifications of bankruptcy laws (Jackson, 1982), the same prospect may be said to weigh in favor of group lawsuits in cases involving limited funds.

11. A Paretian Defense of Aggregation

Figure 1 The Normative Economics of Group Litigation

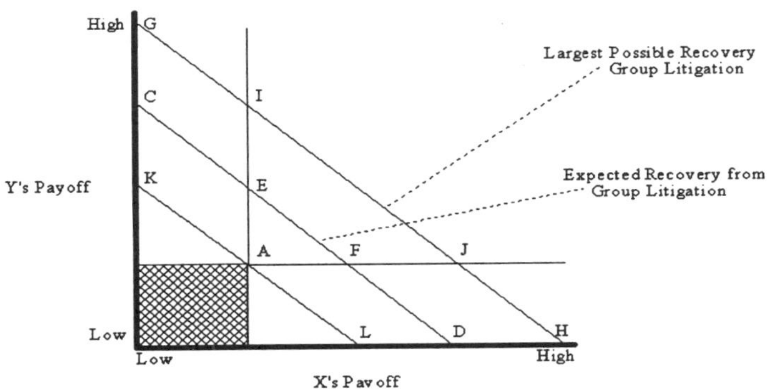

Figure 1 displays the basic economic logic of group litigation. Where X and Y are potential co-plaintiffs, point A represents their expected joint payoff if each sues the common defendant in a separate lawsuit. The space defined by triangle OGH contains all possible joint payoffs if X and Y combine forces and sue as a group. The smaller triangle AIJ within OGH is the set of possible payoffs from group litigation that are Pareto Superior to A. Curve CD contains all possible divisions between X and Y of the expected joint payoff from group litigation. EF is the set of possible divisions of the expected joint payoff that are Pareto Superior to A. A simple normative economic argument for group litigation is that, by joining forces and sharing costs, co-plaintiffs hope to move themselves from A to a point on EF.

12. Why Require Participation? Transaction Costs and Free-Riding

Figure 1 raises an important question about non-consensual group lawsuits. Why are they permitted? When plaintiffs stand to gain by joining forces, they can be expected to form groups voluntarily. Presumptively, a plaintiff's refusal to join a litigation group would indicate that, in the plaintiff's opinion, any gains that may to flow from cooperation fail to offset the expected costs and risks. It is therefore reasonable to ask why class suits and consolidations should ever occur without the consent of absent plaintiffs.

One answer is that class actions and consolidations facilitate mutually beneficial cooperation that is normally frustrated by the high cost of transacting. Transaction costs are a serious problem when a wrongdoer's conduct inflicts small losses on the members of a large victim population. For example, suppose that a credit card company overcharges millions of cardholders a few dollars apiece by calculating interest incorrectly. For cardholders as a group, the loss is large enough to be worth pursuing, but no individual cardholder has an incentive to organize the group. The prospect of recovering a few dollars would not justify the time or effort even if the likelihood of winning were great.

The same problem arises in injunctive cases where litigation may prevent small harms from occurring. Suppose that the members of a large population are exposed to individually small health risks when a toxic substance is disposed of improperly. A lawsuit brought to force the wrongdoer to clean up the waste would protect the entire community and be cost-justified in view of the risk. However, the expected gain to any individual will likely be too small to motivate anyone to bear the expense of organizing a community-wide lawsuit.

Class action rules enable plaintiffs to avoid start-up costs that prevent litigation groups from forming. A single named plaintiff can initiate a class action on behalf of all persons with similar claims just by filing an appropriate complaint. However, in keeping with the belief that non-consensual lawsuits are permissible only when start-up costs are high, the rules permit named plaintiffs to use this gambit only when it is impracticable to join absent plaintiffs as parties voluntarily. This may be because the group's members are numerous and geographically dispersed, because claims are too small to motivate anyone to bear the cost of locating and bargaining with potential plaintiffs, or because group members identities are unknown or change over time. By minimizing transaction costs, class action rules enable named plaintiffs to wage advantageous group lawsuits that would not otherwise be brought.

Free-riding can also impede the formation of voluntary groups when the object of litigation is a non-exclusive good, that is, a good that will be available to group members and non-members alike. Structural reform lawsuits and other injunctive actions provide the best examples. Structural reforms, including improvements in public housing conditions, increased funding for public schools, and changes in hiring and promotional practices by an employer, automatically benefit everyone who suffered under prior arrangements. Consequently, potential plaintiffs may find it economically rational to free-ride on the efforts of others in these cases. If the lawsuit succeeds, the free-rider obtains the benefit without charge. If the lawsuit fails, the free-rider foregoes the benefit but avoids litigation costs, including the risk of being singled out for recrimination or retaliation by people who oppose the lawsuit. Either way, the free-rider is better off not cooperating. The exceptional case in which a free-rider's contribution can make the difference between the success and failure of a group lawsuit occurs too rarely to worry about.

Free-riding can also be a rational strategy when plaintiffs seek damages, even though a money judgment is an exclusive good. Suppose that X, who is one of one thousand claimants, believes that it is important to preserve the going-concern value of a defendant's operations, and that X also believes that piecemeal liquidation will not occur if any group containing at least 500 claimants forms. These beliefs may lead X to regard his own participation in a litigation group as inessential and to remain apart from a group if there is any advantage to doing so. If all claimants think like X, there may be no litigation group despite the opportunity for collective gain.

Opportunities to gain free information may also cause free-riding. Suppose that X and Y are both injured by the same defective product, that X sues the manufacturer, and that X invites Y to join the suit. If Y is confident that X will prosecute the lawsuit whether or not Y joins, Y may decide to let X sue alone. X's lawsuit then will be a valuable source of information for Y. Whether X wins, recovers a substantial settlement, or loses, Y will be better able to assess the value of Y's claim. Y may also be able to take advantage of favorable factual or legal rulings made in the course of X's suit, as in times past the class action device enabled Y to recover under the judgment obtained by X. The possibility of capitalizing on X's lawsuit creates opportunities for Y to gain an advantage by waiting on the sidelines.

13. Non-Paretian Justifications for Non-Consensual Proceedings

One also can argue for non-consensual group lawsuits on a variety of non-Paretian grounds. An obvious alternative is a Kaldor-Hicks approach on which the gains of some, be they group members or others, more than offset any losses some plaintiffs incur. The Kaldor-Hicks standard is often described as a potential Pareto improvement (Cooter and Ulen, 1988).

An argument of this sort can be grounded in the desire to conserve the resources of the legal system. The claim here is that one would squander judges' time by requiring them to process related claims individually. The force of this argument is a function of the number of claims and the extent to which they are related. The larger the number and the closer the factual and legal connection, the more society can gain through aggregation (Bernstein, 1978). This insight has spurred many efforts to consolidate related tort lawsuits, such as those arising out of occupational exposure to asbestos (Hensler et al., 1985).

The judicial efficiency argument has merit when plaintiffs' claims are large enough to justify the expense of separate lawsuits. Then, economies of scale can be gained by using a class action or a consolidation to streamline the processing of claims. When plaintiffs' claims are small, however, the judicial efficiency argument may or may not be persuasive, depending on how it is framed. The distinctive contemporary function of the class suit is to facilitate litigation by claimants who hold small shares of a large controversy, shares that are too small to be litigated individually (Kalven and Rosenfield, 1941). By performing this service, class actions consume judicial resources that would otherwise be spared, it being irrational for individual plaintiffs to sue on their own. A single-minded concern save judicial resources would therefore cause one to oppose small-claim class actions. A slightly different and socially more appropriate concern - a desire that judges' time be used efficiently would lead to the opposite conclusion. As explained above, certified class actions consume eleven times as many hours as conventional lawsuits, but they increase the rate at which judges can resolve claims hundreds or thousands of times, more than offsetting their marginally greater cost (Willging, Hooper and Niemic, 1996).

One must also consider other social costs that would be incurred if wrongs that visit small losses on large numbers of individuals were not policed. Losses imposed on third parties are externalities that producers will ignore unless forced to account for them. By bringing widely dispersed losses home to producers, the class action discourages them from acting in ways that are socially inefficient. It forces them to consider public as well as private production costs (Rosenberg, 1984, 1987; Wright, 1969).

The cost-internalization function of the class action is independent of its compensatory function and may be served when the latter cannot. Difficulties relating to the identification of class members, the measurement of their individual damages, or the cost of fine-tuning payments, may make it impossible or impracticable to restore claimants to the positions they would have come to but for the wrong. Even so, it may often be possible to deter wrongdoers by measuring aggregate social costs and imposing them on malfeasant defendants. It being as important to avoid losses as it is to compensate victims, an inability to compensate should not by itself prevent a class action from proceeding. Alternatives such as fluid class recoveries and escheat of unclaimed funds should instead be explored.

D. A Digression on the Law of Restitution

14. Why Pay Class Counsel?

The preceding sections examined the propriety of drawing plaintiffs into class actions without their consent. This section considers a related issue: why require absent plaintiffs to pay attorneys they never agreed to hire? The answer may seem simple. Unless attorneys are paid to represent absent plaintiffs, they will not do so and there will be no class actions. However, in a legal system committed to freedom of contract, more must be said than this. The usual rule is that people need not pay for services they do not ask to receive. Restitution is rarely required, especially when a provider acts pursuant to a contract with another, as an attorney representing a named plaintiff does. B, who enjoys looking at A's beautiful yard, has no duty to compensate A's gardener. The gardener's only right is to receive the contracted for amount from A.

It has been seriously maintained that the practice of allowing class counsel to recover fees from common funds over and above the amounts they agree to accept from named plaintiffs violates the law of restitution (Dawson, 1975). The argument has not persuaded judges to abandon the practice, which is as entrenched as ever. The desire to cure unjust enrichment has led judges to permit attorneys to claim compensation in limited circumstances. Their efforts must confer benefits on non-clients. It must be infeasible or impracticable for them to bargain with non-clients in advance. And it must be difficult for them to prevent non-clients from deriving benefit from their work. These requirements often are met when an attorney brings a class action to a successful close (Silver, 1991a; see also Levmore, 1985).

The restitutionary approach caps class counsel's fee at the market rate or the size of the recovered fund, whichever is less. It allows judges to use any payment formula employed in the private market, including percentages, hourly rates, and hybrids of the two. Percentage compensation has long been the norm in common fund class actions. Federal judges began a shift to the hourly-rate based lodestar method in the 1970s, but the experience proved disappointing and most federal courts have shifted back to the percentage approach. The emerging practice is to base fee awards on an established benchmark, usually 25 percent of the recovered fund, and to use the lodestar to make small deviations from this figure in exceptional cases.

E. Disadvantages of Aggregation

15. Paretian Misfires

Group lawsuits often have the potential to make litigants worse off than they would expect to be suing on their own. In Figure 1, A represents the expected joint payoff if X and Y wage separate lawsuits. A thus serves as a boundary for Paretian claims about the affects of group lawsuits, but it is not a practical boundary of any kind. It does not restrict the actual allocation of relief. Figure 1 shows this in two ways. First, OGH, the set of possible outcomes of group litigation, includes points that are Pareto Inferior to A. The darkened area to the southwest of A is the set of possible Pareto Inferior payoffs. That such points exist when plaintiffs' claims have positive expected values in conventional litigation is not controversial. Second, OGH also includes many points that are Pareto Noncomparable to A. When a group secures relief equal to or greater than A, the fruits can be divided between X and Y in a manner that leaves one of them worse off than he or she would have been at A. Thus, X is worse off at C than at A, and Y is worse off at D than at A, even though the expected recovery from group litigation is obtained at both C and D. The rectangles AKGI and ALHJ are the sets of possible Pareto Noncomparable results.

The Pareto noncomparable and Pareto inferior outcomes are more than academically interesting. There is good reason to fear they often occur. Empirical evidence shows that class actions often settle for amounts that seem small in relation to the losses claimants incur (Carleton, Weisbach and Weiss, 1996; Martin et al., 1996). Anecdotal evidence further suggests that judges frequently approve distribution plans that divide settlement funds other than in proportion to the size and strength of class members' claims (Coffee, 1998, 1987a; Koniak, 1995).

16. Agency Failures and Sub-Optimal Recoveries

Whether the goal is compensation or deterrence, the importance of regulating class actions in ways that encourage attorneys to maximize the value of plaintiffs' claims is clear. If class suits settle too cheaply or plaintiffs lose at trial more often than they should, wrongdoers will escape some of the social costs of their behaviors. Undercompensation and underdeterrence will be the results.

A central thesis in the literature is that class actions often settle for too little (Coffee, 1986; Hay, 1997a). There also is evidence that defendants win class-wide trials more often than one would expect. Both results are thought to be due to agency failures that plague class actions. These failures have several sources, including defective incentives, inadequate monitoring, economic asymmetries that favor defendants, lack of market discipline, certification for settlement of classes that could not be certified for trial, and conflicts involving settlements of inventories of signed clients.

17. Defective Incentives and Opportunism

The impact of fee arrangements on lawyers' incentives has been widely studied (Clermont and Currivan, 1978; Johnson, 1980-81), and there is broad agreement that many shortcomings of class action practice can be traced to judges' use of inappropriate fee arrangements. The lodestar fee formula, which bases compensation on time expended and hourly rates, is a primary culprit. By rewarding effort instead of results, it discourages lawyers from maximizing the value of plaintiffs' claims and encourages sweetheart deals that make class counsel and defendants better off at absent plaintiffs' expense (Coffee, 1986, 1995a; Silver, 1992).

An ideal fee arrangement would be self-policing. It would harmonize the interests of absent plaintiffs and lawyers, making it in lawyers' interest to prosecute class actions zealously, as duty requires. The lodestar method fails to align interest with duty. It relies on monitoring to encourage superior performance instead of incentives.

A self-interested class member would want to maximize his recovery net of expenses. He would be perfectly willing to pay a larger fee when this would yield a larger expected net recovery. Otherwise, he would prefer to keep for himself money that could be transferred to his attorneys.

The lodestar method does not reflect this preference. It transfers money from a class member to an attorney whenever the attorney works more, whether or not the exchange of time for money leaves the class member better off. Moreover, under the lodestar method, even a class member who profits from a forced transaction may have a valid complaint. Work by the hour can be done poorly or well, and class members may find it advantageous to pay far more for the latter than the former. Suppose a class could offer a lawyer $1000 for an hour of top-quality work that would increase its expected recovery by $5000 or $200 for an hour of mediocre work that would yield an expected return of $201. Both transactions would leave class members better off, but they would rationally prefer a surplus of $4000 to a surplus of $1. Unfortunately, the lodestar prevents class members from choosing between these exchanges. By holding compensation per hour constant, it motivates a lawyer to perform at the lowest quality level sufficient to generate the stipulated fee.

The conventional wisdom is that class members often lose by exchanging money for time when the lodestar method is employed. When a judge decides which hours will be compensated and the hourly rate exceeds a lawyer's opportunity cost, a lawyer's incentive is to bill as many hours as a judge is likely to allow. For example, suppose that a lawyer with an opportunity cost of $150 per hour expects a judge to authorize payment at $200 per hour for up to 1000 hours of work. It would be irrational for the lawyer to charge for less than the full 1000 hours. Any time diverted from the class action to other matters would cost the lawyer $50 an hour. The incentive to bill the entire 1000 hours will exist even if the last 100 hours contribute nothing of value to the class.

In the example just described, the lawyer could do even better by committing fraud. If the lawyer spent 900 hours on the class action, billed the class for 1000, and spent the 100 hours saved on other cases, the lawyer would gain an additional $15,000 by working on the other cases. Thus does the lodestar method encourage lawyers to falsify billing records and create a related need for monitoring.

Unfortunately, if also understandably, in most class actions no one is likely to monitor class counsel closely or well. Judges are reluctant to make careful evaluations of fee records, expenses and lawyers' activities, especially in the absence of serious complaints from absent plaintiffs. The task is subjective, arbitrary and time-consuming. Absent plaintiffs also lack incentives to bear the cost monitoring entails, and they confront the logic of collective action as well.

Scholars have proposed many improvements on the lodestar method, the simplest of which is increased use of contingent percentage compensation arrangements and decreased use of the lodestar. Unfortunately, certain ways of applying the percentage-based approach share the lodestar's defects because they too sever the connection between reward and return. When class actions settle, attorneys are always paid in cash but absent plaintiffs sometimes receive discount coupons or other in-kind relief (Miller and Singer,

1998). The economic value of this relief is difficult to gauge, especially when coupons are not actively traded. To help judges assign the relief a value and justify their requested fees, plaintiffs' attorneys offer experts' assessments. Often, these are based on assumptions about utilization rates that are wildly optimistic. Coupon settlements typically benefit class members far less than experts predict (Borenstein, 1996; In Camera, May-June 1993, July-August 1993).

By weakening or severing the connection between fees and results, the lodestar method and coupon settlements create opportunities for 'sweetheart deals' that are good for defendants and class counsel but bad for absent plaintiffs. Suppose that class counsel expects to win a judgment for $10 million at trial, $2.5 million of which will be paid to counsel as fees. Now suppose the defendant, who privately agrees with the $10 million estimate, offers coupons worth $5 million in settlement of class members' claims and an additional $3 million in fees. By making the offer, the defendant can save $2 million. By accepting the offer, class counsel can gain $500,000. The loss comes at the expense of class members whose recovery net of fees fall from $7.5 million to $5 million. Not knowing that the negotiators think the case is worth $2 million more, the judge is likely to go along with the deal, especially when expert testimony inflating the value of the coupons is offered.

An alternative to the coupon deal is an early settlement at a low price. Suppose a defendant who expects to lose $20 million at trial offers $10 million in settlement, including $3 million in fees, shortly after the complaint is filed. The defendant also threatens to litigate aggressively if the offer is declined. Class counsel will find the offer attractive. Why risk $3 million in fees today in order to win a somewhat larger amount, say, $5 million, two years from now after an expensive fight? If the lawyer has not logged hours sufficient to justify a $3 million fee, announcement of the settlement can be delayed, allowing time for more discovery.

A third type of sweetheart deal expands the class definition or broadens the release to make a settlement more valuable for a defendant. When settling, a defendant naturally wants to free itself from liability to the fullest possible extent. To accomplish this, a defendant may ask class counsel to bring additional claimants into a class or to release claims a class was not asserting. For example, a defendant may want to include personal injury claimants in the settlement of a property damage class action, or a defendant may want claims released over which other courts have exclusive jurisdiction. In return, the defendant will offer a small fee increase that, from class counsel's perspective, will be an unearned bonus (Coffee, 1995a).

A fourth type of sweetheart deal uses a reversion to make a defendant's obligation appear larger than it is. A defendant promises to make a large fund available, say, $20 million, subject to the condition that funds not claimed by class members revert to the defendant. The attorneys' fee is then based on the $20 million. Because claim rates in class actions tend to be low, the defendant is likely to keep a good deal of its money and the attorneys' fee per dollar of relief actually received by class members is likely to be high.

Percentages that vary inversely with settlement size also discourage lawyers from maximizing claim values. Suppose that a lawyer would receive 30 percent of the first $10 million won by a class, 25 percent of the second $10 million, and 20 percent of the third $10 million. Now suppose the defendant offers $20 million in settlement but that class counsel thinks the case is worth $30 million. To reject the offer, class counsel must be willing to risk $5.5 million in fees to win an additional $2 million. On the reasonable assumptions that the higher dollars are riskier than lower dollars, the gamble will attract only risk-preferring attorneys.

As a group, plaintiffs' attorneys are risk-averse. Consequently, they must be paid more to recover risky dollars than dollars that are easy to come by. They must also be paid more in large cases that require great financial commitments and that entail risks that are hard for plaintiffs' attorneys to diversify. A good fee arrangement would therefore vary directly with the amount of the recovery rather than inversely to it, increasing the fee percentage at the margin as the recovery grows (Stock and Wise, 1993). Such an arrangement would also partially offset the declining marginal value money has for attorneys, a problem of great importance in cases where hundreds of millions or billions of dollars in damages are at stake.

A final but fundamental incentive-related shortcoming derives from the possibility of parallel litigation, which prevents class counsel from obtaining a property right in a certified class action. To appreciate this problem, it must be understood that the first class action to settle moots all other similar class actions and that only the attorney handling the settled case is likely to earn a fee.

Suppose that two class actions alleging the same violations and brought on behalf of the same individuals are filed in separate courts against the same defendant. Now suppose the defendant makes two low-ball settlement offers, one in each case, subject to the condition that when either offer is accepted the other lapses. Unless the plaintiffs' attorneys handling the cases collude, a race to settle is likely to occur because only the attorney who accepts first will be paid.

To make matters worse, collusion is nearly impossible. If both attorneys reject the low-ball offer, the defendant can simply find a third lawyer, offer him the deal, and agree to settle a class action filed by that lawyer. For collusion to work, it must involve all plaintiffs' lawyers, an impossibly large coalition.

It may seem unlikely that a defendant would search for an attorney to represent a class. Yet the phenomenon has happened often enough to have a name: the reverse auction (Coffee, 1995a). The name reflects the defendant's desire to find the attorney who will sell it immunity from litigation at the lowest price. In a reverse auction, the low bidder gets the sale.

18. Inadequate Monitoring

No incentive arrangement can wholly eliminate opportunities for agents to benefit at principals' expense. It is therefore important for principals to monitor agents. In class actions, absent plaintiffs are unlikely to monitor class counsel as carefully as they should. Monitoring by absent plaintiffs may also lead to undesirable results when it occurs. For these reasons, judges have a duty to examine how class actions are handled. Unfortunately, even they miss many instances of opportunism.

There are only four candidates for the job of monitor in a class action: the defendant, the named and absent plaintiffs, the presiding judge, and third parties, such as uninvolved attorneys, who may keep track of the case.

The defendant can be ruled out immediately. A party that stands to gain from class counsel's opportunistic acts cannot be trusted to police them.

Nor are named plaintiffs necessarily good monitors. Having chosen or been chosen by the attorneys who lead the class, named plaintiffs may too often give them the benefit of the doubt. Named plaintiffs also, and properly, benefit disproportionately from class settlements. They often receive incentive payments that are intended to compensate them for special risks and costs they incur (Krislov, 1990; Solovy, Kaster and Jiganti, 1990). The availability of these payments may color their judgment.

Although harmed by opportunism, absent plaintiffs also cannot be expected to monitor class counsel efficiently. Many or most absent plaintiffs hold stakes that are too small to warrant the expense. It would be irrational to spend \$100 monitoring a lawsuit in which one has a \$100 interest, but to oversee class counsel effectively an investment of thousands could be required. When expected recoveries are small to begin with, as in class actions they usually are, only class members who ignore economic factors will monitor class counsel actively.

Class members with sizeable claims may also be discouraged. First, they often learn that class actions are pending late in the day when settlement notices are delivered. They then face the daunting and expensive task of reconstructing events and finding signs of collusion, an undertaking in which they can expect no help from class counsel or the settling defendant. Second, an absent plaintiff who uncovers wrongdoing cannot privatize the entire return. If the size of the settlement should ultimately increase, all class members will share the gain. The private cost of monitoring may exceed the expected private gain even when the expected class-wide return would be far greater. Third, the inability to privatize returns on monitoring creates a free-rider problem within a class. When any absent plaintiff bears the cost of monitoring, all profit. Why, then, should any particular absent plaintiff bear the expense instead of free-riding on others who choose to do so?

A further difficulty with relying on absent plaintiffs is that they too can be bought off. A class member who takes a special interest in a case can be made a named plaintiff by class counsel and offered an incentive bonus. Or a defendant can offer to allocate settlement benefits in a way that favors an involved class member. Because the interests of particular plaintiffs always diverge from those of others, an absent plaintiff who serves as a monitor may himself have to be watched.

In theory, judges could be excellent monitors. They understand legal and factual issues better than claimants are likely to, and they are increasingly likely to have experience managing complex litigation. In practice, the quality of judicial monitoring is uneven because judges lack appropriate incentives and have limited fact-gathering capabilities. Many judges are overworked, underpaid, and subjected to strong institutional pressures to move cases along. It is unreasonable to expect them to divert time from live matters to class actions that are all but settled. Judges also have to rely on others for most of their information. Yet their usual sources class counsel and defendants - cannot be relied upon to pinpoint evidence that would scuttle a deal. To make matters worse, in many cases the data judges need to answer the crucial question - Is the money enough? - do not exist. The history of previously settled cases may be thin or no one may have collected it. Often, the most comparable cases are other settled class actions that also may be tainted.

Many judges are poorly placed to serve as monitors because they are architects of the agreements they are asked to review. Often, judges structure rulings to encourage settlement negotiations, they (and the magistrates or masters they appoint) become deeply involved in the negotiation process, and they use powerful signals about future rulings to soften plaintiffs' and defendants' bargaining positions (Resnik, 1982; Schuck, 1986, 1987). This behavior may be motivated by a jumble of forces, including solicitude for plaintiffs facing extraordinary trial delays, pressure to clear dockets, personality quirks, and a desire for the prestige enjoyed by judges who settle big cases. Because trial judges who orchestrate settlements can be expected to approve them, the primary monitors of such settlements must appellate judges.

Judicial scrutiny of fee requests is also uneven. Monitoring is crucial under the lodestar method, which encourages lawyers to inflate hours and claim excessive hourly rates. It is also tedious and time consuming (Silver, 1992; Tomkins and Willging, 1986). Judges must cast themselves as auditors and examine lawyers' time sheets and expenses line by line. Many judges short-circuit this process. They either approve fee applications as submitted or they make rough-cut reductions. Some judges also intentionally deviate from market standards when setting hourly rates, believing that market rates are too high. Judicial monitoring is not an especially good means of policing fee-related misconduct (Coffee, 1986; Silver, 1992).

Finally, consider other third parties. These may be attorneys whose clients are absent class members who object to a settlement. Or they may be public interest lawyers or public officials, such as attorneys general or consumer protection agencies. There are many cases in which third parties have become beneficially involved, but as a general matter they are in short supply. Class members usually lack incentives to get them engaged. Moreover, private lawyers can usually protect clients with large claims by opting them out. This being the cheaper course, it is the one usually taken.

The participation of third parties also can raise several difficulties. First, public officials may intervene to advance political agendas or interests that have little to do with claimants' welfare. For example, they may oppose certain kinds of lawsuits and, assuming the guise of consumer advocates, they may challenge fee awards to discourage lawyers from bringing more cases. Second, class counsel may co-opt third parties, especially lawyers representing claimaints, by making them co-counsel and offering them fees. Third, third parties may intervene solely to be bought off. There are many lawyers, colloquially referred to as 'bottom feeders', who use objections to extort payments. They hold up settlements unless and until class counsel offers to share fees with them, effectively paying them to withdraw. Public officials can also extort payments. They may want settling parties to place funds under their control or to assist them with other endeavors by donating services or cash. One can never be certain that third parties' motives are pure.

Because none of the available candidates has incentives to monitor appropriately, it should not be surprising that objections to proposed class settlement are both rare and rarely successful. Judges approve settlements without modification in 90 percent of the cases where objections are filed. This is true whether an objection concerns the adequacy of a settlement or a proposed award of attorneys' fees (Willging, Hooper and Niemic, 1996b). What the statistics cannot show may be equally important. Many objections that succeed in altering or forestalling settlements may be strategic or otherwise unwarranted.

19. Unresolved Economic Asymmetries

Fee awards in class actions average just above one-third of the amount recovered. Rarely do they exceed 50 percent (Martin et al., 1996; Willging, Hooper and Niemic, 1996b). Many judges also reduce the size of a fee as a percentage as the size of the recovery rises (Lynk, 1990, 1994). These practices tend to tip the balance of economic power against claimant groups and in favor of defendants.

As a practical matter, class members can spend only about 33 cents out of every dollar in controversy to prosecute a lawsuit. This is the amount they can offer their lawyers as fees. By contrast, defendants can spend 100 cents on the dollar or more. Judges do not control defendants' spending. Because the amount one spends affects one's chances of winning, free-spending defendants will predictably gain an edge over class members. This advantage should manifest itself at trial, where plaintiffs should lose relatively often, and in settlement, where bargains reflect one's prospects at trial.

Differences in ability to diversify risks and manage litigation costs should strengthen the spending advantage defendants enjoy. Plaintiffs' attorneys practice mainly in small firms of 10 or fewer lawyers. Plaintiffs' firms with 25 or more lawyers are exceedingly rare (Stock and Wise, 1993). Firms of this size have limited capital to invest and great difficulty diversifying large risks. For them, class actions, which require cash outlays of $500,000 on average, demand lawyer time worth far more, and take longer than conventional lawsuits to settle, can be bet-the-firm cases. To protect themselves, plaintiffs' attorneys spend conservatively and otherwise minimize their financial commitments to class actions. They are low-cost operators because they have to be (Coffee, 1986).

Defendants find class actions easier to manage. Only large businesses, governmental entities, and other well-heeled institutions are likely to be targets for class actions because only they have the resources or insurance needed to pay large judgments. But the size and wealth that make them attractive targets also enable them to tolerate and diversify litigation risks more easily than plaintiffs' attorneys can.

Being relatively wealthy, defendants usually pay lawyers to defend class actions wholly or partly on the basis of hourly rates. They also reimburse their lawyers for expenses. With their clients absorbing the costs and risks of litigation, defense lawyers have every incentive to turn class actions into protracted lawsuits and frequently do. Every motion a defense lawyer files, every discovery objection and request, every interlocutory appeal, and every other dilatory tactic forces plaintiffs counsel to consume scarce resources. The incentive to force plaintiffs' counsel to bankrupt themselves may partly explain why class actions consume so much more of judges' time than other lawsuits.

Defendants also can take advantage of political connections that are not available to plaintiffs. For example, insurance companies faced with class actions have sought protection from insurance regulators and legislators. In effect, they have sought to cut short litigation by acting in other forums where they enjoy significant advantages. When success outside the courtroom can be a 'silver bullet' that puts a conclusive end to litigation, plaintiffs' attorneys have to respond. But doing so requires more political savvy, greater financial resources and better connections than many of them possess.

There are some economic asymmetries that favor plaintiffs. For example, plaintiffs who survive early dispositive motions are entitled to discovery on the merits, and defendants usually possess far more discoverable information than group members do. By requesting this information via discovery requests that are themselves inexpensive to produce, plaintiffs' attorneys can force defendants to bear the considerable cost of locating, reviewing, and producing it. Particularly costly to defendants is lost managerial time that interrupts its business.

Defendants can do little to expose group members to offsetting costs, which means that once discovery gets underway, plaintiffs possess unique leverage. Recognizing this, defendants work hard to prevent discovery from starting and, when their efforts fail, they often settle to avoid discovery costs, whatever the merits of plaintiffs' claims may be. This threat advantage is a temporary one - it decreases in size as discovery is taken and future costs are converted to sunk costs. Its size also bears no necessary relation to the value of class members' claims. Finally, defendants can offset plaintiffs' leverage somewhat by producing documents and witnesses in volume. A plaintiffs' attorney who is swamped with information may lack the resources needed to sort the wheat from the chaff.

20. Lack of Market Discipline

Many of the forces that encourage agents to represent principals well in other contexts are absent from class actions and consolidations. For example, claimants have little or no power to hire or fire lead attorneys or to decide how much they will be paid. Claimants may not control the settlement decision. They cannot sell their claims when they are disappointed with counsel's performance, as owners who are dissatisfied with managers can sell their shares. Nor in the litigation realm is there an analogue to the takeover market. Attorneys who fail to maximize the value of assets cannot easily be dethroned.

Because so many market checks are missing, the quality controls that do exist must operate especially well. Primary among these are the choice of counsel itself and counsel's compensation arrangement. As explained, the latter often misfires because judges use the lodestar method or otherwise fail to compensate counsel appropriately.

It is difficult to overstate the importance of the attorney chosen to lead a litigation group. This person must marshal the resources needed to prosecute a case, see that they are used efficiently, and decide important matters of strategy. When a consensual litigation group is built via a referral market, there is reason to expect a qualified person to be given these tasks. Referring lawyers, who serve as brokers for their clients, have an interest in selecting competent lead lawyers who will maximize referral fees by maximizing claimants' recoveries. Referring lawyers also are potential monitors and sources of future business. Lead lawyers who shirk or settle cheaply can expect criticism from referring lawyers. Lead lawyers who develop bad reputations can expect to be denied future work (Resnik, Curtis and Hensler, 1996; Spurr, 1988).

When a judge selects a lead attorney, the danger is greater that an unsuitable individual will be chosen. A judge has no stake in the amount class members recover. Consequently, a judge has no particular interest in selecting a lawyer who can be expected to maximize the value of their claims. Absent a contest for control, a judge has no reason to do other than appoint the attorney who files the class action complaint.

Sometimes, it is safe to assume that the attorney who files a complaint is the wrong lawyer for a class. This is true, for example, when *a defendant* recruits lead counsel. Defendants facing large numbers of individual claimants sometimes see the class action as a means of resolving all their legal difficulties in a single forum at a bargain price. With this goal in mind, they approach one plaintiffs' firm after another until they find a lawyer who is willing to negotiate a cheap package deal. This is another example of the reverse auction.

The law requires judges to cure the problem of inadequate lead counsel. More accurately, it permits them to allow class actions to proceed only when absent plaintiffs are adequately represented. This includes representation by adequate counsel. It is clear that judges can appoint substitute counsel when a defect of counsel is all that stands in the way of class certification.

Judges are reluctant to assert this power, for several reasons. First, they rarely see lawyers they recognize as bad apples. Lawyers tend to file lawsuits in courts where they are liked and respected. They also enlist respected local lawyers as co-counsel when they are forced to litigate in unfamiliar courts. A lawyer who is a judge's favorite or has a judge's favorite in tow stands a high likelihood of winning appointment.

Second, many judges like lawyers who are deferential and respectful and who help them by settling cases. It is unreasonable to expect these judges to prefer aggressive lawyers to passive ones. The preference for cooperative attorneys may explain why judges so often give the role of lead counsel to plaintiffs' lawyers who negotiate settlements before seeking class certification. One study reported that 'a proposed settlement was submitted to the court before or simultaneously with the first motion to certify' in 49 percent of class actions certified for settlement (Willging, Hooper and Niemic, 1996b). It also may explain why judges frequently re-appoint certain prominent lawyers who are notorious for settling quickly (Tidmarsh, 1998).

Third, judges are rightly concerned about denying lawyers who uncover wrongdoing the reward of serving as class counsel. Unless lawyers are compensated for time spent inventing liability theories and investigating misconduct, they will be discouraged from doing so. The privilege of being appointed class counsel and the contingent right to compensation that comes with the position maintain the incentive to police wrongdoing.

Some judges have attempted to stimulate competition for the role of lead counsel and to reduce attorneys' fees by auctioning the right to represent a class (Macey and Miller, 1991, 1993). The results have been mixed. A judge cannot sell a class action to the highest bidder, a transaction that might be predicted to identify the attorney who can derive the greatest value from a set of claims. They can auction only the right to control the class and, in the event of success, to be paid. The temptation is to sell the lead counsel position to the lawyer willing to handle a case for the smallest fee.

This is a serious mistake. The cheapest lawyer is likely to be the one whose opportunity cost is lowest because he cannot attract other business. Such a lawyer would be a poor candidate to represent a class.

An attorney who represents an individual client with a large stake, such as an institutional investor, would be better suited for the task. Sophisticated clients with large claims are likely to pick good lawyers. Because they can be expected to perform quality control for themselves, they can provide the same service for a class. A lawyer who represents a large number of clients with small stakes could also be a good choice. The lawyer's success in the referral market would show that other attorneys think he or she has the ability to run a group suit. Great financial wealth, a history of committing significant resources to lawsuits, and a record of success in high-stakes litigation are also important. Judges should consider indicia of quality in addition to price.

Two other quality controls that remain in most class actions are the right to object to proposed settlements and the right to opt out. These rights are not especially meaningful.

Absent plaintiffs are likely to object only when the cost of objecting is less than the expected gain. The cost of making anything more than a perfunctory objection can be quite large. An absent class member must retain counsel to canvass the record, attempt discovery of class counsel, and argue against approval of a settlement in court. By contrast, the expected payoff from objecting usually is small. It is the difference between the amount being offered and the amount one might recover under a more favorable settlement or trial judgment. Because objectors rarely succeed in changing settlements, the gain is likely to be worth the cost only for plaintiffs whose claims are very large. Even they may be discouraged by the logic of collective action, which creates pressure to free-ride.

In most situations, procedural rules entitle absent claimants to exclude themselves from class actions by filing opt out forms. This opt out right bears the same relation to objecting that exit bears to voice (Hirschmann, 1970). In theory, claimants could use their opt out right to guarantee themselves at least the expected value of their claims in conventional litigation (A in Figure 1). Some claimants have significantly increased their recoveries by opting out of class actions and filing conventional lawsuits (Tidmarsh, 1998).

The right to opt out may be more efficacious than the right to object, but it generally means that a claimant must litigate alone rather than as part of a second class action that is more efficiently run. For plaintiffs with small claims, this is impracticable, and for plaintiffs with large claims it may be disadvantageous. The empirical findings that class members rarely opt out and that those who do so overwhelmingly have large claims and are represented by counsel are not surprising (Willging, Hooper and Niemic, 1996b). Finally, by opting out absent plaintiffs protect only themselves. Other class members remain exposed to exploitation.

21. Certification of 'Settlement-Only' Classes

Class actions often are certified and settled at the same time. In approximately one-third of all cases where certification is granted, it is for settlement only (Willging, Hooper and Niemic, 1996b).

The set of class actions that are certified for settlement contains two subsets: class actions that would be certified for trial because they meet all the criteria for certification, and class actions that would not be certified for trial because they do not meet the criteria. For shorthand, the latter will be referred to as 'settlement-only classes'. Sell-outs are especially likely in these cases.

To see why, one must understand that plaintiffs' attorneys need defendants' cooperation to get settlement-only classes certified. These cases do not meet the requirements for certification. Consequently, certification would be denied in these cases if defendants were to object. To obtain defendants' acquiescence, plaintiffs' attorneys must make concessions.

The magnitude of the concession depends on the size of the fee interest putative class counsel has in the individual cases that will proceed in the absence of a class action. Assume the following: 100 individual plaintiffs will file cases; the attorney seeking to act as class counsel will represent 10 of these; each plaintiff's case has a settlement value of $500,000; and the attorney will contract with each plaintiff for a 25 percent contingent fee. In this example, the attorney expects to earn $125,000 in fees per case times 10 cases, a total of $1.25 million. The attorney will make nothing off the remaining 90 cases because other lawyers will handle them. Clearly, a class-wide settlement of all 100 cases yielding a fee greater than $1.25 million would be better for the attorney. For example, a fee award of $2.5 million in a class action would be an increase of 100 percent.

Therein lies the rub. At a rate of 25 percent, a class-wide recovery in the amount of $10 million would generate a $2.5 million fee. But a $10 million settlement would grossly undervalue the 100 claims, which would generate $50 million in winnings if tried separately. Settlement-only classes create opportunities for defendants to pay class counsel huge premiums while saving themselves enormous sums.

Defendants' opportunities to save money and to purchase class counsel's cooperation are especially great in so-called 'futures' class actions. These lawsuits cover persons whose injuries are latent. For example, persons exposed to a disease-causing substance who are asymptomatic could fall within a futures class. Although many of these persons can be predicted to sue after their injuries ripen, few are likely to retain counsel during the latency period. A futures class action offers a defendant an opportunity to settle all possible claims cheaply before any symptoms appear. By offering a bribe to an attorney who is willing to serve as class counsel, a defendant can settle immature claims for pennies on the dollar.

22. Settlements of Inventories of Signed Clients

Attorneys who handle class actions often have inventories of signed clients. In principle, this is good. An attorney who manages to build a client base in a litigation area where other lawyers are competing for business has convinced the market that he is a competent lawyer. The inference of quality is especially strong when an attorney has acquired clients by referral from other lawyers.

Concerns arise when an attorney settles a client inventory apart from and on terms that differ from those he negotiates for a class. This is accomplished by excluding the attorney's signed clients from the class action. For example, the class definition may cover only persons who file complaints after a certain date. If class counsel's signed clients filed before that date, a class-wide settlement would not cover them.

When a class action and a block of signed clients settle separately, there is reason to fear that one group may benefit at the other's expense. Usually, the worry is that the signed clients will exploit the unsigned class members. A wealth transfer from the latter to the former will benefit counsel if fees in the signed clients' cases are higher than those typically awarded in class actions. A transfer may also smooth the process of settling the client inventory by creating a surplus that can be used to buy off disgruntled clients or to reward lawyers or organizations, such as labor unions, who provided referrals (Coffee, 1995a; Koniak, 1995; Nagareda, 1996b).

23. Maximization-Related Conflicts

A subject neglected in the scholarly literature on class actions is the inevitability of conflicts in the process of preparing cases for trial. Although class counsel can often advance all absent plaintiffs' interests concurrently by supplying them with joint goods, even related claims invariably have idiosyncratic aspects that require individual attention and targeted expenditures. By devoting time and resources to these issues, class counsel neglects the interests of class members who claims lack these characteristics and who would prefer that counsel's time and resources be spent in ways more likely to be of benefit to them (Rhode, 1982a; Silver and Baker, 1998).

Resource allocations on common issues can also require inter-claimant trade-offs, and usually do. Class members with small compensatory claims, such as employees who were recently hired at discriminatorily low wages, may be best off if litigation resources are devoted mainly to the pursuit of punitive damages, pay increases and promotions. This use of resources may not appeal to class members with large compensatory claims, such as long-time employees. They may benefit most from efforts to model the impact of wage discrimination on their lifetime income and retirement plans. Other class members, such as future job applicants, may care only about new job openings.

By rejecting a settlement offer, class counsel also trades off the interests of some class members against those of others. Every litigation group contains members with different attitudes toward risk, with different views on the time-value of money, and with different desires for relief. By pursuing a high-risk/high-reward approach to litigation or a low-risk/low-reward approach, class counsel necessarily decides which class members' preferences will be favored. Class counsel does the same thing by deciding to settle for a larger amount tomorrow instead of a smaller amount today and by pressing for dollars rather than in-kind relief or symbolic vindication. Every decision to use time or money for one purpose rather than another or to adopt one litigation strategy instead of another necessarily resolves conflicts among class members' interests.

Maximization-related conflicts inhere in all class actions because there is nothing like the stock market that claimants can use to ameliorate them. Shareholders can freely and cheaply move between different companies and different investments so that their portfolios accommodate their risk preferences, attitudes toward the time value of money, and so on. Claimants cannot move from one class action to another to achieve the same result.

F. Inappropriate Settlement Allocations

A recovery can be allocated equitably or inequitably. From a Paretian perspective, allocations on CE and FD in Figure 1 would be inequitable despite being efficient. They would leave some class members worse off than they would have expected to be had they sued on their own.

A nascent but developing literature examines the equity of settlement allocations in class actions and other group lawsuits (Coffee 1998; Hay, 1997b; Hazard, 1995; Koniak, 1995; Menkel-Meadow, 1995; Silver and Baker, 1998). Even scholars who care mainly about deterrence agree that it is important to compensate plaintiffs fairly when that can be done at reasonable expense (Rosenberg, 1987, 1996).

There is a tendency in the literature to run allocation issues and efficiency issues together. When certain claimants are shortchanged, it may be because others receive too much, because a settlement fund is too small, or because others receive too much and a settlement is was too small. The unique contribution of equity is to set standards for dividing funds, not for overall fund size.

24. Allocation-Related Conflicts Inhere In All Class Actions

When it comes to dividing settlement funds, class members' interests always conflict. In Figure 1, X and Y share an interest in moving away from A in the direction of GH, but they have opposing preferences concerning where on GH they wind up. X prefers divisions to the northwest; Y prefers divisions to the southeast. A group lawsuit is a mixed-motive game in which the interest in cooperating for mutual gain is in tension with the interest in getting as much as possible for oneself. The tension exists whether a group seeks injunctive or monetary relief.

The number of ways of allocating recoveries and the conflicts they generate make clear the need for standards. If a class containing only members X and Y were to recover $1000, the entire range of options from ($1000,$0) through ($0,$1000) would be available. If member Z were added to the group, the number of possible allocations would expand exponentially. To avoid arbitrariness, judges and lawyers require normative allocation guidelines.

Unfortunately, there is no widely accepted, general account of the equity of class action settlements. There are instead many assessments of particular allocations that commentators either found deficient or wished to defend. Many of these assessments rest on deeper principles of equity or distributive justice that are neither made explicit nor carefully examined. For example, a scholar may criticize an allocation plan for ignoring differences in the size and strength of claims without explaining why these differences should matter.

Also missing is a cost-benefit analysis of equity. It is more expensive to pay claimants amounts that roughly reflect the size and strength of their claims than it is to engage in damages averaging and pay them equal amounts, and it is more expensive still to distribute payments that reflect fine differences between claimants (Coffee, 1987a, 1998; Silver and Baker, 1998). One therefore wants to know how much cost should be borne to obtain a marginal increase in equity. There is general agreement that the importance of equity increases with claim size. There is also a growing consensus that because class settlements yield less than $400 per claimant on average, often the game is not worth the candle. Between the extremes of large claims and small recoveries, however, there is little agreement as to how much equity is enough. This dissensus has important practical ramifications.

25. Causes of Arbitrary Allocations

Class counsel and defendants design allocation plans. In effect, they serve as agenda setters, deciding which of many possible allocations are presented to courts and claimants for consideration. Like other agenda setters, they have considerable power to control outcomes.

On the surface, this power may seem wasted on class counsel. Because allocation formulas do not affect the size of fee awards, class counsel might not seem to care how relief is divided. Reality is more complicated than this. Class counsel will receive no fee until a settlement is judicially approved. Approval depends, among other things, upon the judge's views and the reaction of the class. Class counsel therefore has an interest in selecting allocations that satisfy these constituencies. Class settlements also frequently contain 'walk away' provisions that condition settlement on an agreed level of claimant participation. When allocating common funds, class counsel may keep the required level of participation in mind.

As explained, only class members with large claims are likely to object or opt out. This is why 'walk away' provisions usually target large-claim plaintiffs. A rational strategy for class counsel may therefore be to over-compensate large-claim plaintiffs and to shortchange everyone else. This approach enables class counsel to mollify large-claim plaintiffs without risking a revolt by small-claim plaintiffs, who rarely complain.

The desire to avoid objections can also lead to class counsel to overcompensate class members who belong to organizations. For example, an asbestos class action may include workers who are union members and workers who are not. Because a union can be an effective advocate of its members' interests, it may contest a settlement that treats them poorly. Class counsel may therefore be inclined to involve the union in the design and administration of the settlement and to overcompensate its members.

A separate dynamic can cause class members with large claims to be underpaid. The typical class contains a small number of persons with sizeable claims and a far larger number whose claims are comparatively small or weak. The latter claims may add little value to the group lawsuit, but they increase greatly the number of mouths to be fed. Unfortunately for class members with large claims, judges are reluctant to deny any subgroup of absent plaintiffs a share of settlement benefits, especially a subgroup that is large. The price of feeding everyone is that plaintiffs with large claims receive less than they should.

The weak may also beggar the strong in litigation groups simply because the weak have less at stake. In bargaining situations, the player who stands to lose the most from the failure to reach an agreement can be expected to give up the most to salvage a deal. Plaintiffs with large claims have more at stake than plaintiffs with small claims, often far more. Small-claim plaintiffs can therefore take advantage of them. Risk aversion will predictably cause plaintiffs with large claims to sacrifice even more because the risks attached to large claims are harder to diversify and because large claims constitute a more sizeable portion of plaintiffs' wealth.

Defendants also may have interests in skewing allocation formulas. For example, they may want to direct as much money as possible to claimants who are current customers, suppliers, employees, or shareholders and as little as possible to others (Coffee, 1998). A plaintiffs' attorney who is indifferent to the manner of allocation will have no reason to resist a defendant's efforts to direct funds to its favorites.

26. Possible Allocation Standards

The possibility of arbitrary allocation plans makes plain the need for concrete normative guidelines. Many scholars seem to embrace a Paretian standard of equity according to which class members should receive at least the expected value of their claims in conventional litigation. This probably includes most scholars who criticize allocations that ignore factors bearing on the size and strength of claims or that take account of irrelevant factors (Coffee, 1995a; Cramton, 1995; Koniak, 1995; Menkel-Meadow, 1995). They seem to assume that size and strength have the greatest impact on claim values in conventional litigation, and they therefore conclude that when size and strength are ignored, claimants are shortchanged.

The merit of the Paretian standard is that it respects the intuition that rational persons would not join litigation groups hoping to make themselves worse off than they are on their own. They would do so expecting collective action to enhance the value of their claims.

There are many difficulties with the Paretian standard, however. One is that the value of claims in conventional litigation is not self-evident. It must be assigned, and the data needed to make the assessment may be unavailable. A second is that the proper baseline to begin with may not be the expected value of claims in conventional litigation. Instead, one could start with a claim's highest expected value in any possible coalition of claimants. Needless to say, this value is not self-evident either. A third is that a commitment to Paretianism may not lead to the conclusion that allocations should reflect only the size and strength of claims. Other factors could also affect the value claims have in conventional litigation, including factors that may have nothing to do with the merits such as sex, age, race, or jury appeal. It is an empirical question which factors matter in particular cases. A fourth difficulty is that a Paretian standard does not tell one how to divide any surplus that exists above the chosen baseline. This shortcoming is especially problematic when class actions include some or solely claims that are too small to litigate individually, as most do.

A fifth problem is that claimants who participate in consensual group lawsuits rarely take steps in advance to identify or protect anything that might serve as a baseline for Pareto comparisons. Most such plaintiffs do nothing to provide for the division of settlement funds. They trust their fates to the discretion of their attorneys, reserving only the right to veto settlements as a means of protecting themselves. The veto right is often more illusory than real, however, because plaintiffs rarely have independent counsel to advise them how to use it.

Scholars who embrace Paretian standards must also consider how shortfalls should be dealt with. Settlements yield actual values, and actual values may be smaller than expected values even when class actions are run efficiently. When a group-wide settlement is too small to pay everyone the amount required by the Paretian baseline, some or all claimants must be shortchanged. The difficulty is in deciding which claimants and how much. Again, the number of possible allocations is exceedingly great.

27. Reform Proposals

There is broad agreement that judges should change certain aspects of the way they manage class actions. For example, whether an auction, a contingent percentage or even the lodestar method is used to set fees, most scholars encourage judges to set the terms of compensation up front. Today, judges often delay this matter until class actions settle. This practice requires class counsel to devote significant economic resources to a risky venture with no formal understanding as to the expected return. It also complicates settlement negotiations by leaving an additional and sizeable matter for the negotiators to resolve. The practice also burdens class counsel with a conflict of interests by creating the possibility that an impasse over fees may block an attractive settlement on the merits.

Investors in risky undertakings rarely tolerate this degree of uncertainty or conflict. They provide in advance for the division of returns, even when there may be no returns to divide. By doing so, they encourage their agents to work hard for their benefit. Judges presiding over class actions should mimic the market in this regard (Federal Judicial Center, 1995).

The practice of setting fees at the end also skews fee awards downward. In hindsight, the risk of loss will naturally seem smaller than it was. It is also more difficult to award large fees when the precise amount of the fee is known. This problem disappears when fees are set before any money is offered in settlement.

Another way to improve the class action to use percentage compensation instead of the lodestar method whenever possible and to increase percentages at the margin as the amount recovered rises. By offsetting risk aversion and the declining marginal value of money, this will encourage class counsel to strive for larger recoveries instead of being satisfied with smaller ones.

Other reform proposals include giving class members the right to opt out of all settlements (Rutherglen, 1996), forced fee sharing between class counsel and lawyers representing clients who opt out (Coffee, 1987b), improved notice (Woolley, 1997), allowing absent plaintiffs to sue class counsel for malpractice and collusion (Koniak and Cohen, 1996), encouraging judges to decide merits issues before motions for class certification (Berry,

1980; Priest, 1997), increased use of injunctions to prevent parallel class litigation (Miller, 1996), restricting opt-out rights (Perino, 1997), and alternative fee arrangements that link counsel's compensation to fees paid in individual representations (Hay, 1997b).

G. Conclusions

28. The Potential for Good

The class action is a procedural device with extraordinary potential for good. It can force product manufacturers and service providers to take account of externalities that they would otherwise ignore, encouraging them to perform more efficiently and compensating victims who would otherwise lack remedies. It can make the procedural system operate more efficiently by enabling judges to process related claims en masse at less cost per claim. It can save claimants' and defendants' money by enabling both to take maximum advantage of economies of scale. It can align the stakes of defendants and claimants so that litigation investments are more nearly equal and settlement bargains better reflect the merits of claims.

29. The Potential for Bad

The class action also entails important risks and dangers. Conflicts among claimants inhere in all class actions and must be resolved as cases are prepared for trial and settled. Lack of market oversight and improper judicial regulation create opportunities for class counsel and defendants to collude. This can frustrate the cost-internalization function of the class action by enabling wrongdoers to escape the social costs of their conduct. It can frustrate the compensatory function as well by shortchanging claimants. The latter can occur independently of the former as a result of improper allocation plans.

30. The Need for Dispassionate Analysis

At the microeconomic level, class actions are fascinating and truly intricate. Agency problems abound, and strategies for dealing with them are often subject to counter-strategies that are difficult to plan for in advance. Compounding the problem is the fact that judges do not always understand or even care about the impact their decisions have on the microstructure of the class action. Many decisions, such as those that require individual notice in small-claim class actions and those that announce the homogeneity of injunctive class actions, are patently flawed. Politics also takes a toll, especially when it comes to lawyers' fees, a subject of great partisan debate in the United States. If the atmosphere surrounding the class action ever cools, it may be possible to reform the device and avoid many excesses.

Acknowledgements

Lynn Baker, Sam Issacharoff, John Leubsdorf, Tom Rowe and Patrick Woolley provided helpful comments on this chapter, as did an anonymous reviewer. Vanessa Pogue's research assistance and Suzanne Hassler's help preparing the bibliography and proofreading everything were invaluable.

Bibliography on Class Actions - Representative Proceedings (7600)

Abraham, Kenneth S. (1987), 'Individual Action and Collective Responsibility: The Dilemma of Mass Tort Reform', **73** *Virginia Law Review*, 845-907.

Administrative Office of the United States Courts (1997), *Judicial Business of the United States Courts*, Washington, DC, The Administrative Office of the United States, 386 p.

Alexander, Janet Cooper (1991), 'Do the Merits Matter? A Study of Settlements in Securities Class Actions', **43** *Stanford Law Review*, 497-598.

Alexander, Janet Cooper (1998), 'Contingent Fees and Class Actions', **47** *DePaul Law Review*, 347-361.

Baughman, Steve (1991), 'Class Actions in the Asbestos Context: Balancing the Due Process Considerations Implicated by the Right to Opt Out', **70** *Texas Law Review*, 211-241.

Bernstein, Roger (1978), 'Judicial Economy and Class Actions', **7** *Journal of Legal Studies*, 349-370.

Berry, Stephen (1980), 'Ending Substance's Indenture to Procedure: The Imperative for Comprehensive Revision of the Class Damage Action', **80** *Columbia Law Review*, 299-344.

Bertelsen, Bruce I., Calfee, Mary S. and Connor, Gerald W. (1974), 'The Rule 23(b)(3) Class Action: An Empirical Study', **62** *Georgetown Law Journal*, 1123-1172.

Bohn, James and Choi, Stephen (1996), 'Fraud in the New-Issues Market: Empirical Evidence on Securities Class Actions', **144** *University of Pennsylvania Law Review*, 903-982.

Bone, Robert G. (1990), 'Personal and Impersonal Litigative Forms: Reconceiving the History of Adjudicative Representation', **70** *Boston University Law Review*, 213-307.

Bone, Robert G. (1993), 'Statistical Adjudication: Rights, Justice, and Utility in a World of Process Scarcity', **46** *Vanderbilt Law Review*, 561-662.

Bone, Robert G. (1994), 'Rule 23 Redux: Empowering the Federal Class Action', **14** *Review of Litigation*, 79-112.

Bordens, Kenneth S. and Horowitz, Irwin A. (1989), 'Mass Tort Civil Litigation: The Impact of Procedural Changes on Jury Decisions', **73** *Judicature*, 22–27.

Bordens, Kenneth S. and Horowitz, Irwin A. (1998), 'The Limits of Sampling and Consolidation in Mass Tort Trials: Justice Improved or Justice Altered?', **22** *Law and Psychology Review*, 43-66.

Borenstein, Severin (1996), 'Settling for Coupons: Discount Contracts as Compensation and Punishment in Antitrust Lawsuits,' **39** *Journal of Law and Economics*, 379-404.

Brunt, Maureen and Fels, Alan (1982), 'Economics of Class Actions: A Research Design', in Cranston, Ross and Schick, Anne (eds), *Law and Economics*, Canberra, Australian National University, 1-9.

Buckley, Colin Hugh (1985), 'Note: A Suggested Remedy for Toxic Injury: Class Actions, Epidemiology, and Economic Efficiency', **26** *William and Mary Law Review*, 497-543.

Bundy, Stephen McG. and Elhauge, Einer Richard (1991), 'Do Lawyers Improve the Adversary System? A General Theory of Litigation Advice and its Regulation', **79** *California Law Review*, 313-420.

Carleton, William T., Weisbach, Michael S. and Weiss, Elliott J. (1996), 'Securities Class Action Lawsuits: A Descriptive Study', **38** *Arizona Law Review*, 491-511.

Carr, Jack and Mathewson, Frank, (1990), 'The Economics of Law Firms: A Study in the Legal Organization of the Firm', **33** *Journal of Law and Economics*, 307-330.

Cerminara, Kathy L. (1998), 'The Class Action Suit as a Method of Patient Empowerment in the Managed Care Setting', **24** *American Journal of Law and Medicine*, 7-58.

Clermont, Kevin M. and Currivan, John D. (1978), 'Improving the Contingent Fee', **63** *Cornell Law Review*, 529-639.

Coffee, John C., Jr (1983), 'Rescuing the Private Attorney General: Why the Model of the Lawyer as Bounty Hunter is Not Working', **42** *Maryland Law Review*, 215-288.

Coffee, John C., Jr (1986), 'Understanding the Plaintiff's Attorney: the Implications of Economic Theory for Private Enforcement of Law through Class and Derivative Actions', **86** *Columbia Law Review*, 669-727.

Coffee, John C., Jr (1987a), 'The Regulation of Entrepreneurial Litigation: Balancing Fairness And Efficiency in the Large Class Action', **54** *University of Chicago Law Review*, 877-937.

Coffee, John C., Jr (1987b), 'Rethinking the Class Action: A Policy Primer on Reform', **62** *Indiana Law Journal*, 625-664.

Coffee, John C., Jr (1995a), 'Class Wars: The Dilemma of the Mass Tort Class Action', **95** *Columbia Law Review*, 1343-1465.

Coffee, John C., Jr (1995b), 'The Corruption of the Class Action: The New Technology of Collusion', **80** *Cornell Law Review*, 851-857.

Coffee, John C., Jr (1998), 'Conflicts, Consent, and Allocation after *AmchemProducts* - or, Why Attorneys Still Need Consent to Give Away Their Clients' Money', **84** *University of Virginia Law Review*.

Coleman, Jules L. and Silver, Charles (1986), 'Justice in Settlements', **4** *Social Philosophy and Policy*, 102-144.

Cooper, Edward H. (1996), 'Rule 23: Challenges to the Rulemaking Process', **71** *New York University Law Review*, 13-73.

Cooter, Robert (1989), 'Economics of Bargaining Towards a Market in Unmatured Tort Claims', **75** *Virginia Law Review*, 383-411.

Cooter, Robert and Ulen, Thomas (1988), *Law and Economics*, United States, Harper Collins Publishers, 644 p.

Cox, James D. (1997), 'Making Securities Fraud Class Actions Virtuous', **39** *Arizona Law Review*, 497-524.

Cramton, Roger C. (1995), 'Individualized Justice, Mass Torts, and "Settlement Class Actions": An Introduction', **80** *Cornell Law Review*, 811-836.

Dam, Kenneth W. (1974), 'Class Action Notice: Who Needs It?', *The Supreme Court Review*, 97-125.

Dam, Kenneth W. (1975), 'Class Actions: Efficiency, Compensation, Deterrence, and Conflict of Interest', **4** *Journal of Legal Studies*, 47-73.

Dawson, John P. (1974a), 'Lawyers and Involuntary Clients: Attorney Fees from Funds', **87** *Harvard Law Review* 1597-1654.

Dawson, John P. (1974b), 'The Self-Serving Intermeddler', **87** *Harvard Law Review*, 1409-1458.

Dawson, John P. (1975), 'Lawyers and Involuntary Clients in Public Interest Litigation', **88** *Harvard Law Review*, 849-930.

Dewees, Donald N., Prichard, J. Robert S. and Trebilock, Michael J. (1981), 'An Economic Analysis of Cost and Fee Rules for Class Actions', **10** *Journal of Legal Studies*, 155-185.

Dole, Richard F., Jr (1971), 'The Settlement of Class Actions for Damages', **71** *Columbia Law Review*, 971-1006.

Durand, Anna L. (1981), 'An Economic Analysis of Fluid Class Recovery Mechanisms', **34** *Stanford Law Review*, 173-201.

Elhauge, Einer R. (1991), 'Does Interest Group Theory Justify More Intrusive Judicial Review', **101** *Yale Law Journal*, 31-110.

Estreicher, Samuel (1996), 'Federal Class Actions after 30 Years', **71** *New York University Law Review*, 1-12.

Federal Judicial Center (1995), *Manual (Third) for Complex Litigation*, St Pauls, West Publishing, 568 p.

Friedman, David (1996), 'More Justice For Less Money: A Step Beyond *Cimino*', **39** *Journal of Law and Economics*, 211-240.

Garth, Bryant G. (1987), 'Studying Civil Litigation Through the Class Action', **62** *Indiana Law Journal*, 497-505.

Garth, Bryant G., Nagel, Ilene H. and Plager, S. Jay (1988), 'The Institution of the Private Attorney General: Perspectives from an Empirical Study of Class Action Litigation', **61** *Southern California Law Review*, 353–398.

Garth, Bryant G. (1992), 'Power and Legal Artifice: The Federal Class Action', **26** *Law and Society Review*, 237-271.

Galanter, Marc and Cahill, Mia (1994), ''Most Cases Settle': Judicial Promotion and Regulation of Settlements', **46** *Stanford Law Review*, 1339-1391.

George, Edward I. and Wecker, William E. (1985), 'Estimating Damages in a Class Action Litigation', **3** *Journal of Business and Economic Statistics*, 132-139.

Gerard, Robert B. and Johnson, Scott A. (January 1998), 'The Role of the Objector in Class Action Settlements: A Case Study of the General Motors Truck "Side Saddle" Fuel Tank Litigation', **31** *Loyola of Los Angeles Law Review*, 409-435.

Goldberg, Michael J. (1988), 'The Propensity to Sue and the Duty of Fair Representation: A Second Point of View [Tactical Use of the Union's Duty of Fair Representation: An Empirical Analysis]', **41** *Industrial and Labor Relations Review*, 456-461.

Green, Eric D. (1997a), 'What Will We Do When Adjudication Ends? We'll Settle in Bunches: Bringing Rule 23 into the Twenty-First Century', **44** *University of California at Los Angeles Law Review*, 1773-1801.

Green, Eric D. (1997b), 'Advancing Individual Rights Through Group Justice', **30** *University of California at Davis Law Review*, 791-804.

Gross, Samuel R. and Syverud, Kent D. (1991), 'Getting to No: A Study of Settlement Negotiations and the Selection of Cases for Trial', **90** *Michigan Law Review*, 319-393.

Grundfest, Joseph A. and Perino, Michael A. (1996), 'The Pentium Papers: A Case Study of Collective Institutional Investor Activism in Litigation', **38** *Arizona Law Review*, 559-622.

Hardin, Russell (1982), *Collective Action*, Baltimore, MD, Johns Hopkins University Press, 248 p.

Hartman, Raymond S. and Doane, Michael J. (1987), 'The Use of Hedonic Analysis for Certification and Damage Calculations in Class Action Complaints', **3** *Journal of Law, Economics, and Organization*, 351-372.

Hay, Bruce L. (1996), 'Contingent Fees and Agency Costs', **25** *Journal of Legal Studies*, 503-533.

Hay, Bruce L. (1997a), 'Asymmetric Rewards: Why Class Actions (May) Settle for Too Little', **48** *Hastings Law Journal*, 479-509.

Hay, Bruce L. (1997b), 'The Theory of Fee Regulation in Class Action Settlements', **46** *American University Law Review*, 1429-1474.

Hazard, Geoffrey C., Jr (1995), 'The Settlement Black Box', **75** *Boston University Law Review*, 1257-1272.

Henderson, James A., Jr (1995), 'Comment: Settlement Class Actions and the Limits of Adjudication', **80** *Cornell Law Review*, 1014-1021.

Hensler, Deborah R. (1989), 'Resolving Mass Toxic Torts: Myths and Realities', **89** *University of Illinois Law Review*, 89-104.

Hensler, Deborah R. and Peterson, Mark A (1993), 'Understanding Mass Personal Injury Litigation: A Socio-Legal Analysis', **59** *Brooklyn Law Review*, 961-1061.

Hensler, Deborah R., Felstiner, William L.F., Selvin, Molly and Ebener, Patricia A. (1985), *Asbestos in the Courts: The Challenge of Mass Toxic Torts*, Santa Monica, CA, Rand Institute for Civil Justice, 128 p.

Hirschmann, Albert O. (1970), *Exit, Voice and Loyalty*, Cambridge, MA, Harvard University Press, 162 p.

Hutchinson, Diane Wood. (1983), 'Class Actions: Joinder or Representational Device?', **1983** *Supreme Court Review*, 459-507.

In Camera (May-June 1993), **16** *Class Action Reports*, 3:250-253.

In Camera (July-August 1993), **16** *Class Action Reports*, 4:244-249.

Issacharoff, Samuel (1991), 'Administering Damage Awards in Mass-Tort Litigation, **10** *Review of Litigation*, 463, 470-80.

Issacharoff, Samuel (1997), 'Class Action Conflicts', **30** *University of California at Davis Law Review*, 805–833.

Jackson, Thomas (1982), 'Bankruptcy, Non-Bankruptcy Entitlements, and the Creditors' Bargain', **91** *Yale Law Journal*, 857–907.

Jensen, Michael C. and Meckling, William H. (1976), 'Theory of the Firm: Managerial Behavior, Agency Costs and Ownership Structure', **3** *Journal of Financial Economics*, 305-311.

Johnson., Earl, Jr (1980-81), 'Lawyers' Choice: A Theoretical Appraisal of Litigation Investment Decisions', **15** *Law and Society Review*, 567–610, 883-910.

Kahan, Marcel and Silberman, Linda (1996), 'Matsushita and Beyond: The Role of State Courts in Class Actions Involving Exclusive Federal Claims', **1996** *Supreme Court Review*, 219–283.

Kahan, Marcel and Silberman, Linda (1998), 'The Inadequate Search for "Adequacy" in Class Actions: A Critique of Epstein v. MCA, Inc'., **73** *New York University Law Review*, 765-792.

Kalven, Harry, Jr and Rosenfield, Maurice (1941), 'The Contemporary Function of the Class Suit', **8** *University of Chicago Law Review*, 684-721.

Kane, Mary Kay (1987), 'Of Carrots and Sticks: Evaluating the Role of the Class Action Lawyer', **66** *Texas Law Review*, 385-409.

Knight, Thomas R. (1988), 'The Propensity to Sue and the Duty of Fair Representation: Reply', **41** *Industrial and Labor Relations Review*, 461-464.

Koniak, Susan P. (1995), 'Feasting While the Widow Weeps: Georgine v. Amchem Products, Inc.', **80** *Cornell Law Review* (May), 1045-1158.

Koniak, Susan P. and Cohen, George M. (1996), 'Under Cloak of Settlement', **82** *Virginia Law Review*, 10510-1280.

Kornhauser, Lewis A. (1983), 'Control of Conflicts of Interest in Class-Action Suits', **41** *Public Choice*, 145-175.

Kraakman, Reinier, Park, Hyun and Shavell, Steven (1994), 'When are Shareholder Suits in Shareholders' Interests', **82** *Georgetown Law Review*, 1733-1775.

Krislov, Clinton A. (1990), 'Scrutiny of the Bounty: Incentive Awards for Plaintiffs in Class Litigation', **78** *Illinois Bar Journal*, 286-290.

Levmore, Saul (1985), 'Explaining Restitution', **71** *Virginia Law Review*, 65-124.

Leubsdorf, John (1995), 'Co-Opting the Class Action', **80** *Cornell Law Review*, 1222-1227.

Lynk, William J. (1990), 'The Courts and the Market: An Economic Analysis of Contingent Fees in Class-Action Litigation', **19** *Journal of Legal Studies*, 247–260.

Lynk, William J. (1994), 'The Courts and the Plaintiff's Bar: Awarding the Attorney's Fee in Class-Action Litigation', **23** *Journal of Legal Studies*, 185-209.

Macey, Jonathan R. (1994), 'Judicial Preferences, Public Choice, and the Rules of Procedure', **23** *Journal of Legal Studies*, 627-646.

Macey, Jonathan R. and Miller, Geoffrey P. (1991), 'The Plaintiffs' Attorney's Role in Class Action and Derivative Litigation: Economic Analysis and Recommendations for Reform', **58** *University of Chicago Law Review*, 1-118.

Macey, Jonathan R. and Miller, Geoffrey P. (1993), 'Auctioning Class Action and Derivative Suits: A Rejoinder', **87** *Northwestern University Law Review*, 458-470.

Macey, Jonathan R. and Miller, Geoffrey P. (1995), 'A Market Approach to Tort Reform Via Rule 23', **80** *Cornell Law Review*, 909-917.

Marcus, Richard L. (1995a), 'They Can't Do That, Can They? Tort Reform via Rule 23', **80** *Cornell Law Review*, 858-908.

Marcus, Richard L. (1995b), 'Confronting the Consolidation Conundrum', **95** *Brigham Young University Law Review*, 879-924.

Marshall, Robert C., Meurer, Michael J. and Richard, Jean Francois (1994), 'Multiple Litigants with a Public Good Remedy', **16** *Research in Law and Economics*, 151-173.

Martin, Denise N., Juneja, Vinita M., Foster, Todd S. and Dunbar, Frederick C. (1996), 'Recent Trends IV: What Explains Filings and Settlements in Shareholder Class Actions?', White Plains, NY, National Economic Research Associates, 88 p.

McCoid, John C. (1976), 'A Single Package for Multiparty Disputes', **28** *Stanford Law Review*, 707-728.

McGovern, Francis E. (1989), 'Resolving Mature Mass Tort Litigation', **69** *Boston University Law Review*, 659-694.

Menkel-Meadow, Carrie (1995), 'Ethics and the Settlements of Mass Torts: When the Rules Meet the Road', **80** *Cornell Law Review*, 1159-1221.

Miller, Geoffrey P. (1996), 'Overlapping Class Actions', **71** *New York University Law Review*, 514-546.

Miller, Geoffrey (1998), 'Class Actions', in Newman, Peter (ed.), *The New Palgrave Dictionary of Economics and the Law*, New York, Stockton Press, Vol. 1 pp. 257–261.

Miller, Geoffrey and Singer, Lori (1998), 'Nonpecuniary Class Action Settlements', **60** *Law and Contemporary Problems*, 97-155.

Monaghan, Henry Paul (1998), 'Antisuit Injunctions and Preclusion Against Absent Nonresident Class Members', **98** *Columbia Law Review*, 1148-1202.

Morawetz, Nancy (1996), 'Underinclusive Class Actions', **71** *New York University Law Review*, 402-438.

Mullenix, Linda S. (1991a), 'Beyond Consolidation: Postaggregative Procedure in Asbestos Mass Tort Litigation', **32** *William and Mary Law Review*, 475–585.

Mullenix, Linda S. (1991b), 'Problems in Complex Litigation', **10** *Review of Litigation*, 213–230.

Mullenix, Linda S. (1994), 'The Pervasive Myth of Pervasive Discovery Abuse and the Consequences for Unfounded Rulemaking', **46** *Stanford Law Review*, 1393-1445.

Mullenix, Linda S. (1995), 'Class Actions, Personal Jurisdiction, and Plaintiffs' Due Process: Implications for Mass Tort Litigation', **28** *University of California at Davis Law Review*, 871-916.

Nagareda Richard A. (1996a), 'In the Aftermath of the Mass Tort Class Action', **85** *Georgetown Law Journal*, 295-368.

Nagareda, Richard A. (1996b), 'Turning From Tort to Administration', **94** *Michigan Law Review*, 899-981.

Perino, Michael A. (1997), 'Class Action Chaos?: The Theory of the Core and an Analysis of Opt Out Rights in Mass Tort Class Actions', **46** *Emory Law Journal*, 85–161.

Polinsky, A. Mitchell and Shavell, Steven (1981), 'Contribution and Claim Reduction among Antitrust Defendants: An Economic Analysis', **33** *Stanford Law Review*, 447-471.

Priest, George L. (1997), 'Procedural versus Substantive Controls of Mass Tort Class Actions', **26** *Journal of Legal Studies*, 521-573.

Rabin, Robert L. (1995), 'Continuing Tensions in the Resolution of Mass Toxic Harm Cases: A Comment', **80** *Cornell Law Review*, 1037-1044.

Ratliff, Jack (1988), 'Offensive Collateral Estoppel and the Option Effect', **67** *Texas Law Review*, 63-101.

Resnik, Judith (1982), 'Managerial Judges', **96** *Harvard Law Review*, 374-448.

Resnik, Judith (1991), 'Modern Civil Procedure: Issues in Controversy, from "Cases" to "Litigation"', **54** *Law and Contemporary Problems*, 5-68.

Resnik, Judith (1995), 'Aggregation, Settlement, and Dismay', **80** *Cornell Law Review*, 918-940.

Resnik, Judith, Curtis, Dennis E. and Hensler, Deborah R. (1996), 'Individuals within the Aggregate: Relationships, Representation, and Fees', **71** *New York University Law Review*, 296-401.

Rheingold, Paul D. (1968), 'The MER/29 Story - An Instance of Successful Mass Disaster Litigation', **56** *California Law Review*, 116-148.

Rhode, Deborah L. (1982a), 'Class Conflicts in Class Actions', **34** *Stanford Law Review*, 1183-1262.

Rhode, Deborah L. (1982b), *Conflicts of Interest in Educational Reform Litigation, Project Report No. 82-A6*, Stanford University, CA, Institute for Research on Educational Finance and Governance, 65 p.

Robinson, Glen O. and Abraham, Kenneth S. (1992), 'Collective Justice in Tort Law', **78** *Virginia Law Review*, 1481-1519.

Rosenberg, David (1984), 'The Causal Connection in Mass Exposure Cases: A "Public Law" Vision of the Tort System', **97** *Harvard Law Review*, 849-929.

Rosenberg, David (1987), 'Class Actions for Mass Torts: Doing Individual Justice by Collective Means', **62** *Indiana Law Journal*, 561–596.

Rosenberg, David (1989), 'Of End Games and Openings in Mass Tort Cases: Lessons from a Special Master', **69** *Boston University Law Review*, 695-730.

Rosenberg, David (1996), 'Individual Justice and Collectivizing Risk-Based Claims in Mass- Exposure Cases', **71** *New York University Law Review*, 210-257.

Rosenfield, Andrew (1976), 'An Empirical Test of Class-Action Settlement', **5** *Journal of Legal Studies*, 113-120.

Rowe, Thomas D., Jr (1982), 'The Legal Theory of Attorney Fee Shifting: A Critical Overview', **1982** *Duke Law Journal*, 651-680.

Rowe, Thomas D., Jr (1989), 'Study on Paths to a "Better Way": Litigation, Alternatives, and Accommodation', **89** *Duke Law Journal*, 824-902.

Rowe, Thomas D., Jr (1996), 'Beyond the Class Action Rule: An Inventory of Statutory Possibilities to Improve the Federal Class Action', **71** *New York University Law Review*, 186–209.

Rubin, Julie (1997), 'Auctioning Class Actions: Turning the Tables on Plaintiffs' Lawyers' Abuse or Stripping the Plaintiff Wizards of Their Curtain', **52** *Business Lawyer*, 1441-1467.

Rutherglen, George (1996), 'Better Late Than Never: Notice and Opt Out at the Settlement Stage of Class Actions', **71** *New York University Law Review*, 258-295.

Sachnoff, Lowell E. and Gilbert, Jeffrey T. (1997), 'Auctioning the Role of Lead Counsel in Class Action Cases to the Lowest Bidder', in *Postgraduate Course in Federal Securities Law*, Philadelphia, PA, Amercan Law Institute, 537-543.

Saks, Michael J. (1992), 'Do We Really Know Anything About the Behavior of the Tort Litigation System - and Why Not?', **140** *University of Pennsylvania Law Review*, 1147-1289.

Saks, Michael J. and Blanck, Peter David (1992), 'Justice Improved: The Unrecognized Benefits of Aggregation and Sampling in the Trial of Mass Torts', **44** *Stanford Law Review*, 815-851.

Sappington, David E.M. (1991), 'Incentives in Principal-Agent Relationships', **5** *Journal of Economic Perspectives*, 45-66.

Schuck, Peter (1986), 'The Role of Judges in Settling Complex Cases: The Agent Orange Example', **53** *University of Chicago Law Review*, 337-365.

Schuck, Peter H. (1987), *Agent Orange on Trial: Mass Toxic Disasters in the Court*, Cambridge, MA, Belknap Press of Harvard University Press, 363p.

Schuck, Peter (1995), 'Mass Torts: An Institutional Evolutionist Perspective', **80** *Cornell Law Review* (May), 941-989.

Schwartz, Alan (1989), 'Commentary on "Towards a Market in Unmatured Tort Claims": A Long Way Yet to Go', **75** *Virginia Law Review*, 423-430.

Schwartz, Gary T. (1994), 'Punitive Damages and Mass Torts: A Comment', **39** *Villanova Law Review*, 415-431.

Schwarzer, William W. (1995), 'Settlement of Mass Tort Class Actions: Order Out of Chaos', **80** *Cornell Law Review*, 837-844.

Shapiro, David L. (1998), 'Class Actions: The Class as Party and Client', **73** *Notre Dame Law Review*, 913-961.

Sherman, Edward F. (1987), 'Class Actions and Duplicative Litigation', **62** *Indiana Law Journal*, 507–559.

Sherman, Edward F. (1991), 'Aggregate Disposition of Related Cases: The Policy Issues', **10** *Review of Litigation*, 231 272.

Siliciano, John A. (1995), 'Mass Torts and the Rhetoric of Crisis', **80** *Cornell Law Review*, 990-1013.

Silver, Charles (1991a) 'A Restitutionary Theory of Attorney's Fees in Class Actions', **76** *Cornell Law Review*, 656-721.

Silver, Charles (1991b), 'Comparing Class Actions and Consolidations', **10** *Review of Litigation*, 495-520.

Silver, Charles (1992), 'Unloading the Lodestar: Toward a New Fee Award Procedure', **70** *Texas Law Review*, 865-969.

Silver, Charles (1993), 'Incoherence and Irrationality in the Law of Attorneys' Fees', **12** *Review of Litigation*, 301-341.

Silver, Charles and Baker, Lynn A. (1997) 'Mass Lawsuits and the Aggregate Settlement Rule', **32** *Wake Forest Law Review*, 733-780.

Silver, Charles and Baker, Lynn A. (1998), 'I Cut, You Chose: The Role of the Plaintiffs' Attorney in Allocating Settlement Proceeds', **84** *University of Virginia Law Review*, 1465-1540.

Simon, William (1972), 'Class Actions - Useful Tool or Engine of Destruction', **55** *Federal Rules Decisions*, 375–394.

Smith, Thomas A. (1994), 'A Capital Markets Approach to Mass Tort Bankruptcy', **104** *Yale Law Journal*, 367-434.

Solovy, Jerold S., Kaster, Laura A. and Jiganti, Jeanine M. (1990), 'The Head of the Class', *National Law Journal* (August 27), 13.

Spurr, Stephen J. (1988), 'Referral Practices Among Lawyers: A Theoretical and Empirical Analysis', **13** *Journal of Law and Social Inquiry*, 87-109.

Steinman, Joan (1995a), 'The Effects of Case Consolidation on the Procedural Rights of Litigants: What They Are, What They Might Be Part I: Justiciability and Jurisdiction (Original and Appellate)', **42** *University of California at Los Angeles Law Review* (February), 717-836.

Steinman, Joan (1995b), 'The Effects of Case Consolidation on the Procedural Rights of Litigants: What They Are, What They Might Be Part II: Non-Jurisdictional Matters', **42** *University of California at Los Angeles Law Review* (April), 967-1068.

Stiglitz, Joseph E. (1987), 'Principal and Agent', in Eatwell, John, Milgate, Murray and Newman, Peter (eds), *The New Palgrave Dictionary of Economics*, Stockton Press, New York, Vol. 3 pp. 966-972.

Stock, James H. and Wise, David A. (1993), 'Market Compensation in Class Actions Suits: A Summary of Basic Ideas and Results', **16** *Class Action Reports*, 584-604.

Strahan, Philip E. (1998), 'Securities Class Actions, Corporate Governance and Managerial Agency Problems', Federal Reserve Bank of New York, 1-41.

Sugarman, Stephen D. (1985), 'Doing Away with Tort Law', **73** *California Law Review*, 555-664.

Thomas, Randall S. and Hansen, Robert G. (1993), 'Auctioning Class Action and Derivative Lawsuits: A Critical Analysis', **87** *Northwestern University Law Review*, 423-457.

Tidmarsh, Jay (1998), *Mass Tort Settlement Class Actions: Five Cases Studies*, Washington, DC, Federal Judicial Center, 100 p.

Tomkins, Alan J. and Willging, Thomas E. (1986), *Taxation of Attorneys' Fees: Practices in English, Alaskan, and Federal Courts*, Washington, DC, Federal Judicial Center, 145 p.

Trangsrud, Roger H. (1985), 'Joinder Alternatives in Mass Tort Litigation', **70** *Cornell Law Review*, 779-849.

Trangsrud, Roger H. (1989), *'Mass Trials in Mass Tort Cases: A Dissent', **89** University of Illinois Law Review*, 69-88.

Vairo, Georgene M. (1997), 'Georgine, the Dalkon Shield Claimants Trust, and the Rhetoric of Mass Tort Claims Resolution', **31** *Loyola of Los Angeles Law Review*, 79–166.

Weinstein, Jack B. (1985), 'The Role of the Court in Toxic Tort Litigation', **73** *Georgetown Law Journal*, 1389-1392.

Weiss, Elliott J. and Beckerman, John S. (1995), 'Let the Money do the Monitoring: How Institutional Investors can Reduce Agency Costs in Securities Class Actions', **104** *Yale Law Journal*, 2053-2127.

Willging, Thomas E., Hooper, Laural L. and Niemic, Robert J. (1996a), 'An Empirical Analysis of Rule 23 to Address the Rulemaking Challenges', **71** *New York University Law Review* (April-May), 74-185.

Willging, Thomas E., Hooper, Laural L. and Niemic, Robert J. (1996), *Empirical Study of Class Actions in Four Federal District Courts*, Washington, DC, Federal Judicial Center, 200 p.

Wolfman, Brian (1998), 'Forward: The National Association of Consumer Advocates' Standards and Guidelines for Litigating and Settling Class Actions', **176** *Federal Rules Decisions*, 370-374.

Wolfman, Brian and Morrison, Alan B. (1996), 'Representing the Unrepresented in Class Actions Seeking Monetary Relief', **71** *New York University Law Review*, 439-513.

Wolfram, Charles W. (1995), 'Mass Torts - Messy Ethics', **80** *Cornell Law Review*, 1228-1235.

Wood, Diane P. (1987), 'Adjudicatory Jurisdiction and Class Actions', **62** *Indiana Law Journal*, 597-624.

Woolley, Patrick (1997), 'Rethinking the Adequacy of Adequate Representation', **75** *Texas Law Review*, 571-630.

Wright, Gerald A. (1969), 'The Cost-Internalization Case for Class Actions', **21** *Stanford Law Review*, 383-419.

Wright, Scott O. and Colussi, Joseph A. (1984), 'The Successful Use of the Class Action Device in the Management of the *Skywalks* Mass Tort Litigation', **52** *University of Missouri at Kansas City Law Review*, 141–150.

X (1982), 'Conflicts in Class Actions and Protection of Absent Class Members', **91** *Yale Law Journal*, 590-614.

X (1996), 'Back to The Drawing Board: The Settlement Class Action and the Limits of Rule 23', **109** *Harvard Law Review*, 828-845.

X (1996), 'In-Kind Class Action Settlements', **109** *Harvard Law Review*, 810-827.

Yeazell, Stephen C. (1987), *From Medieval Group Litigation to the Modern Class Action*, New Haven, CT, Yale University Press, 306 p.

Yeazell, Stephen C. (1989), 'Collective Litigation as Collective Action', **43** *University of Illinois Law Review*, 43-44.

Yeazell, Stephen C. (1997), 'The Past and Future of Defendant and Settlement Classes in Collective Litigation', **39** *Arizona Law Review*, 687-704.

7700
CRIMINAL PROCEDURE

Peter Lewisch
Professor of Criminal and Constitutional Law
University of Vienna - School of Law

Abstract

This chapter discusses the economic interpretation of pre-trial settlement and in particular of the 'plea-bargain', a procedural instrument aiming at the conservation of enforcement resources and providing a screening device *vis-à-vis* the guilt of possible wrongdoers. In this respect, the paper suggests an institutional comparison with continental legal systems and an analysis of those procedural instruments employed there. Apart from the economic interpretation of pre-trial settlement, the paper presents a more encompassing institutional approach to the criminal procedure covering, inter alia, an economically based interpretation of judicial behavior, evidence, appeals, and also of procedural issues of justice.
JEL classification: K40, K42
Keywords: Plea Bargain, Screening Device, Punishment Dilemma, Context Dependant Choices, Appeals, Economics of Justice

1. Introduction

Criminal procedure is generally understood as that body of law governing the legal treatment of a criminal deed from the offence until an unappealable decision (acquittal or conviction). The thus defined rules describe the process, by which the guilt of a possible wrongdoer may be legitimately established and a criminal sanction attributed. These rules encompass, inter alia, the determination of factual evidence (the facts of the case in the light of a possible responsibility of a wrongdoer), the proper interpretation of the substantive law applicable to this case, and the sentencing decision, which is the determination of the sanction fitting both the crime and the criminal in the light of requirements of deterrence. Since criminal proceedings concern the attribution of a sanction to an alleged wrongdoer, the lawmaker has to cope with two types of errors; namely type one errors, that is to convict the innocent, and type two errors, that is to acquit the guilty. Most of the legal rules concerning due process, evidence, and appeal can be interpreted in the light of this dichotomy, regularly being based in favor of an avoidance of unwarranted convictions.

Boundaries between the 'criminal procedure' and adjacent areas of the criminal law are amorphous: in many legal systems it is substantive, not procedural law that both assigns the right of prosecution, to either the attorney general and/or the infringed individual, and defines requirements of proof. More generally, substantive law defines the elements constituting the crime and thereby what is to be proven (regularly: beyond reasonable doubt) in the criminal proceedings. By her deliberate definition of the crime, the lawmaker, therefore, enjoys considerable discretion in enlarging or reducing the impact and relevance of procedural rules. In this light, one may characterize the Anglo-American law as being more concerned with procedural guaranties than with substantive ones; the latter playing a key role within the continental system (where the principle of nulla poena sine lege is of paramount importance).

Whereas the criminal procedure, almost by definition, presupposes an institutionalized process, by which the responsibility of the alleged wrongdoer is established, many ancient legal systems have lacked the concept both of a public enforcement of criminal deeds and of a regular formalized procedure to be followed when sanctioning. Due to the then existing 'technological' infeasibility of properly determining factual truth (the guilt of a wrongdoer), procedural aspects did not reach beyond a few elementary rules: whereas originally many offences were defined such that hardly any determination of factual truth was required ('Die Tat tötet den Mann' = 'the deed kills the man'), subsequent - still ancient - procedures followed, in their rules on evidence, the so-called 'gebundene Beweiswürdigung' ('fixed rules determining evidence'). Further, (criminal) law was originally enforced primarily or even solely by private individuals. Only in subsequent times, criminal procedure turned to an inquisitorial orientation. The type of criminal procedure now predominantly employed is the result of a relatively short history only, commencing with enlightenment and subsequent refinements during the nineteenth century.

2. The Economic Approach to the Criminal Procedure

The law and economics contributions to the analysis of criminal procedure are highly economic in spirit being predominantly written by economists, not lawyers. Most of the literature focuses on the enforcement decisions taken by the prosecuting authority and, in close relation therewith, on the economics of the plea bargaining system prevailing in the US. These contributions apply standard economic maximization exercises to procedural issues, but are less concerned with an evaluation and comparison of existing and possible alternative procedural rules in their potential to accomplish certain policy goals. This lack of a genuinely institutional concern for procedural issues beyond plea bargaining is characteristic for both American and European contributions with the notable exception of Tullock (1980) who provides a systematic economic treatment of the criminal procedure, covering the investigative part of the procedure, rules of evidence, expertise, and appeal.

Issues also covered in this volume that relate to this chapter are: Civil Procedure: General (7000), Judicial Administration (7100), Settlement (7400), Evidence (7900), the economics of crime and punishment (8000-8600), and the production of legal rules and precedent (9000-9200).

The overview presented in this article covers the focus of the pertinent literature. Therefore, major attention will be attributed to the economics of the plea bargaining system in the US (Section 3). Other issues, among those the role of judges and juries, evidence and appeal, are dealt with in the subsequent part (Section 4) of the chapter.

3. The Law and Economics of the Plea Bargaining System

The economic literature's interest with the criminal procedure is inspired by the basic empirical fact that most criminal cases are not decided in a trial but either dismissed in an early stage or ended by pre-trial settlement. Within this first part of the investigative process, regularly being of inquisitorial nature (see Tullock, 1980, p. 137), a government official (the prosecutor) decides on the pursuit of the case in the light of its 'strength' (primarily in terms of the evidence available) so that the defendant has little opportunity to influence outcomes by investment in defense resources. Prosecutorial decisions and possible pretrial settlements are, however, done 'in the shadow of current court practices' and are, hence, the consequence of (relatively accurate) predictions on the side of the prosecutor as to how courts would decide the case.

General

The plea bargain is the most prominent form of pre-trial settlement: The accused agrees to plead guilty for (a) certain crime(s) in exchange for a penalty that is considerably lower than that to be expected after trial (normally this reduction already stems from the fact that the accused pleads guilty only for a minor offence or for one single offence out of many more charged; say manslaughter instead of murder). The basic institutional feature behind the plea bargaining system is the prosecutor's unlimited legal discretion to acquit a case, to settle it or to bring it to trial (see Landes, 1971; Adelstein, 1978a, 1978b, 1979, 1981b). Whereas the prosecutor is legally unconstrained in his enforcement choices, he is controlled by means of the budget assigned to him. The pertinent literature, therefore, views the prosecutor's decision to enforce the law in a particular case as a maximization activity subject to constraints, namely as one of economizing on resources while aiming, at least in the light of the classic articles, at the maximum degree of overall deterrence. Whereas the mainstream legal interpretation considers the plea bargain as a necessary evil in an overburdened system of criminal law enforcement, prominent law and economics scholars (Landes, 1971; Adelstein, 1981b, and Easterbrook, 1983) suggest an interpretation of the plea bargain as an institutional device congenial for the task of merging the criminal law's ultimate goal, namely that of being a 'pricing device' for crimes, with the scarcity constraint expressed in the limited prosecutorial budget. Since the plea bargain, in any case, requires the consent of the accused, it can, moreover, be conceived as a voluntary transaction, whereby both sides improve their position *vis-à-vis* the status quo; insofar standard settlement theory, as developed in civil procedure, is applicable. If one perceives the criminal procedure as a market system, see Easterbrook (1983), the plea bargain provides a contractual settlement, whereby the parties agree on the price of the offence. Since, moreover, the probability of a conviction in trial depends on the observable strength of the case and not on factual, but unperceivable innocence, even an innocent defendant may rationally accept such bargain, if she is unlikely to prevail in trial.

The law and economics literature does not only analyze the working properties of the plea bargaining system and the influence of certain factors (for example, severity of the crime) on the likelihood of a bargained settlement, but has also suggested to interpret the plea bargaining system as a screening device that allows for a separation of guilty and innocent individuals. Further, the economic contributions are also concerned with a normative evaluation of the plea bargain and with an assessment of possible avenues of its institutional reform.

Details

Most economic contributions interpret the criminal sanction as the 'punishment price' for the criminal act, reflecting the full social cost imposed by these acts. Following this standard economic approach, the optimal price for the offence is defined as the equivalent to the entire harm generated by the offence (see Landes, 1971; Adelstein, 1981b). Both sides, prosecutor and defendant, therefore, orient themselves in their procedural strategies on expected sentences as the (current) prices for the respective crime. Operating under a resource constraint regarding the enforcement and pursuit of criminal cases, they maximize their utility subject to these constraints that exist in terms of their resources (endowments) available. Whereas either side can influence the probability of conviction by resources invested into the case, the plea bargain allows both sides to economize on these resources: The defendant, on the one hand, needs to invest resources for his defense; ultimately, he will expend resources up to the point where marginal benefits equal marginal costs. The prosecutor, on her turn, seeks to maximize the expected number of convictions weighted by their respective sentences, again subject to her budget constraint, in particular Landes (1971) and Easterbrook (1983). The prosecutor, therefore, allocates resources to those cases where outcomes in terms of sentences are more responsive to changes in resources invested and to those where the overall sentence is greater. Provided for the said budget constraint, the prosecutor will dismiss 'weak' cases and try to settle cases by plea bargains in order to free resources that he could then shift to cases that are more promising in terms of expected sentences. On this basis, both sides can improve their situation in relation to their expected trial outcome by the settlement of the criminal case outside of courts. Such a settlement is feasible if a certain penalty acceptable to the defendant exceeds the prosecutor's minimum offer; within this broad bargaining range, the relative strength of the parties will decide upon the negotiated sentence.

Consequences

The just described general framework, in which the plea bargain is primarily seen as a conservation of resource problem, allows for some concrete conclusions with respect to the influence on a bargained outcome of the probability of conviction in trial, the severity of the crime, each side's resources and their productivity, the costs of trial and settlement, and ultimately the attitudes toward risk (see Landes, 1971). First, the higher the stakes (expected penalties) in the criminal case, the less important are the costs of trial, that is, as stakes become higher, ceteris paribus, settlements become more difficult. A settlement is, therefore, more probable, the smaller is the sentence in case of a conviction at trial and the more substantial trial costs are *vis-à-vis* those at a settlement. Second, under the assumption that both prosecutor and defendant hold identical views on the expected outcome of a trial, only risklovers would opt for trial (this result is further increased if the defendant's estimates of the probability of conviction exceed the prosecutor's). Third, the more expensive a trial is, the more attractive becomes the plea bargain (that is, the more resources a settlement saves, the more likely is its occurrence). An increase in the defendant's wealth (see Landes, 1971; see also Kobayashi and Lott, 1996), would also increase resources spent on her defense, reducing thus the probability of conviction, so that, regarding plea bargains, a lower negotiated sentence would be predicted; in the special case of risk neutrality the wealthy defendant's choice will depend on whether she expects the penalty to be a jail sentence (then: greater investments) or a money fine (then: smaller investments). Regarding the impact of the bail system, those defendants detained during trial are burdened with increased costs of defense so that they face a higher conviction probability in trial and a longer sentence in a settlement, respectively. The thus increased opportunity costs of trial would also lead to an increased settlement rate of detained defendants.

Empirical Results

Apart from its theoretical analysis, the Landes paper has sparked a series of empirical research both on an individual and the aggregated level, whose results, albeit in the overall consistent with the above mentioned theoretical claims, are not fully conclusive. Landes' own work (see Landes, 1971), showed that a reduction in the differential between trial costs and settlement costs would yield a higher number of trials. The assumption that higher resource costs of a trial would generate more plea bargains (the propensity to stand trial is higher for defendants released on bail) was only weakly confirmed. Subsequent work by Rhodes (1976), devoting attention to the aggregated level, found that both higher penalty offers in the bargaining process and higher defense resource expenditures increase the likelihood of a trial. Similar research by Weimer (1978) confirmed these results. Focusing on the duration of the prosecutorial pursuit of a case, Forst and Brosi (1977) confirmed the (quite apparent) claim that the 'strength of the case' in terms of the evidence against the defendant determines the prosecutor's attitude towards trial (but did not confirm the authors' - theoretically inconclusive - claim that prosecutors would direct their resources towards the prosecution of defendants with extensive arrest records). Elder (1989) could show that those factors that reduce the parties' disagreement on the estimated outcome, increase settlement (in particular, estimates on the 'strength of the case'). Further, increases in the stakes of the case enhance the likelihood of trial. In contrast, personal characteristics (sex, drug abuse, and so on, except for race) do not significantly affect the settlement decision. Elder's study, moreover, could not confirm the influence of bail and of a publicly provided defense counsel on the likelihood of trial.

Plea Bargaining as a Screening Device

An influential economic interpretation of the plea bargaining system beyond that of economizing on resources has been advanced by Grossmann and Katz (1983). The authors propose to view the plea bargaining process as a screening device that separates between innocent and guilty defendants (their further suggestion to view the plea bargain as an insurance device that reduces the scope of errors which would cause greater harm when regular trials are conducted is not deepened here): under the assumption of asymmetric information with respect to actual guilt (the accused is assumed to be systematically better informed than the prosecutor), the plea bargaining system generates a process of self selection of the truly guilty.

In the world of this model, all defendants are initially assumed equally risk averse irrespective of their factual guilt. Prosecutors are unable to identify beforehand actual guilt, but may estimate the percentage of actual guilty individuals among the accused. In such a world, the optimal plea bargain will always induce the truly guilty to accept the prosecutor's offer: Defendants self select such that only the innocent will choose trial whereas guilty defendants reveal their guilt by acceptance of the plea offer. Results change, however, if defendants exhibit different degrees of risk aversion: risk-averse innocent defendants may still improve their position by accepting the plea offer in comparison to a regular trial so that for them the possibility of pre-trial settlement is still attractive. Since these highly risk-averse innocent defendants would not exhibit any behavioral difference to a less risk-averse guilty defendant, both types of defendants would accept the same plea offer. Therefore, if defendants are not equally risk averse, the above described screening property is reduced.

In a variant of this approach, Reinganum (1988) examines plea bargains with particular emphasis on asymmetric information regarding the 'strength of the case' in terms of the likelihood of conviction. This analysis yields the result that sufficiently weak cases are dismissed not in consideration of resource costs, but of type one and type two error costs. Those cases not dismissed, however, exhibit a higher likelihood of a negotiated guilty plea, the weaker their 'relative strength' is. Similarly to the Grossmann and Katz model, also this variant predicts a screening outcome in the sense that (when prosecutor types pool) the defendants separate such that only the guilty accept the plea and only the innocent stand trial. Further, since the strength of a case reflects in the sentence offered in a guilty plea and defendants are more likely to reject higher sentence offers, the likelihood of a trial in fact increases with the strength of the case.

If, hence, innocent defendants are, as it appears to be empirically the case, more risk averse than guilty defendants, this screening effect will disappear: Innocent defendants may incorrectly plead guilty only for the sake of avoiding the uncertain penalty pending from trial. It is here where the contribution by Kobayashi and Lott (1996) comes in: the authors demonstrate that the systematic disparity in criminal defence expenditures existing between guilty and innocent defendants allows for a preservation of efficient screening. Analogizing the procedure to a two-stage contest, the authors show that both defense and prosecution expenditures depend on the strength of the defendant's case. Since innocent defendants enjoy lower defense expenditures, they are less likely to falsely plead guilty in order to avoid trial. It is this mechanism that enlarges the range in which efficient sorting is preserved.

Normative Evaluation of the Plea Bargain

Economic contributions on the criminal procedure, starting with Landes, have emphasized the linkage of the plea bargaining system with the criminal law's overall pricing structure. Subsequent contributions have generated both critique and refinements of the original Landes paper and have sparked a more general discussion of the value, strengths, shortcomings, and the specific institutional framework of the plea bargain, and of possible avenues of reform.

Easterbrook (1983) has suggested refinements of the Landes paper by proposing to view the criminal procedure as a 'market system' constituted by an institutional framework whose essential elements are prosecutorial (and sentencing) discretion and plea bargaining. Following the original Landes position Easterbrook interprets prosecutorial behavior as a maximization activity (ultimately aimed at maximizing the 'deterrent punch' out of those resources committed to crime prevention), whereby the prosecutor, in her specific situation, equalizes marginal returns from resources spent in the prosecution of a variety of individual cases. The 'mix' of resource inputs into these cases is not determined in abstracto, but depends on current rates of apprehension, the frequency of certain offences and of the respective probabilities of conviction. Changes in this factors influence, therefore, the allocation of prosecutorial resources. The plea bargain is congenial to this system, since it facilitates the market like determination and imposition of the current 'price of the crime'. On the one hand, the plea bargaining system is thus flexible enough for quick adjustments to changing conditions in terms of current penalty prices. On the other hand, it constitutes a necessary element in the attempt to maximize deterrence out of a given prosecutorial budget. In this view the plea bargain is even superior to the regular trial, since the plea bargain reflects the probabilities case by case and allows for rapid adjustments as conditions determining the price (for example, frequences of offense) change. The discretion in the criminal procedure, in particular by means of a plea bargain, allows the system to produce deterrence with a minimum of allocative inefficiency.

This view, inspired by a 'market-oriented' general background, has, however become in itself the subject of economically inspired criticism (Schulhofer, 1988). On the one hand, Schulhofer challenges the radical skepticism about the truth value of trials arguing that the proper institutional role of trials within the system of the administration of justice is not to merely distribute acquittals and convictions according to expected probabilities of conviction, but to reveal factual truth; it is this factual accuracy that represents an important factor in the overall administration of the criminal justice system. On the other hand, the criminal procedure in itself is not a market system, but a 'political system'. Framed as a principal-agent problem, this critique is twofold: most importantly the plea bargaining system allows the prosecutors to use and misuse their prosecutorial discretion in many ways, and the pursuit of their self interest will only rarely harmonize with the public interest irrespective of how this public interest is defined. A certain diversity of incentives with respect to the attractiveness of plea bargain deals also holds true with respect to the defendant's side: the basic reason for this diversity of interests between the defendant himself and her defense counsel is the fee structure in the US, whereby most defense lawyers work for a fee below market rates and, hence, have a clear selective interest to finish the case earlier rather then later. They will favor a plea bargain. The said critique also affects the fairness properties of plea bargains in general: to be sure, any concluded bargain makes at least one party to the deal better off without harming the position of the other party; otherwise the parties would not have agreed. If we, however, acknowledge a principal-agent problem on the side of the prosecutor (law enforcement as a public good being entrusted to some agency) and a comparable misrepresentation in the defense lawyer-client relation, it becomes less obvious whether those deals concluded by the agents are always in the true interests of their principals. The scope by which this principal-agent problem actually plagues the fairness of concluded plea bargains remains an empirical question though.

A more institution-oriented and still highly economic interpretation of the plea bargaining system has been advanced by Adelstein (1981b). Since the precise determination of the 'punishment price' (direct material and moral cost of crime), as performed in the criminal procedure, is in itself costly, the cost of this price exaction, in an economic perspective, should be smaller than the crime's social cost: it is pre-trial settlement, as exemplified in the plea bargain, that constitutes a device for steady innovations in reducing these procedural costs. Seen as a process of continuous adaptations and modifications on punishment prices, the plea bargaining system also allows for a more sophisticated - and more institution oriented - treatment of prosecutorial behavior than under the 'penalty maximizing' position advanced by Landes: under the US system, the prosecutor is not an authority entrusted with the goal of maximizing penalties, but with that of promoting justice in terms of penalties that fit the crime. Moreover, the Landes approach tacitly assumes that the prosecutor considers all defendants guilty (or, at least, that the prosecutor is uninterested in the defendants' actual guilt). Since prosecutors are legally bound to pursue criminal cases such that only guilty individuals are sentenced with a due penalty, the prosecutorial behavior is likely to differ from a simple maximization of output in terms of years sentenced, but to follow the more complex mechanism of steady adaptations described above.

Institutional Comparison

The economically inspired skepticism towards the American system of the plea bargain does not amount to a general critique of all settlement institutions. Whereas this critique acknowledges the necessity of some such settlement procedure in the light of the costliness of full-scale criminal proceedings, it argues for a systematic reconsideration of all of its institutional details in order to identify the potential of institutional improvement. Such an analysis, in particular the contribution by Adelstein on the comparison to the British settlement system and that by Alschuler (1983), suggests that the current

American system of plea bargains may be suboptimal and that various ways of improvement of the institutional status quo exist.

Apart from Adelstein's (1981b) insightful comparison between the American plea bargain and its English equivalent, Alschuler (1983) and Schulhofer (1988) have discussed similarities and differences between the American and the European continental, in particular German, system. Their contributions have, inter alia, emphasized the variety of legal institutions which would allow for a more subtle way of settling those cases that do not deserve a full and costly trial and the actual existence of these institutions even under the continental system that, in principle, is characterized by a strict principle of legality regarding prosecutorial enforcement. Despite the existence of some such comparative research, much more remains to be done. Insofar as these settlement devices involve savings in resources, one has, however, to be aware of the fact that these savings exist (only) in the prosecutor's time and trouble costs, since under the continental system the prosecutor is not endowed with a budget to be invested at his sole discretion.

There are in particular two avenues for further research: hardly any systematic studies exist with respect to various informal ways of settlements under the continental system; not the least because of a lack of official data. Apart from those settlement institutions that are formalized parts of the regular legal system (for example, 'diversion'), other ('grey') variants of settlement only exist in the shadow of the law. Due to the different institutional framework of the continental system, in which the prosecutor is obligated to enforce the law, such 'negotiated penalties' are usually performed under inclusion of the judges in regular trials, that is, by an explicit or tacit agreement of all parties involved regarding the negotiated outcome of the trial. The systematic economic treatment of such behavior has to be developed under the rigorous assumption of self-interested motivation by all parties involved, that is, by the judge, the prosecutor, the defendant and his lawyer. Viewed thus it becomes apparent that as long as expectations regarding the expected outcome of the trial overlap, a 'negotiated' outcome should be in the self-interest of each party involved: in such a case the judge does not run the risk of reversal in the instance, the prosecutor may grant a discount due to the confession and yet remain within the limits of the agency's policy of treating like offences alike, and the defendant may obtain a favorable treatment. Since the system would suffer from cheating on the previously agreed upon sanction (say, the judge returns a penalty harsher than that negotiated or the attorney files an appeal despite his prior agreement to the sanction), it requires, for perfect functioning, repeated games with identical players. These conditions are perfectly met, for example, at the Viennese criminal court, where a few specialized lawyers deal with specialized judges and prosecutors. In the shadow of the law, most trials at this Court are in fact negotiated prior to their commencement.

Little attention has been devoted to the relation of settlement procedures to substantive law. Under the continental system, the principle of strict enforcement does not allow the prosecutor to leave certain offences or (sub)groups of offences unforced. Therefore, the 'political decision' to decriminalize certain offenses, has to be taken by the legislator, not the judiciary (closer observation, however, reveals that even the continental system is open to some such adaptation by the law enforcing institutions). In contrast, under the Anglo-American system, the prosecutor may refrain, by his deliberate choice, from enforcing offences, so that the respective behavior is effectively decriminalized. The prosecutors' deliberate enforcement policy may render a whole set of offences practically obsolete. Within the Anglo-American world, criminal offences, as they exist on paper, may, therefore, be radically different from those actually enforced (this is the case for example regarding sexual offences). These alternative systems (and, inter alia, the institutional fact that under the continental system neither prosecutors nor judges are elected) require careful examination in an economic and in particular public choice perspective.

4. Courts and Judges

The Punishment Dilemma

Under most procedural systems, courts (judges and/or juries) decide on the defendant's guilt and determine the penalty. It is these individuals (professional judges and jurors) who carry out the punishment task. To the extent that such meting out of a penalty is not only experienced as a 'good' (say, by deriving some utility from the satisfaction of retributory concepts of punishment), but rather an 'intrinsic bad' (intrinsic disutility of inflicting harm on someone), the 'punishment dilemma' arises if punishment is seen solely in a response setting (Buchanan, 1975). In her sentencing behavior, the individual encharged with the punishment task will seek to avoid or reduce the intrinsic disutility of punishment that - in this *ex post* perspective - appears as the arbitrary infliction of harm: whereas the public good of law compliance by deterrence can only be secured by this infliction of punishment *ex post*, the temptation to punish too leniently in relation to that level of punishment chosen under a 'constitutional' perspective is always likely to prevail in a response setting.

The very existence of the above described punishment dilemma has consequences both for the individual punishment decision and for the institutional choice of punishment institutions (Buchanan, 1975; Lewisch, 1995, 1997). First, as regards the individual's punishment decision, the individual judge will weigh the costs and benefits of punishment according to her own perspective, that is, according to her discounting rate. Although hard facts are missing, empirical observations seem to suggest that the discounting rate of lay judges, who are not professionally trained in considering the long-term deterrent effects of punishment on law compliance, expresses rather current motivations and drives, so that lay judges tend to punish more leniently than their professional peers on the bench (the precise determination of the juries' sentencing behavior, depends, however, on the relation of the punishment dilemma to possible retributive concerns). This perspective also explains why jurors seek to avoid returning a penalty that they consider excessively harsh and prosecutors, aware of this fact, may reduce charges to increase the likelihood of a verdict, preferring a less severe charge with high likelihood of success over a more severe charge that is unlikely to be sentenced. Second, regarding institutional choice, the community would be unable to deter potential criminals if it confines itself, in its punishment institutions, to the response of violations of law, once committed: unduly light punishment would result. Punishment institutions, therefore, must be chosen strategically on the constitutional level (Buchanan, 1975). In particular, taking account of the above dilemma, the seemingly puzzling institutional feature to assign those individuals in a society with the punishment tasks (that is, professional judges) who, in their sentencing behavior, are harsher than the average man in the street, is economically sound.

Apart from the punishment dilemma, the selection and the sentencing behavior of juries has only partially attracted attention. Regarding jury conscription, both the criteria and procedures employed for the selection process are the object of economic interest ('keyman-suggestion versus random selection'). In a particularly economic contribution, Martin (1972) has studied the welfare effects of the jury system that does not pay conscripts according to their opportunity income, analogizing the economic working properties of the respective institutional arrangement to that of army conscription (see also Bowles, 1980). The decision-making mechanism of the jury under alternative voting rules (unanimity and supermajority rules) has, however, not been examined by the published law and economics literature (pertinent working papers are in circulation though). An analytical comparison of legal choices made by single judges and penals has been provided, with reference to work by Condorcet, by the literature on civil procedure (see Schäfer, 1998); particular contributions on the criminal justice system are lacking. For an overview of the use of lay judges in Germany, see Casper and Zeisel (1972).

Context Dependent Choices

Choices by jurors have found increasing attention by the economically inspired psychological literature (see Kelman, Rottenstreich and Tversky, 1996). This literature investigates, notably by means of experiments, to what extent legal evaluations and choices depend on the set of available judgements. Experiments show that generally observed 'violations' of context-independent choices are also present in the realm of judicial choices: experimental data confirm that choices made by jurors exhibit both compromise effects (the same option is evaluated more favorably when seen as an intermediate within the array of options) and contrast effects (an option is evaluated more favorably in the presence of similar options clearly inferior to it than in the absence of such options). In this light, choices by jurors depend, for example, on whether the available options comprise only manslaughter and murder or manslaughter, (regular) murder, and murder under special circumstances. These findings also suggest, as another example of the close linkage of substantive and procedural aspects of criminal law, that a legislative 'splitting up' of a crime in distinguishable new categories alters choice behavior by judges regarding previous categories.

5. Evidence

Regarding evidence, also on issues of standard of proof and burden of proof, see the contribution by Parker and Kobayashi (in this volume Chapter 7900).

With respect to an analysis of specific procedural rules on evidence, it should be emphasized, however, that rules of evidence are not identical for civil and criminal proceedings in most (not all, so the notable exception of the US) legal systems. Differences stem from the more restrictive use of 'suspect' evidence in criminal cases (as embodied in the respective constitutional rights/amendments), which, albeit only partially, can be explained on grounds of the increased costliness of type one errors in criminal than in civil cases.

Economically inspired literature on the subject is not abundant: Tullock (1980, p. 148) suggests an economic categorization of rules of evidence in criminal proceedings (see Chapter 7900). The thus proposed distinction identifies separate categories of 'outlawed' evidence: one group of rules aims at reducing error costs by prohibiting evidence that, being of poor quality, is likely to mislead the court (for example, hearsay or the use of the lie detector). In an economic evaluation, Tullock suggests, however, to admit this 'poor evidence' to the trial, but to give it the appropriate (low) weight. A second category of rules seeks to reduce direct costs of the proceedings, in particular those in terms of wasting the court's time (for example, rules allowing to exclude not-relevant evidence). Category 3 contains rules that serve specific purposes extraneous to the proceedings, for example, the prohibition of torture, the unjustified opening of letters, the unlawful seizure of evidence, or the violation of evidentiary privileges.

Regarding this third category, rules of evidence are used to enforce other parts of the law. The justification for such an exclusion and its legitimate scope are, however, disputed even within the law and economics literature. On the one hand, one may argue, as Tullock (1980), that, if both the judicial and police system are unable to sufficiently enforce the pertinent substantive rules (that is, those protecting the outside interest), some such exclusionary evidence rule can be argued for in an economic perspective. On the other hand, one may favor a strict distinction between the proper enforcement of the respective substantive rules and the usage of evidence gained in violation of these rules. In this respect, Posner (1982) considers excessive the exclusion of evidence in a criminal trial seized in violation of the Fourth Amendment (which forbids unreasonable searches and seizures): the costs of exclusion of the thus acquired evidence (in terms of the inability to obtain a conviction on this basis) is likely to exceed the social (in this view of Posner: often negligible) costs of misconduct. According to Posner, the respective exclusionary rules can only be explained on the basis of the 'technological' infeasibility of earlier times to properly enforce regulations on searches and seizures. In our times, these (in earlier days infeasible) tort sanctions are available, and their usage would suffice to deter violations. In the example of an unauthorized search in the defendant's home, Posner proposes to confine 'legal sanctions' to a tort remedy aimed at recovering the clean up costs of the apartment. In turn, wherever the illegally gathered evidence was not only unlawfully collected, but is in itself unreliable (such as coerced confessions and involuntary guilty pleas), a ban on its use in criminal trials is economically sound. For a well informed criticism of Posner's interpretation of exclusionary rules as an excessive sanction for governmental misconduct, see Morris (1982).

6. Arrest, Bail, and Sentencing Behavior

On arrest and bail, see Landes (1974), Myers (1981), on issues of court delay Levin (1975), on the statistical analysis of courts' sentencing behavior Tiffany, Avichai and Peters (1975).

7. Appeals

Neither the institution of appeals in the criminal proceedings as such nor specific technical procedural issues have been thoroughly discussed from an economic standpoint. We may refer, however, to the general economic analysis of appeals, as developed in civil proceedings, notably by Tullock (1980, p. 162) and Shavell (1995): when designing a court system with the task of minimizing trial costs plus expected error costs, choice has to be made between investments in the reliability of courts of first instance (by investing resources in, say, the education of trial court judges or the usage of panels) and/or by investments in the accuracy of the appeals courts. Policy choices are regularly a mix between investments on both levels of adjudication. An economic explanation for the use of a second instance is that, whereas costs in the first instance are to be borne in every legal case, the costs of appeal only materialize if an appeal is actually filed: this will only be done by those disappointed litigants who consider such an appeal cost-justified, leading thereby to a separation within disappointed litigants. The specific institutional mix of courts of first instance and of courts of appeal in criminal cases is due to the predominant concern of avoiding type one errors. For the task of correctly determining the facts of the case relatively more resources are invested in courts of first instance than in civil cases. Accordingly, since courts of appeal are unlikely to possess superior knowledge regarding fact finding, errors of fact are largely excluded from revision in the appeal's process (the opposite generally hold true where the collection of evidence is performed on a less rigorous basis at first instance, as is the case for petty offences). Even the increased accuracy of the trial proceeding, however, cannot fully substitute for the use of the appeal's process which is more focused on error of law. Whereas the appeal's process is entrusted, in civil cases, solely to disappointed litigants, the characteristics of the criminal law suggest a review of court rulings of first instance also on a more objectivized ('ex offo') basis allowing the courts of instance to review (some) legal mistakes even if they have not been brought up by either side (defendant or prosecutor) in their court motions. The respective institutional arrangements can regularly be observed in various national procedural rules.

The regular exclusion of interrogatory appeals in criminal procedure can be explained in the light of the argument by Shavell (1995) that violations of procedural rules, in particular with respect to the gathering of evidence, can best be considered on the basis of the final judgement. If court rulings prior to the final judgement, however, impose particular costs on the defendant, as is the case with arrest, and warrants of arrest, appeals against these court orders are regularly admitted. Insofar as the avoidance of legal mistakes and harmonization of the law within a jurisdiction is concerned, again criminal proceedings differ from civil proceedings: whereas in civil cases, any correction of a judgment, once unappealable, imposes high costs on the prevailing party trusting the validity of the final court judgment, in criminal cases a particular interest exists in finding the accurate judgement. It follows that judicial review of sentences is facilitated in criminal cases even if (already) unappealable; in particular for the sake of eliminating type one errors.

8. Criminal Procedure and the Economics of Justice

Economic theories of justice, in particular contractarian contributions (Rawls, 1971; Brennan and Buchanan, 1985), propose to frame the normative discussion regarding the fairness of legal (and also procedural) rules by means of the 'veil of ignorance' experiment. If individuals are put behind a veil of ignorance thick enough to screen out all their distinctive properties and features in real life, so that they are unable to identify how their own position will be affected by the rules contemplated, they will opt, based on their own self interest, for rules that can be considered 'fair'. Whereas the veil as such is only an analytical device, the mechanism behind it may be mimicked in real life when the choice setting for institutional choices is designed such that the principles of generality and extended time dimension are observed. If an individual is likely to assume all feasible positions under a legal rule (today she is plaintiff, tomorrow defendant), there is no room for biased choices; hence the individual will design rules, again based on her own interest in a non-discriminatory manner. In the light of this analytical framework, it is possible to evaluate the fairness properties of procedural rules. Similarly to a comparable exercise undertaken for civil procedural law (see Lewisch, 1998), the normative requirements for a just ('fair') criminal procedure, as is enshrined in Article 6 of the European Convention on Human Rights, can be derived from a veil perspective. Research specifically devoted to criminal procedure is, however, necessary.

Bibliography on Criminal Procedure (7700)

Adelstein, Richard P. (1978a), 'The Plea Bargain in Theory: A Behavioral Model of the Negotiated Guilty Plea', **44** *Southern Economic Journal*, 488-503.

Adelstein, Richard P. (1978b), 'The Negotiated Guilty Plea: A Framework for Analysis', **53** *New York University Law Review*, 783-833.

Adelstein, Richard P. (1979), 'Informational Paradox and the Pricing of Crime: Capital Sentencing Standards in Economic Perspective', **70** *Journal of Criminal Law and Criminology*, 281-298.

Adelstein, Richard P. (1981a), 'Institutional Function and Evolution in the Criminal Process', **76** *Northwestern University Law Review*, 1-99.

Adelstein, Richard P. (1981b), 'The Plea Bargain in England and America: A Comparative Institutional View', in Burrows, Paul and Veljanovski, Cento G. (eds), *The Economic Approach to Law*, London, Butterworths, 226-252.

Aghion, Philippe, Hart, Oliver D. and Moore, John (1992), 'The Economics of Bankruptcy Reform', **8** *Journal of Law, Economics, and Organization*, 523-546.

Alschuler, Albert W. (1968), 'The Prosecutor's Role in Plea Bargaining', **36** *University of Chicago Law Review*, 50-112.

Alschuler, Albert W. (1983), 'Implementing the Criminal Defendant's Right to Trial: Alternatives to the Plea Bargaining System', **50** *University of Chicago Law Review*, 931-1050.

Bebchuk, Lucian Arye and Chang, Howard F. (1992), 'Bargaining and the Division of Value in Corporate Reorganization', **8** *Journal of Law, Economics, and Organization*, 253-279.

Becker, Gary S. (1968), 'Crime and Punishment: An Economic Approach', **76** *Journal of Political Economy*, 169-217.

Boari, Nicola (1997), 'On the Efficiency of Penal Systems: Several Lessons from the Italian Experience', **17** *International Review of Law and Economics*, 115-126.

Bowles, Roger A. (1980), 'Juries, Incentives and Self-Selection', **20** *British Journal of Criminology*, 368-376.

Brennan, Geoffrey and Buchanan, James M. (1985), *The Reason of Rules - Constitutional Political Economy*, Cambridge, Cambridge University Press.

Buchanan, James M. (1975), *The Limits of Liberty: Between Anarchy and Leviathan*, Miami.

Casper, Gerhard and Zeisel, Hans (1972), 'Lay Judges in the German Criminal Courts', **1** *Journal of Legal Studies*, 135-191.

Chu, C.Y. Cyrus (1991), 'An Economic Analysis of the Criminal Proceedings in Civil Law Countries', **11(1)** *International Review of Law and Economics*, 111-116.

Easterbrook, Frank H. (1983), 'Criminal Procedure as a Market System', **12** *Journal of Legal Studies*, 289-332.

Elder, Harold W. (1987), 'Property Rights Structures and Criminal Courts: An Analysis of State Criminal Courts', **7** *International Review of Law and Economics*, 21-32.

Elder, Harold W. (1989), 'Trials and Settlements in the Criminal Courts: An Empirical Analysis of Dispositions and Sentencing', **18** *Journal of Legal Studies*, 191-208.

Forst, Brian and Brosi, Kathleen B. (1977), 'A Theoretical and Empirical Analysis of the Prosecutor', **6** *Journal of Legal Studies*, 177-191.

Froeb, Luke M. (1990), 'The Adverse Seletion of Cases for Trial', **13** *International Review of Law and Economics*, 317-324.

Gentry, James Theodore (1986), 'The Panopticon Revisited: The Problem of Monitoring Private Prisons', **96** *Yale Law Journal*, 353-375.

Gould, John P. (1971), 'The Economics of Legal Conflicts', **2** *Journal of Legal Studies*, 279-300.

Grossman, Gene M. and Katz, Michael L. (1983), 'Plea Bargaining and Social Welfare', **73** *American Economic Review*, 749-757.

Kaplow, Louis (1994), 'The Value of Accuracy in Adjudication: An Economic Analysis', **23** *Journal of Legal Studies*, 307-401.

Kaplow, Louis and Shavell, Steven (1994), 'Accuracy in the Determination of Liability', **37** *Journal of Law and Economics*, 1-15.

Katz, Avery (1988), 'Judicial Decisionmaking and Litigation Expenditure', **8** *International Review of Law and Economics*, 124-143.

Kelman, Mark G., Rottenstreich Yuval and Tversky, Amos (1996), 'Context-Dependence in Legal Decision Making', **25** *Journal of Legal Studies*, 287-318.

Kobayashi, Bruce H. (1992), 'Deterrence with Multiple Defendants: An Explanation for "Unfair" Plea Bargains', **23** *Rand Journal of Economics*, 507-517.

Kobayashi, Bruce H. and Lott, John R., Jr (1992), 'Low Probability-High Penalty Enforcement Strategies and the Efficient Operation of the Plea Bargaining System', **12** *International Review of Law and Economics*, 69-77.

Kobayashi, Bruce H. and Lott, J.R., Jr (1996), 'In Defense of Criminal Defense Expenditures and Plea Bargaining', **16** *International Review of Law and Economics*, 397-415.

Landes, William M. (1971), 'An Economic Analysis of the Courts', **14** *Journal of Law and Economics*, 61-108.

Landes, William M. (1974), 'Legality and Reality: Some Evidence on Criminal Procedure', **3** *Journal of Legal Studies*, 287-337.

Langbein, John H. (1978), 'Torture and Plea Bargaining', **46** *University of Chicago Law Review*, 3-22.

Leder, Mathias (1996), 'Kommentar zu "Plea-bargaining - der Deal im Strafprozeß" von Claus Ott/Hans-Bernd Schäfer (Comment on Claus Ott/Hans-Bernd Schäfer, Plea-bargaining - the "deal" in criminal proceedings)', **15** *Jahrbuch für Neue Politische Ökonomie*, 132-134.

Levin, Martin A. (1975), 'Delay in Five Criminal Courts', **4** *Journal of Legal Studies*, 83-131.

Lewisch, Peter (1992), 'A Case Study on the Legal Regulation of Shoplifting in Austria and the "Criminal Tourism" from the East', **12** *International Review of Law and Economics*, 439-455.

Lewisch, Peter (1995), *Punishment, Public Enforcement and the Protective State*, Wien, New York, Springer.

Lewisch, Peter (1997), 'Doorkeepers of Justice? The Legal Services of Judges and Lawyers in an Economic Perspective', **18** *Rechtstheorie*, 1-11.

Lewisch, Peter (1998), 'Ökonomische Analyse des Zivilprozesses (Economic Analysis of Civil Procedure)', in Mayr, Peter (ed), *100 Jahre österreichische Zivilprozessgesetze*, 155-178.

Lott, J.R., Jr (1987), 'Should the Wealthy be Able to "Buy Justice"?', **95** *Journal of Political Economy*, 1307-1316.

Martin, Donald L. (1972), 'The Economics of Jury Conscription', **80** *Journal of Political Economy*, 680-702.

Miceli, Thomas J. (1990), 'Optimal Prosecution of Defendants Whose Guilt is Uncertain', **6** *Journal of Law, Economics, and Organization*, 189-201.

Miceli, Thomas J. (1991), 'Optimal Criminal Procedure: Fairness and Deterrence', **11** *International Review of Law and Economics*, 3-10.

Morris, Arval A. (1982), 'The Exclusionary Rule, Deterrence and Posner's Economic Analysis of Law', **57** *Washington Law Review*, 647-667.

Myers, Samuel L., Jr (1981), 'The Economies of Bail Jumping', **10** *Journal of Legal Studies*, 381-392.

Noam, Eli M. (1981), 'A Cost-benefit Model of Criminal Courts', **3** *Research in Law and Economics*, 173-183.

Ott, Claus and Schäfer, Hans-Bernd (1996), '"Plea-Bargaining", der "Deal" im Strafprozeß (Plea-Bargaining)', in Schenk, Karl-Ernst, Schmidtchen, Dieter and Streit, Manfred E. (eds), *Vom Hoheitsstaat zum Konsensualstaat, Neue Formen der Kooperation zwischen Staat und Privaten Jahrbuch für Neue Politische Ökonomie 15*, Tübingen, Mohr, 107-126.

Palmer, John P. (1984), 'An Economic Analysis of the Right to a Jury Trial', **4** *International Review of Law and Economics*, 29-53.

Parker, Jeffrey S. and Kobayashi, Bruce H. (1999), 'Evidence' , in Bouckaert, B. and De Geest, G. (eds), *Encyclopedia of Law and Economics*, Aldershot, Edward Elgar.

Pastor, Santos (1990), 'Economia de la Justicia (I) y (II) (Economics of the Judicature)', **5-6** *Revista de Economía Pública*.

Pastor, Santos (1991), 'Informe Sobre la Litigación, Recursos y Acceso de los Cuidadanos a la Justicie (Report on Litigation, Courts Inputs and Access to Justice)', in Ministerio De Justicia (ed), *Materiales Para una Reforma Procesal*, Madrid.

Phillips, Llad (1981), 'The Criminal Justice System: Its Technology and Inefficiencies', **10** *Journal of Legal Studies*, 363-380.

Polinsky, A. Mitchell and Shavell, Steven (1979), 'The Optimal Tradeoff between the Probability and Magnitude of Fines', **69** *American Economic Review*, 880-891.

Polinsky, A. Mitchell and Shavell, Steven (1984), 'The Optimal Use of Fines and Imprisonment', **24** *Journal of Public Economics*, 89-99.

Posner Richard A. (1973), 'An Economic Approach to Legal Procedure and Judicial Administration', **2** *Journal of Legal Studies*, 399-458.

Posner, Richard A. (1982), 'Excessive Sanctions for Governmental Misconduct in Criminal Cases' (transcript)', **57** *Washington Law Review*, 635-646.

Rawls, John (1971), *A Theory of Justice*, Cambridge, Cambridge University Press.

Reinganum, Jennifer F. (1988), 'Plea Bargaining and Prosecutorial Discretion', **78** *American Economic Review*, 713-728.

Rhodes, William M. (1976), 'The Economics of Criminal Courts: A Theoretical and Empirical Investigation', **5** *Journal of Legal Studies*, 311-340.

Rhodes, William M. (1977), 'A Study of Sentencing in the Hennepin County and Ramsey County District Courts', **6** *Journal of Legal Studies*, 333-353.

Rubinfeld, Daniel L. and Sappington, David E.M. (1987), 'Efficient Awards and Standards of Proof in Judicial Proceedings', **18** *Rand Journal of Economics*, 303-318.

Schäfer, Hans-Bernd (1998), 'Kein Geld für die Justiz - Was ist uns der Rechtsfrieden wert? (No Money for the Courts - How much Do We Value "Rechtsfrieden")', in Bundesministerium für Justiz, Lewisch, Peter and Rechberger Walter (eds), *100 Jahre ZPO - Ökonomische Analyse des Zivilprozesses (100 Years Civil Procedural Code - Economic Analysis of the Civil Procedure*, 251-274.

Schrag, Joel and Scotchmer, Suzanne (1994), 'Crime and Prejudice: The Use of Character Evidence in Criminal Trials', **10** *Journal of Law, Economics, and Organization*, 319-342.

Schulhofer, Stephen J. (1988), 'Criminal Justice Discretion as a Regulatory System', **17** *Journal of Legal Studies*, 43-82.

Shavell Steven (1995), 'The Appeals Process as a Means of Error Correction', **24** *Journal of Legal Studies*, 379-426.

Steenhuis, D.W. (1984), 'Strafrechtelijk Optreden: Stapje Terug en een Sprong Voorwaarts (Criminal Policy: A Step Backwards and a Jump Ahead)', in X (ed), *Delikt en Delinkwent*, Arnhem, Gouda Quint, 4-5.

Stuntz, William J. (1991), 'Warrants and Fourth Amendment Remedies', **77** *Virginia Law Review*, 881-943.

Tiffany, Lawrence P., Avichai, Yakov and Peters, Geoffrey W. (1975), 'A Statistical Analysis of Sentencing in Federal Courts: Defendants Convicted After Trial, 1967-1968', **4** *Journal of Legal Studies*, 369-390.

Tullock, Gordon (1980), *Trials on Trial: The Pure Theory of Legal Procedure*, New York, Columbia University Press.

Veljanovski, Cento G. (1986), 'The Economics of Criminal Law and Procedure', **23** *Coexistence*, 137-153.

Weimer, David L. (1978), 'Plea Bargaining and the Decision to go to Trial: The Application of a Rational Choice Model', **10** *Policy Sciences*, 124 ff.

White, Michelle J. (1994), 'Corporate Bankruptcy as a Filtering Device: Chapter 11 Reorganizations and Out-of-Court Debt Restructurings', **10** *Journal of Law, Economics, and Organization*, 268-295.

Wils, Wouter P.J. (1997), 'The Commission Notice on the Non-Imposition of Fines in Cartel Cases: A Legal and Economic Analysis', **22** *European Law Review*, 125-140.

Wittman, Donald A. (1974), 'Two Views of Procedure', **3** *Journal of Legal Studies*, 249-256.

7800
BANKRUPTCY PROCEEDINGS

Francisco Cabrillo
Professor of Economics
Universidad Complutense de Madrid

Ben W.F. Depoorter
Researcher
University of Ghent, Faculty of Law

Abstract

Bankruptcy has become a crucial legal institution in market economies all over the world. We try to explain some aspects of bankruptcy law and discover that economic theory provides explanation for many, but not all, attributes of bankruptcy law. Both legal and economic scholars have been engaged in a long series of discussions on the meaning of these attributes.
JEL classification: K22, K40
Keywords: Bankruptcy, Liquidation, Reorganization

1. Introduction

The word 'bankruptcy' originates from the Italian word 'banca rotta', an old expression that indicated that the bench of a trader was broken when he was not able to pay his creditors. For a long time bankruptcy has been an important legal institution in market economies. It enables the market system to dispose of inefficient firms and reallocate the assets of insolvent debtors. Also, the possibility of becoming bankrupt has been considered to be a positive incentive for behaving in an efficient way, both for individual traders and company managers.

Bankruptcy law has traditionally been researched by lawyers, not economists. But in the last two decades many studies on the economics of bankruptcy proceedings have been published. Behind the technicalities of the legal regulation of bankruptcy lies a clear economic rationality. At the origin of a bankruptcy proceeding there is a financial crisis of an individual or company. Economists analyze bankruptcy law as the legal instrument to achieve the best possible outcome, which implies a minimization of social costs. Traditional legal theory, however, usually focuses its analysis on the fairness and equity aspects of bankruptcy. From a law and economics perspective the efficiency of the bankruptcy procedures are the core of the analysis.

Bankruptcy law, as it exists in most countries, can also be understood as a device to increase the efficiency of commercial relationships. In any contract the parties could introduce clauses regulating what should happen in case of default and how the assets of the bankrupt company should be managed. However, the transaction costs of writing and implementing such contracts would be very high. And, since a firm's balance sheet is something dynamic that changes every day, creditors would be forced to renegotiate their contracts every time new creditors make claims against the debtor's estate or every time the debtor acquires new assets or pays his previous debts. Therefore, it may be considered efficient to have standard procedures regulating the possible outcomes of a firm's default (see Aghion, Hart and Moore, 1992).

This chapter studies the efficiency of the most relevant aspects of bankruptcy law. Although most bankruptcy codes share many characteristics in their way of dealing with bankruptcy proceedings, each legal system has its own peculiarities and no international economic organization has yet been able to draft an international bankruptcy code. Therefore, this chapter will not focus on any specific national bankruptcy law, but rather will discuss the most relevant general issues while occasionally commenting on some particular national institutions. Also, our main attention will go to business bankruptcy. The issue of personal bankruptcy is touched sporadically, for example in the discussion on discharge in Section 3 (for more on personal bankruptcy, see Apilado, Dauton and Smith, 1978; Shiers and Williamson, 1987; Warren, Sullivan and Westbrook, 1988, 1989, 1994a).

The second section of this chapter presents bankruptcy proceedings as a collective action of creditors to recover their credits in the most efficient way. In Sections 3 and 4 the main objectives of bankruptcy and the most relevant costs of a liquidation proceeding are discussed. Sections 5, 6, 7 and 8 deal with some of the economic agents involved in bankruptcy proceedings: the debtor, the creditors and employees. A specific section is devoted to the role of employees as a special type of creditor. The liquidation-reorganization dilemma is discussed in Sections 9 and 10. The final section comments on the possible alternatives to the existing bankruptcy proceedings. The problems of secured credits and bankruptcy priority rights will be taken into account occasionally; they are treated elsewehere in Volume II (Chapter 1500, Security Interests, Creditors' Priorities and Bankruptcy) and in Volume III (Chapter 5660, Regulation of the Securities Market).

2. The Collective Action of Creditors

The meeting of creditors, in most bankruptcy legislation a prerequisite before adopting any final decision concerning the bankrupt firm, may be a good example of the various efficiency aspects in bankruptcy procedure. From a law and economics perspective this compulsory meeting can be understood as a useful means to reduce transaction costs in collective action. Negotiations between various creditors are often difficult and expensive. Although an agreement is certainly not guaranteed in this meeting, procedure costs may be substantially reduced.

In more general terms, bankruptcy law can be defined as a set of rules that institutionalizes collective action in debt collection (Jackson, 1986a). When collecting their credits out of a bankruptcy procedure creditors play a non-cooperative game, in which each individual maximizing strategy produces an inefficient outcome. Social costs will increase when each creditor tries to get the highest possible percentage of his credit. These individual strategies cannot raise the value of the debtor's estate. On the contrary, they reduce the net value of the assets to be distributed among the creditors will be reduced. However, the principle of collective action seems to conflict with another generally accepted principle of bankruptcy law, the existence of secured credit, and the principle according to which bankruptcy law should not change the previous structure of the debtor's liabilities.

An important characteristic of some secured credits - mortgages, for instance - is that creditors can sell off part of the company's assets, aside from the normal bankruptcy proceedings, in order to collect their credits beforehand. This possibility not only breaks the principle of collective action - such secured creditors are usually not interested in what may happen to other creditors - but may also reduce the net value of the bankrupt company because of piecemeal liquidation.

The possible conflict of these two principles should be one of the basic problems to be discussed by any economic analysis of bankruptcy law. Most lawyers and economists acknowledge the existence of such a conflict. Bankruptcy law should offer a solution. In some cases collaterals can be substracted from the assets to be distributed and secured creditors denied the vote in the bankruptcy proceedings. In other cases bankruptcy law can provide the receiver or the administrator the option of paying secured credits by selling assets if the goods given as collateral are considered to be essential for an efficient reorganization or for selling the company as a going concern. The existence of secured credits does not mean, therefore, that the principle of collective action has to be abandoned.

3. The Objectives of Bankruptcy Law

The major objective of bankruptcy law is supposed to be the (*ex post*) maximization of the proceeds. Assuming that more is preferred to less, economic theory holds that bankruptcy law should maximize the total value of the firm *ex post*.

Although an efficient allocation of the debtor's assets is usually its main objective, bankruptcy law may have other purposes. One objective may be to impose costs on individuals and firm managers, in order to provide them (*ex ante*) with adequate incentives to perform well (Easterbrook, 1990). Historically these costs were imposed by criminal sanctions to the bankruptcy debtor. Bankrupts went to prison or, in cases of fraudulent bankruptcies, even to the galleys of the scaffold. Contemporary scholars justified these stern measures against fraudulent bankrupts in terms of a rational crime theory. According to Becker (1968) the expected cost of crime has two elements for the criminal: the sanction and the probability of this sanction being imposed. If criminals are risk neutral, a low probability of conviction should be matched to a severe sanction. Adam Smith argued in favor of the highest sanction - the death penalty - for fraudulent bankrupts because, as he puts it, 'there is no fraud which is more easily committed without being discovered' (see Cabrillo, 1986). Although imprisonment for insolvency disappeared in the nineteenth century, most criminal codes still attach penalties of imprisonment to certain frauds committed in bankruptcy procedures.

Note that these two objectives may conflict with each other (Berkovitch et al., 1993). If only the *ex ante* objective mattered, there would be nothing wrong with closing down bankrupt firms. From an *ex post* viewpoint this might be a very bad idea. Even well-managed firms sometimes go bankrupt, due to uncertainty or external factors. Bankruptcy law should de designed to strike the right balance between both objectives (Aghion, Hart and Moore, 1992).

In bankruptcy procedures creditors try to capture the highest possible percentage of the value of their credit. Without the rules of bankruptcy law, creditors would adopt non-cooperative strategies which generate an outcome resembling that under a prisoner's dilemma (on creditor misbehavior and secured credit as a sensible response to the common pool problem, see Picker, 1992). In each case, the dominant strategy, directed to raise the probability of recovering their credits, is non-cooperative. Creditors will waste resources trying to be the first to seize their collateral or to obtain a judgement against the debtor (Jackson, 1986a). This race may lead to premature liquidation of the firm's assets, which may cause a loss of value for all creditors if the firm is worth more as a whole that as a collection of pieces (the insight of the 'collective action' problem in bankruptcy was raised by Jackson, 1982). Therefore, the virtue of bankruptcy law is that it initiates a collective legal procedure by which all claims against the firm are settled in an orderly fashion (Baird and Jackson, 1985; Ang and Chua, 1980; Bulow and Shoven, 1978; White, 1980). However, critics argue that the common pool argument is overstated because in practice debtors react to threats of loss and dissipate assets prior to bankruptcy, leaving nothing to divide (Bowers, 1990, for empirical support, see LoPucki and Whitford, 1993, and Gilson, 1996). Others have argued that any *ex-post* collective action problem can be eliminated by the use of *ex-ante* optimal credit contracts (Adler, 1993), security devices (Picker, 1992) or by relying on the existing nonbankruptcy default rules of secured credit (Bowers, 1991).

Another objective of bankruptcy law may be what is generally referred to as 'discharge of the debtor'. Discharge, the doctrine that frees the debtor's future income from the chain of previous debt, is a characteristic institution of British and American bankruptcy law, but is rarely encountered in continental law. Discharge was first introduced in England in the Statute of 1906, passed to protect honest bankrupts from the greed of their creditors and in particular to keep them from rotting away in jail. With the certificate of discharge the bankrupt was freed from his debts and allowed to keep a part of his estate to help him make a fresh start (Hoppit, 1987, pp. 19-24). Later the discharge of the debtor became an important chapter of American bankruptcy law and received a significant reinforcement under the Bankruptcy Reform Act of 1978.

Discharge may be understood not only as a measure to help the honest debtor, but also as an efficient incentive to avoid asset concealment. Search and transaction costs may be reduced and the efficiency of the procedure is increased.

Jackson (1985) uses analytics from psychology and economics to find support of the non waivable right of discharge in several of the characteristics of human behavior. Another justification would be that it eliminates the incentive structure that causes the debtor to become less productive once a large part of his wages start flowing to creditors. Discharge has also been approached as a supplement to the welfare system. The non waivable right to discharge discourages people to use assets that are essential to the minimal wellbeing. By prohibiting the use of welfare payments as collaterals, discharge law renders 'necessary assets' valueless (Jackson, 1986b; Posner, 1995, 1997). Also, it discourages high-risk behavior that would be induced by welfare. The right of discharge forces creditors to raise interest rates, because of the weaker position the creditors find themselves in, which discourages some debtors to engage in risky behavior that would be externalized by the taxpayer (Jackson, 1986b).

Some effects of discharge of the debtor remain controversial. Discharge seems to discriminate in favor of debtors with a relatively high stock of human capital and against bankrupts with a relatively high stock of physical capital. Physical assets - and their future returns - are appropriated by creditors. But the future returns of human capital - a substantial part of the debtor's wages - remain the bankrupt's property.

Distribution of the costs of discharge is also controversial. Debtors, like creditors, want to minimize costs. The right to discharge increases the cost of credit. The fact that creditors will be prevented from collecting some of their debts will be reflected in higher interest rates. Higher risks for creditors will raise the interest rates (on the adverse selection and moral hazard effects of higher interest rates, see Stiglitz and Weiss, 1981). Creditors do not possess the relevant information in order to discriminate between low-risk and high-risk debtors. Therefore, they will pass higher costs to all consumers. Part of these higher costs, caused by high-risk debtors, will therefore be passed on to low-risk, more reliable debtors. Although favored by those who already have a lot of debt (*ex post*), the non waivable right of discharge will (*ex ante*) be rejected by the vast majority of people (Dye, 1986).

There is some debate among bankruptcy scholars whether a bankruptcy procedure should preserve the absolute priority of claims (Buckley, 1986; Adler, 1993; Triantis, 1992). Under the absolute priority rule each priority class is paid in full, to the extent that sufficient assets are available, before the next class is paid. General creditors, without security interests or priority status, receive payment if any assets are left over (for effeciency justifications of the instrument of security interests, see Scott, 1977; Jackson and Kronman, 1979; White, 1980, 1989; Buckley, 1986; Triantis, 1992, 1994; Adler, 1993; dissenting, Schwartz, 1981; LoPucki, 1994; see Chapter 1500 for an overview of the debate on the 'secured credit puzzle'). If the structure of debt priority, as agreed upon by parties, could be violated within bankruptcy, people will be reluctant to invest (Meckling, 1977). Secured creditors, for example, paid for their specific security entitlement by accepting a lower rate of return and should, therefore, be enabled to retain the benefits of their original bargain by receiving an equivalent value for their collateral in bankruptcy (Scott, 1986). Critics argue that the absolute priority rule will induce management, acting on the behalf of shareholders, to engage in risky behavior when a company is close to bankruptcy (on entrenchment and investment incentives, see Chapter 1500, section 28). If things go badly creditors bear the losses. If the firm does well equity holders will reap the profits.

Another objective of bankruptcy law is the redistribution among groups of claimants. Redistribution is promoted through the dynamics of a reorganization procedure (Eisenberg, 1989, p. 133; on the redistributive nature of the US bankruptcy code, see, for instance, Bowers, 1991). The 'objective' rationale would be that by preserving the going concern value of the company reorganization may enable creditors to capture a higher value than would be possible under liquidation (see Clark, 1981). Although Chapter 11 of the American Bankruptcy law is the best known rehabilitation procedure, most countries have already introduced reorganization procedures in their bankruptcy laws. The positive and negative aspects of reorganization have been widely discussed. Sections 9 and 10 of this chapter will deal with the reorganization-liquidation dilemma.

Finally, according to Bufford (1994), bankruptcy serves an important role as a safety net for economies. It prevents secured creditors from collectively initiating a downward spiral of foreclosures and bank faillures which would result in worldwide economic depression, such as in 1933. From this viewpoint, bankruptcy protects imperfect markets and weak economies by allowing debtors to wait out an economic downturn.

4. Reallocation of Assets through Bankruptcy: The Costs of a Liquidation Procedure

An efficient legal procedure should minimize social costs. There are three main costs to a liquidation procedure. First of all, the social value of specific - both physical and human - capital assets is reduced when the new allocation of productive resources takes place. Secondly, productive resources remain unemployed during the legal proceedings. Thirdly, a liquidation procedure involves certain litigation expenditures.

The bankrupt firm can be sold piecemeal or as a going concern. In piecemeal liquidations, assets are sold in the market and employees move from a bankrupt firm to a more efficient one. This increases social productivity of both physical and human capital. However, part of the value of these capital goods and of employees' human capital is lost in such a procedure. This loss of value is mainly due to the fact that the productivity of capital invested in a given asset, integrated within a production process, is reduced when this asset is sold piecemeal, as the market value of used capital goods does not reflect the discounted value of the asset's expected yields in its original production process. Also, there can be a loss of human capital inasmuch as there is a loss of specific knowledge regarding the handling of specific assets under certain conditions. This loss of value of both physical and human capital is used as an argument in favor of reorganization and against liquidation.

These costs are considerably lower when the bankrupt company is sold as a going concern. In a world of perfect information and perfect capital markets this would then be the best liquidation procedure for any firm (Baird,

1986). Any individual or company interested in the insolvent firm would be able to raise all the necessary capital - even if the bankrupt firm is a big public corporation - to buy it. However, in a world of information costs and imperfect capital markets, it may prove very difficult to find partners or banks willing to offer enough capital to buy the firm - especially if it is a big corporation - and piecemeal liquidation will be the outcome of many bankruptcy proceedings of companies that would have survived under new ownership and management.

The second cost is created by unemployment of productive resources. If bankruptcy implies that the firm is closed while its assets are being sold, assets will be left idle during the proceedings. The longer the duration of the procedure, the higher the social costs associated to it (on the administrative costs of corporate bankruptcy, Ang, Chua and McConnell, 1982). There is another source of social loss: the obsolescence of capital assets. Replacement value of high technology capital assets - computers, for instance - decreases every day. And again, the longer the duration of the procedure, the higher will be the social costs of unemployment of productive assets because of obsolescence will be.

Litigation expenditures are also an important part of the social costs associated with bankruptcies. In any other legal procedure, higher expenses on legal services are assumed to increase the probability of a favorable decision from the court. However, in bankruptcy proceedings, the net value of the debtor's estate cannot be increased through litigation. High litigation expenditures lower the total net value available for distribution among the creditors.

Social costs of litigation in bankruptcy proceedings may be higher if these expenditures are partially paid by government through public subsidies. The overall positive external effect - a reduction of uncertainty and, therefore, reduction of future litigation - explains why partial subsidies paid by government may be efficient. But at the same time subsidies present lower costs to the litigators and thereby provide an incentive to increase litigation in the short run.

5. The Debtor in a Bankruptcy Procedure

Originally, bankruptcy law was established to protect the creditor's interests and proceedings were always initiated by a creditor's petition. It was not until the nineteenth century when voluntary bankruptcy was introduced in most countries. At present, a substantial number of petitions are filed by debtors; and in some countries, with legal provisions generous to debtors, this number exceeds 50 percent (in Spain, for instance, during the period of 1982-

86, debtors initiated more than 80 percent of all bankruptcy proceedings, see Cabrillo, 1986, pp. 75-76).

The risk of bankruptcy provides a positive incentive to management. They want to avoid bankruptcy (it creates a bad reputation, and so on) and therefore it is in their own interest to prevent the firm from having large deficits. Both private and public sector enterprises can go bankrupt. Bankruptcies of public sector enterprises are extremely rare. In fact, the absence of the bankrupt threat is one of the most important differences in the incentives for efficient management of private and public enterprises.

Normally, a bankruptcy proceeding finds its origin in a financial disequilibrium that compels the debtor to suspend payments. The financial structure of the firm, and more precisely the ratio liabilities/equity, is an important factor to determine the probability of an economic crisis of a firm that might end in bankruptcy. According to the Modigliani-Miller theorem (Modigliani and Miller, 1958), under certain assumptions, the market value of a firm is independent from its capital structure. The risk of insolvency, and therefore of bankruptcy, depends substantially on the value of its current liabilities relative to the value of its liquid assets. If the ratio liabilities/equity increases, the risk of bankruptcy will increase. Ceteris paribus, the rise of this ratio in firms will increase the number of bankruptcy proceedings.

Managers and firm owners usually prefer to have debt as a significant part of the firm's capital structure and not to finance its business just through equity. There are several reasons for this preference. First, a mixed capital structure allows different risks and different returns from the capital invested in the firm. In absence of default risk, the leverage effect of a higher amount of debt would allow higher returns to equity holders. But when default risk is introduced into the model, leverage is associated with a higher probability of bankruptcy. Managers and firm owners try to determine an optimal debt-equity ratio, taking into account both the profits of the leverage effect and the probability of bankruptcy.

Secondly, governments are not neutral when it comes down to the assessment of firms' capital structure. The corporation income tax is imposed on the net income of corporations. Net income is defined as revenues minus costs. This way the fiscal regime actually creates incentives to debt financing of corporations.

It can also be argued that a capital structure based on both equity and debt, under the limited liability principle, allows managers and corporation owners to pass a part of the bankruptcy losses to creditors. Thus, in this respect, bankruptcy creates negative externalities. Rational creditors will discount the cost of these negative externalities - the value of the debt multiplied by the probability of default - and charge higher prices and interest rates - or the cost of insurance - to their customers. Debtors, as a class, will internalize these externalities. In a world where information is imperfect, unreliable debtors, who have a higher probability of default than average, will pass a part of these costs to reliable debtors.

6. Creditors in a Bankruptcy Procedure

Most credits or commercial deals involve a risk of default. Although risks are inevitable, they can be reduced through monitoring or transferred to a third party through insurance. Creditors may follow two different strategies when they face the risk of losses caused by bankruptcies. Self-insurance, where a fund to cover possible losses is created, may be one option. Banks and large companies employ self-insurance for bankruptcy losses by having a large number of customers which allows them to pool the risks. Another option is the purchase of credit insurance from an insurance company, which pools the risks of various firms. Such a service is commonly offered in Europe. Insurance companies that specialize in bankruptcy risks usually offer their customers informational services on the financial reliability of their potential clients. Firms that purchase this kind of insurance profit from the economies of scale which are generated by the large number of customers. Insurance companies often share their data on insolvent debtors or debtors with a high default risk.

In a stable commercial relationship the risk assumed by the creditor may change at every moment and might be very different from the risk at the beginning of such a relationship. The basic problem for the creditor is how to adopt the most efficient strategy when the risk of losing his credit increases, due to the probability of bankruptcy of the debtor. When the debtor suspects that the probability of bankruptcy is rising, he may try to raise the total value of his debts in order to solve his short-run financial problems. The new debt may reduce the risk of default as it may be able to prevent bankruptcy in the short run. However, at the same time, the overall debt increases and there is some danger of 'risk alternation' - the debtor may behave in riskier fashion as a result of the additional obligation (see Kanda and Levmore, 1994). It is uncertain whether the product of the amount of credit times the risk of default will increase or decrease.

In a world of perfect information the optimal strategy of a creditor would be to minimize the value of this product when making the decision to offer new credit to his client or to refrain from doing so. But in the real world information is imperfect and asymmetrical. The debtor can discriminate among creditors to help some of them and, at the same time, cause bigger losses to others. Furthermore, all credits are not equal in bankruptcy proceedings.

Creditors' strategies are therefore more complex than they would be in the case of perfect information and the non-existence of secured credits.

There are clear incentives for both the debtor and some creditors to reach agreements that are harmful to other creditors before bankruptcy proceedings begin. Creditors can raise the probability of getting their money back; and the debtor can maximize the expected value of his commercial relationship, discriminating in favor of those creditors that will be able to help him in other businesses.

In most legal systems discriminated creditors can file a petition to the court for annulment of payments to other creditors or changes of unsecured credits into secured credits. Usually the formal declaration of bankruptcy has retrospective effect and annuls these agreements. These retrospective effects may impose high costs on both the owners and the managers of the bankrupt firm. Bankruptcy petitions can be used as a threat to force the debtor not to favor some specific creditors and harm others. These threats often play a significant role in creditors' strategies as there is always uncertainty regarding the relevance of the retrospective effects.

When a creditor files a bankruptcy petition, he usually tries to improve his position and recover at least part if his credits. He expects that, at the end of the bankruptcy proceeding the value of his recovered credits will be higher that the procedure costs he will have to pay. More precisely, a creditor will file a bankruptcy petition only if $X.P / (1 + r)^t > E$, where X represents the value of the credit, P the percentage of the credit that he expects to recover if he wins and E the procedure expenditures. The very low value of P for unsecured creditors in many bankruptcy proceedings explains why many creditors decide not to go to court, even in cases where there are illegal agreements between the debtor and some creditors.

However, some secured creditors - and especially insurance companies representing unsecured creditors - file the bankruptcy petition and go to court even in cases where the value of E is expected to be higher than the value of the recovered credits. The best explanation for this behavior is to qualify these creditors - especially insurance companies - as long-run utility maximizers. They are prepared to lose money in a single bankruptcy case if these losses allow them to build a reputation of going to court in cases of suspected fraud (Mitchell, 1993).

Government can also exert influence on a creditor's behavior. Firstly, the corporation tax reduces the creditors' losses caused by bankruptcy. With this tax government shares the risks of companies. The deduction for losses against other income reduces the losses caused by other firms' bankruptcies in the percentage of the corporation income tax that the company is obliged to pay.

A second result of the corporation income tax is its effect on risk behavior of companies. There is some dissension over the effects of the corporation income tax on risk taking; but most economist think that, if the tax is not progressive and there are no limitations in the magnitude of losses that can be offset, it increases risky behavior by firms. Under this assumption, we should expect two effects on creditors' behavior. First, creditors should be ready to assume a higher risk and offer more credit to a debtor to help him avoid bankruptcy. Secondly, if there is uncertainty about the distribution of the debtor's estate or fraud by the debtor, creditors would have an incentive to go to court to recover their credit. Assume that, according to the model sketched in the previous paragraph, when the creditor renounces to go to court he loses the total amount of his credit, X, but can lose $X + E$. Going to court to recover a credit in bankruptcy proceedings is, therefore, a risky decision, and, when assuming the previous conclusions about taxation and risk taking, we should expect an incentive to go to court as a result of the corporation income tax.

7. Employees in Bankruptcy Proceedings

The foundations of current bankruptcy law were developed within an economic framework characterized by private contracts freely undertaken by all parties, often accompanied by only a low level of government control on economic activity. Such is the way that this institution is modeled even today in the majority of countries. However, it would be tantamount to turning a blind eye to reality not to acknowledge that important changes have taken place in the framework of bankruptcy law. Government control and intervention has modified the original concept of most commercial relationships.

The position of employees in relation to their company has become very different from the relation of the firm with the rest of its creditors. Employees not only prefer payment of credits for non-paid salaries, but also expect the right to a part of the company assets as indemnity for the loss of their jobs. Some bankruptcy laws even allow employees to levy separate execution against the company by seizure of its assets to assure payment of these credits.

The relationship between firms and employees can be explained in terms of the implicit contracts model. According to this approach, implicit contracts within the company-employee relationship protect the employees against fluctuations of their salary. Insurance premiums, a part of these wages, permit them to receive the corresponding indemnity if the situation were to become unfavorable.

When we assume that employees are risk averse, they would prefer to contract this implicit insurance policy as it guarantees them indemnity in case they lose their job when the company goes bankrupt. Therefore, the employee is willing to 'sacrifice' a given fraction of his salary for insurance premiums.

The economic rationality of the lay-off compensation that employees receive in case of bankruptcy implies two requisites. In the first place, we assume that the employee suffers economic losses from losing his job when the firm is liquidated. Secondly, in the absence of alternatives on the market, the companies themselves are in the best position to play the role of insurer.

The damages incurred by a employee when losing his job can be the result of several factors. First of all, transaction costs are inevitable when searching the job market. In a situation of prolonged disequilibrium in the labor market laid off employees may face long periods of unemployment. In some countries the law admits only two forms of lay-offs, either dismissal as a sanction or unjustified lay-off with indemnity. Economically, this indemnity reflects the price that the company pays in order to buy the employee's 'property rights'.

Another possible way in which the employee might experience damages in case of bankruptcy is through the loss of his company-specific human capital. The employee might, for instance, have been an expert in working a specific machine that only the liquidated firm used. The loss of this type of human capital causes a reduction of the employee's marginal productivity of labor and consequentially the wages he could negotiate with other companies.

The second point to be considered is why the law compels companies to assume, at least partially, the risk of lay-offs. The answer to this question lies in the fact that no company in the market is willing to insure these risks. Thus, we are faced with a problem of risk allocation within the framework of a bilateral contractual relationship.

According to this implicit contract model, throughout the period of contract duration, each employee creates a fund through payment of his implicit insurance premiums. The company has at its disposal the sum of the funds corresponding with all employees and acts as an insurance company in its relationship with them. Because of its capacity to reduce risks by means of pooling, it is best placed to provide the insurance in this contractual relationship. Consequently, it is in the interest of efficiency that the employees transfer at least partially their risk of unemployment to the company. In this perspective indemnity to employees in cases of liquidation of the firm in a bankruptcy procedure can be explained in terms of efficiency.

In a similar way preferences in payments of both credits for debited salaries and lay-off indemnities can be explained. Preference in collection of credit basically means an increase in the probability of a specific credit to be paid. If this probability is lower than 1 (as it is always in the case of bankruptcy), the variables to be taken into consideration by employees will no longer be the salary and the prospective indemnity for lay-off, but rather these variables multiplied by the probability of them being actually obtained. Any increase of this probability would permit the firm, therefore, to pay lower wages. Risk-averse employees would, expected values being equal, prefer combinations of higher probabilities and lower wages. With other creditors - banks, large companies or small traders - the risk of insolvencies in credits would be reflected in higher interest rates or higher prices charged to the clients. This would permit each creditor to create his own fund of self-insurance or to contract an insurance policy for unpaid credits under the conditions offered by the insurance markets. Firms are in the best position to provide insurance to the employees. Preference in collection of credits in case of bankruptcy would thus lend weight to the argument that the transfer of risk from employees to companies is efficient in situations in which the profitability of collection is lower than 1.

8. The Liquidation-Reorganization Dilemma

The reform of bankruptcy law has been widely discussed in Europe and the United States in recent years and one outcome of these debates has been the substantial development of the reorganization procedures for bankrupt companies. Advocates of reorganization present it as an efficient procedure that avoids many unnecessary liquidations and reduces the social costs of bankruptcy. However, critics of reorganization find it to be an inefficient procedure that deprives bankruptcy from its main objective, the reallocation of the debtor's assets to more productive employments through creditors' collective action. Reorganization, they argue, raises the social costs of default, instead of reducing them (see Section 9).

Reorganization basically consists of the implementation of a rehabilitation plan in order to allow a firm to stay in business. Although the best known bankruptcy provisions for reorganization are those contained in Chapter 11 of the American Bankruptcy Code, similar provisions can be found in other countries. In Britain reorganization is referred to as 'administration', in Germany 'vergleich', in France it is termed 'reglement aimable' and 'redressement judicaire' and in Italy 'administrazione controllata'.

Each reorganization procedure has its own peculiarities. Some bankruptcy codes (the American Bankruptcy Code, for instance) permit the original management to stay in charge of the firm in most cases. Others, for example the British Insolvency Act of 1986, appoint an administrator to lead the company during the bankruptcy proceedings. The role of creditors in the proceedings may also differ. Some procedures require the conversion of the debt into stock, while others offer diverse alternatives to the creditors. Credit priorities do not always receive the same treatment. Differences also exist between the voting systems on asset sales or postponement grants to the debtor. Employees play a relevant role in some reorganization proceedings, and almost none in others. But in every case, the main object of the procedure is to put the company on a solid base and to try to guarantee its survival.

Should liquidation or reorganization be the main concern of courts and judges in bankruptcy cases? Some codes consider liquidation and reorganization of the firm as alternatives, without showing any special preference for one or the other. Other codes - such as the French law passed in 1985 - favor the rehabilitation of the firm.

In any bankruptcy procedure it is essential to valuate the firm's assets and liabilities in the most accurate way, since the decision between liquidation and reorganization usually depends on this valuation. Most bankruptcy codes are, however, very vague when dealing with the value of a company (on the problem of valuation which is inherent to the fictional sale under reorganization, see Bebchuk, 1988). Judges have therefore significant discretionary powers in a subject they usually know little about. For instance, there is substantial evidence to suggest that, in the United States, the valuation of bankrupt firms by judges in order to consider its possibilities for rehabilitation is systematically too high (Jackson, 1986a, p. 220). This concern has led a number of scholars to seek alternative procedures that provide market-based estimates of a firm's value (see Section 10).

There are two main methods to valuate an insolvent firm: the balance method and the feasibility method. The balance method is static. It uses the market value of assets and liabilities in order to determine whether the company has a positive or negative net worth. A negative net worth would imply liquidation, while a positive net worth would pave the way for reorganization. This method has two inherent problems: first, there is the usual problem with valuation of equipments and inventories when they may have to be sold in the short run. This possibility requires that these evaluations should be made as cautious as possible. For instance, if inventories can be valued at the original cost or at the present market value, the lowest one should be used.

Second, the fact that there is a net worth does not guarantee the future survival of the firm in the market. A company whose net worth is positive because it owns expensive equipment or valuable buildings should be liquidated if there is no demand for its product in the market.

The feasibility method is dynamic. It does not focus on the static value of the firm's assets and liabilities but rather on the probability of survival that a reorganized company would have in a specific market. According to this method a firm should be rehabilitated if the discounted value of its future returns flow is expected to be positive. There are two problems with this method. First of all, the subjective judgements, unavoidable in these evaluations, permit different interest groups to seek rents (more on this in the following section of this article). The second problem is the question how to distribute the stock or debts of the reorganized company to the creditors, when the firm is rehabilitated.

However, the use of either method, does not exclude the application of the other. Assume a bankrupt company proposes a reorganization plan. In order to evaluate the plan a feasibility study should be made. If the court opinionated that the company can be rehabilitated the plan will be implemented and the assets can be evaluated as parts of an ongoing business. If, however, the court should not make a feasibility finding, the court should opt for liquidation. In that case the assets should then be valued according to their market value.

9. Why Reorganization?

American data from the late 1980s show that as many as nine out of ten small and middle-sized firms fail after going into a Chapter 11 reorganization (for data on firms under reorganization, see Franks and Torous, 1989). Italian 'administrazione controllata' has been criticized as a useless and expensive prologue to liquidation or even as a procedure that anaesthetizes creditors. In France the 1985 law is not working as was hoped. And in Britain, where 'administration' has been considered to be an improvement of the old bankruptcy law, its relative success has been due to a most efficient system of liquidation that allows the new managers to sell the profitable divisions of the bankrupt firm for better prices.

Bankruptcy scholars claim that reorganization is time-consuming, that it involves high administrative costs and often reduces the company's value (Baird, 1986; Bradley, 1992; Cutler and Summers, 1988; Lopucki and Whitford, 1990, 1993 and Weiss, 1990). It has been debated on philosophical, political and economic grounds because of its role in increasing the accessibility and attractiveness of bankruptcy (DiPieto and Katz, 1983; Lunnie, 1984; Oswald, 1984; for data on the increase in the incidence of business bankruptcy in the United States since the passage of Chapter 11, see Johnson, 1986, p. 668) .

Efficiency arguments fail to explain why so many firms with such low probabilities of survival are being reorganized. The existence of interest groups and rent-seeking behavior, often disguised as public interest efforts, provide one possible explanation.

A firm may be conceived as a framework of interests and property rights. Property implies three different rights over the firm: the right to control it; the ownership of the firm's assets; and the right to take possession of the firm's profits. According to a complex net of legal provisions and contracts owners have to share these rights with creditors, employees and the government.

Discussions over priorities in the use of these rights are a characteristic feature of bankruptcy procedure. Business experience reveals that the preference for reorganization or liquidation is often determined by the property right framework, as defined by law. The interests of secured creditors may be very different from those of unsecured creditors when faced with a choice between liquidation or reorganization. Employees and unions may think that reorganization is the most beneficial outcome for their interests. The incumbent managers may prefer reorganization if the procedure allows them to stay in charge of the reorganized firm (Gilson, 1990; on the motivation of managers to initiate a bankruptcy proceeding, see Baird, 1991; Berkovitz, Israel and Zender, 1993; Rose-Ackerman, 1991). They might be opposed to reorganization if it seems likely that an external administrator will be appointed to lead the firm.

All these property rights and interests collide in bankruptcy procedures and each group employs its own strategies. Their relative success will depend on the value of their credits, the nature of the applicable bankruptcy law and the public support they can secure for their demands.

Suppose that employees believe - which they almost always do - that reorganization is the most convenient outcome for them. They will follow a strategy that puts pressure on decision makers, local politicians and the media, in order to keep the firm in business. Some laws, like the French bankruptcy code of 1985, goes one step further and assigns an active role to employees in the negotiations. Public choice and rent-seeking models (see, Buchanan, Tollison and Tullock, 1980) offer plausible explanations for the possible success of this strategy and account for the public subsidies that some companies receive in case of reorganization.

It is quite common to present the liquidation-reorganization dilemma as a private vs. public interest problem. The complex framework of property rights and interests should be enlarged to include some kind of public interest in the survival of the bankrupt company. Unemployment or deindustrialization in a depressed area, for instance, are the most common arguments which are advanced to justify the public interest in avoiding the liquidation of insolvent private firms. From an efficiency perspective it may be hard to justify these arguments. Bankruptcy law is not the best instrument to deal with problems such as unemployment or deindustrialization. There is no reason to consider the interests of unemployed employees or local interest groups more 'public' or 'social' than the welfare of the creditors, the taxpayers or the whole society - which will eventually pay for the misallocation of production factors. The costs of liquidation and reorganization are often misperceived. It may be easy to estimate the short-run social costs of the liquidation of a firm, especially in cases of high rates of unemployment. It is, however, more difficult to assert the long-run costs of an inefficient allocation of the social production factors. These long-run costs are usually downgraded by the public opinion, and public interest arguments often prevail over the efficiency arguments. Thus, the dilemma of reorganization is that, while it may allow some efficient firms to continue, it facilitates the reorganization of inefficient firms that should be liquidated (White, 1989, pp. 136-137).

10. Alternative Procedures

The bargaining based-approach of reorganization, such as found in Chapter 11 of the US Bankruptcy Code, has been criticized extentsively in the literature. Equity holders, have been demonstrated to extract significant value, even in cases where the debt increased the value of the reorganization value (Franks and Torous, 1989). The power of equity holders to block or delay the approval of a reorganization plan would bring about deviations from contractual priority (on the deviations from contractual priority under the existing rules, see Eberhart, Moore and Roenfeldt, 1999; Weiss, 1990; for a formalized model on the mechanisms that underlie the bargaining process, see Bebchuk and Chang, 1992; Baird and Picker, 1991).

10.1 Auctions

Alternative solutions to the bargaining based-approach have been suggested to improve the alleged poor results of the reorganization procedure. One possible alternative is to merge the liquidation and reorganization procedures. Several proposals follow this path. It would be possible to sell every bankrupt firm as a going concern, free of debt and pay the creditors, according to the absolute priority rule, with the proceeds. Baird (1986) and Jackson (1986a) argue that bankruptcy reorganizations should be eliminated and replaced by a mandatory auction of the failed firm. (The merits (Hansen and Randall, 1998; Schleifer and Vishny, 1992) and imperfections (Baird, 1993; Cramton and Schwartz, 1991) of an auction regime have received consideration in the litrature.) Roe (1983) suggests an initial public offering of 10 percent of the firms's new equity on the market to provide the market's estimate of the value of the firm.

10.2 Options

Other proposals suggest that bankruptcy should involve an automatic financial restructuring, where all debts would be converted into equity. The decision whether to liquidate or reorganize would then be left to the incumbent management (Bebchuk, 1988).

The Aghion-Hart-Moore procedure is considered to be one of the most interesting alternatives advanced in the literature the past ten years (Aghion, Hart and Moore, 1992, 1994, 1995). This procedure, drawing upon the innovative mechanical scheme of distribution by Bebchuk (1988), consists of cancellation of all of the company's debt and to offer the creditors the stock of the new all-equity company. The creditors become shareholders in the new all-equity company. (For a critique on the debt-equity swap and the A-H-M scheme, see Bufford, 1994, pp. 844-846.)

A second version of the model proposes to leave the status of secured creditors unaltered if the value of the collateral is higher than these credits. Only unsecured credits would be transferred into debt. The essence of the procedure remains unaltered. In both cases the bankrupt company becomes solvent and creditors take the decisions concerning the firm as shareholders with voting rights. A trustee would supervise the process, solicit cash and noncash bids for the new all-equity company and allocate the right to shares in this company. In the final step the shareholders vote to select the various cash and noncash bids.

These, and other new proposals can certainly add to improved bankruptcy proceedings and to increase the efficiency of bankruptcy law.

11. Conclusion

It is impossible to know how bankruptcy law will change in the next few decades. Especially in Europe, the predisposition in favor of reorganization procedures in legislative reform seem to be weakened. For instance, in France, the country with one of the most reorganization-favored bankruptcy codes in Europe, new reforms are initiated to reduce the excessive pro-rehabilitation bias of the 1985 law. Changing the foundations of traditional bankruptcy law has proven to be much more complicated than expected by most reformers.

Acknowledgements

We would like to thank two anonymous referees for fruitful comments and suggestions on an earlier draft.

Bibliography on Bankruptcy Proceedings (7800)

Adler, Barry E. (1992), 'Bankruptcy and Risk Allocation', **77** *Cornell Law Review*, 439ff ff.

Adler, Barry E. (1993a), 'An Equity Agency Solution to the Bankruptcy Priority Puzzle', **22** *Journal of Legal Studies*, 73-98.

Adler, Barry E. (1993b), 'Financial and Political Theories of American Corporate Bankruptcy', **45** *Stanford Law Review*, 311 ff.

Aghion, Philippe, Hart, Oliver D. and Moore, John (1992), 'The Economics of Bankruptcy Reform', **8** *Journal of Law, Economics, and Organization*, 523-546.

Aghion, Philippe, Hart, Oliver D. and Moore, John (1994), 'Improving Bankruptcy Procedure', **72** *Washington University Law Quarterly*, 811-827.

Aghion, Philippe, Hart, Oliver D. and Moore, John (1995), 'Insolvency Reform in the UK: A Revised Proposal', **11** *Insolvency Law and Practice*, 4-11.

Aivazian, Varouj A. and Callen, Jeffrey L. (1983), 'Reorganization in Bankruptcy and the Issue of Strategic Risk', **7** *Journal of Banking and Finance*, 119-133.

Altman, Edward I. (1969), 'Bankrupt Firms Equity Securities as an Investment Alternative', **25** *Financial Analysts Journal*, 129-135.

Altman, Edward I. (1984), 'A Further Empirical Investigation of the Bankruptcy Cost Question', **39** *Journal of Finance*, 1067 ff.

Ang, James S. and Chua, Jess H. (1980), 'Coalitions, the Me-First Rule, and the Liquidation Decision', **11** *Bell Journal of Economics*, 355-359.

Ang, James S., Chua, Jess H. and McConnell, John J. (1982), 'The Administrative Costs of Corporate Bankruptcy', **37** *Journal of Finance*, 219-226.

Apilado, Vincent P., Dauten, Joel J. and Smith, Douglas E. (1978), 'Personal Bankruptcies', **7** *Journal of Legal Studies*, 371-392.

Aumann, Robert J. and Maschler, Michael (1985), 'Game Theoretic Analysis of a Bankruptcy Problem from the Talmud', **36** *Journal of Economic Theory*, 195-213.

Baird, Douglas G. (1986), 'The Uneasy Case for Corporate Reorganization', **15** *Journal of Legal Studies*, 127-147.

Baird, Douglas G. (1987a), 'A World Without Bankruptcy', *Law and Contemporary Problems*, 173 ff.

Baird, Douglas G. (1987b), 'Loss Distribution, Forum Shopping and Bankruptcy. A Reply to Warren', **54** *University of Chicago Law Review*, 815-834.

Baird, Douglas G. (1991), 'The Initiation Problem in Bankruptcy', **11** *International Review of Law and Economics*, 223-232.

Baird, Douglas G. (1992), *The Elements of Bankruptcy*, New York, Foundation.

Baird, Douglas G. (1993), 'Revisiting Auctions in Chapter 11', **36** *Journal of Law and Economics*, 633-653.

Baird, Douglas G. and Jackson, Thomas H. (1984), 'Corporate Reorganizations and the Treatment of Diverse Ownership Interests: A Comment on Adequate Protection of Secured Creditors in Bankruptcy', **51** *University of Chicago Law Review*, 97-130.

Baird, Douglas G. and Jackson, Thomas H. (1985), *Cases, Problems and Materials on Bankruptcy*, Boston, Little Brown.

Baird, Douglas G. and Jackson, Thomas H. (1987), *Cases, Problems, and Materials on Security Interests in Personal Property*, Mineola, NY, Foundation Press, 889 p.

Baird, Douglas G. and Jackson, Thomas H. (1988), 'Bargaining after the Fall and the Contours of the Absolute Priority Rule', **55** *University of Chicago Law Review*, 738-789.

Baird, Douglas G. and Picker, Ronald C. (1991), 'A Simple Noncooperative Bargaining Model of Corporate Reorganizations', **20** *Journal of Legal Studies*, 311-349.

Bebchuck, Lucian Arye (1988), 'A New Approach to Corporate Reorganizations', **101** *Harvard Law Review*, 775-804.

Bebchuck, Lucian Arye and Chang, H. (1992), 'Bargaining and the Devision of Value in Corporate Reorganization', **8** *Journal of Law, Economics and Organiszation*, 253-79.

Bernanke, Ben S. (1981), 'Bankruptcy, Liquidation and Recession', **71** *American Economic Review. Papers and Proceedings*, 135-159.

Berkovitch, E., Israel, R. and Zender, J. (1993), *The Design of Bankruptcy Law: A Case for Management Bias in Bankruptcy Reorganizations*, Mimeo, University of Michigan.

Betker, Brian L. (1995), 'Management's Incentives, Equity's Bargaining Power and Deviations from Absolute Priority Rule in Chapter 11 Bankruptcies', **68** *Journal of Business*, 161-183.

Bisbal, Joaquím (1986), *La Empresa en Crisis y el Derecho de Quiebras* (The Crisis of the Firm and Bankruptcy Law), Bolonia, Real Colegio de España, 383 p.

Bisbal Méndez, Joaquim (1994), 'La Insoportable Levedad del Derecho Concursal (The Unbearable Lightness of Bankruptcy Law)', **214** *Revista de Derecho Mercantil*, 843-872.

Bowers, James W. (1990), 'Groping and Coping in the Shadow of Murphy's Law: Bankruptcy Theory and the Elementary Economics of Failure', **88** *Michigan Law Review*, 2097 ff.

Bowers, James W. (1991), 'Whither What Hits the Fan? Murphy's Law, Bankruptcy Theory, and the Elementary Economics of Loss Distribution', **26** *Georgia Law Review*, 27 ff.

Bowers, James W. (1993), 'The Fantastic Wisconsylvania Zero-Bureaucratic-Cost School of Bankruptcy Theory: A Comment', **91** *Michigan Law Review*, 1773 ff.

Bowers, James W. (1994), 'Rehabilitation, Redistribution or Dissipation: The Evidence for Choosing Among Bankruptcy Hypotheses', **72** *Washington University Law Quarterly*, 955 ff.

Bowers, James W. (1995), 'Of Bureaucrats' Brothers-in-Law and Bankruptcy Taxes: The Article 9 Filing System and the Market for Information', **79** *Minnesota Law Review*, 721 ff.

Boyes, William J. and Faith, Roger L. (1986), 'Some Effects of the Bankruptcy Reform Act of 1978', **29** *Journal of Law and Economics*, 139-149.

Bradley, Michael D. (1992), 'The Untenable Case for Chapter 11', **101** *Yale Law Journal*, 1043-1095.

Bratton, Dale (1985), 'Note: The California Agricultural Producer's Lien, Processing Company Insolvencies, and Federal Bankruptcy Law: An Evaluation and Alternative Methods of Protecting Farmers', **36** *Hastings Law Journal*, 609-644.

Brimmer, Andrew (1981), 'Economic Implications of Personal Bankruptcies', **35** *Personal Finance Law Quarterly Report*, 187-191.

Buckley, F.H. (1986), 'The Bankruptcy Priority Puzzle', **72** *Virginia Law Review*, 1393-1442.

Bufford, Samuel L. (1994), 'What's Right about Bankruptcy and Wrong About it's Critics', **72** *Washington University Law Quarterly*, 829-848.

Bulow, Jeremy I. and Shoven, John B. (1978), 'The Bankruptcy Decision', **9** *Bell Journal of Economics*, 437-456.

Cabrillo, Francisco (1986), 'Adam Smith on Bankruptcy Law? New Law and Economics in the Glasgow Lectures?', **8(1)** *History of Economics Society Bulletin*, 40-41.

Cabrillo, Francisco (1987), *Análisis Económico del Derecho Concursal Español* (An Economic Analysis of Spanish Bankruptcy Law), Madrid, Fundación Juan March.

Cabrillo, Francisco (1989), *Quiebra y Liquidación de Empresas* (Bankruptcy and Closing Down of Firms), Madrid, Unión Editorial, 151 p.

Cabrillo, Francisco (1993), 'La teoría económica de la reorganización de las empresas en quiebra (Economic Theory of the Reorganization of Bankrupty Firms)', **58** *Economistas*, 62-67.

Carlson, David Gray (1987), 'Is Fraudulent Conveyance Law Efficient?', **9** *Cardozo Law Review*, 643-683.

Carlson, David Gray (1987), 'Philosophy in Bankruptcy', **85** *Michigan Law Review*, 1341-1389.

Chiang, Raymond C. and Finkelstein, John M. (1982), 'An Incentive Framework for Evaluating the Impact of Loan Provisions on Default Risk', **49** *Southern Economic Journal*, 962-969.

Chow, Garland and Gritta, Richard D. (1988), 'Estimating Bankruptcy Risks Facing Class I and II Motor Carriers: An Industry-Specific Approach', **55** *Transportation Practitioners Journal*, 352-363.

Clark, E. (1981), 'The Interdisciplinary Study of Legal Evolution', **90** *Yale Law Journal*, 1252-1254.

Cooter, Robert D. (1985), 'Defective Warnings, Remote Causes, and Bankruptcy: Comment on Schwartz', **14** *Journal of Legal Studies*, 737-750.

Countryman, Vern (1985), 'The Concept of Voidable Preference in Bankruptcy', **38** *Vanderbilt Law Review*, 713-828.

Curme, Michael and Kahn, Lawrence (1990), 'The Impact of the Threat of Bankruptcy on the Structure of Compensation', **8** *Journal of Labor Economics*, 419-447.

Cutler, David M. and Summers, Lawrence H. (1988), 'The Costs of Conflict Resolution and Financial Distress: Evidence from the Texaco-Pennzoil Litigation', **19** *Rand Journal of Economics*, 157-172.

Daigle, Katherine H. and Maloney, Michael T. (1994), 'Residual Claims in Bankruptcy: An Agency Theory Explanation', **37** *Journal of Law and Economics*, 157-192.

DiPieto and Katz (1983), 'Chapter 11 of The Bankruptcy Code-Use or Abuse?', **57** *Connecticut Bar Journal*.

Domowitz, Ian and Eovaldi, Thomas L. (1993), 'The Impact of the Bankruptcy Reform Act of 1978 on Consumer Bankruptcy', **36** *Journal of Law and Economics*, 803-835.

Dye, Ronald A. (1986), 'An Economic Analysis of Bankruptcy Statutes', **24** *Economic Inquiry*, 417-428.

Easterbrook, F.H. (1990), 'Is Corporate Bankruptcy Efficient?', **27** *Journal of Financial Economics*, 411-18.

Eberhart, A.C., Moore, W.T. and Roenfeldt, R.L. (1990), 'Security Pricing and Deviations from the Absolute Priority Rule in Bankruptcy Proceedings, **45** *Journal of Finance*, 1457-70.

Eisenberg, Theodore (1981), 'Bankruptcy Law in Perspective', **28** *UCLA Law Review*, 953-999.

Eisenberg, Theodore (1987), 'Bankruptcy in the Administrative State', **50(2)** *Law and Contemporary Problems*, 3-52.

Eisenberg, Theodore (1989), 'Commentary on "On the Nature of Bankruptcy": Bankruptcy and Bargaining', **75** *Virginia Law Review*, 205-218.

Eisenberg, Theodore and Tagashira, Shoichi (1994), 'Should We Abolish Chapter 11? The Evidence from Japan', **23** *Journal of Legal Studies*, 111-157.

Fisher, Timothy C.G. and Martel, Jocelyn (1995), 'The Creditors' Financial Reorganization Decision: New Evidence from Canadian Data', **11** *Journal of Law, Economics, and Organization*, 112-126.

Fletcher, Ian F. (1984), 'Bankruptcy Notices: Perils and Perplexities', *Journal of Business Law*, 355-357.

Franks, Julian and Torous, Walter (1989), 'An Empirical Investigation of U.S. Firms in Reorganization', **44** *Journal of Finance*, 747-769.

Franks, Julian and Torous, Walter (1994), 'A Comparison of Financial Recontracting in Distressed Exchanges and Chapter 11 Reorganizations', **35** *Journal of Financial Economics*, 349-370.

Frost, Christopher (1992), 'Running the Asylum: Governance Problems in Bankruptcy Reorganizations', **34** *Arizona Law Review*, 89 ff.

Frost, Christopher (1993), 'Organizational Form, Misappropriation Risk and the Substantive Consolidation of Corporate Groups', **44** *Hastings Law Journal*, 449 ff.

Frost, Christopher (1995a), 'The Bankruptcy Reform Act of 1994 and the Balance of Power in Corporate Reorganizations', *Annual Survey Bankruptcy Law*, 297 ff.

Frost, Christopher (1995b), 'Bankruptcy Redistributive Policies and the Limits of the Judicial Process', **74** *North Carolina Law Review*, 449 ff.

Gertner, Robert H. and Scharfstein, David (1991), 'A Theory of Workouts and the Effects of Reorganization Law', **46** *Journal of Financial Economics*, 1189 ff.

Gilson, S. (1988), 'Management Turnover and Financial Distress', **25** *Journal of Financial Economics*, 241-62.

Gilson, S. (1990), 'Bankruptcy, Boards and Blockholders', **27** *Journal of Financial Economics*, 355-378.

Gilson, S. (1991), 'Managing Default: Some Evidence on how Firms Choose between Workouts and Chapter 11', **4** *Journal of Applied Corporate Finance*, 62-70.

Gilson, S., John, K. and Lang, L. (1989), 'Troubled Debt Restructuring: An Empirical Study of Private Reorganization of Firms in Default', **26** *Journal of Financial Economics*, 315-353.

Golbe, D.L. (1981), 'The Effects of Imminent Bankruptcy on Stockholder Risk Preferences and Behavior', **12** *Bell Journal of Economics*, 321-328.

Goldberg, Victor P. (1985), 'Economic Aspects of Bankruptcy Law: Comment', **141** *Journal of Institutional and Theoretical Economics*, 99-103.

Guatri, Luigi (1986), *Crisi e Risanamento delle Imprese* (Crisis and Reorganization of the Firms), Milano, Giuffrè, 339 p.

Guttentag, Jack and Herring, Richard (1982), 'The Insolvency of Financial Institutions. Assessments and Regulatory Disposition', in Wachtel, P. (ed), *Crisis in Economic and Fianncial Structure*, Lexington, MA, Heath.

Hansen, R.G. and Randall, S. Thomas (1998), 'Auctions in Bankruptcy: Theoretical Analysis and Practical Guidance', **18(2)** *International Review of Law and Economics*, 159-186.

Harris, Richard A. (1978), 'The Consequences of Costly Default', **16** *Economic Inquiry*, 477-496.

Harris, Steven (1982), 'A Reply to Theodore Eisenberg's Bankruptcy Law in Perspective', **30** *UCLA Law Review*, 327-365.

Hart, Oliver D. (1995), *Firms, Contracts and Financial Structure*, Oxford, Clarendon.

Hax, Herbert (1985), 'Economic Aspects of Bankruptcy Law', **141** *Journal of Institutional and Theoretical Economics*, 80-98.

Hudson, John (1990), 'The Corporate Bankruptcy Decision: Comment', **4** *Journal of Economic Perspectives*, 209-211.

Hudson, John (1992), 'The Impact of the New Bankruptcy Code upon the Average Liability of Bankrupt Firms', **16** *Journal of Banking and Finance*, 351-371.

Ingberman, Daniel E. (1994), 'Triggers and Priority: An Integrated Model of the Effects of Bankruptcy Law on Overinvestment and Underinvestment', **72(3)** *Washington University Law Quarterly*, 1341-1377.

Iwicki, Matthew L. (1990), 'Accounting for Relational Financing in the Creditors' *Ex ante* Bargain: Beyond the General Average Model', **76** *Virginia Law Review*, 815-851.

Jackson, Thomas H. (1982), 'Bankruptcy, Non-Bankruptcy Entitlements, and the Creditors' Bargain', **91** *Yale Law Journal*, 857-907.

Jackson, Thomas H. (1984), 'Avoiding Powers in Bankruptcy', **36** *Stanford Law Review*, 725-787.

Jackson, Thomas H. (1985a), 'The Fresh-Start Policy in Bankruptcy Law', **98** *Harvard Law Review*, 1393-1448.

Jackson, Thomas H. (1985b), 'Translating Assets and Liabilities to the Bankruptcy Forum', **14** *Journal of Legal Studies*, 73-114.

Jackson, Thomas H. (1986a), *The Logic and Limits of Bankruptcy Law*, Cambridge (MA), Harvard University Press, 287 p.

Jackson, Thomas H. (1986b), 'Of Liquidation, Continuation, and Delay: An Analysis of Bankruptcy Policy and Nonbankruptcy Rules', **60** *American Bankruptcy Law Journal*, 399-428.

Jackson, Thomas H. (1993), 'Revisiting Auctions in Chapter 11: Comment', **36** *Journal of Law and Economics*, 655-696.

Jackson, Thomas, H. and Kronman, Anthony T. (1979), 'Secured Financing and Priorities Among Creditors', **88** *Yale Law Journal*, 1143-1182.

Jackson, Thomas H. and Scott, Robert E. (1989), 'On the Nature of Bankruptcy: An Essay on Bankruptcy Sharing and the Creditors' Bargain', **75** *Virginia Law Review*, 155-204.

Jensen, M. (1991), 'Corporate Control and the Politics of Finance', **4** *Journal of Apllied Corporate Finance*, 13-33.

Johnson, Steven B. (1986), 'Bankruptcy Reform and Its International Competitive Implications', **9** *Harvard Journal of Law and Public Policy*, 667-681.

Kanda, Hideki and Levmore, Saul (1994), 'Explaining Creditor Priorities', **80** *Virginia Law Review*, 2103-2154.

Kelly, Thomas O. III (1983), 'Compensation for Time Value as Part of the Adequate Protection during the Automatic Stay in Bankruptcy', **50** *University of Chicago Law Review*, 305-325.

Korobkin, Donald R. (1991), 'Rehabilitating Values: A Jurisprudence of Bankruptcy', **91** *Columbia Law Review*, 717-789.

Landers, Jonathan M. (1975), 'A Unified Approach to Parent, Subsidiairy and Affiliate Questions in Bankruptcy', **42** *University of Chicago Law Review*, 589-652.

Leff, Arthur A. (1970), 'Injury, Ignorance and Spite - the Dynamics of Coercive Collection', **80** *Yale Law Journal*, 1-46. Reprinted in Kronman, Anthony T. and Posner, Richard A. *(eds), The Economics of Contract Law*, Boston, Little Brown, 1979, 175-181.

Levmore, Saul and Kanda, Hideki (1994), 'Explaining Creditor Priorities', **80** *Virginia Law Review*, 2103-2154.

Lopucki, Lynn M. (1982), 'A General Theory of the Dynamics of the State Remedies/Bankruptcy System', **58** *Wisconsin Law Review*, 311-372.

Lopucki, Lynn M. (1983), 'The Debtor in Full Control. Systems Failure notwithstanding Chapter 11 of the Bankruptcy Code?', **57** *American Bankruptcy Law Journal*, 99-126.

Lopucki, Lynn M. (1994), 'The Unsecured Creditor's Bargain', **80** *Virginia Law Review*, 1887-1965.

Lopucki, Lynn M. and Whitford, William C. (1990), 'Bargaining over Equity's Share in the Bankruptcy Reorganization of Large, Publicly Held Companies', **139** *University of Pennsylvania Law Review*, 125-196.

Lopucki, Lynn and Whitford,William C (1991), 'Venue Choice and Forum Shopping in the Bankruptcy Reorganization of Large, Publicly Held Companies', **11** *Wisconsin Law Review*.

Lopucki, Lynn M. and Whitford, William C. (1993), 'Corporate Governance in the Bankruptcy Reorganization of Large, Publicly Held Companies', **141** *University of Pennsylvania Law Review*, 699-800.

Lopucki, Lynn M. and George G. Triantis (1994), 'A Systems Approach to Comparing U.S. and Canadian Reorganization of Financially Distressed Companies', **35** *Harvard International Law Journal*, 268-343.

McCoid, John C. II (1981), 'Bankruptcy, Preferences, and Efficiency: An Expression of Doubt', **67** *Virginia Law Review*, 249-273.

Meckling, William H. (1977), 'Financial Markets, Default and Bankruptcy: The Role of the State', **41(4)** *Law and Contemporary Problems*, 13-38.

Miller, Geoffrey P. (1995), 'Das Kapital: Solvency Regulation of the American Business Enterprise', University of Chicago Law and Economics Working Paper.

Miller, Merton H. (1977), 'The Wealth Transfers and Bankruptcy: Some Illustrative Examples', **41(4)** *Law and Contemporary Problems*, 39-46.

Mitchell, Jean (1993), 'Creditor Passivity and Bankruptcy: Implications for Economic Reform', in Mayer, C. and Vives, X. (eds), *Capital Markets and Financial Intermediation*, Cambridge, Cambridge University Press.

Modigliani, Franco and Miller, Merton H. (1958), 'The Cost of Capital, Corporation Finance and the Theory of Investment', **48** *American Economic Review*, 261-297.

Morris, C. Robert, Jr (1970), 'Bankruptcy Law Reform: Preferences, Secret Liens and Floating Liens', **54** *Minnesota Law Review*, 737-774.

Nelson, Philip B. (1979), 'Contracts Between a Firm and Its Constituents during Bankruptcy Crises', **13** *Journal of Economic Issues*, 583-604.

Nelson, Philip (1981), *Corporations in Crisis: Behavioral Observations for Bankruptcy Policy*, New York, Praeger.

Oswald (1984), 'The Effect of Chapter 11 on Collective Bargaining', **35** *Lab. Law Journal*.

Peterson, Richard L. and Aoki, Kiyomi (1984), 'Bankruptcy Filings before and after Implementation of the Bankruptcy Reform Law', **36** *Journal of Economics and Business*, 95-105.

Posner, Eric, A. (1995), 'Contract Law in the Welfare State: A Defense of the Unconscionabilty Doctrine, Usury Laws, and Related Limitations to Freedom of Contract', **24** *Journal of Legal Studies*, 307-08.

Posner, Eric A. (1997), 'The Political Economy of the Bankruptcy Reform Act of 1978', **96** *Michigan Law Review*.

Rasmussen, Robert K. (1992), 'Debtor's Choice: A Menu Approach to Corporate Bankruptcy', **71** *Texas Law Review*, 51 ff.

Rasmussen, Robert K. (1994), 'The *Ex ante* Effects of Bankruptcy Reform on Investment Incentives', **72** *Washington University Law Quarterly*, 1159 ff.

Rea, Samuel A., Jr (1984), 'Arm-breaking, Consumer Credit, and Personal Bankruptcy', *Economic Inquiry*, 188-208.

Roe, Mark J. (1983), 'Bankruptcy and Debt: A New Model for Corporate Reorganization', **83** *Columbia Law Review*, 527-602.

Roe, Mark J. (1989), 'Commentary on "On the Nature of Bankruptcy": Bankruptcy, Priority, and Economics', **75** *Virginia Law Review*, 219-240.

Rose-Ackerman, Susan (1991), 'Risk Taking and Ruin: Bankruptcy and Investment Choice', **20** *Journal of Legal Studies*, 277-310.

Rowley, Charles, A.I. Ogus (1984), *Prepayments and Insolvency*, London, Office of Fair Trading.

Sayag, Alain and Serbat, Henri (1982), *L'Application du Droit de la Faillite. Eléments pour un Bilan* (The Application of Bankruptcy Law. Data for an Evaluation), Paris, Librairies Techniques.

Schleifer, A. and Vishny, Robert W. (1986), 'Liquidation Values and Debt Capacity: A Market Equilibrium Approach', **47** *Journal of Finance*, 1343-1366.

Schleifer, A. and Vishny, R.W. (1992), 'Liquidation Values and Debt Capacity: A Market Equilibrum Approach', **47** *Journal of Finance*, 1343-66.

Schwartz, Alan (1981), 'Security Interests and Bankruptcy Priorities: A Review of Current Theories', **10** *Journal of Legal Studies*, 1-37.

Schwartz, Alan (1985), 'Products Liability, Corporate Structure, and Bankruptcy: Toxic Substances and the Remote Risk Relationship', **14** *Journal of Legal Studies*, 689-736.

Schwartz, Alan (1993), 'Bankruptcy Workouts and Debt Contracts', **36** *Journal of Law and Economics*, 595-632.

Schwartz, Alan (1997), 'Contracting About Bankruptcy', **13** *Journal of Law, Economics, and Organization*, 127-146.

Scott, James H., Jr. (1977), 'Bankruptcy, Secured Debt, and Optimal Capital Structure', **32** *Journal of Finance*, 1-19.

Scott, Robert E. (1986), 'Through Bankruptcy with the Creditors' Bargain Heuristic', **53** *University of Chicago Law Review*, 690-708.

Scott, Robert E. (1989), 'Sharing the Risks of Bankruptcy: Timbers, Ahlers, and Beyond', *Columbia Business Law Review*, 183-194.

Shepard, Lawrence (1984), 'Personal Failures and the Bankruptcy Reform Act of 1978', **27** *Journal of Law and Economics*, 419-437.

Shiers, Alden F. and Williamson, Daniel P. (1987), 'Nonbusiness Bankruptcies and the Law: Some Empirical Results', **21** *Journal of Consumer Affairs*, 277-292.

Slain, John J. and Kripke, Homer (1973), 'The Interface between Securities Regulation and Bankruptcy: Allocating the Risk of Illegal Securities Issuance between Securityholders and the Issuer's Creditors', **48** *New York University Law Review*, 261-300.

Spier, Kathryn E. and Sykes, Alan O. (1996), *Capital Structure, Priority Rules, and the Settlement of Civil Claims*, Mimeo, August 1996.

Stern, Jeffrey (1990), 'Note: Failed Markets and Failed Solutions: The Unwitting Formulation of the Corporate Reorganization Technique', **90** *Columbia Law Review*, 783 ff.

Stiglitz, Joseph E. (1972), 'Some Aspects of the Pure Theory of Corporate Finance: Bankruptcies and Take-Overs', **3** *Bell Journal of Economics*, 458-482.

Sullivan, A. Charlene and Worden, Debra Drecnik (1990), 'Rehabilitation or Liquidation: Consumers' Choices in Bankruptcy', **24** *Journal of Consumer Affairs*, 69-88.

Sullivan, Teresa A., Warren, Elizabeth and Westbrook, Jay Lawrence (1987), 'The Use of Empirical Data in Formulating Bankruptcy Policy', **50(2)** *Law and Contemporary Problems*, 195-235.

Sundgren, Stefan (1995), *Bankruptcy Costs and Bankruptcy Code*, Helsinki, Swedish School of Economics and Business Administration.

Sward, Ellen E. (1987), 'Resolving Conflicts between Bankruptcy Law and the State Police Power', **63** *Wisconsin Law Review*, 403-453.

Symposium (1977), 'The Economics of Bankruptcy Reform', **41(4)** *Law and Contemporary Problems*, Duke University, School of Law.

Tarzia, Giuseppe (1983), 'Credito Bancario e Risanamento dell'Impresa nella Procedura di Amministrazione Straordinaria' (Credit and the Reorganization of the Firm)', *Giurisprudenza Commerciale*, 340-352.

Triantis, George G. (1992), 'Secured Debt Under Conditions of Imperfect Information', **21** *Journal of Legal Studies*, 234-55.

Triantis, George G. (1993), 'A Theory of the Regulation of Debtor-in-Possession Financing', **46** *Vanderbilt Law Review*, 901-935.

Triantis, George G. (1993), 'A Theory of the Regulation of Debtor-in-Possession Financing', **46** *Vanderbilt Law Review*, 901-935.

Triantis, George G. (1994), 'A Free-Cash-Flow Theory of Secured Debt and Creditor Priorities', **80** *Virginia Law Review*, 2155-2168.

Triantis, George G. (1996), 'The Interplay between Liquidation and Reorganization in Bankruptcy: The Role of Screens, Gatekeepers and Guillotines', **16** *International Review of Law and Economics*, 101-119.

Triantis, George G. and Ronald J. Daniels (1995), 'The Role of Debt in Interactive Corporate Governance', **83** *California Law Review*, 1073-1113.

Trost, J. Ronald (1973), 'Corporate Bankruptcy Reorganization for the Benefit of Creditors or Stockholders?', **21** *UCLA Law Review*, 540-552.

Trost, J. Ronald (1979), 'Business Reorganizations under Chapter 11 of the New Bankruptcy Code', **34** *Business Lawyer*, 1309-1346.

Tussing, Dale A. (1967), 'The Case for Bank Failure', **10** *Journal of Law and Economics*, 129-147.

Warner, Jerold B. (1977a), 'Bankruptcy Absolute Priority Rule and Pricing of Risky Debt Claims', **4** *Journal of Financial Economics*, 239-276.

Warner, Jerold B. (1977b), 'Bankruptcy Costs: Some Evidence', **32** *Journal of Finance*, 337 ff.

Warren, Elizabeth (1984), 'Reducing Bankruptcy Protection for Consumers: A Response', **72** *Georgetown Law Journal*, 1333-1357.

Warren, Elizabeth (1987), 'Bankruptcy Policy', **54** *University of Chicago Law Review*, 775-814. Reprinted in *Bankruptcy: Legal and Financial Papers*, Bhandari (ed.) Cambridge University Press, 1994 and Reprinted in *Company Law*, Wheeler, S. (ed.) Dartmouth Publishing United Kingdom.

Warren, Elizabeth (1991), 'A Theory of Absolute Priority', *New York University Annual Survey of American Law*, 9 ff.

Warren, Elizabeth (1992), 'The Untenable Case for Repeal of Chapter 11', **102** *Yale Law Journal*, 437-479.

Warren, Elizabeth (1992), 'Why Have a Federal Bankruptcy System?', **77** *Cornell Law Review*, 1093 ff.

Warren, Elizabeth (1993), 'Bankruptcy Policymaking in an Imperfect World', **92** *Michigan Law Review*, 336 ff.

Warren, Elizabeth, Sullivan, Teresa and Westbrook, Jay (1983), 'Limiting Access to Bankruptcy Discharge: An Analysis of the Creditors' Data', **59** *Wisconsin Law Review*, 1091 ff.

Warren, Elizabeth, Sullivan, Teresa and Westbrook, Jay (1986), 'Folklore and Facts: A Preliminary Report from The Consumer Bankruptcy Project', **60** *American Bankruptcy Law Journal*, 293 ff.

Warren, Elizabeth, Sullivan, Teresa and Westbrook, Jay (1987), 'The Role of Empirical Data in Formulating a National Bankruptcy Policy', **50** *Law and Contemporary Problems*, 195 ff.

Warren, Elizabeth, Sullivan, Teresa and Westbrook, Jay (1988), 'Laws, Models, and Real People', **13** *Law and Social Inquiry*, 661 ff.

Warren, Elizabeth, Sullivan, Teresa and Westbrook, Jay (1989), *As We Forgive Our Debtors: Consumer Credit and Bankruptcy in America*, Oxford, Oxford University Press.

Warren, Elizabeth, Sullivan, Teresa and Westbrook, Jay (1994a), 'Consumer Debtors Ten Years Later: A Financial Comparison of Consumer Bankrupts 1981-91', **68** *American Bankruptcy Law Journal*, 121 ff.

Warren, Elizabeth, Sullivan, Teresa and Westbrook, Jay (1994b), 'The Persistence of Local Legal Culture: Twenty Years of Evidence from the Bankruptcy Courts', **17** *Harvard Journal of Law and Public Policy*, 801 ff.

Warren, Elizabeth and Westbrook, Jay (1994c), 'Searching for Reorganization Realities', **72** *Washington University Law Quarterly*, 3001 ff.

Webb, David C. (1987), 'The Importance of Incomplete Information in Explaining the Existence of Costly Bankruptcy', **54** *Economica*, 137-151.

Webb, David C. (1991), 'An Economic Evaluation of Insolvency Procedures in the United Kingdom: Does the 1986 Insolvency Act Satisfy the Creditor's Bargain?', **43** *Oxford Economic Papers*, 139-157.

Weiss, L.A. (1990), 'Bankruptcy Resolution: Direct Costs and Violation of Priority of Claims', **27** *Journal of Financial Economics*, 285-314.

Weistart, John C. (1977), 'The Costs of Bankruptcy', **41(4)** *Law and Contemporary Problems*, 107-122.

Weston, Fred J. (1977), 'Some Economic Fundamentals for an Analysis of Bankruptcy', **41(4)** *Law and Contemporary Problems*, 47-65.

White, Michelle J. (1980), 'Public Policy toward Bankruptcy: Me-First and Other Priority Rules', **11** *Bell Journal of Economics*, 550-564.

White, Michelle J. (1983), 'Bankruptcy Costs and the New Bankruptcy Code', **38** *Journal of Finance*, 477-504.

White, Michelle J. (1984), 'Bankruptcy Liquidation and Reorganization', in Logue, D.E. (1984) (ed.), *Handbook of Modern Finance*, Boston, Warren, Gorham and Lamont.

White, Michelle J. (1987), 'Personal Bankruptcy Under the 1978 Bankruptcy Code: An Economic Analysis', **63** *Indiana Law Journal*, 1-53.

White, Michelle J. (1989), 'The Corporate Bankruptcy Decision', **3** *Journal of Economic Perspectives*, 129-151.

White, Michelle J. (1984), 'Corporate Bankruptcy as a Filtering Device: Chapter 11 Reorganizations and Out-of-Court Debt Restructerings', **10** *Journal of Law, Economics and Organization*, 268-295.

White, Michelle J. (1995), 'The Costs of Corporate Bankruptcy: A U.S.-European Comparison', in Bhandari, Jagdeep S. (ed.), *Bankruptcy: Economic and Legal Perspectives*.

X (1987), 'Note: "Adequate Protection" and the Availability of Postpetition Interest to Undersecured Creditors in Bankruptcy', **100** *Harvard Law Review*, 1106-1124.

Other References

Becker, Gary S. (1968), 'Crime and Punishment: An Economic Approach', **76** *Journal of Political Economy*,169-217.

Buchanan, James M., Tollison, Robert D. and Tullock, G. (1980), *Towards a Theory of the Rent-seeking Society*, College Station, Texas A&M, University Press.

Hoppit, Julian (1987), *Risk and Failure in English Business, 1700-1800*, Cambridge; New York, Cambridge University Press.

Stiglitz, Joseph, E. and Weiss, Andrew (1981), 'Credit Rationing in Markets with Imperfect Information', **71** *American Economic Review*, 393-410.

7900
EVIDENCE

Jeffrey S. Parker
Professor of Law
George Mason University School of Law

Bruce H. Kobayashi
Associate Professor of Law
George Mason University School of Law

Abstract

The economic analysis of evidence law is relatively less developed than other areas of the law and economics literature, notwithstanding this subject's close relationship to other well-developed areas, most notably the economic analysis of procedural rules. This chapter first will develop some of the general issues raised by the economic analysis of evidence within the Anglo-American tradition of adversarial presentation. We will then proceed to consider the existing literature on specific topics in the law of evidence and related problems of pre-trial discovery and trial error.
JEL classification: K41, K42
Keywords: Pre-Trial Discovery, Burden of Proof, Accuracy, Hearsay

1. Introduction

The economic analysis of evidence law is relatively less developed than other areas of the law and economics literature, notwithstanding this subject's close relationship to other well-developed areas, most notably the economic analysis of procedural rules (see Friedman, 1998). This state of affairs may be due to the inherent complexity of the subject, as combining the economics of procedural rules with the economics of information, as well as to the diversity of legal approaches to the problems of evidence across different legal traditions and across different jurisdictions within the same legal tradition.

Accordingly, this chapter first will develop some of the general issues raised by the economic analysis of evidence within the Anglo-American tradition of adversarial presentation (Section 2), starting from the analysis of our companion chapter on Civil Procedure: General (Chapter 7000). We will then proceed to consider the existing literature on specific topics in the law of evidence (Section 3) and related problems of pre-trial discovery and trial error (Section 4).

Related topics are treated elsewhere in this volume by the companion chapter on civil procedure: general (7000), and by the chapters on fee shifting (7300), the litigation/settlement decision (7400), and class actions (7600); the organization of the courts, including jurisdictional issues (7100-7200); criminal procedure (7700); the economics of crime and punishment (8000-8600); arbitration and the private enforcement of law (7500); bankruptcy proceedings (7800); legal error, rules versus standards, and accuracy in adjudication (7900), punitive damages (Volume III, 3700), the computing of damages, including the allocations of damages via contribution and indemnity rules (Volume III, 3500); and the production of legal rules and precedent (9000-9900).

A. General Considerations

In this part, we first survey evidence law doctrine as evolved within the Anglo-American tradition of adversarial presentation, and then develop the basic economic analysis of evidence law within such a tradition, as an outgrowth of the general concern of procedural rules with minimizing the sum of direct costs and error costs, as supplemented by a more extensive consideration of the effects of evidence rules on the production, supply and use of information both within the litigation process and externally.

2. Anglo-American Evidence Law Doctrine

Within the Anglo-American legal tradition, evidence law doctrine evolved initially through common-law development. However, in the United States at the present time, evidence law largely has been codified through the vehicle of the Federal Rules of Evidence (FRE), which were adopted in 1975 for use in the US federal courts and, through their adoption in the Uniform Rules of Evidence, now also are substantially in force in the court systems of some 35 of the 50 States, with some variations. (See *Uniform Laws Annotated* for a list of adopting jurisdictions and treatment of variations.) This provides a degree of uniformity within US evidence law, though some important state court systems continue to follow the common-law approach (as in New York) or have their own distinctive evidence codes (as in California). In this chapter, we will relate evidence law doctrine primarily to the provisions of the FRE.

Anglo-American evidence law doctrine concerns itself primarily with questions of *admissibility* (that is, whether a given item of evidence will be admitted to or excluded from consideration by the trier of facts, be it judge or jury), and secondarily with questions of *proof and presumptions* (determining which litigant will bear the burdens of producing evidence and persuading the finder of fact on a particular issue).

Admissibility rules comprise three categories:

(1) rules of relevancy, which measure the relationship between offered evidence and the legal issues involved in the litigation (FRE art. 4);
(2) rules of 'reliability', which regulate the mechanisms and forms by which evidence may be presented, both through witnesses (FRE arts. 6 and 7) and documents (FRE arts. 9 and 10), and include the general rule against hearsay evidence and the exceptions to that rule (FRE art. 8). This usage of the term 'reliability' in reference to this family of rules is not uniform in legal sources, but follows the US Supreme Court's usage in *Daubert v. Merrell Dow Pharmaceuticals*. Other authorities may refer to these rules simply as 'admissibility' rules, or in some cases as 'competency' or 'foundational' rules;
(3) so-called 'extrinsic' policies of exclusion, most notably the evidentiary privileges for confidential or proprietary information (left by FRE art. 5 to common-law development but codified in most state counterparts).

The basic rule of relevancy is a minimal requirement satisfied by a logical argument that a given item of evidence has non-zero probative value, in the Bayesian sense that its admission will affect the probability of a fact of consequence to the litigation (FRE 401). Relevant evidence is presumptively admissible, unless excluded by another rule (FRE 402). Within the doctrine of relevance, minimally relevant evidence may be excluded if its probative value is outweighed by one or more costs, including delay or waste of time, confusion of jurors, or unfairly prejudicial effect. In addition to a general power in the court to exclude relevant evidence on such grounds (FRE 403), the law gives specific treatment to several categories of evidence ordinarily so excluded, including evidence of 'character', meaning an individual's propensity to act in certain ways (FRE 404-406, 412; but see FRE 413-15 (reversing the traditional rule for allegations of sexual assault or child molestation in both civil and criminal cases), evidence of subsequent changes to an injury-causing condition (FRE 407), and evidence of settlement or plea negotiations, liability insurance coverage, and the like (FRE 408-411).

Reliability rules also can exclude minimally relevant evidence that fails to conform to requirements of admissible form or source. This category includes two basic types of rules, the first being 'threshold' showings - sometimes referred to as 'competency' or 'foundational' requirements - that the evidence stems from a 'reliable' source, which in the case of witnesses requires that testimony be limited to personal sense impressions ('first-hand' or 'personal' knowledge) and generally excludes non-expert opinion (FRE 602, 701), and in the case of documents requires 'authentication' of the document (FRE art. 9) and prefers original documents to secondary evidence of their contents (FRE art. 10, the 'Best Evidence' rule). The second type of rule in this category is the general rule against hearsay, defined as an out-of-court statement offered to prove the truth of the matter asserted by the statement (FRE 801-802) and its many exceptions (see FRE 803-807) that admit statements made under conditions thought to provide 'circumstantial guarantees of trustworthiness' (FRE 807, stating the open-ended 'residual' exception to the hearsay rule). Both types of reliability rules, and especially the hearsay rule, are rationalized and developed in legal authority by reference to the value of in-court (or some instances, pre-trial) adversarial testing of the credibility of evidentiary sources.

Extrinsic policies of exclusion - paradigmatically, the evidentiary privileges - may exclude otherwise relevant and reliable evidence in order to encourage or protect some relationship or activity 'extrinsic' to the issues in litigation, such as certain governmental functions, the provision of confidential legal, medical, or personal advice, or the productive use of private or commercial information. In this instance, the rule of exclusion explicitly recognizes a tradeoff between the accuracy of litigation fact-finding and a perceived external benefit, or in some instances an offsetting internal benefit, such as improving the quality of legal representation. In addition to the evidentiary privileges, some of the special rules of relevancy excluding evidence of subsequent remedial measures, insurance, compromise negotiations, or the like, are sometimes rationalized by reference to an extrinsic policy of encouraging safety, insurance against risk, settlement, and so on.

Proof and presumption rules (see FRE art. 3) are concerned with the allocation and procedural effect of burdens and standards of proof. Generally speaking, the substantive law casts the burden of proof for every element of a claim upon the complaining party (the plaintiff in civil cases and the government in criminal cases) in both of two senses: (1) the burden of production or 'going forward', which allocates the burden of adducing some evidence on the point in question (though this burden can be shifted by operation of a 'presumption'); and (2) the burden of persuasion, or 'risk of non-persuasion', which specifies the party who will lose in the event that the quality of evidence falls beneath the pertinent standard of proof. Aside from specifying the verbal formulae to be used in instructing the trier of fact, and the procedural effects of legally deficient failures of proof, the Anglo-American law of evidence (and procedure) has virtually nothing to say on the subject of proof as distinguished from admissibility. Unless the issue is resolved as a matter of law, determinations of fact by juries are formally unreviewable by either trial or appellate judges in the United States, and determinations of fact by trial court judges are reviewed under a highly deferential standard on appeal. The concept of the rules is sharply to distinguish determinations of fact from determinations of law.

3. General Economic Analysis of Evidence Law

As a species of procedural rule, evidence rules can be approached initially through the economic framework postulated by Posner (1973) of minimizing the sum of error costs and direct costs, both public and private. As with procedural rules in general, the coercive and sequential aspects of the litigation process present potential strategic use of evidence rules by litigants to influence opposing litigants' costs or to degrade the accuracy of judicial determinations (see Friedman, 1992), perhaps resulting in excessive expenditures by both the litigants and the court (see Posner, 1992, p. 586), as well as inaccurate decisions (see Tullock, 1980).

However, evidence rules are distinguished from other procedural rules by being focused solely upon the fact-finding aspect of the litigation process. This characteristic has two major implications for the economic analysis of evidence rules that have been identified in the literature: (1) the internalization of most factual error costs; and (2) the effect of evidence rules on information supply, both within litigation and externally.

3.1 Internalization of Error Costs

Aside from the precedential effect of evidentiary rulings themselves, error costs associated with inaccurate fact-finding in litigation tend to be internalized to the immediate parties, thus diminishing the social interest in the accuracy of any particular litigated outcome, unless such errors are systematically biased (see Kaplow, 1994; Kaplow and Shavell, 1994, 1996; Parker, 1995; Rasmusen, 1995). Furthermore, in the absence of external effects, and with the competitive provision of evidence to the court by adversarial parties motivated by symmetrical stakes, there is reason to doubt whether relying on information provided by interested parties systematically degrades the accuracy of factual determinations, even assuming strategic behaviors. Milgrom and Roberts (1986) demonstrate this result under the assumption of symmetrical and costless access to information by the parties. The same theoretical result is extended to symmetrical but costly access by Froeb and Kobayashi (1993, 1996) (see also McAfee and Reny, 1992; Shin, 1998; and Lewis and Poitevin, 1997), and is consistent with recent experimental findings comparing adversarial with non-adversarial presentation in terms of both revelation of hidden information and accuracy of litigated outcomes (Block et al., 1998; Parker and Lewisch, 1998). However, these results are qualified by reference to the assumption of symmetrical access and verification of parties' reports, which highlights the potential importance of the pretrial discovery process as eliminating or diminishing the case of private asymmetrical information in one party (see, for example, Cooter and Rubinfeld, 1994; Hay, 1994; Jost, 1995; Sobel, 1989; and the discussion in the companion Chapter 7000 of this work). Subject to those qualifications, the economic analysis of evidence law has tended to focus on the functions of evidence rules in regulating either direct costs to the parties and the court, or a different class of error costs occasioned by systematic bias or other agency costs on the part of the public decision-maker. From this perspective, many aspects of both proof and the admissibility rules of relevancy and reliability have been explained (or criticized) in terms of their operation on the marginal product of parties' and courts' expenditures (see Posner, 1973, 1992, § 21.8; Gibbons and Hutchinson, 1982; Rubinfeld and Sappington, 1987; Miceli, 1990; Friedman, 1992; Davis, 1994; Hay and Spier, 1997), as reinforcing the institutional specialization implied by the division of decision-making authority within tribunals, including the internalization of fact-finding error by design (Parker, 1995), or as controlling bias on the part of decision makers (Posner, 1992, p. 521; Shrag and Scotchmer, 1994).

3.2 Effects on Information Supply

The second major distinguishing feature of the economic analysis of evidence law concerns the effects of evidence rules (and related rules of pre-trial discovery) on the supply of information both within litigation and externally. This is most transparent in the case of evidentiary privileges, which are based explicitly upon considerations of encouraging the generation of certain types of information by protecting against compelled disçlosure, and as such define a class of intellectual property (Easterbrook, 1981; see also Gould, 1980; Kitch, 1980; and Stigler, 1980). While some evidentiary privilege rules may have entirely external effects on information production (as balanced against direct and error costs internally), both the attorney-client privilege and the related 'work product' doctrine (which protects against compelled disclosure of the fruits of litigation inputs by litigants and lawyers) appear to be endogenous to the litigation fact-finding process, and therefore may contribute either positively or negatively to direct costs and error costs. Existing literature expresses differing points of view on the social consequences of these effects (see Allen et al., 1994; Bundy and Elhauge, 1991; Kaplow and Shavell, 1989, 1990, 1992; Shavell, 1988).

However, the effect of evidence and discovery rules on information supply is more general than the rules of privilege. First, compelled disclosure of information in litigation can affect the incentives of both parties and non-parties to produce information *ex ante*. Thus, rules compelling an interested party to disclose harmful information to the court or adversary (either by formal order or by default on a burden of proof) may reduce incentives to produce any information, or bias the production function (see Kobayashi, Parker and Ribstein, 1996; Shavell, 1989), and, by extension, one or both incentives may also affect even disinterested non-parties, essentially by imposing a 'tax' on information through its expropriation in the litigation process (see Parker, 1995). Second, even in the absence of compulsion, as in the case of compensated expert testimony, the rules of admissibility can affect the external supply of information available for use in litigation, by influencing the marginal incentives of prospective expert witnesses to produce certain forms of expert opinion (Parker, 1995; see also Elliott, 1989).

B. Specific Topics in the Economic Analysis of Evidence Law

In this section, we will survey the existing law and economics literature by reference to the main problems addressed in Anglo-American evidence law doctrine, under the following divisions: (a) relevance and prejudice; (b) statistical evidence; (c) burdens of proof, presumptions, and accuracy; (d) knowledge, opinion, and expert testimony; (e) the hearsay rule; and (f) evidentiary privilege. As will be demonstrated by this survey, relatively few of the institutional details of the law of evidence have been analyzed by the law and economics literature to date.

4. Relevance and Prejudice

The doctrine of relevancy and its counterweights (discussed in section II.A above) appears designed to operate upon both error costs and direct costs to the parties and the court, by focusing all evidence on the matters of fact identified as decisive by the substantive law (FRE 401). Presumably, this improves the efficiency of law enforcement and contributes positively to the accuracy of adjudication (see generally Kaplow, 1994). In addition, relevancy standards may operate to reduce agency costs in the form of fact-finder bias, by depriving the fact-finder of access to information on non-relevant grounds of decision (see Posner, 1992, p. 521).

This same concept of controlling agency cost in the form of bias is carried over into the joint case of evidence that has both probative value and 'prejudicial' effect (conceived for this analysis as extrinsic grounds of decision), for which the law (FRE 403) requires the judge to make an explicit cost-benefit analysis (see Gibbons and Hutchinson, 1982, discussing the

British counterpart to FRE 403). In addition, more specific rules carry the same concept into identified types of evidence, most notably the general rule against 'character' (propensity) evidence (FRE 404) and the recent exception for sex crimes (FRE 412-415), which is analyzed within this framework by Schrag and Scotchmer (1994). Similar considerations may underlay the additional rules disfavoring the admission of evidence of remedial measures taken after an injury-producing event, settlement negotiations, and the like (FRE 407-411) (see Daughety and Reinganum, 1995; Rasmusen, 1998). Alternatively, those rules could be analyzed in whole or in part by analogy to rules of evidentiary privilege, as seeking to reduce the 'taxation' effect of admissibility on the conduct in question, which produces both information and other goods that may have external benefits, as in the case of remedial measures improving safety (FRE 407), or endogenous benefits to the litigation process, as in the case of settlement negotiations (FRE 408), for which both non-disclosure and inadmissibility may contribute positively to the quality of legal representation (see generally Allen et al., 1990).

Relevancy rules may also operate on direct costs as constraining strategic behaviors by litigants that could result in excessive trial expenditures (see Posner, 1992, pp. 564-566; Tullock, 1980), or as one of several mechanisms for rationing access to trial time. Under the traditional Anglo-American system, parties can present evidence at trial without general limit, except through the rules of relevance, under which the judge may exclude even relevant evidence as cumulative or a 'waste of time' (FRE 403). In more recent years, this function has been supplemented by more extensive case 'management' by American trial judges, both before and at trial (see the companion Chapter 7000 of this work).

5. Statistical Evidence

There is a large body of interdisciplinary literature, mostly outside the law and economics field, discussing the use of probabilistic reasoning and statistical methods in assessing both admissibility and proof (for example, Cohen, 1981; Fairley, 1973; Fienberg, 1989; Finkelstein and Fairley, 1970; Kaye, 1979, 1981; Kornstein, 1975; Lempert, 1977; Nesson, 1985; Schum, 1986; Shaviro, 1989; Tillers and Schum, 1988; Tribe, 1971; see generally Anderson and Twining, 1991; Schum, 1994). As part of this literature, there is debate concerning whether and to what extent statistical findings should be admitted into evidence, especially in criminal cases of disputed identification.

In American law, this problem has been addressed through the standards applicable to expert testimony (see Part D, below) and as an application of the relevancy-prejudice balancing analysis of FRE 403. The relatively hostile attitude of American courts toward admissibility may reflect the bias inherent in the selection of disputes for litigation, and for trial versus settlement (see generally Gould, 1973; Priest and Klein, 1984). Statistical methods generally assume random events, while litigation selects unique events non-randomly, and substantive law generally attaches significance to unique events rather than mean outcomes, though it has been argued that this may be inefficient in some settings (see Kaplow and Shavell, 1996). However, where the substantive law effectively requires all events to be random as to some variable (as perhaps in alleged discrimination in jury selection, employment, or the like), or states a standard related to mean outcomes rather than unique non-random events, then the case for admission of statistical findings is stronger.

6. Burdens of Proof, Presumptions, and Accuracy

The debate noted in the previous subsection also embraces questions concerning the evaluation whether a body of evidence meets specified standards of proof, which tend to be stated in terms suggesting probabilistic analysis, as in 'more probable than not' (the 'preponderance' standard applicable in most civil cases), 'clear and convincing evidence' (a higher standard for certain civil cases such as fraud that may have external effects on reputation), and 'beyond a reasonable doubt' (the highest standard, applied in criminal cases). (See the sources cited above and Lombardero (1996), which considers joint probability determinations.) Strictly speaking, this debate has limited significance to the law of evidence or the law of procedure, especially in jury cases, because the sufficiency of evidence to meet a particular standard is evaluated legally through the rule of 'substantial evidence', which essentially asks whether a jury rationally could accept the evidence as sufficient - a highly deferential rule that insulates all but the most egregious factual errors from review by trial or appellate judges, thus minimizing the law's concern with factual accuracy in particular cases.

In contrast, the selection of standards of proof is considered a legal question, which from the economic perspective appears to rest upon whether error costs are symmetrical, with the higher standards predicated on the assumption that false positive errors are more costly than false negative errors in certain settings (see Kaplow, 1994; Kaplow and Shavell, 1994; Posner, 1992, p. 553). However, error costs may also depend upon factors other than the standard of proof (see Davis, 1994, arguing that both the parameters of the underlying population and characteristics of fact-finding technology may affect the optimal standard of proof).

Distinguishable from the standard or quality of proof is the selection of which party bears the burden of proof in terms of both ultimate persuasion and initial production of evidence (see Rubinfeld and Sappington, 1987; Miceli, 1990; Hay and Spier, 1997; Sanchirico, 1997b). The casting of the burden of proof may affect both error costs and direct costs. The general rule of casting the burdens of both production and persuasion upon plaintiffs may operate to reduce direct costs by providing an incentive to avoid litigation in the first instance (see Posner, 1992), and may operate within the litigation to reduce incentives for strategic behavior by forcing plaintiffs to internalize more of the direct cost of obtaining the transfer payment they seek, though the advent of compelled pre-trial discovery from the adversary tends to re-introduce both strategic behavior and moral hazard problems (see, for example, Cooter and Rubinfeld, 1994; Easterbrook, 1989). Even aside from discovery procedures, casting the burden of production on the party bearing relatively higher costs of production may increase both direct and error costs.

Presumptions, under the standard analysis (see FRE 301-302), operate to shift the burden of production rather than persuasion, usually by allowing the party bearing the burden to substitute proof of a different 'basic fact' for direct proof of the 'presumed fact' required by substantive law (see Epstein, 1973). From an economic perspective, presumptions would appear to be based upon both a high factual correlation between the basic and presumed facts, coupled with a disparity in the costs of producing evidence of the two facts, at least in some circumstances.

7. Knowledge, Opinion and Expert Testimony

The 'reliability' rules of admissibility also can operate on both error costs and direct costs (see Gross, 1987), though they also may have effects on information supply and in some instances may be influenced by the interest in policing strategic behaviors by litigants. The basic reliability rules of 'competency' and 'authentication' require that witness testimony be confined to 'facts' based upon the witness's first-hand 'knowledge' (personal sense impression) as distinguished from 'opinion', and that documents be shown to be authentic before their contents may be considered. In both instances, the evidence is required to meet a threshold 'quality' standard before it is admitted to consideration. Thus, these rules can operate both on error costs (assuming that the legal standard of quality is positively related to accuracy) and on direct costs, by channeling the litigants' efforts away from lower quality evidence and toward higher quality evidence, thus increasing the productivity of the parties' expenditures at trial and reducing strategic behaviors consisting of introducing 'low quality' evidence that imposes rebuttal costs on the adverse litigant (see Posner, 1992, pp. 564-566).

The most significant of these rules is the requirement that witness testimony be based upon first-hand knowledge (FRE 602) and its negative correlative in the rule generally excluding non-expert opinion (FRE 701). One economic explanation for these rules is that they embody the economic logic of specialization within the institutional setting of trial, by separating raw information inputs from the inferential function performed by the trier of fact (see Parker, 1995), thus arguably reducing both error costs (if juries and judges are more accurate in drawing conclusions than witnesses) and direct costs, to the extent that litigants are prevented from introducing the 'lower quality' second-hand information or witness conclusions.

The rules permitting expert testimony (see FRE 702-705), generally cast in the form of opinion, may be based upon the similar logic that experts, within their fields of professional specialization, may possess a comparative advantage over juries and judges in drawing conclusions from the available data (see Parker, 1995). However, the standards defining the permitted scope of expert testimony have been controversial. By the logic of permitting expert testimony, neither judges not juries are well-equipped to evaluate when it actually provides a comparative advantage in fact-finding, and so there has been a tendency to look toward external standards of 'general acceptance' in the expert's field. These rules in turn have been criticized as permitting strategic behavior by parties within the litigation (see Elliott, 1989) and as encouraging rent-seeking behaviors by both litigants and testifying experts (Parker, 1995), and recently have been modified by the US Supreme Court in *Daubert v. Merrell Dow Pharmaceuticals*, to place more emphasis on internalized admissibility standards and adversarial testing of scientific expert testimony.

An alternative to exclusive reliance upon adversarial presentation is provided by the court's authority to appoint its own 'neutral' expert (FRE 706). However, Froeb and Kobayashi (1993, 1996) have shown theoretically that the court-appointed expert does not reduce either direct or error costs from the alternative of competitive and selective presentation by adverse parties, even if the fact-finder is both naive and biased. Furthermore, their analysis suppresses considerations of public-choice problems or agency costs in the judge or expert, which would tend to strengthen their results in the direction of favoring adversarial presentation. Their assumption of symmetrical access in the parties does not appear to be a severe limitation in the context of expert opinion testimony, which by definition does not rest upon private factual information and is supplied in an explicit competitive labor market.

8. The Hearsay Rule

Like the other 'reliability' rules, the rule against hearsay evidence (an out-of-court statement offered to prove the truth of the matter asserted by the statement) (see FRE 801-802) appears designed to reduce by direct and error costs by preferring in-court testimony (presumably of higher quality, see Tribe, 1974, for a legal treatment of quality issues) to the secondary 'hearsay' evidence, and by requiring the proponent of the evidence to bear the higher cost of producing the higher quality of evidence. The status of the hearsay rule as a rule of preference rather than a rule of absolute exclusion is indicated by the many exceptions to the general rule (FRE 803-807) and important categories of defined non-hearsay statements (FRE 801(d)), notably including statements by adverse litigants, former testimony, business or governmental records, and spontaneous declarations, among others.

However, the rationale of the basic rule has been criticized by Friedman (1992), who argues that the cost of producing the higher-quality non-hearsay evidence should be placed upon the opposing party, in order to reduce strategic uses of hearsay objections to exclude evidence having some net probative value (see also Kaplow, 1980). This analysis assumes that hearsay evidence passing the relevancy balancing test of FRE 403 will contribute positively to accuracy, and that the proponent is not uniquely advantaged over the opponent in the cost of producing the non-hearsay evidence, and does not address strategic behaviors by proponents under this alternative regime, or consider possible effects on external supply.

9. Evidentiary Privileges

The law of evidentiary privileges explicitly incurs some measure of direct and error costs within litigation fact-finding in order to achieve the 'extrinsic' benefit of encouraging information production by securing property rights against compelled disclosure of information generated in the course of specified relationships or activities. The protected activities traditionally included confidential communications between attorney and client, physician or psychotherapist and patient, priest and penitent, law enforcement officers and informants, and between spouses, as well as trade secrets and government secrets. Recent legislation in some US jurisdictions has extended such protection to news reports and their sources and a wide of counseling relationships. More broadly conceived, this category of rules might be thought to include the constitutional privilege against self-incrimination and the exclusionary rule applied to evidence obtained through illegal search and seizure by the government, though those topics conventionally are treated as part of the law of criminal procedure (see Chapter 7500 of this volume).

Within the law and economics literature, only the attorney-client privilege and the related 'work product' doctrine (protecting against compelled disclosure of litigation inputs by lawyers and litigants) have received extensive consideration. These rules may have differing and more complex characteristics than the other types of privilege, which are most conceived as having only negative influences on the cost and accuracy of litigation fact-finding, to be balanced against positive external benefits widely diffused throughout the society. In contrast with that simpler analysis, both the attorney-client privilege and the work product doctrine may operate to improve the quality of legal representation, and in that way reduce both error costs and direct costs within litigation, in addition to whatever external benefits (or costs) ensue (see Allen et al., 1990; Bundy and Elhauge, 1991; Kobayashi, Parker and Ribstein, 1996).

Suppressing these possible internal benefits to the litigation process itself, a series of papers by Shavell (1988) and Kaplow and Shavell (1989, 1990) questions the social desirability of protecting the confidentiality of legal advice in a variety of settings. The Kaplow-Shavell analysis is criticized by Allen et al. (1990), on the ground that it overlooks the constructive role of confidential client communications in assisting lawyers' development of alternative legal grounds for the litigant's case, which might not be discovered and developed in the absence of the privilege. They advance a similar analysis of the work product doctrine as enabling lawyers to overcome a 'joint production' problem (that is, that lawyers' investment may produce both positive and negative information regarding the client), extending the previous work by Easterbrook (1981) treating the work product doctrine as a species of intellectual property protection.

Bibliography on Evidence (7900)

Allen, Ronald J., Grady, Mark F., Polsby, Daniel and Yashko, Michael S. (1990), 'A Positive Theory of the Attorney Client Privilege and the Work Product Doctrine', **19(2)** *Journal of Legal Studies*, 359-397.

Anderson, Terence and Twining, William (1991), *Analysis of Evidence*, Boston, Little Brown.

Block, Michael K., Parker, Jeffrey S., Vyborna, Olga and Dusek, Libor (1998), *Fact-Finding Efficiency in Legal Procedure: An Experimental Comparison of Adversarial Versus Inquisitorial Regimes*, George Mason University School of Law, Working Papers in Law and Economics, No. 98-3.

Boari, Nicola (1997), 'On the Efficiency of Penal Systems: Several Lessons from the Italian Experience', **17** *International Review of Law and Economics*, 115-126.

Bundy, Stephen M. and Elhauge, Einer Richard (1991), 'Do Lawyers Improve the Adversary System? A General Theory of Litigation Advice and Its Regulation', **79** *California Law Review*, 313-420.

Cohen, L. Jonathan (1981), 'Subjective Probability and the Paradox of the Gatecrasher', *Arizona State Law Journal*, 627 ff.

Cooper, Edward H. (1994), 'Discovery Cost Allocation: Comment', **23** *Journal of Legal Studies*, 465-480.

Cooter, Robert D. and Rubinfeld, Daniel L. (1994), 'An Economic Model of Legal Discovery in the U.S.', **23** *Journal of Legal Studies*, 435-463.

Daughety, Andrew F. and Reinganum, Jennifer F. (1995), 'Keeping Society in the Dark: On the Admissibility of Pretrial Negotiations as Evidence in Court', **26** *Rand Journal of Economics*, 203-221.

Davis, Michael L. (1994), 'The Value of Truth and the Optimal Standard of Proof in Legal Disputes', **10** *Journal of Law, Economics, and Organization*, 343-359.

Easterbrook, Frank H. (1981), 'Insider Trading, Secret Agents, Evidentiary Privileges, and the Production of Information', **1981** *Supreme Court Review*, 309-365.

Easterbrook, Frank H. (1989), 'Comment: Discovery as Abuse', **69** *Boston University Law Review*, 635-648.

Elliott, E. Donald (1989), 'Toward Incentive-Based Procedure: Three Approaches for Regulating Scientific Evidence', **69** *Boston University Law Review*, 487-511.

Epstein, Richard A. (1973), 'Pleadings and Presumptions', **40** *University of Chicago Law Review*, 556 ff.

Fairley, William B. (1973), 'Probabilistic Analysis of Identification Evidence', **2** *Journal of Legal Studies*, 493-513.

Fienberg, Stephen E. (ed.) (1989), *The Evolving Role of Statistical Assessments as Evidence in the Courts*, New York, Springer, 357 p.

Finkelstein, M.O. and Fairley, William B. (1970), 'A Bayesian Approach to Identification Evidence', **83** *Harvard Law Review*, 489 ff.

Friedman, Richard D. (1992), 'Toward a Partial Economic, Game Theoretic Analysis of Hearsay', **76** *Minnesota Law Review*, 723-796.

Friedman, Richard D. (1998), 'Economic Analysis of Evidentiary Law: An Underused Tool, an Underplowed Field', **19** *Cardozo Law Review*.

Froeb, Luke M. and Kobayashi, Bruce H. (1993), *Competition in the Production of Costly Information: An Economic Analysis of Adversarial versus Court-Appointed Presentation of Expert Testimony*, George Mason University School of Law, Working Papers in Law and Economics, No.93-5.

Froeb, Luke M. and Kobayashi, Bruce H. (1996), 'Naive, Biased, Yet Bayesian: Can Juries Interpret Selectively Produced Evidence?', **12** *Journal of Law, Economics, and Organization*, 257-276.

Gibbons, T. and Hutchinson, A.C. (1982), 'The Practice and Theory of Evidence Law - A Note', **2** *International Review of Law and Economics*, 119-126.

Gould, John P. (1973), 'The Economics of Legal Conflicts', **2** *Journal of Legal Studies*, 279-300.

Gould, John P. (1980), 'Privacy and the Economics of Information', **9** *Journal of Legal Studies*, 827 ff.

Grady, Mark F., Allen, Ronald J. and Polsby, Daniel (1990), 'A Positive Theory of the Attorney-Client Privilege and the Work-Product Doctrine', **19** *Journal of Legal Studies*, 359 ff.

Gross, Samuel R. (1987), 'Loss of Innocence: Eyewitness Identification and Proof of Guilt', **16** *Journal of Legal Studies*, 395-453.

Hay, Bruce L. (1994), 'Civil Discovery: Its Effects and Optimal Scope', **23** *Journal of Legal Studies*, 481-515.

Hay, Bruce L. and Spier, Kathryn E. (1997), 'Burdens of Production in Civil Litigation: An Economic Perspective', **26** *Journal of Legal Studies*, 413-432.

Holm, Hakan J. (1995), 'Computational Cost of Verifying Enforceable Contracts', **15** *International Review of Law and Economics*, 127-140.

Huber, Peter W. (1989), 'A Comment on "Toward Incentive-Based Procedure: Three Approaches for Regulating Scientific Evidence" by E. Donald Elliott', **69** *Boston University Law Review*, 513-516.

Jost, Peter J. (1995), 'Disclosure of Information and Incentives for Care', **15** *International Review of Law and Economics*, 65-85.

Kaplow, Louis (1980), 'Note, the Theoretical Foundation of the Hearsay Rules', **93** *Harvard Law Review*, 1786-1815.

Kaplow, Louis (1994), 'The Value of Accuracy in Adjudication: An Economic Analysis', **23** *Journal of Legal Studies*, 307-401.

Kaplow, Louis and Shavell, Steven (1989), 'Legal Advice about Information to Present in Litigation: Its Effects and Social Desirability', **102** *Harvard Law Review*, 565-615.

Kaplow, Louis and Shavell, Steven (1990), 'Legal Advice about Acts Already Committed', **10** *International Review of Law and Economics*, 149-159.

Kaplow, Louis and Shavell Steven (1992), 'Private versus Socially Optimal Provision of Ex-Ante Legal Advice', **8** *Journal of Law, Economics, and Organization*, 306-320.

Kaplow, Louis and Shavell Steven (1994), 'Accuracy in the Assessment of Liability', **37(1)** *Journal of Law and Economics*, 1-16.

Kaplow, Louis and Shavell, Steven (1996), 'Accuracy in the Assessment of Damages', **39** *Journal of Law and Economics*, 191-209.

Kaye, David (1979), 'The Laws of Probability and the Law of the Land', **47** *University of Chicago Law Review*, 34 ff.

Kaye, David (1981), 'Paradoxes, Gedanken Experiments and the Burden of Proof: A Response to Dr. Cohen's Reply', *Arizona State Law Journal*, 635 ff.

Kitch, Edmund W. (1980), 'The Law and Economics of Rights in Valuable Information', **9** *Journal of Legal Studies*, 683 ff.

Kobayashi, Bruce H., Parker, Jeffrey S. and Ribstein, Larry E. (1996), *The Process of Procedural Reform: Centralized Uniformity versus Local Experimentation*, George Mason University School of Law Working Papers in Law and Economics.

Kornstein, Daniel J. (1975), 'A Bayesian Model of Harmless Error', **5(1)** *Journal of Legal Studies*, 121-145.

Lempert, Richard (1977), 'Modeling Relevance', **75** *Michigan Law Review*, 1021 ff.

Levmore, Saul and Stuntz, William J. (1990), 'Remedies and Incentives in Private and Public Law: A Comparative Essay', **66** *Wisconsin Law Review*, 483-499.

Lewis, Donald E. (1983), 'Economic Aspects of the Parole Decision', **22** *Australian Economic Papers*, 259-279.

Lewis, Tracy and Poitevin, Michel (1997), 'Disclosure of Information in Regulatory Proceedings', **13** *Journal of Law, Economics, and Organization*, 50-74.

Lombardero, David A. (1996), 'Do Special Verdicts Improve the Structure of Jury Decision Making?', **36** *Jurimetrics Journal*, 275-324.

McAfee, R. Preston and Reny, Philip J. (1992), 'Correlated Information and Mechanism Design', **60** *Econometrica*, 395-421.

Miceli, Thomas J. (1990), 'Optimal Prosecution of Defendants Whose Guilt Is Uncertain', **6** *Journal of Law, Economics, and Organization*, 189-202.

Milgrom, P. and Roberts, John (1986), 'Relying on the Information of Interested Parties', **17** *Rand Journal of Economics*, 18-32.

Nesson, Charles R. (1985), 'The Evidence or the Event? On Judicial Proof and the Acceptability of Verdicts', **98** *Harvard Law Review*, 1357 ff.

Parker, Jeffrey S. (1995), 'Daubert's Debut: The Supreme Court, the Economics of Scientific Evidence, and the Adversarial System', **4** *Supreme Court Economic Review*, 1-56.

Parker, Jeffrey S. and Lewisch, Peter (1998), 'Materielle Wahrheitsfindung im Zivilprozess (The Revelation of Truth in Civil Procedure)', in X (ed.), *100 Jahre ZPO: Okonomische Analyse des Zivilprozesses*, Wien, Manz.

Posner Richard A. (1973), 'An Economic Approach to Legal Procedure and Judicial Administration', **2** *Journal of Legal Studies*, 399-458.

Posner Richard A. (1992), *Economic Analysis of Law* (4th edn), Boston, Little Brown.

Priest, George W. and Klein, Benjamin (1984), 'The Selection of Disputes for Litigation', **13** *Journal of Legal Studies*, 1-55.

Raeder, Myrna S. (1998), 'Cost-Benefit Analysis, Unintended Consequences and Evidentiary Policy: A Critique and a Rethinking of the Application of a Single Set of Evidence Rules to Civil and Criminal Cases', **19** *Cardozo Law Review*.

Rasmusen, Eric (1995), 'Predictable and Unpredictable Error in Tort Awards: The Effect of Plaintiff Self-Selection and Signaling', **15** *International Review of Law and Economics*, 323-345.

Rasmusen, Eric (1998), 'Mezzanatto and the Economics of Self-Incrimination', **19** *Cardozo Law Review*.

Rubinfeld, Daniel L. and Sappington, David E.M. (1987), 'Efficient Awards and Standards of Proof in Judicial Proceedings', **18** *Rand Journal of Economics*, 308-315.

Sanchirico, Chris William (1997a), 'The Burden of Proof in Civil Litigation: A Simple Model of Mechanism Design', **17** *International Review of Law and Economics*, 431-447.

Sanchirico, Chris William (1997b), 'Evidence Production, Adversarial Process and the Private Instigation of Suits', mimeo, Columbia University Economics Department.

Sanchirico, Chris William (1997c), *Enforcement by Hearing: An Integrated Model of Evidence Production*, mimeo, Columbia University Economics Department.

Schrag, Joel and Scotchmer, Suzanne (1994), 'Crime and Prejudice: The Use of Character Evidence in Criminal Trials', **10** *Journal of Law, Economics, and Organization*, 319-342.

Schum, David A. (1986), 'Probability and the Processes of Discovery, Proof, and Choice', **66** *Boston University Law Review*, 825-876.

Schum, David A. (1994), *The Evidential Foundations of Probabilistic Reasoning*, New York, John Wiley.

Schwartz, Robert L. (1989), 'There is no Archbishop of Science - A Comment on Elliott's Toward Incentive-Based Procedure: Three Approaches for Regulating Scientific Evidence', **69** *Boston University Law Review*, 517-525.

Setear, John K. (1989), 'The Barrister and the Bomb: The Dynamics of Cooperation, Nuclear Deterrence, and Discovery Abuse', **69** *Boston University Law Review*, 569-633.

Shapira, Ron A. (1998), 'Economic Analysis of the Law of Evidence: A Caveat', **19** *Cardozo Law Review*.

Shavell, Steven (1988), 'Legal Advice About Contemplated Acts: The Decision to Obtain Advice, its Social Desirability, and the Protection of Confidentiality', **17** *Journal of Legal Studies*, 123-150.

Shavell, Steven (1989), 'Optimal Sanctions and the Incentive to Provide Evidence to Legal Tribunals', **9** *International Review of Law and Economics*, 3-11.

Shaviro, Daniel N. (1989), 'Statistical Probability Evidence and the Appearance of Justice', **103** *Harvard Law Review*, 530-554.

Shaviro, Daniel N. and Koehler, Jonathan J. (1990), 'Veridical Verdicts: Increasing Verdict Accuracy Through the Use of Overtly Probabilistic Evidence and Methods', **75** *Cornell Law Review*, 247-279.

Shin, Hyun Song (1998), 'Adversarial and Inquisitorial Procedures in Arbitration', **29** *Rand Journal of Economics*, 378-405.

Sobel, Joel (1989), 'An Analysis of Discovery Rules', **52(1)** *Law and Contemporary Problems*, 133-160.

Spier, Kathryn E. and Hay, Bruce L. (1996), 'Burdens of Production in Civil Litigation: An Economic Perspective', **26** *Journal of Legal Studies*.

Spiotto, James E. (1973), 'Search and Seizure: An Empirical Study of the Exclusionary Rule and its Alternatives', **2** *Journal of Legal Studies*, 243-278.

Stigler, George J. (1980), 'An Introduction to Privacy in Economics and Politics', **9** *Journal of Legal Studies*, 623 ff.

Tillers, Peter and Schum, David A. (1988), 'Charting New Territory in Judicial Proof: Beyond Wigmore', **9(3)** *Cardozo Law Review*, 907-966.

Tribe, Laurence H. (1971), 'Trial by Mathematics: Precision and Ritual in the Legal Process', **84** *Harvard Law Review*, 1329-1393.

Tribe, Laurence H. (1974), 'Triangulating Hearsay', **87** *Harvard Law Review*, 957 ff.

Tullock, Gordon (1980), *Trials on Trial*, New York, Columbia University Press.

Tullock, Gordon (1988), 'Defending the Napoleontic Code over the Common Law', **2** *Research in Law and Policy Studies*, 3-27.

Weinstein, Jack B. (1989), 'What Discovery Abuse? A Comment on John Setear's the Barrister and the Bomb', **69** *Boston University Law Review*, 649-657.

X (1980), 'Note: The Theoretical Foundation of the Hearsay Rules', **93** *Harvard Law Review*, 1786-1815.

Cases

Daubert v. Merrell Dow Pharmaceuticals, Inc., 509 U.S. 579 (1993)

8000
PUBLIC ENFORCEMENT OF LAW

A. Mitchell Polinsky
Stanford University

Steven Shavell
Harvard University

Abstract

This chapter discusses the theory of the public enforcement of law - the use of public agents (inspectors, tax auditors, police, prosecutors) to detect and to sanction violators of legal rules. We first present the basic elements of the theory, focusing on the probability of imposition of sanctions, the magnitude and form of sanctions, and the rule of liability. We then examine a variety of extensions of the central theory, including accidental harms, costs of imposing fines, mistake, marginal deterrence, settlement, self-reporting, repeat offenses and incapacitation.
JEL classification: K14, K42
Keywords: Law Enforcement, Crime, Deterrence

1. Introduction

In this chapter we consider the theory of the public enforcement of law - the use of public agents (inspectors, tax auditors, police, prosecutors) to detect and to sanction violators of legal rules. Of course, private parties also play an important role in law enforcement, by providing information to public authorities and also by initiating their own legal actions (notably, tort suits), but to maintain focus we restrict attention here to public enforcement activity. (On private enforcement, see generally Landes and Posner, 1987, and Shavell, 1987c; and on private versus public enforcement, see Becker and Stigler, 1974; Landes and Posner, 1975, and Polinsky, 1980a.)

In Sections 2 through 4, we present the basic elements of the theory of public enforcement of law. Our concern is with the probability of imposition of sanctions, the magnitude and form of sanctions, and the rule of liability. In Sections 5 through 16 we then examine a variety of extensions of the central theory, including accidental harms, costs of imposing fines, mistake, marginal deterrence, settlement, self-reporting, repeat offenses and incapacitation.

Before proceeding, we note that economically-oriented analysis of public law enforcement dates from the eighteenth century contributions of Montesquieu (1748), Beccaria (1770), and, especially, Bentham (1789), whose analysis of deterrence was sophisticated and expansive. But, curiously, after Bentham (1789), the subject of enforcement lay essentially dormant in economic scholarship until the late 1960s, when Becker (1968) published a highly influential article, which has led to a voluminous literature.

2. The Basic Framework

An individual (or a firm) chooses whether to commit an act that for simplicity is assumed to cause harm with certainty (see Section 5 on uncertain harm). If he commits the act, he obtains some gain, and also faces the risk of being caught, found liable and sanctioned. The rule of liability could be either strict - under which the individual is definitely sanctioned - or fault-based - under which he is sanctioned only if his behavior fell below a fault standard. The sanction that he suffers could be a monetary fine, a prison term, or a combination of the two.

Whether an individual commits a harmful act is determined by an expected utility calculation. He will commit the act if that would raise his expected utility, taking into account the gain he would derive and the probability, form, and level of sanction that he would then face. We will usually first examine the assumption that individuals are risk neutral with respect to sanctions, that is, that they treat an uncertain sanction as equivalent to its expected value; but we will also consider alternative assumptions.

Social welfare generally is presumed to equal the sum of individuals' expected utilities. An individual's expected utility depends on whether he commits a harmful act, on whether he is a victim of someone else's harmful act, and on his tax payment, which will reflect the costs of law enforcement, less any fine revenue collected. If individuals are risk neutral, social welfare can be expressed simply as the gains individuals obtain from committing their acts, less the harms caused, and less the costs of law enforcement. (The assumption that individuals' gains always are credited in social welfare could be relaxed without affecting most of our conclusions. The principal difference that altering the assumption would make is that more acts would be treated as socially undesirable and that optimal sanctions and enforcement effort would increase.)

We assume, as is conventional, that fines are socially costless to employ because they are mere transfers of money (but in Section 6 we consider fines that are costly to impose), whereas imprisonment involves positive social costs because of the expense associated with the operation of prisons and the disutility due to imprisonment (which is not naturally balanced by gains to others).

The enforcement authority's problem is to maximize social welfare by choosing enforcement expenditures or, equivalently, a probability of detection, the level of sanctions and their form (a fine, prison term, or combination), and the rule of liability (strict or fault-based).

3. Optimal Enforcement Given the Probability of Detection

We consider here optimal enforcement given the assumption that the probability of detection is fixed (the probability will be treated as a policy instrument in the next section). Thus, we ask about the optimal form and level of sanctions under strict and fault-based liability, and about how the two liability rules compare.

Strict Liability

Assume initially that fines are the form of sanction and that individuals are risk neutral. Then the optimal fine is the harm h divided by the probability of detection p, that is, h/p; for then the expected fine equals the harm (observe that $p(h/p) = h$). If, for example, the harm is $1,000 and the probability of detection is 25 percent, the optimal fine is $4,000, and the expected fine is $1,000. This fine is optimal because, when the expected fine equals the harm, an individual will commit a harmful act if, but only if, the gain he would derive from it exceeds the harm he would cause. Essentially this basic and fundamental formula was noted by Bentham (1789, p. 173) and it has been observed by many others since.

If individuals are risk averse with regard to fines, one would expect the optimal fine to be lower than in the risk-neutral case for two reasons. First, this reduces the bearing of risk by individuals who commit the harmful act. Second, because risk-averse individuals are more easily deterred than risk-neutral individuals, the fine does not need to be as high as before to achieve any desired degree of deterrence. (However, for subtle reasons that we will not address here, the optimal fine could, in principle, be higher when individuals are risk averse.)

Next assume that imprisonment is the form of sanction, with social costs incurred in imposing sanctions. In this case, there is not a simple formula for the optimal imprisonment term (see Polinsky and Shavell, 1984). The optimal term could be such that there is either underdeterrence or overdeterrence, compared to socially ideal behavior. On one hand, a relatively low imprisonment term, implying underdeterrence, might be socially desirable because it means that imprisonment costs are reduced for those individuals who commit harmful acts. On the other hand, a relatively high term, implying overdeterrence, might be socially desirable because it means that imprisonment costs are reduced due to fewer individuals committing harmful acts, even if some of these deterred individuals would have obtained gains exceeding the harm. (The possible optimality of overdeterrence strikes us as more theoretical than real, however.)

Now consider the combined use of fines and imprisonment. Here, the main point is that fines should be employed to the maximum extent feasible before resort is made to imprisonment. In other words, it is not optimal to impose a positive imprisonment term unless the fine is maximal. (The maximal fine might be interpreted as the wealth of an individual.) The rationale for this conclusion is that fines are socially costless to impose, whereas imprisonment is socially costly, so deterrence should be achieved through the cheaper form of sanction first. This point is noted by Bentham (1789, p. 183) and Becker (1968, p. 193); see also Polinsky and Shavell (1984). To amplify, suppose that the fine f is less than the maximal fine f_m and that a positive prison term t is employed. Raise f toward f_m and lower t so as to keep the disutility of the combined sanctions constant. Then deterrence and the amount of harm will not change, but the cost of imposing the imprisonment sanction will fall, raising social welfare. Hence, it must be optimal for the fine to be maximal before imprisonment is used. (Observe that this argument holds regardless of individuals' attitudes toward risk of either fines or imprisonment.)

Fault-Based Liability

Assume again that fines are the form of liability. Then the same formula for the fine that we said was optimal under strict liability - namely, h/p, the harm divided by the probability of detection - will lead to compliance with the fault standard (assuming that the fault standard is optimally selected). For example, suppose that the harm is \$1,000, and that an individual would be found at fault if he failed to take a precaution costing less than \$1,000 that could have prevented the harm. Furthermore, suppose such a precaution exists that costs \$700. If the probability of detection is 25 percent, then a fine of \$4,000 for being at fault would induce the individual to take a precaution costing less than \$1,000; in particular, he would prefer to spend \$700 on the precaution and escape liability than not to take the precaution and bear an expected fine of \$1,000.

Observe that the optimal fine of \$4,000 in the preceding example is not unique. Any higher fine also would induce compliance with the fault standard, as would some lower fines (as long as the expected value of the fine exceeds \$700, or whatever is the expense of the precaution that costs less than \$1,000). Note that higher fines do not lead to a problem of overdeterrence because parties can escape fines by complying with the fault standard. (However, if mistakes occur in the legal process, they might be induced to spend excessively on precautions; see Section 8 below).

If individuals are risk averse, they are more easily deterred than if they are risk neutral, so the fine does not need to be as high to induce compliance with the fault standard. Moreover, assuming that compliance occurs, no one actually is sanctioned because no one is found at fault (assuming, as we do here, that there are no mistakes). Thus, fault-based liability has the attractive feature that it can accomplish desired deterrence of harm-creating conduct without imposing risk on risk-averse individuals (Shavell, 1982).

Next, consider imprisonment as the sanction; see Shavell (1987a). Here, for essentially the reasons given in the case of fines, any sanction above a threshold level will ensure compliance with the fault standard, and the minimum sanction necessary to induce compliance is higher the lower is the probability of detection. Also (Shavell, 1985), fault-based liability again can accomplish deterrence without the actual imposition of sanctions, which would be socially costly.

Finally, consider the joint use of fines and imprisonment. In this case, it does not matter what the combination of sanctions is, provided that the sanctions achieve compliance with the fault standard. In particular, it is not advantageous for society to employ maximal fines before resorting to imprisonment because compliance means that sanctions are never imposed.

Comparison of Liability Rules

Because sanctions are not imposed under fault-based liability (in the absence of mistakes), this form of liability has an advantage over strict liability when the sanction is the fine and individuals are risk-averse, or when the sanction is imprisonment. However, fault-based liability is more difficult to administer. Namely, to apply fault-based liability, the enforcement authority must have more information than under strict liability: it must be able to calculate optimal behavior to determine the fault standard and it must ascertain whether the fault standard was met. Under strict liability, the authority need only ascertain harm. (Moreover, for reasons we discuss in Section 7 below, strict liability encourages better decisions by injurers regarding their level of participation in harm-creating activities.)

4. Optimal Enforcement Including the Probability of Detection

We now consider the optimal system of enforcement when expenditures on enforcement, and hence the probability of detection, are allowed to vary. Consideration of this issue originated with Becker (1968); the early writers on enforcement (including Bentham, 1789) did not examine the issue of the choice of enforcement effort.

Strict Liability

Assume first that the sanction is a fine and that individuals are risk neutral. Then the optimal level of the fine is maximal and the optimal probability is low (in a sense to be described). The basic explanation for this conclusion is that if the fine were not maximal, society could save enforcement costs by simultaneously raising the fine and lowering the probability without affecting the level of deterrence. Suppose, for example, that the fine initially is \$4,000 and that the probability of detection is 25 percent. Now raise the fine to \$10,000, presuming that the maximal fine is at least this high, and lower the probability of detection to 10 percent. Then the expected fine remains equal to \$1,000, so that deterrence is maintained, but expenditures on enforcement are significantly reduced, implying that social welfare rises. This process can be continued, and social welfare augmented, as long as the fine is below the maximal level f_m. Becker (1968) suggested this result (although much of his analysis implicitly presumes that the fine is not maximal); Carr-Hill and Stern (1979, pp. 280-309) and Polinsky and Shavell (1979) note it explicitly.

The optimal probability is low in that there is some underdeterrence; that is, the optimal p is such that the expected fine pf_m is less than the harm h (Polinsky and Shavell, 1984). The reason for this result is that if pf_m equals h, behavior will be ideal, meaning that the individuals who are just deterred obtain gains essentially equal to the harm. These are the individuals who would be led to commit the harmful act if p were lowered slightly. That in turn must be socially beneficial because these individuals cause no net social losses (because their gains essentially equal the harm), but reducing p saves enforcement costs. How much pf_m should be lowered below h depends on the saving in enforcement costs from reducing p compared to the net social costs of underdeterrence that will result if p is lowered non-trivially.

If individuals are risk averse, the optimal fine generally is less than maximal, as first shown in Polinsky and Shavell (1979) (and elaborated upon in Kaplow, 1992). This is because the use of a very high fine would impose a substantial risk-bearing cost on individuals who commit the harmful act. Another more particular explanation involves reconsidering the argument that we used in the risk-neutral case. If the fine f is less than f_m, it is still true that f can be raised and p lowered so as to maintain deterrence, but because of risk aversion, this implies that pf falls, meaning that fine revenue falls. The reduction in fine revenue reflects the disutility caused by imposing greater risk on risk-averse individuals. If individuals are sufficiently risk averse, the decline in fine revenue associated with greater risk-bearing could more than offset the savings in enforcement expenditures from reducing the probability of detection, implying that social welfare would be lower.

Next, assume that the sanction is imprisonment and that individuals are risk neutral in imprisonment, that is, the disutility of imprisonment is the same for each additional year. (We did not discuss individuals' attitudes toward the risk of imprisonment in Section 3 because the points we made there did not depend on this consideration.) Then the optimal imprisonment term is maximal (Shavell,

1991b). The reasoning behind this result parallels that used to show that the optimal fine is maximal when individuals are risk neutral in fines. Specifically, if the imprisonment term is raised and the probability of detection lowered so as to keep the expected sanction constant, neither individual behavior nor the costs of imposing imprisonment are affected (by construction, the expected prison term is the same), but enforcement expenditures fall.

Suppose instead that individuals are risk averse in imprisonment. In other words, the disutility of each year of imprisonment grows with the number of years in prison, perhaps because imprisonment becomes increasingly difficult to tolerate. In this case there is a stronger argument for setting the imprisonment sanction maximally than when individuals are risk neutral (Polinsky and Shavell, 1997). This is because, when the imprisonment term is raised, the probability of detection can be lowered even more than in the risk-neutral case without reducing deterrence. Thus, not only are there greater savings in enforcement expenditures, but also the social costs of imposing imprisonment sanctions decline because the expected prison term falls.

Last, suppose that individuals are risk preferring in imprisonment, that is, the disutility of each year of imprisonment falls with the number of years in prison. This assumption seems particularly important: the first years of imprisonment may create special disutility, due to brutalization of the prisoner, or due to the stigma effect of having been imprisoned at all. Additionally, the fact that individuals discount the future disutility of imprisonment makes earlier years of imprisonment more important than later ones. If individuals are risk preferring in imprisonment, the optimal sanction may well be less than maximal (Polinsky and Shavell, 1997). In particular, the type of argument used above does not necessarily apply. When the sanction is raised, the probability that maintains deterrence cannot be lowered proportionally, implying that the expected prison term rises. Because the resulting increased cost of imposing imprisonment sanctions might exceed the savings in enforcement expenditures from lowering the probability, the optimal prison term might not be maximal.

When the probability of detection is set optimally, together with the imprisonment term, underdeterrence may well result, not only to save enforcement expenditures, but also to reduce the costs of imposing imprisonment sanctions. (In theory, however, overdeterrence could be optimal for the reason mentioned in Section 3 - that overdeterrence could reduce the costs of imprisonment.)

Now consider the situation when both fines and imprisonment are employed as sanctions. Recall that under the optimal enforcement policy, the fine must be maximal, for otherwise it cannot be desirable to employ imprisonment. The main point we wish to make is that, unlike when imprisonment is used alone, the optimal imprisonment term may not be maximal even if individuals are risk neutral or risk averse in imprisonment. Suppose that individuals are risk neutral in imprisonment and fines. Then if the imprisonment term is raised and the probability of detection is lowered so as to keep the expected imprisonment term constant, deterrence declines because the expected fine falls (due to the reduction in the probability). Hence, to maintain deterrence, the probability cannot fall proportionally. But this implies that the expected prison term, and the costs of imposing imprisonment, are higher than previously. Only if the savings in enforcement costs are sufficiently large, therefore, is it socially desirable to raise the imprisonment sanction.

Fault-Based Liability

The least expensive way to accomplish compliance with the fault standard is to use the highest possible sanction and, given this sanction, the lowest probability of detection that deters individuals who would be at fault. The reason is that, if all individuals who would be at fault are deterred, the only cost incurred is associated with the setting of the probability; this cost is minimized by using the maximal sanction and a correspondingly low probability. Note that this is true regardless of whether the sanction is a fine or imprisonment and regardless of individuals' attitudes toward the risk of fines or of imprisonment.

Comparison of Rules

As we emphasized earlier, under fault-based liability sanctions are not actually imposed (in the absence of mistakes), which is an advantage over strict liability when the sanction is a fine and individuals are risk averse, and is always an advantage when the sanction is imprisonment. Moreover, this advantage of fault-based liability implies a second advantage: it may allow a further savings in enforcement expenditures over that under strict liability. For example, suppose that the sanction is a fine and that injurers are risk averse. Then, as we have emphasized, the optimal fine under strict liability generally is not maximal, due to risk-bearing by injurers. This implies that the probability of detection needed to achieve any given level of deterrence is higher than if the fine were maximal. Under fault-based liability, however, the optimal fine is maximal despite the risk aversion of injurers (because the fine is not actually imposed), meaning that a lower probability can be employed. However, to decide which liability rule is preferable, these advantages of fault-based liability would have to be weighed against the disadvantages of this rule relative to strict liability that we mentioned at the end of Section 3 (one of which, as noted, will be discussed in Section 7). This concludes the presentation of the basic theory of public enforcement of law. We now turn to various extensions and refinements of the analysis.

5. Accidental Harms

As we noted at the outset, we assumed that individuals decide whether or not to commit acts that cause harm with certainty, that is, they decide whether or not to cause intentional harms. In many circumstances, however, harms are accidental - they occur only with a probability. For instance, if a driver speeds, he only creates a likelihood of a collision; or if a firm stores toxic chemicals in a substandard tank, the firm only creates the probability of a harmful spill.

Essentially all that we have said above applies in a straightforward way when harms are accidental. If individuals are risk neutral, sanctions are monetary, and the expected sanction equals harm, then induced behavior will be socially optimal; further, the optimal magnitude of sanctions is maximal if individuals are risk neutral because this allows enforcement costs to be saved; and so forth. Our general conclusions from above can thus be interpreted to apply both when harms are intentional and cause harm for sure, as well as when actions alter the risk of harm.

There is, however, an additional issue that arises when harm is uncertain: a sanction can be imposed either on the basis of the commission of a dangerous *act* that increases the chance of harm - storing chemicals in a substandard tank - or on the basis of the *actual occurrence of harm* - only if the tank ruptures and results in a spill. In principle, either approach can achieve optimal deterrence. To illustrate, suppose that the substandard tank has a 10 percent chance of rupturing, in which case the harm would be $10 million; the expected harm from using the tank therefore is $1 million. If injurers are risk neutral and sanctions are imposed only when harm occurs, deterrence will be optimal if, as usual, the expected sanction equals the harm of $10 million. Alternatively, if sanctions are imposed on the basis of the dangerous act of using the substandard tank, deterrence will be optimal if the owner of the tank faces an expected sanction equal to the expected harm due to his use of the substandard tank, $1 million.

Several factors are relevant to the choice between act-based and harm-based sanctions (Shavell, 1993). First, act-based sanctions need not be as high to accomplish a given level of deterrence, and thus offer an underlying advantage over harm-based sanctions because of limitations in parties' assets. In the example in the preceding paragraph, the owner of the storage tank might be able to pay the $1 million required if sanctions are act-based but not the $10 million required if sanctions are harm-based. Second, and closely related, because act-based sanctions need not be as high to accomplish deterrence, they offer an advantage over harm-based sanctions when parties are risk averse. Third, act-based sanctions and harm-based sanctions may differ in the ease with which they can be applied. In some circumstances, act-based sanctions may be simpler to impose (it might be less difficult to determine whether an oil shipper properly maintains its vessels' holding tanks than to detect whether one of the vessels leaked oil into the ocean); in other circumstances, harm-based sanctions may be easier (a driver who causes harm might be caught without difficulty, but not one who speeds). Fourth, it may be hard to calculate the expected harm due to an act, but relatively easy to ascertain the actual harm if it eventuates; if so, this constitutes an advantage of harm-based liability.

6. Costs of Imposing Fines

We inquire in this section about the implications of costs borne by enforcement authorities in imposing fines. Our principal observation is that such costs should raise the level of the fine.

We assume for simplicity that the probability of detection is fixed, that liability is strict, and that individuals are risk neutral. In this setting, recall from Section 3 that the optimal fine is h/p, the harm divided by the probability of detection.

Now let there be a public cost k of imposing a fine. The optimal fine then becomes $h/p + k$; the cost k should be added to the fine that would otherwise be desirable (Becker, 1968, p. 192 and Polinsky and Shavell, 1992). The intuition behind this result is that, if an individual commits a harmful act, he causes society to bear not only the immediate harm h, but also, with probability p, the cost k of imposing the fine - that is, his act results in an expected total social cost of $h + pk$. If the fine is $h/p + k$, the individual's expected fine is $p[(h/p) + k] = h + pk$, leading him to commit the harmful act if and only if his gain exceeds the expected total social cost of his act.

For example, suppose the harm is $1,000, the probability of detection is 25 percent, and the cost of imposing the fine is $500. An individual's harmful act causes society to bear expected total social costs of $1,125 - the harm of $1,000 plus a 25 percent chance of the $500 cost of imposing a fine. If the fine is set equal to $4,500, the individual's expected fine also will equal $1,125.

Additionally, observe that, not only does the state bear costs when fines are imposed, so do individuals who pay the fines (such as legal defense expenses). The costs borne by individuals, however, do not affect the formula for the optimal fine. Individuals properly take these costs into account, because they bear them.

7. Level of Activity

We have been assuming that the sole decision that an individual makes is whether to act in a way that causes harm when engaging in some activity. In many contexts, however, an individual also makes a choice about his *activity level* - that is, not only does he choose whether to commit a harmful act when engaging in an activity, he also chooses whether to engage in that activity or, more generally, at what level to do so. For example, besides deciding how to behave when driving (whether to exercise care in changing lanes), an individual also chooses how many miles to drive; the number of miles driven is the individual's level of activity. Similarly, not only does a firm decide how to conduct its operations during production (whether to pollute), it also chooses its level of production; the output of the firm is its level of activity.

The socially optimal activity level is such that the individual's marginal utility from the activity just equals the marginal expected harm caused by the activity. Thus, the optimal number of miles driven is the level at which the marginal utility of driving an extra mile just equals the marginal expected harm per mile driven. The determination of the optimal level of activity presumes that individuals act optimally when engaging in the activity - for example, that they drive with appropriate care. Thus, in determining the optimal level of activity, an individual's marginal utility from the activity is compared to the expected harm that results when he acts appropriately when engaging in the activity. Often this expected harm is positive even when a party acts optimally, because the cost of precautions (or, equivalently, the gain or savings from not taking precautions) exceeds the expected reduction in harm that taking the precautions would bring about.

Will parties' choices about their activity levels be socially correct under the two major forms of liability? The answer is that under strict liability, their choices about activity levels will be correct, but under fault-based liability, they generally will participate in activities to a socially excessive extent. Under strict liability, parties will choose the optimal level of activity because they will pay for all harm done. They will choose the optimal number of miles to drive because they will pay for all harm per mile driven. Under fault-based liability, however, parties generally do not pay for the harm they cause because, as we have discussed, they will be induced to behave so as not to be found at fault. Consequently, when deciding on their level of activity, they will choose an excessive level. They will not take into account the harm that each additional mile of driving causes, and therefore they will drive too much.

The interpretation of the preceding points in relation to firms is that under strict liability the product price will reflect the expected harm caused by production, so that the price will reflect the full social cost of production. Hence, the amount purchased, and thus the level of production, will tend to be socially optimal. However, under fault-based liability, the product price will not reflect harm, but only the cost of precautions; thus, the amount sold, and the level of production, will be excessive.

A related comment is that safety regulations and other regulatory requirements are often framed as standards of care that have to be met, but which, if met, free the regulated party from liability. Hence, regulations of this character are subject to the criticism that they lead to excessive levels of the regulated activity. Making parties strictly liable for harm would be superior to safety regulation with respect to inducing socially correct activity levels.

The tendency of parties to choose an excessive level of activity under fault-based liability, but not under strict liability, constitutes a fundamental advantage of strict liability; it was first emphasized in Shavell (1980) and Polinsky (1980b). This advantage, note, is stronger the greater is the harm engendered by engaging in the activity (given that behavior is optimal when engaging in the activity). Thus, for activities for which expected harm is likely to be substantial, the disadvantage of fault-based liability will be significant.

8. Mistakes

Errors of the two classic types can occur in public enforcement of law. First, an individual who should be found liable might mistakenly not be found liable - a Type I error. Second, an individual who should not be found liable might mistakenly be found liable - a Type II error. For an individual who has been detected, let the probabilities of these errors be ϵ_1 and ϵ_2, respectively.

Given the probability of detection p and the chances of Type I and Type II errors, an individual will commit the wrongful act if and only if his gain g net of his expected fine if he does commit it exceeds his expected fine if he does not commit it, namely, when $g - p(1 - \epsilon_1)f > - p\epsilon_2 f$, or, equivalently, when $g > (1 - \epsilon_1 - \epsilon_2)pf$.

The first point to note is that, as emphasized in Png (1986), *both* types of error reduce deterrence: the term $(1 - \epsilon_1 - \epsilon_2)pf$ is declining in both ϵ_1 and ϵ_2. The first type of error diminishes deterrence because it lowers the expected fine if an individual violates the law. The second type of error, when an individual is mistakenly found liable, also lowers deterrence because it reduces the difference between the expected fine from violating the law and not violating it. In other words, the greater is ϵ_2, the smaller the increase in the expected fine if one violates the law, making a violation less costly to the individual.

Because mistakes dilute deterrence, they reduce social welfare (see generally Kaplow and Shavell, 1994a). Specifically, to achieve any level of deterrence, the probability p must be higher to offset the effect of errors. It should also be noted that, were one to take into account an individual's decision whether to engage in an activity (like driving), Type II errors have the additional effect of discouraging socially desirable participation in the activity.

Now consider the optimal choice of the fine. Given any probability of detection, the dilution in deterrence caused by errors requires a higher fine to restore deterrence. If the probability and the fine are variable, then, as explained in Section 4, the optimal fine is maximal. Somewhat surprisingly, the optimal fine remains maximal despite mistakes, by essentially the argument used previously: if the fine f were less than maximal, then f could be raised and the probability p lowered so as to keep deterrence constant, but saving enforcement costs.

Now consider the possible risk aversion of individuals. As we emphasized in Section 4, the optimal fine under strict liability generally is less than maximal when individuals are risk averse, because lowering the fine from the maximum level reduces the bearing of risk. Introducing the possibility of mistakes may increase the desirability of lowering the fine because, due to Type II errors, individuals who do not violate the law are subject to the risk of having to pay a fine (Block and Sidak, 1980). Indeed, because the number of persons who do not violate the law often would far exceed the number who do, the desire to avoid imposing risk on the former group can lead to a substantial reduction in the optimal fine.

Next, consider imprisonment and mistake. In this regard, our conclusions parallel those with respect to fines in several respects. Notably, mistakes of both types dilute the deterrent effects of imprisonment; and the optimal imprisonment term is maximal if individuals are risk neutral or risk averse in imprisonment but generally is not maximal if they are risk preferring in imprisonment.

We have not yet commented on fault-based liability. Here, an important implication of mistake is that some individuals will bear sanctions even if they comply with the fault standard. Hence, the results regarding the optimal probability of detection and the sanction under strict liability apply to some extent under fault-based liability as well. Moreover, as stressed by Craswell and Calfee (1986), individuals will often have a motive to take excessive precautions in order to reduce the chance of being found erroneously at fault.

Finally, observe that, although we have treated the probabilities of error as fixed, they can be influenced by procedural choices. For example, prosecutorial resources can be increased in order to reduce the probability of a Type I error, or the standard of proof can be raised to reduce the chance of a Type II error (although this presumably increases Type I errors). Because the reduction of both types of error increase deterrence, expenditures made to reduce errors may be socially beneficial (Kaplow and Shavell, 1994a).

9. General Enforcement

In many settings, enforcement may be said to be *general* in the sense that several different types of violations will be detected by an enforcement agent's activity. For example, a police officer waiting at the roadside may notice a driver who litters as well as one who goes through a red light or who speeds, and a tax auditor may detect a variety of infractions when he examines a tax return. To investigate such situations, suppose that a single probability of detection applies uniformly to all harmful acts, regardless of the magnitude of the harm. (The contrasting assumption is that enforcement is *specific*, meaning that the probability is chosen independently for each type of harmful act.)

The main point that we want to make is that in contexts in which enforcement is general, the optimal sanction rises with the severity of the harm and is maximal only for relatively high harms; this point was first made in Shavell (1991b) (Mookherjee and Png, 1992a is closely related). To see this, assume that liability is strict, the sanction is a fine, and injurers are risk neutral. Let $f(h)$ be the fine given harm h. Then, for any given general probability of detection p, the optimal fine schedule is h/p, provided that h/p is feasible; otherwise - for high h (all h such that $h/p > f_m$) - the optimal fine is maximal. This schedule is obviously optimal given p because it implies that the expected fine equals harm, thereby inducing ideal behavior, whenever that is possible.

The question remains whether it would be desirable to lower p and raise fines to the maximal level for the low-harm acts for which h/p is less than maximal. The answer is that if p is reduced for the relatively low-harm acts (and the fine raised for them), then p - being general - is *also* reduced for the high-harm acts for which the fine is already maximal, resulting in lower deterrence of these acts. The decline in deterrence of high-harm acts may cause a greater social loss than the savings in enforcement costs from lowering p. To express this point differently, p must be sufficiently high to avoid significant underdeterrence of high-harm acts (for which fines are maximal). But since this p also applies to less harmful acts, the fines for them do not need to be maximal in order to appropriately deter them.

The result that, when enforcement is general, sanctions should rise with the severity of harm up to a maximum also holds if the sanction is imprisonment and if liability is fault-based. The underlying reasoning is the same as that given above.

10. Marginal Deterrence

In many circumstances, a person may consider which of *several* harmful acts to commit, for example, whether to release only a small amount of a pollutant into a river or a large amount, or whether to kidnap a person or also to kill the kidnap victim. In such contexts, the threat of sanctions plays a role in addition to the usual one of attempting to deter individuals from committing harmful acts: for individuals who are not deterred, sanctions influence which harmful acts individuals choose to commit. Notably, such individuals will have a reason to commit less harmful rather than more harmful acts if expected sanctions rise with harm. Deterrence of a more harmful act because its sanction exceeds that for a less harmful act is sometimes referred to as *marginal deterrence* (it apparently was so named by Stigler, 1970).

Other things being equal, as observed by Beccaria (1770, p. 32) and Bentham (1789, p. 171), it is socially desirable that enforcement policy creates marginal deterrence, so that those who are not deterred from committing harmful acts have a reason to moderate the amount of harm that they cause. This suggests that sanctions should rise with the magnitude of harm and, therefore, that sanctions should not generally be maximal. However, fostering marginal deterrence may conflict with achieving deterrence generally: in order for the schedule of sanctions to rise steeply enough to accomplish marginal deterrence, sanctions for less harmful acts may have to be so low that individuals are not deterred from committing some harmful act.

We have two additional observations to make about marginal deterrence. First, marginal deterrence can be promoted by increasing the probability of detection as well as the magnitude of sanctions. For example, kidnappers can be better deterred from killing their victims if more police resources are devoted to apprehending kidnappers who murder their victims than to those who do not. (But in circumstances in which enforcement is general, the probability of detection cannot be independently altered for acts that cause different degrees of harm.) Second, marginal deterrence is naturally accomplished if the expected sanction equals harm for all levels of harm; for if a person is paying for harm done, he will have to pay appropriately more if he does greater harm. Thus, for instance, if a polluter's expected fine would rise from \$100 to \$500 if he dumps five gallons instead of one gallon of waste into a lake, where each gallon causes \$100 of harm, his marginal incentives to pollute will be correct. For formal analyses of marginal deterrence, see Shavell (1992), Wilde (1992), and Mookherjee and Png (1994).

11. Principal-Agent Relationship

Although we have assumed that an injurer is a single actor, injurers often are more appropriately characterized as collective entities, and specifically as a principal and the principal's agent. For example, the principal could be a firm and the agent an employee; or the principal could be a contractor and the agent a subcontractor.

When harm is caused by the behavior of principals and agents, many of the conclusions of our prior analysis are not fundamentally altered; they simply carry over to the sanctioning of principals. Notably, if a risk-neutral principal faces an expected fine equal to harm done, he will in effect be in the same position *vis-à-vis* his agent as society is *vis-à-vis* a single potential violator of law (see Newman and Wright, 1990 on a closely related point). Consequently, the principal will behave socially optimally in controlling his agents, and in particular will contract with them and monitor them in ways that will give the agents socially appropriate incentives to reduce harm (but see Arlen, 1994). Another result that carries over to the principal-agent context is that it often will be desirable for society to tolerate some degree of underdeterrence in order to conserve enforcement resources.

A question about enforcement that arises when there are principals and agents is the allocation of financial sanctions between the two parties. It is apparent, however, that the particular allocation of sanctions does not matter when, as would be the natural presumption, the parties can reallocate the sanctions through their own contract. For example, if the agent finds that he faces a large fine but is more risk averse than the principal, the principal can assume it; conversely, if the fine is imposed on the principal, he will retain it and not impose an internal sanction on the agent. Thus, the post-contract sanctions that the agent bears are not affected by the particular division of sanctions initially selected by the enforcement authority.

The allocation of monetary sanctions between principals and agents would matter, however, if some allocations allow the pair to reduce their total burden. An important example is when a fine is imposed only on the agent and he is unable to pay it because his assets are less than the fine (see Sykes, 1981, and Kornhauser, 1982). Then, he and the principal (who often would have higher assets) would jointly escape part of the fine, diluting deterrence. The fine therefore should be imposed on the principal rather than on the agent (or at least the part of the fine that the agent cannot pay).

A closely related point is that the imposition of imprisonment sanctions on agents may be desirable when their assets are less than the harm that they can cause, even if the principal's assets are sufficient to pay the optimal fine (see Polinsky and Shavell, 1993). The fact that an agent's assets are limited means that the principal may be unable to control him adequately through use of contractually-determined penalties, which can only be monetary. For example, a firm may not be able, despite the threat of salary reduction or dismissal, to induce its employees never to rig bids. In such circumstances, it may be socially valuable to use the threat of personal criminal liability and a jail sentence to better control agents' misconduct.

12. Settlements

Although we have thus far assumed that when a liable injurer is discovered he is sanctioned in some automatic fashion, in practice he must be found civilly or criminally liable in a trial, and before this occurs, he commonly settles in lieu of trial. (In the criminal context, the settlement usually takes the form of a *plea bargain*, an agreement in which the injurer pleads guilty to a reduced charge.) Given the prevalence of settlements, it is important to consider how they affect deterrence and the optimal system of public enforcement, and whether settlements are socially desirable.

There are two general reasons why parties might prefer an out-of-court settlement to a trial (see generally the survey by Cooter and Rubinfeld, 1989; and for some recent discussions of plea bargaining, see, for example, Reinganum, 1988, and Miceli, 1996). First, a trial is costly to the parties in terms of time and/or money. Second, settlements eliminate the risks inherent in the trial outcome, a benefit to parties who are averse to such risks. These advantages of settlement to the parties suggest that settlement is socially valuable, but the effect of settlement on deterrence is a complicating factor.

Specifically, settlements dilute deterrence: for if injurers desire to settle, it must be because the expected disutility of sanctions is lowered for them (see generally Polinsky and Rubinfeld, 1988). The state may be able to offset this settlement-related reduction in deterrence by increasing the level of sanctions; if so, settlements need not compromise the overall level of deterrence.

Settlements may have other socially undesirable consequences. First, they may result in sanctions that are not as well tailored to harmful acts as would be true of court-determined sanctions. For example, if injurers have private information about the harm that they have caused, settlements will tend to reflect the average harm caused, whereas trial outcomes may better approximate the actual harm. Thus, the distribution of sanctions meted out through settlements will not be as good in terms of inducing injurers to take proper precautions (high-harm injurers will be underdeterred, and vice versa). Second, settlements hinder the amplification and development of the law through the setting of precedents, a factor of occasional relevance; and settlements also sometimes allow defendants to keep aspects of their behavior secret, which can reduce deterrence. Third, settlements for prison terms can result in increases in public expenditures on jail if defendants are risk averse in imprisonment. On the social desirability of settlement, see, for example, Shavell (1997a) and Spier (1997).

13. Self-Reporting

We have assumed that individuals are subject to sanctions only if they are detected by an enforcement agent, but in fact parties sometimes disclose their own violations to enforcement authorities. For example, firms often report violations of environmental and safety regulations, individuals usually notify police of their involvement in traffic accidents, and even criminals occasionally turn themselves in.

We explain here why it is generally socially desirable for the structure of enforcement to be such as to encourage self-reporting (see Kaplow and Shavell, 1994b). Self-reporting can be induced by lowering the sanction for individuals who disclose their own infractions. Moreover, the reward for self-reporting can be made small enough that deterrence is only negligibly reduced.

To amplify, assume for simplicity that the sanction is a fine f, that the probability of detection is p, and that individuals are risk neutral. If an individual commits a violation and does not self report, his expected fine is pf. Suppose the fine if an individual self-reports is set just below pf, say at $pf - \epsilon$, where $\epsilon > 0$ is arbitrarily small. Then the individual will want to self-report but the deterrent effect of the sanction will be (approximately) the same as if he did not self-report. For example, suppose that the fine if an individual does not self report is \$1,000 and that the probability of detection is 10 percent, so the expected fine is \$100. If the fine for self-reporting is slightly below \$100, such as \$95, or even \$99, individuals will self-report but deterrence will barely be reduced.

Given that self-reporting can be induced essentially without compromising deterrence, why is self-reporting socially advantageous? There are two basic reasons. First, self-reporting reduces enforcement costs because, when it occurs, the enforcement authority does not have to identify and prove who the violator was. If a company reports that it caused pollution, environmental enforcers do not need to spend as much effort trying to detect pollution and establishing its source. Second, self-reporting reduces risk, and thus is advantageous if injurers are risk averse. Drivers bear less risk because they know that if they cause an accident, they can (and will be led to) report this to the police and suffer a lower and certain sanction, rather than face a substantially higher sanction (for hit and run driving) imposed only with some probability.

14. Repeat Offenders

In practice, the law often sanctions repeat offenders more severely than first-time offenders. We explain here why such a policy may be socially desirable.

Note first that sanctioning repeat offenders more severely cannot be socially advantageous if deterrence always induces first-best behavior. If the sanction for polluting and causing a \$1,000 harm is \$1,000, then any person who pollutes and pays \$1,000 is a person whose gain from polluting (say the savings from not installing pollution control equipment) must have exceeded \$1,000. Social welfare therefore is higher as a result of his polluting. If such an individual polluted and was sanctioned in the past, that only means that it was socially desirable for him to have polluted previously. Raising the current sanction because of his having a record of sanctions would overdeter him now.

Accordingly, only if deterrence is inadequate is it possibly desirable to condition sanctions on offense history to increase deterrence. But deterrence often will be inadequate because, as we emphasized in Section 4, it will usually be worthwhile for the state to tolerate some underdeterrence in order to reduce enforcement expenses.

Given that there is underdeterrence, making sanctions depend on offense history may be beneficial for two reasons. First, as developed in Polinsky and Shavell (1996), the use of offense history may create an additional incentive not to violate the law: if getting caught violating the law implies not only an immediate sanction, but also a higher sanction for any future violation, an individual will be more deterred from committing a violation presently. Second, as studied, for example, in Rubinstein (1979) and Polinsky and Rubinfeld (1991), making sanctions depend on offense history allows society to take advantage of information about the dangerousness of individuals and the need to deter them: individuals with offense histories may be more likely than average to commit future violations, which might make it desirable for purposes of deterrence to impose higher sanctions on them.

There is also an incapacitation-based (see Section 16) reason for making sanctions depend on offense history. Repeat offenders are more likely to have higher propensities to commit violations in the future and thus more likely to be worth incapacitating by imprisonment.

15. Imperfect Knowledge about the Probability and Magnitude of Sanctions

Although we have implicitly assumed that injurers know the probability and magnitude of sanctions, this is not always the case. Individuals frequently have imperfect knowledge of these variables; that is, they have estimates, or more likely, subjective probability distributions, describing the true probability of a sanction and its true magnitude. They might not know the true probability of a sanction for several reasons: because the enforcement authority refrains from publishing information about the probability (perhaps hoping that individuals will believe it to be higher than it is in fact); because the probability is variable, depending on factors that individuals do not fully understand (the probability of a tax audit, for example, is influenced by a large number of considerations); and because probabilities seem to be difficult for individuals to assess. Also, individuals may have incomplete knowledge of the true magnitude of sanctions, particularly if the magnitudes of sanctions are not fixed by law, but are to some degree discretionary.

The implications of injurers' imperfect knowledge are straightforward. First, to predict how individuals behave, what is relevant, of course, is not the actual probability and magnitude of a sanction, but the perceived levels or distributions of these variables.

Second, to determine the optimal probability and magnitude of a sanction, account must be taken of the relationship between the actual and the perceived variables (on which, see, for instance, Bebchuk and Kaplow, 1992, and see Kaplow, 1990b, on learning about sanctions). For example, suppose that there is a delay of at least a year before individuals fully comprehend a change in the probability of enforcement. Then if enforcement resources are increased so as to make the probability, say, 15 percent rather than 10 percent, there might not be a significant increase in deterrence for some time, making such an investment less worthwhile. Or, for instance, suppose that the sanction for some act, such as robbery, is variable (say from one month of jail time to 10 years), and that individuals' perceptions are quite rough, not based on true averages but more on the possible range. Then increasing the average sentence might have very little effect on deterrence, but increasing the probability substantially might still augment deterrence. The psychology and learning process (see Sah, 1991) by which individuals assimilate and formulate perceived probabilities of sanctions and their magnitude are important, therefore, to determining how deterrence works and what optimal policy is.

16. Incapacitation

Our discussion of public enforcement has presumed that the threat of sanctions reduces harm by discouraging individuals from causing harm - that is, by deterring them. However, an entirely different way for society to reduce harm is by imposing sanctions that remove parties from positions in which they are able to cause harm - that is, by *incapacitating* them. Imprisonment is the primary incapacitative sanction, although there are other examples: individuals can lose their drivers licenses, preventing them from doing harm while driving; businesses can lose their right to operate in certain domains, and the like. We focus here on imprisonment, but what we say applies to incapacitative sanctions generally; on the economic theory of incapacitation, see Shavell (1987b).

To better understand the role of public enforcement when sanctions are incapacitative, suppose that the sole function of sanctions is to incapacitate; that is, sanctions do not deter. (Deterrence might not occur if, for instance, individuals' gains from harmful acts exceed the expected sanctions, given the relevant range of the probabilities and magnitudes of the sanctions.) We assume that the social goal is as before, to maximize gains from acts less harm, and less the costs of enforcement and sanctions, including the costs of keeping individuals in prison.

The optimal sanction to impose on an individual who is apprehended is determined by comparing the expected harm, net of gains, he would cause if not in prison to the private and public costs of imprisonment. If the expected net harm exceeds the costs of imprisonment, he should be put in prison and kept there as long as this condition holds. Thus, the optimal sanction as a function of expected net harm is zero up to a threshold - the point at which expected net harm equals the costs of imprisonment - and then rises discontinuously to the length of time during which the person's net expected harm exceeds imprisonment costs. Jail should only be used to incapacitate individuals whose net harm is relatively high.

Two points about the incapacitative rationale are worth making. First, there is evidence that suggests that the expected harm caused by individuals declines with their age. Thus, from the incapacitative standpoint, individuals should be released from jail when their dangerousness falls below the cost of incapacitation. Second, as a matter of logic, the incapacitative rationale might imply that a person should be put in jail even if he has not committed a crime - because his danger to society makes incapacitating him worthwhile. This would be true, for example, if there were some means accurately to predict a person's dangerousness independently of his actual behavior. In practice, however, the fact that a person has committed a harmful act may be the best basis for predicting his future behavior, in which case the incapacitation rationale would suggest imposing a jail term only if the individual has committed an especially harmful act.

Last, we comment on the relationship between optimal enforcement when incapacitation is the goal versus when deterrence is the goal. First, when incapacitation is the goal, the optimal magnitude of the sanction is independent of the probability of apprehension. In contrast, when deterrence is the goal, the optimal sanction depends on the probability - the sanction generally is higher the lower is the probability. Second, when incapacitation is the goal, the sanction rises discontinuously with the magnitude of harm (from zero to a positive amount), but when deterrence is the goal the sanction rises continuously with harm. Third, when deterrence is the goal, the probability and magnitude of sanctions depend on the ability to deter, and if this ability is limited (as, for instance, with the enraged), a low expected sanction may be optimal. However, a high expected sanction still might be called for to incapacitate.

17. Conclusion

It may be worthwhile summarizing the main points that we have made in this chapter:

(a) When the probability of detection is for some reason fixed, the benchmark level of the optimal fine is the harm divided by the probability of detection, for this results in an expected fine equal to the harm. However, costs incurred by the public in collecting the fine should be added to the benchmark level of the fine, and risk aversion of injurers should usually lower the level of the fine.

(b) When the probability of detection may be varied, high sanctions may be optimal, for this allows a relatively low probability to be employed and thereby saves enforcement costs. Indeed, the optimal fine is in principle maximal for this reason if individuals are risk neutral in wealth, and the optimal imprisonment term is maximal if individuals are risk neutral or risk averse in imprisonment. More realistically, optimal sanctions are not maximal when individuals are risk averse in wealth or risk preferring in imprisonment (as well as for the general enforcement reasons discussed in Section 9), although the motive to set sanctions at relatively high levels in order to reduce enforcement costs still applies.

(c) Optimal enforcement tends to be characterized by some degree of underdeterrence relative to first-best behavior, because this conserves enforcement resources. More precisely, by lowering the probability of detection from a level that would lead to first-best behavior, the state reduces enforcement costs, and although more individuals commit the harmful act, these individuals do not cause social welfare to decline substantially because their gains are nearly equal to the harm.

(d) The use of fines should be exhausted before resort is made to costlier sanctions, notably imprisonment.

(e) An advantage of fault-based liability over strict liability is that costly sanctions - fines when individuals are risk averse, and imprisonment - are imposed less often: under fault-based liability, injurers generally are induced (in the absence of mistakes) to obey fault standards, and therefore ordinarily do not bear sanctions. Under strict liability, however, injurers are sanctioned whenever they are caught.

(f) An advantage of strict liability over fault-based liability is that it is easier to apply. Another advantage is that injurers' activity-level decisions generally will be better: under strict liability, injurers' activity levels will tend to be optimal because injurers will pay for harm that they cause. But under fault-based liability, their activity levels will tend to be excessive because they generally will not pay for harm that they cause (because they will be led to behave without fault).

These and other basic conclusions about the public enforcement of law that we have described in this essay are now, for the most part, well-established in the economic literature on enforcement. However, an important aspect of this subject that has received relatively little attention is the behavior of public enforcers themselves. Because our focus was on deriving socially optimal public enforcement policies, we assumed, as is conventional, that public enforcers act so as to maximize social welfare. A logical step to take next would be to re-examine optimal enforcement policies when public enforcers behave in a self-interested manner. Although some effort already has been devoted to this inquiry, much remains to be done.

Acknowledgments

Polinsky's research was supported by the Center for Advanced Study in the Behavioral Sciences (through National Science Foundation grant #SBR-960123) and the John M. Olin Program in Law and Economics at Stanford Law School. Shavell's research was supported by the John M. Olin Center for Law, Economics, and Business at Harvard Law School. This essay previously appeared with a less comprehensive bibliography in Peter Newman (ed.), *The New Palgrave Dictionary of Economics and The Law*, London, Macmillan Reference Ltd. (1998).

Bibliography on Public Enforcement of Law (8000)

Adelstein, Richard and Miceli, Thomas J. (1997), 'Toward a Comparative Economics of Plea Bargaining', Manuscript.

Allingham, Michael G. and Sandmo, Agnar (1972), 'Income Tax Evasion: A Theoretical Analysis', **1** *Journal of Public Economics*, 323-338.

Altrogge, Phyllis and Shughart, William F. (1984), 'The Regressive Nature of Civil Penalties', **4** *International Review of Law and Economics*, 55-66.

Andenaes, Johannes (1966), 'The General Preventive Effects of Punishment', **114** *University of Pennsylvania Law Review*, 949-983.

Andenaes, Johannes (1971), 'Deterrence and Specific Offenses', **38** *University of Chicago Law Review*, 537-553.

Andenaes, Johannes (1974), *Punishment and Deterrence*, Ann Arbor, University of Michigan Press.

Anderson, Lee G. and Lee, Dwight R. (1986), 'Optimal Governing Instrument, Operation Level, and Enforcement in Natural Resource Regulation: The Case of the Fishery', **68** *American Journal of Agricultural Economics*, 678-690.

Andreoni, James (1991), 'Reasonable Doubt and the Optimal Magnitude of Fines: Should the Penalty Fit the Crime?', **22** *RAND Journal of Economics*, 385-395.

Andreoni, James, Erard, Brian and Feinstein, Jonathan (1998), 'Tax Compliance', *Journal of Economic Literature*, forthcoming.

Arlen, Jennifer A. (1994), 'The Potentially Perverse Effects of Corporate Criminal Liability', **23** *Journal of Legal Studies*, 833-867.

Arlen, Jennifer. (1997), 'Corporate Crime and Its Control', U.S.C. Law School Working Paper Series, Working Paper No. 97-2, forthcoming in *The New Palgrave Dictionary of Economics and the Law*.

Arlen, Jennifer and Kraakman, Reinier (1997), 'Controlling Corporate Misconduct: An Analysis of Corporate Liability Regimes', **72** *New York University Law Review*, 687-779.

Avio, Kenneth L. (1975), 'Recidivism in the Economic Model of Crime', **13** *Economic Inquiry*, 450-456.

Avio, Kenneth L. (1987), 'Clemency in Economic and Retributive Models of Punishment', **7** *International Review of Law and Economics*, 79-88.

Avio, Kenneth L. and Clark, C. Scott (1976), *Property Crime in Canada: An Econometric Study*, Toronto, University of Toronto Press.

Ayres, Ian and Levitt, Steven D. (1998), 'Measuring the Positive Externalities from Unobservable Victim Precaution: An Empirical Analysis of Lojack', *Quarterly Journal of Economics*, forthcoming.

Baldry, Jonathan C. (1980), 'Crimes Punishable by Imprisonment: A Note', **9** *Journal of Legal Studies*, 617-619.

Baldry, J.C. (1984), 'The Enforcement of Income Tax Laws: Efficiency Implications', **60** *Economic Record*, 156-159.

Basu, Kaushik, Bhattacharya, Sudipto and Mishra, Ajit (1992), 'Notes on Bribery and the Control of Corruption', **48** *Journal of Public Economics*, 349-359.

Bebchuk, Lucian Arye and Kaplow, Louis (1992), 'Optimal Sanctions When Individuals Are Imperfectly Informed About the Probability of Apprehension', **21** *Journal of Legal Studies*, 365-370.

Bebchuk, Lucian Arye and Kaplow, Louis (1993), 'Optimal Sanctions and Differences in Individuals' Likelihood of Avoiding Detection', **13** *International Review of Law and Economics*, 217-224.

Beccaria, Cesare (1770), *On Crimes and Punishments, and Other Writings*. Bellamy, Richard (ed.), Davies, Richard, et al. (trans.), New York, Cambridge University Press, 1995.

Becker, Gary S. (1968), 'Crime and Punishment: An Economic Approach', **76** *Journal of Political Economy*, 169-217.

Becker, Gary S. and Landes, William M. (eds) (1974), *Essays in the Economics of Crime and Punishment*, New York, Columbia University Press.

Becker, Gary S. and Stigler, George J. (1974), 'Law Enforcement, Malfeasance, and Compensation of Enforcers', **3** *Journal of Legal Studies*, 1-18.

Ben-Shahar, Omri (1997), 'Playing Without a Rulebook: Optimal Enforcement When Individuals Learn the Penalty Only by Committing the Crime', **17** *International Review of Law and Economics*, 409-421.

Ben-Shahar, Omri and Harel, Alon (1995), 'Blaming the Victim: Optimal Incentives for Private Precautions Against Crime', **11** *Journal of Law, Economics, and Organization*, 434-455.

Ben-Shahar, Omri and Harel, Alon (1996), 'The Economics of the Law of Criminal Attempts: A Victim-Centered Perspective', **145** *University of Pennsylvania Law Review*, 299-351.

Benson, Bruce L. and Baden, John (1985), 'The Political Economy of Government Corruption: The Logic of Underground Government', **14** *Journal of Legal Studies*, 391-410.

Benson, Bruce L., Kim, Iljoong and Rasmussen, David W. (1994), 'Estimating Deterrence Effects: A Public Choice Perspective on the Economics of Crime Literature', **61** *Southern Economic Journal*, 161-168.

Bentham, Jeremy (1789), 'An Introduction to the Principles of Morals and Legislation', in *The Utilitarians*, Rept. Garden City, NY, Anchor Books, 1973.

Besanko, David and Spulber, Daniel F. (1989), 'Delegated Law Enforcement and Noncooperative Behavior', **5** *Journal of Law, Economics, and Organization*, 25-52.

Block, Michael K. (1991), 'Optimal Penalties, Criminal Law and the Control of Corporate Behavior', **71** *Boston University Law Review*, 395-419.

Block, Michael K. and Feinstein, Jonathan S. (1986), 'The Spillover Effect of Antitrust Enforcement', **68** *Review of Economics and Statistics*, 122-131.

Block, Michael K. and Lind, Robert C. (1975a), 'Crime and Punishment Reconsidered', **4** *Journal of Legal Studies*, 241-247.

Block, Michael K. and Lind, Robert C. (1975b), 'An Economic Analysis of Crimes Punishable by Imprisonment', **4** *Journal of Legal Studies*, 479-492.

Block, Michael K. and Sidak, Joseph Gregory (1980), 'The Cost of Antitrust Deterrence: Why Not Hang a Price Fixer Now and Then?', **68** *Georgetown Law Journal*, 1131-1139.

Block, Michael Kent, Nold, Frederick Carl and Sidak, Joseph Gregory (1981), 'The Deterrent Effect of Antitrust Enforcement', **89** *Journal of Political Economy*, 429-445.

Bone, John (1985), 'On Substituting a Socially Costless Penalty for Costly Crime', **5** *International Review of Law and Economics*, 239-246.

Bose, Pinaki (1995a), 'Anticipatory Compliance and Effective Regulatory Activity', **15** *International Review of Law and Economics*, 151-159.

Bose, Pinaki (1995b), 'Regulatory Errors, Optimal Fines, and the Level of Compliance', **56** *Journal of Public Economics*, 475-484.

Bowles, Roger and Garoupa, Nuno (1997), 'Casual Police Corruption and the Economics of Crime', **17** *International Review of Law and Economics*, 75-87.

Brown, William W. and Reynolds, Morgan O. (1973), 'Crime and "Punishment": Risk Implications', **6** *Journal of Economic Theory*, 508-514.

Burnovski, Moshe and Safra, Zvi (1994), 'Deterrence Effects of Sequential Punishment Policies: Should Repeat Offenders be More Severely Punished?', **14** *International Review of Law and Economics*, 341-350.

Cadot, Olivier (1987), 'Corruption as a Gamble', **33** *Journal of Public Economics*, 223-244.

Cameron, Samuel (1988), 'The Economics of Crime Deterrence: A Survey of Theory and Evidence', **41** *Kyklos*, 301-323.

Cameron, Samuel (1989), 'On the Welfare Economics of Capital Punishment', **28** *Australian Economic Papers*, 253-266.

Campbell, Donald T. and Ross, H. Laurence (1988), 'The Connecticut Crackdown on Speeding: Time-Series Data in Quasi-experimental Analysis', in Overman, E. Samuel (ed.), *Methodology and Epistemology of Social Science: Selected Papers*, Chicago and London, University of Chicago Press, 222-237.

Carlin, Paul and Sandy, Robert (1990), 'The Value of Time and the Effect of Fines on Child Car Safety Seat Usage', **22** *Applied Economics*, 463-476.

Carr-Hill, R.A. and Stern, N.H. (1979), *Crime, the Police and Criminal Statistics: An Analysis of Official Statistics for England and Wales Using Econometric Methods*, London, Academic Press.

Chu, C.Y. Cyrus (1979), 'Crime and Punishment with Possible Post-Offense Compromise', **17** *Academia Economic Papers*, 131-167.

Chu, C.Y. Cyrus (1990), 'Plea Bargaining with the IRS', **41** *Journal of Public Economics*, 319-333.

Chu, C.Y. Cyrus (1991), 'An Economic Analysis of the Criminal Proceedings in Civil-Law Countries', **11** *International Review of Law and Economics*, 111-116.

Chu, C.Y. Cyrus (1993), 'Oscillatory vs. Stationary Enforcement of Law', **13** *International Review of Law and Economics*, 303-315.

Chu, C.Y. Cyrus and Jiang, Neville (1993), 'Are Fines More Efficient than Imprisonment?', **51** *Journal of Public Economics*, 391-413.

Chu, C.Y. Cyrus, Hu, Sheng-cheng and Huang, Ting-yuan (1997), 'Punishing Repeat Offenders More Severely!', Manuscript.

Chwe, Michael Suk-Young (1990), 'Why Were Workers Whipped? Pain in a Principal-Agent Model', **100** *Economic Journal*, 1109-1121.

Clotfelter, Charles T. (1977), 'Public Services, Private Substitutes, and the Demand for Protection Against Crime', **67** *American Economic Review*, 867-877.

Clotfelter, Charles T. (1983), 'Tax Evasion and Tax Rates: An Analysis of Individual Returns', **65** *Review of Economics and Statistics*, 363-373.

Coffee, John C., Jr (1980), 'Corporate Crime and Punishment: A Non-Chicago View of the Economics of Criminal Sanctions', **17** *American Criminal Law Review*, 419-476.

Cohen, Mark A. (1986), 'The Costs and Benefits of Oil Spill Prevention and Enforcement', **13** *Journal of Environmental Economics and Management*, 167-188.

Cohen, Mark A. (1987), 'Optimal Enforcement Strategy to Prevent Oil Spills: An Application of a Principal-Agent Model with Moral Hazard', **30** *Journal of Law and Economics*, 23-51.

Cohen, Mark A. (1989a), 'The Role of Criminal Sanctions in Antitrust Enforcement', **7** *Contemporary Policy Issues*, 36-46.

Cohen, Mark A. (1989b), 'Corporate Crime and Punishment: A Study of Social Harm and Sentencing Practice in the Federal Courts, 1984-1987', **26** *American Criminal Law Review*, 605-660.

Cohen, Mark A. (1992), 'Environmental Crime and Punishment: Legal/Economic Theory and Empirical Evidence on Enforcement of Federal Environmental Statutes', **82** *Journal of Criminal Law and Criminology*, 1054-1108.

Cook, Philip J. (1977), 'Punishment and Crime: A Critique of Current Findings Concerning the Preventative Effects of Punishment', **41** *Law and Contemporary Problems*, 164-209.

Cook, Philip J. (1980), 'Research in Criminal Deterrence: Laying the Groundwork for the Second Decade', in Morris, Norval and Tonry, Michael (eds), **2** *Crime and Justice: An Annual Review of Research*, University of Chicago Press, 211-268.

Cook, Philip J. (1983), 'Costs of Crime', in Kadish, Sanford H. (ed.), **1** *Encyclopedia of Crime and Justice*, New York, The Free Press, 373-378.

Cook, Philip J. (1986), 'The Relationship Between Victim Resistance and Injury in Noncommercial Robbery', **15** *Journal of Legal Studies*, 405-416.

Cook, Philip J. (1987), 'The Economics of Criminal Sanctions', in Friedland, M.L. (ed.), *Sanctions and Rewards in the Legal System: A Multidisciplinary Approach*, Toronto, University of Toronto Press, 50-78.

Cook, Philip J., Molliconi, Stephanie and Cole, Thomas B. (1995), 'Regulating Gun Markets', **86** *Journal of Criminal Law and Criminology*, 59-92.

Cooter, Robert D. and Rubinfeld, Daniel L. (1989), 'Economic Analysis of Legal Disputes and Their Resolution', **27** *Journal of Economic Literature*, 1067-1097.

Cox, Gary W. (1994), 'A Note on Crime and Punishment', **78** *Public Choice*, 115-124.

Craswell, Richard and Calfee, John E. (1986), 'Deterrence and Uncertain Legal Standards', **2** *Journal of Law, Economics, and Organization*, 279-303.

Daniel, Kermit, and Lott, John R., Jr (1995), 'Should Criminal Penalties Include Third-Party Avoidance Costs?', **24** *Journal of Legal Studies*, 523-534.

Das-Gupta, Arindam and Mookherjee, Dilip (1995), 'Tax Amnesties in India: An Empirical Evaluation', Institute for Economic Development, Boston University, Discussion Paper No. 53.

Dau-Schmidt, Kenneth G. (1990), 'An Economic Analysis of the Criminal Law as a Preference-Shaping Policy', *Duke Law Journal*, 1-38.

Davis, Michael L. (1988), 'Time and Punishment: An Intertemporal Model of Crime', **96** *Journal of Political Economy*, 383-390.

Dickens, William T. (1986), 'Crime and Punishment Again: The Economic Approach with a Psychological Twist', **30** *Journal of Public Economics*, 97-107.

Diver, Colin S. (1980), 'A Theory of Regulatory Enforcement', **28** *Public Policy*, 257-299.

Dye, Ronald A. (1986), 'Optimal Monitoring Policies in Agencies', **17** *RAND Journal of Economics*, 339-350.

Earnhart, Dietrich (1997), 'Enforcement of Environmental Protection Laws Under Communism and Democracy', **40** *Journal of Law and Economics*, 377-402.

Ehrlich, Isaac (1972a), 'The Deterrent Effect of Criminal Law Enforcement', **1** *Journal of Legal Studies*, 259-276.

Ehrlich, Isaac (1972b), 'Participation in Illegitimate Activities: A Theoretical and Empirical Investigation', **80** *Journal of Political Economy*, 521-565.

Ehrlich, Isaac (1975), 'The Deterrent Effect of Capital Punishment: A Question of Life and Death', **65** *American Economic Review*, 397-417.

Ehrlich, Isaac (1981), 'On the Usefulness of Controlling Individuals: An Economic Analysis of Rehabilitation, Incapacitation and Deterrence', **71** *American Economic Review*, 307-332.

Ehrlich, Isaac (1982), 'The Optimum Enforcement of Laws and the Concept of Justice: A Positive Analysis', **2** *International Review of Law and Economics*, 3-27.

Ehrlich, Isaac (1996), 'Crime, Punishment, and the Market for Offenses', **10** *Journal of Economic Perspectives*, 43-67.

Ehrlich, Isaac and Brower, George D. (1987), 'On the Issue of Causality in the Economic Model of Crime and Law Enforcement: Some Theoretical Considerations and Experimental Evidence', **77** *AEA Papers and Proceedings*, 99-106

Eide, Erling (1994), *Economics of Crime: Deterrence and the Rational Offender*, Amsterdam, Elsevier.

Eide, Erling (1995), 'RDEU Models of Crime', University of Oslo Working Papers, WP No. C1.

Eide, Erling (1997), 'Economics of Criminal Behavior: Survey and Bibliography', University of Oslo Working Papers, WP No. C5.

Elzinga, Kenneth G. and Breit, William (1976), *The Antitrust Penalties: A Study in Law and Economics*, New Haven, Yale University Press.

Epple, Dennis and Visscher, Michael (1984), 'Environmental Pollution: Modeling Occurrence, Detection, and Deterrence', **27** *Journal of Law and Economics*, 29-60.

Evans, William N., Neville, Doreen and Graham, John D. (1991), 'General Deterrence of Drunk Driving: Evaluation of Recent American Policies', **11** *Risk Analysis*, 279-289.

Faith, Roger L. and Tollison, Robert D. (1983), 'The Pricing of Surrogate Crime and Law Enforcement', **12** *Journal of Legal Studies*, 401-411.

Feinstein, Jonathan S. (1990), 'Detection Controlled Estimation', **33** *Journal of Law and Economics*, 233-276.

Fenn, Paul and Veljanovski, Cento G. (1988), 'A Positive Economic Theory of Regulatory Enforcement', **98** *Economic Journal*, 1055-1070.

Forst, Brian and Brosi, Kathleen B. (1977), 'A Theoretical and Empirical Analysis of the Prosecutor', **6** *Journal of Legal Studies*, 177-191.

Fowles, Richard and Loeb, Peter D. (1989), 'Speeding, Coordination, and the 55-MPH Limit: Comment', **79** *American Economic Review*, 916-921.

Franzoni, Luigi Alberto (1995), 'Negotiated Enforcement and Criminal Deterrence', University of Bologna, Manuscript.

Franzoni, Luigi Alberto (1997a), 'Amnesties, Settlements and Optimal Tax Enforcement', University of Bologna, Manuscript.

Franzoni, Luigi Alberto (1997b), 'Tax Evasion and Tax Compliance', preliminary version, forthcoming in *International Encyclopedia of Law and Economics*.

Franzoni, Luigi Alberto (forthcoming), 'Punishment and Grace: On the Economics of Permanent Amnesties', *Public Finance/Finances Publiques*.

Friedman, David D. (1981), 'Reflections on Optimal Punishment, or: Should the Rich Pay Higher Fines?', **3** *Research in Law and Economics*, 185-205.

Friedman, David and Sjostrom, William (1993), 'Hanged for a Sheep - The Economics of Marginal Deterrence', **22** *Journal of Legal Studies*, 345-366.

Furlong, William J. (1987), 'A General Equilibrium Model of Crime Commission and Prevention', **34** *Journal of Public Economics*, 87-103.

Garoupa, Nuno (1995), 'Optimal Law Enforcement and Imperfect Information', University of York, Discussion Paper 95/96.

Garoupa, Nuno (1997a), 'The Theory of Optimal Law Enforcement', **11** *Journal of Economic Surveys*, 267-295.

Garoupa, Nuno (1997b), 'The Economics of Organized Crime and Optimal Law Enforcement: the Urge for a Tougher Policy', Universitat Pompeu Fabra, Barcelona, Manuscript.

Garoupa, Nuno (1997c), 'The Role of Moral Values in the Economic Analysis of Crime: A General Equilibrium Approach', Universitat Pompeu Fabra, Barcelona, Manuscript.

Garoupa, Nuno (forthcoming), 'Prison, Parole and the Criminal Justice Act 1991', **18** *Research in Law and Economics*.

Gibbons, Thomas (1982), 'The Utility of Economic Analysis of Crime', **2** *International Review of Law and Economics*, 173-191.

Gibbs, Jack P. (1975), *Crime, Punishment and Deterrence*, New York, Elsevier.

Goel, Rajeev K. and Rich, Daniel P. (1989), 'On the Economic Incentives for Taking Bribes', **61** *Public Choice*, 269-275.

Graetz, Michael J., Reinganum, Jennifer F. and Wilde, Louis L. (1986), 'The Tax Compliance Game: Toward an Interactive Theory of Law Enforcement', **2** *Journal of Law, Economics, and Organization*, 1-32.

Graves, Philip E., Lee, Dwight R. and Sexton, Robert L. (1989), 'Statutes Versus Enforcement: The Case of the Optimal Speed Limit', **79** *American Economic Review*, 932-936.

Graves, Philip E., Lee, Dwight R. and Sexton, Robert L. (1990), 'A Note on Drinking, Driving and Enforcement Costs', **56** *Southern Economic Journal*, 793-796.

Greenberg, Joseph (1984), 'Avoiding Tax Avoidance: A (Repeated) Game Theoretic Approach', **32** *Journal of Economic Theory*, 1-13.

Grieson, Ronald E. and Singh, Nirvikar (1990), 'Regulating Externalities Through Testing', **41** *Journal of Public Economics*, 369-387.

Grossman, Gene M. and Katz, Michael L. (1983), 'Plea Bargaining and Social Welfare', **73** *American Economic Review*, 749-757.

Gyapong, Anthony O. and Gyimah Brempong, Kwabena (1988), 'Factor Substitution, Price Elasticity of Factor Demand and Returns to Scale in Police Production: Evidence from Michigan', **54** *Southern Economic Journal*, 863-878.

Gyimah Brempong, Kwabena (1987), 'Economies of Scale in Municipal Police Departments: The Case of Florida', **69** *Review of Economics and Statistics*, 352-356.

Gyimah Brempong, Kwabena (1989), 'Functional Substitution Among Crimes: Some Evidence', **15** *Eastern Economic Journal*, 129-140.

Hannan, Timothy H. (1982), 'Bank Robberies and Bank Security Precautions', **11** *Journal of Legal Studies*, 83-92.

Harel, Alon (1994), 'Efficiency and Fairness in Criminal Law: The Case for a Criminal Law Principle of Comparative Fault', **82** *California Law Review*, 1181-1229.

Harris, Milton and Raviv, Artur (1978), 'Some Results on Incentive Contracts with Applications to Education and Employment, Health Insurance, and Law Enforcement', **68** *American Economic Review*, 20-30.

Hawkins, Gordon (1969), 'Punishment and Deterrence: The Educative, Moralizing, and Habituative Effects', **1969** *Wisconsin Law Review*, 550-565.

Hawkins, Keith O. (1982), *Environment and Enforcement*, Oxford, Oxford University Press.

Hellman, Daryl A. (1980), *The Economics of Crime*, New York, St. Martin's Press.

Hellman, Daryl A. and Alper, Neil O. (1990), *Economics of Crime: Theory and Practice*, Needham Heights, Simon and Schuster, Ginn Press.

Henszey, Benjamin N. and Roadarmel, Richard L. (1981), 'A Comparative Analysis of State Individual Income Tax Enforcement Procedures', **34** *National Tax Journal*, 207-216.

Hui-Wen, Koo and Png, I.P.L. (1994), 'Private Security: Deterrent or Diversion?', **14** *International Review of Law and Economics*, 87-101.

Hylton, Keith N. (1996), 'Optimal Law Enforcement and Victim Precaution', **27** *RAND Journal of Economics*, 197-206.

Jacob, Herbert (1980), 'Deterrent Effects of Formal and Informal Sanctions', **2** *Law and Policy Quarterly*, 61-80.

Jones, Carol Adaire (1989), 'Standard Setting with Incomplete Enforcement Revisited', **8** *Journal of Policy Analysis and Management*, 72-87.

Kahan, Dan M. (1997), 'Social Influence, Social Meaning, and Deterrence', **83** *Virginia Law Review*, 349-395.

Kambhu, John (1989), 'Regulatory Standards, Noncompliance and Enforcement', **1** *Journal of Regulatory Economics*, 103-114.

Kan, Steven S. (1996), 'Corporal Punishments and Optimal Incapacitation', **25** *Journal of Legal Studies*, 121-130.

Kaplow, Louis (1990a), 'A Note on the Optimal Use of Nonmonetary Sanctions,' **42** *Journal of Public Economics*, 245-247.

Kaplow, Louis (1990b), 'Optimal Deterrence, Uninformed Individuals, and Acquiring Information about Whether Acts are Subject to Sanctions', **6** *Journal of Law, Economics, and Organization*, 93-128.

Kaplow, Louis (1990c), 'Optimal Taxation with Costly Enforcement and Evasion', **43** *Journal of Public Economics*, 221-236.

Kaplow, Louis (1992), 'The Optimal Probability and Magnitude of Fines for Acts that Definitely are Undesirable', **12** *International Review of Law and Economics*, 3-11.

Kaplow, Louis (1994), 'The Value of Accuracy in Adjudication: An Economic Analysis', **23** *Journal of Legal Studies*, 307-401.

Kaplow, Louis (1996), 'How Tax Complexity and Enforcement Affect the Equity and Efficiency of the Income Tax', **49** *National Tax Journal*, 135-149.

Kaplow, Louis and Shavell, Steven (1994a), 'Accuracy in the Determination of Liability', **37** *Journal of Law and Economics*, 1-15.

Kaplow, Louis and Shavell, Steven (1994b), 'Optimal Law Enforcement with Self-Reporting of Behavior', **102** *Journal of Political Economy*, 583-606.

Karpoff, Jonathan M. and Lott, John R., Jr (1993), 'The Reputational Penalty Firms Bear from Committing Criminal Fraud', **36** *Journal of Law and Economics*, 757-802.

Katyal, Neal Kumar (1997), 'Deterrence's Difficulty', **95** *Michigan Law Review*, 2385-2476.

Keeler, Theodore E. (1994), 'Highway Safety, Economic Behavior, and Driving Environment', **84** *American Economic Review*, 684-693.

Keenan, Donald C. and Rubin, Paul H. (1982), 'Criminal Violations and Civil Violations', **11** *Journal of Legal Studies*, 365-377.

Kenkel, Donald S. (1993a), 'Do Drunk Drivers Pay Their Way? A Note on Optimal Penalties for Drunk Driving', **12** *Journal of Health Economics*, 137-149.

Kenkel, Donald S. (1993b), 'Drinking, Driving, and Deterrence: The Effectiveness and Social Costs of Alternative Policies', **36** *Journal of Law and Economics*, 877-913.

Klevorick, Alvin K. (1985a), 'Legal Theory and the Economic Analysis of Torts and Crimes', **85** *Columbia Law Review*, 905-920.

Klevorick, Alvin K. (1985b), 'On the Economic Theory of Crime', in Pennock, J. Roland and Chapman, John W. (eds), *Nomos XXVII: Criminal Justice*, New York, New York University Press, 289-309.

Klitgaard, Robert (1988), *Controlling Corruption*, Berkeley, University of California Press.

Knoeber, Charles R. (1978), 'Penalties and Compensation for Auto Accidents', **7** *Journal of Legal Studies*, 263-278.

Kobayashi, Bruce H. (1992), 'Deterrence with Multiple Defendants', **23** *RAND Journal of Economics*, 507-517.

Kobayashi, Bruce H. and Lott, John R., Jr (1992), 'Low-Probability-High-Penalty Enforcement Strategies and the Efficient Operation of the Plea-Bargaining System', **12** *International Review of Law and Economics*, 69-77.

Kobayashi, Bruce H. and Lott, John R., Jr (1996), 'In Defense of Criminal Defense Expenditures and Plea Bargaining', **16** *International Review of Law and Economics*, 397-416.

Kornhauser, Lewis A. (1982), 'An Economic Analysis of the Choice Between Enterprise and Personal Liability for Accidents', **70** *California Law Review*, 1345-1392.

Kraakman, Reinier (1986), 'Gatekeepers: The Anatomy of a Third-Party Enforcement Strategy', **2** *Journal of Law, Economics, and Organization*, 53-104.

Kramer, Samuel (1990), 'An Economic Analysis of Criminal Attempt: Marginal Deterrence and the Optimal Structure of Sanctions', **81** *Journal of Criminal Law and Criminology*, 398-417.

Landes, William M. (1971), 'An Economic Analysis of the Courts', **4** *Journal of Law and Economics*, 61-107.

Landes, William M. and Posner, Richard A. (1975), 'The Private Enforcement of Law', **4** *Journal of Legal Studies*, 1-46.

Landes, William M. and Posner, Richard A. (1987), *The Economic Structure of Tort Law*, Cambridge, MA, Harvard University Press.

Landsberger, Michael and Meilijson, Isaac (1982), 'Incentive Generating State Dependent Penalty System: The Case of Income Tax Evasion', **19** *Journal of Public Economics*, 333-352.

Lave, Charles A. (1985), 'Speeding, Coordination, and the 55 MPH Limit', **75** *American Economic Review*, 1159-1164.

Lave, Charles A. (1989), 'Speeding, Coordination, and the 55 MPH Limit: Reply', **79** *American Economic Review*, 926-931.

Layton, Allan P. (1983), 'The Impact of Increased Penalties on Australian Drink/Driving Behaviour', **19** *Logistics and Transportation Review*, 261-266.

Layton, Allan P. (1984), 'The Impact of Increased Penalties on Australian Drink/Driving Behavior - A Procedural Note', **20** *Logistics and Transportation Review*, 187-189.

Lee, Dwight R. (1983), 'On Substituting a Socially Costless Penalty for Costly Detection', **3** *International Review of Law and Economics*, 179-185.

Lee, Dwight R. (1985), 'Policing Cost, Evasion Cost, and the Optimal Speed Limit', **52** *Southern Economic Journal*, 34-45.

Leung, Siu Fai (1991), 'How to Make the Fine Fit the Corporate Crime? An Analysis of Static and Dynamical Optimal Punishment Theories', **45** *Journal of Public Economics*, 243-256.

Leung, Siu Fai (1995), 'Dynamic Deterrence Theory', **62** *Economica*, 65-87.

Levitt, Steven D. (1997a), 'Private Information as an Explanation for the Use of Jail Sentences Instead of Fines', **17** *International Review of Law and Economics*, 179-192.

Levitt, Steven D. (1997b), 'Using Electoral Cycles in Police Hiring to Estimate the Effect of Police on Crime', **87** *American Economic Review*, 270-290.

Levitt, Steven D. (forthcoming a), 'Juvenile Crime and Punishment', *Journal of Political Economy*.

Levitt, Steven D. (forthcoming b), 'Why do Increased Arrest Rates Appear to Reduce Crime: Deterrence, Incapacitation, or Measurement Error?', *Economic Inquiry*.

Levy, David T. and Asch, Peter (1989), 'Speeding, Coordination, and the 55 MPH Limit: Comment', **79** *American Economic Review*, 913-915.

Lewin, Jeff L. and Trumbull, William N. (1990), 'The Social Value of Crime?', **10** *International Review of Law and Economics*, 271-284.

Linder, Stephen H. and McBride, Mark E. (1984), 'Enforcement Costs and Regulatory Reform: The Agency and Firm Response', **11** *Journal of Environmental Economics and Management*, 327-346.

Lott, John R., Jr (1987), 'Should the Wealthy be Able to "Buy Justice"?', **95** *Journal of Political Economy*, 1307-1316.

Lott, John R., Jr (1990a), 'The Effect of Conviction on the Legitimate Income of Criminals', **34** *Economics Letters*, 381-385.

Lott, John R., Jr (1990b), 'A Transaction-Costs Explanation for Why the Poor Are More Likely to Commit Crime', **19** *Journal of Legal Studies*, 243-245.

Lott, John R., Jr (1991), 'When Does Learning about a Crime Produce External Benefits?', The Wharton School, University of Pennsylvania, Manuscript.

Lott, John R., Jr (1992a), 'An Attempt at Measuring the Total Monetary Penalty from Drug Convictions: The Importance of an Individual's Reputation', **21** *Journal of Legal Studies*, 159-187.

Lott, John R., Jr (1992b), 'Do we Punish High Income Criminals too Heavily?', **30** *Economic Inquiry*, 583-608.

Lott, John R., Jr and Roberts, Russell D. (1989), 'Why Comply: One-Sided Enforcement of Price Controls and Victimless Crime Laws', **18** *Journal of Legal Studies*, 403-414.

Lott, John R., Jr and Roberts, Russell D. (1995), 'The Expected Penalty for Committing a Crime: An Analysis of Minimum Wage Violations', **30** *Journal of Human Resources*, 397-408.

Lui, Francis T. (1986), 'A Dynamic Model of Corruption Deterrence', **31** *Journal of Public Economics*, 215-236.

Luksetich, William and White, Michael (1982), *Crime and Public Policy: An Economic Approach*, Boston, Little, Brown.

McChesney, Fred S. (1980), 'On the Economics of Antitrust Enforcement', **68** *Georgetown Law Journal*, 1103-1111.

McPheters, Lee R. and Stronge, William B. (eds) (1976), *The Economics of Crime and Law Enforcement*, Springfield, IL, Thomas.

Malik, Arun S. (1990), 'Avoidance, Screening and Optimum Enforcement', **21** *RAND Journal of Economics*, 341-353.

Malik, Arun S. (1992), 'Enforcement Costs and the Choice of Policy Instruments for Controlling Pollution', **30** *Economic Inquiry*, 714-720.

Melumad, Nahum D. and Mookherjee, Dilip (1989), 'Delegation as Commitment: The Case of Income Tax Audits', **20** *RAND Journal of Economics*, 139-163.

Miceli, Thomas J. (1991), 'Optimal Criminal Procedure: Fairness and Deterrence', **11** *International Review of Law and Economics*, 3-10.

Miceli, Thomas J. (1994), 'Prison and Parole: Minimizing the Cost of Non-monetary Sanctions as Deterrents', **16** *Research in Law and Economics*, 197-211.

Miceli, Thomas J. (1996), 'Plea Bargaining and Deterrence: An Institutional Approach', **3** *European Journal of Law and Economics*, 249-264.

Montesquieu, Charles (1748), *The Spirit of the Laws*, Rept. edn, Berkeley, University of California Press, 1977.

Mookherjee, Dilip (1997), 'The Economics of Enforcement', in Bose, Amitava, Rakshit, Mihir and Sinha, Anup (eds), *Issues in Economic Theory and Policy, Essays in Honor of Tapas Majumdar*, New Delhi, Oxford University Press, 202-249.

Mookherjee, Dilip and Png, Ivan (1989), 'Optimal Auditing, Insurance, and Redistribution', **104** *Quarterly Journal of Economics*, 399-415.

Mookherjee, Dilip, and Png, I.P.L. (1990a), 'Eliminating Corruption: An End in Itself?', John E. Anderson Graduate School of Management at UCLA, Business Economics Working Paper No. 90-23.

Mookherjee, Dilip and Png, I.P.L. (1990b), 'Enforcement Costs and the Optimal Progressivity of Income Taxes', **6** *Journal of Law, Economics, and Organization*, 411-431.

Mookherjee, Dilip and Png, I.P.L. (1992a), 'Monitoring vis-à-vis Investigation in Enforcement of Law', **82** *American Economic Review*, 556-565.

Mookherjee, Dilip, and Png, I.P.L. (1992b), 'Rights and Regulations: How and How Much to Enforce?', John E. Anderson Graduate School of Management at UCLA, Business Economics Working Paper No. 92-1.

Mookherjee, Dilip and Png, I.P.L. (1994), 'Marginal Deterrence in Enforcement of Law', **102** *Journal of Political Economy*, 1039-1066.

Mookherjee, Dilip, and Png, I.P.L. (1995), 'Corruptible Law Enforcers: How Should they be Compensated?', **105** *Economic Journal*, 145-159.

Nagin, Daniel and Waldfogel, Joel (1995), 'The Effects of Criminality and Conviction on the Labor Market Status of Young British Offenders', **15** *International Review of Law and Economics*, 109-126.

Nash, John (1991), 'To Make the Punishment Fit the Crime: The Theory and Statistical Estimation of a Multi-Period Optimal Deterrence Model', **11** *International Review of Law and Economics*, 101-110.

Newman, Harry A. and Wright, David W. (1990), 'Strict Liability in a Principal-Agent Model', **10** *International Review of Law and Economics*, 219-231.

Ordeshook, Peter C. (1990), 'Crime and Punishment: Are One-Shot, Two-Person Games Enough?', **84** *American Political Science Review*, 573-575.

Parker, Jeffrey S. (1989), 'Criminal Sentencing Policy for Organizations: The Unifying Approach of Optimal Penalties', **26** *American Criminal Law Review*, 513-593.

Pashigian, B. Peter (1975), 'On the Control of Crime and Bribery', **4** *Journal of Legal Studies*, 311-326.

Png, I.P.L. (1986), 'Optimal Subsidies and Damages in the Presence of Judicial Error', **6** *International Review of Law and Economics*, 101-105.

Png, Ivan P.L. and Zolt, Eric (1989), 'Efficient Deterrence and the Tax Treatment of Monetary Sanctions', **9** *International Review of Law and Economics*, 209-217.

Polinsky, A. Mitchell (1980a), 'Private versus Public Enforcement of Fines', **9** *Journal of Legal Studies*, 105-127.

Polinsky, A. Mitchell (1980b), 'Strict Liability vs. Negligence in a Market Setting', **70** *American Economic Review*, 363-370.

Polinsky, A. Mitchell and Rubinfeld, Daniel L. (1988), 'The Deterrent Effects of Settlements and Trials', **8** *International Review of Law and Economics*, 109-116.

Polinsky, A. Mitchell and Rubinfeld, Daniel L. (1989), 'A Note on Optimal Public Enforcement with Settlements and Litigation Costs', **12** *Research in Law and Economics*, 1-8.

Polinsky, A. Mitchell and Rubinfeld, Daniel L. (1991), 'A Model of Optimal Fines for Repeat Offenders', **46** *Journal of Public Economics*, 291-306.

Polinsky, A. Mitchell and Shavell, Steven (1979), 'The Optimal Tradeoff between the Probability and Magnitude of Fines', **69** *American Economic Review*, 880-891.

Polinsky, A. Mitchell and Shavell, Steven (1984), 'The Optimal Use of Fines and Imprisonment', **24** *Journal of Public Economics*, 89-99.

Polinsky, A. Mitchell and Shavell, Steven (1991), 'A Note on Optimal Fines When Wealth Varies Among Individuals', **81** *American Economic Review*, 618-621.

Polinsky, A. Mitchell and Shavell, Steven (1992), 'Enforcement Costs and the Optimal Magnitude and Probability of Fines', **35** *Journal of Law and Economics*, 133-148.

Polinsky, A. Mitchell and Shavell, Steven (1993), 'Should Employees Be Subject to Fines and Imprisonment Given Existence of Corporate Liability?', **13** *International Review of Law and Economics*, 239-257.

Polinsky, A. Mitchell and Shavell, Steven (1996), 'Repeat Offenders and the Theory of Deterrence', John M. Olin Center for Law, Economics, and Business, Harvard Law School, Discussion Paper No. 188; John M. Olin Program in Law and Economics, Stanford Law School, Working Paper No. 134.

Polinsky, A. Mitchell and Shavell, Steven (1997), 'On the Disutility and Discounting of Imprisonment and the Theory of Deterrence', John M. Olin Center for Law, Economics and Business, Harvard Law School, Discussion Paper No. 213; John M. Olin Program in Law and Econ., Stanford Law School, Working Paper No. 146; Forthcoming in *Journal of Legal Studies*.

Posner, Richard A. (1980a), 'Optimal Sentences for White-Collar Criminals', **17** *American Criminal Law Review*, 409-418.

Posner, Richard A. (1980b), 'Retribution and Related Concepts of Punishment', **9** *Journal of Legal Studies*, 71-92.

Posner, Richard A. (1985), 'An Economic Theory of the Criminal Law', **85** *Columbia Law Review*, 1193-1231.

Pyle, David J (1983), *The Economics of Crime and Law Enforcement*, London, Macmillan.

Pyle, D.J. (1995), 'The Economic Approach to Crime and Punishment', **6** *Journal of Interdisciplinary Economics*, 1-22.

Rasmusen, Eric (1995), 'How Optimal Penalties Change with the Amount of Harm', **15** *International Review of Law and Economics*, 101-108.

Rasmusen, Eric (1996), 'Stigma and Self-Fulfilling Expectations of Criminality', **39** *Journal of Law and Economics*, 519-543.

Ray, Subhash C. (1989), 'Legal Control of Drunken Driving: A Time Series Study of California Data', **5** *International Journal of Forecasting*, 515-522.

Reder, M.W. (1974), 'Citizen Rights and the Cost of Law Enforcement', **3** *Journal of Legal Studies*, 435-455.

Reinganum, Jennifer F. (1988), 'Plea Bargaining and Prosecutorial Discretion', **78** *American Economic Review*, 713-728.

Reinganum, Jennifer F. (1993), 'The Law Enforcement Process and Criminal Choice', **13** *International Review of Law and Economics*, 115-134.

Reinganum, Jennifer F. and Wilde, Louis L. (1984), 'An Equilibrium Model of Tax Compliance with a Bayesian Auditor and Some "Honest" Taxpayers', California Institute of Technology, Social Science Working Paper.

Reinganum, Jennifer F. and Wilde, Louis L. (1985), 'Income Tax Compliance in a Principal-Agent Framework', **26** *Journal of Public Economics*, 1-18.

Reinganum, Jennifer F. and Wilde, Louis L. (1988), 'A Note on Enforcement Uncertainty and Taxpayer Compliance', **103** *Quarterly Journal of Economics*, 793-798.

Reynolds, Robert J. (1980), 'The Economics of Antitrust Enforcement: Theory and Measurement', **68** *Georgetown Law Journal*, 1121-1130.

Rose-Ackerman, Susan (1975), 'The Economics of Corruption', **4** *Journal of Public Economics*, 187-203.

Rose-Ackerman, Susan (1978), *Corruption: A Study in Political Economy*, New York, Academic Press.

Ross, H. Laurence (1975), 'The Scandinavian Myth: The Effectiveness of Drinking-and-Driving Legislating in Sweden and Norway', **4** *Journal of Legal Studies*, 285-310.

Ross, H. Laurence (1977), 'Deterrence Regained: The Cheshire Constabulary's "Breathalyser Blitz"', **6** *Journal of Legal Studies*, 241-249.

Ross, H. Laurence (1984), 'Social Control Through Deterrence: Drinking-and-Driving Laws', **10** *American Review of Sociology*, 21-35.

Ross, H. Laurence (1992), 'The Law and Drunk Driving', **26** *Law and Society Review*, 219-230.

Ross, H. Laurence and Blumenthal, Murray (1974), 'Sanctions for the Drinking Driver: An Experimental Study', **3** *Journal of Legal Studies*, 53-61.

Rottenberg, Simon (ed.) (1973), *The Economics of Crime and Punishment*, Washington, American Enterprise Institute for Public Policy Research.

Rubin, Paul H. and Zwirb, Robert (1987), 'The Economics of Civil RICO', **20** *U.C. Davis Law Review*, 883-912.

Rubinstein, Ariel (1979), 'An Optimal Conviction Policy for Offenses that May Have Been Committed by Accident', in Brams, S.J., Schotter, A. and Schwödiauer, G. (eds), *Applied Game Theory*, Wurzburg, Physica-Verlag, 406-413.

Rubinstein, Ariel (1980), 'On an Anomaly of the Deterrent Effect of Punishment', **6** *Economics Letters*, 89-94.

Russell, Clifford S., Harrington, Winston and Vaughan, William J. (1986), *Enforcing Pollution Control Laws*, Washington, DC, Resources for the Future.

Sah, Raaj K. (1991), 'Social Osmosis and Patterns of Crime', **99** *Journal of Political Economy* , 1272-1295.

Schmidt, Peter and Witte, Ann D. (1984), *An Economic Analysis of Crime and Justice: Theory, Methods, and Applications*, New York, Academic Press.

Schroyen, Fred (1997), 'Pareto Efficient Income Taxation Under Costly Monitoring', **65** *Journal of Public Economics*, 343-366.

Schwartz, Warren F. (1980), 'An Overview of the Economics of Antitrust Enforcement', **68** *Georgetown Law Journal*, 1075-1102.

Scotchmer, Suzanne (1987), 'Audit Classes and Tax Enforcement Policy', **77** *American Economic Review*, 229-233.

Scotchmer, Suzanne and Slemrod, Joel (1987), 'Optimal Obfuscation in Tax Enforcement', Graduate School of Public Policy, University of California, Berkeley, Working Paper.

Segerson, Kathleen and Tietenberg, Tom (1992a), 'Defining Efficient Sanctions', in Tietenberg, T.H. (ed.), *Innovation in Environmental Policy*, Aldershot, Edward Elgar, 53-73.

Segerson, Kathleen and Tietenberg, Tom (1992b), 'The Structure of Penalties in Environmental Enforcement: An Economic Analysis', **23** *Journal of Environmental Economics and Management*, 179-200.

Seidman, Louis Michael (1984), 'Soldiers, Martyrs, and Criminals: Utilitarian Theory and the Problem of Crime Control', **94** *Yale Law Journal*, 315-349.

Shapiro, Perry and Votey, Harold L., Jr (1984), 'Deterrence and Subjective Probabilities of Arrest: Modeling Individual Decisions to Drink and Drive in Sweden', **18** *Law and Society Review*, 583-604.

Shavell, Steven (1980), 'Strict Liability versus Negligence', **9** *Journal of Legal Studies*, 1-25.

Shavell, Steven (1982), 'On Liability and Insurance', **13** *Bell Journal of Economics*, 120-132.

Shavell, Steven (1985), 'Criminal Law and the Optimal Use of Nonmonetary Sanctions as a Deterrent', **85** *Columbia Law Review*, 1232-1262.

Shavell, Steven (1987a), 'The Optimal Use of Nonmonetary Sanctions as a Deterrent', **77** *American Economic Review*, 584-592.

Shavell, Steven (1987b), 'A Model of Optimal Incapacitation', **77** *American Economic Review* , 107-110.

Shavell, Steven (1987c), *Economic Analysis of Accident Law*, Cambridge, MA, Harvard University Press.

Shavell, Steven (1990), 'Deterrence and the Punishment of Attempts', **19** *Journal of Legal Studies*, 435-466.

Shavell, Steven (1991a), 'Individual Precautions to Prevent Theft: Private versus Socially Optimal Behavior', **11** *International Review of Law and Economics*, 123-132.

Shavell, Steven (1991b), 'Specific versus General Enforcement of Law', **99** *Journal of Political Economy*, 1088-1108.

Shavell, Steven (1992), 'A Note on Marginal Deterrence', **12** *International Review of Law and Economics*, 345-355.

Shavell, Steven (1993), 'The Optimal Structure of Law Enforcement', **36** *Journal of Law and Economics*, 255-287.

Shavell, Steven (1997a), 'The Fundamental Divergence between the Private and the Social Motive to Use the Legal System', **26** *Journal of Legal Studies*, 575-612.

Shavell, Steven (1997b), 'The Optimal Level of Corporate Liability Given the Limited Ability of Corporations to Penalize Their Employees', **17** *International Review of Law and Economics*, 203-213.

Shleifer, Andrei and Vishny, Robert W. (1993), 'Corruption', **108** *Quarterly Journal of Economics*, 599-617.

Sigman, Hilary (1995), 'Midnight Dumping: An Empirical Analysis of Illegal Waste Oil Disposal', Department of Economics, UCLA, Manuscript.

Skogh, Göran (1973), 'A Note on Gary Becker's "Crime and Punishment: An Economic Approach"', **75** *Swedish Journal of Economics*, 305-311.

Skogh, Göran and Stuart, Charles (1982a), 'A Contractarian Theory of Property Rights and Crime', **84** *Scandinavian Journal of Economics*, 27-40.

Skogh, Göran and Stuart, Charles (1982b), 'An Economic Analysis of Crime Rates, Punishment, and the Social Consequences of Crime', **38** *Public Choice*, 171-179.

Slemrod, Joel and Yitzhaki, Shlomo (1987), 'The Optimal Size of a Tax Collection Agency', **89** *Scandinavian Journal of Economics*, 183-192.

Sloan, Frank A., Reilly, Bridget A. and Schenzler, Christoph M. (1994), 'Tort Liability versus Other Approaches for Deterring Careless Driving', **14** *International Review of Law and Economics*, 53-71.

Snyder, Donald (1989), 'Speeding, Coordination, and the 55-MPH Limit: Comment', **79** *American Economic Review*, 922-925.

Snyder, Edward A. (1990), 'The Effect of Higher Criminal Penalties on Antitrust Enforcement', **33** *Journal of Law and Economics*, 439-462.

Spier, Kathryn E. (1997), 'A Note on the Divergence between the Private and the Social Motive to Settle under a Negligence Rule', **26** *Journal of Legal Studies*, 613-621.

Stigler, George J. (1970), 'The Optimum Enforcement of Laws', **78** *Journal of Political Economy*, 526-536.

Swanson, Timothy M. (1991), 'Enforcement of Environmental Regulation', in Weigel, Wolfgang (ed.), *Economic Analysis of Law - A Collection of Applications*, Vienna, Österreichischer Wirtschaftsverlag, 67-78.

Sykes, Alan O. (1981), 'An Efficiency Analysis of Vicarious Liability under the Law of Agency', **91** *Yale Law Journal*, 168-206.

Tauchen, Helen, Witte, Ann Dryden and Griesinger, Harriet (1994), 'Criminal Deterrence: Revisiting the Issue with a Birth Cohort', **76** *Review of Economics and Statistics*, 399-412.

Thurow, Lester (1970), 'Equity vs. Efficiency in Law Enforcement', **18** *Public Policy*, 451-459.

Tullock, Gordon (1967), 'The Welfare Costs of Tariffs, Monopolies and Theft', **5** *Western Economic Review*, 224-232.

Tullock, Gordon (1969), 'An Economic Approach to Crime', **50** *Social Science Quarterly*, 59-71.

Tullock, Gordon (1974), 'Does Punishment Deter Crime?', **36** *The Public Interest*, 103-11.

United States Sentencing Commission (1995), *Federal Sentencing Guidelines Manual, 1995 Edition*, St. Paul, MN, West Publishing.

Usher, Dan (1987), 'Theft as a Paradigm for Departures from Efficiency', **39** *Oxford Economic Papers*, 235-252.

van den Haag, Ernest (1982), 'The Criminal Law as a Threat System', **73** *Journal of Criminal Law and Criminology*, 769-785.

Veljanovski, C.G. (1982), 'The Market for Regulatory Enforcement', *Economic Journal*, Supplement, 123-129.

Veljanovski, Cento G. (1983), 'Regulatory Enforcement - An Economic Case Study of the British Factory Inspectorate', **5** *Law and Policy Quarterly*, 75-96.

Veljanovski, Cento G. (1984), 'The Economics of Regulatory Enforcement', in Hawkins, Keith and Thomas, John M. (eds), *Enforcing Regulation*, Boston, Kluwer-Nijhoff, 171-188.

Viscusi, W. Kip (1986a), 'Market Incentives for Criminal Behavior', in Freeman, Richard B. and Holzer, Harry J. (eds), *The Black Youth Employment Crisis*, Chicago, University of Chicago Press, 301-346.

Viscusi, W. Kip (1986b), 'The Risks and Rewards of Criminal Activity: A Comprehensive Test of Criminal Deterrence', **4** *Journal of Labor Economics*, 317-340.

Votey, Harold L., Jr (1982), 'Scandinavian Drinking-Driving Control: Myth or Intuition?', **11** *Journal of Legal Studies*, 93-116.

Votey, Harold L., Jr and Phillips, Llad (1972), 'Police Effectiveness and the Production Function for Law Enforcement', **1** *Journal of Legal Studies*, 423-436.

Waldfogel, Joel (1993), 'Criminal Sentences as Endogenous Taxes: Are They "Just" or "Efficient"?', **36** *Journal of Law and Economics*, 139-151.

Waldfogel, Joel (1995), 'Are Fines and Prison Terms Used Efficiently? Evidence on Federal Fraud Offenders', **38** *Journal of Law and Economics*, 107-139.

Weinblatt, J., Spiegel, Uriel, Hakim, Simon and Ben-Zion, Uri (1983), 'Crime Prevention Policies and Externalities: A Theoretical Analysis', **38** *Public Finance*, 110-131.

Wilde, Louis L. (1992), 'Criminal Choice, Nonmonetary Sanctions, and Marginal Deterrence: A Normative Analysis', **12** *International Review of Law and Economics*, 333-344.

Wilkinson, James T. (1987), 'Reducing Drunken Driving: Which Policies are Most Effective?', **54** *Southern Economic Journal*, 322-334.

Wilson, James Q. (1983), *Thinking About Crime*, 2nd edn, New York, Basic Books.

Wilson, James Q. and Herrnstein, Richard J. (1985), *Crime and Human Nature*, New York, Simon and Schuster.

Witte, Ann D. and Woodbury, Diane F. (1985), 'The Effect of Tax Laws and Tax Administration on Tax Compliance: The Case of the U.S. Individual Income Tax', **38** *National Tax Journal*, 1-14.

Yohe, Gary W. (1982), 'Fines as Economic Incentives - An Alternative Variable Control', **2** *International Review of Law and Economics*, 95-109.

Zolt, Eric M. (1989), 'Deterrence via Taxation: A Critical Analysis of Tax Penalty Provisions', **37** *UCLA Law Review*, 343-387.

8100
Economics of Criminal Behavior

Erling Eide
Professor, Faculty of Law, University of Oslo

Abstract

Models of criminal behavior, where a person is assumed to act rationally on the basis of costs and benefits of legal and illegal opportunities, are presented in this chapter. Most of these models are similar to models of portfolio choice and of supply of labor. The empirical studies that are surveyed use various types of regression analyses and employ data from states and police regions down to campuses and individuals. Most studies corroborate the hypothesis that the probability of punishment, and to a lesser degree also the severity of punishment, has a deterrent effect on crime. The effects of various economic factors are less clear, although unemployment seems to increase crime. Methodological problems relating to the assumption of rationality, to statistical identification of equations, to measurement errors, and to operationalization of theoretical variables are discussed.
JEL classification: K42
Keywords: Crime, Punishment, Sanctions, Rational Choice

1. Introduction

Theories of crime are abundant. Various mental, physical, developmental, economic, social, cultural, and other causes have been launched as explanations of why people offend. Concepts like depravity, insanity, abnormality, deviance and deprivation are used to characterize those who commit crimes. During the last 30 years economists have invaded the field using their all-embracing model of individual rational behavior, where a criminal act is preferred and chosen if the total pay-off, including that of sanctions and other costs, is higher than that of legal alternatives. Offenders are primarily not regarded as deviant individuals with atypical motivations, but rather as simple, normal persons like the rest of us. The theory of deterrence thus obtained is regarded as nothing but a special case of the general theory of rational behavior under uncertainty. Assuming that individual preferences are constant, the model can be used to predict how changes in the probability and severity of sanctions and in various socioeconomic factors may affect the amount of crime. Even if most of those who violate certain laws differ systematically from those who abide by the same laws, the former, like the latter, do respond to incentives, that is, to sanctions and economic conditions. Empirical tests with increasing statistical rigour and refinement have been carried out on the basis of this theory.

Whereas the general preventive effects of sanctions for a long time have occupied a main position in penal legislation and sentencing policy, such effects were almost totally neglected in criminology and modern sociology until the late 1960s. Criminologists have been more interested in rehabilitation and treatment, and many are still reluctant to accept studies of deterrence in general and models of criminal behavior based on rational choice in particular. However, scholars who are reluctant to accept the assumption of rational choice, still find interest in the rather rigorous empirical studies in the economics of crime literature (Andenaes, 1975), and sociologists have in recent years been inspired to carry out similar research. Below, mainly studies made by economists are included.

2. The Basic Model

Theories of criminal behavior based more or less on the assumption of rational choice were proposed by Beccaria and Bentham. Bentham ([1788] 1843, p. 399) wrote that 'the profit of the crime is the force which urges man to delinquency: the pain of the punishment is the force employed to restrain him from it. If the first of these forces be the greater, the crime will be committed; if the second, the crime will not be committed.' From the beginning of this century interest in their point of view dwindled as a plethora of other theories were developed. The main idea of Bentham was vitalized and modernized in the pathbreaking article on *Crime and Punishment* by Becker (1968), who suggests that 'a useful theory of criminal behavior can dispense with special theories of anomie, psychological inadequacies, or inheritance of special traits and simply extend the economist's usual analysis of choice' (p. 170). He argues that criminals are like anyone else, and assumes that an individual behaves as if he is a rational utility maximizer. As the total outcome of a criminal act is uncertain, Becker employs the usual assumption that people act as if they were maximizing expected utility, and also that utility is a positive function of income. The individual's expected utility $E[U]$ from committing an offense is:

$$E[U] = PU(Y - f) + (1 - P)U(Y), \tag{1}$$

where $U(\cdot)$ is the individual's von Neumann-Morgenstern utility function, P is the subjective probability of being caught and convicted, Y is the monetary plus psychic income (that is, the monetary equivalent) from an offense, and f is the monetary equivalent of the punishment. The individual will commit the offense if the expected utility is positive, and he will not if it is negative. The common assumption of stable preferences provides a solid foundation for generating predictions about responses to various changes in parameters and, according to Becker, prevents the analyst from succumbing to the temptation of simply postulating the required shift in preferences in order to 'explain' all apparent contradictions to his predictions. Analysis of comparative statics shows that increases in either the probability or the severity of punishment might change the expected utility from being positive to being negative. For society as a whole Becker introduces a 'supply of offense function', where the two factors have an effect on the total amount of crime.

Whereas Becker considers the income and punishment equivalents of an offense separated from other income, later authors, in accordance with Brown and Reynolds (1973), take the individual's initial income position as a point of reference. Expected utility becomes

$$E[U] = PU(W - f) + (1 - P)U(W+g), \tag{2}$$

where W is present income and g is gains from crime. Here, the crime will be committed if the expected utility is higher than the utility of the initial income W. Furthermore, it is sometimes assumed that the offender in case of conviction might retain some gain from the offense. Becker demonstrated that if the elasticity of the expected utility with respect to the probability of punishment exceeded the elasticity of the expected utility with respect to conviction (both in absolute values), the offenders were risk lovers. Empirical studies by Becker and others corroborated this result. As shown by Brown and Reynolds (1973) equation (2), at variance with equation (1), does not imply such a conclusion.

3. Extensions of the Basic Model

Later, several types of economic models of crime have been developed, all of which draw on the theory of supply and the theory of behavior towards risk. The simplest one is very similar to models of portfolio choice, where a person's wealth is allocated between various risky and non-risky projects. In the economics of crime version of this model the illegal alternatives are considered as risky mainly because of uncertainty about punishment. Allingham and Sandmo (1972), Kolm (1973), and Singh (1973) have constructed such models for tax evasion, where the individual is confronted with the problem of deciding what proportion of income not to report to the tax authorities. At variance with Becker's model where the income of crime is a parameter, here the income of criminal activity is a function of the proportion of the exogenous income not reported.

Both the probability and the severity of punishment are found to deter crime for a risk averse person. For risk lovers, the effect of the severity of punishment is uncertain. An increase in the severity will have similar effects for illegal activities as a wage decrease in labor supply models will have for legal activities. Two effects obtain: a substitution effect and an income effect. The substitution effect of a more severe punishment will consist in less crime. The sign of the income effect will depend on individual attitude towards risk. For a risk lover the income effect is positive, and the total effect on crime of a change in severity becomes indeterminate. The effects of changes in gains from crime and in exogenous income depend on whether there is decrease or increase in the risk aversion or risk preference. For the common assumption of decreasing absolute risk aversion an individual will allocate a larger proportion of his income to tax cheating the higher his exogenous income and the higher the gains from crime.

Heineke (1978) has presented a somewhat different type of model where the individual allocates his time (and not his wealth or income) between legal and illegal activities. The individual's income is assumed to be equal to the sum of three elements: exogenous income, the monetary and monetized benefits and costs of legal activities, and the monetary and monetized benefits and costs of illegal activities. (Monetization implicitly takes place if an individual, having to choose between actions involving non-monetary gains and losses, acts rationally according to certain axioms.) If convicted, this income is reduced by a factor that represents the monetary and monetized costs of crime. Here, some of the individuals may choose to specialize in either legal or illegal activities, whereas others may choose a mix of the two. A marginal increase in the probability or the severity of sanctions will affect the optimal mix of activities, whereas such an increase may be insufficient to have an effect on individuals who have specialized in one of the two activities. Assuming leisure time not to be fixed, the same comparative statics results as for the portfolio choice model are obtained. The reason for this similarity is the monetization of psychic benefits, and the high degree of independence between the types of activities. In addition, for some attitudes towards risk, it turns out that an increase in returns to legal activity increases time allocated to both types of activities.

Several authors, first and foremost Ehrlich (1973), have studied the latter type of model, but with the additional restriction that time allocated to leisure is fixed (and thus independent of returns and costs for legal and illegal activities). The assumption of a fixed leisure time obviously requires that the time allocated to legal and illegal activity changes in opposite direction (and with equal amounts), but the effects of changes in some of the parameters are also different from the previous model. Whereas the effects on crime of changes in exogenous income and gains to crime are the same as above, the effects of changes in the severity of sanctions become inconclusive without further restrictions on some parameters.

The portfolio model of time allocation with non-fixed leisure time has been somewhat extended by Wolpin (1978) and by Schmidt and Witte (1984), who have introduced four possible criminal justice states, each taking place with a certain probability. In these models the effects of changes in sanctions, and in gains and losses of crime become more ambiguous than in the previous models. Especially, and somewhat surprisingly, illegal activity will decrease with increasing unemployment under the standard assumption of decreasing absolute risk aversion. The explanation is that unemployment implies a lower income, and therefore a higher risk aversion, and then again a lower expected utility of crime. Under risk neutrality time allocated to illegal activity is not affected by a change in the expected employment rate. Baldry (1974) introduces the assumption that a person has to choose between zero or a given number of hours of legal work per week. Transforming the Ehrlich model into a nonlinear programming model, he obtains unambiguous predictions of the effects on crime of changes in sanctions and economic variables.

If one is not willing to accept the assumption that all psychic factors associated with legal and illegal activities can be monetized, one has to use utility functions where time allocations and their attributes are introduced explicitly. Block and Heineke (1975a) have studied a model where a vector of attributes of the penalty, interpreted as the length of sentence, is included in the utility function. In this model one obtains considerably more ambiguous results than for the previous models. Unless one is willing to make strong assumptions about individual preferences, it is not possible to decide whether criminal activity will decrease or increase as a result of changes in the probability of punishment, of changes in returns to legal and to illegal activity, and of changes in exogenous income.

Block and Heineke (1975a) have shown that changes in legal and illegal remuneration lead to changes in illegal activity that are composed of stochastic counterparts of the substitution and income effects of traditional supply and demand theory. But the similarity is not close. Even if one assumes that illegal activity is inferior (that is, that such activity is decreasing with income), it is not possible to sign the relevant terms. Increasing the penalty, for instance, will not unambiguously deter crime.

Witte (1980, p. 59) and Schmidt and Witte (1984) have studied a simplified version of their several sanctions model where time spent in legal income-generating activity (work), time spent in illegal income-generating activity (theft, and so on), time spent in legal consumption activities, and time spent in illegal consumption activities (drug use, assaultive activities, and so on) are separate arguments in the individual's utility function. Here too, similar inconclusive results are obtained. When benefits and costs of legal activities are risky, even more ambiguous results are obtained.

The standard assumption that people maximize *expected* utility is appealing because it follows from the von Neumann-Morgenstern axioms of individual behavior that many scholars regard as reasonable, or at least as a fruitful hypothesis. However, many laboratory experiments have shown that people do not always choose in accordance with these axioms, in particular Lattimore, Baker and Witte (1992), who included burglaries in a set of risky prospects to choose between. As a result, various alternative forms of preference functions that are non-linear in the probabilities have been proposed. Eide (1995) has substituted the assumption of rank-dependent expected utility for the ordinary expected utility in various models of criminal behavior. In the latter study it is shown that the qualitative results of comparative statics analyses are the same for both types of assumptions.

Summing up the comparative static results so far, an increase in the probability of clear-up or arrest has, regardless of the sign of the attitude towards risk, a negative effect on the supply of crime. The effect of an increase in the conviction rate, given arrest, is indeterminate without further assumptions, and the same holds true for an increase in the probability of imprisonment given conviction. However, reasonable assumptions will produce the same conclusions as for the unconditional probability of arrest or conviction. These results constitute a certain support for the probability part of the deterrence hypothesis.

For any attitude towards risk in Beckers's model, an increase in the severity of punishment has a negative effect on the supply of crime. For the group of portfolio choice models as a whole the severity part of the deterrence hypothesis hinges upon the question of attitude towards risk. The effect of more severe sanctions is especially uncertain for risk lovers, whereas risk averters in most models offend less when sanctions increase. Furthermore, a positive shift in punishment in the several-sanctions model and in the labor supply model with non-monetized attributes can cause an increase in crime for any attitude towards risk. In the latter model, the restriction necessary to generate this effect is that the income effects must be greater than the substitution effects. The labor supply models with non-monetized attributes give inconclusive effects also for changes in the other parameters that are studied. For the other models the effects of changes in the gains to crime, in exogenous income, and in income from legal activities depend on the individual's attitude towards risk.

As a whole, one may conclude that the effects of changes in the environment depend on the individual's attitude towards risk. If one is willing to stick to the rather common assumption of decreasing absolute risk aversion, and also that psychic effects can be monetized, and that there is just one type of sanctions, the effects are clear: crime is deterred by increases in the probability and in the severity of punishment, and enhanced by increases in exogenous income, and in gains from both legal and illegal activities. The reason why increases in various incomes and gains increases crime is that punishment in the case of decreasing absolute risk aversion produces a smaller reduction in expected (total) income. For risk-neutral people an increase in the probability or severity of punishment and a decrease in the gains to crime will reduce the supply of crime, whereas changes in exogenous income, and in the remuneration of legal activity have no effect. Here, changes in the latter income components do not change the bite of punishment.

A crucial assumption in the studies mentioned above seems to be the Bernoulli distribution of the probability of punishment. Introducing a more general distribution of risk into the Becker-type model of Block and Lind (1975a), Baldry (1980) concludes that the 'standard' deterrence results cannot be derived.

A good survey of the main contributions to the development of the economic models of crime is found in Schmidt and Witte (1984).

4. The Benefits and Costs of Crime

Various studies have elaborated on the benefits and costs of crime. The gains and losses included in the economic models of criminal behavior are usually meant to represent all kinds of benefits and costs that have an effect on the people's decisions. People are assumed to allocate time to criminal activity until marginal benefits equal marginal costs. For some people marginal benefits are probably always lower than marginal costs, and we then have a law-abiding person. Others will specialize in crime, whereas most of us possibly commit an offense now and then.

The kinds of gains obtained from a criminal act vary, depending on the type of crime and the individual criminal: some are monetary, obtained from theft, robbery, insurance fraud, and so on. Others are psychic, such as the thrill of danger, peer approval, retribution (bank robbery), sense of accomplishment, or 'pure' satisfaction of wants (rape). For some property crimes the prices obtained on markets of stolen goods are of importance.

Among the costs one may distinguish between material costs (equipment, guns, vehicles), psychic costs (guilt, anxiety, fear, dislike of risk), expected punishment costs and opportunity costs.

The punishment costs include all formal and informal sanctions, as well as pecuniary costs arising from lawsuits (lost income and lawyer's fee). The formal sanctions include fines, various forms of incarceration, and so on. The more severe these sanctions are, the higher the cost. The informal sanctions include any personal inconveniences connected with arrest, suit and conviction. The sanctions related to the social stigma caused by arrest and formal sanctions must be added. The nuisance associated with appearing in court, and the reactions of employer, family and friends, might have a stronger effect than formal sanctions.

The opportunity cost of crime consists of the net benefit (gross benefit minus cost) of the legal activity forgone while planning, performing and concealing the criminal act. The lower an individual's level of income, the lower is his opportunity cost of engaging in illegal activity.

The amount a person can earn in the legal sector may depend upon age, sex, race, education, training, region, rate of unemployment, IQ, and so on. People able to earn only a rather low wage will have a low opportunity cost of crime, the cost of giving up legal income. We would therefore expect that among criminals there are more young people, men, blacks, low-paid workers, and so on than in the population at large. This is in fact what crime statistics tell us, but more refined empirical studies are necessary to substantiate such relationships.

Many individual characteristics might have an effect on benefits and costs. Individual rates of discount might be important. The gains from crime often occur immediately, whereas punishment is something that might come in the future, and stretched over a long period of time. A high discount rate will therefore tend to increase crime. The probability of punishment will be different for different people. Some are more clever than others at concealing the offense and eluding the police. There are also differences in abilities of defending oneself in court, or in engaging good lawyers. The attitude towards risk will also have an effect.

A high rate of recidivism is in accordance with the model of rational choice. If for an offender preferences are stable and the opportunities available remain the same, the degree of criminal activity will not tend to decrease after a conviction. Recidivism is thus not necessarily a result of erratic behavior or lack of self-control, but rather a result of rational choice. Moreover, several factors that count in favor of crime are increased by imprisonment: additional criminal skills are acquired, and opportunities of legal income are reduced. If it was rational to commit a crime in the first place, it is all the more so after having served a prison sentence. If the sentence has increased the criminal's evaluation of how probable or severe sanctions might be, or if he or she has obtained some benefit from prison education schemes, the tendency to recidivism will be counterbalanced.

5. Are Criminals Really Rational?

Exaggerating somewhat the differences between sociologists and economists, one may say that the first consider crime as deviant behavior whereas the latter consider it as rational. Figure 1 illustrates the main elements characterizing an individual's choice situation according to the theory of rational choice. The individual has a feasible set of courses of action, some of which are illegal. The environment, including sanctions and wages, determines the outcomes of the various courses of action. The individual is assumed to choose the course of action that best satisfies its preferences. Preferences include not only wants, but also norms. The guilt of acting in conflict with norms is part of the costs of crime.

Figure 1 Rational Choice With Norms

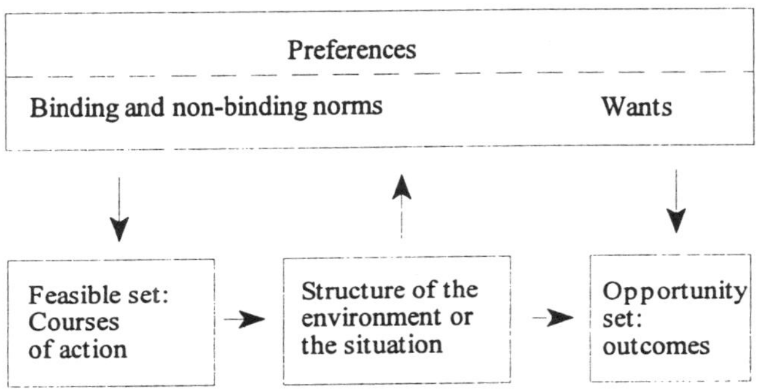

In theories of economics of crime, norms are seldom studied, or even mentioned. Preferences as a whole are usually assumed to be constant, and authors do not find it necessary, or do not feel competent to discuss norms. Traditional criminological theories, on the other hand, suggest that the individual's environment has a significant impact on people's preferences, especially on norms, but also on wants. Theories about culture conflict, cultural deviance, anomie and learning relate individual preferences to various characteristics of the society. Other theories suggest that preferences are inherited or dependent on age, gender, race, intelligence and other personal characteristics. In the literature of economics of crime these various theories are often neglected, and the main question studied is how the environment produces incentives to commit, or not to commit, crimes.

In a very broad sense a deterrent is any factor that exerts a preventive force against crime. Sanctions may have an effect on crime either by causing fear or by influencing norms. The combination of these effects is in parts of the literature on crime called 'general prevention' (Andenaes, 1975). In economics of crime one focuses on the effects of law enforcement on the *outcomes* of actions, and thereby on illegal behavior. This is the deterrence mechanism in the narrow sense. The possibility that law enforcement or other aspects of the environment might affect individual norms and wants, for example, by conditioned aversion as suggested by the behavioral perspective, is given less attention.

An interesting question is whether the model of rational choice is in conflict with, a substitute for, a supplement to, or a general framework for other theories of crime. Carr-Hill and Stern (1979) emphasize that the economic and criminological approaches should be seen as complementary rather than conflicting. They maintain that the economic approach isolates the importance of the probabilities and magnitude of reward and punishment, and shows how they can be treated formally. The criminological approach takes these for granted and indicates how different groups might view and react to these probabilities, rewards, and punishments.

These two approaches are related to the issue of opportunity vs. motivation as explanation of crime. Economists and others who focus on costs and benefits of crime in a rational choice framework, also take into account that crime presupposes potential victims. The better the opportunities of hitting valuable and low-risk targets, the more crime there is. Those who more or less explicitly dismiss the theory of rational choice often focus on the motivation of individuals, assuming that behavior is determined by individual characteristics and by the norms of the groups to which they belong.

The opportunity approach is an element in the market models of crime, where the number of offenses is determined by the interaction of potential offenders, who are seeking the best targets, and potential victims, who by measures of private protection seek to be less attractive or vulnerable to crime (compare Ehrlich, 1981, 1982, 1996, and Cook, 1986).

Several authors have discussed whether people have sufficient information about the environment and about outcomes of actions to make rational choices. Becker and others maintain that even if choices are based on subjective beliefs that are wrong, the choices are meaningful from a subjective point of view, and behavior can be explained and understood on this basis. One may argue that this is not a satisfactory answer to the claim that people have cognitive limitations, and that they stick to 'satisficing' and not to maximization. The studies of Caroll and Weaver (1986), Tunnell (1992), and Nagin and Paternoster (1993) suggest that Simon's theory of bounded rationality might be a better representation of offenders' behavior than the rational choice theory, a conclusion that is supported by Niggli (1994).

It has also been argued that the simple rational choice theory is inadequate because people's behavior is determined by procedural rationality, in which an individual is portrayed as a follower of rules established by history or social relations, or by expressive rationality, in which an individual, through symbolic acts, demonstrates to himself and others his self-conception and worth. There is disagreement about how serious such criticism is for the use of the rational choice theory in studies of crime. Ehrlich (1973, p. 532) maintains that '[s]ince those who hate need not respond to incentives any differently than those who love or are indifferent to the well-being of others, the analysis ... would apply ... to crimes against the person as well as to crime involving material gains'.

6. Empirical Studies

In a great number of empirical studies the theoretical models of criminal behavior have been tested, and the effect on crime of the probability and severity of punishment, and of benefits and costs of legal and illegal activities has been estimated. The influence of norms, tastes, and abilities, corresponding to constitutional and acquired individual characteristics, have in some cases been studied indirectly by including variables like age, race, gender, and so on. A variety of equation specifications and estimation techniques have been used, and the studies have been based on data from countries and states down to municipalities, campuses, and individuals.

Analogously to the terms psychometric studies, cliometric studies, and so on it seems appropriate to introduce the term 'criminometric studies' to characterize this field of research. The subject matter is crime, and it gives the field a somewhat distorted and too limited range to call these studies econometric, although this is what is usually done. The studies are rooted in a general theory of rational choice, and not in some rational choice theory presumably limited to economics.

In the framework of norm-guided rational behavior norms may depend on the environment. In most criminometric studies norms, as well as wants, are assumed to be constant, and often also equal among individuals. Becker (1976, p. 5) expresses a rather common attitude by stating that '[s]ince economists generally have little to contribute, especially in recent times, to the understanding of how preferences are formed, preferences are assumed not to be very different between wealthy and poor persons, or even between persons in different societies and cultures'. With this assumption it is relatively easy to test other parts of the theory, such as hypotheses about the effect of sanctions, and of gains and losses of legal and illegal activities. If preferences differ among individuals, estimates of the effects of sanctions will be relevant for an 'average' person. The explicit assumption that individual preferences are constant, distinguish criminometric studies from most other studies in criminology.

There are good reasons to carry out empirical studies of criminal behavior at the individual level instead of an aggregated level. In the first place it is at best controversial to posit that behavior is anything but individual. Second, the theoretical models that are developed are based on individual rational choice. Third, as will be discussed below, studies based on aggregated data require a number of additional assumptions of questionable validity. Fourth, the statistical identification problem is less serious when individual behavior is studied. Using aggregated data one faces the problem of distinguishing between the effect of the probability of arrest on the amount of crime and the effect of the amount of crime on the probability of arrest. In empirical studies at the individual level it can reasonably be assumed that the probability and severity of punishment is determined without being influenced by the actions of a given individual. Thus, the deterrence variables can be considered to be exogenous to the individual's choices, and the problem of simultaneity inherent in macro studies is absent. Unfortunately, empirical tests of these models by use of information on individuals are few. The application of the theoretical models to empirical studies is intricate (Manski, 1978), and suitable data are scarce. The data we have are mainly self-reports on criminal activity, and records of criminal activity compiled by the criminal justice system. The most serious problem with the latter type of data is that they do not constitute representative samples of the population, but are biased in the sense that only convicted persons are included. It is hardly possible to test a general theory of rational criminal behavior by studying only one subgroup of the offenders. A related problem is that most available data sources include information only about choices made, and not about those available, but not chosen. It is difficult, if not impossible, to test a theory of rational choice if the choice set in this way is limited. Whereas such data are of limited interest for studies of general deterrence, that is, of effects on people in general, they are useful for studies of special deterrence, that is, of effects on the individuals that are punished.

The bulk of criminometric studies consists of cross-section regression analyses based on macro data. Some of them are rather broad, including many types of regional areas, estimation techniques and types of crime, whereas others concentrate on particular types of crime, such as property crimes or hijacking. A few of them address special questions, such as the effect of police 'aggressiveness' in patrolling, or the influence of income differentials. Time series studies are less numerous, and employ mostly data on total crime.

The majority of these empirical studies of crime have been evaluated in various surveys. In an annotated bibliography Beyleveld (1980) reviews a number of investigations of correlations between crime and deterrence variables, in addition to 35 cross-sectional and 31 time-series econometric studies of crime. A thorough review of the empirical evidence of general deterrence is also given by Nagin (1978), who comments on 24 correlation and econometric studies, all but two also covered by Beyleveld. Taylor (1978) concentrates upon six major econometric studies, whereas Pyle (1983) reviews the same studies and about 15 others. A shorter, but somewhat more up to date review is Cameron (1988), and a more recent comprehensive survey is found in Eide (1994). Reviews of certain parts of the literature are found in Passell and Taylor (1977), Fisher and Nagin (1978), Klein, Forst and Filatov (1978), Nagin (1978), Vandaele (1978).

6.1 Empirical Effects of Punishment Variables

In empirical studies the measures used to represent the probability of punishment include the probabilities of arrest, of clearance, of conviction, and of conviction given arrest. The severity of punishment is represented by fines, by the length of sentence, or by time served. Witte (1980) and Schmidt and Witte (1984) have employed individual data on post-release activities of a random sample of 641 men released from prison in North Carolina. The effects on crime of measures of both the probability and the severity of punishment are found to be more or less negative. Myers (1983), using a sample of 2127 individuals released from US Federal prisons, finds that severity of punishment has a statistically significant negative effect on crime, whereas the probability measure (the ratio of previous prison commitments to previous convictions) has a positive effect. Higher wages are found to reduce recidivism. Trumbull (1989) has used data on about 2000 offenders released from prisons in North Carolina to study recidivism and special deterrence. He finds that none of the deterrence variables (probabilities of arrest, conviction and imprisonment, and length of sentence) are statistically significant. Trumbull finds this result natural, since the sample consists only of individuals who, whatever the probability and severity of punishment, have chosen to engage in illegitimate activities. However, an increase in an offender's own previous sentence length has a significant negative effect on crime, a result that corroborates the hypothesis of special deterrence. Higher earnings on the first job after release has a negative effect on crime. Quite unexpectedly, so has unemployment. Viscusi (1986b) uses an approach common in labor economics in the studies of hazardous jobs to estimate the risk/reward trade-off for illegal activities. In labor markets increasing health risks are often rewarded by some amounts of money in addition to non-risk wages. Treating the probability and severity of punishment in the same manner as the probability and severity of injury are treated in analyses of hazardous jobs, Viscusi is able to estimate the effects of changes in these variables. A survey of 2358 inner-city minority youths from Boston, Chicago and Philadelphia constitutes the data employed. Viscusi finds that the premiums obtained for criminal risks are strong and quite robust. In his framework this is interpreted as a corroboration of the general deterrence hypothesis.

Studies of tax cheating based on individual data by Clotfelter (1983), Slemrod (1985), Witte and Woodbury (1985) and Klepper and Nagin (1989a) all conclude that both the probability and the severity of punishment have negative effects upon crime.

Many studies of correlation between crime rates and punishment based on aggregated data appeared in the late 1960s and early 1970s. Using mostly US data on the state or municipal level these studies indicate a negative association between the certainty of arrest and the crime rate for different crime categories. But crime rates are not generally found to vary with the severity of imprisonment, although in some studies a deterrent effect is obtained for homicide and a couple of other crime categories.

A necessary condition for interpreting the results of these correlation studies, mostly carried out by sociologists, as estimates of deterrence is, of course, that there is a one-way causation from punishment to crime, and none in the opposite direction. The many subsequent cross-section criminometric studies allowed for a two-way causation by various specifications of the general model

$$C = f(P, S, Z_j), \tag{3}$$

$$P = g(C, R, Z_k), \tag{4}$$

$$R = h(C, Z_l), \tag{5}$$

where C = crime rate (number of crimes per population), P = probability of punishment, S = severity of punishment, R = resources per capita of the Criminal Justice System (CJS), and Z_j, Z_k, Z_l = vectors of socioeconomic factors. The crime function (3) assumes that the crime rate is a function of the probability and the severity of punishment; equation (4) assumes that the probability of punishment is a function of the crime rate and the resources allocated to the CJS; and equation (5) assumes that the resources allocated to the CJS is a function of the crime rate. Various socioeconomic factors are included as explanatory variables in all three equations. In some studies police resources is included as an explanatory variable in the crime function.

Among the first simultaneous regression analyses in this field we find Ehrlich (1972), Phillips and Votey (1972) and Orsagh (1973). The first major cross-section study appearing after Becker's theoretical article was Ehrlich (1973). He studies seven types of crimes in the US based on data for all states from 1940, 1950 and 1960. He finds that the probability of imprisonment has a statistically significant negative effect on all types of crime, and, except for murder, not less for crimes against the person than for other crimes. The severity of punishment has a similar effect, but here only about half of the estimates are statistically significant. Crime is also found to be positively related to median family income (presumably more assets to steal) and to income differentials. Ehrlich's study has been thoroughly scrutinized by several authors, some of whom have given harsh evaluations of his work. Revisions, replications and extensions of Ehrlich's studies by Forst (1976), Vandaele (1978), and Nagin (1978) resulted in more moderate deterrent effects of the probability and severity of punishment. Moreover, Forst found that by introducing variables thought to be correlated with the punishment variables, such as population migration and population density, the punishment variables became statistically insignificant. Nagin found that incapacitation could explain a large part of the apparent deterrent effect. In a fierce attack on Ehrlich's study Brier and Fienberg (1980) conclude an empirical investigation of the Ehrlich type that no deterrence effect of sanctions were found. A response to the criticism from these and other authors is found in Ehrlich and Mark (1977). Despite critical remarks by various authors, there is now a long list of studies similar to the one by Ehrlich.

The great majority of correlation studies and cross-section regression analyses show a clear negative association between punishment variables and the crime rate. Almost without exception the coefficients of the punishment variables (which usually are the elasticities of the crime rates with respect to the punishment variables) are negative, and in most of the cases significantly so. Furthermore, the estimated elasticities have rather high values. Eide (1994) summarizes such estimates of 20 cross-section studies based on a variety of model specifications, types of data and regression techniques (Ehrlich, 1973; Sjoquist, 1973; Swimmer, 1974; Danziger and Wheeler, 1975; Phillips and Votey, 1975, 1981; Chapman, 1976; Forst, 1976; Mathieson and Passell, 1976; Blumstein and Nagin, 1977; Thaler, 1977; Avio and Clark, 1978; Heineke, 1978; Holtman and Yap, 1978; Mathur, 1978; Vandaele, 1978; Wilson and Boland, 1978; Carr-Hill and Stern, 1979; Myers, 1980, 1982; Furlong and Mehay, 1981; Sesnowitz and Hexter, 1982; Willis, 1983; Schuller, 1986; Trumbull, 1989). Eide finds the median value of the 118 estimates of elasticities of crime rates with respect to various measures of the probability of punishment to be about −0.7. The median of the somewhat fewer severity elasticities is about −0.4. The rates of clearance by arrest are usually considered to be better measures of the certainty of sanction than the rates of conviction (Andenaes, 1975, p. 347). The median of the elasticities of arrest is found to be somewhat smaller than the median of the elasticities of conviction, but the difference is not great.

Almost all criminometric time series studies give additional firm support to the hypothesis that the probability of punishment has a preventive effect on crime. The results concerning the effect of the severity of punishment is somewhat less conclusive. Wahlroos (1981), using Finnish data, finds that the severity of punishment has a statistically significant deterrent effect on larceny, but not on robbery. Cloninger and Sartorius (1979), using data from the city of Houston in the US, obtains a negative, but not statistically significant effect of the mean sentence length. Wolpin (1978), using a time-series for England and Wales in the period 1894-1967, finds that the estimates of the effects of the length of sentences differ among types of crime, and are often not statistically significant. Schuller (1986) on the other hand, using Swedish data, finds a negative effect of the average time in prison. In an international comparison of crime between Japan, England and the US, Wolpin (1980) obtains firm support for the deterrent effect of the severity of punishment. These diverging results are not surprising. The theories surveyed above tell us that if there is a significant proportion of risk lovers in the population, and/or if the income effect is greater than the substitution effect, and/or the effects of legal activities are risky, and/or household protection expenditures are inversely related to the severity of punishment, an increase in the severity of punishment may well cause crime to increase on the macro level. If, however, in spite of these crime increasing effects, macro studies show that crime is reduced when punishment becomes more severe, there is all the more reason to believe in a deterrent and/or a norm formation effect of punishment.

Among the several empirical studies concentrating on just one type of crime, it is worth noticing that Landes (1978) obtained firm support for the deterrence hypothesis for hijacking. In a study of draft evasion in the US, Blumstein and Nagin (1977) avoid four of the main objections against criminometric studies (see discussion of objections below): draft evaders are likely to be well informed about possible sanctions; data are relatively error free; as draft evasion can happen only once, there is no danger of confounding incapacitation effects with deterrence effects; simultaneity problems caused by over-taxing of the Criminal Justice System are unlikely because draft evasion was given priority in the relatively well staffed federal courts. The authors consider that their results provide an important statistical confirmation of the existence of a deterrent effect. They find, however, that the severity of the formal sanction has a modest effect on draft evasion compared to the stigma effect of being arrested and convicted.

The economic model of crime suggests that changes in benefits and costs of committing a particular type of crime might have effects on other types of crime. If, for instance, the probability of being convicted for robbery increases, some robbers might shift to burglary. One crime is substituted for another, just as people buy more apples instead of oranges when the price of oranges goes up. Such substitution effects between crimes have been estimated by Heineke (1978), Holtman and Yap (1978) and Cameron (1987b). A certain number of statistically significant effects are found, indicating that some crimes are substitutes whereas others are alternatives.

As a whole, criminometric studies clearly indicate a negative association between crime and the probability and severity of punishment. The result may be regarded as a rather firm corroboration of the deterrence explanation obtained from the theory of rational behavior: an increase in the probability or severity of punishment will decrease the expected utility of criminal acts, and thereby the level of crime. It should be remembered, however, that in some studies the effect of an increase in the severity of punishment is not statistically different from zero, and a statistically significant positive effect has also occasionally been obtained.

6.2 Empirical Effects of Income, Norm and Taste Variables

In accordance with the theoretical models, most criminometric studies contain income variables representing some of the benefits and costs of legal and/or illegal activities. Looking first at the benefits of legal activities, the great variety of proxies applied is striking: median family income, median income, labor income to manufacturing workers, mean family income, mean income per tax unit, mean income per capita, and so on. No systematic relationship appears between the income measures applied and the estimates obtained. Although the hypothesis that an increase in legal income opportunities decreases crime is not rejected in most of the studies, others would not reject the inverse hypothesis that an increase in legal income opportunities would increase crime. This ambiguity in results might be due to the fact that the income measures used represent benefits not only of legal activities, but also of illegal ones: Higher legal incomes (mostly wages) tend to make work more attractive than crime, but to the extent that higher legal income in a region produces a greater number of more profitable targets for crime, the same empirical income measure may be positively correlated with criminal activity. In addition, high legal incomes also mean high incomes foregone when incarcerated, a cost of crime that will have a negative effect on crime. If these mechanisms are at work simultaneously, and their relative strength not universally constant, it is not surprising that the results of various studies differ. The theory is not necessarily deficient, but the methods applied do not distinguish between the two mechanisms. The main problem is that the incomes of legal and illegal activities are highly correlated, and that it is difficult (or impossible?) to find empirical measures that with enough precision can distinguish between their effects. The impact of income is further obfuscated by the fact that private security measures increase with income, while higher income probably reduces the marginal utility of each piece of property, and therefore also the measures taken to protect property. These problems of correlation are not present in studies where individual data are employed, such as Witte (1980) and Myers (1980).

The estimates of the effects of gains to crime underscore the problem of finding good empirical measures for theoretical variables. Whereas Ehrlich uses median family income as a measure of *gains to crime*, other authors use the same measure to represent *legal income opportunities*. A variety of other measures of gains have been used, with diverse estimated effects on crime.

A large income differential may indicate that crime is a comparatively rewarding activity for the very low income group (that may find a lot to steal from the very rich). Estimates of the effect on crime of income differentials also vary across studies. It is interesting to note, however, that a study which includes variables of both legal and illegal income opportunities in addition to one of income differential (Holtman and Yap, 1978), obtains significant estimates of the expected signs for all three variables. Also Freeman (1995) finds that wages from legitimate work and measures of inequality have the expected effects on crime.

Unemployment is usually included in criminometric studies as a proxy for (lack of) legal income opportunities. Unemployment will make crime more attractive if the alternative is a life in poverty. The estimates of the effect of unemployment on crime, however, are positive in some studies, and negative in others. A comprehensive survey by Chiricos (1987) demonstrates that unemployment in most studies seems to increase crime. He has reviewed 63 aggregate studies published in major journals of economics, sociology and criminology containing 288 estimates of the relationship between unemployment and crime. He finds that 31 percent of the estimates were positive and statistically significant, whereas only 2 percent were negative and statistically significant. Most of the non-significant estimates were positive. A similar conclusion is obtained in a survey by Freeman (1995). Chiricos finds little support for the hypothesis that unemployment decreases the opportunity for criminal activity because of fewer and better protected criminal targets, an hypothesis that has been launched in order to explain why in some studies a negative relationship is obtained. Another explanation of such a negative association, suggested by Carr-Hill and Stern (1973), is that unemployed fathers stay at home and keep an eye on their delinquent sons. Furthermore, differences in results might be the variability in unemployment insurance schemes. In some places unemployment insurance is only slightly below ordinary legal income, and in addition, some of the formally unemployed receive income from short term jobs. According to economic models of crime, the number of offenses will then not increase when unemployment increases. A decrease may even occur. But if unemployment hits people without such income opportunities, crime will increase.

According to criminal statistics the well-to-do are less likely to commit crimes than the poor. Lott (1990c) provides a survey of various explanations of this fact. In an empirical study of ex-convicts Lott (1992a) finds that the reduction in income from conviction is extremely progressive, a result that corroborates the hypothesis that an increase in the costs of committing crimes has a negative effect on the amount of crime.

6.3 Effects of Norm and Taste Variables

In most studies various sociodemographic variables have been included. Unfortunately, the reasons for including many of these variables are often not thoroughly discussed. For instance, an explanation of how differences in preferences (tastes) for legal and illegal activities may vary between groups of people are often lacking. The various choices of empirical measures probably reflect the availability of data. The estimated coefficients on the proportion of non-whites in the population are usually found to be positive. It is difficult to decide whether this result reflects differences in norms, in tastes, in abilities, or in income opportunities. The high proportion of non-whites might also be the result of a tendency among the police to concentrate search for offenders to this group.

The predominance of young people among those arrested and convicted suggest that age would be a very important factor in explaining crime. In many studies such an effect is not found. One reason might be that there is not enough variability in the proportion of youth between statistical units to produce precise estimates. Also possible is that crime among young people is not a consequence of their preferences (lack of socialization, and so on), but of their meager legal income opportunities that possibly is adequately represented by other variables. Young people are perhaps not different, just poorer.

Population density is in most cases found to be a statistically significant explanatory variable. Population density may reflect various phenomena, such as differences in social control, psychic diseases, and so on. The studies reviewed are hardly suitable for a discussion of which of these mechanisms may be at work.

Some studies use police expenditures or the number of police officers as possible deterrent variables instead of measures of probability and/or severity of punishment. Many of these studies show that police activity has a negligible, and sometimes positive, effect on crime. On the other hand, Buck et al. (1983), including both police presence and arrest rates as explanatory variables, find that the former rather than the latter has a deterrent effect. The studies concluding that police activities have a minor effect have tempted some authors to dismiss deterrence as an efficient means against crime. It must be kept in mind, however, that in the theoretical models the deterrence variables are the probability and the severity of punishment, and not the police. There are at least two interpretations of the minor effect on crime of expenditures on the police. Either these expenditures do not have a noticeable effect on the probability of punishment, or such expenditures result in a higher proportion recorded of crimes, a fact that decreases the probability of punishment registered in the data used.

In some studies routine activity and situational opportunity are included as main explanations of crime (compare Cohen, Felson and Land, 1980). Chapman (1976), for instance, finds that the female participation rate in the labor market, a proxy for the proportion of unguarded homes, has a significant positive effect.

It has been argued that the rational choice framework might be relevant for certain property crimes, but not for violent crimes that are considered to be 'expressive' and not 'instrumental'. Undoubtedly, the degree of 'expressiveness' differs among crimes. Many empirical studies may be interpreted as support for the view that threat of punishment also has a preventive effect on expressive crime. At least substantial elements of rationality are revealed in a study of mugging by Lejeune (1977), in a study of rape and homicide by Athens (1980), and in a study of spouse abuse by Dobash and Dobash (1984). Although the effect of punishment may differ among types of crime, evidence so far indicates that the rational choice framework is relevant for all types of crime, and that analyses rejecting a priori that some particular types of crime are deterrable are inadequate.

7. Methodological Problems and Criticism

Objections to economic studies of criminal behavior have been many and occasionally fierce, see for example, Blumstein, Cohen and Nagin (1978), Orsagh (1979), Brier and Fienberg (1980), Prisching (1982), and Cameron (1988). In particular, studies based on aggregated data have been criticized. In addition to attacks on the assumption of rational behavior, the main criticism relates to interpretations of empirical results, to statistical identification of equations and unobserved heterogeneity, to measurement errors, and to operationalization of theoretical variables.

7.1 Interpretation of Empirical Results

It has been argued that many studies do not take into consideration that more certain or more severe punishment may prevent crime by two different mechanisms: either directly as a cost, or indirectly through norm formation. A type of crime that is cleared up more and more seldom, or sanctioned more and more leniently, will easily be considered as not very serious by the population. Individual norms may adjust accordingly, people's crime aversion decrease, and consequently the level of crime increases. It seems true that in most empirical studies no effort is made to distinguish between this mechanism and the more direct deterrence effect of an increase in punishment. Results are often interpreted as a deterrent effect, and not as a general prevention effect where also the indirect norm formation mechanism is included.

Can criminometric studies possibly distinguish between the two mechanisms? In cross-section studies one can imagine that people living in regions where the clear-up probability is low tend to consider crime as less serious than do people in other regions. If such differences in norm formation exist, they are probably more predominant the longer the distance between the regions that are compared, for instance in international comparisons, or in studies of states in the US. It is not probable that norm formation differ among the districts within a rather small region, especially if news about punishment can be assumed to be more or less the same, and mobility of people is high. The effect on crime of variation in the severity of punishment found in studies using data from rather small areas within a region can therefore hardly be explained by a norm formation mechanism. Where one obtains a negative relationship between the crime rate and the clear-up probability when data representing counties of only one state (Chapman, 1976; Avio and Clark, 1978; Trumbull, 1989), or of police districts in a metropolitan area (Mathieson and Passell, 1976; Thaler, 1977; Furlong and Mehay, 1981), one will have reason to believe that the norm formation mechanism must be of minor importance. The same holds true for some studies of substitution of crime which show that an increase in punishment of one type of property crime will have a statistically significant effect on the number of other property crimes. It is not probable that a higher probability of being punished for burglary has any effect on the norms regarding robbery. It is more reasonable to think that robbery is substituted for burglary because of a change in relative costs.

Even if the importance of each mechanism is regarded as uncertain, the estimates obtained in various studies are still of interest. Not only from a political point of view, but also from a scholarly one, it may be useful to know that the probability of punishment has a certain negative effect on crime, notwithstanding the mechanism(s) involved.

Another possible uncertainty concerning the evaluation of results is that there might exist an underlying phenomenon, unknown and/or not studied, a phenomenon that at the same time produces a low crime rate and a high probability of punishment. Individual norms may create such a relationship. If people in one region appreciate each others' welfare more than on average, they will both have a relatively strong aversion against criminal infringements against others, and a high interest in clearing up crimes in order to decrease crime in general. If such differences in norms exist, they must be rooted in cultural differences of some kind. Possibly, such differences can develop if regions are situated far from each other, or if distance in time is substantial. For the smaller regions, such differences seem less realistic.

Theories of criminal behavior show that a whole series of 'causes' may be involved, and that recorded differences in crime between regions, gender, races, drug abuse, and so on might be related to more fundamental explanations of crime, involving norms, wants, opportunities and circumstances. The intricacy of relationships shows the difficulty in interpreting the estimates of the effects on crime of such variables.

7.2 Identification and Unobserved Heterogeneity

If, in an empirical study, one finds that crime rates and probabilities of punishment are negatively correlated, one cannot easily distinguish between the hypothesis that higher probabilities of punishment cause lower crime rates (equation (3)), or the hypothesis that higher crime rates cause lower probabilities of punishment (because of police overloading, equation (4)). If such a simultaeneity exists it is not acceptable to use the method of ordinary least squares (OLS) to estimate each equation. Using the Hausman test Layson (1985) and Trumbull (1989) have for homicide found that simultaneity was not a problem in their data, and OLS could be applied. If simultaneity is present, the standard procedure to identify the first relation, the crime function, consists of introducing exogenous variables that have an effect on the probability of punishment, but not on the crime rate. In an excellent discussion of the (im)possibility of identifying the crime function in macro studies, Fisher and Nagin (1978, p. 379) declare that they know of no such variables. The consequence of this view is that all attempts of identification in empirical macro studies are illusory. The equations may be technically identified, but by false assumptions. Using panel data for police districts, Aasness, Eide and Skjerpen (1994) claim to have solved this problem. In studies based on individual data, the question of identification is much less serious, see above.

It is interesting to note that in the cross-section studies reviewed by Eide (1994) the method of ordinary least squares tend to give smaller estimates of the elasticities of crime with respect to the probability and severity of sanctions than do the methods of 2 stages least squares, full information maximum likelihood, and other more advanced methods. This is what might be expected if a simultaneous equation bias is present. The difference in estimates is, however, not great.

Cornwell and Trumbull (1994) point to the fact that aggregate cross-section econometric techniques do not control for unobserved heterogeneity. Addressing this problem by use of a panel dataset of North Carolina counties, they obtain more modest deterrent effects of the arrest and conviction rates than those obtained from cross-section estimation.

7.3 Measurement Errors

Since a substantial part of all crimes is not registered by the police, one may have serious doubts about the results of empirical studies based on official statistics. However, the problem of underreporting is not damaging to empirical research if the rate at which actual crimes are reported is constant across regions (in cross-section studies) or over the years (in time-series studies). This seems to be an implicit assumption in most studies. Blumstein, Cohen and Nagin (1978) explain how differences in 'dark numbers' between observational units create a spurious negative association between the recorded crime rate and the probability of clearance. Aasness, Eide and Skjerpen (1994) introduce, in addition to the recorded crime rate, a latent variable for the real crime rate, and relates the latter to the former by a linear function and a stochastic term. By this procedure measurement errors are given an explicit stochastic treatment, that allows for a distribution of 'dark numbers' among police districts.

The existence of a substantial dark number of crime, has fostered a certain interest in using victimization studies to obtain more reliable data. These studies give more or less similar results as those based on recorded crimes. A prominent example is Goldberg and Nold (1980) who find that the reporting rate, and thus the probability of clearance, has a great impact on the amount of burglaries. Another comprehensive study is Myers (1982) who obtains almost the same estimates of the effects of sanction variables by correcting crime rates by victimization data.

7.4 Wrong Beliefs

If people have wrong beliefs, one may also question the validity of estimates of the effects of punishment variables and various socio-economic factors. Presumably, the true risk of sanction is not known to the individual. Empirical studies suggest that people tend to overestimate the average risk, while at the same time believing that the risk they themselves run is lower than average. Offenders, however, seem to be better informed. Wilson and Herrnstein (1985, p. 392) refer to a study where over two thousand inmates of jails and prisons in California, Michigan and Texas were interviewed about their criminal careers. The study revealed a close correspondence between the actual and perceived risk of imprisonment in Michigan and Texas, whereas a somewhat weaker correspondence was found in California. The study further corroborated the theoretical result that an increase in the probability of imprisonment will decrease crime.

Even if beliefs to some extent are wrong, macro studies might still be of some value. It may well be that some persons do not observe a given change, and also that they have been mistaken in their beliefs. But the gradual change from very lenient to very harsh punishment will certainly be registered by at least a part of the population, and behavior will change, more or less, as already explained.

7.5 Various Operationalizations

Many studies give weak arguments for the choice of theoretical variables (for example, of variables of punishment, benefits and costs), and of their empirical measures. Orsagh (1979) argues that the great diversity of variables in empirical criminology shows that no good theory exists, and that macro studies of the usual kind have little interest. The objection is certainly relevant, but the consequence is not necessarily that such analyses should be avoided. Problems of operationalization do not make a theory irrelevant. Better than to drop such studies is to continue the theoretical discussion about determinants of crime, and produce more empirical studies, in order to improve the foundation for choosing acceptable measures of theoretical constructs. If various operationalizations produce similar results, there is reason to believe that the theory is robust to such differences. Then, one might even conclude that the theory is quite good, despite the fact that each and every formal test of significance is of limited value.

The studies reviewed above reveal quite consistent results as far as the sign of effects of the punishment variables is concerned. The insensitivity of these results to various operationalizations is comforting. The effects of income variables are less consistent, a result that might either imply that economic factors do not have a uniform effect on crime or that some, or all, of the operationalizations tried so far are unacceptable.

Several measures of punishment variables have been employed. When only one type of sanctions is included, one would expect that the effect assigned to this variable really includes effects of punishment variables correlated with the one included. A better alternative is to use several sanctions simultaneously, as proposed and employed by Witte (1980) and others.

8. Future Research

The reasons why people are more or less law-abiding are manifold. The norm-guided rational choice framework seems to provide a suitable framework for discussing various theories of crime, including characteristics of individuals and circumstances (Cornish and Clarke, 1986, p. 10). The framework allows for a simultaneous consideration of many possible determinants of crime. The abstract model is a means of gaining insight into the elements of rational behavior, and it permits filling bits of information into a broader context. In criminometric studies it might be useful to distinguish between norm variables (representing desires for various courses of action), want (or taste) variables (representing preferences for various outcomes), ability variables (representing intellectual, psychic and physical characteristics), punishment variables (representing the probability and severity of punishment), individual economic variables (representing legal and illegal income opportunities) and environmental variables (other than punishment and economic variables). A survey of variables used in various empirical studies of crime organized according to this typology is given in Eide (1994). Variations in crime among individuals are traditionally related to gender, age, race, and so on. A deeper understanding must be sought in variations in norms and wants, in abilities, and in the opportunities, rewards and costs determined by the environment. Variations in crime among individuals may be caused by differences in all these elements of the rational choice framework. Certain individuals may have more crime-prone (or less crime-averse) norms than others. The special norm structure may be a result of genetic, biological or psychological characteristics, an effect of lack of socialization, or a consequence of cultural conflict, cultural deviance, or anomie. Inherited or acquired abilities may restrict legal activities more than illegal ones. In an empirical study of college students Nagin and Paternoster (1993) found that both individual differences (poor self-control) and the costs and benefits of crime were significantly related to crime. The formidable task for the future may be found in a proposition for social science research by the Nobel Prize Winner Niko Tinbergen (who should not be confused with J. Tinbergen who has won the Nobel Memorial Prize in economics) that four levels of analysis should be put together: the biological (genetical), the developmental (how an individual is socialized), the situational (how the environment influences behavior), and the adaptive (how a person responds to the benefits and costs of alternative courses of action).

Bibliography on Economics of Criminal Behaviour (8100)

Aasness, Jörgen, Eide, Erling and Skjerpen, Terje (1992), 'A Criminometric Study Using Panel Data and Latent Variables', **74** *Central Bureau of Statistics Oslo, Discussion Paper*.

Aasness, Jörgen, Eide, Erling and Skjerpen, Terje (1993), 'Criminometrics, Latent Variables, and Panel Data', in Haagen, K., Bartholomew, D.J. and Deistler, M. (eds), *Statistical Modelling and Latent Variables*, Amsterdam, North-Holland, 1-16.

Aasness, Jürgen, Eide, Erling and Skjerpen, Terje (1994), 'Criminometrics, Latent Variables, Panel Data, and Different Types of Crime', **124** *Statistics Norway, Discussion paper*.

Adams, Michael (1992a), 'Den Teufel mit Belzebub Austreiben - Wie man den Markt für Rauschgifte Zerstört', **12** *Kriminalistik, Zeitschrift für die Gesamte Kriminalistische Wissenschaft und Praxis*, 757-761.

Adams, Michael (1992b), 'Drugs Supply', **20(8)** *Garda Review*, 14-15. Reprinted in **1** *The Police Journal*, 1993, 42-47.

Adams, Michael (1993), 'Drug Enforcement in Germany and Abroad - A New Way to Destroy the Market for Drugs', **17(1)** *International Journal of Comparative and Applied Criminal Justice*, 203-210.

Adams, Michael and Shavell, Steven (1990), 'Zur Strafbarkeit des Versuchs', *Goltdammer's Archiv für Strafrecht*, 337-386.

Adelstein, Richard P. (1978a), 'The Negotiated Guilty Plea: A Framework for Analysis', **53** *New York University Law Review*, 783-833.

Adelstein, Richard P. (1978b), 'The Plea Bargain in Theory: A Behavioral Model of the Negotiated Guilty Plea', **44** *Southern Economic Journal*, 488-503.

Adelstein, Richard P. (1979), 'The Moral Costs of Crime: Prices, Information and Organization', in Gray, Charles M. (ed), *The Costs of Crime*, Beverly Hills, CA, Sage Publications, 233-252.

Ahamad, B. (1967), 'An Analysis of Crimes by the Method of Principal Components', **16** *Applied Statistics*, 17-35.

Allingham, Michael G. and Sandmo, Agnar (1972), 'Income Tax Evasion: A Theoretical Analysis', **1** *Journal of Public Economics*, 323-338.

Allison, John P. (1972), 'Economic Factors and the Rate of Crime', **48** *Land Economics*, 193-196.

Andenaes, Johannes (1975), 'General Prevention Revisited: Research and Policy Implications', **66** *Journal of Criminal Law and Criminology*, 338-365.

Anderson, A.B., Harris, A.R. and Miller, J. (1983), 'Models of Deterrence Theory', **12** *Social Science Research*, 236-262.

Anderson, R.W. (1976), *The Economics of Crime*, London, Macmillan, 71 p.

Andreoni, J. (1995), 'Criminal Deterrence in the Reduced Form: A New Perspective on Ehrlich's Seminal Study', **33** *Economic Inquiry*, 476-483.

Andreano, Ralph and Siegfried, John J. (eds) (1980), *The Economics of Crime*, Cambridge, Schenkman, 426 p.

Antunes, G. and Hunt, A. Lee (1973), 'The Deterrent Impact of Criminal Sanctions: Some Implications for Criminal Justice Policy', **51** *Journal of Urban Law*, 145-161.

Antunes, George and Hunt, A. Lee (1973), 'The Impact of Certainty and Severity of Punishment on Levels of Crime in American States: An Extended Analysis', **64** *Journal of Criminal Law and Criminology*, 486-493.

Asch, Peter and Levy, David T. (1987a), 'The Drinking Age and Traffic Safety', **11(2)** *Regulation*, 48-52.

Asch, Peter and Levy, David T. (1987b), 'Does the Minimum Drinking Age Affect Traffic Fatalities?', **6** *Journal of Policy Analysis and Management*, 180-192.

Athens, Lonnie H. (1980), *Violent Criminal Acts and Actors: A Symbolic Interactionist Study*, Boston, Routledge and Kegan Paul, 104 p.

Avio, Kenneth L. (1973), 'An Economic Analysis of Criminal Corrections: The Canadian Case', **6** *Canadian Journal of Economics*, 164-178.

Avio, Kenneth L. (1975), 'Recidivism in the Economic Model of Crime', **13** *Economic Inquiry*, 450-456.

Avio, Kenneth L. (1979), 'Capital Punishment in Canada: A Time-Series Analysis of the Deterrent Hypothesis', **12** *Canadian Journal of Economics*, 647-676.

Avio, Kenneth L. and Clark, C. Scott (1976), *Property Crime in Canada: An Econometric Study*, Toronto, University of Toronto Press.

Avio, Kenneth L. and Clark, C. Scott (1978), 'The Supply of Property Offences in Ontario: Evidence on the Deterrent Effect of Punishment', **11** *Canadian Journal of Economics*, 1-19.

Badford, R.S. (1989), 'Going to the Island: A Legal and Economic Analysis of the Medieval Icelandic Duel', **67** *Southern California Law Review*, 615-644.

Bailey, William C. (1978), 'The Deterrent Effect of Arrest and Conviction on Crime Rates in Indian States and Territories', **17** *Annales Internationales de Criminologie*, 21-50.

Baldry, Jonathan C. (1974), 'Positive Economic Analysis of Criminal Behaviour', in Ceujler, A.J. (ed), *Economic Policies and Social Goals*, London, Martin Robertson, p171-198.

Baldry, Jonathan C. (1980), 'Crimes Punishable by Imprisonment: A Note', **9** *Journal of Legal Studies*, 617-619.

Baldus, D. and Cole, J.W. (1975), 'A Comparison of the Work of Torsten Sellin and Isach Ehrlich on the Deterrent Effect of Capital Punishment', **85** *Yale Law Journal*, 170-186.

Balkin, Steven and McDonald, John F. (1981), 'The Market for Street Crime: An Economic Analysis of Victim-Offender Interaction', **10** *Journal of Urban Economics*, 390-405.

Barnett, Arnold (1978), 'Crime and Capital Punishment: Some Recent Studies', **6** *Journal of Criminal Justice*, 291-303.

Barnett, Harold C. (1976), 'The Economics of Crime - A Comment', **34** *Review of Social Economy*, 81-87.

Barnett, Randy E. and Hagel, John III (1977), *Assessing the Criminal. Restitution, Retribution, and the Legal Process*, Cambridge, Ballinger Publishing, 403 p.

Bartel, Ann P. (1975), 'An Analysis of Firm Demand for Protection Against Crime', **4** *Journal of Legal Studies*, 443-478.

Bartel, Ann P. (1979), 'Women and Crime: An Economic Analysis', **17** *Economic Inquiry*, 29-51.

Barthold, Thomas A. and Hochman, Harold M. (1988), 'Addiction as Extreme Seeking', **26** *Economic Inquiry*, 89-106.

Beccaria, C. (1971), 'On Crime and Punishment (1764)', in Grupp, S.E. (ed.), *Theories of Punishment*, Bloomington, IN, Indiana University Press, 117-137.

Beccaria-Bonesara, C. (1958), *An Essay on Crime and Punishment*, New York, Oceania Pub. (1764).

Becker, Gary S. (1962), 'Irrational Behavior and Economic Theory', **70** *Journal of Political Economy*, 1-13.

Becker, Gary S. (1968), 'Crime and Punishment: An Economic Approach', **76** *Journal of Political Economy*, 169-217.

Becker, Gary (1976), *The Economic Approach to Human Behavior*, Chicago, University of Chicago Press.

Becker, Gary S. and Landes, William M. (eds) (1974), *Essays in the Economics of Crime and Punishment*, New York, Columbia University Press, 268 p.

Becker, Gary S. and Stigler, George J. (1974), 'Law Enforcement, Malfeasance, and Compensation of Enforcers', **3** *Journal of Legal Studies*, 1-18.

Ben-Shahar, Omri and Harel, A. (1996), 'The Economics of the Law of Criminal Attempts: a Victim-Centered Perspective', **145(1)** *University of Pennsylvania Law Review*, p299-351.

Benson, Bruce L. (1981), 'A Note on Corruption of Public Officials: The Black Market for Property Rights', **5** *Journal of Libertarian Studies*, 305-311.

Benson, Bruce L. (1984), 'Guns for Protection and Other Private Sector Responses to the Fear of Violent Crime', in Kates, Don, Jr (ed), *Firearms and Violence: Issues of Regulation*, Cambridge, MA, Ballinger Press, 329-356.

Benson, Bruce L. (1986), 'Guns for Protection and Other Private Sector Responses to Government's Failure to Control Increasing Violent Crime', **8** *Journal of Libertarian Studies*, 75-109.

Benson, Bruce L. (1995), 'Privatization in Criminal Justice', in *Independent Policy Report*, Oakland, Independent Institute.

Benson, Bruce L. and Baden, John (1985), 'The Political Economy of Government Corruption: The Logic of Underground Government', **14** *Journal of Legal Studies*, 391-410.

Benson, Bruce L. and Rasmussen, David W. (1991), 'The Relationship Between Illicit Drug Enforcement Policy and Property Crimes', **9** *Contemporary Policy Issues*, 106-115.

Benson, Bruce L. and Rasmussen, David W. (1992), 'Illinois' War on Drugs: Some Uninbeuded Consequences', **48** *Heartland Policy Study*, Chicago, Heartland Institute.

Benson, Bruce L. and Rasmussen, David W. (1995a), 'Illicit Drugs and Crime', in *Independent Policy Report*, Oakland, Independent Institute, 56 p.

Benson, Bruce L. and Rasmussen, David W. (1995b), 'Crime and Punishment', in Denslow, David A., Scoggins, J.F. and Shermyen, Anne (eds), *The Economy of Florida*, Gainesville, FL, Bureau of Economic and Business Research, 99-116.

Benson, Bruce L., Kim, Iljoong and Rasmussen, David W. (1994), 'Estimating Deterrence Effects: A Public Choice Perspective on the Economics of Crime Literature', **61** *Southern Economic Journal*, 161-168.

Benson, Bruce L., Kim, Iljoong, Rasmussen, David W. and Zuehlke, Thomas W. (1992), 'Is Property Crime Caused by Drug Use or Drug Enforcement Policy?', **24** *Applied Economics*, 679-692.

Benson, Bruce L., Kim, Iljoong, Rasmussen, David W. and Zuehlke, Thomas W. (1993), 'An Economic Analysis of Recidivism Among Drug Offenders', **60** *Southern Economic Journal*, 169-183.

Bentham, Jeremy ([1788] 1843), 'Principles of Penal Law', **1** *Works*, 399 ff.

Beron, Kurt J. (1988), 'Applying the Economic Model of Crime to Child Support Enforcement: A Theoretical and Empirical Analysis', **70** *Review of Economics and Statistics*, 382-390.

Beyleveld, Deryck (1980), *A Bibliography on General Deterrence Research*, Westmead, Saxon House.

Block, Michael K. and Gerety, Vernon E. (1995), 'Some Experimental Evidence on Differences between Student and Prisoner Reactions to Monetary Penalties and Risk', **24** *Journal of Legal Studies*, 123-138.

Block, Michael K. and Heineke, J.M. (1975a), 'A Labor Theoretic Analysis of the Criminal Choice', **65** *American Economic Review*, 314-325.

Block, Michael K. and Heineke, J.M. (1975b), 'Factor Allocation under Uncertainty: An Extension', **41** *Southern Economic Journal*, 526-530.

Block, Michael K. and Lind, Robert C. (1975a), 'An Economic Analysis of Crimes Punishable by Imprisonment', **4** *Journal of Legal Studies*, 479-492.

Block, Michael K. and Lind, Robert C. (1975b), 'Crime and Punishment Reconsidered', **4** *Journal of Legal Studies*, 241-247.

Blumstein, Alfred and Nagin, Daniel S. (1977), 'The Deterrent Effect of Legal Sanctions on Draft Evasion', **29** *Stanford Law Review*, 241-276.

Blumstein, Alfred, Cohen, Jacqueline and Nagin, Daniel (eds) (1978), *Deterrence and Incapacitation: Estimating the Effects of Criminal Sanctions on Crime Rates*, Washington, DC, National Academy of Sciences.

Bowers, William J. (1974), 'A Causal Framework for the Analysis of Deterrence and Related Processes', in Akers, Ronald L. and Sagarin, Edward (eds), *Crime Prevention and Social Control*, New York, Praeger Publishers, 22-38.

Bowers, William J. and Pierce, Glenn L. (1975), 'The Illusion of Deterrence in Isach Ehrlich's Research on Capital Punishment', **85** *Yale Law Journal*, 187-208.

Bowers, William J. and Salem, Richard G. (1972), 'Severity of Formal Sanctions as a Repressive Response to Deviant Behaviour', **7** *Law and Society Review*, 427-441.

Brier, Stephen S. and Fienberg, Stephen E. (1980), 'Recent Econometric Modeling of Crime and Punishment: Support for the Deterrence Hypothesis', **4** *Evaluation Review*, 147-191.

Brotman, B.A. and Fox P. (1988), 'The Impact of Economic Conditions on the Incidence of Arson: Comment', **55** *Journal of Risk and Insurance*, 751-754.

Brown, William W. and Reynolds, Morgan O. (1973), 'Crime and "Punishment": Risk Implications', **6** *Journal of Economic Theory*, 508-514.

Brumm, H.J. and Cloninger D.O. (1995), 'Violent Crime and Punishment: An Application of the LISREL Model', **27** *Applied Economics*, 719-725.

Buck, Andrew J. et al. (1987a), 'A Disaggregated Study of Police Clear-up Rates for England and Wales', **16** *Journal of Behavioral Economics*, 1-18.

Buck, Andrew J. et al. (1987b), 'Substitution Between Offence Categories in the Supply of Property Crimes: Some New Evidence', **11** *International Journal of Social Economics*, 48-60.

Buck, Andrew J. and Hakim, Simon (1981), 'A Simultaneous Equation System of Crime and Police', **3** *Statistica*, 449-457.

Buck, Andrew J., Hakim, Simon and Spiegel, Uriel (1985), 'The Natural Rate of Crime by Type of Community'', **43** *Review of Social Economy*, 245-259.

Buck, Andrew J., Gross, Meir, Hakim, Simon and Weinblatt, J. (1983), 'The Deterrence Hypothesis Revisited', **13** *Regional Science and Urban Economics*, 471-486.

Burnovski, M. and Safra, Z. (1994), 'Deterrence Effects of Sequential Punishment Policies: Should Repeat Offenders be more Severely Punished?', **14** *International Journal of Industrial Organization*, 341-350.

Bustos Gisbert, Antonio (1995), *El Debate sobre la Legalización de las Drogas Blandas: un Análisis Formalizado* (Making Drugs Legal: A Formal Analysis), 155 p.

Cameron, Samuel (1986), 'An Empirical Study of Malicious False Fire Alarm Calls', **6** *International Review of Law and Economics*, 33-44.

Cameron, Samuel (1987a), 'A Disaggregated Study of Police Clear Up Rates for England and Wales', **16(4)** *Journal of Behavioral Economics*, 1-18.

Cameron, Samuel (1987b), 'Substitution between Offence Categories in the Supply of Property Crime: Some New Evidence', **14(11)** *International Journal of Social Economics*, 48-60.

Cameron, Samuel (1988), 'The Economics of Crime Deterrence: A Survey of Theory and Evidence', **41** *Kyklos*, 301-323.

Cameron, Samuel (1989a), 'Police Cost Function Estimates for England and Wales', **21** *Applied Economics*, 1279-1289.

Cameron, Samuel (1989b), 'Victim Compensation does not Increase the Supply of Crime', **16** *Journal of Economic Studies*, 52-59.

Cameron, Samuel (1991), 'Non-monotonic Supply of Crime Functions: A Replicatory Study', **131** *Cahier Economique de Bruxelles*, 305-317.

Carlin, Paul and Sandy, Robert (1990), 'The Value of Time and the Effect of Fines on Child Car Safety Seat Usage', **22** *Applied Economics*, 463-476.

Caroll, J. and Weaver, F. (1986), 'Shoplifters' Perceptions of Crime Opportunities: A Process-tracing Study', in Cornish, D.B. and Clarke, R.V. (eds), *The Reasoning Criminal*, New York, Berlin, Heidelberg, Tokyo, Springer-Verlag, 18-38.

Carr-Hill, R.A. and Stern, N.H. (1973), 'An Econometric Model of the Supply and Control of Recorded Offences in England and Wales', **2** *Journal of Public Economics*, 289-318.

Carr-Hill, R.A. and Stern, H.H. (1979), *Crime, The Police and Criminal Statistics*, London, Academic Press.

Cassone, Alberto and Marchese, Carla (1995), 'Tax Amnesties as Special Sales Offers: the Italian Experience', **50** *Public Finance/Finances Publiques*, 51-66.

Chalmers, J.A. and Shelton, R.B. (1975), 'An Economic Analysis of Riot Participation', **13** *Economic Inquiry*, 322-336.

Chaloupka, Frank J., Saffer, Henry and Grossman, Michael (1993), 'Alcohol Control Policies and Motor-Vehicle Fatalities', **22** *Journal of Legal Studies*, 161-186.

Chapman, Jeffrey I. (1976), 'An Economic Model of Crime and Police: Some Empirical Results', *Journal of Research in Crime and Delinquency*, 48-63.

Chiricos, Theodore G. (1987), 'Rates of Crime and Unemployment: An Analysis of Aggregate Research Evidence', **34** *Social Problems*, 187-212.

Chu, C.Y.C (1993), 'Oscillatory vs. Stationary Enforcement of Law', **13** *International Review of Law and Economics*, 303-315.

Cloninger, Dale O. (1975), 'The Deterrence Effect of Law Enforcement: An Evaluation of Recent Findings and Some New Evidence', **34** *American Journal of Economics and Sociology*, 323-335.

Cloninger, Dale O. (1987), 'Capital Punishment and Deterrence: A Revision', **16(4)** *Journal of Behavioral Economics*, 55-57.

Cloninger, Dale O. (1991), 'Lethal Police Response as a Crime Deterrent: 57-City Study Suggests a Decrease in Certain Crimes', **50** *American Journal of Economics and Sociology*, 59-69.

Cloninger, Dale O. (1992), 'Capital Punishment and Deterrence: a Portfolio Approach', **24** *Applied Economics*, 635-645.

Cloninger, Dale O. (1994), 'Enforcement Risk and Deterrence: A Re-examination', **23** *Journal of Socio-Economics*, 273-285.

Cloninger, Dale O. and Sartorius, Lester (1979), 'Crime Rates, Clearance Rates and Enforcement Effort: The Case of Houston, Texas', **4** *American Journal of Economics and Sociology*, 389-402.

Clotfelter, C.T. (1983), 'Tax Evasion and Tax Rates: An Analysis of Individual Returns', **65** *Review of Economics and Statistics*, 363-373.

Coate, Douglas and Grossman, Michael (1988), 'Effects of Alcoholic Beverage Prices and Legal Drinking Ages on Youth Alcohol Use', **31** *Journal of Law and Economics*, 145-171.

Coelen, Stephen P. and McIntyre, Robert J. (1986), 'An Econometric Model of Pronatalist and Abortion Policies', **94** *Journal of Political Economy*, 1077-1101.

Cohen, Jacqueline (1978), 'The Incapacitative Effect of Imprisonment: A Critical Review of the Literature', in Blumstein, Cohen and Nagin (eds), *Deterrence and Incapacitation: Estimating the Effects of Criminal Sanctions on Crime Rates*, Washington, DC, National Academy of Sciences, 187-243.

Cohen, Lawrence E., Felson, Marcus and Land, Kenneth (1980), 'Property Crime Rates in the United States: A Macrodynamic Analysis 1947-1977 with Ex Ante Forecasts for the Mid-1980s', **86** *American Journal of Sociology*, 90-118.

Cohen, Mark A. (1987), 'Optimal Enforcement Strategy to Prevent Oil Spills: An Application of a Principal-Agent Model with Moral Hazard', **30** *Journal of Law and Economics*, 23-51.

Cohen, Mark A. (1990), 'A Note on the Cost of Crime to Victims', **27** *Urban Studies*, 139-146.

Cohen, Mark A. (1992), 'Environmental Crime and Punishment: Legal/Economic Theory and Empirical Evidence on Enforcement of Federal Environmental Statutes', **82** *Journal of Criminal Law and Criminology*, 1054-1108.

Cohen, Mark A. and Alexander, Cindy R. (1996), 'New Evidence on the Origins of Corporate Crime', **17** *Managerial and Decision Economics*, 421-435.

Cohen, Mark A. and Simpson, Sally S. (1997), 'The Origins of Corporate Criminality: Rational Individual and Organizational Actors', in Lofquist, William S., Cohen, Mark A. and Rabe, Gary (eds), *Debating Corporate Crime*, Cincinnati, OH, Anderson Publishing.

Cohen, Mark A., Lofquist, William S. and Rabe, Gary (eds) (1997), *Debating Corporate Crime*, Cincinnati, OH, Anderson Publishing.

Coleman, Jules L. (1985), 'Crime, Kickers and Transaction Structures', in Pennock, Roland J. and Chapman, John W. (eds), *Nomos XXVII: Criminal Justice*, Granite Impex.

Confraria, João (1989), 'Aspectos de Abordagem Economica do Comportamento Criminal (Aspects of the Economic Analysis of Criminal Behaviour)', *Scientia Juridica*, 171-182.

Cook, Philip J. (1977), 'Punishment and Crime: A Critique of Current findings Concerning the Preventative Effects of Punishment', **41(1)** *Law and Contemporary Problems*, 164-209.

Cook, Philip J. (1986), 'The Demand and Supply of Criminal Opportunities', in Tonry, Michael and Morris, Norval (eds), *Crime and Justice: An Annual Review of Research*, Chicago and London, The University of Chicago Press, 1-28.

Cook, Philip J. and Zarkin, Gary A. (1985), 'Crime and the Business Cycle', **14** *Journal of Legal Studies*, 115-128.

Cooter, Robert D. (1991), 'Lapses, Conflict, and Akrasia in Torts and Crimes: Towards An Economic Theory of the Will', **11** *International Review of Law and Economics*, 149-164.

Corman, Hope and Joyce, Theodore (1990), 'Urban Crime Control: Violent Crimes in New York City', **71** *Social Science Quarterly*, 567-584.

Corman, Hope, Joyce, Theodore and Lovitch, Norman (1987), 'Crime, Deterrence and the Business Cycle in New York City: A VAR Approach', **69** *Review of Economics and Statistics*, 695-700.

Cornish, Derek B. and Clarke, Ronald V. (eds) (1986), *The Reasoning Criminal: Rational Choice Perspectives on Offending*, New York, Berlin, Heidelberg, Tokyo, Springer-Verlag.

Cornwell, C. and Trumbull, W.N. (1994), 'Estimating the Economic Model of Crime with Panel Data', **76** *Review of Economics and Statistics*, 360-366.

Cowell, Frank A. (1990), *Cheating the Government: The Economics of Evasion*, Cambridge, MIT Press, 267 p.

Cox, G.W. (1994), 'A Note on Crime and Punishment', **78** *Public Choice*, 115-124.

Craig, Steven G. (1987), 'The Deterrent Impact of Police: An Examination of a Locally Provided Public Service', **21** *Journal of Urban Economics*, 298-311.

Craig, Steven G. and Heikkila, Eric J. (1989), 'Urban Safety in Vancouver: Allocation and Production of a Congestible Public Good', **22** *Canadian Journal of Economics*, 867-884.

Curran, Christopher and Dwyer, Gerald P., Jr (1989), 'The Effect of the Double Nickel Speed Limit on Death Rates', in Faure, Michael and Van den Bergh, Roger (eds), *Essays in Law and Economics: Corporations, Accident Prevention and Compensation for Losses*, Antwerpen, Maklu, 117-156.

Danziger, Sheldon and Wheeler, David (1975), 'The Economics of Crime: Punishment or Income Distribution', **33** *Review of Social Economy*, 113-131.

Darrough, M.N. and Heineke, J.M. (1979), 'Law Enforcement Agencies as Multi-Product Firms: An Econometric Investigation of Production Costs', **34** *Public Finance*, 176-195.

Dau-Schmidt, Kenneth G. (1984), 'Sentencing Antitrust Offenders: Reconciling Economic Theory with Legal Theory', **9** *Wm. Mitchell Law Review*, 75 ff.

Dau-Schmidt, Kenneth G. (1990), 'An Economic Analysis of the Criminal Law as a Preference Shaping Policy', **40** *Duke Law Journal*, 1-38.

Davis, Michael L. (1988), 'Time and Punishment: An Intertemporal Model of Crime', **96** *Journal of Political Economy*, 383-390.

De Albuquerque, Klaus (1984), 'A Comparative Analysis of Violent Crime in the Caribbean', **33(3)** *Social and Economic Studies*, 93-142.

Deutsch, Joseph, Hakim, Simon and Spiegel, Uriel (1990a), 'Learning by Criming: Theoretical Analysis and Empirical Evidence', **45** *Public Finance*, 59-69.

Deutsch, Joseph, Hakim, Simon and Spiegel, Uriel (1990b), 'The Effects of Criminal Experience on the Incidence of Crime', **49** *American Journal of Economics and Sociology*, 1-5.

Deutsch, Joseph, Hakim, Simon and Weinblatt, J. (1987), 'A Micro Model of the Criminal's Location Choice', **22** *Journal of Urban Economics*, 198-208.

Deutsch, Joseph, Spiegel, Uriel and Templeman, J. (1992), 'Crime and Income Inequality: An Economic Approach', **201** *Atlantic Economic Journal*, 46-54.

Dickens, William T. (1986), 'Crime and Punishment Again: The Economic Approach with a Psychological Twist', **30** *Journal of Public Economics*, 97-107.

Diiulio, John J., Jr (1996), 'Help Wanted: Economists, Crime and Public Policy', **10** *Journal of Economic Perspectives*, 3-24.

Dobash, R.E. and Dobash, R.P. (1984), 'The Nature and Antecedents of Violent Events', **24** *British Journal of Criminology*, 269-288.

Du Bois, W.E.B. (1987), 'The Negro Criminal', **16(1-2)** *Review of Black Political Economy*, 17-31.

Ehrlich, Isaac (1979), 'The Economic Approach to Crime', *Criminology Review Yearbook, vol. 1*, Messinger, S.L. and Brittner E. (eds), Beverley Hills, Sage Publications, 25-60.

Ehrlich, Isaac (1972), 'The Deterrent Effect of Criminal Law Enforcement', **1** *Journal of Legal Studies*, 259-276.

Ehrlich, Isaac (1973), 'Participation in Illegitimate Activities: A Theoretical and Empirical Investigation', **81** *Journal of Political Economy*, 521-565.

Ehrlich, Isaac (1975a), 'The Deterrent Effect of Capital Punishment: A Question of Life and Death', **65** *American Economic Review*, 397-417.

Ehrlich, Isaac (1975b), 'Deterrence: Evidence and Inference', **85** *Yale Law Journal*, 209-227.

Ehrlich, Isaac (1976), 'Rejoinder', **85** *Yale Law Journal*, 368-369.

Ehrlich, Isaac (1977a), 'Capital Punishment and Deterrence: Some Further Thoughts and Additional Evidence', **85** *Journal of Political Economy*, 741-788.

Ehrlich, Isaac (1977b), 'The Deterrent Effect of Capital Punishment: Reply', **67** *American Economic Review*, 452-458.

Ehrlich, Isaac (1981), 'On the Usefulness of Controlling Individuals: An Economic Analysis of Rehabilitation, Incapacitation, and Deterrence', **71** *American Economic Review*, 307-322.

Ehrlich, Isaac (1982), 'The Market for Offences and the Public Enforcement of Laws: An Equilibrium Analysis', **21** *British Journal of Psychology*.

Ehrlich, Isaac (1996), 'Crime, Punishment and the Market for Offenses', **10** *Journal of Economic Perspectives*, 43-67.

Ehrlich, Isaac and Brower, George D. (1987), 'On the Issue of Causality in the Economic Model of Crime and the Law Enforcement: Some Theoretical Considerations and Experimental Evidence', **77** *American Economic Review. Papers and Proceedings*, 99-110.

Ehrlich, Isaac and Gibbons, Joel C. (1977), 'On the Measurement of the Deterrent Effect of Capital Punishment and the Theory of Deterrence', **6** *Journal of Legal Studies*, 35-50.

Ehrlich, Isaac and Randall, Mark (1978), 'Deterrence and Economics: A Perspective on Theory and Evidence', in Yinger, J.M. and Cutler, S.J. (eds), *Major Social Issues*, New York, 172-188.

Ehrlich, Isaac in co-operation with Mark, R. et al. (1977), 'Fear of Deterrence: A Critical Evaluation of the "Report of the Panel on Research on Deterrent and Incapacitative Effects"', **6** *Journal of Legal Studies*, 293-316.

Eide, Erling (1981), 'Kritikk av Noen Forutsetninger i Kriminalmeldingen (Critique of Some Assumptions in the Report on Crime)', *Lov og Rett*, 312-323.

Eide, Erling (1994), *Kriminal¢konomi* (Economics of Crime), Stavanger, Rogaland Mediesenter, 158 p.

Eide, Erling (1995), 'RDEU Models of Crime', Institutt for Privatrett, University of Oslo, Working Paper Law and Economics, C1.

Eide, Erling, in cooperation with Jørgen Aasness and Terje Skjerpen (1994), *Economics of Crime: Deterrence and the Rational Offender, Contributions to Economic Analysis*, Amsterdam, Oxford and Tokyo, North-Holland, 334 p.

Ellickson, R.C. (1996), 'Controlling Chronic Misconduct in City Spaces: Of Panhandlers, Skid Rows, and Public-Space Zoning', **105** *Yale Law Journal*, 1165-1248.

Entorf, von Horst (1996), 'Kriminalität und Ökonomie: Übersicht und neue Evidenz (Crime and Economy: Survey and New Evidence)', **116** *Zeitschrift für Wirtschafts- und Sozialwissenschaften*, 417-450.

Fadaei Tehrani, Reza (1989), 'The Costs of Crime: Unemployment and Poverty', **16(12)** *International Journal of Social Economics*, 34-243.

Fattah, E.A. (1983), 'Critique of Deterrence Research with Particular Reference to the Economic Approach', **25** *Canadian Journal of Criminology*, 79-90.

Feichtinger, G., Forst, Ch.V. and Piccardi, C. (1993), 'A Nonlinear Dynamic Model for the Dynastic Cycle', **165** *Forschungsbericht/Research Memorandum*.

Fisher, Franklin M. and Nagin, D. (1978), 'On the Feasibility of Identifying the Crime Function in a Simultaneous Model of Crime Rates and Sanction Levels', in Blumstein, Cohen and Nagin (eds), *Deterrence and Incapacitation: Estimating the Effects of Criminal Sanctions on Crime Rates*, Washington, DC, National Academy of Sciences, 361-399.

Fisher, Sethard (1987), 'Economic Development and Crime: Two May Be Associated as an Adaptation to Industrialism in Social Revolution', **46** *American Journal of Economics and Sociology*, 17-34.

Fleisher, B. (1966), *The Economics of Delinquency*, New York, Quadrangle.

Forst, Brian (1976), 'Participation in Illegitimate Activities: Further Empirical Findings', **2** *Policy Analysis*, 477-492.

Forst, Brian (1977), 'The Deterrent Effect of Capital Punishment: A Cross-State Analysis of the 1960's', **5** *Minnesota Law Review*, 743-767.

Fox, J.A. (ed.) (1981), *Methods in Quantitative Criminology*, New York, London, Academic Press.

Freeman, Richard B. (1987), 'The Relation of Criminal Activity to Black Youth Employment', **16(1-2)** *Review of Black Political Economy*, 99-107.

Freeman, Richard B. (1995), 'The Labor Market', in Wilson, James Q. and Petersilia, Joan (eds), *Crime*, San Fransisco, Institute for Contemporary Studies, 171-191.

Freeman, Richard B. (1996), 'Why do so many Young American Men Commit Crimes and What Might we do About it?', **10** *Journal of Economic Perspectives*, 25-42.

Frey, Bruno S. (1988), 'Fighting Political Terrorism by Refusing Recognition', **7** *Journal of Public Policy*, 179-188.

Frey, Bruno S. and Buhofer, Heinz (1988), 'Prisoners and Property Rights', **31** *Journal of Law and Economics*, 19-46.

Friedman, D.D. (1991), 'Impossibility, Subjective Probability, and Punishment for Attempts', **20** *Journal of Legal Studies*, 1790-1860.

Friedman, D. and Sjostrom, W. (1993), 'Hanged for a Sheep - The Economics of Marginal Deterrence', **22** *Journal of Legal Studies*, 165-192.

Friedman, Joseph, Hakim, Simon and Spiegel, Uriel (1989), 'The Difference between Short and Long Run Effects of Police Outlays on Crime: Policing Deters Criminals Initially, but Later They May Learn by Doing', **48** *American Journal of Economics and Sociology*, 177-191.

Friedman, Lee S. (1979a), 'The Use of Multiple Regression Analysis to Test for a Deterrent Effect of Capital Punishment: Prospects and Problems', in Messinger, Sheldon L. and Bittner, Egon (eds), *Criminology Review Yearbook 1*, Beverly Hills, Sage Publications.

Friedman, Lee S. (1979b), 'The Use of Multiple Regression Analysis to Test for a Deterrent Effect of Capital Punishment: Prospects and Problems', in Messinger, Sheldon L. and Bittner, Egon (eds), *Criminology Review Yearbook*, Beverly Hills, Sage Publications, 61-87.

Furlong, William J. (1987), 'A General Equilibrium Model of Crime Commission and Prevention', **34** *Journal of Public Economics*, 87-103.

Furlong, William J. and Mehay, Stephen L. (1981), 'Urban Law Enforcement in Canada: an Empirical Analysis', **14** *Canadian Journal of Economics*, 44-57.

Gallo, Joseph C., Dau-Schmidt, Kenneth G. and Craycraft, Joseph (1997), 'The First Century of Department of Justice Antitrust Enforcement', **12** *Review of Industrial Organization*.

Garoupa, Nuno (1996), 'Prison, Parole and the Criminal Justice Act 1991', **18** *Research in Law and Economics*.

Garoupa, Nuno (1997), 'A Note on Private Enforcement and Type I Error', **17** *International Review of Law and Economics*, 423-429.

Garoupa, Nuno and Bowles, R. (1997), 'Casual Police Corruption and the Economics of Crime', **17** *International Review of Law and Economics*, 75-87.

Geyikdagi, Yasar M. and Geyikdagi, Necla V. (1986), 'The Economics of Street Crime', **33** *Rivista Internazionale di Scienze Economiche e Commerciali*, 813-818.

Ghali, Moheb A. et al. (1983), 'Economic Factors and the Composition of Juvenile Property Crimes', **15** *Applied Economics*, 267-281.

Gibbons, T. (1982), 'The Utility of Economic Analysis of Crime', **2** *International Review of Law and Economics*, 173-191.

Gibbs, J. (1975), *Crime, Punishment and Deterrence*, New York, Elsevier.

Ginsburg, Douglas H. and Shechtman, P. (1993), 'Blackmail: An Economic Analysis of the Law', **141** *University of Pennsylvania Law Review*, 1849 ff.

Glaeser, E.L., Sacerdote, B. and Scheinkman, J.A. (1996), 'Crime and Social Interactions', **11** *Quarterly Journal of Economics*, 274-279.

Goff, B.L. and Tollison R.D. (1993), 'Using (Im)perfect Markets to Catch Criminals', **21** *Journal of Economic Behavior and Organization*, 31-41.

Goldberg, Itzhak and Nold, Frederik C. (1980), 'Does Reporting Deter Burglars? An Empirical Analysis of Risk and Return in Crime', *Review of Economics and Statistics*, 424-431.

Good, David H. and Pirog Good, Maureen A. (1987a), 'A Simultaneous Probit Model of Crime and Employment for Black and White Teenage Males', **16(1-2)** *Review of Black Political Economy*, 109-127.

Good, David H. and Pirog Good, Maureen A. (1987b), 'Employment, Crime, and Race', **5(4)** *Contemporary Policy Issues*, 91-104.

Good, David H., Pirog Good, Maureen A. and Sickles, Robin C. (1986), 'An Analysis of Youth Crime and Employment Patterns', **2** *Journal of Quantitative Criminology*, 219-236.

Graves, Philip E., Lee, Dwight R. and Sexton, Robert L. (1989), 'Statutes versus Enforcement: The Case of the Optimal Speed Limit', **79** *American Economic Review*, 932-936.

Greenberg, David F. and Kessler, Ronald C. (1981), 'Panel Models in Criminology', in Fox, J.A. (ed), *Methods in Quantitive Criminology*, New York, London, Academic Press.

Greenberg, David F., Kessler, Ronald C. and Logan, Charles H. (1979), 'A Panel Model of Crime Rates and Arrest Rates', *American Sociological Review*, 843-850.

Greenberg, Stephanie W. and Rohe, William M. (1986), 'Informal Social Control and Crime Prevention in Modern Urban Neighborhoods', in Taylor, Ralph B. (ed), *Urban Neighborhoods: Research and Policy*, New York, Praeger Publishers, 79-118.

Greenwood, Michael J. and Wadycki, Walter J. (1973), 'Crime Rates and Public Expenditures for Police Protection: Their Interaction', **31** *Review of Social Economics*, 138-151.

Greenwood, Michael J. and Wadycki, Walter J. (1975), 'Crime Rates and Public Expenditures for Police Protection: A Reply', **33** *Review of Social Economics*, 81-84.

Grogger, Jeffrey (1990), 'The Deterrent Effect of Capital Punishment: An Analysis of Daily Homicide Counts', **85** *Journal of the American Statistical Association*, 295-303.

Grogger, Jeffrey (1991), 'Certainty vs. Severity of Punishment', **29** *Economic Inquiry*, 297-309.

Gyimah Brempong, Kwabena (1986), 'Empirical Models of Criminal Behavior: How Significant a Factor is Race?', **15** *Review of Black Political Economy*, 27-43.

Hann, Robert G. (1976), *Deterrence and the Death Penalty: A Critical Review of the Research of Isaac Ehrlich*, Ottawa, Ontario, Research Division of the Solicitor-General of Canada.

Hashimoto, Masanori (1987), 'The Minimum Wage Law and Youth Crimes: Time-Series Evidence', **30** *Journal of Law and Economics*, 443-464.

Hawkins, Gordon (1971), 'Punishment and Deterrence: The Educative, Moralising and Habituative Effects', in Stanley E. Grupp (ed), *Theories of Punishment*, Bloomington, IN, Indiana University Press, 163-180.

Heineke, J.M. (1975), 'A Note on Modelling the Criminal Choice Problem', **10** *Journal of Economic Theory*, 113-116.

Heineke, J.M. (ed) (1978), *Economic Models of Criminal Behaviour*, Amsterdam, North-Holland, 391 p.

Hellman, D.A. (1980), *The Economics of Crime*, New York, St. Martin's Press.

Hellman, Daryl A. and Alper, Neil O. (1990), *Economics of Crime: Theory and Practice*, Needham Heights, Simon and Schuster, Ginn Press, 226 p.

Hersch, Philip L. and Netter, Jeffrey M. (1984), 'The Effects of Crime Rates on Time Served in Prison: An Empirical Analysis', **39** *Public Finance*, 314-320.

Hershbarger, R.A. and Miller, R.K. (1988), 'The Impact of Economic Conditions on the Incidence of Arson: A Reply', **55** *Journal of Risk and Insurance*, 755-757.

Hill, John K. and Pearce, James E. (1990), 'The Incidence of Sanctions against Employers of Illegal Aliens', **98** *Journal of Political Economy*, 28-44.

Hirsch, Werner Z. and Rufolo, Anthony M. (1985), 'Economic Effects of Residence Laws on Municipal Police', **17** *Journal of Urban Economics*, 335-348.

Hoenack, Stephen A. and Weiler, William (1980), 'A Structural Model of Murder Behavior', **70** *American Economic Review*, 327-341.

Hoenack, Stephen A., Kurdle, Robert and Sjøquist, David (1978), 'The Deterrent Effect of Capital Punishment: A Question of Identification', **4** *Policy Analysis*, 491-527.

Holtmann, A.G. and Yap, L. (1978), 'Does Punishment Pay?', **33** *Public Finance*, 90-97.

Howsen, Roy M. and Jarrell, Stephen B. (1987), 'Some Determinants of Property Crime: Economic Factors Influence Criminal Behavior but Cannot Completely Explain the Syndrome', **46** *American Journal of Economics and Sociology*, 445-457.

Hull, B.B. and Bold, F. (1995), 'Preaching Matters: Replication and Extension', **27** *Journal of Economic Behavior and Organization*, 143-149.

Jarrell, Stephen B. and Howsen, Roy M. (1990), 'Transient Crowding and Crime: The More 'Strangers' in an Area, the More Crime Except for Murder, Assault and Rape', **49** *American Journal of Economics and Sociology*, 483-494.

Kaplan, L.J. and Kessler, P. (eds) (1976), *An Economic Analysis of Crime: Selected Readings*, Springfield, Charles Thomas.

Karpoff, Jonathan M. and Lott, John R., Jr (1993), 'The Reputational Penalty Firms Bear from Committing Criminal Fraud', **36** *Journal of Law and Economics*, 757-802.

Kenkel, Donald S. (1993), 'Drinking, Driving, and Deterrence: The Effectiveness and Social Costs of Alternative Policies', **36** *Journal of Law and Economics*, 877-913.

Klein, Lawrene R., Forst, Brian and Filatov, Victor (1978), 'The Deterrent Effect of Capital Punishment : An Assessment of the Estimates', in Blumstein, Cohen and Nagin (eds), *Deterrence and Incapacitation : Estimating the Effects of Criminal Sanctions on Crime Rates*, Washington, DC, National Academy of Sciences, 336-360.

Klepper, Stephen and Nagin, Daniel S. (1989a), 'The Criminal Deterrence Literature: Implications for Research on Taxpayer Compliance', in J.T. Scholz et al. (eds), *Paying Taxes: An Agenda for Compliance Research*, Philadelphia, University of Philadelphia.

Klepper, Steven and Nagin, Daniel S. (1989b), 'The Anatomy of Tax Evasion', **5** *Journal of Law, Economics, and Organization*, 1-24.

Klevorick, Alvin K. (1985), 'On the Economic Theory of Crime', in Pennock, J. Roland and Chapman, John W. (eds), *Nomos XXVII: Criminal Justice*, Granite Impex Ltd, 289-312.

Kobayashi, Bruce H. (1992), 'Deterrence with Multiple Defendants: an Explanation for "Unfair" Plea Bargaining', **23** *Rand Journal of Economics*, 507-515.

Kobayashi, Bruce H. and Lott, John R., Jr (1992), 'Low Probability-High Penalty Enforcement Strategies and the Efficient Operation of the Plea-Bargaining System', **12** *International Review of Law and Economics*, 69-77.

Kobayashi, Bruce H. and Lott, John R., Jr (1996), 'In Defense of Criminal Defense Expenditures and Plea Bargaining', **16** *International Review of Law and Economics*.

Kolm, S.-C. (1973), 'A Note on Optimal Tax Evasion', **2** *Journal of Public Economics*, 265-270.

Komesar, Neil K. (1973), 'A Theoretical and Empirical Study of Victims of Crime', **2** *Journal of Legal Studies*, 301-321.

Koskela, Erkki and Viren, Matti (1993), 'An Economic Model of Auto Thefts in Finland', **13** *International Review of Law and Economics*, 179-191.

Landes, William M. (1978), 'An Economic Study of U.S. Aircraft Hijacking, 1961-1976', **21** *Journal of Law and Economics*, 1-31.

Lattimore, P.K. (1992), 'The Influence of Probability on Risky Choice: A Parametric Examination', **17** *Journal of Economics, Behavior and Organization*, 377-400.

Lattimore P.K., Baker, J.R. and Witte, A.D. (1992), 'The Influence of Probability on Risky Choice: A Parametric Examination', **17** *Journal of Economic Behavior and Organization*, 377-400.

Layson, Stephen K. (1983), 'Homicide and Deterrence: Another View of the Canadian Time Series Evidence', **16** *Canadian Journal of Economics*, 52-73.

Layson, Stephen K. (1985), 'Homicide and Deterrence: A Reexamination of the United States Time Series Evidence', **52** *Southern Economic Journal*, 68-89.

Layton, Allan P. (1983), 'The Impact of Increased Penalties on Australian Drink/Driving Behaviour', **19** *Logistics and Transportation Review*, 261-266.

Lazos, Vaios (1996), 'E Kambyle Adiaforias enos Eglematos (The Indifference Curve of a Crime)', **6** *Aissymnetes*.

Lejeune, R. (1977), 'Management of a Mugging', **6** *Urban Life*, 123-148.

Leung, S.F. (1995), 'Dynamic Deterrence Theory', **6** *Economica*, 65-87.

Lewin, Jeff L. and Trumbull, William N. (1993), 'Neither Boxed in nor Circular: A Reply', **13** *International Review of Law and Economics*, 233-235.

Lewisch, Peter (1992), 'A Case Study on the Legal Regulation of Shoplifting in Austria and the "Criminal Tourism" from the East', **12** *International Review of Law and Economics*, 439-455.

Liu, Yih Wu and Bee, Richard H. (1983), 'Modeling Criminal Activity in an Area in Economic Decline: Local Economic Conditions are a Major Factor in Local Property Crimes', **42** *American Journal of Economics and Sociology*, 385-392.

Loftin, Colin and McDowall, David (1982), 'The Police, Crime and Economic Theory: An Assessment', *American Sociological Review*, 393-401.

Logan. Charles H. (1975), 'Arrest Rates and Deterrence', **56** *Social Science Quarterly*, 76-89.

Logan, Charles H. (1982), 'Problems in Ratio Correlation: The Case of Deterrence Research', **60** *Social Force*, 791-810.

Lott, John R., Jr (1987), 'Juvenile Delinquency and Education: A Comparison of Public and Private Provision', **7** *International Review of Law and Economics*, 163-175.

Lott, John R., Jr (1990a), 'Getting Tough on White-Collar Criminals', **13(1)** *Regulation*, 18-19.

Lott, John R., Jr (1990b), 'The Effect of Conviction on the Legitimate Income of Criminals', **34** *Economic Letters*, 381-385.

Lott, John R., Jr (1990c), 'A Transaction-Costs Explanation for Why the Poor are More Likely to Commit Crime', **19** *Journal of Legal Studies*, 243-245.

Lott, John R., Jr (1992a), 'Do we Punish High Income Criminals too Heavily?', **30** *Economic Inquiry*, 583-608.

Lott, John R., Jr (199b2), 'An Attempt at Measuring the Total Monetary Penalty from Drug Convictions: The Importance of an Individual's Reputation', **21** *Journal of Legal Studies*, 159-187.

Lott, J.R., Jr and Roberts, R.D. (1995), 'The Expected Penalty for Committing a Crime: An Analysis of Minimum Wage Violations', **30** *Journal of Human Resources*, 397-408.

Lupia, Arthur and McCubbins, Mathew D. (1994), 'Learning from Oversight: Fire Alarms and Police Patrols Reconstructed', **10** *Journal of Law, Economics, and Organization*, 96-125.

Manski, Charles, F. (1978), 'Prospects for Inference on Deterrence through Empirical Analysis of Individual Criminal Behaviour', in Blumstein, Cohen and Nagin (eds), *Deterrence and Incapacitation: Estimating the Effects of Criminal Sanctions on Crime Rates*, Washington, DC, National Academy of Sciences, 400-424.

Marceau, Nicolas (1997), 'Self-Selection and Violence in the Market for Crime', **17** *International Review of Law and Economics*, 193-201.

Mathieson, Donald and Passell, Peter (1976), 'Homicide and Robbery in New York City: An Economic Model', **5** *Journal of Legal Studies*, 83-98.

Mathur, Vijay K. (1978), 'Economics of Crime: An Investigation of the Deterrent Hypothesis for Urban Areas', **60** *Review of Economics and Statistics*, 459-466.

McChesney, Fred S. (1993), 'Boxed in: Economists and Benefits from Crime', **13** *International Review of Law and Economics*, 225-231.

McCormick, Robert E. and Tollison, Robert D. (1986), 'Crime and Income Distribution in a Basketball Economy', **6** *International Review of Law and Economics*, 115-124.

McPheters, Lee R. (1978), 'Econometric Analysis of Factors Influencing Crime on the Campus', **6** *Journal of Criminal Justice*, 47-52.

McPheters, Lee R. and Strange, W.B. (eds) (1976), *The Economics of Crime and Law Enforcement*, Springfield, Charles R. Thomas.

McPheters, Lee R., Mann, Robert and Schlagenhauf, Don E. (1984), 'Economic Response to a Crime Deterrence Program: Mandatory Sentencing for Robbery with a Firearm', **22** *Economic Inquiry*, 550-570.

Meera, A.K. and Jayakumar M.D. (1995), 'Determinants of Crime in a Developing Country: A Regression Model', **27** *Applied Economics*, 455-460.

Meier, R.F. (ed) (1985), *Theoretical Methods in Criminology*, Beverly Hills, Sage Publications.

Melossi, Dario (1987), 'Political Business Cycles and Imprisonment Rates in Italy: Report on a Work in Progress', **16(1-2)** *Review of Black Political Economy*, 211-218.

Miceli, Thomas J. (1996), 'Plea Bargaining and Deterrence: An Institutional Approach', **3** *European Journal of Law and Economics*, 249-264.

Michaels, Robert J. (1976), 'Noncriminal Deviance and Mental Hospitalization: Economic Theory and Evidence', **5** *Journal of Legal Studies*, 387-433.

Michaels, Robert J. (1988), 'Addiction, Compulsion, and the Technology of Consumption', **26** *Economic Inquiry*, 75-88.

Myers, Samuel L., Jr (1980), 'Why are Crimes Underreported? What is the Crime Rate? Does it Really Matter?', **6** *Social Science Quarterly*, 23-43.

Myers, Samuel L., Jr (1982), 'Crime in Urban Areas: New Evidence and Results', **11** *Journal of Urban Economics*, 148-158.

Myers, Samuel L., Jr (1983), 'Estimating the Economic Model of Crime: Employment versus Punishment Effects', *Quarterly Journal of Economics*, 157-175.

Myers, Samuel L., Jr (1984a), 'Do Better Wages Reduce Crime? A Research Note', **43** *American Journal of Economics and Sociology*, 191-195.

Myers, Samuel L., Jr (1984b), 'Race and Punishment: Directions for Economic Research', **74** *American Economic Review*, 288-292.

Nagin, Daniel S. (1978), 'General Deterrence: A Review of the Empirical Evidence', in Blumstein, Cohen and Nagin (eds), *Deterrence and Incapacitation: Estimating the*

Effects of Criminal Sanctions on Crime Rates, Washington, DC, National Academy of Sciences, 95-139.

Nagin, Daniel S. and Paternoster, Raymond (1991a), 'The Preventive Effects of the Perceived Risk of Arrest: Testing an Expanded Conception of Deterrence', **29** *Criminology*, 561-587.

Nagin, Daniel S. and Paternoster, Raymond (1991b), 'On the Relationship of Past to Future Participation in Delinquency', **29** *Criminology*, 169-189.

Nagin, Daniel S. and Paternoster, R.A. (1993), 'Enduring Individual Differences and Rational Choice Theories of Crime', **27** *Law and Society Review*, 467-496.

Nagin, Daniel S. and Waldfogel, Joel (1995), 'The Effects of Criminality and Conviction on the Labor Market Status of Young British Offenders', **15** *International Review of Law and Economics*, 109-126.

Neher, Philip A. (1978), 'The Pure Theory of Muggery', **68** *American Economic Review*, 437-445.

Nickerson, Gary W. (1983), 'Analytical Problems in Explaining Criminal Behavior: Neoclassical and Radical Economic Theories and an Alternative Formulation', **15(4)** *Review of Radical Political Economy*, 1-23.

Niggli, Marcel Alexander (1994), 'Rational Choice Theory and Crime Prevention', **3** *Studies on Crime and Crime Prevention*, 83-103.

Opp, Karl Dieter (1989), 'The Economics of Crime and the Sociology of Deviant Behaviour: A Theoretical Confrontation of Basic Propositions', **42** *Kyklos*, 405-430.

Orsagh, Thomas (1973), 'Crime, Sanctions and Scientific Explanation', **64** *Journal of Criminal Law and Criminology*, 354-361.

Orsagh, Thomas (1979), 'Empirical Criminology: Interpreting Results Derived from Aggregate Data', **16** *Journal of Research in Crime and Delinquency*, 294-306.

Otto, Hans-Jochen (1982), *Generalprävention und externe Verhaltenskontrolle, Wandel vom sociologischen zum ökonomischen Paradigma in der nordamerikanischen Kriminologie?* (General Prevention and External Control of Behavior, Evolution from Sociological to Economic Paradigm in the North American Criminology?), Freiburg, Max-Planck-Institut für ausländisches und internationales Strafrecht, 323 p.

Ozenne, Tim (1974), 'The Economics of Bank Robbery', **3** *Journal of Legal Studies*, 19-51.

Packer, Herbert L. (1968), *The Limits of the Criminal Sanction*, Stanford, Hoover Institute Press, Stanford University, 366 p.

Palmer, Jan (1977), 'Economic Analysis of the Deterrent Effect of Punishment: A Review', **14** *Journal of Research in Crime and Delinquency*, 4-21.

Parker, Robert N. and Horwitz, Allan V. (1986), 'Unemployment, Crime, and Imprisonment: A Panel Approach', **24** *Criminology*, 751-771.

Passell, Peter (1975), 'The Deterrent Effect of the Death Penalty: A Statistical Test', **28** *Stanford Law Review*, 61-80.

Passell, Peter and Taylor, John B. (1977), 'The Deterrent Effect of Capital Punishment: Another View', **67** *American Economic Review*, 445-451.

Pastor, Santos (1994), 'La Exigibilidad de las Normas y la Resolución de Conflictos (Law Enforcement and Dispute Resolution)', **3** *Iuris: Quaderns de Política Jurídica*, 155-174.

Paternoster, Raymond, Saltzman, Linda E., Chiricos, Theodore E. and Waldo, Gordon P. (1982), 'Perceived Risk and Deterrence: Methodological Artifacts in Perceptual Deterrence Research', **73** *Journal of Criminal Law and Criminology*, 1238-1258.

Payne, M. and Furnham, A. (1990), 'Perceptions of Crime and Delinquency in Barbados', **39** *Social and Economic Studies*, 135-150.

Peltzman, Sam (1989), 'The Failure of Enforcement', *British Journal of Addiction.*

Phillips, D. (1980), 'The Deterrent Effect of Capital Punishment: New Evidence and Old Controversy', **86** *American Journal of Sociology*, 81-139.

Phillips, Llad (1987), 'Race and Crime: Comments', **16** *Review of Black Political Economy*, 219-221.

Phillips, Llad and Votey, Harold L., Jr (1972), 'An Economic Analysis of the Deterrent Effect of Law Enforcement on Criminal Activity', **63** *Journal of Criminal Law, Criminology and Police Science*, 330-342.

Phillips, Llad and Votey, Harold L., Jr (1975), 'Crime Control in California', **4** *Journal of Legal Studies*, 327-349.

Phillips, Llad and Votey, Harold L., Jr (1981), *The Economics of Crime Control*, Beverly Hills, CA, Sage Publications.

Phillips, Llad and Votey, Harold L., Jr (1984), 'Black Women, Economic Disadvantage, and Incentives to Crime', **74** *American Economic Review*, 293-297.

Phillips, Llad and Votey, Harold L., Jr (1987a), 'Crimes by Youth: Deterrence and Moral Compliance with the Law', **5(4)** *Contemporary Policy Issues*, 73-90.

Phillips, Llad and Votey, Harold L., Jr (1987b), 'Rational Choice Models of Crimes by Youth', **16** *Review of Black Political Economy*, 129-187.

Phillips, Llad, Votey, Harold L., Jr and Howell, John (1976), 'Handguns and Homocide: Minimizing Losses and the Costs of Control', **5** *Journal of Legal Studies*, 463-478.

Phillips, Llad, Votey, Harold L., Jr and Maxwell, Darold (1972), 'Crime, Youth and the Labor Market: An Economic Study', **80** *Journal of Political Economy*, 491-504.

Png, Ivan Paak-Liang (1987), 'Litigation, Liability, and Incentives for Care', **34** *Journal of Public Economics*, 61-85.

Png, Ivan Paak-Liang and Mookherjee, D. (1992), 'Monitoring vis-à-vis Investigation in Enforcement of Law', **82** *American Economic Review*, 556-565.

Png, Ivan Paak-Liang and Mookherjee, D. (1994), 'Marginal Deterrence in Enforcement of Law', **102** *Journal of Political Economy*, 1039-1066.

Png, Ivan Paak-Liang and Mookherjee, D. (1995), 'Corruptible Law Enforcers: How Should They be Compensated?', **105** *Economic Journal*, 145-159.

Pogue, Thomas F. (1975), 'Effects of Police Expenditure on Crime Rates: Some Evidence', **3** *Public Finance Quarterly*, 14-44.

Polinsky, A. Mitchell and Shavell, Steven (1979), 'The Optimal Tradeoff between the Probability and Magnitude of Fines', **69** *American Economic Review*, 880-891.

Polinsky, Mitchell A. (1978), '[Economics and Law:] Discussion', **68** *American Economic Review: Papers and Proceedings*, 435-436.

Prisching, Manfred (1982), 'Sozioökonomische Bedingungen der Kriminalität. Über empirische Divergenzen und theoretische Kontroversen (Socio-economic Conditions of Criminality. On Empirical Divergencies and Theoretical Controversies)', **65** *Monatsschrift für Kriminologie und Strafrechtsreform*, 163-176.

Pyle, David J. (1979a), 'Crime Rates and Police Expenditure', in Maunder, P. (ed), *Case Studies in the Economics of Social Issues*, London, Heinemann, 61-76.

Pyle, David J. (1979b), *The Economics of Crime and Law Enforcement: A Selective Biblipography (+ Supplement 1980)*, SSRC Public Sector Study Group, Bibliography Series No. 1, 216 p.

Pyle, David J. (1983), *The Economics of Crime and Law Enforcement*, London, Macmillan, 216 p.

Radford, R.S. (1989), 'Going to the Island: A Legal and Economic Analysis of the Medieval Icelandic Duel', **62** *Southern California Law Review*, 615 ff.

Rasmussen, David W. and Benson, Bruce L. (eds) (1994), *The Economic Anatomy of a Drug War: Criminal Justice in the Commons*, Lanham, MD, Rowman and Littlefield.

Rasmussen, David W., Benson, Bruce L. and Sollars, David L. (1993), 'Spatial Competition in Illicit Drug Markets: The Consequences of Increased Drug Enforcement', **23** *Review of Regional Studies*, 219-236.

Rizzo, Mario J. (1979), 'The Cost of Crime to Victims: An Empirical Analysis', **8** *Journal of Legal Studies*, 177-205.

Robert, Philippe and Godefroy, Thierry (1977), *Le Coût du Crime ou l'Economie Poursuivant le Crime* (The Cost of Crime or Economics Prosecuting Crime), Genève, Masson, 225 p.

Rogers, A.J. III(1973), *The Economics of Crime*, Illinois, Dryden Press.

Ross, H. Laurence (1977), 'Deterrence Regained: The Cheshire Constabulary's "Breathalyser Blitz"', **6** *Journal of Legal Studies*, 241-249.

Ross, H. Laurence and LaFree, Gary D. (1986), 'Deterrence in Criminology and Social Policy', in Smelser, Neil J. and Gerstein, Dean R. (eds), *Behavioral and Social Science: Fifty Years of Discovery*, Washington, DC, National Academy Press, 129-152.

Ross, Laurence H. (1975), 'The Scandinavian Myth: The Effectiveness of Drinking-and-Driving Legislating in Sweden and Norway', **4** *Journal of Legal Studies*, 285-310.

Rottenberg, Simon (ed) (1973), *The Economics of Crime and Punishment*, Washington, DC, American Enterprise Institute for Public Policy Research, 232 p.

Rovens, R. and Prinsen, P.J. (1984), 'Extra Politie-inzet en Rijden onder Invloed (More Police and Drunken Driving)', **52** *WODC*.

Rubin, Paul H. and Kau, James B. (1975), 'Economic and Ideological Factors in Political Decision Making: The 1980 Election', **24** *Public Choice*, 385-388.

Saffer, Henry and Chaloupka, Frank J. (1989), 'Breath Testing and Highway Fatality Rates', **21** *Applied Economics*, 901-912.

Saffer, Henry and Grossman, Michael (1987a), 'Beer Taxes, the Legal Drinking Age, and Youth Motor Vehicle Fatalities', **16** *Journal of Legal Studies*, 351-374.

Saffer, Henry and Grossman, Michael (1987b), 'Drinking Age Laws and Highway Mortality Rates: Cause and Effect', **25** *Economic Inquiry*, 403-417.

Sah, R.K. (1991), 'Social Osmosis and Patterns of Crime', **99** *Journal of Political Economy*, 1272-1295.

Sandelin, Bo and Skogh, Göran (1986), 'Property Crimes and the Police: An Empirical Analysis of Swedish Data', **88** *Scandinavian Journal of Economics*, 547-561.

Sansarricq, Frank (1990), 'Crime and Economic Development in a Small, Open Economy', **27** *Keio Economic Studies*, 41-49.

Schmidt, Peter and Witte, Ann D. (1984), *An Economic Analysis of Crime and Justice: Theory, Methods, and Applications*, New York, Academic Press, 416 p.

Schmidt, Peter and Witte, Ann D. (1989), 'Predicting Criminal Recidivism Using "Split Population" Survival Time Models', **40** *Journal of Econometrics*, 141-159.

Schuller, Bernd-Joachim (1986), *Ekonomi och Kriminalitet: En Empirisk Undersöking av Brottsligheten i Sverige* (Economics and Criminality: Empirical Research in Sweden), Economiska studier utgivna av Nationalekonomiska institutionen vid Göteborgs Universitet, 17 ff.

Schwartz, Warren F., Baxter, Keith and Ryan, David (1984), 'The Duel: Can These Gentlemen be Acting Efficiently?', **13** *Journal of Legal Studies*, 321-335.

Sesnowitz, Michael L. and Hexter, Lawrence (1982), 'Economic Determinants of Theft: Some Empirical Results', **10** *Public Finance Quarterly*, 489-498.

Shavell, Steven (1989), 'Specific versus General Enforcement of Law', Program in Law and Economics, Harvard Law School, Disc. Paper No. 58.

Shavell, Steven (1990), 'Deterrence and the Punishment of Attempts', **19** *Journal of Legal Studies*, 435-466.

Shavell, Steven (1992), 'A Note on Marginal Deterrence', **12** *International Review of Law and Economics*, 345-355.

Silver, Morris (1975), 'A Critical Survey of the Recent Econometric Literature on Deterrence', in Ernest van den Haag and Robert Martinson (eds), *Crime Deterrence and Offender Career*, New York, City College of the City University of New York, 136-172.

Singh, B. (1973), 'Making Honesty the Best Policy', *Journal of Public Economics*, 257-263.

Sjoquist, David Lawrence (1973), 'Property Crime and Economic Behavior: Some Empirical Results', **63** *American Economic Review*, 439-446.

Skogh, Göran (1973), 'A Note on Becker's "Crime and Punishment: An Economic Approach"', **75** *Swedish Journal of Economics*, 305-311.

Skogh, Göran and Stuart, Charles (1982a), 'A Contractarian Theory of Property Rights and Crime', **84** *Scandinavian Journal of Economics*, 27-40.

Skogh, Göran and Stuart, Charles (1982b), 'An Economic Analysis of Crime Rates, Punishments and the Consequences of Crime', **38** *Public Choice*, 171-179.

Slemrod, J. (1985), 'An Empirical Test of Tax Evasion', **67** *Review of Economics and Statistics*, 67, 232-238.

Sloan, Frank A., Reilly, Bridget A. and Schenzler, Christoph M. (1995), 'Effects of Tort Liability and Insurance on Heavy Drinking and Drinking and Driving', **38** *Journal of Law and Economics*, 49-77.

Snyder, Edward A. (1990), 'The Effect of Higher Criminal Penalties on Antritrust Enforcement', **33** *Journal of Law and Economics*, 439-462.

Sollars, David L., Benson, Bruce L. and Rasmussen, David W. (1994), 'Drug Enforcement and Deterrence of Property Crime Among Local Jurisdictions', **22** *Public Finance Quarterly*, 22-45.

Soloman, H. (1977), 'The Economist's Perspectives on Economic Crime', **14** *American Criminal Law Review*, 641-649.

Solow, R.M. (1977), 'Leff's Swindling and Selling: the Spanish Prisoner and Other Bargains', **8** *Bell Journal of Economics*, 627-629.

Sommers, Paul M. (1985), 'Drinking Age and the 55 MPH Speed Limit', **13(1)** *Atlantic Economic Journal*, 43-48.

Stevans, Lonnie K. (1988), 'An Empirical Model of Property Crime: Deterrence versus Redistribution', **10** *Journal of Post Keynesian Economics*, 572-584.

Sullivan, R.F. (1973), 'The Economics of Crime: An Introduction to the Literature', **19** *Crime and Delinquency*, 138-149.

Sutinen, Jon G. and Andersen, Peder (1985), 'The Economics of Fisheries Law Enforcement', **61** *Land Economics*, 387-397.

Swimmer, Eugene R. (1974), 'Measurement of the Effectiveness of Urban Law Enforcement - A Simultaneous Approach', **40** *Southern Economic Journal*, 618-630.

Tauchen, Helen and Witte, Ann Dryden (1995), 'The Dynamics of Domestic Violence', **85** *American Economic Review. Papers and Proceedings*, 414-418.

Tauchen, Helen, Witte, Ann D. and Griesinger, Harriet (1994), 'Criminal Deterrence: Revisiting the Issue With a Birth Cohort', **76** *Review of Economics and Statistics*, 399-412.

Taylor, J.B. (1978), 'Econometric Models of Criminal Behavior: A Review', in Heineke, J.M. (ed.), *Economic Models of Criminal Behavior*, Amsterdam, North-Holland, 35-81.

Thaler, Richard H. (1977), 'An Econometrie Analysis Of Property Crime: Interaction Between Police and Criminals', **8** *Journal of Public Economics*, 37-51.

Theroux, Richard and Umbeck, John R. (1987), 'Drunken Driving, Hit-and-Runs, and Bribery', **11(2)** *Regulation*, 44-47.

Thompson, James W. and Cataldo, James (1986), 'Market Incentives for Criminal Behavior: Comment', in Freeman, Richard B. and Holzer, Harry J. (eds), *The Black Youth Employment Crisis*, Chicago, IL, University of Chicago Press, 347-351.

Tittle, Charles R. (1978), 'Comment on "Deterrence: Theory versus Practice"', **16** *Criminology*, 31-35.

Tittle, Charles R. and Logan, Charles H. (1973), 'Sanctions and Deviance: Evidence and Remaining Questions', **7** *Law and Society Review*, 371-392.

Tittle, Charles R. and Rowe, A.R. (1974), 'Certainty of Arrest and Crime Rates: A Further Test of the Deterrence Hypothesis', **52** *Social Forces*, 455-462.

Tittle, Charles R. and Rowe, Alan R. (1978), 'Arrest and Crime: More on the Deterrence Problem', in Flynn, Edith Elisabeth and Conrad John P. (eds), *The New and the Old Criminology*, New York, Praeger, 85-95.

Trumbull, William N. (1989), 'Estimations of the Economic Model of Crime Using Aggregate and Individual Level Data', **56** *Southern Economic Journal*, 423-439.

Tulder, Frank Van (1985), *Criminaliteit, Pakkans en Politie* (Criminality, Chance of Being Caught and Police), Sociaal Cultureel Planbureau, Cahier no. 45, s-Gravenhage, Staatsdrukkerij.

Tulder, Frank Van (1986), 'Kosten en Baten van Twee Vormen van Criminaliteitsbestrijding (Costs and Benefits of Two Types of Crime Combat)', **71** *Economisch-Statistische Berichten*, 172-179.

Tullock, Gordon (1969), 'An Economic Approach to Crime', **50** *Social Science Quarterly*, 59-71.

Tullock, Gordon (1974), 'Does Punishment Deter Crime?', *The Public Interest*, 103-111.

Tullock, Gordon (1976), 'The Economics of Crime: Punishment or Income Redistribution - Comment', **34** *Review of Social Economy*, 81-82.

Tunnell, K.D. (1992), *Choosing Crime: The Criminal Calculus of Property Offenders*, Chicago, Nelson-Hall.

Usher, Dan (1986), 'Police, Punishment, and Public Goods', **41** *Public Finance*, 96-115.

Van den Haag, Ernest (1975), 'Deterrence, Deterrability and Effective Sanctions', in Van den Haag, Ernest and Martinson, Robert (eds), *Crime Deterrence and Offender Career*, New York, City College of the City University of New York, 1-99.

Van den Haag, Ernest and Martinson, Robert (eds) (1975), *Crime Deterrence and Offender Career*, New York, City College of the City University of New York.

Vandaele, Walter (1978), 'Participation in Illegitimate Activities: Ehrlich Revisited', in Blumstein, Cohen and Nagin (eds), *Deterrence and Incapacitation: Estimating the Effects of Criminal Sanctions on Crime Rates*, Washington, DC, National Academy of Sciences, 270-335.

Viren, Matti (1990), 'A Note on Finnish Property Criminality', **17** *International Journal of Social Economics*, 55-59.

Viren, Matti (1994), 'A Test of an Economics of Crime Model', **14** *International Review of Law and Economics*, 363-370.

Viscusi, W. Kip (1986a), 'Market Incentives for Criminal Behavior', in Freeman, Richard B. and Holzer, Harry J. (eds), *The Black Youth Employment Crisis*, Chicago, IL, University of Chicago Press, 301-346.

Viscusi, W. Kip (1986b), 'The Risks and Rewards of Criminal Activity: A Comprehensive Test of Criminal Deterrence', **4** *Journal of Labor Economics*, 317-340.

Votey, Harold L., Jr (1969), *Economic Crimes: Their Generation, Deterrence and* Control, Washington, DC, US Department of Commerce.

Votey, Harold L., Jr (1982), 'Scandinavian Drinking-Driving Control: Myth or Intuition ?', **11** *Journal of Legal Studies*, 93-116.

Votey, Harold L., Jr and Phillips, Llad (1973), 'Social Goals and Appropriate Policy for Corrections: An Economic Appraisal', **1** *Journal of Criminal Justice*, 219-240.

Votey, Harold L., Jr and Phillips, Llad (1974), 'The Control of Criminal Activity: An Economic Analysis', in Claser, Daniel (ed), *Handbook of Criminology*, Chicago, Rand McNally & Co., 1055-1093.

Wadycki, Walter J. and Balkin, Steven (1979), 'Participation in Illegitimate Activities - Forst's Model Revisited', **8** *Journal of Behavioral Economics*, 151-163.

Wahlroos, Björn (1981), 'On Finnish Property Criminality: An Empirical Analysis of the Post War Era Using an Ehrlich Model', **83** *Scandinavian Journal of Economics*, 553-562.

Waldfogel, Joel (1994), 'Does Conviction Have a Persistent Effect on Income and Employment?', **14** *International Review of Law and Economics*, 103-119.

Wang, William K.S. (1976), 'The Metaphysics of Punishment - An Exercise in Futility', **13** *San Diego Law Review*, 306-330.

Weissel, Erwin (1994), 'Der Rechtsbruch als Regel- oder Sonderfall (Unlawfulness as a Normal or a Special Case)', **6** *Zeitschrift für Rechtsvergleichung*.

Wickström, Bengt-Arne (1989), 'Comment: The Speed Limit as Life Saver', in Faure, Michael and Van den Bergh, Roger (eds), *Essays in Law and Economics: Corporations, Accident Prevention and Compensation for Losses*, Antwerpen, Maklu, 157-161.

Wilde, L.L. (1992), 'Criminal Choice, Nonmonetary Sanctions, and Marginal Deterrence: A Normative Analysis', **12** *International Review of Law and Economics*, 333-344.

Williams, Allan F., Rich, Robert F., Zador, Paul L. and Robertson, Leon S. (1975), 'The Legal Minimum Drinking Age and Fatal Motor Vehicle Crashes', **4** *Journal of Legal Studies*, 219-239.

Williams, Allan F., Zador, Paul L., Harris, Sandra S. and Karpf, Ronald S. (1983), 'The Effect of Raising the Legal Minimum Drinking Age on Involvement in Fatal Crashes', **12** *Journal of Legal Studies*, 169-179.

Willis, K.G. (1983), 'Spatial Variations in Crime in England and Wales: Testing an Economic Model', **17** *Regional Studies*, 261-272.

Wilson, James Q. and Boland, Barbara (1978), 'The Effect of the Police on Crime', **12** *Law and Society Review*, 367-390.

Wilson, James Q. and Herrnstein, Richard J. (1985), *Crime and Human Nature*, New York, Simon and Schuster, 639 p.

Withers, Glenn (1984), 'Crime, Punishment and Deterrence in Australia: An Empirical Investigation', **60** *Economic Record*, 176-185.

Witte, Ann Dryden (1980), 'Estimating the Economic Model of Crime with Individual Data', **94** *Quarterly Journal of Economics*, 57-84.

Witte, Ann Dryden (1983), 'Estimating the Economic Model of Crime: Reply [to Myers]', **98** *Quarterly Journal of Economics*, 167-175.

Witte, Ann Dryden and Tauchen, Helen (1994), 'Work and Crime: An Exploration Using Panel Data', **49** *Public Finance (suppl.)*, 155-167.

Witte, Ann Dryden and Woodbury, Diane (1985), 'The Effect of Tax Laws and Tax Administration on Tax Compliance: The Case of the U.S. Individual Income Tax', **38** *National Tax Journal*, 1-13.

Wittman, Donald A. (1982), 'Efficient Rules in Highway Safety and Sports Activity', **72** *American Economic Review*, 78-90.

Wolpin, Kenneth I. (1978), 'An Economic Analysis of Crime and Punishment in England and Wales, 1894-1967', **86** *Journal of Political Economy*, 815-840.

Wolpin, Kenneth I. (1978), 'Capital Punishment and Homicide in England: A Summary of Results', **68** *American Economic Review. Papers and Proceedings*, 422-427.

Wolpin, Kenneth I. (1980), 'A Time Series-Cross Section Analysis of International Variation in Crime and Punishment', **62** *Review of Economics and Statistics*, 417-423.

Yaniv, Gideon (1988), 'Crime and Punishment: A Note on Instrumental Violence', **17** *Journal of Behavioral Economics*, 143-148.

Young, T. J. (1993), 'Unemployment and Property Crime: Not a Simple Relationship', **52** *American Journal of Economics and Sociology*, 413-415.

Zimring, Franklin E. (1972), 'The Medium is the Message: Firearm Caliber as a Determinant of Death from Assault', **1** *Journal of Legal Studies*, 97-123.

Zimring, Franklin E. (1975), 'Firearms and Federal Law: The Gun Control Act of 1968', **4** *Journal of Legal Studies*, 133-198.

Zimring, Franklin E. (1977), 'Determinants of the Death Rate from Robbery: A Detroit Time Study', **6** *Journal of Legal Studies*, 317-323.

Zimring, Franklin E. (1984), 'Youth Homicide in New York: A Preliminary Analysis', **13** *Journal of Legal Studies*, 81-99.

Zimring, Franklin E. and Zuehl, James (1986), 'Victim Injury and Death in Urban Robbery: A Chicago Study', **15** *Journal of Legal Studies*, 1-40.

8200
ALTERNATIVE SANCTIONS. CRUEL SANCTIONS

Bibliography Collected by the Editors

Adams, Michael (1994), 'Heroin vom Staat - Kollektiver Wahnsinn oder das gesuchte Konzept zur Zerstörung des Drogenmarktes? (Provision of Heroin by the State - Social Madness or a Concept to Destroy the Drug Market?)', **März** *Zeitschrift für Rechtspolitik*, 106-111.

Adelstein, Richard P. (1979), 'Informational Paradox and the Pricing of Crime: Capital Sentencing Standards in Economic Perspective', **70** *Journal of Criminal Law and Criminology*, 281-298.

Avio, Kenneth L. (1979), 'Capital Punishment in Canada: A Time-Series Analysis of the Deterrent Hypothesis', **12** *Canadian Journal of Economics*, 647-676.

Avio, Kenneth L. (1987a), 'Clemency in Economic and Retributive Models of Punishment', **7** *International Review of Law and Economics*, 79-88.

Avio, Kenneth L. (1987b), 'The Quality of Mercy: Exercise of the Royal Prerogative in Canada', **13** *Canadian Public Policy*, 366-379.

Avio, Kenneth L. (1988a), 'Measurement Errors and Capital Punishment', **20** *Applied Economics*, 1253-1262.

Avio, Kenneth L. (1988b), 'Capital Punishment: Statistical Evidence and Constitutional Issues', **30** *Canadian Journal of Criminology*, 331-349.

Avio, Kenneth L. (1990), 'Retribution, Wealth Maximization, and Capital Punishment: A Law and Economics Approach', **19** *Stetson Law Review*, 373-409.

Avio, Kenneth L. (1993), 'Economic, Retributive and Contractarian Conceptions of Punishment', **12** *Law and Philosophy*, 249-286.

Avio, Kenneth L. (1995), 'Economic, Contractarian and Discourse Arguments against Efficient Torture', in Peczenik, Aleksander and Karlsson, Mikael M. (eds), *Archives on Rights and Social Philosophy 58, 'Law, Justice and the State:I'*, Stuttgart, Franz Steiner, 265-272.

Bartling, Hartwig (1974), 'Zur Ökonomie der Kriminalitätsbekämpfung. Eine Integration der Resozialisierung in die Kriminalökonomie (On the Economics of Criminal Policy: An Integration of Resocialization)', *Zeitschrift für Wirtschafts- und Sozialwissenschaften*, 313-333.

Benson, Bruce L. (1984), 'Guns for Protection and Other Private Sector Responses to the Fear of Violent Crime', in Kates, Don, Jr (ed.), *Firearms and Violence: Issues of Regulation*, Cambridge, MA, Ballinger, 329-356.

Benson, Bruce L. (1986), 'Guns for Protection and Other Private Sector Responses to Government's Failure to Control Increasing Violent Crime', **8** *Journal of Libertarian Studies*, 75-109.

Benson, Bruce L. (1986), 'The Lost Victim and Other Failures of the Public Law Experiment', **9** *Harvard Journal of Law and Public Policy*, 399-427.

Benson, Bruce L. (1992), 'The Development of Criminal Law and Its Enforcement: Public Interest or Political Transfers', **3** *Journal des Economistes et des Etudes Humaines*, 79-108.

Benson, Bruce L. (1994), 'Are Public Goods Really Common Pools: Considerations of the Evolution of Policing and Highways in England', **39** *Economic Inquiry*, 249-271.

Benson, Bruce L. (1995a), 'Appendix Oakland, Independent Institute', in Brakel, Samuel Jan (ed.), *Prisons and Corrections*, Independent Policy Report.

Benson, Bruce L. (1995b), *Privatization in Criminal Justice*, Independent Policy Report, Oakland, Independent Institute.

Benson, Bruce L. (1996), 'Restitution in Theory and in Practice', **12** *Journal of Libertarian Studies*, 75-98.

Benson, Bruce L. and Rasmussen, David W. (1991), 'The Relationship Between Illicit Drug Enforcement Policy and Property Crimes', **9** *Contemporary Policy Issues*, 106-115.

Benson, Bruce L. and Rasmussen, David W. (1992), *Illinois' War on Drugs: Some Unintended Consequences*, Heartland Policy Study, Chicago, Heartland Institute, No. 48.

Benson, Bruce L. and Rasmussen, David W. (1995), *Illicit Drugs and Crime*, Independent Policy Report, Oakland, Independent Institute.

Benson, Bruce L. and Rasmussen, David W. (1995), 'Crime and Punishment', in Denslow, David A., Scoggins, J.F. and Shermyen, Anne (eds), *The Economy of Florida*, Gainesville, FL, Bureau of Economic and Business Research, 99-116.

Benson, Bruce L., Kim, Iljoong, Rasmussen, David W. and Zuehlke, Thomas W. (1993), 'An Economic Analysis of Recidivism Among Drug Offenders', **60** *Southern Economic Journal*, 169-183.

Benson, Bruce L., Rasmussen, David W. and Sollars, David L. (1995), 'Police Bureaucrats, Their Incentives, and the War on Drugs', **83** *Public Choice*, 21-45.

Bergstrom, T. (ed.) (1990), 'On the Economics of Crime and Confiscation', **4(3)** *Journal of Economic Perspectives*, 171-178.

Cameron, Samuel (1989), 'On the Welfare Economics of Capital Punishment', **28** *Australian Economic Papers*, 253-266.

Cameron, Samuel (1993), 'The Demand for Capital Punishment', **13** *International Review of Law and Economics*, 47-59.

Cassone, Alberto and Marchese, Carla (1995), 'Tax Amnesties as Special Sales Offers: the Italian Experience', **50** *Public Finance/Finances Publiques*, 51-66.

Chressanthis, George A. (1989), 'Capital Punishment and the Deterrent Effect Revisited: Recent Time Series Econometric Evidence', **18(2)** *Journal of Behavioral Economics*, 81-97.

Clarf, Stevens H., Freeman, Jean L. and Koch, Gary G. (1976), 'Bail Risk: A Multivariate Analysis', **5** *Journal of Legal Studies*, 341-385.

Cloninger, Dale O. (1987), 'Capital Punishment and Deterrence: A Revision', **16(4)** *Journal of Behavioral Economics*, 55-57.

Cook, Philip J. (1977), 'Punishment and Crime: A Critique of Current Findings Concerning the Preventative Effects of Punishment', **41(1)** *Law and Contemporary Problems*, 164-209.

Cover, James Peery and Thistle, Paul D. (1988), 'Time Series, Homicide, and the Deterrent Effect of Capital Punishment', **54** *Southern Economic Journal*, 615-622.

Daniel, S. (1979), 'Social Science and Death Penalty Cases', **1** *Law and Policy Quarterly*, 336-372.

Donohue, John J. III (1981), *An Evaluation of the Constitutionality of S. 114, the Proposed Federal Death Penalty Statute*, Hearings before the U.S. Senate Judiciary Committee.

Ehrlich, Isaac (1975), 'The Deterrent Effect of Capital Punishment: A Question of Life and Death', **65** *American Economic Review*, 397-417.

Ehrlich, Isaac (1981), 'On the Usefulness of Controlling Individuals: An Economic Analysis of Rehabilitation, Incapacitation and Deterrence', **71** *American Economic Review*, 307-332.

Ehrlich, Isaac and Gibbons, Joel C. (1977), 'On the Measurement of the Deterrent Effect of Capital Punishment and the Theory of Deterrence', **6** *Journal of Legal Studies*, 35-50.

Ehrlich, Isaac and Randall, Mark (1977), 'Fear of Deterrence: A Critical Evaluation of the "Report of the Panel on Research on Deterrent and Incapacitative Effects"', **6** *Journal of Legal Studies*, 293-316.

Friedman, David D. (1981), 'Reflections on Optimal Punishment or: Should the Rich Pay Higher Fines?', **3** *Research in Law and Economics*, 185-205.

Garland, David (1990), *Punishment in Modern Society: A Study in Social Theory*, Chicago, University of Chicago Press.

Garoupa, Nuno (1996), 'Prison, Parole and the Criminal Justice Act 1991', **18** *Research in Law and Economics*.

Grogger, Jeffrey (1990), 'The Deterrent Effect of Capital Punishment: An Analysis of Daily Homicide Counts', **85** *Journal of the American Statistical Association*, 295-303.

Kan, Steven S. (1996), 'Corporal Punishments and Optimal Incapacitation', **15** *Journal of Legal Studies*, 121-130.

Kaplow, Louis (1990), 'A Note on the Optimal Use of Nonmonetary Sanctions', **42** *Journal of Public Economics*, 245-247.

Landes, William M. (1973), 'The Bail System: An Economic Approach', **2** *Journal of Legal Studies*, 79-105.

Lang, Kevin and Bell, Duran (1987), 'An Economic Model of the Intake Disposition of Juvenile Offenders', **32** *Journal of Public Economics*, 79-99.

Langbein, John H. (1976), 'The Historical Origins of the Sanction of Imprisonment for Serious Crime', **5** *Journal of Legal Studies*, 35-60.

Lempert, Richard O. (1981), 'Desert and Deterrence: An Assessment of the Moral Basis for Capital Punishment', **79** *Michigan Law Review*, 1177-1231.

Lott, John R., Jr (1990), 'The Effect of Conviction on the Legitimate Income of Criminals', **34** *Economic Letters*, 381-385.

Macho-Stadler, I. (1987), 'Contratos Basados en Mecanismos de Control y Sanciones Severas: Modelización y Limitaciones (Contracts Based on Monitoring and Severe Punishment)', **4(2)** *Revista Española de Economía*, 291-310.

Macho-Stadler, I. (1993), 'Penalties within the Moral Hazard Problem', **44(3)** *Metroeconomica*, 239-257.

McAleer, Michael and Veall, Michael R. (1989), 'How Fragile are Fragile Inferences? A Re-evaluation of the Deterrent Effect of Capital Punishment', **71** *Review of Economics and Statistics*, 99-106.

Miceli, Thomas J. (1994), 'Prison and Parole: Minimizing the Cost of Non-monetary Sanctions as Deterrents', **16** *Research in Law and Economics*, 197-211.

Michaels, Robert J. (1976), 'Noncriminal Deviance and Mental Hospitalization: Economic Theory and Evidence', **5** *Journal of Legal Studies*, 387-433.

Myers, Samuel L., Jr (1981), 'The Economies of Bail Jumping', **10** *Journal of Legal Studies*, 381-392.

Palmer, John P. (1977), 'Economic Analysis of the Deterrent Effect of Punishment: A Review', **14** *Journal of Research in Crime and Delinquency*, 4-21.

Posner, Richard A. (1980), 'Retribution and Related Concepts of Punishment', **9** *Journal of Legal Studies*, 71-92.

Rasmussen, David W. and Benson, Bruce L. (eds) (1994), *The Economic Anatomy of a Drug War: Criminal Justice in the Commons*, Lanham, MD, Rowman and Littlefield..

Rasmussen, David W., Benson, Bruce L. and Sollars, David L. (1993), 'Spatial Competition in Illicit Drug Markets: The Consequences of Increased Drug Enforcement', **23** *Review of Regional Studies*, 219-236.

Schneider, A.L. and Ervin, L. (1990), 'Specific Deterrence, Rational Choice, and Decision Heuristics: Applications in Juvenile Justice', **71** *Social Science Quarterly*, 585-601.

Shavell, Steven (1985), 'Criminal Law and the Optimal Use of Nonmonetary Sanctions as a Deterrent', **85** *Columbia Law Review*, 1232-1262.

Shavell, Steven (1987), 'A Model of Optimal Incapacitation', **77** *American Economic Review*, 107-110.

Shavell, Steven (1987), 'The Optimal Use of Nonmonetary Sanctions as a Deterrent', **77** *American Economic Review*, 584-592.

Sollars, David L., Benson, Bruce L. and Rasmussen, David W. (1994), 'Drug Enforcement and Deterrence of Property Crime Among Local Jurisdictions', **22** *Public Finance Quarterly*, 22-45.

Votey, Harold L., Jr (1979), 'Detention of Heroin Addicts, Job Opportunities, and Deterrence', **8** *Journal of Legal Studies*, 585-606.

Wolpin, Kenneth I. (1978), 'Capital Punishment and Homicide in England: A Summary of Results', **68** *American Economic Review. Papers and Proceedings*, 422-427.

8300
THE ECONOMICS OF PRISONS

Kenneth L. Avio
Professor of Economics, University of Victoria

Abstract

This chapter scans the English language research on prisons published since Becker's (1968) seminal paper. After first describing the economic nature of prison and parole, issues concerning comparative institutional analysis and organizational design are discussed, including the role of private prisons. Empirical evidence on production functions for prisons, recidivism and offender rehabilitation programs is reviewed. A brief overview of policy issues and suggestions for future research concludes the survey.
JEL classification: K14
Keywords: Economics of Crime, Prisons, Corrections, Recidivism, Rehabilitation

1. Introduction

From a public policy perspective, the normative theory of the economics of crime may be interpreted in terms of the following questions: (1) How many resources should be devoted to the criminal justice system? (2) How should those resources be allocated between the various branches of the system (police, courts, and so on)? (3) How should each branch allocate its resources amongst competing uses? Conceptually these questions are addressed by simultaneously choosing values of policy control variables to minimize the overall social cost of crime, defined as the (net) direct harm from offenses plus the cost of operating the criminal justice system, subject to the various subsystem production functions and the supply of offenses functions (Becker, 1968). This chapter highlights the third question in the efficiency hierarchy as applied to prisons (correctional institutions), with explicit consideration given to the institutional framework within which the question is posed.

Alternatives exist to the model alluded to in the previous paragraph. Ehrlich (1982) permits goals such as retribution to be reflected in the social cost function, with the degree of retribution related to the number of unpunished offenders and to the severity of their crimes (also see Miceli, 1991). Other economists (notably Shoup, 1964 and Thurow, 1970) emphasize conflicts between efficiency and equity in the provision of protection services. The optimization framework itself is inconsistent with the classical retributive justification of punishment. Adam Smith ([1791] 1976, pp. 79, 87-91) suggestively remarks that the private demand for punishment is independent of any consideration of social advantage. In contrast to economic models, Kantian inspired retributive ('just desert') models and their cousins (for example, the 'restorative' theory of Cragg, 1992; the Rawlsian-inspired 'rectification' theory of Adler, 1991; the 'restitutive' theory of Barnett, 1977, 1998, Ch. 8, 10, 11) generally argue that punishment can and must be justified independent of the consequences as measured in a social cost function (Duff, 1986, 1996). Economic and retributive models each have difficulty rationalizing certain policies adopted or at least acknowledged by most modern penal systems: economic prescriptions appear inconsistent with constitutional constraints on cruel and unusual punishments; classical retributive models specify punishments which may be insufficient for deterrence. Constitutional contractarian models applied to punishment can rationalize independent constraints on social cost minimization (Avio, 1993b), and will be implicitly assumed in what follows.

A seemingly natural way to organize this survey is in accordance with the individual purposes of imprisonment: incapacitation, rehabilitation, specific deterrence (the deterrent effect on released offenders of having served an imprisonment term), general deterrence and retribution. The problem is that the literature cannot be easily sorted in this way (consider, for example, how the topic of prison privatization might fit within such a framework). The alternative adopted here is to organize the survey in terms of the 'operational' topics treated in the literature, beginning with the economic nature of prisons and parole. Issues concerning comparative institutional analysis and organizational design are then discussed, followed by various empirical topics including production functions for correctional institutions, recidivism (a variously defined measure related to the criminal activity of released inmates), offender rehabilitation programs, and labor markets for former prison inmates. An overview of policy issues concludes the survey. Discussion is limited for the most part to research by economists and/or to authors taking a law and economic perspective. The reader is forewarned that general deterrence is not systematically covered here, as this would entail surveying the vast theoretical and empirical literature on offender supply functions, and undertaking that would greatly increase the lenght and scope of this chapter.

2. Prisons Conceptualized

Prisons provide protection services to society. In principle, these services could be replaced or supplemented by a less resource absorbing system of monetary penalties and/or corporal punishments, the sanctions of choice throughout most of human history. But constitutional constraints in modern democracies limit corporal punishments, and the wealth constraints of most offenders relative to the social value of the harm they create renders sole reliance on fines inefficient (Polinsky and Shavell, 1984; Shavell, 1985, 1987a, 1987b; Garoupa, 1997). Moreover, Levitt (1997) notes that the authorities may not even know the wealth level of offenders, and may be unable to distinguish between individuals with different subjective disutilities of prison terms. This latter fact is important because the threat of imprisonment must ultimately lie behind any fine. Since the typical criminal has a relatively low disutility of prison term, 'the fine must be low relative to the jail sentence to be incentive compatible' (ibid., 1997, p. 181). But relatively low fines will induce other types of agents to become offenders. Nevertheless, a case can be made that fines are underutilized in Western societies, although less so in Europe than in the US. Benson (1996) favors a system of fines as restitution for victims. He argues that the coerced supply of offender labor services may overcome the wealth constraint (at a cost), while the incentive for victims to cooperate in the prosecution of offenders increases the effectiveness of the police and courts. Conversely, convicted offenders may be induced to commit more crimes to pay off their initial fine, and the promise of fines as restitution may lead to overzealous prosecution by victims. For the remainder of this essay, the relative efficiency of incarceration as a criminal sanction is assumed.

Modern prisons may be viewed as multi-product firms providing incarceration days and rehabilitation opportunities (Avio, 1973). The threat of incarceration has a putative general deterrent effect on prospective offenders (Lewis, 1986) whereas incarceration prevents inmates from committing crimes against those outside the prison walls. This incapacitation effect may be partly offset by an increased number of 'new' criminals if the returns to crime increase as incarcerated offenders are temporarily removed from the criminal market (Cook, 1977; Ehrlich, 1981). The rehabilitation effect acknowledges that a convicted offender's proclivity for crime may decrease as a result of the incarceration experience, as well as by virtue of the fact that age has an independent effect upon criminality. The school for crime syndrome, criminal stigmatization and the natural depreciation of human capital while offenders are incarcerated all pull in the opposite direction. Thus the rehabilitation effect may more properly be labelled a 'training' effect, which from a social standpoint may be either positive or negative. Insofar as this is forecasted by potential offenders, the actual discounted expected costs of engaging in current crime may increase or decrease. This result is tempered by the widely held belief that offenders as a whole tend to discount the future more heavily than non-offenders (Herrnstein, 1983; Wilson, 1983, pp. 223-249; Wilson and Herrnstein, 1985, pp. 166-172, 416-422; Gill, 1994).

3. Parole

Miceli (1994) presents a model of the prison where the optimal lengths of the incarceration and parole periods for individual offenders are chosen by a central authority. The goal is to minimize the cost of a given level of deterrence, conditional upon a predetermined probability of conviction. Parole reduces social costs by prompting prison inmates to behave and by decreasing the number of person-days of incarceration supplied. On the other hand, a system utilizing parole and/or probation reduces the costs of crime to potential offenders and reduces the incapacitation effect. The efficient punishment balances these costs and benefits, and typically requires a period of imprisonment followed by supervised release, as opposed to either probation (immediate release) or unconditional release following incarceration. Miceli demonstrates that the socially optimal policy varies across individual offenders. Garoupa (1996) generalizes these results in a model which includes the net gains to offenders in the social welfare calculation.

The information and coordination requirements in the Miceli model are substantial. This point is brought home in the recognition that the model may be understood in terms of either a determinate or an indeterminate sentencing regime. (In the latter, the trial judge sentences offenders to prison for an indefinite period; parole authorities determine when the inmate is to be released.) The behavior of all agents is invariant to the institutional framework given the rational expectations assumption: potential offenders know *prior to committing offenses* the incarceration/parole mix they will receive if convicted, and the effort they will exert to comply with prison rules. Introducing informational imperfections in the form of a failure on the part of the authorities to correctly perceive the good behaviour efforts of confined inmates does not change the basic results of the Miceli model (Garoupa, 1996, p. 26). An analysis assuming a random component in the relationship between good behavior effort and subsequent proclivity to recidivate would presumably yield similar qualitative implications.

Miceli concludes that a grid-style sentencing scheme such as that promulgated by the US Sentencing Commission, which leaves little room for consideration of the full range of offender-specific characteristics, increases the cost of providing a given level of deterrence. These costs are defined to exclude consideration of retribution and disparities in punishment, factors which in part motivate grid-type sentencing systems (Parker and Block, 1989; Parker, 1989; see Easterbrook, 1983, for a market-analogy argument favoring discretion in sentencing). In a somewhat different context, Garoupa's (1996) model is used to examine the effects of the UK Criminal Justice Act, 1991, which raised the upper and lower bounds for the proportion of the sentence that may be served on parole. The social welfare effects of the law are found to be ambiguous.

Lewis (1979, 1983), in an attempt to provide an empirically feasible guide to parole officials, seeks to establish the optimal parole period given exogenously determined conviction rates *and* original sentence lengths. The maximand consists of 'the expected cost to society ... during the period of the original sentence as a function of the number of months served prior to parole' (Lewis, 1979, p. 382). The model is simulated under a range of assumptions concerning the impact of time served in prison on the rate at which released offenders return to crime (the recidivism rate) while on parole.

Neither Lewis (1979, 1983), Miceli (1994) nor Garoupa (1996) account for the impact and effects of inmate training on the rate at which released offenders return to crime. This consideration requires abandoning Becker's (1968) static framework, and including social investments in inmate training as a new choice variable (Avio, 1975). Limited progress has been made with highly stylized two-period models of punishment (Rubenstein, 1980; Davis, 1988; Polinsky and Rubinfeld, 1991; Nash, 1991; Burnovski and Safra, 1994). These papers explicitly or implicitly assume that punishment is by fine, and ignore recidivistic behaviour. The theme of dynamic efficiency and recidivism is taken up in Flinn (1986) and Leung (1995), but in-prison investments in human capital and their impact on recidivism remain unanalyzed. A dynamic general equilibrium model has yet to be developed.

4. Organizational Design

Several commentators note that the current decentralized criminal justice system is not expected to be efficient. Insofar as the decision variables at issue (overall prison budget, sentence lengths, training opportunities, parole release) are chosen by different decision centers, each with a different mandate, it is unlikely that the resulting product mix would be efficient. With the legislature setting the overall prison budget and the courts and parole authorities determining the level of confinement days, prisons are left with zero degrees of freedom in selecting the level of support that affects post-release behavior. The product mix could be efficient if the courts and parole authorities were to select appropriate sentence lengths for the given budget. But since the mandate of the courts is weighted more toward the provision of retribution (indeed, in some regimes judges are determined by popular vote), and the parole authorities have limited flexibility in determining the actual length of stay of prisoners, the decreed sentence lengths and consequent level of rehabilitation services would not in general be expected to be efficient for any given budget.

A system of indeterminate sentences alleviates the coordination and informational problems inherent in a decentralized penal system (Avio, 1973), while remaining consistent with the efficiency thrust of the Miceli (1994) model.

The confinement and training decisions become centralized, and maximum incentives for offenders to avail themselves of rehabilitation opportunities are provided. The general rejection of such programs for all but repeat violent offenders is based upon several factors: the difficulties with protecting the civil rights of inmates under such a regime; the frustrations arising from several decades of inconclusive research on inmate rehabilitation; a perceived lack of success in predicting recidivism on an individual offender basis; and an increased emphasis on retribution as the primary goal of punishment.

Former UK Home Secretary Howard (1996) proposed a hybrid determinate/indeterminate sentencing scheme reminiscent of 'three strikes and you're out' regimes while retaining the benefits of 'marginal deterrence' (Stigler, 1970). Under this scheme, repeat violent offenders would automatically receive life sentences, while the trial judge sets a minimum period intended to satisfy the need for retribution and deterrence. Once that period is served, penal authorities would determine whether and when the inmate is released. Upon release, offenders would be subject to recall for the rest of their lives.

An earlier proposal for a two-part penalty scheme was proposed by Tabasz (1974) to alleviate the retribution-rehabilitation conflict. The first part of the sentence targets retribution. It would be determinate, independent of offender characteristics, of relatively short duration and served in an environment devoid of amenities. The offender would then pass on to a different environment to serve out the second, indeterminate stage directed to the rehabilitation goal. Again the purpose of the indeterminate sentence is to align the incentives of the offender with society's goal of minimizing the overall time-discounted social costs of crime. Tabasz suggests that the condition for release be some readily visible sign of achievement on the part of the offender such as the attainment of a definable educational or vocational training goal.

One difficulty with two-part penalty schemes is that the various penal functions (retribution, rehabilitation, deterrence) do not map separately into the determinate and indeterminate portions of the sentence. Any 'hardening' of the inmate during the first stage would presumably have to be rectified during the second, and since loss of liberty represents an important component of incarcerative punishment, the retributive function is in play during both phases. If the first phase is thought to fulfill the offender's debt to society, then imposition of the second may be constitutionally impermissible. Of course, this latter objection may apply to any sentencing scheme that incorporates goals other than retribution, a term (like 'debt to society') of art.

Roper (1986) proposes a different solution to the decentralization-coordination problem. He conceptualizes prison output as the delivery of a crime-free offender over the period of the court-rendered sentence. Taking this period as a constraint, Roper's prison decides whether to keep the offender in custody over the entire sentence or to release him early. As Roper puts it, 'the essence of the [prison's] role [is] to assess the risks uniquely associated with the probability of a given offender reoffending' (ibid., p. 91). The author goes on to suggest that the prison enter into contracts with prospective parolees; the prisoner agrees to desist from criminal activities for the duration of the sentence, while the authorities provide financial support, rehabilitation services, employment assistance, and so on, and release the inmate on parole. If the released offender violates a contract term, then he or she is liable not only for the new criminal charge, if any, but also for a civil contracts suit. The argument is presented in terms of a private (for-profit) prison, but a state operated prison could function in the same manner.

While Roper's proposal represents an interesting attempt to correct the principal-agent problem between the state and the offender, as well as the decentralization problem, substantial difficulties remain. First, since most prisoners are judgement proof, the contract remedy must stipulate a return to prison. This penalty would be independent of any sentence levied for the crime causing the contract violation. But it is unlikely that the courts would permit such a remedy. As an alternative, the contract could promise a financial reward subject to forfeit. This avoids the dubious remedy of confinement, but may serve to entice prospective offenders into committing crime in the first place. Second, independent of remedy, the courts may not recognize the validity of such contracts; what economists define as a *voluntary* transaction may not fall within the range recognized by the courts, given that the offender is bargaining for his freedom and *ipso facto* is under duress.

Nardulli (1984) and Giertz and Nardulli (1985) take up the decentralization issue from the perspective of the fiscal federalism literature (also see Benson and Wollan (1989) and Benson (1990, 1994a), where the common pool/property rights nature of the decentralization problem is identified). These authors view judges as rendering inefficiently severe sentences as the result of a free-rider problem emanating from a misalignment of incentives and cost-bearing. Citizens of the local government derive benefits (protection and retribution) from longer sentences, which happen to be specified by local authorities. However, the costs of providing prison services may be partly shifted from one sentencing jurisdiction onto another via prison financing by a senior level of government. Thus the local demand for confinement is not fully constrained by the cost of delivery. The tendency to prison overcrowding in the federal part of the system, and underbuilding in the local part, follows directly.

The short-run solution proposed by Giertz and Nardulli (1985) is to allocate total available prison space to individual sentencing jurisdictions, while continuing with the current division of cost and sentencing responsibilities. This would to an extent defuse free-riding behavior, but one could imagine disagreeable (and constitutionally questionable) inequities in sentencing arising from the constraint. For example, suppose only shoplifters are predicted to appear before a court during some period, so that relatively harsh sentences are compatible with the given space allocation. Then if an armed robber unexpectedly appears in court, he will either receive a comparatively light sentence or else one of the previously convicted shoplifters must be released earlier than expected. Unless judges accurately forecast the distribution of upcoming cases, a shortage or surplus of prison space would develop, leading to disparities in sentences actually served for offenders committing the same crime. This argument could apply to a senior administrative jurisdiction as well, but the greater number of cases reduces the risk of prediction errors. The *long-run* solution offered by Giertz and Nardulli is to hold local jurisdictions responsible for their full share of the cost of incarceration. An alternative is for the senior fiscal authority to impose a mandatory grid sentencing scheme upon all courts within its jurisdiction, thus to some extent negating the free-rider problem.

Gillespie (1983) proposes a market for prison space administered by a centralized correctional authority. This market would facilitate the efficient transfer of prison space from local jurisdictions with excess supply to those with excess demand. Jurisdictions comprised of citizens with relatively heavy demand for long-term sentences backed by a willingness to pay would purchase access to penal space from other jurisdictions. Not only would the pricing mechanism overcome the short-run deficits or surpluses but the market-determined price would signal the social value of new prison space, and hence rationalize the construction of new correctional facilities. Gillespie argues that equity concerns can be addressed by altering the initial allocation according to whatever equity criterion is adopted. With appropriately identified prices and initial allocations, this system appears similar to one giving local authorities a portion of the state budget to be spent by them as they desire: on penal space at the state institution, on space at the local level, or on some other public expenditure (Nardulli, 1984).

Would the Gillespie proposal lead to the same results as a centralized sentencing and prison-supply agency? Probably not, simply because income distribution across the local political units would affect the demands for prison space. For given sentences, the various market-oriented systems should cost less than the standard first-come, first-served, free-rider system. But regardless of the efficiency implications, introducing a market for prison space would predictably exacerbate inequities in sentencing across jurisdictions. Other things equal, low-income sub-units would presumably impose relatively short sentences and sell their space allocations to high-income sub-units, which would impose relatively severe sentences. A general equilibrium formulation of Gillespie's model would also have to consider the possibility that offenders might change their geographical areas of operation in response to differential expected punishments.

5. Privatization

A more fundamental argument for the inefficiency of publicly-operated prisons stems directly from the theory of bureaucracy/public choice literature. Profit-maximization, and its concomitant for non-market production, cost minimization, may not be adopted as the operational goal of the public entity. Some models of bureaucratic behavior assume or imply cost efficiency, whereas other do not. Niskanen (1971) argues that bureaus seek to maximize bureau size, and hence overproduce; but whatever output they provide will be at least cost if the bureau is budget-constrained. Other models (for example, Williamson, 1964) posit that bureau heads will optimize with respect to private objectives, and therefore cost minimization cannot be expected. The debate over private prisons typically draws on the latter genre of models, deemphasizing decentralization and informational difficulties. Privatization and the profit motive, it is argued, removes the wedge between output and returns for public employees, thus reducing agency costs.

The standard private prison contract bases remuneration for the corporate prison upon the number of person-days of confinement supplied, subject to the provision of some standard level of amenities. Thus the corporate prison has no incentive to provide rehabilitation opportunities, except insofar as the latter act to decrease the current cost of confinement (Schmidt and Witte, 1984, pp. 345-346). If rehabilitation activities affect post-release criminality, then regardless of market structure the standard per-diem contract is inferior to one that pays the private prison in accordance with the recidivism success of its releasees (Avio, 1993a). Appropriately designed remuneration schemes harness the power of the market to stimulate the discovery of imprisonment methods that minimize long-run social costs.

The argument has been extended to incorporate the possibility that the corporate prison operating under the traditional remuneration scheme might perversely seek to stimulate recidivism (Gentry, 1986; Avio, 1991). Under the standard contract provisions, the value of the prison corporation depends to an extent upon the continued influx of inmates, which could be enhanced by (clandestinely) providing negative training. A flow of new offenders sufficient to keep individual prisons operating at the minimum of their average cost curves, while simultaneously requiring the construction of new facilities, would maximize profit opportunities. This argument is conditional upon the exercise of market power. Established prison firms would seem to be in an advantageous position to capture managerial and construction contracts for new prisons. Of course, the incentive structure embedded in the public prison system may be equally inimical to social welfare.

Whether the weak or the strong form of the argument against per-diem contracts is applied, the debate over private prisons exhibits a kind of symmetry:

private prisons are socially superior to public prisons because the former seek efficiencies in the drive to maximize profits; public prisons are superior to private prisons because they are *not* driven by the profit motive. Some privatization advocates recognize the difficulty with the standard prison contract, but attempts to explain away this quasi-paradox are unsatisfactory and reveal the inconsistency: Logan (1987, p. 39) argues that rather than maximizing profits, private prisons really seek to maximize convenience subject to some minimal profit constraint; Brakel (1988, p. 34, n.92) argues that line employees of the private prison, whose actions have the greatest potential to affect post-release behavior, are too distant from profit centers to act in accordance with the profit motive. But in the same breath, adherence to the profit motive with the attendant efficiencies is given as the overarching rationale for prison privatization.

The increasing popularity of private prisons in policy circles is attributable to more than the general privatization fashion alone. The modern conceptualization of prisons as a benign warehouse has replaced the 'corrections' model in professional circles. This follows the retrenchment on treatment oriented programs in the 1980s. The prison-as-warehouse conceptualization is consistent with both the static neoclassical and the Kantian-inspired retributive models discussed earlier. In the former, prisons are simply the institutions society employs to effect the restriction of liberty necessary to attain the efficient amount of crime through deterrence and incapacitation. In Kantian retributive models, justice requires punishment in a rights-respecting environment; the moral autonomy of the individual demands that no attempt be made to 'force' rehabilitation. The underlying function of prisons remains the same, a function that could equally well be provided by an institution operating under market incentives.

Non-economic arguments may ultimately decide the scope that private prisons are allowed to play. A feeling of unease accompanies the thought of government delegating to private individuals the authority to punish (Dilulio, 1988, 1990). Regulations such as those included in the American Bar Association's Model Code and Model Statute for Private Incarceration may be necessary to protect the civil liberties of offenders (Robbins, 1989). Benson (1990, 1994b) extends the argument. The potential for success with prison privatization in terms of technological efficiency is so great, that once bureaucratic resistance and other obstacles to private prisons are overcome, society may increasingly come to rely on incarceration as a means of social control. For example, special interest groups may press for the expanded imprisonnment of illegal aliens to control labor supply (Benson, 1994b, pp. 66-72). Prison privatization then poses a threat to both overall allocative efficiency and to individual liberty.

To date, the empirical evidence comparing private and public management of adult secure facilities has been scant and somewhat unsatisfactory. The number of surveys of these studies (McDonald, 1990; Thomas and Logan, 1993; Sellers, 1993, Ch. 4; Sichor, 1995, Ch. 9; USGAO, 1991, 1996) nearly equals the number of studies, simultaneously reflecting the youthfulness of the private prison industry (the first modern adult secure facility went under private management in 1983), the difficulty of the research, and interest in the topic. The studies typically consist of cost and quality comparisons of matched institutions (see, for example, Edwards, 1996). Thomas (1996) notes that comparisons of similarly designed facilities will not necessarily account for the cost-saving innovations that private prisons should bring, as design is itself a major source of efficiencies. Also, recidivism rates of the various institutions are typically ignored (see Hatry, 1989, for an exception). Econometric work on private prisons has yet to be undertaken. Given the growth of the industry (from fewer than 3,000 [rated capacity] beds under contract in 1983 to over 84,000 in the US, UK and Australia at the end of 1996), the time is ripe for sophisticated quantitative research.

6. Linear Programming Models

The empirical test of propositions relating to correctional institutions requires *a priori* modelling. Although unmodified linear programming imposes severe technology constraints, interesting questions can be addressed using this technique. In the tradition of a systems analysis of prisons (Blumstein and Larson, 1969), Tabasz (1975) constructs a linear programming model of the US Federal Bureau of Prisons. The goal is to allocate different types of offenders to different types of institutions and to different sentence lengths in a manner that maximizes net social benefits subject to the capacity of the prison system and the flow of convicted offenders. In all, 2,700 decision variables are specified. Only benefits to incapacitation and rehabilitation are imputed, and the capital costs of prisons are ignored. The results indicate that prison resources should be concentrated on relatively young and dangerous offenders: inmates over 45 years of age are assigned to 'probation' (immediate release). The model cannot directly indicate how many resources should be allocated to the prison system, but it does give an approximation to the benefit-cost ratio potentially generated by prisons (8.51 in the 'standard' version of the model applying 1973 data (ibid., p. 129)). This estimate, which at face value rationalizes the build-up in prison capacity that began in the US in the 1970s (Blumstein, 1995), should not be taken too seriously. The relatively primitive nature of the data available to Tabasz required strong assumptions, particularly those related to the rates of crime commission, the social costs of crime, and the rehabilitative effects of incarceration. The methodology also imposes an interpretive constraint: the results do not necessarily reflect actual net benefits attained, but the *potential* benefits if decision variables are chosen optimally. Nonetheless, this study anticipates later attempts to evaluate the prison system as a whole (see Section 12 below).

Linear programming may also be used to identify the relative efficiency levels of individual prisons. The operations research tool known as Data Envelopment Analysis, a non-stochastic frontier methodology, is applied by Ganley and Cubbin (1992, Ch. 5) for this purpose. The underlying linear program is constructed to embody a varying returns to scale technology. Analysis of 33 UK local prisons and remand centers for the financial year 1984-85 suggests that 13 of the establishments were 'technically inefficient relative to the peer prisons on the cost frontier' (ibid., p. 66). On average the operating costs of the inefficient institutions could be reduced by about 12 percent. Prison cost studies comparing this method with the econometric methods discussed below would be helpful.

7. Econometric Models of Prisons

A major policy issue illuminated by economic theory concerns the appropriate size of prisons. For example, in Canada in the 1960s new prisons were built to accommodate about 450 inmates. In the next decade several government reports advocated even smaller institutions. Since little was known about the cost-effectiveness of prisons, this debate occurred in what was largely an empirical vacuum. Conceptualizing the prison as an economic entity leads to traditional cost and production analysis with the potential to systematically address questions such as returns to scale in the provision of prison services.

Block and Ulen (1979) estimate long- and short-run prison cost functions for the state of California using elementary functional forms. The short-run results (using time-series data for each of two maximum security institutions) suggest that average costs are minimized at surprisingly large inmate populations (for example, 5,700 for San Quentin, as estimated over the years 1948-1964 (Block and Ulen, 1979, p. 200)). A 1971-1972 cross-section of jails yields a long-run cost curve indicating approximately constant returns to scale. Both the short- and long-run analyses abstract from the rehabilitative dimension of prison output; expenditures specifically earmarked for rehabilitation are eliminated from the cost data.

Schmidt and Witte (1984) (also see McGuire and Witte, 1978; Trumball and Witte, 1981-82a,1981-82b; Kritzer, 1981-82) present a comprehensive econometric analysis of US federal and California prison systems from the mid- to late-1970s. Short- and long-run average cost functions are derived. The short-run results for each of 22 federal and 8 California prisons are derived from estimated labor demand equations corresponding to homothetic generalized Cobb-Douglas production functions. Several of the cost functions are found to be inconsistent with economic theory. The authors ascribe this result to altered operating methods within given institutions over the sample period. For those institutions conforming to economic theory, the majority are found to have short-run average costs which decrease as inmate populations increase. This finding is particularly robust for older, fortress-type institutions. While economies of scale are indicated, it would be imprudent to draw policy implications concerning the crowded conditions in many institutions today as crowding was not a widespread phenomenon during the sample period. The impact of rehabilitation activities on costs is diverse, and 'may depend critically on the nature of the particular institution being studied' (Schmidt and Witte, 1984, p. 335). The authors summarize their results for the entire sample of federal and California institutions: 'costs generally increase until a certain level of rehabilitative activities is provided and then decline thereafter' (ibid., p. 345). Anecdotal evidence suggests that prison work experience uniquely reduces the level of violence within prisons, probably by fostering a prisoner sub-culture that rewards co-operative behavior (Fleisher, 1989, pp. 26-27; 1995, pp. 262-270). Unfortunately Schmidt and Witte lump prison work experience with educational programs and counselling services in constructing the rehabilitation activities variable (Schmidt and Witte, 1984, p. 305).

A long-run cost function is estimated using pooled quarterly data over the mid-1970s for a subset of six federal institutions found to possess similar technologies. Estimated average costs are asymmetrically U-shaped, with a higher penalty on institutions housing fewer than the efficient capacity of 1075 inmates. In this subset of prisons, rehabilitation activities are found to have no statistically significant impact on long-run average costs. This result is puzzling, especially since all but one of these institutions have short-run cost functions sensitive to this variable. Several service quality variables are found to be significant. The authors conclude that 'the minimum-cost-sized prison will probably house between 700 and 1500 inmates' (Schmidt and Witte, 1984, p. 363) and that 'providing single cells for inmates and rather substantial amounts of living space may actually decrease the cost of operating prisons' (ibid., p. 362).

Taken as a whole, these studies are indicative of the important role that econometric analysis can play in analyzing policy questions related to the management of prisons. Several extensions come easily to mind. Comparison of the costs and technologies of private and public prisons would be helpful in the ongoing privatization debate. Econometric studies of the cost-effectiveness of prison industries should be undertaken. Linking rehabilitation *outcomes* with current costs would enhance the value of the studies. The data requirements for this latter task would be substantial but not impossible, as the next two sections suggest.

8. Statistical Models of Recidivism

Serving time in prison, as well as participating in various prison and post-release programs, may have either a positive or negative effect upon the activities of released prison inmates. Nailing down the specifics of the relationships is clearly an important factor in evaluating overall social policies towards crime as well as in evaluating specific programs for incarcerated and paroled offenders. If, for example, predictions of future behavior of individual convicted offenders prove to be sufficiently reliable, then a program of 'selective incapacitation' becomes feasible, if not ethically acceptable (Greenwood and Turner, 1987). The extensive literature addressing criminal recidivism has for the most part been the preserve of criminologists, sociologists and psychologists. Here the contributions of economists Peter Schmidt and Anne Witte are noted (also see Myers, 1980a, 1983).

In a series of articles (Witte and Schmidt, 1977, 1979; Sickles, Schmidt and Witte, 1979; Schmidt and Witte, 1980, 1989) and books (Schmidt and Witte 1984, 1988), Schmidt and Witte and their associates exhaustively analyze follow-up microdata on releasees from North Carolina prisons. Since the theoretically relevant dependent variables - time devoted to criminal activity and the intensity thereof - cannot be observed, a number of proxy recidivism variables are employed. These include the traditional binary 'success-failure' measure, categories of crimes leading to reconviction, seriousness of crimes leading to reconviction, total length of prison sentences received during the follow-up period, length of time from release to first arrest leading to conviction, and length of time from release to first return to prison. Different statistical models (qualitative variable models, survival time models) are used as appropriate for the different dependent variables studied.

The polytymous logit model is used to analyze a random sample of 641 inmates in North Carolina prisons in 1969 and 1971, with follow-up periods averaging 37 months (Schmidt and Witte, 1984, Ch. 3). The seriousness of criminal activity, as measured by whether the most serious reconviction (if any) was a misdemeanour or a felony, and the type of criminal activity (crime against the person, against property, or 'other', including drug crime) are analyzed with respect to various personal characteristics and histories of individual inmates (excluding, for some unstated reason, time served for the sample sentence). The likelihood of reconviction is found to vary significantly with the number of previous convictions, age at release (older offenders have lower probabilities of reconviction), length of the follow-up period, and alcohol or hard drug use (ibid., p. 45). Surprisingly, none of these same variables are significant predictors of the type and the seriousness of offenses for which reconvictions are obtained. On the other hand, the type and the seriousness of previous offenses are found to be related to the type and seriousness respectively of subsequent convictions, but not the overall probability of reconviction. Consistent with the criminal career syndrome, some evidence of offenders switching from property crime to personal crime is found.

A more refined indicator of the seriousness of new offenses, the total length of time sentenced for recidivist offenses, is analyzed by the same authors (Schmidt and Witte, 1984, Ch. 5) using two samples: that used in the previously reported research, and a cohort group consisting of all individuals released in North Carolina during the first six months of 1975 (25-31 month follow-up). The censored nature of the dependent variable suggests a Tobit analysis. In both samples, the dependent variable is found to vary in the predicted direction with the youthfulness of the offender, a history of alcohol abuse, the number of previous convictions, unsupervised release, and a sample incarceration for a crime against property (Schmidt and Witte, 1984, p. 73). The estimation sample is used to predict the dependent variable for a validation sample. Separating the samples into various race, gender and age groupings substantially improves the prediction reliability for most subgroups, as there appears to be considerable variability in the significance of different explanatory variables across the subgroups. The predicted total time sentenced for the entire validation sample using the best model for each subgroup is insignificantly different from the actual value of total time sentenced, suggesting an important tool for correctional planning. The overall results show the superiority of the more sophisticated models as compared with binary 'success-failure' models.

The second set of models employed by Schmidt and Witte treat survival time - the length of time from release to recidivism. Not only is this variable of interest in itself, but ignoring information on length of time to recidivism (however defined) is statistically inefficient. The authors' extensive analyses (the present discussion is limited to Schmidt and Witte, 1988) utilize various formulations found in the increasingly sophisticated criminogenic literature. Carr-Hill and Carr-Hill (1972) apparently were the first authors to apply survival models in this context, as well as innovations of their own. The data consist of two cohorts of approximately 9,500 individuals each released from all state prisons in North Carolina in separate 12 month periods, with follow-ups ranging from 46 to 81 months. Data limitations, as well as the needs of the correctional authorities supplying the data, dictated the dependent variable: the length of time from release to return to prison. (The length of time from release to first rearrest leading to conviction is analyzed in Schmidt and Witte, 1984, Ch. 7.) Estimation using distributions with monotonic hazard rates proved inadequate. This is unsurprising since recidivism hazard rates first rise and then rather quickly fall. The best overall results apply individual characteristics as explanatory variables to 'split population' models, thereby permitting the probability of recidivism to follow a generating process distinct from that for recidivist survival times. The best fit is found for 'a logit lognormal model, in which the probability of eventual recidivism follows a logit model and the timing of return follows a lognormal distribution' (Schmidt and Witte, 1988, p. 19). Those models which utilize individual characteristics as explanatory variables for each of the two recidivism outcomes yield the following results: race and gender affect the probability of eventual recidivism but not its timing, whereas indicators of the nature of the previous offense affect the timing of recidivism but not its probability (ibid., p. vii); age on release, the number of prior convictions and a history of alcohol abuse affect in the predicted direction both the probability of eventual recidivism and the mean time until recidivism; finally, the length of the sample incarceration increases the probability of a return to crime and shortens survival time. These latter results appear consistent with the school for crime theory (see Myers, 1980a, for a qualitatively similar conclusion with a sample of parolee data) but selectivity bias renders this interpretation somewhat problematic.

The authors recommend the use of non-parametric methods (Cox's proportional hazards model) to first identify the appropriate explanatory variables, and then the use of parametric models to yield the best predictions. The predictions are generally superior to those elsewhere in the literature (Schmidt and Witte, 1988, p. 15), although the use of explanatory variables does not improve predictions for random samples of releasees. Moreover, the authors emphasize that their best models (predicting false positive rates of 47 percent and false negatives of 28 percent) are unsatisfactory for implementing a policy of selective incapacitation. One can conclude that there is value in using sophisticated models in predicting recidivism for random samples of released offenders, but that the models are not yet sufficiently refined for application to individuals.

Schmidt and Witte note that further experimentation with non-linear formulations of the explanatory variables will probably lead to explaining a higher degree of the variation in the dependent variables (about 10 percent in the current study), and thus boost prediction accuracy (Schmidt and Witte, 1988, p.150). Another suggestion is to take more seriously the economic model of crime by including explanatory variables measuring the certainty and severity of punishment as well as environmental variables representing legitimate and illegitimate opportunities. Suppose, for example, that during the follow-up period there is variation across the relevant geographic jurisdictions and/or over time in police activity. Further, suppose that this leads to variation in the objective probability of arrest. The economic model suggests that the pattern of criminal behavior of released inmates as well as that of individuals with no previous criminal record would be affected. Prediction accuracy could be impaired (and the model mispecified) if the standard criminal justice control variables are excluded. Data limitations may intrude (ibid., p. 85). But even if the local communities in which released offenders reside are unobserved, risk and punishment variables can probably be constructed on an aggregated geographical basis for each period during the follow-up. Examples of survival-time recidivism research employing environmental variables are Visher, Lattimore and Linster (1991) studying paroled California youths, and Kim et al., (1993) examining Florida drug offenders. On a more micro level, Schmidt and Witte (1988, pp. 9-11) note that the complexion of their research results could be attributable in part to police and prosecutors targeting offenders with certain personal characteristics, as well as to the characteristics themselves affecting criminal activity. Sorting out the simultaneity problems remains an important part of the research agenda in the economics of prisons.

9. The Evaluation of In-Prison Rehabilitation Programs

Psychologists, criminologists, sociologists and public policy commentators have contributed to the extensive literature on the rehabilitation of convicted offenders. This topic shades into a discussion of the overall causes of crime. No attempt will be made here to address the larger question, nor should the discussion be considered a survey of anything but a select subsample of the rehabilitation literature. The limited number of contributions by economists on the direct evaluation of rehabilitation programs is taken up in this section and the next.

On the important question of research design, laboratory-like experiments comparing outcomes for randomly selected program and control groups are generally not possible in the criminal justice context (some exceptions are discussed below). Researchers typically are forced to resort to quasi-experimental designs, which designate 'a group of individuals (the comparison group) that is as much like the group of program participants studied as possible' (Grizzle and Witte, 1980, p. 259). The difficulty is that subjects in the two groups may differ in some characteristic that affects post-release activities. This dictates that the researcher must have in mind an underlying model of criminal and recidivistic behavior. In this section a quasi-experimental program evaluation is contrasted with one employing a 'predicted-versus-actual' method.

Witte (1977) employs a quasi-experimental design to evaluate a program in which a non-random sample of inmates in North Carolina prisons work on day-passes with various local industries. The sample consists of men on the 'work release' program in 1969 or 1971. The experiences of the evaluation group are compared with those of a nonparticipating group who appear to be equally eligible for the program. Multiple regression techniques are used to correct for differences in personal characteristics across the two samples. The author finds no programmatic impact on the decision to return to crime, but a marked beneficial effect on the seriousness of crimes committed during the follow-up period. This latter result is confirmed by the logit and tobit analyses of Schmidt and Witte (1984, pp. 34-35, 68) utilizing work release as a binary explanatory variable. The results here further indicate that participation in work release is significantly related to neither the type of post-release criminal activity (crime against the person or against property), nor to survival time.

Schmidt and Witte (1979, 1980, 1984, Ch. 8) use a statistical model estimated from a data set consisting of information on all 4,881 inmates released from North Carolina prisons during the first six months of 1975 to evaluate a comprehensive release program for youthful offenders in North Carolina (the Sandhills Vocational Evaluation and Job/Educational Development program). The estimated model is employed to predict criminality indicators for each of the Sandhills participants (489 participants released over the period February 21, 1975 through February 21, 1977); program evaluation proceeds from a comparison of the predicted effects with the actual criminality indicators for participants. The advantage of this 'predicted versus actual' method is that no matched comparison group is needed. But as the authors stress, the reliability of the evaluation depends crucially on the accuracy of the model and on the implicit assumption that the relevant prison unit does not differ significantly 'from the system norm in a way not controlled for by our models' (Schmidt and Witte, 1984, p. 135). Some weak statistical evidence is found suggesting that the Sandhills program reduces the amount of recidivism during the first six months of the follow-up period. (Using a smaller sample from a different estimation, the authors also find that the program reduces the total time sentenced during the follow-up period, that is, the seriousness of follow-up criminal activity (ibid., pp. 130-133.) This study conveys what can be accomplished by way of program evaluation with suitably specified statistical models. In their later study (Schmidt and Witte, 1988, Ch. 8), however, the view is less optimistic. Here an estimated model is again used to predict survival times for nonrepresentative subsamples, including participants in the previously discussed work-release program. The results significantly underpredict recidivism for this group (ibid., p. 138). The authors attribute this not to program effects, but rather to 'work release participants hav[ing] different characteristics than nonparticipants ... our model does not adequately capture the effects of these characteristics on time until recidivism' (ibid., p. 138).

As Schmidt and Witte note, perhaps the safest and most efficient use of the predicted versus actual models is in conjunction with experiments: such models can be used to justify the initiation of costly experimental studies, as well as to indicate the factors that must be controlled. In the event that true- or quasi-experiments are impractical, the predicted versus actual approach provides a relatively low-cost but not altogether reliable alternative. Research refining and systematizing this method is called for.

Turning from methodological to substantive issues, what kinds of in-prison rehabilitative programs work, if any? The 'Nothing Works' doctrine initiated in

Martinson's well-known paper (Martinson, 1974, previewing Lipton, Martinson and Wilks, 1975) ushered in an era of pessimism in penology. After reviewing the results of 231 papers (the majority dealing with programs of a therapeutic nature) published between 1945 and 1967, Martinson concluded that there was little evidence that rehabilitation programs work. This sweeping generalization was echoed by the Panel of Research on Rehabilitative Techniques of the National Research Council (US), which restated Martinson's conclusion: 'it appears that nothing works or at least that there have not been any consistent and persuasive demonstrations of anything that works' (Sechrest, White and Brown, 1979, p. 27). This conclusion has not gone unchallenged (for example, Halleck and Witte, 1977; Gendreau and Ross, 1987; Mair, 1991), but 'Nothing Works' remains a part of penological lore.

One response follows the lead of the second report of the Panel of Research on Rehabilitative Techniques (Martin, Sechrest and Redner, 1981) in questioning whether the strength and degree of implementation of in-prison programs are sufficient for definitive tests. Lattimore and Witte (1985), responding to Englander (1983) (also see Englander, 1985), note that many vocational programs are poorly designed, rather weak in intervention (for example, a training program of short duration), and poorly and incompletely implemented (for example, inmates dropping in and out of programs). Lattimore, Witte and Baker (1990) attempt to evaluate a vocational rehabilitation program for young property offenders in which care is taken to address these difficulties. The program consists of six integrated in-prison sub-programs (ibid., p. 120, Table 1) any or all of which may have been completed by members of the sample. The sample consists of 591 selected North Carolina male inmates aged 18-22 enrolled in the umbrella project sometime between June 1983 and May 1986. The subjects were randomly partitioned by prison officials into an experimental group and a control group. The two groups differed in their exposure to the various parts of the umbrella project and in their completion records for the various component parts of the project. Only 16 percent of the experimental group began all of the program components, that is, the umbrella program was only weakly implemented. Nevertheless, some programmatic effects were still evident: an examination of survival times indicates that the program reduced post-release arrests by about 10 percentage points for releasees who had been out over about 600 days (ibid., p. 128, Fig. 2). Moreover, the survival history of those who completed a vocational program was significantly better than for those who did not, a result the authors could not account for in terms of their sociodemographic and criminality measures. Unfortunately, doubts were recently cast on these results by one of the co-authors of the original paper: 'unpublished longer-term follow-up results show no significant differences in criminal activities between the experimental and the control groups' (Witte, 1997, p. 226).

10. Manpower Programs for Former Prison Inmates

Perhaps partly in response to the 'Nothing Works' dialogue, the attention of economists has largely shifted from in-prison rehabilitation programs to assistance programs for released prisoners. Cook (1975) (also see Hardin, 1975; Marks and Vining, 1986), after reviewing various labor market studies of parolees, as well as his own study utilizing a data set (collected and analyzed by Evans, 1968) consisting of 327 male parolees from Massachusetts penitentiaries in 1959, notes that (1) 'discrimination is not an important factor in the work experience of parolees' (Cook, 1975, p. 18); (2) the quality of jobs, and not the quantity, is crucial in determining the employment record of released offenders; (3) success in the job market for released offenders leads to lower recidivism rates; and (4) in-prison therapeutic, educational and job-skills programs have little effect upon post-release success. Even though remedial education and vocational training programs 'have demonstrated success in providing prisoners and parolees with measurably increased academic and vocational skill' (ibid., pp. 47-48), they have typically not been successful in reducing recidivism rates. (Witte and Reid, 1980, obtain similarly pessimistic results in examining the labor market performance of a group of ex-inmates not limited to parolees.) The survey by Long and Witte (1981, p. 128) is unequivocal: 'Evaluations of vocational training and remedial education programs in prison, parole, or probation settings have almost uniformly found that such programs have insignificant effects on both labor market performance and criminality.' The hypothesis is that the programs have not improved the job-opportunities of offenders, even though they have improved their skill levels. Released offenders either are unable to find the better jobs or, if found, they cannot keep them because of inadequate preparation for the demands of such work. Cook (echoed by Witte and Reid, 1980) concludes that the evidence suggests job search and on-the-job training programs should be given priority. Whether the prospect of improved legitimate job opportunities would act to reduce the initial deterrent effectiveness of punishment remains a concern. Cook notes that increasing the probability of punishment may be an appropriate offset. Such a substitution would not be costless, however, and again points to an analysis stressing the dynamic and general equilibrium modelling of crime.

Borus, Hardin and Terry (1976) (also see Hardin, 1975) utilize a quasi-experimental design to evaluate a Michigan job-placement program for selected parolees. The authors find that program participants did not fair better in terms of various indicators of job-market success, and in fact 'fared worse, on the average ... as to hours employed, gross earnings, and take-home pay' (Borus, Hardin and Terry, 1976, p. 394). Apparently no attempt was made to directly compare the recidivism experience of program participants with non-participants.

This aspect was addressed in the following study, yielding a similarly pessimistic conclusion.

Mallar and Thornton (1978) report on a program (LIFE - 'Living Insurance for Ex-Offenders') seeking to establish whether transitional aid programs and/or job-placement assistance for ex-prisoners reduce recidivism for theft crimes (also see Myers, 1983). A non-random sample of 432 high-risk prisoners from Maryland's state prisons released into the Baltimore area in the early 1970s was randomly partitioned into four treatment groups: one receiving direct financial aid ($60/week for three months); one receiving job-placement assistance (for up to one year); one receiving both; and a control group receiving no assistance of either type. The authors conclude: 'The provision of financial aid led to a large and statistically significant reduction in theft rearrests, while the provision of job-placement services proved to be singularly ineffective in reducing recidivism' (Mallar and Thornton, 1978, p. 224). Subjects in the financial aid group were less likely to be employed full time, especially during the first quarter after release, and more likely to be enrolled in school or a training program. The authors speculate that this apparent investment in human capital may widen the differential in recidivism response over time. It also appears that the transitional aid group achieved higher paying jobs, leading the authors to suggest that transitional aid permitted subjects to invest more in job search. Finally, the authors demonstrate the benefit/cost viability of the direct aid program.

Broadly similar results with respect to the job-placement component were obtained in an expanded version of the LIFE program (named TARP, 'Transitional Aid Research Project'; see Rossi, Berk and Lenihan, 1980). This program applied a controlled experimental design to all released inmates (not just parolees) from Georgia and Texas state prisons. The transitional aid component also appeared to be unsuccessful, but the authors attribute this to work disincentive effects not in place for the LIFE program (for additional comment see Long and Witte, 1981, pp. 129-130, and Englander, 1983, pp. 28-29). Again, these studies do not address the question whether the prospect of transitional financial aid would eventually reduce the initial deterrent effectiveness of punishment.

The National Supported Work Program (Hollister, Kemper and Maynard, 1984; Couch, 1992) placed subjects in a variety of supportive and subsidized work environments commensurate with their backgrounds. The emphasis was on developing work habits in accordance with a graduated stress concept of job-market preparation. As one author describes it: 'Stress within the working environment increased gradually during the training period until it simulated the workplace norms of the private sector. At that point, not more than 18 months after entry, individuals who received the services ... had to attempt a transition to unsubsidized employment' (Couch, 1992, p. 381). Over the period from March 1975 to July 1977, 2,276 ex-offenders, one of four subject groups, were randomly assigned to either an experimental group or a control group, with regular nine-month follow-ups extending to three years. All subjects had been incarcerated sometime during the six months preceeding enrollment in the program, and the average length of time served was four years. Less than 10 percent of this group exhausted the allowable time in the program. The results indicate no reduction in recidivism among the ex-offender experimental group as a whole, and no measurable labor market effects (Piliavin and Gartner, 1984). An eight year follow-up (Couch, 1992) indicates no improvement in labor market success for disadvantaged youths (the ex-offender group did not receive the long-term follow-up). Other large-scale studies (for example, the Mathematica Policy Research, Inc. study of the Job Corps (Mallar et al., 1982) and the Abt Associates review of the Job Training Partnership Act (JTPA) programs (Orr et al., 1996)) do not identify an ex-inmate subgroup for analysis.

As the concluding sections of this chapter attest, the rich research possibilities inherent in large longitudinal data sets are ushering in a new era of empirical research on criminal behavior (see, for example, Tauchen, Witte and Griesinger, 1994) and recidivism. At the same time, the research design of experimental studies will continue to improve (Witte, 1993). Weitekamp and Kerner (1994) sensibly call for an integration of longitudinal and experimental studies. This method would seem to have considerable potential for evaluating specific programs for inmates and ex-inmates. Pending the outcome of these hybrid studies, the conflicting results found in even the limited subsample of the literature discussed above suggests that a magic one-size-fits-all rehabilitation bullet does not exist. Offenders differ in their motivations as well as in their abilities, proclivities and backgrounds. Moreover, 'success' itself will only be found by choosing carefully from amongst different outcome measures, and then measured only in small magnitudes. Finally, it bears noting that even if 'Something Works', the corresponding implementation may be globally suboptimal either because of high direct program costs, or because of the implicit added incentive for individuals to enter the criminal market.

11. Criminal and Legitimate Labor Markets for Former Prison Inmates

Results obtained from specific in-prison rehabilitation programs and manpower programs for released offenders have been weak and inconsistent. This, coupled with the substantial increase in the proportion of the US population incarcerated over the last two decades makes the wide-scale implementation of costly rehabilitation programs unlikely. Consequently, recent economic research focuses on the general effects of incarceration, independent of prison programs, on subsequent criminal and legitimate labor market activities of released offenders. Various kinds of empirical information and estimation strategies are employed.

Grogger (1991) uses panel data on California arrestees to attempt to determine the effect of imprisonment on future criminality as well as to estimate the incapacitative effect of prison. Since estimates of the proportion of all young California males arrested at some point reach as high as one-third, the sample of arrestees offers a more representative picture than data on prison releasees alone (see Witte, 1980 and Myers, 1983). Grogger's empirical results suggest that imprisonment has a criminogenic effect ('each additional month spent in prison increases average arrests by about 2 percent' (Grogger, 1991, p. 304)) which may be attributed to either negative training or negative labor market signalling. Moreover, under the assumption that sanction expectations are formed entirely from one's own historical involvement with the justice system (that is, 'specific' as opposed to 'general' deterrence), 'the criminogenic effect of imprisonment is nearly three times as great as the deterrent effect' (ibid.). Prison is also found to have an incapacitative effect - each month reduces the average individual's criminal activity roughly in proportion to the time spent in prison. As Grogger notes (ibid., p. 299), the interpretation of the results depends crucially upon whether arrests are an appropriate measure of criminal activity. In addition, unobserved fixed characteristics could also bias the results. For example, a penchant for violence could be correlated with both longer sentences for any given crime category as well as with greater post-incarceration criminality. The following studies address this type of complication.

Freeman (1992) employs the National Longitudinal Survey of Youth and other surveys to estimate the long-run impact of incarceration on future legitimate employment of young US males. After standardizing for observed personal characteristics of individuals in the sample, he finds that incarceration in 1980 had a substantial negative impact on whether one was employed in any given subsequent year (to 1988) and on the total number of subsequent weeks worked. 'For the entire eight-year period, incarceration in 1980 reduced subsequent work weeks by 27 percent for blacks and 22 percent for all youth' (ibid., p. 217). Only one-third of the negative employment effect is attributed to the exclusionary impact of current incarceration on currrent employment. Freeman tests whether his results might be due to some unobserved characteristic correlated with both criminality and labor market fitness (such as functional illiteracy) by utilizing data on the pre- and post-incarceration employment experience of individuals. Adapting an omitted variables regression model, Freeman finds that incarceration continues to have a substantial impact on subsequent employment, although the impact is reduced by up to one-half (ibid., p. 225). Freeman cautions that these results do not imply that a random person assigned a criminal record would necessarily have the predicted subsequent employment experience. Rather, the statistics indicate what happened to those who *chose* crime. In other words, the data remain consistent with rational decision making by far-sighted individuals facing the risk of incarceration and the potential loss of legitimate income.

Freeman's results may be compared with those of Grogger (1995), who again studies a sample of young male California arrestees. All individuals in the sample were arrested at least once between 1973 and early 1987. Grogger seeks to determine the effects of contact with the criminal justice system on subsequent legitimate labor market outcomes. He obtains a comparison sample of non-offenders by partitioning the sample in accordance with the date of first arrest. The treatment sample consists of young California males first arrested prior to 1985, and the comparison sample consists of those first arrested in 1985 or later. Quarterly data on earnings and employment from 1980 through 1984 are merged with each individual's criminal justice history. To eliminate the impact of unobserved variables correlated with arrests, Grogger applies the fixed-effects estimator to a distributed lag model. Unobserved correlated factors are found to have a large effect on labour market outcomes, whereas arrests are found to have a relatively modest and short-lived impact on earnings and employment. ('After six-quarters the effect (of an arrest) is insignificantly different from zero' (ibid. p. 61).) The impact of incarceration is also noted, although the results here are somewhat unreliable because the relatively long prison sentences may lead to regression results that simply reflect a contemporaneous enforced exclusion from the labor market. The results relating to jail sentences are more reliable, as their duration is typically of one year or less. Jail sentences are found to have an impact on subsequent earnings and employment, but again these are characterized as relatively short-lasting when compared with Freeman's results. Grogger notes (ibid., p. 70) that this may be due to the differences in sentence lengths for the two sample: long sentences (Freeman's sample) may have long-lasting effects, whereas short sentences (Grogger's sample) have relatively short-lasting effects. Insofar as the empirical results *do* conflict, different rationalizations of criminal activity would be in order. Freeman's results may be interpreted as indicating a relatively moderate impact of arrests and incarceration on labor market prospects. Studies using empirical measures of actual sentence lengths served would be helpful in determining whether the supply-side argument or the demand-side argument is stronger.

Other papers bearing on the impact of incarceration on earnings and employment stress the independent deterrent effect of criminal stigmatization, a byproduct of contact with the criminal justice system. Rasmussen (1996) presents two models of criminal stigmatization. The moral hazard model has employers unwilling to pay the market wage to ex-offenders because of their lower net productivity (contribution to product less thievery from the firm and other destructive behaviors), whereas in the adverse selection model a criminal record signals exogenously lower *gross* productivity (for example, lower intelligence). Applied to the economics of prisons, the moral hazard effect reflects the negative training discussed earlier: time spent in prison increases the offender's productivity as a criminal. Any deterrent effect of stigmatization would be expected to be greater for those with the highest education and greatest job market prospects. Lott (1992b) finds for a sample of US federal larceny and theft offenders (typically involving government property or postal offenses) that 'a one-month increase in sentence length causes a 5.5 to 32 percent greater reduction in postconviction income' (ibid., p. 597). Waldfogel (1994a) similarly employs a sample of white-collar criminals to demonstrate that the reduction in job market prospects from imprisonment is due primarily to stigma, and not stalled experience growth or job displacement. Waldfogel cautions that his results may not be generalizable to offenders whose pre-conviction jobs do not involve substantial trust, and whose convictions are for crimes other than fraud and larceny. (For example, Lott (1992a) finds that longer sentences do not affect the post-imprisonment legitimate income of drug offenders.) To the extent that crime becomes more concentrated in an underclass composed of individuals who have little in the way of job market aspirations and opportunities, the deterrent effect of any criminal stigma may become insignificant. As well, the stigma measured by the disapproval of one's friends and neighbours will probably fall as the proportion of the population incarcerated increases, thus decreasing the deterrent effectiveness of punishment (Freeman, 1996, pp. 32-33). Other papers more relevant to the impact of conviction than incarceration include Lott (1990), Freeman (1986), Grogger (1992), Waldfogel (1994b) and Nagin and Waldfogel (1995).

12. Public Policy Broadly Conceived

Is the criminal justice system administering sentence lengths that might be considered efficient? Waldfogel (1993) constructs a static model of optimal sentencing where the planner chooses sentences to minimize the direct social harm from crime and the cost of imposing punishment. Optimal sentences are derived after making strong simplifying assumptions on functional forms and the relationships between variables. The results (corrected to account for an interpretive error noted in Pyle, 1995, p. 13), suggest that actual sentences in the US for 1984 are somewhat shorter than optimal sentences, but nevertheless are closer to the optimum than would be called for by a strictly retributive (proportionate to the harm) sentencing scheme. Alternatively, using relatively weak assumptions one can infer the social values of the harms imposed by crimes as implicit in current sentences. Waldfogel (1993) finds these implicit valuations correspond closely with estimates of actual harms as given by Cohen (1988).

Since Waldfogel (1993) takes the probabilities of punishment as exogenous, his analysis does not reach the question of whether the optimal number of offenders is incarcerated. A more comprehensive analysis is needed to address what is perhaps the most important public policy issue concerning the economics of prisons: Do prisons pay? Piehl and DiIulio (1995) (also see DiIulio and Piehl, 1991) review the literature and present some estimates. The idea is to use self-reports of incarcerated offenders to estimate the amount of crime such offenders would have committed if not incarcerated, and then, after pricing these crimes, to compare the 'saved' social costs attributable to incarceration with the direct costs (capital and operating) of incarceration. The self-reports come from surveys constructed to minimize biased and inaccurate reporting. (The earliest reliable surveys were completed by the Rand Corporation (see the discussion in Visher, 1986).) Since the distribution of offender reports are heavily skewed, the result depends upon whether the experience of the median, mean or whichever other offender's experience is taken as the basis for the estimate. For example, in one recent report (Piehl and DiIulio, 1995, p. 25, Table 3), the benefit-cost ratio for prisons ranges from 64.02 to 0.07, depending upon where in the distribution the sampling is done. Moreover, this method does not impart a social value to retribution, nor does it capture deterrent and replacement effects. It takes as a baseline the unlikely prospect that offenders would simply be released unsupervised if not incarcerated. The omission of replacement effects is particularly troubling since it works in an opposite direction to that of the deterrent, retribution and incapacitation effects. The implication is that the derived benefit-cost ratios are not necessarily a lower bound for whatever part of the distribution is sampled. Limiting the estimates to crime categories with low replacement rates should give more reliable estimates, but identifying these categories is a problem. Whereas incarcerated drug dealers are rapidly replaced on the streets, and intra-familial murderers are not, the situation is not so clear with respect to many other crimes. Moreover, there are undoubtedly differences in prison populations across geographical jurisdictions. The age-distribution of offenders, the crime mix, and so on ... are all affected by numerous variables (legitimate labor market opportunities, the allocation of police resources) not accounted for in the analysis, thus making inferences for jurisdictions other than that from which the sample was obtained, or indeed for the same jurisdiction at a different time, somewhat problematic. Since age markedly affects the proclivity for crime, the criminal career profile should also be taken into account (Blumstein and Cohen, 1987). For example, a sampled offender on the downward slope of the age-criminality curve will report crime figures that, if extrapolated forward, will lead to an upwardly biased estimate of the benefits from incarceration. Finally, all downstream costs related to incarceration are ignored in this type of analysis. If offenders form their expectations of the risk and costs of punishment primarily from their own experiences, then failing to incarcerate the sampled offender would lower his perception of the riskiness of criminal activity, and lead to increases in the amount of future crime. The training effects (whether positive or negative) of imprisonment and any stigma and job-market effects are also included from considaration. Very few self-report studies attempt to adjust for all present concerns except deterrence and downstreams effects. His 'best guess' point estimate of the incarceration elasticity of aggregate crime is 0.16 (Spelman, 1994, p. 220). That is, a 1 percent increase in the prison population is predicted to reduce the level of crime by about 0.16 percent.

An alternative methodology more in keeping with the economic model is presented in Levitt (1996) (also see Marvell and Moody, 1994). Levitt estimates offense supply functions using (a proxy for) prison population as an explanatory variable. If prison populations were exogenous, in principle the coefficient could be used to capture incapacitation, deterrence and replacement effects. But Levitt rightly notes that prison populations depend to an extent upon the level of offenses, so that simultaneity problems intrude (Hersch and Netter, 1984, and Cameron, 1989, attempt to estimate the impact of offenses on sentence lengths and prison populations). Levitt employs instrumental variables reflecting prison overcrowding legislation, and thus attempts to isolate the one-way impact of incarceration on crime rates. The estimation indicates that 'each additional prisoner leads to a reduction of between five and six reported crimes. Including unreported crimes raises the total to fifteen' (Levitt, 1996, p. 345). This number is very close to the median numbers obtained from self-report surveys, although only incapacitation effects are accounted for in the latter studies. Levitt demonstrates that his estimates lead to a benefit-cost ratio for the marginal prisoner that exceeds unity, and suggests that the current level of imprisonment (in the US) is 'roughly efficient' (ibid., p. 324).

Levitt's paper will undoubtedly excite controversy (see, for example, Donohue and Siegelman, 1998). If the various subsystems of the criminal justice system do not adjust rapidly to exogenous shifts, then lagged offense rates would be expected to have an impact upon the demand for overcrowding litigation. This would call into question a crucial assumption in the model. Levitt presents numbers indicating otherwise (Levitt, 1996, pp. 334-336), and presents econometric tests supporting the overidentifying restrictions (ibid., p. 340). Perhaps an equally important consideration is whether Levitt has faithfully interpreted the model he seeks to implement. For Ehrlich (1973) as for Becker (1968), the supply of offenses function includes offender risk variables. Thus the appropriate imprisonment variable included in the offense supply equations is a measure of the expected cost of punishment, conditional upon conviction. Proxies typically used for this theoretical measure are based upon average sentence lengths received or served, not prison populations *per se.* While not implausible, the argument that potential offenders form their sanction expectations on the basis of observations of prison populations requires independent justification.

Donohue and Siegelman (1998) employ both the incapacitation and aggregate offense-supply models to calculate cost-benefit ratios from imprisonment in the U.S. The goal is to establish whether a continuation of the huge run-up in the proportion of the population incarcerated over the last quarter century is cost justified. The authors, after reviewing the applicable studies, adopt offense elasticities of approximately 0.15 (also see Wilson, 1994). Attaching cost figures to these estimates suggests that further increases in the proportion incarcerated is unjustified for the US, but recent levels may be justified. These calculations do not take into account the possible criminogenic impact of current incarcerations. If imprisonment increases the criminality of released prisoners, then the US may be incarcerating at excessive rates. Donohue and Siegelman (1998) argue that certain pre-school enrichment programs are a more cost efficient alternative for reducing the level of crime.

13. Additional Topics

This chapter has not attempted to canvass all topics that could be included in a survey of the economics of prisons. Notable exclusions are prison industries (Barnes, 1921; Auerbach et al., 1988), industrial relations in prisons (Staudohar, 1976; Wynne, 1978; Peterson, 1981; Zimmer and Jacobs, 1981), litigation of prisoner suits (Brown, 1992), racial disparities in the prison population and in recidivism (Myers, 1980a, 1980b, 1992; Freeman, 1986, 1988; Myers and Sabol, 1988; Cameron, 1989; Dilulio, 1994; Langan, 1994), class-based models of prison use (Andrews, 1993), various alternatives to imprisonment and to standard methods of incarceration (fines, community-based sanctions, electronic monitoring, bootcamps, corporal punishments (Langbein, 1977; Polinsky and Shavell, 1984; Waldfogel, 1995; Benson and Rasmussen, 1995; Avio, 1995; Kan, 1996)) and economic factors in the origins of prison systems (Langbein, 1976; Conley, 1981; Lewis, 1988, 1990; Nicholas, 1990).

The economics of prisons has come a long way since Becker (1968) regenerated the interest of economists in crime. Further progress will require developments in both theoretical and empirical spheres, including the specification and estimation of dynamic structural models of criminal behaviour. The many simplifying assumptions of existing models must be relaxed, and the relationships between the various crime categories and between criminal and legitimate labour markets better understood. Studies of countries other than the US are necessary for establishing the generality of the empirical findings. 'Protracted prospective' longitudinal data sets (Janson, 1994) must be constructed on representative individuals, with information that includes sentence lengths actually served and activities undertaken while imprisoned, as well as on the more standard variables.

In general, one could argue that the punishment theories developed by economists and within which the economics of prisons is embedded need to pay more attention to the stylized facts uncovered by longitudinal studies: (i) most crimes are committed by youths; (ii) only a small number of these youths persist in criminal activity as they age; but (iii) these same people are responsible for the bulk of serious crimes (for discussion see Farrington, Ohlin and Wilson, 1986; Moffitt, 1994). The theoretical models developed in economics do not appear to satisfactorily address these facts. One policy implication is that more attention is paid to influencing the lifetime profile of established criminals than attending to the prevention of such careers in the first place. Similarly, the underlying legal and social institutions providing the background environment for criminal activity require careful examination (Witte, 1993). Akerlof and Yellen (1994) provide an illustrative model that points in the right direction (also see Becker, 1996), a model which implicates 'community policing' (Campbell, 1994). Finally, given their comparative advantage, economists have quite naturally confined themselves to the impact of the law and its administration on the incentives implicit in fixed preferences, that is, to short-run 'carrot and stick' approaches to modifying criminal behavior. Perhaps a more complete picture of human nature than that depicted in the economic model of crime is warranted. It may now be time to explore the long-run preference-shaping impact of the law (Dau-Schmidt, 1990; Friedman, 1993; Robinson, 1994) and education (Witte, 1996, 1997; Usher, 1997), along with the role of habituation in that process (Wilson, 1994; Dilulio, 1996). We know little about how and why a shared moral order is developed and maintained (Robinson, 1994). This change in perspective, calling as it does for an examination of the relationship between socialization and individuation, suggests a return to a relatively neglected part of the research program laid out in Adam Smith ([1791] 1976). Analysis of the social institutions that inculcate self-command, and which otherwise function as civilizing forces in our society (Muller, 1993; Wilson, 1993), should be part and parcel of the research strategy adopted by social scientists to help understand and control crime.

Bibliography on the Economics of Prisons (8300)

Adler, Jacob (1991), *The Urgings of Conscience: A Theory of Punishment*, Philadelphia, PA, Temple University Press.

Akerlof, George A. and Yellen, Janet L. (1994), 'Gang Behavior, Law Enforcement, and Community Values', in Aaron, Henry J., Mann, Thomas E. and Taylor, Timothy (eds), *Values and Public Policy*, Washington, DC, The Brookings Institution, 173-209.

Andrews, Marcellus (1993), 'Schools, Jails and the Dynamics of an Educational Underclass: Some Dreadful Social Arithmetic', **22** *Journal of Economic Behavior and Organization*, 121-132.

Auerbach, Barbara J., Sexton, George E., Farrow, Franklin C. and Lawson, Robert H. (1988), *Work in American Prisons: the Private Sector Gets Involved*, Washington, DC, U.S. Department of Justice, National Institute of Justice, Office of Communication and Research Utilization (prepared by Criminal Justice Associates under subcontract from Abt Associates, Inc.).

Avio, Kenneth L. (1973), 'An Economic Analysis of Criminal Corrections: The Canadian Case', **6** *Canadian Journal of Economics*, 164-178.

Avio, Kenneth L. (1975), 'Recidivism in the Economic Model of Crime', **13** *Economic Inquiry*, 450-456.

Avio, Kenneth L. (1991), 'On Private Prisons: An Economic Analysis of the Model Contract and Model Statute for Private Incarceration', **17** *New England Journal on Criminal and Civil Confinement*, 265-300.

Avio, Kenneth L. (1993a), 'Remuneration Regimes for Private Prisons', **13** *International Review of Law and Economics*, 35-45.

Avio, Kenneth L. (1993b), 'Economic, Retributive and Contractarian Conceptions of Punishment', **12** *Law and Philosophy*, 249-286.

Avio, Kenneth L. (1995), 'Economic, Contractarian and Discourse Arguments against Efficient Torture', in Peczenik, Aleksander and Karlsson, Mikael M. (eds), **58** *Archives on Rights and Social Philosophy, 'Law, Justice and the State: I'*, Stuttgart, Franz Steiner Verlag, 265-272.

Barnes, Harry Elmer (1921), 'The Economics of American Penology as Illustrated by the Experience of the State of Pennsylvania', **8** *Journal of Political Economy*, 617-642.

Barnett, Randy E. (1977), 'Restitution: a New Paradigm of Criminal Justice', **87** *Ethics*, 279-301.

Barnett, Randy E. (1998), *The Structure of Liberty: Justice and the Rule of Law*, Oxford, Oxford University Press.

Becker, Gary S. (1968), 'Crime and Punishment: An Economic Approach', **76** *Journal of Political Economy*, 169-217.

Becker, Gary S. (1996), 'Norms and the Formation of Preferences', in Becker, Gary S. (ed), *Accounting for Tastes*, Cambridge, MA, Harvard University Press, 225-230.

Benson, Bruce L (1990), *The Enterprise of Law: Justice Without the State*, San Francisco, Pacific Research Institute for Public Policy.

Benson, Bruce L. (1994a), 'Are Public Goods Really Common Pools? Considerations of the Evolution of Policing and Highways in England', **32** *Economic Inquiry*, 249-271.

Benson, Bruce L. (1994b), 'Third Thoughts on Contracting Out', **11** *Journal of Libertarian Studies*, 44-78.

Benson, Bruce L. (1996), 'Restitution in Theory and in Practice', **13** *Journal of Libertarian Studies*, 44-78.

Benson, Bruce L. and Rasmussen, David W. (1995), 'Crime and Punishment', in Denslow, David A., Scoggins, J.F. and Shermyen, Anne (eds), *The Economy of Florida*, Gainesville, FL, Bureau of Economic and Business Research, 99-116.

Benson, Bruce L. and Wollan, Laurin A., Jr (1989), 'Prison Overcrowding and Judicial Incentives', **3** *Madison Paper Series*, 1-22.

Block, Michael K. and Lind, Robert C. (1975), 'An Economic Analysis of Crimes Punishable by Imprisonment', **4** *Journal of Legal Studies*, 479-492.

Block, Michael K. and Ulen, Thomas S. (1979), 'Cost Functions for Correctional Institutions', in Gray, Charles M. (ed.), *The Costs of Crime*, Beverly Hills, CA, Sage Publications, 187-209.

Blumstein, Alfred (1995), 'Prisons', in Wilson, James Q. and Petersilia, Joan (eds), *Crime*, San Francisco, ICS Press, 387-419.

Blumstein, Alfred and Cohen, Jacqueline (1987), 'Characterizing Criminal Careers', **237** *Science*, 985-991.

Blumstein, Alfred and Larson, Richard (1969), 'Models of a Total Criminal Justice System', **17** *Operations Research*, 199-232.

Borus, Michael E., Hardin, Einar and Terry, Patterson A. (1976), 'Job-Placement Services for Ex-Offenders: An Evaluation of the Michigan Comprehensive Offender Manpower Program (COMP) Job-Placement Efforts', **11** *Journal of Human Resources*, 391-401.

Bowman, Gary W., Hakim, Simon and Seidenstat, Paul (eds) (1992), *Privatizing the United States Justice System: Police, Adjudication and Corrections Services from the Private Sector*, Jefferson, NC, Transaction Publishers.

Bowman, Gary W., Hakim, Simon and Seidenstat, Paul (eds) (1993), *Privitazing Correctional Institutions*, New Brunswick, NJ, Transaction Publishers.

Brakel, Samuel J. (1988), 'Privatization' in Corrections: Radical Prison Chic or Mainstream Americana?', **14** *New England Journal on Criminal and Civil Confinement*, 1-39.

Brown, Jennifer G. (1992), 'Posner, Prisoners, and Pragmatism', **66** *Tulane Law Review*, 1117-1178.

Burnovski, Moshe and Safra, Zvi (1994), 'Deterrence Effects of Sequential Punishment Policies: Should Repeat Offenders be More Severely Punished?', **14** *International Review of Law and Economics*, 341-350.

Cameron, Samuel (1989), 'Determinants of the Prison Population: An Empirical Analysis', **16(8)** *International Journal of Social Economics*, 17-25.

Campbell, John (1994), 'Policing Crime', **4** *Federal Reserve Bank of Boston Regional Review*, 6-11.

Carr-Hill, G.A. and Carr-Hill, R.A. (1972), 'Reconviction as a Process', **12** *British Journal of Criminology*, 35-43.

Cohen, Mark (1988), 'Pain, Suffering and Jury Awards: A Study of the Cost of Crime to Victims', **22** *Law and Society Review*, 537-556.

Conley, John A. (1981), 'Revising Conceptions about the Origin of Prisons: The Importance of Economic Considerations', **62** *Social Science Quarterly*, 247-258.

Cook, Philip J. (1975), 'The Correctional Carrot: Better Jobs for Parolees', **1** *Policy-Analysis*, 11-54.

Cook, Philip J. (1977), 'Punishment and Crime: A Critique of Current Findings Concerning the Preventative Effects of Punishment', **41(1)** *Law and Contemporary Problems*, 164-209.

Couch, Kenneth A. (1992), 'New Evidence on the Long-Term Effects on Employment Training Programs', **10** *Journal of Labor Economics*, 380-388.

Cragg, Wesley (1992), *The Practice of Punishment: Towards a Theory of Restorative Justice*, London, Routledge & Kegan Paul.

Dau-Schmidt, Kenneth G. (1990), 'An Economic Analysis of the Criminal Law as a Preference Shaping Policy', **40** *Duke Law Journal*, 1-38.

Davis, Michael (1988), 'Time and Punishment: An Intertemporal Model of Crime', **96** *Journal of Political Economy*, 383-390.

Dilulio, John J., Jr (1988), 'What's Wrong with Private Prisons?', **92** *Public Interest*, 66-83.

Dilulio, John J., Jr (1990), 'The Duty to Govern: A Critical Perspective on the Private Management of Prisons and Jails', in McDonald, Douglas C. (ed), *Private Prisons and the Public Interest*, New Brunswick, Rutgers University Press.

Dilulio, John J., Jr (1994), 'The Question of Black Crime', **117** *The Public Interest*, 3-32.

Dilulio, John J., Jr (1996), 'Help Wanted: Economists, Crime and Public Policy', **10** *Journal of Economic Perspectives*, 3-24.

Dilulio, John J., Jr and Piehl, Anne Morrison (1991), 'Does Prison Pay?', **9** *Brookings Review*, 28-35.

Donohue, John J., III and Siegelman, Peter (1998), 'Allocating Resources Among Prisons and Social Programs in the Battle Against Crime', **27** *Journal of Legal Studies*, 1-43.

Duff, R.A. (1986), *Trials and Punishment*, Cambridge, Cambridge University Press.

Duff, R.A. (1996), 'Penal Communications: Recent Work in the Philosophy of Punishment', **20** *Crime and Justice: A Review of Research*, 1-97.

Easterbrook, Frank H. (1983), 'Criminal Procedure as a Market System', **12** *Journal of Legal Studies*, 289-332.

Edwards, Glyn (1996), 'Public Crime, Private Punishment: Prison Privatization in Queensland', **23** *International Journal of Social Economics*, 391-408.

Ehrlich, Isaac (1973), 'Participation in Illegitimate Activities: A Theoretical and Empirical Investigation', **81** *Journal of Political Economy*, 521-565.

Ehrlich, Isaac (1981), 'On the Usefulness of Controlling Individuals: An Economic Analysis of Rehabilitation, Incapacitation and Deterrence', **71** *American Economic Review*, 307-332.

Ehrlich, Isaac (1982), 'The Optimum Enforcement of Laws and the Concept of Justice: A Positive Analysis', **2** *International Review of Law and Economics*, 3-27.

Englander, Frederick (1983), 'Helping Ex-offenders enter the Labor Market', **106** *Monthly Labor Review*, 25-30.

Englander, Frederick (1985), 'Reply', **108A** *Monthly Labor Review*, 49-50.

Evans, Robert, Jr (1968), 'The Labor Market and Parole Success', **3** *Journal of Human Resources*, 201-212.

Farrington, David P., Ohlin, Lloyd E. and Wilson, James Q. (1986), *Understanding and Controlling Crime: Toward a New Research Strategy*, New York, Springer-Verlag.

Fleisher, Mark S. (1989), *Warehousing Violence*, Newbury Park, CA, Sage Publications.

Fleisher, Mark S. (1995), *Beggars and Thieves*, Madison, WI, University of Wisconsin Press.

Flinn, Christopher (1986), 'Dynamic Models of Criminal Careers', in Blumstein, Alfred, Cohen, Jacqueline, Roth, Jeffrey A. and Visher, Christy A. (eds), *Criminal Careers and "Career Criminals", Vol. II*, Washington, DC, National Academy Press, 356-379.

Freeman, Richard B. (1983), 'Crime and Unemployment', in Wilson, James Q. (ed), *Crime and Public Policy*, San Francisco, Institute for Contemporary Studies Press, 89-106.

Freeman, Richard B. (1986), 'Who Escapes? The Relation Between Churchgoing and Other Background Factors to the Socioeconomic Performance of Black Male Youths from Inner-City Tracts', in Freeman, Richard B. and Holzer, Harry J. (eds), *The Black Youth Employment Crisis*, Chicago, University of Chicago Press, 353-376.

Freeman, Richard B. (1988), 'The Relation of Criminal Activity to Black Youth Employment', in Simms, Margaret C. and Myers, Samuel L., Jr (eds), *The Economics of Race and Crime*, New Brunswick, Transaction Books, 99-107.

Freeman, Richard B. (1992), 'Crime and the Employment of Disadvantaged Youths', in Peterson, George E. and Vronman, Wayne (eds), *Urban Labor Markets and Job Opportunity*, Washington, DC, Urban Institute Press, 201-237.

Freeman, Richard B. (1995), 'Crime and the Job Market', in Wilson, James Q. and Petersilia, Joan (eds), *Crime*, San Francisco, CA, ICS Press.

Freeman, Richard B. (1996), 'Why Do So Many Young American Men Commit Crimes and What Might We Do About It?', **10** *Journal of Economic Perspectives*, 25-42.

Friedman, Lawrence M. (1993), *Crime and Punishment in American History*, New York, Basic Books.

Funke, G.S. (1985), 'The Economics of Prison Crowding', **478** *Annals of the American Academy of Political and Social Science*, 86-99.

Ganley, J.A. and Cubbin, J.S. (1992), *Public Sector Efficiency Measurement: Applications of Data Development Analysis*, Amsterdam, North-Holland.

Garoupa, Nuno (1996), *Prison, Parole and the Criminal Justice Act 1991*, Manuscript, University of York.

Garoupo, Nuno (1997), 'The Theory of Optimal Law Enforcement', **11** *Journal of Economic Surveys*, 267-295.

Gendreau, Paul and Ross, Robert R. (1987), 'Revivification of Rehabilitation: Evidence from the 1980s', **4** *Justice Quarterly*, 349-407.

Gentry, James Theodore (1986), 'The Panopticon Revisited: The Problem of Monitoring Private Prisons', **96** *Yale Law Journal*, 353-375.

Giertz, J. Fred and Nardulli, Peter F. (1985), 'Prison Overcrowding', **46(1)** *Public Choice*, 71-78.

Gill, Richard T. (1994), 'The Importance of Deterrence', **117** *Public Interest*, 51-56.

Gillespie, Robert F. (1983), 'Allocating Prison Space: An Economic Approach Incorporating Efficiency and Equity', **40** *Illinois Business Review*, 3-11.

Greenwood, Peter and Turner, Susan (1987), *Selective Incapacitation Revisited*, Santa Monica, Rand Corporation.

Grizzle, Gloria A. and Witte, Ann D. (1980), 'Criminal Justice Evaluation Techniques: Methods Other Than Random Assignment', in Kleenin, Malcolm W. and Teilmann, Katherine S. (eds), *Handbook of Criminal Justice Evaluation*, Beverly Hills, CA, Sage Publications, 259-302.

Grogger, Jeffrey (1991), 'Certainty vs. Severity of Punishment', **29** *Economic Inquiry*, 279-309.

Grogger, Jeffrey (1992), 'Arrests, Persistent Youth Joblesness, and Black/White Employment Differentials', **74** *Review of Economics and Statistics*, 100-106.

Grogger, Jeffrey (1995), 'The Effect of Arrests on the Employment and Earning of Young Men', **110** *Quarterly Journal of Economics*, 51-71.

Grogger, Jeffrey (1997), 'Incarceration-Related Costs of Early Childbearing', in Maynard, Rebecca A. (ed), *Kids Having Kids: Economic Costs and Social Consequences of Teen Pregnancy*, Washington, DC, The Urban Institute Press.

Halleck, Seymour L. and Witte, Ann D. (1977), 'Is Rehabilitation Dead?', **23** *Crime and Delinquency*, 372-382.

Hardin, Einar (1975), 'Human Capital and the Labor Market Success of New Parolees', in, *1975 Proceedings of the Business and Economics Section*, American Statistical Association, 330-335.

Hatry, Harry P. (Principal investigator) (1989), 'Comparison of Privately and Publicly Operated Corrections Facilities in Kentucky and Massachusetts', prepared by The Urban Institute under grant from the Office of National Institute of Justice, US Department of Justice, Washington, DC.

Herrnstein, Richard J. (1983), 'Some Criminogenic Traits in Offenders', in Wilson, James Q. (ed), *Crime and Public Policy*, San Francisco, Institute for Contemporary Studies Press, 31-49.

Hersch, Philip L. and Netter, Jeffrey M. (1984), 'The Effects of Crime Rates on Time Served in Prison: An Empirical Analysis', **39** *Public Finance*, 314-320.

Hollister, Robinson G., Kemper, Peter and Maynard, Rebecca A. (1984), *The National Supported Work Demonstration*, Madison, WI, University of Wisconsin Press.

Howard, Michael (1996), 'In Defence of Prisons', **June 22nd** *The Economist*, 56-57.

Janson, Carl-Gunner (1994), 'A Case for a Longitudinal Study', in Weitekamp, Elmar G. and Kerner, Hans-Jürgen (eds), *Cross-National Longitudinal Research on Human Development and Criminal Behavior*, Dordrecht, Kluwer Academic Publishers, 409-422.

Kan, Steven S. (1996), 'Corporal Punishments and Optimal Incapacitation', **15** *Journal of Legal Studies*, 121-130.

Kaplow, Louis (1990), 'A Note on the Optimal Use of Nonmonetary Sanctions', **42** *Journal of Public Economics*, 245-247.

Kim, Il Joong, et al. (1993), 'An Economic Analysis of Recidivism among Drug Offenders', **60** *Southern Economic Journal*, 169-183.

Kritzer, Herbert M. (1981-1982), 'Problems in Estimating the Optimal-Costs Prison Size: A Comment', **16** *Law and Society Review*, 139-142.

Langan, Patrick A. (1994), 'No Racism in the Justice System', **117** *Public Interest*, 48-51.

Langbein, John H. (1976), 'The Historical Origins of the Sanction of Imprisonment for Serious Crime', **5** *Journal of Legal Studies*, 35-60.

Langbein, John H. (1977), *Torture and the Law of Proof: Europe and England in the Ancient Regime*, Chicago, IL, University of Chicago Press.

Lattimore, Pamela K. and Witte, Ann D. (1985), 'Programs to aid Ex-offenders: We don't know "Nothing Works"', **108A** *Monthly Labor Review*, 46-50.

Lattimore, Pamela K., Witte, Ann D. and Baker, Joanna R. (1990), 'Experimental Assessment of the Effect of Vocational Training on Youthful Property Offenders', **14** *Evaluation Review*, 115-133.

Lee, Tahirih V. and Searle-White, Joshua (1991), 'Prisoner's Dilemma Meets Glasnost: A Comparative Advantage Solution to the United States Prison Crisis', **24** *Cornell International Law Journal*, 25-56.

Leung, Siu Fai (1995), 'Dynamic Deterrence Theory', **62** *Economica*, 65-87.

Levitt, Steven D. (1996), 'The Effect of Prison Population Size on Crime Rates: Evidence From Prison Overcrowding Litigation', **107** *Quarterly Journal of Economics*, 319-351.

Levitt, Steven D. (1997), 'Incentive Compatibility Constraints as an Explaination for the Use of Prison Sentences Instead of Fines', **17** *International Review of Law and Economics*, 179-192.

Lewis, Donald E. (1979), 'The Optimal Parole Period', **2** *Economics Letters*, 381-386.

Lewis, Donald E. (1983), 'Economic Aspects of the Parole Decision', **22** *Australian Economic Papers*, 259-279.

Lewis, Donald E. (1986), 'The General Deterrent Effect of Longer Sentences', **26** *British Journal of Criminology*, 47-62

Lewis, Frank D. (1988), 'The Cost of Convict Transportation from Britain to Australia, 1796-1810', **41** *Economic History Review, Second Series*, 507-524.

Lewis, Frank D. (1990), 'Australia: An Economical Prison? A Reply', **43** *Economic History Review, Second Series*, 477-482.

Lipton, Douglas W., Martinson, Robert and Wilks, Judith (1975), *The Effectiveness of Correctional Treatment: A Survey of Treatment Evaluation Studies*, New York, Praeger Publishers.

Logan, Charles H. (1987), 'The Propriety of Proprietary Prisons', **51** *Feceral Probation*, 35-40.

Long, Sharon K. and Witte, Ann D. (1981), 'Current Economic Trends: Implications for Crime and Criminal Justice', in Wright, Kevin N. (ed), *Crime and Criminal Justice in a Declining Economy*, Cambridge, MA, Oelgeschlager, Gunn and Hain, 69-143.

Lott, John R., Jr (1990), 'The Effect of Conviction on the Legitimate Income of Criminals', **34** *Economic Letters*, 381-385.

Lott, John R., Jr (1992a), 'An Attempt at Measuring the Total Monetary Penalty from Drug Convictions: The Importance of an Individual's Reputation', **21** *Journal of Legal Studies*, 159-187.

Lott, John R., Jr (1992b), 'Do We Punish High Income Criminals too Heavy?', **30** *Economic Inquiry, 583-608.*

Mair, George (1991), 'What Works - Nothing or Everything? Measuring the Effectiveness of Sentences', **30** *Home Office Research Bulletin*, 3-8.

Mallar, Charles D., Kerachsky, Stuart, Thornton, Craig and Long, David (1982), *Evaluation of the Economic Impact of the Job Corps Program: Third Follow-up Report*, Princeton, NJ, Mathematica Policy Research, Inc. (Final Report).

Mallar, Charles D. and Thornton, Craig V.D. (1978), 'Transitional Aid for Released Prisoners: Evidence from the LIFE Experiment', **13** *Journal of Human Resources*, 208-236.

Marks, Denton and Vining, Aidan R. (1986), 'Prison Labor Markets: The Supply Issue', **19(1)** *Policy Sciences*, 83-111.

Martin, Susan E., Sechrest, Lee B. and Redner, Robin (eds) (1981), *New Directions in the Rehabilitation of Criminal Offenders*, National Research Council, Washington, DC, National Academy Press.

Martinson, Robert (1974), ''What Works' - Questions and Answers about Prison Reform', **25** *Public Interest*, 22-54.

Marvel, Thomas and Moody, Carlisle (1994), 'Prison Population Growth and Crime Reduction', **10** *Journal of Quantitative Criminology*, 109-140.

McDonald, Douglas C. (1990), 'The Cost of operating Public and Private Correctional Facilities' in McDonald, Douglas C. (ed), *Private Prisons and the Public Interest*, New Brunswick, NJ, Rutgers University Press.

McGuire, William J. and Witte, Ann D. (1978), 'An Estimate of an Average Cost Curve for Large Scale Correctional Institutions', Working Paper, Department of Economics, University of North Carolina.

Melossi, Dario (1987), 'Political Business Cycles and Imprisonment Rates in Italy: Report on a Work in Progress', **16(1-2)** *Review of Black Political Economy*, 211-218.

Miceli, Thomas J. (1991), 'Optimal Criminal Procedure: Fairness and Deterrence', **11** *International Review of Law and Economics*, 3-10.

Miceli, Thomas J. (1994), 'Prison and Parole: Minimizing the Cost of Non-monetary Sanctions as Deterrents', **16** *Research in Law and Economics*, 197-211.

Moffitt, Terrie E. (1994), 'Natural Histories of Delinquency', in Weitekamp, Elmar G. and Kerner, Hans-Jürgen (eds), *Cross-National Longitudinal Research on Human Development and Criminal Behavior*, Dordrecht, Kluwer, 3-61.

Morris, Norval (1974), *The Future of Imprisonment*, Chicago, IL, University of Chicago Press, 144 ff.

Moyle, Paul (ed) (1994), *Private Prisons and Police:Recent Australian Trends*, Leichhardt, NSW, Pluto Press.

Muller, Jerry Z. (1993), *Adam Smith in his Time and Ours: Resigning the Decent Society*, New York, The Free Press.

Myers, Samuel L., Jr (1980a), 'The Rehabilitation Effect of Punishment', **18** *Economic Inquiry*, 353-366.

Myers, Samuel L., Jr (1980b), 'Black-White Differentials in Crime Rates', **10** *Review of Black Political Economy*, 133-152.

Myers, Samuel L., Jr (1983), 'Estimating the Economic Model of Crime: Employment versus Punishment Effects', **94** *Quarterly Journal of Economics*, 157-166.

Myers, Samuel L., Jr (1992), 'Crime, Entrepreneurship, and Labor Force Withdrawal', **10** *Contemporal Policy Issues*, 84-97.

Myers, Samuel L., Jr and Sabol, William J. (1988), 'Unemployment and Racial Differences in Imprisonment', in Simms, Margaret C. and Myers, Samuel L., Jr (eds), *The Economics of Race and Crime*, New Brunswick, NJ, Transactions Books, 189-209.

Nagin, Daniel and Waldfogel, Joel (1995), 'The Effects of Criminality and Conviction on the Labor Market Status of Young British Offenders', **15** *International Review of Law and Economics*, 109-126.

Nardulli, Peter F. (1984), 'The Misalignment of Penal Responsibilities and State Prison Crises: Costs, Consequences, and Corrective Actions', **17** *University of Illinois Law Review*, 365-387.

Nash, John F. (1991), 'To Make the Punishment Fit the Crime: The Theory and Statistical Estimation of a Multi-Period Optimal Deterrence Model', **11** *International Review of Law and Economics*, 101-110.

Nicholas, Stephen (1990), 'Australia: An Economical Prison? Comments', **43(3)** *Economic History Review, Second Series*, 470-476.

Niskanen, William A. (1971), *Bureaucracy and Representative Government*, Chicago, Aldine-Atherton.

Orr, Larry R., Bloom, Howard S., Bell, Stephen H., Doolittle, Fred, Lin, Winston and Cave, George (1996), *Does Training for the Disadvantaged Work? Evidence from the National JTPA Study*, An Abt Associates Study, Washington, DC, Urban Institute Press.

Parker, Jeffrey S. (1989), 'Criminal Sentencing Policy for Organizations: The Unifying Approach of Optimal Penalties', **26** *American Criminal Law Review*, 513-604.

Parker, Jeffrey S. and Block, Michael K. (1989), 'The Sentencing Commission, P.M. (Post-Mistretta). Sunshine or Sunset?', **27** *American Criminal Law Review*, 289-329.

Pastor, Santos (1994), 'La Exigibilidad de las Normas y la Resolución de Conflictos (Law Enforcement and Dispute Resolution)', **3** *Iuris: Quaderns de Política Jurídica*, 155-174.

Peterson, Andrew A. (1981), 'Deterring Strikes by Public Employees: New York's Two for One Salary Penalty and the 1979 Prison Guard Strike', **34(4)** *Industrial and Labor Relations Review*, 545-562.

Piehl, Anne Morrison and DiIulio, John J., Jr (1995), 'Does Prison Pay? Revisited', **13** *Brookings Review*, 21-25.

Piliavin, Irving and Gartner, Rosemary (1984), 'The Impacts of Supported Work on Ex-offenders', in Hollister, Robinson G. Jr, Kemper, Peter and Maynard, Rebecca A. (eds), *The National Supported Work Demonstration*, Madison, WI, University of Wisconsin Press.

Polinsky, A. Mitchell and Rubinfeld, Daniel L. (1991), 'A Model of Optimal Fines for Repeat Offenders', **46** *Journal of Public Economics*, 491 ff.

Polinsky, A. Mitchell and Shavell, Steven (1984), 'The Optimal Use of Fines and Imprisonment', **24** *Journal of Public Economics*, 89-99.

Pyle, D.J. (1995), 'The Economic Approach to Crime and Punishment', **6** *Journal of Interdisciplinary Economics*, 1-22.

Rasmussen, David W. and Benson, Bruce L. (eds) (1994), *The Economic Anatomy of a Drug War: Criminal Justice in the Commons*, Lanham, MD, Rowman and Littlefield.

Rasmussen, Eric (1996), 'Stigma and Self-Fulfilling Expectations of Criminality', **39** *Journal of Law and Economics*, 519-543.

Reiss, Albert J., Jr and Roth, Jeffrey A. (eds) (1993), *Understanding and Preventing Violence*, V. 1-4, Panel on the Understanding and Control of Violent Behavior, National Research Council, Washington, DC, National Academy Press.

Robbins, Ira R. (1989), 'The Legal Dimensions of Private Incarceration', **38** *American University Law Review*, 531-854.

Robinson, Paul H. (1994), 'A Failure of Moral Courage', **117** *Public Interest*, 40-48.

Roper, Brian A. (1986), 'Market Forces, Privatisation and Prisons: A Polar Case for Government Policy', **13** *International Journal of Social Economics*, 77-92.

Rossi, Peter H., Berk, Richard A. and Lenihan, Kenneth J. (1980), *Money, Work, and Crime: Experimental Evidence*, New York, Academic Press.

Rubenstein, Ariel (1980), 'On an Anomaly of the Deterrent Effect of Punishment', **6** *Economics Letters*, 89-94.

Schmidt, Peter and Witte, Ann D. (1979), 'Models of Recidivism and an Illustration of Their Use in Evaluating Correctional Programs', in Sechrest, Lee, White, Susan D. and Brown, Elizabeth D. (eds), *The Rehabilitation of Criminal Offenders: Problems and Prospects*, Washington, DC, National Academy of Sciences, 210-224.

Schmidt, Peter and Witte, Ann D. (1980), 'Evaluating Correctional Programs: Models of Criminal Recidivism and an Illustration of their Use', **4** *Evaluation Review*, 585-600.

Schmidt, Peter and Witte, Ann D. (1984), *An Economic Analysis of Crime and Justice: Theory, Methods, and Applications*, New York, Academic Press, 416 ff.

Schmidt, Peter and Witte, Ann D. (1988), *Predicting Criminal Recidivism Using Survival Models*, New York, Springer-Verlag.

Schmidt, Peter and Witte, Ann D. (1989), 'Predicting Criminal Recidivism Using "Split Population" Survival Time Models', **40** *Journal of Econometrics*, 141-159.

Sechrest, Lee, White, Susan D. and Brown, Elizabeth D. (eds) (1979), *The Rehabilitation of Criminal Offenders: Problems and Prospects*, Washington, DC, National Academy of Sciences.

Sellers, Martin P. (1993), *The History and Politics of Private Prisons: A Comparative Analysis*, Rutherford, NJ, Fairleigh Dickinson University Press.

Shavell, Steven (1985), 'Criminal Law and the Optimal Use of Nonmonetary Sanctions as a Deterrent', **85** *Columbia Law Review*, 1232-1262.

Shavell, Steven (1987a), 'A Model of Optimal Incapacitation', **77** *American Economic Review*, 107-110.

Shavell, Steven (1987b), 'The Optimal Use of Nonmonetary Sanctions as a Deterrent', **77** *American Economic Review*, 584-592.

Shoup, Carl S. (1964), 'Standards for Distributing a Free Govermental Service: Crime Prevention', **19** *Public Finance*, 383-392.

Sichor, David (1995), *Punishment for Profit: Private Prisons/Public Concerns*, Thousand Oaks, CA, Sage Publications.

Sickles, Robin C., Schmidt, Peter and Witte, Ann D. (1979), 'An Application of the Simultaneous Tobit Model: A Study of the Determinants of Criminal Recidivism', **31** *Journal of Economics and Business*, 166-171.

Smith, Adam ([1791] 1976), 'The Theory of Moral Sentiments', in D.D. Raphael and A.L. Macfie (eds), *Volume I of The Glasgow Edition of the Works and Correspondence of Adam Smith*, Oxford, Oxford University Press.

Spelman, William (1994), *Criminal Incapacitation*, New York, Plenum Press.

Staudohar, Paul D. (1976), 'Prison Guard Labor Relations in Ohio', **15(2)** *Industrial Relations*, 177-190.

Stigler, George J. (1970), 'The Optimum Enforcement of Law', **78** *Journal of Political Economy*, 526-536.

Tabasz, Thomas F. (1974), 'Penology, Economics, and the Public: Toward an Agreement', **5** *Policy Sciences*, 47-55.

Tabasz, Thomas F. (1975), *Toward an Economics of Prisons*, Lexington, KY, Heath.

Tauchen, Helen, Witte, Ann D. and Griesinger, Harriet (1994), 'Criminal Deterrence: Revisiting the Issue With a Birth Cohort', **76** *Review of Economics and Statistics*, 399-412.

Thomas, Charles W. (1996), Letter to the Subcommittee on Crime, Committee on the Judiciary, House of Representatives, Washington, DC.

Thomas, Charles W. and Logan, Charles, H. (1993), 'The Development, Present Status, and Future Potential of Correctional Privatization in America', in Bowman, Gary W., Hakim, Simon and Seidenstat, Paul (eds), *Privatizing Correctional Institutions*, New Brunswick, Transaction Publishers, 213-240.

Thurman, Quint (1988), 'Taxpayer Noncompliance and Attribution Theory: An Experimental Vignette Approach', **43(1)** *Public Finance*, 147-156.

Thurow, L. (1970), 'Equity vs. Efficiency in Law Enforcement', **18** *Public Policy*, 451-459.

Trumball, William N. and Witte, Ann D. (1981-82a), 'Determinants of the Costs of Operating Large-Scale Prisons with Implications for the Cost of Correctional Standards', **16** *Law and Society Review*, 115-146.

Trumball, William N. and Witte, Ann D. (1981-82b), 'Problems in Estimating the Optimal-Cost Prison Size: A Reply', **16** *Law and Society Review*, 143-146.

United States Government Accounting Office (USGAO) (1991), *Private Prisons: Cost Savings and BOP's Statutory Authority Need to be Resolved*, Report to the Subcommittee on Crime, Committee on the Judiciary, House of Representatives, Letter Report, GAO/GGD-91-21.

United States Government Accounting Office (USGAO) (1996), *Private and Public Prisons: Studies Comparing Operational Costs and/or Quality of Service*, Report to the Subcommittee on Crime, Committee on the Judiciary, House of Representatives, Letter Report, GAO/GGD-96-158.

Usher, Dan (1997), 'Education as a Deterrent to Crime', **30** *Canadian Journal of Economics*, 367-384.

Viscusi, W. Kip (1986), 'The Risks and Rewards of Criminal Activity: A Comprehensive Test of Criminal Deterrence', **4** *Journal of Labor Economics*, 317-340.

Visher, Christy A. (1986), 'The Rand Inmate Survey: A Reanalysis', in Blumstein, Alfred, Cohen, Jacqueline and Roth, Jeffrey A. (eds), *Career Criminals and 'Criminal Careers', Vol. II*, Washington, DC, National Academy Press, 161-211.

Visher, Christy A., Lattimore, Pamela K. and Linster, Richard L. (1991), 'Predicting the Recidivism of Serious Youthful Offenders Using Survival Models', **29** *Criminology*, 329-366.

Waldfogel, Joel (1993), 'Criminal Sentences as Exogenous Taxes: Are they "Just" or "Efficient"?' **36** *Journal of Law and Economics*, 139-151.

Waldfogel, Joel (1994a), 'The Effect of Criminal Conviction on Income and the Trust "Reposed in the Workmen"', **29(1)** *Journal of Human Resources*, 162-181.

Waldfogel, Joel (1994b), 'Does Conviction Have a Persistent Effect on Income and Employment?', **14** *International Review of Law and Economics*, 103-119.

Waldfogel, Joel (1995), 'Are Fines and Prison Terms Used Efficiently? Evidence on Federal Fraud Offenders', **38** *Journal of Law and Economics*, 107-139.

Weitekamp, Elmar G.M. and Kerner, Hans-Jürgen (1994), *Cross-National Longitudinal Research on Human Development and Criminal Behavior*, Dordrecht, Kluwer.

Werden, Gregory J. and Simon, Marilyn J. (1987), 'Why Price Fixers should go to Prison', **32(4)** *Antitrust Bulletin*, 917-937.

Wilde, Louis L. (1992), 'Criminal Choice, Nonmonetary Sanctions, and Marginal Deterrence: A Normative Analysis', **12** *International Review of Law and Economics*, 333-344.

Williamson, Oliver E. (1964), *The Economics of Discretionary Behavior: Managerial Objectives in a Theory of the Firm*, Englewood Cliffs, NJ, Prentice-Hall.

Wilson, James Q. (1983), *Thinking About Crime*, New York, Basic Books.

Wilson, James Q. (1993), *The Moral Sense*, New York, The Free Press.

Wilson, James Q. (1994), 'Culture, Incentives, and the Underclass', in Aaron, Henry J., Mann, Thomas E. and Taylor, Timothy (eds), *Values and Public Policy*, Washington, DC, The Brookings Institution, 54-80.

Wilson, James Q. and Herrnstein, Richard J. (1985), *Crime and Human Nature*, New York, Simon and Schuster.

Witte, Ann D. (1977), 'Work Release in North Carolina - A Program That Works!', **41** *Law and Contemporary Problems*, 230-251.

Witte, Ann D. (1980), 'Estimating the Economic Model of Crime with Individual Data', **94** *Quarterly Journal of Economics*, 57-84.

Witte, Ann D. (1993), 'Some Thoughts on the Future of Research in Crime and Delinquency', **30** *Journal of Research in Crime and Delinquency*, 513-525.

Witte, Ann D. (1995a), 'Crime and Education', Wellesley College Working Paper.

Witte, Ann D. (1995b), 'Urban Crime: Issues and Policies', Wellesley College Working Paper.

Witte, Ann D. (1996), 'Urban Crime: Issues and Policies', **7** *Housing Policy Debate*, 731-748.

Witte, Ann D. (1997), 'Crime' in Jere, Behrman and Nevzer, Stacey (eds), *The Social Benefits of Education*, Ann Arbor, University of Michigan Press, 219-246.

Witte, Ann D. and Reid, Pamela A. (1980), 'An Exploration of the Determinants of Labor Market Performance for Prison Releasees', **8(3)** *Journal of Urban Economics*, 313-329.

Witte, Ann D. and Schmidt, Peter (1977), 'An Analysis of Recidivism, using the Truncated Lognormal Distribution', **26** *Journal of the Royal Statistical Society*, 302-311.

Witte, Ann D. and Schmidt, Peter (1979), 'An Analysis of the Type of Criminal Activity Using the Logit Model', **16** *Journal of Research in Crime and Delinquency*, 164-179.

Wynne, John M. (1978), 'Unions and Bargaining among Employees of State Prisons', **101** *Monthly Labor Review*, 10-16.

Zimmer, Lynn and Jacobs, James B. (1981), 'Challenging the Taylor Law: Prison Guards on Strike', **34(4)** *Industrial and Labor Relations Review*, 531-544.

8400
ORGANIZED CRIME AND ILLEGAL MARKETS

Gianluca Fiorentini
Dipartimento di Scienze Economiche
Università di Bologna

Abstract

This chapter discusses some of the most influential definitions of organized crime focusing on the differences between ordinary illegal firms and governance structures which supply public services such as the protection of property rights and the enforcement of contracts. The chapter further investigates the relations between the structural features of organized crime and the basic working rules of illegal markets. In this respect, the economic justifications to make markets illegal are discussed as second-best policies in serious cases of asymmetric information and externalities. To understand the origin of organized crime we analyze the implications of the proprietary theory of government. Moreover, to understand the internal structure of organized crime we concentrate on the role of input specificity in performing illegal transactions. A brief discussion of the deterrence policies against organized crime concludes the chapter.
JEL classification: K14, K40, K42
Keywords: Illegal Behavior, Enforcement of Law, Illegal Markets, Rent Seeking

1. Introduction

After a brief description of the plan of the work the next section analyzes some influential economic definitions of organized crime. We start focusing on the differences between ordinary illegal firms and governance structures. The former supply private goods in illegal or irregular markets while the latter provide public goods such as the protection of property rights and the enforcement of contracts. On this basis we analyze the relations between the structural features of organized crime and the basic working rules of illegal markets. The purpose of Section 3 is to explore the implications of the proprietary theory of government for the analysis of organized crime. Building on the rent-seeking literature we also discuss contributions on the competition between organizations for the control of a given area. The starting point of such models is that if property rights are weakly enforced by the legitimate government there will be greater incentives to invest in destructive activities against other criminal organizations or legal firms exposed to violent threats. Finally, we show how such a rent-seeking approach to the origin of organized crime allows one to draw some implications on its role in influencing the long-run growth of the economy.

Section 4 investigates the relations between different forms of regulatory intervention of the legitimate government and the firms' choice to shift their activities to irregular markets. To develop this point, we consider the related literature on the empirical analysis of the irregular markets building on direct surveys and on indirect monetary methods. In Section 5, we deal with the role of organized crime in illegal markets when it completely substitutes legitimate governments in most of their basic functions. In this area the literature suggests that there is a positive relation between the volume of transactions in illegal markets and the influence of organized crime in legitimate business activities. For this reason, we report on the economic justifications to limit transactions in illegal markets. In particular, we focus on the contributions explaining prohibitions to exchange goods in terms of second-best policies in serious cases of asymmetric information and externalities. In Section 6, we discuss how organized crime is involved in legal markets. In this respect we concentrate on three distinct activities: the supply of illegal inputs to legal firms, the manipulation of public funds and the joint production of legitimate and illegitimate outputs.

In Section 7, we focus on the internal structure of organized crime in the supply of basic inputs required to compete in illegal markets such as protection from police enforcement and money laundering. As for the internal structure, much work has dealt with the enforcement of secrecy codes in shaping the internal rules of organized crime. Similarly, the literature on vertical integration deals primarily with the degree of specificity of the inputs to explain different organizational models. In this setting particular attention is paid to understand how the authority is distributed between downstream firms active in the markets for illegal outputs and upstream governance structures specialized in supplying protection services. Section 8 analyzes some of the main deterrence policies taken up against organized crime. We start discussing the classic defense of organized crime as a monopolistic supplier of illegal goods based on its interest in minimizing the use of violence and in restricting the output levels. To further understand this issue, we briefly describe the effects of the legalization of illegal markets on the barriers to entry and on the equilibrium output. Taking as given the border between legal and illegal markets, we examine some more specific policy issues. In this area, we discuss the relative costs and benefits of addressing deterrence activities against suppliers and purchasers of illegal goods and the merits of enforcement policies exploiting conflicts between the two parties.

Finally, we report on the literature dealing with the broad theme of policy design against organized crime with specific reference to the cases when different organizations interact strategically.

2. Definitions of Organized Crime

Fiorentini and Peltzman (1995b) discuss three main economic definitions of organized crime. Here we follow broadly their discussion, but we add a fourth definition that builds on the differences between Schelling (1971) and Gambetta (1988). One of the first definitions can be traced back in the report of the President's Commission on Law Enforcement and Administration of Justice (1967). According to such a definition the core business of organized crime is the supply of illegal goods and services. More specifically, Cressey (1967) - one of the experts working for the Commission - suggests that the differences between ordinary illegal firms and organized crime is that the latter specializes in activities for which there is an autonomous demand, while the former more often undertake purely predatory activities. As a whole, the report admits that organized crime practices coercion against other agents (firms, unions, police agencies) but this is more related to its activities in legal markets that are relatively marginal. In this respect, an occasional use of violence can be explained with the need to invest in military technology to protect property rights in illegal markets, and with the relatively low marginal costs in using such assets once they are in place.

The above definition correctly points at the crucial relation between illegal markets and the more general influence of organized crime on the allocation of resources in illegal activities. However, it suffers from three limitations. First, it is purely descriptive and does not provide a convincing economic explanation for such a relation. Second, it builds on an idea of organized crime as a highly integrated firm - both vertically and horizontally – that operates monopolies in various stages of the production and distribution of illegal commodities. Third, it misses the difference between the role of organized crime as a firm supplying illegal goods to final consumers and as a governance structure imposing regulations and supplying public goods to independent illegal firms. Starting from these criticisms, Schelling (1971) suggests that the core business of organized crime is to impose its protection to other legal and illegal firms under the threat of violence. To practice extortion organized crime must reach a monopolistic control over the supply of violence, at least in a limited area, as its services necessarily include protection against other competing organizations. Similarly, those who provide protection services have to control the supply of corruption to local police agencies to reduce the threat of competing organizations calling for police intervention against them.

To explain the main differences between illegal firms and organized crime, Schelling (1971) discusses the features of those markets where the latter typically develops a governmental authority. The first feature of such markets is that victimized firms should be unable to protect themselves. This explains why illegal or irregular markets are privileged areas for the control of organized crime as illegal firms are less likely to call for police protection. Second, victims should find it difficult to hide themselves. Accordingly, organized crime concentrates most of its extortion on illegal firms that supply goods to final consumers and not on other organizations specialized in appropriative activities. Third, organized crime is more likely to impose extortion on firms whose profits are easily observable. In fact, without an independent auditing authority, monitoring problems may lead to continuous conflicts. Fourth, Schelling notices that organized crime is more likely to practice extortion on illegal firms the higher their asset specificity both in terms of site specificity and of capital embodied in customer relations. For this reason, independent restaurants and shops operating at a local level are often victims of organized crime. Fifth, illegal or legal firms are more likely to end up under the control of organized crime if the payments imposed are tax deductible, imposed on all competitors and if they can be shifted onto the final consumers. This explains why organized crime often covers its core business with legitimate commercial activities as this allows levying taxes supplying overpriced inputs to the victimized firms. Finally, organized crime typically succeeds in becoming a governance structure if the victims of extortion are individuals or small firms. This is because the risk of police intervention increases more than proportionally with the number of agents who know the details of the extortion.

At the end of his paper, Schelling (1971) introduces a qualification of his thesis, which has been developed by Gambetta (1993), and constitutes the basis for a third definition of organized crime. Schelling notices that often illegal firms call for organized crime intervention to provide the public services required to stay in business (for example, corruption of police officers or enforcement of collusive agreements). In this perspective, the tax levied on the protected firms represents the price voluntarily paid for the above services. Gambetta (1993) builds on this intuition and argues that organized crime operates as a governance structure mostly addressed to the underworld so that its activities cannot be reduced to the supply of illegal goods. Compared to Schelling, Gambetta goes further in denying the coercive character of the relationships between organized crime and illegal firms, and suggests that its core business is the supply of trust, that is of a more stable institutional setting for illegal firms. Such supply does not involve only the protection of property rights and the enforcement of contracts, but also the provision of barriers against entry and the organization of collusive agreements. Since there is a voluntary demand for these services, the coercive elements in the relations between organized crime and illegal firms are in its need to use violence occasionally to preserve its reputation as an authority to solve disputes or to enforce contracts.

The idea that organized crime does not only supply illegal goods to final consumers and that behind extortion one can see implicit contracts with illegal firms is coherent with the available evidence on its internal organization (Anderson, 1979). In particular, this study shows that organized crime operates as a firm mainly to cover up its governance activities, but even such role is limited to the provision of intermediate inputs to other small illegal firms. Moreover, to extract most of the rents accruing to the firms using its services organized crime usually enforces a strict control on the number of competitors under its protection.

More recently Alexander (1997) proposes three settings to describe the relationships between organized crime and the firms under its control which differ for the degree of coercion imposed by the former. First, a 'leviathan' model where a racketeer can extract surplus from small competitive firms. Second, a model where a 'dominant firm' colludes with a racketeer in imposing coercion over smaller competitors. Third, a 'cartel' model where groups of legal firms demand the enforcement services of organized crime. The 'leviathan' model builds on the idea that when organized crime acts as a racketeer it can force all firms to adopt a monopolistic price in the downstream market because its information set is complete and its threats are credible (Rubin, 1973). Hence, the 'leviathan' can extract all profits through firm-specific sales taxes and lump-sum taxes negatively related with each firm's marginal costs. This model predicts that organized crime will levy higher firm-specific taxes on the most efficient firms to force them to a greater reduction of their output. The 'dominant firm' model builds on the idea that large firms often may be interested in calling for the intervention of a racketeer to impose sales taxes on rival firms. To maximize profits, tax rates are set to a level that the surviving fringe firms have marginal costs just below those of the dominant firm. It follows that the latter extracts more rents from the taxes than from producing the fringe output. Finally, the 'cartel' model builds on some evidence that legal firms in different industries establish associations and acquire the services of organized crime as an enforcer of collusive agreements.

Comparing these different settings with the available data on the tax levied by organized crime on legal firms, Alexander finds out that the former often imposes a two-part tax. The first component is a lump-sum tax creating an entry barrier for relatively small new entrants and the second is a sales tax to control for overproduction. However, the relatively low level of both rates, and especially of the sales tax, is interpreted as evidence of weak or no discrimination against more efficient firms, and therefore is more easily reconciled with the 'cartel' model. Moreover, the organization enforcing the cartel charges legal firms for the purchase of packaging labels thereby monitoring the market shares of the participants. Finally, the reported evidence indicates that firms belonging to the association, and therefore purchasing the cartel enforcement services, are more stable over the long run. Hence, the levy imposed by organized crime is compensated in terms of higher and/or more stable profits over time.

Reuter (1983) provides a fourth definition of organized crime as a hierarchical structure characterized by long-run horizon, and with an involvement in multiple illegal activities. Such an inductive definition relies more on the author's empirical studies of organized crime activities in different industries than on an attempt to deduct new elements to build a general theory. In this respect, Reuter denies that organized crime can be seen as a firm active in illegal markets since its protection extends to legal firms, its activities include the control of public procurements, and its investments in legal businesses often represent the largest share of its assets. Analogously, Reuter does not fully accept Schelling's idea of organized crime as an authority with a coercive control over the allocation of resources in illegal and irregular markets. Indeed, in his empirical work Reuter shows how difficult it is for a central authority to control entry in such markets and more generally to regulate illegal firms. This is because entry barriers are often low, the costs of monitoring decentralized firms are high, and the threat of such firms calling for police intervention against large organizations is often credible. Arguably, the main lesson that can be drawn from Reuter's contributions is that there are a few economic elements which can be used to characterize organized crime (hierarchy, economies of scale and scope, specific capital assets, durability). However, such elements cannot be used to design deterrence policies against organized crime without a careful investigation of its internal structure and of the fundamentals of the specific markets involved.

3. The Proprietary Theory of the State and the Origin of Organized Crime

After Schelling (1971) who put forward the view of organized crime as a governance structure, other authors analyzed the relations between the origin of organized crime and the different activities of legitimate government. In this respect, Anderson (1995) suggests that there are three main factors for the emergence of organized crime: the investment in military technology to enforce legislation, the definition of regulatory measures including direct public intervention, and the legislative definition of illegal markets.

In this section we discuss the effects of a relatively weak investment in military technology on the origin of criminal organizations specialized in predatory activities. To do so, we follow the analysis of those economists who applied to the activities of legitimate government the same conceptual framework used by Schelling for organized crime. For instance, Baumol (1990) proposes a proprietary theory of the government where the ruling class is made of agents whose objective is to extract rents from their subjects under given institutional constraints such as winning the next elections and/or preserving their tax base. To meet these constraints, legitimate governments have to provide at least some public services in exchange for the taxes they levy. Such services are those primarily required for a system of decentralized markets to operate (protection of property rights and enforcement of contracts) and are the same as those supplied by organized crime to firms in irregular or illegal activities. Hence, Grossman (1995), following Gambetta (1993), builds his model on the close analogy between the taxes levied by the legitimate government and the extortionary duties levied by organized crime, as both share some elements of coercion and of voluntary transactions.

More precisely, Grossman (1995) assumes that firms and individuals can purchase the above public services from the legitimate government or from organized crime. In such a setting, the emergence of organized crime has a positive effect as it reduces the monopolistic power of the legitimate government. However, it may have negative consequences in terms of resources wasted in the competitive process to establish the monopoly over coercion. One of the worst possibilities for the victimized firms is when the two enforcers collude imposing revenue-maximizing taxes to their subjects. On the normative side, Grossman shows that as the ruling class appropriates the tax revenue there will be no widespread opposition to the growth of organized crime that reduces the fiscal pressure. Conversely, if the contest between organized crime and the government makes it possible for the former to become the new ruling class, it is rational for the victims to oppose its growth because it will eventually restore a monopolistic supply of public goods.

In the proprietary theory of government, organized crime becomes a competitor in setting taxes and providing public goods only because the latter has been unable or unwilling to invest enough resources in military technology. Baumol (1990) notices that in doing so the government indirectly provides incentives to other groups to specialize in appropriative activities rather than in productive ones. The most frequently used framework to investigate appropriative activities is that of rent-seeking contests (Hirschleifer, 1988). In these models competitors invest their resources to win the exclusive right to extract economic rents through extortion. Hence, if the monopolistic control over the supply of violence is relatively weak, entrepreneurs will invest in appropriative activities as long as they are more profitable than productive ones.

Skaperdas and Syropoulos (1995) combine this rent-seeking literature with the proprietary theory of government to investigate the origin of organized crime. In their model agents can choose to invest in appropriative or productive activities in an anarchy situation where none has the exclusive right to use coercive means and where agents are characterized by a comparative advantage in one of the two activities. The possibility to appropriate other agents' property is modeled in a rent-seeking contest where the larger the asymmetry between agents' productivity in military technology, the smaller the overall investment in such technology. This is because agents with a lower productivity are aware that their investment has little or no effect on their final share of resources. The outcome of the static game with no exit is that agents specialized in productive activities end up with a smaller share of the total output. Furthermore, in a more sophisticated setting, where agents with a comparative advantage in productive activities have an exit option, there is a progressive self-selection of agents in more homogeneous communities with a loss of productive capacity in those with a greater proportion of agents specialized in appropriative activities. When agents specialized in productive activities are complements to each other, they have a greater bargaining power as their exit further reduces the size of the pie. Finally, in a dynamic setting if there is no clear competitive advantage in the use of the military technology, all agents have strong incentives to invest in such technology. Here, the ongoing conflict reduces the effective protection of property rights and the returns from productive activities. In its turn, this induces exit or deters entry of new agents specialized in productive activities. Even this process does not provide sufficient incentives to reduce the investment in military technology as cooperative agreements do not represent equilibria of the rent-seeking game. Indeed, small initial differences in investment bring about large differences in the final pay-off. Hence, the model suggests that, due to the high returns of investing in violence at the beginning of the interaction, it is crucial that a group of agents emerges from the beginning as the most productive in using the military technology to deter other groups' initiatives.

4. Regulatory Policies and Irregular Markets

Anderson (1995) suggests a second relation between the activities of legitimate government and those of organized crime based on the features of the regulatory regime imposed on legal firms. There are two institutional elements involved in this relation. First, a high degree of regulation increases the compliance costs for legal firms and may induce them to switch some activities to irregular markets where property rights are defined and contracts are enforced by organized crime. Moreover, as firms operating in irregular markets often increase their market shares due to their lower costs this brings larger parts of the productive system under the control of organized crime. Second, as noticed by Tanzi (1995), regulation is usually coupled with a high degree of bureaucratic discretion and this provides strong incentives to shift potentially productive resources into corruption. Since the supply of corruption is more efficiently managed through monopolies or collusive agreements to avoid a dissipation of resources, this represents an incentive for criminal organizations to acquire some control over the allocation of public resources.

Along these lines, Smith (1976) investigates the effects of regulation on the size of the irregular markets building on the assumption that there is an unavoidable conflict between the objectives of the government in passing legislation and those of the economic agents who strive to minimize costs. The main purpose of the model is to show that the effects of any regulatory measure can be understood only taking into account the incentives of the regulated agents to shift resources into irregular markets. More specifically, Smith focuses on taxation as an instance of cost-increasing regulation because it is relatively easy to be measured and because of greater data availability. He elaborates a relatively simple two-market model, where goods in the legal and irregular markets are imperfect substitutes for consumers due to an expected sanction if discovered trading in the latter. In this setting Smith analyzes the effects of changes in taxation and in enforcement activities over the equilibrium in both legal and irregular markets. The reduction in the output level in the legal market, due to an increase in taxation, is understated if one does not take into account the possibility for producers to trade in irregular markets. Moreover, no clear effects of a tax increase can be derived for the equilibrium price in both legal and irregular markets. This is because legal and illegal goods are substitutes in consumption and in production so that a change in the price on the legal market (due to increased regulation) has effects on the shape of the demand and supply curves in both markets. Overall, the effect of a tax increase on the profit levels for firms dealing in both markets depends on how they distribute their output across the two. More definite results can be obtained only for firms dealing exclusively in the legal market as an increase in production costs reduces, ceteris paribus, the unitary profits. Smith also provides an empirical analysis of the effects of an increase in regulatory standards on the volumes traded in both legal and irregular markets for distilled spirits. The main result is that demand and supply respond more to changes in tax rates than to changes in market prices with no relation with government regulation. Indeed, both consumers and producers substitute between legal and irregular markets after a change in the regulatory costs. Smith also finds a positive correlation between tax rates and prices in the legal market: the shift of producers and consumers to the illegal market has a greater effect on the supply curve (shifting it upward) than on demand (shifting it downward) in the legal market.

In a similar vein, Anderson (1995) examines other regulatory measures that provide incentives for legal firms to invest in irregular markets and therefore to create a market for the public services supplied by organized crime. First, there is regulation aimed at increasing quality standards which often involves a limited supply of licenses or permits (building, commercial, professional, polluting) or other entry barriers. In these circumstances organized crime tries to control the distribution of the licenses using its comparative advantage in centralizing corruption and/or in enforcing cartels among incumbent firms. Second, there is price control regulation or interventions to set subsidies, quotas or other constraints to exchange. In these cases organized crime avoids quality standards and/or reports non-existing output taking advantage of its protection against the enforcement of police agencies. According to the New York State 'Organized Crime Task Force' Report (1989) the involvement of organized crime in the allocation of public funds is a consequence of two distinct sources of comparative advantage. First, in bribing and threatening public officers and, second, in coordinating collusive agreements between firms and the public administration. When such collusive agreements take place, organized crime succeeds in extracting rents from both public purchasers and private suppliers. According to Grossman (1995), in these collusive agreements greater stability is often obtained when electoral support is provided in exchange for a reduction in the enforcement efforts. In these circumstances the criminal organization can also manage to direct the enforcement activities against its rivals. It follows that while the enforcement agencies meet their targets in terms of quantitative indicators, the incumbent obtains further positive externalities. Moreover, both sides strengthen their fiduciary relationships and reduce the incentives to act opportunistically. On similar lines, Tanzi (1995) observes that collusive agreements between local politicians and criminal organizations become less stable in case of fiscal crises as the latter reduce the possibility to activate public expenditure without a corresponding increase in the fiscal pressure. In such a case it is unlikely that public administrations succeed in appropriating large rents from direct interventions without reducing their electoral support. A greater political instability may therefore decrease the incentives for criminal organizations to collude with politicians as their expected stay in power is shortened.

To measure the size of irregular markets and the potential threat they represent for the activities of the legitimate government some authors attempted to overcome the complex methodological problems due to a lack of reliable data. In this perspective, Feige (1994) proposes a definition of the illegal economy which includes all transactions that violate specific statutory rules concerning the scope of what is regarded as legitimate trade. On the other hand, irregular activities include all transactions which belong to the area of the legal economy as defined above, but violate statutory and/or administrative rules related to one or more of the following areas: property relationships, commercial licensing, labor contracts, torts, financial credit and social security. Feige describes two lines of research aimed at measuring the size of the irregular markets. First, the direct approach based on the analysis of tax auditing and other reports concerning the level of compliance with fiscal legislation and regulatory standards as a whole. Second, the indirect approach based on the analysis of macroeconomic indexes over time. As for the latter, Tanzi (1983) develops a currency approach which builds on the assumption that irregular transactions are mostly undertaken via cash payments. Accordingly, one can detect changes in the irregular transactions observing, ceteris paribus, changes in the demand for liquidity. Similar in spirit is the approach proposed by Feige (1989) which builds on the assumption that the Fischer quantity equation holds through time. On this basis, knowing the amount of liquidity, the level of prices, and the velocity of rotation, one obtains relatively good estimates of the total transactions taking place in the system. Comparing such total transactions with the nominal GDP one could approximate the transaction volume in the irregular markets. Feige also discusses other lines of research that adopt an indirect approach but rely on real variables from national accounts and labor market data. In this group of contributions, Macafee (1982) and Park (1979) propose a quantitative analysis of the irregular markets which relies on the discrepancy between national expenditure and national income as it can be related to unreported income from illegal or irregular transactions. Analogously, Contini (1981) tries to estimate the overall size of the irregular markets looking at changes in the labor force participation rate with respect to a standard level which is assumed to be observable in the absence of illegal or irregular activities.

Although the above authors admit that the lack of reliable data represents a serious obstacle to measure the size of the informal economy, building on these results Schneider (1994) proposes an approach to investigate how that size is related to the overall burden of taxation and to the level of regulation. More precisely, Schneider shows that increases in fiscal pressure or in regulatory intensity (the number of existing laws) and in the complexity of the tax system (a Herfindahl-Hirschman concentration measure of the revenue sources) are all strongly related the size of the illegal and irregular markets.

Moreover, Schneider's results suggest that even a decline in the fiscal pressure is not a sufficient condition for a reduction of the size of the irregular economy if it is not followed by a fall in the indexes of regulatory complexity and intensity. Related to this literature on the size of the shadow economy, Reuter (1984) tries to quantify the multiplier effect of the expenditure in illegal markets on the economy as a whole. In a first model he assumes that illegal goods are produced by foreign criminal agents and therefore can be regarded as imports in national accounts. For this reason, purchases of illegal goods have no impact on national income. Then Reuter assumes that the producers of illegal goods are domestic so that the expenditure on such goods becomes an export to another country, as they do not emerge in official statistics. In such a case an increase in the demand for illegal goods is similar to a purely exogenous demand shock as it originates outside the regular economy. Assuming that the expenditures in illegal goods result in income for the domestic producers, the multiplier is lower because it depends negatively on the differences in saving propensities between producers and consumers of illegal goods.

5. Organized Crime and Illegal Markets

The neo-institutional literature focuses on the effects of different mechanisms for defining and protecting property rights and for enforcing contracts to explain market performances. In one of the leading contributions to this literature Demsetz (1967) notices that the participants in illegal markets should in principle self-protect their property rights. Indeed, if the government does not provide the basic services required to support the working of decentralized markets private agents willing to trade have to substitute it. As most rent-seeking literature suggests, in similar situations it is likely that after a competition among private agents or groups one of them will emerge as the specialized supplier. Schelling (1971) notices that after such an authority becomes established it is likely that its activities will also include the use of violence and corruption and the provision of inputs at regulated prices. Furthermore, when illegal organizations with large specific assets protect themselves from the police and from other opportunistic behaviors they often generate a positive spillover to other producers not only in the same line of product but also in related markets. It follows that they will find it convenient to exploit these economies of scale and scope. Eventually, when large investments are sunk in protecting property rights and enforcing contracts, such organizations may have sufficient incentives to compete with the legitimate government for the right to provide the above services even for agents active in legal markets.

Building on this perspective, Paul and Wilhite (1994) show that the full social cost of making goods or services illegal should also take into account the dissipation of resources invested in the attempt to establish a monopoly in the supply of protection and enforcement services. In this respect, even agents not interested in obtaining a monopoly position but willing to protect their endowments are forced to invest intensively in that direction. In order to derive their main result, Paul and Wilhite discuss Becker and Stigler's (1974) claim that an increased enforcement against producers of illegal goods on average increases their profits. The authors argue that to draw such a clear-cut conclusion one should address directly the effects on producers' costs of the increased enforcement and, more to our point, on the resources wasted in the attempt to monopolize the illegal market. Paul and Wilhite claim that producers are not attracted by the price increase brought about by the government-induced supply restriction, but by the perspective to obtain rents from the monopolistic control of the illegal markets. Hence, the main consequence of a lack of public enforcement of property rights is to increase the investment in military technology and in corruption. Given these negative consequences, different economic justifications have been offered to explain relatively low levels of public enforcement. Traditionally, authors like Buchanan (1973) or Rubin (1973) stress that in most instances markets are made illegal for paternalistic reasons, that is because consumers do not fully understand the consequences of their actions. According to this view, such markets would have usually reached an efficient equilibrium as agents transact voluntarily and there are no significant imperfections such as external effects from production or consumption.

In a different perspective, Rose-Ackerman (1985) explains the decision of making transactions illegal as a second-best policy to reduce the negative effects of market imperfections. Rose-Ackerman proposes two arguments to limit the rights of exchange on efficiency grounds, and a third argument which has to do with the intrinsic limits of the technology used to enforce the ban. First, goods such as body organs or human blood need costly quality controls which make it difficult for purchasers to evaluate the available alternatives. Moreover, even if purchasers were able to discriminate, such goods are often demanded in such an urgency that their bargaining power is negligible. Hence, Rose-Ackerman argues that to avoid excessive *ex post* litigation over the terms, the government might declare such contracts illegal on efficiency grounds. Following this argument, one could object that if the government's objective is to increase the standards of quality, measures aimed at reducing entry but not blocking it completely (for example, licenses) should be used to deter producers who would specialize in low quality supply. However, licensing practices tend to discourage particularly low-income consumers and to shift their demand to irregular markets where non-licensed suppliers operate. Hence, the government's ban could be further rationalized as a measure to avoid negative redistributive effects from the attempt to regulate such markets.

The second efficiency argument to make markets illegal is that the production and/or consumption of illegal goods with a voluntary demand can give rise to negative external effects, which are not accounted for by the parties involved. For instance, the consumption of heavy drugs may lead to the impossibility for consumers to face their obligations using their legal incomes and therefore increase the number of thefts and other predatory crimes. In its turn, this would force other agents to invest in defensive measures that increase the opportunity costs of holding property and trading. Moreover, the consumption of drugs may lead to a worsening of consumers' health conditions to a point that they cannot cover the resulting medical expenses and therefore require some sort of public or charitable intervention. Rose-Ackerman also suggests an additional and subtler source of externality arising from the imperfections of the enforcement mechanisms. Her example is centered on the trade of species in danger of extinction. In such a case the purpose of the ban is to deter further killing of endangered animals and, on efficiency grounds, this should not be extended to animals killed in the past. However, due to the impossibility of detecting differences between animals killed in different periods of time, all transactions are banned. In this respect, the suppliers of new animals in danger of extinction create a negative externality for the owners of animals killed in the past. The example could be regarded as trivial due to the relatively small dimension of such a market compared to other illegal markets, but its logic can be extended to cover other interesting cases. For instance, in the market for illegal drugs, a similar external effect can be relevant as most economists (Moore, 1973; White and Luksetich, 1983) suggest that an appropriate regulatory practice would be to increase the price only for new consumers to discourage their consumption. At the same time the deterrence policy should interfere less with the market price for old consumers not to create rents for producers and traders. However, as most illegal drugs are characterized by very small hoarding costs, it is virtually impossible to enforce a discriminatory regime against new consumers, as the old ones would have too great incentives to enter the trade. As arbitrage would then be declared illegal, it is likely that organized crime would take over from old consumers at least for the large-scale trade.

6. Organized Crime and Legal Markets

Although most economists agree that the larger share of activities of organized crime is linked with the provision of governance services for firms involved in irregular or illegal markets, some influential contributions investigate its intervention in legal markets. For instance, Reuter (1987) and Gambetta and Reuter (1995) investigate the enforcement of cartel agreements in industries with auction markets managed by public administrations (for example, waste disposal, road construction, building). Such markets are often highly competitive due to the relatively low level of specific inputs and cartel agreements are unstable as it is difficult to detect and to sanction defections. The role of organized crime is therefore to increase the stability of such agreements threatening to punish the firms who defect. On similar lines, Gambetta (1988) suggests that a separate service provided by organized crime to legal firms is protection from entry of new competitors. This is because it is neither in the interest of the incumbent firms nor of organized crime to allow entry, since this would ultimately reduce the rents that are at least in part appropriated by the latter.

Organized crime activities in legal markets extend also to the direct investment and management of legitimate businesses. In this respect, Anderson (1979) suggests that the main reason for organized crime to start legitimate business activities is that these activities allow organized crime to exploit economies of scale and scope related to its illegal activities. First, members of the organize crime need a source of legitimate income to hide their true business. Analogously, in the supply of illegal goods or services there is a need for places to trade so that small shops, bars and restaurants are used to cover activities related to loan-sharking or illegal betting. Second, illegal activities often produce outputs or use inputs that are also needed in the legal ones (transportation, communications, warehousing) so that it is profitable to integrate the two. Third, organized crime needs to launder at least part of its profits. To do so through a business activity under its control reduces the risks involved in money laundering. Fourth, the legitimate business can be seen as an occasion to diversify the organization's portfolio with investments characterized by a different mix of risk and returns. Fiorentini and Peltzman (1995b), following Schelling (1967), discuss the features of the legitimate activities in which it is more likely to observe direct investments by organized crime. In this respect, profits from illegal activities are often invested in industries with relatively mature technologies and protected from international competition. In more competitive settings the comparative advantages of organized crime in legal businesses (monopolistic control of the input markets and especially of the labor unions, availability of capital at low cost and direct threats to rival firms) are not likely to be relevant. For instance, large multinational firms active in open markets often compete over product and process innovations and/or financial diversification. Also Gambetta and Reuter (1995) discuss the market features more likely to elicit the intervention of organized crime, reaching similar conclusions. In particular, they find that such intervention can be observed in markets with low barriers to entry both in terms of sunk capital and product differentiation.

Anderson (1979) notices that in the debate on organized crime's legitimate activities opinions differ on how much coercion is used against legal firms. According to the report of the President's Commission on Law Enforcement and Administration of Justice (1967), organized crime disrupts competition through predatory practices and represents a serious threat for all legal firms involved. On the contrary, MacMichael (1971) suggests that the possibility for organized crime to take advantage of these practices is limited by the greater visibility of legal activities. Indeed, there are increasing risks of losing profits from both legal and illegal activities due to a more active police enforcement as legal firms are more likely to call for its intervention. More generally, although an increase in the transactions under control of organized crime has negative consequences for the development of a given area, it may not be always appropriate to concentrate deterrence efforts to prevent money laundering. Fiorentini and Peltzman (1995b) suggest that when criminal organizations obtain a high level of illegal profits one should compare the relative social losses from their investment in other illegal activities or in legal ones. This is because, even if an extremely costly deterrence mechanism could prevent their laundering, illegal profits would be invested in other illegal activities or in other countries. Hence, for a given level of enforcement, one must face a trade-off between reducing the area of legal transactions under control of criminal organizations and reducing the area of the illegal transactions.

7. Internal Structure and Vertical Integration of Organized Crime

One of the first studies of the internal structure of organized crime is Jennings (1984). In his view, the central function of organized crime is to require its members to take an oath not to cooperate with the police and to enforce such an oath by punishing those who fail to comply with it. However, since the relative monitoring and enforcing costs are high and rapidly increasing with the number of members and markets involved, organized crime core business is concentrated in relatively few activities. Moreover, Jennings shows that the enforcement of the oath is valuable only if the illegal activities of organized crime require specialized agents working in teams and running substantial risks if one betrays the others. On the contrary, if the illegal activities are mainly performed individually, the enforcement of the oath is relatively useless. Also Gambetta (1988) draws attention to the relevance of secrecy in shaping the internal structure of organized crime not only to avoid detection from the police, but also to manage different sources of intelligence which can be used to maximize its profits. In this respect, Gambetta notices that the comparative advantage of organized crime in selling its protection services is much greater when those on the demand side know little of its internal structure as the organization would be more exposed to police intervention. A recent development in the analysis of the internal structure of organized crime is Polo (1995) who models the latter as a hierarchical organization where the principal hire agents to carry out tasks usually requiring to commit serious crimes. The main problem of the principal is to design a set of incentives constraining agents' opportunistic behavior in absence of legal contracts. To solve this problem the principal offers contracts where the enforcement of the terms depends on the credibility of the mechanism to sanction the agents who defect.

More generally, the economic literature on the vertical structure of organized crime begins with Schelling (1971) who suggests that the latter integrates downstream with illegal firms' markets when one or more of the following conditions apply: First, when the downstream markets are natural monopolies so that the implicit contracts described in Polo (1995) are particularly subjected to the opportunistic behavior of the illegal firms that might threaten the governance role of organized crime. Second, when there are external effects mainly due to the need to supply violence and corruption which can be internalized through integration. In these circumstances a centralized control avoids duplications of costs and reduces the dissipation of resource in appropriative activities. Third, when financing illegal firms' activities through an integrated structure allows for a more efficient portfolio strategy (Rubin, 1973). Fourth, when contracts may become source of evidence against the agents who sign them. In other words, the impossibility to use detailed contracts in dealing with complex transactions reduces the advantages of the market over an integrated structure. Fifth, when the illegal firms enjoy large informative advantages and are able to hide most of their profits.

However, some authors (Reuter, 1983; New York State Organized Crime Task Force, 1989) stress that there are limits to the benefits of increasing the area of economic transactions directly managed by a centralized organization. According to Reuter, the main limit of such organization has to do with the rapidly increasing costs of monitoring and coordinating agents with conflicting interests. In this respect, the need to keep a centralized control over the use of violence and the fact that police agencies invest more intensively against large-scale organizations might explain the emergence of relatively small local monopolies. Indeed, the first condition provides incentives to reach a monopolistic control while the second limits it to a local area. Second, precisely because the property rights over resources used in illegal activities can only be enforced at very high costs, to concentrate such rights in a centralized organization increases the negative consequences of police enforcement. An analogous reasoning holds for the human capital integrated in large organizations which is at greater risk in case of violation of the secrecy code. Third, in some illegal markets it is virtually impossible to impose a centralized control because of the low level of the barriers to entry. Finally, there might be a structural instability in the financial flows used in illegal activities due to the police enforcement against money laundering which can discourage large-scale sunk investments even by risk-neutral agents.

More recently Dick (1995) develops a framework to analyze the issue of the vertical integration in different institutional settings. In particular, Dick focuses on the illegal firms' choice between buying protection from a specialized organization and producing it internally. To investigate such issue, Dick suggests an decomposing the total transaction costs between production and organizational costs. Production costs are typically lower in a specialized organization due to economies of scale and scope and would call for market supply by a non-integrated producer. On the contrary, the organizational costs to coordinate inputs in specific uses and to adjust to unforeseen contingencies are lower in an integrated structure because of the high specificity of the assets involved. Building on this general framework, Dick (1995) suggests that small firms active in illegal markets are usually interested in buying protection from organized crime only if the latter is not specific to the local market. In such a case protection is more efficiently provided inside the illegal firms so that one of them will enforce the rules underlying the working of the illegal markets. Conversely, illegal firms will buy protection from specialized organizations when their expected time horizon is sufficiently long so that it is worthwhile to define and enforce complex market transactions. Such a longer time horizon is often observed when illegal firms and organized crime share a common culture, for instance due to ethnic networks, so that transaction costs are low and self-enforcing agreements are more likely to be feasible. Finally, illegal firms will self-supply protection if there is a high degree of uncertainty over the terms of the transactions. This explains why organized crime supplies protection to illegal firms dealing with victimless activities where the activities are easily observable, while self-protection is the rule for organizations involved in appropriative activities.

8. Normative Analysis

Buchanan (1973) introduces a controversial argument in the analysis of the deterrence strategies against organized crime. His basic assumption is that organized crime tends to control, directly or indirectly, the allocation of resources in illegal markets. In such a role it operates approximately as a monopolist whose interest is to block entry of new competitors and to limit output. Accordingly, a legislator willing to minimize the level of transactions in illegal markets should not target its deterrence policies against organized crime, which helps to pursue a similar objective. Buchanan also evaluates the distributive effects of a monopolistic structure characterized by a large share of surplus invested in other illegal activities. In his view, such distributive effects do not represent a sufficient reason to concentrate deterrence efforts against organized crime. Indeed, if there are economies of scale in the production of illegal goods a monopoly reduces the opportunity costs as it requires fewer resources per unit of output. Buchanan's analysis deals only with the role of organized crime in illegal markets and not in predatory activities. This means that his model does not address the negative effects of organized crime's supply of violence and corruption. This notwithstanding, compared to other supply structures one can argue that illegal monopolists prefer lower levels of violence and corruption precisely because they internalize such external effects.

Schelling (1967), building on his analysis of organized crime as a coercive authority, suggests that the first priority of any deterrence policy should be to legalize as many illegal markets as possible. The idea behind this is that only by reducing the rents available in the illegal markets can one limit organized crime's role as a governance structure for firms active in legal, irregular and illegal activities. Moreover, among the social costs of making some markets illegal one should consider that profits are used to bribe enforcement agencies and the public administration and that potential victims are led to invest in appropriative activities. To strengthen his thesis Schelling suggests that organized crime is unlikely to keep its control of the legalized markets since they are not characterized by high barriers to entry. Following the same reasoning, Tanzi (1995) proposes reducing the areas of direct public intervention because they are often run through auction markets where organized crime operates as the enforcer of collusive agreements between legal firms and the public administration.

Given the particular relevance of the features of police interventions in explaining the size of illegal markets, several economists analyzed the specific deterrence policies adopted against the criminal organizations running such markets. In this respect, Fiorentini and Peltzman (1995b) report that in most illegal markets (drugs, betting, loan sharking, prostitution, smuggling, counterfeiting) police agencies concentrate their efforts on agents involved in productive and trading activities more than on consumers. This is probably due to the recognition that demand is voluntary, and therefore if consumption gives rise to relatively low negative externalities, to target consumers would impose on them a rather high welfare loss. Moreover, if one takes into account the enforcement costs, consumers are often too many and too dispersed to be an efficient target for effective deterrence efforts. On similar lines, most empirical studies on industries where irregular activities involve a large size of resources show relatively low levels of entry barriers and asset specificity (New York State Organized Crime Task Force, 1989). This makes it difficult to design a deterrence policy against producers or traders as they are easily replaced by new organizations. To reduce the consequences of this problem Lott and Roberts (1989) suggest that the police should try to exploit the conflicts between parties involved in illegal transactions. This follows the analogy with those irregular markets where transactions violate price or safety regulations (house rents, loan sharking) and where one of the two contracting parties can be given enough incentives to denounce the other. A similar strategy, centered upon the use of potential conflicts between agents in the same organization, has been extensively used in fighting organized crime through informants' protection schemes.

These difficulties in targeting small illegal firms can explain why most resources are used to contrast the organizations involved in large-scale trading of illegal goods, in financing other illegal firms' activities, in laundering the profits from such activities and in bribing public officials. Indeed, all these activities involve human and physical capital assets extremely specific and rather difficult to be replaced in the short run. However, large organizations are also more reactive against the enforcement activities of the legitimate government as they have much more at stake. Hence, especially if such reactions take the form of increased corruption and violence against the police agencies (Fiorentini, 1995) it might be advisable to address part of the deterrence efforts against consumption strengthening the enforcement on the demand side. This is especially so if such policies are targeted against markets with a high demand elasticity (Becker and Murphy, 1988).

To specify appropriate deterrence policies aimed at reducing illegal transactions, agencies should also consider the strategic interactions between criminal organizations. In this respect, if there is a monopolistic or oligopolistic supply the allocative and distributive effects of an increase in the deterrence effort depend on the market structure emerging after the enforcement. For instance, if the market becomes competitive and barriers to entry are eliminated, in the long run more illegal goods will be traded at the new equilibrium (Buchanan, 1973). On the contrary, if the entry barriers are not lowered, strong enforcement activities against an incumbent may favor the surviving organizations increasing their profitability and therefore their capacity to supply violence and corruption (Cellentani, Marelli and Martina, 1995). In similar situations it is likely that an increased deterrence effort will lead to greater resources invested in corruption and violence.

Finally, the design of effective deterrence policies should take into account that organized crime's supply of services to legal, irregular and illegal firms is a relevant source of income in areas with large-scale unemployment. For this reason, although the aggregate negative consequences of organized crime activities on the growth of the legal economy are extremely large, there are problems in eliciting continuous support for the fight against it. This is not only because organized crime can directly threaten its opponents and corrupt police agencies, but also because it can buy support with distributive policies implemented jointly with local politicians (Grossman, 1995). Accordingly, most communities where organized crime plays a relevant role can be described using a prisoners' dilemma framework where individual agents are damaged in the short run by its disappearance and are therefore unable to coordinate themselves to reach more efficient outcomes.

Bibliography on Organized Crime and Illegal Markets (8400)

Adams, Michael (1991), 'Wie Zerstört man den Markt für Rauschgifte?', *Zeitschrift für Rechtspolitik*, 202-204. Reprinted in **9** *Zeitschrift für die Polizei*, 1992, p. 4-6.

Adams, Michael (1993), 'Neues vom Drogenmarkt?', **12** *Kriminalistik, Zeitschrift für die gesamte kriminalistische Wissenschaft und Praxis*, 755-757.

Adams, Michael (1994), 'Heroin an Süchtige? - Ein Abschliessender Schlagabtausch', *Zeitschrift für Rechtspolitik*, 421-426.

Alexander B. (1997), 'The Rational Racketeer: Pasta Protection in Depression Era Chicago', **40** *Journal of Law and Economics*, 175-202.

Anderson A. (1979), *The Business of Organized Crime: A Cosa Nostra Family*, Stanford, Hoover Institute Press, Stanford University.

Anderson A. (1995), 'Organized Crime, Mafias and Governments', in Fiorentini, Gianluca and Peltzman, Sam (eds), *The Economics of Organized Crime*, Cambridge, Cambridge University Press.

Arlacchi, Pino (1987), 'Effects of the New Anti-Mafia Law on the Proceeds of Crime and on the Italian Economy', in Alessandrini, Sergio and Dallago, Bruno (eds), *The Unofficial Economy: Consequences and Perspectives in Different Economic Systems*, Aldershot, Gower, 247-255.

Atkinson, Scott E., Sandler, Todd and Tschirhart, John (1987), 'Terrorism in a Bargaining Framework', **30** *Journal of Law and Economics*, 1-21.

Backhaus, Jürgen G. (1979), 'Defending Organized Crime? A Note', **8** *Journal of Legal Studies*, 623-631.

Backhaus, Jürgen G. (1980), 'Kein Aufruf zur Verteidigung des Organisierten Verbrechens (With English Summary) (No Call in Defense of Organized Crime)', **136** *Journal of Institutional and Theoretical Economics*, 658-672.

Baumol, William J. (1990), 'Entrepreneurship: Productive, Unproductive, and Destructive', **98(5)** *Journal of Political Economy*, 893-921.

Becker, G. and Murphy K. (1988), 'A Theory of Rational Addiction', **96** *Journal of Political Economy*, 675-700.

Becker, G. and Stigler, George J. (1974), 'Law Enforcement, Malfeasance, and Compensation of Enforcers', **3** *Journal of Legal Studies*, 1-18.

Benson, Bruce L. (1994), 'Third Thoughts on Contracting Out', **11** *Journal of Libertarian Studies*, 44-78.

Benson, Bruce L. and Baden, John A. (1985), 'The Political Economy of Government Corruption: The Logic of Underground Government', **14** *Journal of Legal Studies*, 391-410.

Benson, Bruce L. and Rasmussen, David W. (1991), 'The Relationship Between Illicit Drug Enforcement Policy and Property Crimes', **9** *Contemporary Policy Issues*, 106-115.

Benson, Bruce L. and Rasmussen, David W. (1992), *Illinois' War on Drugs: Some Unintended Consequences*, Heartland Policy Study, Chicago, Heartland Institute, No. 48.

Benson, Bruce L. and Rasmussen, David W. (1995), *Illicit Drugs and Crime*, Independent Policy Report, Oakland, Independent Institute.

Benson, Bruce L., Kim, Iljoong, Rasmussen, David W. and Zuehlke, Thomas W. (1992), 'Is Property Crime Caused by Drug Use or Drug Enforcement Policy?', **24** *Applied Economics*, 679-692.

Benson, Bruce L., Kim, Iljoong, Rasmussen, David W. and Zuehlke, Thomas W. (1993), 'An Economic Analysis of Recidivism Among Drug Offenders', **60** *Southern Economic Journal*, 169-183.

Benson, Bruce L., Rasmussen, David W. and Sollars, David L. (1995), 'Police Bureaucrats, Their Incentives, and the War on Drugs', **83** *Public Choice*, 21-45.

Brenner, Reuven (1990), 'The Long Road from Serfdom, and how to Shorten it', **17(2)** *Canadian Business Law Journal*, 195-226. Reprinted in Maruyana, M. (ed.)(1993), *Management Reform in Eastern and Central Europe*, Aldershot, Dartmouth, 81-109.

Brenner, Reuven (1994), *Labyrinths of Prosperity*, Ann Arbor, University of Michigan Press.

Brenner, Reuven and Brenner, Gabrielle A. (1990), *Gambling and Speculation*, Cambridge, Cambridge University Press. Reprinted in French edition by Presses Universitaires de France, 1993.

Buchanan, James M. (1973), 'A Defense of Organized Crime', in Andreano, Ralph and Siegfried, John J. (eds), *The Economics of Crime*, Cambridge, Schenkman.

Cellentani G., Marrelli, M. and Martina, Riccardo (1995), 'Cartel Stability and 'Optimal' Deterrence Policy', in Fiorentini, Gianluca and Peltzman, Sam (eds), *The Economics of Organized Crime*, Cambridge, Cambridge University Press.

Contini, Bruno (1981), 'Labor Market Segmentation and the Development of the Parallels Economy', **33** *Oxford Economic Papers*, 401-412.

Cressey D. (1967), *The Structure and Functions of Criminal Syndicates*, Washington, Government Printing Office. Appendix A of the President's Commission on Law Enforcement and Administration of Justice, Task Force Report: Organized Crime.

D'Antonio, Mariano and Scarlato, Margherita (1993a), 'L'Économia del Crimine. Parte I: Il Ruolo Economico (The Economics of Crime. Part I: Economic Role)', **27(3)** *Economia e Lavoro*, 107-122.

D'Antonio, Mariano and Scarlato, Margherita (1993b), 'L'Économia del Crimine. Parte II: La Dimensione del Mercato (With English Summary) (The Economy of Crime: Part II: Market Dimension)', **27(4)** *Economia e Lavoro*, 3-29.

Dawid, H. and Feichtinger, G. (1995), *On the Persistence of Corruption/Forschungsbericht*, Research Memorandum, Vienna, Institute for Econometrics, Operation Research and Systems Theory, University of Technology, No. 186.

Demsetz, H. (1967), 'Toward a Theory of Property Rights', **57** *American Economic Review*, 347-359.

Dick, Andrew R. (1995), 'When Does Organized Crime Pay? A Transaction Cost Analysis', **15** *International Review of Law and Economics*, 25-45.

Ehrlich, Isaac (1972), 'Participation in Illegitimate Activities: A Theoretical and Empirical Investigation', **80** *Journal of Political Economy*, 521-565.

Feige, Edgar L. (1989), *The Underground Economies: Tax Evasion and Information Distortion*, Cambridge, Cambridge University Press.

Feige, Edgar L. (1994), 'The Underground Economy and the Currency Enigma', **49** *Public Finance*, 119-136.

Fiorentini, Gianluca (1995), 'Oligopolistic Competition in Illegal Markets', in Fiorentini, Gianluca and Peltzman, Sam (eds), *The Economics of Organized Crime*, Cambridge, Cambridge University Press.

Fiorentini, Gianluca and Peltzman, Sam (1995a), 'Introduction', in Fiorentini, Gianluca and Peltzman, Sam (eds), *The Economics of Organized Crime*, Cambridge, Cambridge University Press.

Fiorentini, Gianluca and Peltzman, Sam (eds) (1995b), *The Economics of Organized Crime*, Cambridge, Cambridge University Press.

Fletcher, George P. (1985), 'A Transaction Cost Theory of Crime?', **85** *Columbia Law Review*, 921-930.

Gambetta, Diego (1988), 'Fragments of an Economic theory of the Mafia', **29** *Archives Européennes De Sociologie*, 127-145.

Gambetta, Diego (1993), 'The Sicilian Mafia: The Business of Private Protection', Cambridge, Harvard University Press.

Gambetta, Diego and Reuter, Peter (1995), 'Conspiracy Among the Many: Organized Crime in Legitimate Industries', in Fiorentini, Gianluca and Peltzman, Sam (eds), *The Economics of Organized Crime*, Cambridge, Cambridge University Press.

Giusti, Jorge (1991), 'The Economic and Social Significance of Narcotics', **0(45)** *Cepal Review*, 137-167.

Gragnani, A., Feichtinger, G. and Rinaldi, S. (1994), 'Dynamics of Drug Consumption: A Theoretical Model', **94-77** Working Paper.

Gragnani, A., Rinaldi, S. and Feichtinger, G. (1995), 'Slow-Fast Limit Cycles in Controlled Drug Markets', **185** *Forschungsbericht/Research Memorandum*.

Grossman, Herschel I. (1995), 'Rival Kleptocracies: The Mafia versus the State', in Fiorentini, Gianluca and Peltzman, Sam (eds), *The Economics of Organized Crime*, Cambridge, Cambridge University Press.

Hirschleifer, J. (1988), 'The Analytics of Continuing Conflict', **76** *Synthese*, 201-233.

Ichniowski, Casey and Preston, Anne (1989), 'The Persistence of Organized Crime in New York City Construction: Economic Perspective', **42(4)** *Industrial and Labor Relations Review*, 549-565.

Im, Eric Iksoon, Cauley, Jon and Sandler, Todd (1987), 'Cycles and Substitutions in Terrorist Activities: A Spectral Approach', **40** *Kyklos*, 238-255.

Jennings, William P., Jr (1984), 'A Note on the Economics of Organized Crime', **10(3)** *Eastern Economic Journal*, 315-321.

Johnson, Bruce M. (1985), *Taking Care of Business: The Economics of Crime by Heroin Abusers*, Lexington, MA, Lexington Books, 278 p.

Kleiman, Mark A.R. (1989), *Marijuana: Costs of Abuse, Costs of Control*, Westport, Greenwood, 197 p.

Landes, William M. (1978), 'An Economic Study of U.S. Aircraft Hijacking, 1961-1976', **21** *Journal of Law and Economics*, 1-31.

Lee, Barbara A. and Chelius, James R. (1989), 'Government Regulation of Labor Management Corruption: The Casino Industry Experience in New Jersey', **42(4)** *Industrial and Labor Relations Review*, 536-548.

Levine, Daniel, Stoloff, Peter and Spruill, Nancy (1976), 'Public Drug Treatment and Addict Crime', **5** *Journal of Legal Studies*, 435-462.

Levy, Peter B. (1989), 'The Waterfront Commission of the Port of New York: A History and Appraisal', **42(4)** *Industrial and Labor Relations Review*, 508-523.

Lott, John R., Jr (1992), 'An Attempt at Measuring the Total Monetary Penalty from Drug Convictions: The Importance of an Individual's Reputation', **21** *Journal of Legal Studies*, 159-187.

Lott, John R., Jr and Roberts, R.D. (1989), 'Why Comply: One-Sided Enforcement of Price Control and Victimless Crime Laws', **18** *Journal of Legal Studies*, 405-414.

Macafee (1982), 'A Glimpse of the Hidden Economy in the National Accounts', **316** *Economic Trends*, 81-87.

MacMichael D. (1971), *The Criminals as Businessmen: A Discussion of the Legitimate Business Operation of Organized Crime Figures*, Mimeo, Stanford Research Institute.

Magaddino, Joseph P. and Medoff, Marshall H. (1982), 'A Reanalysis of Deterrence and Gun Control', **10(2)** *Atlantic Economic Journal*, 50-53.

Miron, Jeffrey A. and Zwiebel, Jeffrey (1991), 'Alcohol Consumption During Prohibition', **81** *American Economic Review. Papers and Proceedings*, 242-247.

Moore M. (1973), 'Policies to Achieve Discrimination on the Effective Price of Heroin', **63** *American Economic Review*, 378-396.

Morselli, Ricardo and Vannini, Marco (1997), 'Estimating a Crime Equation in the Presence of Organized Crime: Evidence from Italy', **17** *International Review of Law and Economics*, 89-113.

New York State Organized Crime Task Force (1989), *Corruption and Racketeering in the New York City Construction Industry*, New York.

Norton, Desmond A.G. (1988), 'On the Economic Theory of Smuggling', **55** *Economica*, 107-118.

Ozenne, Tim (1974), 'The Economics of Bank Robbery', **3** *Journal of Legal Studies*, 19-51.

Park T. (1979), *Reconciliating Between Personal Income and Taxable Income*, Washington, DC, Bureau of Economic Analysis.

Pashigian, B. Peter (1975), 'On the Control of Crime and Bribery', **4** *Journal of Legal Studies*, 311-326.

Pastor, Santos (1986), 'Heroína y Política Criminal: Un Enfoque Alternativo (Heroin and Criminal Policy: An Alternative Approach)', in X (ed.), *La Problemática de la Droga en España; Análisis y Propuestas Político-Criminales*, Madrid, IUC y Edersa.

Pastor, Santos (1987), 'Liberty versus Security: Should Drugs be Illegal?', in Rolston, B. and Tomlinson, M. (eds), *Civil Rights, Public Opinion and the State*, Belfast, European Group for the Study of Deviance and Social Control.

Paul C. and Wilhite A. (1994), 'Illegal Markets and the Social Costs of Rent-seeking', **79** *Public Choice*, 105-115.

Polo M. (1995), 'Internal Cohesion and Competition among Criminal Organizations', in Fiorentini, Gianluca and Peltzman, Sam (eds), *The Economics of Organized Crime*, Cambridge, Cambridge University Press.

President's Commission on Law Enforcement and Administration of Justice (1967), *The Challenge of Crime in a Free Society*, Washington.

Ramseyer, J. Mark (1991), 'Indentured Prostitution in Imperial Japan: Credible Commitments in the Commercial Sex Industry', **7** *Journal of Law, Economics, and Organization*, 89-116.

Rasmussen, David W. and Benson, Bruce L. (eds) (1994), *The Economic Anatomy of a Drug War: Criminal Justice in the Commons*, Lanham, MD, Rowman and Littlefield.

Rasmussen, David W., Benson, Bruce L. and Sollars, David L. (1993), 'Spatial Competition in Illicit Drug Markets: The Consequences of Increased Drug Enforcement', **23** *Review of Regional Studies*, 219-236.

Reuter, Peter (1983), *Disorganized Crime: The Economics of the Visible Hand*, London, MIT Press, 233 p.

Reuter, Peter (1984), 'The Economic Significance of Illegal Markets in the United States: Some Observations', **1** *Economia e Lavoro*, 135-142.

Reuter, Peter (1987), *Racketeering in Legitimate Industries: A Study in the Economics of Intimidation*, Santa Monica, Rand Corporation.

Rose-Ackerman, Susan (1985), 'Inalienability and the Theory of Property Rights', **85** *Columbia Law Review*, 931-969.

Rubin, Paul H. (1973), 'The Economic Theory of the Criminal Firm', in Rottenberg, Simon (ed.), *The Economics of Crime and Punishment*, Washington, American Enterprise Institute for Public Policy Research, 155-166.

Savona, Ernesto (1990), 'Un Settore Trascurato: l'Análisi Economica della Criminalità, del Diritto Penale e del Sistema di Giustizia Penale (A Neglected Sector: Economic Analysis of Crime, Criminal Law and the System of Criminal Justice)', *Sociologia del Diritto*, 255-277.

Schavell, Steven and Spier, Kathryn E. (1996), 'Threats Without Binding Commitment', **5461** National Bureau of Economic Research Working Paper.

Schelling, Thomas C. (1967), 'Economic Analysis and the Criminal Enterprise', **7** *Public Interest*, 61-78.

Schelling, Thomas C. (1971), 'What is the Business of organized crime?', **20** *Journal of Public Law*, 71-84.

Schelling, Thomas C. (1976), 'Economic Analysis of Organized Crime', in Kaplan, L.J. and Kessler, D. (eds), *An Economic Analysis of Crime: Selected Readings*, Springfield, Charles Thomas.

Schneider, Friedrich (1994), Can the Shadow Economy be Reduced through Major Tax Reforms', **49** *Public Finance*, 137-152.

Skaperdas, S. and Syropoulos, C. (1995), 'Gangs as Primitive States', in Fiorentini, Gianluca and Peltzman, Sam (eds), *The Economics of Organized Crime*, Cambridge, Cambridge University Press.

Smith, R. (1976), 'The Legal and Illegal Markets for Taxed Goods: Pure Theory and Application to State Government Taxation of Distilled Spirits', **27** *Journal of Law and Economics*, 393-435.

Sollars, David L., Benson, Bruce L. and Rasmussen, David W. (1994), 'Drug Enforcement and Deterrence of Property Crime Among Local Jurisdictions', **22** *Public Finance Quarterly*, 22-45.

Sommers, Paul M. (1982), 'Deterrence and Gun Control: A Reply', **10(2)** *Atlantic Economic Journal*, 54-57.

Sommers, Paul M. (1984), 'The Effect of Gun Control Laws on Suicide Rates', **12(1)** *Atlantic Economic Journal*, 67-69.

Spier, Kathryn E. and Shavell, Steven (1996), 'Threats Without Binding Commitment', National Bureau of Economic Research Working Paper.

Tanzi, V. (1983), 'The Underground Economy in the United States', *IMF Staff Papers*, 238-305.

Tanzi, V. (1995), 'Corruption: Arm's Length Relationships and Markets', in Fiorentini, Gianluca and Peltzman, Sam (eds), *The Economics of Organized Crime*, Cambridge, Cambridge University Press.

Taylor, Robert (1995), 'A Game Theoretic Model of Gun Control', **15** *International Review of Law and Economics*, 269-288.

Templeman, Joseph (1984), 'The Effect of Gun Control Laws on Suicide Rates: A Comment', **12(4)** *Atlantic Economic Journal*, 71 ff.

Wagstaff, Adam and Maynard, Alan (1988), *Economic Aspects of the Illicit Drug Market and Drug Enforcement Policies in the United Kingdom*, London, Her Majesty's Stationary Office, 156 p.

Weichman, Dennis, Green, Gary and Bae, Ronald (1987), 'The Death Penalty: A Study in General Deterrence', **1** *Research in Law and Policy Studies*, 187-194.

White M. and Luksetich, William (1983), 'Heroin, Price Elasticity and Enforcement Strategies', **21** *Economic Inquiry*, 557-564.

8500
CORRUPTION

Roger Bowles
School of Social Sciences
University of Bath

Abstract

This chapter reviews the literature on corruption, which is both vast and diverse. Analytically, corruption has been of great interest to economic theorists in recent years because it is an archetypal problem of asymmetric information involving collusion between agents and 'outsiders' against principals, or between supervisors and agents against principals. Most of the models up to now have been essentially static, but recent papers have shown that there is a real prospect of developing dynamic models which can explain the persistence of corruption.
JEL classification: K14, K42
Keywords: Bureaucratic Corruption, Private Sector Corruption, Illegal Behaviour

1. Introduction

Corruption has been around for just about as long as institutions of any sort. In the times of the Greek and Roman empires, for example, corruption was widespread (MacMullen, 1988). Indeed, the corruption of tax officials was so common at that time that it was found expedient to 'privatize' tax collection by auctioning rights to collect taxes (Webber and Wildavsky, 1986). Modern democratic government emerged from earlier structures which were 'rotten to the core', and the professionalisation of the civil service in the nineteenth century in England was aimed in part at eliminating the sapping effects of corruption on public servants. In the present day, corruption 'scandals' are widely reported in the press from almost all walks of life including politics, government and business. The sums involved can range from tiny payments or even small personal favours to bribes running into millions of dollars.

Corruption can be distinguished from '*fraud*', '*embezzlement*' and '*extortion*'. The essence of corruption is that two individuals or groups act in concert to further their own interests at the expense of a third party. Fraud, or extortion, by contrast involves an individual or group acting unilaterally to further their own interests at the expense of others. In the language of principal-agent theory this entails collusion between the agent and supervisor against the principal. There are, nevertheless, many everday situations in which such *collusion* occurs, even when it is at the expense of the principal, where there would be no (legal) presumption that *corruption* has occurred. A patient and doctor, for example, may 'collude' against the insurer responsible for the costs of treatment by agreeing for the patient to have more costly medicine than is necessary. This might be considered corrupt if the doctor has a financial interest in the provision of medicine, but otherwise it would probably be called just another 'agency cost' (Bowles and Rickman, 1998). A good deal of 'corporate hospitality' involves the provision of private benefits to individuals in the hope that the closer personal relationships it fosters will prove a 'worthwhile investment'.

Another everday instance of the 'grey area' between honest and corrupt transactions is where a consumer can benefit by paying 'over the odds' for additional service which directly benefits the employee of a firm but not the firm itself. In some service sectors, such as hairdressing or hotels, gratuities are regarded as normal and acceptable. In other sectors, such as refuse collection, gratuities may be discouraged or even prohibited.

In many jurisdictions corruption is a criminal offence, although it is clear from the relevant legislation that there are difficulties in defining it and in setting standards of evidence for it as an offence. In England and Wales, for example, the Prevention of Corruption Act 1916 (the act which governs public sector corruption in Britain today) coverage extends to members, officers or servants of a public body. Any 'gift, loan, fee, reward, or advantage whatever' will count as corruption if it is in consideration of any act or admission by the public servant. The penalties for the offence can amount to seven years imprisonment or a fine or both, in addition to repaying the amount involved. On a second offence a person stands to lose various rights to vote and may lose any compensation or pension rights to which a public position might otherwise entitle them. As a measure of the response of the legislature to difficulties in seeking successful convictions for the offence, in some circumstances the burden of proof lies on a public employee who has received a payment to show that a suspicious transaction was not corrupt.

Under US law the position is a little different. There is not an outright ban on receiving rewards. The US Department of Defense directive 55007 allows gratuities when they are a 'part of a customary exchange of social amenities between personal friends and relatives when motivated by such relationships and extended on a personal basis' (Adams, 1981).

Though there are many countries in which bribing officials is illegal, it was only in 1997 that 34 countries signed an agreement aimed at eradicating bribery of foreign officials by making such payments a criminal offence and ceasing the practice of making them tax deductible (Tanzi and Davoodi, 1998).

In many countries there may be conflict between social custom and practice on the one hand and the letter of the law on the other. Many cultures rely on the giving of gifts as a symbol of a mutuality of interest. The dividing line between recognising a mutual obligation of support and doing favours expressly in exchange for a reward can be a fine one (Klitgaard, 1991). It is in part because of this ambiguity that some authors have argued that the definition of corruption should be refined to include a wider morality and allow for obligations to others (Palmier, 1983; Lewis, 1996).

In everday use corruption is a term which conveys an element of moral disapproval. It represents an unwelcome deviation from some desired state of the world. Officials or politicians taking bribes are portrayed as ruthless and selfish people exploiting their office for their own private interests at the expense of the wider public good. It is implicit in most discussion of this kind that elimination of corrupt transactions would self-evidently improve welfare. Corruption in this kind of sense is widely recognized as a 'problem' in many countries today. Indices measuring the degree of corruption in the countries of the world are widely published: Business International and Political Risk Services publishes an annual index, International Country Risk Guide; see also Business International Corporation (1984).

In an academic context corruption is a term used in many disciplines (including anthropology, sociology, politics, public administration and development studies) and can refer to a very wide diversity of activities and states of affairs. Shleifer and Vishny (1993), for example, 'define government corruption as the sale by government officials of government property for personal gain'. But this is a much narrower definition of corruption than the classical authors of political theory such as Plato and Aristotle used (Bouckaert, 1996). For them, and for some more recent authors such as Andreski (1978), corruption was not so much a class of illegal practices as a kind of complete subversion to which states and civilisations were vulnerable. In this more classical sense corruption conveys the idea of wrecking or destroying institutions. The more recent use of the term does not have this same connotation, although authors differ widely in the moral content they give the term. For purposes of this review we take a 'middle of the road' view, by defining corruption more widely than Shleifer and Vishny but less broadly than Plato and Aristotle. We include private sector institutions but make rather little reference to the corruption by rulers of the basic machinery of the state.

2. The Literature on Corruption

The literature on corruption is both vast and diverse. There is a journal (*Corruption and Reform*) which has been running since 1987 for which it represents a focus of study, whilst a number of journals have devoted special issues to the subject, some recent examples being: *Stato e Mercato* (April 1992); *Crime, Law and Social Change* (1994-95); *Informacion Comercial Espanola* (May 1995); *Indian Journal of Public Administration* (July-September, 1995); *European Journal on Criminal Policy and Research* (vol 3(2), 1995); and *Journal of Law and Society* (March 1996).

Over the past decade corruption has attracted attention also within the mainstream economics literature as theorists have become increasingly interested in the structure of organizations and agency problems. The impetus for the rapidly growing interest in corruption on the part of economists in recent years is usually traced back to the pioneering work of Rose-Ackerman (1975, 1978a). Texts on microeconomics and on the economics of organisations are increasingly likely to contain discussion of agency problems (Katz and Rosen, 1994) and even corruption itself (Brickley, Smith and Zimmerman, 1996).

It is this strand of literature on which we focus here for the most part. In contemporary economics the notion of corruption is often used in a fairly narrow and technical way to refer to a particular type of opportunistic behaviour which rational agents will follow. In particular corruption results as a cooperative outcome in games involving three or more players, where two (or more) players can collude at the expense of a third party. Bribes to officials are thus readily explained as transactions in which both buyer and seller of a favour benefit at the expense of the organisation or hierarchy within which the official works. This same basic principal-agent model has many applications, such as to the 'agency problems' resulting from the divorce between ownership and control of firms. Lazy managers indulging their workers' preferences for an easy life make life more agreeable for both the manager and the workers at the expense of the profits remaining for the firm's shareholders (Katz and Rosen, 1994). Such behaviour is often described as collusion rather than as corruption, even though it meets most definitions of corruption (Tirole, 1986, 1992).

A survey of the literature on corruption could be organised in many ways. It could be based on discipline or on the type of corruption or on dimensions of corruption such as causes and consequences. We opt here for organisation around various strands in the economics literature on the topic. Sections 3 and 4 set out a basic, or generic, model of corruption giving a flavour of contemporary work in the field. Section 5 explores the Public Choice approach. Section 6 explores some of the applications of corruption models to private sector firms. Section 7 reviews bureaucratic corruption and Section 8 concentrates on political corruption. Section 9 is concerned with 'macro' models of corruption which focus on the consequences of corruption for investment levels, growth rates and so on. Section 10 reviews policy to combat corruption. Section 11 reviews the analysis of corruption in LDCs and Section 12 concludes.

3. Basic Economic Analysis of Corruption

A natural starting point for the economic analysis of corruption is to treat it as any other crime and to apply to it the standard economic model of crime developed originally in Becker (1968) and extended subsequently by many authors such as Polinsky and Shavell (1979, 1984). In this basic model the persons contemplating corruption take account of the expected benefits in the form of bribes, favours or payment in kind and compare the monetary equivalent of these gains with the expected costs in the form of a probability that they will be detected and the monetary sum (or equivalent) of the punishment should they be convicted. Such a formulation has close parallels with the application of the Becker model to the economics of tax evasion by Allingham and Sandmo (1972). Corruption is predicted to occur if the net expected gain is positive.

The important element in corruption which is missing in the earlier applications of the Becker model is, of course, that both sides to a corrupt transaction are ususally committing a crime and not just one side. In the tax evasion model the taxpayer has private information not available to the tax official and all that is entailed analytically is a calculation on the part of the taxpayer as to whether, or how much of the information, to disclose. In a corruption model, *each* side has to be persuaded that it is worthwhile for *both* sides to collude in sharing information which will not be disclosed to third parties.

A simple algebraic formulation helps crystalize ideas on this basic model and forms a useful base on which more sophisticated models can be constructed. We suppose that a citizen stands to enjoy a rent, R. The 'rent' can take a great many forms: it might be an unpaid tax liability, or avoidance of a term of imprisonment, or the supernormal profits from the receipt of monopoly rights and so on: it could be as simple as the gain from having a document processed. A bureaucrat (or regulator or politician or another citizen) is in a position to decide whether or not the rent is to be enjoyed by the citizen. In exchange for a bribe B the bureaucrat promises to bestow the monopoly right, to process the document or to keep the incriminating information secret or whatever. There is nevertheless a risk, in the form of a probability, p, known to both the citizen and the bureaucrat, that payment of the bribe will be detected by a third party in which case both parties to the corruption will be liable for punishment. For the citizen, discovery will mean liability to pay a fine F whilst for the bureaucrat it will mean liability to pay a fine G and to repay the bribe B.

To keep the model simple, assume both parties are risk neutral so that the calculation of expected gains and losses need contain no reference to utility levels. Assume also that both parties to the corruption are sincere, so that we can ignore both the possibility that the citizen is trying to lure the bureaucrat into an illegal act and also any fear the citizen might have that the bureaucrat will renege on the corrupt agreement and spill the beans after taking the bribe.

For the citizen, payment of a bribe will be worthwhile iff:

$$(1 - p)(R - B) - p(F + B) \geq 0 \tag{1}$$

The first term refers to the case where the bribe goes undetected so that the citizen enjoys the rent net of the bribe paid. The second term refers to the case where the bribe is detected and the citizen, who has already paid a (non-recoverable) bribe, is fined for corruption. Condition (1) can be rearranged in the form of an upper bound, B^U, on the size of bribe the citizen will find it worthwhile paying:

$$B^U \leq R(1 - p) - pF \tag{2}$$

For the bureaucrat, the calculation is that taking the bribe is worthwhile provided that:

$$(1 - p)B - pG \geq 0, \tag{3}$$

where, again, the first term refers to the case where the bribe is undetected and the second term to the consequence of detection. We asume that the bureaucrat assigns the same value, p, to the probability of detection as does the citizen. The condition can then be rearranged in the form of a lower bound, B^L, on the bribe which will induce the bureaucrat to conspire in the corruption:

$$B^L \geq pG / (1 - \mathrm{p}) \tag{4}$$

Corruption is assumed to occur in this simple model if there exists a bribe at which the citizen and the official both find themselves better off. This condition is satisfied if and only if the upper bound for the citizen exceeds the lower bound for the official, that is $B^U > B^L$. This is equivalent to the requirement that:

$R(1 - p) - pF > pG / (1 - p)$, or that:

$$R > [pG + pF(1 - p)] / [(1 - p)^2] \tag{5}$$

The 'enforcement parameters' p, F and G describing the probability of detection and the size of the punishment, have to be viewed against the prospective gain to the citizen from corruption. Corruption occurs so long as the rent at stake is sufficiently large to offset the expected punishment.

4. Implications of the Basic Model

Many of the main findings from the corruption literature are at least implicit in the formulation of the previous section, namely:

1. There is nothing to prevent a 'rotten core'. Corruption will occur if the lower bound from (4) is below the upper bound on willingness to pay a bribe derived in (2).
2. As condition (5) indicates, this is equivalent to requiring that the rent at issue is sufficiently high relative to the parameters p, F and G defining the probability of detection and the punishment structure. In policy oriented models it is common to specify either the fines as related in some way to the size of the rent at issue and/or to consider a group of citizens across whom the value of R varies. In this way it is possible to model the *extent* of corruption rather than modelling a (binary) choice problem for an isolated citizen who either indulges in corruption or avoids it;
3. Increasing the fine for citizens, F, will tend to reduce corruption since it raises the cost of detection and thus reduces the net pay-off from corruption: B^U falls while B^L remains constant;
4. Likewise for the penalty, G, imposed on officials: this time B^L rises while B^U remains constant, with the result that corruption again becomes less profitable;
5. Increasing the probability of detection, p, simultaneously reduces B^L and raises B^U and thus erodes the difference $(B^U - B^L)$ on which corruption depends;
6. There is in the transaction at least some of the character of a bilateral monopoly, so long as neither side can readily contact alternative buyers or sellers. The size of the bribe may thus be indeterminate, requiring the introduction of some assumption about the bargaining which will take place between the citizen and the bureaucrat;
7. Introducing competition into the model, for example through allowing the citizen to canvass a range of (corruptible) bureaucrats, may result in Bertrand competition between officials driving bribes down to the competitive level. Corrupt officials try to attract bribes by offering more attractive or cheaper terms than their competitors with the result that the bribe gets driven down close to zero (Shleifer and Vishny, 1993).

We consider some of these findings and further extensions in sections below concerned with more sophisticated models of corruption. One obvious extension is to consider the monetary cost to the bureaucrat of being detected not just in the form of a court-imposed fine, but as putting at risk the bureaucrat's pension rights and any wage premium (relative to available alternative job openings) she is earning as a bureaucrat (see Becker and Stigler, 1974).

A second line of development is to introduce a layer of officials (supervisors or auditors) whose responsibility is to detect corruption by 'front-line' officials. In these multi-tier hierarchies it is possible to specify different kinds of 'supervisory technology' and to distinguish 'systemic' corruption from corruption specific to a single tier (Bac, 1998).

Another extension is to consider corruption in a dynamic model rather than in a purely static way. Individuals who sense that corruption is potentially profitable for them may seek to 'regularize' corrupt arrangements so as to minimize the risk of being surprised by detection and to reduce transactions costs to a minimum. The systematic corruption of police by organized criminals can be interpreted in this way as can various political arrangements, including bureaucratic corruption in the 'old Soviet' type of economy (Shleifer and Vishny, 1992).

From a policy perspective the central question to which this basic model can most readily be applied is the choice of an optimal level of resources to put into the detection of corruption and the choice of an optimal fine. As in other areas, the tendency of this optimal law enforcement model, as pioneered by Becker (1968) and reviewed recently by Garoupa (1997), is to produce solutions suggesting high, possibly maximal, fines and comparatively low probabilities of detection. There are two reasons why these sorts of results tend to emerge. First, fines represent transfer payments rather than real resource costs so that, other things equal, it is usually judged better to rely on the deterrent power of the fine rather than on a high probability of being caught (Polinsky and Shavell, 1984). Secondly, in an area such as corruption where the incentives to report the crime are small, if not non-existent, it is likely to be extremely costly to raise the probability of detection significantly.

One drawback of this model, albeit one which is shared by most models of corruption, is the difficulty of collecting empirical data which could be used to test it. The probability of detection, for example, would require information about the proportion of offences involving corruption in which an individual is detected and convicted. But one of the central features of corruption is that it is, in essence, a cooperative venture which both participants have every incentive to keep secret. It is thus extremely difficult to identify either particular instances of it or its extent in aggregate. From an analytical perspective the question becomes one of how individuals might construct or update (subjective) estimates of probabilities in such circumstances, a matter which is discussed in some of the literature on information, and particularly on the value of message services (see ch. 5 of Hirshleifer and Riley, 1992). There are very obvious parallels with the analysis of the 'underground' or 'black' economy:

ingenious indirect methods may be used to make estimates of how widespread are the transactions at issue, but nobody really knows (Pyle, 1992).

5. Corruption and Public Choice

Whilst the analysis of behaviour under uncertainty has provided a comparatively straightforward line of approach, as we have shown in the previous two sections, there has been a parallel line of intellectual enquiry which has also been influential in the development of our understanding of corruption. The application of economic reasoning to public bodies and political processes has resulted in the development of an analysis of government and bureaucracy which stresses the critical role played by individual interests and objectives in the shaping of these institutions. The formulation of ideas which came to be known as the theory of public choice showed a recognition that public policy could not be thought of simply as the pursuit by pure-minded automata of 'the public interest' but rather represented the outcome of decisions by individuals (be they politicians, bureaucrats or interest groups) with their own interests and their own agenda. Early analyses in this vein were the work of Downs (1957) on the motives of politicians and of Niskanen (1974) on bureaucrats.

The 'public choice' approach emphasizes the role played by the private interests of all the players involved in the formulation and execution of policy. For surveys of the public choice approach see Mueller (1979), or Cullis and Jones (1992). The capture of politicians by interest groups is studied by Becker (1983). Corruption is something which fits very naturally into a picture of the world in which politicians, bureaucrats and citizens are all busily searching for strategies for pursuing their own private motives at the expense of others, whether they be taxpayers, other citizens or whatever. It might be noted also that principal-agent models of the kind reviewed in Section 2 above are quite close in spirit to the Public Choice approach, although they tend to a higher degree of abstraction.

The analysis of rent seeking provides a fertile ground for creating a motivation for corruption. Standard references on rent seeking are Tullock (1967), Kreuger (1974), Posner (1975), Bhagwati (1982) and Tollison (1982). For applications of rent-seeking to corruption see Blomqvist and Mohammad (1986) and Mbaku (1992). Rational individuals assumed to be maximizing their own net benefits without further reference to ethical constraints may come to regard corruption almost as a moral imperative. The individual seeking monopoly rights will probably consider corruption as a possible substitute for (or complement to) other tactics such as political lobbying or capturing bureaucrats. Corruption comes then to be chosen if it represents part of a cost-minimizing strategy. A natural extension of this rent-seeking approach to the analysis of corruption is suggested in Bowles (1998) in which a citizen seeking rents considers various possible 'pathways' to achieve her goal. The more pathways there are, the more opportunity there is to acquire the rent at a lower cost, such as corrupting an official or a politician or whatever may be regarded as alternatives to seeking the rents through some 'legitimate' channel such as legislative change or the exercise of an official's discretion.

Are there any limits to this pursuit of individual self interest other than possibly rather ineffective external controls? Is corruption inevitable if it pays? Just about the only device through which any such limits can be imposed is to suppose that individuals may incur some subjective costs or 'stigma' when acting dishonestly. This approach borrows the term coined by analysts seeking to explain apparently irrational instances of honesty in other spheres, as in Akerlof (1980) and Benjamini and Maital (1985). It may look contrived, but it is often the only practicable way of filling the 'moral vacuum' created by the economic approach and explaining why people may desist from corruption even when it appears 'profitable'.

6. Private Sector Corruption

Within what one might term the 'purely private' sector, corruption has been studied rather less than its public sector counterpart, although that is not necessarily a reason for supposing that it is less widespread than in the public sector. A private sector engineering contractor, for example, may find it expedient to pay bribes to a prospective private sector buyer for just the same reasons they pay bribes to government officials or politicians. Data deficiencies are particularly acute in this field, since it is only really from reports of court cases that remotely reliable evidence is likely to emerge. Whilst a public body might seek to publicize anti-corruption efforts and successes to demonstrate a tough anti-corruption policy, the private firm might prefer to resolve matters away from the public eye in order to avoid the bad publicity and loss of reputation which disclosures of corruption might bring. There are many different forms corruption in the private sector can take: we review a brief selection here.

Insider trading scandals occur from time to time on most of the major financial markets, and they sometimes involve corruption. The insider, say the accountant of a major company or a senior executive of the firm who has seen the firm's provisional profit results, holds information which when published will, or at least might, move the firm's share price. Rather than trade in the shares herself, the accountant or executive might contemplate selling the relevant information to a third party who is in a position to make profitable, but less obvious, use of it by buying or selling shares in the firm. Any such sale of information would be regarded in most countries as corrupt, even though there are some economists who would regard such transactions as being conducive of market efficiency for the most part, and would argue that the main beneficiaries of a prohibition of a ban on insider information are financial market professionals rather than the firm's shareholders (Manne, 1966; Baye, 1997).

Valuation of goods, services or assets is clearly an area where there is scope for corruption. The valuer can 'create a rent' by overvaluing an item, since the owner of the item might stand to gain in creditworthiness as a result or might get a better price if selling the item. This creates an opportunity for collusion between the owner and the valuer of the item at the expense of the buyer. Examples of this kind of collusion can be found in markets for sports players, where the manager of a club buying a player takes a bribe from the club selling a player (or from the player's agent) to overestimate the player's value. They can be found also in the financial markets where a stock analyst is entertained lavishly by a firm hoping that the analyst will publish a positive report about the prospects for the firm's share price. In a somewhat similar vein was the 'payola' scandal in which record companies used to pay bribes to DJs for playing records by the company's artists on the radio. Pechlivanos (1995) refers to the example of the American Honda Motor Company whose managers received kickbacks from prospective franchisees.

Andvig's study (1995) of the North Sea Oil industry makes use of reports from six trials in the British courts of so-called 'information brokers'. Ten of the thirteen defendants in these trials were found guilty: punishments ranged from six months to three years in prison plus fines and compensation orders from about £40,000 to £500,000. Spending on the procurement of equipment for the North Sea is very high, at around £13 billion per annum. Those involved in the award of contracts for the supply of this equipment have information about bids and tenders which is potentially of substantial value to the firms competing for supply contracts.

Monopoly power is likely to be a pre-condition for private sector corruption. A well informed competitive market will leave little room for it since, at least in the longer run, corrupt firms will have higher costs and thus be unable to survive. But a privatized utility might, for example, enjoy a local monopoly in the provision of some service. It is quite imaginable that the employee of the utility will exploit this monopoly for private gain, say, by arranging connection to a power or telephone network unusually quickly for a premium. A number of commentators in the literature on privatization have, indeed, argued that the elimination of waste and inefficiency on the part of public utilities requires not only a transfer of assets from public to private hands but also the introduction of elements of competition to break down the local monopoly power which is what enables the utilitity's employees to 'hold up' their customers (Kay and Thompson, 1986).

7. Bureaucratic Corruption

Public sector bureaucracies often have considerable powers and areas of discretion: they are often in a monopoly supply position and their employees are often tempted to make strategic use of these advantages for their own ends. Anecdotes are legion. There is the immigration official checking papers who can be persuaded with a $20 tip to ignore some real or imaginary inconsistency. There are ships which cannot enter certain ports until they supply customs officials with amounts of whisky and cigarettes as spelled out on a schedule sent in advance of their arrival. There are hospitals in some countries where patients cannot get drugs without paying bribes to staff. And so on.

A hard-bitten economist, or world traveller for that matter, would think it naive to imagine anything else. Even the less cynical would agree that there are dangers that the pursuit of the ideal of public interest might sometimes slip in favour of the pursuit by bureaucrats of their private goals. It is perhaps inevitable then that public administration should have a rather tainted reputation when it comes to corruption. But as the examples above illustrate, in many cases the corruption is not an occasional lapse by an official but a deeply-embedded *modus vivendi*. We consider in this section two particular areas of bureacracy where allegations are often made and a good deal has been written.

7.1 Corruption of Tax Officials

Tax evasion has been widely studied, and it has for long been known that tax administrations are particularly vulnerable to collusion between taxpayers who underdeclare their income and tax officials who may be bribed to overlook these underdeclarations when reporting to the tax authority. As we remarked in Section 1 above, corruption of this kind was the motivation for the development of 'tax farming' from the days of the Greek and Roman empires until comparitively recently.

To give a sense of how deep-seated tax corruption might be, Chu (1990) reports the results of a 1981 survey by the city government of Taipei in which 94 percent of the taxpayers polled admitted to paying off tax officials in exchange for collusion in tax evasion. Interviews with the group of accountants involved in the preparation of tax returns appeared to confirm that taxpayer dishonesty was widespread and that almost a half of the tax officials with whom the accountants dealt would actively solicit payoff.

Contemporary models of corruption of tax administration are usually constructed in two stages. At stage 1, the taxpayer makes a declaration of income following the standard Allingam and Sandmo (1972) approach, that is by comparing the expected costs and benefits of declaring different proportions of true income. The tax administration, meanwhile, selects an audit probability for the taxpayer (which may be declaration-dependent) to maximize its revenue net of the costs of audit. In the Graetz-Reinganum-Wilde (1986) model, a Nash equilibrium is established which makes the policies followed by the taxpayer and the tax administration mutually compatible.

At stage 2 the possibility is introduced that the tax auditor can suppress the result of audits and thereby shield the taxpayer from a penalty for underdeclaring income (Cadot, 1987; Chander and Wilde, 1992). The auditor who chooses to take a bribe herself runs the risk of detection. The tax administration thus has two layers of auditing: audit of the taxpayer and audit of the auditors. Auditing of either kind is costly, and the administration's problem is to figure out how best to split its resources between the two kinds of audit work.

Models of this kind are inevitably rather complex, since there are many sets of assumptions the analyst can make and there are many interactions which can be explored. For example the split of the taxpayer's gain from underdeclaration between the taxpayer and the auditor can be treated as exogenous, as in Chander and Wilde (1992) but is endogenized in other models such as Virmani (1987), Goswami, Sanyal and Gang (1991) and Besley and Maclaren (1993) (see also Flatters and MacLeod, 1995 and Toma and Toma, 1992).

Despite their analytical sophistication, these models gloss over many important practical problems. The ease with which tax auditors can be investigated, for example, will depend on the quality of information and record keeping. If taxpayer files can be (strategically) lost, if tax auditors have discretion about which taxpayer returns to investigate or if the auditor is subject to influence via the political system, then the model misses important interactions. But this demonstrates simply that the tax official has to maintain a delicate balance between various forces. The contemporary models have made a good start on modelling this tension, but there remains plenty of scope for 'fine tuning'. Tirole (1996), for example, has developed a model in which a reputation for corruption may be difficult to shake off, and this is a development which might have an interesting application in the tax field.

7.2 Police Corruption

Police enjoy the same privilege as tax officials, namely access to public resources with which to investigate illegal activities or earnings which individuals wish to keep secret. The temptations to collude in keeping the secret may be very great and there have undoubtedly been occasions when police corruption has been widespread. An early economic study of corruption was the work of Becker and Stigler (1974) who had been asked to find ways of reducing corruption amongst Chicago police (for a recent summary of their work see Brickley, Smith and Zimmerman, 1996).

Models of police corruption can be distinguished by whether they deal with 'one-off' or repeated incidents of corruption. Bowles and Garoupa (1997), for example, treat 'casual' police corruption as a one-shot game, involving isolated instances of a citizen and a police officer who are strangers to each other. There are many instances, however, where it is alleged that corruption is not of a 'one off' kind but is more deeply embedded in a continuing relationship. Schelling (1967) gives as an example an illegal wire-service gambling syndicate in Miami. Regular payments were made to police not only in respect of protection of syndicate members from arrest but also in exchange for systematic intimidation by police of bookmakers outside the syndicate.

Another example is the illegal drugs market where producers and suppliers may establish a regular working relationship with enforcement agents (see Klitgaart, 1988, and Lupsha, 1991).

These dynamic elements call for a repeat play treatment. There are interesting parallels between continuing corrupt relationships and the discussion of alternative forms of contracting between firms using the notion of transactions costs (Williamson, 1979; Deakin and Michie, 1997). Corruption cannot be supported by legally enforceable contracts and yet corrupt agents are clearly able to sustain viable long-term relationships.

8. Political Corruption

The powers of government to create and/or to protect rents have been a rich source of study for those interested in corruption. It was Lord Acton who famously claimed that 'Power tends to corrupt and absolute power corrupts absolutely'.

The power to enact legislation carries with it the possibility of creating rents. The prospect for the amoral individual of being able to participate in the processes by which rents are created and distributed may express itself in a wide variety of ways, some at least of which can be regarded as corrupt. Abuse of this power has occurred frequently, most notably with monarchs and autocratic (often military) governments rather than with democratic governments. Kings in mediaeval England, for example, would grant trading and many other monopolies simply to raise cash for their own purposes, whether noble or otherwise. Similar sorts of claims have sometimes been made about socialist economies and about countries with military governments. For review of these and other issues in the sphere of political corruption (see Amuwo,

1986; Benson, 1978, Brooks, 1978 and other contributors to Heidenheimer, 1978; and Coldham, 1995).

In a modern democracy politicians are not usually in a position to be able to enact legislation purely for their own private benefit. But they may be able to wield influence over the legislative process, and such influence makes them vulnerable to corruption by those groups who will be affected.

The asking of leading questions in the legislature and the exploitation of membership of influential committees or subcommittees are two of the more obvious ways of exerting pressure on the shape of legislation. The corruption element obviously arises when the politician 'sells' this influence to an interested party. The grey area between explicit selling of influence and more subtle routes through which influence can be exploited is sometimes referred to as 'sleaze'. It is in an effort to counter this kind of sleaze which has prompted the Nolan Committee to press for greater disclosure of the outside interests of British Members of Parliament. Consultancies and sponsorship can significantly undermine the credibility of the claim by politicians that they are pursuing the public interest.

The power to enforce legislation is likewise open to manipulation and abuse. Governments make decisions all the time about the public resources to be made available for the agencies responsible for enforcing legislation. Influence over the way the resources are used and over agency priorities will often have a market value since a greater intensity of enforcement is likely to be of advantage to some party. Pressure for law enforcement is, of itself, entirely legitimate. But if the pressure is wielded in return for payments of some kind then we have corruption.

The power to influence public sector contracting with the private sector for the provision of goods and services is an area where corruption is sometimes alleged to occur. In large-scale civil engineering projects, 'political factors' sometimes play a role in deciding which contractor gets the job as well as more traditional criteria such as tender price or track record. Giving a role to such factors is a way of creating a space for political influence to carry weight and thus a market value. In effect it is allowing the politician to collude with outside interests against the bureaucrats responsible for procurement. It thus creates the possibility of corruption since it gives the outsider the incentive to bribe the politician to wield power over the bureaucrat (Becker, 1983).

This is a subtly different form of corruption from the one considered in the 'regulatory capture' tradition in which the regulator (the bureaucrat) and the outside interest collude against the politician or the public interest. Collusion between regulators and regulated industries, in the form of regulatory capture, against the interests of consumers and/or taxpayers has been explored by Stigler (1971), Peltzman (1976) and many others. Corruption in this context, as elsewhere, could range from the payment of cash bribes through to regulators expecting employment in the regulated industry on retirement from the public service: the 'revolving doors' arrangement, on which see Adams (1981) and Breyer and Steward (1979).

The expanding literature on public sector procurement has concerned itself with the structure of contracts and incentives in these 'hierarchical' models, where there are three or more parties involved and a number of forms collusion could take. The standard theoretical work in microeconomics in this area is Laffont and Tirole (1993), which draws on earlier work on multilevel hierarchies by Tirole (1986, 1992), Laffont (1990) and Koffman and Lawarree (1993).

9. Consequences of Corruption

Many 'macro' studies of corruption have been concerned with the causes and consequences of corruption at an aggregate level. These studies can be thought of as complements to, rather than as alternatives to, the essentially micro models of behaviour reviewed here thus far. The consequences of corruption have been widely discussed and authors have reached widely differing conclusions.

The conventional wisdom is that corruption is harmful, and for some authors this seems almost self-evidently to be the case. A recent paper, for example, Tanzi and Davoodi (1998) carries the title 'Road to Nowhere: How Corruption in Public Investment Hurts Growth' (see further Alam, 1990; Ades and Di Tella, 1995, 1998; Mauro, 1995, 1998, and Klitgaard, 1998). The general thrust of the argument is that corruption harms growth by reducing the incentives to invest. This distorts the allocation of resources and leads to underinvestment and poor growth rates.

Some authors, however, argue that corruption may be as good a device for screening projects as anything else. In this view the most profitable amongst a group of competing projects will generate the greatest possible bribe and thus have the best chance of succeeding. The only difference is that most of the monopoly profits are appropriated by the corrupt persons choosing between the projects rather than by the firms proposing them. More technically, this 'neutrality' view suggests that corruption is not inefficient but may redistribute income.

Yet others argue that corruption may be positively beneficial (Leff, 1964). Corrupt bureaucrats who respond to payments for services rendered may work harder and process matters more quickly than they would if they relied purely on their public services salary. But it should be stressed that this is rather a minority view.

Even if the *outcomes* of selection processes for projects will be the same whether or not corruption occurs, it is more efficient to use an honest procedure because of the resource costs of secrecy. Bribes themselves may be only transfer payments and thus irrelevant from an allocative perspective, but real resources are involved in arranging and protecting bribe offers, and these represent real costs which could be avoided. Making corruption illegal raises the costs of corruption and thus some of the rents potentially created by projects get dissipated by rent-seeking behaviour (Shleifer and Vishny, 1993). There are parallels with the continuing debate about the resource costs of rent-seeking more generally: see for example the debate about how transfers are treated in cost-benefit analysis, about how the costs of crime are to be treated and about the distortion of the results of cost-benefit analysis by vested interests in the decision-making processes of government (see Weingast, Shepsle and Johnsen, 1981; Lee, 1983; Lewin and Trumbell, 1993; McChesney, 1993, and Jones and Cullis, 1996).

As well as theoretical arguments about corruption being harmful, there has been some empirical literature pointing in the same direction. Mauro (1995), using data for a wide cross-section of countries, argues that, holding income constant, countries with higher rates of corruption (as measured by the standard business indicators of corruption referred to above) have a lower ratio of both total and private sector investment to income. Tanzi and Davoodi (1998) take a rather different tack in arguing that countries with high levels of corruption will engage in particularly high rates of public investment, and will be particularly subject to low rates of return on these investments. The argument is that corruption may encourage projects which are inefficient but rewarding to corrupt politicians.

10. Control of Corruption

When it comes to measures to control corruption, results tend to be dictated by the structure of the model of behaviour employed. Nevertheless there are a number of recurring strands in discussion of the strategies which can be used to combat corruption.

The basic principal-agent model of corruption rather naturally inclines to the search for 'top-down' solutions. The victim in these models is the principal (the government) and the corrupt parties are bureaucrats and citizens. Principals who suspect themselves to be vulnerable to 'agency problems' can, speaking in general, take various kinds of defensive action (Ross, 1973; Grossman and Hart, 1983; and Hirshleifer and Riley, 1992). The 'Mechanism Design' literature invites the principal to design a grand scheme of things which anticipates the corrupt behaviour and makes it unprofitable. This scheme is implemented through contracts for bureaucrats which are constructed in a way which would make it irrational for the bureaucrat to take bribes (Lui, 1986; Cadot, 1987; and

Mookherjee and Png, 1995). Methods for 'designing corruption out of the system' have long been sought. The 'selling the store' solution (see Rasmusen, 1994) is a rather extreme example, but has relevant historical parallels in the use of 'tax farming' contracts by tax revenue departments for many centuries. The literature also recognizes that there are some circumstances in which it will either be infeasible to prevent corruption (Koffman and Lawarree, 1993) or non-optimal (Olsen and Torsvik, undated).

A second common theme is the use of auditing methods to monitor the quality of the reporting behaviour of agents in hierarchies. Many tax and police authorities have a 'vigilance' or 'special investigations' branch with the express task of identifying and pursuing corrupt officers. This approach has its drawbacks because most of the factors which encourage 'front line' officers to behave corruptly apply equally when it comes to an auditing tier. The audit reveals potentially valuable information which someone is prepared to pay bribes to suppress (Border and Sobell, 1987). Likewise, if corruption is endemic within an institution then it is likely that any findings of corruption will be liable to suppression (see Bac, 1996a, 1996b, 1998).

An early application of this approach is the argument of Becker and Stigler (1974) that by paying police a salary higher than the prevailing market wage it would be possible to create an incentive on the part of officers to retain their job. In such an environment, the prospect of being found guilty of taking bribes acts as a powerful threat since it would result in loss, over the rest of the officer's career, of the rents created by the wage premium. The excess supply of prospective police officers this premium would cause is dealt with by 'selling' the posts. This payment can be interpreted as a bond posted by the officer: the honest officer keeps the bond in the form of a premium wage whilst the dishonest officer forfeits it.

A third theme which recurs quite commonly is the introduction of competition as a means of attacking corruption. In this view, corruption is fostered wherever there is a single source of supply. By opening up alternatives, the capacity of the bureaucrat or tax official to hold up the citizen is reduced and the willingness to pay bribes correspondingly lowered. This might entail opening 'multiple windows', so that a citizen can contact a different official if the first one tries to elicit a bribe (Shleifer and Vishny, 1993). It might equally entail opening up an economy to foreign trade in order to prevent a domestic producer wielding monopoly power (Ades and Di Tella, 1995).

A fourth theme is the use of administrative devices within organisations to discourage corruption. Many police and tax departments have a policy of moving officers around quite frequently in order to prevent them from becoming too familiar with an area. In terms of the relational contracting literature this can be interpreted as an effort to raise the transactions costs of dealing corruptly rather than honestly. By frequently disrupting the pattern it may be possible, at the cost of having to give on-the-job training more frequently, to impose higher 'set-up' costs on those wishing to corrupt officers.

11. Corruption in LDCs

In their folklore at least, many developing countries experience substantial corruption. Many contributions have been made by sociologists and other policy analysts (including some work by economists) to what has become a substantial literature on the subject of corruption in LDCs: for general reviews see Beenstock (1979), Winston (1979), Macrae (1982), Jagannathan (1986, 1988), Andvig (1989), Ward (1989), Alam (1989, 1990, 1995) and Charlick (1992).

An obvious question, of course, is whether there is anything about corruption in developing countries to distinguish it from corruption elswehere. The short answer to this is probably no: the institutions involved are the same (business, bureaucracies and governments) and the incentives for the individuals concerned are similar. The same kind of analysis can thus, at least in principle, be applied.

But this is probably too glib. There are special reasons why corruption in LDCs is of particular concern and there are also reasons why it may take a rather different form and may impose greater costs than its counterpart in the North. Development aid has in many cases been diverted for their own private use by corrupt politicians and bureaucrats. Partly as a defensive measure against criticisms from the taxpayers funding aid budgets, a quest for 'good governance' is now high on the priority list of many international agencies, and anti-corruption programmes have become an essential item for many of the poorer countries (see, for example, United Nations, 1989; World Bank, 1992; Doig, 1995).

This quest can be problematic, however. There are some countries where corruption has become deeply embedded, in part as a response to very low civil service salaries. Just to survive and support their families, officials may need to moonlight or to take bribes. Clearly any serious effort to reduce corruption in such an environment can only work if part of the policy is to raise civil service salary levels. But this tends to raise public expenditure and, other things equal, may intensify what is already a serious debt problem. One could argue, therefore, that in countries where it is difficult to raise money through taxes to pay officials a little bribery is no bad thing because it is one way of getting citizens to support public sector officials. This is not a very attractive argument to economists looking for first best equilibria or to moral crusaders but it probably helps explain why corruption is sometimes tolerated.

A further reason for treating corruption as a 'special' problem for LDCs is that institutional differences resulting from different cultural and political traditions can create some ambiguity about the definition of corruption. Critics have argued that much of the literature of the 1950s and 1960s was judgmental and morally critical, and that care is needed when studying corruption in LDCs to avoid an ethnocentric view in which corruption is viewed as an aberration of post-colonial societies which would eventually disappear as these countries evolved towards a more Western form (Clarke, 1983; Werner, 1983; and Lewis, 1996).

Many of the studies have been concerned with particular countries or regions: Kaufer (1989), Kennedy (1989), Sands (1989, 1990), Kolenda (1990); Rocca (1992), and Wong (1992)on China; Halayya (1985), Goswami, Sanyal and Gang, 1991), Wade (1982) on India; Carino (1986) and Gleason (1995) on Asia; Grayson (1984) on Mexico; Maingot (1994) on the Southern Hemisphere; Werlin (1973) and Le Vine (1975) on Ghana; Amuwo (1986) on Niger; Reno (1995) on Sierra Leone; Ouma (1991) on Uganda; Gould (1980) and Szeftel (1983) on Zaire; Makumbe (1994) on Zimbabwe; Ekpo (1979) on Sub-Saharan Africa and Kotecha and Adams (1981), Theobald (1993) and Mbaku (1994) on Africa more generally.

12. Concluding Remarks

Corruption is a very widespread phenomenon and takes a great variety of forms. It is difficult, for this reason, to define very exactly. It is also something which is very difficult to prevent. It is illegal virtually everywhere, in some of its forms, but its victims often are unaware that it is taking place. Both parties to a corrupt transaction have an incentive to avoid disclosure since both will usually have been acting illegally. Thus, even establishing that it has occurred may be very costly. Even when corruption is suspected it is very often difficult to adduce legally convincing evidence since parties to corrupt transactions can comparatively easily cover their tracks by using tactics which offer ambiguity and are susceptible to multiple explanations. It is not, however, in any respect a 'victimless crime'.

Analytically, corruption has been of great interest to economic theorists in recent years because it is an archetypal problem of asymmetric information involving collusion between agents and 'outsiders' against principals, or between supervisors and agents against principals. Most of the models up to now have been essentially static, but recent papers have shown that there is a real prospect of developing dynamic models which can explain the persistence of corruption. Much of the future for application of these models will probably be in the fields of the economic analysis of the operation of government and political institutions. But corruption remains an area which will continue to be of interest to scholars of law and economics because it raises fascinating issues about the enforcement of law in the broadest sense.

Acknowledgments

The author gratefully acknowledges detailed and constructive comments on an earlier draft from three referees. The usual disclaimer applies.

Bibliography on Corruption (8500)

Adams, G. (1981), *The Politics of Defense Contracting - The Iron Triangle*, New Brunswick, NJ, Transaction.

Adams, G. (1991), *Odious Debts - Loose Lending, Corruption and the Third World's Environmental Legacy*, London, Earthscan Publications.

Adediji, O. (1991), 'Role of Government in Bureaucratic Corruption in the Case of Politicisation of the Civil Service', **25** *Quarterly Journal of Admininistration*, 208-219.

Ades, A. and Di Tella, R. (1995), *Competition and Corruption*, **169** Applied Economics Discussion Paper, University of Oxford, UK.

Ades, A. and Di Tella, R. (1998), 'National Champions and Corruption: Some Unpleasant Interventionist Arithmetic', **108** *Economic Journal*.

Alam, M. Shahid (1989), 'Anatomy of Corruption: An Approach to the Political Economy of Underdevelopment', **48** *American Journal of Economics and Sociology*, 441-456.

Alam, M. Shahid (1990), 'Some Economic Costs of Corruption in LDCs', **27** *Journal of Development Studies*, 89-97.

Alam, M. Shahid (1995), 'A Theory of Limits on Corruption and Some Applications', **48** *Kyklos*, 419-435.

Alatas, S.H. (1990), *Corruption - its Nature, Causes and Functions*, Aldershot, Avebury.

Ali, S. (1985), *Corruption: a Third World Perspective*, Lahore, Aziz Publishers.

Amuwo, K. (1986), 'Military-Inspired Anti-Bureaucratic Corruption Campaigns: an Appraisal of Niger's Experience', **24** *Journal of Modern African Studies*, 285-301.

Andreski, S. (1978), 'Kleptocracy as a System of Government in Africa', in Heidenheimer, Arnold J., Jophnson, Michael and Le Vine, Victor (eds), *Political Corruption: A Handbook*, New Brunswick, NJ, Transaction Press.

Andvig, Jens C. (1989), 'Korrupsjon i Utviklingsland (Corruption in Developing Countries)', **23** *Nordisk Tidsskrift für Politisk Ekonomi*, 51-70.

Andvig, Jens C. (1991), 'The Economics of Corruption: A Survey', **46** *Studi Economici*, 57-94.

Andvig, Jens C. (1995), 'Corruption in the North Sea Oil Industry: Issues and Assessments', **23** *Crime, Law and Social Change*, 289-313.

Andvig, Jens C. and Moene, Karl Ove (1990), 'How Corruption May Corrupt', **13** *Journal of Economic Behavior and Organization*, 63-76.

Anechiarico, F. and Jacobs, James B. (1994), 'Visions of Corruption Control and the Evolution of American Public Administration', **54** *Public Administration Review*, 465-473.

Antoci, Angelo and Sacco, Pier Luigi (1995), 'A Public Contracting Evolutionary Game with Corruption', **61** *Journal of Economics (Zeitschrift für Nationalökonomie)*, 89-122.

Bac, M. (1996a), 'Corruption and Supervision Costs in Hierarchies', **22** *Journal of Comparative Economics*, 99-118.

Bac, M. (1996b), 'Corruption, Supervision and the Structure of Hierarchies', **12** *Journal of Law, Economics and Organization*.

Bac, M. (1998), 'The Scope, Timing, and Type of Corruption', **12** *International Review of Law and Economics*.

Banfield, Edward C. (1975), 'Corruption as a Feature of Governmental Organization', **18** *Journal of Law and Economics*, 587-605.

Basu, Kaushik, Bhattacharya, Sudipto and Mishra, Ajit (1992), 'Notes on Bribery and the Control of Corruption', **48** *Journal of Public Economics*, 349-359.

Beck, P.J. and Maher, M.W. (1986), 'A Comparison of Bribery and Bidding in Thin Markets', **20** *Economics Letters*, 1-5.

Beenstock, Michael (1979), 'Corruption and Development', **7** *World Development*, 15-24.

Benson, Bruce L. (1981), 'A Note on Corruption of Public Officials: The Black Market for Property Rights', **5** *Journal of Libertarian Studies*, 305-311.

Benson, Bruce L. (1988a), 'An Institutional Explanation for Corruption of Criminal Justice Officials', **8** *Cato Journal*, 139-163.

Benson, Bruce L. (1988b), 'Corruption in Law Enforcement: One Consequence of 'The Tragedy of the Commons' Arising with Public Allocation Processes', **8** *International Review of Law and Economics*, 73-84.

Benson, Bruce L. and Baden, John (1985), 'The Political Economy of Government Corruption: The Logic of Underground Government', **14** *Journal of Legal Studies*, 391-410.

Benson, Bruce L. and Rasmussen, David W. (1995), *Illicit Drugs and Crime*, Independent Policy Report, Oakland, Independent Institute.

Benson, G.C.S. (1978), *Political Corruption in America*, Lexington, MA, Lexington Books.

Besley, T. and McClaren, J. (1993), 'Taxes and Bribery: the Role of Wage Incentives', **103** *Economic Journal*, 119-141.

Blomqvist, Ake and Mohammad, Sharif (1986), 'Controls, Corruption, and Competitive Rent Seeking in LDCs', **21** *Journal of Development Economics*, 161-180.

Bouckaert, Boudewijn (1996), 'Political Corruption', **Sept. 96** Mimeo.

Bowles, Roger A. (1998), 'Minimising Corruption in Tax Affairs', in Sandford, Cedric (ed.), *More Key Issues in Tax Reform*, Bath, Fiscal Publications.

Bowles, Roger A. and Garoupa, Nuno (1997), 'Casual Police Corruption and the Economics of Crime', **17** *International Review of Law and Economics*, 85-87.

Brenner, Reuven (1994), *Labyrinths of Prosperity*, Ann Arbor, University of Michigan Press.

Brooks, R.C. (1978), 'The Nature of Political Corruption', in Heidenheimer, Arnold J., Jophnson, Michael and Le Vine, Victor (eds), *Political Corruption: A Handbook*, New Brunswick, NJ, Transaction Press.

Buscaglia, Edgardo (1995), 'Judicial Reform in Latin America: The Obstacles Ahead', **4** *Journal of Latin American Affairs*, 8-16.

Cadot, Olivier (1987), 'Corruption as a Gamble', **33** *Journal of Public Economics*, 223-244.

Carino, Ledivina V. (ed.) (1986), *Bureaucratic Corruption in Asia: Causes, Consequences, and Controls*, Quezon City, Philippines, JMC Press.

Chander, Parkash and Wilde, Louis L. (1992), 'Corruption in Tax Administration', **49** *Journal of Public Economics*, 333-349.

Chang, Ching Hsi (1995), 'Party Enterprises, Members' Ethics, and Party Corruption: An Application of the Rotten Kid Theorem (In Chinese, with English summary)', **23** *Taiwan Economic Review*, 25-42.

Charlick, R. (1992), 'Combatting Corruption in an Era of Political Liberalization - Implications for Donor Agencies', **7** *Corruption and Reform*, 283 ff.

Chu, C.Y.C. (1990), 'Income Tax Evasion with Venal Tax Officials - the Case of Developing Countries', **45** *Public Finance*, 392-408.

Clarke, M. (ed.) (1983), *Corruption: Causes, Consequences and Control*, London, Frances Pinter.

Clutterbuck, R. (1995), *Drugs, Crime and Corruption: Thinking the Unthinkable*, Basingstoke, Macmillan.

Coldham, S. (1995), 'Legal Responses to State Corruption in Commonwealth Africa', **39** *Journal of African Law*, 115-126.

Dernburg, Thomas F. (1992), 'A Note on Data Corruption and Monetary Fiscal Policy Regimes', **16** *Journal of Economics and Finance*, 147-153.

Dey, Harendra Kanti (1989), 'The Genesis and Spread of Economic Corruption: A Microtheoretic Interpretation', **17** *World Development*, 503-511.

Deysine, A. (1980), 'Political Corruption: a Review of the Literature', **8** *European Journal of Political Research*, 447-462.

Doig, A. (1995), 'Good Government and Sustainable Anti-corruption Strategies: a Role for Independent Anti-Corruption Agencies?', **15** *Public Administration and Development*, 151-166.

Dudley, Leonard and Montmarquette, Claude (1987), 'Bureaucratic Corruption as a Constraint on Voter Choice', **55** *Public Choice*, 127-160.

Ekpo, M. (1979), *Bureaucratic Corruption in Sub-Saharan Africa: Toward a Search of Causes and Consequences*, Washington, University Press of America.

Elliott, K. (ed.) (1997), *Corruption in the World Economy*, Washington, DC, Institute for International Economics.

Farrell, A. (1992), *Crime, Class and Corruption - the Politics of the Police*, London, Bookmarks.

Feichtinger, Gustav and Wirl, Franz (1994), 'On the Stability and Potential Cyclicity of Corruption in Governments Subject to Popularity Constraints', **28** *Mathematical Social Sciences*, 113-131.

Fennell, P. (1983), 'Local Government Corruption in England and Wales', in Clarke, M. (ed.), *Corruption: Causes, Consequences and Control*, London, Frances Pinter.

Fennell, P. and Thomas, P. (1983), 'Corruption in England and Wales: an Historical Analysis', **11** *International Journal of the Sociology of Law*, 167-189.

Flatters, Frank and MacLeod, W. Bentley (1995), 'Administrative Corruption and Taxation', **2** *International Tax and Public Finance*, 397-417.

Franklin, Daniel (1981), 'Bribery and Corruption in East West Trade', **23** *ACES Bulletin*, 1-71.

Friedman, Alan E. and Schwartz, T. (1990), 'Power and Greed - Inside the Teamsters Empire of Corruption', **5** *Corruption and Reform*.

Galasi, Péter and Kertesi, Gábor (1990), 'Korrupció és Tulajdon, Tanulmány a Tulajdonjogok Közgazdaságtanának Köreből (Corruption and Property)', **4** *Közgazdasági Szemle*, 389-425.

Galeotti, Ginaluigi and Merlo, A. (1994), 'Political Collusion and Corruption in a Representative Democracy', **49** *Public Finance*, 232-243.

Gambetta, Diego (1993), *The Sicilian Mafia: The Business of Private Protection*, Cambridge, MA, Harvard University Press.

Gardiner, J. A. (1986), 'Controlling Official Corruption and Fraud [in the US]: Bureaucratic Incentives and Disincentives', **1** *Corruption and Reform*, 33-50.

Garoupa, Nuno and Bowles, R. (1997), 'Casual Police Corruption and the Economics of Crime', **17** *International Review of Law and Economics*, 1-16.

Gleason, G. (1995), 'Corruption, Decolonization and Development in Central Asia', **3** *European Journal on Criminal Policy and Research*, 38-47.

Goodman, Timothy (1994), 'Political Corruption: The Payoff Diminishes', **5** *American Enterprise*, 19-27.

Goswami, O., Sanyal, A. and Gang, I.N. (1991), *Taxes, Corruption and Bribes - a Model of Indian Public Finance in Markets in Developing Countries - Parallel, Fragmented and Black*, San Francisco, ICS Press.

Gould, David J. (1980), *Bureaucratic Corruption and Underdevelopment in the Third World: the Case of Zaire*, New York, Pergamon Press.

Gould, David J. and Amaro Reyes, Jose A. (1983), *The Effects of Corruption on Administrative Performance*, World Bank Staff Working Paper, Washington, DC, The World Bank, No. 580.

Graetz, Michael J., Reinganum, Jennifer F. and Wilde, L.L. (1986), 'The Tax Compliance Game: Toward an Interactive Theory of Law Enforcement', **22** *Journal of Law, Economics and Organization*, 1-32.

Gray, C.W. and Kaufmann, D. (1998), 'Corruption and Development', **35** *Finance and Development*, 7-10.

Grayson, G.M. (1984), 'An Overdose of Corruption: the Domestic Politics of Mexican Oil', **13** *Caribbean Review*, 22-49.

Halayya, M. (1985), *Corruption in India*, New Delhi, Affiliated East-West Press.

Hasen, Richard L. (1993), 'An Enriched Economic Model of Political Patronage and Campaign Contributions: Revising Supreme Court Jurisprudence', **14** *Cardozo Law Review*, 1311 ff.

Heidenheimer, A.J. (1978), *Political Corruption: Readings in Comparitive Analysis*, New York, Rinehart and Winston.

Hepworth, N. (1995), 'Fraud and Corruption', **15** *Public Money and Management*, 4-6.

Huang, Peter H. and Wu, Ho-Mou (1994), 'More Order without More Law: A Theory of Social Norms and Organizational Cultures', **10** *Journal of Law, Economics, and Organization*, 390-406.

Hutchinson, John (1969), 'The Anatomy of Corruption in Trade Unions', **8** *Industrial Relations*, 135-150.

Jacobs, James B. and Thacher, Thomas D., II (1989), 'Attacking Corruption in Union Management Relations: A Symposium', **42** *Industrial and Labor Relations Review*, 501-507.

Jacoby, N., Nehemkis, P. and Eells, R. (1977), *Bribery and Extortion in World Business*, New York, Macmillan.

Jagannathan, N. Vijay (1986), 'Corruption, Delivery Systems, and Property Rights', **14** *World Development*, 127-132.

Jagannathan, N. Vijay (1988), 'Corruption, Delivery Systems and Property Rights: Rejoinder', **16** *World Development*, 1393-1394.

Jain, R.B. (1983), 'Fighting Political Corruption: the Indian Experience', **3** *Calcutta Journal of Political Studies*, 1-22.

Jones, P. (1993), *Combatting Fraud and Corruption in the Public Sector*, London, Chapman and Hall.

Kaminsky, A.Z. (1989), 'Coercion, Corruption and Reform - State and Society in the Soviet-type Socialist Regime', **1** *Journal of Theoretical Politics*, 77-102.

Kaufer, Erich (1989), 'Market Clearing by Corruption: The Political Economy of China's Recent Economic Reforms: Comment', **145** *Journal of Institutional and Theoretical Economics*, 127-129.

Kennedy, William P. (1989), 'Market Clearing by Corruption: The Political Economy of China's Recent Economic Reforms: Comment', **145** *Journal of Institutional and Theoretical Economics*, 130-132.

Klitgaard, Robert (1984), 'Managing the Fight against Corruption: a Case Study', **4** *Public Administration and Development*, 77-98.

Klitgaard, Robert (1988), *Controlling Corruption*, Berkeley, University of California Press, 220 p.

Klitgaard, Robert (1990), *Tropical Gangsters*, New York, Basic Books.

Klitgaard, Robert (1991), 'Gifts and Bribes', in Zeckhauser, R. (ed.), *Strategy and Choice*, Cambridge, MA, MIT Press.

Klitgaard, Robert (1998), 'International Cooperation Against Corruption', **35** *Finance and Development*, 3-6.

Kolenda, H. (1990), 'One Party, Two Systems - Corruption in the People's Republic of China and Attempts to Control it', **4** *Journal of Chinese Law*, 187-232.

Kotecha, K.C. and Adams, R.W. (1981), *African Politics: the Corruption of Power*, Washington, University Press of America.

Kowalewski, D., Leitko, T. and Leonard Rosen (1991), 'Revolving Doors, Corporate Performance and Corruption of Markets', **18** *Critical Sociology*, 92-110.

Kurer, Oskar (1993), 'Clientelism, Corruption, and the Allocation of Resources', **77** *Public Choice*, 259-273.

Laffont, J.J. (1990), 'Analysis of Hidden Gaming in a Three Level Hierarchy', **6** *Journal of Law, Economics and Organization*.

Lambert-Mogiliansky, A. (1995), 'Indirect Monitoring and Corruption', Mimeo, Stockholm University.

Le Vine, V. T. (1975), *Political Corruption: the Ghana Case*, Stanford, Hoover Institute Press, Stanford University.

Lee, Barbara A. and Chelius, James R. (1989), 'Government Regulation of Labor Management Corruption: The Casino Industry Experience in New Jersey', **42** *Industrial and Labor Relations Review*, 536-548.

Leff, N. (1964), 'Economic Development through Bureaucratic Corruption', **1964** *American Behavioral Scientist*, 8-14.

Lewis, D.J. (1996), *Political Corruption: the Ghana Case*, Occasional Paper, Centre for Development Studies, University of Bath.

Lien, Da Hsiang Donald (1987), 'Asymmetric Information in Competitive Bribery Games', **23** *Economics Letters*, 153-156.

Lien, Da Hsiang Donald (1990), 'Corruption and Allocation Efficiency', **33** *Journal of Development Economics*, 153-164.

Lui, Francis T. (1985), 'An Equilibrium Queuing Model of Bribery', **93** *Journal of Political Economy*, 760-781.

Lui, Francis T. (1986), 'A Dynamic Model of Corruption Deterrence', **31** *Journal of Public Economics*, 215-236.

Lupsha, P.A. (1991), 'Drug Lords and Narco-Corruption - the Players Change but the Game Continues', **16** *Crime, Law and Social Change*, 41-58.

MacRae, John (1982), 'Underdevelopment and the Economics of Corruption: A Game Theory Approach', **10** *World Development*, 677-687.

Magnusson, Lars (1989), 'Corruption and Civic Order Natural Law and Economic Discourse in Sweden during the Age of Freedom', **37** *Scandinavian Economic History Review*, 78-105.

Maingot, Anthony P. (1994), 'Confronting Corruption in the Hemisphere: A Sociological Perspective', **36** *Journal of Interamerican Studies and World Affairs*, 49-74.

Makumbe, J. (1994), 'Bureaucratic Corruption in Zimbabwe: Causes and Magnitude of the Problem', **19** *Africa Development*, 45-60.

Marjit, S. (1997), 'On Controlling Crime with Corrupt Officials', **34** *Journal of Economic Behavior and Organization*, 163-172.

Mauro, Paolo (1995), 'Corruption and Growth', **110** *Quarterly Journal of Economics*, 681-712.

Mauro, Paolo (1996), *The Effects of Corruption on Growth, Investment, and Government Expenditure*, IMF Working Paper, Washington, IMF, No. 96/98. Elliott (1997) (ed.) op. cit.

Mauro, Paolo (1998), 'Corruption: Causes, Consequences, and Agenda for Further Research', **35** *Finance and Development*, 11-14.

Mbaku, John Mukum (1992), 'Bureaucratic Corruption as Rent Seeking Behavior', **38** *Konjunkturpolitik*, 247-265.

Mbaku, John Mukum (1994), 'Bureaucratic Corruption and Policy Reform in Africa', **19** *Journal of Social, Political and Economic Studies*, 149-176.

Mills, Edwin S. (1987), 'Bureaucratic Corruption as a Constraint on Voter Choice: Comments', **55** *Public Choice*, 161-162.

Mookherjee, D. and Png, Ivan Paak-Liang (1995), 'Corruptible Law Enforcers: How should they be compensated?', **105** *Economic Journal*, 145-159.

Morris, S.D. (1991), *Corruption and Politics in Contemporary Mexico*, Tuscaloosa, University of Alabama Press.

Moteiro, J.B. (1966), *Corruption: Control of Maladministration*, Bombay, Manaktalas.

Murphy, Kevein M., Shleifer, Andre and Vishny, Robert W. (1993), 'Why is Rent Seeking so Costly to Growth?', **83** *American Economic Review. Papers and Proceedings*, 409-420.

Myerson, Roger B. (1993), 'Effectiveness of Electoral Systems for Reducing Government Corruption: A Game Theoretic Analysis', **5** *Games and Economic Behavior*, 118-132.

Myrdal, Gunnar (1989), 'Corruption as a Hindrance to Modernization in South Asia', in Heidenheimer, Arnold J., Jophnson, Michael and Le Vine, Victor (eds), *Political Corruption: A Handbook*, New Brunswick, NJ, Transaction Press, 406-407.

Nas, Tevfik F., Price, Albert C. and Webber, Charles T. (1986), 'A Policy oriented Theory of Corruption', **80** *American Political Science Review*, 107-119.

Olsen, T. and Torsvik, G. 'Collusion and Renegotiation in Hierarchies: the Case of Beneficial Corruption', Mimeo, University of Bergen, Bergen, Norway.

Ouma, S.O.A. (1991), 'Corruption in Public Policy and its Impact on Development: the Case of Uganda since 1979', **11** *Public Administration and Development*, 473-490.

Palmier, L. (1983), 'Bureaucratic Corruption and its Remedies', in Clarke, M. (ed.), *Corruption: Causes, Consequences and Control*, London, Frances Pinter.

Palmier, L. (1989), 'Corruption in the West Pacific', **2** *Pacific Reviewv*, 11-23.

Pechlivanos, L. (1995), 'Sustainability of Corruption and Optimal Deterrence', Mimeo, Boston University.

Peters, John G. and Welch, Susan (1980), 'The Effects of Charges of Corruption on Voting Behavior in Congressional Elections', **74** *American Political Science Review*, 697-708.

Png, Ivan Paak-Liang and Mookherjee, D. (1995), 'Corruptible Law Enforcers: How Should They Be Compensated?', **105** *Economic Journal*, 145-159.

Punch, M., van der Vijer, K. and van Vliet, K. (1993), *Coping with Corruption in a Borderless World*, Boston, Kluwer.

Quansah, E.K. (1994), 'The Corruption and Economic Crime Act, 1994 of Botswana', **38** *Journal of African Law*, 191-196.

Ragazzi, Giorgio (1993), 'I Confini della Corruzione Politica (The Boundaries of Political Corruption. With English summary)', **48** *Studi Economici*, 125-150.

Rasmusen, Eric (1994), *Games and Information*, 2nd edn, Cambridge, MA and Oxford, Blackwell.

Rasmusen, Eric and Ramseyer, J. Mark (1994), 'Cheap Bribes and the Corruption Ban: A Coordination Game among Rational Legislators', **78** *Public Choice*, 305-327.

Rasmussen, David W. and Benson, Bruce L. (eds) (1994), *The Economic Anatomy of a Drug War: Criminal Justice in the Commons*, Lanham, MD, Rowman and Littlefield.

Reder, Melvin W. (1975), 'Corruption as a Feature of Governmental Organization: Comment', **18** *Journal of Law and Economics*, 607-609.

Reno, W.S.K. (1995), *Corruption and State Politics in Sierra Leone*, Cambridge, Cambridge University Press.

Rinaldi, S., Feichtinger, G. and Wirl, F. (1994), 'Corruption Dynamics in Democratic Systems', **168** *Forschungsbericht/Research Memorandum*.

Rocca, Jean Louis (1992), 'Corruption and Its Shadow: An Anthropological View of Corruption in China', **0** *China Quarterly*, 402-416.

Rose-Ackerman, Susan (1975), 'The Economics of Corruption', **4** *Journal of Public Economics*, 187-203.

Rose-Ackerman, Susan (1978a), *Corruption: A Study in Political Economy*, New York, Academic Press.

Rose-Ackerman, Susan (1978b), *Corruption: A Study in Political Economy*, New York, Academic Press. Reprinted as 'Problem Der Ökonomischen Theorie', in C. Fleck and Helmut Kuzmics (eds), Korruption: Zur Soziologie.

Rose-Ackerman, Susan (1994), 'Reducing Bribery in the Public Sector', in Trang, Duc V. (ed.), *Corruption and Democracy*, Budapest, Institute for Constitutional and Legislative Policy, 21-28.

Rose-Ackerman, Susan (1995), 'Second Generation Issues in Transition: Corruption', in Bruno, Michael and Pleskovic, Boris (eds), *Proceedings of The World Bank Annual Conference on Development Economics 1995*, Washington, 373-380.

Rose-Ackerman, Susan and Montias, J.M., 'Corruption in Soviet Type Economies: Theoretical Considerations', in Rosefielde, Steven (ed.), *Economic Welfare and the Economics of Soviet Socialism: Essays in Honor of Abram Bergson*, Cambridge, Cambridge University Press.

Rottenberg, Simon (1975), 'Corruption as a Feature of Governmental Organization: Comment', **18** *Journal of Law and Economics*, 611-615.

Ruggiero, V. (1994), 'Corruption in Italy: an Attempt to Identify the Victims', **33** *Howard Journal of Criminal Justice*, 319-337.

Sah, R.K. (1987), *Persistence and Pervasiveness of Corruption,* The World Bank, Conference on Political Economy: Theory and Policy Implications, June 17-19, 1987, Washington, DC, The World Bank.

Sands, Barbara N. (1989), 'Market Clearing by Corruption: The Political Economy of China's Recent Economic Reforms', **145** *Journal of Institutional and Theoretical Economics*, 116-126.

Sands, Barbara N. (1990), 'Decentralizing an Economy: The Role of Bureaucratic Corruption in China's Economic Reforms', **65** *Public Choice*, 85-91.

Santhanam Committee (1994), *Report by the Committee on Prevention of Corruption*, Government of India, Ministry of Home Affairs.

Schaffer, B. (1986), 'Access: a Theory of Corruption and Bureaucracy', **6** *Public Administration and Development*, 357-376.

Schelling, T. (1967), 'Criminal Enterprise' in '*Task Force Report: Organised Crime*', President's Commission on Law Enforcement and Administration of Justice, Washington, DC.

Schmidt, Kurt (1969), 'Zur Okonomik der Korruption (On the Economics of Corruption. With English summary)', **89** *Schmollers Jahrbuch für Wirtschafts und Sozialwissenschaften*, 129-149.

Schwalbe, Ulrich (1994), 'Gewerkschaften und Korruption (Corruption and Trade Unions. With English summary)', **114** *Zeitschrift für Wirtschafts- und Sozialwissenschaften*, 617-634.

Seagull, L.M. (1994), 'Whistleblowing and Corruption Control: the GE case22', **(4)** *Crime, Law and Social Change*, 381-390.

Sexton, Jean (1989), 'Controlling Corruption in the Construction Industry: The Quebec Approach', **42** *Industrial and Labor Relations Review*, 524-535.

Shavell, Steven and Spier, Kathryn E. (1996), 'Threats Without Binding Commitment', **5461** *National Bureau of Economic Research Working Paper*.

Shleifer, A. and Vishny, Robert W. (1992), 'Pervasive Shortages under Socialism', **23** *Rand Journal of Economics*.

Shleifer, A. and Vishny, Robert W. (1994), 'Politicians and Firms',**109** *Quarterly Journal of Economics*.

Shleifer, Andrei and Vishny, Robert W. (1993), 'Corruption', **108** *Quarterly Journal of Economics*, 599-617.

Sisk, David E. (1982), 'Police Corruption and Criminal Monopoly: Victimless Crimes', **11** *Journal of Legal Studies*, 395-403.

Spier, Kathryn E. and Shavell, Steven (1996), 'Threats Without Binding Commitment', National Bureau of Economic Research Working Paper.

Spiller, P. (1990), 'Politicians, Interest Groups, and Regulators: A Multi-Principals Agency Theory of Regulation (or 'let them be bribed')', **33** *Journal of Law and Economics*, 65-101.

Strauss, D.A. (1994), 'Corruption, Equality and Campaign Finance Reform', **94** *Columbia Law Review*, 1369-1389.

Szeftel, M. (1983), 'Corruption and the Spoils System in Zambia', in Clarke, M. (ed.), *Corruption: Causes, Consequences and Control*, London, Frances Pinter.

Szymanderski, Jacek (1995), 'Moral Order and Corruption in Transition to the Market: Popular Beliefs and Their Underpinnings', **7** *Communist Economies and Economic Transformation*, 249-257.

Tanzi, V. (1995), 'Corruption, Governmental Activities, and Markets', **32** *Finance and Development*, 24-26.

Tanzi, V. and Davoodi, H. (1998), 'Roads to Nowhere: How Corruption in Public Investment Hurts Growth', **12** *Economic Issues, IMF*.

Theobald, R. (1990), *Corruption, Development and Underdevelopment*, Basingstoke, Macmillan.

Theobald, R. (1993), 'Lancing the Swollen African State: Will it Alleviate the Problems of Corruption?', **32** *Journal of Modern African Studies*, 701-706.

Tirole, Jean (1996), 'A Theory of Collective Reputations (with applications to the persistence of corruption and to firm quality)', **63** *Review of Economic Studies*, 1-22.

Toma, Eugenia Froedge and Toma, Mark (1992), 'Tax Collection with Agency Costs: Private Contracting or Government Bureaucrats?', **59** *Economica*, 107-120.

Trivedi, Vishwapati (1988), 'Corruption, Delivery Systems and Property Rights: A Comment', **16** *World Development*, 1389-1391.

Tunstall, Allan W. (1992), 'Corruption! At Flemington Markets? A Case Study in Public Policy', **60** *Review of Marketing and Agricultural Economics*, 57-67.

United Nations (1989), *Corruption in Government*, New York, United Nations.

van de Mortel, E. and Cornelisse, P.A. (1994), 'The Dynamics of Corruption and Black Markets: an Application of Catastrophe Theory', **49** *Public Finance*, 195-210.

Vance, M.A. (1982), *Corruption in Politics in the US: a bibliography*, Monticello, IL, Vance Bibliographies.

Virmani, Arvind (1987), 'Tax Evasion, Corruption and Administration: Monitoring the People's Agents under Symmetric Dishonesty', Mimeo, Development Research Department, The World Bank, Washington, DC.

Wade, Robert (1982), 'The System of Administrative and Political Corruption: Canal Irrigation in South India', **18** *Journal of Development Studies*, 287-328.

Ward, Peter M. (ed.) (1989), *Corruption, Development and Inequality: Soft Touch or Hard Graft?*, London, Routledge, 191 p.

Werlin, Herbert H. (1973), 'The Consequences of Corruption: The Ghanaian Experience', **88** *Political Science Quarterly*, 71-85.

Werner, S.B. (1983), 'New Directions in the Study of Administrative Corruption', **1983** *Public Administration Review*, 146-154.

Williams, R.J. (1981), 'Political Corruption in the United States', **29** *Political Studies*, 126-129.

Winston, Gordon C. (1979), 'The Appeal of Inappropriate Technologies: Self Inflicted Wages, Ethnic Price and Corruption', **7** *World Development*, 835-845.

Wong, Kar Yiu (1992), 'Inflation, Corruption, and Income Distribution: The Recent Price Reform in China', **14** *Journal of Macroeconomics*, 105-123.

Other References

Akerlof, G.A. (1980), 'A Theory of Social Custom of which Unemployment may be One Consequence', **94** *Quarterly Journal of Economics*, 749-795.

Allingham, M. and Sandmo, A. (1972), 'Income Tax Evasion: A Theoretical Analysis', **1** *Journal of Public Economics*, 323-38.

Barzel, Y. (1996), 'Parliament as a Wealth Maximizing Institution: the Right to the Residual and the Right to Vote', mimeo, presented at European Association of Law and Economics Conference, Haifa, Israel.

Baye, M.R. (1997), *Managerial Economics and Business Strategy*, Chicago, Irwin.

Becker, G.S. (1968), 'Crime and Punishment: an Economic Approach', **76** *Journal of Political Economy*, 169-217.

Becker, G.S. (1983), 'A Theory of Competition among Pressure Groups for Political Influence', **98** *Quarterly Journal of Economics*, 371-400.

Becker, G. and Stigler, G. (1974), 'Law Enforcement, Malfeasance, and the Compensation of Enforcers', **3** *Journal of Legal Studies*, 1-18.

Benjamini, Y. and Maital, S. (1985), 'Optimal Tax Evasion and Optimal Tax Evasion Policy', in Gartner, W. and Wenig, A. (eds), *The Economics of the Shadow Economy*, Berlin, Springer Verlag, 245-264.

Bhagwati, J. (1982), 'Directly Unproductive Profit-Seeking (DUP) Activities', **90** *Journal of Political Economy*, 1982.

Border, K.C. and Sobell, J. (1987), 'Samurai Accountant: A Theory of Auditing and Plunder', **54** *Review of Economic Studies*, 525-540.

Bowles, R.A. (1997), 'Reform of Legal Aid and the Solicitors' Profession', **5** *Hume Papers*, 1997.

Bowles, R.A. and Rickman, N. (1998), 'Asymmetric Information, Moral Hazard and the Insurance of Legal Expenses', **23** *Geneva Papers on Risk and Insurance*, 196-209.

Breyer, S. and Steward, R. (1979), *Administrative Law and Regulatory Policy*, Boston: Little, Brown & Co.

Brickley, J.A., Smith, C.W. and Zimmerman, J.L. (1996), *Organizational Architecture: A Managerial Economics Approach*, Chicago, Irwin.

Business International Corporation (1984), *Introduction to the Country Assessment Service*, New York, BIC.

Calvo, G.A. and Wellisz, S.H. (1978), 'Supervision, Loss of Control and the Optimal Size of the Firm', **86** *Journal of Political Economy*, 943-952.

Cohen, S. and Eimicke, W.B. (1995), 'Ethics and the Public Administrator', **537** *Annals of the American Academy of Political and Social Sciences*, 97-108.

Cullis, J.G. and Jones, P.R. (1992), *Public Finance and Public Choice*, London, McGraw-Hill.

Deakin, S. and Michie, J. (eds) (1997), *Contracts, Co-operation and Competition*, Oxford, Oxford University Press.

DeSouza, P. (1985), 'Regulating Fraud in Military Procurement: A Legal Process Model', **95** *Yale Law Journal*, 390-413.

Downs, A. (1957), *An Economic Theory of Democracy*, New York, Harper & Row.

Eide, E. (1994), *Economics of Crime: Deterrence and the Rational Offender*, North Holland.

EMF Foundation (1991), *World Competitiveness Report*, Cologny/Geneva, EMF Foundation.

Garoupa, N. (1997), 'The Theory of Optimal Law Enforcement', **11** *Journal of Economic Surveys*, 267-295.

Grossman, S. and Hart, O. (1983), 'An Analysis of the Principal Agent Problem', **52** *Econometrica*, 1-45.

Hirshleifer and Riley (1992), *The Analytics of Information and Uncertainty*, Cambridge, Cambridge University Press.

Jabbra, J.G. and Dwivedi, O.P. (ed.) (1989), *Public Sector Accountability*, Connecticut, Kumatian Press.

Jones, P.R. and Cullis, J.G. (1996), 'Legitimate and Illegitimate Transfers: Dealing with 'Political' Cost-Benefit Analysis', **16** *International Review of Law and Economics*, 247-258.

Katz and Rosen (1994), *Microeconomics*, Illinois, Irwin.

Kay, J.A. and Thompson, D.J. (1986), 'Privatisation: a Policy in Search of a Rationale', **96** *Economic Journal*, 18-32.

Koffman, F. and Lawarree, J. (1993), 'Collusion in Hierarchical Agency', **61** *Econometrica*, 629-656.

Krueger, A.O. (1974), 'The Political Economy of the Rent-Seeking Society', **64** *American Economic Review*, 291-303.

Laffont, J.-J. and Tirole, J. (1993), *A Theory of Incentives in Procurement and Regulation*, Cambridge, MA, MIT Press.

Lee, D.R. (1983), 'Monitoring and Budget Maximization in the Control of Pollution', **21** *Economic Inquiry*, 565 ff.

Lewin, J.L. and Trumbell, W.N. (1993), 'Neither Boxed in nor Circular: a Reply to Professor McChesney', **13** *International Review of Law and Economics*, 233 ff.

MacMullen, R. (1988), *Corruption and the Decline of Rome*, New Haven, Yale University Press.

Manne, H. (1966), *Insider Trading and the Stock Market*, New York City, The Free Press.

McChesney, F.S. (1993), 'Boxed in: Economists and benefits from crime', **3** *International Review of Law and Economics*, 225-232.

Mueller, D. (1979), *Public Choice*, Cambridge, Cambridge University Press.

Myrdal, G. (1968), *Asian Drama: An Inquiry into the Poverty of Nations*, vol II, New York, Pantheon.

Niskanen, W.A. (1974), *Bureaucracy and Representative Government*, Chicago, Aldine.

Pauly, M. (1970), 'Efficiency, Incentives and Reimbursement for Health Care', **7** *Inquiry*, 114-131.

Peltzman, S. (1976), 'Toward a More General Theory of Regulation', **19** *Journal of Law and Economics*, 211-40.

Polinsky, A.M. and Shavell, S. (1979), 'The Optimal Trade-off between the Probability and Magnitude of Fines', **69** *American Economic Review*, 880-891.

Polinsky, A.M. and Shavell, S. (1984), 'The Optimal Use of Fines and Imprisonment', **69** *Journal of Public Economics*, 880-891.

Posner, R. (1975), 'The Social Costs of Monopoly and Regulation', **83** *Journal of Political Economy*.

Pyle, D.J. (1992), 'The Economics of Taxpayer Compliance', **5** *Journal of Economic Surveys*, 163-198.

Ross, S. (1973), 'The Economic Theory of Agency: The Principal's Problem', **63** *American Economic Review*, 134-139.

Stigler, G.J. (1971), 'The Economic Theory of Regulation', **2** *Bell Journal of Economics and Management Science*, 3-21.

Tirole, J. (1986), 'Hierarchies and Bureaucracies: On the Role of Collusion in Organizations', **2** *Journal of Law, Economics and Organization*, 181-214.

Tirole, J. (1992), 'Collusion and the Theory of Organizations', in Laffont, J.-J. (ed.), *Advances in Economic Theory: Sixth World Congress*, vol II, Econometric Society Monographs, no. 21, Cambridge, Cambridge University Press.

Tirole, J. (1994), 'The Internal Organization of Government', **46** *Oxford Economic Papers*, 1-29.

Tollison, R.D. (1982), 'Rent Seeking: a Survey', **35** *Kyklos*, 575-602.

Tullock, G. (1967), 'The Welfare Costs of Tariffs, Monopolies and Theft', **5** *Western Economic Journal*.

Webber, C. and Wildavsky, A. (1986), *A History of Taxation and Expenditure in the Western World*, New York, Simon & Schuster.

Weingast, B.R., Shepsle, K.A. and Johnsen, C. (1981), 'The Political Economy of Costs and Benefits: A Neoclassical Approach to Distribution Politics', **89** *Journal of Political Economy*, 642 ff.

Williamson, O.E. (1979), *Transaction Cost Economics: The Governance of Contractual Relations*, New York, Free Press.

Wilson, J.Q. (1989), *Bureaucracy: What Government Agencies Do and Why They Do It*, New York, Basic Books.

World Bank (1992), *Governance and Development*, Washington, DC, World Bank.

8600
CORPORATE CRIMINAL LIABILITY

John R. Lott, Jr
John M. Olin Visiting Law and Economics Fellow
University of Chicago Law School

Abstract

This chapter reviews the economic literature on corporate crime. Economists have discussed and answered a number of questions about corporate crime in only few years time span. Perhaps this unusual success is due to the questions involving corporations being so similar to other crime issues, previously analysed. However, a number of questions remain largely unexplored. Why do certain firms commit crimes while others do not? What are the social costs imposed by the very high corporate criminal penalties? How does the criminal justice process shape the organisation of firms?
JEL classification: K22, K14, K42
Keywords: Corporate Crime, Firm, US Sentencing Guidelines

1. Introduction

The economic analysis of corporate crime only started gaining momentum during the last half dozen years. Of course, one notable exception to this rule is Posner's textbook on the *Economic Analysis of Law* (1992), though the discussion of corporate criminality is relegated to issues such as whether firms should obey the law or maximise profits. (It is also puzzling to report how economists still fail in providing a conclusive definition of a firm. For example, while I am sure that it is not done intentionally, definitions of organised crime appear to be interchangeable with definition of firms (see, for example, Dick, 1995)).

The catalyst for this was the debate over and the subsequent adoption in 1991 of the US government's corporate sentencing guidelines. The research itself has largely focused on theoretical questions raised by the guidelines (for example, what should be included in calculating the social cost of crimes committed by corporations or whether it should be the firm and/or its managers who are penalised), descriptive empirical evidence on how corporate penalties have changed over time, and some evidence indicating what factors predispose firms to violate the law.

2. The Theory

The basic principle behind the economics view of legally imposed sanctions is to ensure that those who break the law internalise the externalities that they impose upon others. Several questions arise in this context: (1) how large is the externality, (2) upon whom should the penalty be imposed, and (3) should the penalty take the form of criminal or civil sanctions or possibly just through the loss of reputation.

While the issue of criminal harm is the same for crimes by firms and individuals (see for example Becker, 1968 or Friedman, 1981), the debate among economists over what should be included in corporate penalties largely arises from the sentencing commission's guidelines, which explicitly include some notion of the third-party spillover effects from crimes like financial or consumer fraud (United States Sentencing Commission, Chapter Eight - Sentencing of Organisations, U.S.S.C. § 8 C5.5, November 1, 1991). In part this interest arises because fraud cases involve almost half of all corporate crimes (Alexander and Cohen, 1996a, p. 427). Upward departures from the guidelines are also required when any corporate crime involves a 'substantial risk to the integrity or continued existence of a market' (United States Sentencing Commission, Chapter Eight - Sentencing of Organisations, U.S.S.C. Proposed Addition to the Sentencing Guidelines, § 8.12, July, 1988).

Some economists, such as Tom Ulen (1996), defend the theory behind the guidelines by arguing that criminal penalties are required to ensure that offending firms internalize the losses imposed on buyers because frauds cause both consumers and firms to take costly defensive actions. In this discussion, fraud affects third parties like a tax, raising both the costs of production by firms and lowering the price that consumers are willing to pay. While Ulen accepts that there is an optimal amount of fraud, criminal penalties should account for these third party losses whenever there is more than the 'socially optimal amount of fraud taking place' (p. 358). How one knows when these frauds are greater than the optimal number is not clear, though most of this discussion identifies dead-weight losses whenever frauds effect third-party behaviour. The question of how large the criminal penalties should be are then a function of those parameters that determine the dead-weight loss from taxes (for example, the elasticity of demand).

An alternative position argues that third parties should normally be seen as benefiting from the frauds committed against others (Daniel and Lott, 1995; Lott, 1996). For example, if after a fraud other firms' customers desire that they acquire more reputation because the customers learn that the existing level of reputation produced less quality assurance than they had previously believed, the revelation of the fraud allows them to better equate the marginal benefits and costs from buying quality assurance. The distinction drawn here is whether the fraud changes the underlying probability with which other frauds will occur or whether it merely provides other firms' customers with better information to evaluate their own situation. Given that few frauds are likely to innovate new methods of perpetrating the deception that will then be copied by imitators, few frauds will alter the underlying probability of other frauds occurring.

An interesting debate concerns whether it might be more efficient to impose penalties on the principals instead of simply holding agents directly liable for their actions.

Kraakman (1984b) suggests that part of the reason may have to do with monitoring costs. For example, corporate liability may be efficient if the government is better at monitoring corporations and these corporations are good at monitoring agents. Salzburg (1991) and Polinsky and Shavell (1993) point out that the penalties imposed upon the firm may not always be large enough to produce the efficient level of deterrence, thus justifying an additional penalty being imposed upon the agents (while Salzburg merely provides a verbal argument on this issue, Polinsky and Shavell provide the formal model behind this reasoning). Salzburg (1991) also advocates prosecuting corporations because it reduces the prosecutor's burden of investigation and conviction and avoids various preceived procedural problems, though in the end this argument amounts to little more than a claim that both firms and individuals should be prosecuted because it is possible to do so.

Arlen (1994) suggests that penalties on principles may have the unintended effect of inducing principals to expend less effort monitoring, since their own monitoring of principals may increase the likelihood of detection. Unless corporations are compensated for its monitoring efforts through penalty reductions that offset the higher probability of prosecutions that result from the internal monitoring, the private return to monitoring will fall below the social return. Davis (1996) raises the issue of how the possibility that agents' actions can create liability for a firm's principals thus alter agents' compensation. He asks whether agents actually prefer government rules that increase their liability. His conclusion is that there are reasonable assumptions about the agent's risk neutrality and how the earning depend on legal and illegal profits, where agents will prefer legal liability.

However, whatever the answer to these questions, the central question still remains: should corporate criminality even exist. While there are philosophical arguments over whether a corporation as compared to individuals can have intent (Parker, 1996), economists have largely debated whether criminal sanctions are necessary to ensure that corporations internalize the externalities that their illegal behaviour creates. Block (1991), Karpoff and Lott (1993), Fischel and Sykes (1996) and Parker (1996), ask whether civil penalties might be preferred. Not only do criminal proceedings require higher levels of proof than civil proceedings but, for firms, the ultimate penalty is the same in either case: fines. Civil prosecution provides other benefits ranging from compensation of victims, law enforcement efficiencies, and the ability of apparently obtaining the same stigma produced by criminal prosecution though at a lower cost (Parker, 1996, pp. 387-389).

One question still persists: might the government be better suited to imposing particularly large penalties on individuals because the government can use imprisonment while private firms are limited to monetary damages? While this is true, it misses the central point. Criminal charges can still be pursued against individual agents even if the case against the firm is handled civilly (Fischel and Sykes, 1996).

3. Empirical Evidence

Empirical corporate crime studies take several forms. Either they measure the size of the criminal penalties and how the US Sentencing Guidelines have altered these penalties, test which characteristics are exhibited by firms engaging in crime, measure firm profitability from crime, or examine whether the US Sentencing Guidelines have moved penalties closer towards efficiency.

Penalties prior to the guidelines appear to have exhibited many patterns consistent with optimal penalty theory (Cohen, 1996). Not only did firms creating greater harm face greater sanctions, but individual liability was also greater when the organisation was unable to compensate for the harm done. Interestingly, for the crimes with the largest losses, the penalty that the courts imposed suggested a belief that the probability of detection was higher for those crimes (Cohen, 1991 and Lott, 1991, p. 440). An easy optimal penalty explanation appears to exist for this. For example, large oil spills are virtually certain to be detected, but tiny ones (for example, the discharging of ballast) are most likely to be unnoticed.

The sentencing guidelines turned much of this pre-existing structure on its head, with the multiple now instead increasing with the size of the harm. The guidelines also have dramatically increased criminal penalties. Early estimates indicated increases of 20, 30 or 40 times over previous penalties, and changes as high as 50 to 100 fold for a few select crimes (Cohen, 1991). Others produced estimates of at least twenty-fold (Block, 1991 and Lott, 1991).

With fraud being the largest category of corporate crime and one of the areas with the biggest increases in penalties under the guidelines, much of the recent empirical evidence has focused on it. Analysing the Sentencing

Commission's concerns that the penalties for fraud have been too low, economists sought to investigate whether traditional emphasis on legally imposed penalties underestimated the true penalty. To evaluate this, Karpoff and Lott (1993) measured the extent of reputational penalties for fraudulent firms prior to the 1991 corporate guidelines. An allegation that a corporation had defrauded stakeholders or the government corresponds to an economically and statistically significant loss in the market value of the common stock. On average, very little of this loss, in the order of 6.5 percent, can be attributed to the accused firm's expected legal fees and penalties. It is possible to compute larger portions of the loss that could reflect higher expected penalties for future frauds and the lost value of the cheating firm's profits from committing fraud. But even under extremely unrealistic assumptions, one third of the loss remains. (Yet, firms are not the only entities to suffer from reduced earnings when they commit fraud. White collar criminal face large reductions in legitimate earnings when they are convicted of fraud (Lott, 1992). The average criminal convicted of fraud faces almost a 40 percent drop in legitimate earnings when he returns to the workforce. Similar drops are also observed for embezzlement, larceny and theft.)

Large reputational penalties are associated with frauds committed against stakeholders, government agencies, and investors. In contrast, the reputational loss for frauds involving regulatory violations, in which firms have not violated an implicit or explicit contract with a stakeholder or investor, is negligible (see also Block, 1991). The evidence is consistent with the market penalty for fraud being systematically related to the cost imposed on parties with whom the firm does business. Because of their large size, reputational effects play an important role in disciplining firms that commit fraud. There appear to be very similar reputational penalties when either criminal or civil cases are filed (Block, 1991).

For fraud, the average decrease in common stock value exceeds the US Sentencing Commission's estimates of victim losses by more than 100 times. The Sentencing Commission reports that Department of Justice prosecutors believe the probability of convicting a corporate fraud is between 20 and 57 percent, implying an optimal ratio of actual penalty to social costs of between 1.75 and 5 (Lott, 1996, pp. 374-375). Yet, as mentioned above, the expected *total* penalty far exceeds the Commission's estimated loss borne by the victims, and this holds even at 1980's levels of criminal fines. Thus, unless these numbers are off by a very large magnitude, the past efforts to substantially increase criminal penalties for corporate fraud were completely misguided.

Some evidence indicates that managers conceal bad news from the market (Arlen and Carney, 1992), indirectly supporting a 'last period hypothesis', in which misconduct results from poor performance on the part of the firm. Yet, other findings suggest no actual or expected deterioration in firm profitability prior to a fraud (Karpoff and Lott, 1993). A study by Alexander and Cohen (1996a) examines other aspects of firms' performance prior to a fraud, as measured by the firm's assets, employment and sales. With the exception of environmental crimes, they find no relationship between these measures and whether a fraud is going to occurs.

Antitrust penalties have been studied extensively by economists, and up until recently, when it was displaced by environmental crimes, it involved the second largest number of cases. Asch and Seneca (1975, 1976) provided the earliest evidence in this area by investigating whether the prior performance of firms charged with antitrust violations differed relative to their Fortune 500 counterparts. Surprisingly, Asch and Seneca found a significant negative relationship between collusion and several alternative measures of performance such as growth in sales and return on assets over the five years before the date of the relevant plea or court finding. Staw and Szwajkowski (1975) attempt to explain this result as lower profitability leading to collusion. (However, since these studies rely on actual government suits, there is always the nagging question of whether the government can accurately tell which firms if any are engaging in antitrust violations.)

Game theory has also suggested essentially limitless explanations for firm behavior. A number of recent game-theoretic models suggest that with asymmetric information it can be profitable for some firms to acquire a reputation for toughness in order to discourage later entry. One may view these models as providing a method of understanding what factors increase the likelihood that firms commit crimes, though initial empirical evidence provides little support that these models will be particularly useful. Lott and Opler (1996) identify institutional arrangements that firms must undertake to ensure the credibility of any predatory commitments. Simply hiring managers who value market share or output maximisation is not sufficient if the manager can be removed whenever it actually becomes necessary to engage in predation. It is also required that the firms make removing the manager difficult. In addition, the incumbent manager should be rewarded for increasing output as opposed to increasing short-term profits. A study of firms charged with predation failed to yield any support that allegedly predatory firms are organised as these game-theoretic models imply. If anything, the reverse seems to be frequently true.

Alleged predators more often are large firms with managerial compensation schemes relying heavily on short-term profits (Lott and Opler, 1996, pp. 362-363), with this last fact hardly seeming consistent with any known notion of predation. Just as Bork (1978, pp. 347-364) argues, the general picture is consistent with the laws being used to harass large profitable firms.

4. Conclusion

Economists have discussed and answered a number of questions about corporate crime in only few years time span. Perhaps this unusual success is due to the questions involving corporations being so similar to other crime issues, previously analysed. However, a number of questions remain largely unexplored. Why do certain firms commit crimes while others do not? What are the social costs imposed by the very high corporate criminal penalties? How does the criminal justice process shape the organisation of firms? These are areas that should lend themselves to very interesting future research.

Bibliography on Corporate Criminal Liability (8600)

Alexander, Cindy R. and Cohen, Mark A (1996a), 'New Evidence on the Origins of Corporate Crime', **17** *Managerial and Decision Economics*, 421-435.

Alexander, Cindy R. and Cohen, Mark A. (1996b), *Why Do Corporations Become Criminals? An Agency Explanation*, Working paper.

Arlen, Jennifer H. (1991), 'Controlling Corporate Torts: Strict Liability Versus Negligence Reconsidered', Working Paper Version.

Arlen, Jennifer H. (1994), 'The Potentially Perverse Effects of Corporate Criminal Liability', **23** *Journal of Legal Studies*, 832-867.

Arlen, Jennifer H. (1995), 'Commentary on Rewarding Whistleblowers: The Costs and Benefits of an Incentive-Based Compliance Strategy', in Daniels, Ronald and Morck, Randall (eds), *Corporate Decision-Making in Canada*, 635-647.

Arlen, Jennifer H. and Carney, William J. (1992), 'Vicarious Liability for Fraud on Securities Markets: Theory and Evidence', **25** *University of Illinois Law Review*, 691-740. Reprinted in Andersen, Peder, Vibeke, Jensen and Mortensen, Jørgen Birk (eds) (1993), *Governance by Legal and Economic Measures*, Copenhagen, Gad.

Arlen, Jennifer H. and Kraakman, Reinier H. (1997), 'Controlling Corporate Misconduct: A Comparative Analysis of Alternative Corporate Incentive Regimes', **72** *New York University Law Review*, 687-779.

Asch, Peter and Seneca, J.J. (1975), 'Characteristics of Collusive Firms', **23** *Journal of Industrial Economics*, 223-237.

Asch, Peter and Seneca, J.J. (1976), 'Is Collusion Profitable?', **58** *Review of Economics and Statistics*, 1-12.

Baysinger, G. (1991), 'Organization Theory and the Criminal Liability of Organizations', **71** *Boston University Law Review*, 341-376.

Becker, Gary S. (1968), 'Crime and Punishment: An Economic Approach', **76** *Journal of Political Economy*, 169-217.

Becker, Gary S. and Stigler, George J. (1974), 'Law Enforcement, Malfeasance and Compensation of Enforcers', **3** *Journal of Legal Studies*, 1 ff.

Block, Michael K. (1991), 'Optimal Penalties, Criminal Law, and the Control of Corporate Behaviour', **71** *Boston University Law Review*, 395-420.

Bork, Robert H. (1978), *The Antitrust Paradox: A Policy at War Itself*, New York, Basic Books.

Braithwaite, John (1986), 'Consumers as Victims of Corporate Crime', in Wheelwright, Ted (ed.), *Consumers, Transnational Corporations and Development*, Sydney, University of Sydney, Transnational Corporations Research Project, 331-342.

Byam, John I. (1982), 'The Economic Inefficiency of Corporate Criminal Liability', **73** *Journal of Criminal Law and Criminology*, 582-603.

Cochran, Philip L. and Nigh, Douglas (1987), 'Illegal Corporate Behavior and the Question of Moral Agency: An Empirical Examination', in Frederick, William C. (ed.), *Empirical Studies of Business Ethics and Values. V*, Greenwich, CT, JAI Press, 73-91.

Coffee, John C., Jr (1980), 'Corporate Crime and Punishment: A Non-Chicago View of the Economics of Criminal Sanctions', **17** *American Criminal Law Review*, 419-476.

Coffee, John C. (1981), ''No Soul to Damn: No Body to Kick': An Unscandalized Inquiry Into the Problem of Corporate Punishment', **79** *Michigan Law Review*, 386 ff.

Coffee, John C. (1991), 'Does 'Unlawful' Mean 'Criminal'?: Reflections of the Disappearing Tort/Crime Distiction in American Law', **71** *Boston University Law Review*, 193 ff.

Cohen, Mark A. (1989), 'Corporate Crime and Punishment: A Study of Social Harm and Sentencing Practice in the Federal Courts, 1984-1987', **26** *American Criminal Law Review*, 605-660.

Cohen, Mark A. (1991), 'Corporate Crime and Punishment: An Update on Sentencing Practice in the Federal Courts, 1988-1990', **71(2)** *Boston University Law Review*, 247-280.

Cohen, Mark A. (1992a), 'Sentencing Guidelines and Corporate Criminal Liability in the US', **4** *Business and the Contemporary World*, 140-157.

Cohen, Mark A. (1992b), 'Environmental Crime and Punishment: Legal/Economic Theory and Empirical Evidence on Enforcement of Federal Environmental Statutes', **82** *Journal of Criminal Law and Criminology*, 1054-1108.

Cohen, Mark A. (1996), 'Theories of Punishment and Empirical Trends in Corporate Criminal Sanctions', **17** *Managerial and Decision Economics*, 399-412.

Cohen, Mark A., Ho, Chih-Chin, Jones, Edward D. III. and Schleich, Laura M. (1988), 'Organizations as Defendants in Federal Court: A Preliminary Analysis of Prosecutions, Convictions and Sanctions, 1984-1987', **10** *Whittier Law Review*, 103-124.

Dana, D. (1996), 'The Perverse Incentives of Environmental Audit Immunity', **81** *Iowa Law Review*, 969 ff.

Daniel, Kermit and Lott, J.R. Jr (1995), 'Should Criminal Penalties Include Third Party Avoidance Costs?' **24** *Jounal of Legal Studies*, 523-534.

Daniels, Ronald J. and Howse, Robert (1995), 'Rewarding Whistleblowers: The Costs and Benefits of an Incentive-Based Compliance Strategy', in Daniels, Ronald and Morck, Randall (eds), *Corporate Decision-Making in Canada*, Calgary, University of Calgary Press, 525-549.

Dau-Schmidt, Kenneth G. (1984), 'Sentencing Antitrust Offenders: Reconciling Economic Theory with Legal Theory', **9** *Wm. Mitchell Law Review*, 75 ff.

Davis, Mike L. (1996), 'The Impact of Rules Allocating Legal Responsibilities between Principals and Agents', **17** *Managerial and Decision Economics*, 413-420.

Dick, Andrew R. (1995), 'When Does Organised Crime Pay? A Transaction Cost Analysis', **15** *International Review of Law and Economics*, 25-46.

Dickens, William T. (1989), 'Employee Crime and the Monitoring Puzzle', **7** *Journal of Labor Economics*, 331-347.

Eaton, B. Curtis and White, William D. (1982), 'Agent Compensation and the Limits of Bonding', **20** *Economic Inquiry*, 330 ff.

Fischel, Daniel R. and Sykes, Alan O. (1996), 'Corporate Crime', **25** *Journal of Legal Studies*, 319-350.

Friedman, David D. (1981), 'Reflections on Optimal Punishment, Or: Should the Rich Pay Higher Fines?', in Zerbe, Richard O. (ed.), *Research in Law and Economics, Vol.. 3*, Greenwich, CT, JAI Press, 185-230.

Gallo, Joseph C., Dau-Schmidt, Kenneth G. and Craycraft, Joseph (1997), 'The First Century of Department of Justice Antitrust Enforcement', **12** *Review of Industrial Organization*.

Karpoff, Jonathan M. and Lott, J.R., Jr (1993), 'The Reputational Penalty Firms Bear from Committing Criminal Fraud', **36(2)** *Journal of Law and Economics*, 757-802.

Kornhauser, Lewis A. (1982), 'An Economic Analysis of the Choice Between Entreprise and Personal Liability for Accidents', **70** *California Law Review*, 1345 ff.

Kraakman, Reinier H. (1984a), 'The Economic Functions of Corporate Liability', in Hopt, Klaus J. and Teubner, Gunther (eds), *Corporate Governance and Directors' Liabilities*, New York, de Gruyter, 178-207.

Kraakman, Reinier H. (1984b), 'Corporate Liability Strategies and the Costs of Legal Controls', **93** *Yale Law Journal*, 857 ff.

Kraakman, Reinier H. (1986), 'Gatekeepers: The Anatomy of a Third-Party Enforcement Strategy', **2** *Journal of Law, Economics, and Organization*, 53 ff.

Landes, William M. (1983), 'Optimal Sanctions for Antitrust Violations', **50** *University of Chicago Law Review*, 652-678.

Leung, S.F. (1991), 'How to Make the Fine Fit the Corporate Crime? An Analysis of Static and Dynamic Optimal Punishment Theories', **45** *Journal of Public Economics*, 243-256.

Levmore, Saul (1982), 'Monitors and Freeriders in Commercial and Corporate Settings', **92** *Yale Law Journal*, 49-83.

Lofquist, William S., Cohen, Madeline and Rabe, Gary (1996), *Debating Corporate Crime: An Interdisciplinary Examination of the Causes and Control of Corporate Misconduct*, Cincinnati, OH, Anderson Publishing.

Lott, J.R., Jr (1991), 'Optimal Penalties versus Minimising the Level of Crime: Does it Matter Who is Correct?', **71** *Boston University Law Review*, 439-446.

Lott, J.R., Jr (1992), 'Do We Punish High Income Criminals Too Heavily?', **30** *Economic Inquiry*, 583-608.

Lott, J.R., Jr (1996), 'The Level of Optimal Fines to Prevent Fraud When Reputations Exist and Penalty Clauses are Unenforceable', **17** *Managerial and Decision Economics*, 363-380.

Lott, John R. and Opler, Tim C. (1996), 'Testing Whether Predatory Commitments are Credible', **69** *Journal of Business*, 339-382.

Macey, Jonathan R. (1991), 'Agency Theory and the Criminal Liability of Organizations', **71** *Boston University Law Review*, 315 ff.

Metzger, Michael R. (1984), 'Corporate Criminal Liability for Defective Products: Policies, Problems, and Prospects', **73** *Georgetown Law Journal*, 1-88.

Newman, Harry A. and Wright, David W. (1990), 'Strict Liability in a Principal-Agent Model', **10** *International Review of Law and Economics*, 219 ff.

Parker, Jeffrey S. (1989), 'Criminal Sentencing Policy for Organizations: The Unifying Approach of Optimal Penalties', **26** *American Criminal Law Review*, 513-604.

Parker, Jeffrey S. (1996), 'Doctrine for Destruction: The Case of Corporate Criminal Liability', **17** *Managerial and Decision Economics*, 381-398.

Polinsky, A. Mitchell and Shavell, Steven (1993), 'Should Employees be Subject to Fines and Imprisonment Given the Existence of Corporate Liability?', **13** *International Review of Law and Economics*, 239-257.

Posner Richard A. (1992), *Economic Analysis of Law* (4th edn), Boston, Little, Brown and Company.

Ryan, Patrick J. (1991), 'Strange Bedfellows: Corporate Fiduciaries and the General Law Compliance Obligation in Section 2.01(a) of the American Law Institute's Principle of Corporate Governance', **66** *Washington Law Review*, 413-502.

Salzburg, Stephen A. (1991), 'The Control of Criminal Conduct in Organisations', **71** *Boston University Law Review*, 421-438.

Segerson, Karen and Tietenberg, Thomas (1992), 'The Structure of Penalties in Environmental Enforcement: An Economic Analysis', **23** *Journal of Environmental Economics and Management*, 179-200.

Shavell Steven (1997), 'The Optimal Level of Corporate Liability Given the Limited Ability of Corporations to Penalize Their Employees', **17** *International Review of Law and Economics*.

Snyder, Edward A. (1990), 'The Effects of Higher Criminal Penalties on Antitrust Enforcement', **33** *Journal of Law and Economics*, 439-462.

Staw, B.M. and Szwajkowski, E. (1975), 'The Scarcity-munificence Component of Organisational Environments and the Commission of Illegal Acts', **20** *Administrative Science Quarterly*, 345-354.

Stone, C. (1975), *Where the Law Ends: The Social Control of Corporate Behavior*, New York, Harper and Row.

Stone, C. (1980), 'The Place of Entreprise Liability in Controlling Corporate Conduct', **90** *Yale Law Journal*, 1-77.

Straachan, J.L., Smith, D.B. and Beedles, W.L. (1983), 'The Price Reaction to (Alleged) Corporate Crime', **18** *Financial Review*, 121-132.

Sykes, Alan O. (1981), 'An Efficiency Analysis of Vicarous Liability Under the Law of Agency', **91** *Yale Law Journal*, 168 ff.

Sykes, Alan O. (1984), 'The Economics of Vicarous Liability', **93** *Yale Law Journal*, 1231 ff.

Ulen, Thomas S. (1996), 'The Economics of Corporate Criminal Liability', **17** *Managerial and Decision Economics*, 351-362.

Van Altena, A.R., Schippers, Joop J. and Siegers, Jacques J. (1990), 'Rechtseconomie en Economisch Strafrecht (Law and Economics and Economic Criminal Law)', in X (ed.), *Facetten van Economisch Strafrecht: Opstellen over Economisch Strafrecht*, Arnhem, Gouda Quint, 163-182.

9000
GENERAL CHARACTERISTICS OF RULES

Louis Kaplow
Harvard Law School and National Bureau of Economic Research

Abstract

This chapter addresses two fundamental characteristics of rules. The first concerns the degree of precision, detail, or complexity they embody: how finely are different sorts of behavior to be distinguished? A second aspect of legal commands concerns *when* a given level of detail is provided - at the time of promulgation ('rules') or subsequent to individuals' actions, in the context of adjudication ('standards'). These aspects of rules are considered from a perspective that focuses upon information costs and dissemination: different sorts of legal commands involve differing costs of formulation and application by private parties (deciding upon their own conduct) and adjudicators, and the character of laws also influences how well parties actually will understand the law and conform their conduct accordingly. The discussion encompasses related questions involving the role of precedent, the evolution of the law over time, legal uncertainty and accuracy in adjudication. This chapter also addresses the separate problem of how changes in legal rules should apply to prior behavior or preexisting investments - issues of retroactivity and transition.
JEL classification: K40
Keywords: Rules, Precision, Complexity, Transitions, Retroactivity, Standards

1. Introduction

Legal rules serve many functions: channeling behavior (for example, tort law, environmental law, criminal law), providing background rules (much of contract, commercial and corporate law), and defining obligations and eligibility for benefits (tax law, social welfare provisions). This chapter, following existing research, focuses on the first type of law. The relevance (or irrelevance) of the analysis to other types of law will usually be apparent, and some comments about the differences in contexts will be noted.

The most commonly noted characteristic of rules concerns the degree of precision, detail, or complexity they embody: how finely are different sorts of behavior to be distinguished? Such matters may arise in defining the scope of a legal command, providing for exceptions, adjusting sanctions based upon aggravating and mitigating circumstances, and so on. A related aspect of legal commands concerns *when* a given level of detail is provided - at the time of promulgation ('rules') or subsequent to individuals' actions, in the context of adjudication ('standards'). These aspects of rules are considered from a perspective that focuses upon information costs and dissemination: different sorts of legal commands involve differing costs of formulation and application by private parties (deciding upon their own conduct) and adjudicators, and the character of laws also influences how well parties actually will understand them and conform their conduct accordingly. This approach is used to illuminate choices about the degree of precision (or complexity) with which legal commands are formulated and between rules and standards. These subjects, in turn, encompass related questions involving the role of precedent, the evolution of the law over time, legal uncertainty and accuracy in adjudication.

After outlining the main ideas concerning these topics, this chapter addresses the separate problem of how changes in the law should apply to prior behavior or preexisting investments - issues of retroactivity and transition - and considers some other aspects of rules that have been addressed in the economic analysis of law.

A. Precision of the Law

2. Precision of the Law: The Problem

The precision of a legal command is taken here to refer to the degree of detail or differentiation involved. For example, an environmental regulation is more precise if more types of pollutants or sources of pollution are distinguished. A negligence regime is more precise if the standard of care is more finely tailored to different types of actors in different contexts. A damages scheme is more precise the greater the extent to which damages are designed to reflect the particular harm done to a particular victim.

The greater the degree of precision, the greater will be the costs of formulating legal commands and applying them in adjudication and of parties interpreting them for purposes of deciding how to conform behavior to the law. But it does not follow that the costs of precision - any more than costs of litigation or of pollution control - should be minimized: the simplest rules might permit all acts, require equal reduction of pollutants regardless of their toxicity, or require the same speed limits on all roads. Rather, the degree of precision should be optimized, which makes an economic analysis particularly useful.

Before proceeding, it is worth noting that greater precision in legal commands - higher levels of detail, more distinctions recognized in rules and exceptions - is a primary source of legal complexity, which is broadly condemned. The subject of the next section, whether a legal command is formulated as a rule or a standard (the latter leaving more open to subsequent adjudication and thus being more difficult to interpret), also may bear on what is often described as legal complexity. A number of other sources of complexity could be considered, but they have received little attention in the literature. Most obviously, poorly drafted laws and legal opinions will be more confusing; it will be more costly to extract less information. Although this problem is often serious, analysis of it is straightforward. More subtle are problems like those confronted under tax laws wherein parties may devise complicated schemes to circumvent simple legal commands. In this setting, complexity may be unavoidable. Moreover, it is possible that greater complexity will reduce costs: if a more complex regime successfully discourages transactional manipulations, parties might in the end spend less in learning the intricacies of legal rules and in making convoluted arrangements.

3. Effects of Precision on Legal Costs and on Behavior

The presentation here follows most closely the model in Kaplow (1995a) (see also Ehrlich and Posner, 1974; Diver, 1983). First, we can consider the effects of precision on legal costs. It is straightforward that greater precision tends to increase them: more detailed laws tend to be more costly for the government to promulgate, for parties to interpret, and for enforcers to apply. The second factor - private interpretation costs - involves some subtlety, because parties will incur such costs only if they find it in their interest to do so. For example, extremely complex details may be ignored by almost everyone.

Second, more precise commands - those that differentiate behavior more precisely - will generally result in better behavior. If pollutants are differentiated and subject to particularized sanctions, rather than grouped together and subject to a single sanction (reflecting, say, the average harm they cause), there will be two beneficial results. Activities that are more harmful will be subject to higher sanctions than otherwise, which will efficiently deter additional undesirable activity. Similarly, less harmful activities will face lower sanctions, avoiding inefficient overdeterrence.

These behavioral benefits are related to private legal costs, because the benefits can arise only if private actors expend the resources necessary to learn whether their particular activity is of a more or less harmful type, and thus subject to a higher or lower sanction. If the cost of determining the relevant sanction - which may involve learning about the content of legal commands or about the nature of one's own activity (such as by testing the chemical content of discharges) - is too high, individuals will not learn about the legal rules. Individuals with rather low benefits may simply forgo activities, even though there is some chance that they may be subject to low sanctions or no sanction, in which case their activities would be worth undertaking. Individuals with high benefits may simply act, even though there is some chance that they may face a very high sanction, in which case they will regret their decision. Individuals with intermediate benefits, however, will tend to acquire information and then to act accordingly - that is, to proceed if the sanction is low and abstain if the sanction is high.

Given the nature of this problem, it is natural to ask whether private parties' incentives to acquire information will be socially appropriate. It turns out that in the simplest case, in which liability is strict and there are no predictable errors in adjudication, private and social incentives are aligned (for the familiar reason that private actors bear all the social costs of their activities, here including the cost of acquiring information). More generally - if there is legal error, if individuals may misestimate the value of information, if information facilitates circumvention of legal sanctions, or if a negligence regime governs - private incentives may be excessive or inadequate (see Shavell, 1988a; Kaplow, 1990; Kaplow and Shavell, 1992).

Having stated how parties will behave and what costs will be incurred when laws are more detailed, it is possible to characterize when greater precision is desirable. At the broadest level, the lower the information costs and the greater the variation in harm caused by different individuals' actions, the larger will be the net benefit of precision in legal commands. To offer more insight, it is helpful to consider some special cases.

First, suppose that formulation costs are low (perhaps because a single rule will apply to a large number of actions) and that adjudication costs are low (perhaps because harm occurs only with a low probability or because violations are enforced with a low probability/high sanction strategy, as suggested by Becker, 1968). In this case, more precise laws tend to be desirable as long as information is not prohibitively costly for actors to obtain. The reason is that the actors have the option of not obtaining information. Those who do make expenditures to become informed will be only those for whom the expected behavioral benefit is large - individuals whose acts will be significantly desirable if they are not in fact very harmful but significantly undesirable if they are of the more harmful type. For example, consider a complex rule scheme that regulates routes over which hazardous substances may be transported. Most drivers - those who never or rarely carry significant amounts of such substances - will ignore the rules. Those who regularly transport hazardous materials, however, will undertake the necessary effort to learn the rules and conform their behavior. Their information costs may be high, but the benefits from better controlling their activity will be even larger.

One implication of this analysis is that the existence of high total compliance expenditures is not an unambiguous sign of excessively detailed or complex rules. Low total expenditures may indicate that few individuals bother to learn the details of the law, in which case any additional formulation or adjudication costs would largely be wasted. High total expenditures, on the other hand, reflect that many individuals contemplate actions the desirability of which is contingent upon the type of their act; in this case, saving compliance costs by eliminating the law's precision may be a mistake because significant behavioral benefits will be sacrificed. Another implication of the analysis is that widespread noncompliance need not indicate that rules are unduly complex; as long as the few for whom the rules are most important do learn the details, the benefits of precision will be achieved at little cost with regard to others.

As a second case, suppose that private information costs are low (perhaps most individuals already know the details of their actions and how they might be sanctioned) but that the cost of differentiating acts in adjudication would be high (because it is hard for the state to learn the details of individuals' behavior). In this case, more refined legal commands may or may not be desirable. For example, additional costs may be repeatedly incurred in adjudication even though few individuals' behavior would be affected as a result of greater detail in the law. The distinction between this case and the foregoing one is that the state must make additional expenditures on adjudication even when the *ex ante* benefit of improved behavior would be small, because the state will not know when this is true; by contrast, when only *ex ante* information costs are high, private parties will incur them selectively.

4. Relationship of the Precision of the Law to the Accuracy of Adjudication

The precision of the law has a direct connection to the accuracy of adjudication, a topic explored in Kaplow (1994a) and Kaplow and Shavell (1994, 1996a). The former subject can be taken to refer to the precision of the law on the books and the latter question to the precision with which the law actually is applied. At the time they act, individuals will be induced to become more informed about the details of their situation only if, in a subsequent adjudication, their behavior will in fact be differentiated from that of others. If, instead, individuals' acts will be assigned to different legal categories largely at random, or if no effort will be made to refine the classification of acts, the situation is much as if the law itself did not make the refined distinctions in the first place. Many topics of procedure - discovery, the use of experts, evidentiary rules, summary judgment, juries, appeals, burdens of proof - and many substantive rules - notably, concerning which categories of damages may be established and whether damages are determined by individualized evidence or by standardized tables - may thus be illuminated by analysis similar to that presented here. A central concern when assessing these features of adjudication is parties' incentives in litigation to make expenditures on their own behalf: it often may be the case that parties, if freely permitted to undertake further efforts in litigation, will spend excessively because the private benefits from favorably influencing the outcome will exceed any social benefits from enhanced precision in applying legal rules.

5. Related Issues and Literature

The preceding discussion may be extended in a number of ways. Spier (1994) incorporates *settlement* bargaining. The interesting complication is that application of a more precise rule in adjudication may make information that is possessed by only one party relevant to the outcome. By thereby creating a situation involving asymmetric information, settlement becomes less likely. Thus, greater precision may be accompanied by increased litigation costs.

Kaplow (1995a) briefly considers *costly sanctions* - monetary payments made by risk-averse individuals and nonmonetary sanctions. Few generalizations are possible. For risk-averse actors who do not become informed, greater differentiation may increase risk-bearing costs, although, as noted in Kaplow and Shavell (1996a), more precise damage awards may reduce the risks borne by uninsured victims.

Kaplow (1990) examines the case in which some individuals know how the law differentiates among acts but others do not. In this case, there is no general deterrence rationale favoring lower sanctions for *individuals who mistakenly commit violations*, but reducing their sanctions may be optimal when sanctions are socially costly, because the lower rate of compliance by mistaken individuals results in sanctions being imposed more often.

Kaplow (1995a) extends the analysis to regimes of *self-reporting*, as is common with much environmental and safety regulation as well as with many forms of taxation. Self-reporting tends to be efficient when individuals' information costs are much lower than the government's; increasing precision in a self-reporting regime has the confounding effect of inducing some individuals to acquire information not to determine how better to behave but solely to determine how best to report their conduct.

Most applied work on complexity and compliance costs is in the field of *taxation*. Empirical work is extensive: see, for example, Long and Swingen (1987), Arthur D. Little (1988), Slemrod (1989), Blumenthal and Slemrod (1992). Analysis of the benefits of precision in the tax context is qualitatively different from that presented here because the benefits of fine-tuning taxpayers' payments typically involve matters of distributive equity and minimizing adverse incentive effects of taxation rather than of optimally controlling harm-causing behavior (see, for example, Yitzhaki, 1979; Kaplow, 1994c, 1996). The most obvious simplifying devices in the United States income tax code are the standard deduction (which taxpayers may take instead of itemizing particular deductions) and the use of floors (which forbid small amounts of deductions); they are analyzed in Kaplow (1994b) and Slemrod and Yitzhaki (1994).

The discussion here, like much analysis in law and economics, emphasizes the role of legal commands in providing incentives to govern parties' behavior *ex ante*. Modifications to the analysis would be required when adjudication concerns *future behavior*, as in the granting of licenses, enjoining harm-causing behavior, incarcerating dangerous individuals, or determining eligibility for government benefits. In particular, the benefit of precision in adjudication will be greater than otherwise because the outcome will affect future activity directly (perhaps in addition to influencing *ex ante* incentives), and concerns about whether individuals will learn the relevant details of the law may be less relevant.

Finally, it is worth noting that the benefits of more detailed rules are relevant to wholly *private ordering*, as in contractual arrangements (contingencies can be distinguished more precisely, and provisions may provide reasonably complete specifications or be more open-ended) or in the internal organization of firms. As a result, work on the economics of contracting and organizations, wholly apart from analysis of the law, can illuminate issues concerning the design of legal rules, and conversely.

B. Rules versus Standards

6. Rules versus Standards: The Problem

The choice between rules and standards has long received attention from legal commentators and more recently has been addressed from an economic perspective. The presentation here will follow Kaplow (1992a); a number of the points, particularly concerning the effects of rules and standards on legal costs and on behavior, can also be found in the prior economic analyses by Ehrlich and Posner (1974) and Diver (1983).

An initial obstacle in analyzing rules and standards involves matters of definition. Usage varies greatly (which is no surprise since most dictionaries offer definitions of each term that use the other), and logically distinct issues are often combined or confused. For purposes of economic analysis, it is useful to define the difference between rules and standards as involving exclusively the distinction between whether the law is given content *ex ante* or *ex post*. Thus, a rule might list hazardous substances that may not be released into the water supply whereas a standard may only proscribe releases of hazardous substances, leaving the determination of which substances are hazardous to adjudication, after releases have occurred.

This distinction between rules and standards is obviously one of degree, although it often is convenient to discuss it as an all-or-nothing choice. A law is more rule-like the greater the extent to which it provides advance guidance: it may, for example, provide a partial list or state criteria to be used, either of which will ease the application of the legal norm to particular behavior. Moreover, even a given formal specification will have a different character depending upon what is understood about the mode of adjudication and upon what other information is available in advance. For example, if everyone knows that an adjudicator is likely to rely upon a recent government study that indicates the degree of danger posed by potentially hazardous substances, the situation will be almost the same as that under a rule that incorporated the study's results. For present purposes, such a situation will be viewed as essentially rule-like, as the economic analysis depends upon the extent to which content - as understood by private parties and adjudicators - has actually been provided in advance, not upon the wording of legal commands. (It thus can be seen that the generation and dissemination of information, even when not explicitly embodied in a legal rule, is an important aspect of the law.)

Finally, it is important to distinguish the question of the degree to which content is determined *ex ante* from the preceding subject, which concerns the degree of precision with which a law is formulated or applied. Often, commentators assume that standards are inherently more precise or subtle than rules because standards leave open the possibility of considering all possible factors whereas rules, no matter how detailed, provide a definitive resolution that is not open to reconsideration. But this assumption implicitly contemplates that adjudicators will devote virtually unlimited resources in applying standards. Such an outcome is irrational, implausible, and inconsistent with the actual operation of legal systems. For example, tax codes and many safety regulations are far more detailed and context-dependent than, say, the results that would be produced by a jury that was presented with the open-ended question of what tax payment or safety regime was appropriate. As a result of law, custom, or the application of common sense, an adjudicator may well consider far less than all conceivably relevant factors. In an ordinary negligence dispute involving modest stakes, parties will not commission numerous expert studies; nor will the adjudicator commit substantial time to consider all possibilities.

Thus, it is a matter of choice how much detail will be incorporated in rules and standards, and it is hardly the case that rule-like systems tend to be particularly simple and standard-like schemes extremely precise in actual operation. The main point for present purposes is that the question of how much refinement is optimal when formulating and applying the law - legal precision - is logically and, to a great extent, practically distinct from the question whether a given degree of precision is best specified in advance (rules) or left to adjudication (standards). In the end, one can combine the following analysis of rules versus standards with the preceding analysis of the optimal precision of the law to determine what sort of legal command is best.

7. Effects of Rules and Standards on Legal Costs and on Behavior

Rules are defined as legal commands that provide greater specification in advance. Hence, the initial cost of formulating rules will be greater than the cost of formulating standards. It will be necessary, for example, to undertake studies to determine which substances are hazardous and to determine appropriate thresholds of safety if a rule listing hazardous substances is to be promulgated. Such efforts can be avoided (for the moment) under a standard that merely proscribes the release of hazardous substances and leaves their determination to subsequent proceedings.

On the other hand, rules will be cheaper for private parties to interpret when deciding upon their own conduct and for adjudicators to apply to past behavior. Precisely because more has been determined in advance, there will be less need for parties to conduct their own studies and to predict legal outcomes and for adjudicators to devote effort to determine whether a violation should be deemed to have occurred. If a rule specifies which substances may be discharged, actors and adjudicators need merely consult the list to apply a rule, whereas substantial inquiry may be necessary under a standard.

The same reasoning concerning the ease of application suggests that rules will tend to produce behavior more in conformity with legal norms than would equivalent standards. Because parties will be able to learn the governing norms more cheaply and accurately in advance, they will tend to behave more in accord with such norms. (This raises the question, explored in Kaplow and Shavell (1992) and noted above, whether private parties' incentives to learn about the law will be socially appropriate.) When guidance is easier to obtain, fewer parties will be deterred from behavior that actually is not objectionable, because they will have greater confidence that such behavior will not be subject to legal sanctions. More parties will be deterred from truly undesirable behavior because they are less likely to proceed in the mistaken belief that the prospect of being sanctioned is remote. It is important to observe that the desirable effect of rules on behavior may hold even when standards turn out to be more precise in actual adjudication, for any refinement embodied in the application of standards will influence behavior only to the extent parties are able to predict the relevant details in advance, and often parties will not make such precise predictions. (The point that details tend to be helpful only when parties find it in their interest to learn them was emphasized in the preceding section on the precision of legal rules.)

Combining these effects, one can see that rules tend to be preferable when particular activities are frequent, and standards do best when behavior varies so greatly that any particular scenario is relatively rare. The reason is that the added cost of rules, at the formulation stage, is borne once, whereas the relative benefits of rules - lower costs and greater compliance for private actors and lower costs of adjudication - may arise often or almost never, as the case may be. Thus, for dry cleaning and automotive fluids, it would be best to specify permitted disposal techniques in advance, for the many small establishments would be unlikely to be able to determine the effects on their own and, even if they could, the costs of each obtaining information on the matter would be great; also, redundant costs would be incurred in inevitable enforcement proceedings. But in the case substances that are rarely used, it may not be worthwhile to specify the range of permitted and prohibited disposal techniques in advance because most scenarios involving potentially hazardous action may never arise.

In this regard, it should be noted that the frequency of activity may be great even if reported adjudications in a field are few. For example, rules might lead countless individuals to comply with the law at very low cost. Even when compliance is imperfect (or when harm nonetheless arises and is subject to a regime of strict liability), there may be little adjudication despite frequent activity because the probability of harm is low, detection of harm is unlikely, or most legal disputes are quickly settled. Conversely, disputes may appear to be frequent but not indicate that conditions are favorable to the use of rules. For example, there are many negligence disputes but some types may involve unique situations that, *ex ante*, were unlikely ever to arise.

Finally, the costs and benefits of rules and standards are important for determining the optimal effort to devote to formulating rules and to applying rules and standards in adjudication. All else equal, the greater the frequency of the behavior to be governed, the more valuable it will be to formulate the law with greater care. Conversely, to the extent that an adjudication is relevant to only a single case, it will not be very valuable to expend substantial resources to consider myriad factors in order to reach a precise determination - unless a precedent is to be set, as discussed below. That individuals may have difficulty predicting refined decisions with any accuracy will strengthen this point. These considerations reinforce the previous observation that, in fact, rules often will be more precise and subtle than standards, taking into account how the latter will actually be applied.

8. Precedent, Other Legal Interpretations, and the Evolution of Legal Commands

Precedent may be seen as the (perhaps partial) conversion of a standard into a rule. Whether after accumulated experience or as a result of hearing a single case, a tribunal may issue a statement that will govern future adjudication. At that point, and to that extent, a rule will have been established. Similarly, even less authoritative legal interpretations, ranging from discussions in judicial opinions to public statements of enforcement agencies, will tend to guide future behavior and adjudications to some degree. Once the analysis of standards - the state of affairs before the precedent - and of rules - after the precedent - is understood, the study of precedent (and other legal interpretations) is straightforward. A few particular factors, however, deserve some elaboration.

It is worth asking why the use of precedent is superior to an earlier announcement of rules. After all, the primary burden of using a rule, incurring additional formulation costs, is ultimately borne when the precedent is established. But in the interim, before the precedent is announced, the benefits - of cheaper and better guidance of behavior and simpler adjudication - are forgone. This point is particularly striking when an important, open legal question is identified many years or decades before a precedent is finally announced. The primary advantage of delay is that more information may be collected in the interim - information about the optimal legal command or about the importance of resolving an issue. But many precedents are announced with little more information than existed initially. Moreover, the most efficient way to collect information may be to commission a study in the first place rather than to wait until a case happens to appear before the relevant tribunal (when all that is then learned is the single data point from that case or perhaps a handful of data points). Also, once more information does become available through whatever means, it is not clear why the legal system should not make an announcement immediately rather than waiting still further.

It should be noted that making initial legal commands more rule-like does not imply that they cannot be changed if new information becomes available. The prospect of change does reduce the benefit of rules, but it does not follow that there will be no benefit from providing guidance in the interim. Indeed, many detailed regimes that are designed by regulatory agencies have a more rule-like character, with occasional revision, and detailed statutes, such as tax codes, are made precise but often revised later. (And, of course, precedents themselves are extended, narrowed, and reversed.) With standards, change may occur implicitly, but the prospect of change will accordingly increase the cost and difficulty of prediction. Substantial developments that call for significantly different legal commands may be apparent, making prediction under standards easier, but also presenting a clear case for adjusting rules. It is hardly the case that operative legal commands in heavily rule-governed domains (like tax and environmental regulation) and the interpretation of important precedents change slowly compared, say, to applications of the negligence rule.

For prior economic analyses of precedent, emphasizing that the body of precedent can be analogized to a capital stock that depreciates over time, see Landes and Posner (1976) and Posner (1992). See also Landes and Posner's (1994) discussion of the related subject of anticipatory adjudication, in which a party may seek a legal decision before undertaking an activity, so as to avoid the need to wait for a precedent.

9. Related Issues and Literature

Other law and economics work that is addressed directly to the subjects considered herein includes Ogus (1981) (discussing rules formulated in quantitative terms), and Ogus (1992) (emphasizing private actors greater ability to predict rules than standards).

The choice between rules and standards is closely related to the problem of *legal uncertainty*. Indeed, if rules are defined as the extent to which legal commands are given content *ex ante* and thus the ease with which private parties can predict how the law will apply to their conduct, legal uncertainty might be viewed as simply a measure of the extent to which a legal command is standard-like. Uncertainty about the negligence rule has received the greatest attention in the literature (see Calfee and Craswell, 1984; Craswell and Calfee, 1986, and Shavell, 1987). Because the negligence rule has an all-or-nothing (discontinuous) character - taking slightly more care will exonerate an actor from what otherwise would be significant liability - uncertainty about the legal standard may tend to produce excessive care (although it is also possible that great uncertainty will produce too little care). The suggestion that malpractice liability results in overly defensive medicine is one example. For empirical evidence, see Kessler and McClellan (1996). Kahan (1989) shows that these issues would not arise if negligent actors were not responsible for all the harm they caused, but only for the incremental increase in harm due to their negligence. Also, in considering legal uncertainty, it would be appropriate to extend the present analysis and that in prior work on the negligence rule to take explicit account of risk-bearing costs.

As noted when addressing legal precision, the discussion here focuses on the role of law in providing incentives to control parties' *ex ante* behavior. When *future behavior* (licenses, injunctions, incarceration, benefit eligibility) is involved, the analysis will differ. Indeed, the difference between *ex ante* and *ex post* formulation may be moot, as a definitive resolution will in any event precede the relevant effect of a legal decision. There are, nonetheless, similar questions about the benefits of wholesale decision making, as in stating a rule for a class of cases rather than adjudicating the same question repeatedly. And the foregoing analysis remains applicable to the extent adjudication will influence *ex ante* incentives in addition to regulating future behavior (such as in the case of incarceration).

There are other functions of law as well. Much of *contract law* and related fields is concerned with providing rules of form or background rules that leave parties free to transact as they wish (see, for example, Baird and Weisberg, 1982). Because the purpose of such law is different - law is largely facilitating rather than constraining - the analysis would have to be different. Nonetheless, it seems that in contexts where transactions are frequent, the benefit of greater *ex ante* formulation - through rules - would be larger.

Yet another concern with some bodies of law is to constrain *fraud*. In some instances (notably, tax evasion) greater specificity in advance might be problematic because parties will better be able to evade legal norms. Both uncertainty and complexity, discussed previously, may be desirable precisely because parties will be less able to predict the law.

Apart from normative analysis, one can inquire into *lawyers' and legal institutions incentives to formulate legal commands*. In this regard, conflicts between private and social interest may be noted. For example, lower legal costs save social resources but may reduce the demand for lawyers (see, for example, White, 1992). And legislation might be designed with an eye to attracting campaign contributions rather than serving the public interest (see, for example, Doernberg and McChesney, 1987). Regulators may be more concerned with their own costs in formulating and applying rules than in private costs (see, for example, Diver, 1983).

Finally, the present discussion may be situated in the large literatures in the areas of *legal philosophy* and *public choice* which examine the rule of law and in particular address the use of rules to constrain official discretion. For a reasonably comprehensive treatment of rules that attends to functional concerns, see Schauer (1991).

C. Changes in Legal Rules: Transitions and Retroactivity

10. Transitions and Retroactivity: The Problem

Transition rules, including a determination of whether a law is to apply retroactively, concern not the form and content of substantive legal commands but instead how the problem of legal change is to be addressed. The most common problem of legal change concerns the fact that investments and other actions often have effects in the future, at which time the governing legal regime may be different. Changes in the law will affect, positively or negatively as the case may be, the returns from prior actions. This raises the question whether losses from legal change should be compensated or otherwise mitigated (as through grandfather provisions that exempt prior investments or phase-ins that implement the change only gradually) and, analogously, whether gains from legal change should be subject to windfall taxation or otherwise reduced.

As first analyzed carefully in the context of tax reform by Graetz (1977), these problems arise even when new legislation is nominally prospective. For example, if a tax subsidy is repealed, a prior investment that benefited on a continuing basis from the subsidy will become less valuable even if none of the prior subsidy payments must be returned to the government. The possibility of explicit retroactivity does, however, expand the potential scope for transition issues: even completed transactions might subsequently be rewarded or penalized when laws change.

The general problem of transition, analyzed in Hale (1927), Samuels (1974), and Kaplow (1986, 1987, 1992b), arises much more widely and with more common elements than is usually appreciated. Basically, whenever there is uncertainty concerning government policy - about statutory change, new regulation or deregulation, court decisions, government spending priorities, takings of private property for public use, tariffs, and so on - the resolution of the uncertainty will create winners and losers. Thus, all government action (unless fully anticipated), government inaction (that is not fully anticipated - that is, when change had a positive probability that was not realized), and even changes in the prospect for action in the future, will tend to affect the value of prior investments. The potentially affected investments include physical and financial assets, investments in human capital, and choices of location and occupation, among others.

As this general description suggests, an important aspect of the transition problem concerns the *ex ante* choice of private actors - individuals and firms - under uncertainty. The prospect of legal change (like that of any other change) will affect both investment incentives and the imposition of risk, and these incentive effects and risk-bearing costs will in turn be influenced by whether transition relief is anticipated and provided. The immediately following analysis considers the question of optimal government transition policy, taking as given the actual change in the law that might occur and its desirability. The focus is on how transition relief affects the behavior and wellbeing of private parties and, accordingly, its effect on social welfare. Subsequent discussion will take up concerns about possible government misbehavior in changing the law and how different transition policies may influence government activity.

11. Effects of Transitions and Transition Relief on Private Actors' Incentives and on Risk-bearing Costs

Begin by considering the case in which private actors are risk-neutral (which may be approximately true for large, widely-owned enterprises that are the subject of much legal regulation). Suppose that there is some prospect, say, a 50 percent chance, of an adverse legal change: a firm's product might be banned if it turns out that the product is dangerous. Anticipating such a possibility - and assuming for the moment that there will be no compensation, exemption, or other relief to those investing prior to the transition - private parties will invest less than they would otherwise. Half the time they will earn some positive return and the other half of the time they will earn no return (and, indeed, they may lose their initial investment).

Now suppose instead that investors anticipate that there will be complete transition relief, say, full compensation. In this case, investors expect a positive return for sure, so they are more likely to invest - or to invest at a larger scale - than if there were to be no relief. As Blume, Rubinfeld and Shapiro (1984) first showed formally in the takings context, the prospect of such relief induces inefficient overinvestment. The key point is that a private loss in such instances corresponds to a real social loss. If a product is too dangerous and must be banned, sunk investments that are valuable only for producing such a product will be of no subsequent social value. Hence, insulating investors from such risks is inefficient, just as it would be inefficient to insulate investors from the prospect that their products might become obsolete or lose out to better products of competitors. As noted by Hale (1927), Samuels (1974), Graetz (1977), and Kaplow (1986, 1987, 1992b), from the perspective of investors, the risk of future government action is similar to various market risks and natural risks (earthquakes, hurricanes). Private decisions are efficient when actors bear the full costs and benefits of their actions. Transition relief thus does not correct an externality; it creates one.

This analysis of transition relief may be extended to determine when retroactive application of legal changes is efficient (see Kaplow, 1986, 1987, 1992b). If a product is banned because it is discovered to be dangerous, it is probably the case that past production of the product resulted in danger as well. Thus, imposing retrospective liability will tend to be efficient, in order for investors *ex ante* to have had the proper incentives to take safety into account. By contrast, if a pollutant is to be regulated because it damages a newly introduced crop strain, there is no reason to impose retrospective liability, for the decision to regulate the pollutant does not suggest that the pollutant previously caused some social harm. To generalize, when the government discovers new information about conditions that have long been in existence, retroactive application in some form will often be necessary to provide the right *ex ante* incentives, but when there is a change in circumstances that makes future use undesirable without affecting the desirability of past conduct, retroactivity will be inefficient.

Similar reasoning suggests that transition relief is inefficient even when private actors are risk averse (see Kaplow, 1986, 1987, 1992b). In this case, relief has the advantage of reducing risk-bearing costs. But private arrangements - diversified ownership, insurance, contractual risk allocations, and the like - also may be available. Moreover, these mechanisms have systematic advantages over transition relief. First, they often are implemented in ways that preserve incentives, in full or in part. For example, insurance premiums are greater the more assets are covered, so investors contemplating expansion in the face of some risk will bear the expected loss *ex ante* through higher insurance payments. In other cases, private risk mitigation is partial precisely to preserve incentives; absent other market imperfections (notably, adverse selection), private risk-sharing arrangements tend to be efficient. Transition relief generally lacks these features. Second, even if transition relief were only partial, private parties would undertake actions to further mitigate risk; such actions may worsen their incentives (moral hazard), but some of the resulting cost would be borne by the government. Again the analogy to market risks can be made: just as government relief (as in the case of disaster relief) tends to be inefficient for ordinary risks (see Arnott and Stiglitz, 1991; Kaplow, 1991), so government relief against government-created risks tends to be inefficient with regard to private investment and risk-mitigation incentives.

12. Related Issues

The analysis assumes that transition policy will be *anticipated* by investors and actually *implemented* by the government. To the extent such policy is embodied in constitutional provisions or strong norms that guide legal reform, the assumption is plausible. More generally, a government is unlikely to succeed in the long run in getting investors to expect one transition policy while often implementing another. Problems of credible commitment may make it difficult to establish a desired transition policy. To consider a familiar analogy, some governments regularly offer *ex post* relief when natural disasters strike, which has the effect of encouraging individuals to, say, invest excessively in building on flood plains. A possible solution to this political commitment problem is for the government either to regulate such activity (limiting investment in high-risk areas) or to compel the purchase of insurance in advance at actuarially fair rates (the insurance premiums would discourage excessive investment and the fact that victims have paid for compensation in advance would eliminate the pressure for *ex post* relief).

Most of the discussion here, like most in various literatures that address transition issues - ranging from tax reform to deregulation - emphasizes the case in which investors suffer transition *losses*. But it was noted at the outset that transition *gains* arise with similar frequency. The analysis of both possibilities is symmetric: just as providing relief for losses will encourage overinvestment, imposing windfall taxes on gains (or otherwise reducing them) will produce underinvestment. Few if any windfall gains - or losses - are really pure windfalls.

It tends to be best for investors to bear all the gains and losses they cause, with any risk mitigation being contractually arranged to provide for the most effective limitation of adverse incentive effects.

Another question of transition policy concerns the *means* of relief. One can compensate losers (and tax winners) in whole or in part, grandfather prior investors (that is, provide some exemption from new rules), or curtail the new policy (as by delay or phase-in or implementing reform only partially). With regard to *ex ante* incentives and mitigation of risk, all of these approaches are similar, to the extent that they provide the same degree of effective relief. (For example, a phase-in that reduces gains and losses by half has effects like that of 50 percent compensation and 50 percent windfall taxation.) With regard to future behavior, however, compensation and windfall taxation are generally superior to other forms of relief. Grandfathering, for example, might exempt existing producers of dangerous products, allowing the danger to continue (but perhaps not to grow); delaying implementation would similarly permit some future harm. By contrast, immediate elimination of the danger accompanied by compensation would avoid this difficulty.

As in the discussion of rule formulation, the present analysis is most applicable to *laws that regulate behavior*. Contract rules that serve as defaults are quite different. If a default rule is changed, it may well be that the prior rule should govern preexisting contracts, for parties may have failed to make special provision in their contracts precisely because they knew they could rely upon background rules. On the other hand, if a default is changed because new analysis suggests that most parties have a different preference than previously suspected, and if many contracts are silent simply because of the cost of making special provision, it could be best to apply the new default to preexisting agreements.

13. Effects on Government Behavior of Requiring Transition Relief

The foregoing analysis takes as given a particular legal change, assumes that it is well conceived, and asks how transition relief affects private behavior. But it cannot be assumed that government always acts appropriately, and transition relief may affect the behavior of government.

One familiar argument is that transition relief - in particular, requiring compensation - *provides the government proper incentives* because then government bears the full costs of its actions. One can make the analogy to tort liability when both injurers' and victims' behavior affects accident costs. For analysis of this tort problem, see Shavell (1980), and for application to the transition context see Kaplow (1986, 1987); for a similar discussion, see Blume, Rubinfeld and Shapiro (1984). No liability - or schemes that provide no compensation when injurers behave well, a negligence-type rule, or that deny compensation when victims behave improperly, contributory or comparative negligence rules - is best for victims' incentives (like investors' incentives, above), whereas full liability - strict or otherwise - is best for injurers' incentives. If one can assume that the government (the 'injurer') always behaves properly, then a regime that denies compensation is best for the incentives of investors (the 'victims'). But if one cannot make this assumption about government behavior, one may wish to impose liability on the government - for example, by requiring compensation. Unless some tribunal can determine when the government or investors misbehaved, which is likely to be very difficult in most transition contexts (and which involves courts second-guessing legislative, executive, agency, or their own actions), it must be recognized that any solution will be a compromise: if some relief is required, government's incentives may improve but investors' incentives will be worse.

This argument, however, is incomplete (see Kaplow, 1986, 1987). The implicit assumption is that the government, like a private investor, receives the benefits from its actions. But the benefits of most government action - banning hazardous products, improving tort rules, building highways - are received by private citizens. Thus, making the legislature or an agency pay for transition losses (in addition to paying for direct costs, as in building a highway) when few if any of the benefits are directly received might systematically skew decisions against any change. Once benefits as well as costs are considered, it is not obvious that even a highly imperfect government is generally biased in favor of change when no compensation or other relief is required. For any bias - whether for or against change - to exist, there must be some *asymmetry* in the government's treatment of costs and benefits. Some theories of government action (see Downs, 1957 and Olson, 1965), suggest that the most effective political interest groups are those on whom gains or losses are concentrated. Other theories are concerned with the majority exploiting the minority. Still others (see Niskanen, 1971), emphasize bureaucrats' desire to enhance their budget or prestige. Thus, whether requiring compensation would make government behavior better or worse depends upon which theories of government behavior are most plausible, whether it is the benefits or the costs that are more concentrated, and other factors (see also Quinn and Trebilcock, 1982).

Another concern with government behavior involves the problem of pure *expropriation* (see Kaplow, 1987). It is familiar from public economics that the most efficient government tax is a one-time capital levy, in which capital (more broadly, savings, assets in any form) is taken and the government promises never to repeat the action. As long as the expropriation is wholly unanticipated, there will be no adverse *ex ante* incentive effects; likewise, if it will never be repeated, there will be no future distortions in behavior. Levmore (1993) offers this as a basis for a more favorable view toward retroactive taxation. But it has long been recognized that governments would find it difficult to engage in such inconsistent behavior. Rather, there needs to be some commitment - whether through constitutional means or long-established norms - that the government will not expropriate, and governments that deviate from such a path will be unlikely to be able to provide investors with confidence for the future.

In principle, expropriation can be distinguished from other government action. As noted when addressing private incentives, it is efficient for investors to anticipate and respond to the prospect that new information or changed circumstances will affect what government regulation is optimal, just as new developments will influence the market directly in ways that investors should take into account. Anticipating expropriation, however, is inefficient *ex ante*. The benefit arises from transferring resources to the government, not from providing proper incentives for private behavior. To be sure, some taxation is required, to fund public goods and services and to accomplish redistribution. Particularly with regard to redistribution, it would improve efficiency if taxpayers did not anticipate having to pay taxes, as such anticipation results in distortion of behavior. But this problem is largely unavoidable.

Successful economies seem to have succeeded, for the most part, in avoiding expropriation. The mechanism by which this is accomplished is not that clear; no system prohibits taxation or legal changes, and constitutional or other strong compensation requirements are limited. (For example, in the United States, the government must compensate a landowner whose building is taken for a highway, but a high capital income or wealth tax is not legally proscribed.) The development of strong norms seems to play a greater role in successful economies, but such norms cannot succeed unless the relevant audience can understand which legal reforms are improper in the relevant respect.

A variant of the expropriation problem arises when the government is involved with ordinary *contractual behavior* and related activity. In fact, most governments accomplish many of their purposes - building roads, procuring military equipment, hiring employees - through ordinary market transactions. (In some countries, state enterprises are common; these too, however, often use ordinary contractual means of paying workers and purchasing other necessary inputs.) Moreover, most governments, despite the availability of sovereign immunity from private suits, voluntarily subject themselves to a legal regime under which their contracts have a binding effect similar to that of private contracts. This avoids problems of opportunism, both large and small.

Some commentators have analogized legislation and other government law-making to government contracts (see, for example, Graetz, 1977; Kaplow, 1986, 1987; Ramseyer and Nakazato, 1989; Logue, 1996). Thus, sometimes the government uses subsidies to induce certain behavior rather than explicit contracts under which it pays for a promise to undertake certain activity. If the subsidy is terminated, this might be viewed as a breach of an implicit contract. Of course, subsidies are routinely terminated. When governments use ongoing subsidies to encourage an activity rather than entering into a long-term contract to pay for a given amount of the activity, they are choosing to use a more flexible mechanism, allowing the possibility of change without compensation. To impose a norm or constitutional requirement that all law be treated as if it were a binding contract would not add to the government's options; it would eliminate one. (Actually, it may have no effect at all, as laws could simply be written to expire unless extended or with some other loophole providing the government a way to avoid any binding obligation.)

14. Additional Issues

Transition relief is sometimes favored because it may make it politically feasible to implement desirable reform. For example, efficient deregulation might be opposed by protected incumbents, who could be bought out with compensation (see Tullock, 1978; see also Usher, 1995, addressing compensation for takings). The problem is that, *ex ante*, special interest groups would have a greater incentive to seek inefficient rules, knowing that even if the rules were subsequently repealed they would benefit from transition relief (see Kitch, 1977; Quinn and Trebilcock, 1982; McKenzie, 1986; Kaplow, 1987, 1992b). Thus, it is not obvious that a policy of buying out such political opposition would in the long run produce better or worse laws and lead to more or less resources being wasted on rent-seeking activity.

Another problem concerns changes in political power that may produce legal changes that do not reflect real changes in information or circumstances (although legal reforms may reflect shifts in perceptions or in value judgments). Small changes in beliefs may produce large legal changes (as when an opposition party gains a few percentage points in support and comes into power), and such change may be frequent. *Ex ante* behavior that is desirable from the perspective of one party's policies may be undesirable from the perspective of the other's. Use of transition relief will tend to cause investors to put more weight on the status quo, something unlikely to be favored by a subsequent regime seeking change. Analysis of social welfare in such instances is difficult.

15. Literature

The first careful analysis of many issues concerning legal transitions appears to be Hale (1927). For a general analysis of changing legal rules in a variety of contexts, see Kaplow (1986, 1987, 1992b).

Most writing by legal academics on the subject focuses on takings or on tax reform. With respect to takings, Michelman (1967) offers an important early analysis, although it does not take the economic approach as far as subsequent work. Baxter and Altree (1972) advance a 'first-in-time' approach to address the problem of airport noise; they are among the first to pursue directly the problem of the adverse incentive effects of compensation. Blume, Rubinfeld and Shapiro (1984) analyze incentive effects of compensation in a formal model and Blume and Rubinfeld (1984) consider risk, although these authors do not integrate the two analyses or systematically consider private risk mitigation. Kaplow (1986, 1987) discusses takings in the context of analyzing the transition problem more generally. For additional work, with emphasis on the problem of the government's incentives, see, for example, Fischel and Shapiro (1989) and Hermalin (1995). For an empirical analysis of the effect of requiring compensation on government behavior, see Cordes and Weisbrod (1979).

Feldstein (1976a, 1976b) and Graetz (1977) offer the first substantial treatments of tax transitions, followed by Kaplow (1986, 1987, 1992b), who more explicitly analyzes effects of relief on investors' incentives and private risk mitigation, compares alternative transition mechanisms, and addresses institutional problems with government decision making. This latter problem is also considered by Ramseyer and Nakazato (1989) and Logue (1996), who are both favorable toward relief because of concerns about government misbehavior. Levmore (1993) is more favorable to (uncompensated) retroactivity because of the possibility of an efficient capital levy. The particular problem of transition to a consumption tax is addressed in Graetz (1979), Kaplow (1986, 1987, 1995b), Sarkar and Zodrow (1993) and Bradford (1996).

Another subject receiving increased attention is deregulation and other regulatory changes (see Quinn and Trebilcock, 1982; Kolbe, Tye and Myers, 1993; Kaplow, 1993).

D. Additional Topics

16. Additional Topics

There are a number of other dimensions along which many legal rules vary that are sufficiently general to warrant independent study. Because these subjects are addressed in other fields within law and economics, the present discussion will be brief. Each of the topics considered involves the general question whether laws should identify certain conduct as permitted or prohibited or should instead impose fines, provide for private liability, or use other means of aligning private and social interests so as to induce parties to make efficient choices on their own.

Strict Liability Versus Negligence
The choice between strict liability and negligence has received much attention. Similar issues arise involving defenses based upon victim behavior. And other areas of law present analogous questions: namely, is a party responsible for all harm caused, or is the party responsible only if behavior was improper (and, then, only to the extent of any additional harm caused by the inappropriate action)? The latter type of law requires both defining a norm of behavior (which may be done *ex ante*, as a rule, or *ex post*, as a standard, and which may be done in a simple or precise manner), and both types of law require provisions governing the measurement of harm. This sort of choice involves many of the issues considered here, as well as concerns for the frequency of litigation, victims' incentives, and other factors (see Brown, 1973; Shavell, 1980, and Chapter 3100 on strict liability versus negligence in tort).

Property Versus Liability Rules
The distinction between property and liability rules involves remedies: if one party wishes to infringe the legal rights of another, must the acting party first obtain permission (or else be subject to extreme sanctions and the possibility of injunction, if feasible) - a property rule - or may the party simply act and pay damages - a liability rule? This scheme is first explored in detail by Calabresi and Melamed (1972) and has subsequently been expanded in Kaplow and Shavell (1996b). Other relevant work includes Ellickson (1973), Polinsky (1979, 1980) and Krier and Schwab (1995). The problem of bargaining under asymmetric information has attracted disproportionate attention, beginning with Samuelson (1985) and followed, for example, by Farrell (1987), Shavell (1988b), Johnston (1995), Ayres and Talley (1995a, 1995b) and Kaplow and Shavell (1995, 1996b). See Chapter 3800 on property versus liability rules.

Acknowledgments

I am grateful for comments from Steven Shavell and the referees, research assistance from Enrique Arana, Judson Berkey and Jerry Fang, and support from the John M. Olin Center for Law, Economics and Business at Harvard Law School.

Bibliography on General Characteristics of Rules (9000)

Arthur D. Little (1988), *Development of Methodology for Estimating the Taxpayer Paperwork Burden, Final Report to the Department of the Treasury*, Washington, DC, Internal Revenue Service.

Baird, Douglas G. and Weisberg, Robert (1982), 'Rules, Standards and the Battle of the Forms: A Reassessment of §2-207', **68** *Virginia Law Review*, 1217-1262.

Baxter, William F. and Altree, Lillian R. (1972), 'Legal Aspects of Airport Noise', **15** *Journal of Law and Economics*, 1-113.

Blume, Lawrence and Rubinfeld, Daniel L. (1984), 'Compensation for Takings: An Economic Analysis', **72** *California Law Review*, 569-628.

Blume, Lawrence, Rubinfeld, Daniel L. and Shapiro, Perry (1984), 'The Taking of Land. When Should Compensation be Paid?', **99** *Quarterly Journal of Economics*, 71-92.

Blumenthal, Marsha and Slemrod, Joel B. (1992), 'The Compliance Cost of the U.S. Individual Income Tax System: A Second Look After Tax Reform', **45** *National Tax Journal*, 185-202.

Bouckaert, Boudewijn and Schäfer, Hans-Bernd (1995), 'Mistake of Law and the Economics of Legal Information', in Bouckaert, Boudewijn and De Geest, Gerrit (eds), *Essays in Law and Economics II: Contract Law, Regulation, and Reflections on Law and Economics*, Antwerpen, Maklu, 217-245.

Bradford, David F. (1996), 'Consumption Taxes: Some Fundamental Transition Issues', in Boskin, Michael J. (ed.), *Frontiers of Tax Reform*, Stanford, Hoover Institution Press.

Calfee, John E. and Craswell, Richard (1984), 'Some Effects of Uncertainty on Compliance with Legal Standards', **70** *Virginia Law Review*, 965-1003.

Cordes, Joseph J. and Weisbrod, Burton A. (1979), 'Governmental Behavior in Response to Compensation Requirements', **11** *Journal of Public Economics*, 47-58.

Coulange, Pierre (1990), 'La Production de Droit (The Production of Legal Rules)', **3** *Journal des Economistes et des Etudes Humaines*, 277-302.

Coulange, Pierre (1990), *Analyse Économique de la Production de Droit* (Economic Analysis of the Production of Legal Rules), PhD, Aix-en-Provence, Université d'Aix-Marseille III, Faculté d'Economie Appliquée.

Craswell, Richard and Calfee, John E. (1986), 'Deterrence and Uncertain Legal Standards', **2** *Journal of Law, Economics and Organization*, 279-303.

Diver, Colin S. (1983), 'The Optimal Precision of Administrative Rules', **93** *Yale Law Journal*, 65-109.

Doernberg, Richard L. and McChesney, Fred S. (1987), 'On the Accelerating Rate and Decreasing Durability of Tax Reform', **71** *Minnesota Law Review*, 913-962.

Ehrlich, Isaac and Posner, Richard A. (1974), 'An Economic Analysis of Legal Rulemaking', **3** *Journal of Legal Studies*, 257-286.

Feldstein, Martin (1976a), 'On the Theory of Tax Reform', **6** *Journal of Public Economics*, 77-104.

Feldstein, Martin (1976b), 'Compensation in Tax Reform', **29** *National Tax Journal*, 123-130.

Fisch, Jill E. (1997), 'Retroactivity and Legal Change: An Equilibrium Approach', **110** *Harvard Law Review*, 1055-1123.

Fischel, William A. and Shapiro, Perry (1989), 'A Constitutional Choice Model of Compensation for Takings', **9** *International Review of Law and Economics*, 115-128.

Graetz, Michael J. (1977), 'Legal Transitions: The Case of Retroactivity in Income Tax Revision', **126** *University of Pennsylvania Law Review*, 47-87.

Graetz, Michael J. (1979), 'Implementing a Progressive Consumption Tax', **92** *Harvard Law Review*, 1575-1661.

Graetz, Michael J. (1985), 'Retroactivity Revisited', **98** *Harvard Law Review*, 1820-1841.

Hale, Robert L. (1927), 'Value and Vested Rights', **27** *Columbia Law Review*, 523-529.

Hermalin, Benjamin E. (1995), 'An Economic Analysis of Takings', **11** *Journal of Law, Economics and Organization*, 64-86.

Hutter, Michael (1989), *Die Produktion von Recht. Eine selb streferentielle Theorie der Wirtschaft, angewandt auf den Fall des Arzneimittelpatentrechts* (The Production of Law. A Selfreferential Theory of the Economy, applied to the Case of Pharmaceutical Patent Law), Tübingen, J.C.B. Mohr, p. 213.

Kahan, Marcel (1989), 'Causation and Incentives to Take Care Under the Negligence Rule', **18** *Journal of Legal Studies*, 427-447.

Kaplow, Louis (1986), 'An Economic Analysis of Legal Transitions', **99** *Harvard Law Review*, 509-617.

Kaplow, Louis (1987), *Optimal Transition Policy: Replacing Horizontal Equity With an Ex Ante Incentives Perspective*, dissertation accepted by Harvard University Department of Economics, Cambridge, MA.

Kaplow, Louis (1990), 'Optimal Deterrence, Uninformed Individuals, and Acquiring Information About Whether Acts are Subject to Sanctions', **6** *Journal of Law, Economics and Organization*, 93-128.

Kaplow, Louis (1992a), 'Rules versus Standards: An Economic Analysis', **42** *Duke Law Journal*, 557-629.

Kaplow, Louis (1992b), 'Government Relief for Risk Associated with Government Action', **94** *Scandinavian Journal of Economics*, 525-541.

Kaplow, Louis (1993), 'An Ex Ante Perspective on Deregulation, Viewed ex post', **15** *Resource and Energy Economics*, 153-173.

Kaplow, Louis (1994a), 'The Value of Accuracy in Adjudication: An Economic Analysis', **23** *Journal of Legal Studies*, 307-401.

Kaplow, Louis (1994b), 'The Standard Deduction and Floors in the Income Tax', **50** *Tax Law Review*, 1-31.

Kaplow, Louis (1994c), 'Accuracy, Complexity, and the Income Tax', Working Paper No. 4631, Cambridge, MA, National Bureau of Economic Research.

Kaplow, Louis (1995a), 'A Model of the Optimal Complexity of Legal Rules', **11** *Journal of Law, Economics and Organization*, 150-163.

Kaplow, Louis (1995b), 'Recovery of Pre-Enactment Basis Under a Consumption Tax: The USA Tax System', **68** *Tax Notes*, 1109-1118.

Kaplow, Louis (1996), 'How Tax Complexity and Enforcement Affect the Equity and Efficiency of the Income Tax', **49** *National Tax Journal*, 135-150.

Kaplow, Louis and Shavell, Steven (1992), 'Private versus Socially Optimal Provision of Ex Ante Legal Advice', **8** *Journal of Law, Economics and Organization*, 306-320.

Kaplow, Louis and Shavell, Steven (1994), 'Accuracy in the Determination of Liability', **37** *Journal of Law and Economics*, 1-15.

Kaplow, Louis and Shavell, Steven (1996a), 'Accuracy in the Assessment of Damages', **39** *Journal of Law and Economics*, 191-210.

Kessler, Daniel and McClellan, Mark (1996), 'Do Doctors Practice Defensive Medicine?', **111** *Quarterly Journal of Economics*, 352-390.

Kitch, Edmund W. (1977), 'Can We Buy Our Way Out of Harmful Regulation?', in Martin, Donald L. and Schwartz, Warren F. (eds), *Deregulating American Industry: Legal and Economic Problems*, Lexington, MA, Lexington Books.

Kolbe, A. Lawrence, Tye, William B. and Myers, Stewart C. (1993), *Regulatory Risk: Economic Principles and Applications to Natural Gas Pipelines and Other Industries*, Boston, Kluwer Academic Press.

Landes, William M. and Posner, Richard A. (1976), 'Legal Precedent: A Theoretical and Empirical Analysis', **19** *Journal of Law and Economics*, 249-307.

Landes, William M. and Posner, Richard A. (1994), 'The Economics of Anticipatory Adjudication', **23** *Journal of Legal Studies*, 683-719.

Levmore, Saul (1993), 'The Case for Retroactive Taxation', **22** *Journal of Legal Studies*, 265-307.

Logue, Kyle D. (1996), 'Tax Treatments, Opportunistic Retroactivity, and the Benefits of Government Precommitment', **94** *Michigan Law Review*, 1129-1196.

Long, Susan B. and Swingen, Judyth A. (1987), 'An Approach to the Measurement of Tax Law Complexity', **8** *Journal of the American Tax Association*, 22-36.

MacKaay, Ejan (1979), 'Les Notions Floues ou l'Economie de l'Imprécision (Fuzzy Concepts or the Economics of Imprecision)', **12** *Langages*, 33-50.

MacKaay, Ejan (1980), 'Le Nozione "Fluide" Ovvero l'Economia Dell'Imprecisione (Fuzzy Concepts or the Economics of Imprecision)', *Informatica e Diritto*, 253-274.

McKenzie, Richard B. (1986), 'Tax/Compensation Schemes: Misleading Advice in a Rent-Seeking Society', **48** *Public Choice*, 189-194.

Michelman, Frank I. (1967), 'Property, Utility and Fairness: Comments on the Ethical Foundations of 'Just Compensation' Law', **80** *Harvard Law Review*, 1165-1258.

Munzer, Stephen R. (1977), 'Retroactive Law', **6** *Journal of Legal Studies*, 373-397.

Ogus, Anthony I. (1981), 'Quantitative Rules and Judicial Decision Making', in Burrows, Paul and Veljanovski, Cento G. (eds), *The Economic Approach to Law*, London, Butterworths, 210-225.

Ogus, Anthony I. (1992), 'Information, Error Costs and Regulation', **12** *International Review of Law and Economics*, 411-421.

Posner, Richard A. (1992), *Economic Analysis of Law* (4th edn), Boston, Little, Brown and Company.

Quinn, John and Trebilcock, Michael J. (1982), 'Compensation, Transition Costs, and Regulatory Change', **32** *University of Toronto Law Journal*, 117-175.

Ramseyer, J. Mark and Nakazato, Minoru (1989), 'Tax Transitions and the Protection Racket: A Reply to Professors Graetz and Kaplow', **75** *Virginia Law Review*, 1155-1175.

Russell, A.M. and Rickard, J.A. (1987), 'A Model of Tax Evasion Incorporating Income Variation and Retroactive Penalities', **26** *Australian Economic Papers*, 254-264.

Samuels, Warren J. (1974), 'Commentary: An Economic Perspective on the Compensation Problem', **21** *Wayne Law Review*, 113-134.

Sarkar, Shounak and Zodrow, George R. (1993), 'Transitional Issues in Moving to a Direct Consumption Tax', **46** *National Tax Journal*, 359-376.

Schauer, Frederick (1991), *Playing by the Rules: A Philosophical Examination of Rule-Based Decisionmaking in Law and in Life*, New York, Oxford University Press.

Schwartz, Gary T. (1983), 'New Products, Old Products, Evolving Law, Retroactive Law', **58** *New York University Law Review*, 796-852.

Shavell, Steven (1988a), 'Legal Advice about Contemplated Acts: The Decision to Obtain Advice, Its Social Desirability, and the Protection of Confidentiality', **17** *Journal of Legal Studies*, 123-150.

Shavell, Steven (1988b), 'Property Rights and the Rule of Liability in a Simple Bargaining Model', unpublished manuscript, on file with the Harvard Law School Library, Cambridge, MA.

Skogh, Göran (1985), 'Rättssäkerhet I Marknadsekonomin (Legal Certainty in the Market Economy)', in X. (ed.), *Rättssäkerhet och Demokrati*, Ratios förlag.

Slemrod, Joel B. (1989), 'Complexity, Compliance Costs, and Tax Evasion', in Roth, Jeffrey A. and Scholz, John T. (eds), *Taxpayer Compliance, Volume 2: Social Science Perspectives*, Philadelphia, University of Pennsylvania Press.

Slemrod, Joel B. and Yitzhaki, Shlomo (1994), 'Analyzing the Standard Deduction as a Presumptive Tax', **1** *International Tax and Public Finance*, 25-34.

Slot, P.J. (1983), *Regelen en Ontregelen. Oratie Leiden* (Regulating and De-regulating), Kluwer, Deventer.

Spier, Kathryn E. (1994), 'Settlement Bargaining and the Design of Damage Awards', **10** *Journal of Law, Economics and Organization*, 84-95.

Tullock, Gordon (1978), 'Achieving Deregulation - A Public Choice Perspective', **2** *Regulation*, 50-54.

Usher, Dan (1995), 'Victimization, Rent-Seeking and Just Compensation', **83** *Public Choice*, 1-20.

Walz, W. Rainer (1988), 'Rechtssicherheit und Risikozuweisung bei Steuerrechtsänderungen - Verbotene Rückwirkung, gebotene Übergangsregelung, richterliche Vertragsanpassung' (Legal Certainty and Risk Allocation for Changes in Tax Law - Illegal Retroaction, Transitional Rules), *Recht und Risiko*, 252-286.

White, Michelle J. (1992), 'Legal Complexity and Lawyers' Benefit from Litigation', **12** *International Review of Law and Economics*, 381-395.

Yitzhaki, Shlomo (1979), 'A Note on Optimal Taxation and Administrative Costs', **69** *American Economic Review*, 475-480.

Other References

Arnott, Richard and Stiglitz, Joseph E. (1991), 'Moral Hazard and Nonmarket Institutions: Dysfunctional Crowding Out or Peer Monitoring?', **81** *American Economic Review*, 179-190.

Ayres, Ian and Talley, Eric (1995a), 'Solomonic Bargaining: Dividing a Legal Entitlement to Facilitate a Coasean Trade', **104** *Yale Law Journal*, 1027-1117.

Ayres, Ian and Talley, Eric (1995b), 'Distinguishing Between Consensual and Nonconsensual Advantages of Liability Rules', **105** *Yale Law Journal*, 235-253.

Becker, Gary S. (1968), 'Crime and Punishment: An Economic Approach', **76** *Journal of Political Economy*, 169-217.

Brown, John (1973), 'Toward an Economic Theory of Liability', **2** *Journal of Legal Studies*, 323-350.

Calabresi, Guido and Melamed, A. Douglas (1972), 'Property Rules, Liability Rules, and Inalienability: One View of the Cathedral', **85** *Harvard Law Review*, 1089-1128.

Downs, Anthony (1957), *An Economic Theory of Democracy*, New York, Harper.

Ellickson, Robert C. (1973), 'Alternatives to Zoning: Covenants, Nuisance Rules, and Fines as Land Use Controls', **40** *University of Chicago Law Review*, 681-781.

Farrell, Joseph (1987), 'Information and the Coase Theorem', **1** *Journal of Economic Perspectives*, 113-129.

Johnston, Jason Scott (1995), 'Bargaining Under Rules versus Standards', **11** *Journal of Law, Economics and Organization*, 256-281.

Kaplow, Louis (1991), 'Incentives and Government Relief for Risk', **4** *Journal of Risk and Uncertainty*, 167-175.

Kaplow, Louis and Shavell, Steven (1995), 'Do Liability Rules Facilitate Bargaining? A Reply to Ayres and Talley', **105** *Yale Law Journal*, 221-233.

Kaplow, Louis and Shavell, Steven (1996b), 'Property Rules versus Liability Rules: An Economic Analysis', **109** *Harvard Law Review*, 713-790.

Krier, James E. and Schwab, Stewart J. (1995), 'Property Rules and Liability Rules: The Cathedral in Another Light', **70** *New York University Law Review*, 440-483.

Niskanen, William A. (1971), *Bureaucracy and Representative Government*, Chicago, Aldine, Atherton.

Olson, Mancur (1965), *The Logic of Collective Action; Public Goods and the Theory of Groups*, Cambridge, MA, Harvard University Press.

Polinsky, A. Mitchell (1979), 'Controlling Externalities and Protecting Entitlements: Property Right, Liability Rule, and Tax-Subsidy Approaches', **8** *Journal of Legal Studies*, 1-48.

Polinsky, A. Mitchell (1980), 'Resolving Nuisance Disputes: The Simple Economics of Injunctive and Damage Remedies', **32** *Stanford Law Review*, 1075-1112.

Samuelson, William (1985), 'A Comment on the Coase Theorem', in Roth, Alvin E. (ed.), *Game-Theoretic Models of Bargaining*, New York, Cambridge University Press.

Shavell, Steven (1980), 'Strict Liability Versus Negligence', **9** *Journal of Legal Studies*, 1-25.

Shavell, Steven (1987), *Economic Analysis of Accident Law*, Cambridge, MA, Harvard University Press.

9100
CONSTITUTIONAL LAW

Stefan Voigt
Max-Planck-Institute for Research into Economic Systems, Jena (Germany)

Abstract

The chapter discusses both the normative and the positive approach towards the economic analysis of constitutional law. With regard to the normative branch, Buchanan's approach is shortly presented and evaluated. With regard to the positive branch, it is differentiated between research which is interested in explaining the choice of constitutional rules on the one hand and research which is interested in explaining the outcomes that (alternative) constitutional rules bring about on the other. Concerning the first research direction, a distinction between explicit and implicit constitutional change is proposed. Concerning the second direction, concepts such as the separation of powers, unicameral vs. bicameral systems and direct-democratic institutions are discussed. The entry closes with a proposal to complement the two existing branches with an 'art of constitutional political economy' which is conjectured to make the economic analysis of constitutional law more relevant in real world processes of constitutional choice.
JEL classification: K0
Keywords: Normative Constitutional Economics, Positive Constitutional Economics, Constitutional Rights, Economic Growth

1. Introduction

The economic analysis of constitutional law has not been one of the most researched topics within law and economics. The special issue of the *International Review of Law and Economics* on 'Constitutional Law and Economics' (1992) is rather exceptional. The research program known as 'constitutional economics' or 'constitutional political economy' has primarily been developed by scholars emanating from public choice, that is, 'the application of economics to political science' (Mueller, 1989, p. 1). James M. Buchanan, the most prominent proponent of constitutional economics, has described law and economics as a related subdiscipline that remained, however, closer to orthodox economic theory because the standard efficiency norm remains central to it (Buchanan, 1987a, p. 586). Scholars of constitutional economics have broadened the standard research program of economics:

Standard economics is interested in the analysis of choices within rules, thus assuming rules to be exogenously given and fixed. Constitutional economics broadens this research program by analyzing the choice of rules using the standard method of economics, that is, rational choice.

Buchanan defines constitutions in their most basic sense as 'a set of rules which constrain the activities of persons and agents in the pursuits of their own ends and objectives' (Buchanan, 1977, p. 292). Defined as such, quite a few rule systems could be analyzed as constitutions: a firm's partnership agreement as well as the statute of a church. Although such rule systems have indeed been analyzed from the point of view of constitutional economics (for a firm's constitution, see Gifford, 1991, or Vanberg, 1992), the rule system analyzed most often remains the constitution of the state. Two broad avenues in the economic analysis of constitutions can be conceived of: (1) The normative branch of the research program is interested in legitimizing the state and the actions of its representatives. In other words: it is interested in identifying conditions under which the outcomes of collective choices can be judged as 'fair' or 'efficient'. (2) The positive branch of the research program is interested in explaining (a) the emergence and modification of constitutional rules and (b) the outcomes that are the consequence of (alternative) constitutional rules (for a similar demarcation of the topic, see Mueller, 1996).

The chapter is organized as follows: Part A will be devoted to normative constitutional economics whereas Part B will deal with positive constitutional economics. The chapter closes with an outlook.

A. Normative Constitutional Economics

2. Methodological Foundations

Normative constitutional economics could deal with a variety of questions, for example: (1) How should societies proceed in order to bring about constitutional rules that fulfill some criterion like being 'just' or 'efficient'? (2) What contents should the constitutional rules have? (3) Which issues should be dealt with in the constitution - and which should be left to sub-constitutional choice? (4) What characteristics should constitutional rules have? and many more. Buchanan answers none of these questions directly but hopes to offer a conceptual frame that would make them answerable. The frame is based on social contract theory as developed most prominently by Hobbes. According to Buchanan (1987b, 249), the purpose of this contractarian approach is justificatory in the sense that 'it offers a basis for normative evaluation. Could the observed rules that constrain the activity of ordinary polititics have emerged from agreement in constitutional contract? To the extent that this question can be affirmatively answered, we have established a legitimating linkage between the individual and the state.'

The value-judgment that nobody's goals and values should a priori be more important than those of anybody else, that is, normative individualism, is the basis of Buchanan's entire model. One implication of this norm is that societal goals cannot exist. According to this view, every single individual has the right to pursue her or his own ends within the frame of collectively agreed upon rules. Therefore, a collective evaluation criterion that compared the societal 'is' with some 'ought' cannot exist since there is no such thing as a societal 'ought'. But it is possible to derive a procedural norm from the value judgment stated. Buchanan borrowed this idea from Wicksell (1896): agreements to exchange private goods are judged as advantageous if the involved parties agree voluntarily. The agreement is supposed to be 'efficient', 'good' or 'advantageous' because the involved parties expect to be better off with the agreement than without it. Often, the exchange activities are considered to be taking place only between two parties, the seller and the buyer. Buchanan follows Wicksell who had demanded the same evaluation criterion for decisions that affect more than two parties, at the extreme an entire society. Rules that have consequences for every single member of a society can only be looked upon as advantageous if every single member of that society has voluntarily agreed to them. This is the Pareto criterion applied to collectivities. Deviations from the unanimity principle could occur during a decision process on the production of collective goods, but this would only be within the realm of the Buchanan model as long as the constitution itself provided for a decision rule below unanimity. Deviations from the unanimity rule would have to be based on a provision that was brought about unanimously.

3. Giving Efficiency Another Meaning

Normative constitutional economics thus re-interprets the Pareto criterion in a twofold way: it is not outcomes but rules or procedures that lead to outcomes which are evaluated using the criterion. The evaluation is not carried out by an omniscient scientist or politician but by the concerned individuals themselves: 'In a sense, the political economist is concerned with "what people want"' (Buchanan, 1959, p. 137). In order to find out what people want Buchanan proposes to carry out a consensus test. The specification of this test will be crucial as to which rules can be considered legitimate. In 1959, Buchanan had factual unanimity in mind and those citizens that expect to be worse off due to some rule changes would have to be factually compensated. This test would thus be equivalent to a modified Kaldor-Hicks-criterion. In the meantime, Buchanan seems to have changed his position: hypothetical consent deduced by an economist will do in order to legitimize some rule (see, for example, Buchanan 1977, 1978, 1986). This position can be criticized because a large variety of rules seem to be legitimizable depending on the assumptions of the scientist who does the process. Scientists arguing in favor of an extensive welfare state will most likely assume risk-averse individuals while scientists who argue for cuts in the welfare budgets will assume people to be risk-neutral.

4. Critical Evaluation of Normative Constitutional Economics

The possibility of hypothetical consent crucially depends on the information assumptions. Buchanan and Tullock (1962, p. 78) introduced the veil of uncertainty in which the individual cannot make any long-term predictions on her or his future socioeconomic position. Rawls' (1971) veil of ignorance is more radical because the consenting individuals are asked to decide on proposed rules *as if* they did not have any knowledge on their individual fate. Rawls' veil is thus more demanding on the individuals. Both veils assume a rather curious asymmetry concerning certain kinds of knowledge: on the one hand, the citizens are supposed to know very little about their own socioeconomic position, but on the other, they are supposed to have at their disposal a consistent theory concerning the working properties of alternative constitutional rules (Reisman, 1990, pp. 23-30 describes the differences between the two conceptions of the veil).

In order to discuss the usefulness of the conceptual frame, suppose for a moment that it is impossible to legitimize a currently valid constitutional rule and that some constitutional economist has proposed an alternative rule for which she has ascertained a hypothetical consent. Further suppose that it is impossible to transform the hypothetical consent into majorities with which the constitution could be changed. Clearly, the non-legitimizable *status quo* would prevail over the legitimate constitutional rule.

B. Positive Constitutional Economics

Positive constitutional economics can be divided into two parts. On the one hand, it is interested in explaining the outcomes that result from (alternative) rule sets. Here, constitutional rules are part of the *explanans*. On the other hand, it is interested in explaining the emergence and modification of constitutional rules. In that case, they are the *explanandum*.

5. Constitutional Rules as Explanandum

5.1 Procedures for Generating Constitutional Rules

Constitutional rules can be analyzed as the outcome of certain procedures used to bring them about. Elster's (1991, 1993) research program concerning constitutional economics puts a strong emphasis on hypotheses of this kind. He inquires about the consequences of time limits for constitutional conventions, about how constitutional conventions that simultaneously serve as legislature allocate their time between the two functions, about which effects the regular information of the public concerning the progress of the constitutional negotiations has and about how certain supermajorities and election rules can determine the outcome of conventions (Elster, 1991, p. 30). Some of Riker's articles (1983, 1984) can also be interpreted as an encouragement to search for hypotheses of this kind. He calls for an extension of traditional rational-choice theory pointing to the fact that in its traditional form it is incapable of taking into account dynamic and creative processes which structure the decision room of the actors.

This part of constitutional economics does not offer a general perspective on the process of constitution-making (Elster, 1993, p. 174). There is, however, a large number of case studies (see, for example, the volume edited by Goldwin and Kaufman, 1988).

5.2 The Relevance of Preferences and Restrictions for Generating Constitutional Rules

Procedures are a modus of aggregating inputs and can therefore never bring about constitutional rules by themselves. It is therefore only a logical step to analyze whether a bunch of potentially relevant variables can explain the choice of certain constitutional rules. There are good reasons - and some empirical evidence - to assume that (1) the individual preferences of the members of constitutional conventions will directly enter into the deliberations, and that (2) the preferences of all the citizens concerned will be recognized in the final document in quite diverse ways. This would mean that rent-seeking does play a role even on the constitutional level, a conjecture that is often excluded by representatives of normative constitutional economics.

McGuire and Ohsfeldt (1986, 1989a, 1989b) have tried to explain the voting behavior of the Philadelphia delegates as well as those of the delegates to the 13 state ratifying conventions that led to the US Constitution. Their statistical results show that merchants, western landowners, financiers and large public-securities holders, *ceteris paribus*, supported the new constitution, whereas debtors and slave owners, *ceteris paribus*, opposed it (ibid., 1989a, p.175).

5.3 Explicit Constitutional Change

The two approaches towards constitutions as *explananda* just sketched are rather static. A third approach focuses on explaining the modifications of constitutions over time. Constitutional change that results in a modified document will be called explicit constitutional change here whereas constitutional change that does not result in a modified document - that is, change that is due to a different interpretation of formally unaltered rules - will be called implicit constitutional change.

One approach towards explaining long-run explicit constitutional change focuses on changes of the relative bargaining power of organized groups. Due to a comparative advantage in using violence (see North, 1981), an autocrat is able to establish government and secure a rent from that activity. As soon as an (organized) group is convinced that its own cooperation with the autocrat is crucial for the maintenance of the rent, it will seek negotiations with the autocrat. Since the current constitution is the basis for the autocrat's ability to appropriate a rent, the opposition will strive after changing it. In this approach, bargaining power is defined as the capability to inflict costs on your opponent. The prediction of this approach is that a change in (relative) bargaining power will lead to modified constitutional rules (Voigt, 1997).

Explicit constitutional change can be sought by interest groups who try to convince legislators to change the constitution. If constitutional change is only sought in a disequilibrium, the interest group seeking change must perceive its own relevance as having changed. Boudreaux and Pritchard (1993) analyze the hitherto 27 amendments to the US Constitution from an economic perspective. They begin with the conjecture that a lobby-group interested in constitutional change principally has two possibilities of seeking its realization: it can either lobby for a simple law or it can lobby for constitutional change. The second option is, however, more expensive. The trivial prediction of rational choice theory is that the group will choose the option with the higher expected utility. In order to be able to make predictions about the option chosen, it is therefore necessary to specify the cost and benefit categories implied. Boudreaux and Pritchard specify two categories and predict a demand for constitutional change in cases in which the costs of maintaining an interest group over time are high, and today's opposition is weak but expected to be strong in the future.

5.4 Implicit Constitutional Change

Implicit constitutional change has been defined as a changed constitutional interpretation that occurs although the formal constitutional document remains unchanged. This means that the conceptual separation between choice of rules on the one hand and choice within rules on the other has been factually blurred. This possibility must be disturbing to the proponents of normative constitutional economics. To adherents of positive constitutional economics, it amounts to an analytical difficulty because the identification of what is analyzed as the valid 'constitution' either as *explanandum* or as *explanans* becomes more difficult. At the same time, the possibility of implicit constitutional change also becomes an object of inquiry. It can be asked which variables determine the scope and extent of the implicit constitutional change to be expected.

Suppose a constitution in the sense of constitutionalism exists and the government branches are legislature, executive and judiciary. If all government representatives have at their disposal a certain latitude concerning the interpretation of the constitution, it can be argued that all branches can bring about implicit constitutional change. If an independent judiciary exists, it seems plausible to assume that it has most latitude in causing implicit constitutional change because it has the power to judge the constitutional conformity of the actions of the other two government branches. It can now be argued that the judiciary is subject to a number of constraints among which those laid down in the original constitutional document play a rather marginal role. Instead, the current preferences of the other branches are more relevant restrictions. There are various factors that determine the latitude that justices have in bringing about implicit constitutional change. Cooter and Ginsburg (1996) show that it depends on the number of chambers whose consent is needed to pass fresh legislation. The higher its number, the more difficult it will be for the other branches to correct implicit constitutional change by changing the constitutional document explicitly. They further show (ibid.) that it depends on the existence of a 'dominant disciplined party'. If such a party exists, it will be more difficult for the justices to bring about implicit constitutional change. Other variables that influence the amount of implicit constitutional change include the following: (1) If implicit constitutional change can only be prevented by changing the document explicitly, the necessary majority becomes a factor. The more inclusive it is, the more difficult it will be to prevent such change. (2) The possibility of referenda should be another explanatory variable. If the population at large can overturn the justices, they have an incentive not to deviate too drastically from the preferences of the median voter. (3) The extent of implicit constitutional change should be higher in common-law systems than in continental-law systems because in the first group decisions by justices become directly applicable law (see also Voigt, 1999).

6. Constitutional Rules as Explanans

In the previous section of this chapter, constitutional rules have been analyzed as *explananda*. Such an analysis is only of interest if it can be shown that constitutional rules are themselves relevant to bringing about certain results or patterns that concern economists or social scientists in general, in other words: if constitutions matter. Possible *explananda* include per capita income, its growth rate, but also income distribution.

6.1 The Separation of Powers

The analysis of economically relevant consequences of the separation of powers has long been neglected almost entirely. In a survey article, Posner (1987) writes that the separation of powers increases the transaction costs of governing. This would hold for welfare-enhancing as well as for redistributive or even exploitative measures. North and Weingast (1989) use the British case of the seventeenth century to demonstrate that the separation of powers can secure property rights because it is one way for the governing to credibly commit themselves.

Brennan and Hamlin (1994) develop a 'revisionist view' of the separation of powers. To make their point, they draw on standard monopoly models used in economics and distinguish between a horizontal and a vertical separation of powers. Starting out with a monopoly, the introduction of the horizontal separation amounts to two (or more) suppliers competing for demand and thus to the introduction of duopoly (or oligopoly). The equilibrium price will then be below the monopoly price and consumer rent will subsequently increase. A vertical separation of powers also entails a division of the original monopoly, albeit in a different way: now single functions of the process are divided; there is, for example, one monopolistic firm that produces certain goods and a second monopolistic firm that distributes it. Brennan and Hamlin call this functional separation of powers too. The (individually) maximizing strategies of the vertically separated firms will at best lead to the monopoly price, but usually the price will even be higher and the accruing consumer rent will thus be lower than in the original monopoly. Brennan and Hamlin argue that the separation of powers doctrine as conventionally understood is equivalent to the functional separation of powers and will therefore not protect citizens from exploitation by the governed. The horizontal separation of powers could, instead, have beneficial results. In order to unfold, it needs to entail an 'exit' option for citizens as well as the absence of strong externalities between competing states.

6.2 Unicameral vs. Bicameral Systems

A first attempt to compare the differential effects of unicameral and bicameral legislatures dates back to Buchanan and Tullock (1962, Ch. 16). In their analytical frame, that decision rule is optimal which leads to a minimum of interdependence costs which are defined as the sum of decision-making costs and those external costs an actor has to bear in case his individually most preferred outcome is not the outcome of the collective choice. They conjecture that in comparison with unicameral systems bicameral systems have higher decision costs and continue:

'on the other hand, if the basis of representation can be made significantly different in the two houses, the institutions of the bicameral legislature may prove to be an effective means of securing a substantial reduction in the expected external costs of collective action without incurring as much added decision-making costs as a more inclusive rule would involve in a single house' (ibid., p. 235f.). The larger the majority required to reach a certain decision, the lower the external costs connected with that decision because the number of opponents to a decision is negatively correlated with the required majority. On the other hand, it will become increasingly difficult to reach a decision at all because the decision costs are positively correlated with the required majority. One possibility of keeping the external costs down is to require a supermajority (say of 3/4 or 5/6) in the single-house system. Supermajorities in a single-house system and simple majorities in a two-house system can thus be considered as alternatives. Buchanan and Tullock now conjecture that - given identical external costs - the decision costs would be lower in a bicameral than in a unicameral system.

Miller and Hammond (1989) inquire into the effects of bicameralism and the executive veto - which is sometimes simply considered the third chamber - on stability in the sense that it reduces the probability of cycling majorities à la Condorcet or Arrow (1951). They conclude that bicameralism and the executive veto increase stability. The stability-enhancing effect of bicameralism depends on some preference difference between the two chambers.

Levmore (1992) somewhat changes the focus of the analysis when he conjectures that a bicameral system might be better suited than a corresponding qualified majority in a unicameral system to reduce the power of the agenda setter. Bicameral systems are often interpreted as a break against overly active legislatures. Levmore relates this interpretation to the concept of federalism in a double sense: First, all federations have a bicameral legislature. Secondly, '(f)ederalism is likely to increase the chance of regulation because federal arrangements nearly always create some overlap in jurisdictional responsibilities so that there are multiple sources of regulation' (ibid., p. 159). According to Levmore, federations tend to produce active legislatures but come systematically along with bicameral systems which tend to reduce legislator activism.

Concerning the effects of bicameral systems, one could analyze whether the legislative activity in bicameral systems is indeed lower than in unicameral ones, whether this is reflected in government consumption of economic output and whether there are even different growth rates. For a clear-cut comparative analysis of institutions the description of the exact functioning of the institutions to be compared is, however, primordial. One would have to inquire how a mediation committee influences the functioning of a bicameral system and how a presidential veto influences the decision and the external costs. More general inquiries into the (economic) effects of the separation of powers could try to proceed by way of comparative institutional analysis, that is, by comparing common features of constitutions which do know a separation of powers with those which do not.

6.3 Direct-Democratic vs. Representative Institutions

Representatives of normative constitutional economics ask on what rules the members of a society could agree behind a veil of uncertainty. If they agree on a democratic constitution, they would further have to specify whether and to what extent they want to combine representative with direct-democratic elements. In order to make an informed decision, the citizens would be interested to know whether there are systematic relationships between these institutions and the patterns that they are interested in.

In a number of papers, Bruno Frey and his various co-authors argue that referenda are a feasible and effective institution for having the preferences of a society's members reflected in the public goods bundle produced by the politicians. Referenda could make politicians' cartels directed against the voters ineffective (Frey, 1994, p. 338). In 39 percent of the referenda that took place in Switzerland between 1848 and 1990, the majority among the population was different from the majority in Parliament (Frey and Bohnet, 1994, p. 73) which is interpreted as a proof of the hypothesis of a better reflection of voters preferences via referenda. Pommerehne already showed in 1978 that *ceteris paribus* tax rates are lower when taxpayers decide for themselves on the bundle of public goods supplied (for an overview over comparative studies, see Pommerehne, 1990). Additionally, taxpayer honesty is positively correlated with voters' chances to participate directly in the choice of the bundle of public goods to be supplied (Pommerehne and Frey, 1992).

6.4 Individual Rights and Economic Growth

The question of whether societies whose constitutions grant individual rights to their citizens grow faster than societies that do not has often been answered using 'democracy' as a proxy for individual rights. The results of those studies have been mixed at best (for a survey, see Przeworski and Limongi, 1993). Bhalla (1994) proposes to search for a relationship not between democracy and growth rates but between political, civil and economic rights on the one hand and growth rates on the other. He finds a positive correlation not only between individual liberty and economic growth but also between political and civil rights and enrollment in secondary schools and a negative one between political and civil rights and infantile mortality. Bhalla shows that the availability of human capital is a necessary but not a sufficient condition for sustained economic growth. This will only occur if economic liberties come along with human capital. His study is thus also a challenge of the so-called new growth theory. Up to now, the most comprehensive study on the relationship between individual economic liberties and growth is due to Gwartney, Lawson and Block (1996). For the period between 1975 and 1995, 103 countries are evaluated on an index comprising 17 components that puts special emphasis on the security of property rights and the freedom to contract. Two results are of special interest in this context: (1) There is a clearcut positive relation between individual economic liberty and per-capita income. There is reason to hypothesize that this not merely a correlation but also a causality: countries scoring best on the index of economic liberties first carried out liberalization and became wealthy only later on. (2) Economic liberties are also significantly correlated with a society's rates of economic growth. Countries that liberalized most between 1975 and 1995 without exception secured positive growth rates.

To sum up: Economic liberties seem to enhance economic growth. Direct-democratic rights tend to make sure that citizen preferences are better reflected in policy outcomes. A federal structure might help to tame Leviathan and make the economic liberties more secure. Some normative conclusions thus almost seem to suggest themselves. Before drawing them, one needs, however, to clarify the conditions that have to be fulfilled in order to implement any of the above institutions successfully.

C. Outlook

John Neville Keynes proposed a tripartite division of political economy, introducing the 'art of political economy' besides the more standard positive and normative branches. This art deals with possibilities of reducing differences between 'Is' and 'Ought' (Keynes, 1955). It almost suggests itself to conceive of an 'art of constitutional political economy' analogously. This art would itself have to have a positive foundation: knowledge about the possibilities to modify constitutions intentionally is primordial for such a third branch. If one thinks that constitutional economics is potentially relevant for real world constitution writers, then one must be disappointed with the degree to which insights from this research program have entered into the newly written constitutions of Central and Eastern Europe. In order to become more relevant, it seems essential to work on the third branch.

A central presumption of both branches presented in Sections 2 and 3 is that constitutional rules constrain human behavior and that they can therefore be relevant for explaining it. Representatives of the new institutional economics would broaden this presumption and claim that institutions in general constrain human behavior. It thus almost suggests itself to plead for an integration of constitutional economics into the new institutional economics. Whereas Brennan and Hamlin (1995) argue that one can conceptualize the 'new institutionalism' as a subordinate research program, one can also argue exactly the other way round: if one does not start with the assumption that constitutional design is possible to a large extent and if one is furthermore critical of the assumed hierarchy of rules, and rather points to the complex interdependence between informal constraints and formal rules (North, 1990) or between internal and external institutions (Kiwit and Voigt, 1995), one would tend to conceptualize constitutional economics as part of the new institutional economics.

Bibliography on Constitutional Law (9100)

Arrow, Kenneth (1951), *Social Choice and Individual Values*, New York, Wiley.

Bhalla, Surjit (1994), *Freedom and Economic Growth: A Virtuous Cycle?*, Nobel Symposium, Uppsala University.

Boudreaux, Donald J. and Pritchard, A.C. (1993), 'Rewriting the Constitution: An Economic Analysis of the Constitutional Amendment Process', **62** *Fordham Law Review*, 111-162.

Brennan, Geoffrey and Hamlin, Alan (1994), 'A Revisionist View of the Separation of Powes', **6(3)** *Journal of Theoretical Politics*, 345-368.

Brennan, Geoffrey and Hamlin, Alan (1995), 'Constitutional Political Economy: The Political Philosophy of Homo Economicus?', **3(3)** *The Journal of Political Philosophy*, 280-303.

Buchanan, James M. (1959), 'Positive Economics, Welfare Economics, and Political Economy', **2** *Journal of Law and Economics*, 124-38.

Buchanan, James M. (1975), *The Limits of Liberty - Between Anarchy and Leviathan*, Chicago, University of Chicago Press.

Buchanan, James M. (1977), *Freedom in Constitutional Contract - Perspectives of a Political Economist*, College Station and London, Texas A&M University Press.

Buchanan, James (1978), 'A Contractarian Perspective on Anarchy', in Pennock, J. Roland and Chapman, John W. (eds), *Anarchism: Nomos XIX*, New York, New York University Press, 29-42.

Buchanan, James (1986), 'Political Economy and Social Philosophy', in Buchanan, James M., *Liberty, Market and State - Political Economy in the 1980s*, New York, 261-274.

Buchanan, James M. (1987a), 'Constitutional Economics', in Eatwell, J., Milgate, M. and Newman, P. (eds), *The New Palgrave - A Dictionary of Economics*, London and Basingstoke, Macmillan, Vol. 1, 585-588.

Buchanan, James M. (1987b), 'The Constitution of Economic Policy', **77** *American Economic Review*, 243-250.

Buchanan, James M. and Tullock, Gordon (1962), *The Calculus of Consent - Logical Foundations of Constitutional Democracy*, Ann Arbor, University of Michigan Press.

Cooter, Robert D. and Ginsburg, Tom (1996), 'Comparative Judicial Discretion: An Empirical Test of Economic Models', **16(3)** *International Review of Law and Economics*, 295-313.

Elster, Jon (1991), *Arguing and Bargaining in two Constituent Assemblies*, The Storrs Lectures.

Elster, Jon (1993), 'Constitution-Making in Eastern Europe: Rebuilding the Boat in the Open Sea', **71(1/2)** *Public Administration*, 169-217.

Frey, Bruno S. (1994), 'Direct Democracy: Politico-Economic Lessons from Swiss Experience', **84** *American Economic Review*, 338-342.

Frey, Bruno S. and Bohnet, Iris (1994), 'Democracy by Competition: Referenda and Federalism in Switzerland'.

Gifford, Adam (1991), 'A Constitutional Interpretation of the Firm', **68** *Public Choice*, 91-106.

Goldwin, Robert A. and Kaufman, Art (eds) (1988), *Constitution-Makers on Constitution-Making*, Washington, DC, American Enterprise Institute.

Gwartney, James, Lawson, Robert, and Block, Walter (1996), *Economic Freedom of the World: 1975 - 1995*. Vancouver et al., The Fraser Institute et al.

International Review of Law and Economics (1992), Special Issue on Constitutional Law and Economics **12(2)**.

Keynes, John Neville (1955), *The Scope and Method of Political Economy*, New York, Kelley.

Kiwit, Daniel and Voigt, Stefan (1995), 'Überlegungen zum Institutionellen Wandel unter Berücksichtigung des Verhältnisses interner und Externer Institutionen', **46** *ORDO*, 117-147.

Levmore, Saul (1992), 'Bicameralism: When are Two Decisions Better than One?', **12** *International Review of Law and Economics*, 145-162.

McGuire, Robert A. and Ohsfeldt, Robert L. (1986), 'An Economic Model of Voting Behavior over Specific Issues at the Constitutional Convention of 1787', **46** *Journal of Economic History*, 79-111.

McGuire, Robert A. and Ohsfeldt, Robert L. (1989a), 'self-Interest, Agency Theory, and Political Voting Behavior: The Ratification of the United States Constitution', **79** *American Economic Review*, 219-234.

McGuire, Robert A. and Ohsfeldt, Robert L. (1989b), 'Public Choice Analysis and the Ratification of the Constitution', in Grofman, Bernard and Wittman, Donald (eds), *The Federalist Papers and the New Institutionalism*, New York, Agathon, 175-204.

Miller, Gary J. and Hammond, Thomas H. (1989), 'stability and Efficiency in a Separation-of-Powers Constitutional System', in Grofman, B. and Wittman, Donald (eds), *The Federalist Papers and the New Institutionalism,* New York, Agathon Press, 85-99.

Mueller, Dennis C. (1989), *Public Choice II*, Cambridge, Cambridge University Press.

Mueller, Dennis C. (1991), 'Constitutional Rights', **7** *Journal of Law, Economics, and Organisation*, 313-333.

Mueller, Dennis C. (1996), 'Constitutional Public Choice', in Mueller, Dennis C. (ed.), *Perspectives on Public Choice*, Cambridge, Cambridge University Press, 124-146.

North, Douglass C. (1981), *Structure and Change in Economic History*, New York, Norton.

North, Douglass C. (1990), *Institutions, Institutional Change and Economic Performance*, Cambridge, Cambrdige University Press.

North, Douglass C. and Weingast, Barry W. (1989), 'The Evolution of Institutions Governing Public Choice in 17th Century England', **49** *Journal of Economic History*, 803-832.

Pommerehne, Werner W. (1990), 'The Empirical Relevance of Comparative Institutional Analysis', **34** *European Economic Review*, 458-468.

Pommerehne, Werner W. and Frey, Bruno S. (1992), 'The Effects of Tax Administration on Tax Morale', paper presented at the Conference on Tax Administration and Tax Evasion of the International Seminar in Public Economics (ISPE), El Escorial (June).

Posner, Richard A. (1987), 'The Constitution as an Economic Document', **56(1)** *George Washington Law Review*, 4-38.

Przeworski, Adam, Limongi, F. (1993), 'Political Regimes and Economic Growth', **7(3)** *Journal of Economic Perspectives*, 51-69.

Rawls, John (1971), *A Theory of Justice*, Cambridge, Belknap.

Reisman, David (1990), *The Political Economy of James Buchanan*, College Station, Texas A & M.

Riker, William H. (1983), 'Political Theory and the Art of Heresthetics', in A. Finifter (ed.), *Political Science: the State of the Discipline*, Washington, DC, American Political Science Association, 47-67.

Riker, William H. (1984), 'The Heresthetics of Constitution-Making: The Presidency in 1787, with Comments on Determinism and Rational Choice', **78** *American Political Science Review*, 1-16.

Vanberg, Viktor J. (1992), 'Organizations as Constitutional Systems', **3** *Constitutional Political Economy*, 223-253.

Voigt, Stefan (1997), 'Bargaining for Constitutional Change', Discussion Paper 02/97 of the Max-Planck-Institute for Research Into Economic Systems, Jena, Germany.

Voigt, Stefan (1999), 'Implicit Constitutional Change - Changing the Meaning of the Constitution Without Changing the Text of the Document', **8** *Journal of Law and Economics*.

Wicksell, Knut (1896), *Finanztheoretische Untersuchungen*, Jena, Fischer.

9200
JUDGE-MADE LAW

Paul H. Rubin
Department of Economics, Emory University

Abstract

A major positive claim in the law and economics literature, due first to Posner, is that the common law is economically efficient. However, mechanisms to explain this putative efficiency are lacking. Posner's hypothesis is that judges gain utility from efficient decisions, and are constrained so that other decision criteria are limited. Evolutionary models of the law were devised to provide another mechanism for such efficiency, but these models, while proving very useful for some purposes, have not achieved this goal. Indeed, there are now evolutionary models of legal change driven by rent seeking by lawyers and others which lead to inefficient results. There is also a literature on multi-judge interactions, showing conditions under which such interactions will or will not lead to consistent results.

> At the heart of economic analysis of law is a mystery that is also an embarrassment: how to explain judicial behavior in economic terms....Posner (1993, p. 2)

JEL classification: K00, K41
Keywords: Common Law, Judges, Legal Evolution, Legal Efficiency, Efficiency of the Common Law

1. Introduction

As the quotation in the abstract indicates, explanation of the behavior of judges is one of the most important but also most difficult problems facing law and economics scholars. This is because judicial opinions are the result of utility-maximizing behavior and economists are unable to specify the details of judges' (or anyone else's) utility functions. Consequently, it has proven difficult to develop a theory that explains why judges make the decisions that we observe, though, as we discuss below, many have tried. Because of the difficulty of explaining decisions in terms of utility functions, there have also been attempts to use evolutionary models to explain outcomes. In these models, the form of law is due to factors involving wealth-maximizing behavior of actors in the legal process such as litigants or attorneys, and judges play a minor role.

The structure of this chapter is as follows: I first consider briefly arguments regarding the efficiency of common law. I then discuss utility-maximizing models of judicial behavior. I next consider the evolutionary models. The following section discusses models of multi-judge behavior.

2. Efficiency of Common Law

A basic question for law and economics is the efficiency of law. Hayek (1960, 1973), although writing before the law and economics movement and writing from another perspective, had argued that common or judge made law was better than statute law (see Christiansen, 1990, for an attempt to reconcile Hayekian arguments with law and economics). More recently, Posner (1992) has of course argued often and forcefully that the common law is efficient. His arguments are based on examination of particular legal doctrines. The difficulty of this method is that often the conclusion regarding the efficiency of a particular rule depends on unmeasured transactions costs of various sorts; if Posner's intuition about relative magnitudes of costs is incorrect, then doctrines he claims are efficient may not be so. Nonetheless, his analysis has been the intellectual spark behind the growth of law and economics, and questions of efficiency of the sort he was the first to raise have dominated the literature. Much of this literature may be considered as detailed attempts to answer the positive efficiency question first posed by Posner, and much of the rest aims at deriving normative conclusions as to what is efficient.

Others are less certain that common law is efficient. Tullock (1971, 1980) has long argued that the English common law process is less efficient than Continental processes. Rizzo (1980a, 1980b) argues from an Austrian perspective that the amount of information needed for judges to achieve efficiency is excessive, although Rubin (1980) in a critique argues that Rizzo's criticism might apply to efficiency in all of economics, not merely in law and economics. Aranson (1992) argues that it is impossible for judges to seek efficiency because the calculations required are equivalent to those required to make central planning work. Hadfield (1992b) has argued that because judges see only a biased sample of potential cases, depending on the rules in existence, it is impossible for judges to move towards efficiency, even if they desire to do so. Much of the literature in law and economics consists of attempts to examine particular legal doctrines and attempt to determine if they are efficient. (Much of my own work is of this type; see for example Rubin, 1983.) This method of analysis is fundamentally different from efficiency analysis in other branches of economics. There, a process (market competition) is postulated and it is shown that the process leads to efficient outcomes. Economists do not generally examine consumers to see if they are equating ratios of marginal utilities to prices, or firms to see if they are charging marginal cost. Rather, the process by which outcomes are generated is shown to lead to efficiency. It is for this reason that many economists are uncomfortable with the efficiency arguments of law and economics. Nonetheless, because this is the standard method in law and economics, any analysis of the efficiency of any particular body of law can be considered as evidence for or against Posner's hypothesis. If some law is found efficient, then this is evidence for the hypothesis. If some law is found inefficient, or if there are proposals for reform, then this is evidence against the hypothesis. In this sense, all of law and economics is aimed at testing this fundamental hypothesis.

Scholars are of course aware of this difficulty, and have sought to identify a process that would lead to efficiency. The two candidates are utility maximization by judges and evolutionary models. I discuss each. As we will see, there is no definitive demonstration in the literature of a mechanism that would lead to efficiency. This has led many to conclude that the law is not so efficient as Posner believes.

3. Utility Maximization

The first argument regarding utility maximization by judges was in Posner (1992, first edition, 1973). The argument (elaborated in Posner, 1993) is that judges are so insulated from personal factors and from interest group and other pressures that the only remaining decision factor is efficiency. The only other candidate is income redistribution, and judges lack the tools needed for such redistribution. This explanation was and is not terribly convincing to economists because it ultimately relies on judicial tastes for efficiency and economists prefer not to explain behavior on this basis.

There have been some attempts to model judicial utility functions in terms of economically relevant and observable variables. The first such effort was by Higgins and Rubin (1980). They argued that promotion to a higher position was an element of judicial utility functions, that promotion was more likely if the judge was reversed less, and that the value of promotion was reduced as the judge became older. However, in their sample they were unable to find any relation between age or any other factor and reversal, and only a weak relation between reversal and promotion.

In two articles, Cohen continued to examine promotion possibilities for federal judges. His argument was that if the Justice Department recommended a judge, then promotion was more likely. In Cohen (1991) he examined voting on the constitutionality of the US Sentencing Commission and found that judges voting for constitutionality were more likely to be promoted; the Justice Department favored this position. In Cohen (1992) he found that judges who imposed more severe antitrust sanctions, again in line with the desires of the

Department, were more likely to be promoted. Thus, there is evidence for normal utility maximization by judges. The problem is that it is difficult to see how these results generalize to explain other types of decisions, including common law decisions. Macey (1994) has argued that many rules of procedure are aimed at maximizing judicial utility - for example by emphasizing procedure, where judges have a comparative advantage, over substance, where they do not.

Landes and Posner (1980) examined differences between state court judges and federal court judges. Their hypothesis was that since federal judges are paid more and have life tenure, we would expect higher quality people to occupy these positions and write better opinions. Their measures of quality had to do with citations to opinions as discussed in Landes and Posner (1976) and with use of opinions in legal casebooks. Except for the last measure, they found little difference. Other variables such as age and the political party appointing the judge also had little influence. Ashenfelter, Eisenberg and Schwab (1995) examined the extent to which judicial decisions are influenced by the political party appointing the judge and other elements of the judges' personal background. They find little or no influence. Thus, if we believe that these characteristics influence the judges' utility function, this may be taken as an argument that this aspect of utility has little impact.

It is apparent that there is little evidence regarding the effect of utility maximization on the mass of case outcomes. This is clearly an area for future research.

4. Evolutionary Models

The evolutionary models are attempts to explain judicial behavior without resort to utility functions. Initially, these models aimed at explaining Posner's putative observation that the common law was efficient. It is fair to say that the models failed in this endeavor, perhaps because the law is not so efficient as Posner argued. Nonetheless, these models have had an important impact on the literature because they have called attention to forces other than judicial preferences in explaining the law. The evolutionary models are ultimately based on the model of the litigation process first set forth by Landes (1971).

The first paper applying an evolutionary model to the common law was Rubin (1977). Following Landes (1971) Rubin argued that most cases are settled, rather than litigated, and that it is only litigated cases that can lead to legal change. Cases are settled when the expected value to the plaintiff of a case is less than the expected cost to the defendant, which is generally true if stakes are symmetric. However, inefficient laws can sometimes create asymmetric stakes because the inefficiency means that there are deadweight losses that cannot be bargained away in the settlement process. That is, an inefficient rule creates a loss to one party that is greater than the gain to the other because of future stakes in similar type cases. Thus, litigation becomes more likely when rules are inefficient, and so inefficient rules are subject to greater selection pressure, and more likely to be overturned. (Note that this model, like many of its successors, depends on parties having ongoing interests in disputes of a certain sort, rather than merely in the matter at hand.)

Following this initial contribution were several extensions and modifications. Priest (1977) argued that inefficient rules generated larger stakes and so were more likely to be litigated, again subjecting them to increased selection pressure. Goodman (1979) argued that efficient precedents were worth more to parties who would benefit than inefficient precedents were worth to their beneficiaries, and that parties to whom a decision was worth more would spend more litigating and so would be more likely to win. In other words, efficient precedents were more likely to win in litigation and survive than were inefficient precedents. Katz (1988) expanded on this notion in the context of presenting a model of litigation expenditures. Terrebonne (1981) also presented a model of efficient legal evolution.

Other scholars began critically examining these models. Landes and Posner (1979) in a symposium paper published in the *Journal of Legal Studies* argued that the earlier models had erred by modeling precedent as an all or nothing issue, when the proper question was whether a precedent was stronger or weaker. That is, litigation might strengthen or weaken a precedent without overturning it completely. Thus a party with an interest in overturning an inefficient precedent would also have to consider the possibility that litigation could strengthen as well as weaken the precedent. This consideration greatly weakens the evolutionary pressures for efficiency. Parsons (1983) combined Priest's point (that inefficient precedents would lead to increasing litigation) with the Landes and Posner point (that precedents that were litigated might become entrenched) to argue that there is a tendency for the common law to become 'reckless' - to favor rules that inefficiently lead to increased accidents.

Cooter et al. (1979) presented a model in which movement towards efficiency could only occur if judges sought such a movement. In a more elaborate examination of the issue, Cooter and Kornhauser (1980) present a complex evolutionary model in which there are some tendencies towards efficiency, but in which both efficient and inefficient rules will be observed at any time. This model, and alternative definitions and implications of efficiency, are discussed in Kornhauser (1980). Von Wagenheim (1993) presents a model with similar results.

Hirshleifer (1982), building on Rubin's discussion of inefficiency when stakes in precedent are asymmetric, provided what may be the most useful and influential criticism of the evolutionary models. Recall that in the original Rubin (1977) model and in some others, including Goodman (1979) and Landes and Posner (1979) evolutionary forces moved the law towards efficiency only if the party with an interest in efficiency had an ongoing interest in the form of the law.

Hirshleifer generalized this point to show that the law could come to favor whichever party could most easily organize and mobilize resources for litigation of unfavorable precedents. This movement would be independent of efficiency. Rubin (1982) uses this point to argue that common law was more like statute law than many want to admit: interest groups could use either common or statute law to achieve their goals. He argued that the apparent efficiency of the common law was because most common law was developed at a time when organization of interest groups was expensive, and that more recently both common and statute law have been subject to interest group pressures. Crew and Twight (1990) expanded on this point and found common law less subject to rent seeking than statute law. Rowley and Brough (1987) find that contract and property might be expected to be efficient, but not tort. Bailey and Rubin (1994) have extended this theme in a formal model of the influence of interest groups on the law, and Rubin and Bailey (1994) have shown that plaintiffs' attorneys have been responsible for the shape of modern tort law, using an evolutionary mechanism to shape the law. An interesting question worthy of future exploration is the extent to which other interest groups have found litigating for precedent worthwhile.

Heiner (1986) explains stare decisis and other features of the law as a result of human imperfect decision making. Because attempts to achieve optimality in each decision might lead to erroneous decisions in many cases, it may be more efficient to rely on rather simple rules that minimize the potential costs of error.

An interesting set of hypotheses regarding legal evolution is in Roe (1996). Roe argues that the notion of evolution towards efficiency is an important determinant of legal form, but it is not the only determinant. He incorporates three subsidiary notions into an efficiency framework - the importance of initial conditions (borrowed from chaos theory), path dependence and evolutionary accidents. The result of these processes would be that laws would be well but not perfectly adapted. However, while these notions are interesting, as Roe himself admits, they do not as of yet provide refutable hypotheses. It would be interesting to see if these propositions can be generalized to provide some implications.

What can we say about the evolutionary models? They have not succeeded in the original task of providing an explanation for common law efficiency. However, by demonstrating the difficulty of achieving this goal, they have helped understand when the law may be efficient and when it is likely not to be efficient. Moreover, an important component of the evolutionary models was their focus on the litigation decision as driving legal evolution. Other models of legal evolution, both economic and non-economic, either leave mechanisms for evolution unspecified or assume that the preferences of judges are the driving forces. The economic models were the first to focus on the motives of litigants, realizing that judges can decide only those cases that come before them.

As Elliott (1985, p. 71), in an important study of the history of evolutionary models, indicates: 'Moreover, the economic school of evolution has broadened our view of the legal system to include the role of litigants, as well as judges, in making law.' The literature associated with Priest and Klein (1984) on selectivity bias in case selection is a result of the focus on litigants' decisions, which has come out of the evolutionary models; for a discussion, see Priest (1980). (For an analysis of theories of legal evolution from 1880-1940 (which thus omits analysis of the economic theories) see Hovenkamp, 1985.)

Aranson (1986) summarizes the assumptions of several of the evolutionary models. He shows that many combinations of assumptions have not been examined, and thus provides clues for further research. There is much useful research to be done on evolutionary models of legal change.

5. Multi-Judge Interactions

Matters become more complex when more than one judge is involved in a decision or sequence of decisions. Multiple judges may be involved because a judicial panel may consist of more than one judge; because different judges may hear similar cases at different times; or because the appellate process may involve judges at different levels of a judicial hierarchy hearing the same case.

One issue that appears when panels of judges hear a matter is the potential for inconsistency. Easterbrook (1982) was the first to point out that the Arrow theorem (which shows that there is no way of aggregating preferences that is not subject to some flaw, and that, for example, majority voting can lead to cycles: A defeats B, B defeats C, C defeats A) also applies to judicial voting; see also Easterbrook (1984).

Kornhauser has written extensively on issues that arise in multi-judge settings, both alone and with Sager. Kornhauser and Sager (1986) apply the Condorcet Jury Theorem to the context of judicial panels and show that increasing the number of judges on a panel will increase the accuracy of the outcome. In addition, they argue that multi-judge panels can act consistently (in the sense of avoiding cycles) but that multi-judge panels may act incoherently, in the sense that the pattern of decision will not satisfy community principles of coherent explanation.

In two related papers Kornhauser (1992a, 1992b) investigated several additional characteristics of collegial courts. He emphasized the dichotomous nature of common law adjudication. He argued further that judges had to respect the results rather than the rules or rationales of prior decisions. In this context, he showed that, except under implausible conditions, a legal system will be path dependent; that is, the state of the law at any time will be a result of the order in which the court has heard disputes. This path dependence, however, will not lead to inconsistency if the legal system observes strict stare decisis.

Next, Kornhauser observed that common law practice incorporates two distinct ways of aggregating judgments of multiple judges: courts may resolve matters on a case-by-case or on an issue-by-issue basis. Kornhauser shows that there is a 'doctrinal paradox' in that these two methods may lead to different outcomes. He shows that the doctrinal paradox is distinct from the Condorcet paradox. Kornhauser and Sager (1993) extend the analysis of the doctrinal paradox in several ways. They observe, for instance, that in actual practice each judge decides how to aggregate the votes of other members on the court and that this may affect the outcome.

Kornhauser (1995) considers the hierarchical structure of courts systems. It explains many of the features of the US judicial system through a simple production model. Kornhauser assumes that judges in the system form a team, in that they all want the same goal, the maximization of the 'number of correct answers subject to its resource constraint'. Then the structure of the production function explains the pattern of precedent observed and the specialization of trial courts to fact finding and appellate courts to review of law. Other features, such as the lack of specialization of courts by subject matter, are not explained by the model.

Miceli and Cosgel (1994) and Rasmusen (1994) have argued that judges' behavior is based on a tradeoff between writing decisions they prefer and the possibility of reversal, either by higher courts or by future judges. O'Hara (1993) analyzes why appellate judges choose to follow precedents in the absence of any formal rule mandating adherence to precedent. She explains this behavior as the result of a repeated game between different appellate judges, each of whom follows the precedents established by his or her colleagues' decisions in order to avoid triggering a 'punishment' phase. In this punishment phase the precedents established by the errant judge's decisions are ignored by his or her colleagues. Shavell (1995) argues that the structure of the appellate process is a low cost method of error correction, since only a subset of cases are examined for error through an appeal.

Bibliography on Judge-Made Law (9200)

Alexander, Janet Cooper (1994), 'Judges' Self Interest and Procedural Rules: Comment', **23** *Journal of Legal Studies*, 647-665.

Alpa, Guido, Pulitini, Francesco, Rodota, Stefano and Romani, Franco (1982), *Interpretazione Giuridica e Analisi Economica* (Legal Interpretation and Economic Analysis), Milano, Giuffrè, 662 p.

Aranson, Peter H. (1986), 'Economic Efficiency and the Common Law: A Critical Survey', in Graf von der Schulenburg, J.-Matthias and Skogh, Göran (eds), *Law and Economics and the Economics of Legal Regulation*, Dordrecht, Kluwer, 51-84.

Aranson, Peter H. (1992), 'The Common Law as Central Economic Planning', **3** *Constitutional Political Economy*, 289-317.

Armitage, Thomas C. (1985), 'Economic Efficiency as a Legal Norm', **7** *Research in Law and Economics*, 1-27.

Ashenfelter, Orley, Eisenberg, Theodore and Schwab, Stewart J. (1995), 'Politics and the Judiciary: The Influence of Judicial Background on Case Outcomes', **24** *Journal of Legal Studies*, 257-81.

Backhaus, Jürgen G. (1989), 'Efficient Statute Law', in Faure, Michael and Van den Bergh, Roger (eds), *Essays in Law and Economics. Corporations, Accident Prevention and Compensation for Losses*, Antwerpen, Maklu, 23-32.

Bailey, Martin J. and Rubin, Paul H. (1994), 'A Positive Theory of Legal Change', **14** *International Review of Law and Economics*, 467-77.

Benson, Bruce L. (1990), *The Enterprise of Law: Justice Without the State*, San Francisco, Pacific Research Institute for Public Policy.

Benson, Bruce L. (1992), 'Market Failure versus Government Failure in the Production of Adjudication', in Bowman, Gary, Hakim, Simon and Seidenstat, Paul (eds), *Privatizing the United States Justice System: Police, Adjudication, and Corrections Services from the Private Sector*, Jefferson, NC, McFarland & Co., 203-225.

Benson, Bruce L. (1995), 'An Exploration of the Impact of Modern Arbitration Statutes on the Development of Arbitration in the United States', **11** *Journal of Law, Economics, and Organization*, 479-501.

Benson, Bruce L. (1996), 'Uncertainty, the Race for Property Rights, and Rent Dissipation due to Judicial Changes in Product Liability Tort Law', *Cultural Dynamics*.

Benson, Bruce L. and Wollan, Laurin A., Jr (1991), 'Increasing Judicial Responsibility can Reduce Prison Overcrowding', in Tipp, Stacey L. (ed.), *America's Prisons: Opposing Viewpoints*, San Diego, Greenhaven Press, 139-144.

Blume, Lawrence E. and Rubinfeld, Daniel L. (1982), 'The Dynamics of the Legal Process', **11** *Journal of Legal Studies*, 405-420.

Bruce, Christopher J. (1984), 'Testing the Hypothesis of Common Law Efficiency: The Doctrine of Informed Consent', **6** *Research in Law and Economics*, 227-265.

Bruce, Christopher J. (1988), 'The Adjudication of Labor Disputes as a Private Good', **8** *International Review of Law and Economics*, 3-19.

Buchanan, James M. (1978), 'Law and the Invisible Hand', in Siegan, Bernard H. (ed.), *The Interaction of Economics and the Law*, Lexington, Lexington Books.

Carrington, Paul D. (1979), 'Adjudication as a Private Good: A Comment', **8** *Journal of Legal Studies*, 303-317.

Che, Yeon Koo and Yi, Jong Goo (1993), 'The Role of Precedents in Repeated Litigation', **9** *Journal of Law, Economics and Organization*, 399-424.

Christiansen, Gregory B. (1990), 'Law as a Discovery Procedure', **9** *Cato Journal*, 497-530.

Chubb, Larry L. (1989), 'Economic Analysis in the Courts: Limits and Constraints', **64** *Indiana Law Journal*, 769-801.

Clark, Robert C. (1981), 'The Interdisciplinary Study of "Legal Evolution"', **90** *Yale Law Journal*, 1238-1274.

Cohen, George M. (1985), 'Posnerian Jurisprudence and Economic Analysis of Law: The View from the Bench', **133** *University of Pennsylvania Law Review*, 1117-1166.

Cohen, Mark A. (1991), 'Explaining Judicial Behavior or What's "Unconstitutional" about the Sentencing Commission?', **7** *Journal of Law, Economics, and Organization*, 183-199.

Cohen, Mark A. (1992), 'The Motives of Judges: Empirical Evidence from Antitrust Sentencing', **12** *International Review of Law and Economics*, 13 ff.

Cooter, Robert D. (1983), 'The Objectives of Private and Public Judges', **41** *Public Choice*, 107-132.

Cooter, Robert D. (1987), 'Liberty, Efficiency, and Law', **50 (4)** *Law and Contemporary*

Problems, 141-163.

Cooter, Robert D. (1990), *The Structural Approach to Adjudicating Social Norms: Evolution of the Common Law Reconsidered*, Working Paper, School of Law, University of California at Berkeley.

Cooter, Robert (1992), 'The Minimax Constitution as Democracy', **12 (2)** *International Review of Law and Economics*, 292-94.

Cooter, Robert D. and Kornhauser, Lewis A. (1980), 'Can Litigation Improve the Law without the Help of Judges?', **9** *Journal of Legal Studies*,139-163.

Cooter, Robert D. and Rubinfeld, Daniel L. (1989), 'Economic Analysis of Legal Disputes and Their Resolution,' **27 (3)** *Journal of Economic Literature*, 1092 ff.

Cooter, Robert D., Kornhauser, Lewis A. and Lane, D. (1979), 'Liability Rules, Limited Information, and the Role of Precedent', **10** *Bell Journal of Economics*, 366-373.

Cramton, Roger C. (1959), 'The Supreme Court and the Decline of State Power', **2** *Journal of Law and Economics*, 175-189.

Crew, Michael A. and Twight, Charlotte (1990), 'On the Efficiency of Law: A Public Choice Perspective', **66** *Public Choice*, 15-136.

Culp, Jerome M. (1987), 'Judex Economicus', **50(4)** *Law and Contemporary Problems*, 95-140.

Davis, Otto A. (1979), 'Public and Private Characteristics of a Legal Process: A Comment', **8** *Journal of Legal Studies*, 285-293.

Daynard, Richard A. (1971), 'Use of Social Policy in Judicial Decision-Making', **56** *Carnell Law Review*, 919-950.

De Alessi, Louis (1985), 'Property Rights and the Judiciary', **4** *Cato Journal*, 805-811. Reprinted in Dorn, James A. and Manne, Henry G. (eds) (1987), *Economic Liberties and the Judiciary*, Fairfax, George Mason University Press, 175-181.

Denzau, Arthur (1979), 'Litigation Expenditures as Private Determinants of Judicial Decisions: A Comment', **8** *Journal of Legal Studies*, 295-302.

Dicke, Hugo and Hartung, Hans (1986), 'Externe Kosten von Rechtsvorschriften (External Effects of Legal Rules)', in *Möglichkeiten und Grenzen der ökonomischen Gesetzesanalyse*, Tübingen, J.C.B. Mohr, 123 ff.

Easterbrook, Frank H. (1982), 'Ways of Criticizing the Court', **95** *Harvard Law Review*, 802 ff.

Easterbrook, Frank H. (1984), 'The Supreme Court, 1983 Term, Foreword: The Court and the Economic System', **98** *Harvard Law Review*, 4-60.

Easterbrook, Frank H. (1992), 'Some Tasks in Understanding Law through the Lens of Public Choice: General Panel Commentary', **12** *International Review of Law and Economics*, 284-288.

Eisenberg, Melvin Aron (1988), *The Nature of the Common Law*, Cambridge, MA, Harvard University Press, 204 ff.

Ellickson, Robert C. (1989), 'A Hypothesis of Wealth-Maximizing Norms: Evidence from the Whaling Industry', **5** *Journal of Law, Economics, and Organization*, 83-97.

Elliott, E. Donald (1985), 'The Evolutionary Tradition in Jurisprudence', **85** *Columbia Law Review*, 38-94.

Epstein, Richard A. (1980), 'The Static Conception of the Common Law', **9** *Journal of Legal Studies*, 253-275.

Epstein, Richard A. (1982), 'The Social Consequences of Common Law Rules', **95** *Harvard Law Review*, 1717-1751.

Epstein, Richard A. (1987), 'Judicial Review: Reckoning on Two Kinds of Error', in Dorn, James A. and Manne, Henry G. (eds), *Economic Liberties and the Judiciary*, Fairfax,

George Mason University Press, 39-46.
Fox, Eleanor M. (1986), 'The Politics of Law and Economics in Judicial Decision Making: Antitrust as a Window', **61** *New York University Law Review*, 554-588.
Friedman, David (1979), 'Private Creation and Enforcement of Law: A Historical Case', **8** *Journal of Legal Studies*, 399-415.
Gerhart, Peter M. (1982), 'The Supreme Court and Antitrust Analysis: The (Near) Triumph of the Chicago School', **1982** *Supreme Court Review*, 319-349.
Goldberg, Victor P. (ed.) (1979), 'Discussion by Seminar Participants', **8** *Journal of Legal Studies*, 323-398.
Golbert, J.P. and Lowenstein, Paul (1982), 'The Court and the Marketplace: Who Should Regulate Whom?', **34** *Baylor Law Review*, 39-65.
Goodman, John C. (1979), 'An Economic Theory of the Evolution of the Common Law', **7** *Journal of Legal Studies*, 235 ff.
Greenwalt, Kent (1977), 'Policy, Rights and Judicial Decision', **11** *Georgia Law Review*, 991-1053.
Hadfield, Gillian K. (1992a), 'Incomplete Contracts and Statutes: Commentary', **12** *International Review of Law and Economics*, 257-259.
Hadfield, Gillian K. (1992b), 'Biases in the Evolution of Legal Rules,' **80** *Georgetown Law Journal*, 583-616.
Harris, Peter (1985), 'Difficult Cases and the Display of Authority', **1** *Journal of Law, Economics, and Organization*, 209-221.
Hayek, Friedrich A. (1960), *The Constitution of Liberty*, Chicago, University of Chicago Press.
Hayek, Friedrich A. (1973), *Law, Legislation, and Liberty*, **1** *Rules and Order*, Chicago, University of Chicago Press.
Hazard, Geoffrey C., Jr (1979), 'Adjudication as a Private Good: A Comment', **8** *Journal of Legal Studies*, 319-321.
Heiner, Ronald A. (1986), 'Imperfect Decisions and the Law: On the Evolution of Legal Precedent and Rules', **15** *Journal of Legal Studies*, 227-261.
Higgins, Richard S. and Rubin, Paul H. (1980), 'Judicial Discretion', **9** *Journal of Legal Studies*, 129-138.
Hirshleifer, Jack (1982), 'Evolutionary Models in Economics and Law', **4** *Research in Law and Economics*.
Holmes, Oliver Wendell (1880), *The Common Law*, Boston, Little Brown.
Hovenkamp, Herbert (1985), 'Evolutionary Models in Jurisprudence,' **64** *Texas Law Review*, 645-685.
Kaplow, Louis (1987), 'Antitrust, Law and Economics, and the Courts', **50 (4)** *Law and Contemporary Problems*, 181-216.
Katz, Avery (1988), 'Judicial Decisionmaking and Litigation Expenditure', **8** *International Review of Law and Economics*, 127-143.
Kennedy, Duncan (1981), 'Cost-Reduction Theory as Legitimation', **90** *Yale Law Journal*, 1275-1283.
Kenny, Paul (1982), 'Economic Analysis and Efficiency in the Common Law', in Cranston, Ross and Schick, Anne (eds), *Law and Economics*, Canberra, Australian National University, 42-58.
Kobayashi, Bruce H. and Lott, John R., Jr (1994), 'Judicial Reputation and the Efficiency of the Common Law', mimeo, George Mason University.
Kornhauser, Lewis A. (1980), 'A Guide to the Perplexed Claims of Efficiency in the Law', **8** *Hofstra Law Review*, 591-639.

Kornhauser, Lewis A. (1989a), 'An Economic Perspective of Stare Decisis', **65** *Chicago-Kent Law Review*, 63-92.

Kornhauser, Lewis A. (1989b), 'Response to Macey', **65** *Chicago-Kent Law Review*, 115-122.

Kornhauser, Lewis A. (1992a), 'Modeling Collegial Courts I: Path Dependence', **12** *International Review of Law and Economics*, 169-185.

Kornhauser, Lewis A. (1992b), 'Modeling Collegial Courts. II. Legal Doctrine', **8** *Journal of Law, Economics and Organization*, 441-470.

Kornhauser, Lewis (1995), 'Adjudication by a Resource-Constrained Team: Hierarchy and Precedent in a Judicial System', **68** *Southern California Law Review*, 1605 ff.

Kornhauser, Lewis (1996), 'Notes on the Logic of Legal Change', in David Braybrooke (ed.), *Social Rules: Origin, Character, Logic, Change*, Westview Press.

Kornhauser, Lewis and Sager, L. (1986), 'Unpacking the Court', **96** *Yale Law Journal*, 82ff.

Kornhauser, Lewis A. and Sager, Lawrence G. (1993), 'The One and the Many: Adjudication in Collegial Courts', **81** *California Law Review*, 1 ff.

Kornhauser, Lewis, Cooter, Robert and Lane, D. (1979), 'Liability Rules, Limited Information, and the Role of Precedent', **10** *Bell Journal of Economics*, 366 ff.

Kübler, Friedrich (1990), 'Effizienz als Rechtsprinzip - Überlegungen zum rechtspraktischen Gebrauch ökonomischer Argumente (Efficiency as Legal Principle - Considerations for the Legal Practice Use of Economic Arguments)', in Baur, Jürgen F., Hopt, Klaus J. and Mailänder, Peter K. (eds), *Festschrift für Ernst Steindorff*, Berlin, de Gruyter, 687-704.

Landes, William M. (1971), 'An Economic Analysis of the Courts', **14** *Journal of Law and Economics*, 61-107.

Landes, William M. and Posner, Richard A. (1976), 'Legal Precedent: A Theoretical and Empirical Analysis', **19** *Journal of Law and Economics*, 249-307.

Landes, William M. and Posner, Richard A. (1979), 'Adjudication as a Private Good', **8** *Journal of Legal Studies*, 235-284.

Landes, William and Posner , Richard (1980), 'Legal Change, Judicial Behavior, and the Diversity Jurisdiction, **9** *Journal of Legal Studies*, 367-386.

Landes, William and Posner, Richard (1987), *The Economic Structure of Tort Law*, Cambridge, Harvard University Press.

Latin, Howard (1987), 'Legal and Economic Considerations in the Decisions of Judge Breyer', **50 (4)** *Law and Contemporary Problems*, 57-86.

Liebeler, Wesley J. (1985), 'A Property Rights Approach to Judicial Decision Making', **4** *Cato Journal*, 783-804. Reprinted in Dorn, James A. and Manne, Henry G. (eds) (1987), *Economic Liberties and the Judiciary*, Fairfax, George Mason University Press, 153-174.

Liebermann, Yehoshua (1986), 'Economic Efficiency and Making of the Law: The Case of Transaction Costs in Jewish Law', **15** *Journal of Legal Studies*, 387-404.

Linder, Douglas O. (1989), 'Some Doubts Concerning the Selection Hypothesis of George Priest', **37** *University of Kansas Law Review*, 319-347.

Macey, Jonathan R. (1989), 'The Internal and External Costs and Benefits of Stare Decisis', **65** *Chicago-Kent Law Review*, 93-113.

Macey, Jonathan R. (1994), 'Judicial Preferences, Public Choice, and the Rules of Procedure', **23** *Journal of Legal Studies*, 627-46.

Magat, Wesley A. (1987), 'Howard Latin's Analysis of the Legal and Economic Considerations in the Decisions of Judge Breyer', **50** *Law and Contemporary Problems*, 87-93.

Mcnollgast (1992), 'The Theory of Interpretive Canon and Legislative Behavior:

Commentary', **12** *International Review of Law and Economics*, 235-238.

Mendelson, Wallace (1961), 'The Politics of Judicial Supremacy', **4** *Journal of Law and Economics*, 175-185.

Miceli, Thomas J. and Cosgel, Metin M. (1994), 'Reputation and Judicial Decision-Making', **23** *Journal of Economic Behavior and Organization*, 31-51.

Michelman, Frank I. (1978), 'Norms and Normativity in the Economic Theory of Law', **62** *Minnesota Law Review*, 1015-1048.

Miller, Geoffrey P. (1989), 'Comment: Some Thoughts on the Equilibrium Hypothesis', **69** *Boston University Law Review*, 561-568.

O'Hara, Erin (1993), 'Social Constraint or Implicit Collusion?: Toward a Game Theoretic Analysis of Stare Decisis', **24** *Seton Hall Law Review*, 736-778.

Parsons, Wes (Student Contribution) (1983), 'The Inefficient Common Law', **92** *Yale Law Journal*, 863-887.

Polinsky, A. Mitchell and Rubinfeld, Daniel L. (1988), 'The Deterrent Effects of Settlements and Trials', **8** *International Review of Law and Economics*, 109-116.

Pollock, Stewart G. (1988), 'Economic Analysis at Work in Judicial Decision-Making', *Annual Survey of American Law*, 133-136.

Posner, Richard A. (1980), 'The Ethical and Political Basis of the Efficiency Norm in Common Law Adjudication', **8** *Hofstra Law Review*, 487-507.

Posner, Richard A. (1981a), 'A Reply to Some Recent Criticisms of the Efficiency Theory of the Common Law', **9** *Hofstra Law Review*, 775 ff.

Posner, Richard A. (1981b), 'The Present Situation in Legal Scholarship', **90** *Yale Law Journal*, 1113-1130.

Posner, Richard A. (1985), *The Federal Courts: Crisis and Reform*, Cambridge, MA, Harvard University Press, 365 ff.

Posner, Richard A. (1992), *Economic Analysis of Law*, 4th edn, Little, Brown, Boston.

Posner, Richard A. (1993), 'What do Judges Maximize? (The Same Thing Everybody Else Does),' **3** *Supreme Court Economic Review*, 1-41.

Priest, George L. (1977), 'The Common Law Process and the Selection of Efficient Rules', **6** *Journal of Legal Studies*, 65-82.

Priest, George L. (1980), 'Selective Characteristics of Litigation', **9** *Journal of Legal Studies*, 399 ff.

Priest, George L. (1981b), 'The New Scientism in Legal Scholarship: A Comment on Clark and Posner', **90** *Yale Law Journal*, 1284-1295.

Priest, George (1985), 'The Invention of Enterprise Liability: A Critical History of the Intellectual Foundations of Modern Tort Law', **14** *Journal of Legal Studies*, 461-528.

Priest, George L. (1987), 'Measuring Legal Change', **3** *Journal of Law, Economics, and Organization*, 193-225.

Priest, George L. and Klein, Benjamin (1984), 'The Selection of Disputes for Litigation', **13** *Journal of Legal Studies*, 1 ff.

Rasmusen, Eric (1994), 'Judicial Legitimacy as a Repeated Game', **10** *Journal of Law, Economics and Organization*, 63-83.

Richter, Rudolf (1987), 'The Efficiency of the Common Law: A New Institutional Economics Perspective: Comment', in Pethig, Rudiger and Schlieper, Ulrich (eds), *Efficiency, Institutions, and Economic Policy: Proceedings of a Workshop Held by the Sonderforschungsbereich 5 at the University of Mannheim*, June 1986, New York, Springer, 123-125.

Rizzo, Mario J. (1979), 'Uncertainty, Subjectivity and the Economic Analysis of Law', in Rizzo, Mario J. (ed.), *Time, Uncertainty and Disequilibrium*, Lexington, Lexington

Books, 71-89.

Rizzo, Mario J. (1980a), 'The Mirage of Efficiency', **8** *Hofstra Law Review*, 641-658.

Rizzo, Mario J. (1980b), 'Law Amid Flux: The Economics of Negligence and Strict Liability in Tort', **9** *Journal of Legal Studies*, 291 ff.

Rizzo, Mario J. (ed.) (1980c), 'Symposium: Change in the Common Law: Legal and Economic Perspectives. A Symposium Sponsored by The Institute for Humane Studies and the Liberty Fund', **9** *Journal of Legal Studies*, 189-427.

Rizzo, Mario J. (1980d), 'Can There be a Principle of Explanation in Common Law Decisions? A Comment on Priest', **9** *Journal of Legal Studies*, 423-427.

Rizzo, Mario J. (1985), 'Rules versus Cost-Benefit Analysis in the Common Law', **4** *Cato Journal*, 865-884. Reprinted in Dorn, James A. and Manne, Henry G. (eds) (1987), *Economic Liberties and the Judiciary*, Fairfax, George Mason University Press, 1987, 225-244.

Rizzo, Mario J. and Arnold, Frank S. (1987), 'An Economic Framework for Statutory Interpretation', **50** *Law and Contemporary Problems*, 165-180.

Roberts, Neal A. (1980), 'Beaches: The Efficiency of the Common Law and Other Fairy Tales', **28** *UCLA Law Review*, 169-196.

Roe, Mark J. (1996), 'Chaos and Evolution in Law and Economics', **109** *Harvard Law Review*, 641-668.

Romano, Roberta (1992), 'Judicial Choice of Legal Doctrines: Comment', **8** *Journal of Law, Economics and Organization*, 47-58.

Rose-Ackerman, Susan (1987), 'Tullock and the Inefficiency of the Common Law', in Rowley, Charles K. (ed.), *Democracy and Public Choice: Essays in Honor of Gordon Tullock*, Oxford, Blackwell, 181-185.

Rowley, Charles K. (1987), 'Comment: A Public Choice Perspective on Judicial Pragmactivism', in Dorn, James A. and Manne, Henry G. (eds), *Economic Liberties and the Judiciary*, Fairfax, George Mason University Press, 219-224.

Rowley, Charles K. and Brough, Wayne (1987), 'The Efficiency of the Common Law: A New Institutional Economics Perspective', in Pethig, Rudiger and Schlieper, Ulrich (eds), *Efficiency, Institutions, and Economic Policy: Proceedings of a Workshop Held by the Sonderforschungsbereich 5 at the University of Mannheim*, New York, Springer, 103-121.

Rubin, Paul H. (1977), 'Why is the Common Law Efficient?', **6** *Journal of Legal Studies*, 51-63.

Rubin, Paul H. (1980), 'Decision Making and the Efficiency of Law: A Comment on Rizzo', **9** *Journal of Legal Studies*, 319-334.

Rubin, Paul H. (1982), 'Common Law and Statute Law', **11** *Journal of Legal Studies*, 205-223.

Rubin, Paul H. (1983), *Business Firms and the Common Law. The Evolution of Efficient Rules*, New York, Praeger, 189 ff.

Rubin, Paul H. and Bailey, Martin J. (1994), 'The Role of Lawyers in Changing the Law', **23** *Journal of Legal Studies*, 807 ff.

Sajó, András (1981), 'A Gazdaság jogi Szabályozásának egy Lehetséges útja (A Possible Way of Legal Regulation of the Economy)', **4** *Jogtudományi Közlöny*, 297-308.

Sajó, András (1987), 'A jog a Gazdaság Szabályozástechnikái Közt (Law as One of the Regulating Means of the Economy)', **3** *Jogtudományi Közlöny*, 126-132.

Samuels, Warren J. and Mercuro, Nicholas (1984), 'Posnerian Law and Economics on the Bench', **4** *International Review of Law and Economics*, 107-130.

Samuels, Warren J. and Mercuro, Nicholas (1986), 'Wealth Maximization and Judicial

Decision-Making: The Issues Further Clarified', **6** *International Review of Law and Economics*, 133-137.

Schäfer, Hans-Bernd (1989), 'Allokationseffizienz als Grundprinzip des Zivilrechts (Allocative Efficiency as Basic Principle of Civil Law)', in Ott, Claus and Schäfer, Hans-Bernd (eds), *Allokationseffizienz in der Rechtsordnung*, Berlin, Springer, 1-24.

Scheppele, Kim Lane (1988), *Legal Secrets, Equality and Efficiency in the Common Law*, Chicago, University of Chicago Press, 363 ff.

Schwartz, Edward P. (1992), 'Policy, Precedent, and Power: A Positive Theory of Supreme Court Decision Making', **8** *Journal of Law, Economics and Organization*, 219-252.

Shapiro, Martin (1972), 'Toward a Theory of Stare Decisis', **1** *Journal of Legal Studies*, 125-134.

Shavell, Steven (1995), 'The Appeals Process as a Means of Error Correction', **24** *Journal of Legal Studies*, 379 ff.

Shepsle, Kenneth A. (1992), 'Congress is a "They", not an "It": Legislative Intent as Oxymoron', **12** *International Review of Law and Economics*, 239-256.

Simpson, A.W.B. (1979), 'The Horwitz Thesis and the History of Contracts', **46** *University of Chicago Law Review*, 533-601.

Sinder, Janet (1987), 'Economists as Judges: A Selective, Annotated Bibliography', **50 (4)** *Law and Contemporary Problems*, 279-286.

Smith, Steven D. (1984), 'Rhetoric and Rationality in the Law of Negligence', **69** *Minnesota Law Review*, 277-323.

Spiller, Pablo T. and Spitzer, Matthew L. (1992), 'Judicial Choice of Legal Doctrines', **8** *Journal of Law, Economics and Organization*, 8-46.

Spitzer, Matthew L. (1992), 'Jurisprudence and Formal Models', **12** *International Review of Law and Economics*, 295-296.

Sunstein, Cass R. (1992), 'Public Choice, Endogenous Preferences', **12** *International Review of Law and Economics*, 289-291.

Terrebonne, R. Peter (1981), 'A Strictly Evolutionary Model of Common Law', **10** *Journal of Legal Studies*, 397 ff.

Tullock, Gordon (1971), *The Logic of the Law*, New York, Basic Books.

Tullock, Gordon (1980), *Trials on Trial: The Pure Theory of Legal Procedure*, New York, Columbia University Press.

Varat, Jonathan D. (1986), 'Review Essay: Economic Ideology and the Federal Judicial Task (Review of The Federal Courts: Crisis and Reform by Richard A. Posner), **74** *California Law Review*, 649-674.

Veljanovski, Cento G. (1985), 'The Role of Economics in the Common Law', **7** *Research in Law and Economics*, 41-64.

Von Wangenheim, Georg (1993), 'The Evolution of Judge Made Law', **13** *International Review of Law and Economics*, 381-411.

Wald, Patricia M. (1987), 'Limits on the Use of Economic Analysis in Judicial Decisionmaking', **50 (4)** *Law and Contemporary Problems*, 225-244.

Whichard, Willis P. (1987), 'A Common Law Judge's View of the Appropriate Use of Economics in Common Law Adjudication', **50 (4)** *Law and Contemporary Problems*, 253-263.

Williams, Stephen F. (1980), 'The Static Conception of the Common Law: A Comment', **9** *Journal of Legal Studies*, 277-289.

Wilson, James G. (1986), 'Justice Diffused: A Comparison of Edmund Burke's Conservatism with the Views of Five Conservative, Academic Judges', **40** *University of Miami Law Review*, 913-975.

Wittman, Donald (1989), 'Why Democracies Produce Efficient Results', **97** *Journal of Political Economy*, 1395-1424.

X (1987), 'Note: Judge Frank H. Easterbrook: A Faithful Adherent of the Law and Economics Approach Advocates by Professor Frank H. Easterbrook', **50 (4)** *Law and Contemporary Problems*, 265-277.

9300
PRODUCTION OF LEGAL RULES BY AGENCIES AND BUREAUCRACIES

Georg von Wangenheim
University of Hamburg

Abstract

The main questions which the literature on rule production by agencies and bureaucracies deals with are: To what extent should legislators delegate rule making to bureaucracy? How can procedural rules curb an agency's discretion in making substantive rules? Do legislators select bureaucratic decisions for oversight randomly or on the basis of complaints? Who exactly controls bureaucracy: some and which elements in the legislature or the judiciary? How does the process of bureaucratic rule making work inside an agency? This article reviews the literature with a special emphasis on the effect of procedural rules and on the spatial representation of the interplay between the bureaucracy and the legislature. It concludes by pointing out that more research should be conducted on the process of rule making within agencies and the underlying preferences.
JEL classification: D73, H11, K23, K29
Keywords: Theory of Bureaucracy, Spatial Approaches to Politics, Procedural vs Substantive Rules, Principal-Agent Theory

1. Introduction

The central question posed in the literature on the production of rules by agencies is how the discretion of law-making agencies can be curbed. The political preferences of bureaucracies are most often taken to be exogenously given. These may be the personal political preferences of the director of the single agency or may reflect the influence of interest groups. The influence of interest groups is hardly ever modeled explicitly in this literature. Based on more or less complete answers to the central question, explanations are given for why a legislator may want to delegate law-making power to bureaucracies and how control of this delegated power is to be organized. The key normative question is how much delegation there ought to be. However, answers given to this question barely rely on the positive analyses mentioned herein.

Current positive law and economics analyses of how agencies and bureaucracies (these two terms are used as synonyms herein) produce legal rules differ substantially from approaches applied to other law-making institutions. These analyses do not follow the Public Choice approach commonly used to explain the production of legal rules by legislators; nor do they follow the evolutionary approaches mostly used to explain production of rules by the court system. Theories dealing with bureaucratic law making do not derive, accordingly, one utility maximizing position of the bureaucratic decision makers (which are hardly ever modeled as multiple individuals); nor do these theories rely on the assumption that inefficient legal rules are challenged more often than efficient ones (so that the average of legal rules evolves towards a rather efficient state.) Only if the study of production of rules by the legislator concentrates on consequences of more than one institution needed to pass a law, do strong similarities with the approaches to bureaucratic rule production arise; no such similarities occur between theories of bureaucratic rule making and the evolutionary approach.

Comparing the literature on decision making by agencies and bureaucracies with the research on the production of legal rules by the legislator on the one side, and rule production by the judiciary on the other, not only demonstrates how the approaches to very similar problems differ, but also underlines a problem which only seems to be purely semantic: bureaucratic rule making and bureaucratic adjudication are analytically distinct, as are legislative rule making and judicial adjudication. If bureaucratic decisions are rule making, the Public Choice approach suggests itself for tackling bureaucratic rule making; if they are adjudication, an evolutionary approach seems to be more appropriate. The problem arises in much of the theoretical literature and holds true for many empirical studies. Single bureaucratic decisions or entire classes of bureaucratic decisions are often analyzed without having any thought about whether these decisions are rule making or adjudication.

The reason for the reluctance to distinguish between rule making and adjudication may be that the distinction is not as clear in American administrative law (see, for example, Rugge, 1987), as it would seem from the Administrative Procedures Act (5 U.S.C. §551 (4)-(7)). This lack of clarity may be a problem in other jurisdictions as well. As a result, very few authors in the field reviewed here mention the distinction at all (for example, Lupia and McCubbins, 1994b). It is therefore often not possible to restrict this review to the literature on bureaucratic rule making; research with regard to decisions made in single cases has to be referred to in many places. Likewise, some of the literature reviewed here may overlap with the literature discussed in the articles on regulation of contracts and on environmental regulation. Yet the emphasis of this chapter will be different: it deals with the 'production of legal rules by agencies and bureaucracies', that is, with the rule-making activities of agencies and bureaucracies. I will, however, avoid making too many references to scholarly works on bureaucracies in general, if there is no specific relation to rule making (for an overview of this literature with special reference to Public Choice arguments see Benson, 1995).

The chapter is organized as follows: Sections 2 and 3, respectively, review the literature that describes how procedural rules, by framing the production of substantive rules by agencies, facilitate the control of agencies by their principal, that is, the legislator, and writings comparing the different ways in which the legislator is able to control a rule-making agency. The following two sections, 4 and 5, concentrate on the literature breaking down the legislator into its different institutions, including the courts in the analysis of constraints to bureaucratic rule production. Section 4 deals with econometric studies while Section 5 presents the spatial approach to the topic. Section 6 surveys works that ask normatively whether there ought to be delegation of rule production to agencies and bureaucracies at all. Section 7 reviews the few inquiries into the interior process of agencies which produce rules and Section 8 concludes.

2. Curbing Bureaucratic Discretion by Procedural Rules

Two distinct phenomena bring about bureaucratic discretion: one, the inability of legislative institutions to control perfectly the activities of bureaucracies at reasonable costs; the other, the need for cooperative action by legislative institutions, to sanction an agency or to replace bureaucratic rules by new statutory rules. Although a clear distinction between these phenomena cannot be maintained in reviewing all the publications, the first phenomenon is dealt with in this and the next section; the second in Sections 4 and 5.

As stressed by McCubbins, Noll and Weingast (1987) ('McNollgast'), the principal-agent relationship between legislators and bureaucracies cannot be dealt with appropriately by the mere reference to general principal-agent models of the Laffont-Tirole-Holmström-Milgrom type. The reason is that *ex post* sanctions, which are imposed after the bureaucracy deviates from the political preferences of the politicians, are far too limited, in view of low probabilities of detection, high monitoring costs, and the costs which legislators themselves must bear to impose sanctions (work, political backlash for poorly working agencies, further deterioration of the agency's work). Note however, that Mitnick (1975) emphasizes that one has to be careful with short- and long-run costs and benefits from control here: strict control by the principal may run up more costs than benefits in the short run, but be profitable in the long run because agents become 'educated' by control, and strict control may result in a self-selection of 'good' agents. In McCubbins, Noll and Weingast (1989), the authors extend the reasons for the inappropriateness of the general principal-agent model to embrace the phenomenon to be discussed extensively in Section 5 of this chapter: the need for coordination among several institutions if control of bureaucratic rule production is to be exercised by the shadow of overriding statutory legislation.

McNollgast argue that the remaining, large problems of compliance may be partly solved by procedural rules. In this respect, procedural rules governing the agency's soliciting of information and the consequences of not doing so properly are most important: they may ensure that agencies base their decisions on large sets of information which would also be sufficient for legislative control. Soliciting information can only be successful if those who are better informed have enough incentives to disclose their information. This is, of course, the case if the stakes of affected groups in an issue are high or the issue is highly controversial. These variables, however, fail to be within the control of the legislator. The legislator is forced, thus, to concentrate on enacting procedural rules that modify the costs and the effectiveness of providing information to the bureaucracy.

McNollgast study such procedural rules. Public disclosure requirements facilitate political intervention of interest groups at early stages in the rule-making process, even earlier than in the legislative process. Thus, political intervention of interest groups may allow *ex ante* control of bureaucratic rule production. Elaborate rules of procedure result in high costs of rent seeking and, accordingly, favor those groups which have large resources to spend on representation. On the other hand, budget subsidies for poorly represented groups favor these groups, instead. Next, the discretion of the agency is limited by evidentiary standards, which refer to how evidence must be processed to come to a decision. Burden-of-proof rules may favor or hamper groups which base arguments on unclear cause-effect relationships. Further, '*ex parte*' rules serve to prohibit direct informal communication between private parties and an agency during the formal rule-making process. These rules variously provide for sanctions against prohibited *ex parte* communications, that run a gamut up to, at the extreme, imposing a final decision against the infringing group. *Ex parte* rules enable politicians to participate in the rule-making process, at least as brokers of communication. Also, politicians may exert direct pressure on agencies. For all these procedural rules to enable politicians to exert *ex ante* control, a judicial remedy for their infringement must be sufficiently likely to occur. This can be achieved by decentralized enforcement of these rules if private parties are able to sue at low costs.

McNollgast not only examine ways in which procedural rules and interest groups interact to curb decision making by bureaucrats and agencies, but also argue that politicians are not constrained to granting a policy which is currently favorable to some interest groups. McNollgast suggest politicians are able to ensure, for the future, that changes of legal (agency-made) rules are favorable to the interest groups which constitute the original coalition. This 'autopilot' for future decisions relieves the enacting coalition of the problem that future political majorities might favor other interest groups. The problem of 'slack' of future legislators as being opposed to regulatory slack in rule making is particularly stressed by Horn and Shepsle (1989) and by Steunenberg (1992). They emphasize that there is a trade-off between these two kinds of slack because constraints on either the agency or future legislators require freedom to act by the other institution.

McNollgast allow, against the thrust of their argument, that the control of agencies exercised by the interest groups may evolve in an unexpected direction, or be impeded altogether, if the interest groups that are engaged in the original deal with the legislator cease to exist. Macey (1992) discounts the importance of this caveat for three reasons, all related to the design of a newly-formed agency, and thus strengthens the thrust of McNollgast's argument: first, when interest groups agree with the legislator to institute a regulatory agency, the agreement is likely to cover institutional rules about what parties may influence the future agency's decisions and the ways influence can be exerted. For example, the influence of poorly organized groups may be secured by facilitating access, to individuals with an interest, to agency hearings or judicial review of agency decisions. Levine (1992) criticizes this argument on the basis that, while one may predict that liberalized standing will increase the degree of interference of the courts with regulatory drift, one is unable to predict easily the direction of this interference. This argument apparently neglects the results of evolutionary approaches to the common law (compare the literature following Rubin, 1977 and Priest, 1977), where predictions on the directions of judicial rule making are certainly possible, even if the court system is not systematically biased in some direction. If the court system is known to be biased, it is obvious that one may predict in what direction judge-made law will evolve.

Second, limiting the jurisdiction of a newly-installed agency to the regulation of a small number of industries, or even to part of a single industry, assures that expertise in the agency in this specialized field mainly will be recruited from the same industries or part of an industry. As a result, the points of view held by the agency and industry will usually concur. Accordingly, at least regulation in favor of the regulated industry is stable over time.

Third, when agencies compete for jurisdiction with each other, they seek out the support of constituents and hence will not deviate from the preferences of their constituency. The agency and its constituent interest group(s) thus mutually support each other in order to further their own *raison d'être* and improve their chances to survive over time. This mutual support together with the procedural rules mentioned above serve as an autopilot for rule making by the agency. A similar argument had already been forwarded by Benson (1981), Benson (1983a), and Benson (1983b) although Benson did not set forth the argument in terms of curbing regulative drift. Benson focuses on the size of the bureau and the problem of over-regulation. Johnson and Libecap (1994) drive home the argument that the rank and file of bureaucrats are interested in the duration of their agency to a point that they become an influential interest group in shaping long-run trends in bureaucratic institutions. With particular reference to the third argument (mutual support of regulator and regulated industry), Macey (1992) rejects Shepsle's (1992) view (also expressed by Horn and Shepsle, 1989, and by Steunenberg, 1992), that more emphasis should be placed on the trade-off between the regulatory and legislative slack. Macey claims that there is no such trade-off, but interest groups with political clout, which participate in the original, political decision to set up an agency, retain their political power by this mutual support and continue to exert a like influence on the legislator as well as on the agency.

Although both of the papers of McNollgast give case studies as empirical examples of their theory, Robinson (1989) casts severe doubts on the empirical relevance of McNollgast's argument. McNollgast argue that procedural provisions serve mainly as a curb on the discretion of agencies. Robinson points out that even most of the examples cited by McNollgast do not support their theory, much less do the examples introduced by Robinson himself. He contends, however, that McNollgast's approach could be very useful. If the empirical relevance of the argument were shown, it could substantially change and advance the understanding of the legal-administrative process.

In a related study, Rose-Ackermann (1995) compares how procedural rules enable interested (third) parties to control and interfere with bureaucratic rule making in Germany and the US. Contrary to the situation in the US, in Germany individual citizens hardly have any chance to control rule production by bureaucracies; this control only extends to applications of the rules. Rule making by bureaucracies in Germany is typically under the influence of well-organized interest groups, in the same informal way as statutory legislation is in both countries. Only in the US do procedural rules give the power to control bureaucratic rule making to interested parties which are not politically powerful in the legislative process anyway.

Hamilton and Schroeder (1994) call into question this entire line of reasoning. They ask why agencies would follow procedural rules more strictly than substantive rules. Though they do not enter into a theoretical discussion of the point of view, they do provide some empirical evidence that procedural rules are, in fact, circumvented. Agencies leave substantive rules incomplete and fill the gaps with extensive directives, guidance documents and policy memoranda, which fail to be rules in a formal sense and are not subject to formal rule-making procedures that require the participation of interest groups, in particular of those groups which are protected by procedural rules.

3. Police-Patrol Control versus Fire-Alarm Control

An issue closely related to the question of how procedural rules give control over bureaucratic rule making to third parties is the question of how legislators can best control agencies. The problem posed is whether legislators want to take a random sample of bureaucratic activity (including its rule-making activity) in the same manner in which a police patrol randomly inspects the streets; or whether legislators want to look at bureaucratic decisions only when and where someone protests against a particular decision with vehemence, in the same manner in which the fire department takes action only after someone sounds a fire alarm. I refer to this question as the optimal-type-of-control problem.

The leading articles that discuss the optimal-type-of-control problem (for an overview of the consequential literature until 1990 see Ogul and Rockmann, 1990) are McCubbins and Schwartz (1984) and Weingast (1984). These articles argue that, in general, Congress prefers fire-alarm to police-patrol oversight, because the costs of the monitoring activities are partly transferred from Congress itself to interested groups and individuals. However, citizens harmed by violations of legislative goals are not always represented by well-organized groups and, accordingly, are unable to sound alarms loud enough to obtain redress of grievances. The authors answer this criticism by referring to arguments like those in the previous section herein: disadvantaged groups often have public spokesmen; problems of collective action are overcome by legislation which favors the organization of interest groups, particularly affected by collective action problems; extensive constituent-service by congress(wo)men opens up review procedures.

In the optimal-type-of-control literature, there is no discussion of the social costs of fire-alarm oversight, but one might speculate that it is socially cheaper. With fire-alarm oversight, individuals, who are affected by bureaucratic rule making and will notice it anyway, detect regulatory slack;

with police-patrol oversight, legislators must fund specialized individuals to scrutinize bureaucratic decisions for which they have little inherent regard. The argument might, however, be weakened if one takes into account a problem like dispersed damages in tort law: the adverse effects of regulatory slack may be so dispersed, that sounding a fire alarm is too costly for anyone other than specialists hired to search for regulatory slack. This assumption, again, throws the argument partly back to the discussion of the previous section herein.

It is, however, unclear whether asymmetric degrees of organization among opposing interest groups can be completely offset by procedural rules. Hopenhayn and Lohmann (1996) study the results of asymmetric access to review procedures for a particular kind of fire-alarm oversight, where an agency's decision can be (partly) controlled before adverse effects on social welfare occur. A fire alarm can be sounded either: (i) only if the agency has allowed some regulated activity although the activity decreases social welfare; or (ii) in addition to this condition also if the agency prohibits a regulated activity although the activity would increase social welfare. If the political institutions rely on this kind of fire-alarm oversight, less activities will be allowed in case (i) than in case (ii). Hence, there may be adverse social welfare effects due to reliance on fire-alarm oversight, as opposed to some symmetric oversight system, possibly a police-patrol system.

Aberbach (1990) questions the theoretical findings of McCubbins and Schwartz (1984) and Weingast (1984) on factual grounds. They argue that Congress prefers fire-alarm to police-patrol oversight; he offers empirical evidence that Congress has increasingly used police-patrol oversight instead of only fire-alarm oversight. Ogul and Rockmann (1990) explain this finding by pointing to the greater resources employed by Congress (in particular more staff) to scrutinize agencies, where less means are allocated to new legislative activity because congress(wo)men have, in general, fewer opportunities to obtain name recognition through new legislation.

Lupia and McCubbins (1994a, 1994b) develop formal models of both police-patrol and fire-alarm oversight. They explore under what conditions each kind of control is superior to no oversight from the viewpoint of Congress-as-principal. The hardly surprising conditions they derive for police-patrol oversight being superior to no oversight are: large differences between an agency's and legislators' preferences; and low costs of oversight. Fire-alarm oversight is superior to no oversight: when high penalties are imposed for false fire alarms; or where the preferences of legislators and of interested groups or individuals that may pull the fire alarm are close to each other. Due to the disparate structure of their two models, Lupia and McCubbins fail to compare the two kinds of oversight with one another. After making exactly this point (Bawn, 1994), Bawn (1997) constructs another formal model to carry out this comparison. This model again mainly restates the arguments of McCubbins and Schwartz (1984) in a formal way. By emphasizing that marginal costs of oversight are lower for members of the committee with jurisdiction over the agency than for other members of the chamber, she adds, however, the insight that the latter will prefer more fire-alarm-like or (as Bawn calls it in a slightly broader sense) statutory control.

Both Lindsay (1976) and Holmström and Milgrom (1991) express fundamental doubts as to whether an optimal degree of control over agencies can be defined merely by taking into account direct costs of control. They stress that agents that have multiple tasks, which the principal can monitor to different degrees, tend to carry out only tasks for which they will get credit, namely those tasks which the principal can monitor. Such agents neglect the tasks which the principal cannot monitor. By distorting the allocation of the agent's efforts, additional oversight may thus lead to indirect costs. As there is no common denominator in which to measure the net benefits reaped in the public sector, such as profits, the problem they discuss is particularly relevant to government bureaucracies.

4. Who Controls Bureaucratic Discretion: Econometric Approaches

While the literature discussed so far concentrates on how to overcome bureaucratic discretion by assuming a dichotomy between agencies and the legislature (as a unitary actor), many authors also ask who exactly controls the bureaucracy: which particular institution among several engaged in the legislative process? Or none of them, but an independent judiciary? Two strands of literature, only loosely intertwined, must be distinguished: econometric studies (discussed in this section) and theoretical arguments based on sequential games which describe strategic choices made between policies, represented by different points in a given policy space (discussed in Section 5).

Among the econometric approaches this article surveys, some authors ask which of several possible institutions controls an agency. Other authors test whether a particular institution controls an agency's decisions or not. A typical and prominent example for the first type of approach is Moe (1985) (also compare Moe, 1987). He takes the National Labor Relations Board (NLRB) as an example of an agency which could be influenced by the political preferences of the President of Congress and of the courts. His analysis clearly shows that all these institutions are important (changes in political orientation have a significant impact on the decisions of the NLRB), but the President has the most impact on the NLRB. The NLRB is not a prominent example of rule production by agencies because its decisions are nearly all adjudicatory. Notwithstanding this limitation, Moe's paper may well be labeled as path-breaking: it lays ground for later econometric studies to inquire which institutions wield the most power over agencies that makes rules.

Beck (1987) employs a model less ambitious in comparing the power wielded over agencies by different institutions but more directly focused on rule production. He studies to what extent the US President is able to influence rule making within the Federal Reserve. In particular, he tests whether monetary policy of the Federal Reserve supports a political business cycle favorable to incumbent presidents. His findings are that the Fed does not actively support such cycles by inducing political monetary cycles but that it passively accepts such cycles induced by fiscal policy. Accordingly, Beck asserts that the President of the US exerts a certain but limited degree of power to control the Fed.

Probably the most extensive and detailed econometric study of bureaucratic rule production is conducted by Magat, Krupnick and Harrington (1986, p. 8). Their book aims at clarifying which factors influence bureaucratic decisions with regard to rule making. They test fourteen hypotheses derived from different theoretical approaches to bureaucratic rule making. Unfortunately, few of the results of the study are statistically significant, but most parameters do have the sign which should be expected from the theoretical argument. The same caveat holds for the work of Hamilton and Schroeder (1994), who study how much an agency will resort to 'informal' rule making (in the form of directives, guidance documents and policy memoranda issued by an agency) in order to avoid the control of formalized rule-making procedures.

Based on studies of the Food and Drug Administration (FDA), Olson (1995, 1996) compares not so much which political institutions exert power in controlling agencies; rather she contrasts different approaches to predict bureaucratic behavior. In particular, she compares capture theory (agencies are controlled by the industries they are supposed to regulate), public interest theory (agencies are the benevolent pursuers of social welfare), and Congressional control theory (legislative institutions, modeled by Olson as a unitary actor, control agencies). She finds that the behavior of one and the same agency is best explained by different theories or even by different combinations of theories for different industries which are regulated. Accordingly, she suggests that unless subsequent empirical studies focus on the micro-level trade-offs which face regulators, it is impossible to get a clear answer as to what are the important incentives in bureaucratic rule production. In order to formulate better explanations or even predictions of bureaucratic behavior, future research must be more sensitive to different regulatory actions and their specific constraints and trade-offs for the regulator.

Hammond and Knott (1996) altogether reject econometric analyses of which institutions control the bureaucracy based on the correlation between, on the one hand, changes in preferences of an institution, and on the other hand, changes in policy of the agency. As they point out, it is impossible for one institution to control an agency without the cooperation of the other institutions. Thus, future empirical work on political control should incorporate the interplay of preferences of the controlling institutions. These authors do not develop, however, an operational measure of the power wielded by institutions over agencies, although they consider such a measure to be indispensable to conduct empirical studies.

5. Who Controls Bureaucratic Discretion: Spatial Approaches

The literature reviewed in Sections 2 and 3 explained the discretion exercised by bureaucrats by highlighting the superior information which agencies possess and explored the ways in which control of the bureaucracy is achieved. The literature discussed in this section takes a game-theoretic approach. This approach is based on preferences in a given policy space to show that bureaucratic discretion exists even without asymmetric information. The basic idea developed in this body of literature is that an agency can be sanctioned, for example, by new legislation that overrules decisions of an agency or interferes with the resources of the agency, only if more than one of the institutions agree to apply sanctions. If n institutions are needed to sanction an agency and every institution has single-peaked preferences in the policy space, Pareto sets of dimension $n - 1$ or less result. Within these Pareto sets, the agency is free to act because every change in policy makes at least one institution better off; accordingly, this 'winning' institution will be reluctant to sanction the agency. As legislative procedures become more complicated than simple acceptance by all relevant institutions, the models are formed as sequential games. In these games, institutions can veto, accept or amend proposals from institutions with the right to take the initiative, according to (a simplified version of) the constitution.

The starting point for this discussion is the paper by Weingast (1981). He develops a spatial policy model (one and two policy dimensions) that explains the bounds of agencies' decisions on regulation. Based on three examples (airlines, telecommunications and nuclear power), he studies the interplay between possibly more than one Congressional (sub)committee; interest groups which form the clientele of both the (sub)committee(s) and the agency controlled by the (sub)committee(s); and sometimes (namely if he makes appointments to the agency himself) the President. Weingast shows how this interplay restricts the range of discretion of the agency. Weingast and Moran (1983) take the same approach to explain why there is scant evidence of Congressional oversight. They put forth this approach as an alternative to the dominant view in the literature at the time that this lack of evidence is due to major imperfections in the oversight exercised by Congress, due to Congress's lack of information. This approach argues, alternatively, that Congressional oversight is near perfect; accordingly, agencies do not even attempt to deviate from the preferences of the legislature. Weingast and Moran demonstrate that their theory explains better than an imperfect-oversight theory would why Congress was extraordinarily active in its oversight of the Federal Trade Commission (FTC) in 1979-80, after a turnover in the members of the appropriate Senate subcommittee: the FTC temporarily lacked sufficient information on new constraints imposed on its discretion by new Senate subcommittee members, and the FTC deviated involuntarily from the preferences of the subcommittee. Finally, Weingast and Moran test their theory econometrically. Their econometric analysis is challenged by Muris (1986) and successfully defended by Weingast and Moran (1986). Econometric support for their theory is also offered in the paper of Faith, Leavens and Tollison (1982). They reject the claim of Katzmann (1980) (who relies exclusively on a non-statistical analysis of interviews conducted on members of the FTC) that the decisions of the FTC are independent of Congressional influence and of efforts to maximize the budget of the Commission. Instead, they offer compelling econometric evidence that both the House and the Senate have a substantial impact on the selection of cases by the FTC, though the impact of the Senate seems to vanish after sweeping reforms were carried out in 1970 on the FTC.

In ensuing years, the approach of Weingast has been criticized, mainly for its simplifying assumptions on Congressional legislative procedures (see for example, Moe, 1987). Complicating assumptions, however, were only introduced into the model in the early 1990s. Two papers, by Ferejohn and Shipan (1990) and Gely and Spiller (1990), written independently of each other, incorporate in the model judicial review of administrative decisions, as well as Presidential veto to Congressional override of both decisions of agencies and judicial review of decisions of agencies. The preferences of agencies are assumed to be identical to those of the President (this flaw is overcome by Steunenberg, 1992). Ferejohn and Shipan allow for an override of a Presidential veto by a two-thirds majority in Congress which is modeled as a unicameral legislative body. In a different vein, Gely and Spiller abstract from the opportunity to override a Presidential veto but treat the House and the Senate as two different (unitary) agents and extend the model to a two-dimensional policy space. A final important difference between the two models is that judicial control is restricted to replacing the agency's issuance of new rules by the *status quo ante* in the paper of Ferejohn and Shipan. In variations of the model of Gely and Spiller, the courts act as a kind of super-agency able to replace the agency's choice of a new rule with whatever policy the courts prefer most (subject to the threat of new legislation).

Ferejohn and Shipan deduce that the next (namely judicial) step in the control of policy making by agencies restricts the power of agencies, and makes agencies more responsive to the preferences of the current (not the originally enacting) legislature. In a comment to this article, Spitzer (1990) studies some cases in which agencies have preferences which differ from those of the President. In another comment, Rose-Ackerman (1990) expresses the criticism that it is unclear why Congress should allow its own committee to deviate as much from Congress's own preferences as is assumed in the Ferejohn and Shipan paper and, more related to the general approach adopted by Ferejohn and Shipan, that it might substantially increase the agency's and the court's discretion and influence to abandon the assumption of costless Congressional action.

The paper by Gely and Spiller yields the same result with respect to judicial control over an agency: the reduction in the discretion of an agency is substantially greater if courts are able to impose the policy they prefer most. Allowing the President to have preferences different from those of an agency forces Gely and Spiller to introduce a second dimension in the policy space. Only then can they demonstrate how an increase in the number of institutions that must cooperate to enact a statute increases the dimension of the Pareto set which defines the discretion of an agency. They apply their model to two cases decided by the Supreme Court. The examples show how the ruling of an agency changes after and due to a change in the preferences of the legislature.

Formalizing the presentation of the spatial approach, thus far most often based on a graphical exposition, Hammond and Knott (1996) show that any number of dimensions of the policy space and a complete model of US institutions are tractable by this approach. They set forth a formal model. They include all five institutions most relevant to American legislation: the House, the Senate, the relevant committees of both (some multi-person institutions are even divided into their members) and the President. They include two alternative procedures of legislation: majority of House and Senate and approval by President as well as 2/3 majority of the House and Senate. The judiciary is added in an informal way, which may be more appropriate than the alternative approaches chosen by Ferejohn and Shipan (1990) and Gely and Spiller (1990). The power of the judiciary is reduced to stretch the set of legal policies constraining the agency in the direction preferred by the judiciary. And Hammond and Knott include in their model the President's ability or inability to fire an agency director. Complicating the assumptions in the analysis does not provide new insights into how, in theory, bureaucratic discretion changes when additional institutions are included in the model. But they offer the insight that the results of less comprehensive models are not due to their simplifying assumptions. The stress in the paper of Hammond and Knott is, however, laid on the conclusion that it is impossible to give a clear answer to the question of who really controls an agency; control is exerted by the interplay of institutions. Thus, they reject empirical studies into the power of controlling institutions if such studies are based on correlations between changes in the preferences of the allegedly controlling institutions and agency policy.

A general problem in the literature is, of course, that the assumptions on information about the preferences of other agents are as strong as they are for most models of sequential games. One should not overemphasize this problem, though, because spatial approaches to bureaucratic discretion have to be seen as a complement to the literature basing the explanation of bureaucratic discretion on incomplete information.

While the earlier articles, which take spatial approaches (this section) or optimal-type-of-control approaches (Section 3) to bureaucratic discretion include but references to the other approach, only Epstein and O'Halloran (1995) integrate both spatial and optimal-type-of-control approaches in one formal model. These authors assume that only interest groups and the agency are completely informed about the state of the world and hence know what policy they prefer most. The legislator (modeled as a unitary actor and thus re-simplified as compared to the newer spatial literature) only knows its most preferred policy as a function of the true state of the world. When an agency proposes a policy change to the legislator, the legislator may accept or reject the proposal, but not amend it. From the legislator's perfect knowledge of the preferences of the other actors, the rule proposed by the agency, and the reaction of the interest groups (which sound a fire alarm or not), the legislator is able to deduce a piece of information about the true state of the world and react accordingly. The most important result derived from this model is that the legislator can deduce the most information from the reaction of an interest group if the legislators' most preferred policy lies between those of the agency and the interest group. Less information can be deduced if the interest groups' most preferred policy is at the center. No information can be deduced if the agency's most preferred policy is at the center. The reaction of more interest groups increases the information deduced by the legislator only if the interests of the additional groups differ more than, and in the same direction as, the preferences of the legislators differ from the most preferred policy of the agency.

6. Ought there be a Delegation of Rule-Making Power to Agencies and Bureaucracies?

While the literature discussed thus far looks at the positive questions of how bureaucratic discretion in rule production can best be controlled by the legislature (Sections 2 and 3) and which particular institution controls agencies (Sections 4 and 5), other authors ask more fundamentally whether there ought to be delegation of rule making to the bureaucracy from the point of view of the legislature or society. Since answers to the positive questions mentioned above are mostly based on fire-alarms control by the same interest groups which influence the legislation, most authors neglect the problems discussed by the capture theory of regulation. They do not even perceive them as problems, if capture works in favor of the same groups in both legislation and bureaucratic rule making. This is different for the normative question discussed in this section.

Imperfect control of agencies can only be used as an argument against having a delegation of rule-making authority from the legislator to the bureaucracy for three reasons: (1) a bureaucrat (agency director) has political preferences differing from those of the legislator; (2) a bureaucrat (agency director) exploits his superior knowledge for his own non-political advantage as described by Niskanen (1971, 1975) (also compare Migué and Belanger, 1974); (3) an agency gets captured by the regulated industry more than the legislator. The first reason vanishes if the legislator can choose the bureaucrat. The second reason either coincides with the third or does not systematically interfere with the content of rules produced by agencies except for the case where some rules allow collusion of an agency with the regulated industry or firm and consequential rent sharing while other rules do not allow this. An example for such a case is discussed by Laffont and Tirole (1990). They conclude that for the case of price regulation it might be reasonable not to delegate to the agency the decision between (average-)cost-plus pricing and marginal-cost pricing with a transfer to the firm(s) covering the fixed costs.

The third reason is discussed more extensively. Contradicting Page (1981), Wiley (1986) argues (the argument is reinforced in Wiley, 1988) that there is no general evidence that regulated entities have a disproportionate influence upon regulatory agencies. Accordingly, the decision to delegate regulatory rule making to an agency ought to rest mainly on the agency's advantages and disadvantages in dealing with specific rule production as compared to the legislator himself. This argument is refuted by Spitzer (1988) who claims with reference to Fiorina (1977, pp. 15-29) that rule making by agencies is more apt to capture by interest groups than rule making by the legislator because the latter uses the agency to shirk responsibility for the costs imposed by regulation, while claiming credit for the benefits at the same time (also compare Vaubel, 1991, who applies the same argument to the supranational European legislative institutions; and Moe, 1989). Wiley (1988) points to the many other reasons for a legislator to delegate specific rule making to a bureaucracy in order to reduce the importance of the argument of Spitzer (1988). Referring to better responsiveness of the law to specific local conditions, Mashaw (1985) supports this pro-delegation position. Bawn (1995) compares costs and benefits faced by the legislator from delegation of rule making in a formal model. She shows that the legislator will balance marginal costs incurred as a result of a loss of control through the delegation with marginal benefits reaped as a result of the better fit between agency decisions and specific cases. Her model uses quite specific functional forms but can be generalized easily.

Spulber and Besanko (1992) argue that a problem similar to capture may arise from the way the regulator and the regulated firm or industry interact. If the former is able to commit to some environmental quality standard, that is, if the regulator is a Stackelberg leader, then it is sufficient to choose an agency director with political preferences similar to those of the legislator. However, if the regulator is unable to commit to a specific environmental quality standard but is likely to adapt the standard to the firm's or industry's activities (levels of output and levels of pollution), that is, if the relationship between regulator and regulated industry or firm is Nash, then an optimizing legislator will choose an agency director with preferences deviating from its own and will enact statutory limits to bureaucratic standard setting. The answer which Spulber and Besanko give to the question as to whether or not statutory limits ought to be imposed on regulatory discretion depends upon whether the relationship between the regulator and the regulated firm or industry is Stackelberg or Nash. In addition, their answer to the question *in what direction* these limits should be erected also depends on the circumstances of the specific case. As stressed by Arvan (1992), the ambiguities can only be cleared up by empirical studies. The result of Spulber and Besanko (1992) are ambiguous even though they abstract from important aspects influencing the degree of *ex ante* statutory constraints on regulatory agencies, such as judicial review, problems of incomplete information on the technology (legislators have to know the technology up to one parameter which does not influence complementarity or substitutiveness of pollution abatement and production costs), and incomplete knowledge of the preferences of other political actors (Ross, 1992).

If non-delegation is assumed to be the only alternative, the question whether there ought to be a delegation of rule-making power to agencies and bureaucracies is only incompletely answered. In his structural approach to law, Cooter (1996a) (also 1994a, 1996b) argues that, among rule-making bodies, agencies should make as few rules as possible because they do not follow social norms to the extent that courts do or at least ought to. Following social norms which evolve from efficient incentive structures (that is, social settings in which spillovers to groups not engaged in the social formation of the norms do not exist nor do evolutionary traps resulting from non-convexities exist) are better than rules issued by law makers such as legislators or regulatory agencies and bureaucracies (that is, constructivist law makers in a Hayekian sense.)

Kaplow (1992), too, deals with the role of the courts in the question of whether to delegate rule-making authority to agencies. Yet he does not see rule production by courts as an alternative to rule production by agencies. Rather, he emphasizes that non-delegation is only possible if the legislator includes overly general clauses in statutes. Thus, courts are forced to deduce concrete standards from the general clauses and do so necessarily after the regulated firm or industry has acted, whereas rules set by agencies are promulgated before a regulated firm or industry acts. Regulation by *ex post* standards is inferior to (bureaucratic) regulation by rules if and only if the costs measured per case of formulating *ex ante* rules which are readily applicable outweigh the costs which result from less precise standards. Thus, if and only if the law under review is relevant to frequent behavior of a clearly distinguishable type, bureaucratic regulation through rules will be superior to regulation by standards which courts interpret from statutes.

With the same problem in mind, Fiorina (1982, 1986) tries to develop a model that shows how legislative decisions to delegate rule interpretation (and thereby making of new, less abstract rules) to the courts or to an agency depend on the substantive preferences of the legislators. Unfortunately, all his results depend on incorrect graphical representations of expected utilities of legislators and, in the 1982 article, also on the assumption of bell-shaped utility functions of legislators (compare also Nichols, 1982). Accordingly, the results are not reported herein.

Finally, Rubin and Cohen (1985) mention a third alternative to delegation of rule making to agencies. Law (in particular regulatory statutes) should be made more concrete and enforced by private firms and not by state agencies for several reasons: the legislator (the state) must merely formulate policies on a general, aggregate level and does not have to deal with specific technologies. These technologies can be decided upon by the private law enforcer who signs a contract to pay some (positive or negative) per unit tax on the aggregate level of pollution or safety or other regulatory targets. Then, he may require firms to abide by a standard or to pay a fee sufficient to cover the tax. Hence, which technology is used becomes a decision subject to market forces. The private enforcer has stronger (monetary) incentives than an agency. The rules governing the relationship between the firms and the enforcer become more efficient because evolutionary theory of efficient common law is applicable as both sides have long-lasting economic stakes in these rules. The basic idea of the paper is to make existing substantive regulation a property right (entitlement) of the private enforcement agency, and the absence of some regulation a property right of the regulated industry. The property right becomes valuable for the enforcer by paying him some money for avoided (statistical) damages (for example, saved statistical lives) and making the enforcer liable for (statistical) damages. Property rights being thus clearly defined will be reallocated in a Pareto-optimal way by Coasean bargaining.

7. The Rule-Production Process Itself

Little has been written in the law and economics literature on how rules are actually produced by agencies and bureaucracies, although taking this approach might substantially clarify the relevance of different arguments with respect to control of bureaucratic rule production by the legislator and its branches. One of the few examples of this approach is the paper contributed by McCubbins and Page (1986). They conclude that decentralized incentives within agencies are too flexible for congress(wo)men who want close control over an agency and, perhaps more importantly, that incentives in an agency are such that agencies do not strive for positive overall results but for countable 'beans' (for example, a ban on dioxin instead of the improvement of public health). If research were to take these insights into account, the models constructed to predict the degree and relevance of bureaucratic discretion would gain in explanatory power.

In developing concise models of bureaucratic rule production, law and economics scholars might have to take a close look at general descriptions of the rule-making process, such as the book of Kerwin (1992) and case studies like those of Fox (1987) and McGarity (1991). And more descriptive studies of this kind might be needed. Kerwin thoroughly describes the legal background and actual process of rule making at the federal level in the US. Though he does not make a consistent theoretical approach, let alone rely on economic theory, his study is very helpful as a starter and as background knowledge for any scholar not wholly familiar with the US institutions. On the basis of three cases, Fox describes how decision making in the FTC changes with the chairman of the Commission. McGarity studies the effects of having different types of employees working for regulatory agencies. He contrasts the 'techno-bureaucratic rationality' for rule making of one group of employees with the 'comprehensive analytical rationality' of the other. The former group, professionals who typically have technical or legal training, draft rules without paying much attention to economic trade-offs. The latter group, young economists trained in an anti-regulative atmosphere, entered agencies during the 1970s. McGarity uses the term 'comprehensive' to stress that the ideal pursued by this second group is an open-ended decision-making process based on the quantitative comparison of all possible routes to a goal, which in turn may be defined as quantitative cost-benefit analysis. Based on a large number of case studies, he discusses different institutional settings within bureaucracies which may promote or hinder the relevance of cost-benefit analysis to bureaucratic rule making. Yet McGarity notes that at first, many of the analysts with thorough microeconomic training went too far in replacing pro-regulation biases of techno-bureaucrats with anti-regulation biases. In his opinion, the different but equally-strong biases of the young economists neither furthered their goals nor overcame traditional and still-dominant engineering and legal orientations to bureaucratic rule making. Were case studies such as those of Fox and McGarity to be turned into models of bureaucratic behavior (adding the preference side to the constraints thus far discussed in the literature), much would be gained in understanding, predicting and evaluating rule production by agencies.

An early theoretical approach, which unfortunately did not find many followers, is the study conducted by Breton and Winetrobe (1982). They explain the reason for the lack of economic discussion of what happens inside bureaucracies (both public and private!) is a seeming absence of property rights and competition in bureaucratic interactions. Introducing a theory of trust as an instrument which backs intertemporal contracts, they succeed in establishing an analogy to a pure barter economy. Concentrating on Schumpeterian competition instead of neoclassical price competition, they even construct market-like 'networks' within bureaucracies. By combining trust and Schumpeterian competition, they can explain not only many of the alleged inefficiencies in bureaucracies but also the existence of particularly efficient bureaucratic organizations which replace market exchanges to a greater degree than transaction cost arguments are able to justify. Unfortunately, it seems that it would be difficult to apply this innovative theory to rule production by public bureaucracies. Johnson and Libecap (1994) make further progress (based on more-standard, neoclassical assumptions) toward understanding what happens inside bureaucracies but, like Breton and Winetrobe, they do not concentrate on rule making.

Notwithstanding these problems with positive approaches, some articles and books deal with normative questions of how rules ought to be made by agencies and on what arguments decisions of agencies should be based. For example, Breyer (1985) emphasizes that it, of course, would be most appropriate to base regulation entirely on simple economic models, but that this is often impossible because resulting policies would lack practicability.

Still, economic models ought to be used to organize regulators' analyses and focus their attention on the relevant questions (McGarity, 1991 is clearly supportive of this point).

Ribstein and Kobayashi (1996a, 1996b) discuss a different kind of rule production by agencies. These authors look at agencies which only draft rules which a legislator subsequently may enact or amend. In particular, they discuss the effects and the efficiency of the National Conference of Commissioners on Uniform State Laws (NCCUSL), which provides fully-formulated drafts of statutes to state legislatures. They claim that this procedure may have advantages over enacting federal laws but that it is clearly worse than free competition among diverse state laws, which would result in an evolution towards the most efficient laws (for example, other jurisdictions copy provisions out of corporations code of Delaware because many firms choose to incorporate in that jurisdiction). These authors allow that model codes facilitate competition between jurisdictions and overall law making by exploiting economies of scale. Yet they point out that private institutions such as the American Bar Association draft model laws more dispassionately. Agencies like the NCCUSL are claimed to be too easily influenced by interest groups. The reviewer comments that the reference which these authors make to capture theory is relevant only if the agencies have a monopoly of the supply of model laws for if they do not, private institutions are free to provide *additional* competing drafts.

8. Conclusion

Both the positive and the normative literature on the rule production by agencies and bureaucracies is still incomplete, and further work is necessary and seems to be promising. Substantial progress has been made in the positive literature concerning the constraints of regulatory rule production. Yet it is still particularly difficult to derive a complete microeconomic model which describes or predicts the rule-producing behavior of agencies because the political preferences of agencies and bureaucracies have hardly been discussed outside capture theory. Capture theory suffers from weak econometric support and, if taken seriously, would make many of the problems posed in the literature based on positive political theory obsolete. Bureaucratic preferences obviously are not determined by a single individual but are the result of a decision-making process *within* a bureaucracy. Models of this process would substantially facilitate understanding and prediction of the rule-making behavior of agencies.

On the normative side, due to the lack of complete positive theories on bureaucratic decision making constrained by legislative and judicial oversight, arguments often do not seem to be too strong because normative conclusions cannot be based on a clear relationship between institutional settings and their welfare effects. Hence, much of this literature must be based on ideological premises concerning the behavior of agencies and bureaucracies.

Acknowledgements

I am indebted to two anonymous referees who draw my attention to parts of the literature which escaped my eyes and to Juan Javier Del Granado and Elizabeth Sullivan for editing my paper intensely. All remaining errors are, of course, mine.

Bibliography on Production of Legal Rules by Agencies and Bureaucracies (9300)

Aberbach, Joel (1990), *Keeping a Watchful Eye*, Washington, Brookings Institution.

Arvan, Lanny (1992), 'Delegation, Commitment, and the Regulatory Mandate: Comments', **8** *Journal of Law, Economics, and Organization*, 159-164.

Bagnoli, Mark and McKee, Michael (1991), 'Controlling the Game: Political Sponsors and Bureaus', **7** *Journal of Law, Economics, and Organization*, 229-247.

Bainbridge, Stephen M. (1991), 'The Short Life and Resurrection of SEC Rule 19c-4', **69** *Washington University Law Quarterly*, 565 ff. Reprinted in 1992 *Securities Law Review* 377.

Bainbridge, Stephen M. (1995), 'Incorporating State Law Fiduciary Duties Into the Federal Insider Trading Prohibition', **52** *Washington and Lee Law Review*, 1189 ff. Reprinted in *Corporate Practice Commentator*, **38**, 1996, 1.

Bawn, Kathleen (1994), 'Bureaucratic Accountability For Regulatory Decisions: Comment on Lupia and McCubbins', **57** *Law and Contemporary Problems*, 139-142.

Bawn, Kathleen (1995), 'Political Control versus Expertise: Congressional Choices About Administrative Procedures', **89** *American Political Science Review*, 62-73.

Bawn, Kathleen (1997), 'Choosing Strategies to Control the Bureaucracy: Statutory Constraints, Oversight, and the Committee System', **13** *Journal of Law, Economics, and Organization*, 101-126.

Beck, Nathaniel (1987), 'Elections and the Fed: Is there a National Monetary Cycle?', **31** *American Journal of Political Science*, 194-216.

Benson, Bruce L. (1981), 'Why are Congressional Committees Dominated by "High Demand" Legislators?', **48** *Southern Economic Journal*, 68-77.

Benson, Bruce L. (1983a), 'The Economic Theory of Regulation as an Explanation of Policies Toward Bank Mergers and Holding Company Acquisitions', **28** *Antitrust Bulletin*, 839-862.

Benson, Bruce L. (1983b), 'High Demand Legislative Committees and Bureaucratic Output', **11** *Public Finance Quarterly*, 259-281.

Benson, Bruce L. (1989), 'Further Thoughts on Rent Seeking, Bureaucratic Output, and the Price of Complements', **63** *Public Choice*, 279-281.

Benson, Bruce L (1990), *The Enterprise of Law: Justice Without the State*, San Francisco, Pacific Research Institute for Public Policy.

Benson, Bruce L. (1994), 'Third Thoughts on Contracting Out', **11** *Journal of Libertarian Studies*, 44-78.

Benson, Bruce L (1995), 'Understanding Bureaucratic Behavior: Implications from the Public Choice Literature', **13** *Journal of Public Finance and Public Choice/ Economia delle Scelte Pubbliche*, 89-117.

Benson, Bruce L. and Greenhut, Melvin L. (1986), 'Interest Groups, Bureaucrats and Antitrust: An Explanation of the Antitrust Paradox', in Grieson, Ronald E. (ed.), *Antitrust and Regulation*, Lexington, MA, Lexington Books, 53-90.

Benson, Bruce L. and Mitchell, Jean (1988), 'Rent Seekers Who Demand Government Production: Bureaucratic Output and the Price of Complements', **56** *Public Choice*, 3-16.

Benson, Bruce L., Greenhut, Melvin L. and Holcombe, Randall (1987), 'Interest Groups and the Antitrust Paradox', **6** *Cato Journal*, 801-817.

Benson, Bruce L., Rasmussen, David W. and Sollars, David L. (1995), 'Police Bureaucrats, Their Incentives, and the War on Drugs', **83** *Public Choice*, 21-45.

Bos, P.V.F. (1994), 'Van Ontvoogding naar Ontgoocheling of van Interstatelijkheid naar Communautaire Dimensie? (From Guardianship to Illusion or From a State to a Community Perspective)', **69** *Nederlands Juristen Blad*, 906-911.

Breton, Albert and Winetrobe, Ronald (1982), *The Logic of Bureaucratic Conduct*, Cambridge, Cambridge University Press.

Breyer, Stephen G. (1985), 'Economists and Economic Regulation', **47** *University of Pittsburgh Law Review*, 205-218.

Centner, Terence J. (1995), 'Organically-Produced Food Products: Regulations from the European Union and the United States Set the Stage for Imports', **7(4)** *Journal of International Food and Agribusiness Marketing*, 41-58.

Centner, Terence J. and Lathrop, K.W. (1996), 'Differentiating Food Products: Organic Labeling Provisions Facilitate Consumer Choice', **1** *Drake Agricultural Law Review*, 30-50.

Cooter, Robert D. (1994a), 'Structural Adjudication and the New Law Merchant: A Model of Decentralized Law', **14** *International Review of Law and Economics*, 215-231. Reprinted under the title, 'The Structural Approach to Decentralizing Law: A Theory of Games and Norms', in a book edited by Gerard Hertig.

Cooter, Robert D. (1994b), 'Decentralized Law for a Complex Economy', **23** *Southwestern Law Review, Hayek Symposium*, 443-451.

Cooter, Robert D. (1996a), 'Decentralized Law for a Complex Economy: The Structural Approach to Adjudicating the New Law Merchant', **144** *University of Pennsylvania Law Review*.

Cooter, Robert D. (1996b), 'The Theory of Market Modernization of Law', **16** *International Review of Law and Economics*, 141-172.

Eckert, Ross D. (1981), 'The Life Cycle of Regulatory Commissioners', **24** *Journal of Law and Economics*, 113-120.

Eijlander, Ph. (1996), 'Regulering van de Kwaliteit van Zorginstellingen (Regulating the Quality of Care Organizations)', in Gestel, R.A.J. van et al. (eds), *Markt en Wet*, Deventer, W.E.J. Tjeenk Willink, 209-219.

Epstein, David and O'Halloran, Sharyn (1995), 'Theory of Strategic Oversight: Congress, Lobbyists, and the Bureaucracy', **11** *Journal of Law, Economics, and Organization*, 227-255.

Faith, Roger L., Leavens, Donald R. and Tollison, Roger D. (1982), 'Antitrust Pork Barrel', **25** *Journal of Law and Economics*, 329-342.

Ferejohn, John A. (1987), 'On a Structuring Principle for Administrative Agencies', in McCubbins, Mathew D. and Sullivan, Terry (eds), *Congress: Structure and Policy*, Cambridge, Cambridge University Press.

Ferejohn, John A. and Shipan, Charles (1990), 'Congressional Influence on Bureaucracy', **6(S)** *Journal of Law, Economics, and Organization*, 1-20.

Fiorina, Morris P. (1977), *Congress: Keystone of the Washington Establishment*, New Haven, CT, Yale University Press.

Fiorina, Morris P. (1982), 'Legislative Choice of Regulatory Forms: Legal Process or Administrative Process?', **39** *Public Choice*, 33-66.

Fiorina, Morris P. (1986), 'Legislator Uncertainty, Legislative Control, and the Delegation of Legislative Power', **2** *Journal of Law, Economics, and Organization*, 33-51.

Fox, Eleanor M. (1987), 'Chairman Miller, the Federal Trade Commission, Economics, and Rashomon', **50(4)** *Law and Contemporary Problems*, 33-55.

Frech, H. Edward III and Samprone, Joseph C., Jr (1980), 'The Welfare Loss of Excess Nonprice Competition: The Case of Property-Liability Insurance Regulation', **13** *Journal of Law and Economics*, 429-440.

Fuchs, Edward Paul and Anderson, James E. (1987), 'Institutinalizing Cost-Benefit Analysis in Regulatory Agencies', in Nagel, Stuart S. (ed.), *Research in Public Policy Analysis and Management, Volume 4*, Greenwich, CT, JAI Press, 187-211.

Gely, Rafael and Spiller, Pablo T. (1990), 'A Rational Choice Theory of Supreme Court Statutory Decisions with Applications to the State Farm and Grove City Cases', **6** *Journal of Law, Economics, and Organization*, 263-300.

Greenhut, Melvin L. and Benson, Bruce L. (1989), *American Antitrust Law in Theory and in Practice*, Aldershot, Avebury.

Grier, Kevin (1984), *The Political Economy of Monetary Policy*, PhD dissertation.

Hamilton, James T. and Schroeder, Christopher H. (1994), 'Strategic Regulators and the Choice of Rulemaking Procedures: The Selection of Formal vs. Informal Rules in Regulating Hazardous Waste', **57** *Law and Contemporary Problems*, 111-160.

Hammond, Thomas H. and Knott, Jack H. (1996), 'Who Controls the Bureaucracy?: Presidential Power, Congressional Dominance, Legal Constraints and Bureaucratic Autonomy in a Model of Multi-Institutional Policy-Making', **12** *Journal of Law, Economics, and Organization*, 119-166.

Hatzis, Aristides N. (1998), 'Mancur Olson, Jr (1932-1998)', **1** *Episteme and Koinonia*.

Hatzis, Aristides N. (1999), 'Rent-Seeking and Vested Interests', in O'Hara, Phillip (ed.), *Encyclopedia of Political Economy*, London, Routledge.

Holmström, Bengt and Milgrom, Paul R. (1991), 'Multitask Principal-Agent Analysis: Incentive Contracts, Asset Ownership, and Job Design', **7** *Journal of Law, Economics, and Organization*, 24-52.

Hopenhayn, Hugo and Lohmann, Susanne (1996), 'Fire Alarm Signals and the Political Oversight of Regulatory Agencies', **12** *Journal of Law, Economics, and Organization*, 196-213.

Horn, Murray J. (1995), *The Political Economy of Public Administration - Institutional Choice in the Public Sector*, Cambridge, Cambridge University Press.

Horn, Murray J. and Shepsle, Kenneth A. (1989), 'Commentary: Administrative Process and Organizational Form as Legislative Responses to Agency Costs', **75** *Virginia Law Review*, 499-508.

Johnson, Ronald N. and Libecap, Gary D. (1994), *The Federal Civil Service System and the Problem of Bureaucracy*, Chicago, University of Chicago Press.

Kaplow, Louis (1992), 'Rules Versus Standards: An Economic Analysis', **42** *Duke Law Journal*, 557-629.

Kaplow, Louis (1995), 'A Model of the Optimal Complexity of Legal Rules', **11** *Journal of Law, Economics, and Organization*, 150-163.

Katzmann, Robert A. (1980), *Regulatory Bureaucracy: The Federal Trade Commission and Antitrust Policy*, Cambridge, MA, MIT Press.

Kerwin, Cornelius (1992), *Rulemaking: How Government Agencies Write Law and Make Policy*, Washington, DC, CQ Press.

Kobayashi, Bruce H. and Ribstein, Larry E. (1996), 'Evolution and Spontaneous Uniformity: Evidence from the Evolution of the Limited Liability Company', **34** *Economic Inquiry*.

Laffont, Jean-Jacques and Tirole, Jean (1990), 'The Politics of Government Decision Making: Regulatory Institutions', **6** *Journal of Law, Economics, and Organization*, 1-31.

Landy, Marc K., Roberts, Mark J. and Thomas, Stephen R. (1990), *The Environmental Protection Agency: Asking the Wrong Questions*, Oxford, Oxford University Press, 309 p.

Lemieux, Vincent (1991), *Les Relations de Pouvoir dans les Lois - Comparaison entre les Gouvernements du Québec de 1944 à 1985* (Power Relations in Laws - Comparison Between Quebec Governments from 1944 to 1985), Sainte-Foy, Presses de l'Université Laval.

Levine, Michael E. (1992), 'Organizational Design and Political Control of Administrative Agencies: Comment', **8** *Journal of Law, Economics, and Organization*, 119-125.

Lewis, Tracy and Poitevin, Michel (1997), 'Disclosure of Information in Regulatory Proceedings', **13** *Journal of Law, Economics, and Organization*, 50-73.

Lindsay, Cotton M. (1976), 'A Theory of Government Enterprise', **84** *Journal of Political Economy*, 1061-1077.

Lupia, Arthur and McCubbins, Mathew D. (1994a), 'Learning from Oversight: Fire Alarms and Police Patrols Reconstructed', **10** *Journal of Law, Economics, and Organization*, 96-125.

Lupia, Arthur and McCubbins, Mathew D. (1994b), 'Designing Bureaucratic Accountability', **57** *Law and Contemporary Problems*, 91-126.

Macey, Jonathan R. (1992), 'Organizational Design and Political Control of Administrative Agencies', **8** *Journal of Law, Economics, and Organization*, 93-110.

MacKay, Robert J., Miller, James C., III and Yandle, Bruce (1987a), 'Public Choice and Regulation: An Overview', in MacKay, Robert J., Miller, James C., III and Yandle,

Bruce (eds), *Public Choice and Regulation: A View from Inside the Federal Trade Commission*, Stanford, Hoover Institute Press, Stanford University, 3-12.

MacKay, Robert J., Miller, James C., III and Yandle, Bruce (eds) (1987b), *Public Choice and Regulation: A View from Inside the Federal Trade Commission*, Stanford, Hoover Institute Press, Stanford University, 363 p.

Magat, Wesley A., Krupnick, A. and Harrington, W. (1986), *Rules in the Making: A Statistical Analysis of Regulatory Agency Behavior*, Washington, Resources for the Future.

Mashaw, Jerry L. (1985), 'Prodelegation: Why Administrators Should Make Political Decisions', **1** *Journal of Law, Economics, and Organization*, 81-100.

McCubbins, Mathew D. and Page, Talbot (1986), 'The Congressional Foundations of Agency Performance', **51** *Public Choice*, 173-190.

McCubbins, Mathew D. and Page, Talbot (1987), 'A Theory of Congressional Delegation', in McCubbins, Mathew D. and Sullivan, Terry (eds), *Congress: Structure and Policy*, Cambridge, Cambridge University Press.

McCubbins, Mathew D. and Schwartz, T. (1984), 'Congressional Oversight Overlooked: Policy Patrols vs. Fire Alarms', **28** *American Journal of Political Science*, 165-179.

McCubbins, Mathew D., Noll, Roger G. and Weingast, Barry R. (1987), 'Administrative Procedures as Instruments of Political Control', **3** *Journal of Law, Economics and Organization*, 243-277.

McCubbins, Mathew D., Noll, Roger G. and Weingast, Barry R. (1989), 'Structure and Process, Politics and Policy: Administrative Arrangements and the Political Control of Agencies', **75** *Virginia Law Review*, 431-482.

McGarity, Thomas O. (1991), *Reinventing Rationality - The Role of Regulatory Analysis in the Federal Bureaucracy*, Cambridge, Cambridge University Press.

Migué, Jean-Luc and Belanger, Gerard (1974), 'Towards a General Theory of Managerial Discretion', **17** *Public Choice*, 27-43.

Miller, James C., III (1989), *The Economist as Reformer: Revamping the FTC, 1981*, Washington, American Enterprise Institute for Public Policy Research, 110 p.

Mitnick, Barry M. (1975), 'The Theory of Agency: The Political Paradox and Regulatory Behaviour', **24** *Public Choice*, 27-47.

Mitnick, Barry M. (1980), *Political-Economy of Regulation*, New York, Columbia University Press.

Moe, Terry M. (1985), 'Control and Feedback in Economic Regulation: The Case of the NLRB', **79** *American Political Science Review*, 1094-1117.

Moe, Terry M. (1987), 'An Assessment of the Positive Theory of Congressional Dominance', **12** *Legislative Studies Quarterly*, 475-520.

Moe, Terry M. (1989), 'The Politics of Bureaucratic Structure', in Chubb, John and Peterson, Paul (eds), *Can the Government Govern?*, Washington, Brookings Institution.

Muris, Timothy J. (1986), 'Regulatory Policymaking at the Federal Trade Commission: The Extent of Congressional Control', **94** *Journal of Political Economy*, 884-889.

Nichols, Albert L. (1982), 'Legislative Choice of Regulatory Forms. A Comment on Fiorina', **39** *Public Choice*, 67-71.

Niskanen, William A. (1971), *Bureaucracy and Represention Government*, Chicago, Aldine-Atherton.

Niskanen, William A. (1975), 'Bureaucracts and Politicians', **18** *Journal of Law and Economics*, 617-643.

Noll, R. (1971), *Reforming Regulation: An Evaluation of the Ash Council Proposals*, Washington, Brookings Institution.

Ogul, Morris S. and Rockmann, Bert A. (1990), 'Overseeing Oversight: New Departures and an Old Problem', **15** *Legislative Studies Quarterly*, 5-24.

Ogus, Anthony I. (1995), 'Economics and Law Reform: Thirty years of Law Commission Endeavor', **11** *Law Quarterly Review*, 407-420.

Olson, Mary (1995), 'Regulatory Agency Discretion among Competing Industries: Inside the FDA', **11** *Journal of Law, Economics, and Organization*, 379-408.

Olson, Mary (1996), 'Substitution in Regulatory Agencies: FDA Enforcement Alternatives', **12** *Journal of Law. Economics, and Organization*, 376-407.

Page, William H. (1981), 'Antitrust, Federalism, and the Regulatory Process: A Reconstruction and Critique of the State Action Exemption After Midcal Aluminium', **61** *Boston University Law Review*, 1099-1138.

Parisi, Francesco (1995), 'Public Choice Theory and International Institutions: One More Comment on Richard Falk', **1** *International Legal Theory*, 45-48.

Parisi, Francesco (1997), *The Market of Votes: Coasian Bargaining in an Arrovian Setting*, George Mason University Law and Economics Working Paper Series, No. 97-05.

Parisi, Francesco (1998a), *A Property-Right Theory of Democratic Voting*, George Mason University Law and Economics Working Paper Series, #98-04.

Parisi, Francesco (1998b), 'The Market for Votes: Coasian Bargaining in an Arrovian Setting', **6** *George Mason Law Review*, 745-766.

Posner, Richard A. (1972), 'The Behavior of Administrative Agencies', **1** *Journal of Legal Studies*, 305-347.

Provopoulos, George and Zambaras, Athanassios (1991), 'Testing for Causality Between Government Spending and Taxation', **68** *Public Choice*, 277-282.

Rasmussen, David W. and Benson, Bruce L. (eds) (1994), *The Economic Anatomy of a Drug War: Criminal Justice in the Commons*, Lanham, MD, Rowman and Littlefield.

Ribstein, Larry E. and Kobayashi, Bruce H. (1996a), 'An Economic Analysis of Uniform State Laws', **25** *Journal of Legal Studies*, 131-199.

Ribstein, Larry E. and Kobayashi, Bruce H. (1996b), 'Uniform Laws, Model Laws and Limited Liability Companies', **66** *University of Colorado Law Review*, 947-999.

Robinson, Glen O. (1989), 'Commentary: Political Uses of Structure and Process', **75** *Virginia Law Review*, 483-498.

Rose, Jonathan (1985), 'Executive Oversight of Rulemaking in Arizona: The Govenor's Regulatory Review Counsel - the First Three Years', *Arizona State Law Journal*, 425-491.

Rose, Jonathan (1985), 'Nonlawyer Practice before Federal Administrative Agencies Should be Encouraged', **37** *Administrative Law Review*, 363-373.

Rose-Ackerman, Susan (1978), *Corruption*, New York, Academic Press.

Rose-Ackerman, Susan (1979), *Political Corruption*, New York, Academic Press.

Rose-Ackerman, Susan (1990), 'Comment (on Ferejohn and Shipan's "Congressional Influence (on Bureaucracy)"', **6(S)** *Journal of Law, Economics, and Organization*, 21-27.

Rose-Ackerman, Susan (1995), *Controlling Environmental Policy*, New Haven and London, Yale University Press.

Ross, Stephen F. (1992), 'Delegation, Commitment, and the Regulatory Mandate: Comment', **8** *Journal of Law, Economics, and Organization*, 155-158.

Rubin, Paul H. and Cohen, Mark A. (1985), 'Private Enforcement of Public Policy', **3(1)** *Yale Journal on Regulation*, 167-193.

Rugge, Dale R. (1987), 'Judicial Review of Environmental Protection Agency Rule Promulgation - Clean Air Act State Implementation Plan Requirement', **27** *Natural Resources Journal*, 723-737.

Shepsle, Kenneth A. (1992), 'Organizational Design and Political Control of Administrative Agencies: A Comment: Bureaucratic Drift, Coalition Drift, and Time Consistency', **8** *Journal of Law, Economics, and Organization*, 111-118.

Simon, Herbert A., Smith, D.W. and Thompson, Victor A. (1950/1991), *Public Administration*, (2nd edn), New York, Alfred A. Knopf.

Smith, Janet Kiholm (1982a), 'Production of Licensing Legislation: An Economic Analysis of Interstate Differences', **11** *Journal of Legal Studies*, 117-137.

Smith, Janet Kiholm (1982b), 'An Analysis of State Regulations Governing Liquor Store Licensees', **25** *Journal of Law and Economics*, 301-320.

Spiller, Pablo T. and Tiller, Emerson H. (1997), 'Decision Costs and the Strategic Design of Administrative Process and Judicial Review', **16** *Journal of Legal Studies*, 347-370.

Spitzer, Matthew L. (1988), 'Antitrust Federalism and Rational Choice Political Economy: A Critique of Capture Theory', **61** *Southern California Law Review*, 1293-1326.

Spitzer, Matthew L. (1990), 'Extensions of Ferejohn and Shipan's Model of Administrative Agency Behavior', **6(S)** *Journal of Law, Economics, and Organization*, 29-43.

Spulber, Daniel F. and Besanko, David A. (1992), 'Delegation, Commitment, and the Regulatory Mandate', **8** *Journal of Law, Economics, and Organization*, 126-154.

Stalon, Charles G. (1986), 'Analysis and Synthesis in Quasi-Judicial Multimember Regulatory Agencies', in Saltzman, Sidney and Schuler, Richard E. (eds), *The Future of Electrical Energy: A Regional Perspective*, New York, Greenwood Press, 330-339.

Steunenberg, Bernard (1992), 'Congress, Bureaucracy, and Regulatory Policy Making', **8** *Journal of Law, Economics, and Organization*, 673-694.

Van Damme, E.E.C. (1996), 'Marktwerking en Herregulering (Markets and Re-regulation)', in Gestel, R.A.J. van et al. (eds), *Markt en Wet*, Deventer, W.E.J. Tjeenk Willink, 19-43

Vaubel, Roland (1991), 'A Public Choice View of International Organizations', in Vaubel, Roland and Willet, Thomas D. (eds), *The Political Economy of International Organizations*, Boulder, CO, Westview Press, 27-45.

Waline, M. (1965), 'Quelques Facteurs Sociologiques de l'Evolution Actuelle du Droit (Some Sociologic Factors of Actual Evolution of Law)', in X (ed.), *Mélanges Offerts à René Savatier*.

Weingast, Barry R. (1981), 'Regulation, Reregulation, and Deregulation: The Political Foundations of Agency Clientele Relationships', **44** *Law and Contemporary Problems*, 147-177.

Weingast, Barry R. (1984), 'The Congressional-Bureaucratic System: A Principal Agent Perspective (With Applications to the SEC)', **44** *Public Choice*, 147-191.

Weingast, Barry R. and Moran, Mark J. (1983), 'Bureaucratic Discretion or Congressional Control? Regulatory Policymaking by the Federal Trade Commission', **91** *Journal of Political Economy*, 765-800. Reprinted in Mackay, Robert J., Miller, James C., III and Yandle, Bruce (eds) (1987), *Public Choice and Regulation: A View form Inside the Federal Trade Commission*, Stanford, Hoover Institution Press, 30-62.

Weingast, Barry R. and Moran, Mark J. (1986), 'Congress and Regulatory Agency Choice: Reply', **94** *Journal of Political Economy*, 890-894.

Wiley, John Shepard, Jr (1986), 'A Capture Theory of Antitrust Federalism', **99** *Harvard Law Review*, 713-789.

Wiley, John Shepard, Jr (1988), 'A Capture Theory of Antitrust Federalism: Reply to Professors Page and Spitzer', **61** *Southern California Law Review*, 1327-1341.

Other References

Rubin, Paul H. (1977), 'Why is the Common Law Efficient', **6** *Journal of Legal Studies,* 51-63.

Priest, George L (1977), 'The Common Law Process and the Selection of Efficient Rules', **6** *Journal of Legal Studies*, 65-82.

9400
SELF-REGULATION

Anthony Ogus
University of Manchester

Abstract

Self-regulation encompasses a wide range of arrangements, from private ordering without resort to legal rules to state-enforced systems of delegated rules. Transaction cost analysis has been used to explain how private ordering emerges, and principal-agency theory to indicate the advantages, but also the difficulties, of state delegation. While public choice theory, as supported by empirical studies, suggests that rent-seeking is inherent in delegated self-regulatory regimes, institutional structures capable of controlling this phenomenon can be envisaged.
JEL classification: D45, D71, K20
Keywords: Self-Regulation, Private Ordering, Decentralized Law-Making, Regulatory Competition

1. Introduction

Self-regulation, understood narrowly as law formulated by private agencies to govern professional and trading activities, has been rigorously criticised by lawyers and economists alike. From a legal perspective, it is seen as an example of modern 'corporatism', the acquisition of power by groups which are not accountable to the body politic through the conventional constitutional channels (Schmitter, 1985). The capacity of such groups to make rules governing the activities of members of an association or profession may itself constitute an abuse if they lack democratic legitimacy (Page, 1986). The potential for abuse may become intolerable if, and to the extent that, the rules affect third parties (Cane, 1987). Further, if the group's functions cover policy formulation, interpretation of the rules, adjudication and enforcement (including the imposition of sanctions) as well as rule making, this conflicts with basic notions of separation of powers (Harden and Lewis, 1986).

For their part, economists have traditionally focused on how self-regulatory powers may be exercised to impede competition on the supply side of the market. Barriers to entry may be created, thereby raising prices and conferring rents on incumbent practitioners; standards governing practice may be devised more to confer utility on suppliers than to meet consumer preferences (Shaked and

Sutton, 1981a). And the prospect of gaining such advantages may lure groups into spending resources to persuade legislatures to grant them self-regulatory powers - a social deadweight loss (Tullock, 1967).

While criticisms such as these may be appropriate in some circumstances, they are based on a very incomplete picture of self-regulation. The modern law and economics literature has been concerned to explore a much broader conception of the phenomenon and in so doing to identify institutional arrangements which may escape, or meet, the traditional criticisms and which thereby may be conducive to allocatively efficient outcomes. A survey of this literature must necessarily begin with an investigation of the nature of self-regulation.

2. The Nature of Self-Regulation

In its most literal sense, and as it used in psychology (Carver and Scheier, 1981), self-regulation means acting according to one's own volition, and not as a response to an external constraint. Thus interpreted, the concept would cover an infinite number of self-imposed behavioural standards, including those determined internally by the management of a firm. Although the latter may have no legal significance, they are not irrelevant to discussions of regulatory systems (Bardach and Kagan, 1982; Cheit, 1990). The internal standards are designed to ensure quality of the kind which will meet consumer preferences. On the assumptions of competition between suppliers, adequate information possessed by consumers and an absence of externalities, there is no need to render the standards legally enforceable.

When used in a legal context, the 'self' in 'self-regulation' is not used in the literal sense. Rather it connotes some degree of collective constraint, other than that directly emanating from government, to engender outcomes which would not be reached by individual market behaviour alone (Black, 1996). It is also normally taken to imply 'a fairly well established and generally recognised set of rules, whether customary or reduced to writing, in accordance with which the activity is regulated' (Cane, 1987).

There is, nevertheless, a multitude of institutional arrangements which fall somewhere between government regulation on the one hand and individual, unconstrained behaviour on the other and which can therefore be treated as self-regulation (Rees, 1988; Cheit, 1990). The possibilities can be considered on two spectra depicting, respectively, degrees of autonomy from government and legal force (Page, 1986; Baggott, 1989). The first ranges from, at one extreme, rules private to firms, groups or organizations to, at the other, those approved by a government minister or some independent public authority; in between, representatives of the public interest may participate in, but not conclusively determine, the decision making. The second encompasses varying degrees of legal force. The rules may be: formally binding, non-compliance leading to public law or private law sanctions; codes of practice which presumptively apply unless an alleged offender can show that some alternative conduct was capable of satisfactorily meeting the regulatory goals; norms the breach of which leads to non-legal sanctions, such as ostracism; or standards compliance with which is purely voluntary.

3. Spontaneous Private Legal Ordering

In its most complete sense, and thus at one end of the spectra described above, self-regulation involves a system of private ordering, without any form of state intervention; that is, without any imposition of rules by those with political power. This phenomenon is covered by other chapters (notably Spontaneous Emergence of Law, 9500, and Non-Legal Sanctions, 0780) and the treatment here is consequently brief - for a valuable overview of the literature, see Klein (1997).

Economic explanations of how informal systems emerge are epitomized by studies of primitive societies (Benson, 1988). The basis is reciprocity: individuals recognise the benefits they will derive from behaving in accordance with others' expectations. Such reciprocity may be reflected in individual agreements but, as standards of behaviour, will spread to other members of a group as property rights when the benefits of doing so exceed the costs of defining those rights. While originally disputes may be resolved by force, individuals will normally find non-violent methods (for example, arbitration or mediation) to be cheaper; and ostracism from the group will generally be an adequate sanction for non-compliance.

Analysis of this kind has been used to explain other historical self-ordering arrangements, including: the Maghribi Traders (Greif, 1989); the Law Merchant (Benson, 1989; Milgrom, North and Weingast, 1990); medieval Iceland (Friedman, 1979); and the mining camps in the American West (Anderson and Hill, 1979; Umbeck, 1981). In more modern contexts, equivalent systems can emerge within groups to reduce the costs of drafting commitments and of establishing and activating enforcement systems (Charny, 1990). The expectation is that such cost savings will be significant where the group is small enough for informal control - generally requiring continuing face-to-face interaction - but where also power is broadly dispersed (Ellickson, 1993). Illustrative studies are those on diamond traders (Bernstein, 1992) and neighbour disputes (Ellickson 1991).

Within a broader social setting decentralized law making encounters the problem that some individuals will tend to free-ride on the enforcement of others. This may be only partly solved by the internalization of norms, and thus public institutions (courts) are necessary to identify situations requiring state-imposed incentives (Cooter, 1996). Nevertheless, informal systems also occur in international trading environments (Benson, 1992; see also Schanze, 1988). Here there is an increased need to accommodate the system to inter-group interaction. The co-existence of groups creates incentives for each to compete to attract or hold members and a form of mutual insurance emerges to prevent individuals taking advantage of other individuals and then escaping to another group (Benson, 1993).

A not insignificant part of the literature addresses the normative issue of choice between public and private ordering. Some (for example, Friedman, 1973; Rothbard, 1973; Benson, 1990) reveal a hostility to almost all instances of state-imposed law, arguing from public choice theory that it is predominantly motivated by pressure for wealth transfers and undermines the incentives of the reciprocity-based system of property rights. But, apart from the important reminder that the consequences of government failure may be more severe than market failure, it is not clear that these contributions add much to the debate which has taken place within the mainstream of law and economics (Katz, 1996), and which has its origin in the Coase Theorem (Coase, 1960). The ability of consensual bargaining to achieve efficient outcomes is a function of transactions costs, thus suggesting that the normative question of when private ordering should prevail should be determined by an analysis of how those costs impact on any given situation. Self-regulation may, therefore, be an appropriate solution where bargaining, at low cost, can occur between risk-creators and those affected; occupational health and safety provides a familiar example (Rees, 1988; Ogus, 1995; though for reservations, see Baldwin, 1987).

4. Self-Regulation as Delegation of State Law-Making Powers

In the previous section, we examined systems of private ordering which emerge independently of state intervention. As a legal phenomenon, self-regulation is more usually analysed as a deliberate delegation of the state's law-making powers to an agency, the membership of which wholly or mainly comprises representatives of the firms or individuals whose activities are being regulated.

Public interest arguments for such delegation can be derived from principal-agent theory (Tuohy and Wolfson, 1978). Once the principal (normally, the legislature) has decided that an activity ought to be regulated on grounds of market failure, for example externalities or information asymmetries, the question arises what form of regulation is appropriate. That can be assessed by reference to such variables as the costs of information upon which the rule-making decisions are to be based and those of monitoring compliance and enforcing the rules. The principal may rationally conclude that these costs would be minimised if the tasks of rule-formulation, monitoring, adjudication and enforcement were to be conferred on a self-regulatory agency (hereafter SRA) (Trebilcock, 1983; Cane, 1987).

Since SRAs typically command a greater degree of expertise and technical knowledge of practices and innovatory possibilities within the relevant area than the principal, information costs for the formulation and interpretation of standards are lower. Secondly, for the same reasons, monitoring and enforcement costs are also reduced, as are the costs to the regulatees of dealing with regulators, given that such interaction is likely to be fostered by mutual trust. This aspect is particularly important where, as with advertising, it is difficult to define the desired behaviour with precision and an adversarial relationship between regulator and regulatee is likely to be counterproductive (Baggott and Harrison, 1986). In addition, to the extent that the processes of, and rules issued by, SRAs are less formalized than those of public regulatory regimes, there are likely to be savings in the costs (including those attributable to delay) of amending rules. Finally, the administrative costs of the regime are normally internalized in the trade or activity which is subject to regulation; in the case of independent, public agencies, they are typically borne by taxpayers.

Delegation to SRAs should thus reduce the principal's costs of regulation; to what extent will they confer benefits of the kind which regulation is supposed to foster? Take a situation in which the quality of products or services cannot be observed by consumers prior to purchase. Although individual firms will be motivated to provide signals of quality (for example, product warranties), this may be very costly or - where the characteristics of quality are not easily definable - not feasible. It then becomes in the joint interest of the suppliers, as represented by the SRA, to maintain quality by self-regulation (Gehrig and Jost, 1995). And since, in such circumstances, attempts by consumers themselves to measure quality will also be costly and/or futile, such regulation will confer a benefit on them by obviating the need for measurement (Barzel, 1982).

Once such a regime of self-regulation has been established, individual suppliers have an incentive to supply (at lower cost) lower quality, but since the reputation of other firms will be affected by defaulters the SRA will be motivated to enforce the standards. On the basis of this analysis, it has been predicted that viable self-regulatory regimes will emerge where monitoring costs for the SRA are low, the number of local markets is small, and customers are relatively mobile as between suppliers (Gehring and Jost, 1995).

At the same time, there is every reason to expect that SRAs will use their law-making power to benefit their members in ways which are not consistent with the public interest (Horowitz, 1980). As has been formally demonstrated (Shaked and Sutton, 1981a), the self-regulatory rules may create barriers to entry and thus confer significant rents on incumbent practitioners. The latter include non-financial benefits, for example, a quiet life, as well as monetary income (Lees, 1966).

Most obviously rent may be obtained where the SRA has the power to issue licences and therefore to determine the qualifications of those who engage in the activity (Moore, 1961). But there are also a variety of other ways in which 'quality' standards may be used to promote the interests of the regulatees, rather than those of the public. For example, most professional associations have, at some time or another, prohibited their members from advertising, ostensibly on the ground that 'touting' for business is incompatible with the ethical nature of professional practice (OECD, 1985). As we have seen, such bans can eliminate wasteful consumer searches on elusive quality characteristics (Barzel, 1982), but they can also inhibit comparative price shopping, thus generating monopoly rents for practitioners (Trebilcock, 1982). Secondly, restrictions can be imposed on the legal form used by professional firms (for example, insisting on partnerships and prohibiting corporations) or on the participation of professionals from other disciplines in the firm (OECD, 1985). Both forms of control can add to client costs insofar as they inhibit productive efficiency of the firm (Evans, 1980) and, in some cases, make it necessary for consumers to deal with two or more firms, rather than one (Quinn, 1982). The quality imposed by SRAs may exceed that which presumptively will meet consumers' preferences and not be justified by externalities; and the excessive cost will be borne by consumers (Trebilcock, 1983). Other welfare losses can arise from the tendency of SRAs to discourage diversity and experimentation (Ostry, 1978; White, 1979).

In the light of public choice theory, rent-seeking explanations of regulation are, of course, commonplace (Tollison, 1982). If rule-making remains with the legislature or an independent agency, interest groups representing the regulatees have the task of exerting influence on those institutions and diverting them away from public interest goals or other, competing private interest claims. Of course, delegation of the regulatory powers to SRAs relieves the groups of this task and the relative absence of accountability and external constraints maximizes the possibilities of rent-seeking - 'with self-regulation, regulatory capture is there from the outset' (Kay, 1988). Governments are motivated to maintain or extend the use of self-regulation because, while they may derive political benefits from measures which appear to benefit consumers and others, the costs are not revealed in any public accounts (Trebilcock, 1983). And it is difficult for the cost-bearers both to determine the amount of wealth transfers and to coordinate their activities in opposing them (Van den Bergh and Faure, 1991).

Although, as we shall see in the next section, there is considerable empirical evidence to support this theory of self-regulation, it has not gone unchallenged. Dingwall and Fenn argue that it cannot explain the persistence and stability of entry restriction; other forces must be at work to prevent pressure from potential entrants building up to an intolerable level (Dingwall and Fenn, 1987). Such forces may lead to the emergence of illegal (or 'informal') markets (De Soto, 1989), or of reasonably close, but unregulated, substitutes (Fisher, 1997). Indeed, it may be an inherent feature of regulation that it cannot control every margin of adjustable behaviour, and thus rents are dissipated as firms seek to trade on these uncontrollable margins (Cheung, 1974).

Weingast also finds it hard to reconcile the theory with the fact that many of the self-imposed restrictions can dissipate rents or seem designed to increase a perception of quality maintenance at the expense of greater rents (Weingast, 1980). Drawing on Arrow's public interest analysis (Arrow, 1963), he sees self-regulation as performing a symbolic informational function: as a consequence of the uncertainties both as to quality in the unregulated market and to the effects of regulation there is a tendency for SRAs to adopt policies which improve observable features of the activity and give the appearance of service uniformity.

5. Sector-Specific Studies

Some studies of self-regulatory systems support the notion of spontaneous, private ordering described above. For example, there are incentives for banks voluntarily to become members of private protective and certifying agencies (Gorton and Mullineaux, 1987; Gehring and Jost, 1995), and for voluntary 'best practice' auditing and other standards to be diffused among different SRAs (Belcher, 1996). In the advertising industry, self-regulation has emerged as the suppliers have perceived the benefit to be obtained from acquiring public creditability for their products and from creating an image of professional responsibility (Baggott and Harrison, 1986). But these researchers also highlight the problem of enforcement: SRAs begin to adopt an aggressive stance only where there was perceived to be a threat of intervention by public agencies. The same phenomenon has been observed with the self-regulation of commodity exchanges (Pirrong, 1995; see also Page, 1987; Fishman, 1993; Black, 1997). Investigations of occupational health and safety systems, as they have increasingly shifted towards decentralised standard-setting by local arrangements between employers and employees, suggest this has been effective when the systems can be related to nationally established standards and are supported by knowledge that the arrangements will be enforced (Dawson et al., 1988). But there has been a decline in protection against risks created by small or non-unionised firms (Baldwin, 1987; Smith and Tombs, 1995).

Beginning with the pioneering work of Friedman and Kuznets (1945), published at the end of the Second World War, most attention has been given to regimes governing the professions (for a valuable survey of studies relating to the medical professions, see Gravelle, 1985). Typically the regimes involve SRAs having the power to issue licences and therefore the ability to restrict entry (see Kessel, 1970, for a study on how control by the SRA was used for the benefit of members of the profession). The prediction that this will enable incumbent practitioners to earn rents is difficult to substantiate because it is necessary to disentangle supra-competitive profits from higher earnings which represent legitimate compensation for higher educational costs and greater responsibilities. Nevertheless when such variables are controlled for, researchers have found strong evidence of rents being earned by eyeglass suppliers (Benham and Benham, 1975), dry cleaners (Plott, 1965), lawyers (Holen, 1965; Lees, 1966; Domberger and Sherr, 1989; Curran, 1993) and dentists (Holen, 1965; Shepard, 1978; Wilson, 1987). Studies on other medical professions (Holen, 1965; White, 1979; Wilson, 1987; Curran, 1993) and architects (Button and Fleming, 1992) are less conclusive. In a general study, Maurizi found that there was a significant correlation between licensing regimes and monetary returns for about half of the systems examined (Maurizi, 1974). Exacerbation of shortages in the supply of practitioners (Hogan, 1979), maldistribution of such supply (Holen, 1965; Boulier, 1980; Pashigian, 1980) and poorer quality of service (Caroll and Gaston, 1979) are other welfare effects found to have resulted from licensing regimes.

Ongoing professional standards, established by SRAs, have also enabled them to protect anti-competitive practices: for example, fee regulation and restrictions on advertising which limit price competition (Benham, 1972; Office of Fair Trading, 1982; Domberger and Sherr, 1989; Van den Bergh and Faure, 1991); and 'professional ethics' which serve the wellbeing of practitioners rather than their clients and mask prohibitions on cost-saving innovation (Gravelle, 1985; Trautwein and Rönnau, 1993).

6. Competitive Self-Regulation

The above discussion suggests that, on certain key assumptions, systems of spontaneous private legal ordering can generate efficient outcomes but that state-delegated systems of self-regulation can lead to adverse welfare effects. The crucial factor which distinguishes the two systems is that the act of state delegation normally involves conferring on the SRA a monopoly power to legally constrain supply in the relevant market.

We have seen (Baggott and Harrison, 1986; Pirrong, 1995) that the threat of state intervention may, to some extent, mitigate the harmful effects of monopolization. A useful analogy may here be drawn with the theory of contestable markets which indicates that, under certain conditions, efficient pricing and production can be forced upon a monopolistic supplier by the threat of competition, just as much as by actual competition (Baumol, Panzar and Willig, 1982). But the necessary conditions - notably the ability of the entrant costlessly to leave the market - are rarely met in practice (Waterson, 1988). Similarly, on cost grounds, SRAs may not regard the threat of state intervention as credible.

An alternative solution to the problem presents itself: if the principal objection to SRAs is that they are able to exploit their monopolistic control of supply so as to enable practitioners to earn rents, then why not force SRAs to compete with one another, so that the rents will be eliminated (Kay and Vickers, 1990; Ogus, 1995)? Such competition would obviously prevent SRAs creating barriers to entry. But it should also constrain SRAs to formulate standards which meet consumer preferences at lowest cost since, assuming consumers have adequate information to make appropriate comparisons, they will choose the combination of price and self-regulatory standards which most closely corresponds to those preferences.

Competition of this kind is inherent in systems of private ordering: suppliers compete to attract consumers by the quality (as well as the price) of their products and services. Quality is, to some extent at least, a consequence of standards and other forms of control imposed internally by the management of a firm. The standards may reflect public regulatory requirements but more often they are voluntary, representing the firm's response to assumed consumer demand and, in some cases, incorporating industry-wide practices. To signal to consumers the relationship between standards and quality, some form of voluntary accreditation or certification can be used (Bardach and Kagan, 1982). Suppliers who aim at different quality standards, and have difficulty in communicating that fact to consumers, will have an incentive to establish a rival certification system. Competing self-regulatory regimes may thus emerge.

Thus envisaged, competitive self-regulation is, in essence, no different from competition between national public regulatory regimes (Bratton et al., 1997). If there is mutual recognition of national standards and freedom of trade, consumers can choose between the different quality standards imposed by the national systems in accordance with their own preferences. Provided that they are informed as to the relevant national compliance certificate, competition between national regulatory regimes should induce standard-setters to meet those preferences (Kay and Vickers, 1990).

The policy implication of this analysis is that where the public interest arguments for the state delegating its regulatory powers are strong (see above), it should not grant monopoly power but rather enable two or more SRAs within a given supplier group to formulate alternative regimes (Ogus, 1995; for the effects of competition between professionals and para-professionals, see Shaked and Sutton, 1981b). Although there is a risk of cartelization, most industries are sufficiently heterogeneous for this purpose. An alternative is to retain the monopoly but force different SRAs to compete *ex ante* to acquire the right to control supply by self-regulation. Competing applicants would be required to include their self-regulatory rules as part of the bid; and, as with other public franchises (Demsetz, 1968), the competition should force applicants to offer regimes consistent with the public interest.

There are, nevertheless, potential problems with these solutions. Consumers - more precisely marginal consumers (Schwartz and Wilde, 1979) - must be able to attribute general quality characteristics to certificates generated by the competing self-regulatory regimes; otherwise there will be a 'race to the bottom' (Akerlof, 1970). Secondly, there must be no significant externalities arising from their purchasing behaviour. The importance of information asymmetries and externalities and, in relation to the franchising solution, the need to scrutinize competing bids suggest that in many areas some residual form of state intervention will be optimal. It remains to consider this issue more generally.

7. Mixed Systems

As was indicated in the discussion of the nature of self-regulation, there is a wide range of possible institutional arrangements between public regulation on the one hand and pure private ordering on the other. In an effort to realize many of the benefits of self-regulation but controlling the costs which result from SRA rent-seeking, some jurisdictions have adopted what has been referred to as 'coregulation' (Grabosky and Braithwaite, 1986): SRAs regulate with some oversight or ratification by government, or officials representing the public interest (see for example Page, 1987). The main problem is that of informational asymmetry between the public agency and the SRA. The latter can withhold vital information unless there is confidence that it will be used to reach regulatory solutions which favour its members (Quirk, 1981). Typically, also, the SRA retains monopolistic control of enforcement.

In an important contribution to the literature, Ayres and Braithwaite argue, instead, for 'enforced self-regulation' (Ayres and Braithwaite, 1992; see also Braithwaite, 1982). Under this model, a public agency negotiates with individual firms regulations that are particularized to each firm, with the threat of an imposition of less tailored standards if it fails to cooperate. While the firm may thus formulate the rules, they are enforced by the public agency. The advantages are clear: as with other privately ordered systems, the rules are tailored to match the firm's circumstances and are less costly to adapt; there are incentives to identify least-cost solutions, which should encourage regulatory innovation; and firms would be more committed to the rules than if imposed externally. Moreover, the very fact of individualization avoids the monopoly problem. On the other hand, the administrative costs would be high. This suggests that, for such a regime to be cost-effective, the firm must be large and the activity to be regulated must be one in which efficiency requires significantly differentiated standards (Latin, 1985).

Acknowledgements

I acknowledge with gratitude the very helpful comments of two anonymous referees.

Bibliography on Self-Regulation (9400)

Adelstein, Richard P. (1992), 'Charles E. Lindblom', in Samuels, Warren J. (ed.), *New Horizons in Economic Thought: Appraisals of Leading Economists*, Cheltenham, Edward Elgar, 202-226.

Anderson, Terry L. and Hill, Peter J. (1979), 'American Experiment in Anarcho-Capitalism: The *Not* so Wild, Wild West', **3** *Journal of Liberation Studies*, 9-19.

Barzel, Yoram (1982), 'Measurement Costs and the Organisation of Markets', **25** *Journal of Law and Economics*, 27-48.

Belcher, Alice (1996), 'The Invention, Innovation and Diffusion of Self-Regulation in Corporate Governance', **47** *Northern Ireland Law Quarterly*, 322-334.

Benham, Lee (1972), 'The Effect of Advertising on the Price of Eyeglasses', **15** *Journal of Law and Economics*, 337-352.

Benham, Lee and Benham, Alexandra (1975), 'Regulating Through the Professions: A Perspective on Information Control', **18** *Journal of Law and Economics*, 421-447.

Benson, Bruce L (1988), 'Legal Evolution in Primitive Societies', **144** *Journal of Institutional and Theoretical Economics*, 772-788.

Benson, Bruce L. (1989), 'The Spontaneous Evolution of Commercial Law', **55** *Southern Economic Journal*, 644-661.

Benson, Bruce L (1990), *The Enterprise of Law: Justice Without the State*, San Francisco, Pacific Research Institute for Public Policy.

Benson, Bruce L. (1992), 'Customary Law as a Social Contract: International Commercial Law', **3** *Constitutional Political Economy*, 1-27.

Benson, Bruce L. (1993), 'The Impetus for Recognizing Private Property and Adopting Ethical Behavior in a Market Economy: Natural Law, Government Law, or Evolving Self-Interest', **6** *Review of Austrian Economics*, 43-80.

Bernstein, Lisa (1992), 'Opting Out of the Legal System: Extralegal Contractual Relations in the Diamond Industry', **21** *Journal of Legal Studies*, 115-158.

Blair, Roger D. and Rubin, Stephen (eds), *Regulating the Professions: A Public-Policy Symposium*, Lexington, MA, Lexington Books.

Boulier, B.L. (1980), 'An Empirical Examination of the Influence of Licensure and Licensure Reform on the Geographical Distribution of Dentists', in Rottenberg, Simon (ed.), *Occupational Licensure and Licensure Regulation*, American Enterprise Institute, 73-97.

Braithwaite, John (1982), 'Enforced Self Regulation: A New Strategy for Corporate Crime', **80** *Michigan Law Review*, 1466-1507.

Button, Kenneth and Fleming, Michael (1992), 'The Effects of Regulatory Reform on the Architectural Profession in the United Kingdom', **12** *International Review of Law and Economics*, 95-116.

Caroll, Sidney L. and Gaston, Robert J. (1979), 'State Occupational Licensing Provisions and Quality of Service: The Real Estate Business', **1** *Research in Law and Economics*, 1-13.

Charny, David (1990), 'Nonlegal Sanctions in Commercial Relationships', **104** *Harvard Law Review*, 373-467.

Cheit, Ross E. (1990), *Setting Safety Standards: Regulation in the Public and Private Sectors*, University of California Press.

Cheung, Steven N.S. (1974), 'A Theory of Price Control', **17** *Journal of Law and Economics*, 53-72.

Cooter, Robert D. (1996), 'Decentralized Law for a Complex Economy: The Structural Approach to Adjudicating the New Law Merchant', **144** *University of Pennsylvania Law Review*.

Curran, Christopher (1993), ' The American Experience with Self-Regulation in the Medical and Legal Professions', in Faure, Micheal, Finsinger, Jörg, Siegers, Hacques and Van den Bergh, Roger (eds), *Regulation of Professions: A Law and Economics Approach to the Regulation of Attorneys and Physicians in the US, Belgium, Netherlands, Germany and the UK*, Maklu, Antwerpen, 47-87.

De Soto, Hernando (1989), *The Other Path: The Invisible Revolution in the Third World*, New York, Harper and Row.

Dingwall, Robert and Fenn, Paul (1987), 'A Respectable Profession? Sociological and Economic Perspectives on the Regulation of Professional Services', **7** *International Review of Law and Economics*, 55-64.

Domberger, Simon and Sherr, Avrom (1989), 'The Impact of Competition on Pricing and Quality of Legal Services', **9** *International Review of Law and Economics*, 41-56.

Ellickson, Robert C. (1991), *Order Without Law: How Neighbours Settle Disputes*, Cambridge, MA, Harvard University Press.

Ellickson, Robert C. (1993), 'Property in Land', **102** *Yale Law Journal*, 1315-1400.

Evans, Robert G. (1980), 'Professionals and the Production Function: Can Competition Policy Improve Efficiency in the Licensed Professions?', in Rottenberg, Simon (ed.), *Occupational Licensure and Regulation*, American Enterprise Institute.

Friedman, David (1973), *The Machinery of Freedom: Guide to Radical Capitalism*, New York, Harper and Row.

Friedman, David (1979), 'Private Creation and Enforcement of Law: A Historical Case', **8** *Journal of Legal Studies*, 399-415.

Friedman, Milton and Kuznets, S. (1945), *Income from Independent Professional Practice*, New York, National Bureau of Economic Research.

Gehrig, Thomas and Jost, Peter J. (1995), 'Quacks, Lemons and Self-Regulation: A Welfare Analysis', **7** *Journal of Regulatory Economics*, 309-235.

Gorton, Gary and Mullineaux, Donald J. (1987), 'The Joint Production of Confidence: Endogenous Regulation and Nineteenth Century Commercial Bank Clearinghouses', **19** *Journal of Money, Credit, and Banking*, 457-468.

Gravelle, Hugh (1985), 'Economic Analysis of Health Service Professions: A Survey', **20** *Social Sciences and Medicine*, 1049-1061.

Greif, Avner (1989), 'Reputation and Coalitions in Midieval Trade: Evidence on the Maghribi Traders', **49** *Journal of Economic History*, 857-882.

Holen, Arlene S. (1965), 'Effects of Professional Licensing Arrangements on Interstate Labor Mobility and Resource Allocation', **73** *Journal of Political Economy*, 492-498.

Horowitz, Ira (1980), 'The Economic Foundations of Self-Regulation in the Professions', in Blair, Roger D. and Rubin, Stephen (eds), *Regulating the Professions: A Public-Policy Symposium*, Lexington, MA, Lexington Books.

Katz, Avery (1996), 'Taking Private Ordering Seriously', **144** *University of Pennsylvania Law Review*, 1754-1763.

Kay, John (1988), 'The Forms of Regulation', in Seldon, Arthur (ed.), *Financial Regulation - or Over-Regulation*, Institute of Economic Affairs, 33-42.

Kessel, Reuben A. (1970), 'The A.M.A. and the Supply of Physicians', **35** *Law and Contemporary Problems*, 267-283.

Klein, Daniel B. (ed.) (1997), *Reputation: Studies in the Voluntary Elicitation of Good Conduct*, University of Michigan Press.

Kissam, P.C. (1980), 'Anti-Trust Law, the First Amendment, and Professional Self-Regulation of Technical Quality', in Blair, Roger D. and Rubin, Stephen (eds), *Regulating the Professions: A Public-Policy Symposium*, Lexington, MA, Lexington Books.

Lees, D.S. (1966), *The Economic Consequences of the Professions*, London, Institute of Economic Affairs, 48 p.

Maurizi, Alex R. (1974), 'Occupational Licensing and the Public Interest', **82** *Journal of Political Economy*, 399-413.

Milgrom, Paul R., North, Douglass, C. and Weingast, Barry R. (1990), 'The Role of Institutions in the Revival of Trade: the Law Merchant, Private Judges, and the Champagne Fairs', **2** *Economics and Politics*, 1-23.

Moore, Thomas G. (1961), 'The Purpose of Licensing', **4** *Journal of Law and Economics*, 93-117.

Ogus, Anthony (1995), 'Rethinking Self-Regulation', **15** *Oxford Journal of Legal Studies*, 97-108.

Ostry, Sylvia (1978), 'Competition Policy and the Self- Regulating Professions', in Slayton, Philip and Trebilcock, Michael J. (eds), *The Professions and Public Policy*, Toronto, University of Toronto Faculty of Law.

Pashigian, B. Peter (1980), 'Has Occupational Licensing Reduced Geographical Mobility and Raised Earnings?', in Rottenberg, Simon (ed.), *Occupational Licensure and Regulation*, American Enterprise Institute.

Paul, Chris W. (1982), 'Competition in the Medical Profession: An Application of the Economic Theory of Regulation', **48** *Southern Economic Journal*, 559-569.

Pirrong, Stephen Craig (1995), 'The Self Regulation of Commodity Exchanges: The Case of Market Manipulation', **38** *Journal of Law and Economics*, 141-206.

Plott, Charles R. (1965), 'Occupational Self-Regulation: A Case-Study of the Oklahoma Dry Cleaners', **8** *Journal of Law and Economics*, 195-222.

Quinn, John (1982), 'Multidisciplinary Legal Services and Preventive Regulation', in Evans, Robert G. and Trebilcock, Michael J. (eds), *Lawyers and the Consumer Interest: Regulating the Market for Legal Services*, London, Butterworths, ch.11.

Rees, Joseph (1988), *Reforming the Workplace: A Study of Self-Regulation in Occupational Safety*, University of Pennsylvania Press.

Rothbard, Murray N. (1973), *For a New Liberty*, London, Macmillan.

Schanze, Erich (1988), 'Regulation by Consensus: The Practice of International Mining Agreements', **144** *Journal of Institutional and Theoretical Economics*, 152-171.

Shaked, Avner and Sutton, John (1981a), 'Heterogeneous Consumers and Product Differentiation in a Market for Professional Services', **15** *European Economic Review*, 159-177.

Shaked, Avner and Sutton, John (1981b), 'The Self-Regulating Profession', **47** *Review of Economic Studies*, 217-234.

Shepard Lawrence (1978), 'Licensing Restrictions and the Cost of Dental Care'', **21** *Journal of Law and Economics*, 187-201.

Smith, Denis and Tombs, Steve (1995), 'Beyond Self-Regulation: Towards a Critique of Self-Regulation as a Control Strategy for Hazardous Activities, **32** *Journal of Management Studies*, 619-636.

Trautwein, Hans-Michael and Rönnau, Andreas (1993), 'Selfregulation of the Medical Profession in Germany: A Survey', in Faure, Michael, Finsinger, Jörg, Siegers, Jacques and Van den Bergh, Roger (eds), *Regulation of Professions: A Law and Economics Approach to the Regulation of Attorneys and Physicians in the US, Belgium, Netherlands, Germany and the UK*, Antwerpen, Maklu, 249-306.

Trebilcock, Michael J. (1982), 'Competitive Advertising', in Evans Robert G. and Trebilcock, Michael J. (eds), *Lawyers and the Consumer Interest: Regulating the Market for Legal Services*, London, Butterworths, ch. 5.

Trebilcock, Michael J. (1983), 'Regulating Service Quality in Professional Markets', in Dewees, Donald N. (ed.), *The Regulation of Quality: Products, Services, Workplaces and The Environment*, Butterworths, ch. 4.

Tuohy, Carolyn and Wolfson, Alan (1978), 'Self-Regulation: Who Qualifies?', in Slayton, Philip and Trebilcock, Michael J. (eds), *The Professions and Public Policy*, Toronto, University of Toronto Faculty of Law.

Umbeck, John (1981), *A Theory of Property Rights with Applications to the Californian Gold Rush*, Iowa State University Press.

Van den Bergh, Roger and Faure, Michael G. (1991), 'Self Regulation of the Professions in Belgium', **11** *International Review of Law and Economics*, 165-182.

Weingast, Barry R. (1980), 'Physicians, DNA Research Scientists, and the Market for Lemons', in Blair, Roger D. and Rubin, Stephen (eds), *Regulating the Professions: A Public-Policy Symposium*, Lexington, MA, Lexington Books.

White, William D. (1979), Dynamic Elements of Regulation: The Case of Occupational Licensure', **1** *Research in Law and Economics*, 15-33.

Wilson, R.A. (1987), 'Returns to Entering the Medical Profession in the UK', **6** *Journal of Health Economics*, 339-363.

Other References

Akerlof, George, A. (1970), 'The Market for "Lemons": Qualitative Uncertainty and the Market Mechanism', **84** *Quarterly Journal of Economics*, 488-500.

Arrow, Kenneth (1963), 'Uncertainty and the Welfare Economics of Medical Care', **53** *American Economic Review*, 941-973.

Ayres, Ian and Braithwaite, John (1992), *Responsive Regulation: Transcending the Deregulation Debate*, Oxford, Oxford University Press.

Baggott, Rob and Harrison, Larry (1986), 'The Politics of Self-Regulation: The Case of Advertising Control', **14** *Policy and Politics*, 143-160.

Baggott, Rob (1989), 'Regulatory Reform in Britain: The Changing Face of Self-Regulation, **67** *Public Administration*, 435-454.

Baldwin, Robert (1987), 'Health and Safety at Work: Consensus and Self-Regulation', in Baldwin, Robert and McCrudden, Christopher (eds), *Regulation and Public Law*, London, Weidenfeld and Nicholson, ch.7.

Bardach, Eugene and Kagan, Robert A. (1982), 'Mixing Public and Private Regulation', in Graymer, LeRoy and Thompson, Frederick (eds), *Reforming Social Regulation: Alternative Public Policy Strategies*, London, Sage Publications, ch.10.

Baumol, William, J., Panzar, John C. and Willig, Robert D. (1982), *Contestable Markets and the Theory of Industry Structure*, New York, Harcourt Brace Jovanovich.

Black, Julia (1996), 'Constitutionalising Self-Regulation', **59** *Modern Law Review*, 24-55.

Black, Julia (1997), *Rules and Regulators*, Oxford, Clarendon Press.

Bratton, William, Mccahery, Joseph, Picciotti, Sol and Scott, Colin (eds) (1997), *International Regulatory Competition and Coordination: Perspectives on Economic Regulation in Europe and the United States*, Oxford, Clarendon Press.

Cane, Peter (1987), 'Self Regulation and Judicial Review', **6** *Civil Justice Quarterly*, 324-347.

Carver, Charles, S. and Scheier, Michael F. (1981), *Attention and Self-regulation: A Control Theory Approach to Human Behavior*, Berlin, Springer-Verlag.

Coase, Ronald H. (1960), 'The Problem of Social Cost', **3** *Journal of Law and Economics*, 1-44.

Dawson, Sheila, Willman, Paul, Clinton, Alan and Bamford, M. (1988), *Safety at Work: The Limits of Self-Regulation*, Cambridge, Cambridge University Press.

Demsetz, Harold (1968), 'Why Regulate Utilities?', **11** *Journal of Law and Economics*, 55-65.

Fisher, Andrew (1997), 'The Licensing of Taxis and Minicabs', **7** *Consumer Policy Review*, 158-161.

Fishman, James J. (1993), 'A Comparison of Enforcement of Securities Law Violations in the UK and US', *Company Lawyer*, 163-172

Grabosky, Peter and Braithwaite, John (1986), *Of Manners Gentle: Enforcement Strategies of Australian Business Regulatory Agencies*, Oxford, Oxford University Press.

Harden, Ian and Lewis, Norman (1986), *The Noble Lie: The British Constitution and the Rule of Law*, New York, Hutchinson.

Hogan, Daniel B. (1979), *Regulation of Psychotherapists: A Study in the Philosophy and Practice of Professional Regulation*, Cambridge, MA, Ballinger.

Kay, John and Vickers, John (1990), 'Regulatory Reform: An Appraisal', in Majone, Giandomenico (ed.), *Deregulation or Re-regulation: Regulatory Reform in Europe and the United States*, London, Frances Pinter.

Latin, Howard (1985), 'Ideal versus Real Regulatory Efficiency: Implementation of Uniform Standards and "Fine-Tuning" Regulatory Reforms', **37** *Stanford Law Review*, 1267-1332.

OECD (1985), *Competition Policy and the Professions*, Paris, Organisation for Economic Co-operation and Development.

Office of Fair Trading (1982), *Opticians and Competition*, HMSO.

Page, Alan C. (1986), 'Self-Regulation: The Constitutional Dimension', **49** *Modern Law Review*, 141-167.

Page, Alan C. (1987), 'Financial Services: The Self-Regulatory Alternative', in Baldwin, Robert and McCrudden, Christopher (eds), *Regulation and Public Law*, London, Weidenfeld and Nicholson, ch.13.

Quirk, Paul J. (1981), *Industry Influence in Federal Regulatory Agencies*, Princeton University Press.

Schmitter, Philippe C. (1985), 'Neo-Corporatism and the State', in Grant, Wyn (ed.), *The Political Economy of Corporatism*, London, Macmillan, 32-62.

Schwartz, Alan and Wilde, Louis L. (1979), 'Intervening in Markets on the Basis of Imperfect Information: A Legal and Economic Analysis', **127** *University of Pennsylvania Law Review*, 630-682.

Tollison, Robert D. (1982), 'Rent Seeking: A Survey', **35** *Kyklos*, 575-602.

Tullock, Gordon (1967), 'The Welfare Costs of Tariffs, Monopolies and Theft', **5** *Western Economic Journal*, 224-232.

Waterson, Michael (1988), *Regulation of the Firm and Natural Monopoly*, Oxford, Basil Blackwell.

9500
SPONTANEOUS EMERGENCE OF LAW: CUSTOMARY LAW

Francesco Parisi
George Mason University School of Law

Abstract

In the 'social contract' framework, customary rules can be regarded as an implied and often non-verbalized exercise of direct legislation by the members of society. Those legal systems that grant direct legal force to customary rules regard custom as a primary, although not exclusive, source of law. In such legal traditions, courts enforce customary rules as if they had been enacted by the proper legislative authority. Custom thus amounts to a spontaneous norm which is recognized by the legal system and granted enforcement as a proper legal rule. Judicial recognition of spontaneous norms amounts to a declaratory (rather than constitutive) function that treats custom as a legal fact. The legal system 'finds' the law by recognizing social norms, but does not 'create' the law. The most notable illustration is the system of international law, where, absent a central legislative authority, custom stands next to treaties as a primary source of law. (See, for example, Article 38 (1) of the *Statute of the International Court of Justice*; and Restatement 102 of the *Foreign Relations Law of the United States.*)

Whenever they are granted legitimate status in a legal system, customary rules are usually given the same effect as other primary sources of law. Although often subordinated to formal legislation, customary rules derive their force from the concurrence of a uniform practice and a subjective belief that adherence to them is obligatory (*opinio iuris*), without necessarily being formally incorporated into any written body of law. For this reason, they are usually classified as 'immaterial' sources of law (Brownlie, 1990). This notion implies that the custom remains the actual source of law even after its judicial recognition. In this setting, the judicial decisions that recognize a custom offer only persuasive evidence of its existence and do not themselves become sources of law. In turn, this prevents the principle of *stare decisis* from crystallizing customary law.

Modern legal systems generally recognize customary rules that have emerged either within the confines of positive legislation (*consuetudo secundum legem*) or in areas that are not disciplined by positive law (*consuetudo praeter legem*). Where custom is in direct conflict with legislation (that is, *custom contra*

legem) the latter normally prevails. In some instances, however, a custom supersedes prior legislation (that is, *abrogative custom*), and some arguments have been made in support of emerging practices that conflict with obsolete provisions of public international law (*desuetudo*, or abrogative practice) (Kontou, 1994). The theoretical and practical significance of these forms of spontaneous social order, which compete with enacted law in influencing human choice, are discussed below.
JEL classification: K00
Keywords: Customary Law, Spontaneous Law, Social Norms

1. Introduction

Legal theorists define custom as a practice that emerges outside of legal constraints, and which individuals and organizations spontaneously follow in the course of their interactions out of a sense of legal obligation. Two categories of social practices are generally distinguished:

(a) Practices that reflect mere behavioural patterns. In legal jargon, such behaviour is a mere usage; in economic terms it simply represents an equilibrium convention. A mere behavioural regularity does not generate a customary rule.
(b) Practices that reflect an internalized belief that the practice is necessary or socially desirable. These practices are considered necessary for social well-being and are treated as proper legal custom, often entering the legal system as primary sources of law.

The terminology used in the legal and economic literature should be contrasted with the terminology employed in sociological literature (see, for example, Weber, 1978, pp. 319-320). What is legally termed a mere usage is defined in sociological literature as a custom (*Sitte*), in the sense of a typically uniform activity that is not considered to be socially necessary. Convention - the sociological notion closest to the legal concept of custom - amounts to conduct manipulated by express approval or disapproval by other members of the group, but lacking the enforceability that characterizes a legal custom.

A. The Theory of Spontaneous Law

2. The Formative Elements of a Customary Rule

According to the theory of customary law, individual actors gradually come to embrace norms that they view as requisite to their collective wellbeing. An enforceable custom emerges from two formative elements: (a) a quantitative element consisting of a general or emerging practice; and (b) a qualitative element reflected in the belief that the norm generates a desired social outcome.

2.1 The Quantitative Element

The quantitative requirements for the formation of customary law concern both the length of time and the universality of the emerging practice. Regarding the time element, there is generally no universally established minimum duration for the emergence of customary rules. Customary rules have evolved from both immemorial practice and a single act. Still, French jurisprudence has traditionally required the passage of forty years for the emergence of an international custom, while German doctrine generally requires thirty years (see Tunkin, 1961; Mateesco, 1947). Naturally, the longer the time required to form a valid practice, the less likely it is for custom to effectively anticipate the intervention of formal legislation, and to adapt to changing circumstances overtime.

Regarding the condition of universality, international legal theory is ambivalent. Charney (1986) suggests that the system of international relations is analogous to a world of individuals in the state of nature, dismissing the idea that unanimous consent by all participants is required before binding customary law is formed. Rather than universality, recent restatements of international law refer to 'consistency' and 'generality' (see D'Amato, 1971). Where it is impossible to identify a general practice because of fluctuations in behavior, the consistency requirement is not met (see *Asylum* (1950) pp. 276-277; and *Wimbledon* (1923), Ser. A, no. 1). Similarly, more recent cases in international law restate the universality requirement in terms of 'increasing and widespread acceptance' (see, for example, *Fisheries Jurisdiction* (1974), pp. 23-26; *North Sea Continental Shelf* (1969), p. 42), allowing special consideration for emerging general norms (or local clusters of spontaneous default rules) that are expected to become evolutionarily stable over time.

With regard to rules at the national or local level, the varying pace with which social norms are transformed suggests that no general time or consistency requirement can be established as an across-the-board condition for the validity of a custom. Some variance in individual observation of the practice should be expected because of the stochastic origin of social norms. A flexible time requirement is particularly necessary in situations of rapid flux, where exogenous changes are likely to affect the incentive structure of the underlying relationship.

2.2 The Qualitative Element

The second formative element of a customary rule is generally identified by the phrase *opinio iuris ac necessitatis*, which describes a widespread belief in the desirability of the norm and the general conviction that the practice represents an essential norm of social conduct. This element is often defined in terms of necessary and obligatory convention. (Kelsen, 1939, 1945; D'Amato, 1971; Walden, 1977). The traditional formulation of *opinio iuris* is problematic because of its circularity. It is quite difficult to conceptualize that law can be born from a practice which is already believed to be required by law.

The practical significance of this requirement is that it narrows the range of enforceable customs: only those practices recognized as socially desirable or necessary will eventually ripen into enforceable customary law. Once there is a general consensus that members of a group ought to conform to a given rule of conduct, a legal custom can be said to have emerged when some level of spontaneous compliance with the rule is obtained. As a result, observable equilibria that are regarded by society as either undesirable (for example, a prisoner's dilemma uncooperative outcome) or unnecessary (for example, a common practice of greeting neighbours cordially) will lack the subjective and qualitative element of legal obligation and, therefore, will not generate enforceable legal rules.

B. The Emergence of Spontaneous Law

According to the traditional legal approach to customary law, two elements are generally required for the emergence of a binding custom: (1) the practice should emerge out of the spontaneous and uncoerced behaviour of various members of a group, and (2) the parties involved must subjectively believe in the obligatory or necessary nature of the emerging practice (*opinio iuris*). To an economist, the first element corresponds to the rather standard assumption of rational choice. The second element may be appraised as a belief of social obligation, emerging in response to game inefficiencies, to support behavioural rules that avoid aggregate losses from strategic behaviour.

The law and economics literature has examined some additional structural conditions for the emergence of customary law, which will briefly be analyzed below. (For a more extensive analysis, see Parisi, 1998b.)

3. Structural Symmetry and Incentive Alignment

The literature on social norms focuses on non-contractual mechanisms and considers the situations that are more easily governed by spontaneous law. Under symmetrical conditions, norms that maximize group welfare also maximize individual expected payoffs. Thus, no one has any reason to challenge the emerging norm. Paradoxically, therefore, there is no need for law or norm enforcement in an environment characterized by perfect incentive alignment, as contracts or relationships are self-enforcing (Klein, 1996).

In the presence of perfect incentive alignment, cooperation will result in both the case of repeated games in which the players are faced with high discount factors, and in one-shot games. It is worth noting that situations characterized by symmetric payoffs or role reversibility do not present an opportunity for strategic preference revelation. The expected costs and benefits of alternative rules are the same among the members of the group. Each individual has an incentive to agree to a set of rules that maximize the aggregate welfare of the group, consequently maximizing his expected share of wealth. True preferences will therefore be revealed in situations of stochastic symmetry. Conversely, strategic choices are more likely to characterize real life situations with misaligned individual incentives.

Additionally, in the absence of perfect incentive alignment, the discount factor plays an important role. In situations where the probability of future interaction is relatively high, the discount factor captures two analytically distinct elements. First, it acts as a function of the players' time preference. Second, the discount factor is a function of the probability of future interactions.

The discount factor's role in evolutionary models is therefore critical. Environments promoting a high probability of future interaction and low time preference are therefore more likely to induce optimizing equilibria. In the case of a one-shot game, on the other hand, the probability of future interaction is zero, so that the expected value of future cooperation is also zero (see, generally, Axelrod, 1984).

Another area of research in the customary law literature considers the role of morality and internalized obligations as a means for inducing cooperation in conflict games (see, for example, Gauthier, 1986; Ullmann-Margalit, 1977). Internalization of the norm is a source of spontaneous compliance. For example, individuals internalize obligations when they disapprove and sanction other individuals' deviations from the rule, or when they directly lose utility when the norm is violated. In this setting, Cooter (1994a) suggests that a legal custom will successfully evolve when the *ex ante* individual incentives are aligned with the collective public interest. Cooter (1994a, p. 224) calls this proposition the 'alignment theorem'.

4. Stochastic Symmetry and Role Reversibility

Traditionally, strategic preference revelation is viewed as a hindrance to the spontaneous emergence of cooperation. Such a problem is likely to be minimized in situations of role reversibility or stochastic symmetry (Parisi, 1995). Similar to a Rawlsian veil of ignorance, role reversibility and stochastic symmetry induce each member to agree to a set of rules that benefits the entire group, thus maximizing her expected share of the wealth.

These conditions in fact occurred during the formative period of the medieval law merchant (*lex mercatoria*), when traveling merchants acted in the dual capacity of buyer and seller. If they articulated a rule of law which was favourable to them as sellers, it could have the opposite effect when they acted as buyers, and vice-versa. This role reversibility changed an otherwise conflicting set of incentives (buyer versus seller) into one that converged toward symmetrical and mutually desirable rules.

The law merchant therefore illustrates a successful system of spontaneous and decentralized law (see Benson, 1989, 1990; Greif, 1989). Fuller (1969, p. 24) observes that frequent role changes foster the emergence of mutually recognized and accepted duties 'in a society of economic traders. By definition the members of such a society enter direct and voluntary relationships of exchange. ... Finally, economic traders frequently exchange roles, now selling, now buying. The duties that arise out of their exchanges are therefore reversible, not only in theory but in practice.'

Certainly, the emergence of consensus for a given rule does not exclude the possibility of subsequent opportunistic deviation by some individuals when roles are later reversed. This is a typical enforcement problem, however, and the possibility of strategic defection does not undermine the rule's qualitative features. The general acceptance of or acquiescence to a custom depends primarily on its anticipated effect on the group. Those strategies that maximize the expected payoff for each participant if reciprocally undertaken evolve into norms. This conception of spontaneous law is examined by Stearns (1994, pp. 1243-1244), who observes that if the participants were unable to devise rules governing future interactions, and unforeseen circumstances placed them in a forced market relationship requiring post-contractual negotiations, courts and legislatures might have a comparative advantage over the participants in devising market facilitating rules. Unlike market participants, courts and legislatures choose from among alternative solutions as if the underlying events had not yet occurred, without attempting to strategically maximize the advantage caused by unforeseen circumstances (see also Shubik, 1987). Where rules are breached following role reversal, norms play a collateral yet crucial role in sanctioning case-by-case opportunism.

Conditions of role reversibility, coupled with norms that generate disincentives to adopt opportunistic double standards, are therefore likely to generate optimal rules via spontaneous processes. The group's ability to impose a sanction obviously depends on an individual's accountability for his past behaviour. Benson (1992d, pp. 5-7) explores the role of reputation in situations of repeated market interaction, observing that reputation serves as a source of collective knowledge regarding past actions.

5. Induced Symmetry and Reciprocity Constraints

Prisoner's dilemma-type games are plagued by the dominance of opportunistic behaviour because of the potential accessibility of off-diagonal, non-cooperative outcomes. Schotter (1981), Lewis (1969) and Leibenstein (1982) analyze the role of conventions in correcting prisoner's dilemma situations.

Among the devices capable of correcting prisoner's dilemma-type games, the players can bind their strategic choices to those of their opponents, drastically changing the equilibrium of the game. Ensuring automatic reciprocity by binding a player's strategy to that of his opponent eliminates access to off-diagonal outcomes and renders the reward for unilateral defection unobtainable. Just as no rational player will employ defection strategies in the hope of obtaining higher payoffs from unilateral cheating, neither will a rational player be induced to select defection strategies as a merely defensive tactic. Automatic reciprocity mechanisms thus guarantee a shift toward optimizing cooperation. As pointed out by Parisi (1997), ancient customs of retaliation, based on conceptions of symmetry and punitive balance, provide an intriguing illustration of the principle of reciprocity at work (see, for example, Exodus 21:23; and Code of Hammurabi Paragraphs 108 and 127). Parisi (1998a) considers another example of a reciprocity constraint. Art. 21 (1)b of the 1969 Vienna Convention, which articulates an established custom of reciprocity, creates a mirror-image mechanism in the case of unilateral reservations in the process of treaty ratification: 'A reservation established with regard to another party ... modifies those provisions to the same extent for that other party in its relations with the reserving state.' The effects of this automatic reciprocity mechanism are similar to a tit-for-tat strategy without the need for active retaliation by states: whenever a treaty is modified unilaterally in favour of one state, the result will be as if all the other states had introduced an identical reservation against the reserving state. By imposing a symmetry constraint on the parties' choices, this rule offers a possible solution to prisoner's dilemma problems.

Parisi (1998a) further observes that, while the principle of reciprocity solves conflict situations characterized by a prisoner's dilemma structure (in both symmetric and asymmetric cases), alone it is incapable of correcting other strategic problems. When a conflict occurs along the diagonal possibilities of the game (such that the obtainable equilibria are already characterized by symmetric strategies), a reciprocity constraint will not eliminate the divergence of interests between the players and will not affect the results of the game. The dynamic process of norm formation may unveil the existence of a 'tilt point' beyond which emerging beliefs become stable and self-sustaining. In light of reciprocal constraints undertaken by other members of the community, individuals who frequently exchange roles in their social interactions have incentives to constrain their behaviour to conform to socially optimal norms of conduct. Buchanan (1975) insightfully anticipated this result, suggesting that an even stronger logic explains the emergence of cooperation in situations of induced reciprocity. In both cases, the non-idealistic and self-interested behaviour of human actors will generate optimal norms.

6. Articulation Theories in the Formation of Customary Law

Notable scholars have considered the conditions under which principles of justice can emerge spontaneously through the voluntary interaction and exchange of individual members of a group. As in a contractarian setting, the reality of customary law formation relies on a voluntary process through which members of a community develop rules that govern their social interaction by voluntarily adhering to emerging behavioural standards. In this setting, Harsanyi (1955) suggests that optimal social norms are those that would emerge through the interaction of individual actors in a social setting with impersonal preferences. The impersonality requirement for individual preferences is satisfied if the decision makers have an equal chance of finding themselves in any one of the initial social positions and they rationally choose a set of rules to maximize their expected welfare. Rawls (1971) employs Harsanyi's model of stochastic ignorance in his theory of justice. However, the Rawlsian 'veil of ignorance' introduces an element of risk aversion in the choice between alternative states of the world, thus altering the outcome achievable under Harsanyi's original model, with a bias toward equal distribution (that is, with results that approximate the Nash criterion of social welfare). Further analysis of the spontaneous formation of norms and principles of morality can be found in Sen (1979), Ullmann-Margalit (1977) and Gauthier (1986).

Legal theorists and practitioners have addressed a similar issue when considering the requirements of *opinio iuris*. In attempting to solve one of the problems associated with the notion of *opinio iuris*, namely the troublesome problem of circularity, legal scholars (notably, D'Amato, 1971) have considered the crucial issue of timing of belief and action in the formation of customary rules. The traditional approach emphasizes the awkward notion that individuals must believe that a practice is already law before it can become law. This approach basically requires the existence of a mistake for the emergence of a custom: the belief that an undertaken practice was required by law, when instead, it was not. Obviously, this approach has its flaws. Placing such reliance on systematic mistakes, the theory fails to explain how customary rules can emerge and evolve overtime in cases where individuals have full knowledge of the state of the law.

In this context, legal theorists have proposed to look past the notions of *opinio iuris* and usage concentrating on the qualitative element of 'articulation'.

Consistent with the predicament of the economic models, articulation theories suggest that greater weight should be given to beliefs that have been expressed prior to the emergence of a conflict.

Here, it is interesting to point out a strong similarity between the legal and the economic models. Articulations that are made prior to the unveiling of conflicting contingencies can be analogized to rules chosen under a Harsanyian veil of uncertainty. States and individuals will have an incentive to articulate and endorse norms that maximize their expected welfare. Given some degree of uncertainty as to the future course of events, the emerging rules will be such as to maximize the expected welfare of the community at large. Conversely, rules that are articulated after an outburst of conflict may be strategically biased. Once the future is disclosed to them, parties will tend to articulate rules that maximize their actual welfare, rather than the expected welfare to be derived from an uncertain future. Thus, *ex ante* norms should be given greater weight in the adjudication process.

This predicament seems to be contradicted by the empirical and anecdotal evidence on commercial customary law. Bernstein (1996) examines customary rules that have developed in various modern commercial trades. Her findings seem to indicate that in the adjudication of business disputes, commercial tribunals tend to enforce customary rules that are quite different from the business norms spontaneously followed by the parties in the course of their relationship. Rather, customary rules develop around practices developed during the conflictual phase of a relationship. In this setting, Bernstein distinguishes between relationship norms and end-of-the-game norms. When adjudicating a case, courts are faced with parties who have reached the end point in their relationship. The end-of-the-game norms of the conflictual phase thus tend to be enforced, while the cooperative norms developed in the course of their relationship remain outside the domain of adjudication.

C. The Failures of Customary Law

According to the popular paradigms of economic analysis, decentralized market processes have a comparative advantage over centralized allocative mechanisms in the creation of efficient equilibria. Customary law formation can be analogized to a decentralized decision making process, with a comparative advantage over centralized processes in the creation of efficient rules.

Customary rules are generally accepted by the community, with a larger share of rules followed spontaneously by the community and a consequent reduction in law enforcement costs. In the decentralized dynamic of spontaneous law, individual decision makers directly perceive the costs and benefits of alternative rules, and reveal their preferences by supporting or opposing their formation.

The formative process of customary law proceeds through a purely inductive accounting of subjective preferences. Through his own action, each individual contributes to the creation of law. The emerging rule thus embodies the aggregate effects of independent choices by various individuals that participate in its formation. This inductive process allows individuals to reveal their preferences through their own action, without the interface of third-party decision makers.

The analogy between customary rules and spontaneous market equilibria, however, calls for an assessment of the potential insufficiencies of the spontaneous processes of law formation. I will proceed by setting out some hypotheses for failure and discussing their potential scope of application in the area of customary law. The literature in this area is relatively thin and much work still needs to be done to develop a coherent theory of spontaneous law.

7. Path Dependence and the Idiosyncracies of Customary Law

Norms and conventions vary from place to place. Any theory about the efficiency of spontaneous law should explain the diversity of norms and conventions across time and space. In my view, there are two primary ways to provide such an explanation.

The first is to look for idiosyncratic environmental or institutional factors which might attribute to the diversity of observed rules. If the underlying social, economic, or historical realities are found to be different from one another, different norms or conventions should be expected. Rules, norms and conventions develop in response to exogenous shocks through a natural process of selection and evolution. This 'survival of the fittest' explanation would suggest that whatever exists in equilibrium is efficient, given the current state of affairs. This belief, borrowed from Darwinian evolutionism, is pervasive in the law and economics literature and, when applied to spontaneous law, risks becoming a tautological profession of faith. Ironically, we should note that the originators of such a claim, socio-biologists, have now widely refuted its validity.

The second way to reconcile the efficiency claim to the observed diversity of spontaneous rules is to consider the role of path dependence in the evolution of norms and conventions. Following Roe (1996) and his definition of path dependence in law, evolution toward efficiency may be seen as taking place with some random component. Random historical and natural events (the random element of chaos theory) determine the choice of the initial path. This may be the case particularly where initial choices are made under imperfect information. Evolution then continues toward efficiency along different paths, with results that are influenced and constrained by the initial random conditions.

If we agree that path dependence has something to do with the emergence and evolution of customary law, we should follow this logic to its conclusion, revisiting the very foundations of the efficiency claim. The main question is whether path dependence could ever lead to inefficient results. According to current research (Roe, 1996), path dependence may lead to inefficient equilibria. Once a community has developed its norms and conventions, the costs of changing them may outweight the benefits. Less efficient rules may persist if the transition to more efficient alternatives is costly. Thus, if one allows for some randomness and path dependence, norms and conventions, although driven by an evolution-toward-efficiency dynamic, may stabilize around points of local, rather than global, maximization. Our history, in this sense, constrains our present choices. We may wish we had developed more efficient customs and institutions, but it would be foolish now to attempt to change them. The claim of efficiency of spontaneous law thus becomes a relative one *vis-à-vis* the other sources of law. The point then becomes that of weighing the relative advantages of spontaneous law-making against the attributes of engineered legislation, taking full account of the pervasive public choice and information problems underlying such alternatives.

8. Rational Abstention and Norm Manipulation

A public choice analysis of customary law should consider the vulnerability of norms and customs to the pressure of special interest groups. This line of analysis - relatively undeveloped in the current literature - should search for parallels between the legislative process and the dynamic of norm formation. In that setting, the opportunity for collective beliefs and customs to be manipulated by special interest groups should be analyzed. Any claim that customary sources are superior to proper legislation will have to rest on a solid understanding of the relative sensibility of each source to possible political failures.

The application of a well-known theorem of public choice to the study of customary law generates very interesting results. Unlike legislation in a representative democracy, customary law rests on the widespread consensus of all individuals affected by the rule. If principal-agent problems are likely to arise in a political world characterized by rational ignorance and rational abstention of voters, no such problems appear to affect customary sources. Individuals are bound by a customary rule only to the extent that they concurred - actively or through voluntary acquiescence - in the formation of the emerging practice.

Imperfect information, however, may induce voluntary acquiescence - or even active concurrence - to an undesirable practice. Economic models of cascade or bandwagon behaviour have shown how inferior paths can be followed by individuals who rely on previous choices undertaken by other subjects, and value such observed choices as signals of revealed preference. Economic models have shown that, when information is incomplete, excessive weight can be attached to the signal generated by others. Others' choices may be followed even when the agent's own perception conflicts with the content of the observed signal. In this way, a biased or mistaken first-mover can generate a cascade of wrong decisions by all his followers, with a result that may prove relatively persistent under a wide array of conditions.

Cascade arguments may also unveil the relative fragility of spontaneous sources of law in light of the possible manipulation of collective beliefs through biased leadership. If information is imperfect, the input of politically biased first-movers may generate undesirable norms. These norms may persist because of the weight attached to the choices of our predecessors. Thus, once generated, wrong beliefs may become stable and widespread in any community of imperfect decision makers.

9. Collective Action Problems in Customary Legal Regimes

Another potential weakness of customary law is revealed by the application of a collective action framework to the study of the formation and enforcement of customary rules. We can start the analysis by observing that legal rules and law enforcement are public goods. In the case of customary rules, collective action problems may thus arise at two distinct stages: first, in the formative process of customary rules; and second, in the enforcement of the emerged customs.

The process of a custom formation relies on the spontaneous and widespread acceptance of a given rule by the members of a group. Individuals often face a private cost when complying with the precepts of the rule, and they generally derive a benefit because of the compliance of others with existing rules. Thus, the formation of customary law can be affected by a public good problem. When discussing the conditions under which customary rules can effectively develop, I illustrated the analysis with a game-theoretic framework. The public good problem considered here is in many respects similar to the strategic tension that we have examined in the context of customary law formation. If individuals face a private cost and generate a public benefit through norm creation, there will be a suboptimal amount of norms created through spontaneous processes. Any individual would like others to observe a higher level of norm compliance than he or she observed. The resulting level of norm compliance would thus be suboptimal. Collective action problems in the formation of customary rules have traditionally been corrected by norms which sanctioned opportunistic double standards, and by metarules imposing reciprocity constraints on the parties.

The issue has only marginally been addressed in the economic literature. The reader may look at Hirshleifer (1982) who discusses enforcement by the sanction of one time retaliation by defection in a prisoner's dilemma setting; and Witt (1986) who discusses enforcement by costly retaliation and other punishment not depending on repeat interactions.

More serious collective action problems emerge in the enforcement of spontaneous norms. If the enforcement of norms is left to the private initiative of individual members of the group, a large number of cases will be characterized by a suboptimal level of enforcement. Punishing violators of a norm creates a public good because of the special and general deterrent effect of the penalty. Yet if imposition of the penalty is left to private initiative, punishers would be willing to enforce norms only to the point at which the private marginal cost of enforcement equals its private marginal benefit. This equilibrium obviously diverges from the social optimum, where enforcement would be carried out until the marginal cost equals the social, rather than private, marginal benefit.

This consideration explains why the customs of ancient societies recognized and sanctioned only a limited category of wrongs. Generally speaking, only those wrongs that had a well-identified victim were likely to be addressed through a system of private law enforcement. For the system of private law enforcement to function properly, it was necessary for the victim or his clan to have a strong interest in carrying out the punishment. This also explains why other categories of wrong with a broader class of victims tend to emerge during more advanced stages of legal development, when law enforcement is delegated to a central authority.

In sum, collective action problems may be pervasive in the enforcement of customary rules, with a consequential risk that enforcement will be suboptimal. This conclusion suggests that the decentralized process of law formation may be successfully coupled with a centralized mechanism of law enforcement. In this way, the advantages that customary sources have in gathering diffuse information will be available, free from the collective action problems that typically affect decentralized processes of law enforcement.

10. Adjudicating Social Norms

According to the theory of spontaneous law, customary law has a comparative advantage over the other institutional sources. The intellectual basis of this claim is related to the proposition that any social arrangement that is voluntarily entered upon by rationally self-interested parties is beneficial to society as a whole.

The inductive process which underlies spontaneous law builds upon the role of individuals giving direct effect to their revealed preferences, without the interface of third-party decision makers. To the extent that social practices have emerged under competitive conditions (that is, so long as there is an implicit cost for indulging in inefficient equilibria) without Pareto-relevant externalities, we may be able to draw plausible conclusions regarding the desirability of emerging customs. It is in this latter sense that custom may reclaim full dignity as a source of law. The evolutionary and game-theoretic appraisals of the law-making process have shed new light on the normative foundations of spontaneous law, but they require an appropriate analysis of the incentive structure in the originating social environment (Cooter, 1992).

Evolutionary theories of cooperation have indeed explained the ability of rationally self-interested individuals to cooperate for the sake of mutual gain. Evolutionarily stable cooperative strategies serve efficiency goals and may emerge as social norms recognized by the community to be obligatory. Once emerged, customary rules generate the expectations of the other members of society and those expectations in turn demand judicial enforcement. In some instances, peer pressure and spontaneous processes of norm internalization will support their enforcement.

The legal system may further this process by recognizing and enforcing welfare-maximizing social norms. In this regard, Cooter (1994a) argues that legal recognition and enforcement should consequently be denied in the case of non-cooperative practices, under a test that amounts to a structural analysis of the social incentives that generated the norm. He further argues that in the process of common law adjudication, a distinction must necessarily be made between cooperative norms and non-cooperative practices. Courts are not specialized in the adjudication of most norms. They must therefore resort to a structural approach, first inquiring into the incentives underlying the social structure that generated the norms, rather than attempting to weigh their costs and benefits directly.

11. Local Information and Evolutionary Traps

When the private incentives of the parties diverge from the collective good and the parties cannot enter into binding and enforceable social contracts, inefficient social interactions may follow. These situations may generate suboptimal Nash equilibria as the benefit pursued by each individual player is insufficient to compensate for the harm suffered by the other players. While at times benefitting a few members of the group, strategies of this kind may result in a net social loss for the collectivity. Generally considered undesirable, they may be condemned from the other members of the group. In this way, rules that are expected to harm the aggregate wellbeing of the community will not be supported by a belief of social necessity. By discouraging the adoption of socially suboptimal strategies, the group ethic may serve to destabilize undesirable stalls in the evolutionary process. Therefore, those societies that foster a strong group ethic will maintain a comparative advantage over others. Whenever the societies operate in an intergroup environment marked by strong competition, competing societies will adopt the norms of societies with the comparatively strong group ethic, or else they will suffer negative selection.

In a different setting, one may also think of a group ethic evolving to correct for evolutionary stalls and to stabilize individual behaviour on a point of global maximization (Hirshleifer, 1982). Figure 1 illustrates a possible scenario for an evolutionary trap, where, even in the absence of any strategic interaction between individuals, global maximization is facilitated by the existence of norms. Whenever the non-convexity of individual preferences does not permit a progressive shift from B to A without a utility loss, the point of local maximization B may be characterized as a behavioural trap. In these situations, individuals face a 'no pain, no gain' dilemma. Individuals are at a point of local maximization and - because of imperfect knowledge or perhaps inertia in their consumption or behavioural habits - are unlikely to shift to a different optimizing point without external incentives. Imperfect information, in this context, implies that individuals may have complete information about where they are, but not necessarily about where they are going - such that the preferences that are revealed through the observed choices of the parties may not be used as an absolute proxy for individual optimization.

Figure 1 The Utility-Enhancing Norm

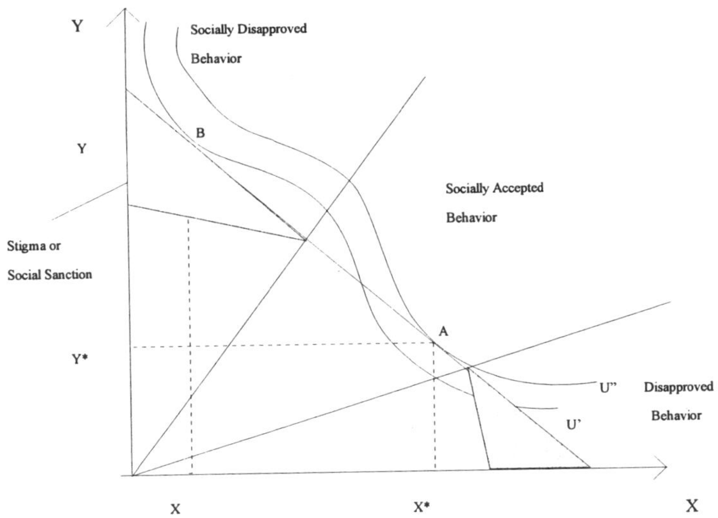

When this type of evolutionary stall persists in a group, social norms of acceptable behaviour may emerge (Levy, 1988). Those who depart from these norms may be subjected to sanctions (condemnation).

Individuals, perhaps even the large majority of individuals in society, may be trapped in behaviour B due to incomplete (ly known) preferences over never-experienced alternatives. It would then be utility enhancing for society (or other members within the group who have obtained information over the alternative states of the world) to influence the consumption choices of other individuals by stigmatization or punishment, in order to lead the individual out of his or her trap. Such stigmatization - one may observe: paternalistic in nature - may well evolve spontaneously in societies because it makes individuals and society as a whole better off. In an evolutionary setting, societies that developed such norms - be them social, ethical, or moral in nature - will enjoy a comparative advantage over other societies.

Despite the general economic motion which views constraints as 'bads' for optimization problems, Figure 1 thus shows the possibility of a utility-enhancing constraint capable of correcting a suboptimal equilibrium obtained in a point of local maximization along a non-convex preference set. Within a local optimization setup, moral constraints may supply information not otherwise revealed by the local surface. Together with social norms and group standards, moral constraints transmit the accumulated wisdom of past experience to individual decision makers. In this framework, norms of tradition, morality, and group ethics do not conflict in any general way with the economic paradigms of efficiency and optimization. Evolution assures that practices which are socially inferior (in the sense that they do not make a cost-justified contribution to human wellbeing) are less frequently adopted because they are labelled as immoral, socially inappropriate, or ethically wrong. Of course, evolutionary processes are never completed, and their task is only stochastically accomplished. Still, the strong correlation between activities and institutions that are efficient, and the community's moral approval of them, should not be underestimated. Many activities that are generally considered immoral (for example, stealing, cheating, lying, and so on) are also inefficient in that they dissipate human wealth. While counterexamples exist in which 'morally condemned' behaviour actually contributes to overall human welfare, social norms and moral principles of the type described above should be considered 'rules of thumb' principles of conduct for individuals who operate in a world of imperfect information and limited cognitive competence (see, Heiner, 1983; Frank, 1987; Parisi, 1995).

Bibliography on Spontaneous Emergence of Law: Customary Law (9500)

Ackerman, Bruce A. (1986), 'Law, Economics and the Problem of Legal Culture', **66** *Duke Law Journal*, 929-947.

Adelstein, Richard P. (1979), 'The Moral Costs of Crime: Prices, Information and Organization', in Gray, Charles M. (ed.), *The Costs of Crime*, Beverly Hills, CA, Sage Publications, 233-252.

Adelstein, Richard P. (1981), 'Institutional Function and Evolution in the Criminal Process', **76** *Northwestern University Law Review*, 1-99.

Adelstein, Richard P. and Peretz, Steven I. (1985), 'The Competition of Technologies in Markets for Ideas: Copyright and Fair Use in Evolutionary Perspective', **5** *International Review of Law and Economics*, 209-238.

Alchian, Armen A. (1950), 'Uncertainty, Evolution and Economic Theory', **58** *Journal of Political Economy*, 211-221.

Arthur, W. Brian (1988), 'Self-Reinforcing Mechanisms in Economics', in Anderson, Philip W. et al. (eds), *The Economy as an Evolving Complex System*, Reading, MA, Addison-Wesley.

Axelrod, R. (1981), 'The Emergence of Cooperation Among Egoists', **75** *American Political Science Review*, 306-318.

Axelrod, R. (1984), *The Evolution of Cooperation*, New York, Basic Books.

Bailey, Martin J. and Rubin, Paul H. (1994), 'A Positive Theory of Legal Change', **14** *International Review of Law and Economics*, 467-477.

Barnes, David W. and Stout, Lynn A. (1992), *Economics of Constitutional Law and Public Choice*, St. Paul's West Publishing.

Barry, B.M. (1995), *Justice as Impartiality*, Oxford, Clarendon.

Bell, John W. (1977), 'Averting a Crisis in Product Liability: An Evolutionary Process of Socioeconomic Justice', **65** *Illinois Bar Journal*, 640-648.

Benson, Bruce L (1990), *The Enterprise of Law: Justice Without the State*, San Francisco, Pacific Research Institute for Public Policy.

Benson, Bruce L. (1988), 'Legal Evolution in Primitive Societies', **144** *Journal of Institutional and Theoretical Economics*, 772-788.

Benson, Bruce L. (1989a), 'The Spontaneous Evolution of Commercial Law', **55** *Southern Economic Journal*, 644-661, reprinted in Klein, Daniel B. (ed.), *Reputation: Studies in the Voluntary Enforcement of Good Behavior*, Ann Arbor, University of Michigan Press.

Benson, Bruce L. (1989b), 'Enforcement of Private Property Rights in Primitive Societies: Law Without Government', **9** *Journal of Libertarian Studies*, 1-26.

Benson, Bruce L. (1990), 'Customary Law With Private Means of Resolving Disputes and Dispensing Justice: A Description of a Modern System of Law and Order Without State Coercion', **9** *Journal of Libertarian Studies*, 25-42. Reprinted in 'Law and Order Without State Coercion', in Veljanovski, Cento (ed.) (1991), *Regulation, Regulators and the Market*, London, Institute of Economic Affairs, 159-179.

Benson, Bruce L. (1991a), 'An Evolutionary Contractarian View of Primitive Law: The Institutions and Incentives Arising Under Customary American Indian Law', **5** *Review of Austrian Economics*, 65-89.

Benson, Bruce L. (1991b), 'Reciprocal Exchange as the Basis for Recognition of Law: Examples from American History', **10** *Journal of Libertarian Studies*, 53-82.

Benson, Bruce L. (1992a), 'Market Failure Versus Government Failure in the Production of Adjudication', in Bowman, Gary W., Hakim, Simon and Seidenstat, Paul (eds), *Privatizing the United States Justice System: Police, Adjudication, and Corrections Services from the Private Sector*, Jefferson, NC, McFarland & Co., 203-225.

Benson, Bruce L. (1992b), 'The Evolution of Values and Institutions in a Free Society: The Under-Pinnings of a Market Economy', **5** *International Journal on the Unity of Sciences*, 411-442. Reprinted in Radnitzky, Gerard and Bouillon, Hardy (eds) (1995), *Values and the Social Order Vol.I*, Aldershot, Avebury, 87-125.

Benson, Bruce L. (1992c), 'The Development of Criminal Law and Its Enforcement: Public Interest or Political Transfers', **3** *Journal des Economistes et des Etudes Humaines*, 79-108.

Benson, Bruce L. (1992d), 'Customary Law as a Social Contract: International Commercial Law', **2** *Constitutional Political Economy*, 1-27.

Benson, Bruce L. (1992e), 'Customary Indian Law: Two Case Studies', in Anderson, Terry L. (ed.), *Property Rights and Indian Economics*, Lanham , MD, Rowman and Littlefield Press.

Benson, Bruce L. (1993), 'The Impetus for Recognizing Private Property and Adopting Ethical Behavior in a Market Economy: Natural Law, Government Law, or Evolving Self-Interest', **6** *Review of Austrian Economics*, 43-80.

Benson, Bruce L. (1994), 'Legal Philosophy', in Boettke, Peter J. (ed.), *The Elgar Companion to Austrian Economics*, London, Edward Elgar, 270-275.

Benson, Bruce L. (1994), 'Emerging from the Hobbesian Jungle: Might Takes and Makes Rights', **5** *Constitutional Political Economy*, 129-158. Translated into Spanish and republished (1995) *Las Instituciones y Los Derechos de Propiedad al Emerger de la Jungla Hobbesiana: La Fuerza Quita los Reprinted Derechos y los Crea Libertas*, 12, 35-75.

Benson, Bruce L. (1995), 'Competition Among Legal Institutions: Implications for the Evolution of Law', in Gerken, Luden (ed.), *Competition Among Institutions*, London, Macmillan, 153-175.

Benson, Bruce L. (1995), 'An Exploration of the Impact of Modern Arbitration Statutes on the Development of Arbitration in the United States', **11** *Journal of Law, Economics, and Organization*, 479-501.

Berlin, I. (1970), 'Two Concepts of Liberty', in Berlin, I. (ed.), *Four Essays on Liberty*, New York, NY, Oxford University Press.

Berman, Harold J. and Dasser, Felix J. (1990), 'The "New" Law Merchant and the "Old": Sources, Content, and Legitimacy', in Carbonneau, Thomas E. (ed.), *Lex Mercatoria and Arbitration: A Discussion of the New Law Merchant*, New York, Dobbs Ferry, Transnational Juris Publications.

Bernstein, Lisa (1996), 'Merchant Law In a Merchant Court: Rethinking the Code's Search for Immanent Business Norms', **144** *University of Pennsylvania Law Review*, 1765 ff.

Binmore, Ken and Samuelson, Larry (1994), 'An Economist's Perspective on the Evolution of Norms', **150** *Journal of Institutional and Theoretical Economics*, 45-63.

Boyd, R. and Richerson, P.J. (1992), 'Punishment Allows the Evolution of Cooperation (or Anything Else) in Sizable Groups', **13** *Ethology and Sociobiology*, 171-195.

Boyd, R. and Richerson, P.J. (1994), 'The Evolution of Norms: An Anthropological View', **150** *Journal of Institutional and Theoretical Economics*, 72-86.

Bromley, Daniel W. (1989), 'Institutional Change and Economic Efficiency', **23** *Journal of Economic Issues*, 735-759.

Brownlie, Ian (1990), *Principles of Public International Law*, 4th edn, Oxford, Clarendon Press.

Buchanan, James M. (1975), *The Limits of Liberty: Between Anarchy and Leviathan*, Chicago, University of Chicago Press.

Buchanan, James M. (1979), 'General Implications of Subjectivism in Economics', in X (ed.), *What Should Economists Do?*, Indianapolis, Liberty Press.

Buchanan, James M. (1991), 'The Foundations for Normative Individualism', in X (ed.), *The Economics and the Ethics of Constitutional Order*, Ann Arbor, University of Michigan Press.

Buchanan, James M. (1994), 'Choosing What to Choose', **150** *Journal of Institutional and Theoretical Economics*, 123-135.

Buxbaum, Hertig and Hirsch, Hopt (1996) (eds), *European Economic and Business Law, Legal and Economic Analyses on Integration and Harmonization*, Berlin, Springer, 401 p.

Cassone, Alberto and Marchese, Carla (1994), 'Indulgenze Religiose: un'Analisi Economica', **2-3** *Economia delle Scelte Pubbliche*, 191-209.

Charney, J.I. (1986), 'The Persistent Objector Rule and the Development of Customary International Law', **56** *British Yearbook of International Law*, 1 ff.

Christiansen, Gregory B. (1990), 'Law as a Discovery Procedure', **9** *Cato Journal*, 497-530.

Clark, Robert C. (1981), 'The Interdisciplinary Study of "Legal Evolution"', **90** *Yale Law Journal*, 1238-1274.

Clay, Karen (1997), 'Trade Without Law: Private-Order Institutions in Mexican California', **13** *Journal of Law, Economics, and Organization*, 202-231.

Coleman, Jules L. (1992), *Risks and Wrongs*, Cambridge, Cambridge University Press.

Contending with Hayek (1994), *On Liberalism, Spontaneous Order and The Post-Communist Societies in Transition*, Bern, Peter Lang.

Cooter, Robert D. (1989), 'Kin Groups and the Common Law Process', in Larmour, Peter (ed.), *Customary Land Tenure: Registration and Decentralisation in Papua New Guinea*, Monograph XXIX, Papua New Guinea Institute of Applied Social and Economic Research, 33-50.

Cooter, Robert D. (1991), 'Inventing Market Property: The Land Courts of Papua New Guinea', **25** *Law and Society Review*, 759-801.

Cooter, Robert D. (1992), 'Against Legal Centrism' **81** *California Law Review*, 425 ff.

Cooter, Robert D. (1993), 'Against Legal Centrism: Review of Robert C. Ellickson's Order Without Law', **81** *California Law Review*, 417 ff.

Cooter, Robert D. (1994a), 'Structural Adjudication and the New Law Merchant: A Model of Decentralized Law', **14** *International Review of Law and Economics*, 215-231. Reprinted under the title, 'The Structural Approach to Decentralizing Law: A Theory of Games and Norms', in a book edited by Gerard Hertig.

Cooter, Robert D. (1994b), 'Decentralized Law for a Complex Economy', **23** *Southwestern Law Review, Hayek Symposium*, 443-451.

Cooter, Robert D. (1996), 'Decentralized Law for a Complex Economy: The Structural Approach to Adjudicating the New Law Merchant', *University of Pennsylvania Law Review*.

D'Amato, A. (1971), *The Concept of Custom in International Law*, Ithaca, NY, Cornell University Press.

Eger, Thomas (1996), 'Die Evolution von Recht als Prozeß der Selbstorganisation (The Evolution of Law as a Process of Self-Organization)', in Priddat, B.P. and Wegner, G. (eds), *Zwischen Institution und Evolution. Neuè Ansätze in der ökonomischen Theorie*, Marburg, Metropolis, 211-244.

Eger, Thomas and Weise, Peter (1995), 'Die Evolution von Normen aus Unordnung, Ein synergetisches Modell (The Evolution of Norms out of Disorder, A Synergetic Model)', in X. (ed.), *Ökonomie und Gesellschaft. Jahrbuch 11, Markt, Norm und Moral*, Frankfurt/New York, 192-209.

Eisenberg, Melvin Aron (1988), *The Nature of the Common Law*, Cambridge, MA, Harvard University Press.

Ellickson, R.C. (1991), *Order Without Law: How Neighbors Settle Disputes*, Cambridge, MA, Harvard University Press.

Ellickson, R.C. (1994), 'The Aim of Order Without Law', **150** *Journal of Institutional and Theoretical Economics*, 97-100.

Elliott, E. Donald (1984), 'Holmes and Evolution: Legal Process as Artificial Intelligence', **13** *Journal of Legal Studies*, 113-146.

Elliott, E. Donald, Ackerman, Bruce A. and Millian, John C. (1985), 'Toward a Theory of Statutory Evolution: The Federaliza tion of Environmental Law', **1** *Journal of Law, Economics, and Organization*, 313-340.

Epstein, Richard A. (1980), 'The Static Conception of the Common Law', **9** *Journal of Legal Studies*, 253-275.

Epstein, Richard A. (1992), 'The Path to the T. J. Hooper: The Theory and History of Custom in the Law of Tort', **21** *Journal of Legal Studies*, 1-38.

Fortier, V. (1991), *La Fonction Normative des Notions Floues* (The Normative Functions of the Vagueness Notions), Aix-Marseille, Presses Universitaires d', 755 p.

Frank, Robert H. (1987), 'If Homo Economicus Could Choose his Utility Function, Would He want one with a Conscience?', **77** *American Economic Review*, 593-604.

Frank, Robert H. (1994), *Passions Within Reason: The Strategic Role of Emotions*, New York, W.W. Norton.

Frech, H. Edward III (1972), 'The Public Choice Theory of Murray N. Rothbard: A Modern Anarchist', **14** *Public Choice*, 143-154.

Fried, Charles, Summers, Robert S., Tullock, Gordon and Arrow, Kenneth J. (1982), 'Commentary on Hirshleifer Paper', **4** *Research in Law and Economics*, 61-208.

Friedman, David D. (1979), 'Private Creation and Enforcement of Law: A Historical Case', **8** *Journal of Legal Studies*, 399-415.

Fudenberg, Drew and Maskin, Eric (1986), 'The Folk Theorem in Repeated Games with Discounting or with Incomplete Information', **54** *Econometrica*, 533-554.

Fuller, Lon L. (1969), *The Morality of Law. Revised Edition*, New Haven, CT, Yale University Press.

Galanter, Marc (1987), 'Conceptualizing Legal Change and Its Effect: A Comment on George Priest's "Measuring Legal Change"', **3** *Journal of Law, Economics, and Organization*, 235-241.

Gauthier, David Peter (1986), *Morals by Agreement*, Oxford, Clarendon.

Goldberg, Victor P. (1974), 'Institutional Change and the Quasi-Invisible Hand', **17** *Journal of Law and Economics*, 461-492. Reprinted in Goldberg, Victor P. (ed.) (1989),

Readings in the Economics of Contract Law, Cambridge, Cambridge University Press, 169-173.

Goodman, John C. (1978), 'An Economic Theory of the Evolution of the Common Law', **7** *Journal of Legal Studies*, 393-406.

Gordon, Wendy J. (1992), 'Of Harms and Benefits: Torts, Restitution, and Intellectual Property', **21** *Journal of Legal Studies*, 449-482.

Grady, Mark F. (1992), 'Toward a Positive Economic Theory of Antitrust', **30** *Economic Inquiry*, 225 ff.

Grady, Mark F. (1995), 'Legal Evolution and Precedent', **3** *Annual Review of Law and Ethics*, 147 ff.

Greif, Avner (1989), 'Reputation and Coalitions in Medieval Trade: Evidence on the Maghribi Traders', **49** *Journal of Economic History*, 857 ff.

Hardin, Garrett (1968), 'The Tragedy of the Commons', **162** *Science*, 1243 ff.

Harsanyi, John C. (1955), 'Cardinal Welfare Individualistic Ethics, and Interpersonal Comparisons of Utility', **63** *Journal of Political Economy*, 315 ff.

Hart, Herbert Lionel A. (1961), *The Concept of Law*, Oxford, Clarendon.

Hayek, Friedrich A. von (1955), *The Counterrevolution of Science*, New York, NY, Free Press.

Hayek, Friedrich A. von (1960), *The Constitution of Liberty*, Chicago, University of Chicago Press.

Hayek, Friedrich A. von (1967), 'The Results of Human Action but not of Human Design', in X (ed.), *Studies in Philosophy, Politics and Economics*, Chicago, University of Chicago Press.

Hayek, Friedrich A. von (1989), *The Fatal Conceit*, Chicago, University of Chicago Press.

Heiner, Ronald A. (1983), 'Origin of Predictable Behavior', **73** *American Economic Review*, 561-595.

Hesse, Günter (1980), 'Der Property-Rights-Ansatz. Eine ökonomische Theorie der Veränderung des Rechts? (The Property Rights Approach. An Economic Theory of Legal Change?)', **195** *Jahrbuch für Nationalökonomie und Statistik*, 481 ff.

Hesse, Günter (1983), 'Zur Erklärung der Änderung von Handlungsrechten mit Hilfe der ökonomischen Theorie (The Explanation of the Change of Property Rights with Aid from Economic Theory)', in Schüller, Alfred (ed.), *Property Rights und Ökonomische Theorie*, München, Vahlen, 79-109.

Hirshleifer, Jack (1982), 'Evolutionary Models in Economics and Law: Cooperation versus Conflict Strategies', **4** *Research in Law and Economics*, 1-60.

Hirshleifer, Jack and Coll Martinez, Juan Carlos (1988), 'What Strategies can Support the Evolutionary Emergence of Cooperation?', **32** *Journal of Conflict Resolution*, 367-398.

Holmes, Oliver Wendell (1980), *The Common Law*, Boston, Little Brown.

Hovenkamp, Herbert J. (1983), 'The Economics of Legal History', **67** *Minnesota Law Review*, 645-697.

Huang, Peter H. and Wu, Ho-Mou (1994), 'More Order without More Law: A Theory of Social Norms and Organizational Cultures', **10** *Journal of Law, Economics, and Organization*, 390-406.

Jaffe, Austin J. (1988), 'Toward an Evolutionary Theory of Trade Associations: The Case of Real Estate Appraisers', **16** *American Real Estate and Urban Economics Association Journal*, 230-256.

Janis, M.W. (1993), *An Introduction to International Law*, New York, Little Brown and Co..

Josserand, L. (1937), *Un Ordre Juridique Nouveau* (A New Juridical Order), Dalloz, 41 p.

Kelsen, Hans (1939), 'Théorie du Droit International Coutumier', **1** *Revue Internationale de la Théorie du Droit (New Series)*, 263 ff.

Kelsen, Hans (1945), *General Theory of Law and State*, New Jersey, Lawbook Exchange.

Kennedy, Duncan (1981), 'Cost-Reduction Theory as Legitimation', **90** *Yale Law Journal*, 1275-1283.

Kitch, Edmund W. (1987), 'Law and the Economic Order', in Lipson, Leon and Wheeler, Stanton (eds), *Law and the Social Sciences*, New York, Russel Sage Foundation, 109-149.

Kitch, Edmund W. (1991), 'Business Organization Law: State or Federal?', in Buxbaum, Richard M., Hertig, Gerard, Hirsch, Alain and Hopt, Klaus J. (eds), *European Business Law*, Berlin, Walter de Gruyter, 35 ff.

Kitch, Edmund W. (1996), 'Competition Between Securities Markets: Good or Bad?', in X (ed.), *The Future for the Securities Market: Legal and Regulatory Aspects*, Oxford, Clarendon, 233 ff.

Klein, B. (1996), 'Why Hold-Ups Occur: The Self-Enforcing Range of Contractual Relationships', **34** *Economic Inquiry*, 444 ff.

Klein, B. and Leffler, K. (1981), 'The Role of Market Forces in Assuring Contractual Performance', **89** *Journal of Political Economy*, 615-641.

Kobayashi, Bruce H. and Ribstein, Larry E. (1996), 'Evolution and Spontaneous Uniformity: Evidence from the Evolution of the Limited Liability Company', **34** *Economic Inquiry*.

Kontou, N. (1994), *The Termination and Revision of Treaties in the Light of New Customary International Law*, Oxford, Clarendon.

Kornhauser, Lewis A. (1992), 'Are There Cracks in the Foundations of Spontaneous Order? Book Review of Ellickson, Order without Law', **67** *New York University Law Review*, 647 ff.

Kraus, Jody S. (1997), 'Segal Design and the Evolution of Commercial Norms', **16** *Journal of Legal Studies*, 377-411.

Krauss, Michael I. (1994), 'La Réglementation Contre le Marché dans le Développement de Normes (Regulation against the Market in Norms Formation)', **5** *Journal des Economistes et des Etudes Humaines*, 573-599.

Kronman, Anthony T. (1985), 'Contract Law and the State of Nature', **1** *Journal of Law, Economics, and Organization*, 5-32.

Kubasek, N. (1985), 'The Artificiality of Economic Models as a Guide for Legal Evolution', **33** *Cleveland State Law Review*, 505-512.

Kunz, Harald (1985), 'Zur Entstehung und Verhaltenswirkung sozialer Normen, mit einigen Argumenten für eine Ökonomisch rationale Kriminalpolitik (On the Evolution and the Incentive Effect of Social Norms, with Some Arguments for an Economic Rational Crime Policy)', **68** *Monatsschrift für Kriminologie und Strafsrechtsreform*, 202-215.

Larmore, Charles E. (1987), 'Liberalism and the Neutrality of the State', in Larmore, Charles E. (ed.), *Patterns of Moral Complexity*, Cambridge, New York.

Lehmann, Michael (1982), 'Ökonomie, Sozialbiologie - Humanwissenschaften. Über die Notwendigkeit und Möglichkeit einer interdisziplinären Grundlagenforschung (Economics, Social Biology - Human Sciences. About the Necessity and Possibility of an Interdisciplinary Fundamental Reform)', *Der Betriebs-Berater*, 1997-2004.

Lehmann, Michael (1986), 'Evolution in Biologie, Ökonomie und Jurisprudenz (Evolution in Biology, Economics and Jurisprudence)', **17** *Rechtstheorie*, 463-477.

Lehmann, Michael (1993), 'Das Prinzip Wettbewerb. Ein gemeinsames Gesetz der Evolution für Biologie, Ökonomie und Wirtschaftsrecht (The Competition Principle. A Common Law of Evolution for Biology. Economics and Commercial Law)', in McGuire, Michael T. (ed.), *Der Faktor Mensch im neuen Europa*, Luchterhand, Neuwied et. al., 241-258.

Leibenstein, Harvey (1982), 'The Prisoners' Dilemma in the Invisible Hand: An Analysis of Intrafirm Productivity', **72** *American Economic Review. Papers and Proceedings*, 92 ff.

Lemieux, Pierre (1983), *Du Libéralisme à l'Anarcho-capitalisme* (From Liberalism to Anarcho-Capitalism), Paris, Presses Universitaires de France (PUF).

Lemieux, Pierre (1988), *L'Anarcho-Capitalisme* (What is Anarcho-Capitalism?), Paris, Presses Universitaires de France (PUF).

Leoni, B. (1991), *Freedom and the Law*, 3rd edn, Indianapolis, Liberty Fund.

Levy, D. (1988), 'Utility-Enhancing Consumption Constraints', **4** *Economics and Philosophy*, 69-88.

Levy, D. (1992), 'Adam Smith and the Texas A&M; Rats', in Levy, D. (ed.), *The Economic Ideas of Ordinary People: From Preferences to Trade*, New York, NY, Routledge.

Lewis, D. (1969), *Convention: A Philosophical Study*, Cambridge, MA, Harvard University Press.

Leyd, L., Leydesdoff, L.A., Besselaar, P.V. and Allen, P.M. (1994), *Evolutionary Economics and Chaos Theory: New Directions in Technology Studies*, New York, St. Martin's Press.

Libecap, Gary D. (1978), 'Economic Variables and the Development of the Law: The Case of Western Mineral Rights', **38** *Journal of Economic History*, 338-362.

Loasby, Brian J. (1976), *Choice, Complexity, and Ignorance: An Enquiry into Economic Theory and the Practice of Decision-Making*, Cambridge, Cambridge University Press.

Mackaay, Ejan (1988), 'L'Ordre Spontané Comme Fondement du Droit - un Survol des Modèles de l'Émergence des Règles dans une Société Civile (Spontaneous Order as Foundation of Law - A Survey of Models of the Emergence of Rules in Civil Society)', **22** *Revue Juridique Themis*, 347-383.

Mackaay, Ejan (1989), 'L'Ordre Spontané comme Fondement du Droit - un Survol des Modèles de l'Emergence des Règles dans la Société Civile (Spontaneous Order as the Foundation of Law - A Survey of Models of the Emergence of Rules in Civil Society)', **3** *Revue Internationale de Droit Economique*, 247-287.

Mackaay, Ejan (1995), 'Mededinging, Welvaart en Federalisme (Competition, Welfare and Federalism)', in Kanning, Walter (ed.), *Liber Amicorum voor Arnold Heertje*, Leiden, Stenfert Kroese, 93-100.

Mateesco, N.M. (1947), *La Coutume dans les Cycles Juridiques Internationaux*, Paris.

McAdams, H. (1997), 'The Origin, Development, and Regulation of Norms', **96** *Michigan Law Review*, 338 ff.

Miller, Geoffrey P. (1993), 'Ritual and Regulation: A Legal Economic Interpretation of Selected Biblical Texts', **22** *Journal of Legal Studies*, 477-501.

Miller, Geoffrey P. (1993), 'Contracts of Genesis', **22** *Journal of Legal Studies*, 15-45.

Miller, Geoffrey P. (1994), 'The Legal-Economic Analysis of Comparative Civil Procedure, the Legal-Economic Approach to Biblical Interpretation', **150** *Journal of Institutional and Theoretical Economics*, 755 ff.

Miller, Geoffrey P. (1995a), 'Verbal Feud in the Hebrew Bible: Judges 3:12-30 and 19-21', **55** *Journal of Near Eastern Studies*, 105 ff.

Miller, Geoffrey P. (1995b), 'J as Constitutionalist: A Legal-Economic Interpretation of Exodus 17:8-16 and Related Texts', **70** *Chicago-Kent Law Review*, 1829 ff. to be republished in Lindgren, James and Miller, Laurent Geoffrey (eds), *Ancient Law: the New Learning* (tentative title) (1996)

Miller, Geoffrey P. (1996a), *A Riposte Form in the Song of Deborah*, Manuscript.

Miller, Geoffrey P. (1996b), 'Foreword: The Development of Ancient Near Eastern Law', **70** *Chicago-Kent Law Review*, 1623 ff.

Miller, Geoffrey P. (1996c), 'Ancient Law: the New Learning (tentative title) (1996) Constitutionalist: A Legal-Economic Interpretation of Exodus 17:8-16 and Related Texts', **70** *Chicago-Kent Law Review*, 1829 ff. To be republished in Lindgren, James and Miller, Lauren Geoffrey (eds).

Miller, Geoffrey P. (1996d), 'The Song of Deborah: A Legal-Economic Analysis', **144** *University of Pennsylvania Law Review*, 2293 ff.

Miller, Geoffrey P. (1998), 'A Riposte Form in the Song of Deborah', in Frymer-Kensky, Tikva, Levinson, Bernard and Matthews, Victor (eds), *Gender and Law in the Hebrew Bible and the Ancient Near East*, Shefheld Academic Press.

Miller, Geoffrey P., Lindgren, James and Laurent Mayali (1995), 'Why Ancient Law?', **70** *Chicago-Kent Law Review*, 1465 ff.

Mueller, Dennis C. (1989), 'A Just Social Contract', in Mueller, Dennis C. (ed.), *Public Choice II*, Cambridge, Cambridge University Press.

Noreau, Pierre (1993), *Droit Préventif - Le Droit au-Delà de la Loi* (Preventive Law - Law Beyond Legislation), Montréal, Éditions Thémis.

O'Driscoll, Gerald P., Jr and Rizzo, Mario J. (1986), 'Subjectivism, Uncertainty, and Rules', in Kirzner, Israel M. (ed.), *Subjectivism, Intelligibility and Economic Understanding. Essays in Honor of Ludwig M. Lachmann on his Eightieth Birthday*, London, Macmillan, 252-267.

Ott, Claus and Schäfer, Hans-Bernd (1991), *Emergence and Construction of Efficient Rules in the Legal System of German Civil Law*, Paper Presented at the European Law and Economics Association.

Parisi, Francesco (1994), 'Autonomy and Private Ordering in Contract Law', **1** *European Journal of Law and Economics*, 213-227.

Parisi, Francesco (1995), 'Toward a Theory of Spontaneous Law', **6** *Constitutional Political Economy*, 211-231.

Parisi, Francesco (1996a), 'Normative Knowledge and Self-Enforcing Rules in International Law', **2** *International Legal Theory*, 27-30.

Parisi, Francesco (1996b), 'Law as a Voluntary Enterprise', in Ratnapala, S. and Moens, G. (eds), *The Jurisprudence of Liberty*, London, Butterworths.

Parisi, Francesco (1997), *The Genesis of Liability in Ancient Law*, George Mason University Law and Economics Working Paper Series, 97-07.

Parisi, Francesco (1998a), 'Customary Law', in Newman, Peter (ed.), *The New Palgrave Dictionary of Economics and the Law*, New York, Macmillan, 572-578.

Parisi, Francesco (1998b), 'The Economics of Customary Law: Lessons From Evolutionary Socio-Biology', in Ott, Claus and von Wangenheim, Georg (eds), *Essays in Law and Economics IV*, Antwerpen, Maklu, 245-269.

Parisi, Francesco (1998c), 'Opinio Iuris Revisited: A Law and Economics Perspective (Forthcoming)', **4** *International Legal Theory*.

Parisi, Francesco (1999), 'The Cost of the Game: A Topology of Social Interactions (Forthcoming)', *European Journal of Law and Economics*.

Parisi, Francesco and Ribstein, Larry E. (1998), *Choice of Law*, New York, Macmillan.

Pollock, F. (1929), *First Book of Jurisprudence*, 6th edn, London, Macmillan.

Popper, Karl R. (1995), *The Open Society and Its Enemies*, 5th edn, London, Routledge.

Posner, Eric A. (1996a), 'Law, Economics and Inefficient Norms', **145** *University of Pennsylvania Law Review*, 1697-1744.

Posner, Eric A. (1996b), 'Norms, Formalities, and the Statute of Frauds: A Comment', **144** *University of Pennsylvania Law Review*, 1971 ff.

Posner, Richard A. (1980), 'A Theory of Primitive Society, with Special Reference to Law', **23** *Journal of Law and Economics*, 1-53.

Posner, Richard A. (1981), *The Economics of Justice*, Cambridge, MA, Harvard University Press, 415 p.

Priest, George L. (1981), 'The New Scientism in Legal Scholarship: A Comment on Clark and Posner', **90** *Yale Law Journal*, 1284-1295.

Priest, George L. (1987), 'Measuring Legal Change', **3** *Journal of Law, Economics, and Organization*, 193-225.

Prigogine, Ilya and Stengers, Isabelle (1984), *Order Out of Chaos: Man's New Dialogue with Nature*, Boulder, CO, New Science Library.

Rapoport, Anatol (1987), 'Prisoner's Dilemma', in X (ed.), *The New Palgrave: A Dictionary of Economics*, New York, McGraw-Hill.

Rawls, John (1971), *A Theory of Justice*, Cambridge, MA, Harvard University Press.

Raz, J. (1986), *The Morality of Freedom*, Oxford, Clarendon.

Reese, David A. (1989), 'Does the Common Law Evolve?', **12** *Hamline Law Review*, 321-353.

Ress, G. (1994), 'Ex Ante Safeguards Against Ex Post Opportunism in International Treaties: Theory and Practice of International Public Law', **150** *Journal of Institutional and Theoretical Economics*, 279-303.

Ribstein, Larry E. and Kobayashi, Bruce H. (1995), 'Uniform Laws, Model Laws and Limited Liability Companies', **66** *University of Colorado Law Review*, 947-999.

Ribstein, Larry E. and Kobayashi, Bruce H. (1996), 'An Economic Analysis of Uniform State Laws', **25** *Journal of Legal Studies*, 131-199.

Ridley, Matt (1997), *Origins of Virtue: Human Instincts and the Evolution of Cooperation*, New York, Viking.

Rizzo, Mario J. (1980), 'Symposium: Change in the Common Law: Legal and Economic Perspectives. A Symposium Sponsored by The Institute for Humane Studies and the Liberty Fund', **9** *Journal of Legal Studies*, 189-427.

Roe, Mark J. (1996), 'Chaos and Evolution in Law and Economics', **109** *Harvard Law Review*, 641-668.

Rubin, Paul H. (1982), 'Symposium: Evolutionary Models in Economics and Law', **4** *Research in Law and Economics*, 218 ff.

Rubin, Paul H. (1983), *Business Firms and the Common Law. The Evolution of Efficient Rules*, New York, Praeger, 189 p.

Rubin, Paul H. (1993), 'Private Mechanisms for the Creation of Efficient Institutions for Market Economies', in Somogyi, Laszlo (ed.), *The Political Economy of The Transition Process in Eastern Europe*, Cheltenham, Edward Elgar.

Rubin, Paul H. (1994), 'Growing A Legal System in the Post-Communist Economies', **27** *Cornell International Law Journal*, 1-47.

Rubin, Paul H. (1996), *Promises, Promises: Contracts in Russia and Other Post-Communist Economies*, Shaftesbury Papers, Edward Elgar and the Locke Institute.

Rubin, Paul H. (in press), *Growing a Legal System, with Special Reference to the Post-Communist Economies' Center for International Reform and the Informal Sector*, Working Paper, No. 63.

Rubin, Paul H. and Tesche, Jean (in press), 'Enforcement of Agreements in Russia, in the Rule of Law and Economic Reform in Russia', in Sachs, Jeffrey (ed.), Boulder, Westview Press, 912 ff.

Ruhl, J.B. and Ruhl, H.J., Jr (1997), 'The Arrow of the Law in Modern Administrative States: Using Complexity Theory to Reveal the Diminishing Returns and Increasing Risks the Burgeoning of Law Poses to Society', **30** *University of California at Davis Law Review*, 405 ff.

Salmond, J.W. (1966), *Jurisprudence* (12th edn), London, Sweet & Maxwell.

Santagata, Walter (1995), 'Istituzioni per il Mercato dell'Arte: Artisti e Mercanti tra Regole, Convenzioni e Allocazioni dei Diritti (Institutions for the Market of Works of Art: Artists and Merchants among Rules, Conventions and Allocation of Rights)', *Economia Pubblica*, 87-115.

Savatier René (1959), *Les Méthamorphoses Economiques et Sociales du Droit Civil Aujourd'hui* (The Economic and Sociologic Metamorphoses of Civil Law Today).

Schlicht, Ekkehart (1993), 'Koordinationskosten und "Social Capital" (Co-ordination Costs and Social Capital)', in Schlieper, Ulrich and Schmidtchen, Dieter (eds), *Makro, Geld & Institutionen*, Tübingen, 95-100.

Schmidt Trenz, Hans Jorg and Schmidtchen, Dieter (1994), 'Theorie optimaler Rechtsräume. Die Regulierung sozialer Beziehungen durch die Kontrolle von Territorium (Theory of Optimum Legal Areas)', **13** *Jahrbuch für Neue Politische Ökonomie*, 7-29.

Schmidtchen, Dieter (1995), 'Die Zwillingsideen der Evolution und der spontanen Bildung einer Ordnung (The Twin Ideas of Evolution and Spontaneous Order)', in Francke, H.-H. (ed.), *Ökonomischer Individualismus und Freiheitliche Verfassung*, Freiburg, 239-271.

Schotter, Andrew (1981), *Economic Theory of Social Institutions*, Cambridge, MA, Harvard University Press.

Schwartz, Warren F. et al. (1984), 'The Duel: Can These Gentlement be Acting Efficiently?', **8** *Journal of Legal Studies*, 321 ff.

Scott Kenneth E. (1994), 'Bounded Rationality and Social Norms', **150** *Journal of Institutional and Theoretical Economics*, 315-319.

Selten, Reinhard (1978), 'The Chain-Store Paradox', **9** *Theory and Decision*, 127-159.

Sen, Amartya K. (1979), 'Rational Fools: A Critique of the Behavioural Foundations of Economic Theory', in Hahn, F. and Hollis, M. (eds), *Philosophy and Economic Theory*, Oxford, Clarendon.

Shubik, Martin (1987), *Game Theory in the Social Sciences: Concepts and Solutions*, 4th edn, Boston, MA, The MIT Press.

Shughart, William F., II and Tollison, Robert D. (1985), 'Corporate Chartering: An Exploration in the Economics of Legal Change', **23** *Economic Inquiry*, 585-599.

Simpson, Alfred William Brian (1979), 'The Horwitz Thesis and the History of Contracts', **46** *University of Chicago Law Review*, 533-601.

Smith, James Charles (1977), 'Book Review of Morton J. Horwitz the Transformation of American Law (1780-1860)', **53** *Wisconsin Law Review*, 1253-1276.

Stearns, M.L. (1994), 'The Misguided Renaissance of Social Choice', **103** *Yale Law Journal*, 1219 ff.

Terrebonne, R. Peter (1981), 'A Strictly Evolutionary Model of Common Law', **10** *Journal of Legal Studies*, 397-407.

Tietzel, Manfred (1986), 'Zur Entstehung des Privateigentums (On the Evolution of Private Property)', **37** *Ordo*, 105-127.

Trakman, Leon E. (1983), *The Law Merchant: The Evolution of Commercial Law*, Littleton, CO, Fred B. Rothman and Company.

Tucker, A.W. (1950), *A Two-Person Dilemma*, Unpublished manuscript. Reprinted in: Straffin, P. (1980) 'The Prisoner's Dilemma', *UMAP Journal*, 101 ff.

Tullock, Gordon (1987), *Private Wants, Public Means - An Economic Analysis of the Desirable Scope of Government*, Lanham (MD), University Press of America.

Tunkin, G.I. (1961), 'Remarks on the Juridical Nature of Customary Norms in International Law', **49** *California Law Review*, 419 ff.

Turnbull, Shann (1977), *Impact of Mining Royalties on Aboriginal Communities in the Northern Territory*, First Report, Parliamentary Paper, Canberra, Australian Government Publishing Service, No. 135/1978, Oct..

Turnbull, Shann (1978), *Economic Development of Aboriginal Communities in the Northern Territory Second Report, Self-sufficiency (with Land Rights)*, Parliamentary Paper, Canberra, Australian Government Publishing Service, No. 438/1978.

Turnbull, Shann (1980), *Economic Development of Aboriginal Communities in the Northern Territory: A Study in Two Parts, Department of Aboriginal Affairs*, Canberra, Australian Government Publishing Service.

Turnbull, Shann (1986), 'When Land Owns People', **43 (4)** *Et cetera: A Review of General Semantics*, 389-392.

Udehn, Lars (1996), *The Limits of Public Choice: A Sociological Critique of the Economic Theory of Politics*, London, Routledge.

Ullman-Margalit, Edna (1977), *The Emergence of Norms*, Oxford, Clarendon.

Vanberg, Viktor J. (1993), 'Rational Choice, Rule-Following and Institutions: An Evolutionary Perspective', in Gustafson, B., Knudsen, C. and Maki, U. (eds), *Rationality, Institutions and Economic Methodology*, London, Routledge, 171-200.

Vaughn, Karen I. (1982), *Can Democratic Society Reform Itself: The Limits of Constructive Change*, George Mason University Working Paper.

Versteeg, J. Russell (1989), 'Law and the Security of Homeric Society (A Response to Richard A. Posner)', **10** *Journal of Legal History*, 265-284.

Voigt, Stefan (1991), 'Die Evolutionsorientierte Theorie der Verfassung - Bemerkungen zum Ansatz von Hayeks (The Evolutionary Theory of Constitution. Remarks on Hayek's Approach)', **40** *Zeitschrift für Wirtschaftspolitik*, 93-107.

Voigt, Stefan (1993), 'On the Internal Consistency of Hayek's Evolutionary oriented Constitutional Economics - Some General Remarks', **3** *Journal des Economistes et des Etudes Humaines*, 461-476.

Wagner, Richard E. (1992), 'Crafting Social Rules: Common Law vs. Statute Law, Once Again', **3** *Constitutional Political Economy*, 381 ff.

Walden, R.M. (1977), 'The Subjective Element in the Formation of Customary International Law', **12** *Israel Law Review*, 344 ff.

Waldron, Jeremy (1993), 'Theoretical Foundations of Liberalism', in Waldron, Jeremy (ed.), *Liberal Rights: Collected Papers, 1981-1991*, Cambridge, Cambridge University Press.

Wangenheim, Georg v. (1995), *Die Evolution von Recht. Ursachen und Wirkungen haeufigkeitsabhaengigen Verhaltens in der Rechtsfortbildung* (The Evolution of Law. Causes and Effects of Frequency Dependend Behaviour in Legal Evolution), Tübingen, Mohr/Siebeck.

Warren, Elizabeth (1981), 'Trade Usage and Parties in the Trade: An Economic Rationale for an Inflexible Rule', **42** *University of Pittsburgh Law Review*, 515 ff.

Watrin, Christian (1996), 'Der Wettbewerb der Ordnungen als Entdeckungsverfahren für eine nachhaltige Entwicklung (Korreferat) (Sustainable Development and Competition Among Economic Systems as a Discovery Process)', in Gerken, Lüder (ed.), *Ordnungspolitische Grundfragen einer Politik der Nachhaltigkeit/Walter Eucken Institut*, Baden-Baden, 103-113.

Weber, M. (1978), *Economy and Society*, Berkeley, University of California Press.

Weise, Peter (1996), 'Verhaltenskoordination durch soziale Normen und Kräfte (Co-ordination of Behaviour by Social Norms and Forces)', in Priddat, B.P. and Wegner, G. (eds), *Zwischen Institution und Evolution. Neue Ansätze in der ökonomischen Theorie*, Marburg, Metropolis, 187-209.

Weise, Peter and Eger, Thomas (1995), 'Die Evolution von Normen aus Unordnung, Ein synergetisches Modell (The Evolution of Norms out of Disorder, A Synergetic Model)', **11** *Ökonomie und Gesellschaft*, 192-209.

Williams, Stephen F. (1980), 'The Static Conception of the Common Law: A Comment', **9** *Journal of Legal Studies*, 277-289.

Williamson, O.E. (1983), 'Credible Commitments: Using Hostages to Support Exchange', **73** *American Economic Review*, 519 ff.

Wilson, James Q. (1993), *The Moral Sense*, New York, NY, Free Press.

Witt, Ulrich (1986), 'Evolution and Stability of Cooperation without Enforceable Contracts', **39** *Kyklos*, 245-266.

Witt, Ulrich (1988), 'Eine Individualistische Theorie der Entwicklung Ökonomischer Institutionen (An Individualistic Theory of the Evolution of Economic Institutions)', **9** *Jahrbuch für Neue Politische Ökonomie*, 72-95.

Wolfke, K. (1993), *Custom in Present International Law*, 2nd edn, Amsterdam, Kluwer Academic Publishers.

Cases

Fisheries Jurisdiction (U.K. v. Ice), 1974 I.C.J. 3 (July 25).

North Sea Continental Shelf (F.R.G. v. Den.) (F.R.G. v. Neth.), 1969 I.C.J. 3 (Feb. 20).

Asylum (Colom. v. Peru), 1950 I.C.J. 266, 275, 277 (Nov. 20).

S.S. Wimbledon, 1923 P.C.I.J. (ser. A), No. 1, at 25.

9600
Conflict of Laws and Choice of Law

Erin Ann O'Hara and Larry E. Ribstein
George Mason University School of Law

Abstract

We discuss the law and economics of conflict of laws and choice of law, focusing on the law in the US. We first consider choice of law when the parties have not effectively chosen their governing law by contract. We address four questions: (1) Why do courts ever apply anything other than the law of the forum? (2) If a court sometimes applies foreign law, is a rule-based or more modern standard-based approach to its choice preferable? (3) Why have so many states abandoned rule-based approaches in favor of standard-based ones? and (4) Is there any real practical difference between the First Restatement and modern approaches? We then discuss costs and benefits of enforcing parties' contractual choice of law provisions. We conclude that permitting parties to choose the governing law that best fits their transactions and future private disputes can enhance jurisdictional competition and help restore predictability to the conflict of laws problem.
JEL classification: K33
Keywords: Conflict of Laws, Choice of Law, Private International Law

1. Introduction

When a legal dispute involves parties, property or events located in more than one government jurisdiction, and the substantive laws of those jurisdictions differ, whose substantive laws govern the rights and obligations of the parties? As barriers to migration and trade between jurisdictions fall, choice of law increasingly complicates transaction and litigation planning and provides new opportunities for private ordering.

Until approximately forty years ago, all courts in the United States applied the territorial rules embodied in the First Restatement of Conflicts when they resolved inter-jurisdictional disputes. The rules, which address most litigation subjects, are premised on a 'vested rights' theory. A party's rights vest, if at all, at a particular place and point in time. Only that state has the power to create the rights relied on by the plaintiff (Beale, 1935; Brilmayer, 1995). Tort issues, for example, are governed by the law of the 'place of the wrong', which is defined for a variety of tortious activities. Contract validity, necessary forms, and substantial performance issues are treated according to the law of the place of contracting, while details of performance are governed by the place of performance. Property issues are resolved according to the law of the situs of the property (Restatement (First) Conflict of Laws, 1934). Accordingly, although an interstate dispute is litigated in a Massachusetts court, the court might apply the substantive law of another state to resolve that dispute.

Several decades ago, however, conflicts scholars began increasingly to criticize the territorial approach to choice of law. The First Restatement Rules were condemned as arbitrary, because there is no *a priori* reason why states' powers should stop at their borders as prescribed by vested rights theory (Brilmayer, 1995). Indeed, conflicts scholars searched the case law for places where the choice of law under the First Restatement led to intuitively unsatisfying results (Cavers, 1933; Currie, 1958a, 1958b; Ehrenzweig, 1956). Tort immunities as applied to common domiciliaries is one such place (Ely, 1981). Under the First Restatement, a husband's ability to recover for an injury caused by his wife's negligence while they were on vacation in another state is governed by the law of the place of the injury, even though the marital domicile is the only state which really has an interest in compensating this husband or preserving this family's harmony. As another example, some have advocated a place of sale rule for products liability cases to better enable manufacturers to charge customers for the varying levels of care and liability they are subject to in differing places. Because products can be moved anywhere, the First Restatement's place of injury rule ends up causing customers in states with lesser tort protections to help pay for the increased tort protections of customers in other states (Kozyris, 1987; McConnell, 1988; O'Hara and Ribstein, 1997; Solomine, 1989).

Defenders of the First Restatement dismissed these occasional unsatisfying results and instead focussed on the general benefits of rules. Rules promote predictability, uniformity, ease of application, and judicial restraint, while discouraging forum-shopping (Reese, 1972; Rosenberg, 1968). In reality, however, a number of 'escape devices' sometimes enabled courts to avoid First Restatement rules when they really wanted to. One method found in every rule-based system is characterization (North and Fawcett, 1992): how the forum court characterized a case, as one of tort or contract for example, determines the choice of law. Where ambiguities arose, judges were free to choose a more preferred governing law. In addition, a public policy exception in the First Restatement permitted courts to avoid applying any foreign law that violated the public policy of the forum. Critics argued that these and other escape devices deprived the First Restatement rules of the very benefits they purported to confer (Brilmayer, 1995). As discussed later in this section, however, subsequent empirical studies cast some doubt on the strength of critics' claims.

In any event, critics argued that courts should replace the rule-based approach with a more sensible basis for choosing governing law. As detailed later in this section, some advocated maximizing the ability of states to give effect to important policies, while others promoted the use of the better or more 'progressive' states' laws. Still others proffered personal rights-based approaches to choice of law. Most of the critics favored standard over rule-based approaches. As a consequence of widespread First Restatement criticism, a significant majority of US state courts have abandoned the traditional approach in favor of one of several alternative approaches to choice of law. As of 1989, only fourteen US states purported to follow the First Restatement (Solomine, 1989), and each of the others has adopted one of at least four alternative approaches. Consensus has clearly disappeared.

Part A will consider four questions regarding choice of law when the parties have not effectively chosen their governing law by contract. First, why do courts ever apply anything other than the law of the forum? Second, if a court sometimes applies foreign law, is a rule-based or standard-based approach to its choice preferable? Third, why have so many states abandoned rule-based approaches in favor of standard-based ones? Finally, is there any real practical difference between the First Restatement and modern approaches? After all, if the standard-based choices do not differ systematically in practice from the First Restatement, the academic debate seems irrelevant. Moving to contractual choice of law, Part B discusses the costs and benefits of enforcing parties' choice of law. Permitting parties to choose the governing law that best fits their transactions and future private disputes can enhance jurisdictional competition and help restore predictability to the conflicts of law problem.

As indicated in this Introduction, we focus on choice of law by US states. The same basic economic principles apply, of course, to international choice of law. Although a detailed examination is beyond the scope of this article, we note some international comparisons and implications at relevant points of our article. We also note at the outset that choice of law within the US may have very different implications from choice of law in Europe given legal harmonization under European Community directives and regulations.

Nor do we discuss arbitration. An arbitration clause in an agreement is a type of forum selection. The choice of law governing the agreement may be as significant as choice of law in other contexts. On the other hand, the arbitrator may not be bound to apply any specific body of law, especially under the European approach of 'de-localised' arbitration (Dicey, 1980, pp. 583-585).

A. The Conflict of Laws Problem

2. Forum Law: The Costs and Benefits

Forum law has at least two efficiency advantages over applying foreign law. First, it is easier to ascertain. Because the judges and lawyers who are licensed to practice in the jurisdiction have previously made significant capital investments learning the details of forum law, the costs of applying that law to any given case are generally lower than the alternatives. Second, the precedent created by applying forum law provides valuable information to primary actors as well as courts and litigators regarding future legal treatment of the issues. In contrast, an investment in foreign law is less valuable locally because foreign precedent is less binding and therefore less important in guiding local conduct or judicial decisions (Thiel, 1996).

An interesting question thus arises: why should a court ever apply the laws of another state? One reason is to enhance predictability. If actors can rely on the application of the law of a particular state, they can structure transactions and other activities and avoid inappropriate or inefficient laws. This, in turn, forces states to internalize the costs of inferior laws, thereby promoting competition among jurisdictions for more efficient substantive rules (O'Hara and Ribstein, 1997). *Ex ante* reliance on Delaware corporations law, for example, is only attainable if New York courts commit themselves to applying Delaware law to the internal affairs of a Delaware corporation. A *lex fora* approach to choice of law therefore impedes pre-litigation predictability. Conflicts scholars have, however, questioned the benefits of predictability by doubting whether people respond to differing legal standards in such contexts as accidents and child abuse (Sterk, 1994; Symposium, 1997). If governing laws do not provide marginal deterrent value in these contexts, then *ex ante* predictability is not sufficiently valuable to justify the increased costs of applying foreign law. On the other hand, empirical evidence indicates that governing tort standards do affect aggregate behavior (Bruce, 1984; Landes, 1982; Landes and Posner, 1987). In particular, repeat players, including manufacturers and insurance companies, pay careful attention to differing laws. Moreover, the actual uncertainty created when the plaintiff can forum-shop for the applicable law is debatable. Actors can predict that disputes will likely be governed by the most plaintiff-favoring law in the set of possible fora for disputes. And, even if parties cannot be certain which forum will ultimately be chosen, in the event of litigation they can proceed with probabilistic expectations. Although the outcome of a plaintiff's forum-shopping law may not be very predictable *ex ante* in many circumstances, it is often not clearly less predictable than anticipating what law a court will apply under default choice of law standards which, as discussed below, can be vague and open-ended.

Another disadvantage to a forum law rule is that it encourages forum-shopping which can produce inefficiencies. Differing substantive laws create disparities across jurisdictions regarding plaintiffs' expected gains from litigation. Forum shopping is generally regarded as skewing the litigation process toward plaintiffs and distributing litigation unevenly across jurisdictions (Sterk, 1994). States with more plaintiff-favoring laws end up being swamped with litigation, while lawyers in states with relatively more defendant-protecting laws face a lower demand for their services.

A third reason for applying foreign law is to take advantage of foreign jurisdictions' comparative regulatory advantages (Posner, 1992; O'Hara and Ribstein, 1997). Suppose, for example, that a South Carolina driver collides with a Florida driver in New York City. Presumably New York adopts traffic and tort laws to encourage an optimal level of care in New York. If a defendant is sued in South Carolina and the court applies South Carolina traffic and tort laws to the suit, then the effectiveness of New York's laws are watered down, given that drivers from all over the country traverse the streets of New York. If everyone is subject to New York standards of liability, then New York can better tinker with its own laws to encourage the standard of care it seeks.

Brilmayer (1995, p. 15) describes the tendency of courts across the world to sometimes consider foreign law as 'virtually universal'. In the US, only two states, Kentucky and Michigan, explicitly embrace a *lex fora* approach (Solomine, 1989). Indeed, the United States Supreme Court has held that application of forum law is unconstitutional if the forum has no substantial interest or connection to the litigation (*Home Insurance Co. v. Dick*). This result is supported by our conclusion that the benefits of predictability, regulatory efforts and jurisdictional competition probably outweigh the costs of applying forum law in many interstate contexts.

3. Rule vs. Standard-based Approaches

Assuming that a court should sometimes apply foreign law, should choice of law decisions be based on rules or a standard? Rules provide predictability, enhance planning and help ensure uniform treatment of similarly situated litigants. In contrast, standards are often better at generating just results in individual cases. Because the costs of overdeterrence and underdeterrence can differ according to the context, rules may be preferable in some areas, while standards may be preferable in others.

As mentioned earlier, the First Restatement rules seemed arbitrary in some contexts. But will a standard-based approach improve choice of law overall? And if a standard-based approach is preferable, what should the governing standard be? States that have abandoned the First Restatement have usually adopted one of three alternative standards: (1) Leflar's 'better law'; (2) interest analysis; or (3) the 'most significant relationship' test. Leflar (1966a, 1966b) says that courts should give significant weight to the 'better law' when faced with the choice, and the better law is generally the one that achieves the most justice, which is courts' primary obligation.

Interest analysts advocate that choice of law should advance state policies behind their laws. Each state thinks its laws are 'better' in general. Consequently, courts should determine which states have an interest in applying their laws to this dispute, given the domiciles of the parties and the location of property and events leading to litigation. As originally conceived, states intend to protect or compensate only their own domiciliaries with their laws, not foreign residents. And a state has a regulatory interest in conduct occurring only within its borders. Brainard Currie, the originator of interest analysis, argued that the forum always should apply its own law when it is 'interested' in the outcome of the dispute. If no state has an interest in the outcome, the forum should still apply its own law because it is cheaper than applying foreign law. Foreign law should be applied only when the foreign state is interested and the forum state is disinterested (Currie, 1959). Baxter (1963), offered an alternative 'balance of state interests' approach. Under this approach, courts should use interest analysis to maximize the joint effectuation of state policies. If two or more states are 'interested' in the outcome of a dispute, a court should determine which state stands to lose most if its policies are ignored, and then apply the law of that state. In other words, in the face of a conflict, Baxter proposed that courts minimize social costs, as those costs are perceived by the individual interested states.

The drafters of the Second Restatement took a third approach. They concluded that courts should apply the law of the state with 'the most significant relationship' to the parties, property and events involved in the dispute. In making this determination, courts should consider a number of factors, including 'the needs of the interstate and international systems'; 'the relevant policies of the forum'; 'the relevant policies of other interested states and the relative interests of those states in the determination of the particular issue'; 'the protection of justified expectations'; 'the basic policies underlying the particular field of law'; 'certainty, predictability and uniformity of result'; and 'ease in the determination and application of the law to be applied' (Restatement (Second) Conflict of Laws, 1971). This test approach is similar to the 'most significant relationship' test used in Europe, except that the latter provides somewhat more guidance in selecting the applicable jurisdiction (Scoles and Hay, pp. 45-47).

Each of the three standards used in American courts has significant problems. Leflar's approach allows judges significant leeway for application of outcome-determinative choice of law rules. Moreover, judges' varying preferences undermine predictability. The same can be said of the Second Restatement test, which gives no indication of how much weight to give to each of the numerous factors (Brilmayer, 1995).

Interest analysis is more complicated. The narrow range of state interests recognized by Currie fails adequately to promote the purported goal of the standard. A state's substantive goals reach far beyond compensating its plaintiffs or protecting its defendants. Often a state is attempting to achieve a sensitive balance between competing interests. Viewing the state's interests behind its substantive laws ignores important choice of law concerns such as protecting party expectations and interstate harmony and preventing forum shopping (Brilmayer, 1980). On the other hand, while modern interest analysts advocate considering the state's true interests behind its laws (Kramer, 1990, 1991a, 1991b), this reduces any predictability the approach might otherwise provide (Brilmayer, 1995) since many factors can motivate state decision making. Moreover, the idea of state interests becomes problematic from a public choice perspective (O'Hara and Ribstein, 1997). States are not monolithic entities. Individual legislators vote for very different reasons, and the state government officials, including judges, who influence the application of the laws have their own concerns. Interest groups that lobby for laws are often trying to achieve purposes very different from the 'public policies' stated by the legislators themselves.

Baxter's comparative impairment approach to interest analysis further complicates the choice. Baxter advocates applying the law of the state with the most to lose if its laws are ignored. However, this calculation is often impossible. Suppose, for example, that two states have interests in applying their laws to a contract dispute. Under State A's laws, spendthrifts can void their contracts. Under State B's laws, spendthrifts contracts are enforceable against the spendthrifts. C, a spendthrift from state A, borrows money from D, a creditor from state B. C fails to repay the loan and D sues to enforce the loan contract. Under interest analysis, state B has an 'interest' in compensating its creditor, while State A has an interest in protecting its spendthrift. Which state's policy suffers greater impairment if its laws are ignored? If such conflicts arise frequently, at least one of the states necessarily will end up having difficulty protecting its residents.

The standard-based approaches have proved unsatisfying. A better solution might be to retain the First Restatement rules with periodic modifications to avoid frequent arbitrary results. Indeed, Posner (1992) has argued that the First Restatement, for all its faults, had the virtue of enabling states to exercise their comparative regulatory advantages. For example, by defining and then applying the 'place of the wrong' to tort suits, states usually could apply their laws to tortious conduct within their states, and could therefore ensure that actors took optimal levels of care. The First Restatement situs rule for property enabled the state where the land was located to regulate its use. Title questions are also resolved by the law of the place of property, a clear rule easing the tracking of titles and therefore facilitating the transfer of property to its highest valued use. Finally, contract validity issues are governed by the place of contracting, and the detailed rules tended to protect those who contract within their own borders. Those who reached across borders were on notice of being subject to the differing protections outside their states. The rule minimized the costs of gathering personal and legal information for those, such as consumers, who transacted business locally. Details of performance were governed by the state with the greatest regulatory concern, where those details were to be performed.

The choice between rules and standards also may be viewed from a contractual perspective. Part B, below, discusses the enforcement of express choice of law clauses. A related issue is the appropriate default rules to supply in the absence of express contract in order to facilitate private bargaining. Standards provide 'tailored' defaults that fit specific situations, while rules provide 'untailored' defaults that apply across a range of cases (Ayres, 1993). In general, untailored rules can reduce contracting costs by decreasing uncertainty as to the rule applied in the absence of contracting. Tailored defaults, by attempting to anticipate the parties' actual preferences, can reduce the need for costly customized contracting (Whincop and Keyes, 1998, pp. 525-526). But untailored *choice-of-law* rules, because they only choose legal systems rather than specific rules, may actually do a good job of anticipating the parties' preferences in the usual case, as distinguished from the odd cases courts actually decide (Whincop and Keyes, 1998, Ch. 3).

Any choice of law approach should take into account concerns for harmonizing state interests, protecting party expectations, minimizing costs of legal information, as well as allowing states to exercise their comparative regulatory advantages. But a rule-based system under which the drafters take these concerns into account to the extent feasible also could promote uniformity and thereby minimize forum shopping. Compared to the standard-based alternatives that have received court attention, the First Restatement likely provides much greater predictability despite its escape devices, and would be even better if these devices were narrowed.

4. Coordination Problems with Rule-Based Approaches

If the First Restatement approach to choice of law is so superior, why have most states abandoned it? In other words, why have the states been unable in recent decades to coordinate choice of law to achieve increased uniformity and predictability? Unless the states collectively adopt or retain choice of law rules, the primary benefits of those rules are lost. A few conflicts scholars have advocated a return to a rule-based approach that would yield net benefits across states, perhaps with legislative encoding of a new Restatement to foster cooperation (Rosenberg, 1981; Scoles and Hay, 1992). But individual rules do not always benefit the state or judge that is supposed to follow them, and interstate enforcement problems may have led to the breakdown of choice of law rules. In other words, courts face an unresolved prisoner's dilemma in the choice of law context.

In general, as the late Judge Breitel once explained in an unpublished speech (Sterk, 1994), judges first ask themselves who deserves to win. Then they assess how much cost to jurisprudence is likely imposed if they manipulate the system to get that outcome. If costs will be borne by future worthy litigants, judges will apply rules with less preferred outcomes for the present litigants. In other words, future litigants constrain judges in the present case to a general application of rules, including procedural ones. Judges who are nevertheless tempted to violate the precedents of other judges are constrained by reputational sanctions imposed by colleagues and higher courts (O'Hara, 1993).

But choice of law is different. Issues arise in many factual contexts involving people and events from different places, and sufficiently infrequently that the specific issue seldom arises again. Because the precedential value of a given choice of law decision is quite limited, costs to future litigants of reduced predictability in that factual context are slight. And colleagues and higher courts are much less likely to attempt to vigilantly protect choice of law precedents than they are to protect precedents that shape forum substantive law.

Even if rules are generally preferred to standards, formulating a comprehensive set that leaves all states better off than they are under choice of law anarchy might prove difficult to formulate (Sterk, 1994). Perhaps more importantly, judges are always tempted to defect from individual rules in favor of local litigants (Hay, 1992), or to apply more easily ascertained local laws. While other states may suffer as a consequence, they are unlikely to pressure the deciding state to prevent these defections. The classic tit-for-tat enforcement strategies (Axelrod, 1984) would be difficult to implement, especially because monitoring of other states' choice of law decisions is costly. Even with monitoring, escape devices allow states in some contexts to defect while feigning cooperation under the rules. When defections are difficult to detect, enforcement becomes much more difficult, and bargains are likely to unravel for at least a while (Friedman, 1971; Green and Porter, 1984). Moreover, it might be years before an interstate dispute arises in the disadvantaged state enabling retaliation against the state that originally defected. Larger plaintiff-favoring states, which were the first to abandon the First Restatement, have more opportunity to defect because they handle a larger volume of interstate litigation.

In a few areas where cooperation among the states really matters, interstate compacts have been formed on a piecemeal basis. For example, state taxation of corporations and child custody disputes are now treated with relatively uniform choice of law provisions. Where cooperation is important but has proven unsuccessful, Congress can step in and federalize the substantive law, as it has done, for example, regarding both bankruptcy and products liability for vaccine manufacturers. For better or worse, choice of law problems are mooted once the federal government imposes uniform federal laws. Finally, private parties can enhance predictability and uniformity to some extent with choice of law provisions in their contracts (Kobayashi and Ribstein, 1998). What is left may not be worth coordinating, at least on the grand scale of a new Restatement.

Of course, some coordination persists in smaller rural states. The First Restatement states are clustered together in the south, including Maryland, Virginia, West Virginia, Tennessee, Alabama, North Carolina, South Carolina and Georgia (Solomine, 1989). These states share a relatively distinct economy and culture that may limit a majority of interactions to people and events in one of the other First Restatement states, perhaps enhancing cooperation. Alternatively, coordination in these states may have more to do with a shared conservative legal culture. In any event, it is not surprising that the First Restatement broke down across a majority of states as legal realism permeated the law, beginning with the larger, plaintiff-favoring states. The benefits to achieving preferred results in individual cases outweighed the costs to individual judges' preferences of ignoring the settled choice of law rules.

5. Do the Choice of Law Approaches Matter in Practice?

The academic debate over choice of law loses relevance if court decisions do not vary significantly under the alternative regimes. Some commentators have suggested that the approaches to choice of law followed within the US make no difference in the end. (This does not, of course, apply to the different choice of law approaches in the international setting.) Sterk (1994), for example, argues that courts care about ensuring that deserving parties win their cases. In contrast, the choice-of-law theorists concern themselves with a host of issues that do not concern the courts. The courts therefore cannot be expected to take any of the approaches seriously. In fact, Leflar (1977) points out his casual impression that courts often make a choice of law determination, and then rely on the choice of law theories that support the court's conclusion.

Even assuming that each state is committed to a single choice of law approach, systematic differences in chosen law between the modern approaches might be difficult to detect, if the modern approaches leave judges effectively unconstrained. One might predict, then, that results differ between First

Restatement states and states adopting modern approaches, but not among states that have adopted each of the modern approaches. Alternatively, if First Restatement escape devices also leave judges unconstrained, then no differences among states would be found based on choice of law approach. It has also been suggested that the modern approaches are more pro-resident, pro-forum, and pro-recovery in principle than the relatively neutral First Restatement (Brilmayer, 1980) and that, because each of the modern approaches rests on theoretically distinct grounds, some of the modern approaches display these biases more than others (Borchers, 1992).

Three empirical papers have attempted to test for systematic differences across states according to choice of law approaches for torts. Solomine (1989) studied 227 cases retrieved from a Westlaw computer search of all published US state supreme court and federal court of appeal cases that explicitly reviewed choice of law determinations in torts. He compared those decisions made according to the First Restatement with those decided according to one of the modern theories. Solomine found that the modern theories resulted in choices of law that were more likely to favor residents, recovery and forum law than did the First Restatement.

It may seem surprising that Solomine would find differences across jurisdictions, at least with regard to recovery-favoring rules. After all, Priest and Klein (1984) demonstrated convincingly that disputes that are actually litigated are biased toward those that are on the margin. Plaintiff win rates should tend toward 50 percent. Even if they vary due to asymmetric information or stakes, win rates should not vary systematically across courts. But choice of law questions might be sufficiently inexpensive and preliminary in the litigation process that results may vary at the margin across jurisdictions.

Borchers (1992) followed with a more extensive study, and ascertained confidence intervals to test the significance of variations across choice of law methodologies. Borchers classified each state by choice of law approach, and then collected 800 published state and federal cases, including those reported at both the trial and appellate level. In the First Restatement states, he retrieved every case found on-line from 1960. In the modern approach states, he retrieved all cases found subsequent to the shift in methodology. Borchers attempted to ascertain the differences both between the First Restatement and modern states as a group and among the specific methodologies applied in the modern states. When the modern states taken together were compared with the First Restatement states, Borchers' results confirmed Solomine's. The modern approach states were significantly more pro-recovery, resident and forum favoring in their choice of laws. However, Borchers found essentially no statistically significant variations across the modern approaches. He found significant variation only with respect to recovery-favoring rules. The Second Restatement and Leflar states were statistically distinguishable from each other, with the Leflar states generating more recovery-favoring outcomes. Borchers' results were seriously qualified, however, by the fact that neither the Second Restatement nor the Leflar states produced choices statistically distinguishable from interest analysis. Borchers concludes (p. 379), 'Courts do not take the new approaches seriously. Because all of the competitors to the First Restatement start from different analytic premises, if courts were faithful to their tenets they would inevitably generate different result patterns. Yet in practice the outcomes are largely indistinguishable.'

Thiel (1996), a trained econometrician, criticized Borchers' methodology for lacking a regression analysis that could control for legal culture. Pro-recovery and pro-plaintiff results can come partly from the modern choice of law approach, but could also be affected by systematic differences in the general legal culture of the First Restatement and modern approach states. At the same time, the states that have adopted the same choice of law methodology might have positively correlated legal cultures. To separate out these influences on choice of law decisions, Thiel used Borchers' state classifications, and remeasured the differences, using variables that might control the estimates for the influence of legal culture.

Thiel found that while the modern approach states clearly use forum law more often than states using the First Restatement, there was little difference at the margin between the two groups of states with respect to recovery-favoring choice of law determinations. Thiel believes that the results indicate that plaintiffs push lawsuits to where their prospects of prevailing on choice of law rulings are about equal in all states. Thiel's most interesting results are found in comparing states according to modern methodology. Unlike Borchers, Thiel's regressions produced statistically significant variations across the modern approaches with respect to forum and recovery-favoring choice of law. As predicted by theoretical analyses of modern methodologies (Borchers, 1992), the point estimates of the differences indicate that the Leflar states are relatively strongest in their generosity to plaintiffs and preference for forum law. The interest analysis states also show a strong bias toward choice of forum law, and are relatively strongest in favoring local parties.

More empirical studies could help clarify the choice of law debate. In the conflicts field, as least as much as any other, legal academics make bald statements claiming that various approaches or rules will work in particular ways or have specific effects on primary behavior. Those statements are supported at best with slight anecdotal evidence. The field is ripe for empiricists who can cut through the legal and academic thicket to view the landscape.

B. Contractual Choice of Law

We have so far discussed only the default choice of law rules that apply in the absence of contract. Enforcing clauses in contracts that select the applicable law has several possible benefits (Ribstein, 1993; Whincop and Keynes, 1998, Ch. 3).

6. Benefits of Enforcing Contractual Choice of Law

Eliminating Inconsistency
The parties may contract for choice of law in order to eliminate problems that arise when inconsistent mandatory rules otherwise might be applied to different aspects of or parties to the contract, such as shareholder voting rules and the rights of franchisees.

Clarifying the Applicable Law
Contracting for choice of law enables the parties easily to determine what law governs the transaction. Uncertainty about the applicable law that results from the choice of law default rules discussed above prevents the parties from easily determining the standard of conduct to which they should conform or how to price contract rights and duties. Uncertainty at the time of litigation can increase both the costs and frequency of litigation. In particular, the uncertainty may increase the parties' gains from litigating rather than settling (Priest and Klein, 1984). This is not only privately more costly for the parties, but also imposes costs on the judicial system that are borne by taxpayers generally.

Jurisdictional Competition
Enforcing contractual choice of law is particularly useful in fostering jurisdictional competition for more efficient laws across states (Kobayashi and Ribstein, 1998; Ribstein 1993). Competition works both by encouraging states to develop new terms to attract new legal business, and by encouraging states to retain legal business by efficiently revising their laws. Jurisdictional competition was first observed with regard to corporations, where a clear choice of law rule, the internal affairs rule in the US, compels application of the law of the state of incorporation (see Section 8, below). This rule encourages corporations to select the applicable law. Commentators have debated whether this process is a 'race to the bottom' in which the states attract incorporation business by exploiting principal-agent problems resulting from the separation of ownership and control (Cary, 1974) or a 'race to the top' that is disciplined by efficient capital markets (Winter, 1977). For empirical evidence favoring the race to the top hypothesis, see Carney (1993), Romano (1985), Dodd and Leftwich

(1980). For studies of the role of jurisdictional competition in the transition from special chartering to general incorporation, see Shughart and Tollison (1985) and Butler (1985).

As Tiebout recognized, the ability of people and firms to exit jurisdictions whose policies they do not like motivates governments to reflect voters' preferences (Tiebout, 1956; Frey and Eichenberger, 1995; Gerken, 1995; Kerber and Vanberg, 1995). Thus, the demand side of jurisdictional competition requires, among other things, that actors are mobile (Easterbrook, 1983; Tiebout, 1956; Fischel, 1987). For example, with regard to corporations, foreign incorporation imposes registration costs, exposes firms to suits in remote jurisdictions and makes unavailable intrastate financing that is exempt from the federal securities laws. Close corporations ordinarily lack incentives to incur these costs because they can get most of what they want by adapting the default provisions of their resident-state's law (Ayres, 1992a; but see Ribstein, 1995a). Large multistate firms, on the other hand, pay these costs anyway in all but one state in which they transact business and have scale economies that can absorb the costs.

The supply side of state competition requires that states have incentives to compete for formation business (Daniels, 1991). The states provide their law free of charge at taxpayer expense. If states cannot internalize the benefits from efficient contract rules, they may have inadequate incentives to devote legislative and judicial resources to developing and maintaining efficient contract rules. The standard explanation of the state competition for corporate law is based on the states' incentives to earn franchise and related fees from incorporating firms (Romano, 1985). They can also earn revenue if enforcing choice-of-law attracts firms' operations to the state. Either of these mechanisms would, in effect, give the state property rights in application of its law.

In analyzing the supply side of state competition, it is necessary to disaggregate the 'state' and determine what motivates politicians to compete. Contracting parties' ability to exit the state is a necessary but not sufficient basis for efficient competition. It is also necessary that this exit be translated into incentives for politicians. Whatever the benefits to states by participating in interstate competition, it is not clear that taxpayers can motivate state legislators to draft state-of-the-art legislation solely in order to maximize state revenues, particularly given legislators' costs of producing this legislation. No individual taxpayers can capture enough benefits from legislative action to justify expending resources on legislation. Also, legislators may not be able to capture benefits from engaging in the competition because other jurisdictions easily can free-ride on their efforts by copying successful legislation (Rose-Ackerman, 1980). At the same time, legislators incur costs in competing to provide state law. In particular, because legislators can earn contributions and other support from affected parties by brokering changes in mandatory rules, they do not have strong incentives to lead the movement toward more enabling rules. Third, legislators face an unfavorable balance of risks and rewards. They take the risk that the legislation will fail to accomplish its objectives or will alienate groups that otherwise would have supported them, while their successes can be copied easily by other states. For discussions of legislators' weak incentives to innovate, see Rose-Ackerman (1980), Ayres (1992b), Carney (1993), MacIntosh (1993), Ribstein and Kobayashi (1996).

State competition to supply law may, however, be driven by lawyers rather than legislatures (Ribstein, 1994, 1995). Lawyers not only wield the conventional power of a cohesive interest group but, in most states, draft complex business statutes. Lawyers have an incentive to make their state a standard for commercial contracts in order to attract more litigation business to the state's courts and increase the value of advice on and expertise in the state's law. However, as the price for assisting in the competition of state laws, lawyers may reduce the demand for these rules by pressing for rules that favor lawyers, such as by offering open-ended default rules that discourage settlement and increase litigation (Macey and Miller, 1987; White, 1992; Priest and Klein, 1984). Accordingly, lawyers may have an interest in preventing the parties from simplifying choice of law by contracting in advance to be governed by a particular law. On the other hand, lawyers are constrained by jurisdictional competition. In general, lawyers would support rules that reduce demand for law up to the point that the reduction in demand exceeds their benefits from the rules. Demand may be reduced by inefficient legal rules that cause parties to move their legal business to other states, federal courts and arbitrators.

The extent to which states compete to supply non-corporate law depends significantly on whether interest groups in those states can protect their benefits from mandatory rules from erosion by state competition. Under standard interest group theory, state legislation is determined by the relative strength of the various groups that the legislation helps and hurts (Olson, 1965; McCormick and Tollison, 1981; Tollison, 1988). To be sure, states can successfully compete only by making their underlying legal rules generally attractive to contracting parties. Thus, a state could not win a competition to attract, say, franchise law business simply by adopting a pro-franchisee law. However, the state might be able to help franchisees by imposing retroactive burdens on existing franchise contracts. Groups helped by such laws might oppose vigorous choice-of-law competition. States' incentives to compete therefore depend on how well organized are groups that favor mandatory rules, the costs and benefits to competing groups of applying contract-friendly enabling rules rather than protective mandatory rules, and lawyers' benefits from competing for law business. Thus, for example, Delaware may be in a good position to compete to supply law in part because it has a highly organized commercial bar but no well-organized competing groups.

The quantity and quality of state competition ultimately depend on the legal rules regarding contractual choice of law. Politicians may protect themselves by, for example, restricting enforcement of contractual choice law. While the courts may have considerable discretion to interpret the legislature's statutes, they can do little in the face of a statute that explicitly invalidates choice of law clauses. Even if the statute does not invalidate exit by choice of law, judges may have their own incentives to maximize the value of interest group deals by protecting them from dilution by party choice of law. After all, judges clearly have some incentive to respond to legislators' interests to the extent that the latter control judges' salary and tenure. If so, judges can be expected to act to increase the durability and value of legislators' interest group deals by enforcing them within the state (Anderson et al., 1989; Crain and Tollison, 1979; Landes and Posner, 1975).

Although legislators and judges may attempt to block contractual choice of law, contracting parties to some extent have the last say. They may, among other things, choose the fora in which disputes are decided and completely exit jurisdictions that are hostile to contractual choice of law. These moves, in turn, put pressure on courts and legislators to enforce contractual choice (Kobayashi and Ribstein, 1998).

Jurisdictional Competition and Evolutionary Theories

Contractual choice of law may lead to a process of legal evolution. As to legal evolution generally, see Benson (1995), Kerber and Vanberg (1995). Alchian (1950) observed that a study of the 'adaptive mechanism' of the market may be more fruitful than that of 'individual motivation and foresight'. Under this theory, individuals and firms who have an incentive to minimize their transaction and information costs and an ability to choose legal regimes that accomplish this goal will cause the law to move toward efficiency. For example, corporate law evolved from the sale of corporate charters by state legislators to largely enabling statutes and alternative forms of limited liability business forms because of the pressure of jurisdictional competition (Butler, 1985; Shughart and Tollison, 1985). There is also evidence of such evolution with respect to the demand for statutory forms (Ribstein, 1995a) and the demand for uniform statutory provisions (Kobayashi and Ribstein, 1996). This evolutionary theory suggests that the conditions for efficiency may exist even if this outcome could not be predicted *ex ante* based on a study of the incentives of legislators or other key actors.

It may be indeterminate whether the mechanisms for efficient competition are in place, and therefore impossible to determine *ex ante* whether competition among unknown alternatives will produce more efficient results than applying a centralized rule. Nevertheless, it may be more efficient to facilitate jurisdictional competition by enforcing contractual choice of law in order to promote a process of discovering more efficient alternatives (Hayek, 1948; Vihanto, 1992; Kobayashi, Parker and Ribstein, 1994; Gerken, 1995). Contractual choice of law is also likely to be superior to other alternatives, such as the adoption of uniform or national laws, precisely because differing state laws foster experimentation (Ribstein and Kobayashi, 1996; Kobayashi and Ribstein, 1996). Moreover, diverse environments may suggest differing optimal rules, and choice of law enables parties to choose the rule that fits best with their contracting situation (Posner and Scott, 1980; Easterbrook, 1983; Baysinger and Butler, 1985; Romano, 1985).

On the other hand, enforcing contractual choice of law might not lead to efficient competition if state legislators engage in 'herd' behavior' by ignoring their private information generated by other states' experiences and simply adopting prior laws. (For theoretical treatments of herd behavior, see Banerjee, 1992; Bikhchandani, Hirshleifer and Welch, 1992; Scharfstein and Stein, 1990.) However, evidence from the evolution of statutory forms for closely-held firms indicates that legislators do not simply follow-the-leader but rather apply new information in adopting legislation (Ribstein, 1995a).

7. Costs of Contractual Choice of Law

Notwithstanding the above arguments, there are also reasons why enforcing contractual law may lead to inefficient results (Ribstein, 1993).

Evasion of Mandatory Rules

Enforcing contractual choice of law arguably can lead to externalization of costs where it permits contracting parties to evade mandatory rules that are intended to address specific bargaining problems that can lead to such externalization. This may be the case, for example, where the parties are attempting to escape prohibitions on contract terms such as fiduciary duty waivers, usurious interest rates, termination-at-will or noncompetition provisions.

The argument against enforcing the contractual choice-of-law in these situations may seem to be precisely the same as that supporting the mandatory rule itself. However, there are several reasons for permitting the parties to opt out of locally mandatory rules by contractually choosing the applicable law or forum. First, where several jurisdictions' laws may apply, the parties' choice of law is not obviously less appropriate than any other basis of selecting the applicable law.

Second, evasion of mandatory rules is constrained by the fact that avoidance requires applying a state law rather than solely the voluntary act of contracting parties. That the chosen state's law applies to its own residents reduces state legislators' incentives to engage in this sort of conduct. Accordingly, this danger of enforcing contractual choice of law exists mainly where most victims live outside the state.

Third, the enacting legislature may not have intended to preclude contracting for the applicable law or forum. In particular, a mandatory rule may not make sense to the extent that it precludes efficient bargains. The parties arguably indicate that the mandatory rule is costly when applied to them by their willingness to incur the costs of contracting for choice of law. Thus, courts generally should enforce contractual choice of law or forum even to the extent that it overrides a locally mandatory rule (Buckley and Ribstein, 1998; Whincop and Keyes, 1998a, Ch. 4, 1998b).

Information Assymmetry and Protecting Contracting Parties

Enforcing contractual choice of law arguably may lead to externalization of costs because the party responsible for the term is probably more well-informed concerning the chosen law. Indeed, such information asymmetries may skew interstate competition because states may tailor their rules to suit the more informed party. However, information asymmetry is arguably not a problem where the effect of the law selection clause is to choose a legal regime that literally enforces the contract; in long-term contracts negotiated by sophisticated and knowledgeable parties who have the ability and incentive to read the contract carefully or hire an attorney to do so; or where firms are subject to market incentives to disclose and to constraints on cheating (Schwartz and Wilde, 1979). In any event, regulators could minimize information costs by mandating disclosure of unusual and significant law-selection terms in some circumstances.

Similarly, enforcing contractual choice of law is arguably inefficient where the choice-of-law clause can be characterized as an 'adhesion' contract imposed by one party on another. This argument also has been used to justify broad regulation of corporate governance. However, this is not the case merely because of the parties' acceptance of a standard term, particularly where the contract chooses the entire local law of a particular jurisdiction. A state's entire law as to a complex contract probably will not operate unfairly against one of the parties on all or most of the many issues that could arise in the future.

8. Enforcement of Contractual Choice of Law

This section considers the extent to which choice of law provisions are enforced in United States courts.

Common Law

The common law, as summarized in Restatement (1971), § 187(1) provides for enforcement of the parties' contractual choice of law as to interpretation issues the parties could have resolved by contract. Under Restatement § 187(2), the contract is not enforced as to issues such as validity, where choice of law matters most, if:

(a) the chosen state has no substantial relationship to the parties or the transaction and there is no other reasonable basis for the parties' choice, or
(b) application of the law of the chosen state would be contrary to a fundamental policy of a state which has a materially greater interest than the chosen state in the determination of the particular issue and which, under the rule of §188, would be the state of the applicable law in the absence of an effective choice of law by the parties.

Courts and commentators have not clearly articulated a rationale for these limitations on enforcement of contractual choice of law (Ribstein, 1993). The 'substantial relationship' test in subsection (a) seems to have no function other than to increase the parties' cost of exit from mandatory rules and, therefore, to reduce the likelihood of efficient interstate competition. For example, it is not clear why any mutually agreed choice would not be prima facie 'reasonable'. The test conceivably could be defended on the ground that it addresses externalization of costs by states whose law is applied. But even if the particular contract at issue does not relate to the contractually selected state, the state might still be subject to market discipline where the applied law has substantial application within the applying state. In other situations, such as corporate law, the state is otherwise subject to market discipline in formulating its law. With respect to the vague 'fundamental policy' exception in subsection (b), the Restatement gives as examples 'illegal' contracts or rules 'designed to protect a person against the oppressive use of superior bargaining power' (Restatement, 1971, p. 568). This appears to track potential concerns about bargaining power and information asymmetries (see Section 7, above). Alternatively, this ground for non-enforcement may just invite courts to determine and effectuate the underlying goal of the interest groups that promoted the law.

In general, courts applying the US Restatement (Second) rule have quite generally enforced contractual choice of law (Ribstein, 1993). Thus, in practice, the US rule is close to the rule favoring enforcement articulated in the leading UK case of *Vita Food Products Inc. v. Unus Shipping Co.*. That case enforced a provision applying English law though there was nothing to connect the contract with England except the choice of law clause.

Statutory Law

Several states, including California, Illinois, Delaware, New York and Texas, have promulgated statutes that, to varying degrees, clarify the enforcement of contractual choice of law clauses (Ribstein, 1994). These choice-of-law statutes provide some evidence both of jurisdictional competition to supply law and of the determinants of such competition. The laws do not generate obvious gains for legislators. They do not generate franchise fee or other obvious income for the state. Nor do they even appear to benefit firms and individuals residing or doing business in the enacting states since such parties do not need the statute to secure jurisdiction in or to justify contractual enforcement of the law of the enacting states. However, the laws are understandable in light of the role of lawyers in promoting jurisdictional competition (see Section 6). Lawyers' role also helps explain differences among the four statutes. The broadest statute is in Delaware, where lawyers clearly dominate. In the larger commercial states such as Texas, other powerful interest groups clearly would want to protect local mandatory laws from erosion by interstate competition.

Corporate Internal Affairs Rule

In contrast to the rule applied to other contractual relationships, the parties' rights regarding the internal governance of a corporation usually are determined by the law selected by the parties - that is, the law of the state of incorporation (Restatement, 1971, § 302(2). The conflicts rules that apply to corporations therefore differ substantially from those which apply to non-corporate contracts. This ignores the fact that corporations and other types of firms are fundamentally similar in the sense of being alternative devices for minimizing transaction costs (Williamson, 1985; Coase, 1937). Nor do the costs and benefits of applying contractual choice of law discussed above differ significantly according to whether corporate or non-corporate contracts are involved (Ribstein, 1993). For example, parties to non-corporate contracts, like those to corporations, would benefit from being permitted to shop for the applicable law, from the certainty of applying a contractually selected law, and from applying the same law to all parties to interstate contracts. On the other side of the ledger, corporations present the same potential problems as other contracts regarding potential evasion of mandatory rules, as indicated by commentators such as Cary (1974) who have condemned interstate competition for corporate law as a 'race to the bottom'. Although corporations do clearly identify the applicable law through their centrally filed certificates or articles of incorporation, this does no more than justify analogous requirements for non-corporate contracts. The fact that corporate shares are traded on efficient securities markets that discount significant contract terms plainly does not justify a distinction between closely held corporations and other types of contracts.

The different treatment of corporations and other types of contracts with regard to enforcement of contractual choice of law may be due at least partly to the long acceptance of the legal fiction that a corporation is a legal 'person' created and endowed with certain attributes by the chartering state (Ribstein, 1995b). This characterization is conducive to application of contractual choice of law because it seems to give greater weight to the parties' jurisdictional choice than would characterizing the corporation as a mere contract. The entity theory helped create a legal momentum toward enforcement of contractual choice of law in corporations that has never been opposed by coordinated interest groups. In other words, the special choice-of-law rule for corporations, which has been instrumental in ensuring efficient state default rules and enforcement of contracts in firms, ironically may be attributable to the fact that the corporation traditionally has been viewed as a legal person rather than an ordinary contract.

There is a potential tension between the corporate internal affairs rule and the choice of law statutes discussed above. Those statutes arguably permit the parties to a corporation to select the law *other than* of the state of incorporation. This raises the question of whether states should be able to, in effect, bundle their lawmaking and adjudication services by insisting that their corporate law applies only to parties who have formally incorporated in the state and, therefore, paid the franchise tax (Ribstein, 1994). Fees and taxes arguably play a role in giving states an incentive to compete to provide law, depending on the role of lawyers in promoting in this competition (see Section 6, above).

Constitutional law

The federal government in a federal system has an important role with respect to contractual choice of law. For broad-based discussions of the economics of federalism, see Hayek (1948), Riker (1964), Shapiro (1972), Rose Ackerman (1980, 1981), Cover (1981), Kitch (1981), Macey (1990) and Carney (1993). This section discusses Constitutional provisions that mandate enforcement of choice of law contracts. Other potential effects of federal law are discussed below.

The commerce clause of the US Constitution, §8, cl.3, provides in part that Congress has the power '[t]o regulate Commerce ... among the several states'. The 'negative implication' of this clause is that *only* Congress, and not the individual states, can regulate such commerce (see *Cooley v. Board of Wardens*). The Supreme Court has endorsed an exportation-of-costs theory of the commerce clause which holds that if the costs of state regulation fall mostly on interest groups outside the state while the benefits accrue to those within it, the legislature lacks incentives to consider both costs and benefits in enacting laws (Posner, 1992, pp. 638-644; Fischel, 1987; Levmore, 1983). From an efficiency standpoint, cost exportation subverts interest group interaction within the enacting jurisdiction that otherwise would cause laws to tend toward Kaldor-Hicks efficiency.

The cost-exportation theory arguably justifies invalidation under the commerce clause of state statutes to the extent that they prevent enforcement of choice-of-law clauses. This targets a particular application of state law that generally tends to benefit concentrated in-state groups while imposing costs on out-of-state firms or interest groups (Ribstein, 1993). It is significant in that regard that such clauses tend not to be enforced when they are in form contracts that are used on a national scale rather than within a single state (Ribstein, 1993). This theory is arguably supported by two Supreme Court cases on state anti-takeover laws, *Edgar v. Mite Corp.* and *CTS Corp. v. Dynamics Corp. of America*. *Edgar* struck down on Commerce Clause grounds a state law which imposed conditions, including approval by a state agency, on interstate tender offers, while *CTS* held under the commerce clause that an interstate tender offer *could* be regulated by the law of the state of incorporation. These cases are best rationalized on the basis that regulation of a corporate contract which is inconsistent with the law of the contractually selected state - that is, the law of the state of incorporation - is invalid under the commerce clause.

Even if the commerce clause technically applies in this situation, its application may be unnecessary in the long run. Costs ultimately may be borne inside the state even if they initially fall on nonresidents (Kitch, 1981), and laws hurt out-of-state groups invite retaliation by other states (Levmore, 1983).

The full faith and credit clause, US Constitution art. IV, §1, provides in part that 'Full Faith and Credit shall be given in each State to the public Acts, Records, and judicial Proceedings of every other State'. This requires states to respect the laws of other states at least to the extent of having a principled basis for refusing to the follow the law in a particular case (see *Allstate Insurance Co v. Hague*). However, this principle does not directly protect individuals' rights to freedom of contract.

Some early 'full faith and credit' cases involving fraternal benefit associations held that the association's formation state law or charter must apply in order to ensure that a single legal regime applies to all association members (see, for example, *Supreme Council of the Royal Arcanum v. Green*, enforcing increase in assessment rate pursuant to association's constitution). However, given the limited objectives of the full faith and credit clause discussed above, it is unlikely that this authority would be broadly applied today to compel enforcement of choice of law clauses. At most, these cases might justify applying a single rule, such as the law of the one state that has overwhelming contacts with the transaction even if this is not the law the parties selected.

Federal Law

Congress is explicitly empowered under the full faith and credit and commerce clauses to regulate choice of law. A federal choice of law rule could preserve state power and reinforce private contracts similar to commerce clause protection of contractual choice of law. However, any Congressional action would have to emerge from a competition among interest groups. There is probably no group that would gain enough from a general rule validating choice-of-law clauses to organize support for such a law. Congress may fail to act only to avoid negative interest group pressure (Macey, 1990) rather than because action would be inefficient. This suggests that it may be better to rely on the Supreme Court's power under the Constitution to lift state burdens on interstate commerce.

Bibliography on Conflict of Laws and Choice of Law (9600)

Anderson, Gary M. et al. (1989), 'On the Incentives of Judges to Enforce Legislative Wealth Transfers', **32** *Journal of Law and Economics*, 215 ff.

Ayres, Ian (1992a), 'Judging Close Corporations in the Age of Statutes', **70** *Washington University Law Quarterly*, 365 ff.

Ayres, Ian (1992b), 'Making a Difference: The Contractual Contributions of Easterbrook and Fischel', **59** *University of Chicago Law Review*, 1391 ff.

Ayres, Ian (1993), 'Preliminary thoughts on Optimal Tailoring of Contractual Rules', **3** *Southern California Interdisciplinary Law Journal*, 1 ff.

Bainbridge, Stephen M. (1984), 'Trade Usages in International Sales of Goods: An Analysis of the 1964 and 1980 Sales Conventions', **24** *Virginia Journal of International Law*, 619 ff.

Bainbridge, Stephen M. (1986), 'Comity and Sovereign Debt Litigation: A Bankruptcy Analogy', **10** *Maryland Journal of International Law and Trade*, 1 ff.

Baxter, William F. (1963), 'Choice of Law and the Federal System', **16** *Stanford Law Review*, 1 ff.

Beale, Joseph H. (1935), *A Treatise on the Conflict of Laws*.

Benson, Bruce L. (1992), 'Customary Law as a Social Contract: International Commercial Law', **2** *Constitutional Political Economy*, 1-27.

Benson, Bruce L. (1995), 'Competition Among Legal Institutions: Implications for the Evolution of Law', in Gerken, Luden (ed.), *Competition Among Institutions*, London, Macmillan, 153-175.

Borchers, Patrick (1992), 'The Choice of Law Revolution: An Empirical Study', **49** *Washington and Lee Law Review*, 357 ff.

Boyd, James (1996), 'Environmental Liability Reform and Privatization in Central and Eastern Europe', **3** *European Journal of Law and Economics*.

Brilmayer, Lea (1980), 'Interest Analysis and the Myth of Legislative Intent', **78** *Michigan Law Review*, 392 ff.

Brilmayer, Lea (1995), *Conflict of Laws*, Boston, Little Brown.

Bruce, Christopher J. (1984), 'The Deterrent Effects of Automobile Insurance and Tort Law: A Survey of the Empirical Literature', **6** *Law and Policy*, 67 ff.

Buckley, Francis H. and Ribstein, Larry E. (1998), *Marriage and Choice of Law* (Unpublished manuscript).

Butler, Henry N. (1985), 'Nineteenth-Century Jurisdictional Competition in the Granting of Corporate Privileges', **14** *Journal of Legal Studies*, 129 ff.

Carney, William J. (1993), 'The ALI's Corporate Governance Project: the Death of Property Rights?' **61** *George Washington Law Review*, 898 ff.

Carney, William J. (1997), 'The Political Economy of Competition for Corporate Charters', **26** *Journal of Legal Studies*, 303 ff.

Cary, William L. (1974), 'Federalism and Corporate Law: Reflections upon Delaware', **83** *Yale Law Journal*, 663 ff.

Cavers, David (1933), 'A Critique of the Choice-of-Law Problem', **47** *Harvard Law Review*, 173 ff.

Coase, Ronald H. (1937), 'The Nature of the Firm', **4** *Economica*, 386-405.

Cover, Robert M. (1981), 'The Uses of Jurisdictional Redundancy: Interest Ideology and Innovation', **22** *William and Mary Law Review*, 639 ff.

Crain, W. Mark and Tollison, R.D. (1979), 'Constitutional Change in an Interest Group Perspective', **8** *Journal of Legal Studies*, 165 ff.

Currie, Brainard (1958a), 'Survival of Actions: Adjudication versus Automation in the Conflict of Laws', **10** *Stanford Law Review*, 205 ff.

Currie, Brainard (1958b), 'Married Women's Contracts: A Study in Conflict-of-Laws Method', **24** *University of Chicago Law Review*, 227 ff.

Currie, Brainard (1959), 'Notes on Methods and Objectives in the Conflict of Laws', **1959** *Duke Law Journal*, 171 ff.

Daniels, Ronald J. (1991), 'Should Provinces Compete: The Case for a Competitive Corporate Law Market', **36** *McGill Law Journal*, 130 ff.

Dezalay, Yves and Garth, Bryant G. (1995), 'Merchants of Law as Mortal Entrepreneurs: Constructing International Justice from the Competition for Trasnational Business Disputes', **29** *Law and Society Review*, 27-64.

Dicey, Albert Venn (1980), *Dicey and Morris on the Conflict of Laws*, London, Stevens.

Dodd, Peter and Leftwich, Richard (1980), 'The Market for Corporate Charters: Unhealthy Competition versus Federal Regulation', **53** *Journal of Business*, 259 ff.

Easterbrook, Frank H. (1983), 'Antitrust and the Economics of Federalism', **26** *Journal of Law and Economics*, 23 ff.

Ehrenzweig, Albert (1956), 'Parental Immunity in the Conflict of Laws: Law and Reason versus the Restatement', **23** *University of Chicago Law Review*, 474 ff.

Ely, John Hart (1981), 'Choice of Law and the State's Interest in Protecting Its Own', **23** *William and Mary Law Review*, 173-217.

Fischel, Daniel R. (1987), 'From MITE to CTS: State Anti-Takeover Statutes, the Williams Act, the Commerce Clause, and Insider Trading', **47** *Supreme Court Review*.

Frey, Brumo S. and Eichenberger, Reiner (1995), 'Competition among Jurisdictions: The Idea of FOCJ', in Gerken, Luden (ed.), *Competition Among Institutions*, London, Macmillan, 209-229.

Green, Edward J. and Porter, Robert H. (1984), 'Noncooperative Collusion Under Imperfect Price Information', **52** *Econometrica*, 87 ff.

Hay, Bruce L. (1992), 'Conflicts of Laws and State Competition in the Product Liability System', **80** *Georgetown Law Journal*, 617 ff.

Henry, Sherrye P. and Bainbridge, Stephen M. (1984), 'Nationalizations - Standard of Compensation', **24** *Virginia Journal of International Law*, 993 ff.

Joustra, Carla (1992), 'Cross Border Consumer Complaints in Private International Law', **15(4)** *Journal of Consumer Policy*, 431-443.

Kitch, Edmund W. (1981), 'Regulation and the American Common Market', in Tarlock, A. Dan (ed.), *Regulation, Federalism and Interstate Commerce 9.*

Kobayashi, Bruce H. and Ribstein, Larry E. (1996), 'Evolution and Spontaneous Uniformity: Evidence from the Evolution of the Limited Liability Company', **34** *Economic Inquiry.*

Kobayashi, Bruce H. and Ribstein, Larry E. (1998), 'Contract and Jurisdictional Competition', in Buckley, F.H. (ed.), *Fall and Rise of Freedom of Contract*, NC, Duke Univ Press.

Kobayashi, Bruce H., Parker, Jeffrey S. and Ribstein, Larry E. (1994), *The Process of Procedural Reform*, George Mason University Law and Economics Working Paper, 96-5.

Kötz, Hein (1986), 'Rechtsvereinheitlichung - Nutzen, Kosten, Methoden, Ziele (Law Harmonization - Benefits, Costs, Methods, Goals)', **50** *Rabels Zeitschrift für Ausländisches und Internationales Privatrecht*, 483-507.

Kozyris, John P. (1987), 'Choice of Law for Products Liability: Whither Ohio?', **48** *Ohio State Law Journal*, 377 ff.

Kramer, Larry (1990), 'Rethinking Choice of Law', **90** *Columbia Law Review*, 277 ff.

Kramer, Larry (1991a), 'Return of the Renvoi', **66** *New York University Law Review*, 979 ff.

Kramer, Larry (1991b), 'More Notes on Methods and Objectives in the Conflict of Laws', **24** *Cornell International Law Journal*, 245 ff.

Leflar, Robert (1966a), 'Choice-Influencing Considerations in Conflicts Law', **41** *New York University Law Review*, 267 ff.

Leflar, Robert (1966b), 'Conflicts Law: More On Choice Influencing Considerations', **54** *California Law Review*, 1584 ff.

Leflar, Robert (1977), 'Choice of Law: A Well-watered Plateau', **41** *Law and Contemporary Problems*, 10 ff.

Levmore, Saul (1983), 'Interstate Exploitation and Judicial Intervention', **69** *Vanderbilt Law Review*, 568-569.

Macey, Jonathan R. (1990), 'Federal Deference to Local Regulators and the Economic Theory of Regulation: Toward a Public Choice Explanation of Federalism', **76** *Vanderbilt Law Review*, 265 ff.

Macey, Jonathan R. and Miller, Geoffrey P. (1987), 'Toward an Interest-Group Theory of Delaware Corporate Law', **65** *Texas Law Review*, 469 ff.

MacIntosh, Jeffrey G. (1993), *The Role of Interjurisdictional Competition in Shaping Canadian Corporate Law: A Second Look*, University of Toronto Law and Economics Working Paper Series, WPS 18.

Malysiak, James T. (1973), 'Toward a Substantive Private International Law of Trademarks: The Lessons of the Carl Zeiss Litigation', **82(5)** *Yale Law Journal*, 1072-1091.

McConnell, Michael W. (1988), 'A Choice of Law Approach to Products-Liability Reform', in Olson, Walter (ed.), *New Directions in Liability Law*, New York, The Academy of Political Science.

Nagel, Bernhard (1992), 'Von der Lex Mercatoria zur Lex Laboris, zur Rechtlichen Bewältigung der Internationalen Arbeitsbeziehungen (Lex Mercatoria and Lex Laboris.

On the Legal Analysis of International Work Relations)', in Däubler, Wolfgang, Bobke, Manfred and Kehrmann, Karl (ed.), *Festschrift für Albert Gnade*, Köln, Bund-Verlag.

North, P.M. and Fawcett, J.J. (1992), *Cheshire and North's Private International Law*, London, Butterworths.

O'Hara, Erin and Ribstein, Larry E. (1997), 'Interest Groups, Contracts and Interest Analysis', **48** *Mercer Law Review*, 765-774.

Parisi, Francesco (1995), 'Toward a Theory of Spontaneous Law', **6** *Constitutional Political Economy*, 211-231.

Parisi, Francesco (1996a), 'Normative Knowledge and Self-Enforcing Rule in International Law', **2** *International Legal Theory*, 27-30.

Parisi, Francesco (1996b), 'Law as a Voluntary Enterprise', in Ratnapala, S. and Moens, G. (eds), *The Jurisprudence of Liberty*, London, Butterworths, 111-128.

Parisi, Francesco (1997), 'The Economics of Customary Law: Lessons From Evolutionary Socio-Biology', in Ott, Claus and von Wangenheim, Georg (eds), *Essays in Law and Economics IV*, Antwerpen, Maklu.

Parisi, Francesco (1998a), 'Customary Law', in Newman, Peter (ed.), *The New Palgrave Dictionary of Economics and the Law*, London, Macmillan.

Parisi, Francesco (1998b), 'The Cost of the Game: A Topology of Social Interactions', **6** *European Journal of Law and Economics*.

Parisi, Francesco (1998c), 'Spontaneous Emergence of Law: Customary Law', in X., *Encyclopedia of Law and Economics*, Cheltenham, Edward Elgar and University of Gent.

Reese, Willis (1972), 'Choice of Law: Rules or Approach', **57** *Cornell Law Review*, 315 ff.

Ribstein, Larry E. (1993), 'Choosing Law by Contract', **18** *Journal of Corporation Law*, 245 ff.

Ribstein, Larry E. (1994), 'Delaware, Lawyers and Choice of Law', **19** *Delaware Journal of Corporate Law*, 999 ff.

Ribstein, Larry E. (1995a), 'Statutory Forms for Closely Held Firms: Theories and Evidence from LLCs', **73** *Washington University Law Quarterly*, 369 ff.

Ribstein, Larry E. (1995b), 'A Critique of the Uniform Limited Liability Company Act', **25** *Stetson Law Review*, 313 ff.

Ribstein, Larry E. (1995c), 'The Constitutional Conception of the Corporation', **4** *Supreme Court Economic Review*, 95 ff.

Ribstein, Larry E. and Kobayashi, Bruce H. (1995), 'Uniform Laws, Model Laws and Limited Liability Companies', **66** *University of Colorado Law Review*, 947-999.

Ribstein, Larry E. and Kobayashi, Bruce H. (1996), 'Economic Analysis of Uniform State Laws', **25** *Journal of Legal Studies*, 131 ff.

Riker, William H. (1964), *Federalism: Origin, Operation, Significance*, Boston, Little Brown .

Romano, Roberta (1985), 'Law as Product: Some Pieces of the Incorporation Puzzle', **1** *Journal of Law, Economics, and Organization*, 225 ff.

Rose-Ackerman, Susan (1980), 'Risk Taking and Reelection: Does Federalism Promote Innovation?', **9** *Journal of Legal Studies*, 593 ff.

Rose-Ackerman, Susan (1981), 'Does Federalism Matter? Political Choice in a Federal Republic', **89** *Journal of Political Economy*, 152 ff.

Rosenberg, Maurice (1968), 'Comments on Reich v. Purcell', **15** *UCLA Law Review*, 641-647.

Rosenberg, Maurice (1981), 'The Comeback of Choice-of-Law Rules', **81** *Columbia Law Review*, 946 ff.

Rubin, Paul H. (1993), 'Private Mechanisms for the Creation of Efficient Institutions for Market Economies', in Somogyi, Laszlo (ed.), The Political Economy of the Transition Process in Eastern Europe, Cheltenham, Edward Elgar.

Rubin, Paul H. (1994), 'Growing A Legal System in the Post-Communist Economies', **27** *Cornell International Law Journal*, 1-47.

Santagata, Walter (1995), 'Istituzioni per il Mercato dell'Arte: Artisti e Mercanti tra Regole, Convenzioni e Allocazioni dei Diritti (Institutions for the Market of Works of Art: Artists and Merchants among Rules, Conventions and Allocation of Rights)', *Economia Publica*, 87-115.

Schenk, Karl-Ernst (1978), 'Grenzüberschreitende Unternehmensformen in den Ost-West-Wirtschaftsbeziehungen (Transnational forms of Enterprises in East-West Economic Relations, with A. Wass von Czege)', in Schiller, Karl (ed.), *Technologietransfer durch Ost-West-Kooperation, Ökonomische Studien aus den Institut für Außenhandel und Überseewirtschaft, Bd. 27*, Stuttgart/New York, 1-12.

Schenk, Karl-Ernst (1988), 'Technologietransfer, Joint Ventures und Transaktionskosten. Möglichkeiten und Grenzen strategischer Allianzen von Unternehmen in und zwischen Ost und West (Transfer of Technologies, Joint Ventures and Transaction Costs. Opportunities and Boundaries of Strategic Alliances by Enterprises of East and West)', in Dürr, E. and Sieber, H. (eds), *Weltwirtschaft im Wandel, Festgabe für E. Tuchtfeldt*, Bern-Stuttgart, 595-606.

Schenk, Karl-Ernst (1991), 'Internationale Kooperationen und Joint Ventures. Theoretische und strategische Grundlagen ((International Cooperations and Joint Ventures. Theoretical and Strategical Foundations)', in Schoppe, S.G. (ed.), *Kompendium der Internationalen Betriebswirtschaftslehre*, München-Wien, 153-184.

Schmidt Trenz, Hans Jorg (1990), *Außenhandel und Territorialität des Rechts. Grundlegung einer Neuen Institutionenökonomik des Außenhandels* (Trade and Territoriality of Law), Baden-Baden, Nomos.

Schmidtchen, Dieter (1993), 'Neue Institutionenökonomik internationaler Transaktionen (New Institutional Economics of International Transaktions)', in Schlieper, Ulrich and Schmidtchen, Dieter (eds), *Makro, Geld and Institutionen*, Tübingen, 57-84.

Schmidtchen, Dieter (1995), 'Territorialität des Rechts, Internationales Privatrecht und die privatautonome Regelung internationaler Sachverhalte. Grundlagen eines interdisziplinären Forschungsprogramms (Territoriality of Law, International Private Law, and Private Autonomous Order of International Relations)', **59(1)** *Rabels Zeitschrift für Ausländisches und Internationales Privatrecht*, 56-112.

Schmidtchen, Dieter and Schmidt-Trenz, Hans-Jorg (1990), 'The Division of Labor is Limited by the Extent of the Law: A Constitutional Approach to International Private Law', **1(3)** *Constitutional Political Economy*, 49-71.

Schmidtchen, Dieter and Schmidt-Trenz, H.-J. (1990), 'The Division of Labor is Limited by the Extent of the Law. A Constitutional Economics Approach to International Private Law', **1(3)** *Constitutional Political Economy*, 49-71.

Scoles, Eugene and Hay, Peter (1992), *Conflict of Laws*, St. Paul, Minn.,West Publishing Co.

Shapiro, Martin M. (1972), 'Toward a Theory of Stare Decisis', **1** *Journal of Legal Studies*, 125 ff.

Shughart, William F., II and Tollison R.D. (1985), 'Corporate Chartering: An Exploration in the Economics of Legal Change', **23** *Economic Inquiry*, 585 ff.

Solomine, Michael (1989), 'An Economic and Empirical Analysis of Choice of Law', **24** *Georgia Law Review*, 49 ff.

Sterk, Stewart E. (1994), 'The Marginal Relevance of Choice of Law Theory', **142** *University of Pennsylvania Law Review*, 949 ff.

Streit, Manfred E. and Voigt, Stefan (1993), 'The Economics of Conflict Resolution in International Trade', in Friedmann, D. and Mestmäcker, E.J. (eds), *Conflict Resolution in International Trade*, Baden-Baden, Nomos, 39-77.

Symposium (1997), 'Choice of Law: How It Ought to Be', **48** *Mercer Law Review*, 623 ff.

Thiel, Stuart E. (1996), *Choice of Law and the Home Court Advantage: Evidence* (Unpublished Manuscript).

Vihanto, Martti (1992), 'Competition Between Local Governments as a Discovery Procedure', **148** *Journal of Institutional and Theoretical Economics*, 411 ff.

Voigt, Stefan (1992), *Die Welthandelsordnung zwischen Konflikt und Stabilität - Konfliktpotentiale und Konfliktlösungsmechanismen* (The World Trade System between Conflict and Stability), Freiburg.

Watson, Alan (1974), *Legal Transplants: An Approach to Comparative Law*, Cambridge, MA, Harvard University Press.

Whincop, Michael J. (1997), 'Putting the "Private" Back into Private International Law: Default Rules and the Proper Law of the Contract', **21** *Melbourne University Law Review*, 515 ff.

Whincop, Michael J. (1998), 'Statutes' Domains in Private International Law: An Economic Theory of the Limits of Mandatory Rules', **20** *Sydney Law Review*, 435 ff.

Whincop, Michael J. and Keyes, Mary E. (1998), *Policy and Pragmatism in the Conflict of Laws* (Unpublished Manuscript).

White, Michelle J. (1992), 'Legal Complexity and Lawyers' Benefit from Litigation', **12** *International Review of Law and Economics*, 381 ff.

Williamson, Oliver E. (1985), *The Economic Institutions of Capitalism*, New York, NY, Free Press.

Winter, Ralph A. (1977), 'State Law, Shareholder Protection, and the Theory of the Corporation', **6** *Journal of Legal Studies*, 251 ff.

Other References

Alchian, Armen A. (1950), 'Uncertainty, Evolution, and Economic Theory', **58** *Journal of Political Economy*, 211 ff.

Axelrod, Robert (1984), *The Evolution of Cooperation*, New York, Basic Books.

Banerjee, Abhijit (1992), 'A Simple Model of Herd Behavior', **107** *Quarterly Journal of Economics*, 797-817.

Baysinger, Barry D. and Butler, Henry N. (1985), 'The Role of Corporate Law in the Theory of the Firm', **28** *Journal of Law and Economics*, 179 ff.

Bikhchandani, Sushil, Hirshleifer, David and Welch, Ivo (1992), 'A Theory of Fads, Fashion, Custom, and Cultural Change as Informational Cascades', **100** *Journal of Political Economy*, 992 ff.

Friedman, James (1971), 'A Non-cooperative Equilibrium for Supergames', **28** *Review of Economic Studies,* 1 ff.

Gerken, Luder (ed.) (1995), *Institutional Competition: An Orientative Framework, in Competition among Institutions*, 1-31.

Hayek, F.A. (1948), *Individualism and Economic Order*, Chicago, University of Chicago Press.

Kerber, Wolfgang and Vanberg, Viktor (1995), 'Competition among Institutions: Evolution within Constraints', in Gerken, Luder (ed.), *Institutional Competition: An Orientative Framework, in Competition among Institutions*, 33-64 .

Landes, Elisabeth (1982), 'Insurance, Liability and Accidents: A Theoretical and Empirical Investigation of the Effect of No-Fault Accidents', **25** *Journal of Law and Economics*, 49 ff.

Landes, William M. and Posner, Richard A. (1975), 'The Independent Judiciary in an Interest Group Perspective', **18** *Journal of Law and Economics*, 875 ff.

Landes, William M. and Posner, Richard A. (1987), *The Economic Structure of Tort Law*, Cambridge, MA, Harvard Univ. Press, 14-19.

McCormick, R. and Tollison, R. (1981), *Politicians, Legislations and the Economy, an Inquiry into the Interest-GroupTheory of Government*, Boston, M. Nijhoff-Kluwer.

O'Hara, Erin (1993), 'Social Constraint or Implicit Collusion: Toward A Game Theoretic Analysis of Stare Decisis', **24** *Seton Hall Law Review,* 736 ff.

Olson, Mancur (1965), *The Logic of Collective Action*, Boston, MA, Harvard University Press.

Posner, Richard A. (1992), *Economic Analysis of Law*, 4th edn, Boston, Little Brown.

Posner, Richard A. and Scott, Kenneth (1980) (eds), *Economics of Corporation Law and Securities Regulation*, Boston, Little Brown, 384 p.

Priest, George and Klein, Benjamin (1984), 'The Selection of Disputes for Litigation', **13** *Journal of Legal Studies*, 1 ff.

Restatement (First), Conflict of Laws (1934).

Restatement (Second), Conflict of Laws (1971).

Scharfstein, David and Stein, J. (1990), 'Herd Behavior and Investment', **80** *American Economic Review*, 465 ff.

Schwartz, Alan, and Wilde, Louis A. (1979), 'Intervening in Markets on the Basis of Imperfect Information: A Legal and Economic Analysis', **127** *University of Pennsylvania Law Review*, 630-638.

Tiebout, Charles M. (1956), 'A Pure Theory of Local Expenditure', **64** *Journal of Political Economy*, 416 ff.

Tollison, Robert (1988), 'Public Choice and Legislation', **74** *Virginia Law Review*, 339 ff.

Cases

Cooley v. Board of Wardens, 53 U.S. 299 (1851)

Supreme Council of the Royal Arcanum v. Green, 237 U.S. 531 (1915)

Home Insurance Co. v. Dick, 281 U.S. 397 (1930)

Vita Food Products Inc. v. Unus Shipping Co. A.C. 277 (1939)

Allstate Insurance Co v. Hague, 449 U.S. 302 (1981)

Edgar v. Mite Corp., 457 U.S. 624 (1982)

CTS Corp. v. Dynamics Corp. of America, 481 U.S. 69 (1987).

9700
FEDERALISM

Robert P. Inman
Professor of Finance and Economics, Wharton School, University of Pennsylvania

Daniel L. Rubinfeld
Robert L. Bridges Professor of Law and Professor of Economics, University of California, Berkeley

Abstract

With a topic such as federalism that has been so widely debated from so many perspectives, it would be impossible to provide a comprehensive review of the literature. Rather, we provide a particular perspective, one that balances the twin goals of political participation and economic welfare. To fashion such a balance, we first review the potential virtues of each federalist structure. We conclude that political participation rises with increased decentralization, but economic efficiency first rises and then falls. It is when efficiency declines that we face a trade-off. The choice of an 'optimal' level of decentralization ultimately depends upon the relative importance one places upon the competing federalist values of economic efficiency and political participation.
JEL classification: K33, H11
Keywords: Political Participation, Voting by Feet, Tiebout, Decentralization

1. Introduction

Federalism is today a topic of intense intellectual debate in many countries throughout the world. In Europe, the former Soviet Union, South Africa and elsewhere the view that good government will involve a blending of local and central governmental decision making is now well accepted. With a topic such as federalism that has been so widely debated from so many perspectives, it would be impossible to provide a comprehensive review of the literature. Rather, we provide a particular perspective, one that balances the twin goals of political participation and economic welfare. A carefully-specified theory of federalism has many useful applications: to government expenditure policy (Martinez-Vasquez, 1994), to tax policy (Inman and Rubinfeld, 1996), to deficit policies (Inman, 1990), or to regulatory policy (Rose-Ackerman and Mashaw, 1984).

Confederations of small governments have been praised by many - from Plato and Aristotle, through Rousseau, Montesquieu, Smith and Mills, to contemporary federalist legal and economic scholars - as that political institution most likely to encourage a trio of social virtues: political participation, protection of the sovereign rights of citizens and economic efficiency. On participation and the virtues of small governments see Pateman (1970, pp. 46, 110, 111 and Frug (1980). On economic efficiency and the positive role of small governments see Smith (1776) and Tiebout (1956). Other scholars have been more skeptical. *The Federalist Papers* (particularly at No. 47), the intellectual blueprint for the US Constitution, raises serious doubts about the virtues of loose confederations of small governments. Leading contemporary social scientists from political science (Robert Dahl and William Riker) and economics (Joseph Schumpeter and Paul Samuelson) have lent theoretical support to the Federalists' concerns. On small governments and their consequences for meaningful political participation, see Schumpeter (1943), Dahl (1956), and Dahl and Tufte (1973). On the potential inability of small governments to protect group rights, see Riker (1964). For a discussion of why small governments might be economically inefficient, see Samuelson (1954). Like the Federalists, these scholars have argued that a strong, democratically elected central government is generally the more effective means to ensure political participation, protection of the rights of citizens, and more efficient and equitable resource allocations.

Which level of government is best suited to make public policies, given that we want those policies to be democratically decided, respectful of personal rights, and economically efficient? A considered answer - whether for Europe's new Economic Union, the new South African Constitution, or to the regulation of anticompetitive firm behavior within the United States or the Economic Union - requires a careful balancing of the benefits and costs of decentralized and centralized political structures. To fashion such a balance, it is essential that we first review the potential virtues of each federalist structure.

We begin by defining what is meant by decentralized and centralized federalist structures. In this chapter, governments will be defined as 'decentralized and state' or 'centralized and national' according to the combination of two constitutional decisions. The first decision - called the *partition decision* - divides the single national citizenry into states. Following the partition decision, there will be a group of separate state governments and one central government to which each state will send (for simplicity) one representative to a central legislature, the single policymaking body of the central government. Policy decisions made by state governments will be decided by their separate legislatures. Adding another legislative chamber or an executive with a veto to our analysis will only improve the ability of federalist systems to meet the participation, sovereignty and efficiency objectives. For an analysis of the effects of bicameral legislatures on government performance, see Levmore (1992). For an analysis of the effects of a president with veto powers on government performance, see Fitts and Inman (1992).

Courts and legislatures are concerned with the second constitutional decision - the *assignment decision* - which allocates final political responsibility for choices over a social or economic policy to either the legislature of the central government or to the legislatures of each of the separate states. If the assignment decision allocates ultimate responsibility for a social or economic policy to the states (or their localities), then we describe policymaking for this class of government decisions as 'state' or 'decentralized'. In contrast, if the assignment decision gives final responsibility for a social or economic policy to the central government, then we describe policymaking for these assigned responsibilities as 'national' or 'centralized'. Together, these two constitutional decisions define the essential federalist - decentralized or centralized - structure of the government. We realize, of course, that federalist structures may have decentralized and centralized components, as, for example, when the central government mandates the form and function of certain decentralized government activities.

The much debated virtues of these decentralized or centralized governmental structures include democratic political participation and enhanced economic efficiency. Which federalist structure or combination of structures favors which virtues given the realities of the political and economic marketplace? We review the arguments and the contemporary evidence in Parts A (participation) and B (economic efficiency) below. Not surprisingly, neither a centralized nor a decentralized structure maximizes public participation and economic efficiency all the time. Which structure is preferred turns on a balancing of these values. In Part C we discuss briefly how a society might set that balance.

A. Political Participation

2. The Benefits of Participation

Political participation is defined as 'actions through which ordinary citizens of a political system influence or attempt to influence (political) outcomes' (Nagel, 1980, p. 1). Actions include voting, debating, marching, picketing, contributing, and passive and armed resistance. The aim of these actions is to influence the direction of government policy. Active citizens may be successful in moving public policies closer to their preferred outcomes because of their participation. In this case, citizens are said to have influence. Or active citizens may be unsuccessful, their political actions having no effect on policy outcomes. In this case, the citizens have attempted, but failed, to influence political outcomes.

The benefits to citizens of their own, and others', participation can be divided into three categories: instrumental or utilitarian, developmental or educative, and intrinsic or consumptive. In the utilitarian view, perhaps argued most directly in the work of Bentham and James Mill, political participation serves a specific function; to ensure that government maximizes aggregated citizen utility or welfare. In democratic societies, political participation is the necessary check on abuses of citizen welfare by ill-informed or even greedy elected officials. Political participation guarantees that abusive elected officials will be exposed and defeated at the next election. For the utilitarians, political participation's value is fundamentally instrumental; it plays, in the words of Pateman (1970), a 'protective function' for the public welfare.

For Jean-Jacques Rousseau and John Stuart Mill, political participation was instrumental to another, perhaps more important, end: it protected citizen liberties. While both Rousseau and Mill acknowledged the instrumental value of participation in protecting private economic interests and ensuring good (efficient) government, they extended the argument of the utilitarians to include participation's protective value for personal freedom as well. Participation ensures that no one individual or group is master over any other - 'The rights and interests of every or any person are only secure from being disregarded, when the person interested is himself able, and habitually disposed, to stand up for them' (Mill, 1960, p. 186; see Pateman, 1970, Chapter 2, particularly pp. 26-27, for a summary of the arguments of J.S. Mill and J. Rousseau in favor of political participation).

For many scholars, however, participation does much more than just protect private economic interests and personal liberties. Aristotle, Rousseau, J.S. Mill, de Tocqueville, and contemporary commentators such as Dewey and Pateman view citizen political participation as serving an important educative function as well. By participating in the political process the individual learns that his private interests are intimately linked to the interests of others. This knowledge leads to a willingness to compromise, to put private interests aside and to call upon values of justice and common good when making public choices. There may be beneficial spillovers to private decision making, too. Having recognized and accepted the validity of others' interests in the public arena, we may be more accepting of those interests in our private dealings. Simply put, we may be different people - more tolerant, less selfish - after political participation.

Finally, political participation may provide direct consumptive benefits to those who participate. From those who simply like to hear the sound of their own voice or revel in controlling others, to those who take genuine satisfaction in having contributed to a cause they feel is worthy, the act of political participation offers many a personal consumption benefit. How else might we explain widespread voting in national elections? (Ordeshook and Riker, 1973, Ch. 3). While perhaps not the most compelling argument for increased political participation, it should not be ignored.

3. Metrics of Political Participation

If political participation is an activity to be valued, how do we know if there is more or less of it within society? The instrumental, or influence, effects of individual political participation can be measured by a metric of political *power*. At one extreme, the individual fully controls the outcome, while at the other the individual has no influence over the outcome. If one person controls the outcome, then, of course, all others must be powerless (see Nagel, 1975, for a detailed discussion). The participatory, or 'actions', effects of political participation can be measured by a metric of political *effort*. One plausible effort metric would be the hours, or the hourly equivalent of dollar contributions, given by the individual to political activity.

Whether an individual engages in political activity and whether those activities translate into political influence depends on the individual's personal desires to participate and to have power, and on how society's political environment translates individual participatory activity into influence. Important attributes of the political environment will include the political institutions that define voting rights, freedom of expression and access to elected officials and the legislature. Also important is the number of citizens who can participate in public decision making.

As a theoretical matter, one would expect that participation would be higher in local politics simply because the benefits of influence are greater the fewer the number of disparate constituents. However, individual political effort is not so easily predicted. When participatory effort is more productive in producing political influence, as it is likely to be in small democratic states, individuals might actually participate for fewer hours, choosing to allocate some of their increased 'political productivity' into other, non-political activities. Ultimately, how political institutions and the population of the nation and its states affect political influence and political effort is an empirical question. Certainly the early (Aristotle, Rousseau, J.S. Mill) and contemporary (Pateman, Frug) advocates of participatory politics see the small, democratic state as most conducive to high values of influence and effort for the average citizen.

4. Measuring Participation

How will the two constitutional decisions central to setting the federalist structure - the partition decision and the assignment decision - affect the level of political participation in a society? The answer is ultimately empirical: How do political influence and participatory effort change as political decision-making moves from large central governments to smaller, decentralized states and local polities? Participation theorists have not hesitated to make predictions, typically arguing that a federalist system with a large number of small states with substantial policy responsibilities will increase the political influence of each citizen and generate increased political effort as well. There is little doubt that this is true for political influence, especially in societies with strong guarantees of equal political rights. Less certain, however, is the relationship between political effort and the size of states with decision making power; it is not difficult to present arguments that effort may rise, fall, or even remain unchanged as federalist systems become more decentralized.

The empirical evidence on how political influence and participatory effort change as the governmental structure becomes decentralized is sparse, but what is available generally supports the prediction that both influence and effort will rise as the size of government declines. Within-country comparisons of political influence and effort across small and large governments seem the most appropriate testing ground of the participation hypothesis. (See Dahl and Tufte, 1973, pp. 44-53, for a review and critique of the cross-national evidence on size and participation.) First, citizens surveyed in five countries (United States, Britain, West Germany, Italy, and Mexico) all reported making greater effort to understand, and having more success in understanding, local rather than national political issues. In the surveyed countries, citizen efforts to influence government were also typically two to three times higher for local than for national governments. In supporting evidence, a detailed survey of political participation across Swedish cities found average citizens in small communities were more aware of local politics than their counterparts in middle-sized cities and both knew more basic local political facts than large city residents. Second, political effectiveness or influence - at least as perceived by citizens - also seems to increase as governments get smaller in size. Again, the five nation survey finds that citizens feel much more influential at the local than at the national level; typically, half of the citizens in the surveyed countries felt they had no influence over national policies while only 25 to 30 percent felt powerless at the local level. A more detailed analysis of the US subsample showed a significant positive correlation between an index of political powerlessness and size of government (Finifter, 1970, pp. 389-410). Indirect evidence from the Swedish study also implies that citizen influence declines as governments get larger; the gap between the percentage of citizens and the percentage of elected officials who would support a tax increase increases as communities get larger. Finally, evidence from the United States, the Netherlands and Switzerland all show that politics in larger communities, states and cantons are increasingly dominated by organized interest groups or political parties. While such groups make participation easier for some citizens, they may also it more difficult for others. If so, then Rousseau's concern that participation becomes more unequal as governments get larger is confirmed.

Any final conclusions regarding the effects of institutional decentralization on participatory effort and political influence must await more complete empirical analyses. Nonetheless, theoretical argument and the current empirical evidence lead us to the tentative conclusion that smaller governments, and thus more decentralized federalist structures, are likely to encourage the valued goal of greater political participation.

B. Federalism and Economic Efficiency

5. The Pros and Cons of Decentralization

Using the economic efficiency criterion to choose the appropriate federalist structure is a complex endeavor involving a comparison of the economic benefits and costs of assigning responsibility to each level of government: in the US, to the national or central level, the state level, or the local government level. In a federal system there are two important dimensions to economic efficiency. First, *inter*jurisdictional efficiency involves the appropriate allocation of individuals and other resources, such as capital, *among* the different jurisdictions. Interjurisdictional efficiency is achieved when the public activities of these interacting governments satisfy the collective demands of individuals living in different jurisdictions at a minimum economic cost. A full analysis would also include the economic costs of politically deciding what those policies should be and ensuring that the politically decided policies are what the government actually provides. These latter costs have been identified elsewhere as the transactions costs of government. They include the costs of selecting legislators, the decision-making costs of setting a policy, and the monitoring costs of ensuring that the policy is put in place (see Breton and Scott, 1978). Second, *intra*jurisdictional efficiency requires a choice of public activities which satisfies the collective demand *within* a given jurisdiction, measured as the willingness to pay for those activities for all individuals within the jurisdiction, and again does so at minimum costs.

In our complex federal system both interjurisdictional and intrajurisdictional inefficiencies can arise; the former because of *spillovers* - the decisions and actions of individuals within one jurisdiction can have effects on individuals located in other jurisdictions that are not accurately reflected in the marketplace - and the latter because the political process may not generate outcomes within a jurisdiction which maximize the wellbeing of its residents, that is, create *political inefficiencies*. In a broad sense, the choice of the appropriate jurisdiction to be responsible for a government activity involves a trade-off - the larger the jurisdiction the less likely that there will be spillovers from one jurisdiction to the next, but the more likely that the political process will lead to a misallocation of resources within jurisdictions.

A decentralized system of governments is ideal from the point of view of intrajurisdictional efficiency, since assigning economic responsibility to the smaller and more homogeneous of the jurisdictions increases the likelihood that services provided and regulations promulgated will be consistent with the desires of each and every member of the population. In other words, in a decentralized system of governments, local tastes for public goods are likely to be less disparate than national tastes. The resulting reduction in the inefficiency of providing public goods (since citizens with similar tastes would prefer to consumer the same level of public goods) has been characterized as the *decentralization theorem* by Wallace Oates.

Unfortunately, decentralization has its disadvantages, due primarily to the spillovers that are likely to arise when jurisdiction size is small. A less decentralized system with larger jurisdictions can minimize the spillovers involved, while at the same time taking advantage of the lower cost of promulgating and enforcing certain regulations or dispensing the benefits of public programs, and the lower cost of obtaining and using information.

Our analysis of the political economy of federalism begins with a critique of the arguments for a strongly decentralized system. While we agree that a focus on the presence of substantial spillovers is appropriate, we stress the fact that decentralization will not guarantee an optimal public sector mix even when no spillovers are present. We believe that a complete theory of federalism cannot rely solely on the 'Tiebout Model', an ideal model of a fiscal competition between many independent local governments. Appropriately specified, Tiebout's decentralized model of governmental competition is formally analogous to the purely competitive market model with complete information used to study market competition between private firms. In the Tiebout model, government policies are determined by *market*, or economic, exchange alone. Unfortunately, the assumptions needed to ensure that governmental competition is fully analogous to efficient private market competition are very strong, and may not hold in realistic public economies (see, for example, Rubinfeld, 1987.)

A more appropriate analytic framework - based upon political models of state government decision making and interstate bargaining - yields, we feel, more appropriate conclusions as to the likely economic performance of decentralized public environments. In the section that follows we study how such systems are likely to work. We conclude that when viewed as a *political* rather than market process, decentralized federalism may be economically inefficient. This conclusion suggests the need to consider a more centralized environment, using the central, or national, government to set policy. To be consistent, however, the analysis of central government performance must use the same political model that found inefficiencies at the decentralized level. This we do by explaining how central government regulatory policies also might be inefficient - indeed, potentially worse, for political reasons, than the inefficient state and local policies which the central policies had hoped to correct.

6. The Tiebout Approach

According to one view, the world of decentralized, competitive governments will allow for a national regulatory marketplace, in which individuals move among local jurisdictions or states to select the regulatory combination that they most desire. Just as a private market place forces suppliers to produce their goods at the lowest cost, and to provide the goods most desired by consumers, so too will the pressure of taxpayers shopping, through exit and relocation, force governments to be efficient in their provision of public goods and public goods and services.

According to this view, public activities should be decentralized, except when there are significant economic spillovers from the regulating jurisdiction to its neighbors. When spillovers result, decentralized governments may ignore important economic costs or benefits which will lead them to over- or underprovide the activity. In these instances central government review is appropriate.

We must be clear, however, about the assumptions built into the Tiebout model of decentralized governments on which this model relies. Each household and business is highly mobile and chooses to reside in the jurisdiction that offers the tax-expenditure-regulation package that it most prefers. As typically specified, five conditions define the competitive Tiebout public economy:

1. Publicly provided goods, services, and regulatory activities are provided at minimum average cost. (If assumption 1 holds, there is an efficient population size which minimizes the average cost per household of providing that government activity. This rules out using Tiebout competition to allocate 'pure public' goods, those goods where additional users of the government's facility does not reduce the consumption benefits enjoyed by previous users. Typical examples of a pure public good include defense, television or radio signals, and new knowledge. Goods which can be allocated by the Tiebout competitive process are those goods where more users reduce, proportionally, the benefits enjoyed by current users. Rather than *pure* public goods, these goods are *congested* public goods. Education, highways, police protection and parks are examples. The efficient scale of operation for such goods must be sufficiently small (for example, 15,000 in population) so that each household can find a suitable jurisdiction in which to reside. Existing evidence suggests that this constraint can be met for many government services; see, for example, Ladd and Yinger, 1989, pp.83, 85.)
2. There is a perfectly elastic supply of political jurisdictions, each capable of replicating all attractive economic features of its competitors. (This assumption ensures that efficient alternatives exist; this is the task of public sector entrepreneur-politicians who run against, and defeat, inefficient incumbents; competitive political entrepreneurs play a role analogous to take-over 'artists' in the private market. Or public sector entrepreneurs can appear as enterprising real estate developers who build new jurisdictions -

analogous to 'new entrants' in a private market - to draw away dissatisfied residents from inefficient governments; see Epple and Zelenitz, 1981.)
3. Mobility of households and businesses among jurisdictions is costless.
4. Households and businesses are fully informed about the fiscal and regulatory policies of each jurisdiction. (Assumptions 3 and 4 ensure that when possible inefficiencies arise, households and businesses can move to otherwise similar jurisdictions without those inefficiencies.)
5. There are no interjurisdictional externalities or spillovers. (Assumption 5 ensures that all public regulatory activities can be provided within these efficient jurisdictions - larger governments or intergovernmental cooperation is not required. In the end, a regulated economy satisfying assumptions 1 to 5, and organized as a fully decentralized network of competing jurisdictions, will maximize economic efficiency. Citizens and businesses can consume their preferred levels of the public regulatory activity with a minimum expenditure of production and transactions costs.)

7. Critiquing Tiebout

While a useful starting point, the Tiebout model does not provide a complete theory of federalism. The assumptions 1 through 5 may arguably apply to a local public activity such as rent control, which is imposed in California in only a relatively few cities, thereby leaving most households the opportunity to move to non-rent control jurisdictions as they see fit. However, the assumptions are less likely to hold for more centralized activities, where choices are more limited and moving is more costly.

If assumptions 2 through 5 do not hold, we must rethink the optimality of complete decentralization. The model of perfectly competitive *private* markets has long been an appealing paradigm for economists, in part because some real world markets do actually seem to operate in that manner, and in part because if they do, the efficiency consequences seem clear. Neither of these reasons applies without qualification to the Tiebout framework for competitive *governments*, however.

Consider assumption 2, that there is a perfectly elastic supply of political jurisdictions. The model of perfectly competitive markets yields an efficient allocation of resources in part because firms are free to make the efficient choices of inputs and outputs, and in part because entry into and exit from an industry are free. In the Tiebout model, competitive governments fill the role of firms. But governments may be constrained by internal politics when making their input and output choices, and free entry of new governments is by no means assured in actual public goods economies. (See generally, Epple and Zelenitz (1981), arguing that limited entry permits competitive governments to maximize public 'monopoly profits' from the provision of public goods and public regulations and the level and allocation of those profits will be determined politically within the jurisdiction.) For example, an entrepreneur cannot simply invest his capital to build a new city.

If assumption 2 does not hold, four potentially adverse consequences for economic efficiency are likely to arise. First, with a limited supply of jurisdictions each government is likely to contain citizens with different views of what constitutes the government's best policy. If so, local politics becomes important. If local decisions are made by majority rule, the outcome will not necessarily be economically efficient (see Bergstrom et al., 1988). Second, when the economy can no longer replicate attractive local jurisdictions, economic rents can be earned. The presence of these publicly created rents associated with the desirability of some locations over others can in turn create a tension between the fiscal entrepreneurs who wish to develop new communities and the owners of the desirable locations. As a result, there is no guarantee that the market for land and for other scarce resources will be economically efficient.

Third, when private sector job opportunities are not identical in all locations, productive private sector employment may be sacrificed as labor is attracted to less efficient locations for fiscal reasons. The consequence is a less efficient private economy (see Buchanan and Goetz, 1972, for the initial presentation of this argument and the summaries in Boadway and Flatters, 1982, and Wildasin, 1986).

Fourth, once the supply of jurisdictions is fixed, the analogy of the decentralized model of federalism to anonymous free market competition is no longer valid. Each local government may be aware of the potential effect of its action on other jurisdictions. It will then act strategically in making its decisions on the basis of its best guess as to how other jurisdictions will respond. In this framework the actions of each local jurisdiction, even if small, can have a substantial effect on the welfare of the rest of the decentralized world. Essentially, a self-interested decision by those in power in one jurisdiction can result in a series of distortions that arise throughout the effected network of other jurisdictions. For example, a decision by one jurisdiction to offer a tax break to attract new business could lead to a competition in which many jurisdictions offer a variety of tax business tax benefits.

While it is difficult to predict the exact consequence of the rather complex behavioral patterns that can arise when these strategic interactions are taken into account, it seems clear that an efficient outcome is unlikely to arise. States may, for example, underprovide welfare services, or more generally to underprovide public services in which they have particular production advantages and therefore should provide in abundance (see Gramlich and Laren, 1984, on welfare competition among states, and Pestieau, 1977). This could occur because a state realizes that by providing a high level of welfare benefits it is likely to attract new low-income residents from nearby states, thus adding substantially to its cost of providing such benefits. States might also provide substantial tax benefits to attract business, or at least to avoid losing business to other competing states, and in the process undertax business capital and overtax the residential base (see, for example, Break, 1967, pp. 23-24; Oates, 1972, pp. 142-143; for a review of the more recent literature, see Inman and Rubinfeld, 1996).

An equivalent phenomenon can occur with respect to regulatory policies. States might relax their environmental controls to encourage business migration, or simply to forestall the loss of business because other states had or were about to relax their environmental regulations. This argument has been developed by Cumberland (1981); see also Fischel, 1975, p.119), and more generally, Oates and Schwab (1986). Note that the competitive process which leads to a uniformity of regulation among states is not consistent with the advantages of the diversity associated with the Tiebout model, nor is it likely to be efficient. The result could be a 'race to the bottom' resulting in an equilibrium in which environmental regulations are 'undersupplied'. (The uniformity of occupational regulation is described in Stigler, 1971, p. 130.) For a more general argument that the regulatory actions of individual states may not result in an optimal federal system, given the incentives that determine political choice, see Rose-Ackerman (1981), also Revesz (1992).

Assumption 3, that citizens and businesses are costlessly mobile between political jurisdictions, is also problematic. The assumption applies best to suburban jurisdictions among which individuals and firms have a good deal of mobility. When the number of cities and towns within a metropolitan area is substantial, families and firms have significant choice in their provision of public goods and public regulations. Empirical evidence supporting the Tiebout hypothesis has focused entirely on this local public sector. For studies of household relocation, see Gramlich and Rubinfeld (1982), who used survey data for Michigan and concluded that their results were 'reasonably consistent with a Tiebout interpretation: in large metropolitan areas there is quite extensive grouping; in smaller areas, there is some grouping' (pp. 554-555). Oates (1972, pp. 162-179) studied the metropolitan New Jersey region, using tests of the capitalization of public goods differentials into property values, and concluded that public goods preferences could explain migration among neighboring cities and towns. For evidence that businesses are sensitive to local taxes and services when relocating within a metropolitan area, see Bartik (1988) and McConnell and Schwab (1990), suggesting that environmental regulations are not an important factor affecting business location decisions. Activities of local governments in metropolitan areas - save those with significant spillovers - are likely to meet the competitive test (see Courant and Rubinfeld, 1981). Yet much economic activity occurs at the state level, where assumption 3 is unlikely to hold. Studies of migration show that most household moves are within metropolitan areas, not between states. Those who do move between states are typically job motivated, and are not primarily seeking a more attractive public service/public regulation environment (Easterbrook, 1983, pp. 35 n. 28). (See also the detailed evidence on interstate and interregional location of households reviewed in Greenwood, 1986.) If assumption 3 does not apply, then the model cannot guarantee overall (that is, market plus public sector) efficiency.

Assumption 4, that households and businesses are fully informed, presents another problem for the Tiebout argument. Households and firms must have reasonably accurate information about the tax, spending, and regulatory policies of the communities in which they will reside. Yet, it is often difficult for individuals and firms to ascertain the implications of regulations within their own jurisdiction, let alone make a reasonable judgment about the public activities that will exist in other jurisdictions at a future point in time after which they have relocated. Stigler (1971, p. 130) has argued, '(t)he voter's expenditure to learn the merits of individual policy proposals and to express his preferences ... are determined by expected costs and returns' and that, in the case of regulatory policy, this cost-benefit calculus dissuades voters from discovering very much. When we view the location decision as involving a choice of public sector packages, and we take into account the fact that other jurisdictions are likely to be changing those packages over time, the informational demands that must be satisfied for the competitive system of governments to work effectively seem very great.

When assumption 4 no longer holds, that is, when there is incomplete information about the costs and levels of regulatory activity, an important principal-agent problem arises. Households and firms have two options: go it alone and risk being exploited by better informed fiscal entrepreneurs and local factors of production, or hire an agent to protect household and firm interests. Complications arise when information about agent performance is costly and some deceitful agents survive, or when the expertise provided by agents to households and firms cannot itself be kept private. To the extent the market for 'agents' works perfectly - all inefficient or exploitive providers are exposed, and only truthful agents survive - the final outcome will still be efficient, but some fiscal surplus will be allocated to the agents as payment for services performed. Such payments can be made as a contingent fee conditional on the performance of the agent in managing the purchase of the public good, or as a competitively determined lump-sum payment to a previously identified - by reputation or certification - 'truthful' agent. In both instances there will emerge externalities in the market for agents that can cause an inefficient level of information to be provided about the fiscal performance of the Tiebout communities. When information about agent performance or abilities is available at no cost, then agent efforts can be fully monitored (avoiding all problems of moral hazard) and agent abilities will be fully known (avoiding all problems of adverse selection). The agent market can then work perfectly. When information about agents is costly, however, there is no guarantee that the efficient agent market will arise (see Holmstrom, 1985). Similarly, when the information provided by the agents to households cannot be kept private, then there will be externality-caused inefficiency in the information market.

The final assumption, requiring no spillovers, is an important real world violation of the Tiebout framework that may require central government intervention. A spillover or externality arises when the activities of a jurisdiction affect directly the wellbeing of an individual or firm in another jurisdiction and the decision making of the first jurisdiction does not take these effects on others into account. For a discussion of public goods externalities see Williams (1966) and Brainard and Dolbear (1967) among others. This literature is critically reviewed and extended by Pauly (1970). For a discussion of tax externalities see the survey in Inman and Rubinfeld (1996). One occurs when a spillover offers a positive benefit to a neighboring community, for example, through the regulation of socially damaging air pollution emitted by a locally valuable firm. When such positive spillovers exist, state and local governments may provide too little of the activity. The converse case provides a third example. Here a socially productive firm produces only local pollution, for example, a garbage or nuclear waste site. The incentive is for the local community to impose stringent regulations on such a firm so as to force its relocation onto a neighboring community. A negative regulatory externality results. If the neighboring communities respond with similar regulations, the firm may have no place to go, even though it is in the interests of all jurisdictions to have the firm locate in at least one locality. With negative spillovers, there may be too much state and local activity. For an illustration of this point with respect to the regulation of solid wastes, see David and Lester (1989). In these circumstances, a federal or state set of uniform standards may be preferred by all. In fact, uniform national regulation not only can take advantage of economies of scale in administration, it can also produce scale economies of production and distribution for firms, while at the same time reducing their location costs (see Rose-Ackerman, 1994). Augmentation of national standards by states or localities can be allowed, but only if the additional regulations do not generate spillovers by benefiting local households and businesses at the expenses of nonresidents. The general point is clear: when assumption 5 is violated, there is no guarantee that decentralized competition will produce an efficient allocation of public and private resources.

Our review of the assumptions of the Tiebout framework lead us to conclude that the analogy between the model of competitive governments and the model of competitive markets is not sufficiently strong to serve as the basis of a theory of federalism. If we are to have a compelling efficiency basis for drawing the lines between decentralized and centralized governmental policy it must be found in an analysis based upon paradigms other than Tiebout's model of public sector competition. Our discussion in the next two sections seeks to provide that paradigm.

8. The Politics of State Legislative Policy

Economic efficiency demands that state public activities be efficient both with respect to the preferences of residents of the state (*intra*jurisdictional efficiency) and with respect to the preferences of residents outside the state (*inter*jurisdictional efficiency). Separate political institutions exist through which each dimension of efficiency might be achieved. State legislatures and their appointed state agencies are the means through which residents within a state might hope to obtain intrajurisdictional efficiency. Interstate cooperative agreements struck between residents, or their elected agents, of neighboring states are the means to interjurisdictional efficiency. We consider the potential of each, beginning with an analysis of state legislative processes.

When elected representatives join together in a state legislature, they are free to fashion coalitions and set regulatory policies as they wish, subject only to the constraint that decisions receive the approval of a majority of legislators. Majority-rule legislatures making decisions over multiple public policies must resolve a fundamental structural defect: the propensity of the majority-rule process to cycle from one policy outcome to another. This fundamental observation regarding majority rule processes has been well recognized at least since the work of De Condorcet (1785) and is known popularly as the paradox of voting: even though majority rule leads a legislature to vote for policy A over policy B, and for policy B over policy C, it is certainly possible, and often likely, that policy C will be defeat policy A. Arrow (1963) proves that this paradox of voting is a symptom of a more fundamental problem with all democratic processes: there is no guarantee that such processes can find a best outcome or are immune to manipulation. Thus, the design of political institutions will almost inevitably be a search among the second-best. For a survey of this literature in the context of the new political economy, see Inman (1987). When no winning coalition is capable of holding its majority against small policy variations offered by a losing minority, then either no decision will be made or final policy outcomes will be random and uncertain.

If legislatures are to reach decisions, additional legislative institutions must be discovered for overcoming this inherent instability of the majority-rule process. Two institutional approaches are commonly used by legislatures. The first assigns agenda-setting powers to a small subset of members, say the speaker of the house or a key legislative committee. Other members in the legislature then simply vote - up or down - on the items in the approved agenda. Most likely, policies will be approved by a bare majority - a minimal winning coalition - in this strong agenda-setter legislature. For articulation of the general theory of how this process overcomes cycling, see Baron and Ferejohn (1989). For a careful description of what legislative institutions are used to assign agenda control, see Shepsle (1979). There is an extensive literature which tests for the direct influence of agenda-setters - typically congressional committees - on policy outcomes; see Krehbiel (1992) for a critical but balanced review. A second strategy shares agenda-setting powers among all members, giving each legislator a right to select his most preferred policy in that policy area most germane to the legislator's constituents. This second approach to legislative decision making involves each legislator deferring to the preferred policies of all other legislators, provided the other legislators defer to the legislator's own policy requests. The guiding principle here is a norm of deference - 'You scratch my back, I'll scratch yours' - and it typically results in legislative proposals which are approved unanimously. For this reason such legislatures are often called 'universalistic'. The guiding theory can be found in Weingast (1979) and Niou and Ordeshook (1985). The theory has been developed for, and its applications must be limited to, understanding how legislative bodies allocate government projects and government regulations - what has been called *distributive* politics (see Lowi, 1969). A norm of deference is not an appropriate model for predicting how legislatures will decide *re*distributive policies such as welfare or progressive taxation, politics where one group constituents must lose to another. Details regarding the legislative institutions needed to enforce the norm of deference can be found in Weingast and Marshall (1988) for the details of how such a legislative norm of deference might be enforced.

A single legislator uncertain as to whether she will be one of the lucky winners in the bare majority legislature will typically favor the more open rules of the universalistic legislature. Intuitively, the universalistic legislature is preferred because under universalism activities that benefit the legislator's district are nearly certain to be chosen, and a substantial portion of the costs will be borne by other districts. (If benefits exceed average project costs in a majority of districts - a likely case - then a legislature run by a norm of deference will be the preferred legislative institution. Weingast (1979) and Niou and Ordeshook (1985) prove exactly when this outcome holds. See also Schwartz (1989) or Inman and Fitts (1990), both of whom extend the analysis to legislative projects of variable size. The conclusion that legislators prefer universalism to bare-majority rule extends to this more general case.

Universalistic state legislatures operating under a norm of deference run a significant risk that their public activities will be economically inefficient, however. Consider, for example, the typical case of a state regulation which raises industry prices within a state, effectively reducing output below competitive levels. Those who benefit from such a regulation are state residents who own capital and other 'specialized' factors of production employed in the regulated industry. Those who lose are the state's consumers who buy the output of the regulated industry and the state's taxpayers who pay for the regulatory bureaucracy.

Assume further that the industry would be competitive, pricing at marginal cost, if unregulated, but would act as a profit-maximizing cartel if regulated. The cartel would choose to maximize its profits by raising its price above the competitive level, and by reducing its output. Three conclusions follow from this framework. First, industry producers within the state prefer to be at a regulated output near the cartel profit-maximizing level, because as regulation nears this level industry profits, the 'marginal benefits' of regulation to the interest groups that own the specialized inputs that gain from regulation, are maximized. Second, state consumers of industry output prefer the competitive output, for at zero industry regulation, the tax costs and lost consumer benefits from regulation - the 'marginal costs' of regulation - are minimized. Finally, any regulation of a competitive industry is inefficient from the perspective of *all* state residents, because the additional cost to state taxpayers and consumers everywhere greater than the additional benefit to state producers.

How then will a universalistic state legislature set government policy for the state? Under the norm of deference each elected state representative is allowed to propose a state policy which maximizes the returns to his constituents. Consider how one legislator (perhaps with a group of other legislators representing similar districts) might view an activity when all of the benefits, but only a small fraction of the state's costs, are felt within the district(s). In this case, constituents would internalize all of the marginal benefits, while constituents will take into account only a small fraction of the marginal costs. For the affected legislator(s), the preferred activity would be a higher than efficient output. But not all legislators will propose inefficient activities. Only those legislators from districts whose local economy has concentrated benefits will find the activity to be in their interests. When they do, state politics will generate an *intra*jurisdictional inefficiency.

States with strong political parties capable of disciplining party members or states with strong governors capable of mobilizing broad-based citizen support may be able to control these intrajurisdictional inefficiencies of universalistic legislatures, but not perfectly. Consider first the ability of strong political parties to control policy. By definition strong parties form a stable legislative majority. Members who might be tempted to deviate from the party's platform can be disciplined so that deviations will not occur. Government policy will therefore be the policy which is in the interests of the stable, majority party. In this stylized framework, only those producers in legislative districts belonging to the majority party will be favored. Minority party districts will receive no benefits.

When proposing an activity for their constituents, representatives in the majority party will be required by the party to consider the effects of their proposed activity on constituents in all districts controlled by the party. From the perspective of the majority party, therefore, an activity in one district will still provide benefits to party constituents, but will now impose only a fraction (perhaps slightly greater than 50 percent) of the total cost of the activity on party members.

From the majority party's perspective, the preferred activity level in a party-controlled district will be an efficient level, where *party* marginal benefits equal *party* marginal costs. Because the party preferred level internalizes the costs to party members, the inefficiency must be less than the inefficiency created by the universalistic legislature. The loss of intrajurisdictional efficiency declines accordingly. Put simply, by internalizing more of the costs of government activity, strong political parties can improve the efficiency performance of state regulations. For empirical evidence that strong political parties may have controlled legislative inefficiencies, see Inman and Fitts (1990, pp. 111-115). Political parties may even promote full economic efficiency. This limiting case occurs if the political party controls all representatives in the legislature. Here there is an incentive for all districts to elect a representative to the stable majority party, since this is their only way to join the controlling coalition and to receive constituent benefits. With a single stable majority party, therefore, there is strong pressure towards full economic efficiency. Wittman (1989) makes this argument.

Strong governors can also improve the efficiency performance of state regulations. Michael Fitts and Robert Inman present an analysis of executive leadership in economic policy where the executive who has access to needed political resources - appointment powers, control over appropriated budgets, and an executive veto - and with the appropriate political incentive - running in a national or state-wide election - will seek efficient economic reform. Using appointment powers and discretionary executive authority over policies and the budget, the governor can fashion a reform coalition in which each member district agrees to sacrifice its inefficient policy for a compensating *executive-controlled* substitute policy. Facing a universalistic legislature, executive-led reform will improve economic efficiency for all state residents. A successful reform package must share the benefits of this reduced inefficiency with residents in the original district and the rest of the state's taxpayers and consumers. On balance, reform makes all residents in the state better off, thereby increasing the governor's chances for re-election. But only strong governors, those with sufficient executive-controlled resources to pay compensation to those districts made worse off, can hope to achieve reform. Even then reform will typically fall short of full efficiency.

We conclude that state politics will often encourage inefficient governmental activities for state residents, and that these *intra*jurisdictional inefficiencies are likely to be greatest in those states with weak political parties and weak executives. Importantly, these intrajurisdictional inefficiencies occur even when there are no spillovers to citizens outside the state. Matters are even worse, however, when there are spillovers, for here even strong political parties and strong governors will find it politically useful to support the (now nationally) inefficient activity. The case of activities with out-of-state spillovers involves *inter*jurisdictional inefficiency.

As with the case of intrajurisdictional inefficiency, the marginal benefits continue to reflect the benefits to residents within the state. The marginal costs, however, now encompass the national marginal costs to the residents of the state (state marginal costs *plus* the marginal costs of lost consumer benefits to out-of-state residents). These national marginal costs are greater than the statewide marginal costs discussed previously because they reflect the additional lost consumer surplus suffered by out-of-state residents. Government policy remains a political decision within the state, however, set by the balancing of state constituents' marginal benefits and costs.

Large interjurisdictional inefficiencies can remain even when strong parties and strong governors successfully control their own state's intrajurisdictional inefficiencies. Even though the inefficient regulation declines with a strong party (or strong governor), significant interjurisdictional inefficiencies may remain. Even a fully efficient state government setting policy efficiently within the state could impose large interjurisdictional inefficiencies on out-of-state citizens; the 'state' of OPEC is a prominent example.

9. Coasian Interjurisdictional Bargains

Might we imagine a political response from neighboring states to correct these interjurisdictional spillovers? Economists have designed systems of grants (matching and non-matching, specific and general) as well as tax and subsidy arrangements which can greatly increase the effiency of a decentralized system. However, a more distinctive approach, which we pursue in depth here, is the facilitation of interstate agreements, or Coasian bargains, to remove interjurisdictional inefficiencies. The bargain would require the out-of-state residents to 'compensate' the producers from the regulating state for the profits they lose when the inefficient regulation is removed. As Coase and others have pointed out, there are sufficient benefits to in-state and out-of-state consumers and taxpayers harmed by the activity that compensation can be paid to the state-created cartel, with the out-of-state residents remaining better off.

In practice, such compensation would be paid through an interstate agreement with neighboring states paying compensation to the regulating state, with the resulting compensation then passed on by that state's governor or legislature to within state producers. But we expect such a Coasian bargain between out-of-state consumers and within-state producers will be hard to effect. Successful Coasian bargains require five assumptions to be met:

1. there are no, or very small, resource costs associated with the bargaining process;
2. preferences over bargaining outcomes and the resources of households are common knowledge;
3. bargaining agents perfectly represent the economic interests of their constituents;
4. all bargaining agreements are costlessly enforceable; and
5. the parties can agree to a division of the bargaining surplus.

Only when assumptions 1 through 5 hold will interjurisdictional efficiency be achieved. How likely are these assumptions to be valid?

On its face, assumption 1 seems defensible. The institutions for bargaining - elected state officials - are already in place, and the marginal costs of applying these institutions to one additional political agreement are likely to be very small, but only to a point. Legislatures do not solve all problems in every year. The legislative agenda is limited, and at some point it simply does not pay to bring additional policies to the floor for consideration. Those policies which will be excluded are likely to be the marginal problems, those which have only a small effect on the economic wellbeing of voters.

Even if 1 holds, assumptions 2 to 5 may fail. If the preferences of the participants to the bargain are not common knowledge (2 no longer holds), then there may be a strategic advantage to concealing costs and benefits, demanding greater compensation from the agreement if you represent the 'winning' state or offering less compensation if you represent one of the 'losing' states. If both parties adopt the 'conceal' position, however, no agreement may be forthcoming.

In choosing their bargaining strategy, jurisdictions must assess the extent to which other parties are likely to make concessions. In game theoretic terms, the parties try to assess the threat points of the other parties - the minimum offer that they are willing to accept in order to accept a negotiating offer. In addition, they try to estimate the extent to which the other party will be willing to make concessions prior to reaching their threat point. If the parties make poor estimates of each other's threat point, or miscalculate the chances that the other party will accept a compromise offer, they may take a hard line in the bargaining process. Clearly, therefore, Coasian bargainers will not be immune to possibilities for strategic behavior when they negotiate, and to the extent that they succumb, Coasian bargaining may break down (see Polinsky, 1980; Crawford, 1982; and Kreps and Wilson, 1982). Such attempts at free-riding behavior are likely to undo a Coasian bargain when preferences are not common knowledge and the number of states with affected consumers is large. (For the first treatment of the effects of group size on voluntary agreements see Olsen (1965). The effect of group size and other variables on bargaining has been studied extensively through the use of experiments (see, for example, Hoffman and Spitzer, 1982; also Bagnoli and McKee, 1991.

Even if consumer preferences and industry profits are common knowledge, there is no guarantee that state elected officials will choose to make the constituents of the Coasian bargain better off (3 no longer holds). While the favored industry is well represented in its state (why else would there be regulation?), consumers of the product may not be so fortunate in their states. They may be in the minority in a majority rule state. In contrast to private market agreements, here the affected parties are heard only if generally elected representatives choose to make their case.

Assumption 4 is perhaps the least problematic of the five Coase assumptions. *If* states do reach an agreement and sign an interstate compact, typically the agreement is legally enforceable (see Ellickson, 1979). Ellickson discusses the idea of creating a series of public property rights and duties to encourage bargaining solutions to environmental spillovers. Note that monitoring costs, a serious problem in many contracts, are not likely to problem here. States which have agreed to curtail their monopoly overcharge regulation will know if they have been paid compensation. Consumer states which pay compensation will be able to observe if the regulating state has reintroduced regulation. For a discussion of the importance of monitoring costs to contract enforcement, see Williamson (1985). Enforcement difficulties arise only when important contingencies which might affect the agreement cannot be foreseen in advance. For example, if a future event occurs which alters the benefits and costs of a particular policy, then the state choosing the activity may decide to break the previous interstate agreement.

Arguably the most important and perhaps least appreciated source of bargaining failure is the loss of assumption 5. Even if 1 through 4 hold, the parties may not be able to agree as to how the economic surplus generated by the bargaining process can be divided. Each Coasian bargain does two things: it establishes an efficient exchange thereby creating economic surplus, *and* it distributes that surplus among the bargaining parties. Proponents of Coase emphasize the first outcome and have largely ignored the important difficulties of the second. Yet it is well known that the division of any economic pie is a bargaining problem which may have no solution. When redistribution games might have equilibrium outcomes is an important topic of recent economic research; see Rubinstein (1982) and more recently Binmore, Rubinstein and Wolinsky (1986). The often observed result in 'divide-the-pie' games that bargaining breaks down because the proposed division is not 'fair' illustrates the point. In such situations, one state rejects an economically beneficial offer from another state because the proposed offer violates the first state's exogenous, and no doubt politically motivated, sense of economic fairness.

What is seen as an exogenous norm of fairness in a one-time game may be a rational endogenously chosen strategy in a repeated political game. For example, a governor seeking re-election cannot appear 'weak' when bargaining with another state. If the money involved in a regulatory agreement is modest relative to the overall state budget - as it is likely to be - then the political symbolism of the 'share' from the divide-the-pie game may be far more important for re-election prospects than the actual dollars involved. If so, and if both governors must demand more than 50 percent, then agreement will not be possible. (For evidence from the experimental literature that a sense of fairness is crucial to the ability of parties to reach agreement, see Roth, 1985.) Strategic interplay becomes even more complicated, and agreement less likely, as the number of bargaining states increases beyond two. This is true even if preferences are fully known and the free-rider problem is not at issue (see Haller, 1986).

We conclude that economically inefficient policies are likely at the state and local level. Our analysis of state and local political institutions reveals strong political pressures towards favoring narrow, geographically concentrated interests at the expense of more diffused interests. While strong political parties and powerful governors have a political incentive to internalize the costs, even in these states some inefficiencies will remain for residents. For evidence that state regulations are politically motivated, and in particular, are more likely for geographically concentrated industries and occupations, see Stigler (1971). These intrajurisdictional regulatory inefficiencies are compounded when the effects of government activity spill over onto consumers in other states. In these instances, even strong political parties and governors have a political incentive to choose activities. The hope that voluntary interstate compacts might control these interjurisdictional inefficiencies seems to us to be very optimistic. The assumptions required for such Coasian agreements are very demanding and unlikely to hold in practice. This seems particularly so when the efficiency costs on any one individual are small, costs are not common knowledge and are diffused over groups in many states, the affected individuals are themselves a minority within a state, and state politicians treat the division of proceeds from the bargain as a signal of their political 'toughness'. (For evidence of the difficulties states have in fashioning Coasian agreements, even when the number of states is few, see Kolstad and Wolak, 1983, and Coates and Munger, 1995.) When any one of the assumptions 1 to 5 fail to hold, Coasian agreements will not arise and state created interjurisdictional regulatory inefficiencies will remain.

10. The Politics of Central Government Legislative Policy

Within federalist public economies, whenever state and local governments are economically inefficient, it is appropriate to ask whether the central government might do a better job (see, for example, Oates, 1972, particularly chs 1 and 2). But the comparison must be a consistent one, allowing for potential political inefficiencies at both the state and federal levels of government. Deciding whether to centralize regulatory policy at the national level first requires an analysis of how the national legislature will set such policies.

The effects of state regulatory policies on industries and consumers outlined previously generalizes to central government regulatory policymaking as well. In this instance industries are concentrated in particular congressional districts or states: tobacco in North Carolina, defense production in Washington and California, automobiles in Michigan. Like their counterparts in state government, congressional legislators have an incentive to look for central government activities which will benefit households and firms located in their districts. However, such national activities will have significant costs for US taxpayers, costs which may exceed the benefits.

Whether such economically inefficient activities will be legislated in the central authority depends upon the institutions of legislative decision making. If the legislature is 'universalistic', then we can expect it to favor inefficient activities. (For evidence that US congressional institutions have supported a universalistic legislative process, see Weingast and Marshall (1988); see also Silberman and Durden's (1976) study of the labor market regulations and Kalt and Zupan's (1984) study of environmental regulations.) As with state legislatures, reform of policymaking will require strong presidential leadership and/or political parties capable of controlling the inefficient policy demands of members.

Given that state and central legislatures face the same political pressures to choose inefficient activities, and neither seems, at the moment at least, institutionally well-equipped to resist those pressures, we conclude that neither states nor the central government can be preferred unambiguously as the appropriate domain for choosing economic activities. The current evidence shows economic inefficiencies arising from choices at both levels of government.

All this said, there remains a final argument, a variant of Justice Brandeis' famous plea for 'states as laboratories', which we feel tries to tip the balance in favor of decentralizing policy for economic efficiency. Here the laboratory is the state legislature and the experiment is the political ability of a state's governor or a strong political party to control the legislature's excesses. Under our analysis, those states with strong governors or strong political parties will typically have more efficient policies. If so, they become models of 'good government' which other states might copy. Recent research by Besley and Case (1995) suggests that residents do use the economic performance of neighboring states as a 'yardstick' against which to measure the performance of their own political process, typically the governor. Governors who fail to control legislative inefficiencies face a significantly lower chance of re-election. Only the decentralization of regulatory policy to the states will give this process of political 'yardstick' competition a chance to promote efficiency.

C. Balancing Participation and Efficiency in a Federalist System

11. Conclusion

We have concluded to this point that political arguments and the current evidence on participation appear to support the use of small decentralized governments to maximize citizen political participation. However, a more centralized alternative can be supported by economic arguments and evidence concerning the economic efficiency of governmental activity. As a result, trade-offs between the potentially competing values of political participation and economic efficiency may be required when evaluating the optimality of a federalist structure.

How are such choices to be made? The analyses in sections A and B can be used to clarify the potential trade-off between the federalist values of political participation and economic efficiency. Consider how economic efficiency, measured in the dollars of economic output, is likely to change as the public sector becomes more decentralized through the assignment of responsibility to more and more, and thus smaller and smaller, governments. Economic benefits rise as responsibility for policy moves from a single central government to the assignment of responsibility to lower level governments, but only to a point. Efficiency improves because decentralization limits the reach of inefficient government activities; rather than the country as a whole bearing the burden of inefficiency, only residents within a state are so burdened. Further, interstate political competition may point the way to more *intra*jurisdictionally efficient policies. But as we decentralize, we also increase the likelihood of *inter*jurisdictional inefficiencies - that is, spillovers. Moving initially from a centralized structure, the gains from intrajurisdictional efficiencies exceed any losses from interjurisdictional inefficiencies. Eventually, however, inefficient spillovers come to dominate, and the overall performance of the economy declines.

There is a similar relationship between decentralization and the extent of political participation. Consistent with our theoretical and empirical analysis in Part B, greater decentralization is likely to increase political participation, though perhaps at a decreasing rate.

Combining our efficiency and participation analysis, we conclude that political participation rises with increased decentralization, but economic efficiency first rises and then falls. It is when efficiency declines that we face a trade-off. Increasing decentralization initially allows efficiency and participation to both increase, but beyond a point more political participation through decentralization must mean less economic efficiency.

The choice of an 'optimal' level of decentralization ultimately depends upon the relative importance one places upon the competing federalist values of economic efficiency and political participation; alternative weightings for the values of efficiency and participation will dictate different federalist structures. For example, if efficiency is weighted more highly than participation, the optimal federalist structure will move away from a fully decentralized system so as to increase efficiency and reduce participation. We look forward, with anticipation, to seeing how these federalism issues will be resolved in the emerging constitutions throughout the world.

Bibliography on Federalism (9700)

Arrow, A. Kenneth (1963), *Social Choice and Individual Values*, New York, Wiley.

Bagnoli, Mark and McKee, Michael (1991), 'Voluntary Contribution Games: Efficient Provision of Public Goods', **29** *Economic Inquiry*, 351.

Baron, David and Ferejohn, John (1989), 'Bargaining in Legislatures', **83** *American Political Science Review*, 1182.

Bartik, Timothy (1988), 'The Effects of Environmental Regulation on Business Location in the United States', **19** *Growth and Change*, 22-44.

Bergstrom, Theodore, Rubinfeld, Daniel, Roberts, Julia and Shapiro, Perry (1988), 'A Test for Efficiency in the Supply of Public Education', **35** *Journal of Public Economy*, 289.

Besley, Timothy and Case, Anne (1995), 'Incumbent Behavior: Vote-Seeking, Tax-setting, and Yardstick Competition', **85** *American Economic Review*, 25.

Binmore, Kenneth, Rubinstein, Ariel and Wolinsky, Asher (1986), 'The Nash Bargaining Solution in Economic Modelling', **17** *Rand Journal of Economics*, 176-188 .

Boadway, Robin and Flatters, Frank (1982), 'Efficiency and Equalization Payments in a Federal System of Government', **15** *Canadian Journal of Economics*, 613.

Brainard, William C. and Dolbear, F. Trenery (1967), 'The Possibility of Oversupply of Local Public Goods', **75** *Journal of Political Econonomy*, 86.

Break, George (1967), *Intergovernmental Fiscal Relations in the United States*,Washington, DC, Brookings Institute, 23-24.

Breton, Albert and Scott, Anthony (1978), *The Economic Constitution of Federal States*, Toronto, University of Toronto Press.

Buchanan, James M. and Goetz, Charles (1972), 'Efficiency Limits of Fiscal Mobility: An Assessment of the Tiebout Model', **1** *Journal of Pubic Econonomy*, 25.

Coase, Ronald (1960), 'The Problem of Social Costs', *Journal of Law and Economics*, 1-44.

Coates, Dennis and Munger, Michael (1995), 'Strategizing in Small Group Decision-Making: Host State Identification for Radioactive Waste Disposal Among Eight Southern States', **82** *Public Choice*, 1.

Cooter, Robert (1982), 'The Cost of Coase', **11** *Journal of Legal Studies,* 1-34.

Courant, Paul and Rubinfeld, Daniel (1981), 'On the Welfare Effects of Tax Limitation', **16** *Journal of Public Economy,* 289.

Crawford, Vincent (1982), 'A Theory of Disagreement in Bargaining', **50** *Econometrica,* 607.

Cumberland, John (1981), 'Efficiency and Equity in Interregional Environmental Management', **2** *Review of Regional Studies*, 1.

Dahl, Robert (1956), *A Preface to Democratic Theory*, Chicago, University of Chicago Press.

Dahl, Robert and Tufte, Edward (1973), *Size and Democracy,* Stanford, CA, Stanford University Press.

David, Charles E. and Lester, James P. (1989), 'Federalism and Environmental Policy', in Lester, James P. (ed.), *Environmental Politics and Policy: Theories and Evidence,* NC, Duke University Press, 57-59.

De Condorcet, M. (1785), 'Essai sur l'Application de L'Analyse à la Probabilité des Decisions Rendues à la Pluraliste des Voix', Paris.

Easterbrook, Frank (1983), 'Antitrust and the Economics of Federalism', **26** *Journal of Law & Economics,* 23-50.

Ellickson, Robert (1979), 'Public Property Rights: Vicarious Intergovernmental Rights and Liabilities as a Technique for Correcting Intergovernmental Spillovers', in Rubinfeld, Daniel (ed.), *Essays on the Law and Economics of Local Governments.*

Epple, Dennis and Zelenitz, Alan (1981), 'The Implications of Competition Among Jurisdictions: Does Tiebout Need Politics?', **89** *Journal of Public Economy*, 1197.

Finifter, Ada W. (1970), 'Dimensions of Political Alienation', **30** *American Political Science Review.*

Fischel, William (1975), 'Fiscal and Environmental Considerations in the Location of Firms in Suburban Communities', in Mills, Edwin and Oates, Wallace (eds), *Fiscal Zoning and Land Use Controls*, Lexington, MA, Lexington Books, 119.

Fitts, Michael and Inman, Robert P. (1992), 'Controlling Congress: Presidential Influence in Domestic Fiscal Policy', **80** *Georgetown Law Journal,* 1737.

Frug, Gerald (1980), 'The City as a Legal Concept', **93** *Harvard Law Review,* 1059.

Gramlich, Edward M. and Laren, Deborah S. (1984), 'Migration and Income Redistribution Responsibilities', **19** *Journal of Human Resources,* 489.

Gramlich, Edward M. and Rubinfeld, Daniel L. (1982), 'Micro Estimates of Public Spending Demand Functions and Tests of the Tiebout and Median Voter Hypotheses', **90** *Journal of Political Econonomy,* 536.

Greenwood, Michael J. (1986), 'The Factor Market Consequences of U.S. Immigration', **24** *Journal of Economic Literature,* 1738.

Haller, Hans (1986), 'Noncooperative Bargaining of N 3 Players', **22** *Economic Letters,* 11.

Hoffman, Elizabeth and Spitzer, Matthew L. (1982), 'The Coase Theorem: Some Experimental Tests', **25** *Journal of Law and Economics,* 73-98.

Holmstrom, Bengt (1985), 'The Provision of Services in a Market Economy', in Inman, Robert (ed.), *Managing the Service Economy: Prospects and Problems,* Cambridge, MA, Cambridge Univ Pr, 183p.

Inman, Robert (1987), 'Markets, Government, and the New Political Economy', in Auerbach, Alan and Feldstein, Martin (eds), *Handbook of Public Economics*, Vol. II, Cambridge, MA, MIT Press.

Inman, Robert P. (1990), 'Public Debts and Fiscal Politics: How to Decide', **80** *American Economic Review*, 81.

Inman, Robert and Fitts, Michael (1990), 'Political Institutions and Fiscal Policy: Evidence from the U.S. Historical Record', **6** (Special Issue) *Journal of Law, Economics and Organization*, 79-132.

Inman, Robert P. and Rubinfeld, Daniel L. (1996), 'Designing Tax Policies in Federalist Economies: An Overview', **60** *Journal of Public Economics*, 307.

Kalt, Joseph and Zupan, Mark (1984), 'Capture and Ideology in the Economic Theory of Politics', **74** *American Economic Review*, 279-300.

Kolstad, Charles and Wolak, Frank (1983), 'Competition in Interregional Taxation: The Case of Western Coal', **91** *Journal of Political Economy*, 443.

Krehbiel, Keith (1992), *Information and Legislative Organization*, Ann Arbor, The University of Michigan Press.

Kreps, David and Wilson, Robert (1982), 'Reputation and Imperfect Information', **28** *Journal of Economic Theory*, 253.

Ladd, Helen F. and Yinger, John (1989), *America's Ailing Cities*, Baltimore, Johns Hopkins University Press.

Levmore, Saul (1992), 'Bicameralism: When Are Two Decisions Better than One', **12** *International Review of Law and Economics*, 145-162.

Lowi, Theodore J. (1969), *The End of Liberalism*, New York, Norton.

Martinez-Vasquez, J. (1994), 'The Challenge of Expenditure-Assignment Reform in Russia', **12** *Environment and Planet*, 277.

McConnell, Kenneth and Schwab, Robert (1990), 'The Impact of Environmental Regulation on Industry Location Decisions: The Motor Vehicle Industry', **66** *Land and Economics*, 67.

Mill, John Stuart (1960), 'Representative Government', in *Three Essays: On Liberty, Representative Government, The Subjection of Women*, London, Oxford University Press

Nagel, Jack (1975), *The Descriptive Analysis of Power*, New Haven, Yale University Press.

Nagel, Jack (1980), *Participation*, Englewood Cliffs, NJ, Prentice Hall.

Niou, Emerson and Ordeshook, Peter (1985), 'Universalism in Congress', **29** *American Journal of Political Science*, 246.

Oates, Wallace E. (1972), *Fiscal Federalism*, London, Harcourt Brace Jovanovich.

Oates, Wallace E. and Schwab, Robert M. (1986), 'Economic Competition Among Jurisdictions: Efficiency Enhancing or Distortion Inducing?', **35** *Journal of Public Economics*, 333.

Olsen, Mancur (1965), *The Logic of Collective Action*, Cambridge, MA, Harvard University Press

Ordeshook, Peter and Riker, William (1973), *An Introduction to Positive Political Theory*, NJ, Prentice-Hall.

Pateman, Carole (1970), *Participation and Democratic Theory*, Cambridge, Cambridge University Press.

Pauly, Martin (1970), 'Optimality, "Public"' Goods, and Local Governments: A General Theoretical Analysis', **78** *Journal of Political Economy*, 572-586.

Pestieau, Pierre (1977), 'The Optimality Limits of the Tiebout Model', in Oates, Wallace (ed.), *The Politics of Fiscal Federalism*.

Polinsky, A. Mitchell (1980), 'Resolving Nuisance Disputes: The Simple Economics of Injunctive and Damage Remedies', **32** *Stanford Law Review*, 1075-1112.

Revesz, Richard (1992), 'Rehabilitating Interstate Competition: Rethinking the "Race-to-the-Bottom" Rationale for Federal Environmental Regulation', **67** *New York University Law Review*, 1210-1255.

Riker, William (1964), *Federalism: Origins, Operation, Significance*, Boston, Little, Brown, and Co.

Rose-Ackerman, Susan (1981), 'Does Federalism Matter? Political Choice in a Federal Republic' , **89** *Journal of Political Economy*, 152-165.

Rose-Ackerman, Susan (1994), 'Environmental Policy and Federal Structure: A Comparison of the United States and Germany', **47** *Vanderbilt Law Review*, 1587-1622.

Rose-Ackerman, Susan and Mashaw, Jerry (1984), 'Federalism and Regulation', in Eads, George C. and Fix, Michael (eds), *The Reagan Regulatory Strategy: An Assessment*, Washington, DC, Urban Institute Press, 111-152.

Roth, Alvin (1985), 'Towards a Focal Point Theory of Bargaining', in Roth, A.E. (ed.), *Game Theoretic Models of Bargaining*, Cambridge and New York, Cambridge University Press

Rubinfeld, Daniel L. (1987), 'The Economics of the Local Public Sector', in Auerbach, Alan and Feldstein, Martin (eds), *Handbook of Public Economics*, Volume II, North-Holland, Amsterdam, 571-645.

Rubinstein, Ariel (1982), 'Perfect Equilibrium in a Bargaining Model', **50** *Econometrica*, 97-110.

Samuelson, Paul (1954), 'The Pure Theory of Public Expenditure', **36** *Review of Economics and Statistics*, 386-389.

Schumpeter, Joseph (1943), *Capitalism, Socialism, and Democracy*, New York, Harper and Row.

Schwartz, Thomas (1989), 'Representation as Agency and Pork Barrel Paradox', Mimeo, UCLA.

Silberman, Jonathan and Garey Durden (1976), 'Determining Legislative Preferences on Minimum Wage: An Economic Approach', **84** *Journal of Political Economy*, 317.

Shepsle, Kenneth (1979), 'Institutional Arrangements and Equilibrium in Multidimensional Voting Models', **28** *American Journal of Political Science*, 27.

Smith, Adam (1776), *An Inquiry into the Nature and Causes of the Wealth of Nations*.

Stigler, George (1971), 'The Theory of Economic Regulation', **2** *Bell Journal of Economics and Managment Science*, 3-21.

Tiebout, Charles (1956), 'A Pure Theory of Local Expenditures', **64** *Journal of Political Economy*, 416-424.

Weingast, Barry (1979), 'A Rational Choice Perspective on Congressional Norms', **23** *American Journal of Political Science*, 245.

Weingast, Barry R. and Marshall, William (1988), 'The Industrial Organization of Congress', **96** *Journal of Political Economy*, 132.

Wildasin, David E. (1986), *Urban Public Finance*, Chicago, Adademic Publishers, Hartcourt Press.

Williams, Alan (1966), 'The Optimal Provision of Public Goods in a System of Local Governments', **74** *Journal of Political Economy*, 18-33.

Williamson (1985), *The Economic Institutions of Capitalism*, New York, The Free Press.

Wittman, Donald (1989), 'Why Democracies Produce Efficient Result', **97** *Journal of Political Economy*, 1395-1424.

9800
INTERNATIONAL ORGANIZATION

Alexander Thompson and
Duncan Snidal
University of Chicago

Abstract

From the principle of state sovereignty to United Nations bureaucracies, international relations are organized by a variety of norms and institutions. After tracing the history of international organization (IO), as well as the intellectual development of its study, we conceptualize IO in terms three levels of formality: IO as formal organization, IO as regime, and IO as ordering principle. We emphasize rationalist approaches - including cooperation theory, associated theories of regimes, and the new institutional economics - as the ones most closely connected to law and economics. After discussing this broad perspective, we consider emerging approaches to international institutional design. Overall, we document a convergence among economists, political scientists and international legal scholars reflected in methodological approach and substantive interests.
JEL classification: K33, A12, D70, F02, D23
Keywords: International Organizations, Regime Theory, New Economics of Organization, Cooperation Theory, Institutions, International Politics

1. Introduction

The modern history of international organization (IO) reflects an uneven development of both the practice and concept that go under that name. The term is used in differing ways and we apply it to both IO conceived as formal institutional organizations and in a more general sense of order creation. Furthermore, international organization includes not only interstate arrangements but, increasingly, arrangements among non-governmental and transnational actors. Thus, the landscape of international organizations (IOs) includes both inter-governmental organizations (IGOs) and international non-governmental organizations (INGOs). International organization is clearly a very broad concept, which has evolved with the practice of various forms of international governance. Our main task here is to chart the theoretical development of understanding about IO. We emphasize approaches that are most relevant to international law and economics, while noting important contributions and challenges posed by alternative perspectives.

After a descriptive summary of the history and evolution of IOs, we discuss three general conceptions of IO as formal organization, as international ordering principle and as international regime. Cooperation theory then provides a theoretical bridge from the realist ordering principle of anarchy to the neoliberal argument regarding the role of regimes. In turn, elaboration of regime analysis has laid the ground for a reintegration of international law and international relations (IR), an incorporation of various forms of new institutional analysis, a closer concern for specific institutional design principles and, finally, to a new appreciation of the role of formal institutions which had long ago been abandoned in theory if not in practice. Finally, we note the challenges posed by other traditions of international organization and indicate promising future directions for productive theorizing.

A. A Brief History of International Organization

2. Westphalia to Vienna

The signing of the Peace of Westphalia in 1648, reinforced by the Treaty of Utrecht in 1713, established the principle of national sovereignty, thereby placing the states of Europe on equal legal footing. This notion of sovereign equality - endowing each state with territorial integrity and the right to conduct domestic and foreign affairs without outside intervention - represents the first real ordering principle among states. After Westphalia, 'decentralized control by sovereign states' (Falk, 1969, p. 69) provided the basis for a horizontal international order critical to the subsequent development of international organization.

However, it was not until the nineteenth century that actual international organizations began to appear in significant numbers. Though the advent of states as sovereign political units was an important step, preconditions for the creation of IOs were not met during the seventeenth and eighteenth centuries. For example, there was insufficient contact between states, there was little recognition of problems arising from interdependence among states, and there was no perceived need for institutionalized mechanisms to manage international relations (Claude, 1964).

3. Vienna and the Nineteenth Century

The first serious attempt at formal international organization arose with the Congress of Vienna (1814-1815), which established diplomatic foundations for a new European security order following the devastation of the Napoleonic Wars. Some credit the resulting 'Congress system' as a fundamental turning point in the conduct and organization of international relations (Schroeder, 1994). It created a more systematic and institutionalized approach to managing issues of war and peace in the international system. The principal innovation at Vienna was that representatives of states should meet at regular intervals - not just in the wake of war - to discuss diplomatic issues. Accordingly, four major peacetime conferences were held between 1815 and 1822.

After this period, the aspirations of the Congress system gave way to a more informal regime. As characterized by one historian, 'A looser association of the Great Powers continued in existence - an attenuated Congress system limited to dealing with problems as they arose, not seeking to anticipate them or to iron them out of existence' (Hinsley, 1963, 213). This 'Concert of Europe' featured sporadic gatherings throughout the century, mostly in response to wars: Paris in 1856, Vienna in 1864, Prague in 1866, Frankfurt in 1871, Berlin in 1878, Berlin in 1884-1885, and The Hague in 1899 and 1907. These last two conferences went so far as to establish panels of arbitrators to settle international disputes and produced a Convention for the Pacific Settlement of International Disputes. These are the earliest examples of formal IOs designed to manage security issues. The result of the Concert was, indeed, quite a long period of relatively peaceful interstate relations among the great powers of Europe.

Many of the most dramatic developments in international organization during the nineteenth century were not related to the goal of averting war but to an emerging mismatch between the geographic scope of problems versus the scope of state authority. The technological changes brought on by the Industrial Revolution - especially in communication (telegraph) and transportation (steamship and railroad) - created an interdependence among states that required more stable forms of cooperation. A new set of IOs was created to manage international economic transactions which were an increasingly important aspect of interstate relations but were difficult for national governments to manage on a unilateral basis (Woolf, 1916). To facilitate shipping and international trade and to regulate traffic, the littoral states of the Rhine established the Central Commission for the Navigation of the Rhine in 1815 at Vienna. Similar commissions were established for the Danube (1856) and Elbe (1821) rivers. The Zollverein, a customs union of Germanic states established 1834, was the first effort at international economic integration and governance in Europe.

A related set of IOs, the Public International Unions, was also a response to technological change. These were concerned primarily with nonpolitical, technical matters, and included the International Telegraphic Union (1865), the General (later Universal) Postal Union (1874), the International Union of Railway Freight Transportation (1890), and the International Bureau of Weights and Measures (1875). Some of these organizations had elaborate institutional frameworks, including permanent bureaus that represented forerunners of secretariats (Archer, 1983, p. 12). The ultimate purpose of these IOs was to facilitate international trade by establishing market rules and standardization. It should be noted that the improved technology that increased the need for coordination among states also made communicating and convening easier, thus facilitating the process of organization.

4. Versailles and the League of Nations

The periods following the two World Wars saw the greatest proliferation of institutions. Heads of state and diplomats met in 1919 at the Versailles Peace Conference to create a global security IO in the League of Nations. This was the first attempt at collective security - that is, an institution operating on the notion of all against one (Claude, 1962; Kupchan and Kupchan, 1991). Under Article 16 of the League Covenant, all member states were required to come to the aid of a member that was the victim of military aggression. The League was overwhelmingly concerned with fostering peace, though economic and social issues did receive secondary attention. The Covenant further established the Permanent Court of International Justice, the first attempt to create a global forum of justice and predecessor to today's International Court of Justice. All members participated in the General Assembly, while a separate League Council - consisting of five permanent members (the United States, Britain, France, Japan, Italy) and several rotating members - guided the operation of the organization.

Versailles also represented the first instance of widespread participation by national and transnational private interest groups in a large interstate conference. Though the nineteenth century saw the formation of a number of INGOs - concerned with humanitarian, religious, economic, educational, scientific, political, and other matters - it was rare for private organizations to sit at the table next to governments. Two products of this non-governmental participation at Versailles were the establishment of the International Labor Organization and a more formal partnership between member states and the Red Cross (already founded in 1864).

Though President Woodrow Wilson was its chief proponent, the United States never joined the League. Due largely to the lack of US participation, the organization never lived up to its promise. It successfully resolved some small military conflicts, but the Covenant was frequently violated and other mechanisms for resolving disputes were employed at least as often. In the end, of course, the League was not able to avert World War II. Nevertheless, the League of Nations is an important marker in the history of international organization as an attempt to forge a new international order based on a formal institution with universal membership.

5. Post-World War II International Organization

The architects of the postwar system set out to establish an extraordinarily ambitious framework of positive international law and institutions. Though the number of formal IOs increased from about 50 to 80 during the interwar period, in the enthusiasm of the early postwar period they were created on a wide scale until they numbered over 600 by 1980 (Wallace and Singer, 1970; Jacobson, 1984). The most important was the United Nations, whose basic structure was decided by the US, the United Kingdom, the Soviet Union and China at the Dumbarton Oaks meeting of 1944 and the 1945 Yalta Summit. The drafters of the Charter, signed at the San Francisco conference of founding members in June 1945, were conscious of the limits inherent in the idealism of the League of Nations. Rather than count on collective security, 'the UN was to be primarily a peace and security organization based on the concept of the Four Policemen, that is, the USA, USSR, the United Kingdom and China as protectors against a recurrence of Axis aggression' (Archer, 1983, p. 24). Abstinence from unilateral use of force remained the main driving principle, however, and the Security Council was entrusted with primary responsibility for authorizing and overseeing military action. The reality of the Cold War dashed these expectations and rendered the UN ineffective, though not irrelevant, in global security affairs. But demand for an expanded range of UN security services has re-emerged in the post-Cold War era and, despite some failures in recent years, the UN is playing an increasingly important security role (Roberts, 1993; Koskenniemi, 1996, pp. 456-460).

The United Nations is divided into six principal organs, though the General Assembly is clearly 'first among them' (Peterson, 1986). Of the other five, the Secretariat, the Trusteeship Council and the Economic and Social Council report to the General Assembly. The Security Council and International Court of Justice have limited mandates, the former dealing only with situations related to the outbreak or potential outbreak of war, and the latter ruling on legal questions brought to it by member states or other UN bodies. These central components of the UN are surrounded by a cluster of functional agencies, including the International Labor Organization, the UN Educational, Scientific and Cultural Organization, the World Health Organization and the Food and Agricultural Organization. Over the years, there has been a steady proliferation of specialized and affiliated agencies, many designed to deal with development issues (Feld and Jordan, 1988, pp. 19-20; Schachter and Joyner, 1995).

Another set of organizations was created during and following World War II, for the purpose of avoiding economic conflict by, especially, maintaining currency stability and free trade. The Bretton Woods monetary system established the US dollar as the central currency; other currencies would be valued according to the dollar, which in turn was pegged to gold. Two formal IOs were created as part of this system: the International Monetary Fund was charged with monitoring balance of payments while the World Bank supervised economic development and postwar reconstruction. The General Agreement on Tariffs and Trade (GATT) was established in 1947 to maintain open trade based on the principle of non-discrimination. It was replaced in 1995 by the more encompassing and centralized - for instance, it contains strengthened dispute settlement procedures - World Trade Organization.

These economic organizations were established as universal in principle but, in fact, began as closely held institutions of the Western powers. Their universality was overshadowed by the Cold War and, to a lesser extent, by North-South distributive conflicts (Krasner, 1985). These institutions have become more inclusive over time, but effective control - both formal and informal - remains in Western hands.

A further striking development in international organization in the postwar period has been the rise of regional IOs (Taylor, 1993; Nye, 1968). Some perform a range of functions within a given geographical area (the Organization of American States, the Organization of Central American States, the Arab League, the Organization of African Unity, and the Association of South East Asian Nations). Others are specifically security-related, such as the North Atlantic Treaty Organization, the Organization for Security and Cooperation in Europe, and the now defunct Warsaw Treaty Organization. The largest number are economic, including the European Free Trade Association, the North American Free Trade Agreement, the Southern Cone Common Market, the Council for Economic Assistance (formerly the Council for Mutual Economic Assistance), the Andean Common Market, and the Asian-Pacific Economic Cooperation. Of this last category, the European Union (formerly the European Community) has the most developed set of institutions in terms of economics (Eichengreen and Frieden, 1994; Kenen, 1995), law (Armstrong and Bulmer, 1998; Burley and Mattli, 1993; Garrett, 1995), security (Kupchan, 1997) and politics (Moravcsik, 1998; Nugent, 1994).

6. Recent Trends in IO

Despite the frequent assumption that IGOs rarely die once created, fully one-third of the organizations that existed in 1981 were defunct by 1992. Many of those that became inactive were in the former Eastern bloc or were regional development organizations in the developing world. In the 1981-1992 period there was also a 'growing polarization between powerful countries - dominated by the literate, wealthy, and democratic - that establish and control IGOs and countries whose populations and governments are badly off and increasingly disengaged from international organizations' (Shanks, Jacobson and Kaplan, 1996, p. 594).

Parallel to the growth in governmental organizations has been a rapid proliferation of international non-governmental organizations (Skjelsbaek, 1971; Willets, 1982; Castermans et al., 1990; Weiss and Gordenker, 1996; Charnovitz, 1996). The growth in private international associations matched that of public international unions in the second half of the nineteenth century, and has surpassed it in the twentieth century. Indeed, since the late nineteenth century there have been more INGOs than NGOs in existence. From 176 in 1909, there were 1,255 INGOs in 1960 and are now more than 5,500 (UIA, 1997/98, Table 2, Appendix 3). Although these organizations cover countless functional areas, the most important categories are commerce and industry, technology, science, and health and medicine, and human rights. In terms of geographical distribution, almost half were founded in Europe; Africa and Asia account for the greatest number in the developing world (UIA, 1997/98, Table 6.2, Appendix 3).

Today, IOs range in size from small consultative organizations such as the Northwest Atlantic Fisheries Organization to very substantial bureaucracies like the World Bank or European Union with elaborate administrative structures, large budgets, many employees and extensive operational capacities. There has also been a striking, though uneven, development of international judicial bodies, most recently reflected in war tribunals for the former Yugoslavia and Rwanda and in the creation of an International Criminal Court. As this historical summary makes clear, international organization has generally been a response to or manifestation of deeper changes in international relations, not a driver of these changes.

B. Conceptual Approaches to IO

The theory and practice of IO have developed together in the modern era, and especially in the post-World War II period. One consequence of this progressive development is substantial ambiguity in what we mean by 'international organization' since the practice and concept have co-evolved over time. A compensating virtue is that we have developed a richness in terms of different possibilities for organizing international behavior and in terms of different ways of thinking about it. It is useful to distinguish three different conceptions of the term.

7. IO as Formal Organization

The most familiar and straightforward definition of international organization is as formal organizations, usually among states or with states selecting representatives. As noted above, the Congress of Vienna (1815) established the Rhine Commission as the first formal IO, but not until the last third of the nineteenth century did IGOs begin to proliferate rapidly to facilitate expanding commercial and other forms of interdependence among European states. In the current period, formal IOs are exemplified by the United Nations and its agencies, as well as a host of functional and regional organizations.

While early discussions can be found in the writings of Dante Alighieri ([1314] 1957), Henri de Saint-Simon ([1825] 1952), Jeremy Bentham ([1786-89] 1927) and Immanuel Kant ([1784] 1914), the study of formal organizations took off in the early twentieth century, especially as the debacle of World War I led to the creation of the League of Nations. The interwar analysis was heavily descriptive and normative and focused on the legal and organizational structure of emerging or proposed institutions (Yalem, 1966). It suffered from a relative neglect of the actual incentives of states, including their reluctance to transfer sovereignty to federal or supranational organizations. This led to its being labeled as 'idealistic' in distinction to the 'realist' account of international life as being fundamentally driven by the harsh realities of power politics (Carr, 1939; Morgenthau, 1948). Realism continues to view power, not institutions, as the key organizing principle of international affairs, and is skeptical of any significant role for formal organizations.

Despite the failure of the League, the concern for international organizations carried through World War II, although it was significantly changed by David Mitrany's ([1943] 1966) 'functionalist' theory. Technological advancements and the desire to promote welfare concerns were seen as creating a need for interstate cooperation that required both international governmental organizations and non-governmental organizations to manage the necessary technical cooperation. The theory further emphasized the important role of professionals within those formal organizations in effecting international cooperation. 'Neofunctionalism' extended this argument by suggesting that successful collaboration in one area would increase the benefits of cooperation in related areas, and generate joint pressure from domestic interest groups and international officials to extend the realm of cooperation (Haas, 1964; Lindberg and Scheingold 1971; Nye, 1971; Groom and Taylor, 1975). This 'spillover' would then provide the motor for broad international, and especially regional, integration, as exemplified by the development of the European Community. Although this body of literature never took off (see Haas, 1975), it represented an important move away from description towards a theoretical analysis whose ideas continue to be echoed in contemporary discussions.

While these theories argued that formal IOs could perform functions that would lead them to acquire authority, subsequent theory focused on how increasing interdependence was eroding state sovereignty. This trend has not been monotonic, as illustrated by high levels of pre-World War I economic interdependence that declined precipitously in the interwar period and were only surpassed well after World War II. Nevertheless, long-term and increasing interactions among states in all fields of activity - including health, technology, security, environment, culture and economics - mean that even the most powerful states are sensitive to occurrences elsewhere and cannot always achieve their goals by themselves. Small states that are dependent on larger states have even stronger reasons to seek support from such organizations. Moreover, this interdependence takes increasingly complex forms, including the increase in the number of significant transnational actors such as multinational corporations and environmental groups (Keohane and Nye, 1972, 1977). These changes have increased opportunities for formal international organizations but have not necessarily increased the willingness of states to transfer political authority to them.

Indeed, formal international organizations had come to be viewed unfavorably from both practical and theoretical standpoints until quite recently. From a practical perspective, IOs have not always lived up to the high expectations they have raised. This was true with the League of Nations in the 1930s and with the United Nations by the 1970s when the General Assembly and various UN agencies seemed to have become little more than forums for ideological debate (between North and South and between East and West). In the 1980s the UN system faced open hostility from the United States, its most powerful member. Similarly, the high expectations for the European Community appeared to have stalled in this period - both within Europe itself and with regard to transferring the regional community model elsewhere.

In fact, many formal IOs continued to play an important role throughout this period (Karnes and Mingst, 1990). Economic organizations were instrumental in the performance of the global economy, while NATO was the most institutionalized, and probably the most successful, alliance.

In the post-Cold War years, formal organizations have experienced somewhat of a renewal. There has been an effort to make better use of existing organizations as the United States did with the United Nations during the Gulf War, to change organizations such as NATO to address a different set of problems, and to expand the venue of organizations such as the World Bank to address new issues, including the environment. Skepticism regarding the effectiveness of formal IOs is neither over nor unwarranted, but there is new interest in pursuing the possibilities of IOs ranging from the European Union to the World Trade Organization

The theoretical literature is experiencing a similar sharp turnaround from the preceding decades where, in the words of one commentator, there 'has been the steady disengagement of international organization scholars from the study of [formal] organizations, to the point that today one must question whether such a field even exists any longer except in name' (Rochester, 1986). This new attention to IOs should not be understood as a continuation of the earlier tradition, however, but as a reconstitution of a substantive interest, now on stronger theoretical footings. On the one hand, the new literature is decidedly non-idealist and questions of enforcement of agreements and incentives to obey institutions are key concerns of its proponents. On the other hand, the literature is theoretical as it seeks to move well beyond the institutional-descriptive accounts that dominated much of the earlier literature. Indeed, if anything, it can be criticized for being too abstract such that it has lost sight of many of the real institutional variations, including formal IOs, that it should seek to explain (Abbott and Snidal, 1998).

Legal scholarship, especially the doctrinal analysis of the rules and outputs of formal IOs, has continued to provide a rich description of the institutional forms and details of IOs. Although largely non-theoretical (see Virally, 1972 for a partial exception), its implicit emphasis on problem-solving states is highly amenable to rationalist theoretical development. This work examines how similar problems are addressed under different IO arrangements (Amerasinghe, 1996; Dupuy, 1988; Kirgis, 1993) and the best is comparative (Schermers and Blokker, 1995). An especially promising recent development discussed below is the reuniting of the legal concern with detailed arrangements and more theoretical developments in economics (Trachtman, 1996) and international relations (Abbott, 1992; Slaughter, Tulumello and Wood, 1998).

Finally, the emphasis on formal IOs represents a very narrow view of the forms of, and possibilities for, international governance. Indeed, the failure of the 'classic' IO model to live up to an exaggerated promise of managing international affairs in a relatively depoliticized and expert manner has led to its disrepute in many quarters. Improved understandings of governance suggest that formal organizations are only one among numerous institutional possibilities.

8. IO as Ordering Principle

If formal organization provides a narrow view of international organization, the most expansive definitions of international organization are framed in terms of broad ordering principles of the international system. We focus on two here: the realist conception of self-help in anarchy and the English school view of 'society'. We do not consider other ordering principles such as Marxist theories of imperialism (Lenin, [1917] 1939) or of a 'world capitalist system' (Wallerstein, 1979), although the economic logic they describe certainly constitutes an alternative international ordering principle. The two we do consider play a central role in debates regarding the nature of international organization and pose major alternatives to regime theory which we consider below.

Self-Help in Anarchy

The traditional realist view centers on sovereign territorial states in a state of anarchy, with Thomas Hobbes as the relevant intellectual hero. Anarchy is defined primarily in terms of the absence of central authority, not necessarily in terms of war (Milner, 1991, offers a valuable discussion of different meanings of anarchy). However, the realist view does imply that international politics is inherently competitive and conflictual, that survival is the primary goal of states, and that relative power is of central importance.Waltz (1959, 1979), the most influential contemporary realist commentator on anarchy, emphasizes that the fundamental difference between domestic and international politics is that the former is hierarchic while the latter is irreducibly anarchic. This creates some irony with respect to realist reliance on Hobbes as their intellectual forebear since they part ways with him on his central conclusion that actors in a dire state of anarchy would choose a Leviathan, and thus transform anarchy into hierarchy. The best explanation for states' failure to do so is that international anarchy is not as brutish as Hobbes' vision of domestic anarchy (Beitz, 1979).

Nevertheless, given the absence of central authority, the key realist ordering principle is self-help: states must take care of themselves (Waltz, 1979). Security is seen as the overwhelmingly central problem and balance of power provides the unique source of international order. Thus a central focus of realist theory is the relation between the distribution of power and international outcomes, including but not restricted to war - although there are sharp debates over the precise impact of different power distributions (Kaplan, 1957; Gilpin, 1981; Waltz, 1979). Power and security considerations are further seen as the deep source of states' attitudes towards, and arrangements for, other (secondary) issues such as economics, human rights or environment. Thus lower-order institutions - including formal organizations and regimes - are seen as largely epiphenomenal, with the organization of the system explained largely by the balancing of power among states (Mearsheimer, 1994/95; Wight, 1973).

International Society

A very different tradition in the international relations field, inspired by Hugo Grotius ([1625] 1925), focuses on the system of states as an 'international society' that contains persistent elements of order (Bull, 1977; Wight, 1977). According to Bull (1977, p. 13), the most prominent member of this English school, 'states form a society in the sense that they conceive themselves to be bound by a common set of rules in their relations with one another, and share in the working of common institutions'. This framework of rules and institutions guides state behavior in patterned ways. Similarly, Finnemore stresses the notion of 'norms as social structure'. States, embedded in a dense network of social relations that shape their judgments, define their interests according to 'internationally shared norms and values that structure and give meaning to international political life' (Finnemore, 1996a, p. 3). The simple notion of anarchy thus cannot capture the richness and order of the international system. Even in settings of intense security competition such as the Cold War, mutual understandings and 'rules of the game' can provide considerable stability (Gaddis, 1987).

Members of this school have used its insights to critique the rationalist underpinnings of regime theory (next) for failing to capture many of the dynamics of international cooperation and organization. States abide by rules and norms, even when it is not in their material interest, because they have a long-term interest in the maintenance of a 'law-impregnated international community' and share a sense of 'moral community' (Hurrell, 1993). This work, however, has generally attempted to integrate regime theory into the study of international society, arguing, for example, that functional theories of regimes are largely accurate but that international society is a precondition for their development (Buzan, 1993). Hurrell (1993) suggests that the field of international law can provide a bridge for understanding the interaction between normative structure and self-interested cooperation. This recognition that regime theory and the notion of a norm-laden international society are not mutually exclusive offers a promising path for future work in the study of IO and cooperation more generally.

9. IO as Regime

Between the narrow understanding of formal organizations and the extremely broad understanding of ordering principles lies the concept of 'international regime', which has become the most widely used approach to international organization. Regime theory is premised on the twin observations that international politics is highly interdependent (Keohane and Nye, 1977), thus implying mutual interests in cooperation, and that 'international behavior is institutionalized' in a variety of ways (Ruggie, 1975, p. 559). There is agreement over these empirical phenomena, but the approach includes a diverse set of theoretical and methodological orientations. While there is no theoretical consensus, there has been wide adherence to a 'standard' definition of regimes as 'sets of implicit or explicit principles, norms, rules and decision-making procedures around which actors' expectations converge in a given area of international relations' (Krasner, 1983, p. 2). This very broad conception of regimes includes the endpoints as well as the vast middle ground between formal organizations and broader ordering principles in international relations.

The definition of regime has been criticized as being expansive to the point of vagueness (Strange, 1982). An unfortunate consequence is that an inordinate amount of effort has been expended in arguing about whether or not there is an effective regime in a particular area. The corresponding virtue is that this broad definition allows for a broader view of governance possibilities than is suggested by the narrower concern with formal institutions. The various categories in the definition also point towards a greater level of specificity than is often achieved by more ethereal discussions of ordering principles. Finally, the breadth of the definition leaves room for a plurality of approaches - liberal as well as realist, rationalist as well as constructivist. This has provided some unity to the field despite the diversity of approaches sometimes employed.

Regime 'theory' is confusing insofar as it refers to a body of literature including a wide range of different approaches and theories. Nevertheless, the most substantial vein of regime theory relies on rational choice understandings of state behavior, where states are viewed as unified, self-interested actors (Hasenclever, Mayer and Rittberger, 1997). We emphasize rationalist approaches for this reason and because they are closest to the law and economics tradition.

Rational regime theory was a natural outgrowth of the increasing propensity among IR scholars, beginning in the 1970s, to theorize international cooperation problems as analogous to 'market failure'. They used a public choice approach to problems such as public goods provision and externalities at the international level (Russett and Sullivan, 1971; Ruggie, 1972; Snidal, 1979; Fratianni and Pattison, 1982) and applied Coase's theory of property rights to the process of international organization (Conybeare, 1980). But the most important move in the literature emerged from the 'folk theorem' of economics and its result that decentralized cooperation can be an equilibrium outcome when a circumstance is repeated through time. This provided a response to the realist claim that the lack of centralized authority in anarchy prevents international cooperation. Indeed, by taking a Hobbesian specification of anarchy as akin to a prisoner's dilemma (Taylor, 1976), international relations theorists began to develop a theoretical argument that cooperation was not only possible in realist anarchy, it was in some sense likely (Axelrod, 1984). Thus the title of Kenneth Oye's (1986) *Cooperation Under Anarchy* reflected the emerging synthesis in the literature that international order did not require centralized institutions. The articles in Keohane and Ostrom (1995) provide a recent elaboration of this perspective.

Cooperation theory has been challenged in several important ways, especially by disputing whether its underlying assumptions truly apply in international relations. Possibly states, or their leaders, are not properly characterized as rational agents with the capacities or inclinations necessary to maintain decentralized cooperation. An alternative, more realist critique is that states as rational actors seek goals such as power that are different from the goals of economic actors who seek wealth. This latter position has been formalized as the claim that because states seek 'relative gains', cooperation is limited in international affairs (Grieco, 1988), but this argument has been countered by analyses demonstrating that these limits are not great (Snidal, 1991; Powell, 1991). An alternative and more telling criticism of rational cooperation as a theory of international organization is that it has at best a very thin view of institutions. Thus cooperation theory provides a substitute for the need for international organization as centralized enforcement, but it does not provide an account of why any substantial international organization is needed at all.

C. Contemporary Theoretical Approaches to IO

10. Rationalist Regime Theory

The seminal work for the study of rationalist regime theory is Robert Keohane's *After Hegemony* (1984). The book explains the continued existence and increasing strength of international institutions in the wake of declining American hegemony. Drawing on rational choice logic and microeconomic theories, Keohane offers a functional theory of international regimes - in other words, the anticipated benefits to states explain the persistence of the regime and compliance with its rules. 'Political market failure' is a central notion in Keohane's analysis: 'Like imperfect markets, world politics is characterized by institutional deficiencies that inhibit mutually advantageous cooperation' (1984, p. 85). While bargaining could in principle correct these failures (Coase, 1960), Keohane argues that the underlying conditions for Coasean logic to operate - well-defined property rights (that is, a legal framework), perfect information, and zero transactions costs - do not naturally exist in the international system. Regimes, then, serve to fill in these gaps to facilitate cooperation among states on a decentralized basis.

Moreover, '[b]y clustering issues together in the same forums over a long period of time, they [regimes] help to bring governments into continuing interaction with one another, reducing incentives to cheat and enhancing the value of reputation. By establishing legitimate standards of behavior for states to follow and by providing ways to monitor compliance, they create the basis for decentralized enforcement founded on the principle of reciprocity' (Keohane, 1984, p. 145; see also Keohane, 1986). In short, states find it much more efficient to operate within multilateral institutions than to generate cooperation through countless bilateral agreements (Aggarwal, 1985). And since the cost of dealing with an additional issue is much less within a regime, this may explain why they strengthen and expand in scope over time.

Much of the early regimes literature focused on explaining why states create international regimes and demonstrating that they 'matter', that is, that they influence state behavior in a meaningful way. From the beginning, however, regime theorists were addressing issues such as why regimes change or evolve (Young, 1982; Lipson, 1982; Aggarwal, 1983) and how to measure a regime's effectiveness (Young, 1992; Haas, Keohane and Levy, 1993; Bernauer, 1995). They are also concerned with why regimes take particular forms, such as bilateral, minilateral or multilateral (Yarbrough and Yarbrough, 1992; Ruggie, 1993a). In addition, the application of regime theory has been expanded to a wide variety of issue-areas, including international security (Jervis, 1982; McCalla, 1996), trade (Finlayson and Zacher, 1981; Aggarwal, 1985; Yarbrough and Yarbrough, 1987), finance (Cohen, 1982; Lipson, 1985), human rights (Donnelly, 1986), telecommunications (Cowhey, 1990: Zacher, 1996; Sandholtz, 1993), and the environment (Young 1989, 1994; Young and Osherenko, 1993; Haas, 1993; Haas, Keohane and Levy, 1993). International legal scholars have increasingly used regime theory to better understand issues such as international trade law, arms control agreements, and the law of treaties (Abbott, 1985; Abbott, 1993; Smith, 1991; Setear, 1996; see also Aceves, 1997).

Scholars in the regime tradition have also used alternative terminology, including *institutions*, *multilateralism*, and *governance systems*, to describe phenomena of international organization that exist between formal organizations and broader elements of order in the international system. Works centered around the construct of 'international institutions' are closely tied to regime theory and tend to either subsume the concept of a 'regime' (Haas, Keohane and Levy, 1993, p. 5) or employ a definition that is virtually synonymous with the earlier Krasner definition (Young, 1989, pp. 5, 32). Multilateralism has been described as an institutional form that orders state behavior on the basis of generalized principles of conduct (Ruggie, 1993a). However, there is a distinct body of work that relies on the notion of 'governance without government' (Rosenau and Czempiel, 1992; Young, 1994). 'Governance' is distinct from 'government' in that rules are obeyed not because they are backed by the threat of force; rather, it is the perceived legitimacy of rules that leads to compliance (Franck, 1990, 1995; Young, 1979). Actors in the international system recognize certain norms and rules of conduct and feel compelled to oblige by them. Governance, then, is 'order with intentionality' (Rosenau, 1992, p. 5). This normative theory of international organization is thus different from earlier, interest-based theories of international regimes, though their predictions about order are similar.

11. New Institutionalism

A subsequent wave of scholarship studies international organization through the lens of the 'new institutionalism' within several social science fields, including economics (Williamson, 1985; Eggertsson, 1989; Furubotn and Richter, 1991, 1997), sociology (Powell and DiMaggio, 1991), and political science (March and Olsen, 1989; Moe, 1984). Important works, for example, have attempted to apply the sociology of organizations to IOs, describing them as 'live collectivities interacting with their environments' that 'tend to become infused with value' (Ness and Brechin, 1988, p. 247; see also Finnemore, 1996b, and Young, 1994). Armstrong and Bullmer (1998) use historical institutionalism to explain the development of the Single European Market in terms of the interaction between law and politics.

The largest body of literature has begun to integrate the 'new economics of organization' (NEO) - also referred to as 'new institutional economics' or 'transaction costs economics' - into the study of international organization. In the early 1990s, economists began to notice 'striking parallels between the central questions of NEO and those of international relations' (Yarbrough and Yarbrough, 1990). Both literatures focus on the need to establish institutions to facilitate cooperation when independent actions would produce sub-optimal outcomes. Oliver Williamson, for example, stresses the 'feasibility of crafting superior ex ante incentive structures' to promote cooperative behavior (1985, p. 204). Thus, firms arise as a form of private, hierarchic ordering within a market that lacks formal organization or authority (Williamson, 1975, 1985). The emphasis is on non-governmental forms of managing such problems as the provision of public goods and the guarantee of property rights.

An important aspect of this NEO wave is an attempt to theorize about the organizational design of international institutions rather than treating them as black boxes. The assumption is that states do not simply follow the dictates of formal organizations - rather, they create institutions with specific design features intended to be the most effective and focus on the variety of institutional forms that result. In their study of international trade liberalization over time, Yarbrough and Yarbrough (1992, p. 19) show that '[i]nstitutional variety ... (reflects the efficacy of alternate governance structures for different types of trade transactions in different political and economic environments'.

Lake (1996) presents a theory of contracting whereby organizational choice in security relations - which varies on a continuum from anarchic alliances to hierarchic empires - is determined by considerations of transaction costs and the expected costs of opportunism. International lawyers have similarly applied transaction costs economics to explain various governance structures in the international system (Aceves, 1996; Trachtman, 1997). Even the existence of sovereign territorial states themselves, as a form of international institutionalization, has been explained through this lens (Spruyt, 1994).

Though NEO writers tend to focus on formal IOs, this approach is far more theoretical in its objectives than the earlier legal-descriptive tradition in the field of international law. Formal rules are only one aspect of IOs according to the NEO school and they are not the most important determinant of state behavior: 'From the NEO perspective, concentration on formal legal structures may prove not only incomplete but also misleading, since the effective enforcement of rules assumed by the formal approach is often missing, particularly in international relations' (Yarbrough and Yarbrough, 1990, p. 257). Informal institutions and behavioral norms play a prominent role. Much like regime theory, then, NEO applications to IO suggest that the stark dichotomy presented by some IR scholars between a hierarchic and ordered domestic arena and an anarchic international order is misleading.

12. Micro-Design

In much the same spirit as NEO, other international relations and legal scholars have focused on what might be called the micro-design of IOs and international treaties. These writers go beyond explaining the general demand for international regimes (Keohane, 1982, 1984) and focus on the demand and effectiveness of particular regime design features. Though they typically concentrate on formal IOs, they use the detailed study of these organizations to draw broad theoretical implications about international cooperation in a manner that is consistent with the goals of regime theory.

One important vein of this scholarship begins with the assumption that compliance with international agreements is generally high, and that violations are the result of legal ambiguities, inadvertence, or the incapacity of states to comply rather than calculated, self-interested 'cheating' (Chayes and Chayes, 1993, 1995; Mitchell, 1993). Moreover, the incidence of this non-compliance is largely a function of how international treaties and regimes are designed, and thus regime effectiveness can be improved when certain institutional features are present (Mitchell, 1994a, 1994b; Sand, 1990). The resulting theories are thus prescriptive as well as descriptive.

A related literature explains why particular design features or levels of institutionalization are chosen (Sykes, 1990; Lipson, 1991; Staiger, 1995; Mansfield and Milner, 1997) through consideration of the relative bargaining power of states (Garrett, 1992), of domestic factors influencing institutional design (Cowhey, 1990), and of the specific features of the international problems that states face (Kahler, 1996; Koremenos, Lipson and Snidal, 1998). Downs and Rocke (1995, p. 77) argue that uncertainty about future demands from domestic interest groups leads policymakers to design institutions with 'sanctions for noncompliance that are low enough to allow politicians to break the agreement when interest group benefits are great, but high enough to encourage states to obey the agreement most of the time and thereby prevent trade wars' (Graber, 1999). So while these institutions may seem inefficient in that noncompliance is not severely punished, they are in fact an optimal outcome in light of the domestic uncertainty that exists. Finally, other micro-design theorists revert to simple functionalism to explain certain designed features. Garrett and Weingast (1993), for example, argue that the design of the European Union's legal order is accepted by governments because it serves to mitigate various ambiguities that make cooperation difficult, namely, incomplete contracting and monitoring problems.

13. Critiques

The Realist Critique

From its inception, regime theory and its successors have been criticized by 'realist' theorists of international relations arguing that international institutions simply do not 'matter' in any meaningful way. According to the conventional structural critique, regimes have little or no independent effect on state behavior, especially when it comes to important economic and power relationships (Strange, 1982). Regimes, and international cooperation more generally, are readily upset by the logic of security competition because states have an overwhelming concern with power and survival. As a result, regimes are epiphenomenal to international politics: sustained cooperation can only exist when it is consistent with power politics considerations (Gowa, 1994). This logic does not preclude the establishment of cooperative institutions, including military alliances, to satisfy short-term interests, but such forms of organization are merely 'temporary marriages of convenience' (Mearsheimer, 1994/95, p. 11). Not all realists are so pessimistic. Glaser (1994/95) begins with the basic assumptions of structural realism and shows that discord is not the logical consequence under a wide variety of conditions. Institutions that provide information and reduce transaction costs, in particular, are not inconsistent with the exigencies of security competition, though in the end cooperation will normally be based on ad hoc agreements rather than more formal organization.

Globalization

Building from past work on 'transnational relations' (Keohane and Nye, 1972) the literature on globalization stresses the large and growing number of non-state actors in the international system, such as firms, private associations, and religious groups (Cerny, 1990; Krugman, 1995; Risse-Kappen, 1995; Gupta, 1997). The fact that economic and other transactions increasingly take place without regard to national boundaries has important implications for international politics (Rodrik et al., 1998). One conclusion drawn by globalization theorists is that the traditional state has become structurally inappropriate as a political unit, leading some to consider whether globalization has gone too far (Rodrik, 1997). In terms of international organization, Philip Cerny argues that the 'residual state' will no longer be the most important entity driving collective action in the international system and will not be able to provide global public goods, such as the regulation of the world market (Cerny, 1995; see also McGrew and Lewis, 1992; Ruggie, 1993b; Strange, 1996). The result may be increased reliance on private sources of governance that are more flexible and appropriate, such as interfirm alliances (Dunning, 1997) and international non-governmental organizations.

Constructivism

A major limitation of rational regime theory is that it takes both states as unitary actors and their interests as unproblematic. Some 'bottom-up' efforts rectify this situation by incorporating a richer rationalist view of the domestic constraints that states face, notably the 'two-level games' of Putnam (1988) and Milner (1997). Nevertheless, constructivism and other knowledge-based theories argue that the identities and interests of the actors, and how these are determined by the nature of the international community and its institutions, need to be explained rather than assumed (Wendt, 1994; Biersteker and Weber, 1996; Katzenstein, 1996). Some of these approaches can be readily accommodated by rational regime theory insofar as they provide a complementary analysis of why states have particular goals and beliefs (Haas, 1993; Goldstein and Keohane, 1993), or of how particular outcomes become focal points (Garrett and Weingast, 1993).

Other approaches are more sharply contradictory to rational approaches. In part, this is because many constructivists reject the typically positivistic premises of rational regime theory, but fundamentally it is because they reject its individualism. They want to explain international arrangements from a 'top-down' perspective that examines the broader normative structures that constitute international ordering principles (Kratochwil, 1989; Wendt and Duvall,

1989; Finnemore 1996a; Arend, 1998). The broadness of regime theory will allow it to incorporate some of these ideas; the rationalist stream of the theory will rework some of them in terms of its own conceptions of beliefs and information, though surely not to the full satisfaction of constructivist critics. While no agreed synthesis will emerge, the tension between the two approaches is likely to be mutually improving (Hasenclever, Mayer and Rittberger, 1997).

D. Conclusion

Theorists and practitioners have employed a number of differing conceptions of 'international organization'. These conceptions can usefully be thought of as falling into three categories: IO as formal organization, IO as ordering principle in the international system, and IO as regime. The last of these categories has received the most attention recently and has involved a high degree of fruitful theorizing about IO and international cooperation more generally.

Political scientists who study IO have begun in recent years to return to the study of formal organizations, though this time they have done so with explicitly theoretical intentions (Snidal, 1997). At the same time, international legal scholars have sought to meet IR theorists halfway. The result is a self-conscious effort from both sides to integrate the two fields (Abbott, 1989; Burley, 1993; Keohane, 1997). In his treatment of the negotiations on dispute resolution in the Uruguay Round of GATT, for example, Abbott (1992, p. 112) recognizes that 'meaningful analysis of matters like these requires a theoretical framework'. Burley (1993, p. 222; Slaughter, Tulumello and Wood, 1998) offers an historical account of the interaction of the law and IR literatures and suggests some 'components of an institutionalist interdisciplinary dialogue'. This 'dual agenda' includes the study of organizational design, compliance, and international ethics. The overlap between this agenda and much of the NEO agenda is obvious, and this suggests that the future of IO scholarship will be more interdisciplinary than ever before.

Indeed, common concerns and methodology among political scientists, legal scholars and economists increasingly characterize the IO literature. More than ever before, international legal scholars are using modes of analysis drawn from political science and economics to understand international organizations and law (Bhandari and Sykes, 1997; Mock, 1992; Shell, 1995; Aceves, 1996; Chong, 1995; Colombatto and Macey, 1996; Setear 1996). This interdisciplinary movement is clearly evident in substantive work on compliance with international rules and on dispute settlement. Scholars from various traditions have come together to understand why nations comply with international law and institutional rules (Mitchell, 1994a; Keohane, 1992; Downs, Rocke and Barsoom, 1996; Cameron, Werksman and Roderick, 1996; Chayes and Chayes,

1995; Franck, 1990, 1995; Koh, 1997), as well as the development of supranational adjudication in international organizations (Hefler and Slaughter, 1997; Horlich and DeBusk, 1993; Hudec, 1990; Jackson, 1994; Kovenoch and Thursby, 1992; Pescatore, 1993; Yarbrough and Yarbrough, 1997). Through this intellectual interaction, the study of international organization, like the practice of international governance itself, is becoming more energized and, one hopes, more sophisticated.

Acknowledgements

We thank two anonymous reviewers for valuable comments.

Bibliography on International Organization (9800)

Abbott, Kenneth W. (1985), 'The Trading Nation's Dilemma: The Functions of the Law of International Trade', **26** *Harvard International Law Journal*, 501-532.

Abbott, Kenneth W. (1989), 'Modern International Relations Theory: A Prospectus for International Lawyers', **14(2)** *Yale Journal of International Law*, 335-411.

Abbott, Kenneth W. (1992), 'The Uruguay Round and Dispute Resolution: Building a Private-Interests System of Justice', **1** *Columbia Business Law Review*, 111-149.

Abbott, Kenneth W. (1993), 'Trust but Verify': The Production of Information in Arms Control Treaties and Other International Agreements', **26** *Cornell International Law Journal*, 1-58.

Abbott, Kenneth W. and Snidal, Duncan (1998), 'Why States Act Through Formal International Organizations', **41(1)** *Journal of Conflict Resolution*, 3-32.

Aceves, William J. (1996), 'The Economic Analysis of International Law: Transaction Cost Economics and the Concept of State Practice', **17** *University of Pennsylvania Journal of International Economic Law*, 995-1068.

Aceves, William J. (1997), 'Institutionalist Theory and International Legal Scholarship', **12** *American University Journal of International Law and Policy*, 227-266.

Aggarwal, Vinod (1983), 'The Unraveling of the Multi-fiber Arrangement, 1981: An Examination of Regime Change', **37** *International Organization*, 617-645.

Aggarwal, Vinod (1985), *Liberal Protectionism: The International Politics of Organized Textile Trade*, Berkeley, University of California Press.

Alighieri, Dante ([1314] 1957), *On World Government* (trans. by Herbert W. Schneider, 2nd rev. edn), New York, Liberal Arts.

Amerasinghe, Chittharanjan (1996), *Principles of International Law of International Organizations*, Cambridge, Cambridge University Press.

Archer, Clive (1983), *International Organizations*, Winchester, Allen and Unwin.

Arend, Anthony Clark (1998), 'Do Legal Rules Matter? International Law and International Politics', **38** *Virginia Journal of International Law*, 107-153.

Armstrong, Kenneth and Bulmer, Simon (1998), *The Governance of the Single European Act*, New York, Manchester University Press.

Axelrod, R. (1984), *The Evolution of Cooperation*, New York, Basic Books.

Beitz, Charles R. (1979), *Political Theory and International Politics*, Princeton, Princeton University Press.

Ben-Shahar, Omri and Rottem, G. (1996), 'The Credibility of International Enforcement', in Brown-Weiss, E. and Jacobson, H.K. (eds), *Compliance with International Environmental Agreements*, Transnational Press.

Bentham, Jeremy ([1786] 1927), *Plan for a Universal and Perpetual Peace*, London, Grotius Society.

Bernauer, Thomas (1995), 'The Effect of International Environmental Institutions: How we Might Learn More', **49** *International Organization*, 351-377.

Bhandari, Jagdeep S. and Sykes, Alan O. (eds) (1997), *Economic Dimensions in International Law: Comparative and Empirical Perspectives*, Cambridge, Cambridge University Press.

Biersteker, Thomas and Weber, Cynthia (eds) (1996), *State Sovereignty as Social Construct*, New York, Cambridge University Press.

Black, Cyril .E. and Falk, Richard A. (eds) (1969), *The Future of the International Legal Order, Vol. 1 Trends and Patterns*, Princeton, Princeton University Press.

Bull, Hedley (1977), *The Anarchical Society: A Study of Order in World Politics*, New York, Columbia University Press.

Burley, Anne-Marie (1993), 'International Law and International Relations Theory: A Dual Agenda', **87** *American Journal of International Law*, 205-239.

Burley, Anne-Marie and Mattli, Walter (1993), 'Europe Before the Court: A Political Theory of Legal Integration', **47** *International Organization*, 41-76.

Buxbaum, Hertig and Hirsch, Hopt (eds), *European Economic and Business Law, Legal and Economic Analyses on Integration and Harmonization*, Berlin, Springer, 401 p.

Buzan, Barry (1993), 'From International System to International Society: Structural Realism and Regime Theory Meet the English School', **47** *International Organization*, 327-352.

Cameron, James, Werksman, Jacob and Roderick, Peter (eds) (1996), *Improving Compliance with International Environmental Law*, London, Earthscan Publications.

Carr, Edward H. (1939), *The Twenty Years' Crisis, 1919-1939*, London and New Jersey, Zed Books.

Castermans, G. et al. (eds) (1990), *The Role of Non-Governmental Organization in the Promotion and Protection of Human Rights*, Boston, Kluwer Law International.

Cerny, Philip (1990), *The Changing Architecture of Politics: Structure, Agency, and the Future of the State*, London, Sage.

Cerny, Philip (1995), 'Globalization and the Changing Logic of Collective Action', **49** *International Organization*, 595-625.

Charnovitz, Steve (1996), 'Participation of Nongovernmental Organizations in the World Trade Organization', **17** *University of Pennsylvania Journal of International Business Law*, 331-358.

Chayes, Abram and Chayes, Antonio Handler (1993), 'On Compliance', **47(2)** *International Organization*, 175-206.

Chayes, Abram and Chayes, Antonio Handler (1995), *The New Sovereignty: Compliance with International Regulatory Agreements*, Cambridge, MA, Harvard University Press.

Chong, Howard F. (1995), 'An Economic Analysis of Trade Measures to Protect the Global Environment', **83** *Georgetown Law Journal*, 2131 ff.

Claude, I.L. (1962), *Power and International Relations*, New York, Random House.

Claude, I.L. (1964), *Swords into Plowshares,* 3rd edn, London, University of London Press.

Coase, Ronald H. (1960), 'The Problem of Social Cost', **3** *Journal of Law and Economics*, 1-44.

Cohen, Benjamin (1982), 'Balance-of-Payments Financing: Evolution of a Regime', **36(2)** *International Organization*, 457-478.

Colombatto, Enrico and Macey, Jonathan R. (1996), 'A Public Choice Model of International Economic Cooperation and the Decline of the Nation State', **18** *Cardozo Law Review*, 925-956.

Conybeare, John (1980), 'International Organization. and the Theory of Property Rights', **34** *International Organization*, 307-334.

Cowhey, P. (1990), 'The International Telecommunications Regime: The Political Roots of International Regimes for High Technology', **44** *International Organization*, 169-199.

Cox, Robert W. (1996), *Approaches to World Order*, Cambridge, Cambridge University Press.

Cox, Robert W. and Jacobson, H.K. (1974), *The Anatomy of Influence: Decision Making in International Organization*, New Haven, CT, Yale University Press.

Donnelly, Jack (1986), 'International Human Rights: a Regime Analysis', **40** *International Organization*, 599-642.

Downs, George and Rocke, David (1995), *Optimal Imperfection? Domestic Uncertainty and Institutions in International Relations*, Princeton, Princeton University Press.

Downs, George, Rocke, David and Barsoom, Peter (1996), 'Is the Good News about Compliance Good News about Cooperation?', **50** *International Organization*, 379-406.

Dunning, John H. (1997), *Alliance Capitalism and Global Business*, New York, NY, Routledge.

Dupuy, Rene Jean (ed.) (1988), *A Handbook on International Organisations*, Hingham, MA, Kluwer.

Eggertsson, Thrainn (1989), *Economic Behavior and Institutions*, Cambridge, Cambridge University Press.

Eichengreen, Barry and Frieden, Jeffry (1994), *The Political Economy of European Monetary Unification*, Boulder, CO, Westview Press.

Falk, Richard A. (1969), 'The Interplay of Westphalia and Charter Conceptions of International Legal Order', in Black, Cyril E. and Falk, Richard A. (eds), *The Future of the International Legal Order, Vol. 1 Trends and Patterns*, Princeton, Princeton University Press, 32-72.

Fearon, James (1998), 'Bargaining, Enforcement, and International Cooperation', **52** *International Organization*, 269-305.

Feld, Werner J. and Jordan, Robert S. (1988), *International Organizations: A Comparative Approach,* 2nd edn, New York, Praeger.

Finlayson, Jock and Zacher, Mark (1981), 'The GATT and the Regulation of Trade Barriers: Regime Dynamics and Functions', **35(4)** *International Organization*, 561-602.

Finnemore, Martha (1996a), *National Interests in International Society*, Ithaca (NY), Cornell University Press.

Finnemore, Martha (1996b), 'Norms, Culture, and World Politics: Insights from Sociology's Institutionalism', **50(2)** *International Organization*, 325-348.

Franck, Thomas M. (1990), *The Power of Legitimacy among Nations*, Oxford, Oxford University Press.

Franck, Thomas M. (1995), *Fairness in International Law and Institutions*, Oxford, Oxford University Press.

Fratianni, Michele and Pattison, John (1982), 'The Economics of International Organizations', **35** *Kyklos*, 244-262.

Furubotn, Eirik G. and Richter, Rudolf (eds) (1991), *The New Institutional Economics*, College Station, TX, Texas A & M University Press.

Furubotn, Eirik G. and Richter, Rudolf (1997), *Institutions and Economic Theory: The Contribution of the New Institutional Economics*, Ann Arbor, University of Michigan Press.

Gaddis, John L. (1987), *The Long Peace: Inquiries into the History of the Cold War*, New York, NY, Oxford University Press.

Garrett, Geoffrey (1992), 'International Cooperation and Institutional Choice: The European Community's Internal Market', **46(2)** *International Organization*, 533-560.

Garrett, Geoffrey (1995), 'The Politics of Legal Integration in the European Union', **46** *International Organization*, 533-560.

Garrett, Geoffrey and Weingast, B. (1993), 'Ideas, Interests, and Institutions: Constructing the European Community's Internal Market', in Goldstein, J. and Keohane, R. (eds), *Ideas and Foreign Policy: Beliefs, Institutions, and Political Change*, Ithaca, NY, Cornell University Press, 173-206.

Gilpin, Robert (1981), *War and Change in International Politics*, Cambridge, Cambridge University Press.

Glaser, Charles (1994/95), 'Realists as Optimists: Cooperation as Self-Help', **19** *International Security*, 50-90.

Goldstein, Judith and Keohane, Robert O. (1993), *Ideas and Foreign Policy: Beliefs, Institutions, and Political Change*, Ithaca, NY, Cornell University Press.

Gowa, Joanne (1994), *Allies, Adversaries, and International Trade*, Princeton, Princeton University Press.

Graber, Lloyd (1999), *Ruling the World: Power, Politics and the Rise of Supranational Institutions*, Princeton, NJ, Princeton University Press, forthcoming.

Grieco, Joseph (1988), 'Anarchy and the Limits of Cooperation: A Realist Critique of the Newest Liberal Institutionalism', **42** *International Organization*, 485-507.

Groom, A.J.R. and Taylor, Paul G. (1975), *Functionalism: Theory and Practice in International Relations*, London, University of London Press.

Grotius, Hugo ([1625] 1925), *De Jure Belli ac Pacis*, trans. Francis W. Kelsey, Oxford, Clarendon.

Gupta, S. (ed.) (1997), *The Political Economy of Globalization*, Boston, Kluwer.

Haas, Ernst B. (1958), *The Uniting of Europe: Political, Social and Economic Forces, 1950-1957*, Stanford, Stanford University Press.

Haas, Ernst B. (1961), 'International Integration: The European and the Universal Process', **15** *International Organization*, 366-397.

Haas, Ernst B. (1964), *Beyond the Nation-State: Functionalism and International Organization*, Stanford, Stanford University Press.

Haas, Ernst B. (1975), *The Obsolescence of Regional Integration Theory*, Berkeley, University of California Press.

Haas, Peter (ed.) (1993), *Knowledge, Power and International Policy Coordination*, Columbia, SC, University of South Carolina Press.

Haas, Peter, Keohane, Robert O. and Levy, Marc A. (1993), *Institutions for the Earth: Sources of Effective International Environmental Protection*, Cambridge, MA, MIT Press.

Hasenclever, Andreas, Mayer, Peter and Rittberger, Volker (1997), *Theories of International Regimes*, Cambridge, Cambridge University Press.

Hefler, Laurence and Slaughter, Anne Marie (1997), 'Toward a Theory of Effective Supranational Adjudication', **107** *Yale Law Journal*, 273-391.

Hinsley, Francis H. (1963), *Power and the Pursuit of Peace: Theory and Practice in the History of Relations between States*, Cambridge, Cambridge University Press.

Horlick, Gary and DeBusk, Amanda (1993), 'Dispute Resolution under NAFTA: Building on the U.S.-Canada FTA, GATT and ICSID', **27**, *Journal of World Trade*, 21-41.

Hudec, Robert E. (1990), 'Dispute Settlement', in Schott, Jeffrey (ed.), *Completing the Uruguay Round*, Institute for International Economics, 180-204.

Hurrell, Andrew (1993), 'International Society and the Study of Regimes: A Reflective Approach', in Rittberger, Volker (ed.), *Regime Theory and International Relations*, Oxford, Oxford University Press, 49-72.

Jackson, John (1994), 'The World Trade Organization, Dispute Settlement, and Codes of Conduct', in Collins, Susan and Bosworth, Barry (eds), *The New GATT*, Washington, Brookings Institution.

Jacobson, H.K. (1984), *Networks of Interdependence: International Organizations and the Global Political System*, 2n edn, New York, Alfred A. Knopf.

Jervis, Robert (1982), 'Security Regimes', **36(2)** *International Organization*, 357-378.

Kahler, Miles (1996), *International Institutions and the Political Economy of Integration*, Washington, Brookings Institution.

Kant, Immanuel ([1784] 1914), *Eternal Peace and Other International Essays (trans. by William Hastie)*, Boston, World Peace Foundation.

Kaplan, Morton (1957), *System and Process in International Politics*, New York, Wiley.

Karnes, Margaret and Mingst, Karen (1990), *The United States and Multilateral Institutions*, Boston, Unwin Hyman.

Katzenstein, Peter (1996), *The Culture of National Security*, New York, Columbia University Press.

Kenen, Peter (1995), *Economic and Monetary Union in Europe: Moving beyond Maastricht*, Cambridge, Cambridge University Press.

Keohane, Robert O. (1982), 'The Demand for International Regimes', **36(2)** *International Organization*, 325-356.

Keohane, Robert O. (1984), *After Hegemony: Cooperation and Discord in the World Political Economy*, Princeton, Princeton University Press.

Keohane, Robert O. (1986), 'Reciprocity in International Relations', **40** *International Organization*, 1-27.

Keohane, Robert O. (1992), 'Compliance with International Commitments: Politics within a Framework of Law', **86** *American Society of International Law Proceedings*, 176-180.

Keohane, Robert O. (1997), 'International Relations and International Law: Two Optics', **38** *Harvard International Law Journal*, 487-502.

Keohane, Robert O. and Nye, Joseph (eds) (1972), *Transnational Relations and World Politics*, Cambridge, MA, Harvard University Press.

Keohane, Robert O. and Nye, Joseph (1977), *Power and Interdependence: World Politics in Transition*, Boston, Little Brown.

Keohane, Robert O. and Ostrom, Elinor (1995), *Local Commons and Global Interdependence: Heterogeneity and Cooperation in Two Domains*, Thousand Oaks, California, Sage.

Kirgis, Frederic L. Jr. (1993), *International Organizations in Their Legal Setting*, 2nd ed, St. Paul, West Publishing Company.

Koh, Harold (1997), 'Why Do Nations Obey Inernational Law?', **106** *Yale Law Journal*, 2598-2659.

Koremenos, Barbara, Lipson, Charles and Snidal, Duncan (1998), *Rational International Institutions*, Unpublished Manuscript.

Koskenniemi, Martti (1996), 'The Place of Law in Collective Security', **17** *Michigan Journal of International Law*, 455-490.

Kovenoch, Dan and Thursby, Marie (1992), 'GATT, Dispute Settlement and Cooperation', **4** *Economics and Politics*, 151-170.

Krasner, Stephen (1983), *International Regimes*, Ithaca, NY, Cornell University Press.

Krasner, Stephen (1985), *Structural Conflict: The Third World Against Global Liberalism*, Berkeley, University of California Press.

Kratochwil, Friedrich (1989), *Rules, Norms, and Decisions: On the Conditions of Practical and Legal Reasoning in International Relations and Domestic Affaris*, Cambridge, Cambridge University Press.

Kratochwil, Friedrich and Ruggie, John G. (1986), 'International Organization: a State of the Art on an Art of the State', **40(4)** *International Organization*, 753-776.

Krugman, Paul R. (1995), 'Growing World Trade: Causes and Consequences', *Brookings Papers on Economic Activity*, 327-377.

Kupchan, Charles (1997), 'Regionalizing Europe's Security: The Case for a New Mitteleuropa', in Mansfield, Edward and Milner, Helen (eds), 209-239.

Kupchan, Charles and Kupchan, Clifford (1991), 'Concerts, Collective Security, and the Future of Europe', **16(1)** *International Security*, 151-198.

Lake, David (1996), 'Anarchy, Hierarchy, and the Variety of International Relations', **50(1)** *International Organization*, 1-34.

Lenin, Vladimir I. ([1917] 1939), *Imperialism: The Highest Stage of Capitalism*, New York, International Publisher.

Lindberg, Leon N. and Scheingold, Stuart (1971), *Regional Integration: Theory and Research*, Cambridge, MA, Harvard University Press.

Lipson, Charles (1982), 'The Transformation of Trade: the Sources and Effects of Regime Change', **36** *International Organization*, 417-455.

Lipson, Charles (1985), *Standing Guard: Protecting Foreign Capital in the Nineteenth and Twentieth Centuries*, Berkeley, University of California Press.

Lipson, Charles (1991), 'Why Are Some International Agreements Informal?', **45** *International Organization*, 495-538.

Mansfield, Edward and Milner, Helen (eds) (1997), *The Political Economy of Regionalism*, New York, Columbia University Press.

March, James G. and Olsen, Johan (1989), *Rediscovering Institutions: The Organizational Basis of Politics*, New York, NY, Free Press.

McCalla, Robert B. (1996), 'NATO's Persistence after the Cold War', **50** *International Organization*, 445-475.

McGrew, Anthony and Lewis, Paul (1992), *Global Politics: Globalization and the Nation-State*, Cambridge, MA, Blackwell.

Mearsheimer, John ([1994/95), 'The False Promise of International Institutions', **19** *International Security*, 5-49.

Milner, Helen (1991), 'The Assumption of Anarchy in International Relations Theory', **17** *Review of International Studies*, 67-85.

Milner, Helen (1997), *Interests, Institutions and Information*, Princeton, Princeton University Press.

Mitchell, Ronald B. (1993), 'Compliance Theory: A Synthesis', **2** *Review of European Community and International Environmental Law*, 327-334.

Mitchell, Ronald B. (1994a), *Intentional Oil Pollution at Sea: Environmental Policy and Treaty Compliance*, Cambridge, MA, MIT Press.

Mitchell, Ronald B. (1994b), 'Regime Design Matters: Intentional Oil Pollution and Treaty Compliance', **48** *International Organization*, 425-458.

Mitrany, David ([1943] 1966), *A Working Peace System: An Argument for the Functional Development of International Organization*, Chicago, Quadrangle Press.

Mock, William B.T. (1992), 'Game Theory, Signalling, and International Legal Relations', **26** *George Washington Journal of International Law and Economics*, 33-60.

Moe, Terry M. (1984), 'The New Economics of Organization', **28** *American Journal of Political Science*, 739-777.

Moravcsik, Andrew (1998), *The Choice for Europe: Social Purpose and State Power from Messina to Maastricht*, Ithace, NY, Cornell University Press.

Morgenthau, Hans (1948), *Politics Among Nations*, New York, Alfred A. Knopf.

Morrow, James (1994), 'Modeling the Forms of International Cooperation: Distribution versus Information', **48** *International Organization*, 387-424.

Ness, Gayl D. and Brechin, Steven R (1988), 'Bridging the Gap: International Organizations as Organizations', **42(2)** *International Organization*, 245-273.

Nugent, Neill (1994), *The Government and Politics of the European Union*, Durham, NC, Duke University Press.

Nye, Joseph (ed.) (1968), *International Regionalism*, Boston, Little Brown.

Nye, Joseph (1971), *Peace in Parts: Integration and Conflict in Regional Organization*, Boston, Little Brown.

Oye, Kenneth A. (ed.) (1986), *Cooperation under Anarchy*, Princeton, Princeton University Press.

Pescatore, Pierre (1993), 'The GATT Dispute Settlement Mechanism', **27** *Journal of World Trade*, 5-20.

Peterson, M.J. (1986), *The General Assembly in World Politics*, Boston, Unwin Hyman.

Powell, Robert (1991), 'Absolute and Relative Gains in International Relations Theory', **85** *American Political Science Review*, 1303-1320.

Powell, Walter W. and DiMaggio, Paul J. (1991), *The New Institutionalism in Organizational Analysis*, Chicago, University of Chicago Press.

Putman, Robert (1988), 'Diplomacy and Domestic Politics: The Logic of Two-Level Games', **42** *International Organization*, 427-460.

Risse-Kappen, Thomas (1995), *Bringing Transnational Relations Back In: Non-State Actors, Domestic Structures and International Institutions*, Cambridge, Cambridge University Press.

Roberts, Adam (1993), 'The United Nations and International Security', **35(2)** *Survival*, 3-30.

Rochester, J. Martin (1986), 'The Rise and Fall of International Organization as a Field of Study', **40(4)** *International Organization*, 777-813.

Rodrik, Dani (1997), *Has Globalization Gone Too Far?*, Washington, DC, Institute for International Economics.

Rodrik, Dani, Obstfeld, Maurice, Feenstra, Robert and Williamson, Jeffrey (1998), 'Symposium on Globalization in Perspective', **12(4)** *Journal of Economic Perspectives*, 3-72.

Rosenau, James N. (1992), 'Governance, Order, and Change in World Politics', in Czempiel, Ernst-Otto and Rosenau, James (eds), *Global Changes and Theoretical Challenges*, Lexington, MA, Lexington Books, 1-29.

Rosenau, James N. and Czempiel, Ernst-Otto (1992), *Governance Without Government: Order and Change in World Politics*, Cambridge Ontario, Collier-MacMillan.

Ruggie, John G. (1972), 'Collective Goods and Future International Collaboration', **66** *American Political Science Review*, 874-893.

Ruggie, John G. (1975), 'International Responses to Technology: Concepts and Trends', **29** *International Organization*, 557-583.

Ruggie, John G. (1993a), *Multilateralism Matters: The Theory and Praxis of an Institutional Form*, Columbia University Press.

Ruggie, John G. (1993b), 'Territoriality and Beyond: Problematizing Modernity in International Relations', **47** *International Organization*, 139-174.

Russett, Bruce M. and Sullivan, John D. (1971), 'Collective Goods and International Organizations', **25** *International Organization*, 845-865.

Saint-Simon, Henri de ([1825] 1952), 'On Social Organization (trans. F.M.H. Markham)', in Markham, F.M.H. (ed.), *Henri Comte de Saint-Simon (1760-1825): Selected Writings*, Oxford, Basil Blackwell.

Sand, Peter H. (1990), *Lessons Learned in Global Environmental Governance*, Washington, World Resources Institute.

Sandholtz, Wayne (1993), 'Institutions and Collective Action: the New Telecommunications in Western Europe', **45** *World Politics*, 242-270.

Schachter, Oscar and Joyner, Christopher (eds) (1995), *United Nations Legal Order, 2 vols.*, Cambridge, Cambridge University Press.

Schermers, Henry and Blokker, Niels (1995), *International Institutional Law: Unity within Diversity*, 3rd edn, The Hague, Mouton.

Schroeder, Paul W. (1994), *The Transformation of European Politics, 1763-1848*, Oxford, Clarendon.

Setear, John K. (1996), 'An Iterative Perspective on Treaties: A Synthesis of International Relations Theory and International Law', **37** *Harvard International Law Journal*, 139-229.

Shanks, Cheryl, Jacobson, H.K. and Kaplan, Jeffrey H. (1996), 'Inertia and Change in the Constellation of International Governmental Organizations, 1981-1992', **50(4)** *International Organization*, 593-627.

Shell, Richard G. (1995), 'Trade Legalism and International Relations Theory: An Analysis of the World Trade Organization', **44** *Duke Law Journal*, 829-927.

Shermers, Henry and Blokker, Niels (1995), *International Institutional Law: Unity within Diversity*, 3rd edn, The Hague, Nijhoff.

Skjelsbaek, Kjell (1971), 'The Growth of International Nongovernmental Organizations in the Twentieth Century', **25** *International Organization*, 420-442.

Slaughter, Anne-Marie, Tulumello, Andrew and Wood, Stepan (1998), 'International Law and International Relations Theory: A New Generation of Interdisciplinary Scholarship', **92(3)** *American Journal of International Law*, 367-397.

Smith, Edwin M. (1991), 'Understanding Dynamic Obligations: Arms Control Agreements', **64** *Southern California Law Review*, 1549-1606.

Snidal, Duncan (1979), 'Public Goods, Property Rights, and Political Organization', **23(4)** *International Studies Quarterly*, 532-566.

Snidal, Duncan (1985), 'Coordination versus Prisoners' Dilemma: Implications for International Cooperation and Regimes', **79** *American Political Science Review*, 923-943.

Snidal, Duncan (1991), 'Relative Gains and the Pattern of International Cooperation', **85** *American Political Science Review*, 701-726.

Snidal, Duncan (1997), 'International Political Economy Approaches to International Institutions', in Bhandari, Jagdeep S. and Sykes, Alan O. (eds), *Economic Dimensions in International Law: Comparative and Empirical Perspectives*, Cambridge, Cambridge University Press, 477-512.

Spruyt, Hendrik (1994), 'Institutional Selection in International Relations: State Anarchy as Order', **48** *International Organization*, 527-557.

Staiger, Robert (1995), 'International Rules and Institutions for Trade Policy', in Jones, Ronald and Kenen, Peter (eds), *Handbook of International Economics, Vol. 2*, Amsterdam, North-Holland.

Stein, Arthur (1982), 'Coordination and Collaboration Regimes in an Anarchic World', **36** *International Organization*, 299-324.

Strange, Susan (1982), 'Cave! Hic dragones: A Critique of Regime Analysis', **36(2)** *International Organization*, 479-498.

Strange, Susan (1996), *The Retreat of the State*, Cambridge, Cambridge University Press.

Streit, Manfred E. and Voigt, Stefan (1996), 'Toward Ever Closer Union - Or Ever Larger? Or Both? Entry to the European Union from the Perspective of Constitutional Economics', **16** *International Review of Law and Economics*, 385-388.

Sykes, Alan O. (1990), 'Mandatory Retaliation for Breach of Trade Agreements: Some Thoughts on the Strategic Design of Section 301', **8** *Boston University International Law Journal*, 301-331.

Taylor, Michael (1976), *Anarchy and Cooperation*, London, Wiley.

Taylor, Paul G. (1993), *International Organization in the Modern World: The Regional and Global Process*, New York, Pinter Publishers.

Trachtman, J.P. (1996), *The Theory of the Firm and the Theory of International Economic Organization: Toward Comparative Institutional Analysis*, Unpublished Manuscript.

Trachtman, J.P. (1997), 'Externalities and Extraterritoriality: The Law and Economics of Prescriptive Jurisdiction', in Bhandari, Jagdeep and Sykes, Alan (eds), 642-683.

Union of International Associations (UIA) (Multiple dates), *Yearbook of International Organizations 1997/1998*, Munich, K.G. Saur.

Virally, Michel (1972), *L'Organisation Mondiale (Global Organization)*, Paris, Armand Collin.

Wallace, Michael D. and Singer, David J. (1970), 'Intergovernmental Organization in the International System: A Quantitative Assessment', **24** *International Organization*, 239-287.

Wallerstein, Immanuel (1979), *The Capitalist World Economy*, Cambridge, Cambridge University Press.

Waltz, Kenneth N. (1959), *Man, State and War*, New York, Columbia University Press.

Waltz, Kenneth N. (1979), *Theory of International Politics*, Reading, MA, Addison-Wesley.

Weiss, Thomas G. and Gordenker, Leon (1996), *NGOs, the UN, and Global Governance*, Boulder, CO, Lynne Rienner.

Wendt, Alexander (1994), 'Collective Identity Formation and the International State', **88** *American Political Science Review*, 391-425.

Wendt, Alexander (1998), *Social Theory of International Politics*, Unpublished Manuscript.

Wendt, Alexander and Duvall, Robert (1989), 'Institutions and International Order', in Czempiel, Ernst-Otto and Rosenau, James (eds), *Global Changes and Theoretical Challenges*, Lexington, MA, Lexington Books, 51-73.

Wight, Martin (1973), 'The Balance of Power and International Order', in Alan, James (ed.), *The Bases of International Order*, Oxford, Oxford University Press, 85-115.

Wight, Martin (1977), *Systems of States*, Leicester, Leicester University Press.

Willets, Peter (1982), *Pressure Groups in the Global System: The Trasnsnational Relations of Issue-Oriented Non-Governmental Organizations*, New York, St. Martin's Press.

Williamson, Oliver E. (1975), *Markets and Hierarchies: Analysis and Antitrust Implications*, New York, NY, Free Press.

Williamson, Oliver E. (1985), *The Economic Institutions of Capitalism*, New York, NY, Free Press.

Wittman, Donald A. (1991), 'Nations and States: Mergers and Acquisitions; Dissolutions and Divorce', **81** *American Economic Review. Papers and Proceedings*, 126-129.

Woolf, Leonard (1916), *International Government*, 2nd edn, London, Allen and Unwin.

Yalem, Ronald J. (1966), 'The Study of International Organization, 1920-65: A Survey of the Literature', **10** *Background*, 1-56.

Yarbrough, Beth V. and Yarbrough, Robert M. (1987), 'Institutions for the Governance of Opportunism in International Trade', **3** *Journal of Law, Economics, and Organization*, 129-133.

Yarbrough, Beth V. and Yarbrough, Robert M. (1990), 'International Institutions and the New Economics of Organization', **44(2)** *International Organization*, 235-259.

Yarbrough, Beth V. and Yarbrough, Robert M. (1992), *Cooperation and Governance in International Trade*, Princeton, Princeton University Press.

Yarbrough, Beth V. and Yarbrough, Robert M. (1997), 'Dispute Settlement in International Trade: Regionalism and Procedural Coordination', in Mansfield, Edward and Milner, Helen (eds), 134-163.

Young, Oran R. (1979), *Compliance and Public Authority: A Theory with International Implications*, Baltimore, MD, John Hopkins University Press.

Young, Oran R. (1982), 'Regime Dynamics: the Rise and Fall of International Regimes', **36** *International Organization*, 277-297.

Young, Oran R. (1989), *International Cooperation: Building Regimes for Natural Resources and the Environment*, Ithaca, NY, Cornell University Press.

Young, Oran R. (1992), 'The Effectiveness of International Institutions: Hard Cases and Critical Variables', in Czempiel, Ernst-Otto and Rosenau, James (eds), *Global Changes and Theoretical Challenges*, Lexington, MA, Lexington Books.

Young, Oran R. (1994), *International Governance: Protecting the Environment in a Stateless Society*, Ithaca, NY, Cornell University Press.

Young, Oran R. and Osherenko, Gail (1993), *Polar Politics: Creating International Environmental Regimes*, Ithaca, NY, Cornell University Press.

Zacher, Mark with Sutton, Brent (1996), *Governing Global Networks: International Regimes for Transportation and Communications*, Cambridge, Cambridge University Press.